Angelo Kinicki
Arizona State University
Kent State University

Denise Breaux Soignet
University of Arkansas

management
A PRACTICAL INTRODUCTION

TENTH EDITION

Mc
Graw
Hill

MANAGEMENT: A PRACTICAL INTRODUCTION, TENTH EDITION

Published by McGraw Hill Education, 2 Penn Plaza, New York, NY 10121. Copyright © 2022 by McGraw Hill Education. All rights reserved. Printed in the United States of America. Previous editions ©2020, 2018, and 2016. No part of this publication may be reproduced or distributed in any form or by any means, or stored in a database or retrieval system, without the prior written consent of McGraw Hill Education, including, but not limited to, in any network or other electronic storage or transmission, or broadcast for distance learning.

Some ancillaries, including electronic and print components, may not be available to customers outside the United States.

This book is printed on acid-free paper.

2 3 4 5 6 7 8 9 LWI 26 25 24 23 22

ISBN 978-1-260-73516-1 (bound edition)
MHID 1-260-73516-8 (bound edition)
ISBN 978-1-264-26368-4 (loose-leaf edition)
MHID 1-264-26368-6 (loose-leaf edition)

Portfolio Director: *Michael Ablassmeir*
Product Developer: *Anne Ehrenworth*
Executive Marketing Manager: *Debbie Clare*
Content Project Managers: *Harvey Yep (Core)/Keri Johnson (Assessment)*
Buyer: *Susan K. Culbertson*
Design: *Matt Diamond*
Content Licensing Specialists: *Gina Oberbroeckling*
Cover Image: *Kapook2981/iStock/Getty Images*
Compositor: *Aptara®, Inc*

All credits appearing on page or at the end of the book are considered to be an extension of the copyright page.

Library of Congress Control Number: 2020923831

The Internet addresses listed in the text were accurate at the time of publication. The inclusion of a website does not indicate an endorsement by the authors or McGraw Hill Education, and McGraw Hill Education does not guarantee the accuracy of the information presented at these sites.

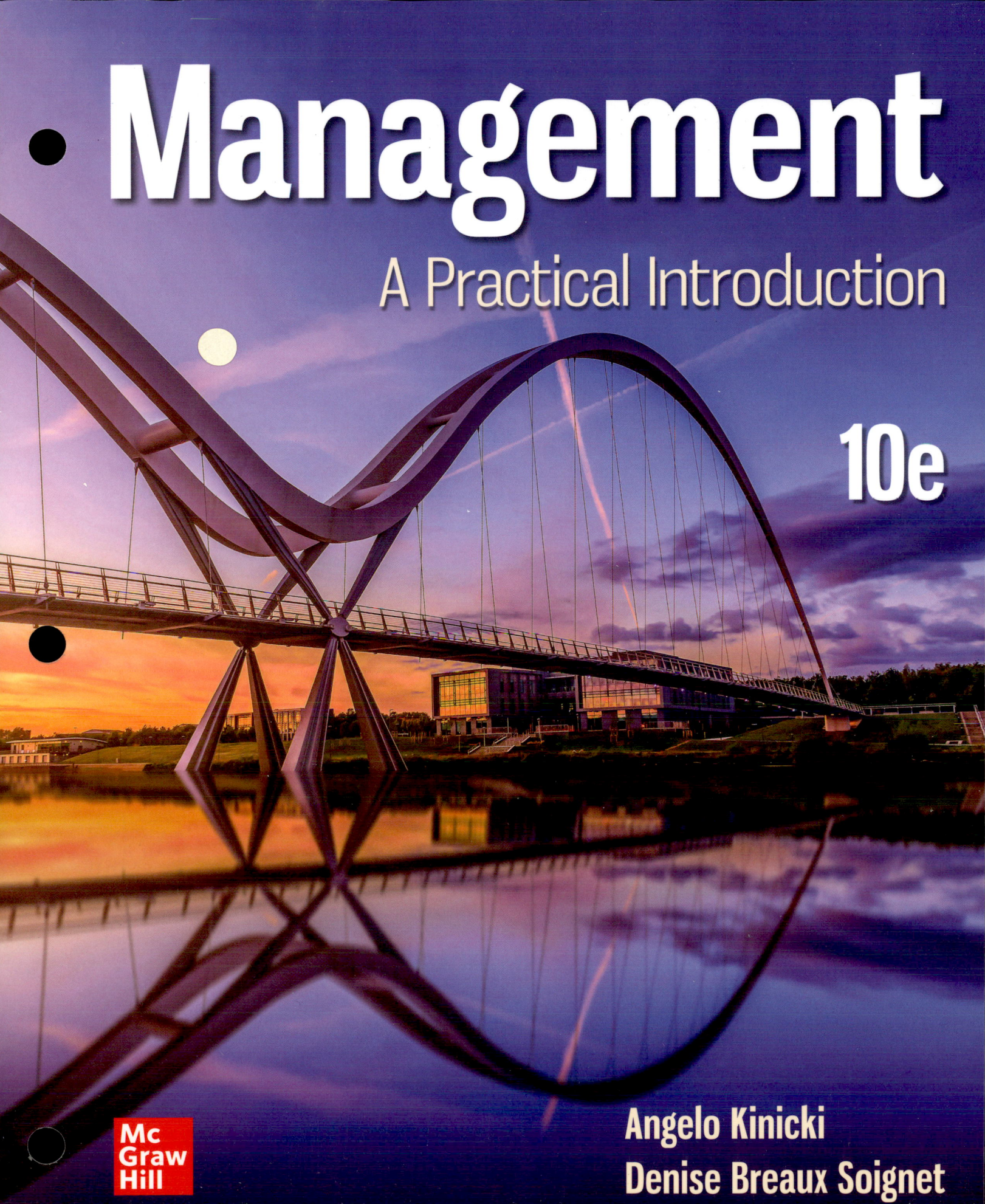

Management

A Practical Introduction

10e

Angelo Kinicki

Denise Breaux Soignet

brief contents

about the authors

Angelo Kinicki is an emeritus professor of management and held the Weatherup/Overby Chair in Leadership from 2005 to 2015 at the W. P. Carey School of Business at Arizona State University. He joined the faculty in 1982, the year he received his doctorate in business administration from Kent State University. He was inducted into the W. P. Carey Faculty Hall of Fame in 2016. Angelo currently is the Dean's Scholar in Residence at Kent State University. He is conducting seminars on the implementation of active learning in the classroom and publishing scholarly research. He also serves on the Dean's National Advisory Board.

Angelo is the recipient of six teaching awards from Arizona State University, where he taught in its nationally ranked undergraduate MBA and PhD programs. He also received several research awards and was selected to serve on the editorial review boards for four scholarly journals. His current research interests focus on the dynamic relationships among leadership, organizational culture, organizational change, and individual, group, and organizational performance. Angelo has published over 95 articles in a variety of academic journals and proceedings and is co-author of eight textbooks (37 including revisions) that are used by hundreds of universities around the world. Several of his books have been translated into multiple languages, and two of his books were awarded revisions of the year by McGraw Hill. Angelo was identified as being among the top 100 most influential (top .6%) Organizational Behavioral authors in 2018 out of a total of 16,289 academics.

Angelo is a busy international consultant and co-founder of Kinicki and Associates, Inc., a management consulting firm that works with top management teams to create organizational change aimed at increasing organizational effectiveness and profitability. He has worked with many Fortune 500 firms as well as numerous entrepreneurial organizations in diverse industries. His expertise includes facilitating strategic/operational planning sessions, diagnosing the causes of organizational and work-unit problems, conducting organizational culture interventions, implementing performance management systems, designing and implementing performance appraisal systems, developing and administering surveys to assess employee attitudes, and leading management/executive education programs. He developed a 360° leadership feedback instrument called the Performance Management Leadership Survey (PMLS) that is used by companies throughout the world.

Angelo and his wife of 39 years, Joyce, have enjoyed living in the beautiful Arizona desert for 38 years. They are both natives of Cleveland, Ohio. They enjoy traveling, hiking, and spending time in the White Mountains with Gracie, their adorable golden retriever. Angelo also has a passion for golfing.

Denise Breaux Soignet is an associate teaching professor of management and director of the Tyson Center for Faith and Spirituality in the Workplace at the Sam M. Walton College of Business at the University of Arkansas. She joined the University of Arkansas faculty in 2010 after receiving her PhD in business administration from Florida State University. Denise has received awards both for her teaching and her work to promote inclusion and diversity within the university and professional communities. She has taught courses in the Walton College's nationally ranked undergraduate and MBA programs, has developed several online undergraduate courses for her department, and sees active learning as a key component of all of her courses,

both face-to-face and online. Denise's research interests include dysfunctional workplace behavior, inclusion and diversity, leadership, social influence, and job stress, and her work has been published in multiple premier management journals.

Denise is a Certified Professional for the Society for Human Resource Management, and she consults with public- and private-sector organizations. Her expertise includes diagnosing the causes of interpersonal problems in the workplace, implementing management solutions that enhance the quality of supervisor-subordinate relationships, assessing workplace religious inclusion and tolerance, and designing and delivering organizational learning and development programs. She also has specialized expertise in resolving the unique interpersonal challenges that arise in poultry production and has years of experience working with managers and technicians at some of the industry's largest firms.

Denise lives in Northwest Arkansas with her husband, Joe, and their two children. They are natives of South Louisiana and Cajuns at heart. They enjoy watching their two favorite football teams—the New Orleans Saints (WHO DAT!) and the Nicholls State University Colonels—and can often be found making food and cocktails for friends, gardening, listening to jazz, and traveling with their kids.

dedication

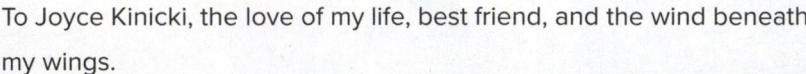

To Joyce Kinicki, the love of my life, best friend, and the wind beneath my wings.

—Angelo

To A and G, my everything. May you always make good choices, be kind to others, and have fun.

—Mom

new to the tenth edition

It all begins with a new author team

This edition brings a 22-year collaboration between Brian Williams and me (Angelo Kinicki) to an end. It was a great partnership and I am proud of what we accomplished and the student lives we influenced over the years. I am very excited about the future and would like to introduce my new co-author, Dr. Denise Breaux Soignet. Based on my 36 years of textbook writing experience, I selected Denise because she possesses all the skills and traits I desire in a co-author. Her content knowledge is vast and stems from exceptional training from academic scholars such as Dr. Pam Perrewé, Dr. Jerry Ferris, and Dr. Ben Tepper. She also is a beautiful writer and an outstanding teacher. She cares deeply about teaching and helping students, and this passion comes through in her commitment to our work. Denise is smart, humble, driven, honest, and hard working. She also pushes back and challenges me when needed. Finally, I like Denise and she's fun to work with. I can't ask for anything more in a co-author.

We are pleased to share these exciting new additions and updates!

All of our changes are based on the goal of providing the most up-to-date theory, research, and practical examples. For instance, we have used 56 examples to illustrate the application of management principles to the context of managing COVID-19 and the associated pandemic of 2020. We also wrote 13 new Management in Action chapter closing cases and replaced or updated 15 of our Legal/Ethical Challenge cases.

The tenth edition incorporates four major changes. The first entailed updating and extending our strategic theme regarding career readiness. The second involved integrated coverage regarding the concepts of creating shared value and sustainable development. The third was to increase the extent to which our examples were inclusive and representative of the diverse body of today's managers, not to mention the diversity of our students. The final change involved an overhaul of our Teaching Resource Manual 2.0 (TRM). Below is a review of these substantive changes.

Updated and Expanded Coverage of Career Readiness

Our ninth edition was the first textbook to introduce a strategic theme on career readiness. Our goal was to help students develop their career readiness competencies so that they would be more employable upon graduation. This was an important theme because research shows that employers believe college graduates are not career ready. We have expanded this theme in the tenth edition.

Our first change involved refining our model of career readiness in Chapter 1 based on recent research findings. The new model starts with seven core competencies—a set of competencies that are vital across jobs, occupations, and industries. We then categorize 20 additional career readiness competencies into four categories: knowledge, soft skills, attitudes, and other characteristics (KSAOs, see Figure 1.4). We have also taken great effort in this edition to link career readiness competencies to their respective chapter content. For example, Table 7.2 illustrates the career readiness competencies needed to effectively use big data across managerial levels.

Creating Shared Value and Sustainable Development

Creating shared value and sustainable development represents a new approach to leading and managing, which replaces more traditional forms of corporate social responsibility (CSR). The core idea underlying the concept of creating shared value (CSV) is that companies can implement policies and operating practices that enhance the competitiveness of a company while simultaneously advancing the economic and social conditions in the communities in which they operate. As such, CSV results in an expanded "pie" or pool of value for the firm as well as for society. This approach toward management is based on a greater-good mentality in which the goals of a business involve more than making money. Executives are encouraged to make decisions that favorably impact all of their stakeholders. The integrations take five forms:

- We introduce the concept in Chapter 1 while discussing the seven challenges to becoming an exceptional manager. We define sustainable development and explain how the 193 members of United Nations adopted a set of 17 Sustainable Development Goals (SDGs) in 2015.
- We reintroduce the concept in Chapter 2's coverage of management history, in a section that discusses contemporary approaches to managing and leading. Students will have a clear understanding how this new approach fits within the historical evolution of management thought.
- We provide further insight into the idea of CSV and sustainable development in Chapter 3 when discussing the social responsibilities required of managers. Students will learn that sustainable development represents one form of social responsibility.
- We present a new Learning Module 1 titled "Shared Value and Sustainable Development: A New Way to Think about Leading and Managing." The module focuses on three learning objectives: (1) describe how the concept of shared value improves upon the traditional approach to corporate social responsibility, (2) discuss the roles various stakeholders play in creating shared value, and (3) explain recommendations for creating shared value in light of current progress and challenges.
- We weave examples in subsequent chapters when appropriate.

> *I incorporate sustainable business practices in all my course [and] the books I use do not cover it. I love this idea! It's about time!*
>
> **—Jack Cichy,**
> *Davenport University*

> *I like the idea of a higher-level concept of sustainable development. It lays the foundation of starting a business with sustainability in mind from the beginning instead of needing to pivot later. And it begins to build that foundation in the minds of the students as they develop their own ideals.*
>
> **—Ronda Taylor,**
> *Ivy Tech Community College*

Inclusiveness and Representativeness

The United States is wonderfully diverse in its ethnic, racial, gender, and age makeup. So are our students. We want to celebrate the fact that some of the most innovative, powerful, and brilliant leaders in modern organizations are women and people of color—groups that have historically been underrepresented both in industry and in textbooks. Throughout this revision your students will find a multitude of wonderful examples. For just a few illustrations, check out the Example box on how Revolution Foods—founded by Kristin Richmond and Kirsten Tobey—creates shared value on pages 136-37 of Learning Module 1; the feature on how Stephanie Lampkin—founder and CEO of Blendoor—is building Artificial Intelligence into the hiring process on pages 398-99 in Chapter 9; and the story of the late Bernard Tyson—former CEO of Kaiser Permanente—and his empowering leadership on page 628-29 of Chapter 14. The tenth edition includes 165 examples of diverse individuals who have made a difference in their organizations. We hope that each one of your students sees themselves represented in this textbook.

Fully Revised Teaching Resource Manual 2.0 (TRM) Provides Complete Guidance for Instructors

The TRM was initially developed to provide instructors with a turnkey solution for implementing active learning with their students. It far exceeds traditional content covered in an instructor's manual by providing suggestions for creatively teaching topics, suggested videos outside of the McGraw Hill arsenal (e.g., YouTube, *The Wall Street Journal,* etc.), group exercises, lecture enhancers, and supplemental exercises that correspond with cases, videos, Self-Assessments, and Application-Based Activities. The TRM has been praised by instructors around the world for its depth, navigation, and experiential-based content. Despite this praise, we decided to undertake a major overhaul of the TRM based on (1) our reading of several recent books that focus on teaching today's students, and (2) feedback from faculty.

Moreover, our decision to overhaul the TRM also was based on our observation that many of us do not have the time to learn and apply the techniques associated with active learning. It takes knowledge, time, and effort to implement active learning in our classes, particularly in a COVID environment in which many of us are teaching online for the first time. We thus decided to further ease your preparation by developing new detailed lesson plans that incorporate active learning for every chapter learning objective for both in-person and online classes. These lesson plans are customized for each learning objective and draw from a wide variety of Connect- and non-Connect-based resources. Our hope is that they will assist you in increasing student engagement, developing career ready graduates, and promoting higher-order thinking skills.

Finally, we provide new web video links for each chapter. These free, short videos allow instructors to illustrate the practical applications of management principles. They are integrated within the detailed lesson plans for each learning objective. We also include new current online article links instructors can use to discuss material that supplements the text.

66 *A very comprehensive TRM compared to the competitors. As a department chair, I strongly recommend the TRM to my new adjuncts.* 99

—**Mark Zarycki,**
Hillsborough Community College (Brandon)

66 *[The TRM] is perhaps the most comprehensive collection of material I have seen.* 99

—**Michael Bento,**
Owens Community College

Completely revamped, revised, and updated chapters

In each chapter, we refreshed examples, research, figures, tables, statistics, and photos, as well as modified the design to accommodate new changes to this tenth edition. We also have largely replaced topics in such popular features as Example boxes, Practical Action boxes, Management in Action cases, and Legal/Ethical Challenge cases.

While the following list does not encompass all the updates and revisions, it does highlight some of the more notable changes.

CHAPTER 1

- Updated Manage U: Using Management Skills for College Success.

- Section 1.1—New Example box on efficiency versus effectiveness discusses how scientists are working to address rising food demands and changing food preferences. Revised discussion of the rewards of studying and practicing management. Updated management pay statistics.

- Section 1.3—Revised Figure 1.2 to include team leaders. Introduced "team leaders" as a new key term and added a discussion of four key elements of successful teams. Updated list of top managers. New examples of general managers. New data in Managers for Three Types of Organizations.

- Section 1.4—Completely revised section on The Manager's Roles incorporating current research on how managers spend their time.

- Section 1.5—Updated statistics in the Practical Action box on developing soft skills.

- Section 1.6—Revised the layout and flow of entire section for enhanced readability. Revised disussion of Managing for

Technological Advances (formerly Managing for Information Technology. Updated e-commerce statistics. New Example box about how direct-to-consumer genetics testing companies have harnessed big data to disrupt the health care industry. Updated discussion of Managing for Inclusion and Diversity to replace "Managing for Diversity." Updated information on Christine Lagarde. Updated details on Volkswagen emissions scandal. New example of Houston Astros ethical scandal. Introduced new key term "sustainable development" in revised discussion of Managing for Sustainable Development (formerly Managing for Sustainability) and the UN Sustainable Development Goals.

- Section 1.7—Major revision to this section included an updated list of most attractive employers, new statistics on students' career readiness, a new model of career readiness, and a new example of resilience featuring 2020 Heisman Trophy winner Joe Burrow.

- Section 1.8—Updated Career Corner on Managing Your Career Readiness with a new section on creating habits.

- New Management in Action case: Fast Fashion—Was Forever 21 Fast Enough?

CHAPTER 2

- Updated Manage U: What Type of Work Environment Do I Prefer?

- Section 2.1—New Example box explores the success of Wegmans Food Markets based on its employee- and customer-focused management. New Figure 2.1 depicts the progression of management perspectives.

- Section 2.2—Expanded coverage of Lillian Gilbreth's contribution to management science.

- Section 2.3—Updated Example box discussing open-plan offices and their impact on productivity.

- Section 2.4—This section was revised to include new coverage of evidence-based management and a new Practical Action box that discusses big data's role in evidence-based management.

- Section 2.5—New Example box illustrates how U.S. Steel uses systems theory to stay competitive.

- Section 2.6—Updated Example box applying the contingency viewpoint with manufacturers "pitching" jobs to parents of college students hoping they'll influence their children to consider open positions after high school graduation.

- Section 2.7—The old 2.7 was replaced with a new section, titled "Contemporary Approaches: The Learning Organization, High-Performance Work Practices, and Sustainable Management." Learning organizations were previously discussed in Section 2.8, and content on high-performance work practices and sustainable management is new. New Example box discusses three organizations that exhibit high-performing work practices. Shifted content on quality management to Chapter 16.

- Section 2.8—Updated Career Corner on Managing Your Career Readiness

- New Management in Action case: Vegan Leather: Earth's Friend or Foe?

- Updated Legal/Ethical Challenge: What Should You Do about an Insubordinate Employee?

CHAPTER 3

- New Manage U: Being Courageous at Work.

- Section 3.1—Updated discussion of the triple bottom line. New statistics regarding younger workers and their search for meaning.

- Section 3.2—Various content updates, including new examples of employees as internal stakeholders and an employee-owned company. Updated statistics on sole proprietorships. Updated research regarding gender diversity on boards of directors.

- Section 3.3— Reconfigured multiple sections throughout for enhanced readability. Updated statistics regarding unions, unemployment, demographic forces, sociocultural forces, and the use of drones. Updated Example box discusses

Amazon's tax breaks. Updated Example box illustrates the Dark Side of Technology. Updated figure showcases the states in which marijuana is legal. Various content updates, including company examples for international forces, special interest groups, strategic allies, and competing firms, and an updated list of "America's Most Hated Companies."

- Section 3.4—Revised introduction with new example on Bombas. Updated Example box featuring Volkswagen and ethics. Redesigned section on ethics and values, including an updated list of the six most common types of ethical misconduct at work and multiple new company examples. Updated discussion of how people learn ethics. New examples of recent SarbOx cases, white-collar crime, conflict of interest, and workplace cheating. New Figure 3.3 on global rates of unethical workplace behavior.

- Section 3.5—Updated Example box on CSR at Salesforce. Updated statistics on CEO dismissals and Bill and Melinda Gates. Updated Table 3.1 with current statistics that show how being ethically and socially responsible pays off.

- Section 3.6—New content on board characteristics, social responsibility, and firms' ethical behaviors/reputations. Introduction of new key term: CSR contracting. New Example box on corporate governance failure at Theranos.

- New Management in Action case: Who's to Blame for the College Admissions Scandal?

- Updated Legal/Ethical Challenge: Should You Apply to Have Your Student Loans Forgiven?

NEW: LEARNING MODULE 1: SHARED VALUE AND SUSTAINABLE DEVELOPMENT

This material is new to the tenth edition:

- Manage U: How Can You Contribute to a More Sustainable Future?

- Section LM 1.1—Introduces the concept of creating shared value (CSV) and explains how it differs from traditional CSR. Figure LM 1.1 introduces a model of shared value creation. A discussion of the new figure includes timely examples that illustrate how organizations create shared value. New Example boxes on shared value creation at Williams-Sonoma and the Campbell Soup Company.

- Section LM 1.2—Discusses the various stakeholders that play a role in CSV, including big and small businesses, entrepreneurs, and business schools. Includes timely examples woven throughout to illustrate the roles of different stakeholders in CSV. Figure LM 1.2 summarizes the UN Sustainable Development Goals (SDGs). New Example box on how the Bill and Melinda Gates Foundation encourages private-sector engagement with the UN SDGs. New Example box on how the start-up Ricult is pursuing CSV to empower rural farmers in developing countries.

- Section LM 1.3—Explores the progress made to date on CSV and the challenges that lie ahead for organizations that wish to pursue shared value creation. Provides recommendations

for how firms can tackle these challenges and forge ahead with CSV. Includes timely company examples woven throughout to illustrate the progress, challenges, and recommended solutions in CSV. New Example box on CSV at Revolution Foods.

CHAPTER 4

- Updated Manage U: Working Successfully Abroad: Developing Cultural Awareness.

- Section 4.1—Updated section opener with new statistics regarding U.S. imports in 2018. Updated Table 4.1 and corresponding content with competitiveness rankings for 2019. Updated Example box featuring international e-commerce company Alibaba.

- Section 4.2—Updated Example box discussing how to get an edge in the global job market.

- Section 4.3—Updated discussion on the foreign manufacturing of Apple products. An updated discussion of why companies expand internationally, including Coca-Cola, Costco, and China Investment Company. Updated examples for how companies expand internationally. Updated examples of global outsourced jobs, including an updated Table 4.2 with top exporting countries through 2018. Updated list of U.S. companies opening franchises overseas, including McDonald's and Marriott.

- Section 4.4—Updated Table 4.3 with the U.S.'s top ten trading partners through 2019. Updated content regarding tariffs with a discussion of the Trump administration as well as updated content pertaining to import quotas, dumping, and embargoes and sanctions. Updated table featuring organizations promoting international trade. Updated discussion on NAFTA and USMCA, the EU, and other trading blocs. Updated Example box to showcase the exchange rates on various common products like rent, movie tickets, and designer jeans. Updated statistics for major economies, including China, India, Brazil, Russia, and South Africa.

- Section 4.5—An updated discussion on language and personal space with a discussion on learning foreign language online and through apps. Updated Practical Action box discussing how to run an international meeting. Updated examples of expropriation, corruption, and labor abuses. An updated discussion on expatriates and why U.S. managers often fail.

- Section 4.6—Updated Career Corner: Managing Your Career Readiness.

- New Management in Action case: The Isolation of a Global Giant, which discusses Huawei.

- Updated Legal/Ethical Challenge: Should Qatar Be Hosting the 2022 World Cup?

CHAPTER 5

- Updated Manage U: Start Your Career Off Right by Planning.

- Section 5.1—New Example box on Burger King's turnaround on the back of effective planning.

- Section 5.2—Value statement content has been updated with an example from SurveyMonkey. Updated Example box on Coca-Cola includes the company's mission, vision, and values statements. An updated Example box discusses Coca-Cola's six long-term strategies.

- Section 5.3—Updated Example box pertaining to long- and short-term goals at Southwest Airlines. New section on executing plans with examples from Katerra and Handshake.

- Section 5.4—Updated table on the three types of objectives used in MBO. Updated Practical Action box on small businesses and goal setting.

- Section 5.5—New Example box applying the planning/control cycle through Pacific Gas and Electric Company.

- Section 5.6—Updated Career Corner: Managing Your Career Readiness.

- New Management in Action case: Amtrak Is on the Wrong Side of the Tracks.

- Updated Legal/Ethical Challenge: Are Profits More Important than Alzheimer's Patients?

CHAPTER 6

- Updated Manage U: Your Personal Brand Requires a Strategy.

- Section 6.1—New examples from Amazon, Fiat, and Dunkin Donuts portraying the levels of strategy. Updated Example box illustrating strategic planning at Evernote and Groove HQ.

- Section 6.2—Updated opening with coverage of Toyota's 2020 recalls. New examples from Microsoft for each of the five steps of the strategic management process.

- Section 6.3—Updated figure on SWOT analysis by changing verbiage to more closely link with organizational environment coverage in Chapter 3. Updated Example box using SWOT to analyze Toyota. Updated VRIO examples with a focus on Toyota. New Example box on Walmart's expansion to India through its purchase of Flipkart. New Figure 6.5 compares benchmarks for nine U.S. airlines.

- Section 6.4—New examples from Lululemon, Tabasco, and Bombardier for corporate strategy. Updated Dell example for discussion of the BCG Matrix.

- Section 6.5—New examples from Netflix to describe Porter's five competitive forces. New examples from companies such as Warby Parker and Viking Cruises to portray Porter's four competitive strategies. New section focuses on an executive's approach toward strategy development. We featured Jack Welch's approach toward strategy development.

- Section 6.6—Renamed Strategic Implementation: Creating, Executing, and Controlling Functional-Level Strategies. The section starts with a discussion of functional strategy using a new Figure 6.7 depicting strategic implementation at Kroger. New examples from Costco and Kroger portraying the three

core processes of business. New content on execution roadblocks as well as an updated Practical Action box on fueling execution in the workplace.

- Section 6.7—Updated Career Corner: Managing Your Career Readiness.

- New Management in Action case: La Croix is Losing the Sparkling Water Wars.

- Updated Legal/Ethical Challenge: Is Your School Selling Your Bank Accounts?

LEARNING MODULE 2: ENTREPRENUER-SHIP (Formerly Learning Module 1)

- Updated Manage U: So You Want to Start a Business?

- Section LM 2.1—New content on social entrepreneurship, highlighting it as a new key term and linking it to the concept of creating shared value. New Example box on Two Blind Brothers, a business that is making a profit and doing good at the same time. Updated with new research and new characteristic of positive intentions and attitudes. Updated small business giants from 2019. Updated Table LM 2.1 with current facts about small businesses.

- Section LM 2.2—New content on franchising that includes its advantages, disadvantages, and how to start one. Updated content on choosing a legal structure. Updated Example box featuring the start and growth of a small business. New content on why entrepreneurial ventures fail, including an introduction of four common themes.

CHAPTER 7

- Updated Manage U: How to Make Good Decisions. Includes a new section on how mindfulness can help managers make better decisions.

- Section 7.1—Updated Example box on how Starbucks used decision making to overcome a crisis. Expanded content on nonrational decision making with addition of hubris as a key term. We also updated Figure 7.2 regarding hindrances to perfectly rational decision making and provided new examples on Carlos Ghosn and Hallmark. Updated research and examples on intuition with updates to Example box on the power of intuition and Practical Action box on how to improve intuition.

- Section 7.2—Expanded content on business ethics that includes a new Figure 7.3 portraying reasons for CEO departures, updated examples of ethical lapses, and new research.

- Section 7.3—Begins with a new discussion of evidence-based decision making and career readiness. New examples of companies using evidenced-based decision making. Updated Example box on using analytics in sports. Expanded coverage of big data with new examples from companies such as Coca-Cola, Credit Suisse, Unilever, and Dallas County. A new Table 7.2 Illustrates the use of big data at

different levels of an organization, and there is a new Example box on Banco Bilbao Vizcaya Argentaria.

- Section 7.4—Content on decision-making styles was moved to Section 7.5, and this section was renamed "Artificial Intelligence Is a Powerful Decision-Making Resource." This new section starts with a discussion of autonomous devices and artificial intelligence using examples from Home Depot. New Table 7.3 demonstrates the types of AI used at six companies, including Ford, Liberty Mutual, and Amtrak. New Figure 7.5 shows the benefits of AI, and a new Practical Action box describes how career readiness skills can facilitate collaboration with robots.

- Section 7.5—Content on decision-making biases was moved to Section 7.6. This section now includes the four general decision-making styles, which was formerly Section 7.4. New examples of leaders portraying different leadership styles, including Terry Jimenez, Ursula Burns, Bob Iger, and Larry Sutton.

- Section 7.6—Content on group decision making was moved to Section 7.7 and this section was renamed "Decision-Making Biases." Biases were updated with new examples and research, as well as the addition of a tenth bias known as the categorical thinking bias.

- Section 7.7—This section now includes group decision making. "Sham participation" is introduced as a new key term under disadvantages of group decision making. New research on characteristics of group decision making. Updated table on the seven rules for brainstorming. Expanded content on project post-mortems, including new research.

- Section 7.8—Updated Career Corner: Managing Your Career Readiness.

- New Management in Action case: Juul Is Going Up in Smoke.

- Updated Legal/Ethical Challenge: Should Emotional Support Pets Be Treated the Same as Service Animals?

CHAPTER 8

- Updated Manage U: How to Get Noticed in a New Job: Fitting into an Organization's Culture in the First 60 Days

- Section 8.1—A new section title, "Aligning Culture, Structure, and Human Resource (HR) Practices to Support Strategy," was used to replace the previous title, "Aligning Strategy, Culture, and Structure." A new Figure 8.1 depicts how an organization's culture, structure, and HR practices support strategic implementation. This figure informs content and discussions throughout the chapter. New discussions of HR practices and how leadership creates alignment between culture, structure, and HR practices. Various content updates including new company examples of HR practices, leadership as a force for alignment, organizational culture, and organizational structure. New Example box on how Patagonia aligns culture, structure, and HR practices to support its strategy.

- Section 8.2—Reconfigured ordering of the discussion within this section for enhanced flow. Introduced new Figure 8.2 on the levels of organizational culture. Updated Figure 8.4: What organizational variables are associated with organizational cultures? Revised discussion of Figure 8.4. A new section titled "Preparing to Assess P-O Fit Before a Job Interview," was used to replace the section previously titled "What Does It Mean to 'Fit'?" Various content updates, including new examples of each of the three levels of culture; the various ways employees learn culture; clan, market, and hierarchy cultures; and person-organization fit. New Figure 8.4 shows meta-analytic relationships between organizational culture and various antecedents and outcomes.

- Section 8.3—This section was refocused to highlight the fact that organizations use multiple change levers simultaneously to create culture change. New examples of 10 of the 12 mechanisms for culture change are presented. New Example box on how Dr. Li Wenliang used the power of a story to change culture. New Example box on how Total used multiple culture change mechanisms to improve its safety culture.

- Section 8.4—Shifted the language used throughout this section (previously Section 8.5) to refer to the "features" of an organization rather than the "elements" of an organization. Restructured discussion of authority and centralization versus decentralization for enhanced readability. New Figure 8.5 illustrates the concept of span of control. Moved Figure 8.6 (organization chart) to this section.

- Section 8.5—Previously Section 8.6, updated title from "Basic Types of Organizational Structure" to "Eight Types of Organizational Structure." Updated Example box on Whole Foods Market's use of a horizontal design. Various content updates including a revised Figure 8.10 on matrix structure and new company examples of modular and virtual structures.

- Section 8.6—Updated Career Corner on Managing Your Career Readiness (formerly Section 8.7). New examples of companies that displayed adaptability.

- Updated Management in Action case: Wells Fargo's Sales Culture Fails the Company.

- Updated Legal/Ethical Challenge: Should Socializing Outside Work Hours Be Mandatory?

CHAPTER 9

- Updated Manage U: How to Prepare for a Job Interview.

- Section 9.1—This section was completely rewritten. Our goal was to explain how HR practices can generate superior firm performance and competitive advantage. The section starts with a new Figure 9.1 that depicts a set of five generic HR practices and illustrates them with examples from multiple companies. A new section discusses how Internal and External HR Fit Promote Strategic HRM and centers on a new Figure 9.2 that shows how HR practices, in combination with organizational culture and organizational structure, drive

successful strategic implementation. New key term, "strategic HRM", and a new example of a company that practices strategic HRM. Updated discussion of human and social capital. New discussion of two approaches to strategic HRM complete with multiple new company examples. New Example box on how T-Mobile used strategic HRM in its customer service function. New examples of HR practices at some of *Fortune's* best places to work.

- Section 9.2—New statistics on the costs of recruitment and selection. Reconfigured sections on recruitment and selection, including multiple new company examples; new data on the use of background information; a new section discussing how Fit figures into recruitment; and three new key terms: "boomerangs," "employee referrals," and "person-job fit." Updated Example box discussing the lies job applicants tell. Updated Example box listing the pros and cons of personality tests and updated information on personality tests. New discussion on the use of criminal and financial background checks in selection.

- Section 9.3—Updated statistics on benefits.

- Section 9.4—Renamed "Onboarding and Learning and Development." Opens with an updated discussion linking onboarding and learning and development to strategic HRM. New Table 9.1 on the effects of positive and negative onboarding experiences and a new discussion of onboarding best practices. Updated discussion of Figure 9.3: Five steps in the learning and development process, including new company examples and a new section on whether learning and development is worth the investment. Updated Example box on Keller Williams and its learning and development program.

- Section 9.5—Renamed "Performance Management." Reconfigured section "Performance Appraisals: Are They Worthwhile?" and revised discussion of forced ranking, with new company examples in both. New Example box on performance management at Regeneron. New content on best practices for 360-degree performance appraisals. New company examples for customer appraisals and 360-degree assessments.

- Section 9.6—Reconfigured discussions of transfers as well as disciplining and demotion for enhanced readability. New content on tips for managing the demotion process. Updated discussion of firings and introduced new key term: "employment at will."

- Section 9.7—Updated statistics on minimum wage, bullying, and workplace discrimination. Updated Example box discussing sexual harassment at work. Reconfigured discussions of bullying and what managers can do to prevent sexual harassment. New examples of affirmative action and a company using AI to reduce discrimination in hiring decisions.

- Section 9.8—Opens with updated statistics on labor unions. Updated Figure 9.5 showing right-to-work states. Updated Table 9.5 on union membership. Updated Table 9.6 on four

kinds of workplace labor arrangements. New company examples of two-tier wage rates and arbitration.

- Section 9.9—Updated Career Corner feature: Managing Your Career Readiness. Revised discussion of becoming a better receiver with new material on listening and self-compassion. Introduced new key terms: self-compassion and psychological capital.

- Updated Management in Action case: Difficulties Attracting and Retaining Human Capital in the Nursing Profession.

- Updated Legal/Ethical Challenge: Should Noncompete Agreements Be Legal? New company example.

CHAPTER 10

- Updated Manage U: How Can I Be More Creative at Work? Introduced new key term: "creativity."

- Section 10.1—New Example box discussing radical change in the movie industry. New example box on reactive change discussing religious practices during COVID-19. Various content updates, including new examples of the supertrends shaping the future of business; proactive change; technological advancements as forces for change; shareholder, customer, and broader stakeholder concerns; and managers' behavior. Updated example of human resource concerns and new data on demographic characteristics as forces for change.

- Section 10.2—Renamed "Forms and Models of Change." New example of very threatening, radically innovative change. New example of Walmart's use of robots in its stores woven throughout discussion of Lewin's Change Model. Reconfigured discussions of force-field analysis and applying the systems model of change for enhanced readability. New company example to illustrate application of the systems model of change.

- Section 10.3—A new section title, "Improving Individual, Team, and Organizational Performance," was used to explain the uses of OD: It replaces the previous title "Managing Conflict." New Example box on career readiness interventions. Reconfigured discussion of how OD works for enhanced readability. New example of conflict in a company and revitalizing organizations.

- Section 10.4—Updated introduction section with new statistics and a new example. Content updates throughout, including new examples of product innovation, process innovation, improvement innovation, new-direction innovation, innovation strategy, commitment from senior leaders, how organizational structure and processes can promote innovation, crowdsourcing, developing the necessary human capital for innovation, and using resources for innovation. New section and example discussing whether innovation can go too far. Updated discussion of the components of an innovation system. Updated discussion of human resource policies, practices, and procedures along with a new company example. Updated Table 10.1: The

world's most innovative companies. Updated Example box: IDEO's Approach to Innovation.

- Section 10.6 —Updated Career Corner feature: Managing Your Career Readiness. Reconfigured discussion of Applying Self-Affirmation Theory.

- New Management in Action case: Were Deadly COVID-19 Outbreaks Aboard Carnival Cruise Ships the Result of Managers' Resistance to Change?

- New Legal/Ethical Challenge: Does Clearview Technology Violate Rights?

CHAPTER 11

- Updated Manage U: Making Positive First Impressions.

- Section 11.1—Opens with updated information and statistics for employment and personality testing and the Big Five personality dimensions. Updated research regarding personality and individual behavior and work attitudes. Expanded content on emotional intelligence with a new table on the traits associated with EI and the related career readiness competencies. Updated Practical Action box on how technology can be used to develop emotional intelligence.

- Section 11.2—Updated research on values and behavior, as well as both research and statistics for attitudes. Updated Practical Action box on using cognitive reframing to reduce cognitive dissonance.

- Section 11.3—Updated research, statistics, and examples pertaining to distortions in perception. Expanded coverage of implicit bias to include its effects on employment decisions, courtroom decisions, utilization of technology. Updated Example box discussing the halo effect and how body weight affects careers. Updated Example box on the Pygmalion effect.

- Section 11.4—Opens with new content on employee engagement and a new Figure 11.3 showing the percentage of fully engaged employees around the world. New coverage of the four ways managers can increase employee engagement: design meaningful work, improve supervisor-employee relations, provide learning and development opportunities, and reduce stressors. Updated research, examples, and statistics on job satisfaction; organizational commitment; and important workplace behaviors like organizational citizenship, counterproductive behavior, performance and productivity, and absenteeism and turnover. Entirely new focus on prosocial behavior and prosocial motivation with a new Figure 11.4 depicting a model of prosocial behavior. "Prosocial behavior (PSB)" and "prosocial motivation (PSM)" are new key terms. This new content includes new research and examples from both the Bill and Melinda Gates Foundation and the coronavirus pandemic. Updated Example box on toxic workplaces.

- Section 11.5—Updated examples, research, and statistics regarding trends in workplace diversity, including age,

gender, race, and sexual orientation. Updated research and examples pertaining to barriers to diversity. Updated Example box showcasing Ultimate Software.

- Section 11.6—Updated research, examples, and statistics on stress and its consequences. New Figure 11.6 shows the relationship between stress and performance. Updated research and examples on sources of stress. Expanded content on employee assistance programs with new statistics. Updated Example box showcasing Google's wellness initiatives.

- Section 11.7—Updated Career Corner: Managing Your Career Readiness.

- New Management in Action case: Emotional Baggage at Away.

- Updated Legal/Ethical Challenge: Should Airlines Accommodate Oversized People?

CHAPTER 12

- Updated Manage U: Managing for Motivation: Building your Own Motivation.

- Section 12.1—Updated introduction section and updated discussion of student loan debt and repayment. New examples of wellness incentives and intrinsic rewards.

- Section 12.2—Reconfigured discussions of Using the Hierarchy of Needs to Motivate Employees, McClelland's Acquired Needs Theory, and Using Two-Factor Theory to Motivate Employees for enhanced readability. New company example of two-factor theory. Updated example for competence and new examples of autonomy and relatedness in discussions of Deci and Ryan's Self-Determination Theory. Updated examples of hygiene factors and motivating factors.

- Section 12.3—New Example box on employee activism. New Example box on Dr. Anne-Marie Imafidon. Reconfigured discussions of equity/justice theory, expectancy theory, stretch goals, and two types of goal orientations for enhanced readability and clarity. Reconfigured discussion of practical results of goal-setting theory along with new company examples. Updated data on CEO compensation and new statistics on the desire for voice. New examples of employee perceptions of injustice, employee voice, appeals process, and instrumentality. New example of valence, discussing the rewards preferred by various generations of workers.

- Section 12.4—Updated introduction with new statistics on the percentage of people who are bored with their jobs. Reconfigured discussion of Fitting Jobs to People and how the Job Characteristics Model works for enhanced readability. New company examples of job enrichment and job redesign.

- Section 12.5—New title of Figure 12.10: "Four types of behavior modification" and a reconfigured discussion throughout this section that centers on behavior modification.

- Section 12.6—Reconfigured discussion of characteristics of the best incentive compensation plans, work-life benefits, and the need for a positive work environment for enhanced readability. Updated examples of companies that use bonuses, profit sharing, and stock options. Updated statistics on learning and development. New title of section "The Need for Personal Growth" to replace title "The Need to Expand Skills." New title of section "The Need for Meaningful Work" to replace title "The Need to Matter—Finding Meaning in Work" along with three new examples in this section.

- Section 12.7—Updated Career Corner feature: Managing Your Career Readiness. Reconfigured discussion of "the self-management process" for enhanced readability and clarity. New discussion of recharging.

- New Management in Action case: What Motivated Workers in the Face of a Pandemic?

- Updated Legal/Ethical Challenge: Are Workplace Wellness Programs Using Proper Motivational Tools?

CHAPTER 13

- Updated Manage U: Managing Team Conflict Like a Pro.

- Section 13.1—Updated research and new examples pertaining to teams. New Example box showcasing T-Mobile's approach to cross-functional teams. Expanded content on virtual teams with new statistics. Updated Practical Action box regarding best practices for virtual teams.

- Section 13.2—Updated content on punctuated equilibrium and its tie to Brexit.

- Section 13.3—Updated examples, research, and statistics on collaboration. Expanded content on trust with the addition of the trust triangle and its drivers. Revised Example box focuses on building trust using the trust triangle. Updated Practical Action box on building effective team norms. Expanded content on team reflexivity by linking with post-mortems.

- Section 13.4—Updated research and examples on conflict. Expanded and updated the discussion on kinds of conflict and included coverage of envy as a source of conflict. Updated Practical Action box on devil's advocacy. New content on career readiness competencies to help you better handle conflict. Updated research on common conflict-handling styles.

- Section 13.5—Updated Career Corner: Managing Your Career Readiness.

- New Management in Action case: Must See Quarantine TV.

- Updated Legal/Ethical Challenge: Recreational Marijuana Use: A Manager's Quandary.

CHAPTER 14

- Updated Manage U: Improving Your Leadership Skills.

- Section 14.1—Reconfigured discussion on "What Is the Difference between Leading and Managing?" for enhanced

readability. Updated Table 14.1 to include coping with complexity and coping with change. Updated discussion of sources of power to include sixth source—informational power. New examples of leadership versus management and all six types of power. New examples of all nine influence tactics in Table 14.2. New title of section "How to Use the Tactics to Influence Outcomes" to replace title "Match Tactics to Influence Outcomes" along with updates to the lessons from research and practice.

- Section 14.2—Updated Table 14.3 to clarify the difference between positive interpersonal attributes and negative interpersonal attributes. Completely revised discussion of "what do we know about gender and leadership," including new examples of female leaders, a new Example box on gender and leadership during a crisis, and updated statistics on gender and leadership. Updated examples of three of the four basic skills for leaders in Table 14.4. New examples of dark triad traits, an organization that uses personality assessments, and a company that values cross-cultural competency.

- Section 14.3—Reconfigured discussion of Behavioral Approaches to focus on task-oriented behavior and relationship-oriented behavior. Moved discussion of transformational and transactional leadership to Section 14.5. New comparison of the results of the Ohio State and University of Michigan studies. New examples of task-oriented and relationship-oriented leadership.

- Section 14.4—Reconfigured discussion of the two leadership orientations in Fiedler's model for enhanced readability. New discussion of what the path–goal theory looks like in practice along with a new example of a leader using this approach.

- Section 14.5—New title "The Full-Range Model: Using Transactional and Transformational Leadership" to replace title "The Uses of Transformational Leadership." Updated discussion in this section to focus on the full-range model, which includes both transactional and transformational leadership. New examples of transactional leadership, transformational leadership, idealized influence, individualized consideration, and intellectual stimulation. New Example box featuring Ann-Marie Campbell as a leader who is both transactional and transformational. Revised discussions of Four Key Behaviors of Transformational Leaders and So What Do We Know about Transformational Leadership for enhanced readability.

- Section 14.6—New title "Contemporary Perspectives and Concepts" to replace "Three Additional Perspectives." Moved discussions of servant leadership, empowering leadership, ethical leadership, and the role of followers to this section. Updated discussions of the LMX model and Humility for enhanced readability. New examples of servant leadership, a humble leader, and ethical leadership. Updated discussion of Satya Nadella as a humble leader and an updated Practical Action box that discusses how to be a good leader by being a good follower. New example of Bernard Tyson woven

throughout discussion of Empowering Leadership. Updated research on ethical leadership. New section on Abusive Supervision as a contemporary leadership concept, including discussions of what causes abusive supervision, how it affects employees, and how organizations might deal with it.

- Section 14.7—Updated Career Corner: Managing Your Career Readiness. Reconfigured section on Becoming More Self-Aware for enhanced readability.

- New Management in Action case: Adam Neumann's Rise and Fall at WeWork.

- Updated Legal/Ethical Challenge: Should Starbucks Have a Corporate Loitering Policy?

CHAPTER 15

- New Manage U: Improving Your Use of Empathy.

- Section 15.1—New coverage of noise focuses on four components: physical, psychological, semantic, and physiological. Updated research on media richness and selecting the best medium. New example involving Captain Brett Crozier regarding the incorrect choice of communication medium. New Example box on how two health systems used the contingency approach to communication.

- Section 15.2—New examples of downward and external communication. New material on four ways managers can reduce negative aspects of the grapevine. Updated research on the grapevine. New Practical Action box offering tips for improving meetings.

- Section 15.3— Revised focus of Table 15.2 to center on how barriers happen in various steps of the communication process. Reconfigured discussions of all of the barriers to communication for enhanced readability. New examples of physical distance and facial expressions as communication barriers. New title "Attentional Issues" to replace title "Faulty Listening Skills" along with an updated discussion and two new suggestions for reducing the impact of these issues on communication. Updated discussion and statistics on generational differences as communication barriers. New Practical Action box on improving your cross-cultural communication fluency. Updated discussion of touch as a communication barrier with new general guidelines for physical affection at work. Revised discussion of gender differences as communication barriers to include a revised Table 15.3 that focuses on masculine and feminine social norms for communication.

- Section 15.4—Completely new content on how social media has changed our lives with new examples and statistics, as well as an updated figure showing the use of social media across various age groups. Updated research on social media and managerial and organizational effectiveness. Updated Practical Action box on building your own social media brand. New examples and research for employee and employer productivity, crowdsourcing, sales and brand recognition,

and reputation. Updated examples, statistics, table, and research pertaining to the downsides of social media, including new content on false information and fake news. New Practical Action box on defending against fake news. Updated table showing elements of an effective social media policy. New Example box illustrating samples of social media policies at IBM, Best Buy, Intel, Walmart, *Washington Post*, and GAP.

- Section 15.5—Reconfigured discussion of Nondefensive Communication for enhanced readability and included three suggestions for avoiding defensive communication and fostering nondefensive communication. Revised discussion of Being an Effective Listener with new points about active listening. Revised discussion of five recommendations for improving your listening skills with new examples throughout. New example of empathy. Revised discussion of Being an Effective Speaker for enhanced readability along with the inclusion of new statistics.

- Section 15.6—Updated Career Corner feature: Managing Your Career Readiness.

- Updated Management in Action case: Fyre and Fury.

- New Legal/Ethical Challenge: The Cost of Speaking Out Against Your Employer.

CHAPTER 16

- Updated Manage U: Mentors Can Help You Control Your Career.

- Section 16.1—New examples on why control is needed from higher education, the coronavirus pandemic, Ford, General Electric, and Amazon. Types of control moved to next section.

- Section 16.2—Renamed "The Control Process and Types of Control." Revamped section opens with new examples and research pertaining to steps in the control process. Updated Example box on how UPS uses control to ensure success. Coverage of the types of control is now in this section with new examples from Southwest, the trucking industry, and Cigna.

- Section 16.3—Renamed "What Should Managers Control?" with a new focus on how the balanced scorecard can be used to effectively control an organization. Section opens with a new introduction and examples from Walmart, United

Airlines, and the coronavirus pandemic. New research and examples for all four perspectives of the balanced scorecard from companies including ExxonMobil, Ritz Carlton, and Phoenix Sintered Metals. The financial perspective includes new content on budgets, financial statements (including coverage of income statements, balance sheets, and statements of cash flows), and financial ratios, as well as a new table depicting select ratios. Customer perspective includes expanded coverage on customer satisfaction and retention. Internal business perspective includes expanded coverage of productivity, benchmarking, best practices, efficiency, quality, and safety. Innovation and learning perspective includes new content on employee attitudes, turnover, resource capabilities, and culture. Updated strategy map for Keurig Dr. Pepper.

- Section 16.4—This section now focuses on total quality management. Opens with an updated example of the 2019 Malcolm Baldrige National Quality Award recipient. Incorporation of content on quality, quality control, and quality assurance that used to be in Chapter 2. Updated research and examples pertaining to core TQM principles. Updated Example box on the Hyundai Genesis. Updated Example box on Kaizen methods. Updated Example box on how Nordstrom and Trader Joe's provide excellent customer service. Updated research, examples, and statistics on TQM tools, techniques, and standards, including six sigma, lean six sigma, and ISO 9000/14000 series.

- Section 16.5—New section titled "Contemporary Control Issues" focuses on artificial intelligence and employee tracking and monitoring. Section opens with new research, statistics, and examples from the CDC, Siemens, and Trenitalia, portraying how artificial intelligence can be used to effectively control an organization. New content on the advantages and disadvantages of employee monitoring and tracking with a new Example box on Three Square Market's practice of microchipping employees.

- Section 16.6—Updated Career Corner: Managing Your Career Readiness.

- New Management in Action case: The U.S. Shale Boom . . . and Bust.

- Updated Legal/Ethical Challenge: Using GPS to Track Employees.

Kinicki/Breaux Soignet, *Management: A Practical Introduction*, 10e, empowers students to develop the management career skills necessary in everyday life through the practical and relevant application of theory. Developed to help students learn management with a purpose, Kinicki/Breaux Soignet 10e takes a student-centered approach. **The revision expands its strategic career readiness theme and includes new coverage on the recently proposed management principle of creating shared value (CSV) and sustainable development.** The hallmark strengths that have made it the market best-seller have been maintained and include:

- A student-centered approach to learning.
- Imaginative writing for readability and reinforcement.
- Emphasis on practicality.
- Resources that work.

Our product covers the principles that most management instructors have come to expect in an Introductory text—planning, organizing, leading, and controlling—plus current issues that students need to be to be aware of to succeed: career readiness, customer focus, globalism, diversity, ethics, social media, entrepreneurship, teams, innovation, artificial intelligence, big data, and person-organization fit.

> ❝ *The textbook does a good job covering the role of a manager. I would recommend [it] to any instructor who is teaching the Principles of Management course.* ❞
>
> **—Jerry D. Stevens,**
> *Texas Tech University*

> ❝ *Written with the modern student in mind. [This] book takes a very practical approach to management theory (and) especially shows how it applies to (someone) just starting a career.* ❞
>
> **—William Belcher,**
> *Troy University*

Based on a wealth of instructor feedback and blending Angelo's scholarship, teaching, publishing, and management-consulting with Denise's academic background and writing ability, we have worked tirelessly to create a research-based yet highly readable, practical, and motivational product for the introductory principles of management course. Our goal is to make a difference in the lives of you and your students.

Focus on Career Readiness

Global research shows that employers are finding it hard to find college graduates who possess the skills needed to be successful. These employers also think that colleges and universities need to do a better job making students career ready. Our goal in 10e is to contribute to overcoming this problem in two ways. First, we expanded and updated the coverage of career readiness in the product. Second, we developed activities for both online and face-to-face teaching that professors can use to develop students career readiness competencies. They are contained in our novel Teaching Resources Manual (TRM).

Building Your Career Readiness

Chapter 1 contains a section devoted to explaining the need, value, and process for becoming career ready. It includes a model of career readiness along with a table of competencies desired by employers.

1.7 Building Your Career Readiness

THE BIG PICTURE

Companies want to hire *career-ready* college graduates. In this section we describe a model of career readiness and offer tips for building your readiness.

LO 1-7

Define the core competencies, knowledge, soft skills, attitudes, and other characteristics needed for career readiness and discuss how they can be developed.

About 53,000 undergraduate students from 218 universities across the United States rated 2019's most attractive employers. The top 10 were (1) Google, (2) JPMorgan Chase, (3) Amazon, (4) Apple, (5) Goldman Sachs, (6) The Walt Disney Company, (7), Nike, (8) Deloitte, (9) Netflix, and (10) EY (Ernst & Young).[132] Would you like to work at these companies or others like them? If so, you need to be career ready.

Career readiness represents the extent to which you possess the knowledge, skills, and attributes desired by employers. How ready do you believe you are? Recent surveys of college students and employers reveal a big gap in the degree of readiness each group perceives in students. *Figure 1.3* shows some key results of a study of 201 employers and 4,213 graduating seniors. The majority of students rated themselves as career-ready on 6 of 7 skills, while the majority of employers perceived students to be well-prepared on only 3 of the skills. The three largest gaps were in professionalism/work ethic, leadership, and oral/written communication, skills that are very important to employers.[133] Other studies have similarly demonstrated that employers see a major skills gap in college students' interpersonal skills.[134]

FIGURE 1.3

Employers and college grads disagree about levels of career readiness

Sources: National Association of Colleges and Employers, "Are College Graduates 'Career Ready?" February 19, 2018, https://www.naceweb.org/career-readiness/competencies/are-college-graduates-career-ready/. Data derived from NACE's "Job Outlook 2018" and "The Class of 2017 Student Survey Report."

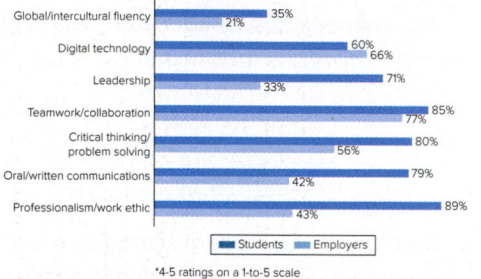

Proportions Saying They/Recent College Graduates Are Proficient in Each Competency*

- Global/intercultural fluency: 35%, 21%
- Digital technology: 60%, 66%
- Leadership: 71%, 33%
- Teamwork/collaboration: 85%, 77%
- Critical thinking/problem solving: 80%, 56%
- Oral/written communications: 79%, 42%
- Professionalism/work ethic: 89%, 43%

■ Students ■ Employers

*4–5 ratings on a 1-to-5 scale

The good news is that merely acknowledging the existence of these gaps will impress potential employers because companies prefer to hire people with realistic self-perceptions. This underscores the need to obtain information about your strengths and weaknesses throughout your career.

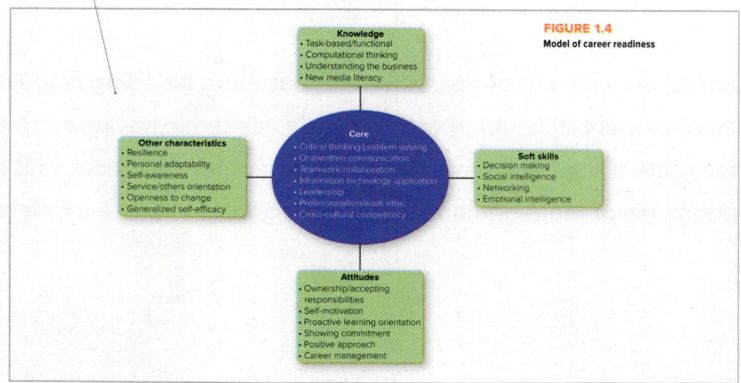

FIGURE 1.4

Model of career readiness

SELF-ASSESSMENT 1.2   CAREER READINESS

To What Extent Do You Accept Responsibility for Your Actions?

People are more likely to work diligently toward accomplishing their goals and accept performance feedback when they accept responsibility for their actions. They also are less likely to blame others for their mistakes or poor performance. This self-assessment allows you to determine your status regarding this important attitude. The survey feedback will help you to maintain or improve your attitude about taking ownership/responsibility for your actions.

Please be prepared to answer these questions if your instructor has assigned Self-Assessment 1.2 in Connect.

1. Do you have a strong attitude about accepting responsibility for your actions? Do you agree with these results? Explain your thinking.

2. What can you do to increase the strength of this attitude?

3. What things would you say during an interview to demonstrate that you possess the career readiness competency of ownership/accepting responsibility?

Self-Assessments

Over 38 Self-Assessments allow students to assess the extent to which they possess aspects of the career readiness competencies desired by employers.

Career Corner

Each chapter concludes with a section entitled "Career Corner: Managing Your Career Readiness." The material provides students with practical tips for developing targeted career readiness competencies. It also explains the linkage between the content covered in the chapter and the career readiness competencies desired by employers.

1.8 Career Corner: Managing Your Career Readiness

The goal of this section is to help you apply what you learn to building your career readiness. Let's begin with three keys to success:

1. It's your responsibility to manage your career. Don't count on others.
2. Personal reflection, motivation, commitment, and experimentation are essential.
3. Success is achieved by following a process. A **process** is defined as a series of actions or steps followed to bring about a desired result.

LO 1-8
Describe the process for managing your career readiness.

A Process for Developing Career Readiness

Figure 1.5 illustrates a process to guide the pursuit of managing your career readiness. We recommend the following four steps:

Step 1.   The first step entails examining the list of career readiness competencies in Table 1.2 and picking two or three that impact your current performance at school, work, or extracurricular activities. You then need to assess your skill level for these competencies. This textbook contains 64 self-assessments you can take for this purpose. The first one was presented on page 29.

Step 2.   The second step requires you to consider how you can use the material covered in a chapter to develop your targeted career readiness competencies. For example, do your targeted competencies at this point relate to any of the four functions of management: planning, organizing, leading, or controlling? If yes, reflect on what you learned while reading material regarding the functions of management and consider how you can apply ideas, concepts, or suggestions that were discussed.

Concept Mastery

New exercises in Connect allow students to demonstrate lower levels of learning regarding career readiness. The TRM provides opportunities for higher levels of learning for career readiness competencies.

Student-Centered Approach to Learning

Our writing style and product design is based on neuroscience research. Greater learning occurs when information is "chunked" to keep student attention. We break down topics into easily digestible portions with purposeful pedagogy to make theories and concepts easier to learn and apply. We made a concerted effort to increase the amount of chunked material in 10e. This accounts for the use of purposeful color, an extensive photo program, bulleted lists, and headings to appeal to the visual sensibilities, time constraints, and diverse learning styles of today's students.

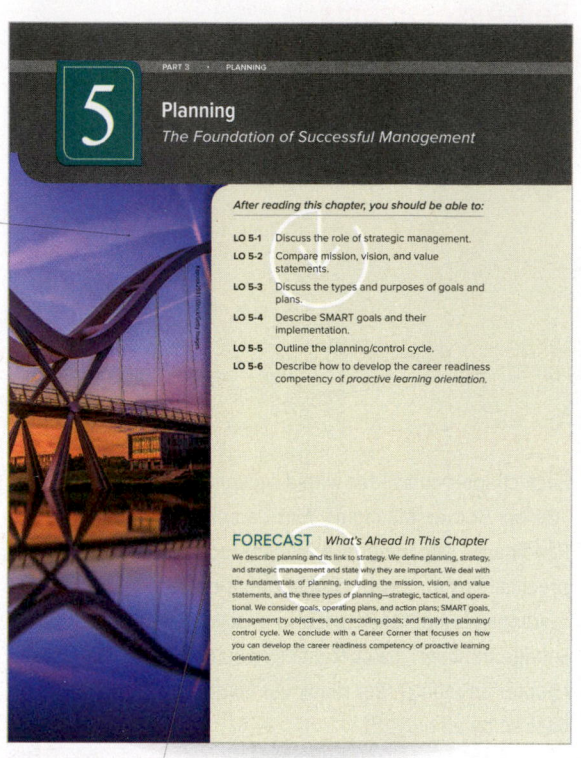

Chapter Openers

Each chapter begins with a list of key learning objectives that appeal to students' concern about "what's in it for me?" and to help them read with purpose.

2.1 Evolving Viewpoints: How We Got to Today's Management Outlook

THE BIG PICTURE

This section provides an overview of management history, starting with an overview of Peter Drucker's four fundamental principles of management. We also review six reasons for studying management theory.

Chapter Sections

Within each chapter, sections are organized according to the major learning objectives. Generous use of headings and bulleted lists provide students with bite-sized chunks of information to facilitate retention. Each section begins with a recap of the **Learning Objective** and includes **The Big Picture**, which presents an overview of how the section addresses the stated objective.

Forecast

Shown below the learning objectives, the forecast provides a high-level of summary of what is covered in the chapter.

> *The good problem to have with this book and related materials is that the resources available . . . enhance student learning.*

—**Gerald Schoenfeld,**
Florida Gulf Coast University

> *The book is well organized and offers a good variety of resources and activities [that can be] used in a face-to-face or online format.*

—**Patricia Lanier,**
University of Louisiana at Lafayette

Imaginative Writing for Readability and Reinforcement

Research shows that products written in an imaginative, story-telling style significantly improve students' ability to retain information. We employ numerous journalistic devices to make the material engaging and relevant to students lives.

Example boxes

We utilize numerous Example boxes to emphasize the practical applications of business. These mini cases use snapshots of real-world companies to explain text concepts. "Your Call" questions stimulate class discussions and help students develop their critical thinking skills.

EXAMPLE   Local Communities as Stakeholders: Does Amazon Really Need Tax Breaks?

The Amazon Spheres at its urban campus in the Belltown neighborhood of Seattle. Paul Christian Gordon/Alamy Stock Photo

Amazon is becoming one of Ohio's largest employers,[43] and in Summer 2019 the company announced it would open two new fulfillment centers in the state, bringing the state's total number of Amazon fulfillment centers up to six.[44] Since 2016 Amazon has received more than $15.8 million in tax credits for its facilities in Ohio. The city of Akron also plans to give Amazon an estimated $17 million dollar tax rebate over 30 years in exchange for the company locating its facility there.[45]

Amazon's tax breaks are not confined to Ohio. In fact, in 2019, Amazon saved at least $171.9 million dollars due to tax incentives it received from its distribution centers across the United States.[46] These tax breaks are popular because "incentives give companies the ability to shop around in various states and ask for breaks," said Adam Michel, Washington, D.C.–based senior policy analyst. He added, "Because of the perceived ability of these firms to choose somewhere else, a lot of local governments feel pressure to give them sweetheart deals to lure them to their locality."[47]

Impacts on Local Economies. New physical facilities bring great economic benefits according to Amazon and others who support the use of tax incentives to lure companies to build warehouses and distribution centers in their locations. Amazon reasons that across its six facilities in Ohio it will have created more than 11,000 jobs in the state.[48] The company also says that its presence in Illinois has resulted in more than $4 billion worth of investments in the state since 2010.[49] Finally, Amazon estimates that it has created at least 7,000 jobs in Illinois outside of Amazon.[50]

Not everyone agrees that these tax incentives create jobs or do much to boost local economies. And since Amazon's infamous decision to retreat from its planned second headquarters in New York (which would have meant $3.4 billion in tax incentives and grants for the company),[51] lawmakers in at least seven states are working on legislation aimed at outlawing these incentives.[52]

Some economists have warned that giving huge tax breaks to incoming businesses does little more than rob cities of resources needed by arguably more important entities like their school, housing, and transportation systems. What's more, these systems also may need expensive upgrades and improvements to accommodate the huge influx of Amazon workers moving in, and existing businesses and individual taxpayers would end up footing the bill.[53]

San Jose, California, had been one of the cities vying for Amazon's second headquarters, but Mayor Sam Liccardo's offer made it clear that the e-commerce giant would receive no tax incentives for locating there. He said, "If you're offering incentives, those are dollars you could use to be building out transit . . . supporting an ecosystem of talent development."[54] Several studies suggest that tax incentives often fail to deliver the benefits they promise, and that in some cases, tax breaks may even harm employment growth and local economies.[55]

YOUR CALL

Do you think tax breaks for big companies like Amazon benefit local communities? Should these companies continue to receive tax breaks when they build new facilities? Why or why not?

> " [Has the] right level of rigor for the course . . . contains a logical structure of material . . . [and] current examples for students to relate to [their] course work. "
>
> **—Jennifer Trout,**
> *Rasmussen College*

> " I devoted several weeks to reviewing textbooks. I started with 12, narrowed it down to 3 and Kinicki came up as my first choice. It is easy to read and not boring. Those are both important to me. "
>
> **—Mihran Aroian,**
> *University of Texas at Austin*

Extended Emphasis on Practicality

Students are more engaged and motivated when they connect with the material being taught. This implies that textbook examples and illustrations must be relevant to readers. We accomplish this by using hundreds of practical examples that are both timely and inclusive. For example, we used 56 examples to illustrate how management principles could be applied to handling the coronavirus pandemic in 2020, and we incorporated 165 examples of diverse individuals who have made a difference in their organizations. Given the diversity of today's students, our use of these examples should resonate with students.

We want this tenth edition to be a cherished resource that students keep as they move into future courses and their future careers. We give students a great deal of practical advice in addition to covering the fundamental concepts of management.

Practical Action boxes Practical Action boxes offer students practical and interesting advice on issues they will face in the workplace.

PRACTICAL ACTION	Setting Goals for a Small Business

Goal setting can seem like an intimidating process, but it's both a necessary and a helpful one for the millions of small businesses (defined as having 500 or fewer employees) in the United States. In fact, a research study of 231 small businesses found that goal setting had a positive impact on the firm's performance.[57] These findings are important, particularly because small businesses account for 44% of U.S. economic activity and two-thirds of the nation's new jobs.[58]

The Great Lakes Brewing Company, Ohio's first craft brewery, is a good example of goal setting in small businesses.[59]

1. **Break large goals down into smaller ones:** Great Lakes developed a five-year strategic plan in 2013 and focused on three "bottom lines": social, economic, and environmental. We'll focus on the social bottom line, which the brewery breaks down into areas such as equitable compensation, safety, and employee wellness. Safety is then broken down into a measurable goal, which is to keep the number of safety-related incidents (recordable incident rate) at or below the industry average for any given year.

2. **Track progress toward goals:** Great Lakes has a safety committee that meets regularly to track the number of safety-related incidents at its factory. For example, in 2013 it was 3.05 and in 2018 it was 2.94. It then compares the incidents to that year's industry average (the industry average in 2018 was 3.1). The company knows it is meeting its goal if its incident rate is below the industry average.

3. **Keep the goal in sight:** The brewery's management knows it must take action to ensure safety goals are met. For example, the company hired a full-time safety manager in 2015 to "give more attention to the development of safety programs and culture." The company also made some changes in 2017 to improve safety, such as changing its chemical storage policies and providing training and equipment for respiratory protection.

4. **Accept that setbacks will happen:** Just because the company strives to make improvements doesn't mean the number of safety-related incidents will always decrease. For example, Great Lakes' incident rate significantly increased from 0.48 in 2017 to 2.94 in 2018. Based on this setback, the company decided to change its safety manager in 2019 and re-evaluate its safety program.

5. **Celebrate success:** Great Lakes celebrated achieving 90% overall goal attainment in 2018. In recognition of this achievement, the company gave employees monetary bonuses.

YOUR CALL

What major goal of your own have you broken into smaller parts? If you have never done this, for what future goal do you think it would be an effective strategy for you?

SELF-ASSESSMENT 13.1   CAREER READINESS

Attitudes toward Teamwork

The following survey was designed to assess your attitude toward teamwork. Please be prepared to answer these questions if your instructor has assigned Self-Assessment 13.1 in Connect.

1. What is your attitude toward teamwork?

2. If you do not have a positive teamwork attitude, consider the reason and identify what you might do to foster a more positive attitude.

3. What might you say during an interview to demonstrate that you possess the competency of teamwork/collaboration?

Self-Assessments Self-Assessment evaluations help students relate what they are learning to their own experiences and promote self-reflection, engagement, and development of their career readiness. Of the 64 total Self-Assessments included, nearly 38 of them pertain to a career readiness competency. For each of these, students are asked to consider how they might display the competency in an employment interview.

Management in Action cases Rather than using stories about companies, the new Management in Action cases now focus on higher levels of learning by asking students to solve real organizational problems using relevant management concepts. They develop students' core career readiness competencies of critical thinking and problem solving.

Management in Action

Amtrak Is on the Wrong Side of the Tracks

The National Railroad Passenger Corporation, better known as Amtrak, began operations in 1971. The railroad has more than 20,000 employees and serves more than 500 destinations in the United States and Canada on more than 21,400 miles of track. Amtrak customers took 32.5 million trips in 2019, setting a record year-over-year increase of 800,000 passengers.[72]

Congress created Amtrak because private railroads were failing. By the 1940s, rail travel became less popular as Americans chose buses, planes, and cars to get around the country. Eventually, the U.S. government consolidated the majority of passenger rail service under Amtrak's umbrella. The federal government is Amtrak's majority stockholder and guarantees its financial support, but the company is operated as a for-profit organization rather than a government entity.

Though it was created to save an unprofitable railroad system, Amtrak itself has never earned a profit since its inception. For example, the company lost $194 million and $170 million in 2017 and 2018, respectively.

Americans continue to choose other modes of transportation over Amtrak, and government subsidies are all that stand between the railroad and bankruptcy.[73]

Let's take a closer look at what's going on at America's only high-speed rail provider.

A LOSING MODEL

One of Amtrak's biggest problems is its price. For example, a four-hour Amtrak train from New York City to Boston is more expensive than hopping on a one-hour flight. Amtrak charges these high fares on popular Northeastern routes because its other routes across the country are either unprofitable or operating at a loss.[74] According to *Virginia Mercury*, ridership may be able to grow if Amtrak's prices were reduced.[75]

Amtrak's other challenge is America's sheer size. It is the fourth largest country in the world with 3.8 million square miles of land. Compare this with Japan's rail service, which has to cover an area smaller than the state of California. All of this rail needs maintenance and repair, which Amtrak can't afford. For example,

Legal/Ethical Challenge cases Legal/Ethical Challenge cases ask students to resolve real ethical challenges faced by managers and organizations. They help develop students' critical thinking and problem-solving skills around ethical issues.

Legal/Ethical Challenge

To Delay or Not to Delay?

You have been hired by a vice president of a national company to create an employee attitude survey, to administer it to all employees, and to interpret the results. You have known this vice president for more than 10 years and have worked for her on several occasions. She trusts and likes you, and you trust and like her. You have completed your work and now are ready to present the findings and your interpretations to the vice president's management team. The vice president has told you that she wants your honest interpretation of the results, because she is planning to make changes based on the results. Based on this discussion, your report clearly identifies several strengths and weaknesses that need to be addressed. For example, employees feel that they are working too hard and that management does not care about providing good customer service. At the meeting you will be presenting the results and your interpretations to a group of 15 managers. You also have known most of these managers for at least five years.

You arrive for the presentation armed with slides, handouts, and specific recommendations. Your slides are loaded on the computer, and most of the participants have arrived. They are drinking coffee and telling you how enthused they are about hearing your presentation. You also are excited to share your insights. Ten minutes before the presentation is set to begin,

however, the vice president takes you out of the meeting room and says she wants to talk with you about your presentation. The two of you go to another office, and she closes the door. She then tells you that her boss's boss decided to come to the presentation unannounced. She thinks that he is coming to the presentation to look solely for negative information in your report. He does not like the vice president and wants to replace her with one of his friends. If you present your results as planned, it will provide this individual with the information he needs to create serious problems for the vice president. Knowing this, the vice president asks you to find some way to postpone your presentation. You have 10 minutes to decide what to do.

SOLVING THE CHALLENGE

What would you do?

1. Deliver the presentation as planned.
2. Give the presentation but skip over the negative results.
3. Go back to the meeting room and announce that your spouse has had an accident at home and you must leave immediately. You tell the group that you just received this message and that you will contact the vice president to schedule a new meeting.
4. Invent other options. Discuss.

Boeing Continuing Case These new cases ask students to synthesize and apply what they've learned across the course to Boeing. Based on reviewer feedback, we've introduced these at the part level.

Boeing Continuing Case connect

Learn more about Boeing's ethical responsibilities in a globalized world, and the impact its decisions had on various stakeholders, including those outside the U.S.

Assess your ability to apply concepts discussed in Chapters 3 and 4 to the case by going to Connect.

> *I'm a huge fan of the self-assessments . . . they [make] students . . . think critically and apply their learning . . . and also make [students] more open to learning if they recognize a weakness in themselves. The overall applicability is so needed.*
>
> **—Kathleen Gosser,**
> *University of Louisville*

Resources That Work

No matter how you teach your course—face-to-face, hybrid, or online—you're in the driver's seat. We offer the most robust set of resources to enhance your Principles of Management course. In addition to our unique Teaching Resource Manual 2.0 (TRM), packed with additional activities and supplemental teaching tools, PowerPoint presentations, and Test Bank questions, we have a wealth of assignable resources available in Connect®.

Connect®

The tenth edition continues to build on the power of Connect and furthers our quest to help students move from comprehension to application. McGraw Hill Connect® is a personalized teaching and learning tool powered by adaptive technologies so your students learn more efficiently, retain more, and achieve better outcomes. We used this platform to create exercises that are auto-graded in order to assist students in developing their career readiness. Here you will find a wide variety of learning resources that develop students' higher-order thinking skills, including:

- **SmartBook 2.0®** An adaptive learning and reading tool, SmartBook 2.0 prompts students with questions based on the material they are studying. By assessing individual answers, SmartBook learns what each student knows and identifies which topics they need to practice. This technology gives each student a personalized learning experience and path to success. SmartBook provides students with a seamless combination of practice, assessment, and remediation.

- **Matching and Multiple Choice** These activities help make the connection between theory and application through matching, ranking, or grouping. Every Career Corner has an exercise to help you assess students understanding about how to improve targeted career readiness competencies.

- **iSeeIt Animated Videos** These brief, contemporary videos offer dynamic student-centered introductions, illustrations, and animations to guide students through challenging concepts. Ideal for before class as an introduction, during class to launch or clarify a topic, or after class for formative assessment.

- **Self-Assessments** Designed to promote student self-awareness and self-reflection, these research-based activities also provide personal and professional development. For this edition, five new assessments were created to measure different career readiness competencies. In addition, new structured feedback explains how students should interpret their scores.

- **Case Analyses and Video Cases** Our assortment of written and video cases challenge students to analyze concepts as they manifest in scenarios related to a real-life product or company, fostering students' ability to think critically in lecture and beyond. Thought-provoking questions check the students' application of the course material and develop their workplace readiness skills.

- **Manager's Hot Seat Videos** These actor-portrayed videos depict real-life situations where a manager is faced with a dilemma that needs to be analyzed based on management concepts. These videos enable students to see how managers in realistic situations deal with employees and complex issues. Students use their critical thinking skills to apply, analyze, and evaluate these managerial challenges, while learning from the manager's mistakes. Each Hot Seat includes follow-up multiple-choice questions that are assignable and auto-gradable.

- **Boeing Continuing Case** Students understand the application of and relationship between different concepts by applying them to the same company throughout the semester. Instructors now have a continuing case on Boeing that can be used as a summary case for each part. Each part-ending case includes multiple-choice questions that are assignable and auto-gradable, as well as essay-based questions.

- **Application-Based Activities** McGraw Hill's Application-Based Activities are highly interactive, automatically graded online exercises that provide students with a safe space to practice using problem-solving skills to apply their knowledge to realistic scenarios. Each scenario addresses key concepts and skills that students must use to work through and solve course-specific problems, resulting in improved critical thinking and relevant workplace skills. Students progress from understanding basic concepts to using their knowledge to analyze complex scenarios and solve real-life problems. Along the way, students see the implications of their decisions and are provided with feedback on how management theory should be informing their actions. They also receive detailed feedback at the conclusion of the activity.

- **Writing Assignment Premium** Available within McGraw Hill Connect® and McGraw Hill Connect® Master, the Writing Assignment tool delivers a learning experience to help students improve their written communication skills and conceptual understanding. As an instructor you can assign, monitor, grade, and provide feedback on writing more efficiently and effectively.

Instructors: Student Success Starts with You

Tools to enhance your unique voice

Want to build your own course? No problem. Prefer to use our turnkey, prebuilt course? Easy. Want to make changes throughout the semester? Sure. And you'll save time with Connect's auto-grading too.

65%
Less Time Grading

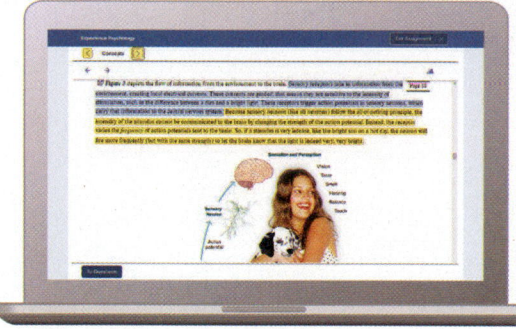

Laptop: McGraw Hill; Woman/dog: George Doyle/Getty Images

Study made personal

Incorporate adaptive study resources like SmartBook® 2.0 into your course and help your students be better prepared in less time. Learn more about the powerful personalized learning experience available in SmartBook 2.0 at **www.mheducation.com/highered/connect/smartbook**

Affordable solutions, added value

Make technology work for you with LMS integration for single sign-on access, mobile access to the digital textbook, and reports to quickly show you how each of your students is doing. And with our Inclusive Access program you can provide all these tools at a discount to your students. Ask your McGraw Hill representative for more information.

Padlock: Jobalou/Getty Images

Solutions for your challenges

A product isn't a solution. Real solutions are affordable, reliable, and come with training and ongoing support when you need it and how you want it. Visit **www.supportateverystep.com** for videos and resources both you and your students can use throughout the semester.

Checkmark: Jobalou/Getty Images

Students: Get Learning that Fits You

Effective tools for efficient studying

Connect is designed to make you more productive with simple, flexible, intuitive tools that maximize your study time and meet your individual learning needs. Get learning that works for you with Connect.

Study anytime, anywhere

Download the free ReadAnywhere app and access your online eBook or SmartBook 2.0 assignments when it's convenient, even if you're offline. And since the app automatically syncs with your eBook and SmartBook 2.0 assignments in Connect, all of your work is available every time you open it. Find out more at **www.mheducation.com/readanywhere**

"I really liked this app—it made it easy to study when you don't have your textbook in front of you."

- Jordan Cunningham, Eastern Washington University

Calendar: owattaphotos/Getty Images

Everything you need in one place

Your Connect course has everything you need—whether reading on your digital eBook or completing assignments for class, Connect makes it easy to get your work done.

Learning for everyone

McGraw Hill works directly with Accessibility Services Departments and faculty to meet the learning needs of all students. Please contact your Accessibility Services Office and ask them to email accessibility@mheducation.com, or visit **www.mheducation.com/about/accessibility** for more information.

acknowledgments

We have the pleasure of working with one of the best teams in the business. Their dedication and effort significantly contribute to the quality of this revision. It all begins with the captain of the team, Michael Ablassmeir. As our editorial director, he provides the internal support to launch and manage the revision process. He also spends much time traveling in support of our products. Thanks for your continuing support over the last 10 years! To Anne Ehrenworth, product developer, thank you for paying attention to the details, keeping us all focused on the schedule, coordinating all the moving pieces, and your timely response to all our questions.

To Debbie Clare, executive marketing manager, you are the energizer bunny who works tirelessly in support of this product. Your creativity, passion, and effort make you the absolute best at your job, and you push us more than anyone to raise our "marketing" game. Thank you! To Harvey Yep, your knowledge and experience with the production process keep us on schedule and responsive to all the change requests. We also appreciate your flexibility and creativity when solving production-related issues.

To Patrick Soleymani, your support as our digital faculty consultant and subject matter expert is invaluable. Your editorial work on 10e was greatly appreciated, as was your collaboration on the Teaching Resource Manual. Thank you for your commitment to our product. To Keri Johnson, assessment content project manager, and Matt Diamond, designer, thanks for all you do to in support of the product. We would also like to thank Cate Rzasa for her editorial assistance, Doreen MacAulay for her work on the Teaching Resource Manual, Jake Heller for the PowerPoint slides, Laci Lyons for her work on the test bank, and Ken Carson for his work on the Self-Assessments for Connect.

We also want to thank Cathy DuBois, Associate Dean at Kent State University's College of Business, for her guidance and support regarding our decision to include new coverage on the topics of creating shared value and sustainable development.

To the McGraw Hill company, a world-class publisher, we are grateful to be members of the family.

Warmest thanks and appreciation go to the individuals who provided valuable input during the developmental stages of this edition, as follows:

Steven Abram,
Kirkwood Community College

Lindy Archambeau,
Warrington College of Business,
University of Florida

Mihran Aroian,
University of Texas at Austin

William Belcher,
Troy University

Michael Bento,
Owens Community College

Audrey Blume,
Wilmington University

Scott Boyar,
University of Alabama–Birmingham

Jack Cichy,
Davenport University

Susie Cox,
University of Louisiana–Monroe

Carrie L. Devone,
Mott Community College

Ed Drozda,
Bryant University

Kathleen Gosser,
University of Louisville

Jacob Heller,
Tarleton State University

Mark Hiatt,
Kennesaw State University

Gregory A. Hoffeditz,
Southern Illinois University–
Carbondale

Aviad Israeli,
Kent State University

Jacquelyn Jacobs,
University of Tennessee

John Kirn,
University of Kentucky

Bobbie Knoblauch,
Wichita State University

Patricia Lanier,
University of Louisiana
at Lafayette

Dave Lanzilla,
College of Central Florida

K. Doreen MacAulay,
University of South Florida

David Kim McKinnon,
Arizona State University

Benjamin David McLarty,
Mississippi State University

Erin McLaughlin,
University of Alabama–Huntsville

Tammy Rich,
Pennsylvania College of Technology

Gerald Schoenfeld,
Florida Gulf Coast University

Michael Shane Spiller,
Western Kentucky University

Jerry Stevens,
Texas Tech University

Ronda Taylor,
Ivy Tech Community College

Jennifer Trout,
Rasmussen College

Kevin Walker,
Eastern Oregon University

Ray D. Walters,
Fayetteville Technical Community
College

Tiffany Woodward,
East Carolina University

Carol Bormann Young,
Metropolitan State University

Mark Zarycki,
Hillsborough Community College
(Brandon)

We would also like to thank the following colleagues who served as manuscript reviewers during the development of previous editions:

G. Stoney Alder,
University of Nevada–Las Vegas

Phyllis C. Alderdice,
Jefferson Community and Technical
College

Laura L. Alderson,
University of Memphis

M. Ruhul Amin,
Bloomsburg University of
Pennsylvania

Danielle Beu Ammeter,
University of Mississippi

William Scott Anchors,
University of Maine at Orono

Jeffrey L. Anderson,
Ohio University

Darlene Andert,
Florida Gulf Coast University

Joel Andexler,
Cuyahoga Community College

John Anstey,
University of Nebraska at Omaha

Joseph Aranyosi,
University of Phoenix

Maria Aria,
Camden County College

Shelly Arneson,
Colorado State University

Lisa Augustyniak,
Lake Michigan College

Mona Bahl,
Illinois State University

Tanya Balcom,
Macomb Community College

Pamela Ball,
Clark State Community College

Amy S. Banta,
Ohio University

Valerie Barnett,
Kansas State University

Lynn Becker,
University of Central Florida

James D. Bell,
Texas State University–San Marcos

Jessie Bellflowers,
Fayetteville Technical Community
College

Victor Berardi,
Kent State University

George Bernard,
Seminole State College of Florida

Patricia Bernson,
County College of Morris

David Bess,
University of Hawaii

Stephen Betts,
William Paterson University

Jim Bishop,
New Mexico State University

Randy Blass,
Florida State University

Larry Bohleber,
University of Southern Indiana

Alison Bolton,
Solano Community College

Melanie Bookout,
Greenville Technical College

Robert S. Boothe,
University of Southern Mississippi

Susan M. Bosco,
Roger Williams University

Anne Brantley,
Central Piedmont Community College

David Allen Brown,
Ferris State University

Roger Brown,
Northwestern Oklahoma State
University

Reginald Bruce,
University of Louisville

Marit Brunsell,
Madison Area Technical College

Jon Bryan,
Bridgewater State University

Becky Bryant,
Texas Woman's University

Paul Buffa,
Jefferson College, Missouri Baptist
University

Mark David Burdsall,
University of Pittsburgh

Neil Burton,
Clemson University

Regina Cannon,
Tarrant County College

Barbara A. Carlin,
University of Houston

Shari Carpenter,
Eastern Oregon University

Tara Carr,
University of Wisconsin–Green Bay

Pamela Carstens,
Coe College

Julie J. Carwile,
John Tyler Community College

Daniel A. Cernas Ortiz,
University of North Texas

Glen Chapuis,
St. Charles Community
College

Rod Christian,
Mesa Community College

Mike Cicero,
Highline College

Anthony Cioffi,
Lorain County Community College

Deborah Clark,
Santa Fe Community College

J. Dana Clark,
Appalachian State University

Dean Cleavenger,
University of Central Florida

Sharon Clinebell,
University of Northern Colorado

Loretta Fergus Cochran,
Arkansas Tech University

Glenda Coleman,
South University

Ron Cooley,
South Suburban College

Melissa M. Cooper,
School of Management, Texas
Woman's University

Gary Corona,
Florida State College

Anastasia Cortes,
Virginia Tech

Keith Credo,
University of Louisiana–Lafayette

Derek E. Crews,
Texas Woman's University

Daniel J. Curtin,
Lakeland Community College

Ajay Das,
Baruch College

Justin L. Davis,
University of West Florida

Tom Deckelman,
Owens Community College

Linda I. DeLong,
University of La Verne

Margaret Deck,
Virginia Tech

Kate Demarest,
University of Baltimore

E. Gordon DeMeritt,
Shepherd University

Kathleen DeNisco,
Erie Community College

Anant R. Deshpande,
SUNY Empire State College

John DeSpagna,
Nassau Community College

Pamela A. Dobies,
University of Missouri–Kansas City

David Dore,
Pima Community College

Lon Doty,
San Jose State University

Ron Dougherty,
Ivy Tech Community College/
Columbus Campus

Scott Droege,
Western Kentucky University

Ken Dunegan,
Cleveland State University

Steven Dunphy,
Indiana University Northwest

Linda Durkin,
Delaware County Community
College

Subhash Durlabhji,
Northwestern State University of
Louisiana

Jack Dustman,
Northern Arizona University

Jennifer Egrie,
Keiser University

Ray Eldridge,
Lipscomb University

Bob Eliason,
James Madison University

Valerie Evans,
Kansas State University

W. Randy Evans,
University of Tennessee at
Chattanooga

Paul A. Fadil,
University of North Florida

Crystal Saric Fashant,
Metropolitan State University

Jud Faurer,
Metropolitan State University of
Denver

Bennie Felts,
North Carolina Wesleyan College

Judy Fitch,
Augusta State University

Carla Flores,
Ball State University

Christopher Flynn,
University of North Florida

David Foote,
Middle Tennessee State University

Lucy R. Ford,
Saint Joseph's University

Charla Fraley,
Columbus State Community College

Gail E. Fraser,
Kean University

Dana Frederick,
Missouri State University

Tony Frontera,
Binghamton University

Dane Galden,
Columbus State Community College

Patricia Galitz,
Southeast Community College

Michael Garcia,
Liberty University

Barbara Garrell,
Delaware County Community College

Evgeniy Gentchev,
Northwood University

Lydia Gilmore,
Columbus State Community College

Terry Girdon,
Pennsylvania College of Technology

James Glasgow,
Villanova University

Ronnie Godshalk,
Penn State University

Connie Golden,
Lakeland Community College

Lacey Gonzalez-Horan,
Lehigh Carbon Community College

Deborah Cain Good,
University of Pittsburgh

Kris Gossett,
Mercyhurst University

Marie Gould,
Horizons University

Tita Gray,
Maryland University of Integrative
Health

Ryan Greenbaum,
Oklahoma State University–
Stillwater

Jan Grimes,
Georgia Southern University

Kevin S. Groves,
Pepperdine University

Joyce Guillory,
Austin Community College

William Habacivch,
Central Penn College

Gordon Haley,
Palm Beach State College

Reggie Hall,
Tarleton State University

Stephen F. Hallam,
University of Akron

Marie D.K. Halvorsen-Ganepola,
University of Notre Dame

Charles T. Harrington,
Pasadena City College

Lisa M. Harris,
Southeast Community College

Joanne Hartsell,
East Carolina University

Santhi Harvey,
Central State University

Ahmad Hassan,
Morehead State University

Karen H. Hawkins,
Miami Dade College, Kendall
Campus

Samuel Hazen,
Tarleton State University

Jack Heinsius,
Modesto Junior College

Duane Helleloid,
University of North Dakota

Cathy Henderson,
Stephen F. Austin State University

Evelyn Hendrix,
Lindenwood University

Nhung Hendy,
Towson University

Kim Hester,
Arkansas State University

Lara Hobson,
Western Michigan University

Anne Hoel,
University of Wisconsin–Stout

Mary Hogue,
Kent State University

David Hollomon,
Victor Valley College

James Hopkins,
University of Georgia

Tammy Hunt,
University of North Carolina–
Wilmington

Perwaiz Ismaili,
Metropolitan State University

Aviad Israeli,
Kent State University

Edward Johnson,
University of North Florida

Nancy M. Johnson,
Madison Area Technical College

Paul D. Johnson,
University of Mississippi

Sue Joiner,
Tarleton State University

Kathleen Jones,
University of North Dakota

Rusty Juban,
Southeastern Louisiana University

Dmitriy Kalyagin,
Chabot College

Heesam Kang,
Trident University International

Marvin Karlins,
University of South Florida

Marcella Kelly,
Santa Monica College

Richard Kimbrough,
University of Nebraska–Lincoln

Renee N. King,
Eastern Illinois University

Shaun C. Knight,
Penn State University

Todd Korol,
Monroe Community College

Leo C. Kotrodimos,
NC Wesleyan College

Sal Kukalis,
California State University–Long
Beach

Chalmer E. Labig Jr.,
Oklahoma State University

Wendy Lam,
Hawaii Pacific University

Barbara Larson,
Northeastern University

Zahir Latheef,
University of Houston–Downtown

Robert L. Laud,
William Paterson University

Blaine Lawlor,
University of West Florida

Rebecca Legleiter,
Tulsa Community College

David Leonard,
Chabot College

Chris Levan,
University of Tennessee–
Chattanooga

David Levy,
United States Air Force Academy

Chi Lo Lim,
Northwest Missouri State University

Natasha Lindsey,
University of North Alabama

Benjamin Lipschutz,
Central Penn College

Beverly Little,
Western Carolina University

Guy Lochiatto,
MassBay Community College

Mary Lou Lockerby,
College of DuPage

Michael Dane Loflin,
York Technical College

Jessica Lofton,
University of Mount Olive

Paul Londrigan,
Charles Stewart Mott Community
College

Tom Loughman,
Columbus State University

Ivan Lowe,
York Technical College

Gregory Luce,
Bucks County Community College

Margaret Lucero,
Texas A&M–Corpus Christi

Charles Lyons,
University of Georgia

Professor Cheryl Macon,
Butler County Community College

Zengie Mangaliso,
University of Massachusetts–
Amherst

James Manicki,
Northwestern College

Christine Marchese,
Nassau Community College

Christine I. Mark,
University of Southern Mississippi

Marcia A. Marriott,
Monroe Community College

Dr. David Matthews,
SUNY Adirondack

Brenda McAleer,
University of Maine at Augusta

Daniel W. McAllister,
University of Nevada–Las Vegas

David McArthur,
Utah Valley University

Tom McFarland,
Mount San Antonio College

Joe McKenna,
Howard Community College

Zack McNeil,
Metropolitan Community College

Jeanne McNett,
Assumption College

Spencer Mehl,
Coastal Carolina Community College

Mary Meredith,
University of Louisiana

Lori Merlak,
Kirkwood Community College

Douglas Micklich,
Illinois State University

Christine Miller,
Tennessee Tech University

Val Miskin,
Washington State University

Lorianne Mitchell,
East Tennessee State University

Kelly Mollica,
University of Memphis

Debra L. Moody,
Virginia Commonwealth University

Gregory Moore,
Middle Tennessee State University

Vivianne Moore,
Davenport University

Rob Moorman,
Elon University

Byron Morgan,
Texas State University

Jaideep Motwani,
Grand Valley State University

Troy Mumford,
Colorado State University

Jennifer Muryn,
Robert Morris University

Robert Myers,
University of Louisville

Christopher P. Neck,
Arizona State University

Patrick J. Nedry,
Monroe County Community
College

Francine Newth,
Providence College

Margie Nicholson,
Columbia College, Chicago

Troy Nielson,
Brigham Young University

Thomas J. Norman,
California State University–
Dominguez Hills

Paul O'Brien,
Keiser University

Nathan Oliver,
University of Alabama at Birmingham

Joanne Orabone,
Community College of Rhode Island

John Orife,
Indiana University of Pennsylvania

Eren Ozgen,
Florida State University–Panama City

Rhonda Palladi,
Georgia State University

Fernando Pargas,
James Madison University

Jack Partlow,
Northern Virginia Community College

Don A. Paxton,
Pasadena City College

John Paxton,
Wayne State College

John Pepper,
University of Kansas

Clifford R. Perry,
Florida International University

Sheila Petcavage,
Cuyahoga Community College–
Western Campus

Barbara Petzall,
Maryville University

Thomas Philippe,
St. Petersburg College

Shaun Pichler,
Mihaylo College of Business,
California State University–Fullerton

Michael Pirson,
Fordham University

Anthony Plunkett,
Harrison College

Beth Polin,
Eastern Kentucky University

Tracy H. Porter,
Cleveland State University

Paula Potter,
Western Kentucky University

Elizabeth Prejean,
Northwestern State University

Cynthia Preston,
University of Northwestern Ohio

Ronald E. Purser,
San Francisco State University

Gregory R. Quinet,
Kennesaw State University

Kenneth Rasheed,
Chattahoochee Technical College

George Redmond,
Franklin University

Deborah Reed,
Benedictine College

Chelsea Hood Reese,
Southeast Community College

Rosemarie Reynolds,
Embry Riddle Aeronautical
University

H. Lynn Richards,
Johnson County Community College

Leah Ritchie,
Salem State College

Gary B. Roberts,
Kennesaw State University

Martha Robinson,
University of Memphis

Sean E. Rogers,
University of Rhode Island

Katherine Rosenbusch,
George Mason University

Barbara Rosenthal,
Miami Dade Community College/
Wolfson Campus

Gary Ross,
Cardinal Stritch University

David Ruderman,
University of Colorado–Denver

Catherine Ruggieri,
St. John's University–Staten Island

Storm Russo,
Valencia Community College

Cindy Ruszkowski,
Illinois State University

William Salyer,
Illinois State University

Diane R. Scott,
Wichita State University

Alex J. Scrimpshire,
Xavier University

Marina Sebastijanovic,
University of Houston

Marianne Sebok,
College of Southern Nevada

Thomas J. Shaughnessy,
Illinois Central College

Joanna Shaw,
Tarleton State University

Sarah Shike,
Western Illinois University

Randi Sims,
Nova Southeastern University

Raj K. Singh,
University of California–Riverside

Frederick J. Slack,
Indiana University of Pennsylvania

Erika E. Small,
Coastal Carolina University

Jim Smas,
Kent State University

Dustin Smith,
Webster University

Gerald F. Smith,
University of Northern Iowa

Joy Turnheim Smith,
Elizabeth City State University

Mark Smith,
University of Southwest Louisiana

Paula Kirch Smith,
Cincinnati State

Jeff Stauffer,
Ventura College

George E. Stevens,
Kent State University

Martin St. John,
Westmoreland County Community
College

Raymond Stoudt,
DeSales University

Barb Stuart,
Daniels College of Business

Robert Scott Taylor,
Moberly Area Community College

Virginia Anne Taylor,
William Patterson University

Wynn Teasley,
University of West Florida

Marguerite Teubner,
Nassau Community College

Jerry Thomas,
Arapahoe Community College

C. Justice Tillman,
Baruch College–City University of
New York

Jody Tolan,
University of Southern California,
Marshall School of Business

Joseph Tomkiewicz,
East Carolina University

Robert Trumble,
Virginia Commonwealth University

Jim Turner,
Davenport University

Isaiah Ugboro,
North Carolina Agricultural & Technical
State University

Brandi Ulrich,
Anne Arundel Community College

Anthony Uremovic,
Joliet Junior College

George Valcho,
Bossier Parish Community College

Barry Van Hook,
Arizona State University

Scot W. Vaver,
University of Wisconsin–Stout

Susan Verhulst,
Grand View University

Annie Viets,
Prince Mohammad Bin
Fahd University

Tom Voigt Jr.,
Judson University

Tim Waid,
University of Missouri

Carolyn Waits,
Cincinnati State

Bruce C. Walker,
University of Louisiana at Monroe

Wendy Walker,
University of North Georgia

Charlene Walters,
Strayer University

Tekle O. Wanorie,
Northwest Missouri State
University

Charles Warren,
Salem State College

Kerry Webb,
Texas Woman's University

Rick Webb,
Johnson County Community
College

Brian D. Webster,
Ball State University

Velvet Weems-Landingham,
Kent State University–Geauga

Allen Weimer,
University of Tampa

Anthony Weinberg,
Daymar College

David A. Wernick,
Florida International University

James Whelan,
Manhattan College

John Whitelock,
Community College of Baltimore/
Catonsville Campus

Eric S. Williams,
University of Alabama–
Tuscaloosa

Wallace Alexander Williams Jr.,
Texas A&M University–Commerce

Joette Wisnieski,
Indiana University of Pennsylvania

Dr. Linsey Willis,
Florida Atlantic University

Colette Wolfson,
Ivy Tech Community College

M. Susan Wurtz,
University of Northern Iowa

Wendy V. Wysocki,
Monroe County Community
College

Ned D. Young,
Sinclair Community College

Jan T. Zantinga,
University of Georgia

Mary E. Zellmer-Bruhn,
University of Minnesota

Mark Zorn,
Butler County Community College

From Angelo –
I would like to thank my wife, Joyce, for being understanding, patient, and encouraging throughout the process of writing this edition. We have been at this for many years, and I could not do what I do without you. Your continued love and support helped me endure the trials of completing this revision.

From Denise –
To the women who have inspired my career as well as many of the specific choices in this revision—Pam Perrewé (an extraordinary mentor to whom I am unspeakably grateful), Sonya Premeaux, Anne O'Leary-Kelly, Lauren Simon, Angèle Gautreaux, Mallorre Dill, Lai Moy, and my late mother. And to my snug harbor, Joe—this revision happened because of your unwavering love and support as a husband and father and I am, as always, in awe of you.

   We hope you enjoy reading and applying the book. Best wishes for success in your career.

Angelo Kinicki

Denise Breaux Soignet

contents

PART 6
Controlling

CHAPTER SIXTEEN

Control Systems and Quality Management: Techniques for Enhancing Organizational Effectiveness 694

1

The Exceptional Manager
What You Do, How You Do It

Kapook2981/iStock/Getty Images

After reading this chapter, you should be able to:

LO 1-1 Identify the rewards of being an exceptional manager.

LO 1-2 List the four principal functions of a manager.

LO 1-3 Describe the levels and areas of management.

LO 1-4 Identify the roles an effective manager must play.

LO 1-5 Discuss the skills of an outstanding manager.

LO 1-6 Identify the seven challenges faced by most managers.

LO 1-7 Define the core competencies, knowledge, soft skills, attitudes, and other characteristics needed for career readiness and discuss how they can be developed.

LO 1-8 Describe the process for managing your career readiness.

FORECAST *What's Ahead in This Chapter*

We describe the rewards, benefits, and privileges managers might expect. We also describe the four principal functions of management—planning, organizing, leading, and controlling. We consider levels and areas of management and describe the three roles managers must play. We describe the three skills required of a manager and discuss seven challenges managers face in today's world. We then focus on a model of career readiness and offer tips for building your career readiness. The chapter concludes with a Career Corner that presents a process that can be used to develop your career readiness.

Using Management Skills for College Success

Our goal is *to make this book as practical as possible for you.* One place we do this is in the "Manage U" feature, like this one, which appears at the beginning of every chapter and offers practical advice for applying the topic of the chapter to your personal life and career. Here, for instance, we show you how to make teamwork one of your job strengths, starting now. This is an important skill that recruiters look for when hiring college graduates.[1]

Functions of Management

In the chapter you will read about the four functions of management—planning, organizing, leading, and controlling. They represent essential activities that all managers undertake in the course of doing their jobs. Although they may sound a little abstract right now, you can use them today to work more successfully on team projects assigned by your professors.

Applying the Functions of Management to School Projects

Consider the students in a Princeton University summer business program. Working in teams, they had 10 weeks to prepare a pitch for a start-up idea and ask for funding. One of the teams ran a four-week pilot after-school program for five Trenton, NJ, girls and asked for $324,000 to scale the program up to include 40 girls on a year-round basis. Their pitch was that the program would help more young women graduate from high school and have a positive effect on the entire community. The students planned their pilot program, its budget, and its schedule and curriculum; they organized the four weeks of activities for the girls they recruited; they led the girls through each day's events; and they used before and after surveys to control (that is, measure) the effects of their efforts. In other words, they relied on the four functions of management to ensure that they worked together to achieve their goals.[2]

Think about how you might make better use of planning and controlling in a team assignment for a course. You might draw up a detailed schedule of tasks and assign them to team members (planning), and then identify checkpoint dates on which you measure progress toward your deadline (controlling). You could set up a way to best use the resources at your disposal, such as time, library materials, personal expertise, and outside experts (organizing), and then use the progress checkpoints to motivate your fellow team members to continue putting forth their best effort (leading). The experience you can gain by using these essential management skills now will serve you well in your studies and throughout your career.

Applying the Functions of Management in Your Personal Life

Consider how you might use the functions of management to run your first 10K race. Your plan would include dates and times to exercise on your Google or Outlook calendar along with distances and ideas for how you will fuel your body on longer runs. You then would make sure you have the resources (time, clothing, support network, nutrition plan) to assist you along your journey (organizing). You also may find it valuable to have a running buddy during some of your workouts (leading). Alternatively, some people may find it motivational to have an accountability partner to review their time and distance totals each week (controlling).

For Discussion Why would employers seek to hire people with good management skills? How can you strive to improve your managerial skills while working on class projects?

1.1 Management: What It Is, What Its Benefits Are

THE BIG PICTURE

Management is defined as the efficient and effective pursuit of organizational goals. Organizations, or people who work together to achieve a specific purpose, value managers because of the multiplier effect: Good managers have an influence on the organization far beyond the results that can be achieved by one person acting alone. Managers are well paid, with the chief executive officers (CEOs) and presidents of even small and midsize businesses earning good salaries and many benefits.

LO 1-1

Identify the rewards of being an exceptional manager.

When chief executive officer Mary Barra took the reins of Detroit-based General Motors (GM) in January 2014, she became the first female CEO of a global automaker anywhere in the world. She also became only the 22nd woman at the helm of a Fortune 500 company, one of those 500 largest U.S. companies that appear on the prestigious annual list compiled by *Fortune* magazine. (Other female CEOs of major companies include Michele Buck of Hershey, Safra Catz of Oracle, and Accenture's Julie Sweet.)

What kind of a person is Barra, a 40-year GM veteran? She has been called "nearly impossible to dislike" and is credited with bringing a much-needed "calm stability" to GM. Among her many people skills is the ability to engage and motivate others, including top executives who may have vied for her job but who have been persuaded to stay and work with her.[3] Are these qualities enough to propel someone to the top of a great organization?

The Rise of a Leader

Barra grew up in suburban Detroit, joined GM at age 18 as an intern on the factory floor, graduated from General Motors Institute (now Kettering University) with a degree in electrical engineering, and then became a plant engineer in GM's Pontiac Division. Spotting her talent, GM gave her a scholarship to Stanford University, where she earned a graduate degree in business. She then began moving up the GM ladder, first as the executive assistant to the CEO and then as the company's head of human resources—formerly often as high as female executives ever got in the auto industry and many others. In 2011, Barra's big break came when she was promoted to lead GM's $15 billion vehicle-development operations, a high-profile role that became the stepping-stone to the CEO spot. In 2016, she was also made chair of the board.[4]

The driving force. One quality that stands out about General Motors CEO Mary Barra is her obvious enthusiasm for cars. She is said to be given to talking excitedly about whatever car she is currently driving and what it demonstrates about GM's product line. Do you think passion about one's work is a necessary quality for managerial success?
Mark Lennihan/AP Images

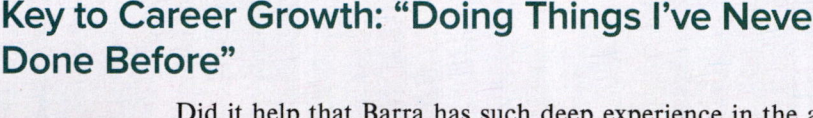

Key to Career Growth: "Doing Things I've Never Done Before"

Did it help that Barra has such deep experience in the auto industry and at GM in particular? No doubt it did. But there is another key to career growth—the ability to take risks. Jeff Bezos, the founder of Amazon.com, was holding down a lucrative job as a Wall Street hedge fund manager in the 1990s when he read that the Internet had recently grown 2,300% in a single year. Even though it meant leaving a stable job with a big bonus on the way, Bezos made the risky leap to the start-up he called Amazon, working out of a garage. "I knew that I might sincerely regret not having participated in this thing called the Internet that I thought was going to be a revolutionizing event," he says. "When I thought about it that way . . . it was incredibly easy to make the decision."[5] Bezos built his company into the largest e-commerce hub in the world and now operates several other businesses and charities as well. He is one of the two or three richest people in the world.

The Art of Management Defined

Is being an exceptional manager a gift, like a musician having perfect pitch? Not exactly. But in good part it may be an art.[6] Fortunately, it is one that is teachable.

Management, said one pioneer of management ideas, is "the art of getting things done through people."[7]

Getting things done. Through people. Thus, managers are task oriented, achievement oriented, and people oriented. And they operate within an ==organization==—a group of people who work together to achieve some specific purpose.

More formally, ==management== is defined as (1) the pursuit of organizational goals efficiently and effectively by (2) integrating the work of people through (3) planning, organizing, leading, and controlling the organization's resources.

Note the words *efficiently* and *effectively,* which basically mean "doing things right."

- *Efficiency—the means.* Efficiency is the means of attaining the organization's goals. To be ==efficient== means to use resources—people, money, raw materials, and the like—wisely and cost-effectively.

- *Effectiveness—the ends.* Effectiveness regards the organization's ends, the goals. To be ==effective== means to achieve results, to make the right decisions, and to successfully carry them out so that they achieve the organization's goals.

Good managers are concerned with trying to achieve both qualities. Often, however, organizations will erroneously strive for efficiency without being effective. Retired U.S. Army general Stanley McChrystal, former commander of all U.S. and coalition forces in Afghanistan, suggests that effectiveness is a more important outcome in today's organizations.[8]

EXAMPLE | Effectiveness versus Efficiency: Have Scientists Found a Viable Solution to Address Rising Demands for Meat?

Current data suggest that 70% of the land on earth suitable for growing crops is currently being used for livestock farming. If this figure sounds high, consider that experts predict a 70% increase in the demand for meat products by 2050 as the earth's population reaches 9 to 10 billion.[9] With younger generations of consumers showing a clear preference for healthier nutrition sources and more sustainable alternatives to traditional livestock production, how should the food industry evolve in order to meet the changing population's needs?

At least 30 start-ups across the globe think they have the answer. Scientists at companies like Mosa Meat, Finless Foods, Memphis Meats, SuperMeat, and Future Meat Technologies are "growing" meat in laboratories using stem-cell samples taken from live animals—no slaughter required.[10] The resulting product is referred to interchangeably as "cultured meat," "clean meat," and "lab-grown meat," and could potentially provide a healthier, less expensive, and more sustainable food source.

Sound crazy? Then you should know these companies have already received investments from billionaires Bill Gates and Richard Branson,[11] and industry giants Cargill[12] and Tyson Foods.[13] In 2019, Israeli-based Future Meat Technologies raised $14 million in funding to build a production plant,[14] and Memphis Meats received $161 million in 2020 for the same reason.[15] It's possible that lab-grown meat products will hit supermarket shelves in as little as one to two years, with some analysts forecasting an $85 billion-dollar market for cultured meats by 2030.[16]

Let's take a look at this issue from both an effectiveness and efficiency perspective.

Effectiveness. If you're currently having visions of Frankenstein, you're not alone. There is evidence that the idea of lab-grown meet feels unnatural and even repulsive to many consumers. Can this product ever be socially acceptable enough to present a viable solution?[17] Clearly if cultured meat producers wish to be successful, then they will need to supply food that consumers are willing to purchase and eat.

For those who aren't completely turned off by the idea of a steak grown from stem cells, there are other concerns. For example, consumers are skeptical of claims that cultured meats will taste the same as the farmed meats they are accustomed to eating. Taste-testers at a Memphis Meats event in San Francisco said they would eat the company's lab-grown chicken product again and that it "pretty much tastes like chicken."[18] Still, many worry that laboratories just won't be able to replicate the taste and texture of traditional animal meat.[19]

There are also widespread fears of unforeseen negative health consequences. According to researchers at Maastricht University in the Netherlands, growing meat in laboratories eliminates the need for antibiotics and gives scientists control over things like cholesterol and fat levels, making these products a healthier option than conventional meats. But a substantial portion of consumers aren't ready to take the risk.[20]

Efficiency.   Lab-grown meat start-ups claim to offer a more environmentally friendly solution to increasing meat demands. For example, according to some research, it may be possible to produce as many as 175 million quarter-pound hamburgers with the stem cells from only one cow. (It currently takes about 440,000 cows to produce the same amount of meat.) Further, both Future Meat Technologies and Mosa Meats say their production processes use 99% less land and 96% less water than livestock production.[21]

But some experts believe that growing meat in labs could foster climate change. "Lab meat doesn't solve anything from an environmental perspective, since the energy emissions are so high," said Marco Springmann, senior environmental researcher at the University of Oxford. He added, "So much money is poured into meat labs, but even with that amount of money, the product still has a carbon footprint that is roughly five times the carbon footprint of chicken and ten times higher than plant-based processed meats." Scientists won't be able to assess the true carbon footprint of cultured meat until production facilities are operational, but some research suggests the potential for high levels of carbon dioxide pollution. This would question the environmental benefit of lab-grown meat, given that CO_2 stays in the atmosphere for several hundred years,

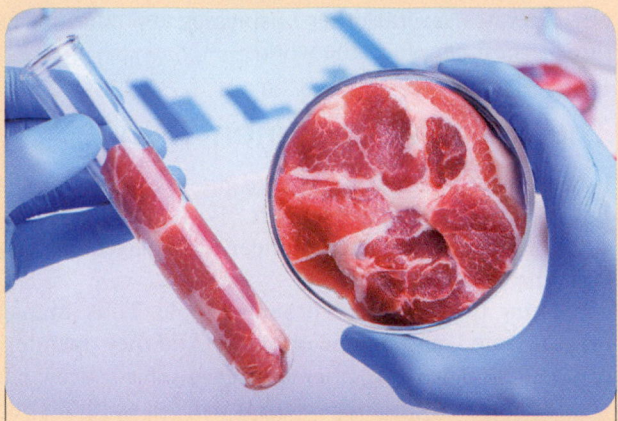

Lab-grown meat. Have scientists found a way to address rising food demands by growing meat in laboratories? Would you be willing to try a burger made from a cow's stem cells? nevodka/Shutterstock

while the methane produced in cattle farming dissipates after about 12 years.[22]

There is also the issue of whether cultured meat products will ever be affordable. In 2013 a pound of lab-grown hamburger meat cost an astonishing $1.2 million, but process and technology improvements have continued to drive these costs down. By 2018 a pound of Memphis Meats ground beef had dropped to around $2,400,[23] and by late 2019, Future Meats could produce a pound of chicken and a pound of beef for $150 and $200, respectively.[24]

Preliminary data surrounding all of these issues—from social acceptability to environmental impacts to costs—are mixed.[25] It will be difficult to answer any of these questions with precision until cultured meats are available to the mass market and more data are available.

YOUR CALL

Do you think that lab-grown meat companies will be effective in reaching their goals? Do you believe their processes will prove to be more or less efficient than traditional livestock production?

Why Organizations Value Managers: The Multiplier Effect

Some great achievements of history, such as scientific discoveries or works of art, were accomplished by individuals working quietly by themselves. But so much more has been achieved by people who were able to leverage their talents and abilities by being managers. For instance, of the top 10 great architectural wonders of the world named by the American Institute of Architects, none was built by just one person. All were triumphs of management, although some reflected the vision of an individual. (The wonders are the Great Wall of China, the Great Pyramid, Machu Picchu, the Acropolis, the Coliseum, the Taj Mahal, the Eiffel Tower, the Brooklyn Bridge, the Empire State Building, and Frank Lloyd Wright's Falling Water house in Pennsylvania.)

Good managers create value. The reason is that in being a manager you have a *multiplier effect:* Your influence on the organization is multiplied far beyond the results that can be achieved by just one person acting alone. Thus, while a solo operator such as a salesperson might accomplish many things and incidentally make a very good living, his or her boss could accomplish a great deal more—and could well earn two to seven times the income. And the manager will undoubtedly have a lot more influence.

What Are the Rewards of Studying and Practicing Management?

Are you studying management but have no plans to be a manager? Or are you trying to learn techniques and concepts that will help you be an exceptional management practitioner? Either way, you will use what you learn. Managerial competencies including time management, people skills, mastery of interpersonal and electronic communication, and the capacity to organize and plan are essential in both managerial and nonmanagerial careers.

The multiplier effect. The Great Wall of China was constructed over thousands of years by hundreds of thousands of workers. Imagine the management required to coordinate such an effort!
axz700/Shutterstock

The Rewards of Studying Management   Students sign up for an introductory management course for all kinds of reasons. Many, of course, are planning business careers, but others are taking it to fulfill a requirement or an elective. Some students are in technical or nonprofit fields—computer science, education, health, and the like—and never expect to have to supervise people.

Here are just a few of the payoffs of studying management as a discipline:

- **You will have an insider's understanding of how to deal with organizations from the outside.** Since we all are in constant interaction with all kinds of organizations, it helps to understand how they work and how the people in them make decisions. Such knowledge may give you skills that you can use in dealing with organizations from the outside, as a customer or investor, for example.

- **You will know from experience how to relate to your supervisors.** Since most of us work in organizations and most of us have bosses, studying management will enable you to understand the pressures managers deal with and how they will best respond to you.

- **You will better interact with co-workers.** The kinds of management policies in place can affect how your co-workers behave. Studying management can give you the understanding of teams and teamwork, cultural differences, conflict and stress, and negotiation and communication skills that will help you get along with fellow employees.

- **You will be able to manage yourself and your career.** Management courses in general, and this book in particular, give you the opportunity to realize insights about yourself—your personality, emotions, values, perceptions, needs, and goals. We help you build your skills in areas such as self-management, listening, handling change, managing stress, avoiding groupthink, and coping with organizational politics.

- **You might make more money during your career.** Managers are well compensated in comparison to other workers. At the lower rungs, managers may make between $33,000 and $87,000 a year; in the middle levels, between $45,000 and $146,000.[26] (For examples of managerial salaries, go to www.bls.gov/ooh/management/home.html.) There are also all kinds of fringe benefits and status rewards that go with being a manager, ranging from health insurance to stock options to large offices. And the higher you ascend in the management hierarchy, the more privileges may come your way.

The Rewards of Practicing Management   Many young people want not only to make money but also to make a difference. As Swarthmore psychology professor Barry Schwartz, author of *Why We Work,* suggests, "We care about more than money. We

These three machinists are using several managerial skills to produce better products. One involves mentoring from the machinist in the middle.
stockbroker/123RF

want work that is challenging and engaging, that enables us to exercise some discretion and control over what we do, and that provides us with opportunities to learn and grow."[27] Becoming a management practitioner offers many rewards apart from money and status, as follows:

- **You and your employees can experience a sense of accomplishment.** Every successful goal accomplished provides you not only with personal satisfaction but also with the satisfaction of all those employees you directed who helped you accomplish it.

- **You can stretch your abilities and magnify your range.** Every promotion up the hierarchy of an organization stretches your abilities, challenges your talents and skills, and magnifies the range of your accomplishments.

- **You can build a catalog of successful products or services.** Every product or service you provide—the personal Eiffel Tower or Empire State Building you build, as it were—becomes a monument to your accomplishments. Indeed, studying management may well help you in running your own business.

- **You can become a mentor and help others.** According to one survey, 75% of executives who had a mentor—an experienced person who provides guidance to someone new to the work world—said the relationship was crucial to advancing their careers.[28] •

1.2 What Managers Do: The Four Principal Functions

THE BIG PICTURE

Management has four functions: *planning, organizing, leading,* and *controlling.*

LO 1-2

List the four principal functions of a manager.

What do you as a manager do to get things done—that is, to achieve the stated goals of the organization you work for? You perform what is known as the management process, also called the **four management functions:** planning, organizing, leading, and controlling. (The abbreviation "POLC" may help you to remember them.) As Figure 1.1 illustrates, all these functions affect one another, are ongoing, and are performed simultaneously.

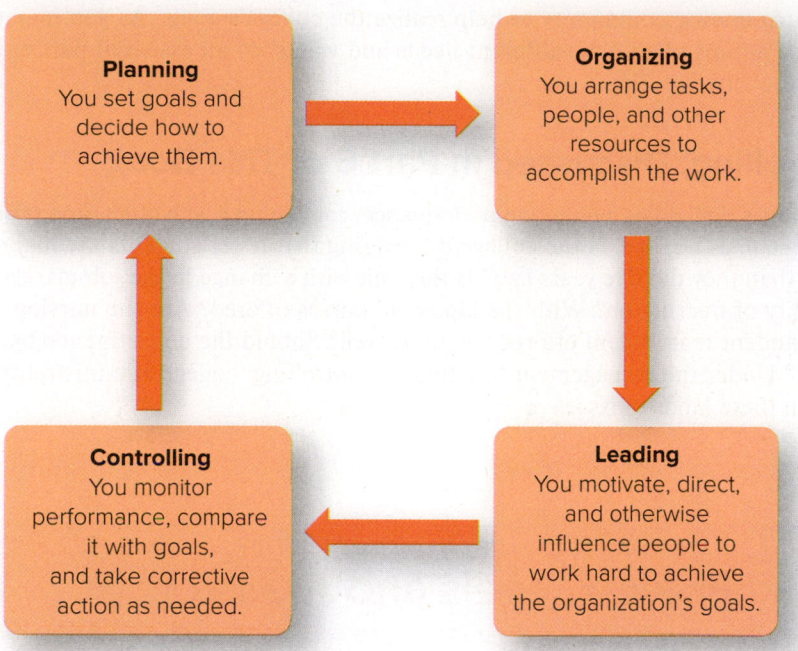

FIGURE 1.1

The management process

What you as a manager do to get things done—to achieve the stated goals of your organization.

Although the process of management can be quite varied, these four functions represent its essential principles. Indeed, as a glance at our text's table of contents shows, they form four of the part divisions of the book. Let's consider what the four functions are, using the management (or "administration," as it is called in nonprofit organizations) of your college to illustrate them.

Planning: Discussed in Part 3 of This Book

Planning is defined as setting goals and deciding how to achieve them. Your college was established for the purpose of educating students, and its present managers, or administrators, now must decide the best way to accomplish this. Which of several possible degree programs should be offered? Should the college be a residential or a commuter campus? What sort of students should be recruited and admitted? What kind of faculty should be hired? What kind of buildings and equipment are needed?

Organizing: Discussed in Part 4 of This Book

Organizing is defined as arranging tasks, people, and other resources to accomplish the work. College administrators must determine the tasks to be done, by whom, and what the reporting hierarchy is to be. Should the institution be organized into schools with departments, with department chairpersons reporting to deans who in return report to vice presidents? Should the college hire more full-time instructors than part-time instructors? Should English professors teach just English literature or also composition, developmental English, and "first-year experience" courses?

Leading: Discussed in Part 5 of This Book

Leading is defined as motivating, directing, and otherwise influencing people to work hard to achieve the organization's goals. At your college, leadership begins, of course, with the president (who would be the CEO in a for-profit organization). He or she is the one who must inspire faculty, staff, students, alumni, wealthy donors, and residents of the surrounding community to help realize the college's goals. As you might imagine, these groups often have different needs and wants, so an essential part of leadership is resolving conflicts.

Controlling: Discussed in Part 6 of This Book

Controlling is defined as monitoring performance, comparing it with goals, and taking corrective action as needed. Is the college discovering that fewer students are majoring in nursing than they did five years ago? Is the fault with a change in the job market? With the quality of instruction? With the kinds of courses offered? Are the nursing department's student recruitment efforts not going well? Should the department's budget be reduced? Under the management function of controlling, college administrators must deal with these kinds of issues. ●

1.3 Pyramid Power: Levels and Areas of Management

THE BIG PICTURE

Within an organization, there are four levels of managers: *top, middle,* and *first-line managers* as well as *team leaders*. Managers may also be *general managers,* or they may be *functional managers,* responsible for just one organizational activity, such as research and development (R&D), marketing, finance, production, or human resources. Managers may work for for-profit, nonprofit, or mutual-benefit organizations.

LO 1-3

Describe the levels and areas of management.

The workplace of the future may resemble a symphony orchestra, famed management theorist Peter Drucker said.[29] Employees, especially so-called knowledge workers—those who have a great deal of technical skills—can be compared to concert musicians. Their managers can be seen as conductors.

In Drucker's analogy, musicians are used for some pieces of music—that is, work projects—and not others, and they are divided into different sections (teams) based on their instruments. The conductor's role is not to play each instrument better than the musicians but to lead them all through the most effective performance of a particular work.

This model differs from the traditional pyramid-like organizational model, where one leader sits at the top, with layers of managers beneath, each of whom must report to and justify their work to the manager above (what's called *accountability,* as we discuss in Chapter 8). We therefore need to take a look at the traditional arrangement first.

The Traditional Management Pyramid: Levels and Areas

A new Silicon Valley technology start-up company staffed by young people in sandals and shorts may be so small and so loosely organized that only one or two members may be said to be a manager. General Motors or the U.S. Army, in contrast, have thousands of managers doing thousands of different things. Is there a picture we can draw that applies to all the different kinds of organizations and describes them in ways that make sense? Yes: by levels and by areas, as the pyramid shows. *(See Figure 1.2.)*

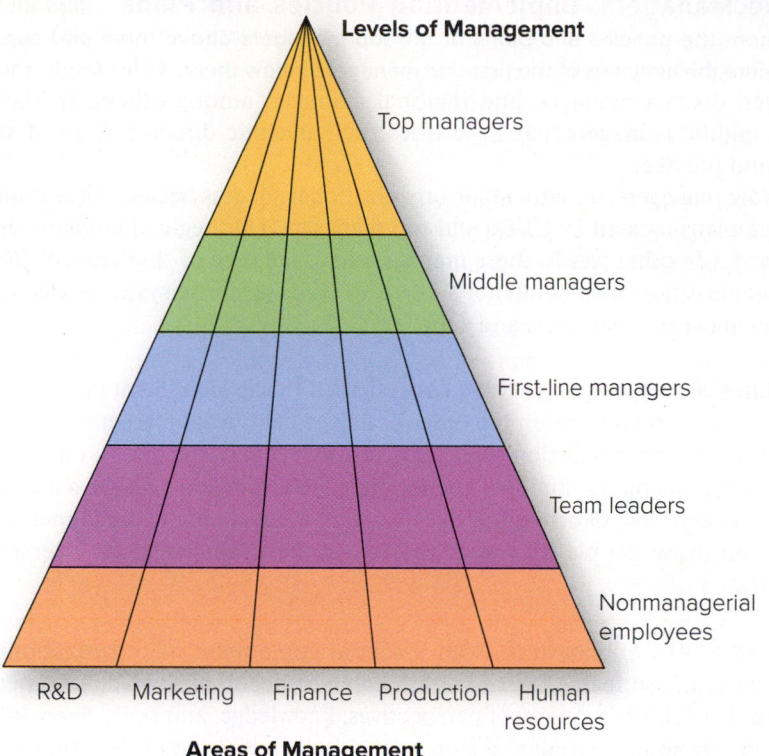

Levels of Management

- Top managers
- Middle managers
- First-line managers
- Team leaders
- Nonmanagerial employees

R&D   Marketing   Finance   Production   Human resources

Areas of Management

FIGURE 1.2

The levels and areas of management

Top managers make long-term decisions, middle-managers implement those decisions, first-line managers make short-term decisions, and team leaders facilitate team activities toward achieving a goal.

Four Levels of Management

Not everyone who works in an organization is a manager, of course, but those who are may be classified into four levels—top, middle, and first-line managers, and team leaders. Nonmanagerial employees represent the foundation of an organizational pyramid.

Top Managers: Determining Overall Direction   Their offices may be equipped with expensive leather chairs and have lofty views. Or, as with one Internet company, they may have plastic lawn chairs in the CEO's office and beat-up furniture in the lobby. Whatever their decor, an organization's top managers tend to have titles such as chief executive officer (CEO), chief operating officer (COO), president, and senior vice president.

Some may be the stars in their fields, the men and women whose pictures appear on the covers of business magazines, people such as Lockheed Martin CEO Marillyn Hewson (now retired), Lucasfilm president Kathleen Kennedy, or Apple CEO Tim Cook, all of whom have appeared on the front of *Fortune*.

Top managers make long-term decisions about the overall direction of the organization and establish the objectives, policies, and strategies for it. They need to pay a lot of attention to the environment outside the organization, being alert for long-run opportunities and problems and devising strategies for dealing with them. Thus, executives at this level must be future oriented, strategic, and able to deal with uncertain, highly competitive conditions.

These people stand at the summit of the management pyramid. But the nature of a pyramid is that the farther you climb, the less space remains at the top. Thus, most pyramid climbers never get to the apex. However, that doesn't mean that you shouldn't try. Indeed, you might end up atop a much smaller pyramid of some other organization than the one you started out in—and happier with the result.

Successful top manager. India-born Satya Nadella, who joined Microsoft in 1992, became CEO of the technology company in early 2014 and has helped transition it to cloud computing. His net worth in 2019 was over $320 million. Do you see yourself joining a company and staying with it for life, as Nadella has (after an earlier job at Sun Microsystems), or is that even possible anymore?
Justin Sullivan/Getty Images

Middle Managers: Implementing Policies and Plans

Middle managers implement the policies and plans of the top managers above them and supervise and coordinate the activities of the first-line managers below them. Titles might include plant manager, district manager, and regional manager, among others. In the nonprofit world, middle managers may have titles such as clinic director, dean of student services, and the like.

Middle managers are critical for organizational success because they implement the strategic plans created by CEOs and top managers. (Strategic planning is discussed in Chapter 6.) In other words, these managers have the type of "high-touch" jobs—dealing with people rather than computer screens or voice-response systems—that can directly affect employees, customers, and suppliers.

First-Line Managers: Directing Daily Tasks

The job titles at this level of the managerial pyramid tend to be on the order of department head, foreperson, or supervisor—clerical supervisor, production supervisor, research supervisor, and so on.

Following the plans of middle and top managers, first-line managers make short-term operating decisions, directing the daily tasks of nonmanagerial personnel, who are, of course, all those people who work directly at their jobs but don't oversee the work of others.

Team Leaders

Teamwork is an essential component of organizational success. Organizations use teams for tasks that can't be accomplished by one person alone because they require a variety of perspectives, knowledge, and skills. Team leaders facilitate team members' activities to help teams achieve their goals. In other words, team leaders see to it that their team members have everything they need to be successful.

Recent research published in *Harvard Business Review* suggests that the most successful teams possess four key elements—compelling direction, strong structure, a supportive context, and a shared mindset—and that team leaders are uniquely positioned to positively impact these elements.[30] Building effective teams is discussed in Chapter 13.

Nonmanagerial Employees

Nonmanagerial employees either work alone on tasks or with others on a variety of teams. They do not formally supervise or manage other people, and they are the bulk of a company's workforce.

Areas of Management: Functional Managers versus General Managers

We can represent the levels of management by slicing the organizational pyramid horizontally. We can also slice the pyramid vertically to represent the organization's departments or functional areas, as we did in Figure 1.2.

In a for-profit technology company, these functional areas might include research and development, marketing, finance, production, and human resources. In a nonprofit college, these might be faculty, student support staff, finance, maintenance, and administration. Whatever the names of the departments, the organization is run by two types of managers—functional and general.

Functional Managers: Responsible for One Activity

If your title is Vice President of Production, Director of Finance, or Administrator for Human Resources, you are a functional manager. A functional manager is responsible for just one organizational activity. Google is particularly noteworthy for its unusual functional management job titles, such as Director of Organic and Softlines, Vice President of Marketing, Mobile, and Wearable Hardware, and Experience Design Lead. Ultimate Software also has unusual functional titles, such as Chief Architect for Emerging Technologies and Identity Access Management Team Lead.

General Managers: Responsible for Several Activities   If you are working in a small organization of, say, 100 people and your title is Executive Vice President, you are probably a general manager over several departments, such as production and finance and human resources. A <mark>general manager</mark> is responsible for several organizational activities.

At the top of the pyramid, general managers are those who seem to be the subject of news stories in magazines such as *Bloomberg Businessweek, Fortune, Forbes,* and *Inc.* Examples are big-company CEOs Mark Clouse of Campbell Soup and Jeff Bezos of Amazon.com, as well as small-company CEOs such as Emily Weiss, who founded Glossier, an online beauty-product retailer. But not all general managers are in for-profit organizations.

Susan L. Solomon is the chief executive officer of the nonprofit New York Stem Cell Foundation. As the parent of a 10-year-old boy diagnosed with Type 1 diabetes, Solomon began reading widely about the disease and came to think that stem cells might transform the understanding and treatment of diabetes, which led her to co-found NYSCF as a research foundation out of her apartment in 2005. As CEO, Solomon has helped to raise $150 million, which makes NYSCF one of the biggest nonprofits dedicated to stem-cell research, employing 45 full-time scientists and funding 75 others around the world. She started her career in law, then went into business and finance, worked for the online auction house Sothebys.com, then formed her own consulting business.[31]

Nonprofit general manager. As CEO of the nonprofit New York Stem Cell Foundation, Susan L. Solomon does a lot of fundraising, directs the activities of the foundation's research scientists, and keeps up with the latest scientific research. "As a lawyer, you learn how to learn about a new field instantly," she says. In addition, she learned how to read quickly. Do you think managerial skills are different for nonprofit and for-profit organizations? D Dipasupil/Getty Images

Managers for Three Types of Organizations: For-Profit, Nonprofit, Mutual-Benefit

There are three types of organizations classified according to the three purposes for which they are formed—*for-profit, nonprofit,* and *mutual-benefit.*

1. **For-Profit Organizations: For Making Money**   For-profit, or business, organizations are formed to make money, or profits, by offering products or services. When most people think of "management," they think of business organizations, ranging from Allstate to Zynga, from Amway to Zagat. There are about 3,600 public companies in the United States today.[32] This is less than half of the 7,400 listed in 1996.[33]

2. **Nonprofit Organizations: For Offering Services**   Managers in nonprofit organizations are often known as administrators. Nonprofit organizations may be either in the public sector, such as the University of California, or in the private sector, such as Stanford University. Either way, their purpose is to offer services to some clients, not to make a profit. Examples of such organizations are hospitals, colleges, and social-welfare agencies (the Salvation Army and the Red Cross). According to the National Center for Charitable Statistics (NCCS), more than 1.4 million nonprofit organizations are registered in the United States. This number includes public charities, private foundations, and other types of nonprofit organizations, including chambers of commerce, fraternal organizations and civic leagues.[34]

   One particular type of nonprofit organization is called the *commonweal organization* (not to be confused with *commonwealth* organization). Unlike nonprofit service organizations, which offer services to *some* clients, commonweal organizations offer services to *all* clients within their jurisdictions. Examples are the military services, the U.S. Postal Service, and your local fire and police departments.

3. **Mutual-Benefit Organizations: For Aiding Members**   Mutual-benefit organizations are voluntary collections of members—political parties, farm cooperatives, labor unions, trade associations, and clubs—whose purpose is to advance members' interests. There are over 9,500 such organizations.[35]

Different Organizations, Different Management?

If you became a manager, would you be doing the same types of things regardless of the type of organization? Generally you would be; that is, you would be performing the four management functions—planning, organizing, leading, and controlling—that we described in Section 1.2.

The single biggest difference, however, is that in a for-profit organization, the measure of success is how much profit (or loss) it generates. In the other two types of organizations, although income and expenditures are very important concerns, the measure of success is usually the effectiveness of the services delivered—how many students were graduated, if you're a college administrator, or how many crimes were prevented or solved, if you're a police chief. ●

1.4 Roles Managers Must Play Successfully

THE BIG PICTURE

Managers tend to work long hours and their time is always in demand; their work is characterized by near constant communication with others; and their jobs require impeccable time-management skills. According to management scholar Henry Mintzberg, managers play three roles—*interpersonal, informational,* and *decisional.* Interpersonal roles include figurehead, leader, and liaison activities. Informational roles are monitor, disseminator, and spokesperson. Decisional roles are entrepreneur, disturbance handler, resource allocator, and negotiator.

LO 1-4

Identify the roles an effective manager must play.

Clearly, being a successful manager requires playing several different roles and exercising several different skills. We discuss managerial roles in this section and key managerial skills in the next.

The Manager's Roles: How Do Managers Spend Their Time?

Maybe, you think, it might be interesting to follow some managers around to see what it is they actually do. That's exactly what management scholar Henry Mintzberg did when, in the late 1960s, he shadowed five chief executives for a week and recorded their working lives.[36] The portrait looked like this:

- "There was no break in the pace of activity during office hours."
- "The mail (average of 36 pieces per day), telephone calls (average of five per day), and meetings (average of eight) accounted for almost every minute from the moment these executives entered their offices in the morning until they departed in the evening."[37]

Although these findings have historical value, times have changed, and they may not reflect today's reality. Two management scholars—Michael Porter and Nitin Nohria—thus decided to update this research by examining how 27 CEOs of multi-billion-dollar companies spent their time on a daily basis over three months.[38]

Here is a summary of some of Porter and Nohria's key findings, important for any prospective manager, along with a discussion of how they compare with Mintzberg's earlier work:

1. Managers Are Always Working and They Are in Constant Demand

Today's managers worked an average of 9.7 hours each weekday. True "breaks" were rare, with most working at least a couple of hours on 79% of their weekend days and 70% of their vacation days. Results showed the typical modern manager clocked a 62.5 hour workweek.

Multitasking. Juggling multiple activities is common for managers—which is why so many managers use their smartphones to keep track of their schedules. Interestingly, although many of us multitask, research shows that very few people are good it. In general, multitasking reduces your productivity. Why do you think this happens? Olivier Lantzendörffer/ Getty Images

Add to this the fact that managers spent most if not all of those 60+ hours satisfying *the demands of others*, and it becomes clear that managing is one tough job. The laundry list of interests demanding a piece of the CEO's time was endless. Both internal constituencies (direct reports, senior leaders, lower-level managers, and nonmanagerial employees) and external constituencies (suppliers, lawyers, service providers, the media, and charitable organizations) continuously vied for a CEO's time.

What's changed for managers since Mintzberg's study many years ago? Not much, it turns out. Mintzberg found that long hours at work were standard, with 50 hours a week being typical and up to 90 hours not unheard of. He also observed that managers almost never had "a true break" from dealing with constituencies—not even on their lunch hours.[39]

2. Managers Spend Virtually All of Their Work Time Communicating with Others

Results showed that CEOs spent 100% of their work time engaged in some form of communication with others. That's right—a full 100% of their work time involved communication! Face-to-face interactions accounted for 61% of managers' work time and electronic communications took up 24%. Managers spent the remaining 15% of their work time on phone calls and reading/responding to letters. Further, many of these communications took place during meetings. Porter and Nohria concluded that these leaders attended a whopping 37 meetings per week, on average.

If we compare these findings with Mintzberg's observations, we see that the role of the manager as a constant communicator was and still is the norm. Much like today, managers in the 1960s spent lots of time in meetings and lots of time communicating. What's changed are the methods of communication available to today's managers and the complexity this adds to an already demanding gig. The telephone conversations that once filled a significant portion of a manager's day have been edged out by e-mail, texting, and social media. Indeed, says Ed Reilly, who heads the American Management Association, all the e-mail, text messaging, and so on can lead people to end up "concentrating on the urgent rather than the important."[40]

Written and oral communication ability is one of the most important career readiness competencies you can develop—it is essential not only for managers but in every single job. We'll explore this and other important career readiness competencies in Section 1.7.

3. Managers Have to Be Purposeful and Proactive about Managing Their Time

Managing means having a full plate at all times. It entails being responsible for multiple departments, locations, decisions, projects, and people; doing multiple things—and feeling the need to be in multiple places—at once; and dealing with constant distractions and interruptions. Even the most impressive managers cannot, and should not, attempt to handle all of these things alone. Rather, skilled management hinges on keeping a rigorous calendar and having the ability to delegate.

Porter and Nohria found that most of the CEOs they studied operated from clear, meticulous agendas. They also observed that CEOs depended a great deal on direct reports—their senior leadership teams—in order to accomplish many tasks. The most effective CEOs also used what the authors termed "broad integrating mechanisms" to enable others in the organization to make the right decisions even in the CEOs' absence. These included strategy, employee development, relationships, and organizational culture—and their existence freed up managers' time for more important tasks.

How do modern managers' workdays compare to those observed in the 1960s? Mintzberg saw workdays characterized by much of the same fragmentation, brevity, and variety we've just described. A 9-minute task here, a 6-minute call there, followed by a 10-minute informal meeting and a 15-minute desk-work session. Only about one-tenth of the managerial activities observed by Mintzberg took more than an hour. "When free time appeared," wrote Mintzberg, "ever-present subordinates quickly usurped it."[41]

No wonder the executive's work time has been characterized as "the interrupt-driven day" and that many managers—such as GM's Mary Barra—are often in their offices by 6 a.m. to take advantage of a brief, quiet period in which to work undisturbed. No wonder that finding balance between work and family lives—work–life balance, as we consider in Chapter 12—is an ongoing concern. No wonder, in fact, that the division between work and nonwork hours is considered almost obsolete in newer industries such as information technology, where people seem to use their smartphones 24/7 to stay linked to their jobs.[42]

It is clear from Porter and Nohria's study and Mintzberg's work that it is easy for managers to get distracted and lose focus and attention during the workday. The practice of mindfulness can help overcome these tendencies (see the Practical Action box).

Mindfulness: How Good Are You at Focusing Your Thoughts, Controlling Your Impulses, and Avoiding Distractions?

How many other things are you trying to do right now, besides reading this chapter? If you are a fan of multitasking, you may want to challenge yourself to try its more effective opposite: practicing mindfulness. If you've never done it before, consider this challenge a practical test of your curiosity; it is an important soft skill.

So what is mindfulness? **Mindfulness is the state of being fully aware of what is happening in the present moment without reacting or applying judgment.**[43] In case you are thinking this sounds like an impractical trait for a busy manager to cultivate, consider that learning how to focus just on the task or conversation at hand is actually an invaluable way to get *more* done. By focusing on one thing at a time, you can complete it fully, put it behind you, and be ready to move on unencumbered by distracting thoughts. Multitasking, on the other hand, divides the mind's attention and actually slows work down.[44]

Snake River at Grand Teton SeanXu/iStock/Getty Images

One of the most effective strategies for increasing your ability to be mindful is meditation, which has also been shown to relieve anxiety and depression and improve sleep.[45] Meditation can literally recharge your brain as well as strengthen your ability to break out of destructive thought patterns that have become habitual.[46] There is even some evidence that meditation can improve your memory.[47] All these are mental traits that will serve anyone well.

Companies that now offer their employees mindfulness training include American Express, Ford, LinkedIn, General Mills, Intel, Goldman Sachs, Apple, Nike, and Target.[48] A study at General Mills showed that after its 7-week program, 80% of participating managers were making better decisions and nearly 90% felt they had become better listeners.[49] Many businesses now believe that mindfulness leads to greater self-awareness, and that this, in turn, makes for stronger leaders who can better manage their own emotions as well as respond more effectively to the concerns of others.[50]

YOUR CALL

Meditation is called a practice because it's a skill that you improve over time. If you're new to it, try repeating this simple method for five minutes a day: Sit still in a quiet place, inhale while counting to seven, hold your breath for seven counts, and exhale for seven counts.[51] Clear your mind, thinking of nothing but your breathing, and if you find other thoughts intruding, don't be discouraged. Put them gently aside and try again. If you find it helpful, place a neutral object in front of you on which to focus, like a candle or a small object that has religious or spiritual meaning for you, or close your eyes.

Three Types of Managerial Roles: Interpersonal, Informational, and Decisional

From his observations and other research, Mintzberg concluded that managers play three broad types of roles or organized sets of behavior: *interpersonal, informational,* and *decisional.* (Porter and Nohria's discussion of the dimensions of the modern CEO role is consistent with the behaviors Mintzberg described).

1. Interpersonal Roles—Figurehead, Leader, and Liaison   In their **interpersonal roles**, managers interact with people inside and outside their work units. The three interpersonal roles include *figurehead, leader,* and *liaison activities.*

2. Informational Roles—Monitor, Disseminator, and Spokesperson   The most important part of a manager's job, Mintzberg believed, is information handling, because accurate information is vital for making intelligent decisions. In their three **informational roles**—as monitor, disseminator, and spokesperson—managers receive and communicate information with other people inside and outside the organization.

At Google, CEO Sundar Pichai scheduled a companywide "town hall" meeting that was abruptly canceled when some employees revealed they were being harassed online because their names and concerns had been leaked to outside websites. Pichai's memo announcing the cancelation needed to communicate clearly and calmly in a tense situation. In it he explained the employees' concerns for their safety and promised to set up several smaller forums "where people can feel comfortable to speak freely." Pichai also acknowledged the many personal meetings and e-mails in which he had heard employees' views and their concerns about being able to speak out. He closed by reminding Googlers that their "desire to build great products" is what unites them and communicating his own excitement about carrying that goal onward.[52]

3. Decisional Roles—Entrepreneur, Disturbance Handler, Resource Allocator, and Negotiator   In their **decisional roles**, managers use information to make decisions to solve problems or take advantage of opportunities. The four decision-making roles are entrepreneur, disturbance handler, resource allocator, and negotiator. These roles are summarized in Table 1.1.

Did anyone say a manager's job is easy? Certainly it's not for people who want to sit on the sidelines of life. Above all else, managers are *doers.* ●

TABLE 1.1   Three Types of Managerial Roles: Interpersonal, Informational, and Decisional

BROAD MANAGERIAL ROLES	TYPES OF ROLES	DESCRIPTION
Interpersonal	Figurehead role	In your *figurehead* role, you show visitors around your company, attend employee birthday parties, and present ethical guidelines to your subordinates. In other words, you perform symbolic tasks that represent your organization.
	Leadership role	In your role of *leader,* you are responsible for the actions of your subordinates, as their successes and failures reflect on you. Your leadership is expressed in your decisions about training, motivating, and disciplining people.
	Liaison role	In your *liaison* role, you must act like a politician, working with other people outside your work unit and organization to develop alliances that will help you achieve your organization's goals.
Informational	Monitor role	As a *monitor,* you should be constantly alert for useful information, whether gathered from newspaper stories about the competition or gathered from snippets of conversation with subordinates you meet in the hallway.
	Disseminator role	Workers complain they never know what's going on? That probably means their supervisor failed in the role of *disseminator.* Managers need to constantly disseminate important information to employees, as via e-mail and meetings.
	Spokesperson role	You are expected, of course, to be a diplomat, to put the best face on the activities of your work unit or organization to people outside it. This is the informational role of *spokesperson.*
Decisional	Entrepreneur role	A good manager is expected to be an *entrepreneur,* to initiate and encourage change and innovation.
	Disturbance handler role	Unforeseen problems—from product defects to international currency crises—require you be a *disturbance handler,* fixing problems.
	Resource allocator role	Because you'll never have enough time, money, and so on, you'll need to be a resource *allocator,* setting priorities about use of resources.
	Negotiator role	To be a manager is to be a continual *negotiator,* working with others inside and outside the organization to accomplish your goals.

1.5 The Skills Exceptional Managers Need

THE BIG PICTURE

Good managers need to work on developing three principal skills. The first is *technical,* the ability to perform a specific job. The second is *conceptual,* the ability to think analytically. The third is *human*, the ability to interact well with people.

LO 1-5

Discuss the skills of an outstanding manager.

Lower- and middle-level managers are a varied lot, but what do top managers have in common? A supportive spouse or partner, suggests one study.[53] Regardless of gender, reaching the top demands a person's all-out commitment to work and career, and someone needs to be there to help with children and laundry. Thus, in 2017, the majority of the 54 Fortune 1000 female CEOs were married and told the Korn Ferry Institute that they had supportive spouses: "Being a CEO, they acknowledge, is not a one-person job; a CEO's partner has to 'lean in' too. The partners of the women CEOs often took primary responsibility on the home front."[54]

General Motors CEO Mary Barra, who is married and the mother of two grown children, has been assisted in her rise by her husband, Tony Barra, a technology consultant. Although female managers with supportive partners are becoming more common, society is still struggling with what it means for men and women to be peers and whether one's career should come first or both should be developed simultaneously.

Whether or not they have support at home, aspiring managers also need to have other kinds of the "right stuff." In the mid-1970s, researcher Robert Katz found that through education and experience managers acquire three principal skills—*technical, conceptual,* and *human.*[55]

1. Technical Skills—The Ability to Perform a Specific Job

Technical skills consist of the job-specific knowledge needed to perform well in a specialized field. Having the requisite technical skills seems to be most important at the lower levels of management—that is, among employees in their first professional job and first-line managers.

Mary Barra has a bachelor's degree in electrical engineering and a master's in business administration and a well-rounded resume that includes important experience as executive assistant to the CEO, being head of midsize car engineering, managing GM's Detroit-Hamtramck plant, and leading the company's human resources division. Then in 2011 she became head of GM's huge worldwide product development, where she "brought order to chaos," according to one account, "mostly by flattening its bureaucracy . . . reducing the number of expensive, global vehicle platforms, and bringing new models to market faster and at lower cost."[56]

Said by her predecessor to be "one of the most gifted executives" he had met in his career, she displays an engineer's enthusiasm for cars, a quality not found among other car-company CEOs promoted from finance operations.[57] Indeed, says one account, "Ms. Barra can often be found on the company's test track putting vehicles through their paces at high speeds."[58]

2. Conceptual Skills—The Ability to Think Analytically

Conceptual skills consist of the ability to think analytically, to visualize an organization as a whole and understand how the parts work together. Conceptual skills are more important as you move up the management ladder, particularly for top managers, who must deal with problems that are ambiguous but that could have far-reaching consequences. Today a top car executive must deal with several radical trends—autonomous (self-driving) cars, electric-powered vehicles, and new business models of start-ups like Uber and Lyft.

Said a GM executive about Barra, "When you put her in a position that's completely new to her, she does an amazing job of getting grounded, understanding what's important and what's not, and executing very well."[59] Or, as Barra said about her management approach, "Problems don't go away when you ignore them—they get bigger. In my experience, it is much better to get the right people together, to make a plan, and to address every challenge head on."[60]

At every stop along the way in rising through GM, Barra analyzed the situation and simplified things. For example, in her product-development job, she streamlined designs by using the same parts in many different models. She also assigned engineers to work in car dealerships to learn more about what customers want in their vehicles.[61] When promoted to CEO, she stepped into the middle of a safety crisis in which GM had to admit to misleading regulators and consumers about a defective ignition switch and agreed to pay a $900 million penalty.[62]

Triple threat. Mary Barra announces that GM will invest $300 million in electric and self-driving vehicles at its Orion Assembly Plant. Barra seems to have the three skills—technical, conceptual, and human—necessary to be a terrific manager in the complex organization that is General Motors. Which skill do you think you need to work on the most? Rebecca Cook/Newscom

Now she is dealing with bigger issues and trying to make GM a more nimble and forward-thinking company. "We know our industry is being disrupted," Barra says. The century-old company is leading the industry in connected-car technology, new electric and hybrid vehicles, and investing in the ride-share service Lyft to prepare for a future in which city residents use self-driving cars to get around.[63]

3. Human Skills—"Soft Skills," the Ability to Interact Well with People

This may well be the most difficult set of skills to master. **Human skills** consist of the ability to work well in cooperation with other people to get things done—especially with people in teams, an important part of today's organizations. Groups and teams are thoroughly discussed in Chapter 13.

Often these are thought of as "soft skills." **Soft skills** are interpersonal "people" skills needed for success at all levels. As discussed in Section 1.7, developing your soft skills is an ongoing, lifelong effort (see the Practical Action box).

During her more than four decades at GM, Barra has demonstrated exceptionally strong soft skills. She has "an ability with people," says her previous boss, that is critical to GM's team-first approach.[64] "She is known inside GM as a consensus builder who calls her staff together on a moment's notice to brainstorm on pressing issues," says another report.[65] "She's fiercely intelligent yet humble and approachable," says a third account. "She's collaborative but is often the person who takes charge. And she's not afraid to make changes."[66]

Among her most significant changes: hiring people with "diverse views, diverse backgrounds, diverse experiences," she says, to try to reshape the company's notoriously insular corporate culture and to bring GM into the age of Apple and Google.

PRACTICAL ACTION   Developing Your Soft Skills

Are you persistent, creative, curious? How do you deal with frustration or anxiety? Do you see yourself as part of a larger whole that gives your work purpose? How do you perceive problems—as temporary and solvable, or as a personal burden you are doomed to bear? Are you a good listener? Your answers will give you an idea about how well developed some of your soft skills are.

More than 90% of respondents to a recent Global Talent Trends survey by LinkedIn identified soft skills like creativity, adaptability, and collaboration as a critical priority.[67] In fact, these skills will become more important than ever as machines assume an increasing number of simple, routine, and manual tasks.[68] Many employers say these skills are hard to find in college graduates, who often value hard skills more highly.[69] Companies are eagerly looking for soft skills as well; Google, for example, now prioritizes social awareness, critical thinking, and problem solving in its hiring process.[70] The good news is that soft skills can be taught. Employers are finding it worth investing money to develop these abilities in their employees. A study conducted by Harvard University, Boston University, and the University of Michigan shows that training employees in soft skills doesn't just marginally improve individual performance and employee retention; it actually betters these metrics enough to provide a 256% return on the financial investment a company makes in training programs.[71]

For firms that can spare their employees for three days, the American Management Association (AMA) offers soft-skills seminars for managers at all levels including front-line supervisors.[72] Among the skills they can gain are the ability to give direction without generating conflict, to lead and motivate groups and teams, to influence others including "difficult" people, to offer effective feedback, and to get things done in an atmosphere of trust and respect. The seminar topics are a comprehensive list of essential soft skills employers look for in college graduates and new hires—and say they seldom find: time management; communication proficiency, which includes presentation and listening skills; self-understanding; social influence and assertiveness; the ability to productively manage conflict; and an understanding of team development and the role of a team player in getting work done.

For those who want to learn online and at their own pace, many inexpensive online classes are available.[73] These short interactive programs are geared for everyone from CEOs to entry-level employees. They cover everything from self-confidence to emotional intelligence, coaching teams, building healthy work relationships, handling business etiquette, resolving conflicts, decision making, reading body language, negotiating, dealing with angry customers, and becoming a successful leader.

YOUR CALL

Look back at the first paragraph in this Practical Action box. Which of the soft skills listed there would you like to improve by the time you graduate, in order to make yourself a more attractive candidate to prospective employers?

The Most Valued Traits in Managers

Clearly, GM's Barra embodies the qualities sought in exceptional managers, especially top managers. "The style for running a company is different from what it used to be," says a top executive recruiter of CEOs. "Companies don't want dictators, kings, or emperors."[74] Instead of someone who gives orders, they want executives who ask probing questions and invite people to participate in decision making and power sharing.

Among the chief skills companies seek in top managers are the following:

- The ability to motivate and engage others.
- The ability to communicate.
- Work experience outside the United States.
- High energy levels to meet the demands of global travel and a 24/7 world.[75] ●

1.6 Seven Challenges to Being an Exceptional Manager

THE BIG PICTURE

Seven challenges face any manager: You need to manage for competitive advantage—to stay ahead of rivals. You need to manage for technological advances—to deal with the "new normal." You need to manage for inclusion and diversity, because the future won't resemble the past. You need to manage for globalization and the expanding management universe. You also must maintain ethical standards, and you need to manage for sustainable development—to practice sound environmental policies. Finally, you need to manage for the achievement of your own happiness and life goals.

Would you agree that the ideal state many people seek is an emotional zone somewhere between boredom and anxiety? That's the view of psychologist Mihaly Csikszentmihalyi (pronounced Me-*high* Chick-sent-me-*high*-ee), founder of the Quality of Life Research Center at Claremont Graduate University.[76]

Boredom, he says, may arise because skills and challenges are mismatched: You are exercising your high level of skill in a job with a low level of challenge, such as licking envelopes. Anxiety arises when someone has low levels of skill but a high level of challenge, such as (for many people) suddenly being called upon to give a rousing speech to strangers.

As a manager, could you achieve a balance between these two states—between boredom and anxiety, or between action and serenity? Certainly managers have enough challenges to keep their lives more than mildly interesting. Let's see what they are.

LO 1-6

Identify the seven challenges faced by most managers.

Challenge #1: Managing for Competitive Advantage—Staying Ahead of Rivals

Competitive advantage is the ability of an organization to produce goods or services more effectively than competitors do, thereby outperforming them. This means an organization must stay ahead in four areas: (1) being responsive to customers, (2) innovation, (3) quality, and (4) efficiency.

1. Being Responsive to Customers   The first law of business is *Take care of the customer.* Without customers—buyers, clients, consumers, shoppers, users, patrons, guests, investors, or whatever they're called—sooner or later there will be no organization. Nonprofit organizations are well advised to be responsive to their "customers," too, whether they're called citizens, members, students, patients, voters, rate-payers, or whatever, because they are the justification for the organizations' existence.

2. Innovation   Finding ways to deliver new or better goods or services is called ==innovation==. No organization, for-profit or nonprofit, can allow itself to become complacent—especially when rivals are coming up with creative ideas. "Innovate or die" is an important adage for any manager. We discuss innovation in Chapter 10.

3. Quality   If your organization is the only one of its kind, customers may put up with products or services that are less than stellar (as they have with some airlines that have a near monopoly on flights out of certain cities), but only because they have no choice. If another organization comes along and offers a better-quality travel experience, TV program, cut of meat, computer software, or whatever, you may find your company falling behind. Making improvements in quality has become an important management idea in recent times, as we shall discuss.

4. Efficiency   A generation ago, organizations rewarded employees for their length of service. Today, however, the emphasis is on efficiency: Companies strive to produce goods or services as quickly as possible using as few employees (and raw materials) as possible. Although a strategy that downgrades the value of employees might ultimately backfire—resulting in the loss of essential experience and skills and even customers—an organization that is overstaffed may not be able to compete with leaner, meaner rivals. This is the reason why, for instance, today many companies rely so much on temp (temporary) workers.

Challenge #2: Managing for Technological Advances—Dealing with the "New Normal"

The challenge of managing for technological advances will require your unflagging attention. Some observers see a Fourth Industrial Revolution on the horizon given the unprecedented speed, scope, and impact of technological breakthroughs in every industry, including artificial intelligence (AI), robotics, self-driving cars, 3D printers, the Internet of Things, and many more innovations.[77]

Some of the implications of technological advances that we will discuss throughout the book are as follows:

- ==**E-commerce**==, or electronic commerce—the buying and selling of goods or services over computer networks—has reshaped entire industries and revamped the very notion of what a company is. U.S. consumers spent more than $550 billion online in 2019, nearly 11% of overall retail spending, and are expected to spend as much as $969 billion by 2023.[78] More important than e-commerce, technological advances have led to the growth of ==e-business==, using the Internet to facilitate every aspect of running a business. Because the Internet so dramatically lowers the cost of communication, it can radically alter any activity that depends heavily on the flow of information. The result is that disruption has become the "new normal," according to Forrester Research.[79]

- **Far-ranging electronic management: e-communication all the time.** Today's managers will be masters of electronic communication, using mobile devices to create powerful messages to motivate and lead teams of specialists all over the world. The next section notes that employers are looking to hire college graduates with information technology application skills. ==Information technology application skills== reflect the extent to which you can effectively use information technology and learn new applications on an ongoing basis. You will clearly want to excel at e-communication.

- **Data, data, and more data: a challenge to decision making.** The digital universe is growing at an incomprehensible speed, one that— according to web-hosting service 100Tb— contains an amount of data so vast it is "impossible for the human mind to quantify."[80] The Internet can assemble astonishing amounts of information and make them available to us instantaneously. This is possible through ==cloud computing==—the storing of software and data on gigantic collections of computers located away from a company's principal site ("in the cloud")—and huge, interconnected ==databases==—computerized collections of interrelated files. This has led to the phenomenon known as ==big data==, stores of data so vast that conventional database management systems cannot handle them, so very sophisticated analysis software and supercomputers are required. The challenge: How do we deal with this massive amount of data to make useful decisions without violating people's right to privacy? We discuss big data in Chapter 7. (Check out the Example box on the use of big data in the health care industry.)

| EXAMPLE | How Direct-to-Consumer Genetics Testing Companies Are Using Big Data to Disrupt the Health Care Industry |

Ancestry and 23andme are competitive rivals that sell genetic testing kits directly to consumers. These companies use sophisticated data analytics and something called genotyping to home in on rich genealogical data and unearth users' ethnicities, family lineage, potential relatives, regions of origin, and fun facts like inherited traits and preferences.[81]

This kind of glimpse into the genome has been largely inaccessible to the everyday person until recently. Advances in analytics along with a 99% decrease in the cost of genetic sequencing over the past decade have opened the door for consumers to be able to access this information quickly and affordably—all it takes is a few weeks, a small sample of saliva, and less than $200.[82]

Direct-to-consumer genetics testing. Having a DNA test is simpler and more affordable than ever. To date, more than 20 million people have been tested through companies like 23and me and Ancestry. What kinds of problems do you think these massive data collections might be used to solve? What kinds of problems might they create? Andrew Brookes/Cultura/Getty Images

Disruption through Data Analytics. But DNA has tremendous potential beyond genealogy. For example, genetic scientists have uncovered thousands of links between genetic variants and diseases, meaning that your DNA has the potential to tell you whether you're likely to develop serious medical conditions as well as whether you're likely to respond to specific treatments.[83] Most people go their entire lives without this information due to the exorbitant costs that prevent insurance companies from approving genetic testing for all but the most seriously ill or high-risk patients.[84] Still, it's hard not to imagine how different the future of health care could be if we shifted our mindset from one of reactive treatment to one of prevention.

Could genetic testing be the missing link in disrupting the health care industry and shifting more knowledge and power into the hands of consumers? Companies like 23andme and Ancestry certainly think so, and both are working to tap into this potential in their massive data sets (combined, the two companies house the DNA of more than 20 million people).[85]

23andme broke through the "wall of the white coat" in 2015 when it received FDA approval to provide health-related genetic reports directly to consumers without a doctor's prescription.[86] It remains the only consumer genetics testing company to offer this option. Reports provide information on users' propensities for blood clots and high cholesterol as well as genetic risks of developing conditions such as Alzheimer's and Parkinson's.[87] Users can also learn whether they carry genetic mutations that may increase their and their offsprings' likelihood of developing diseases such as breast cancer and cystic fibrosis.[88] Ancestry added health-related genetic reports to its menu in 2019, but users must have a physician's orders to obtain them.[89]

Another way these companies are disrupting the health care paradigm is through medical research. Both are sharing data with medical scientists and pharmaceutical giants as they attempt to discover new links between genetics and disease.[90] 23andme has instituted an internal drug discovery unit aimed at developing new drug treatment options for patients suffering with various diseases. GlaxoSmithKline (GSK) recently invested $300 million for an exclusive partnership with 23andme to develop and test new drugs over the next four years.[91]

Ethical Concerns.   Privacy concerns have surfaced in the wake of the consumer genetics testing boom. Recent data breaches at companies like Facebook and First American make clear that databases are susceptible to either malicious or accidental leaks no matter how well protected they are. Users sign waivers and consent forms and have some control over how their data are used and stored, but the fact remains that each user's genetic information is vulnerable.[92]

Further, genetic information stored with Ancestry and 23andme may be subpoenaed by law enforcement agencies in criminal investigations. Even without a subpoena, it is possible for forensic experts to identify perpetrators without the perpetrators' DNA; all that is needed may be the DNA samples of enough of the suspect's close family members, as was the case in the identification and arrest of Golden State Killer Joseph DeAngelo in 2018.[93]

Privacy concerns have also permeated the military. The Pentagon recently issued a statement warning military members to avoid direct-to-consumer DNA tests. The U.S. Defense Department believes this information has the potential to pose security risks and to make covert operations impossible in the future.[94]

The Future of DNA Testing.   Proponents of direct-to-consumer genetics testing praise companies like 23andme and Ancestry for their "democratization of health care" and believe privacy concerns are outweighed by the access to information that these services afford consumers.[95] Still, 2019 saw a marked dip in consumer DNA test sales, and some experts attribute this to increased alarm over recent data breaches and the identification of criminals in high-profile cold cases.[96] But the companies are forging ahead with expanded offerings and new partnerships. For example, 23andme CEO Anne Wojcicki wants to break into the coaching space by using genetic data to tailor health education and training to users.[97]

Consumers seem confident that biotech companies like Ancestry and 23andme will play a critical role in transforming the health care industry and consumers' access to health care.[98]

YOUR CALL

Do you think direct-to-consumer genetics testing companies will gain and sustain significant competitive advantages over existing health care options? If so, how? If not, why? What role will data analytics play in the future of consumer genetics testing?

- **The rise of artificial intelligence: more automation in the workforce. Artificial intelligence (AI)** is the discipline concerned with creating computer systems that simulate human reasoning and sensation, as represented by robots, natural language processing, pattern recognition, and similar technologies. Some people fear that increasingly sophisticated robots will eventually take over even those jobs previously considered too complex for automation, replacing surgeons, writers, lawyers, and airline pilots with AI technology.[99] But others are more optimistic and argue for focusing on what technology has created rather than on what might be lost. Work will be transformed, these observers say, rather than eliminated, and the change will be slow enough for employers, and employees, to adapt.[100] What will be the implications of these events for you as a manager for staffing and training employees and for your own professional development?

- **Organizational changes: shifts in structure, jobs, goals, and management.** Organizations and their employees are no longer as bound by time zones and locations. The "virtual" organization presents a variety of options for how work gets done, including the ability to:
    1. **Telecommute** or work from home or remote locations using a variety of information technologies.
    2. **Videoconference** by using video and audio links along with computers to conduct meetings and allow people in different locations see, hear, and talk with one another.
    3. Deliver and track a variety of functions digitally with programs such as eWorkbench that enable managers to create and track employee goals and deliver feedback.

4. Manage projects using ==project management software== programs for planning and scheduling the people, costs, and resources to complete a project on time.

- **Knowledge management and collaborative computing.** The forms of interaction just described will require managers and employees to be more flexible, and there will be an increased emphasis on ==knowledge management==—the implementing of systems and practices to increase the sharing of knowledge and information throughout an organization. In addition, ==collaborative computing== will help people work better together through state-of-the-art computer software and hardware. Many hospitals, for example, now knit various functions together—patient histories, doctors' orders, lab results, prescription information, billing—in a single information system, parts of which patients can access themselves to schedule appointments, question doctors, and request prescription refills.

Challenge #3: Managing for Inclusion and Diversity—The Future Won't Resemble the Past

In 2018, more than 44 million people in the United States were born in another country, representing 13.7% of the population.[101] That number will exceed 50 million (14.6% of the population) by 2025, and by 2060, over 17% of the U.S. population will be made up of people who were born outside of the United States.[102]

Between the years 2020 and 2060, African American, Asian, and Hispanic individuals will make up increasing proportions of the U.S. population, while the proportion of non-Hispanic white individuals will fall substantially.[103]

In addition, in the coming years there will be a different mix of women, immigrants, and older people in the general population, as well as in the workforce. For instance, in 2030, one in five U.S. residents is expected to be 65 and older. This age group is projected to increase to 94.7 million in 2060, more than doubling the number in 2014 (40.1 million).[104]

Some scholars think that diversity and variety in staffing produce organizational strength, as we will discuss in Chapter 11. Clearly, however, the challenge to the manager of the near future is to maximize the contributions of employees diverse in gender, age, race, ethnicity, and sexual orientation.

Challenge #4: Managing for Globalization—The Expanding Management Universe

When you ask some Russians "How are you?" the response may not be a simple "Fine" but rather the complete truth as to how they really feel—"a blunt pronouncement of dissatisfaction punctuated by, say, the details of any recent digestive troubles," as one American world traveler explained it.[105] And when you meet Cambodians or Burmese and are asked "Have you eaten yet?" you should not mistake this as an invitation to lunch—all it means is "Hello."[106]

The point is this: Verbal expressions and gestures don't mean the same thing to everyone around the world. Failure to understand such differences can affect organizations' ability to manage globally.

U.S. firms have been going out into the world in a major way, even as the world has also been coming to them. This increasingly interconnected nature of business around the word, called globalization, has had economic downsides for workers in some industries, such as clothing, shoe, and toy manufacturing, which have largely moved out of the United States to countries where labor is less expensive. Some critics have therefore pushed back against the idea that globalization is always a good idea, but the fact is that it is likely here to stay.[107] "We know from experience that international cooperation works—from reconstruction after World War II more than 70 years ago to fighting

Cross-border burger business. The manager of this Johnny Rockets hamburger store, which opened in Lagos, Nigeria, in 2012, found that to achieve an authentic, U.S.-style taste he needed to fly in the toppings—onions, mushrooms, and iceberg lettuce—which meant that he had to start prices at $14 for a single-patty burger. Sunday Alamba/AP Images

Ebola just a few years back," says Christine Lagarde, the president of the European Central Bank.[108] Managing for globalization will be a complex, ongoing challenge, as we discuss at length in Chapter 4.[109]

Challenge #5: Managing for Ethical Standards

Under pressure to meet sales, production, and other targets, managers can find themselves confronting ethical dilemmas. What would you do if, as an employee, you discovered that your company was deliberately falsifying data about its product? Consider the following example:

> **Volkswagen Example:** In 2015, Volkswagen was found to have installed, in some 11 million cars sold in the United States, software that deactivated required emissions controls while on the road, releasing many times more emissions than allowed by law, because the controls reduced the cars' advertised fuel economy and drivers might complain. When the vehicles were being tested for compliance with EPA standards, however, their computer systems sensed the test in progress and turned the emissions controls back on, concealing the cars' real environmental cost. Fines and other costs resulting from the scandal are expected to cost VW more than $33 billion.[110] Some executives were forced to resign and at least one was sentenced to jail time.[111]

How far would you go to satisfy demanding customers in a highly competitive international market? In an era of climate change, with increasingly severe storms and rising sea levels, what is your responsibility to "act green"—to avoid company policies that are damaging to the environment?

Ethical behavior is not just a nicety; it is an essential principle to follow in every industry, and one that is even more compelling when you are in a position of power. We hold leaders and managers accountable for unethical behaviors in their organizations even if they are not directly involved. This was evident in the case of the Houston Astros baseball organization.

> **Houston Astros Example:** In early 2020, the Houston Astros fired general manager Jeff Luhnow and manager A.J. Hinch after an investigation revealed that Astros players and personnel had colluded to steal opposing teams' signs using camera footage

during the 2017 and 2018 baseball seasons. Commissioner Robert Manfred acknowledged that Luhnow and Hinch were not directly involved with the scheme, but Manfred stressed that high-ranking officials were responsible for creating cultures where these types of behaviors are not able to take root.[112]

Recent incidents point to serious repercussions when people fail to realize that ethical standards must be followed in every area of life. Clearly ethical lapses have the potential to do great harm, and not only financial harm. How would you behave if you were in a position of power? We consider ethics in Chapter 3 and throughout the book and provide some advice to jumpstart your thinking in the Practical Action box below.

PRACTICAL ACTION   Doing the Right Thing When You're Tempted to Cheat

All kinds of pressures influence people to cheat. Some people may cheat more in the afternoon than in the morning, perhaps because mental fatigue sets in as the day wears on.[113] They may cheat more when technology makes it easy. (Access to copy/paste tools was associated with a higher rate of cheating.)[114] One recent study of 300 college students found that 9 in 10 admitted to cheating, and some believed their instructors did as well.[115]

Of course, just because you may feel okay about cheating doesn't mean it's right, or, from a hard-headed business point of view, even effective—either for you or for the organization you work for.[116] Did you know, for instance, that you can be fired for lying on a job application or resume?

Learning to Be Ethical. Concerned about transgressions in the managerial world, some of the top U.S. researchers in business ethics recently introduced a new website, EthicalSystems.org (*www.ethicalsystems.org*). One of its purposes is to examine the problem that, as one article describes it, "how we think we're going to act when faced with a moral decision and how we really do act are often vastly different."[117] Originally business ethics grew out of the philosophy that ethical behavior was the right thing to do. Now research is uncovering the underlying reasons people act the way they do, to develop a more psychologically realistic approach and learn what tools will nudge people toward right behavior. We include a "Legal/Ethical Challenge" case at the end of every chapter to assist you in developing an ethical orientation.

Doing Right versus Being Liked. When people predict how they're going to act in a given situation, "the 'should' self dominates—we should be fair, we should be generous, we should assert our values," says business ethics professor Ann E. Tenbrunsel. "But when the time for action comes, the 'want' self dominates—I don't want to look like a fool, I don't want to be punished."[118] Thus, you may see some wrong occur (such as an act of cheating) and actually mean to do something about it, but can't quite figure how—and then the moment passes and you let it go and tell yourself that what you did was okay.

YOUR CALL

How can you learn to be ethical? First, recognize the reasons you are tempted to overlook wrongdoing—reluctance to disappoint your friends, worry about what others will think of you, or fear that you'll get in trouble if you speak up. Then realize that the discomfort you're experiencing is a signal that you need to be courageous and act. What will you tell yourself the next time you're tempted to cheat or see someone cheating?

Challenge #6: Managing for Sustainable Development —The Business of Green

Our economic system has brought prosperity for many generations, but in doing so has often assumed an unlimited supply of natural resources. We now believe some of the actions and decisions of the past have caused irreversible damage to the environment, resulting in problems including deforestation, water shortages, and soil pollution.

The United Nations (UN) addressed these issues head-on in 2015 when all 193 members adopted a set of 17 Sustainable Development Goals (SDGs) meant to serve as a blueprint for future economic planning.[119] **Sustainable development** focuses on meeting present needs while simultaneously ensuring that future generations will be able to meet their needs.[120] The UN SDGs include *zero hunger, decent work and economic*

Working to meet the SDGs. A group of professors, ambassadors, and participants at a seminar addressing Taiwan's progress toward meeting the SDGs. SOPA Images Limited/Alamy Stock Photo

growth, affordable and clean energy, and *responsible consumption and production, among others.*

A unique aspect of the UN's approach to sustainable development is that it encourages businesses to pursue strategies that are mutually beneficial to both society and the organizations' bottom lines.[121] The corporate world took notice of this quickly, and by 2016, brands such as The North Face, LEGO, Kimberly-Clark, and Visa had already built one or more of these specific SDGs into their strategic plans.[122]

More recently, the CEOs of some of the most admired and profitable companies in the world (Accenture, Salesforce, Apple, IBM, FedEx, Coca-Cola, and Amazon, to name a few) came together collectively to address sustainable development. These leaders are members of something called Business Roundtable—a public policy advocacy group comprised of CEOs from about 200 leading U.S. companies. In 2019 the group released an updated statement of what it believes to be the purpose of a corporation. This statement was the first since 1997 that did not place shareholders above all other priorities. Instead, it stressed the value of environmental health and widespread economic opportunity, and it expressed that these leaders and their organizations would commit to, among other things, "protect the environment by embracing sustainable practices across our businesses."[123]

The UN has called for an interdisciplinary approach to achieving the SDGs. They emphasize that a sustainable future depends on cities, organizations, educational institutions, governments, and individuals coming together to solve these global issues collaboratively.[124] Clearly sustainable development is a critical issue facing businesses today. We will discuss these issues in depth in Learning Module 1 of the text.

Challenge #7: Managing for Happiness and Meaningfulness

Which would you rather have, a happy life or a meaningful life? We recommend both!

One study found that "Happiness was linked to being a taker rather than a giver, whereas meaningfulness went with being a giver rather than a taker," as a study author put it.[125] Happiness is getting what you want, having your desires fulfilled. Meaningfulness is the sense of "belonging to and serving something that you believe is bigger than the self."[126] In our case, for example, we derive meaning from writing this book because we believe it can enrich your life and help you manage others more effectively. Research clearly shows that a sense of meaningfulness in your life is associated with better health, work and life satisfaction, and performance.[127]

We have three suggestions for building meaning into your life.

1. **Identify activities you love doing.** Try to do more of these activities or find ways to build them into your work role. Employees at St. Jude Children's Research Hospital embody this suggestion. They truly enjoy participating in the St. Jude Marathon weekend because it raises money for the children being treated at the hospital. One employee, a cancer survivor, commented, "Each year it provides me with another opportunity to give back so that we can help countless other children have anniversaries of their own."[128]

2. **Find a way to build your natural strengths into your personal and work life.** Doing this requires that you assess yourself along a host of competencies desired by employers. The next section identifies these competencies and discusses how you might evaluate your strengths and development opportunities.

3. **Go out and help someone.** Research shows that people derive a sense of meaningfulness from helping others.[129] Salesforce, ranked as the second best place to work by *Fortune* in 2019, follows this suggestion.[130] The company donates "subscriptions for its technology to nonprofits and educators, it grants employees seven days off to volunteer each year, and has given away more than $137 million."[131]

Finding meaning at work. Some organizations give their employees paid time off for volunteer work. Would you find it meaningful to put food and drinks into paper bags for charity? LightField Studios/ Shutterstock

How Strong Is Your Motivation to Be a Manager? The First Self-Assessment

As we stated at the beginning of this chapter, it is our desire to make this book *as practical as possible* for you. As an important means of advancing this goal, we developed 64 **self-assessments**—two to four per chapter—that allow you to gauge how you feel about the material you are reading and how you can make use of it.

Go to the self-assessment website at *connect.mheducation.com,* complete the self-assessment, then answer the self-assessment questions in the book. (Note: These self-assessments are available only if your instructor uses *Connect* and assigns them to you.) Taking the self-assessments is a valuable way to develop your self-awareness and career readiness, which is discussed in the next section. The first one assesses your motivation to lead. Do you desire to hold leadership positions? Find out by taking the self-assessment. ●

SELF-ASSESSMENT 1.1   CAREER READINESS

How Strong Is My Motivation to Lead?

Are you motivated to lead others? Please be prepared to answer these questions if your instructor has assigned Self-Assessment 1.1 in *Connect.*

1. Do results match your desire to assume leadership roles at school, work, and home? Explain.

2. Which of the three dimensions do you think is most likely to affect your future success as a leader? Discuss.

3. What things would you say during an interview to demonstrate that you possess the career readiness competency of leadership?

1.7 Building Your Career Readiness

THE BIG PICTURE

Companies want to hire *career-ready* college graduates. In this section we describe a model of career readiness and offer tips for building your readiness.

LO 1-7

Define the core competencies, knowledge, soft skills, attitudes, and other characteristics needed for career readiness and discuss how they can be developed.

About 53,000 undergraduate students from 218 universities across the United States rated 2019's most attractive employers. The top 10 were (1) Google, (2) JPMorgan Chase, (3) Amazon, (4) Apple, (5) Goldman Sachs, (6) The Walt Disney Company, (7), Nike, (8) Deloitte, (9) Netflix, and (10) EY (Ernst & Young).[132] Would you like to work at these companies or others like them? If so, you need to be career ready.

Career readiness represents the extent to which you possess the knowledge, skills, and attributes desired by employers. How ready do you believe you are? Recent surveys of college students and employers reveal a big gap in the degree of readiness each group perceives in students. *Figure 1.3* shows some key results of a study of 201 employers and 4,213 graduating seniors. The majority of students rated themselves as career-ready on 6 of 7 skills, while the majority of employers perceived students to be well-prepared on only 3 of the skills. The three largest gaps were in professionalism/work ethic, leadership, and oral/written communication, skills that are very important to employers.[133] Other studies have similarly demonstrated that employers see a major skills gap in college students' interpersonal skills.[134]

FIGURE 1.3

Employers and college grads disagree about levels of career readiness

Sources: National Association of Colleges and Employers, "Are College Graduates 'Career Ready'?" February 19, 2018, https://www.naceweb.org/career-readiness/competencies/are-college-graduates-career-ready/. Data derived from NACE's "Job Outlook 2018" and "The Class of 2017 Student Survey Report."

Proportions Saying They/Recent College Graduates Are Proficient in Each Competency*

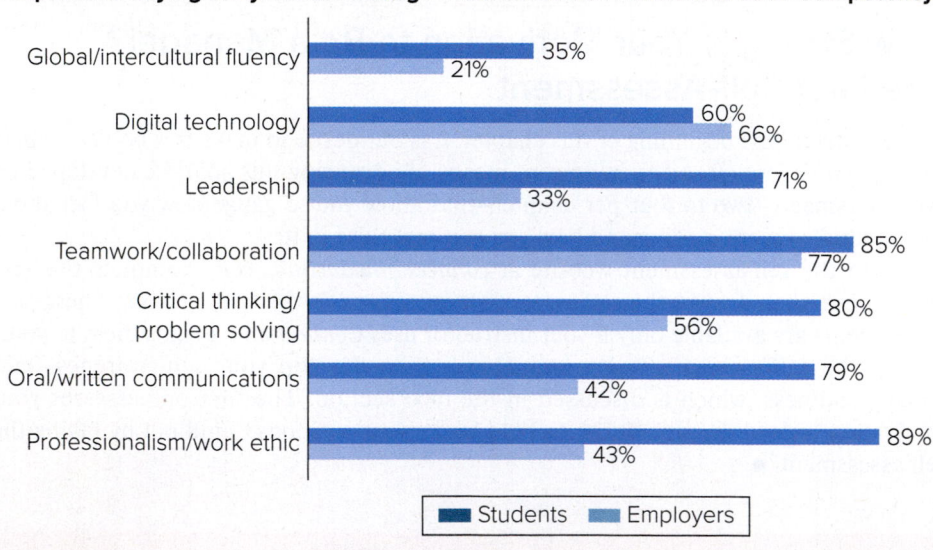

*4-5 ratings on a 1-to-5 scale

The good news is that merely acknowledging the existence of these gaps will impress potential employers because companies prefer to hire people with realistic self-perceptions. This underscores the need to obtain information about your strengths and weaknesses throughout your career.

More importantly, we think your awareness that employers expect more from you in these areas will be valuable for at least two reasons:

1. **You will be motivated to learn.** Studies of human behavior reveal that people won't spend time on personal development unless they feel the need. Overinflated perceptions of career readiness will not motivate you to develop the attributes that

enhance that readiness. Having a realistic picture will increase your motivation to learn and develop. It will also allow you to practice learning, which is something you will need to do throughout your career. You may be surprised to learn that the knowledge you gain from your college degree may be obsolete in as little as five years.[135] This is due to the rapidly changing nature of jobs, and it means that you should approach career readiness as a lifelong process rather than a one-time event that stops after graduation. Authors of the *Future Work Skills 2020* report concluded that individuals "will increasingly be called upon to continually reassess the skills they need, and quickly put together the right resources to develop and update these. Workers in the future need to be adaptable lifelong learners."[136]

2. **You will know where to focus your energy.** As you will learn in the upcoming section, the list of career readiness competencies is quite long, and some of the competencies will be more relevant to your personal career path than others. This can be daunting when you are trying to improve your career readiness—where should you begin? We're here to help. In comparing the results from multiple career readiness studies (including the NACE data presented in Figure 1.3), we noticed there were several competencies that employers consistently rated as essential.[137] We call these *core competencies.* Organizations across the board are on the prowl for employees who possess these basic competencies, many of which are reflected in the "gaps" you just learned about.

Let's consider a model of career readiness and how you can apply it in your life.

A Model of Career Readiness

Being career ready is more encompassing than you might think. It starts with ==core competencies==—a set of competencies that are vital across jobs, occupations, and industries. Four additional categories of competency round out career readiness: knowledge, soft skills, attitudes, and other characteristics (see *Figure 1.4*). Let's look at each component of the model in detail.

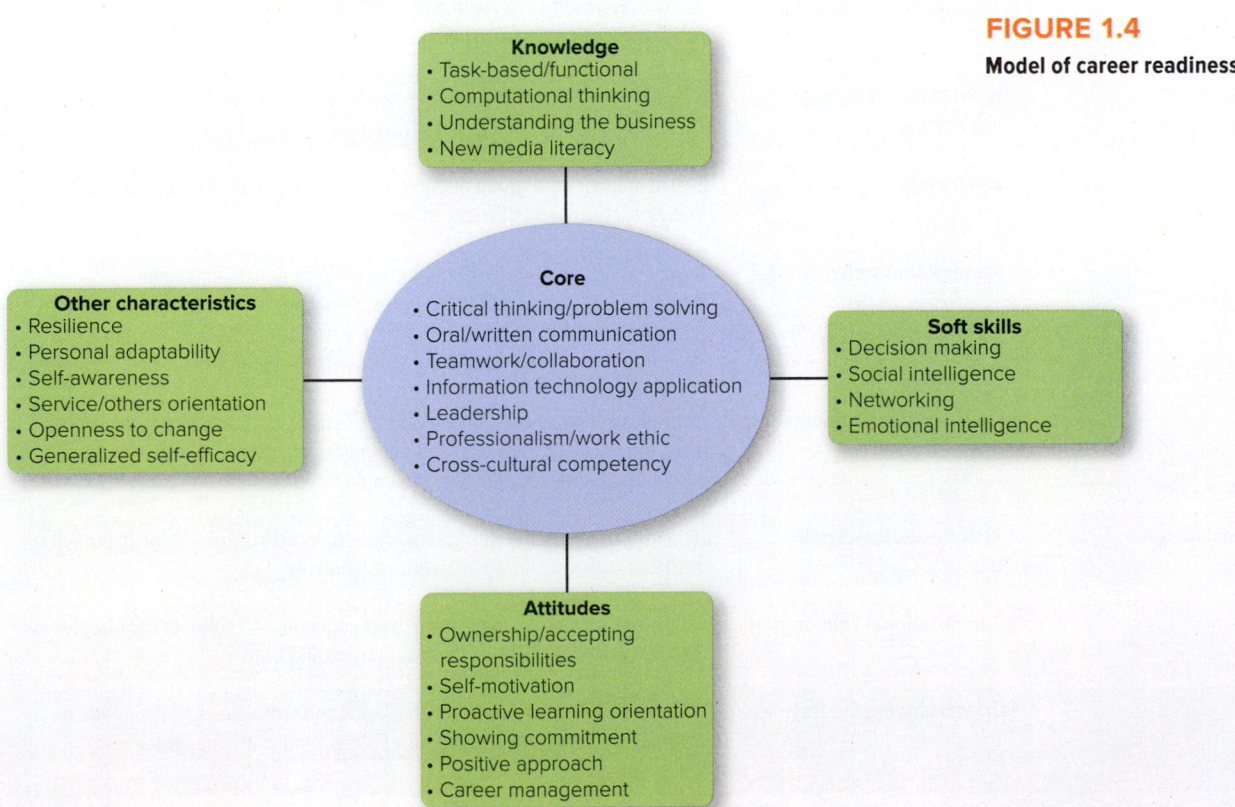

FIGURE 1.4

Model of career readiness

Core Competencies   The seven competencies in the center of the model are necessary for success no matter what career path you pursue. The demand for things like communication and leadership ability, interpersonal skills, and information technology skills is predicted to grow substantially across all industries in the United States and Europe by the year 2030.[138] Still, employers consider many of these competencies to be rare in today's labor market. Kate Davidson, a reporter for *The Wall Street Journal*, concluded that "it is becoming increasingly difficult to find applicants who can communicate clearly, take initiative, problem-solve and get along with co-workers."[139] We think this provides excellent incentive for you to work on increasing your level of these competencies. Your efforts may translate to big advantages on the job market.

Knowledge   Skills in the knowledge category, generally referred to as "hard skills," encompass the basic knowledge employers expect you to possess. They develop from your ability to apply academic and practical knowledge while performing the job. Your grade point average is one way to assess your current level of this type of knowledge.[140] Other types of knowledge desired by employers include computational thinking, understanding the business, and new media literacy (see Table 1.2).

TABLE 1.2   Description of the Competencies Needed for Career Readiness

CATEGORY	COMPETENCY	DESCRIPTION
Core	Critical Thinking/Problem Solving	Sound reasoning to analyze situations, make decisions, and solve problems. Ability to obtain, interpret, and analyze both qualitative and quantitative information while creatively solving problems.
	Oral/Written Communication	Ability to effectively express your thoughts, ideas, and messages to diverse people in oral and written form. Public speaking skills and ability to write/edit e-mails, letters, and technical reports.
	Teamwork/Collaboration	Ability to work effectively with and build collaborative relationships with diverse people, work within a team structure, and manage interpersonal conflict.
	Information Technology Application	Effective use of IT and learning new applications as needed.
	Leadership	Skill at influencing a group of people to achieve common goals. Ability to motivate, coach, and develop others.
	Professionalism/Work Ethic	Accountability and positive work habits such as punctuality, time management, appropriate dress and appearance, and willingness to go beyond a job description or ask for help when needed. Demonstrated integrity, ethical behavior, and concern for the greater good.
	Cross-Cultural Competency	Awareness of cross-cultural differences; respect for diverse cultures, races, ages, genders, and religions; and demonstrated openness, inclusiveness, and ability to interact with diverse people.
Knowledge	Task-Based/Functional	Demonstrated ability to apply academic and practical knowledge in pursuit of organizational and individual goals/assignments.
	Computational Thinking	Ability to use numbers to distill abstract concepts and conduct data-based reasoning. Ability to work with and interpret Big Data.
	Understanding the Business	Understanding of the company's business and strategies and the needs of stakeholders, and ability to see how your work fits into the larger organizational puzzle.

TABLE 1.2   Description of the Competencies Needed for Career Readiness (*Continued*)

CATEGORY	COMPETENCY	DESCRIPTION
	New Media Literacy	Ability to develop, evaluate, and use new media forms, and to apply these media for persuasive communication. Ability to stay up-to-date with the latest media trends and to leverage them in the interest of the organization.
Soft Skills	**Decision Making**	Ability to collect, process, and analyze information in order to identify and choose from alternative solutions that lead to optimal outcomes.
	Social Intelligence	Ability to connect with others in a meaningful way, to recognize and understand another person's feelings and thoughts, and to use this information to stimulate positive relationships and beneficial interactions.
	Networking	Ability to build and maintain a strong, broad professional network of relationships.
	Emotional Intelligence	Ability to monitor your emotions and those of others, to discriminate among them, and to use this information to guide your thinking and behavior.
Attitudes	**Ownership/Accepting Responsibility**	Willingness to accept responsibility for your actions.
	Self-Motivation	Ability to work productively without constant direction, instruction, and praise. Ability to establish and maintain good work habits and consistent focus on organizational goals and personal development.
	Proactive Learning Orientation	Desire to learn and improve your knowledge, soft skills, and other characteristics in pursuit of personal development.
	Showing Commitment	Willingness to support others and positively work toward achieving individual and company goals.
	Positive Approach	Willingness to accept developmental feedback, to try and suggest new ideas, and to maintain a positive attitude at work.
	Career Management	Ability to proactively manage your career and identify opportunities for professional development.
Other Characteristics	**Resilience**	Ability to bounce back from adversity and to remain motivated when confronted with challenges.
	Personal Adaptability	Ability and willingness to adapt to changing situations.
	Self-Awareness	A realistic view of your strengths and weaknesses relative to a specific job and context, and the ability to create and implement a personal development plan.
	Service/Others Orientation	Willingness to put the needs of others over self-interests.
	Openness to Change	Flexibility when confronted with change, ability to see change as a challenge, and willingness to apply new ideas, processes, or directives.
	Generalized Self-Efficacy	Confidence in your ability to perform across a variety of situations.

Sources: Based on material in NACE Staff, "Career Readiness Defined," 2019, https://www.naceweb.org/career-readiness/competencies/career-readiness-defined; Alison Doyle, "Hard Skills vs. Soft Skill: What's the Difference? The Balance Careers, February 4, 2019, https://www.thebalancecareers.com/hard-skills-vs-soft-skills-2063780; Ashita Bhagra and Dinesh Kumar Sharma, "Changing Paradigm of Employability Skills in the Global Business World: A Review," IUP Journal of Soft Skills, 2018, pp. 7–24; and Fatima Suleman, "The Employability Skills of Higher Education Graduates: Insights into Conceptual Frameworks and Methodological Options," Higher Education, 2018, pp. 263–278.

Soft Skills   We defined *soft skills* above as interpersonal or "people" skills needed for success at work. These are not knowledge or technical skills. Soft skills are becoming increasingly important as companies outsource and automate routine tasks. For example, a recent *LinkedIn* survey of global talent trends reported that 92% of talent professionals believed soft skills were as important or more important than hard skills when making hiring decisions. Further, 89% said that identifying someone as a "bad hire" typically came down to a lack of soft skills.[141] You can increase your career readiness by focusing on the four soft skills described in Table 1.2. You will learn more about each one as we progress through this book.

Attitudes   Attitudes are beliefs and feelings directed toward *specific* objects, people, or events. More formally, an **attitude is defined as a learned predisposition toward a given object.** Attitudes are thoroughly discussed in Chapter 11.

Table 1.2 indicates that recruiters prefer to find six attitudes in college graduates they hire. All have a positive and proactive focus. People perceive our attitudes by observing what we do and say. For example, taking ownership or responsibility is a key attitude preferred by recruiters. It reflects the extent to which a person accepts responsibility for his or her actions. We suspect recruiters desire this attitude because it is positively associated with employees' commitment, job satisfaction, and engagement. Feelings of ownership also reduce employees' desire to quit.[142] All told, you can create more favorable impressions during interviews if you demonstrate this attitude. Find out where you stand on this attitude by taking Self-Assessment 1.2. It was designed to enhance your self-awareness about the extent to which you accept responsibility for your actions.

SELF-ASSESSMENT 1.2   CAREER READINESS

To What Extent Do You Accept Responsibility for Your Actions?

People are more likely to work diligently toward accomplishing their goals and accept performance feedback when they accept responsibility for their actions. They also are less likely to blame others for their mistakes or poor performance. This self-assessment allows you to determine your status regarding this important attitude. The survey feedback will help you to maintain or improve your attitude about taking ownership/responsibility for your actions.

Please be prepared to answer these questions if your instructor has assigned Self-Assessment 1.2 in Connect.

1. Do you have a strong attitude about accepting responsibility for your actions? Do you agree with these results? Explain your thinking.

2. What can you do to increase the strength of this attitude?

3. What things would you say during an interview to demonstrate that you possess the career readiness competency of ownership/accepting responsibility?

Other Characteristics   This category contains a host of personal characteristics that prompt positive impressions among others and help you effectively adapt to personal and work-related changes. Consider professionalism/work ethic and resilience. Aaron Michel, cofounder and CEO at PathSource, a career navigation and education software company, believes professionalism/work ethic "cannot be overvalued in the job market." He concluded that "just being on time and behaving responsibly can leave a strong impression."[143] Consider the competency of resilience.

Resilience is the ability to bounce back from adversity and to sustain yourself when faced with a challenge. Research shows that it is a key trait of successful people.[144] Heisman Trophy winner Joe Burrow displayed resilience in his college football career. After being rejected by his dream school Nebraska and then sitting on the bench at Ohio State for two seasons, Burrow suffered a broken thumb and lost his chance to start in the 2018 season.[145] Instead of giving up on his dream he transferred to LSU, where his

Bouncing back from adversity. Joe Burrow (#9), pictured with LSU head coach Ed Orgeron (left) and teammates Grant Delpit (#7), and Patrick Queen (#8), showed tremendous resilience during his college football career, culminating in a 2020 National Championship for the LSU Tigers. Alika Jenner/Getty Images Sport/Getty Images

persistence and dedication led the LSU Tigers to a 2020 National Championship. In describing his path to success, Burrow said, "Adversity is a key component in building the kind of players to succeed at the next level. I'm forever grateful I went through that adversity."[146] This type of cognitive reframing is key to becoming resilient.[147] Can you see why employers want to hire people who are professional and resilient?

Developing Career Readiness

We classify the many ways to develop career readiness into six categories: (1) *build self-awareness,* (2) *learn from educational activities,* (3) *model others possessing the desired competencies,* (4) *learn from on-the-job-activities,* (5) *seek experience from student groups and organizations,* and (6) *experiment.*

1. Build Self-Awareness   There are two ways to gather the data or information you need to make an accurate evaluation of your strengths and developmental opportunities:

- Ask for honest, targeted feedback from fellow students, co-workers, managers, teachers, and family. Find people you trust.
- Take validated self-assessment surveys. This textbook provides 64 self-assessments for this purpose. Each provides developmental feedback, enabling you to devise a path toward improvement of a particular skill.

2. Learn from Educational Activities   To continue the lifelong process of learning, you need a proactive learning orientation. As defined in Table 1.2, a **proactive learning orientation** is the desire to learn and improve your knowledge, soft skills, and other characteristics in pursuit of personal development. This orientation allows you to improve your chances of learning new skills by means of the following:

- Taking courses at your university or attending training seminars that focus on the competencies you need, such as time management or communication.

- Watching training videos and documentaries.
- Reading books, magazines, and research articles in pursuit of developmental ideas.[148] This textbook is a good source. You can also consult the references cited in this book to find more detailed information about a variety of topics.
- Searching the Internet or Amazon for relevant source materials from reputable sources.

3. Model Others Possessing the Targeted Competencies   To learn from others around you, you can:

- Identify role models or mentors who possess the skills or traits you need and then interview them. Try to learn how they execute their competencies.
- Observe people who possess the targeted competency and learn from their behavior.
- Try out new behaviors and then discuss your results with a mentor, coach, or colleague.

4. Learn from On-the-Job Activities   Steps you can take include:

- Seeking new assignments that require you to use one of your targeted competencies.
- Representing a member of management at a meeting or business function.
- Serving as a coach to another employee.
- Asking to serve as a team leader or project manager.
- Making presentations and facilitating meetings.
- Volunteering for special projects or committees.
- Transferring to another job to obtain new skills and experience.

5. Seek Experience from Student Groups and Organizations   The following activities are useful:

- Join student groups and seek leadership positions.
- Join and network at student organizations such as Toastmasters.
- Volunteer at organizations where you can practice your developing skills.
- Enroll in internships, research projects, service learning opportunities, or co-ops. Internships generally last one semester or summer and can be paid or unpaid. Co-ops are paid full-time jobs that typically last 3 to 12 months.[149]
- Make presentations to professional or civic organizations.
- Volunteer in religious, civic, or community organizations.

6. Experiment   Developing soft skills requires you to put new knowledge or information to use. Try these ideas:

- Identify new behaviors you want to master and then practice them. For example, if you want to increase your leadership skills, volunteer to facilitate your next team meeting at school or work. Practice using the influence skills we'll discuss in Chapter 14.
- Keep a career journal. Record the details of your developmental efforts and learn from both success and missteps. Collect stories about your strengths and the improvements you've made and then use them during job interviews.

Let Us Help

Our two overriding goals for writing this book are to (1) assist you in leading a happy and meaningful life and (2) help you become career ready by learning about the principles of management. We thus created a feature for each chapter titled "Career Corner: Managing Your Career Readiness." The purpose of this feature is to help you integrate what you learn in a chapter into the process of building your career readiness. The next section is our first installment. •

1.8 Career Corner: Managing Your Career Readiness

The goal of this section is to help you apply what you learn to building your career readiness. Let's begin with three keys to success:

1. It's your responsibility to manage your career. Don't count on others.
2. Personal reflection, motivation, commitment, and experimentation are essential.
3. Success is achieved by following a process. A **process** is defined as a series of actions or steps followed to bring about a desired result.

LO 1-8

Describe the process for managing your career readiness.

A Process for Developing Career Readiness

Figure 1.5 illustrates a process to guide the pursuit of managing your career readiness. We recommend the following four steps:

Step 1.   The first step entails examining the list of career readiness competencies in Table 1.2 and picking two or three that impact your current performance at school, work, or extracurricular activities. You then need to assess your skill level for these competencies. This textbook contains 64 self-assessments you can take for this purpose. The first one was presented on page 29.

Step 2.   The second step requires you to consider how you can use the material covered in a chapter to develop your targeted career readiness competencies. For example, do your targeted competencies at this point relate to any of the four functions of management: planning, organizing, leading, or controlling? If yes, reflect on what you learned while reading material regarding the functions of management and consider how you can apply ideas, concepts, or suggestions that were discussed.

Step 3.   The third step involves experimenting with small steps aimed at developing your targeted career readiness competencies.

Step 4.   The final step is to evaluate what happened during your small-step experiments. This entails reflecting on what went right and wrong. Remember, you can learn as much from failure as success.

Figure 1.5 shows that *willingness* is at the center of developing your career readiness. This reinforces the point that it's up to you to shape and direct your future. We are confident that you can develop your career readiness by following this process and using the guidance provided at the end of every chapter.[150]

FIGURE 1.5

Process for managing career readiness

Kinicki and Associates, Inc., 2022

Make It a Habit

We know from experience that self-improvement can be a difficult and often disappointing process. If you've ever tried to change something about yourself, you know it too. We want to set you up for success right from the start. With that in mind, here is a simple way to approach the task of managing your career readiness: Make it a habit.

Stanford University behavior scientist Dr. B.J. Fogg says the secret to successfully changing behavior lies in creating habits. You can use Dr. Fogg's three-step process to turn managing your career readiness into a habit.[151]

1. **Identify something specific you want to accomplish.** Be sure to choose something that excites you. Fogg says that if the goal you're working toward is something you truly want to accomplish, then motivation will come naturally. Suppose you really want to get better at the career readiness competency of networking. Perhaps you are energized when you imagine what it would feel like to have a large network of professional contacts at your disposal. (Tickets to that sold-out concert? You'd know just whom to call. A job interview with that exciting new company? You'd be a mere text message away.) An example of a specific outcome related to networking is to "add three new professionals to my contacts list over the next year."

2. **Identify a simple, tiny change you can implement.** Fogg says you should plan to make incremental progress toward your desired outcome through a series of tiny, simple changes. Tiny changes are easy, which means you are more likely to stick with them. Take our previous example. If you want to get better at networking and your ultimate goal is to add three professional contacts to your list, start by identifying all of the little steps that would eventually get you to this goal. Your first tiny change might be as simple as peeking at your local young professionals Instagram account every day. Once you've established this as a habit, your next tiny change might be to bookmark any post

on that account that advertises an upcoming networking event. Again, do this until it becomes habitual. Next you might commit to adding each new bookmarked event to your personal calendar. Before you know it, you'll be attending networking events, meeting new people, and upsizing that professional contacts list.

3. **Attach the tiny change to an existing habit.** Fogg's method relies on the fact that we are already engaging in a slew of habits as part of our daily routines. Try to identify some of your existing habits. Maybe you head straight for the bathroom sink to brush your teeth when you wake up in the morning. Or perhaps you are useless until you get your first cup of coffee. Think about your lunch break—can you make it through without a Sudoku puzzle? It's likely you can easily identify a long list of existing habits; choose one of them to prompt your new, tiny change. In the case of our networking example, if you are a daily coffee drinker, you might start by looking at your local young professionals Instagram account each morning as you sip your latté. Over time, each successive tiny change should move you closer to your ultimate networking goal.

One final note—be sure to celebrate each time you engage in one of these tiny behaviors. It can be as simple as saying "nice job!" to yourself in your head. Fogg says that over time, these moments of positive reinforcement will go a long way toward making your new behaviors automatic, and therefore, toward helping you reach your goals. ●

artificial intelligence (AI) 24

attitude 34

big data 23

career readiness 30

cloud computing 23

collaborative computing 25

competitive advantage 21

conceptual skills 19

controlling 10

core competencies 31

databases 23

decisional roles 17

e-business 22

e-commerce 22

effective 5

efficient 5

first-line managers 12

four management functions 8

functional manager 12

general manager 13

human skills 20

information technology application skills 22

informational roles 17

innovation 22

interpersonal roles 17

knowledge management 25

leading 9

management 5

meaningfulness 28

mentor 8

middle managers 12

mindfulness 16

nonmanagerial employees 12

organization 5

organizing 9

planning 9

proactive learning orientation 35

process 37

project management software 25

resilience 34

soft skills 20

sustainable development 27

team leaders 12

technical skills 19

telecommute 24

top managers 11

videoconference 24

Key Points

1.1 Management: What It Is, What Its Benefits Are

- Management is defined as the pursuit of organizational goals efficiently through wise and cost-effective use of resources, and effectively through planning, organizing, leading, and controlling the organization's resources.

1.2 What Managers Do: The Four Principal Functions

- The management process consists of four functions: Planning, organizing, leading, and controlling.

1.3 Pyramid Power: Levels and Areas of Management

- Within an organization, there are managers at four levels: top managers, middle managers, first-line managers, and team leaders.
- There are three types of organizations—for-profit, nonprofit, and mutual benefit. Each has a different purpose.

1.4 Roles Managers Must Play Successfully

- Porter and Nohria found that managers (1) are always working and in constant demand, (2) spend virtually all of their time at work communicating with others, and (3) have to be purposeful and proactive about managing their time.
- Mintzberg concluded that managers play three broad roles: (1) interpersonal—figurehead, leader, and

liaison; (2) informational—monitor, disseminator, and spokesperson; and (3) decisional—entrepreneur, disturbance handler, resource allocator, and negotiator.

1.5 The Skills Exceptional Managers Need

- The three skills that exceptional managers cultivate are technical, conceptual, and human. Each uses different abilities.

1.6 Seven Challenges to Being an Exceptional Manager

- Managers face seven key challenges. These include managing for (1) competitive advantage, (2) technological advances, (3) inclusion and diversity, (4) globalization, (5) ethical standards, (6) sustainable development, and (7) happiness and meaningfulness.

1.7 Building Your Career Readiness

- Career readiness reflects the extent to which you possess the competencies desired by employers.
- Research uncovered 27 career readiness competencies preferred by employers (see Table 1.2).
- Six actions develop career readiness: (1) Build self-awareness, (2) learn from educational activities, (3) model others possessing the targeted competencies, (4) learn from on-the-job activities, (5) seek experience from student groups and organizations, and (6) experiment.

1.8 Career Corner: Managing Your Career Readiness

- A four-step process is recommended for managing your career readiness: (1) Identify the career readiness competencies you want to develop, (2) determine which concepts are relevant for developing your targeted career readiness competencies, (3) experiment with implementing a few small steps aimed at developing your career readiness competencies, and (4) evaluate the results of your experimental small steps.
- It takes willingness on your part to manage career readiness.
- You can turn developing career readiness into a habit by following three simple steps: (1) identify something specific you want to accomplish; (2) identify a simple, tiny change you can implement; and (3) attach the tiny change to an existing habit.

Understanding the Chapter: What Do I Know?

1. What is the difference between being efficient and being effective?
2. What is the formal, three-part definition of management?
3. How would I define the four functions of management?
4. What are the differences among the four levels of managers in the organizational pyramid?
5. Porter and Nohria's recent study came up with three important findings about a manager's routine. What are they, and how do they compare to what Mintzberg's earlier study found?
6. Mintzberg also found that managers play three important roles. What are they, and what examples can I think of?
7. What are the three skills that exceptional managers need to cultivate, and which one do I probably have to work on most?
8. What are the seven challenges of being a manager, and which one is the one I will probably most have to worry about during my lifetime?
9. What does it mean to be career ready, and what are the attributes that define it?
10. How can I build my level of career readiness?

Management in Action

Fast Fashion—Was Forever 21 Fast Enough?

MR. AND MRS. CHANG

Do Won Chang and Jin Sook Chang arrived in the United States from South Korea in 1981. For three years, the married couple worked hard—he pumped gas and waited tables, she styled hair— and by 1984 they amassed $11,000 in savings that they used to purchase a single retail clothing store in Los Angeles. By 2014 they were billionaires, running one of the most recognizable fashion retailers in the world—Forever 21.[152] And as they required of even their most senior executives, you can call them Mr. and Mrs. Chang.[153]

FAST FASHION, FAST GROWTH

Forever 21 was a pioneer in *fast fashion*. Under this model, companies produce and sell on-trend clothing quickly and cheaply, making most current styles affordable and accessible to a wide range of consumers. Fast fashion is inexpensive and customers have little expectation for quality. Instead, the imperative is to get of-the-moment styles into consumers' hands within weeks or even days of the trends first appearing on reality TV or influencers' social media accounts.[154]

Forever 21 was a massive success, and the company grew very big, very quickly. At one point Forever 21 had almost 500 stores in the United States and more than 800 stores globally.[155] As the so-called retail apocalypse took even the most established brick-and-mortar brands out one-by-one, Forever 21 leaned in. Eventually, having a Forever 21 store became a virtual requirement for any struggling mall that wanted a chance at survival.[156]

CONTROL PROBLEMS

What was it like to work in the upper echelons of such a massive and successful company? Former executives paint a picture of a tightly run ship. The inner circle of executives consisted of the Changs, their daughters Esther and Linda, and their close friends, married couple Alex and Seong Eun Kim Ok. Over the years only a handful of other close confidants entered and left the group, and some senior executives say they don't recall having a single e-mail from or conversation with either of the Changs. The small team operated largely in isolation from the rest of the company, and every decision had to go through Mr. and Mrs. Chang.[157]

These decisions have been scrutinized in recent years as stories of poor planning and mismanagement surfaced. Insiders recall watching huge shipments of inventory stagnate in warehouses as they waited for the Changs to approve the items, then shipping at expensive overnight rates to make up for the lost time. There also are accounts of expensive mistakes in international operations, including shipments of shoes and cosmetics being confiscated at customs because the company hadn't acquired proper import licenses. Much of this inventory wound up in dumpsters.[158]

The Changs were presented with big data, including market trends, previous years' sales figures, and inventory projection, but they seemed to make subsequent decisions without regard for the pertinent data. Orders mostly reflected some combination of the Changs' gut feelings, Western style preferences, and North American weather patterns. In some years this resulted in too much inventory, in others, not enough. It also led to international stores stocked full of clothing that was inappropriate for local weather, norms, and customers.[159] There is little evidence that the Changs made any substantial changes to the company's processes, systems, or supply chain in recent years.

By 2016 the Changs and their daughters had loaned the business at least $20 million and had borrowed another $18 million from a company in the Philippines. Their international stores weren't turning profits, and the company had begun to quietly close some stores and downsize others.[160] It also opened new stores that year and expanded several existing ones.[161]

NOTHING LASTS FOREVER

Retail has changed dramatically in the past 30 years. A young adult's shopping experience in 1986 would be unrecognizable to today's Gen Zers and young Millennials. Data show that the 18- to 24- year-old demographic (Forever 21's target market) continues to increase its preference for online shopping.[162] Young consumers also place significant value on corporate social responsibility.[163] While Forever 21 was busy maintaining laser focus on physical expansion, direct competitors like Zara were adapting with sustainable clothing lines and streamlined online shopping experiences.[164] And some recent players—ASOS and Revolve, for example—ditched the idea of physical stores altogether. Without the weight of retail space, these companies respond to trends almost instantly and can get new fashion into customers' hands in record time.[165] Forever 21 had increasing difficulty staying competitive in this landscape.

WHAT'S NEXT FOR FOREVER 21?

The Forever 21 corporation filed for Chapter 11 bankruptcy protection in September 2019. According to the filing, the Changs owned 99% of the company and Alex Ok owned 1%.[166]

Their decision to file for Chapter 11 bankruptcy provided an opportunity to reconfigure operations as they attempted to stabilize and, hopefully, come back stronger.[167] The company sold hundreds of store locations along with its LA headquarters and distribution center and negotiated over $100 million in deductions to its rent payments.[168] It planned to abandon operations in Europe and Asia altogether and focus instead on its more lucrative markets in Mexico and Latin America.[169]

Some experts worried that the Changs' continued refusal to cede any equity as they negotiated with creditors would ultimately be the company's downfall. Others were confident that Forever 21 would weather the storm.[170] In February 2020, the Changs reached a deal to sell the company's retail stores and e-commerce sites for $81 million.[171] By May 2020 the remaining Forever 21 shell corporation appeared to have little funds left to cover payment plan installments or legal fees, and the United States Trustee Program (an arm of the Department of Justice dedicated to federal bankruptcy cases) recommended that the filing be dismissed or converted to a Chapter 7 bankruptcy (liquidation).[172] As fashion analyst Anusha Couttigane put it, Forever 21's experience should serve "as a cautionary tale for retailers that are slow to innovate and embrace change."[173]

FOR DISCUSSION

Problem-Solving Perspective

1. What is the underlying problem in this case from the perspective of Forever 21's customers and creditors?

2. Why do you think Forever 21 ended up in its current situation?

3. What would you have done differently if you had been a senior executive at Forever 21?

Application of Chapter Content

1. Did Forever 21 operate more from a principle of efficiency or effectiveness? Explain your rationale.

2. Which of the seven challenges to being an exceptional manager did the Changs face as leaders of the company? How did they handle them?

3. Which of the three skills that exceptional managers need did the Changs most lack? Explain your answer.

4. Which career readiness competencies did the Changs display? Which competencies would have benefited the Changs most?

To Delay or Not to Delay?

You have been hired by a vice president of a national company to create an employee attitude survey, to administer it to all employees, and to interpret the results. You have known this vice president for more than 10 years and have worked for her on several occasions. She trusts and likes you, and you trust and like her. You have completed your work and now are ready to present the findings and your interpretations to the vice president's management team. The vice president has told you that she wants your honest interpretation of the results, because she is planning to make changes based on the results. Based on this discussion, your report clearly identifies several strengths and weaknesses that need to be addressed. For example, employees feel that they are working too hard and that management does not care about providing good customer service. At the meeting you will be presenting the results and your interpretations to a group of 15 managers. You also have known most of these managers for at least five years.

You arrive for the presentation armed with slides, handouts, and specific recommendations. Your slides are loaded on the computer, and most of the participants have arrived. They are drinking coffee and telling you how enthused they are about hearing your presentation. You also are excited to share your insights. Ten minutes before the presentation is set to begin,

however, the vice president takes you out of the meeting room and says she wants to talk with you about your presentation. The two of you go to another office, and she closes the door. She then tells you that her boss's boss decided to come to the presentation unannounced. She thinks that he is coming to the presentation to look solely for negative information in your report. He does not like the vice president and wants to replace her with one of his friends. If you present your results as planned, it will provide this individual with the information he needs to create serious problems for the vice president. Knowing this, the vice president asks you to find some way to postpone your presentation. You have 10 minutes to decide what to do.

SOLVING THE CHALLENGE

What would you do?

1. Deliver the presentation as planned.

2. Give the presentation but skip over the negative results.

3. Go back to the meeting room and announce that your spouse has had an accident at home and you must leave immediately. You tell the group that you just received this message and that you will contact the vice president to schedule a new meeting.

4. Invent other options. Discuss.

2

Management Theory

Essential Background for the Successful Manager

Kapook2981/iStock/Getty Images

After reading this chapter, you should be able to:

LO 2-1   Describe the development of current perspectives on management.

LO 2-2   Discuss the insights of the classical view of management.

LO 2-3   Describe the principles of the behavioral view of management.

LO 2-4   Discuss the two quantitative approaches to solving problems.

LO 2-5   Identify takeaways from the systems view of management.

LO 2-6   Explain why there is no one best way to manage in all situations.

LO 2-7   Define how managers foster a learning organization, high-performance work practices, and shared value and sustainable development.

LO 2-8   Describe how to develop the career readiness competency of understanding the business.

FORECAST   *What's Ahead in This Chapter*

This chapter gives you a short overview of the three principal viewpoints on management—classical, behavioral, and quantitative. It then describes three more recent viewpoints—systems, contingency, and contemporary. We also consider the concepts of learning organizations, high-performance work practices, and shared value and sustainable development. We conclude with a Career Corner that focuses on how you can demonstrate the career readiness competency of understanding the business.

What Type of Work Environment Do I Prefer?

You'll see a bit later in this chapter that a manager may assume that employees are capable, creative, responsible, and motivated to work and learn. If so, this manager is practicing Theory Y management. This contrasts sharply with Theory X, which suggests that workers are resistant and unwilling and need to be monitored and controlled in order to achieve anything. Theory Y is obviously a more benevolent and optimistic view of workers, and it has lately given rise to a real-world phenomenon known as the *people-focused organization*.

What Does It Mean for You?

People-focused organizations are guided by the Theory Y view that people are essentially good, trustworthy, and productive, and that they flourish when they are empowered to act independently in an atmosphere that respects their diversity and values their well-being. If you were born after 1996, employees referred to as Gen Z, you will be glad to know that organizations are interested in your well-being and job satisfaction.[1] For example, companies such as Pepsi, Johnson & Johnson, and the NFL are hiring Gen Z consultants to help them better understand the needs of this generation.[2] As *Forbes* magazine notes, "companies have started to figure out that they can stay competitive with customers and in the war for talent if they become more people-focused."[3] The key is for managers to see the company's positive internal culture as a competitive advantage.

For young and entry-level workers, the rise of this new focus on people means there may be more choices about the kind of environment in which you can work. *Self-awareness* is one of the career readiness competencies employers desire in new college graduates. Are you aware of the type of work environment you prefer? While you may not find yourself in an organization with four-day workweeks and almost no managers—two innovations the e-learning company Treehouse briefly experimented with[4]—you might be given some responsibility for deciding how to accomplish your work with less direct oversight

and fewer rules than you are used to. Of course, to succeed in this kind of culture, you need to be self-directed, motivated, and able to quickly identify the questions you need to ask, all competencies associated with career readiness.

How Can You Get a Job in a People-Focused Organization?

Nearly 70% of full-time U.S. college students work while in school.[5] If you are one of these students, or if you are thinking ahead to getting an entry-level job after graduation, you may want to consider how well you would fit into a people-focused organization that takes the optimistic Theory Y view of its employees. For instance, do you like to work independently? That calls for you to set your own goals and figure out how to achieve them on time and on budget. You'll need to develop and demonstrate good organizational and time-management skills, a willingness to contribute to the organization's larger purpose, and the ability to do so without a manager's heavy hand.

Citrix, a publicly traded, multinational software company, is a good example of a people-focused organization. The company isn't just looking to offer perks like free food and babysitting, it is trying to connect people to their work in a unique, digital way. For example, Citrix is building an intelligent workspace that will allow employees to keep all their texts, e-mails, and documents right in front of them. They will also use artificial intelligence to learn what employees need in the workforce over time. For Donna Kimmel, Citrix's executive vice-president and chief people officer, being people-focused is about "marrying culture, technology, and space."[6]

For Discussion Would you like to work for a company that follows a people-focused, Theory Y view of its employees? What questions might you ask a recruiter to determine whether a company believes in a Theory Y or Theory X view of its employees?

2.1 Evolving Viewpoints: How We Got to Today's Management Outlook

THE BIG PICTURE

This section provides an overview of management history, starting with an overview of Peter Drucker's four fundamental principles of management. We also review six reasons for studying management theory.

LO 2-1

Describe the development of current perspectives on management.

"The best way to predict the future is to create it," says Peter Drucker. Understanding management history can assist you in determining the type of management style you prefer in others and the type you want to adopt for yourself in the future. A good grasp of management history also enables you to utilize a host of different managerial perspectives and techniques, thereby improving your ability to manage others.

Creating Modern Management: The Handbook of Peter Drucker

Who is Peter Drucker? "He was the creator and inventor of modern management," says management guru Tom Peters (author of *In Search of Excellence*).[7] *Business.com* suggests that Drucker's management theories "form the bedrock on which corporate America was built."[8]

An Austrian trained in economics and international law, Drucker came to the United States in 1937, where he worked as a correspondent for British newspapers and later became a college professor. In 1954, he published his famous text *The Practice of Management,* in which he proposed the important idea that *management was one of the major social innovations of the 20th century and should be treated as a profession,* like medicine or law.

In this and other books, he introduced several ideas that now underlie the organization and practice of management:

- Workers should be treated as assets.
- The corporation could be considered a human community.
- There is "no business without a customer."
- Institutionalized management practices are preferable to charismatic cult leaders.

Many ideas you will encounter in this book—decentralization, management by objectives, knowledge workers—are directly traceable to Drucker's pen (see the Example box on Wegmans). In our time, Drucker's rational approach has culminated in *evidence-based management,* as we describe in Section 2.4 in this chapter.

True learner. In his 70-year career, Peter Drucker published more than 35 books and numerous other publications, received the U.S. Presidential Medal of Freedom, and achieved near rock-star status for his management ideas. A true learner who constantly expanded his knowledge, Drucker understood that new experiences are key to nurturing new ideas and new ventures. Do you have this kind of curiosity?
Jonathan Alcorn/ZUMAPRESS/Newscom

EXAMPLE   Drucker's Principles in Action: Wegmans Food Markets

Drucker's principles are alive and well in many leading businesses today, including at Wegmans supermarket chain. The organization has more than 100 locations and has been listed as one of *Fortune*'s "Best Companies to Work For" 22 years in a row. The company also boasts a 94% approval rating from current and former employees who rated it on Glassdoor.[9]

Employees are ecstatic about Wegmans because the supermarket chain treats its workforce as assets. Every year, Wegmans invests more than $50 million in employee scholarships, cooking technique certifications, management trainee and leadership development programs, and a whole host of other initiatives. Employees can also take online training seminars

Ecstatic employees. New York City's first Wegmans store opened to employee cheers in October 2019. The company has churned out a cult following among both employees and customers. Brittainy Newman/Redux Pictures

and workshops from the convenience of their homes. The company says, "Wegmans is a place where anybody can love what they do as they thrive in their careers."[10]

The company has seen its investment in its employees provide substantial returns in the form of customer satisfaction.

Wegmans creates a people-focused community, which motivates their employees to go above and beyond. Michael Bush, CEO of Great Place to Work, adds that Wegmans is "giving their employees careers they can be proud of in an environment where they can learn and grow, and their customers love them for it."[11]

Wegmans' customers love them so much that the company ranks #1 for providing the best customer experience of any supermarket in the U.S, according to the 2018 Temkin Experience Ratings. This rating is based on 10,000 consumers rating Wegmans and 317 other companies across 20 industries. Wegmans' senior leadership credits its employees for this result. "We are incredibly proud and know this happens because we all work together and help one another," says Colleen Wegman, the company's president and CEO.[12]

YOUR CALL

Wegmans continues to add locations across the U.S. As it grows, how can it ensure its focus remains on employees and customers? Explain.

Six Practical Reasons for Studying This Chapter

"Theory," say business professors Clayton Christensen and Michael Raynor, "often gets a bum rap among managers because it's associated with the word 'theoretical,' which connotes 'impractical.' But it shouldn't."[13]

No one approach to management is suited for all situations, so what could be more practical than studying different approaches to see which work best?

Indeed, there are six good reasons for studying theoretical perspectives:

1. **Understanding of the present.** "Sound theories help us interpret the present, to understand what is happening and why," say Christensen and Raynor.[14] Or as scholars Scott Montgomery and Daniel Chirot argue, ideas "do not merely matter, they matter immensely, as they have been the source for decisions and actions that have structured the modern world."[15] Understanding history will help you understand why some practices are still favored, whether for right or wrong reasons.

2. **Guide to action.** Good theories help you make predictions and enable you to develop a set of principles that will guide your actions. For example, the theory of supply and demand tells us that prices go up when demand is high and supply is low. This is the situation with respect to the cost of labor in 2020 prior to the COVID-19 pandemic. Firms had to pay more for workers due to the shortage of qualified employees looking for work.

3. **Source of new ideas.** It can also provide new ideas that may be useful to you when you come up against new situations. For example, theories of employee engagement, which are discussed in Chapter 11, offer managers new ideas for how to best engage their workers. Contrary to the notion that compensation drives employee performance, these theories reveal that employees become engaged when an organization has the kind of culture that promotes employee development, recognition, and trust between management and employees.

4. **Clues to the meaning of your managers' decisions.** It can help you understand your firm's focus, where the top managers are "coming from."

5. **Clues to the meaning of outside events.** It may allow you to understand events outside the organization that could affect it or you.

6. **Producing positive results.** It can help you understand why certain management practices—such as setting goals that stretch you to the limit (stretch goals), basing compensation and promotion on performance, and monitoring results—have been so successful for many firms.

The Progression of Management Perspectives

In this chapter, we describe theories of management starting from the most historical to the most recent. *(See Figure 2.1.)* Each of the following sections in this chapter is devoted to exploring these theoretical viewpoints.

FIGURE 2.1

Progression of management perspectives

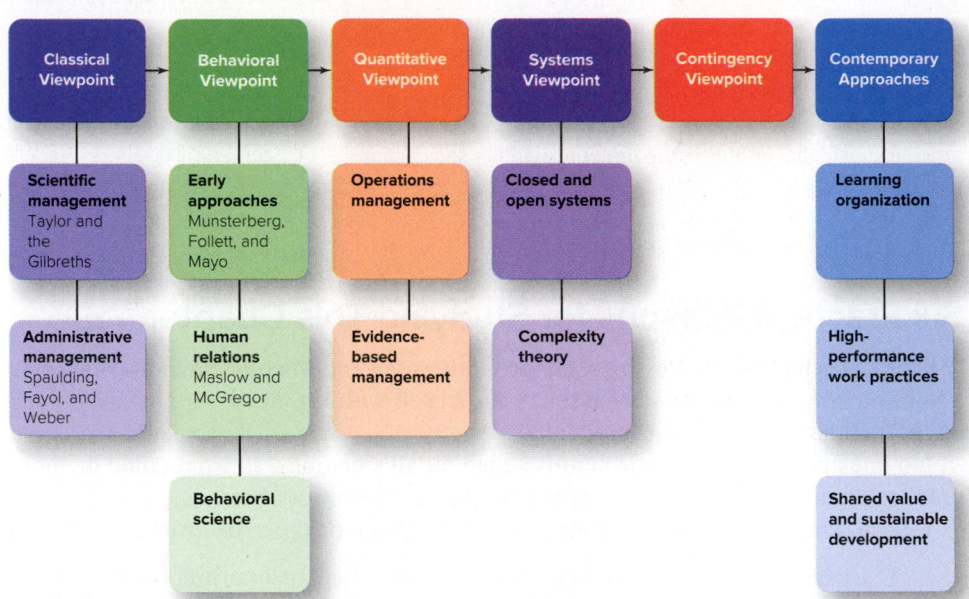

2.2 Classical Viewpoint: Scientific and Administrative Management

THE BIG PICTURE

Here we'll discuss the classical viewpoint, which emphasized ways to manage work more efficiently. This viewpoint had two approaches (a) scientific management and (b) administrative management. *Scientific management* emphasized the scientific study of work methods to improve the productivity of individual workers. *Administrative management* was concerned with managing the total organization.

LO 2-2

Discuss the insights of the classical view of management.

In this section, we describe the classical perspective of management, which originated during the early 1900s. The ==classical viewpoint==, which emphasized finding ways to manage work more efficiently, assumed that people are rational. It had two branches—scientific and administrative—each of which is identified with particular pioneering theorists. Let's compare the two approaches.

Scientific Management: Pioneered by Taylor and the Gilbreths

The problem for which scientific management emerged as a solution was this: In the expansive economy of the early 20th century, labor was in such short supply that managers looked for ways to raise the productivity of workers. ==Scientific management applied the scientific study of work methods to improving the productivity of individual workers.== Two of its chief proponents were Frederick W. Taylor and the team of Frank and Lillian Gilbreth.

Frederick Taylor and the Four Principles of Scientific Management
Known as "the father of scientific management," Taylor was an engineer from Philadelphia who believed managers could improve workers' productivity by applying four principles of science:[16]

Frederick W. Taylor. Called the father of scientific management, Taylor published *The Principles of Management* in 1911. Bettmann/Getty Images

1. Evaluate a task by scientifically studying each part of it (not by using old rule-of-thumb methods). This leads to the establishment of realistic performance goals for a job.

2. Carefully select workers with the right abilities for the task.

3. Give workers the training and incentives to do the task with the proper work methods.

4. Use scientific principles to plan the work methods and ease the way for workers to do their jobs.

Taylor based his system on *motion studies,* in which he broke down each worker's job—for example, moving pig iron at a steel company—into basic physical motions and then trained workers to use the methods of their best-performing co-workers. He suggested employers institute a *differential rate system,* in which more efficient workers earned higher rates of pay. He also was a proponent of setting performance goals for employees.

Why Taylor Is Important: "Taylorism" met considerable resistance from workers, who feared it would lead to lost jobs except for the highly productive few. In fact, Taylor believed that increasing production would benefit both labor and management by increasing profits to the point where they no longer had to quarrel over them. If used correctly, the principles of scientific management can enhance productivity, and innovations like motion studies and differential pay are still used today.

Frank and Lillian Gilbreth and Industrial Engineering
Have you ever heard of a *therblig? Therblig* is a made-up word coined by Frank Gilbreth and is, in fact, "Gilbreth" spelled backward, with the "t" and the "h" reversed. The term refers to 1 of 17 basic motions workers can perform. By identifying the therbligs in a job, such as that of a bricklayer (which he had once been), Gilbreth and his wife, Lillian, were able to help workers eliminate unnecessary motions and reduce their fatigue, thereby increasing productivity.

Frank and Lillian Gilbreth's experiences raising 12 children—to which they applied some of their ideas about improving efficiency—were later popularized in a book, two movies, and a TV sitcom, *Cheaper by the Dozen.* The Gilbreths expanded on Taylor's motion studies, for instance, by using movie cameras to film workers in order to isolate specific parts of a job.

Lillian Gilbreth was a pioneer in her own right. She was the first woman to receive a PhD in industrial psychology and the first to become a member of the Society of Industrial Engineers.[17] She also was a major contributor to management science. Her work focused on finding ways to improve workplace communication, nonfinancial incentive programs, and management training.[18]

Why the Gilbreth's Are Important: The Gilbreths are important because they reinforced the link between studying the physical movements in a job and workers' efficiency.[19] Today, as companies such as Tesla and GM look to automate physical production processes to increase efficiencies, they use the Gilbreths' management principles.

Lillian and Frank Gilbreth with 11 of their dozen children. As industrial engineers, the Gilbreths pioneered time and motion studies that helped workers eliminate unnecessary motions, reduce fatigue, and increase productivity. Bettmann/Getty Images

Administrative Management: Pioneered by Spaulding, Fayol, and Weber

Scientific management is concerned with the jobs of individuals. **Administrative management** is concerned with managing the total organization. Among the pioneering theorists were Charles Clinton Spaulding, Henri Fayol, and Max Weber.

Charles Clinton Spaulding and the "Fundamental Necessities" of Management   Spaulding was the son of a farmer and had 13 siblings. He proposed eight "necessities" of management based on his experiences working in his father's fields as a boy and later leading the North Carolina Mutual Life Insurance Company. He is recognized as the "Father of African-American Management" and published his classic article in the *Pittsburgh Courier* in 1927.[20]

Why Spaulding Is Important: Spaulding's "necessities" went beyond the task orientation of scientific management, thereby broadening the view of what it takes to effectively manage people and organizations. He suggested that considerations such as the need for authority, division of labor, adequate capital, proper budgeting, and cooperation and teamwork were essential for smooth organizational operations. He also was one of the first management practitioners to highlight the need to enrich "the lives of his organizational and community family" while simultaneously focusing on making a profit.[21]

Henri Fayol and the Functions of Management   Fayol was not the first to investigate management behavior, but he was the first to systematize it. A French engineer and industrialist, he became known to American business when his most important work, *General and Industrial Management,* was translated into English in 1930.

Why Fayol Is Important: Fayol was the first to identify the major functions of management—planning, organizing, leading, and controlling, as well as coordinating—the first four of which you'll recognize as the functions providing the framework for this and most other management books.[22]

Max Weber and the Rationality of Bureaucracy   In our time, the word *bureaucracy* has come to have negative associations: impersonality, inflexibility, red tape, a molasses-like response to problems. But to German sociologist Max Weber, a *bureaucracy* was a rational, efficient, ideal organization based on principles of logic. After all, in Weber's Germany in the late 19th century, many people were in positions of authority (particularly in the government) not because of their abilities but because of their social status. The result, Weber wrote, was that they didn't perform effectively.

A better-performing organization, he felt, should have five positive bureaucratic features:

1. A well-defined hierarchy of authority.
2. Formal rules and procedures.
3. A clear division of labor, with parts of a complex job being handled by specialists.
4. Impersonality, without reference or connection to a particular person.
5. Careers based on merit.

Why Weber Is Important: Weber's work was not translated into English until 1947, but it came to have an important influence on the structure of large corporations, such as the Coca-Cola Company.

The Problem with the Classical Viewpoint: Too Mechanistic

A flaw in the classical viewpoint is that it is mechanistic: It tends to view humans as cogs within a machine, not taking into account the importance of human needs. Behavioral theory addressed this problem, as we explain next.

Why the Classical Viewpoint Is Important: The essence of the classical viewpoint was that work activity was amenable to a rational approach, that through the application of scientific methods, time and motion studies, and job specialization it was possible to boost productivity. Indeed, these concepts are still in use today as scientific management is at the center of industries like quick-serve restaurants and manufacturing. The results are visible every time you visit a McDonald's or see images of an auto manufacturing plant. The classical viewpoint also led to such innovations as management by objectives and goal setting. •

Scientific management. Automakers have broken down the manufacturing process into specific tasks, as shown here in an assembly plant. This process reflects the contributions of the school of scientific management. Is there anything wrong with this approach? How could it be improved?
RainerPlendl/iStock/Getty Images

2.3 Behavioral Viewpoint: Behaviorism, Human Relations, and Behavioral Science

THE BIG PICTURE

The behavioral viewpoint emphasized the importance of understanding human behavior and of motivating employees toward achievement. The behavioral viewpoint developed over three phases: (1) *Early behaviorism,* (2) the *human relations movement*, and (3) *behavioral science*.

LO 2-3

Describe the principles of the behavioral view of management.

The **behavioral viewpoint** emphasized the importance of understanding human behavior and of motivating employees toward achievement. The behavioral viewpoint developed over three phases: (1) early behaviorism, (2) the human relations movement, and (3) behavioral science.

Early Behaviorism: Pioneered by Munsterberg, Follett, and Mayo

The three people who pioneered behavioral theory were Hugo Munsterberg, Mary Parker Follett, and Elton Mayo.

Hugo Munsterberg and the First Application of Psychology to Industry

Called "the father of industrial psychology," German-born Hugo Munsterberg had a PhD in psychology and a medical degree and joined the faculty at Harvard University in 1892. Munsterberg suggested that psychologists could contribute to industry in three ways. They could:

1. Study jobs and determine which people are best suited to specific jobs.
2. Identify the psychological conditions under which employees do their best work.
3. Devise management strategies to influence employees to follow management's interests.

Why Munsterberg Is Important: His ideas led to the field of *industrial psychology,* the study of human behavior in workplaces, which is still taught in colleges today.

Mary Parker Follett and Power Sharing among Employees and Managers

A Massachusetts social worker and social philosopher, Mary Parker Follett was lauded on her death in 1933 as a female pioneer in the fields of civics and sociology. Instead of following the usual hierarchical arrangement of managers as order givers and employees as order takers, Follett thought organizations should become more democratic, with managers and employees working cooperatively.

The following ideas were among her most important:

1. Organizations should be operated as "communities," with managers and subordinates working together in harmony.
2. Conflicts should be resolved by having managers and workers talk over differences and find solutions that would satisfy both parties—a process Follett called *integration.*
3. The work process should be under the control of workers with the relevant knowledge, rather than of managers, who should act as facilitators.

Why Follett Is Important: With these and other ideas, Follett anticipated some of today's concepts of "self-managed teams," "worker empowerment," and "interdepartmental teams"—that is, members of different departments working together on joint projects.

Elton Mayo and the Supposed "Hawthorne Effect"

Do you think workers would be more productive if they thought they were receiving special attention? This was the conclusion drawn by a Harvard research group in the late 1920s.

Conducted by Elton Mayo and his associates at Western Electric's Hawthorne plant near Chicago, what came to be called the *Hawthorne studies* began with an investigation into whether workplace lighting level affected worker productivity. (This was the type of study that Taylor or the Gilbreths might have done.) In later experiments, other variables were altered, such as wage levels, rest periods, and length of workday. Worker performance varied but tended to increase over time, leading Mayo and his colleagues to hypothesize what came to be known as the **Hawthorne effect—namely, that employees worked harder if they received added attention, if they thought that managers cared about their welfare, and that supervisors paid special attention to them.**

Elton Mayo. In the 1920s, Elton Mayo (shown with long cigarette holder) and his team conducted studies at Western Electric's Hawthorne Plant near Chicago. Do you think you would perform better in a repetitive job if you thought your supervisor cared about you and paid more attention to you? AP Images

However, later investigators found flaws in the studies, such as variations in ventilation and lighting or inadequate follow-through, which were overlooked by the original researchers. Critics also point out that it's doubtful workers improved their productivity merely on the basis of receiving more attention rather than because of a particular instructional method or social innovation.[23]

Why the Hawthorne Studies Are Important: Ultimately, the Hawthorne studies were faulted for being poorly designed and not having enough empirical data to support the conclusions. Nevertheless, they succeeded in drawing attention to the importance of "social man" (social beings) and how managers using good human relations could improve worker productivity. This in turn led to the so-called human relations movement in the 1950s and 1960s.

The Human Relations Movement: Pioneered by Maslow and McGregor

The two theorists who contributed most to the **human relations movement—which proposed that better human relations could increase worker productivity—were Abraham Maslow and Douglas McGregor.**

Abraham Maslow and the Hierarchy of Needs

What motivates you to perform: Food? Security? Love? Recognition? Self-fulfillment? Probably all of these, Abraham Maslow would say, although some take priority over others. The chairman of the psychology department at Brandeis University and a practicing psychologist, Maslow observed that his patients had certain innate needs that had to be satisfied before they could reach their fullest potential. Based on these observations, he proposed his famous *hierarchy of human needs* (physiological, safety, love, esteem, and self-actualization) in 1943.[24] As a humanist, Maslow advocated that employees have an innate desire to be self-actualized, which means to be all that they can be.[25]

We discuss Maslow's hierarchy in detail in Chapter 12, where we further explain why he is important and how his work has impacted motivation theory.

Douglas McGregor and Theory X versus Theory Y

Having been a college president for a time (at Antioch College in Ohio), Douglas McGregor came to realize that it was not enough for managers to try to be liked; they also needed to be aware of their attitudes toward employees.[26] Basically, McGregor suggested in a 1960 book, these attitudes could be thought of as either "X" or "Y," which we introduced in the chapter opener about people-focused organizations.

Theory X represents a pessimistic, negative view of workers. In this view, workers are considered to be irresponsible, to be resistant to change, to lack ambition, to hate work, and to want to be led rather than to lead.

Theory Y represents a human relations outlook—an optimistic, positive view of workers as capable of accepting responsibility, having self-direction and self-control, and being imaginative and creative.

Why Theory X/Theory Y Is Important: The principal contribution offered by the Theory X/Theory Y perspective is that it helps managers understand how their beliefs affect their behavior. For example, Theory X managers are more likely to micromanage, which leads to employee dissatisfaction, because they believe employees are inherently lazy.

Underlying both Maslow's and McGregor's theories is the notion that more job satisfaction leads to greater worker performance—an idea that is somewhat controversial, as we'll discuss in Chapter 11.

What is your basic view of human nature? Being aware of your perspective is important because it influences your interactions with others and your managerial style. To see the general direction of your outlook, try the following self-assessment if your instructor assigns it to you.

SELF-ASSESSMENT 2.1

What Is Your Orientation: Toward Theory X/ Theory Y?

This self-assessment is designed to reveal your orientation as a manager—whether it tends toward Theory X or Theory Y.

Please be prepared to answer these questions if your instructor has assigned Self-Assessment 2.1 in *Connect*.

1. To what extent do you think your results are an accurate reflection of your beliefs about others? Are you surprised by the results?

2. As a leader of a student or work-related project team, how might your results affect your approach toward leading others? Explain.

3. If an employee doesn't seem to show ambition, can that be changed? Discuss.

The Behavioral Science Approach

The human relations movement was a necessary correction to the sterile approach used within scientific management, but its optimism came to be considered too simplistic for practical use. More recently, the human relations view has been superseded by the behavioral science approach to management. **Behavioral science approach** relies on scientific research for developing theories about human behavior that can be used to provide practical tools for managers. The disciplines of behavioral science include psychology, sociology, anthropology, and economics. •

EXAMPLE   The Open-Plan Office—Does It Really Increase Productivity?

Open plan workspaces. Though a majority of U.S. workplaces have an open floor plan, its effectiveness is still an open question. How would you feel working in such an arrangement? Rawpixel.com/Shutterstock

Roughly 70% of today's offices have an open floor plan,[27] mixing managers and workers in completely open offices, often using shared tables and desks.[28]

When the concept originated in the 1950s, its purpose was to "facilitate communication and idea flow," according to one report.[29] Other goals were to save money (because such spaces are cheap to build)[30] and to increase productivity. The idea was not only that open spaces encourage collaboration but also that workers are discouraged from wasting time if everyone can see them. But do open-plan offices work? The latest results suggest they are a mixed blessing at best.

Noise is one of the biggest distractions of open workspaces. When people are actively collaborating or socializing in a large room without walls, the sound of their conversation is hard to ignore and can even be amplified by the open space. The same goes for the sound of phones ringing and desktop alerts going off, or even worse, the sound of someone eating lunch or having a personal phone conversation. Some workers respond to the stress that can result from such constant distractions and overstimulation by emotionally isolating themselves, using rooms intended for private meetings as their personal offices, or even repeatedly calling in sick or working from home. Headphones are one of the most common ways not only to block out noise distractions but to send the message, "Please don't interrupt me now." All this evidence tends to weigh against the idea that working without walls will encourage people to work together more often, more productively, or more creatively. A recent study, for example, found that an open office reduced face-to-face interactions by around 70%.[31]

"Visual noise" is a distraction, too. As a *Wall Street Journal* article reports, "Visual noise, the activity or movement around the edges of an employee's field of vision, can erode concentration and disrupt analytical thinking or creativity."[32] It's almost impossible, for instance, to see a group of co-workers gathering nearby and not wonder what they are talking about, or to keep your focus when co-workers are visibly and chronically late.

One study of more than 40,000 U.S. workers in 300 different office buildings concluded that the expected benefits of open-plan offices were outweighed by the noise and lack of privacy.[33] Research also suggests that open offices increase the use of e-mail by 67%.[34] It's possible that many companies just aren't designing their open-office plans effectively. A team of researchers studied seating arrangements from more than 2,000 employees of a large technology company. Results showed that 10% of a person's performance spills over to those nearby. If you want to improve your performance, try to get a desk near a high performer. The researchers estimated that "a strategic seating chart" could bring in $1 million in annual profit from greater productivity for an organization of 2,000 workers.[35]

YOUR CALL

What kind of office arrangements do you think would work best and why?

2.4 Quantitative Viewpoints: Operations Management and Evidence-Based Management

THE BIG PICTURE

Quantitative viewpoints emphasize the application of quantitative techniques, such as statistics and computer simulations, to the practice of management. Two approaches of quantitative management are *operations management* and *evidence-based management*.

LO 2-4

Discuss the two quantitative approaches to solving problems.

During the air war known as the Battle of Britain in World War II, a relative few of England's Royal Air Force fighter pilots and planes were able to successfully resist the overwhelming might of the German military machine. How did they do it? Military planners drew on mathematics and statistics to determine how to most effectively allocate use of their limited aircraft.

When the Americans entered the war in 1941, they used the British model to form *operations research (OR)* teams to determine how to deploy troops, submarines, and other military personnel and equipment most effectively. For example, OR techniques were used to establish the optimum pattern that search planes should fly to try to locate enemy ships.

OR techniques have evolved into ==quantitative management==, the application of quantitative techniques, such as statistics and computer simulations, to management. Two branches of quantitative management are operations management and evidence-based management. Today's military continues to use these techniques, but quite differently from the 1940s. For instance, the Army's marketing team is utilizing data analytics and social media to attract potential Gen Z soldiers. "Everything we do in the digital space will be integrated so that we can hyper-target, so that we can deliver a message that we believe will resonate with someone that we're interested in," says Brig. Gen. Alex Fink, who leads this initiative.[36]

Quantitative management is used not only by the military and businesses, but also by sports franchises. For example, the Oakland Athletics baseball team used quantitative management to identify undervalued players by evaluating in-game statistics.[37] The Athletics' executive vice president of baseball operations, Billy Beane, believes that today, numbers dictate a team's strategy more than ever before. "It's just evolution," Beane says.[38] The National Basketball Association (NBA) also uses quantitative management when scheduling games, developing a playoff structure, and setting draft lotteries. Evan Wasch, senior vice president of basketball strategy and analytics for the NBA, says that evidence-based management can prompt small changes that make a big difference.[39]

Pitching quantitative management. Oakland Athletics' Marcus Semien (#10) celebrates with Jurickson Profar (#23) after a home run. These types of celebrations are common for the players because the team's analysis of in-game statistics allowed it to outcompete wealthier teams like the New York Yankees. This method revolutionized professional sports and inspired the movie *Moneyball*. Cody Glenn/Getty Images

Operations Management: Being More Effective

==Operations management== focuses on managing the production and delivery of an organization's products or services more effectively. In the day-to-day running of the company, operations management consists of all the job functions and activities in which managers schedule and delegate work and job training, plan production to meet customer needs, design services customers want and how to deliver them, locate and design company facilities, and choose optimal levels of product inventory to keep costs down and reduce backorders. It governs managers' decisions about how to increase productivity and efficiency, as well as how to achieve the highest possible quality of both goods and services. Another major function of operations management is managing the ==supply chain==, which is the process of creating the product, starting with designing and obtaining raw materials for physical goods or technology for services and going all the way through delivery to customers' hands, and sometimes even beyond to responsible disposal or recycling.

Why Operations Management Is Important: Through the rational management of resources and distribution of goods and services, operations management helps ensure that business operations are efficient and effective.

Evidence-Based Management: Facing Hard Facts, Rejecting Nonsense

==Evidence-based management== entails translating principles based on best evidence into organizational practice, bringing rationality to the decision-making process.

As its two principal proponents, Stanford business scholars Jeffrey Pfeffer and Robert Sutton, put it, evidence-based management is based on the belief that "facing the hard facts about what works and what doesn't, understanding the dangerous half-truths that constitute so much conventional wisdom about management, and rejecting the total nonsense that too often passes for sound advice will help organizations perform better."[40]

Learning to make managerial decisions based on evidence is the approach we hope you will learn to take after studying many other approaches—the perspectives we covered in this chapter. We will consider evidence-based management further, along with analytics and big data, in Chapter 7. ●

PRACTICAL ACTION   Evidence-Based Management: The Role of Big Data

Big data, as the name implies, refers to sets of data so vast and complex that new methods have been developed to analyze them. Businesses and governments will find many applications for the information big data can yield, but harnessing and analyzing large amounts of data continue to challenge organizations. In fact, *Forbes* estimates that 95% of businesses need to manage their unstructured data.[41] Kaiser Permanente, Starbucks, and Amazon are just a few of the companies already using big data in a big way.[42]

Pharmaceutical companies, for instance, use data collected from patients to study different diseases and try to find better treatments and cures.[43] Employment-related search engines use their database to see what skills are in demand, which markets are the most competitive, and where employers are hiring. Intel is developing technology that will allow cars to communicate with each other, giving drivers an opportunity to see three cars in front of, behind, and to each side of them at the same time.[44] Government applications of big data include agriculture management, transportation safety, and poverty reduction.[45]

Privacy is an ongoing issue users of big data must confront. As one writer says, "Transparency and ethical use of data is vital. . . . Companies should do what they can where they can to be transparent and help consumers understand what data they are collecting and for what purpose. The Big Data ecosystem is becoming increasingly complex. . . . Companies who are forthright and build trust will be increasingly important to their customers."[46]

YOUR CALL

Do you think the application of big data could stifle managers' decision-making abilities?

2.5 Systems Viewpoint

THE BIG PICTURE

The *systems viewpoint* sees organizations as a system, either open or closed, with inputs, outputs, transformation processes, and feedback. The systems viewpoint has led to the development of complexity theory, the study of how order and pattern arise from very complicated, apparently chaotic systems.

Being of a presumably practical turn of mind, could you run a present-day organization or a department according to the theories you've just learned? Probably not. The reason: People are complicated and organizations are more complex than ever before. In order to better understand the complexity surrounding today's businesses, we need to break down organizations into separate, but interrelated parts. This is best done using the systems viewpoint of management.

The Systems Viewpoint

The 27 bones in the hand. The monarchy of Great Britain. A weather storm front. Each of these is a system. A **system** is a set of interrelated parts that operate together to achieve a common purpose. Even though a system may not work very well—as in the inefficient way the Italian government collects taxes, for example—it is nevertheless still a system. Furthermore, if managers do not understand how the different parts of an organization come together to achieve its goals, they will not be able to diagnose problems and develop effective solutions.

The **systems viewpoint** regards the organization as a system of interrelated parts. By adopting this point of view, you can look at your organization both as (1) a collection of **subsystems**—parts making up the whole system—and (2) a part of the larger environment. A college, for example, is made up of a collection of academic departments, support staffs, students, and the like. But it also exists as a system within the environment of education, having to be responsive to parents, alumni, legislators, nearby townspeople, and so on.

The Four Parts of a System

The vocabulary of the systems perspective is useful because it gives you a way of understanding many different kinds of organizations. The four parts of a system are defined as follows:

1. **Inputs** are the people, money, information, equipment, and materials required to produce an organization's goods or services. Whatever goes into a system is an input.

2. **Transformational processes** are the organization's capabilities in management, internal processes, and technology that are applied to converting inputs into outputs. The main activity of the organization is to transform inputs into outputs.

3. **Outputs** are the products, services, profits, losses, employee satisfaction or discontent, and the like that are produced by the organization. Whatever comes out of the system is an output.

4. **Feedback** is information about the reaction of the environment to the outputs that affects the inputs. Are the customers buying or not buying the product? That information is feedback.

The four parts of a system are illustrated in *Figure 2.2*.

FIGURE 2.2

The four parts of a system

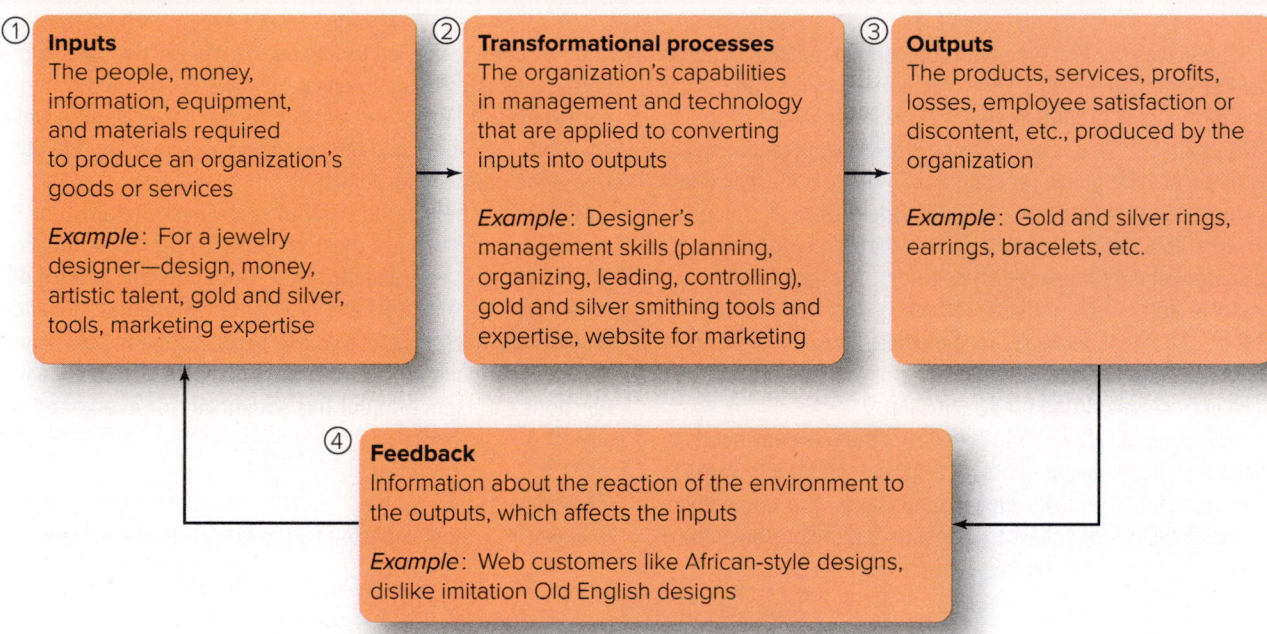

① **Inputs**
The people, money, information, equipment, and materials required to produce an organization's goods or services

Example: For a jewelry designer—design, money, artistic talent, gold and silver, tools, marketing expertise

② **Transformational processes**
The organization's capabilities in management and technology that are applied to converting inputs into outputs

Example: Designer's management skills (planning, organizing, leading, controlling), gold and silver smithing tools and expertise, website for marketing

③ **Outputs**
The products, services, profits, losses, employee satisfaction or discontent, etc., produced by the organization

Example: Gold and silver rings, earrings, bracelets, etc.

④ **Feedback**
Information about the reaction of the environment to the outputs, which affects the inputs

Example: Web customers like African-style designs, dislike imitation Old English designs

Closed Systems, Open Systems, and the Concept of Synergy

A **closed system** has little interaction with its environment; that is, it receives very little feedback from the outside. The classical management viewpoint often considered an organization a closed system. So does the management science perspective, which simplifies organizations for purposes of analysis. However, any organization that ignores feedback from the environment opens itself up to possibly spectacular failures.

An **open system** continually interacts with its environment. Today nearly all organizations are, at least to some degree, open systems rather than closed. Open systems have the potential of producing synergy. **Synergy** (pronounced "sin-ur-jee") is the idea that two or more forces combined create an effect that is greater than the sum of their individual effects, as when a guitarist, drummer, and bassist combine to play a better version of a song than any of them would playing alone. Or a copywriter, art director, and photographer combine to create a magazine ad, each representing various influences from the environment.

Complexity Theory: The Ultimate Open System

The systems viewpoint has led to the development of **complexity theory**, the study of how order and pattern arise from very complicated, apparently chaotic systems. Complexity theory recognizes that all complex systems are networks of many interdependent parts that interact with each other according to certain simple rules. Used in strategic management and organizational studies, the discipline seeks to understand how organizations, considered as relatively simple and partly connected structures, adapt to their environments.

Why the Systems Viewpoint—Particularly the Concept of Open Systems—Is Important: History is full of accounts of products that failed (such as the 1959 Ford Edsel) because they were developed in closed systems and didn't have sufficient feedback. Open systems stress multiple feedback from both inside and outside the organization, resulting in a continuous learning process to try to correct old mistakes and avoid new ones. ●

EXAMPLE   U.S. Steel Uses Systems Theory to Stay Competitive

U.S. Steel was the first American company to reach a $1 billion market valuation in 1901. Over a century later, the company is one of the least profitable steelmakers, with shares dropping 25% in 2019.[47] This is a result of a slowdown in global manufacturing activity, due in part to the U.S.–China trade war, which is decreasing demand for steel. President Donald Trump imposed a 25% tariff on steel imports in 2018 in order to protect U.S. Steel and its domestic competitors, but those tariffs also hurt the automotive industry, which is a major end-user of steel.[48] U.S. Steel also has faced multiple lawsuits for allowing air pollution emissions. It settled one of the class-action lawsuits in December 2019 for $8.5 million.[49]

U.S. Steel CEO David Burritt believes the company needs to make significant investments in its infrastructure if it wants to stay relevant in today's global landscape. The company is spending billions of dollars to renovate and replace equipment that has been in service for decades. "We are investing in our core assets to continue to ensure that we are aligned with our core values of safety and environmental performance, while positively contributing to the communities where we operate," said a company spokesperson.[50]

CEO Burritt believes that the company needs to abandon its outdated ways and make these changes in order to better align with a changing environment. This environment includes a decline in the price of steel and also more stringent air pollution regulations. Burritt wants to make sure that the infrastructure investments make a positive impact across all the company's functions. "This investment has something for everyone," he says.[51]

YOUR CALL

How was U.S. Steel impacted by the four parts of a system?

2.6 Contingency Viewpoint

THE BIG PICTURE

The *contingency viewpoint* emphasizes that a manager's approach should vary according to the individual and environmental situation.

LO 2-6

Explain why there is no one best way to manage in all situations.

The classical viewpoints advanced by Taylor, Spaulding, and Fayol assumed that their approaches had universal applications—that they were "the one best way" to manage organizations. The contingency viewpoint began to develop when managers discovered that under some circumstances better results could be achieved by breaking the one-best-way rule. The contingency viewpoint emphasizes that a manager's approach should vary according to—that is, be contingent on—the individual and the environmental situation.

The beauty, and simplicity, of contingency theory lies in the proposition that there is not one best way to manage. Rather, effective management requires using the most appropriate theory or tool for a specific situation. Consider the example of HSBC's former CEO John Flint. He was fired in 2019 because his decision making was not contingent on the bank's environmental uncertainties and digital challenges. He also failed to make decisions as quickly as the bank's board needed him to.[52] Flint might have been more successful if he had utilized the contingency viewpoint and asked, "What method is the best to use under these particular circumstances?"

The same concept applies to you and your studies. Do you study the same way for every course you take in college? Probably not. Let's say you are taking both anatomy and finance classes this semester. The anatomy course may require you to memorize the different parts of the body and their functions to pass the exam. In contrast, the technique of memorizing may not be as effective in your finance class. Finance requires you to perform calculations so you can master concepts such as the time value of money. In this case, however, you are more likely to obtain a better grade by doing sample problems. The point is that you are more likely to get higher grades in different classes by using methods of study that match the content being taught.

Why the Contingency Viewpoint Is Important: The contingency viewpoint would seem to be the most practical of the viewpoints discussed so far because it addresses problems on a case-by-case basis and provides solutions specific to a certain situation or dilemma.

EXAMPLE | **The Contingency Viewpoint: Manufacturers Pitch Parents to Recruit Their Kids**

Parents around the country are increasingly worried about paying for their children to attend college, and college graduates are worried about getting that first real job in a competitive job market. U.S. manufacturers also are worried about how they're going to fill approximately 470,000 open positions.[53]

Historically, manufacturing jobs were attractive, stable positions. Manufacturing companies presented opportunities for young talent to progress from factory-line positions to top management. This is not the case anymore, possibly because manufacturing jobs do not seem to possess the "cool factor" touted by technology giants Amazon, Google, or Facebook in their job openings and benefits packages. In fact, a study found that 52% of U.S. teens expressed little or no interest in a manufacturing career.[54] Faced with this situation, manufacturing firms are having to take a contingency approach toward recruiting.[55]

Some U.S. manufacturers are taking creative steps to recruit workers for critical and well-paid jobs, including reaching out to the parents of young people they hope to hire. "Parents are the missing part of this," said one economic development manager in Colorado.

One engine parts maker in Colorado hosted a "Parents' Night" at its plant for about 200 people with high-school age children. As the company's vice president of operations (and lifelong employee) explained, "We're really trying to get after the parents—the parents are influential with their kids. Our message was 'there's another option'" to a four-year college degree. Recruiters from Michelin pitched parents at a recent career night hosted by the Greenville, SC, Chamber of Commerce, offering to hire their children part-time while paying their tuition for a two-year technical program at a local college. Graduates of the program can be hired into full-time jobs at Michelin with starting pay of around $55,000 and generous benefits.[56]

One parent who is reconsidering his teenage son's options said, "Well, you know, not everyone is an accountant."

YOUR CALL

Are there any downsides to these appeals to parents by U.S. manufacturers? What other contingency approaches can you suggest to help solve their recruiting problem?

2.7 Contemporary Approaches: The Learning Organization, High-Performance Work Practices, and Shared Value and Sustainable Development

THE BIG PICTURE

Three contemporary approaches include learning organizations, high-performance work practices, and shared value and sustainable development. Learning organizations actively create, acquire, and transfer knowledge within themselves and are able to modify their behavior to reflect new knowledge. High-performance work practices require investment and effective implementation of human resource systems. Shared value and sustainable development look beyond short-term profits and focuses on the environmental and social costs of doing business.

Management theory continues to evolve to tackle the challenges facing companies today. Three contemporary approaches to management include *learning organizations, high-performance work practices,* and *shared value and sustainable development.*

LO 2-7

Define how managers foster a learning organization, high-performance work practices, and shared value and sustainable development.

The Learning Organization: Sharing Knowledge and Modifying Behavior

Ultimately, the lesson we need to take from the theories, perspectives, and viewpoints we have described is this: Keep on learning. Individuals who embrace learning make the organization smarter and contribute to its growth, but managers need to have a reciprocal interest and create a learning ecosystem.[57] A key challenge for managers, therefore, is to establish a culture of shared knowledge and values that will enhance their employees' ability to learn—to build so-called learning organizations. An additional advantage for tomorrow's managers is that Millennials, now the largest generation ever, don't just appreciate but actively *expect* to have learning opportunities at work.[58]

Learning organizations, says Massachusetts Institute of Technology professor Peter Senge, who coined the term, are places "where people continually expand their capacity to create the results they truly desire, where new and expansive patterns of thinking are nurtured, where collective aspiration is set free, and where people are continually learning how to learn together."[59]

More formally, a ==learning organization== is an organization that actively creates, acquires, and transfers knowledge within itself and is able to modify its behavior to reflect new knowledge. Note the three parts of a learning organization:

A learning organization is like a lightbulb. It must be turned on before it creates value. How do you think organizations promote the value of continuous learning? Photodisc/Getty Images

1. **Creating and acquiring knowledge.** In learning organizations, managers try to actively infuse their organizations with new ideas and information, which are the prerequisites for learning. They acquire such knowledge by constantly scanning their external environments, by hiring new talent and expertise when needed, and by devoting significant resources to training and developing their employees. Another helpful strategy is to maintain a learning culture within the organization, which encourages people to ask questions without negative consequences (such as being made to feel ignorant) and recognizes that differences of opinion, when handled with respect, can often lead to new and better ideas.

2. **Transferring knowledge.** Individual managers should actively work to transfer knowledge throughout the organization, reducing barriers to sharing information and ideas among employees. One consultant suggests three strategies for managers: share your personal success story and challenges overcome; be ready to learn any and everything from peers and employees; and align your learning goals for the company with its business goals.[60] Managers should not be afraid to try new technologies to help employees learn. For example, Walmart is using virtual reality to train employees in management and customer service skills.[61]

3. **Modifying behavior.** Learning organizations are nothing if not results oriented. First, managers should make sure the learning or training opportunity meets a real employee or organizational need. Does it solve a specific problem, and how? The link between learning and performance improvement, and the way the improvement will be measured, should be clear to employees as well.[62] Next, both formal and informal learning experiences should be followed up with surveys or other measures to see whether employees are applying the new skills or information or need more coaching or encouragement from management.[63]

Based on the given discussion, do you wonder about the specific behaviors that people exhibit in a learning organization? It would be interesting to determine if you have ever worked for such an organization. The following self-assessment was created to evaluate whether an organization you now work for or formerly worked for could be considered a serious learning organization. The survey items provide a good indication of what it takes to become a learning organization.

Virtual learning. Jeanelle Bass, a Walmart assistant manager in New Jersey, uses virtual reality goggles during a training session. The company's use of this technology allows them to develop their employees' customer service skills before they face real customers. Would you be comfortable training with a computer instead of real people? Julio Cortez/AP Images

High-Performance Work Practices

A focus on high-performance work practices is an extension of the behavioral and systems viewpoints and grew from research done by Jeff Pfeffer and James Collins. Pfeffer, a professor at Stanford, and Collins, a former Stanford professor who became a consultant, promoted the idea that employees are an organization's most important asset and that management should focus on attracting, developing, and motivating the best talent.[64] The job of management, according to this viewpoint, is to create human resource (HR) practices that foster employee development and overall well-being.[65] These practices are called **high-performance work practices (HPWPs)** because they focus on enhancing employees' ability, motivation, and opportunity to contribute, and thus improve an organization's ability to effectively attract, select, hire, develop, and retain high-performing personnel.[66]

High-performance work practices include ability-enhancing, motivation-enhancing, and opportunity-enhancing practices as follows:[67]

- *Ability-enhancing practices:* Formal selection tests, structured interviews, hiring standards or selectivity, high pay, and training opportunities.

- *Motivation-enhancing practices:* Providing rewards based on individual and group performance and use of formal performance evaluation systems and merit-based promotion systems.

- *Opportunity-enhancing practices:* Employee involvement via formal participation processes, ongoing communication and information-sharing practices, and autonomy in making work-related decisions.

Research supports the recommendation that managers should strive to create HPWPs. Findings revealed that HPWPs were associated with lower turnover and absenteeism and higher employee commitment and extra-role behavior. HPWPs also were related to greater organizational performance, financial performance, efficiency, and creativity.[68]

There is one conclusion about this contemporary viewpoint that is important to remember. It's not enough to have one type of HPWP. The best outcomes are obtained when managers integrate bundles of ability-enhancing, motivation-enhancing, and opportunity-enhancing practices into one overall organizational HR system. We discuss High Performance Work Systems in depth in Chapter 9.

Let's consider how three organizations have incorporated high-performance work practices into their HR systems.

High performance work practices are utilized across many different industries. Here are three examples:[69]

Enterprise Rent a Car

As the largest car rental company in the United States, Enterprise understands the importance of recruiting top talent. The company has successfully used selective hiring to recruit "people people," whom they categorize as those with excellent interpersonal skills. Specifically, Enterprise targets college students who are more prone to understanding the importance of working as a team. This includes former athletes and fraternity and sorority members.

Whole Foods

The Amazon-owned supermarket chain known for its high-quality products also provides high- quality rewards for its employees. The company rewards employees with bonuses based on performance, including coming in under budget on labor costs. Whole Foods also reintroduced employee stock options in 2019, which allow employees to share in the company's success.

Ritz-Carlton Hotels

The luxury hotel chain, with more than 100 locations in 30 countries, is known for the high quality of its customer service. Management's approach to customer service includes providing employees with autonomy in decision making. For example, Ritz-Carlton lists gold standards on its website, which include employees being empowered to "create unique, memorable and personal experiences for our guests."[70] How empowered are Ritz employees? They have discretion to spend up to $2,500 if they believe it would benefit the customer and uphold the hotel's mission.

Shared Value and Sustainable Development: Going beyond Profits

Fashion Week 2019 in New York City wasn't just about glitz and glamour. Iconic brands, such as Dior, Louis Vuitton, and Burberry, were focusing on sustainability campaigns. Whether creating new clothes from old fabric or implementing responsible land management for the production of cotton, wool, and hemp, there is a growing consensus in the fashion industry that doing right by the planet makes good business sense.[71] And this industry isn't alone.

Green innovations. Some managers believe sustainable practices can be costly when in fact they can make companies more competitive. Can you think of some sustainable practices that can be profitable for both organizations and the earth? AnjuChoudhary/Shutterstock

Shared value and sustainable development look beyond short-term profits and focuses on the environmental and social costs of doing business. The term *sustainable* was first used by the Club of Rome in 1972, a nonprofit organization that includes politicians, scientists, economists, and business leaders from around the world. Scientists Dennis and Donella Meadows used the term to describe a "state of global equilibrium" in which the world would not have a sudden and uncontrolled collapse, and would be able to satisfy the basic requirements of its people.[72] As we discussed in Chapter 1, sustainable development focuses on meeting the needs of the present without compromising the ability of future generations to meet their own needs.[73]

Harvard Professor Michael Porter argued in 1995 that sustainability "can trigger innovations that lower the total cost of a product or improve its value . . . making companies more competitive, not less."[74] Thus, shared value and sustainable development is where business and sustainability intersect. Organizations that focus on creating value not only for their shareholders but also for their stakeholders position themselves and future members of society to reap rewards. In the decades that followed Porter's statement, more and more organizations started to focus on sustainability as a competitive advantage. Yet, in 2017, 90% of executives said they saw sustainability as important, while only 60% of companies had a sustainability strategy.[75]

Companies have now developed management positions such as chief sustainability officer, VP of corporate responsibility, and environmental program manager to be accountable for a company's sustainability strategy, policies, and initiatives. Shared value and sustainable development is prevalent in a range of industries, as evidenced by companies who have hired staff to support their sustainability goals. These include Kohler, GE Healthcare, and Lands' End.[76]

We'll discuss shared value and sustainable development in depth in Learning Module 1.

Responsible Management Education: The United Nations Takes the Lead

The growing importance of shared value and sustainable development has led the United Nations (UN) to tackle the issue. During the UN's Global Compact Summit in 2007, the organization launched Principles for Responsible Management Education (PRME). The mission of PRME is to "transform business and management education, research and thought leadership globally, while promoting awareness about the Sustainable Development Goals [SDGs], and developing the responsible business leaders of tomorrow."[79] There are 17 SDGs, ranging from poverty to climate action to gender equality. All 193 member states of the UN have adopted a plan to meet the SDGs by 2030.[80]

PRME works with schools and businesses to advance the SDGs in business education. Schools can join this UN initiative and integrate the skills needed to achieve the SDGs into their curriculum. PRME also assists businesses recruiting talent with sustainability mindsets, skills, and abilities.[81] Some notable PRME industry partners include Deloitte and Bertelsmann Stiftung.[82]

As institutions of higher education involved in the development of current and future managers we declare our willingness to progress in the implementation, within our institution, of the following Principles, starting with those that are more relevant to our capacities and mission. We will report on progress to all our stakeholders and exchange effective practices related to these principles with other academic institutions:

Principle 1 | Purpose
We will develop the capabilities of students to be future generators of sustainable value for business and society at large and to work for an inclusive and sustainable global economy.

Principle 2 | Values
We will incorporate into our academic activities, curricula, and organisational practices the values of global social responsibility as portrayed in international initiatives such as the United Nations Global Compact.

Principle 3 | Method
We will create educational frameworks, materials, processes and environments that enable effective learning experiences for responsible leadership.

Principle 4 | Research
We will engage in conceptual and empirical research that advances our understanding about the role, dynamics, and impact of corporations in the creation of sustainable social, environmental and economic value.

Principle 5 | Partnership
We will interact with managers of business corporations to extend our knowledge of their challenges in meeting social and environmental responsibilities and to explore jointly effective approaches to meeting these challenges.

Principle 6 | Dialogue
We will facilitate and support dialog and debate among educators, students, business, government, consumers, media, civil society organisations and other interested groups and stakeholders on critical issues related to global social responsibility and sustainability.

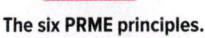

The six PRME principles.
Source: Based on material in "About the Sustainable Development Goals," The United Nations. https://www.un.org/sustainabledevelopment/sustainable-development-goals/.

2.8 Career Corner: Managing Your Career Readiness

Figure 2.3 shows the model of career readiness we discussed in Chapter 1. What does a chapter on management history have to do with your career readiness? How about its application to the **Knowledge** competency of *understanding the business?* This competency was defined in Table 1.2 as the extent to which you understand a company's business and strategies and the needs of its stakeholders. It comes into play whenever you interview for a job.

Recruiters expect you to do some research, just as you would for a class assignment. They want you to act like Sherlock Holmes and do some snooping. That's good for both you and a potential employer because it helps identify the likely level of fit between the two of you. Good fit, in turn, is associated with more positive work attitudes and task performance, lower intentions to quit, and less job-related stress.[83] Moreover, doing your homework on a company makes you a more attractive job candidate. It shows interest on

LO 2-8

Describe how to develop the career readiness competency of understanding the business.

FIGURE 2.3
Model of career readiness

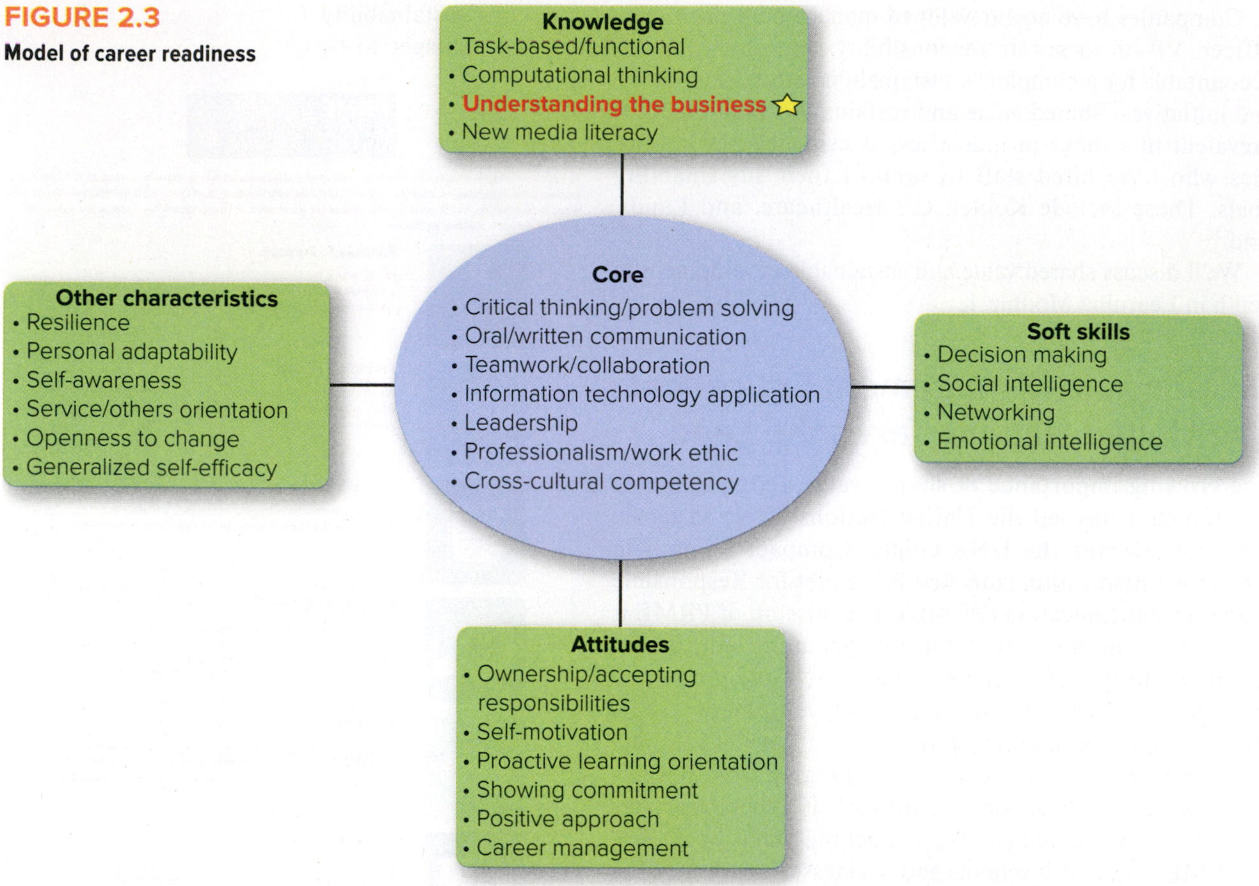

Knowledge
- Task-based/functional
- Computational thinking
- **Understanding the business** ⭐
- New media literacy

Other characteristics
- Resilience
- Personal adaptability
- Self-awareness
- Service/others orientation
- Openness to change
- Generalized self-efficacy

Core
- Critical thinking/problem solving
- Oral/written communication
- Teamwork/collaboration
- Information technology application
- Leadership
- Professionalism/work ethic
- Cross-cultural competency

Soft skills
- Decision making
- Social intelligence
- Networking
- Emotional intelligence

Attitudes
- Ownership/accepting responsibilities
- Self-motivation
- Proactive learning orientation
- Showing commitment
- Positive approach
- Career management

your part, and recruiters are impressed by the fact that you took the time to learn about the business.[84] It also prepares you to ask smart questions, a behavior recruiters want to see. Remember, sometimes it's the small things like this that help land a job.

So, what does it take to demonstrate that you understand a business? We recommend that you learn the following eight things about a company before showing up at a job interview:[85]

1. **The company's mission and vision statements.** These statements tell you why the company exists and what it wants to become or achieve over time. The question to answer is whether you support these pursuits and would like to be part of the journey. If you do, you will be a better fit for the company. This is important because employees are more likely to be productive and stay at a company when they fit in. For example, if you like outdoor activities, you will most likely be a better fit at Recreational Equipment, Inc. (REI), which sells sporting goods, camping gear, and outdoor clothing, than at Whole Foods. You can find this information on the company's website.

2. **The company's core values and culture.** The values an organization endorses represent the foundation of its culture. You can find clues about this by studying a company's website. Try to find a list of company values. What do these values tell you about the company? Next, look for statements that inform you about how the company treats its employees. For example, does the company support empowerment and employee development? Look at any photos posted online and consider what they tell you. If you see pictures only of products and not of people, for instance, it suggests the company really cares about products. What type of goals is the company pursuing? Does the company care about the environment, quality, or customers' opinions?

3. **The history of the company.** When was the company founded? What were the values and background of the founder(s)? Try to find out how the company evolved, grew, or changed over the years.

4. **Key organizational players.** It's important to demonstrate this knowledge during a job interview. Who holds important positions in the company? What are their backgrounds? You can find this out by reading the employer's "About" page and top employees' bios. You might check them out on LinkedIn or read what they say on Twitter.

5. **Who are you interviewing with?** Aside from key organizational players, you should also find out the names and titles of the people you're likely to interview with, particularly those higher up the chain of command. Knowing the interviewers' titles and responsibilities will help you better answer their questions in a way that shows your appreciation for their roles.

6. **The company's products, services, and clients.** What are people saying about the company's products and services? You can explore this by locating reviews or comments about the company's products and services. It would also be useful to try the company's products and services. This would enable you to speak directly from experience. You should also let the interviewer know that you've done your research by sharing three concrete ideas about how you can help the company with its products and services.

7. **Current events and accomplishments.** Look for current news stories about the company and examine its website for a list of accomplishments. Note what this information reveals about the company and decide whether it matches what you learned about the company's mission, vision, stated values, and organizational culture. Inconsistencies are a red flag.

8. **Comments from current or previous employees.** Talk to anyone you know at the company. Ask their opinion about working there and how they feel about management and corporate policies. Search websites like Glassdoor to find inside information such as salary ranges and company reviews.

These activities will increase your career readiness and chances of getting a desired job. They also demonstrate that you care about or even have passion about working at the company. This will distinguish you from others who did not do their research. Remember, it is important to stand out from other applicants when looking for a job. More important, understanding the business will help you determine if you are a good fit for an employer. Go get 'em! ●

You must do research to understand a business. This takes time and attention. At what point in the interview process should you investigate a potential employer?
Kraska/Shutterstock

administrative management 50

behavioral science approach 54

behavioral viewpoint 52

classical viewpoint 48

closed system 59

complexity theory 59

contingency viewpoint 60

evidence-based management 57

feedback 58

Hawthorne effect 53

high-performance work practices (HPWPs) 63

human relations movement 53

inputs 58

learning organization 62

open system 59

operations management 56

outputs 58

quantitative management 56

scientific management 49

subsystems 58

supply chain 57

synergy 59

system 58

systems viewpoint 58

transformational processes 58

Key Points

2.1 Evolving Viewpoints: How We Got to Today's Management Outlook

- Principal management viewpoints include classical, behavioral, and quantitative. More recent viewpoints include systems, contingency, and contemporary.

- Six practical reasons for studying theoretical perspectives are that they provide (1) understanding of the present, (2) a guide to action, (3) a source of new ideas, (4) clues to the meaning of your managers' decisions, (5) clues to the meaning of outside ideas, and (6) understanding as to why certain management practices produce positive outcomes.

2.2 Classical Viewpoint: Scientific and Administrative Management

- The first viewpoint is the classical viewpoint, which emphasized finding ways to manage work more efficiently. It had two branches, scientific management and administrative management.

- Scientific management emphasized the scientific study of work methods to improve productivity by individual workers. It was pioneered by Frederick W. Taylor, who offered four principles of science that could be applied to management, and by Frank and Lillian Gilbreth, who refined motion studies that broke down job tasks into physical motions.

- Administrative management was concerned with managing the total organization. Among its pioneers were Charles Clinton Spaulding, the "Father of African-American Management"; Henri Fayol, who identified the major functions of management (planning, organizing, leading, controlling); and Max Weber, who identified five positive bureaucratic features in a well-performing organization.

2.3 Behavioral Viewpoint: Behaviorism, Human Relations, and Behavioral Science

- The second viewpoint is the behavioral viewpoint, which emphasized the importance of understanding human behavior and of motivating employees toward achievement. It developed over three phases: (1) early behaviorism, (2) the human relations movement, and (3) the behavioral science approach.

- Early behaviorism had three pioneers: (1) Hugo Munsterberg suggested that psychologists could contribute to industry by studying jobs and identifying the psychological conditions for employees to do their best work; (2) Mary Parker Follett thought organizations should be democratic, with employees and managers working together; (3) Elton Mayo hypothesized a so-called Hawthorne effect, suggesting that employees worked harder if they received added attention from managers.

- The human relations movement suggested that better relationships between managers and employees could increase worker productivity. Among its pioneers were Abraham Maslow, who proposed a hierarchy of human needs, and Douglas McGregor, who proposed Theory X (managers have pessimistic view of workers) and Theory Y (managers have positive views of workers).

- The behavioral science approach relies on scientific research for developing theories about human behavior that can be used to provide practical tools for managers.

2.4 Quantitative Viewpoints: Operations Management and Evidence-Based Management

- The third viewpoint is the quantitative viewpoint, which emphasized the application of quantitative techniques to management.

- Two approaches are (1) operations management, which focuses on managing the production and delivery of an organization's products or services more effectively, and (2) evidence-based management, which means translating principles based on best evidence into organizational practice, bringing rationality to the decision-making process.

2.5 Systems Viewpoint

- The systems viewpoint regards the organization as a system of interrelated parts or collection of subsystems that operate together to achieve a common purpose. A system has four parts: inputs, outputs, transformational processes, and feedback.
- A system can be closed, having little interaction with the environment, or open, continually interacting with it.

2.6 Contingency Viewpoint

- The contingency viewpoint emphasizes that a manager's approach should vary according to the individual and the environmental situation.

2.7 Contemporary Approaches: The Learning Organization, High-Performance Work Practices, and Shared Value and Sustainable Development

- A learning organization is one that actively creates, acquires, and transfers knowledge within itself and is able to modify its behavior to reflect new knowledge.

- High-performance work practices improve an organization's ability to effectively attract, select, hire, develop, and retain high-performing personnel.
- Shared value and sustainable development looks beyond short-term profits and focuses on the environmental and social costs of doing business.

2.8 Career Corner: Managing Your Career Readiness

- You can increase the competency of understanding the business by engaging in eight activities: (1) learn the company's mission and vision; (2) identify the company's core values and culture; (3) learn the history of the company; (4) identify the key organizational players; (5) know whom you are talking to; (6) learn about the company's products, services, and clients; (7) study current events and accomplishments about the company; and (8) talk to current or former employees.

Understanding the Chapter: What Do I Know?

1. What are the different management viewpoints?
2. What are six practical reasons for studying theoretical perspectives?
3. What are the contributions of scientific management?
4. How would I summarize the behavioral viewpoint, and what are its contributions?
5. What would be an example of the application of the four parts of a system?

6. What would be an example of the application of the contingency viewpoint?
7. Where have I seen an organization employ evidence-based management?
8. Why should I adopt a shared value and sustainable development perspective?
9. What are three roles I could play as a manager in a learning organization?

Management in Action

Vegan Leather: Earth's Friend or Foe?

Clothes wreak havoc on the environment. Millions of tons of old clothing are sent to landfills or incinerators each year as Americans try to keep up with the latest trends. The clothes that replace what's been disposed of are manufactured by polluting the air and water with chemicals. These chemicals poison our food chain and are responsible for 10% of humanity's greenhouse gases.[86]

Today's fashion consumers are savvier than ever and have taken notice of this danger. According to *Forbes*, professional women pay attention to more than just the quality of their garments; they are focusing on the entire production process and product afterlife.[87] A Nielsen study found that 73% of Millennials are

willing to pay more for sustainable clothing brands. This demand has led to a new market of fashion brands that are fully sustainable.[88] In fact, if you Google "sustainable fashion," you'll get over 280 million results as businesses are stepping up to address sustainability issues in the fashion industry.[89]

A NEW TYPE OF LEATHER

Significant criticism of the fashion industry's sustainability practices focuses on leather. Leather is made from animal skins that are tanned and converted to wearable form. Most tanning substances are made from chromium salts, which can be toxic when tanneries use them in the leather-making process. As a result, tanning agents are hazardous compounds that are difficult to recycle or reuse, and pose a challenge for waste collection. The amount of tannery toxic byproducts is staggering. Take India, for example, home to the most tanneries. The Indian city of Kanpur produces up to 40 million liters (more than 10 million gallons) of tannery wastewater each day.[90] This water is dumped into local farmlands, killing vegetation and entering the city's drinking water. As a result, local residents are developing skin conditions, tuberculosis, blindness, gastrointestinal issues, and having children born with severe mental and physical disabilities.[91]

Criticism of the leather industry isn't only tied to environmental concerns. There are also serious animal rights issues associated with the leather-making process. Leather comes from industrial farms, many of which raise animals in crammed quarters with no natural light. And since they are in such close contact, many of the animals have their teeth, horns, and tails removed.[92]

Vegan, also known as faux or synthetic, leather was developed to address these concerns with the traditional leather-making process. Most vegan leather is made from plastic-based materials, without using animal byproducts. It can be used as an alternative to traditional leather for handbags, belts, wallets, jackets, shoes, and anything else you'd typically use leather for.[93]

Vegan leather is becoming increasingly popular in the United States, not only because of environmental concerns, but also because it is generally less expensive and easier to maintain than traditional leather. The online availability of vegan leather products actually rose 54% from 2018 to 2019. There is also increased demand from the auto industry as more and more carmakers use artificial leather for car interiors. *Bloomberg Businessweek* reports that global demand for vegan leather may grow at a rate of 7%, reaching $45 billion by 2025.[94]

A PIONEER FACES CRITICISM

The vegan leather market may be growing today, but one of its pioneers has been developing these types of products since 2001. Stella McCartney, daughter of Beatles' legend Sir Paul McCartney, operates 51 vegan leather stores in locations such as New York, London, Hollywood, Paris, Milan, and Tokyo. McCartney's collections are also distributed by partner specialty shops and department stores in 77 countries. Moreover, she ships to 100 countries through her online marketplace.[95]

McCartney's business may be growing, but vegan leather is coming under increased scrutiny. The plastics used to create this type of leather, polyurethane and polyvinyl chloride, pose serious environmental threats because they are manufactured from fossil fuels, such as petroleum. Petroleum is "toxic, terrible for the Earth, and fuels climate change," according to

Coveteur.[96] And Greenpeace actually labels polyvinyl chloride as the "single most environmentally damaging type of plastic."[97] As a result of this criticism, McCartney herself has admitted that the plastics used in her products are "not without concern."[98]

The harmful effects of vegan leather don't end at the production process. Plastic leather has a shorter lifespan than traditional leather, meaning consumers dispose of their vegan leather belts, shoes, and other clothing more quickly than long-lasting "hand-me-down" leather products. Furthermore, when trashed, vegan leather may take hundreds of years to decompose in water, if it even does at all.[99] Traditional leather, on the other hand, is biodegradable. Patrick Grant, creative director of Norton & Sons tailors and a materials expert, says designers like McCartney are causing microplastics to enter our waterways. "Eighteen years ago, she had been telling people to switch from leather to polyurethane and now the fish have it inside them," he says.[100]

REAL LEATHER CAN BE SUSTAINABLE, TOO

McCartney's product line isn't just facing skepticism from environmental activists, it is also dealing with eco-friendly changes to the traditional leather-making process. Rachel Garwood, a creative leather technology expert, says that genuine leather is more environmentally friendly due to modern tanning methods. For example, more and more tanneries are using vegetable tanning, which is far less harmful than traditional methods. "Chemical companies and tanners are working closely with brands to offer reassurance of the clean technology and ethics in leather manufacturing," says Garwood.[101]

Other leather companies are using laboratories to go green. Modern Meadow, for example, touts itself as a "biofabrication" company, saying biofabrication is a way of building fabric with cells, DNA, and protein.[102] Modern Meadow's lab-grown leather comes from collagen, the protein that makes animal and human skin. Their products look, feel, and wear much more like leather, and since they are made from collagen, may arguably be genuine. Moreover, biofabrication alleviates some leather production and decomposition concerns.[103]

McCartney continues to innovate in order to stay ahead of not just the leather controversy, but also concerns about other fabrics. During her Spring/Summer 2020 fashion show in Paris, she debuted the world's first "fur-free" fur. The innovative material uses plant-based fibers and recycled polyester, not plastic. McCartney claims it uses 30% less energy and 63% less greenhouse gases than competing plastic brands. Fur-free fur can also be recycled at the end of its life, so it won't end up in a landfill.[104]

Will environmentalists be satisfied?

Problem-Solving Perspective

1. What is the underlying problem in this case from Stella McCartney's perspective?

2. What are the key causes of this problem?

Application of Chapter Content

1. Use the four parts of a system to find a solution to McCartney's environmental challenges. Provide support for your conclusions.

2. Does evidence-based management support McCartney's claims that her products are more eco-friendly than traditional leather? Explain.

3. Is McCartney an example of a leader effectively using shared value and sustainable development? Why or why not?

4. What key lessons from this chapter could McCartney use to improve how her products are perceived by the market? Explain.

Legal/Ethical Challenge

What Should You Do about an Insubordinate Employee?

You are a vice president for a company in the insurance industry, and you supervise five managers. These managers in turn supervise a host of employees working in their departments. Your company is having trouble achieving its sales growth goals and your boss, the president of a division, called a meeting with you and your peers to create a plan of action.

The meeting was a bit volatile because layoffs were proposed, and it was agreed that all vice presidents had to reduce their budgets. This means that you and your peers were not allowed to hire consultants or send employees to training. You also have to reduce your labor costs by $300,000. This means that you must lay off employees. You informed the managers who report to you about these decisions and asked them to come up with a list of potential people to lay off. You suggested that performance should be the key criterion for deciding layoffs.

Two weeks later, one of your reporting managers walked into your office with a worried look. He told you that Jim, one of your other reporting managers, had just hired a consultant to lead a team-building session with his group in another state. Not only did this require significant travel expenses, but the consultant's fees were well outside of your budgeted expenses. Further, your other employees were expressing feelings of unfairness because Jim was taking his team on a team-building trip while they were being forced to cut costs. It also was a bit inconsistent to spend money on team building when impending layoffs were just around the corner.

In terms of layoffs, all your reporting managers submitted a list of potential employees to let go except for Jim. You have no idea why he avoided this task.

Jim's behavior clearly violates the agreement that was made about cost cutting, and you are upset that he has not submitted his list of employees to lay off. You have not yet spoken to him about this insubordination, and now you are wondering what to do.

SOLVING THE CHALLENGE

What would you do?

1. Meet with Jim to review his behavior. Tell him that any more acts of insubordination will result in termination. Don't make a big deal about these events and don't include documentation in his personnel file.

2. Put Jim on the list of people to be laid off. Although the company will have to pay him severance, the money reduces the chance he would file a lawsuit against the company.

3. Call your human resource (HR) representative and discuss the legality of firing Jim. Jim was insubordinate in hiring a consultant and irresponsible for not submitting his list of potential employees to be laid off. If HR agrees, I would fire Jim.

4. Reprimand Jim by putting him on a performance improvement plan (PIP). This plan outlines specific changes Jim needs to make going forward, and it gives him a chance to make up for his poor decisions.

5. Invent other options. Discuss.

Learn more about Boeing's history and management perspectives, starting from the beginning to the company's current challenges in developing the Boeing 737 MAX.

Assess your ability to apply concepts discussed in Chapters 1 and 2 to the case by going to Connect.

3

The Manager's Changing Work Environment and Ethical Responsibilities

Doing the Right Thing

Kapook2981/iStock/Getty Images

After reading this chapter, you should be able to:

LO 3-1 Describe the triple bottom line of people, planet, and profit and its importance to younger workers.

LO 3-2 Identify important stakeholders inside the organization.

LO 3-3 Identify important stakeholders outside the organization.

LO 3-4 Explain the importance of ethics and values in effective management.

LO 3-5 Describe the concept of social responsibility and its role in today's organizations.

LO 3-6 Discuss the role of corporate governance in building ethical and socially responsible organizations.

LO 3-7 Describe how to develop the career readiness competency of professionalism/work ethic.

FORECAST   What's Ahead in This Chapter

The triple bottom line of people, planet, and profit represents a new standard of success for businesses. This helps define the new world in which managers must operate and their responsibilities, including the community of stakeholders, both internal and external, they must deal with. The chapter also considers a manager's ethical and social responsibilities, as well as the importance of corporate governance. We conclude with a Career Corner that focuses on how you can develop the career readiness competency of professionalism/work ethic.

Being Courageous at Work

More than 50% of employees report witnessing unethical behavior at their jobs. This means that workplace ethics violations are common, and it's likely you will find yourself in an unethical work environment at some point in your career. How do you think you would respond if you witnessed someone doing something that was clearly unethical on the job? Would you say something?

Sadly, over one-third of workers who witness unethical workplace behavior never report anything because they think that their voices won't matter—or worse, because they fear that speaking up for what is right will get them into trouble.[1] Doing the right thing requires courage, and recent job postings from companies including Lululemon, Ann Taylor, Coach, Nestlé USA, Toyota, and Kimberly-Clark demonstrate that organizations are actively looking for employees who are ready to exercise courage.[2]

Behaving with **courage** means taking intentional and **deliberate action in the name of a worthy cause and enduring in this act despite the risk of serious personal consequences such as retaliation, disapproval, or rejection.**[3] Here's how you can develop your capacity to behave courageously at work.

1. Practice in a Low-Risk Setting

Executive coach Peter Bregman says the best way to get better at something that scares you is to practice doing it in an environment where the actual risk to you is low. Do you want to be a better negotiator? Try negotiating with your partner or roommate the next time you both want to pick the music station. Are you interested in being more assertive when a co-worker repeatedly interrupts you during meetings? Think about how you'd want to respond, then engage a close friend in a debate over something mundane such as which Starbucks drink is best or why Drew Brees is the greatest QB of all time. Chances are your friend will interrupt you at some point, giving you the opportunity to practice your skill.

Bregman encourages you to allow yourself to feel all of the discomforts that surface as you practice. When the time comes to put your skills into practice in a work situation, he says, these feelings won't surprise or overcome you because you will have experienced them already during your practice sessions.[4]

2. Plan for an Endurance Event

Imagine that you are about to head out into the snow on a freezing day. You'll likely dress in multiple layers of warm clothing to shield your body from the cold, right? Researchers Debra Comer and Leslie Sekerka suggest that you prepare yourself to behave courageously much like you prepare yourself for a day in the snow.

Part of being courageous is the willingness to *endure* hardship.[5] Courage requires a series of courageous acts, rather than a one-time intervention, and you should be prepared for a lengthy and uncomfortable journey that will neither go smoothly nor completely your way. You should also plan to face resistance and unsupportive organizational responses. Anticipating a long and challenging process will "insulate" you from the difficulties that may otherwise cause you to abandon your decision to behave courageously, just like your thermal shirt, down jacket, and warm gloves help you stay out in the snow for a longer period of time.[6]

3. Rely on Self-Regulation after the Act of Courage

If anticipating a difficult journey works like a set of warm and cozy winter layers, then practicing self-regulation *after* a courageous act is akin to a steamy mug of hot cocoa or soup that warms you from the inside out and gives you the strength to go back out in the snow after a brief rest. In other words, self-regulation techniques fortify you each time you grow weary, reinforcing your energy to sustain your convictions in the face of unsupportive responses from your supervisor or organization. Self-regulation helps you to keep going back out into the snow, over and over again.

Comer and Sekerka recommend three self-regulation practices:

- *Self-Affirmation*—One way to keep going when others in the organization are unsupportive is to think about your past accomplishments. These can be anything—from any time in your life. Maybe you finally got through your backlog of class reading or assignments. Or perhaps you ranked first in some type of competition earlier in life such as a spelling bee, swim meet, or debate. Remembering your successes generates positive emotions, and these help you to continue behaving courageously even when others are resisting your attempts.

- *Self-Compassion*—Another way to fortify yourself is to focus on what you can learn from the experience rather than on the lack of organizational support. Avoid the temptation to be consumed by your negative emotions or to abandon your mission. Instead, be kind to yourself the way you would be to a close friend going through the same thing. Remind yourself that you did the "right" thing and that you will adjust to any setbacks and forge ahead on a courageous path.

- *Social Support*—Share your experience with people who support you when you find it difficult to sustain your courageous campaign. These people can be co-workers, other contacts in the organization, or friends and family members. Their willingness to listen and provide advice and encouragement will validate your belief that you are doing the right thing and supply you with the sustenance you need to stay strong.

For Discussion Have you ever wanted to behave courageously but decided to stay silent? What do you think prevented you from acting with courage? What are one or two ways that you can practice courage in a low-risk environment? What can you do to ensure that you will both insulate and fortify yourself when you are confronted with a situation that requires you to behave with courage?

3.1 The Goals of Business: More Than Making Money

THE BIG PICTURE

Many businesses, small and large, are beginning to subscribe to a new standard of success—the triple bottom line, representing people, planet, and profit. This outlook has found favor with many younger workers who are more concerned with finding meaning than material success.

LO 3-1

Describe the triple bottom line of people, planet, and profit and its importance to younger workers.

Siemens USA supports the triple bottom line. CEO Barbara Humpton speaks about what Siemens USA is doing to create value for society at the 2019 Concordia Annual Summit.

Riccardo Savi/Getty Images

The Triple Bottom Line: People, Planet, and Profit

"If you're a company that isn't creating value for society, why do you exist?" asked Siemens USA CEO Barbara Humpton on a recent *Washington Post Live* podcast. In Humpton's view, making money should be only one goal of business. The others are to foster social and environmental consciousness—the two other elements of what's known as the "triple bottom line." The **triple bottom line**—representing people, planet, and profit (the 3 Ps)—measures an organization's social, environmental, and financial performance. In this view of corporate performance, an organization has a responsibility to its employees and to the wider community (people); is committed to sustainable development (planet); and includes the costs of pollution, worker displacement, and other factors in its financial calculations (profit), matters high in the minds of many of today's consumers.[7] Success in these areas can be measured through a **social audit**, a systematic assessment of a company's performance in implementing socially responsible programs, often based on predefined goals.

The Good Bowl in Traverse City, Michigan, for instance, is known for its socially responsible mission. The small Vietnamese restaurant donates $1 to charity for each bowl ordered, and customers can choose from a list of local, national, and international charities. The restaurant opened in 2018 and donated more than $30,000 within one year.[8] Hawaiian jewelry company Nurdle in the Rough crafts all of its items from ocean plastic and recycled silver. Owner Kat Crabill also donates 10% of the company's profits to the Hawaii Wildlife Fund.[9]

But the triple bottom line isn't just to be practiced by small companies. As Deloitte Global CEO Punit Renjen observes, "by their very nature, businesses have the entrepreneurial spirit, operational prowess, and deep bench of talent to help change the world."[10] For instance, Patagonia donated $10 million of its 2018 corporate tax cuts to environmental groups.[11] Ben & Jerry's ice cream, according to its director of social mission, was able to have a bigger impact once it was taken over by global giant Unilever.[12] Its new CEO Matthew McCarthy has pledged to double the ice cream brand's social impact.[13]

Younger Workers' Search for Meaning

Millennials (born between 1981 and 1996) and Gen Zers (born after 1997) care about the triple bottom line. These younger workers now make up more than one-third of the U.S. workforce and could account for as much as 58% by 2029.[15]

In Chapter 1, we mentioned that one of the great challenges for a manager is trying to achieve personal success, whether in striving for a happy life or a meaningful life—or, if possible, both. Younger workers are no different, and they expect more from the organizations they work for and do business with. These generations want things like meaningful work and products that represent their personal values more than older generations ever did.[16] According to a Deloitte study of Millennials and Gen Zs, only 49% of respondents indicated they believed business leaders, in general, are committed to behaving ethically, and only 55% believed businesses have a positive impact on the world. Over 60% believed the average company has "no ambition beyond wanting to make money."[17] Younger workers also are more concerned with having experiences than with owning material possessions, which will impact how companies market to them as consumers and attract them as employees.[18] They also want work–life balance.[19]

In this chapter, we discuss two factors in achieving a meaningful life:

- Understanding the environment in which a manager operates—the community of stakeholders inside and outside the organization.

- The ethical and social responsibilities of being a manager. ●

3.2 The Community of Stakeholders inside the Organization

THE BIG PICTURE

Managers operate in two organizational environments—internal and external—both made up of stakeholders, the people whose interests are affected by the organization. The first, or internal, environment consists of employees, owners, and the board of directors.

Is a company principally responsible only to its stockholders and executives? Or are other groups equal in significance?

Perhaps we need a broader term than "stockholders" to indicate all those with a stake in an organization. That term, appropriately, is **stakeholders**—the people whose interests are affected by an organization's activities.

LO 3-2

Identify important stakeholders inside the organization.

Internal and External Stakeholders

Managers operate in two organizational environments, both made up of various stakeholders. *(See Figure 3.1.)* This section focuses on internal stakeholders.

Internal Stakeholders

Whether small or large, your organization has people in it who have both an important stake in how it performs and the power to shape its future.[20] These **internal stakeholders** consist of employees, owners, and the board of directors, if any. Let us consider each in turn.

FIGURE 3.1

The organization's environment

The two main groups are internal and external stakeholders.

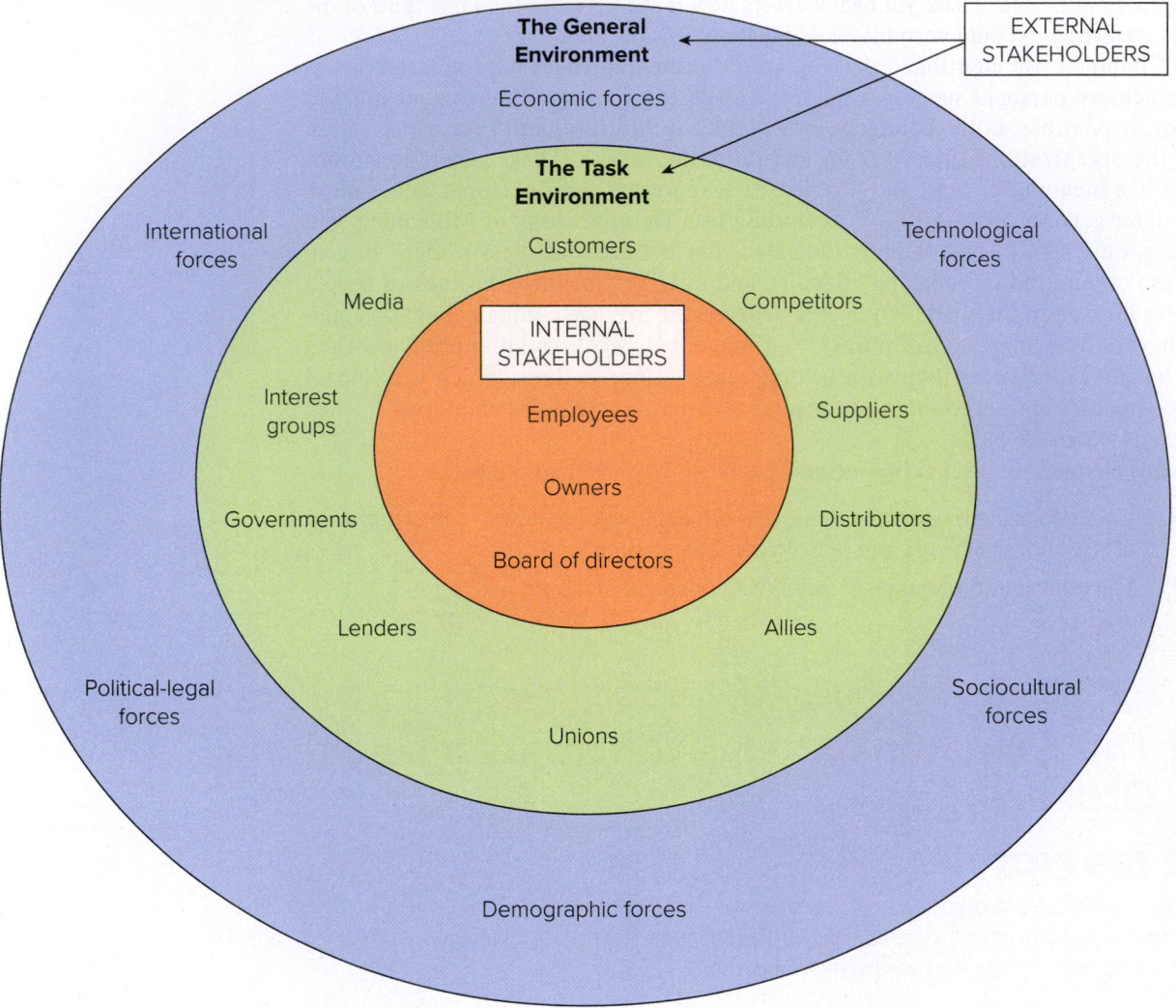

Source: From Diverse Teams at Work *by Lee Gardenswartz. Published by the Society for Human Resource Management.*

Employees   As a manager, could you run your part of the organization if you and your employees were constantly in conflict? Labor history, of course, is full of accounts of just this. But such conflict may lower the company's performance, thereby hurting everyone's stake. In many of today's forward-looking organizations, employees are considered "the talent"—the most important resource.

"We are in a people business—a business that relies upon the talent and passion of our team to deliver incredible experiences to our guests," said Hilton president and CEO Christopher Nassetta. "We do this through our relentless focus on creating an exceptional workplace culture for all."[21] Hilton was ranked No. 1 on *Fortune*'s 2020 list of "100 Best Companies to Work For."[22] The hotel chain treats its employees exceptionally well, as evidenced by a recent *Great Place to Work* Trust Index Survey, which found that "96% of Hilton's employees say that it's a great place to work, 97% say that when you join the company, you are made to feel welcome, and 96% say that they are proud to tell others they work for the company."[23]

As we saw in Chapter 1 (Manager's Challenge #3), the U.S. workforce of the future will consist of employees more diverse in gender, age, race, ethnicity, and sexual orientation than we've been accustomed to. We consider the implications of this further in Chapter 11.

Owners The <mark>owners</mark> of an organization consist of all those who can claim it as their legal property, such as Walmart's stockholders. There are five principal types of ownership.

- **Sole proprietorship:** In the for-profit world, if you're running a one-person graphic design firm, the owner is just you—you're what is known as a sole proprietorship. There are currently more than 17 million sole proprietorships in the United States.[24]

- **Partnership:** If you're in an Internet start-up with your brother-in-law and you're both owners—you're a partnership.

- **Private investors:** If you're a member of a family running a car dealership and you're all owners—you're investors in a privately owned company.

- **Employee owners:** If you work for a company that is more than half owned by its employees (such as Tucson-based Barrio Brewing Company, producer of 15,000 barrels of craft beer per year, or Alton, Illinois–based Alton Steel Company), you are one of the joint owners—you're part of an Employee Stock Ownership Plan (ESOP).[25]

- **Stockholders:** And if you've bought a few shares of stock in a company whose shares are listed for sale on the New York Stock Exchange, such as General Motors, you're one of thousands of owners—you're a stockholder.

In all these examples, of course, the stated goal of the owners is to make a profit.

A Publix store manager leads a cheer at the end of a daily managers' huddle. Store employees' motivation may be enhanced by the fact that Publix is an employee-owned American supermarket. Why would employee ownership fuel employee motivation? Patrick James Miller/Redux Pictures

Board of Directors Who hires the chief executive of a for-profit or nonprofit organization? In a corporation, it is the <mark>board of directors</mark>—the group of people elected to oversee the firm's activities and ensure that management acts in shareholders' best interests. In nonprofit organizations, such as universities or hospitals, the board may be called the *board of trustees* or *board of regents*. Board members are very important in setting the organization's overall strategic goals and in approving the major decisions and salaries of top management.

A large corporation might have eight or so members on its board of directors. Some of these directors (inside directors) may be top executives of the firm. The rest (outside directors) are elected from outside the firm. The board of directors at Facebook, for instance, includes not only insiders CEO Mark Zuckerberg and chief operating officer (COO) Sheryl Sandberg but also executives from outside firms, including PayPal, Dropbox, and General Catalyst.[26]

Boards of directors can play an important role in setting corporate strategy and executive compensation. Research shows that companies with good boards "did not pay CEOs high bonuses for luck." Conscientious boards also prevented self-serving CEOs from skimming corporate profits.[27] Some experts further speculate that balanced gender representation on boards is an important characteristic of a "good" board. A recent study by Credit Suisse suggests there are "strong correlations" between the number of women on a board, share price, and profits.[28] Another study found that boards with more gender diversity are less likely to commit fraud.[29] We clearly have room for improvement, given that women account for only about 25% of board seats in S&P companies.[30]

We consider directors further in Section 3.6, "Corporate Governance." ●

3.3 The Community of Stakeholders outside the Organization

THE BIG PICTURE

The external environment of stakeholders consists of the task environment and the general environment. The task environment consists of customers, competitors, suppliers, distributors, strategic allies, employee associations, local communities, financial institutions, government regulators, and special-interest groups. The general environment consists of economic, technological, sociocultural, demographic, political–legal, and international forces.

LO 3-3

Identify important stakeholders outside the organization.

In the first section, we described the environment inside the organization. Here let's consider the environment outside it, which consists of **external stakeholders**—people or groups in the organization's external environment that are affected by it. This environment consists of:

- The task environment.
- The general environment.

The Task Environment

The **task environment** consists of 10 groups that interact with the organization on a regular basis. The task environment is made up of customers, competitors, suppliers, distributors, strategic allies, employee organizations, local communities, financial institutions, government regulators, and special-interest groups.

1. Customers   The first law of business (even for nonprofits), as we've said, is *take care of the customer*. **Customers** are those who pay to use an organization's goods or services. Many customers are generally frustrated by poor customer relations at airlines, banks, and cable and satellite service providers, in part because many of these companies have few competitors and thus don't have to worry about making customers happy.

Among "America's most hated companies," by one account: Facebook, WeWork, Pacific Gas & Electric (PG&E), Boeing (which you are reading about in the continuing case), Frontier Communication, Wells Fargo, and Juul. The most frequently cited reason for hatred toward these companies is ethical violations, including Facebook's data problems, the former CEO's questionable business decisions at WeWork, PG&E's neglect of safety regulations in California, and Boeing's decision to ignore equipment malfunctions.[31]

2. Competitors   Is there any line of work you could enter in which there would *not* be competitors—people or organizations that compete for customers or resources, such as talented employees or raw materials? We mentioned that some of the most hated companies in America have little competition—but every organization has to be on the lookout for *possible c*ompetitors, even if not yet in sight.

Amazon Example: For example, rapid digital disruption has stimulated intense competition in the food retail industry in recent years. E-commerce retailer Amazon is quickly expanding its AmazonFresh grocery delivery service—free for Prime members—as it competes with Walmart, Target, Instacart, and local supermarkets.[32] The company also has launched its own cashierless grocery stores (Amazon Go) that rely on specially equipped carts, cameras, and other software to facilitate its "just walk out technology."[33]

Werner paddles. Kayaker Dylan McKinny trusted Werner Paddles during the 21st annual Green Race, considered to be one of the most competitive whitewater races in the world. Larry Clouse/Shutterstock

3. Suppliers   A supplier, or vendor, is a person or an organization that provides supplies—that is, raw materials, services, equipment, labor, or energy—to other organizations. Suppliers in turn have their own suppliers. Firms may turn to their suppliers for help with product improvements and innovations.[34]

Werner Paddles Example: For instance, Werner Paddles makes handcrafted kayak paddles from carbon fiber reinforced plastic. When the company wanted to improve the appearance of its product, not usually a priority for components made of carbon fiber, it went to its supplier, KASO Plastics, for help. KASO, in turn, searched out a recycled material made by RTP Company, which was working in partnership with aircraft maker Boeing to reclaim manufacturing scrap from Boeing's 787 Dreamliner. The result was a paddle blade that met Werner's aesthetic criteria at no increase in cost, with the bonus of including recycled content that would appeal to its environmentally conscious customers.[35]

4. Distributors

A **distributor**, sometimes called a middleman, is a person or an organization that helps another organization sell its goods and services to customers. Publishers of magazines, for instance, don't sell directly to newsstands; rather, they go through a distributor, or wholesaler. Tickets to a Lizzo or Billie Eilish concert might be sold to you directly by the concert hall, but they are also sold through such distributors as Ticketmaster, LiveNation, and StubHub.

Distributors can be quite important because in some industries (such as movie theaters and magazines), there is not a lot of competition, and the distributor has a lot of power over the ultimate price of the product. However, the popularity of the Internet has allowed manufacturers of cell phones, for example, to cut out the "middleman"—the distributor—and to sell to customers directly.

5. Strategic Allies

Companies frequently link up with other organizations (even competing ones) in order to realize strategic advantages.[36] The term **strategic allies** describes the relationship of two organizations who join forces to achieve advantages neither can perform as well alone. Strategic alliances allow firms to access new technologies, knowledge, capital, and markets while sharing the costs and risks.[37]

AES and Google Example: The unreliable nature of both wind and sunlight as renewable energy sources has been a major source of frustration in the quest to deliver clean energy on a global scale. AES Corporation recently entered into a ten-year strategic alliance with Google to facilitate widespread expansion of wind and solar power. The relationship will leverage the Google cloud platform to engineer smart grids that are able to manage large-scale renewable energy adoption.[38] According to president and CEO Andrés Gluski, AES is "one of the largest renewables solutions providers and developers in the world." He added, "By combining the capabilities, footprint and experience of both companies, we will be able to provide better and more efficient energy solutions."[39]

6. Employee Organizations: Unions and Associations

As a rule of thumb, labor unions (such as the United Auto Workers or the Teamsters Union) tend to represent hourly workers; professional associations (such as the National Education Association or The Newspaper Guild) tend to represent salaried workers. Nevertheless, during a labor dispute, salary-earning teachers in the American Federation of Teachers might well act in sympathy with the wage-earning janitors in the Service Employees International Union.

In recent years, the percentage of the U.S. labor force represented by unions has steadily declined (from 35% in the 1950s to 10.3% in 2019).[40] In contrast, 23% of the workforce in the European Union is unionized, with a range of 74% in Finland to a low of 8% in France and Lithuania. Unions clearly have a greater influence on managerial decisions in the EU than the United States.[41]

7. Local Communities

Local communities are obviously important stakeholders, which becomes evident not only when a big organization arrives but also when it leaves, sending government officials scrambling to find new industry to replace it. Schools and municipal governments rely on the organization for their tax base. Families and merchants depend on its employee payroll for their livelihoods. In addition, everyone from the United Way to the Little League may rely on it for some financial support. Organizations realize significant benefits when they invest time and resources into understanding and meeting the needs of the local communities surrounding their various locations.[42]

If a community gives a company tax breaks in return for the promise of new jobs and the company fails to deliver, does the community have the right to institute **clawbacks**—rescinding the tax breaks when firms don't deliver promised jobs? Further, should companies be getting these tax breaks to begin with? We explore this second question further in the Example box below.

EXAMPLE   Local Communities as Stakeholders: Does Amazon Really Need Tax Breaks?

The Amazon Spheres at its urban campus in the Belltown neighborhood of Seattle. Paul Christian Gordon/Alamy Stock Photo

Amazon is becoming one of Ohio's largest employers,[43] and in Summer 2019 the company announced it would open two new fulfillment centers in the state, bringing the state's total number of Amazon fulfillment centers up to six.[44] Since 2016 Amazon has received more than $15.8 million in tax credits for its facilities in Ohio. The city of Akron also plans to give Amazon an estimated $17 million dollar tax rebate over 30 years in exchange for the company locating its facility there.[45]

Amazon's tax breaks are not confined to Ohio. In fact, in 2019, Amazon saved at least $171.9 million dollars due to tax incentives it received from its distribution centers across the United States.[46] These tax breaks are popular because "incentives give companies the ability to shop around in various states and ask for breaks," said Adam Michel, Washington, D.C.–based senior policy analyst. He added, "Because of the perceived ability of these firms to choose somewhere else, a lot of local governments feel pressure to give them sweetheart deals to lure them to their locality."[47]

Impacts on Local Economies. New physical facilities bring great economic benefits according to Amazon and others who support the use of tax incentives to lure companies to build warehouses and distribution centers in their locations. Amazon reasons that across its six facilities in Ohio it will have created more than 11,000 jobs in the state.[48] The company also says that its presence in Illinois has resulted in more than $4 billion worth of investments in the state since 2010.[49] Finally, Amazon estimates that it has created at least 7,000 jobs in Illinois outside of Amazon.[50]

Not everyone agrees that these tax incentives create jobs or do much to boost local economies. And since Amazon's infamous decision to retreat from its planned second headquarters in New York (which would have meant $3.4 billion in tax incentives and grants for the company),[51] lawmakers in at least seven states are working on legislation aimed at outlawing these incentives.[52]

Some economists have warned that giving huge tax breaks to incoming businesses does little more than rob cities of resources needed by arguably more important entities like their school, housing, and transportation systems. What's more, these systems also may need expensive upgrades and improvements to accommodate the huge influx of Amazon workers moving in, and existing businesses and individual taxpayers would end up footing the bill.[53]

San Jose, California, had been one of the cities vying for Amazon's second headquarters, but Mayor Sam Liccardo's offer made it clear that the e-commerce giant would receive no tax incentives for locating there. He said, "If you're offering incentives, those are dollars you could use to be building out transit . . . supporting an ecosystem of talent development."[54] Several studies suggest that tax incentives often fail to deliver the benefits they promise, and that in some cases, tax breaks may even harm employment growth and local economies.[55]

YOUR CALL

Do you think tax breaks for big companies like Amazon benefit local communities? Should these companies continue to receive tax breaks when they build new facilities? Why or why not?

---

8. Financial Institutions   Want to launch a small company? Although normally reluctant to make loans to start-ups, financial institutions—banks, savings and loans, and credit unions—may do so if you have a good credit history or can secure the loan with property such as a house. You might also receive help from venture capitalists. **Venture capital is money provided by investors to start-up firms and small businesses with high risk but perceived long-term growth potential, in return for an ownership stake.**

During the Great Recession, when even good customers found loans hard to get, a new kind of financing emerged called **crowdfunding, raising money for a project or venture by obtaining many small amounts of money from many people ("the crowd"), using websites such as Kickstarter.** We discuss crowdfunding further in Chapter 10.

Established companies also often need loans to tide them over when revenues are down or to finance expansion, but they rely on lenders such as commercial banks, investment banks, and insurance companies for assistance.

9. Government Regulators   The preceding groups are external stakeholders in your organization because they are clearly affected by its activities. But why would ==government regulators==—regulatory agencies that establish ground rules under which organizations may operate—be considered stakeholders?

We are talking here about an alphabet soup of agencies, boards, and commissions that have the legal authority to prescribe or proscribe the conditions under which you may conduct business. To these may be added local and state regulators on the one hand and foreign governments and international agencies (such as the World Trade Organization, which oversees international trade and standardization efforts) on the other.

Such government regulators can be said to be stakeholders because not only do they affect the activities of your organization, they are in turn affected by it. The Federal Aviation Agency (FAA), for example, specifies how far planes must stay apart to prevent midair collisions. But when the airlines want to add more flights on certain routes, the FAA may have to add more flight controllers and radar equipment because those are the agency's responsibility.

FAA Example: In recent years the FAA has had to take on the heavy responsibility of regulating the use of drones, which now number more than 1.5 million.[56] New regulations will implement more sophisticated identification and tracking systems, place tighter restrictions on where drones can be flown, and require that all drone users pass an aeronautical knowledge and safety exam.[57]

10. Special-Interest Groups   ==Special-interest groups== are groups whose members try to influence specific issues, some of which may affect your organization. Examples are People for the Ethical Treatment of Animals, Mothers Against Drunk Driving, the National Organization for Women, and the National Rifle Association.

Special-interest groups may try to exert political influence by contributing funds to lawmakers' election campaigns, launching letter-writing efforts to officials, or organizing marches. This was the case in 2019 when 16-year-old Greta Thunberg led millions of students, trade unions, and workers across the globe in the largest climate march in history.[58] Some groups have made striking visual statements, such as the thousands who gathered near Virginia's state capitol wearing tactical gear and carrying pistols and rifles to advocate for gun rights.[59]

The General Environment

Beyond the task environment is the ==general environment==, or ==macroenvironment==—the set of broad, uncontrollable forces in the external environment that impact the organization.

Marching for climate change. Environmental activist Greta Thunberg speaking to climate protestors outside of the White House in Washington, D.C. Nicholas Kamm/AFP/Getty Images

Rallying for gun rights. Virginia citizens rallying against state gun legislation at the state capitol. The legislation would ban guns in some locations and require background checks. Jim Lo Scalzo/Shutterstock

The general environment includes six forces: economic, technological, sociocultural, demographic, political–legal, and international.

You may be able to control some forces in the task environment, but you can't control those in the general environment. Nevertheless, they can profoundly affect your organization's task environment without your knowing it, springing nasty surprises on you. Clearly, then, as a manager you need to keep your eye on the far horizon because these forces of the general environment can affect long-term plans and decisions.

1. Economic Forces

==Economic forces== consist of the general economic conditions and trends—such as unemployment, interest rates, and trade balance—that may affect an organization's performance. These are forces in your world, region, and nation, over which you and your organization probably have no control, as happened in the Great Recession and its aftermath and in the COVID-19 pandemic.

- **Unemployment.** Is the unemployment rate rising? Then maybe you'll have more job applicants to hire from, yet you'll also have fewer customers with money to spend. Conversely, declining unemployment will mean you'll have to vie for top talent (often by offering more competitive wages and benefits), but you may enjoy increased consumer spending. The national unemployment rate hit 3.5% in 2019—the lowest in 50 years—and rose to its highest level since the Great Depression during COVID-19.[60]

- **Interest rates.** Are banks' interest rates going up in the United States? Then it will cost you more to borrow money to open new stores or build new plants. When the Federal Reserve lowers interest, small businesses may be in a better position to expand.[61]

- **Trade balance.** The ==trade balance==, or balance of trade, is the difference between the monetary value of a country's imports and exports.[62] When the United States imports more than it exports it is said to have a *trade deficit*. If exports exceed imports, there is a *trade surplus*. Although the word surplus sounds positive and the word deficit sounds negative, economists generally do not view a trade surplus as inherently good, nor do they view a trade deficit as inherently bad.[63]

These and other economic forces greatly impact organizations,[64] and it is important that managers consider them in concert with one another rather than as isolated indices. For example, low unemployment rates may not boost wages immediately if employers fear impending trade disputes, economic recession, or other factors that would make increased wages difficult to sustain.[65]

2. Technological Forces

==Technological forces== are new developments in methods for transforming resources into goods or services. The way we manufacture goods and provide services has changed dramatically in recent years and will continue to evolve as technologies improve. Technological forces such as artificial intelligence, which is discussed in Chapter 7, have overhauled not only how humans interact with the workplace, but also the amount and type of human interaction that is necessary.[66]

- **Technology and work arrangements.** Flexible working arrangements are important to young generations of workers.[67] Millennials and Gen Zers were raised with technology and fully embrace the idea that productivity and innovation don't always require face-to-face interaction in an office.[68] In fact, the capacity to work remotely means that the potential talent pool for many organizations is no longer limited by geographic boundaries. Companies can search for the absolute best talent, rather than the best available from a local pool. Halo Top ice cream grew its revenues from $230,000 in 2013 to $100 million in 2018—without a corporate office.[69] All of the company's full-time employees worked remotely and used the Slack app to communicate.

- **Technology and automation.** Technological innovations continue to change the types of skills required in the workplace, and employers need to be able to find workers who possess the requisite skill sets as they shift. Skills shifts are not a novel concept, but experts predict that automation will cause these shifts to occur at an unprecedented rate. Rapid advances in robotics and artificial intelligence mean that demands for physical labor and basic cognitive skills will drop, and jobs will increasingly require higher-order cognitive processing, technological skills, and soft skills.[70]

Read more about how technology has changed our lives in the Example box.

EXAMPLE   The Dark Side of Technology

The key fact about technology is its capacity for *disruption*—disruption of how we provide and receive services, how we travel and how we experience art, how we manage our health, and how we access information, and the list goes on.

The Internet of Things. The Internet of Things (IoT) is a set of everyday devices—called *smart devices*—like cars, refrigerators, home security systems, thermostats, medical devices, light bulbs, and even children's toys that are digitally connected and able to receive and share data. How does the IoT work? Your IoT refrigerator, for example, could recognize that you are getting low on cold-pressed juice, order it from the supermarket, and tell your bank to pay for it. One report suggests there will be more than 75 billion such devices in the world by 2025,[71] and another predicts over 60 million "smart" homes in the United States by the time you read this.[72] Businesses are adopting this technology, too, with at least 25% of companies currently employing smart devices.[73]

The IoT has made it possible for us to control many aspects of our personal and professional lives digitally. In other words, it has disrupted the way we live and work. Security and privacy are big concerns, however, and smart devices are finding their way into homes and businesses faster than regulators can keep up.[74] Here are a few major issues related to the IoT:

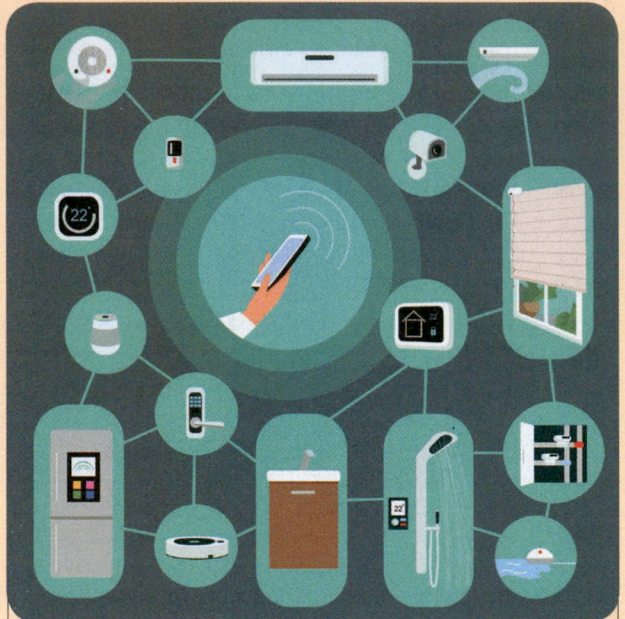

Does connectivity equal vulnerability? Can you imagine the convenience of controlling all of these devices from your smartphone? Would this kind of connectivity make you concerned about the vulnerability of your data? NTL studio/Shutterstock

- **Vulnerability.** The world of smart devices means that everything is linked. For example, a "smart" glucose monitor sends real-time health data to users' phones, allowing various health apps to collect, store, and use the information to alert those with diabetes and other conditions when health concerns arise.[75] This connectivity, while exciting, makes smart technology more vulnerable to data hacks than traditional computers.[76] As one person put it, "I can hack your smart doorbell and end up in your bank account."[77]

- **Permission Granted?** Even if your data are protected from illegal hacks, what about the people you've granted permission to? Each time you download an app to register

a new smart device, you'll likely read (or maybe skim through) a long list of "terms and conditions" and then check the "agree" box as you go on with your day. You also may have set various permissions within these apps to increase your feelings of data security and privacy. But do you really know what you've agreed to? And do you really know who can access your data? One study found that more than 1,300 Android apps were collecting data on users even after those users had denied permission.[78] This is especially concerning when you consider that some smart devices could allow others to listen in to your personal home.[79]

- **What Can Data Be Used for?** Amazon's Ring doorbell alerts you whenever there is motion detected around the door to your home, or whenever someone rings the doorbell. The Ring device captures video day and night and allows you to talk with the people standing at your doorstep.[80] But did you know Amazon partnered with more than 500 police departments to allow police to automatically message people with Ring doorbells if they wanted to request video footage for investigations? More than 30 civil rights groups penned a joint letter to Amazon asking the company to end its partnerships with police forces, citing massive concerns about the creation of a surveillance state and the potential for police to misuse the data. Amazon now allows customers to opt out of receiving notifications from police who are requesting Ring doorbell video footage.

Security through Blockchain. It's expected that blockchain, the encrypted digital ledger system, will soon form a part of the IoT. Blockchain has the potential to greatly increase the security of our personal data on the IoT by eliminating the need for vulnerable, centralized cloud servers.[81]

YOUR CALL

Do you think the IoT is a positive technological change? If so, why? If not, why not? What do you think should be done to better protect users' data in the future?

3. Sociocultural Forces

Sociocultural forces are influences and trends originating in a country's, a society's, or a culture's human relationships and values that may affect an organization or industry. Here are a few examples of industries that have been affected by Millennials and Gen Zers as a sociocultural force:

- **Automotive.** The costs of auto ownership, environmental concerns, and availability of ridesharing services have fostered less interest from younger generations in owning vehicles than their predecessors.[82] Automakers like BMW and Daimler have responded by teaming up on ride-sharing deals.[83]

- **Tourism.** Younger workers are poised to give the travel industry a boost. In particular, ecotourism—travel that is sustainable and supports environmental causes[84]— is on the rise, with one study finding that 41% of Millennials want to book an ecotourism vacation.[85]

- **Weddings.** Millennials and Gen Zers are not experiencing traditional social pressures to get married early in life, and many are predicted to wait until their late 20s and 30s to wed. Wedding registries are changing, too, with gifts like travel becoming more popular than dishes and stemware.[86]

Smoking marijuana is another sociocultural force. It is now legal for medical reasons in 33 states, and for recreational use in 11 states and in the District of Columbia *(see Figure 3.2)*, reflecting the fact that about two-thirds of U.S. adults now support legalization.[87] Federal marijuana legislation is in flux at the time of this writing.

Entire industries have been rocked when the culture underwent a lifestyle change, most notably changes in approaches to health. Some killer diseases, such as measles, whooping cough, and mumps, are creeping back because of an anti-vaccine movement.[88] Obesity rates are also rising, with one study out of Harvard predicting that almost half of the United States population will be obese by 2030.[89] Health professionals and organizations are concerned about the rising medical costs associated with treatment. Estimates suggest that medical costs for obese individuals are $1,429 higher than those for non-obese individuals.[90]

4. Demographic Forces

Demographics derives from the ancient Greek word for "people"—*demos*—and deals with statistics relating to human populations. Age, gender, race, sexual orientation, occupation, income, family size, and the like are known as demographic characteristics when they are used to express measurements of certain groups. **Demographic forces** are influences on an organization arising from changes in the characteristics of a population, such as age, gender, or ethnic origin.

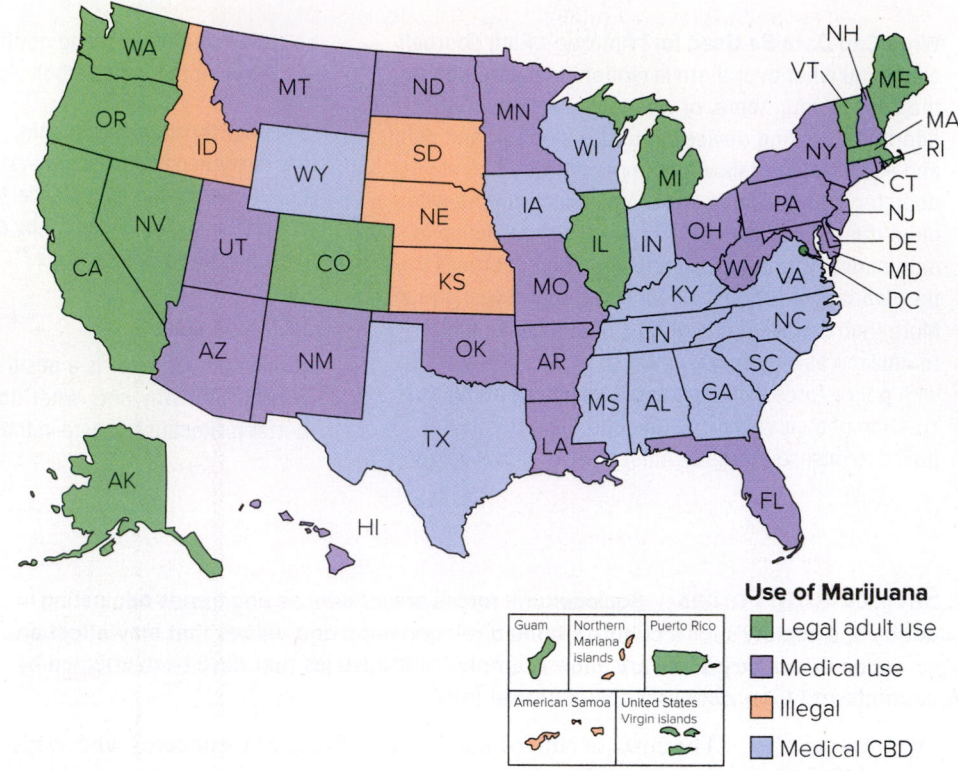

In Chapter 1 we mentioned several instances of major impending shifts in racial and ethnic diversity. Among other recent changes: interracial marriages are increasing, the birth rate is the lowest in 32 years, divorce rates are down, and secularism (being nonreligious) is up.[91] Support for same-sex marriage is rising steadily, and a recent study found that the majority of same-sex couples who cohabitate are now married.[92] Many firms now have chief diversity officers to support increasing workforce diversity.[93] We consider demographic and diversity matters in detail in Chapter 9.

5. Political–Legal Forces

Political–legal forces are changes in the way politics shape laws and laws shape the opportunities for and threats to an organization. In the United States, the currently dominant political view may be reflected in the way the government addresses environmental and sustainable development issues, such as those we described in Chapter 1 and the upcoming Learning Module 1. For instance, should the government pursue an agenda of nationalism and isolation?[94] Should coal mining be allowed on public lands?[95] How should public money be spent on climate change and ocean warming?[96]

As for legal forces, some countries have more fully developed legal systems than others. And some countries have more lawyers per capita. (The United States reportedly has one lawyer for every 300 people versus one for every 1,400 people in France.)[97] U.S. companies may be more willing to use the legal system to advance their interests, as in suing competitors to gain competitive advantage. But they must also watch that others don't do the same to them.

6. International Forces

International forces are changes in the economic, political, legal, and technological global system that may affect an organization. This category represents a huge variety of influences. Two notable recent examples of U.S. businesses being impacted by international forces are:

- **Uber's operations in London.** Uber is one U.S. company to face difficulties overseas; the company lost its license to operate on London's streets due to business irregularities and driver safety issues, to the relief of London's cab drivers and other competitors. The company will continue operating while it appeals the British court's decision, but it is facing increased competition from new entrants such as the Indian firm Ola.[98]

- **Amazon's dealings with Saudi Arabia.** Amazon CEO Jeff Bezos and Saudi Crown Prince Mohammed bin Salman became friends as they worked toward a mutually beneficial business deal. Amazon would build its presence in the Middle East by placing a massive data center in Saudi Arabia, and the Crown Prince would attract more foreign investment. The two men communicated over WhatsApp, and recent forensic analysis suggests that bin Salman's account delivered spyware to Bezos' phone in 2018 that eventually exported more than 6 gigabytes of data.[99] Officials speculate that bin Salman was seeking information to use against Bezos after the *Washington Post* (owned by Bezos) published articles questioning his, and Saudi Arabia's, involvement in the murder of journalist Jamal Khashoggi.[100]

Uber faced unfriendly forces in London. One of the approximately 8,000 London Black Cab drivers that joined a protest against Uber's operations in London.
Tom Nicholson/Shutterstock

Another factor to keep in mind is the need for flexibility when dealing with other countries and cultures. Behaviors as habitual to U.S. employees as asking questions and expressing unsolicited opinions might need to be tailored to fit new circumstances abroad, where these behaviors may seem overbearing. At the same time, ethically charged behaviors like bribery and gift-giving (discussed in the upcoming section) can carry different meanings in different cultures, proving that there is no substitute for learning as much as possible about the countries with which you are dealing.[101]

3.4 The Ethical Responsibilities Required of You as a Manager

THE BIG PICTURE

Managers need to be aware of what constitutes ethics, values, the four approaches to ethical dilemmas, and how organizations can promote ethics.

Would you take supplies from the office supply closet on leaving a job? Would you pocket a company laptop on your last day of work? These may be easy decisions. But how would you handle a choice between paying a client money under the table in order to land a big contract, for example, and losing your job if you didn't? That's a much harder call.

One of a manager's major challenges, as we stated in Chapter 1, is managing for ethical standards. In business, most ethical conflicts are about choosing between *economic performance* and *social performance*.[102] This is known as an **ethical dilemma**, a situation in which you have to decide whether to pursue a course of action that may benefit you or your organization but that is unethical or even illegal. MIT, for example, received $800,000 in donations from billionaire Jeffrey Epstein over the course of 20 years.

LO 3-4

Explain the importance of ethics and values in effective management.

When Epstein was indicted for sex-trafficking in 2019, MIT president L. Rafael Reif announced that the university would not keep the money and would instead donate $800,000 to a charity to benefit sexual abuse victims. Read about another example of an ethical dilemma in the Volkswagen Example box.[103]

Following a tip from puzzled researchers, the Environmental Protection Agency (EPA) discovered in 2014 that Volkswagen had deliberately installed cheating software in more than 500,000 diesel passenger cars sold in the United States. The software allowed the cars' computers to sense when the vehicles were being tested for harmful emissions and to switch, undetected, to a driving mode that artificially reduced nitrogen oxide or NO_x (linked to smog and lung cancer) so the cars could pass the test. Once back on the road, the computers adjusted the driving mode again, permitting drivers to experience the power and mileage the company was touting while allowing some cars to emit as much as 40 times the volume of pollutants permitted by law. Volkswagen had done the same in more than 10 million other cars sold around the world.[104]

How did a venerable and successful company come to commit what one business publication called "a truly brazen act of business malfeasance" in the first place?[105] More stringent controls on NO_x took effect in 1999, and of the two possible ways it could meet them, VW chose the one that did not require a costly reengineering of the interior of its cars. This might have seemed like the right business decision to make, but as a side effect, VW's new NO_x controls dramatically reduced the degree of fuel economy the company was advertising. It was apparently at this point that the decision to rig the cars to falsify emissions tests was made.[106]

The Fallout. The VW emissions scandal resulted in billions of dollars in fines and penalties, multiple prison sentences, and charges that seem to keep coming year after year. Here's a summary of what unethical decision making at VW has caused in different countries:

- *United States.* The U.S. government's case against VW resulted in the company paying out $33 billion in fines, civil and criminal penalties, and restitution. Eight high-ranking executives were charged with crimes and two received prison sentences.[107]

Speaking out against ethical violations. Members of Greenpeace with a sign calling out Volkswagen's cheating scandal in front of London's Royal Courts of Justice. PA Images/Alamy Stock Photo

- *Germany.* German fines totaled $1.2 billion,[108] and in 2019 German prosecutors charged Volkswagen's CEO Herbert Diess, chair Hans Dieter, and former CEO Martin Winterkorn with market manipulation for withholding news of the impending scandal from investors in 2015.[109] On January 14, 2020, VW announced it had achieved record annual sales—on this same day the company also received news that German prosecutors were charging six of its executives with fraud related to the scandal.[110]

- *Canada.* In January 2020, Canadian prosecutors hit the auto manufacturer with $258.3 million (USD) in fines.[111]

YOUR CALL

What is the fundamental ethical dilemma faced by Volkswagen's managers? How well do you think Volkswagen is managing the balance between its economic and its social performance? What could it be doing better?

Solving ethical dilemmas is an important skill, according to a recent investigation of 1001 executives and hiring managers. The study revealed that 77% believed ethical judgment and ethical decision making were among the top-tier skills required of college graduates entering the workforce. Unfortunately, only 43% of the executives and hiring managers surveyed thought college students were prepared to exercise these two skills.[112] To help you develop this skill, we ask you to solve an ethical/legal dilemma at the end of each chapter.

Defining Ethics and Values

A report from the Ethics & Compliance Initiative (ECI) revealed that 47% of U.S. workers surveyed had witnessed some form of ethical misconduct at work. Sadly, 63% of respondents said these behaviors were committed by someone with managerial authority.[113] Most of us assume we know what "ethics" and "values" mean, but do we? Let's consider them.

Ethics   **Ethics** are the standards of right and wrong that influence behavior. These standards may vary among countries and among cultures. **Ethical behavior** is behavior that is accepted as "right" as opposed to "wrong" according to prevailing standards.

Sometimes it's hard to know whether something is right or wrong. A survey of more than 18,000 employees in 18 countries led by the ECI helps to clarify this issue by identifying the six most common workplace behaviors that are considered ethical misconduct (*see Figure 3.3*).[114] They are:

1. **Conflicts of interest.** A conflict of interest occurs when the potential for personal benefit—or benefit to family or friends—makes it difficult for you to make the best decision for the organization you are representing. Conflicts of interest often involve the issue of whether an employee of one organization can accept gifts from another organization.[115]

Global Median Rates of the Most Common Types of Ethical Misconduct in the Workplace

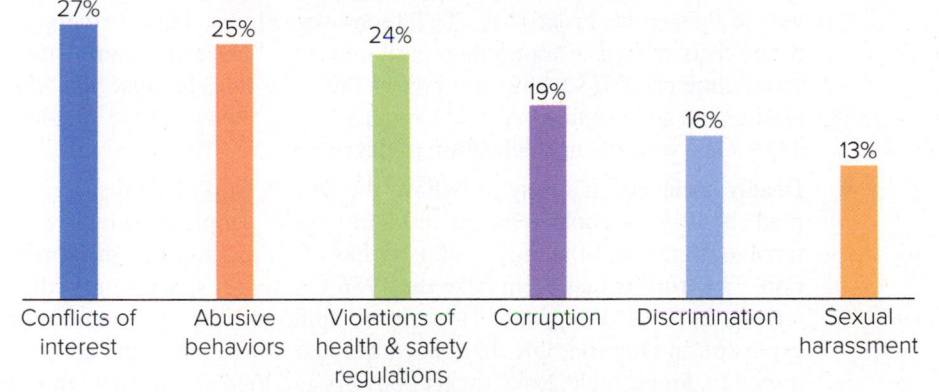

FIGURE 3.3

Global rates of unethical workplace behavior

Source: Ethics & Compliance Initiative, "2019 Global Business Ethics Survey: Workplace Misconduct and Reporting—a Global Look," 2019, https://43wli92bfqd 835mbif2ms9qz-wpengine .netdna-ssl.com/wp-content/ uploads/Global-Business-Ethics-Survey-2019-Third-Report-1.pdf.

Pharmaceutical Example: For example, it is illegal for pharmaceutical companies to pay physicians to prescribe specific drugs. However, doctors can legally accept payments for consulting and speaking engagements.[116] A study conducted by nonprofit ProPublica from 2014 to 2018 found that 2,500 physicians had earned at least $500,000 each from pharmaceutical and medical device companies for these engagements, and more than 700 of the physicians had earned at least $1 million.[117] Do these behaviors represent unethical attempts to influence the sales of drugs? Are these doctors accepting bribes, or are they simply promoting medical knowledge and receiving fair compensation for doing so? Sometimes it is hard to tell the difference between a legitimate business relationship and a conflict of interest.

2. **Abusive behaviors.** These are behaviors that serve to threaten or intimidate others or that contribute to a hostile work environment. One type of abusive workplace behavior is **abusive supervision**, which occurs when supervisors repeatedly display verbal and nonverbal hostility toward their subordinates.[118] Abusive supervision does not include physical contact between supervisors and subordinates; rather, it focuses on behaviors such as public humiliation, insults, shouting, and ignoring subordinates.[119,120]

Examples of abusive supervision include bullying, gossiping, backstabbing, and repeatedly calling people names like "loser," "stupid," or "worthless." This type of behavior erodes employees' self-esteem, engagement, job satisfaction, and performance, and often leads to counterproductive employee behaviors.[121]

One of the ways employees retaliate against abusive supervisors is by stealing company property.[122] We discuss abusive supervision in more detail in Chapter 14.

3. **Violations of health and safety regulations.** Different jobs come with different sets of rules about what constitutes safe and healthy behavior. In a hospital setting, for example, employees must wash their hands frequently and thoroughly; at a construction site, hard hats, goggles, and steel-toed boots are necessary protections. Experts agree that a major contributing factor to accidents and injuries across the board is the *overconfidence* that can accompany violations of health and safety regulations over time. Diane Vaughan, the famed sociologist who studied the *Challenger* space shuttle disaster and many accidents since, calls this the *normalization of deviance,* a phenomenon that occurs when actors become so desensitized to violating a rule without consequences that the violation eventually no longer feels like a violation at all.[123] Consider the following examples:

- **Trampolines.** Did you know that doctors believe that recreational trampolines aren't safe for anyone? Still, trampoline parks have exploded in popularity in recent years, particularly as a place for parents to let young kids blow off their energy. Jumpers (or their guardians) sign legal waivers and read a list of safety rules before they are allowed to jump, but how often do we see these rules broken? In 2017, there were almost 18,000 emergency room visits related to trampoline park injuries.[124] Have you ever visited a trampoline park? If so, have you ever violated the rules because you "do it all the time and nothing bad ever happens"? If so, then you have first-hand experience with the normalization of deviance.

- **Deadly accidents.** It's easy to believe the deadly workplace disasters we read about in textbooks were the result of sinister people knowingly doing terrible things, and the movie industry has often fed into this misconception. The truth is that events like the 1986 *Challenger* space shuttle disaster, the 2010 BP Deepwater Horizon oil spill, and the 2018 natural gas explosion in Quinton, OK, happened because workers became so accustomed to, for example, leaky rocket boosters and loud alarms that ignoring these things eventually ceased to register as a safety violation. According

Did health and safety violations cause the Quinton, OK, natural gas explosion? A jury believed this was the case when it awarded the families of two of the five victims $10 million each after they sued Red Mountain Energy, Patterson-UTI Energy, and National Oilwell Varco.
Christina Goodvoice/AP Images

to an interview with psychologist and accident investigator Sidney Dekker, "Large accidents are more often the result of dozens of tiny contributing factors: misguided assumptions on the part of workers and managers; small, subtly flawed decisions; routine mechanical or digital glitches. Individually, none of these seem particularly noteworthy to the people on the front line—just another day on the job. It's only after the accident that we see how this particular row of dominos toppled."[125]

4. **Corruption.** Corruption occurs when someone uses the power with which they have been entrusted by the organization to achieve personal benefit. Despite many anti-corruption laws, corrupt behaviors such as bribery are still a major problem across the globe. According to a recent report in *Harvard Business Review,* corrupt practices can account for up to $2 trillion of the global economy in a single year.[126] Authors Ravi Venkatesan and Leslie Benton reported that although corporate corruption is prevalent, companies that actively fight against it may have a competitive advantage. Research conducted by the Ethisphere Institute reveals that publicly traded companies with strong corruption prevention programs in place may outperform competitors by between 10.5 and 14.4% over five years.[127]

5. **Discrimination.** Making employment decisions on the basis of employees' protected class status—including their sex, national origin, race, religion, age, or sexual orientation—constitutes discrimination in most cases. There are some exceptions, such as when protected class membership is directly related to job performance—known as a *bona fide occupational qualification*—but for most jobs, membership in one or more protected classes is not related to job performance and should not be used to make decisions about things like hiring, firing, raises, or promotions.

   The EEOC and its partner agencies close more than 100,000 workplace discrimination cases each year, but only 18% result in workers receiving assistance. In addition, EEOC data for the period 2010–2017 reveals that 40% of the workers who filed these discrimination complaints reported being retaliated against by their organizations.[128]

6. **Sexual harassment.** Sexual harassment takes many forms. It includes basing employment decisions on a subordinate's willingness to engage in sexual conduct with a superior. Sexual harassment also includes any behavior of a sexual nature that becomes pervasive enough to create a hostile work environment. This can consist of repeated requests or advances, offensive comments, and physical harassment.

   Sadly, research continues to show that workplace sexual harassment often goes unreported. A recent study of surgical trainees found that almost 50% of respondents had been sexually harassed at least once during training; for female trainees this number was over 70%. Only 7.6% reported the harassment. Reasons for underreporting included the fear that nothing would be done or that the reporter would experience retaliation.[129]

We discuss discrimination and sexual harassment at length in Chapter 9.

Values Ethical dilemmas often take place because of an organization's value system, the pattern of values within an organization. Values are the relatively permanent and deeply held underlying beliefs and attitudes that help determine a person's behavior, such as the belief that "fairness means hiring according to ability, not family background." Values and value systems are the underpinnings for ethics and ethical behavior.[130]

Organizations may have two important value systems that can conflict: (1) the value system stressing financial performance versus (2) the value system stressing cohesion and solidarity in employee relationships.[131]

Hypothetical Example: A car dealership may hire an accounting firm to send an accountant to audit its books, and she works alongside employees of the car dealer for several weeks, establishing cohesion and solidarity. But when a task that she estimated would take 10 hours actually takes 15, the dealership's employees might say, "You charged us more hours than you said you would," and so she might report just 10 hours to her superiors at the accounting firm. This action makes the subordinate look good, and keeps the client happy, thereby improving social cohesion. But, of course, the accounting firm unknowingly takes a loss on financial performance.[132] This kind of value system conflict happens all the time.

Four Approaches to Resolving Ethical Dilemmas

How do alternative values guide people's decisions about ethical behavior? Here are four approaches, which may be taken as guidelines:

1. The Utilitarian Approach: For the Greatest Good

Ethical behavior in the utilitarian approach is guided by what will result in the greatest good for the greatest number of people. Managers often take the utilitarian approach, using financial performance—such as efficiency and profit—as the best definition of what constitutes "the greatest good for the greatest number."[133]

Thus, a utilitarian "cost–benefit" analysis might show that in the short run the firing of thousands of employees may improve a company's bottom line and provide immediate benefits for the stockholders. The drawback of this approach, however, is that it may result in damage to workforce morale and the loss of employees with experience and skills—actions not so readily measurable in dollars.

2. The Individual Approach: For Your Greatest Self-Interest Long Term, which Will Help Others

Ethical behavior in the individual approach is guided by what will result in the individual's best long-term interests, which ultimately are in everyone's self-interest. The assumption here is that you will act ethically in the short run to avoid others harming you in the long run.

The flaw here, however, is that one person's short-term self-gain may *not*, in fact, be good for everyone in the long term. After all, placing a series of eight dams around the Columbia and Snake rivers helped mitigate the effects of water shortages, improved the wheat export process, and bolstered access to food sources, but the fishing industries downstream have ultimately suffered as the increased water temperatures and blocked migration routes have drastically reduced the number of fish. Indeed, this is one reason why Puget Sound Chinook, or king salmon, has been threatened with extinction in the Pacific Northwest.[134]

3. The Moral-Rights Approach: Respecting Fundamental Rights Shared by Everyone

Ethical behavior in the **moral-rights approach** is guided by respect for the fundamental rights of human beings, such as those expressed in the U.S. Constitution's Bill of Rights. We would all tend to agree that denying people the right to life, liberty, privacy, health and safety, and due process is unethical. Thus, most of us would have no difficulty condemning the situation of immigrants illegally brought into the United States and then effectively enslaved—as when made to work seven days a week without adequate compensation or rest.

The difficulty, however, is when rights are in conflict, such as employer and employee rights. Should employees on the job have a guarantee of privacy? Actually, it is legal for employers to listen to business phone calls and monitor all nonverbal personal communications.[135]

4. The Justice Approach: Respecting Impartial Standards of Fairness

Ethical behavior in the **justice approach** is guided by respect for impartial standards of fairness and equity. One consideration here is whether an organization's policies—such as those governing promotions or sexual harassment cases—are administered impartially and fairly regardless of gender, age, sexual orientation, and the like.

Fairness can often be a hot issue. For instance, many employees are loudly resentful when a corporation's CEO is paid a salary and bonuses worth hundreds of times more than what they receive—even when the company performs poorly—and when fired is then given a "golden parachute," or extravagant package of separation pay and benefits.

White-Collar Crime, SarbOx, and Ethical Training

At the beginning of the 21st century, U.S. business erupted in an array of scandals represented in such names as Enron, WorldCom, Tyco, and Adelphia, and their chief executives went to prison on various fraud convictions. Executives' deceits generated a great deal of public outrage, and as a result Congress passed the Sarbanes-Oxley Act, as we'll describe. Did that stop the raft of business scandals? Not quite.

Next to hit the headlines were cases of **insider trading, the illegal trading of a company's stock by people using confidential company information.** The federal government launched a six-year crackdown on insider trading on Wall Street that resulted in 87 convictions (14 of which were dismissed or lost on appeal; one ended in acquittal).[136]

Consider the following two examples of white-collar crime in recent news:

Apple Example: In 2019 Gene Levoff—the attorney in charge of preventing insider trading at Apple—was indicted on charges of insider trading after he used inside financial information to trade stock. In total, Levoff's trades resulted in his avoiding around $377,000 in losses and profiting more than $225,000.[137]

Insys Therapeutics Example: Multiple executives at Insys Therapeutics were indicted and sentenced to federal prison terms for their role in a bribery and fraud scheme, including founder John Kapoor. Insys manufactured a powerful opioid drug called Subsys, which had been FDA approved only for terminal cancer patients whose pain was no longer relieved by other narcotics. Federal investigations revealed that more than 7,000 patients died after overdosing on the drug; all had been prescribed Subsys by their doctors, and none of them had cancer. Off-label

Kapoor convicted. Insys Therapeutics founder John Kapoor leaving a federal court building in Boston during his 2019 trial. Pat Greenhouse/Getty Images

prescribing of medications is not illegal, but it is severely regulated in the case of opioids, and most insurance companies would not have covered off-label Subsys prescriptions. Insys would instead bribe doctors to prescribe the expensive drug, then route the prescriptions through their own reimbursement center that paid workers based on the number of insurance approvals they obtained for Subsys. Workers communicated directly with pharmacies and insurance companies and used what one former employee called "word games" to obtain approvals.[138]

The Sarbanes–Oxley Reform Act   The Sarbanes–Oxley Act of 2002, often shortened to SarbOx, or SOX, established requirements for proper financial record keeping for public companies and penalties of as much as 25 years in prison for noncompliance.[139] Administered by the Securities and Exchange Commission (SEC), SarbOx requires a company's chief executive officer (CEO) and chief financial officer (CFO) to personally certify the organization's financial reports, prohibits them from taking personal loans or lines of credit, and makes them reimburse the organization for bonuses and stock options when required by restatement of corporate profits. It also requires the company to have established procedures and guidelines for audit committees.[140]

> **Comscore Example:** Recently, the SEC charged media analytics company Comscore and its former CEO Serge Matta with exaggerating revenues by $50 million and misleading the public and its investors about company performance. Comscore and Matta settled the case by agreeing to refrain from future violations and paying $5 million and $700,000 in penalties, respectively. Matta will also reimburse Comscore the $2.1 million he received from incentive compensation and stock sales and is barred from serving as a director of or officer for a public company for 10 years.[141]

How Do People Learn Ethics? Kohlberg's Theories   U.S. business history is permeated with occasional malfeasance, from railroad tycoons trying to corner the gold market (the 1872 Crédit Mobilier scandal) to 25-year-old bank customer service representatives swindling elderly customers out of their finances. Legislation such as SarbOx can't head off all such behavior. It is no wonder that now many colleges and universities require more ethics education.

"Schools bear some responsibility for the behavior of executives," says Fred J. Evans, dean of the College of Business and Economics at California State University at Northridge. "If you're making systematic errors in the [business] world, you have to go back to the schools and ask, 'What are you teaching?'"[142]

University of Virginia Darden School of Business Professor Mary Gentile developed an ethics curriculum for business schools called *Giving Voice to Values* (GVV). The GVV program is built on the assumption that the problem in organizations is not necessarily a lack of values, but rather a lack of training in how to voice and act on our existing values successfully. The program centers on giving people the opportunity to practice voicing their values so that they are better prepared to do so when unethical situations arise in the workplace. GVV has been implemented in hundreds of business schools and organizations to date.[143] The good news is that more graduate business schools are changing their curriculums to teach ethics, although there is some question as to effectiveness.[144] The bad news is that students across educational levels are still cheating.

Have you ever lied, scammed, or deceived someone to advance your self-interests? Workplace cheating consists of unethical behaviors that result in employees receiving benefits or advantages to which they are otherwise not entitled.[145] Cheating is far too common among college students. A poll of 30,000 students revealed that about 61% admitted to cheating, and 16.5% didn't regret it.[146] These behaviors may persist because professors don't want to deal with the hassle of reporting cheating, fear legal trouble, or believe they truly have no control over the problem.[147] They also occur in response to performance pressures to deliver results or face negative consequences.[148]

Cheating extends to the workplace. The Georgia State Patrol recently fired an entire class of 30 troopers after it was discovered that they had cheated on an exam as part of their training curriculum.[149]

Of course, students' levels of moral development are likely to be well-established through personalities and upbringing long before they get to college, with some being more advanced than others. Psychologist Laurence Kohlberg has proposed three levels of personal moral development—preconventional, conventional, and postconventional.[150]

- **Level 1, preconventional—follows rules.** People who have achieved this level tend to follow rules and to obey authority to avoid unpleasant consequences. Managers at Level 1 tend to be autocratic or coercive, expecting employees to be obedient for obedience's sake.

- **Level 2, conventional—follows expectations of others.** People whose moral development has reached this level are conformist but not slavish, generally adhering to the expectations of others in their lives. Level 2 managers lead by encouragement and cooperation and are more group and team oriented. Most managers are at this level.

- **Level 3, postconventional—guided by internal values.** The farthest along in moral development, Level 3 managers are independent souls who follow their own values and standards, focusing on the needs of their employees and trying to lead by empowering those working for them. Only about a fifth of American managers are said to reach this level.

What level of moral development do you think you've reached?

How Organizations Can Promote Ethics

Ethics needs to be an everyday affair, not a one-time thing. This is why many large U.S. companies now have a *chief ethics officer*, whose job is to make ethical conduct a priority issue.

There are several ways an organization may promote high ethical standards on the job, as follows.[151]

1. Creating a Strong Ethical Climate
The first step is to foster an ethical climate. An ethical climate represents employees' perceptions about the extent to which work environments support ethical behavior. This climate manifests in employees' shared sense of "how things are done around here." It is important for managers to foster ethical climates because they significantly affect the frequency of ethical behavior, which in turn impacts employee performance and firm profitability.[152] Managers can promote ethical climates through the policies, procedures, and practices that are used on a daily basis.[153]

2. Screening Prospective Employees
Companies try to screen out dishonest, irresponsible employees by checking applicants' resumes and references. Some also use personality and integrity testing to identify potentially dishonest people. Most recently, AI technology is being harnessed to streamline employee screening. For example, bots can quickly analyze candidates' social media accounts, and algorithms can scan interview videos for content, emotional cues, tone of voice, and information about temperament. Experts caution that many AI screening tools need further refinement to address serious validity, privacy, and equal employment opportunity concerns.[154]

3. Instituting Ethics Codes and Training Programs

A **code of ethics** consists of a formal written set of ethical standards guiding an organization's actions. Most codes offer guidance on how to treat customers, suppliers, competitors, and other stakeholders. Their purpose is to clearly state top management's expectations for all employees.[155] As you might expect, most codes prohibit bribes, kickbacks, misappropriation of corporate assets, conflicts of interest, and "cooking the books"—falsifying accounting statements and other records. Other areas frequently covered in ethics codes are political contributions, workforce diversity, and confidentiality of corporate information.

According to the Society for Human Resource Management, 81% of U.S. companies provide ethics training, and 66% include ethical behavior as a measure of employee evaluations.[156]

4. Rewarding Ethical Behavior: Protecting Whistle-Blowers

It's not enough to simply punish bad behavior; managers must also reward ethical behavior, as in encouraging (or at least not discouraging) whistle-blowers.[157]

A **whistle-blower** is an employee, or even an outside consultant, who reports organizational misconduct such as health and safety violations, waste, corruption, or overcharging of customers, to the public.[158] For instance, the law that created the Occupational Safety and Health Administration (OSHA) gives employees and their representatives the right to file a complaint and request an OSHA inspection of their workplace if they believe there is a serious hazard or their employer is not following OSHA standards."[159] In some cases, whistle-blowers may receive a reward; the Internal Revenue Service (IRS), for instance, is authorized to pay tipsters rewards as high as 30% in cases involving large amounts of money.[160]

Whistle-blowing has been on the rise since the Great Recession, and the number of whistle-blower tips received by the Securities and Exchange Commission (SEC), for example, is now over 5,000 a year.[161] Whistle-blowers sometimes risk their jobs by coming forward and thus deserve protection. Federal law prohibits organizations from retaliating against whistleblowers, and the SEC has the authority to impose severe penalties on companies that violate these protections.[162] Still, retaliation against whistle-blowers is not uncommon and includes social rejection, verbal abuse, demotion, and firing.[163]

5. Using a Multi-Faceted Approach

The four suggestions offered above highlight the need for organizations to promote ethical behaviors by addressing both individual factors such as personality, and organizational factors such as training, reward systems, and climate. Indeed, there is abundant evidence to suggest that unethical behaviors stem both from workers' personalities and their work environments.[164] In short, it is not enough to screen out the bad apples—we also must repair the bad barrels and prevent the good barrels from rotting.

All told, it is important for you to learn more about your ethical tendencies. This will help you to behave in ways that are consistent with your values and beliefs, even when your environment isn't ideal. ●

SELF-ASSESSMENT 3.1   CAREER READINESS

Assessing My Perspective on Ethics

This survey is designed to assess your views about ethics. It provides feedback about your status on the Career Readiness "other characteristic" of *professionalism/work ethic.*

Please be prepared to answer these questions if your instructor has assigned Self-Assessment 3.1 in Connect.

1. Are your views more idealistic or more relativistic?
2. What do you think about students cheating on homework assignments in school? What about cheating on exams?
3. Are your answers consistent with your score? Explain.
4. What can you say during an interview to demonstrate an ethical orientation?

3.5 The Social Responsibilities Required of You as a Manager

THE BIG PICTURE

Managers need to be aware of the viewpoints supporting and opposing social responsibility and whether being and doing good pays off financially for the organization.

Is money the be-all and end-all in business? This is the concern behind the triple bottom line discussed earlier. For Bombas, profit must be balanced with the higher purpose of helping homeless individuals, who often lack belongings as simple as a pair of socks. Bombas was founded in 2013 and bolstered by a Shark Tank deal with multi-millionaire investor Daymond John. With the simple idea to donate one pair of socks to a homeless shelter for every pair purchased by a consumer, the company has had great success with the "buy-one, give-one" model pioneered by companies like TOMS. Bombas employees also volunteer every week by distributing socks and serving food at homeless shelters.[165] Said co-founder Randy Goldberg, "You kind of take your socks for granted. They're an afterthought in the design and apparel world. . . . We just got obsessed with this idea that we could help solve a problem through starting a business."[166]

If ethical responsibility is about being a good individual citizen, social responsibility is about being a good *organizational citizen*. More formally, ==social responsibility== is a manager's duty to take actions that will benefit the interests of society as well as of the organization. When generalized beyond the individual to the organization, social responsibility is called ==corporate social responsibility (CSR)==, the notion that corporations are expected to go above and beyond following the law and making a profit. Areas of CSR include the environment, philanthropy, and ethical labor practices.[167]

LO 3-5

Describe the concept of social responsibility and its role in today's organizations.

Bombas gives back. Co-founder and CEO David Heath (right) hands out socks at the Los Angeles Mission. Bombas committed to donating 1 million socks to the shelter. John Sciulli/Getty Images

Corporate Social Responsibility: The Top of the Pyramid

According to University of Georgia business scholar Archie B. Carroll, corporate social responsibility rests at the top of a pyramid of a corporation's obligations, right up there with economic, legal, and ethical obligations. Some people might hold that a company's first and only duty is to make a profit. However, Carroll suggests the responsibilities of an organization in the global economy should take the following priorities, with profit being the most fundamental (base of the pyramid) and corporate citizenship at the top:[168]

- *Be a good global corporate citizen,* as defined by the host country's expectations.
- *Be ethical in its practices,* taking host-country and global standards into consideration.
- *Obey the law* of host countries as well as international law.
- *Make a profit* consistent with expectations for international business.

These priorities are illustrated in the pyramid opposite. *(See Figure 3.4.)*

FIGURE 3.4

Carroll's global corporate social responsibility pyramid

Source: A. Carroll, "Managing Ethically and Global Stakeholders: A Present and Future Challenge," Academy of Management Executive, *May 2004, p. 116.*

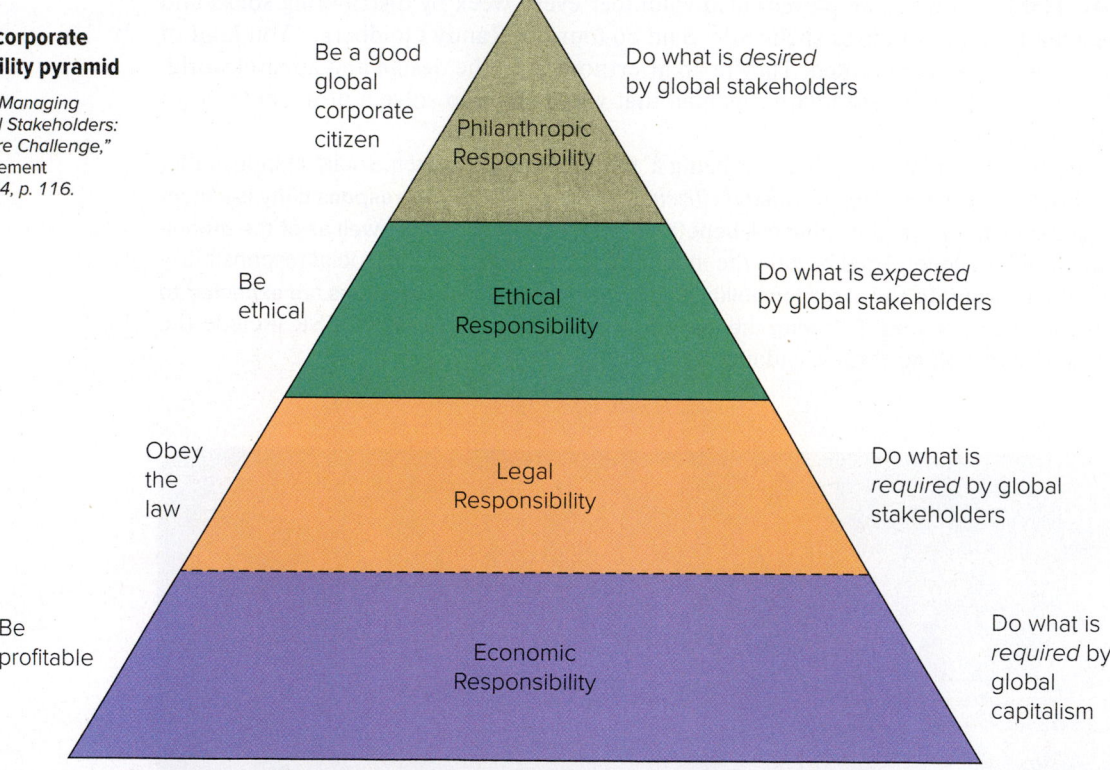

Is Social Responsibility Worthwhile? Opposing and Supporting Viewpoints

In the old days of cutthroat capitalism, social responsibility was hardly a thought. A company's most important goal was to make money pretty much any way it could—consequences be damned. Today, for-profit enterprises in the United States and Europe—along with an increasing number of multinational firms from developing nations—generally make a point of "putting something back" into society in conjunction with taking something out.[169]

Not everyone, however, agrees with these new priorities. Let's consider the two viewpoints.

Against Social Responsibility   "Few trends could so thoroughly undermine the very foundations of our free society," argued the late free-market economist Milton Friedman, "as the acceptance by corporate officials of social responsibility other than to make as much money for their stockholders as possible."[170]

Friedman represents the view that, as he said, "The social responsibility of business is to make profits." That is, unless a company focuses on maximizing profits, it will become distracted and fail to provide goods and services, benefit the stockholders, create jobs, and expand economic growth—the real social justification for the firm's existence.

This view would presumably support the efforts of companies to set up headquarters in name only in offshore tax havens (while keeping their actual headquarters in the United States) in order to minimize their tax burden.

For Social Responsibility   "A large corporation these days not only may engage in social responsibility," said famed economist Paul Samuelson, who passed away in 2009, "it had damned well better try to do so."[171] That is, a company must be concerned for society's welfare as well as for corporate profits.

Beyond ethical obligation, the rationale for social responsibility is the belief that it is good for business, morally appropriate, or important to employees. That is, CEOs support CSR because they think it increases firm performance, provides a favorable signal about firms, or garners positive accolades from internal and external stakeholders.[172] See the Example box for more on CSR.

EXAMPLE	Corporate Social Responsibility: Salesforce Wants to Change the Way the World Works

Corporations approach social responsibility in a variety of ways. Marc Benioff, co-founder and co-CEO of San Francisco–based software company Salesforce, says, "Companies can do more than just make money, they can serve others. The business of business is improving the state of the world."[173] Here are some of the ways Salesforce serves others and improves the world.

Supporting entrepreneurs. Salesforce CEO Marc Benioff (right) pictured with Sound Ventures founding partner Ashton Kutcher; PitchPerfect startup competition judges Matthew McConaughey, Melody McCloskey, Guy Oseary, and Gary Vaynerchuk; and winner Rebecca Liebman. Liebman's startup, LearnLux, provides online personal finance skills training, and her pitch earned investments from Sound Ventures and Benioff. Joe Scarnici/Getty Images

Operating with Integrity. Salesforce has adopted Business Conduct Principles and a Code of Conduct that, among other things, support ethical business practices, anticorruption, antidiscrimination, and rejection of forced or involuntary labor.[174]

"1-1-1" Charitable Giving. When Marc Benioff started Salesforce in 1999, he also created a foundation with a powerful but simple vision: Donate 1% of Salesforce resources, 1% of employees' time, and 1% of the firm's product to improving communities around the world. For instance, in 2018, the company donated $18 million toward San Francisco Bay area causes, including education and homelessness.[175] The company has also helped dramatically increase the enrollment of girls and underrepresented students of color in computer science courses in San Francisco. Girls now account for 47% of students in computer science classes (increased from 25%), and African American, Native American, and LatinX students now account for 35% (increased from 8%).[176]

Journeying to Net-Zero. Although Salesforce does no manufacturing or mining, it still strives to reduce carbon emissions in the operation of its data centers and office buildings, as well as in employee travel. The company has achieved its goal of "net-zero greenhouse gas emissions" and has now committed to work toward relying exclusively on renewable energy sources such as wind power.[177]

Fostering Employee Success. At Salesforce, says the company, "our goal is to deliver a dream job experience for our employees. We are intense, passionate people on a mission to change the way the world works."[178] Salesforce employees receive 56 hours of paid time off for volunteer work each year, the company matches up to $5,000 of charitable giving per employee annually, and employees get $100 per month to use toward personal wellness.[179]

YOUR CALL

Do you believe corporate social responsibility really has benefits? Can you think of any highly profitable and legal businesses that *do not* practice any kind of social responsibility?

One Type of Social Responsibility: Climate Change, Sustainable Development, and Natural Capital

Nearly everyone is aware of the growing threat of climate change and global warming, and for the first time in history, the majority of U.S. adults are highly worried about global warming.[180] Scientists say global warming is a "clear and unequivocal emergency" and that without significant changes, the world will face "untold human suffering."[181] **Climate change** refers to major changes in temperature, precipitation, wind patterns, and similar matters occurring over several decades. **Global warming**, one aspect of climate change, refers to the rise in global average temperature near the Earth's surface, caused mostly by increasing atmospheric concentrations of greenhouse gases, such as carbon emissions from fossil fuels.[182]

Sustainable development, as introduced in Chapter 1, is economic development that meets the needs of the present without compromising the ability of future generations to meet their own needs.[183] The U.N., along with many scholars, has stressed the importance of natural capital accounting for informing sustainable development policy.[184] Indeed, planet (of the triple bottom line people, planet, and profit) is now identified by the name **natural capital**, the value of natural resources, such as topsoil, air, water, and genetic diversity, which humans depend on.

We discuss sustainable development goals at length in Learning Module 1.

Another Type of Social Responsibility: Undertaking Philanthropy, "Not Dying Rich"

"He who dies rich dies thus disgraced," 19th-century steel magnate Andrew Carnegie is supposed to have said, after he turned his interests from making money to **philanthropy**, **making charitable donations to benefit humankind.** Carnegie became well known as a supporter of free libraries.

Marine pollution occurs when chemicals, particles, residential waste, and industrial and agricultural waste enter the oceans or seas. This example comes from the sea in Spain. The majority of marine pollution comes from land. Perry van Munster/Alamy Stock Photo

When Bill Gates, one of the richest people in the world (with a 2019 net worth of $110 billion) stepped down from day-to-day oversight of Microsoft, the company he co-founded, he turned his attention to the Bill and Melinda Gates Foundation, through which he and his wife have pledged to spend billions on health, education, and overcoming poverty.[185] The Gateses have been joined by 169 other billionaires from 22 countries—including Facebook founder Mark Zuckerberg and his wife, Priscilla Chan, oil and gas financier T. Boone Pickens, Berkshire Hathaway chairman Warren Buffett, Chobani yogurt founder Hamdi Ulukaya, and others—in taking the Giving Pledge, a commitment to dedicate a majority of their wealth to philanthropy.[186] The Bill and Melinda Gates Foundation pledged up to $100 million to aid research and response efforts related to the COVID-19 pandemic.[187]

Does Being Good Pay Off?

We answered this question by reviewing relevant research. Our conclusion is that indeed it pays to be ethical and socially responsible. Supportive findings are shown in Table 3.1.

Have you ever considered the degree of importance you place on ethics and social responsibility? An organization's commitment to CSR may be an important factor for you to consider during job searches. Take a few minutes to complete Self-Assessment 3.2 to get a better idea of your attitude toward corporate responsibility. ●

TABLE 3.1   Being Ethical and Socially Responsible Pays Off

	RESEARCH FINDINGS
Employees	- Millennials and Gen Zs are more likely to stay with a company when management is committed to helping society. - Millennials and Gen Zs are highly concerned with diverse representation and fair employment practices.
Interpersonal relationships	- Employees feel confident in doing the right thing when faced with an ethical situation when the organization has an effective ethics and compliance culture. - Employees are less likely to retaliate against one another when the company has an effective ethics and compliance culture.
Customers	- Customers believe it's important to purchase from socially responsible companies. - Customers make purchases and plan to spend more with socially responsible companies in the future.
Revenue	- Investing in responsible companies topped $30 trillion by 2019. - Quality service and ethical behavior are essential for long-term revenue growth.
Stock price	- Stock prices drop an average of 7.27 % after data breaches and are linked to long-term market underperformance. - Infosys shares fell more than 12% on the NYSE in 2019 after the company announced it was investigating complaints against its CEO for unethical behavior.
Profits	- Customers are more satisfied with and loyal to companies that uphold higher ethical standards, and this increases long-term profits. - America's Most Just Companies earn a 6% higher return-on-equity than competition.

Source: Research findings compiled from "The Deloitte Global Millennial Survey 2019," http://www2.deloitte.com/global/en/pages/about-deloitte/articles/millennialsurvey.html, accessed February 17, 2020; M. Defelice, "What Gen Z Wants at Work Will Blow Your Mind," Forbes, October 31, 2019, https://www.forbes.com/sites/ manondefelice/2019/10/31/what-gen-z-wants-at-work-will-blow-your-mind/#1007d227b8e7; "Increasing Employee Reporting Free From Retaliation," ECI Ethics and Compliance Initiative, https://www.ethics.org/knowledge-center/increasing-employee-reporting-free-from-retaliation/, accessed February 17, 2020; "Consumers Expect the Brands they Support to Be Socially Responsible," October 2, 2019, https://www.businesswire.com/news/home/20191002005697/en/Consumers-Expert-Brands-Support-Socially-Responsible; A. M. Anderson, "Do Ethics Really Matter to Today's Consumers?" Forbes, August 20, 2019, https://www.forbes.com/sites/theyec/2019/08/20/do-ethics-really-matter-to-todays-consumers/#50a09aeb2d0e; Bloomberg, "Socially Responsible Investments Reach $30.7 Trillion," InvestmentNews, April 1, 2019, https://www.investmentnews.com/socially-responsible-investments-reach-30-7-trillion-78882; K. Jiang, J. Hu, Y. Hong, H. Liao, and S. Liu, "Do It Well and Do It Right: The Impact of Services Climate and Ethical Climate on Business Performance and the Boundary Conditions," Journal of Applied Psychology, November 2016, pp. 1553–1568; S. Klebnikov, "Companies with Security Fails Don't See Their Stocks Drop as Much, According to Report," Forbes, November 6, 2019, https://www.forbes.com/sites/sergeiklebnikov/2019/11/06/companies-with-security-fails-dont-see-their-stocks-drop-as-much-according-to-report/#177a097862e0; N. Varshney, "Infosys Price Plummets as Company Says It's Investigating CEO's 'Unethical Practices'," Benzinga, October 22, 2019, https://www.benzinga.com/news/19/10/14632952/Infosys-price-plummets-as-company-says-its-investigating-ceos-unethical-practices; K. B. DeTienne, B. R. Agle, C. M. Sands, A. Aleo, and A. Aleo, "Fostering an Ethical Culture on Your Sales Team," Harvard Business Review, June 20, 2019; and "JLL Named One of America's Most JUST Companies for Fourth Year in a Row," Markets Insider, November 12, 2019, https://markets.businessinsider.com/news/stocks/jll-named-one-of-america-s-most-just-companies-for-fourth-year-in-a-row-1028682312

SELF-ASSESSMENT 3.2   CAREER READINESS

Assessing Your Attitudes toward Corporate Responsibility

This self-assessment assesses your attitudes toward corporate responsibility. It partially overlaps with the Career Readiness "other characteristic" of *professionalism/work ethic*. Please be prepared to answer these questions if your instructor has assigned Self-Assessment 3.2 in Connect.

1. Where do you stand on corporate social responsibility?

2. What life events have influenced your attitudes toward corporate social responsibility? Discuss.

3. Based on the three lowest-rated items in the survey, how might you foster a more positive attitude toward social responsibility? Explain.

4. What can you say during an interview to demonstrate a positive attitude toward corporate responsibility?`

3.6 Corporate Governance

THE BIG PICTURE

Good corporate governance can contribute to more ethical and socially responsible organizations. CEO accountability, board composition, and CSR contracting are important governance factors for organizations and their boards to consider.

What, you might ask, were boards of directors doing (or not doing) in the years leading up to fraud allegations, bankruptcy filings, and executive prison terms at Enron, World-Com, Tyco, and Adelphia? Don't stockholders elect directors to ensure that a company is run according to their interests? Indeed, after Enron and related scandals there was renewed interest in what is known as ==corporate governance==—the system of governing a company so that the interests of corporate owners and other stakeholders are protected.

LO 3-6

Discuss the role of corporate governance in building ethical and socially responsible organizations.

Corporate Governance and Ethics

Is there any connection between corporate governance and ethics? Certainly, says scholar Henrik Syse. Corporate governance is about such matters as long-term strategies, sustainable finances, accurate reporting, and positive work environment. All are obviously tied to ethics because they are concerned with how a firm relates to and impacts its internal and external stakeholders.[188]

There is evidence that ethics has become a primary concern for boards of directors and that boards are recognizing the importance of holding CEOs more accountable for their ethical (mis)behaviors. Specifically, the finding that more CEOs were booted from their companies in 2018 for ethical violations than for reasons such as financial performance or problems with the board illustrates a virtual 180-degree turnaround from the minimal thought boards gave to CEO misconduct around the time of the financial crisis. In 2008, only 10% of CEO dismissals were due to unethical conduct, and 52% were due to financial performance.[189]

How organizations approach ethics will vary according to the unique compositions of their boards. Companies should actively seek to build boards with characteristics that are likely to encourage the organization to be more ethical. A recent study in the *Journal of Business Ethics* analyzed 43 publicly traded companies from 13 different countries and found that the presence of board characteristics that reflect stronger oversight and monitoring are positively related to financial firms' ethical reputations.[190] Specifically, companies with boards that are larger, more gender-diverse, and whose members serve—on average—on fewer than three other boards, have better ethical reputations. The authors theorize that these characteristics signal that a board will be more sensitive to and able to focus on ethical issues.

Now, more attention is being paid to two additional trends in board composition. First, there is a move toward increasing the number of board members who are "independent," meaning that they have no employment relationship, family ties, or commercial affiliations with the company and are thus presumably able to be more objective in their judgments. Second, boards are taking proactive steps to elect members with more varied backgrounds and skill sets.[191] Recent research supports this trend and argues for the importance of choosing board members with unique perspectives as a way to enhance the quality of boards' decision making.[192]

Corporate Governance and Social Responsibility

Boards of directors are tasked with designing compensation packages for CEOs and upper-level managers, and modern executive compensation is increasingly likely to be linked to additional metrics beyond traditional performance indicators.[193] In particular, more firms are integrating social responsibility into executive compensation.[194] This practice is often referred to as ==CSR contracting==—the linking of executive compensation to CSR criteria such as environmental and social performance.[195]

A recent analysis of S&P firms over a 10-year period found that CSR contracting is becoming increasingly prevalent and its adoption is linked to some pretty important organizational outcomes. Firms see increases in value, long-term orientation, and engagement in CSR initiatives when boards include CSR criteria in executive compensation. Further, CSR contracting leads to reduced carbon emissions and a stronger pursuit of "green" innovations. Importantly, the study also found that CSR contracting is more effective when a substantial portion of executive compensation is tied to CSR criteria.[196]

Would you agree that factors such as board composition and the inclusion of CSR in executive compensation are important drivers of ethical and socially responsible organizations? Check out the Example box for an example of a corporate governance failure.

EXAMPLE   Theranos: An "Epic Failure" in Corporate Governance

Elizabeth Holmes dropped out of Stanford at 19 years old and founded Theranos, a health technology company that eventually achieved a $9 billion valuation on claims that it had developed the capability to run 30 or more lab tests at once using a single drop of blood.[197] Promises of convenient, affordable, reliable blood testing; a board stacked with government and industry veterans; and a mesmerizing founder with eerie resemblances to Steve Jobs combined to win the company more than $700 million in funding and a host of partnerships with companies like Walgreens, Capital Blue Cross, and Safeway.[198]

The problem was, the company's revolutionary blood testing technology didn't actually exist. Theranos was founded—and funded—on the basis of an utter fabrication. Throughout the company's life, Holmes neither presented any data, nor revealed any information about the effectiveness of the technology, to her investors and partners. The explanation? She was merely protecting the company's trade secrets.[199] In reality there were no such data, because most of the blood tests were run on Siemens equipment rather than on the company's own Edison technology, and the small number of tests Theranos devices were able to handle produced inconsistent, inaccurate results.[200]

Holmes and former COO and president Ramesh "Sunny" Balwani were indicted for federal wire fraud in June 2018 and were awaiting trial as of this writing. The pair were accused of, among other things, scheming to defraud investors, medical professionals, and patients in an "elaborate, years-long fraud."[201]

Elizabeth Holmes. Elizabeth Holmes, CEO of Theranos, speaking at *Fortune's* Most Powerful Women Conference. Neither Holmes nor Theranos have admitted wrongdoing.
Krista Kennell/Shutterstock

Where Was the Board?   How were Holmes and Balwani able to get away with a lie for such a long time? Why did no one take them to task? Investigative reporter John Carreyrou—credited with uncovering the massive fraud—described the saga as "one of the most epic failures in corporate governance in the annals of American capitalism."[202] Here are a few of the ways that corporate governance failed miserably in the case of Theranos:

1. *Little experience, big connections.* The Theranos board was a veritable who's who of American political and corporate influence, including former Secretary of State Henry Kissinger, former Marine Corps General James Mattis, and former Wells Fargo CEO Dick Kovacevich. There were also two former senators, and a grand total of one licensed medical professional. None of the board members had any formal auditing, accounting, or legal expertise, and they certainly were unfit to evaluate laboratory testing innovations. Journalist Jennifer Reingold described the board as being "assembled for its regulatory and governmental connections, not for its understanding of the company or its technology."[203]

2. *Exploitation.* Holmes proved skilled at exploiting both regulations and her board members' trust. The company was in the business of "laboratory-developed tests" which were, conveniently, not subject to strict FDA regulation. Holmes knew that Theranos did not legally have to prove that its bloodwork results were accurate, and she used this to her advantage as she continued to mislead her board. Further, when two

whistle-blowers revealed to the board that Holmes had been dishonest with them, she convinced them to keep her on, then immediately multiplied the voting rights of her stock shares, giving herself 99% of the company's total voting rights.[204]

3. *A culture of secrecy.* Effective boards are those that are able to speak openly and honestly with one another, ask questions, and stand up to leaders with too much power.[205] But Holmes created a culture of secrecy and paranoia that permeated every corner of Theranos. Workers were instructed to stay in their own silos and were not allowed to communicate with one another about what they were working on. Further, Holmes quickly fired any employee who disagreed with or questioned her or the company's technology.[206] The board may have failed to do their job holding Holmes accountable in part because of this culture.

YOUR CALL

How would you describe the board's performance at Theranos? What was the board's responsibility in this case, and how did it fail to meet that responsibility? How could good corporate governance have prevented this fraud from escalating to such epic proportions?

3.7 Career Corner: Managing Your Career Readiness

Figure 3.5 shows the model of career readiness we discussed in Chapter 1. We see one clear link between the content of this chapter and this model. It's the Career Readiness competency of *professionalism/work ethic*. The relevant aspect of this competency for this chapter is "demonstrated integrity, ethical behavior, and concern for the greater good" (look back at Table 1.2).

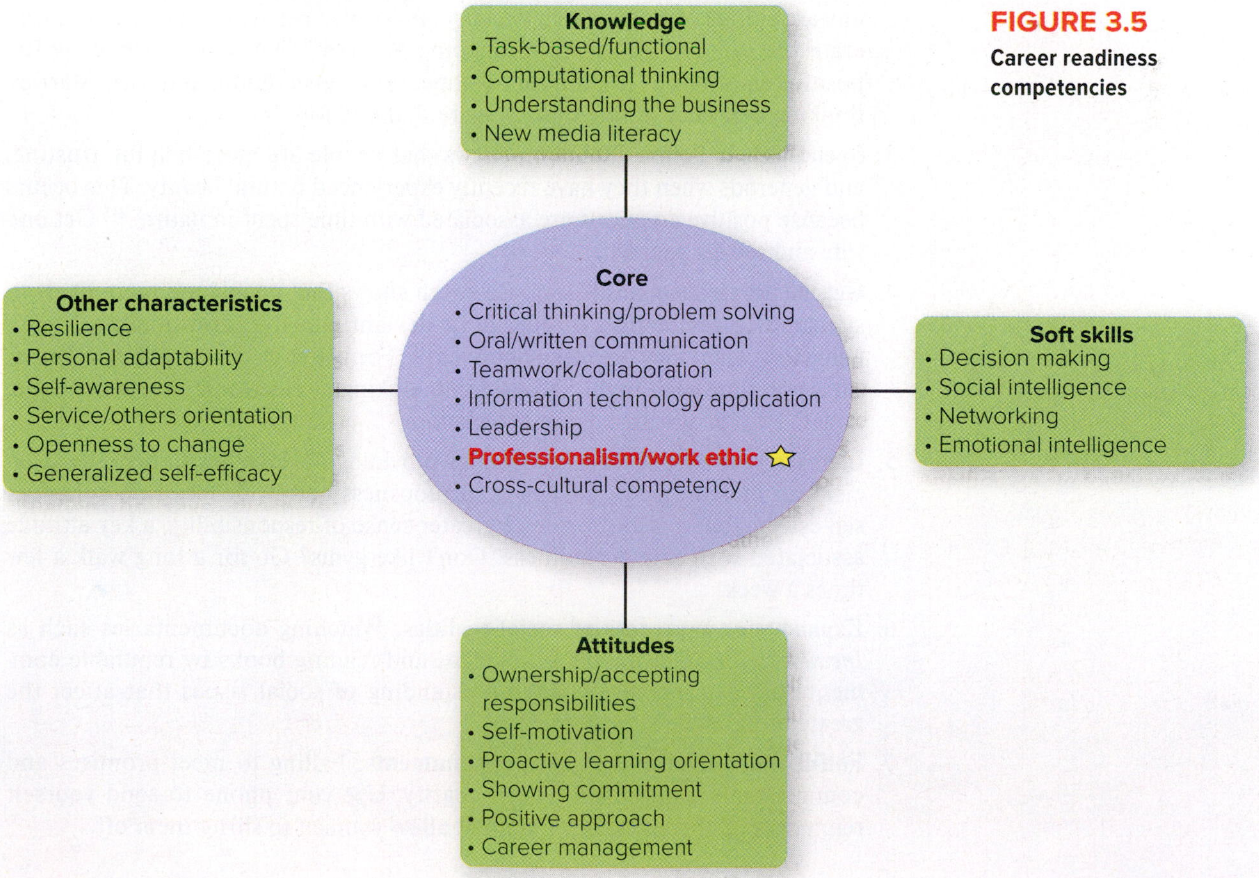

LO 3-7

Describe how to develop the career readiness competency of professionalism/work ethic.

FIGURE 3.5

Career readiness competencies

Knowledge
- Task-based/functional
- Computational thinking
- Understanding the business
- New media literacy

Other characteristics
- Resilience
- Personal adaptability
- Self-awareness
- Service/others orientation
- Openness to change
- Generalized self-efficacy

Core
- Critical thinking/problem solving
- Oral/written communication
- Teamwork/collaboration
- Information technology application
- Leadership
- **Professionalism/work ethic** ☆
- Cross-cultural competency

Soft skills
- Decision making
- Social intelligence
- Networking
- Emotional intelligence

Attitudes
- Ownership/accepting responsibilities
- Self-motivation
- Proactive learning orientation
- Showing commitment
- Positive approach
- Career management

Can you really develop integrity and ethical behavior? We think you can, even though this competency is partly based on stable characteristics like values, moral perspective, and religious beliefs that are all resistant to change. Our goal is not to suggest modifying these fundamental aspects of your life. Rather, we believe this competency is best developed by engaging in activities that facilitate a habit of showing integrity, ethicality, and concern for the greater good. Doing so will give you behavioral examples of your *professionalism/work ethic* to discuss during job interviews.

Focus on the Greater Good and on Being More Ethical

Experiment with implementing some of the following:

1. **Reduce your carbon footprint.** Activities include walking or using public transportation more frequently; turning off lights when you leave a room; unplugging devices that are not in use; using whatever water bottles, jars, and totes you own until they fall apart; eating more plants and less meat; avoiding fast fashion; reducing your use of air conditioning and annually servicing your home's air-conditioning/heating units; and, even better, living in an apartment instead of a house.[207]

2. **Foster positive emotions in yourself and others.** A recent study of workplace interactions found that workers who made an effort to experience genuinely positive feelings toward their co-workers experienced better work relationships and made more progress toward goals than workers who simply "faked it" in order to get through conversations with people they didn't necessarily want to engage with.[208] Positivity and helping others can also beget positivity and helping behavior, thereby enhancing the greater good. Psychologist Barbara Fredrickson said it best, "Beyond the dance of positivity between you and the person you helped, those who witness your good deed may well feel inspired, their hearts uplifted and elevated."[209] This self-reinforcing and perpetuating aspect of positive emotion, and of positivity more generally, is what leads to upward spirals of positivity, in which your positive behaviors and attitudes generate the same in others in an ongoing process.[210] Focus on displaying the positive emotions of joy, gratitude, hope, pride, inspiration, and love. Start by thinking every day of one thing you are thankful for.

3. **Spend time in nature.** Research shows that people are more helpful, trusting, and generous when they have recently experienced natural beauty. This occurs because positive emotions are associated with time spent in nature.[211] Get outside and see for yourself.

4. **Get the proper amount of sleep.** Research shows that people are more likely to succumb to temptation to engage in deviant, abusive, and unethical work behaviors when they are sleep-deprived.[212] For better sleep, try going to bed at the same time each night and avoiding looking at electronic screens (phone, tablet, TV) for at least half an hour before.

5. **Increase your level of exercise.** Besides providing obvious health benefits, exercise can increase your feelings of virtuousness and pride.[213] Pride enhances self-esteem, but it also provides a greater sense of responsibility, a key attitude associated with career readiness. Don't like gyms? Go for a long walk a few times a week.

6. **Expand your awareness of social realities.** Watching documentaries such as *Inequality for All*, available on Netflix, and reading books by reputable commentators can increase your understanding of social issues that affect the greater good.[214]

7. **Fulfill your promises and keep appointments.** Failing to meet promises and commitments undermines your integrity. Use your phone to send yourself reminders of appointments and don't allow yourself to shrug them off.

8. **Avoid people who lack integrity.** People make judgments about you based on those you choose to associate with. Socializing or working with individuals known to be unethical will detract from a positive personal image.[215]

Become an Ethical Consumer

Try these suggestions:

1. **Purchase Fair Trade items.** Purchasing Fair Trade products increases the chances that your money will help provide a decent wage for the people who made them.[216] Low prices often result from producers paying low wages to their workers. Take a look at "Fair Trade USA" (*https://www.fairtradecertified .org/*) to discover where you might find clothing, alcohol, and home goods from producers who treat workers ethically.[217]

2. **Bring your own grocery bags.** You can lower your carbon footprint and reduce the price of goods sold by bringing your own reusable cloth or natural fiber bags when purchasing groceries.

3. **Don't purchase items that aren't ethically made or sourced.** Research where and how a company makes its products. You may pay more for your purchases, but passing on low prices to support more ethical companies supports the greater good.[218]

4. **Don't buy knockoffs.** Cheap counterfeit and illegal merchandise are often made in sweatshop conditions. Although forgoing the low prices on such items may hurt your pocketbook, it's another way you can help the greater good. ●

abusive supervision 91

board of directors 79

clawbacks 82

climate change 102

code of ethics 98

competitors 81

corporate governance 105

corporate social responsibility
(CSR) 99

courage 75

crowdfunding 83

CSR contracting 106

customers 80

demographic forces 87

distributor 82

economic forces 85

ethical behavior 91

ethical climate 97

ethical dilemma 89

ethics 91

external stakeholders 80

general environment 84

global warming 102

government regulators 84

individual approach 94

insider trading 95

internal stakeholders 77

international forces 88

justice approach 95

macroenvironment 84

moral-rights approach 95

natural capital 102

owners 79

philanthropy 102

political–legal forces 88

Sarbanes–Oxley Act of 2002 96

social audit 76

social responsibility 99

sociocultural forces 87

special-interest groups 84

stakeholders 77

strategic allies 82

supplier 81

task environment 80

technological forces 85

trade balance 85

triple bottom line 76

utilitarian approach 94

value system 93

values 93

venture capital 83

whistle-blower 98

workplace cheating 96

Key Points

3.1 The Goals of Business: More Than Making Money

- Many businesses subscribe to a new standard of success—the triple bottom line, representing people, planet, and profit.
- Success in these areas can be measured through a social audit.
- The triple bottom line has particular appeal to younger workers who are less concerned with financial success and material goods than with meaningful work, work–life balances, and experiences.

3.2 The Community of Stakeholders inside the Organization

- Managers operate in two organizational environments—internal and external—both made up of stakeholders.
- The first, or internal, environment includes employees, owners, and the board of directors.

3.3 The Community of Stakeholders outside the Organization

- The external environment of stakeholders consists of the task environment and the general environment.
- The task environment consists of 10 groups that present the manager with daily tasks to deal with: (1) customers, (2) competitors, (3) suppliers,

(4) distributors, (5) strategic allies, (6) employee organizations, (7) local communities, (8) financial institutions, (9) government regulators, and (10) special-interest groups.
- The general environment consists of six forces: (1) economic, (2) technological, (3) sociocultural, (4) demographic, (5) political–legal, and (6) international.

3.4 The Ethical Responsibilities Required of You as a Manager

- Ethics are the standards of right and wrong that influence behavior. Ethical behavior is behavior that is accepted as "right" as opposed to "wrong" according to those standards.
- Ethical dilemmas often take place because of an organization's value system. Values are the relatively permanent and deeply held underlying beliefs and attitudes that help determine a person's behavior.
- There are four approaches to resolving ethical dilemmas: (1) utilitarian, (2) individual, (3) moral-rights, and (4) justice.
- Public outrage over white-collar crime (Enron, Tyco) led to the creation of the Sarbanes–Oxley Act of 2002 (SarbOx)
- Laurence Kohlberg proposed three levels of personal moral development: (1) preconventional, (2) conventional, and (3) postconventional.

- There are five ways an organization can promote high ethical standards: (1) creating a strong ethical climate, (2) screening prospective employees, (3) instituting ethics codes and training programs, (4) rewarding ethical behavior, and (5) using a multi-faceted approach.

3.5 The Social Responsibilities Required of You as a Manager

- Social responsibility is a manager's duty to take actions that will benefit the interests of society as well as of the organization.
- Archie Carroll suggests the responsibilities of an organization in the global economy should have the following priorities: (1) be a good global corporate citizen, (2) be ethical in its practices, (3) obey the law, and (4) make a profit.
- The idea of social responsibility has opposing and supporting viewpoints.
- One type of social responsibility focuses on climate change, sustainable development, and natural capital.
- Another type of social responsibility is undertaking philanthropy.

- Positive ethical behavior and social responsibility can pay off in the form of customer satisfaction, employee and customer loyalty, revenue growth, and enhanced long-term profits.

3.6 Corporate Governance

- Corporate governance is the system of governing a company so that the interests of corporate owners and other stakeholders are protected.
- Ways to use corporate governance to build more ethical and socially responsible organizations include holding CEOs accountable for their ethical (mis)behaviors, ensuring that boards are composed of the mix of people that will encourage the organization to be more ethical, and integrating social responsibility into executive compensation.

3.7 Career Corner: Managing Your Career Readiness

- You can develop the competency of professionalism/work ethic by engaging in activities that facilitate a habit of showing integrity, ethicality, and concern for the greater good.

Understanding the Chapter: What Do I Know?

1. How would you explain the difference between internal and external stakeholders?
2. Among external stakeholders, what's the difference between the task environment and the general environment?
3. Of the 10 groups in the task environment, which five do you consider most important, and why?
4. Of the six groups in the general environment, which one do you think has the least importance, and why?
5. Distinguish among the four approaches to resolving ethical dilemmas.

7. How would you summarize Kohlberg's levels of personal moral development?
8. What are five ways that organizations can promote ethics?
9. Describe the levels in Carroll's corporate social responsibility pyramid. Where does trying to achieve sustainability fit in?
10. What is corporate governance and why is it important? How can good corporate governance be used to build more ethical and socially responsible organizations?

Management in Action

Who's to Blame for the College Admissions Scandal?

In March 2019, news broke that the FBI had uncovered a scheme in which 50 wealthy parents had paid a combined $25 million dollars to get their children admitted to elite universities like Stanford and Yale between 2011 and 2019. The list of people charged included celebrity parents Felicity Huffman and Lori Loughlin, as well as high-profile executives, attorneys, university athletic coaches, an expert test-taker, and standardized testing professionals.[219]

At the center of the scandal was William "Rick" Singer, a college-prep consultant who had masterminded the operation under the cover of his federally registered 501(c)3 charity, Key Worldwide Foundation.[220]

HOW DID IT WORK?

Singer used several strategies to bolster the parents' chances of snagging prestigious university spots for their kids. One tactic was to direct the parents to a psychologist who would evaluate their children for learning disabilities. Singer suggested parents tell their kids to "be stupid . . . be slow . . . be not as bright" in order to receive a diagnosis that would permit the students to have extended or unlimited time as well as an individual room for the ACT and SAT college entrance exams.[221] For some students, this was enough to improve test scores.

Parents who wanted additional help made sizable "charitable donations" to Singer's nonprofit—between $15,000 and $75,000 per test—to have an expert test-taker, now identified as Mark Riddell, complete exams for their kids. This ploy had parents traveling to one of two centers where exam administrators Igor Dvorskiy and Niki Williams would be waiting to pocket $10,000 per test to allow Riddell to either take the exams himself, correct the kids' responses, or feed them the correct answers as they were testing. Riddell also earned approximately $10,000 per test. Many of the children who benefited were unaware of the test-cheating scheme.[222]

Other maneuvers included Singer creating phony athletic profiles for the students, then paying bribes to college coaches for spots on their team rosters. In one case, parents paid Singer $1.2 million to secure their daughter's admission to Yale. Singer created a fake athletic profile for the girl, sent it to Yale soccer coach Rudolph "Rudy" Meredith, and, after she was admitted, cut Meredith a check for $400,000.[223]

GUILTY AS CHARGED

At some point during the investigation, Singer, Riddell, and Meredith agreed to become "cooperating witnesses" for the FBI. They wore wire taps that recorded their conversations with wealthy parents, and they turned over incriminating e-mails related to the scheme. The three agreed to enter guilty pleas and to cooperate fully with the investigation in exchange for what they hoped would be more lenient sentencing.[224]

Singer pleaded guilty to obstruction of justice, money laundering conspiracy, racketeering conspiracy, and conspiracy to defraud the United States.[225] He told U.S. District Court Judge Rya W. Zobel, "I am absolutely responsible for it," adding that "I put everything in place. I put all the people in place and made the payments directly."[226]

Actress Felicity Huffman was the first parent sentenced in the admissions scandal. She pleaded guilty to fraud, and the court ordered that she serve a 14-day jail term, pay a $30,000 fine, and complete 250 hours of community service. John Vandemoer, the former Stanford University sailing coach who had accepted a total of $610,000 in bribes, pleaded guilty to racketeering. The court ordered that he serve one day in prison, spend two years on supervised release, and pay a $10,000 fine.[227] As of this writing, real-estate executive Toby MacFarlane has received the longest prison sentence of anyone involved. The court sentenced MacFarlane to six months in prison, two years of supervised release, 200 hours of community service, and a $150,000 fine for paying $450,000 for athletic spots at USC for his son and daughter.[228]

WHO WAS RESPONSIBLE?

In spite of their guilty pleas, are Singer and these parents, coaches, and administrators the only ones responsible for the largest college admissions scandal in Department of Justice history? It is likely that systemic factors played a role as well.

Many of the parents involved cited the intense pressure surrounding college admissions that plagues both students and parents. Indeed, a lucrative industry of test preparation and tutoring has blossomed in response to this pressure. In spite of research that shows no substantial link between a person's undergraduate degree–granting institution and their subsequent successes, many parents hold tight to the belief that their kids can only truly succeed if they have a degree from an exclusive school.[229] Sadly, the academic achievement race often starts as early as kindergarten, with more and more teachers leaving the teaching profession rather than participate in overly structured, rigorous, testing-focused environments that they believe are akin to child abuse.[230]

And what about the broader system of college admissions? Are current admissions criteria doing a good job of selecting the most promising and most deserving students? Studies suggest that standardized test scores don't predict much more than first-year grades and retention rates, but SAT and ACT scores remain the gold standard in admissions decisions across the spectrum of colleges and universities. Other factors that play a role in students' chances of getting into their school of choice include whether they attended a private high school, their family socioeconomic status, and their gender (females often are victims of discrimination in the college admissions process).[231]

When asked how she felt about the scandal, Mia M., a student at Martin Luther King High, said, "We have created a mentality that we must be the best at all costs. Grades are valued over integrity, and alternative facts prevail over truth. Constant comparisons make us become desperate to be perfect." Alex Lee, a student at Hoggard High School in Wilmington, NC, expressed his sadness over the scandal, saying, "I feel sorry for everyone in this situation. The parents, because they feel as if this is the only way to create happiness for their children, the students because some had no idea, and especially those students who worked so hard and got pushed out by those with more money to spare."[232]

FOR DISCUSSION

Problem-Solving Perspective

1. What is the underlying problem in this case from the perspective of the federal government, the parents, and the prospective college students?

2. Why do you think the parents were willing to play such a significant and risky role in their kids' college admissions?

3. How do you think the higher education system and the government should move forward to prevent the same behavior from occurring in the future?

Application of Chapter Content

1. How do you think the general environment, particularly economic, demographic, international, and sociocultural forces, fed into the admissions scandal?

2. Are the children who were aware of the cheating scheme purely victims in this situation, or should they also be considered unethical? Explain your answer using one of the four approaches to deciding ethical dilemmas.

3. What might universities do to promote higher ethical standards among their admissions departments, coaching staff, and other decision makers?

4. Do you think the punishments handed down in court will be enough to deter similar scams from happening again?

5. Based on what you've learned about Rick Singer, his involvement, and his decision to cooperate in the investigation, where would you place his level of moral development? Explain your answer.

Legal/Ethical Challenge

Should You Apply to Have Your Student Loans Forgiven?

Student loan debt nearly tripled between 2007 and 2017, thanks to increased attendance at for-profit colleges along with rising college tuition and living expenses.[233] For hundreds of thousands buried in student loan debt, a little known 1994 program called "Borrower Defense" or "Defense to Repayment" sponsored by the U.S. Department of Education offers a lifeline.

The program is available for those students who obtained loans from the government's Direct Loan program. "The law says students are entitled to forgiveness of any existing debt—and, possibly, reimbursement of any repaid loans—if they can show that their school violated state law in getting them to take out the debt. (An example might be if a school lied in its advertisements about how many of its graduates landed jobs.) However, it's not clear what documentation the borrower needs to prove fraud."[234]

To date, around 227,000 people have applied to have student loans expunged through the program.[235] The Department of Education has already agreed to forgive nearly $150 million in debt and indicated many more will likely get forgiveness.[236]

Education Secretary Betsy DeVos recently announced that a more stringent set of rules for evaluating borrower defense claims will apply to loans granted from July 2020 forward. Under these new rules, borrowers will have a much higher burden in proving their universities deceived them. There will also be a three-year deadline to apply for the program once a student graduates or leaves the school. Finally, the program will no longer automatically erase borrowers' loans when schools close before students are able to complete their degree programs. Now, these individuals will be required to apply for loan cancelations.[237]

Assume that you recently graduated from a state university. You took the required courses for your bachelor's degree and excelled in your studies. You made the Dean's List each semester of your last two years and interned for a social services organization in your community. You hoped you'd be able to work in your chosen field of psychology and be able to pay off the debt a few years after graduation.

Like many students, you paid for the majority of your education with student loans. Three years after graduation, your career has not turned out as expected. Instead of working in your chosen field of psychology, you have a low-paying job at a retail chain and wait tables on weekends to make ends meet. You weren't aware that psychology positions required a graduate degree. Your student loan debt remains unpaid, and you recently heard about the borrower defense program.

You are considering whether or not to apply for the Borrower Defense program.

SOLVING THE CHALLENGE

What would you do?

1. Apply for loan forgiveness and hope that the broad language of the law will make an exception for your state college education and loan. Besides, what's wrong with asking?

2. Apply for loan forgiveness. After all, you aren't benefiting from your education, someone should have told you that you needed a graduate degree in psychology to get a good job, and there is no clear definition of fraud.

3. Don't apply. You were never promised a job and you made the decision to major in psychology. You could have chosen a field with more job opportunities.

4. Invent other options. Discuss.

Shared Value and Sustainable Development:

A New Way to Think about Leading and Managing

After reading this learning module, you should be able to:

LM 1-1 Describe how the concept of creating shared value improves upon the traditional approach to corporate social responsibility.

LM 1-2 Discuss the roles various stakeholders play in creating shared value.

LM 1-3 Explain recommendations for creating shared value in light of current progress and challenges.

How Can You Contribute to a More Sustainable Future?

It's easy to think that sustainable development is a problem for big businesses and governments to solve, but we all can contribute. The United Nations' "Lazy Person's Guide to Saving the World" suggests activities at four levels, ranging from things you can accomplish during a Netflix binge to things you can try at your job.[1] Here are some of their ideas:

1. Level 1: Things You Can Do from Your Couch.

- **Like and Share**. If you see an interesting social media post about women's rights or climate change, share it so folks in your network see it too. Use the hashtag #globalgoals to share with the UN and give other people ideas about how they can contribute. These efforts can have a big ripple effect.

- **Report online bullies**. If you notice harassment online, flag it. Your willingness to call out the behavior prevents others from being harmed and gives you practice at speaking up when it's important.

- **Stay informed**. Follow local and national news outlets and social media. Doing so means you'll

automatically learn about anything noteworthy when it comes across your feed.

2. Level 2: Things You Can Do at Home.

- **Air dry your clothes**. You'll use less energy and preserve your clothes for longer use. This translates into less carbon and less consumption, with the bonus of saving money.

- **Reconsider the preheat**. Think about whether you really need to preheat your oven. If you're just reheating a plate of leftovers, skip this step and instead stick your plate in as soon as you turn on the oven. This will drastically reduce the amount of energy your oven uses.

3. Level 3: Things You Can Do outside Your House.

- **Purchase ugly foods**. Misfits Market purchases ugly produce (the stuff grocers won't put on their shelves because it doesn't adhere to size, shape, or other appearance standards) from local, organic farmers and bundles it in food subscription boxes that it ships right to your door.[2] This strategy cuts down on food waste and gives farmers a chance to earn something on crops that would otherwise go into the garbage.

- **Shop smart**. Plan your meals so that you don't buy more than you need. The eMeals app takes it a step further by generating a shopping list based on the meals you choose.

4. **Level 4: Things You Can Do at Work.**

- **Share.** If you don't want your apple or snack, don't toss it—send an e-mail on the listserv or offer it to a colleague—people love free stuff—especially food.

- **Speak up**. Raise your voice against discrimination in your office. If you're feeling unsure about how to do this the right way, flip back to the Chapter 3 ManageU feature for advice.

- **Engage locally.** Always be thinking about ways your company may be able to help the local community achieve its goals. Focus on your firm's core business activities for ideas on how your company can create the most impact.

FORECAST

What's Ahead in This Learning Module

This learning module discusses shared value and sustainable development as a new approach to leading and managing, which replaces more traditional forms of corporate social responsibility (CSR). We briefly review CSR and its shortcomings before introducing the concept and model of creating shared value. Next, we explore the roles that various stakeholders play in the creation of shared value, including the United Nations and its set of 17 sustainable development goals. We then examine progress that has been made toward creating shared value and managing for sustainable development and the challenges that have arisen in this process. We conclude with recommendations for managing for shared value and sustainable development.

1.1 From Corporate Social Responsibility to Creating Shared Value

THE BIG PICTURE

Traditional CSR programs are one way organizations have attempted to contribute to society. Creating shared value is a new approach that incorporates capitalism to improve upon the limitations of CSR.

By now you have completed your work on Chapter 2 and hopefully remember a few facts about management history. Do you recall the contemporary perspective on management that says firms should look beyond making short-term profits for shareholders and also consider the environmental and social costs of doing business? Chapter 3 revealed that corporate social responsibility (CSR) captures the idea that organizations have obligations to a much broader group of stakeholders than just the people who own shares of the company's stock.

In this section we take a look at traditional CSR and some of the criticisms of this approach in practice. We then turn our discussion to the concept of shared value.

LM 1-1

Describe how the concept of creating shared value improves upon the traditional approach to corporate social responsibility.

Traditional CSR

CSR is a hot topic for 21st-century corporations. Recent estimates say that Fortune 500 companies funnel an estimated $20 billion into CSR initiatives each year.[3] More and more companies now believe that being socially responsible—attending to the triple bottom line of people, planet, and profit—is simply the "right thing" to do.[4] Here are a couple of examples:

Going carbon-neutral. Occidental Petroleum CEO Vicki Hollub, the first woman to lead a major U.S. oil & gas company, is known for taking risks. Under her leadership, the company has made big investments in carbon-cutting initiatives. Tim Pannell/The Forbes Collection/Contour by Getty Images

Occidental Petroleum Example: The Fortune 500 organization and fifth largest oil and gas company in the United States recently announced that it is working to be completely carbon-neutral in its operations. One analyst noted that environmental initiatives of this magnitude are "largely unheard of" in the oil and gas industry.[5] Occidental CEO Vicki Hollub said the company wants to "help to be part of the solution" to preserving the environment, and she believes that "as a socially responsible company we've got to do the right thing."[6]

Other Industry Examples: The world has generated approximately 8 billion metric tons of plastic since 1950, and almost 80% of it is now in landfills or littering the natural environment. A primary concern is that plastics take hundreds and sometimes thousands of years to decompose, and in the process release microplastics into the soil, oceans, and subsequently the food chain. Research estimates that ocean plastics alone generate economic costs of $13 billion each year in the form of lost tourism and harm to wildlife, ecosystems, and fisheries.[7] Starbucks, McDonald's, Red Lobster, the Walt Disney Company, and Alaska Airlines are just a few on a long list of companies committed to phasing out single-use plastic straws in some or all of their operations in the coming years.[8] Dell intercepts ocean-bound plastics and uses them in product packaging; the company has recycled 27 metric tons of plastic through this program since 2017.[9]

Does Traditional CSR Run Counter to Shareholders' Interests?   What do you think Milton Friedman, one of the most influential economists of the 20th century, would say about the popularity of CSR? Recall from Chapter 3 that Friedman believed the only social responsibility a business should worry about was making profits for shareholders. In Friedman's view, being profitable was the best way for a business to serve society.

You may think that support for Friedman's ideas has faded given the widespread adoption of CSR we see today. But firms remain hesitant to move beyond making minimally acceptable investments in social initiatives. This is because many managers still see CSR as a "necessary expense" and believe that pursuing too much of it is an irresponsible way to spend shareholders' dollars.[10] In this view, there is a "fixed pie" of value available in the marketplace, and by spending money in one area (social responsibility) a company reduces the money available for another area (shareholders).

Moving beyond the "Fixed Pie" Perspective   Do you think organizations are doomed if they "give up" a portion of shareholders' profits and redistribute them as charity in order to be socially responsible? A quick review of Table 3.1 in Chapter 3 will remind you of evidence that suggests some organizations are actually better off financially after engaging in CSR. Perhaps maximizing shareholder wealth and creating social benefit aren't necessarily mutually exclusive propositions. In fact, some organizations are using CSR strategically as a way to solve social problems while growing their organizations. Here are two examples:

Alibaba Example: The Chinese e-commerce giant added a feature to its Auto-Navi map service called the "poverty alleviation map." The feature draws users' attention to restaurants, stores, and gas stations in remote villages and makes it more likely that travelers will venture out to these isolated areas by car. The poverty alleviation map benefits these struggling regions by stimulating their potential for economic growth, and Alibaba benefits by drawing more users to its map service.[11]

Reliance Jio Example: This wireless carrier invested billions of dollars to create a modern 4G network in India in 2016. Prior to this, only about 150 million people in India (out of more than 1 billion) had access to a mobile network, and existing cellular service was unreliable and expensive. By 2020, Reliance Jio had over 388 million subscribers on its network and had attracted huge investments, including $5.7 billion from Facebook in exchange for a 9.9% stake in the company.[12] The company offers data for about five cents per gigabyte (the cheapest rate in the world) and also sells inexpensive smartphones. The existence of a reliable mobile network provides a plethora of opportunities for economic growth in developing regions because businesses have more access to customers, real-time information, and mobile financial services. Reliance Jio's network benefits a huge number of people in India, and the company has experienced unprecedented growth and soaring profits.[13]

Affordable and reliable 4G. A Reliance Jio employee demonstrates the JioTV app that provides live-streaming TV content to its almost 400 million subscribers. The 4G access Reliance Jio provides has transformed India's digital economy. Sara Hylton/Redux Pictures

The firms mentioned above leveraged the power of capitalism to generate financial wealth while simultaneously solving large-scale social problems. And the opportunities created by their initiatives will drive continued economic growth in these once underserved regions. In these examples, the "fixed pie" perspective is replaced by one that allows for the whole pie to get bigger. This new approach requires a major shift in the way we think about capitalism and is the foundation of a new managerial approach referred to as "creating shared value."

Creating Shared Value

According to Harvard Business School professors Michael Porter and Mark Kramer, organizations often miss out on how best to impact society through CSR because they fail to align their CSR initiatives with their core business strategies. This failure, they say, stems from a limited view of capitalism's potential to create value, which in turn generates extensive corporate philanthropy, but few meaningful solutions for long-term societal improvement.[14] Porter and Kramer conclude that, "Businesses acting as businesses, not as charitable donors, are the most powerful force for addressing the pressing issues we face."[15]

Does this mean firms should abandon CSR all together and return to a purely profit-driven mindset? Not exactly. Porter and Kramer propose that managers and leaders instead focus on <mark>creating shared value (CSV)—</mark> implementing policies and operating practices that enhance the competitiveness of a company while simultaneously advancing the economic and social conditions in the communities in which it operates. CSV results in an expanded "pie" or pool of value for the firm as well as for society.

CSV Generates Sustainable Competitive Advantages Firms seeking CSV should evaluate opportunities for social benefit in the same way they evaluate firm-level strategic decisions. This means that managers should only pursue the opportunities that allow their firms to thrive, grow, and create long-term value for shareholders. This is known as generating sustainable competitive advantage, which is discussed in detail in Chapter 6.

The beauty of CSV is that it shifts the concept of CSR from *a way to use profits* toward *a way to make profits*.[16] Successful CSV is strategic—it stems from opportunities that are closely aligned with a firm's specific business. It also requires taking social responsibility out of an isolated CSR department and giving it a prominent seat at the firm's strategy and operations table.[17]

CDW Example: Fortune 500 IT company CDW has received awards for its strategic thinking as well as its commitment to inclusion and diversity. Led by CEO Christine Leahy, the company is deeply committed to improving the communities in which it operates. According to senior program manager Sandy Pierantoni, "Our business was founded on the principle that you 'treat your coworkers the way you want your customers to be treated' and 'everything we do revolves around the customer.'" CDW knows first-hand the importance of aligning social responsibility with business strategy. Said Pierantoni, "We used to be everything to everyone, focusing on so many activities and breadth of focus areas but that just was not sustainable. We were all over the map. So a few years ago we made some hard choices to not support certain organizations that ultimately did not support our bottom line of what our business is about." She added, "We are taking a much more focused approach to our philanthropy that is synonymous with our business goals and objectives as a top global employer and information technology solutions provider."[18]

CSV Is Gaining Traction   In the last 20 years, the private sector has grown increasingly supportive of the idea that firms are uniquely positioned to enact solutions to some of the world's most pressing problems—issues like poverty, poor education, and inequality—while maximizing shareholder value.[19] In 2015, for example, *Fortune* introduced its annual Change the World List to recognize firms that are using their core business models to tackle major societal issues. Editors at *Fortune* say these companies "understand that doing good for society and the planet can help them bring in more revenue, which can help them do more good, in a self-reinforcing loop."[20]

Let's consider how organizations can work toward successful CSV.

A Model of Shared Value Creation

Figure LM 1.1 shows a model of CSV based on Porter and Kramer's work. The figure is structured around the classic Input–Process–Output (IPO) management perspective that shows how key processes transform inputs into outputs. The idea is that managers create desired outputs by fostering a specific set of inputs and processes. As business students and professors, we know that the overarching goal of firms is to provide economic value for shareholders in the form of increased profits. Figure LM 1.1 shows how CSV contributes to this goal.

The model shows that the amount of economic value a firm ultimately produces for shareholders is most directly affected by the extent to which it is able to create shared value. Shared value creation occurs when the firm generates meaningful, lasting benefits for its broader stakeholders in addition to maximizing shareholders' profits. Let's consider the processes and inputs that drive shared value.

Key Processes for Creating Shared Value   As a manager, you need to understand the processes that enable CSV if you want to approach business decisions from a perspective of shared value. Figure LM 1.1 shows that there are three key processes at play:

1. ***Discovery of new products, markets, and opportunities.*** One of the key processes for CSV is the discovery of potential new products and/or services that the firm can offer, new markets the firm can enter, and new opportunities for the firm to reposition or differentiate itself in its current landscape. The following example illustrates this key process:

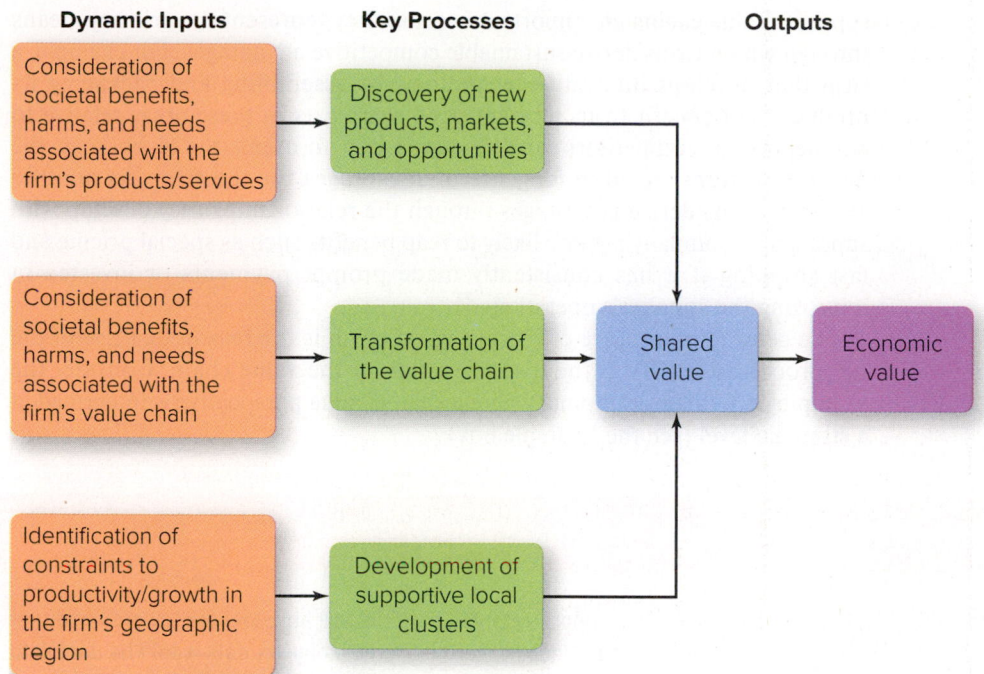

Dynamic Inputs

Key Processes

Outputs

Consideration of societal benefits, harms, and needs associated with the firm's products/services

Discovery of new products, markets, and opportunities

Consideration of societal benefits, harms, and needs associated with the firm's value chain

Transformation of the value chain

Shared value

Economic value

Identification of constraints to productivity/growth in the firm's geographic region

Development of supportive local clusters

FIGURE LM 1.1

A model of creating shared value

Novartis Pharmaceuticals Example: A shared-value approach led Novartis pharmaceuticals to discover a lucrative new market across 14,000 rural villages in India. The company launched a program called Arogya Parivar (Hindi for "healthy family") in 2007 with the goal of increasing access to doctors and medications and improving health literacy for the 32 million residents of these villages. The program enlists health educators familiar with local customs to travel from village to village offering free health camps. The residents, most of whom earn the equivalent of less than $5 a day, gain access to information about things like disease prevention, hygiene, and nutrition. Local doctors often volunteer to join the educators, seeing patients at no cost but gaining potential future patients in the process. The program's corporate wing sells inexpensive medications for conditions that are common in the villages. The increased demand for these medications allowed the program to turn a profit for Novartis after only three years. Villagers' doctor visits tripled in this time, meaning that millions of people—many of whom had never seen a doctor—had increased access to important medical care. Novartis is expanding its program in India and is mobilizing the initiative to Kenya and Vietnam.[21]

Without a shared-value perspective, it is highly unlikely that Novartis would have seen the potential to market its products to millions of people in rural India who had little money for medicine and almost no access to doctors.

2. *Transformation of the value chain*. A value chain consists of all of the processes a company uses to add value to its products or services. The value chain includes activities involved in production, marketing, and ongoing customer

An example of a value chain. All of the activities involved in getting food on the table—from sowing seeds through cooking a meal—are part of the food value chain. One of the ways firms create shared value is by transforming their value chain activities.
elenabs/iStock/Getty Images

support. Value chains are important because they represent the primary means through which firms derive sustainable competitive advantages. For example, a firm that develops innovative technology for assembling and packaging its products can benefit from substantially lower costs in these areas relative to competitors. If competitors can't figure out how to mimic the technology, the innovation translates into longer-term advantages for the firm. As another example, firms derive advantages through the relationships they develop with suppliers. A company is more likely to reap benefits such as special pricing and fast shipping if it has consistently made prompt payments or invested in improving the supplier's operations.[22]

The central importance of a firm's value chain is the reason that one of the key processes in CSV is the transformation of the value chain. Consider the example of Williams-Sonoma, where a shared-value perspective is integrated at a strategic level (see the Example box).

EXAMPLE   Shared Value at Williams-Sonoma

Danielle Jezienicki is the Director of Corporate Social Responsibility for Williams-Sonoma, Inc. She is responsible for ensuring that value-chain activities across eight brands maximize the potential for CSV. In a recent interview, Jezienicki explained what this process looks like in "the life of a towel." First, Williams-Sonoma makes creative designers aware of the environmental drawbacks and benefits of the various fabric production processes its vendors employ. Armed with this information, designers then work with the company's sourcing team to select and procure the most appropriate fabric for the towel—one that maximizes sustainability at acceptable costs. Finally, marketing and branding teams incorporate these explanations into the towel's packaging so that the customer is educated about the benefits they and the environment will derive by choosing this particular towel.

At a broader level, Williams-Sonoma aims to create value across its industry. The company provides resources and support so that its vendors are able to work toward important sustainability certifications. Many vendors would be unable to devote the time and/or money necessary to obtain these credentials without such support. Jezienicki hopes this will help Williams-Sonoma achieve its goal of using 100% responsibly sourced cotton by increasing the available supply. She also believes that over time these efforts will increase the presence of sustainable options in the retail industry.[23] According to Williams-Sonoma president and CEO Laura Alber, the company's efforts have resulted in "big shifts in the way our industry operates, in our customers' choices, and in the well-being of our workers and the communities in which we do business world-wide."[24]

YOUR CALL

How do you think this example demonstrates the key process of transformation of the value chain?

---

3. *Development of supportive local clusters*. The third and final key process that enables CSV is the development of supportive clusters—geographic concentrations of interrelated entities such as competitors, suppliers, universities, and other organizations that result in benefits for the firm in the local operating environment.

Employees in the various firms comprising a cluster are likely to engage in face-to-face interactions because they are near to one another and face similar operational challenges arising from the local operating environment. Over time, these close interactions create trust, and this forms the basis for the open and transparent sharing of ideas, knowledge, and resources that characterizes supportive clusters. Innovation results from working through problems with employees from competing and supporting firms, universities, governments, and trade associations.[25] Cluster-related activities improve the broader local environment in the form of, for example, job creation and larger skilled labor pools.[26]

Deficiencies in local clusters represent constraints to firm productivity and profitability. Cisco learned this first-hand and used a shared-value perspective to address cluster weaknesses.

Cisco Example: A lack of qualified candidates in the local labor pool represented a critical constraint for Cisco's operations in Brazil, South Africa, and other markets. The company addressed this weakness by establishing its Networking Academy—a collaboration with nonprofits, government bodies, schools, and other entities through which Cisco leverages its cloud technology expertise to deliver IT training and education and foster career readiness for students and veterans that may not otherwise have the opportunity to enhance their education or career prospects.

The company also works with talent management software company Futures Inc. to match these underserved populations with jobs in science, technology, engineering, and math (STEM) that align with their skills, training, and career goals. Cisco enjoys the benefit of a stronger cluster enabled by the growing size of its skilled labor pool.[27]

Dynamic Inputs   Figure LM 1.1 shows that each key process is affected by a unique dynamic input. We call these dynamic because organizations' rapidly changing environments create constant opportunities for reassessment and adjustment. Let's consider the dynamic inputs managers can use to promote the processes that create shared value.

1. *Consideration of societal benefits, harms, and needs associated with the firm's products/services.* The first set of dynamic inputs requires that firms continually envision all of the ways their products and services might be used to address current and potential societal needs. This set of dynamic inputs also asks companies to get real about the ways their business might be harming or benefiting society. Figure LM 1.1 shows that this set of inputs drives the key process of discovery of new products, markets, and opportunities.

   HSBC Example: HSBC Bank wanted help with identifying the various social issues related to its business, so it established an internal research group called the Climate Change Center of Excellence. The center works to build a deeper understanding of the effects of climate change and to uncover the strategic opportunities climate change creates for HSBC and its clients.[28]

2. *Consideration of societal benefits, harms, and needs associated with the firm's value chain.* The second set of dynamic inputs requires that firms continually consider all of the current and potential ways their value chain activities meet societal needs and/or and create societal benefit or harm. Figure LM 1.1 shows that this set of inputs drives the key process of transformation of the value chain.

   Experts emphasize the need for firms to be brutally honest with themselves when considering the societal impacts of their value chains. It is highly likely that managers will discover value chain activities that are counterproductive to the goals of CSV. What is important is to acknowledge the existence of these issues and then make a detailed plan for improvement.[29] Walmart is a great example.

   Walmart Example: When Walmart critically examined its value chain, it realized that the benefits it gained by sourcing produce from geographically dispersed industrial farms were overshadowed by transportation costs and constraints in stores' ability to quickly restock fruits and vegetables. The company now maintains a commitment to increased local sourcing and says it has removed multiple days from the time it takes to get produce into its stores. This decision benefits local farmers through increased business, helps customers enjoy produce that lasts longer, and makes a sizable dent in Walmart's carbon footprint.[30]

3. *Identification of constraints to productivity/growth in the firm's geographic region.* The third set of dynamic inputs requires that firms continually monitor their cluster for things that might restrain firm productivity and growth. Figure LM 1.1 shows that this set of inputs drives the key process of development of supportive local clusters. Consider how Mars addressed this input.

> **Mars Example:** Mars was constrained by local conditions in the Cote d'Ivoire that were negatively impacting cocoa yields, reducing the pool of cocoa farmers, and increasing the price of cocoa. The company had already spent years investing in community initiatives and providing educational opportunities in local operating environments, but a re-examination of its cluster conditions revealed the need for a different approach. Mars scientists joined forces with nonprofit, government, and industry partners in the affected regions and ultimately developed higher-yield, disease-resistant cocoa clones. This approach resulted in tripled cocoa yields, reduced cocoa prices, and revitalized local farming communities.[31]

How CSR and CSV Are Fundamentally Different

Historically speaking, CSR approaches have been largely ineffective at addressing large-scale societal problems. This is because CSR initiatives tend to be narrow in scope and misaligned with firms' core businesses. Campbell Soup presents a great example of the difference between a failed CSR effort and a vibrant CSV strategy (see the Example box).

EXAMPLE   A Shift in Perspective at the Campbell Soup Company

CSR at Campbell Soup

In 2010 the Campbell Soup Company announced that it was doing its part to combat heart disease by reducing the sodium content in its soups by up to 45%. It didn't go over well—customers revolted against the loss of flavor and by mid-2011, the company had added most of the sodium back.[32] Campbell Soup made a noble attempt to do the socially responsible thing, but the project only addressed one specific concern and was not implemented as a strategic initiative.

CSV at Campbell Soup

Fast-forward to present day and you'll find Campbell Soup engaged in a full-blown campaign to improve the agricultural supply chain of tomatoes. The company educates its farmers on environmental impact and efficient resource utilization. It encourages and supports the installation of drip irrigation, a strategy that helped the company reduce the amount of water required to produce a pound of tomatoes by 15% between 2012 and 2018. Recently, Campbell Soup expanded its efforts to wheat and has partnered with Land O'Lakes to educate wheat farmers on soil nutrient preservation and optimal fertilizer use. These initiatives benefit local watersheds and increase the long-term viability of soil for wheat production.[33]

Moving from CSR to CSV. For Campbell Soup, the decision to remove salt was socially responsible but not strategically valuable. By focusing instead on the environmental impact of its agricultural supply chains, the company has begun to create shared value. *a*) FoodCollection *b*) David R. Frazier Photolibrary, Inc./Alamy Stock Photo

YOUR CALL

What are the key differences between the two initiatives at Campbell Soup? What additional opportunities might the company have to create shared value through its core business activities?

The contrasting examples within Campbell Soup illustrate the importance that a shift in managers' perspectives can have on a company's ability to create shared value. While CSR focuses on isolated issues or on minimizing or making up for firms' collateral damage to society, CSV places profit maximization at the center of solutions to complex, wide-ranging global challenges.[34]

1.2 The Roles of Various Stakeholders in CSV

THE BIG PICTURE

CSV involves multiple stakeholders. The United Nations introduced the Sustainable Development Goals to help stakeholders across the globe understand how to work together to solve global crises. The stakeholders most relevant to leading and managing for CSV include big and small businesses, entrepreneurs, and business schools.

The world is facing serious problems, and many of them are getting bigger. For example:

- 20% of children in the world live in extreme poverty, and the percentage of people who live with hunger is growing.

- More than 10% of the world's population has no access to safe drinking water, and 2 billion people live in countries with high water stress.

- 90% of people living in urban areas are breathing polluted air, and 25% of urban residents live in slum-like conditions. Rapidly increasing urbanization is adding to these problems.[35]

Do you think businesses and managers can make a difference in these and other global issues? Solving problems of this scale represents a remarkable challenge, and research suggests that societal change efforts can only be successful when a wide range of stakeholders get involved.[36] In this section, we discuss several stakeholder groups that must work together to solve global challenges through the creation of shared value.

LM 1-2

Discuss the roles various stakeholders play in creating shared value.

Global Collaboration: The Role of the United Nations

The United Nations (UN) took an aggressive stance on global issues in 2016 when all 193 member countries agreed to adopt a set of 17 Sustainable Development Goals (SDGs). These goals, introduced in Chapter 1, represent a roadmap for economic planning and development that allows the current population to meet its needs without compromising the ability of future generations to do the same.[37] The SDGs address serious, persistent, global issues such as threats to human and animal life, destruction of the natural environment, and unequal access to basic necessities. We summarize the 17 SDGs in *Figure LM 1.2*.

The SDGs Are an Opportunity for CSV   The SDGs emphasize the need for key stakeholders to join forces in creating mutually beneficial solutions. In other words, the way to achieve the SDGs is to create shared value.[38] Dr. Mark Kramer explained the connection between the SDGs and CSV as "a new revenue model for business," adding, "You can actually quantify the market potential of for-profit business to meet the needs of the SDGs."[39] Good health and well-being—SDG #3—is one goal area in which businesses are striving to create shared value. Here are two examples:

FIGURE LM 1.2

Summary of the 17 UN Sustainable Development Goals

 **1 NO POVERTY** — 10% of the world's population lives in extreme poverty. Economic growth must be inclusive to reduce poverty and provide sustainable jobs.

 **7 AFFORDABLE AND CLEAN ENERGY** — Energy is vital to every challenge and opportunity in the world. Access to clean fuel, technology, and renewable energy is essential for sustainability.

 **13 CLIMATE ACTION** — Climate change is affecting every country, disrupting economies and affecting lives. Renewable energy and emissions reduction are needed to create a low carbon world.

 **2 ZERO HUNGER** — Investments in agriculture and sustainable food production systems are needed to help alleviate hunger.

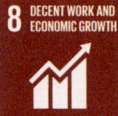 **8 DECENT WORK AND ECONOMIC GROWTH** — Conditions where people have quality jobs that stimulate the economy but don't harm the environment are needed for sustainable economic growth.

 **14 LIFE BELOW WATER** — The world's oceans make the earth habitable for humankind. Careful management including control of overfishing, pollution, and ocean acidification is needed.

 **3 GOOD HEALTH AND WELL-BEING** — Good health for all ages is imperative for sustainable development. Improved sanitation and hygiene as well as access to doctors can save millions.

 **9 INDUSTRY, INNOVATION AND INFRASTRUCTURE** — Transportation, irrigation, energy and information, and communication technology are vital infrastructure needs for sustainable development.

 **15 LIFE ON LAND** — Forests cover 30.7% of the earth and they are key to combating climate change, protecting biodiversity, and combating desertification.

 **4 QUALITY EDUCATION** — A quality education is the foundation for sustainable development. Education equips people with the tools needed to help solve the world's problems.

 **10 REDUCED INEQUALITIES** — Policies that are universal and include the needs of the disadvantaged and marginalized populations need to be created in order to reduce inequality.

 **16 PEACE, JUSTICE AND STRONG INSTITUTIONS** — Sustainable development includes justice for all and effective, accountable institutions. Efficient and transparent regulations are vital.

 **5 GENDER EQUALITY** — Women and girls must be provided with access to equal education, health care and work to create sustainable economies, benefit societies, and humanity at large.

 **11 SUSTAINABLE CITIES AND COMMUNITIES** — Sustainable development requires cities to provide opportunities for all, including clean air, access to basic services, energy, housing, transportation, and more.

 **17 PARTNERSHIPS FOR THE GOALS** — Sustainable development requires partnerships—along with shared goals and visions—between governments, the private sector, and civil society.

 **6 CLEAN WATER AND SANITATION** — 40% of the world's population struggles with water scarcity. Investment in freshwater ecosystems and sanitation facilities is needed to create fresh water for all.

 **12 RESPONSIBLE CONSUMPTION AND PRODUCTION** — Sustainable consumption and production—"doing more and better with less"—reduces resource use, degradation, and pollution while increasing quality of life.

Source: Based on material in "About the Sustainable Development Goals," The United Nations, https://www.un.org/sustainabledevelopment/sustainable-development-goals/.

Nestlé Example: Nestlé strategically aligns its efforts to create shared value with the UN SDGs. The company engages in partnerships with multiple organizations to address issues in its supply chain such as child labor, deforestation, agricultural practices, and dietary health. According to Nestlé's website, "we are particularly focused on encouraging kids around the world to eat nutritious food and get active by creating new and better products, promoting education and conducting industry-leading scientific research. By 2030, our global initiative, Nestlé for Healthier Kids, aims to help 50 million kids lead healthier lives, and we've already reached 8.3 million."[40]

Becton Dickinson Example: Becton Dickinson (BD) created a $2 billion business with its innovative needleless injection technology. The solution has protected millions of health care workers in the world from contracting dangerous infections such as HIV, and nurses' needle-related injuries have declined by more than 50% since its introduction.[41] This technology accounts for 25% of BD's revenue.[42] According to the company's website, "we actively evaluate how we can mobilize and contribute to the achievement of the UN Sustainable Development Goals (SDGs), through our product and service offerings, as well as collaborative efforts across various sectors."

Private-Sector Involvement Is Critical for Achieving the SDGs Did you know that the SDGs were designed specifically to enlist businesses and managers in solving global problems through the creation of shared value?[43] The private sector's participation is essential because it carries unparalleled financial resources and capabilities. For example, in the United States alone, private-sector spending is about seven times more than government spending, and around twenty times more than non-profit spending.[44] According to UN Secretary-General António Guterres, "there is no global goal that cannot benefit from private sector investment."[45] Read more about the importance of the private sector for achieving the SDGs in the Example box.

EXAMPLE | **The Bill & Melinda Gates Foundation Recognizes the Need for Private-Sector Engagement with the SDGs**

The Bill & Melinda Gates Foundation (BMGF) is the largest charitable foundation in the world. Through BMGF, the Gateses have given more than $53 billion to various programs aimed at global health and development.[46] The foundation has adopted the UN SDGs as a framework for its philanthropy and created the *Goalkeepers* initiative to gather world leaders in driving progress toward achieving the goals.[47]

The BMGF recognizes the importance of creating shared value through private sector partnerships. For example, the foundation:

- Collaborates with corporations all over the world to stimulate the growth of agricultural clusters in developing areas.[48]

- Is one of the founding members of the Global Financing Facility (GFF), a fund that aims to stimulate needed investment from the private sector and other parties so that the world is able to achieve the SDGs.[49]

- Provides grants and engages in private-sector partnerships to support pharmaceutical and biotech firms' work toward developing affordable, safe, and effective vaccines and drugs. This work is particularly focused on eradicating diseases responsible for mortality in the world's poorest regions.[50]

According to the BMGF website, "The foundation believes that the private sector can play a catalytic role in making the market work for the poor by drawing on its innovation and technology platforms, entrepreneurial and scientific talent, commercialization and low cost manufacturing, business model validation and access to large pools of capital."[51]

Bill Gates has expressed his belief that while it is possible to meet at least some of the SDGs by 2030, the world is not on track to do so. In March 2020, Gates announced that he would step down from the boards of both Microsoft and Berkshire Hathaway in order to "dedicate more time to philanthropic priorities including global health and development, education, and my increasing engagement in tackling climate change."[52]

YOUR CALL

On which of the SDGs do you think the private sector can have the biggest impact?

The Role of Businesses, Big and Small

We said that meeting the SDGs would be virtually impossible without the help of the private sector. But did we mention what's in it for businesses? According to recent estimates, global CSV initiatives represent a $12 trillion opportunity and carry the potential to create 380 million new jobs across the globe.[53]

Big Businesses   What do GM, Walmart, IBM, and Apple have in common? For starters, and as you've probably already guessed, these are some of the largest and most recognizable companies in the world. But you may be surprised to learn that these firms also share a commitment to shared value creation. They belong to a growing body of industry titans pledging to embrace sustainable business practices by working to benefit *all* of their stakeholders rather than just their shareholders.[54]

This is good news for advocates of shared value and the SDGs for at least two reasons:

1. *Big businesses are influencers*—These firms have the reputations, reach, and social media presence to shine a spotlight on societal issues.[55] Their actions inspire others to follow suit.

2. *Big businesses can mobilize big solutions*—Companies with extensive resources can deliver sizable impact.[56] And collaborations across big businesses have the potential to—quite literally—change the world.

Here are some of the recent strides big businesses have made in creating shared value:

Philips Example: Robert Metzke, Global Head of Sustainability for Philips, a health technology company, said, "Philips has fully aligned its strategy with the UN Sustainable Development Goals (SDGs), because we believe that creating sustainable value for our customers and society are the ultimate and only source of lasting economic growth."[57] At Philips, managers constantly look for opportunities to improve the company's supply chains, operations, and products. The firm ranked number one on *Fortune's* Sustainability All Stars list for its work to limit emissions, use resources responsibly, and generate new solutions to environmental problems. Philips' health care innovations have already improved the lives of more than 1.5 billion people, and the company has a goal to double that number by 2030.[58]

Mastercard Example: The global financial services company wants to remove barriers to financial inclusion for micro and small merchants. The company developed a digital marketplace to provide access to formal financial services for small farmers in developing areas. In the process, Mastercard discovered new markets and increased returns for its shareholders. More than 250,000 farmers are now able to negotiate pricing, payments, quantities, and distribution from mobile devices. Through the platform, merchants also are able to build a record of digital transactions which they can use to gain access to business loans. Financial inclusion means that for the first time these farmers have a chance to grow their businesses and improve their lives and local economies.[59]

Merck Example: CEO Kenneth Frazier believes, "While a fundamental responsibility of business leaders is to create value for shareholders, I think businesses also exist to deliver value to society." Frazier's view of Merck's opportunity to create shared value is that "our salient purpose in the world is to deliver medically important vaccines and medicines that make a huge difference for humanity. The revenue and shareholder value we create are an imperfect proxy for the value we create for patients and society."[60] The pharmaceutical company is currently using its core business strategy and strengths to pursue research on Alzheimer's, a disease predicted to affect at least 30 to 50% of people 85 and older and cost the United States $1 trillion by 2050. A cure for Alzheimer's would have enormous impact on future generations and on the overall economy.[61]

People first, and profits will follow. Merck CEO Kenneth Frazier has shown steadfast commitment to the company's research-focused mission in his leadership. During Frazier's first 10 years as CEO, Merck developed the first FDA approved Ebola virus vaccine and simultaneously doubled shareholder returns.
Mike Cohen/Redux Pictures

Small Businesses   It may be difficult to believe that small businesses can have an impact on global issues after reading examples of large companies improving *billions* of lives with their CSV initiatives. But did you know that small businesses account for about 90% of the economic activity in the world?[62] These companies occupy the front lines for eradicating poverty, boosting income generation, and creating jobs, making them an essential player in shared value creation and sustainable development.[63]

Need more proof that small firms can make big strides? Consider *Fortune's* 2019 Change the World List—it featured nine companies with annual revenues of less than $1 billion.[64] Here are two examples of small businesses creating shared value:

LanzaTech Example: Led by CEO Dr. Jennifer Holmgren, the Illinois-based company developed bacteria capable of converting carbon dioxide and carbon monoxide into sustainable ethanol fuel for use in aviation. In 2018 Virgin Atlantic used the company's recycled carbon fuel for one of its transatlantic flights. LanzaTech recently received a $72 million investment from Novo Holdings after working for 14 years to refine its technology in a lab setting.[65] LanzaTech hopes to one day see its ethanol used in the production of consumer goods.[66]

The English Tea Shop Example: This company made a conscious decision to adopt a shared value perspective in 2008. It cut ties with large plantation tea farmers and began building relationships with a few small suppliers instead. CEO Suranga Herath said that the English Tea Shop "wanted to find a model that empowered people," citing the lack of opportunity and mobility for many hard-working tea farmers. The company now operates in more than 50 markets and it reported revenues of more than $28 million in 2018. The English Tea Shop sponsors educational programs on various management topics for its employees and has seen worker productivity increase by more than 30%.[67]

The Role of Entrepreneurs

According to two experts, "Lasting societal change is catalyzed by starting enterprises." This statement highlights the critical role entrepreneurship plays in creating shared value.[68] In fact, experts believe entrepreneurs are one of the groups that has driven the most progress toward the SDGs to date.[69]

Here are two reasons entrepreneurs are well-positioned to create shared value:

- **Entrepreneurs' environments are less constrained.** Big businesses may have the advantage of deep pockets, but there's one thing they don't have—agility. Recall from the model of shared value in Figure LM 1.1 that societal needs are dynamic. This means organizations must monitor their environments regularly and be poised to respond to new or changing opportunities for CSV as they arise. Unfortunately, large and established companies often suffer from inertia—the tendency for firms to resist change in favor of their current modes of operation—and this is where entrepreneurs have a unique advantage. Unlike large organizations, entrepreneurial ventures are not locked in by pre-existing policies, routines, or expectations, and this enables them to be nimble and responsive to changing needs.[70]

- **Entrepreneurs possess important traits.** CSV is uncharted territory for many firms and doing something completely new is both difficult and scary. Entrepreneurs have two traits that are advantageous in this situation: creativity and risk propensity. (We discuss entrepreneurs' traits in detail in Learning Module 2.)

  1. *Creativity.* Entrepreneurs are more likely to be innovative, which is beneficial when devising solutions to highly complex societal problems for which there is no precedent. Entrepreneurs have a gift for seeing *possibilities* when others see lost causes.

  2. *Risk propensity.* Entrepreneurs are willing to take risks. This means they are more comfortable trying something even though it may not be successful. Their bold moves, in turn, often clear the way for industrywide changes later on.[71]

See the Example box to learn how entrepreneurs at one start-up are using smartphone technology to create shared value.

EXAMPLE   **Ricult Changes the Landscape for Farmers**

Approximately two-thirds of the people in the world now have access to mobile networks, and this number continues to grow.[72] Further, network service and smartphones have become increasingly affordable, and overhead costs associated with mobile business solutions are low. This combination of factors makes smartphone technology a ripe opportunity for entrepreneurs seeking to create shared value.

MIT-based start-up Ricult is using smartphone technology to empower rural farmers in developing countries to break free from a slew of systemic factors that previously held them in poverty.

"Farmers are at the bottom of the pyramid in developing countries, so if you want to drive these countries forward and reduce inequality, you have to transform the agricultural

Transforming agriculture. Farmers like the one pictured here are using Ricult's mobile platform to overcome a multitude of obstacles that arise in agriculture in developing countries. Courtesy of Ricult

sector," said co-founder Aukrit Unahalekhaka. Along with Usman Javaid, Jonathan Stoller, and Gabriel Torres, Unahalekhaka created the service to give farmers direct access to credit, a digital marketplace for farm supplies, and buyers. The farmers also receive personalized advice for their operations based on their unique weather and soil conditions.

So far, farmers using Ricult have seen their yields increase by an average of 50%, and their profits have gone up by 30–40%. This kind of growth is life-changing for the rural farmers the company serves. Unahalekhaka said, "Before the farmer had to decide, 'Should I send my kid to school or should I save that money to pay for food or health care?' All of those things are necessary for a quality life. With more money, they don't have to make those tough choices anymore."[74]

YOUR CALL

What are some other ways that entrepreneurs might use smartphone technology to create shared value?

The Role of Business Schools

Younger generations of workers expect organizations to create shared value. In one recent study, two-thirds of Millennials said they had no interest in working for a company that didn't have a strong commitment to sustainability, and more than 90% of Gen Zers believed the private sector needed to address social and environmental issues.[75] Further, Millennials' values and rising earnings potential are driving financial advising firms to incorporate more socially responsible investments in their portfolios.[76]

In spite of their strong feelings about firms' social responsibilities, younger generations are not well-informed on CSV. For example, one study conducted at Yale found that fewer than 60% of business students had even heard of the UN SDGs.[77] This may be due to the fact that many business schools struggle to weave CSV and sustainable development into their curricula.[78] But evidence suggests business students want their universities to rise to the challenge. During the search for a new dean at Harvard Business School, for example, more than 250 students petitioned the search committee to fill the position with someone who would take "the challenge of revamping the curriculum to reflect environmental and societal challenges seriously."[79] Let's take a look at what we can learn from the business schools leading the charge in shared value and sustainable development education.

Business Schools Take Varied Approaches to Teaching Shared Value   The Association to Advance Collegiate Schools of Business (AACSB) reports that more and more colleges and universities are contributing to advancing the SDGs with innovative and meaningful approaches.[80] Evidence suggests institutes of higher education incorporate these ideas at four levels:

1. **Coursework.** We found various examples of course syllabi that mentioned shared value, sustainable development, and related concepts. For example, the Kellogg School at Northwestern University taught principles of shared value in a course called *Corporate Social Innovation*.[81] At NYU, Jeffrey Hollender—co-founder and former CEO of Seventh Generation—taught about shared value in a course called *Sustainable Business & the New Economy*.[82] There are many more examples of business school coursework focused on these ideas.

2. **Experiential learning.** Another approach for teaching the principles of shared value and sustainable development is to provide students with opportunities for hands-on experience. An example is Ravi Subramanian's *Business Decisions for Sustainability and Shared Value* course at Georgia Tech's Scheller College of Business. In Spring 2019, teams of students in the class partnered with a non-profit called the Center for Sustainable Communities (CSC) to devise creative development plans for a struggling Virginia neighborhood. Subramanian tasked the class with implementing sustainable development ideas in practice and praised students for connecting with people in the community to understand their needs and challenges at a deep level.[83]

Teaching CSV through experiences at Georgia Tech. CSC founder and president Garry A. Harris, Professor Ravi Subramanian, and students in the *Business Decisions for Sustainability and Shared Value* course (all pictured here) worked together to create shared value by transforming a "striving" Virginia community into a "thriving" one.
Courtesy of Georgia Institute of Technology, Scheller College of Business, Ray C. Anderson Center for Sustainable Business

3. **Certificate and degree programs.** Students at the Wisconsin School of Business at the University of Wisconsin–Madison can earn a certificate in Business, Environment, and Social Responsibility. The Lundquist College of Business at the University of Oregon and the Miami Herbert Business School at the University of Miami both offer minors in Sustainable Business.[84]

4. **Cultural infusion.** Some business school leaders embed shared value at a deep, cultural level. For example, Dr. Cathy DuBois leads the Responsible Leadership Initiative at the Kent State University College of Business. The initiative advocates for business as a force for good and weaves the SDGs into research, teaching, and practice activities throughout the college. Through this program, Kent State business students are immersed in principles of shared value. The college integrates the SDGs and related concepts into at least 60 courses for students and offers multiple study abroad programs built around sustainable development and social responsibility. Faculty members participate in workshops and resource groups, and between 2013 and 2018, 36% of faculty research publications related to at least one of the SDGs.

Canada's University of Guelph uses its Sustainable Business Initiative to incorporate societal welfare, shared value, and sustainability into the culture at the Gordon S. Lang School of Business and Economics. The school has dedicated sustainability research centers, and approximately 20 of its faculty members engage in related research. Sustainable development is embedded in a variety of undergraduate and graduate coursework, and responsible business and sustainability is a key learning objective of its bachelor of commerce degree program.

Engaging the next generation of leadership in CSV and sustainable development. In 2020, the World Economic Forum ranked the Gordon S. Lang School of Business and Economics at Canada's University of Guelph as one of the top business schools across the globe for its contributions to solving societal problems. Courtesy of John F. Wood Centre for Business and Student Enterprise at the Lang School of Business and Economics

Your Knowledge of CSV and the SDGs Enhances Your Career Readiness

You can use the knowledge you gain from this learning module to give yourself an advantage on the job market, even if your university hasn't begun to incorporate shared value and/or sustainable development into its formal programs just yet. Recruiters surveyed reported that an increasing number of job applicants are asking about shared value in their job interviews.[85] We suggest taking time to research an organization's history with shared value and sustainable development before your interview. This will increase your career readiness competency of *understanding the business*, and you'll demonstrate to the company that you have a *proactive learning orientation*.

1.3 Progress, Challenges, and Recommendations for CSV

THE BIG PICTURE

In this section we discuss progress to date on shared value and sustainable development, examine the challenges firms face as they work toward shared value creation, and provide recommendations for addressing these challenges and moving forward.

LM 1-3

Explain recommendations for creating shared value in light of current progress and challenges.

Today's organizations are excited and optimistic about changing the world. In a recent article in the *Journal of Management,* a team of experts noted that, "as portrayed in their reports, press releases, websites, and other public statements, businesses intend to do a tremendous amount of good for society through their countless CSR initiatives."[86] A recent study of the 50 largest companies in the United States found that more than half professed public commitments to advancing specific SDGs.[87] It is clear that the private sector is adopting the view that profitable businesses and social change go hand-in-hand.

Current Progress and Challenges in Shared Value and Sustainable Development

Much progress in fostering shared value and sustainable development has occurred in recent years. Organizations, for example, are becoming increasingly comfortable with the notion of CSV and have started to implement shared value in strategic decisions.

Areas of Progress Corporate engagement with shared value and sustainable development is relatively new, but already we see improvements in two broad areas:

1. *Awareness of and engagement with CSV and the SDGs.* A growing number of organizations are updating their existing, outdated CSR programs with the language of shared value and sustainable development.[88] There also is increasing awareness and understanding of shared value and sustainable development in the corporate community,[89] and more CEOs are engaging their organizations with the SDGs at a strategic level.[90] Procter & Gamble and ENGIE are two good examples.

   Procter & Gamble Example: In 2018 Procter & Gamble's CEO David Taylor introduced a platform called *Ambition 2030* that committed the company to making positive social and environmental impacts while creating value for P&G's shareholders. Taylor wants P&G executives and employees to incorporate sustainability into their daily work and said that "we believe P&G can be a force for good and a force for growth, and we are taking a more deliberate approach to delighting consumers while enabling responsible consumption."[91]

   ENGIE Example: ENGIE, the French multinational utility company, has undergone a radical reinvention in the past few years, beginning with then-CEO Isabelle Kocher's announcement that her company would lead the transition to a low-carbon economy.[92] ENGIE sold over $16 billion in assets that did not align with its sustainable development goals and has sharpened its focus on renewable energy. The company will use collaborative partnerships to help the world's corporations, governments, and universities to transition to more sustainable energy consumption. Gwénaëlle Avice-Huet, president and CEO of ENGIE North America, said of the company's recent overhaul, "At the end of the day, our company, it's a new one—a new one, fully dedicated to sustainability commitments."[93]

A renewed focus on sustainable development. ENGIE'S Gwénaëlle Avice-Huet speaks at a press briefing on renewable energy. The company has realigned its business to focus on meeting its sustainable development goals. Romain Gaillard/Redux Pictures

2. *Progress toward specific goals.* Societies have made significant strides toward achieving some of the SDGs. For example:

   - SDG #3: Good Health and Well-Being[94]

       - The global neonatal fatality rate dropped by 41% between 2000 and 2017.
       - Coverage with a critical second dose of the measles vaccine increased to 67% by 2017.
       - Adult HIV (among those 15-49) decreased by 22% between 2010 and 2017.

   - SDG #5: Gender Equality[95]

       - Women increased their representation in national parliaments from 19 to 24% between 2010 and 2019.
       - A record number of women—127 total—served in the 116th U.S. Congress beginning in 2019.

Progress toward gender equality. The Democratic women of the 116th Congress pose with Speaker of the House Nancy Pelosi in front of the U.S. Capitol, Washington, D.C., in 2019—a year that saw a record number of women serving in Congress. Jim Lo Scalzo/Shutterstock

- SDG #8: Decent Work and Economic Growth[96]
    - Global Real GDP per capita—which is used to estimate average standard of living—grew by approximately 2% per year between 2017 and 2020.
    - Economic growth in the least developed countries grew almost 5% annually between 2010 and 2020.
    - Global labor productivity has increased consistently since 2010.

Areas of Concern   The UN's most recent SDG progress report acknowledged the good intentions of private-sector organizations attempting to take a shared value perspective. But experts agree that businesses could and should do a much better job of advancing solutions for important global issues.[97] At this rate, it is unlikely the world will meet the UN's original objective to accomplish the SDGs by 2030.[98] Here are three areas of concern:

1. *More of the same.* One reason we don't see more progress toward CSV in the private sector is that firms are doing the same things they did before. Traditional philanthropy and CSR have been dressed up in fancy new titles. There is an abundance of enthusiasm for adopting a new mindset, but many firms still lack the necessary tools for funneling that energy into a complex plan for creating shared value.[99]

2. *Lack of commitment at the top.* Another roadblock is a lack of CEO engagement with shared value. A recent report on the state of the SDGs suggests the implementation of these goals still ranks fairly low on CEO agendas.[100] Managers also struggle to suppress the impulse to prioritize decisions that maximize short-term profits. Infusing an organization with a shared-value outlook requires a dramatic shift in perspective along with strong commitment, participation, and continual support from the top down.

3. *Misalignment with strategy.* A final concern is that firms are struggling to incorporate shared-value principles with core business strategies.[101] CSV isn't

possible without a nuanced understanding of how core capabilities and strategic objectives align with specific opportunities for addressing societal issues.[102] Outdated organizational policies and procedures that support CSR instead of CSV can further complicate the process.[103]

Recommendations for Transitioning to a Shared-Value Mindset

In this section we offer three recommendations for transitioning to a shared-value mindset and overcoming the challenges discussed above. Managers can use the practical advice and examples we share to help manage with a new CSV lens.

Set Priorities to Overcome Problems with Strategic Alignment

As a manager you will need to prioritize opportunities for shared value creation. Look for opportunities to maximize impact, and don't pursue goals that aren't a good fit for your unique business. Recall from the model of CSV in Figure LM 1.1 that the best opportunities for shared value aren't always immediately obvious. Keep this in mind as you evaluate your firm's potential to make progress on one of the SDGs. Consider the following example:

> **TE Connectivity Example:** TE Connectivity is a $30 billion consumer electronics company that specializes in connectivity and sensor technology. Up until a few years ago, TE's solutions focused on sustainable vehicle technology in the automotive, aerospace, and oil and gas industries. But the company recently created a device-based solution to help the 15 million emergency cardiac patients suffering from a stroke each year. Doctors thread TE microcatheters and guide wires to precise areas of patients' brains, enabling them to stop bleeding or break up blood clots caused by strokes. TE's solution is safer, more accurate, and more effective than traditional pharmaceutical-based options. The innovation has already helped millions of stroke patients, and TE ranked #4 on *Fortune*'s 2019 Change the World List.[104] Managers at TE reevaluate their corporate responsibility strategy on a regular basis because they know how quickly their environment can change. The process includes an assessment of the social, environmental, and economic issues that are most relevant to TE and its stakeholders, solicitation of feedback from multiple parties, an analysis of the UN SDGs, and internal prioritization.

Encourage a Long-Term Mindset to Gain Support across the Organization

Creating shared value requires that companies adopt a longer-term perspective on earnings than they have in the past. Unfortunately, the importance of short-term rewards is deeply embedded in executive compensation systems, and managers face intense pressure to prioritize short-term earnings over other goals.[105] Some experts believe this obsession with the short-term is the reason more firms in the private sector have yet to engage with the SDGs.

Boards of directors and CEOs are encouraged to take a long-term perspective that focuses on multiple stakeholders. This shift in perspective is essential for CSV because projects aimed at achieving the SDGs often won't produce quick returns.[106] Here are two recommendations for building a long-term mindset in your organization:

- *Designate special-purpose funds*. In some firms, investors contribute to separate funds that are earmarked for longer-term opportunities. This provides the chance for investors to adjust to a long-term perspective in a relatively risk-free environment. Over time, investors may become more amenable to additional long-term projects that focus on creating shared value.[107]

- *Reconfigure executive compensation*. Executive pay often revolves around short-term results like stock performance, and this leads managers to prioritize decisions that prop up short-term stock price over decisions that may grow the business.[108] Executives are more likely to adopt a long-term focus if they are rewarded for long-term performance rather than short-term earnings.

Consider the following example of Unilever, a company widely considered to be one of the most sustainable in the world.

Focusing on the long term at Unilever. Paul Polman, former Unilever CEO, speaking about the SDGS at the Concordia Annual Summit in New York, 2017. Riccardo Savi/Getty Images

Unilever Example: When Paul Polman took over as Unilever's CEO in 2009, he decided to make it clear that he wanted the company to focus on long-term solutions for sustainable growth.[109] On his very first day, Polman announced that Unilever would stop issuing quarterly financial reports. Polman knew that these short-term performance indicators would make it impossible to justify investments in sustainable development and carbon reduction. He also knew that his decision would anger some of the company's shareholders. His solution was to communicate to the shareholders, clearly and convincingly, about the benefits of this change. He explained, "transparency builds trust . . . We spent a disproportionate amount of time explaining why a more socially responsible business model is actually also a better model for the shareholders longer term—if you are a long-term shareholder. We made it very clear to shareholders that this model would give them consistency of delivery, where every year we would grow faster than the market, where we would improve stability." Polman promised that his approach would deliver consistent growth every year—and it did.

Paul Polman retired from Unilever in 2018, and new CEO Alan Jope wasted no time doubling down on the company's commitment to shared value. Jope instituted a strategic review of all the company's brands, asking, "Can these brands figure out how to make society or the planet better in a way that lasts for decades?" The company plans to sell off brands that don't make a positive contribution to society.[110]

Break Out of Old Routines by Thinking Bigger   It can be difficult to switch from a traditional CSR business model to a shared-value perspective.[111] In fact, the majority of the firms that have publicly committed to advancing the SDGs through their business activities have failed to make any meaningful changes to their existing CSR frameworks.[112]

As a manager, adopting a shared value and sustainable development approach means that you can no longer view your organization in isolation from its larger environment. Instead, you must consider yourself in conjunction with the larger ecosystem that includes your community, local cluster participants, value chain, and other stakeholders. Creating shared value is virtually impossible without collaboration across the ecosystem.[113]

Consider the case of Revolution Foods in the following Example box.

EXAMPLE   **Revolution Foods Navigates Its Ecosystem to Create Shared Value**

Kristin Richmond and Kirsten Tobey became friends in 2006 in an MBA class at UC Berkeley. The former educators shared a vision of getting nutritious, appetizing, affordable meals into school cafeterias, and Revolution Foods was born. The owners quickly realized they were operating within a complex web of federal government–mandated lunch prices, existing food-service companies, and schools that seemed closed off to changes in their existing routines.

In response, Richmond and Tobey developed a keen understanding of their ecosystem and devised strategies for innovation that relied on collaboration with key stakeholders. For example, Richmond and Tobey figured out that

A school lunch revolution at Revolution Foods. Co-founder, CEO, and chair Kristin Richmond (right) and co-founder and Chief Impact Officer Kirsten Tobey inside their company's food prep operation in Oakland, CA. Jim Wilson/Redux Pictures

maximum, a necessity if they wanted to sell their meals in the public school system.

When they finally got the chance to serve their lunches at a few schools, they experienced immediate pushback from students and administrators because their meals contained whole grains and vegetables instead of chips and sodas. Once again, Richmond and Tobey took the opportunity to collaborate with their stakeholders. They visited the schools and educated lunchroom staff and administrators about nutrition and its impacts on children's behavior and health outcomes. They won their case, and Revolution Foods now provides nutritious meals for 2,500 schools across the country and generates $150 million in annual revenues.[114]

Revolution Foods' success—which can be measured by its progress toward SDG #3 (good health and well-being) and its healthy revenue stream—is the result of strategic collaboration with stakeholders and a nuanced understanding of how Revolution Foods fits into its unique ecosystem. Experts believe that efforts to create shared value and deliver on the SDGs will be most successful if firms collaborate with stakeholders in this fashion.[115]

suppliers were willing to offer big discounts on pricey and nutritious food items because demand from school lunch providers is high and consistent. This discount allowed them to keep their meal prices at or below the $3 federal

YOUR CALL

Why do you think it is so important for companies to understand and collaborate with their ecosystems in order to create shared value?

Conclusion A shared value and sustainable development perspective means that shareholder returns and societal benefit are no longer in competition. Using this approach, businesses can do well while simultaneously doing good, and shared value provides the perfect framework for understanding and achieving the SDGs.[116]

Key Terms Used in This Learning Module

clusters 122
creating shared value (CSV) 119

inertia 129

value chain 121

Key Points

LM 1.1 From Corporate Social Responsibility to Creating Shared Value

- Organizations have traditionally used CSR programs to contribute to societal welfare.
- Creating shared value (CSV) is a new way to think about an organization's role in tackling societal issues.
- CSV is defined as implementing policies and operating practices that enhance the competitiveness of a company while simultaneously advancing the economic and social conditions in the communities in which it operates.

LM 1.2 The Roles of Various Stakeholders in CSV

- Multiple stakeholders are involved in creating shared value.
- The United Nations' 17 Sustainable Development Goals (SDGs) represent the efforts of the multinational organization's 193 member countries to tackle global issues.

- The private sector, entrepreneurs, and business schools are important stakeholders in the process of creating shared value.

LM 1.3 Progress, Challenges, and Recommendations for CSV

- There is more awareness of and engagement with CSV and the SDGs, and there has been progress made toward meeting specific goals.
- Three important areas of concern in CSV are (1) more of the same—organizations not doing enough to change existing CSR programs, (2) lack of commitment at the top, and (3) misalignment with organizational strategies.
- Three recommendations for CSV are (1) set priorities to overcome problems with strategic alignment; (2) encourage a long-term mindset to gain support across the organization, and (3) break out of old routines by thinking bigger.

4

Global Management
Managing across Borders

Kapook2981/iStock/Getty Images

After reading this chapter, you should be able to:

LO 4-1 Identify three influential effects of globalization.

LO 4-2 Describe the characteristics of a successful international manager.

LO 4-3 Outline the ways in which companies can expand internationally.

LO 4-4 Discuss barriers to free trade and ways companies try to overcome them.

LO 4-5 Explain the value to managers of understanding cultural differences.

LO 4-6 Describe how to develop your cross-cultural competency.

FORECAST *What's Ahead in This Chapter*

This chapter covers the impact of globalization—the rise of the global village, of one big market, of both worldwide megafirms and minifirms. We also describe the characteristics of the successful international manager and why and how companies expand internationally. We describe the barriers to free trade and the major organizations promoting trade and the major competitors. We discuss some of the cultural differences you may encounter if you become an international manager, and we conclude with a Career Corner that focuses on how you can develop the career readiness competency of cross-cultural awareness.

Working Successfully Abroad: Developing Cultural Awareness

Whether you travel abroad on your own or on a work assignment for your company, there are many ways to develop cultural awareness, a career readiness competency that can help ensure your international experience enhances your career success.[1] The general idea is to be global in your focus but think in terms of your local environment.

Do Your Research

Don't wait until you arrive to start the process of familiarizing yourself with the culture of your new environment. Start reading books and articles and watching videos well in advance. Study the geography and the transportation systems ahead of time. Talk to people who have been there, and before you leave, begin seeking out and contacting people from the local area who can help you now or in the future. A few general rules always apply when you are the outsider: Learn by listening more than you speak; follow the example of others; and be moderate, open-minded, and humble.

Check Your Attitude

In a recent interview with *Business Insider*, Karoli Hinricks, CEO of Jobbatical, the international tech marketplace, offered some good advice about leaving biased attitudes at home. "Don't move abroad if you're looking to find things to be exactly like they were back home," she says. "Only when you open your mind to the experience and grasp all the quirks that your new home has in store for you, will the journey boost your creativity and become positive." Be ready to embrace the opportunity, and don't let minor problems or the novelty of your experience throw you. Maintain a positive, can-do attitude and overcome the small stuff.

Learn the Appropriate Behavior

Before you go, spend some time learning about patterns of interpersonal communication and interaction. A quick online search can clue you in about expectations in the particular country or areas where you'll be living or working. Pay attention to social customs about such everyday behaviors as making introductions, being introduced, order

of speaking in a meeting or group, use and nonuse of humor, dining etiquette, and the norms for personal space, which can be very different from what you're used to.

Become at Least Minimally Skilled in the Language

Whatever foreign country you're in, at the very least you should learn a few key phrases—such as "hello," "please," and "thank you"—in your host country's language. The effort you make to do this will go a long way to enhancing your relationships with others, even if your grammar and accent aren't perfect.

Global events. A trio of business people chat during an international conference. How would you start a conversation with someone from another country if you were attending such a conference?
Rawpixel.com/Shutterstock

Pack Wisely

Packing wisely means more than just bringing the right clothes for the climate, although you should do that, too. But also inform yourself about the attire that's appropriate for the places you'll visit and the events you'll attend. More conservative clothing is often the norm abroad, and you'll want to be sensitive to your cultural surroundings. Consider, too, that living spaces are often smaller in other countries. Pack light, bring outfits that are versatile and easy to care for, and don't anticipate a walk-in closet.

Finally, Be Prepared

Get a head start on making sure all your paperwork is in order—a valid passport (with an expiration date at least six months in the future), a visa and work permit if needed, debit and credit cards that are accepted in your host country, and health insurance that covers you outside the United States. Know your rights, too; working abroad is not the same as being a tourist. Be prepared for emergencies, such as running out of cash unexpectedly (though you should always have some in reserve), and have a plan that will help you stay calm and focused while you resolve the issue.

For Discussion You've just accepted an internship at a telecommunications company in Seoul, South Korea. Before leaving for Korea, how would you plan on developing your cross-cultural awareness to ensure success?

4.1 Globalization: The Collapse of Time and Distance

THE BIG PICTURE

Globalization, the trend of the world economy toward becoming a more interdependent system, is reflected in three developments: the rise of the "global village" and e-commerce, the trend of the world becoming one big market, and the rise of both megafirms and Internet-enabled minifirms worldwide.

LO 4-1

Identify three influential effects of globalization.

Is everything for sale in the United States now made abroad? What does that mean for U.S. consumers and the economy? Although it is the third-largest exporter in the world, the United States imports more than it exports. In 2019, the nation imported $2.5 trillion in goods and $597 billion in services. Only the European Union imports more. Consumer goods account for almost $654 billion of U.S. imports, mostly consisting of cell phones, TVs, and pharmaceuticals.[2]

Competition and Globalization: Who Will Be No. 1 Tomorrow?

It goes without saying that the world is a competitive place. Where does the United States stand in it? What's our report card?

The United States remained the world's largest economy in 2019,[3] but was it the most competitive? Actually, the World Economic Forum ranks the United States at No. 2, behind Singapore. *(See Table 4.1.)*

The World Economic Forum defines competitiveness as "the set of institutions, policies and factors that determine the level of productivity of a country." It lists 12 themes that influence a country's productivity and long-term growth. As a manager, understanding these themes is important if you decide to enter a foreign market so you can ensure a productive workforce.[4] For example, you wouldn't want to expand your business to a country with a faltering financial system or shrinking market size because both of these themes influence a country's long-term growth.

Is the United States the richest nation? In terms of gross domestic product per capita (the total value of all goods and services produced in the country divided by the population), the International Monetary Fund's annual ranking for 2019 puts the United States at No. 12 in the world. That's behind countries such as Kuwait, Norway, Luxembourg, and Ireland. The richest nation is Qatar.[5]

Another indicator of whether a country is business friendly or not is economic freedom. This is the fundamental right of every human to control his or her own labor and property. Here Hong Kong, part of the People's Republic of China, is No. 1. The United States is No. 12, according to the 2019 Index of Economic Freedom (produced by the Heritage Foundation). Hong Kong and Singapore are considered "free" by this standard; both Canada, at No. 8, and the United States are considered "mostly free."[6]

There are many reasons the winners on these lists achieved their status, but one thing is clear: They didn't do it all by themselves; other countries were involved. We are living in a world being rapidly changed by <mark>globalization</mark>—the trend of the world economy toward becoming a more interdependent system. Time and distance, which have been under assault for 150 years, have now virtually collapsed, as reflected in three important developments we shall discuss:[7]

1. The rise of the "global village" and electronic commerce.
2. The world becoming one market instead of many national ones.
3. The rise of both megafirms and Internet-enabled minifirms worldwide.

TABLE 4.1

Country Rankings for Competitiveness, 2019

1.	Singapore
2.	United States
3.	Hong Kong SAR
4.	Netherlands
5.	Switzerland
6.	Japan
7.	Germany
8.	Sweden
9.	United Kingdom
10.	Denmark

Source: K. Schwab, "Global Competitiveness Report 2019: How to End a Lost Decade of Productivity Growth," World Economic Forum, 2019, https://www.weforum.org/reports/how-to-end-a-decade-of-lost-productivity-growth.

The Rise of the "Global Village" and Electronic Commerce

The hallmark of great civilizations has been their great systems of communications. In the beginning, communication was based on transportation: The Roman Empire had its network of roads, as did other ancient civilizations, such as the Incas. Later, the great European powers had their far-flung navies. In the 19th century, the United States and Canada unified North America by building transcontinental railroads. Later the airplane reduced travel time between continents.

From Transportation to Communication Transportation began to yield to the electronic exchange of information. Beginning in 1844, the telegraph ended the short existence of the Pony Express and, beginning in 1876, found itself in competition with the telephone. The amplifying vacuum tube, invented in 1906, led to commercial radio. Television came into being in England in 1925. During the 1950s and 1960s, as television exploded throughout the world, communications philosopher Marshall McLuhan posed the notion of a "global village," where we all share our hopes, dreams, and fears in a "worldpool" of information. The **global village** refers to the "shrinking" of time and space as air travel and the electronic media have made it easier for the people around the globe to communicate with one another.

Then the world became even faster and smaller. When AT&T launched the first cellular communications system in 1983, it predicted there would be fewer than a million users by 2000. By 2021, there will be around 3.8 billion smartphone users worldwide.[8]

The Net, the Web, and the World Then came the Internet, the worldwide computer-linked "network of networks." Today, of the 7.7 billion people in the world, almost 59% are Internet users.[9] The arrival of the web quickly led to the introduction of **e-commerce**, or electronic commerce, the buying and selling of products and services through computer networks. U.S. online sales of goods surpassed $500 billion in 2018[10] and are projected to reach $970 billion by 2023.[11]

EXAMPLE Alibaba: The "Amazon of China"

The biggest U.S. e-commerce site is Amazon.com, which was started in 1994 by Jeffrey Bezos as an online bookstore and now offers an unimaginable stream of products and services that accounts for 50 cents of every dollar spent online in the United States.[12] If there are any Amazon challengers left in online retail, they may be coming from overseas. Consider Alibaba, the "Amazon of China." This organization is actually the world's largest and fastest-growing e-commerce company based on the total value of items it sells online.[13]

Alibaba was founded in 1999 to serve as a hub for small businesses to sell online and has grown into a leading global wholesale and retail marketplace and provider of cloud computing, digital media, and entertainment services. In a country with more than 800 million Internet users, the company sees itself as "the future infrastructure of commerce" and intends to last "at least 102 years" in order to span three centuries.[14] Hundreds of millions of users frequent its three separate websites, participating in transactions worth about $768 billion a year. That's more sales than Amazon, eBay, and JD.com (another Chinese Internet retailer) recently earned

combined.[15] In addition to its e-commerce sites, Alibaba offers a payment app called Alipay, through which users can pay cab drivers, restaurants, utility companies, and even their landlord.[16] The company also partnered with Ford to develop gigantic vending machines that allow car shoppers to take a car on a three-day test drive. The entire process takes around 10 minutes and customers who want to purchase the vehicle after the test drive can do so on the spot, even if financing is required.[17]

Jack Ma, the founder of Alibaba, stepped down as executive chairman in 2018. A former English teacher and now the richest man in China, Ma was rejected a lot in life. The key, he says, is not to let rejection keep you down for long. "Of course, you are not happy when people say 'no.' Have a good sleep, wake up, try it again."[18]

YOUR CALL

Alibaba does not have much of a presence in the United States. Does it make sense for the company to remain focused on its home market of China? Why or why not?

One Big World Market: The Global Economy

"We are seeing the results of things started in 1988 and 1989," said Rosabeth Moss Kantor of the Harvard Business School, referring to three historic global changes.[19] The first was in the late 1980s when the Berlin Wall came down, signaling the beginning of the end of communism in Eastern Europe. The second was when Asian countries began to open their economies to foreign investors. The third was the worldwide trend of governments deregulating their economies. These three events set up conditions by which goods, people, and money could move more freely throughout the world—a global economy. **The global economy refers to the increasing tendency of the economies of the world to interact with one another as one market instead of many national markets.**

It's no secret the economies of the world are increasingly tied together, connected by information arriving instantaneously through currency traders' screens, CNN news reports, Twitter feeds, text messages, and other technology. Money, represented by digital blips, changes hands globally in a matter of keystrokes. Let's consider the positive and negative effects of globalization.

Positive Effects   A global economy has a number of benefits. In the past, people on different continents could not interact without difficulty. The Internet, high-speed travel, and other innovations have lessened the "friction of distance," shrinking the world and eliminating borders.[20]

Spreading soda. A Coca-Cola employee unloads a truck in Phuket, Thailand. The company sells its products in over 200 countries and territories.
Lou Linwei/Alamy Stock Photo

Faster technological improvements can result from increased communication and information sharing, and as we've seen, many products and services can be produced more cheaply due to innovation and economies of scale.[21] People and information aren't the only two things moving quickly across the globe; money is as well. Electronic transfers and the ability to invest in developing countries has increased access to capital, allowing for greater market growth across different global economies.[22]

In addition, in some industries foreign firms are building plants in the United States, revitalizing some industrial areas. For example, in the automotive industry, megafirm foreign auto companies produce more vehicles in the United States than Ford, GM, and Fiat Chrysler combined.[23] In fact, Japanese automakers alone have invested $51 billion in manufacturing in the United States over the past few decades. This has led to the creation of 94,000 manufacturing jobs at U.S. plants, as well as 1.6 million indirect jobs, such as those at U.S. dealerships and suppliers.[24]

A global economy isn't just good for megafirms like auto manufacturers. Minifirms, which are considered small companies, also are thriving. The Internet and the World Wide Web allow almost anyone to be global, with two important results:

1. **Small companies can get started more easily.** Anyone can put goods or services online and sell on websites such as eBay, Shopify, Poshmark, and Craigslist. This wipes out the former competitive advantages of distribution and scope that large companies used to have.

2. **Small companies can maneuver faster.** Little companies can change direction faster, which gives them an advantage in terms of time and distance over large companies.

Negative Effects   The large-scale effects of the rise of global economy have included much-publicized job losses across the United States. Despite an apparent rise in protectionist sentiment in some of the world's largest economies, some of those jobs will not return. Other negative effects of globalization are more closely tied to individual managers' day-to-day challenges. These include potential threats to information security because data must be shared, possible loss of control over quality and standards because products or components are made hundreds or thousands of miles away, and the risk of hidden or unanticipated costs, especially transportation costs, that can offset some of the savings expected from moving manufacturing to countries with lower labor costs.[25] An interconnected world also has other risks. For example, if a nation is heavily depended on by others, and its economy falters, there can be instant regional or global instability.[26] ●

Craft beers. At Costco, craft beers account for 30% of the company's beer sales. What kind of threat do you think the merger of giant breweries Anheuser-Busch InBev (makers of Budweiser, Corona, Beck's) and SABMiller (Miller, Coors) pose to craft breweries?
David Caudery/Future Publishing/Getty Images

4.2 You and International Management

THE BIG PICTURE

Studying international management prepares you to work with foreign customers or suppliers, for a foreign firm in the United States, or for a U.S. firm overseas. Successful international managers aren't ethnocentric or polycentric but geocentric.

Can you see yourself working overseas? It can definitely be an advantage to your career. According to Hamilton Recruitment, you'll be able to improve your communication skills, gain insights into other cultures, and experience personal growth, among other benefits.[27] The following Example box explores how you might pursue a job overseas.

LO 4-2

Describe the characteristics of a successful international manager.

| EXAMPLE | Managing Your Career: Strategies for Landing That Global Gig |

Were you born between 1997 and 2012? If so, then you may share the global perspective desired by members of Gen Z. A Cite Research survey found that 75% of Gen Z college grads were more likely to work for a company that offers opportunities to work overseas. Moreover, a strong majority of Gen Z college grads are willing to forgo career advancement or financial gain, if it means they can work abroad.[28] If you are someone who wants to work abroad, how can you increase your chances of landing the job?

1. Brush up on your cultural awareness (an important career readiness skill), and your foreign language skills. Being able to converse freely in an overseas environment makes you valuable to employers of all kinds. We'll discuss these concepts in further detail later in the chapter.

2. Demonstrate your flexibility, one of the most important skills you will take abroad with you. A corporate communications intern who worked in Brussels had this to say

about the need for flexibility: "I was on a team with people from all over Europe and Asia, so in addition to a slight language barrier, our ethics, ideas, and methods almost never matched, which made for some challenges in communication. Working abroad taught me how to be flexible, bend what I know about my field, and adapt it to fit any environment or client's needs."[29]

3. If you are already employed, find out whether your current company has positions overseas, and research the responsibilities and requirements of these jobs. See whether your boss will support you or find a mentor in the company who will (this might be someone who currently holds or has recently returned from such an assignment).

4. Build your network of people who work for companies with overseas opportunities and tell them what you're looking for and what you can offer.

5. Look into jobs with entry requirements you may already meet, such as tutoring or teaching English abroad. These may not be the highest-paying openings, but once in a foreign country, you can more easily make local connections to expand your opportunities and use your experience to move up.

YOUR CALL

What are the key challenges in pursuing an international job after graduation?

Foreign experience demonstrates independence, resourcefulness, and entrepreneurship, according to management recruiters. "You are interested in that person who can move quickly and is nimble and has an inquiring mind," says one. People who have worked and supported themselves overseas, she says, tend to be adaptive and inquisitive—valuable skills in today's workplace.[30] This outlook represents the career readiness competency of **cross-cultural awareness, defined as the ability to operate in different cultural settings.** This competency is expected to become more important over the next decade in response to our globally connected world. According to the Institute for the Future, "In a truly globally connected world, a worker's skill set could see them posted in any number of locations. . . . This demands specific content, such as linguistic skills, but also adaptability to changing circumstances and an ability to sense and respond to new contexts."[31]

Why Learn about International Management?

International management is management that oversees the conduct of operations in or with organizations in foreign countries, whether it's through a multinational corporation or a multinational organization.

Multinational Corporations   A **multinational corporation,** or multinational enterprise, is a business firm with operations in several countries. For example, McDonald's is a well-known multinational corporation with more than 36,000 restaurants in over 100 countries.[32] In terms of sales revenue, the 10 largest American multinational corporations in 2019 were Wal-Mart Stores, ExxonMobil, Apple, Berkshire Hathaway, Amazon, UnitedHealth Group, McKesson, CVS Health, AT&T, and AmerisourceBergen.[33] The largest foreign firms were the oil companies SinoPec Group, Royal Dutch Shell (Netherlands), and PetroChina, followed by State Grid (utilities, China). Automakers Volkswagen (Germany) and Toyota Motor (Japan) are also on the list.[34]

Multinational Organizations   A **multinational organization** is a nonprofit organization with operations in several countries. Examples are the World Health Organization, the International Red Cross, and the Church of Latter Day Saints.

Even if in the coming years you never travel to the wider world outside North America (an unlikely proposition, we think), the world will surely come to you. That, in a nutshell, is why you need to learn about international management.

More specifically, consider yourself in the following situations:

You May Deal with Foreign Customers or Partners   While working for a U.S. company you may have to deal with foreign customers. Or you may have to work with a foreign company in some sort of joint venture. The people you're dealing with may be outside the United States or visitors to the country. Either way you would hate to blow a deal—and maybe all future deals—because you were ignorant of some cultural aspects you could have known about.

You May Deal with Foreign Employees or Suppliers   You may have to purchase important components, raw materials, or services for your U.S. employer from a foreign supplier. And you never know where foreign practices may diverge from what you're accustomed to. Many software developer jobs, for instance, have moved outside the United States to places such as India, New Zealand, and Eastern Europe. Among the U.S. tech companies with overseas subsidiaries (and plenty of cash there as well) are Apple, Microsoft, Cisco, Oracle, Alphabet, and Intel.[35]

You May Work for a Foreign Firm in the United States   You may sometime take a job with a foreign firm doing business in the United States, such as an electronics, pharmaceutical, or car company. And you'll have to deal with managers above and below you whose outlook is different from yours. For instance, Japanese companies, with their emphasis on correctness and face saving, operate in significantly different ways from U.S. companies.

Sometimes it is even hard to know whether a U.S. company actually has foreign ownership. For example, among some classic U.S. brands that are now foreign owned are Anheuser-Busch, sold to InBev of Belgium; Ben & Jerry's, owned by multinational giant Unilever; Burger King, purchased by Restaurant Brands International of Canada; Trader Joe's, a subsidiary of German supermarket chain Aldi Nord; General Electric's appliance division, owned by China's Haier, the largest appliance company in the world; American Apparel, bought by Gildan Activewear, a Canadian clothier; and 7-Eleven, owned by the Japanese retail group Seven & I Holdings.[36]

Globalized boardrooms. A group of business people from different countries sit in a board room. Company boards around the world are becoming more and more diverse as foreign ownership of firms increases. What benefits and challenges do you see associated with this shift? Andersen Ross/Blend Images LLC

You May Work for a U.S. Firm outside the United States—or for a Foreign One   You might easily find yourself working abroad in the foreign operation of a U.S. company. Most big U.S. corporations have overseas subsidiaries or divisions. On the other hand, you might also work for a foreign firm in a foreign country, such as a big Indian company in Bangalore or Mumbai.

The Successful International Manager: Geocentric, Not Ethnocentric or Polycentric

Maybe you don't really care that you don't have much understanding of the foreign culture you're dealing with. "What's the point?" you may think. "The main thing is to get the job done." Certainly there are international firms with managers who have this perspective. They are called *ethnocentric*, one of three primary attitudes among international managers, the other two being *polycentric* and *geocentric*.[37]

Ethnocentric Managers—"We Know Best"   What do foreign executives fluent in English think when they hear Americans using an endless array of baseball, basketball, and football phrases (such as "out of left field" or "Hail Mary pass")? **Ethnocentric managers** believe that their native country, culture, language, and behavior are superior to all others. Ethnocentric thinkers tend to believe that they can export the managers and practices of their home countries to anywhere in the world and that they will be more capable and reliable. Often, the ethnocentric viewpoint is less attributable to prejudice than it is to ignorance. For example, people with cross-cultural awareness are less likely to hold ethnocentric viewpoints.[38] Ethnocentrism might also be called **parochialism**—that is, a narrow view in which people see things solely through their own perspective.

Ethnocentric views also affect our purchasing decisions. Some people believe that we should only purchase products made in our home country.[39] What are your views about being an ethnocentric consumer? You can find out by taking Self-Assessment 4.1.

SELF-ASSESSMENT 4.1

Assessing Your Consumer Ethnocentrism

This survey is designed to assess your consumer ethnocentrism. Please be prepared to answer these questions if your instructor has assigned Self-Assessment 4.1 in Connect.

1. Are you surprised by the results? What do they suggest about your purchasing decisions? What are the pros and cons of being an ethnocentric consumer?

2. How do American companies, associations, and unions encourage us to be ethnocentric consumers?

Polycentric Managers—"They Know Best"   **Polycentric managers** take the view that native managers in the foreign offices best understand native personnel and practices, and so the home office should leave them alone. Thus, the attitude of polycentric managers is nearly the opposite of that of ethnocentric managers.

Geocentric Managers—"What's Best Is What's Effective, Regardless of Origin"   **Geocentric managers** accept that there are differences and similarities between home and foreign personnel and practices and that they should use whatever techniques are most effective. Clearly, being an ethno- or polycentric manager takes less work. But the payoff for being a geocentric manager can be far greater. ●

4.3 Why and How Companies Expand Internationally

THE BIG PICTURE

Multinationals expand to take advantage of availability of supplies, new markets, lower labor costs, access to finance capital, or avoidance of tariffs and import quotas. Five ways they do so are by global outsourcing; importing, exporting, and countertrading; licensing and franchising; joint ventures; and wholly owned subsidiaries.

Who makes Apple's iPhone? The iPhone is a good example of the complexity of Apple's supply chain. The accelerometer comes from Germany; the battery comes from China; a Japanese company makes the camera, compass, and LCD screen; the gyroscope comes from Switzerland; and the glass screen, Wi-Fi chip, and audio chips are made in the U.S.[40]

LO 4-3

Outline the ways in which companies can expand internationally.

Where is Netflix going for new business as its U.S. growth slows? Now that it is streaming content in over 190 countries around the world and in 20 different languages, the company has more international than U.S. subscribers.[41]

There are many reasons U.S. companies are going global. Let us consider why and how they are expanding beyond U.S. borders.

Why Companies Expand Internationally

Many a company has made the deliberate decision to restrict selling its product or service to just its own country. Is anything wrong with that?

The answer is: It depends. It would probably have been a serious mistake for NEC, Sony, or Hitachi to have limited their markets solely to Japan during the 1990s, a time when the country was in an economic slump and Japanese consumers weren't consuming. During that same period, however, some American banks might have been

A Middle Eastern Gem. The gross domestic product of Dubai has grown from 82 billion in U.S. dollars in 2008 to 425 billion in 2019. This tremendous economic growth has resulted in the development of the beautiful skyscrapers at the Dubai Marina in the United Arab Emirates. Boule/Shutterstock

better off not making loans abroad, when the U.S. economy was booming but foreign economies were not. Going international or not going international—it can be risky either way.

Why, then, do companies expand internationally? There are at least five reasons, all of which have to do with making or saving money.

1. Availability of Supplies Mining companies, banana growers, sellers of hard woods—all have to go where their basic supplies or raw materials are located. For years oil companies, for example, expanded their activities outside the United States to seek cheaper or more plentiful sources of oil.

2. New Markets Sometimes a company will find, as cigarette makers have, that demand for their product has declined domestically but they can still make money overseas. Or sometimes a company will launch a concerted effort to expand into foreign markets, as Coca-Cola did under the leadership of legendary CEO Robert Goizueta. Costco is another U.S. company that has been successful internationally. Taking advantage of a growing middle class in China, the warehouse opened its first store in Shanghai in August 2019 to crowds so large it was forced to suspend business due to safety concerns. Amazon expanded to Australia in 2017 and opened its third fulfillment center down under in 2019.[42]

3. Lower Labor Costs   The decline in manufacturing jobs in the United States is partly attributable to the fact that U.S. companies have found it cheaper to manufacture outside the States. For example, the rationale for using **maquiladoras**—foreign-owned **manufacturing plants allowed to operate in Mexico with special privileges in return for employing Mexican citizens**—is that they provide less expensive labor for assembling everything from appliances to cars. Sometimes companies even move operations from one foreign country to another in order to reduce labor costs. For example, Apple moved a significant portion of iPhone production from China to India, where production costs are nearly 60% less than in China.[43]

Even professional or service types of jobs, such as computer programming, may be shipped overseas.

4. Access to Finance Capital   Companies may be enticed into going abroad by the prospects of capital put up by foreign companies or subsidies from foreign governments. A sovereign wealth fund is a government-owned investment fund that often invests in foreign assets. China's sovereign wealth fund, China Investment Company (CIC), has started in a joint venture with Goldman Sachs called the China-U.S. Industrial Cooperation Fund. The joint venture aims to invest as much as $5 billion in U.S. industrial firms.[44] However, as CIC and China make more foreign investments, we're seeing the rise of protectionism in some countries and regions, be it the U.S. or Europe. For example, CIC President Ju Weimin said the U.S.–China trade war is causing the sovereign-wealth fund to be "more cautious about investing in the U.S."[45]

5. Avoidance of Tariffs and Import Quotas   Countries place tariffs (fees) on imported goods or impose import quotas—limitations on the numbers of products allowed in—for the purpose of protecting their own domestic industries. For example, Japan imposes tariffs on agricultural products, such as rice, imported from the United States. To avoid these penalties, a company might create a subsidiary to produce the product in the foreign country. Whirlpool, for example, has foreign subsidiaries to produce appliances overseas.

How Companies Expand Internationally

Most companies don't start out to be multinationals. Generally, they edge their way into international business, at first making minimal investments and taking minimal risks. *(See Figure 4.1.)*

Let's consider the five ways of expanding internationally shown in the figure.

FIGURE 4.1

Five ways of expanding internationally

These range from lowest risk and investment (*left*) to highest risk and investment (*right*).

| Global outsourcing | Importing, exporting, & countertrading | Licensing & franchising | Joint ventures | Wholly owned subsidiaries |

Lowest risk & investment ← → *Highest risk & investment*

1. Global Outsourcing

A common practice of many companies, ==outsourcing== is defined as using suppliers outside the company to provide goods and services. For example, airlines farm out a lot of aircraft maintenance to other companies. Management philosopher Peter Drucker believed that in the near future organizations might be outsourcing all work that consists of "support services"—such as information systems—because they don't generate revenue for the company.

Global outsourcing extends this technique outside the United States. ==Global outsourcing==, or ==offshoring==, is defined as using suppliers outside the United States to provide labor, goods, or services. The reason may be that the foreign supplier has resources not available in the United States, such as Italian marble. Or the supplier may have special expertise, such as weavers in Pakistan. Or—more likely these days—the supplier's labor is cheaper than American labor. As a manager, your first business trip outside the United States might be to inspect the production lines of one of your outsourcing suppliers. The nearby Example box discusses jobs that are prone to outsourcing.

However, in a countertrend called "reshoring," some companies are moving production back home in order to respond faster and more flexibly to consumer trends. The Reshoring Institute conducted a survey of global manufacturers in 2019 and found that more than half of the executives surveyed were planning or considering reshoring activities in the next five years.[46] Amgen, a large biopharmaceutical company, announced in 2018 that it was planning to reshore 1,600 manufacturing jobs to the United States. Other large American companies, such as Dow Chemical and Intel, have reshored 2,900 and 4,000 jobs, respectively, between 2010 and 2018.[47]

2. Importing, Exporting, and Countertrading

When ==importing==, a company buys goods outside the country and resells them domestically. Nothing might seem to be more American than Caterpillar tractors, but they are made not only in the United States but also in Mexico, from which they are imported and made available for sale in the United States.[48] Many of the products we use are imported, ranging from LG televisions (South Korea) to Chevron gasoline (Saudi Arabia) to Honda snowblowers (Japan).

EXAMPLE   Global Outsourcing: Which Jobs Have Gone Overseas?

Workers in the United States are rightly concerned about the changing jobs picture, brought about in part by offshoring of work to low-wage countries such as Vietnam, India, and the Philippines. Companies look to reduce their production costs and, thereby, the prices they must charge their customers. Few of the more than 14 million jobs that have been lost will be replaced, and according to the U.S. Bureau of Labor Statistics, less than 8% of U.S. workers are employed in manufacturing today.[49] In a survey of working adults, more than half said it would be "essential for them to get training and develop new skills throughout their work life in order to keep up with changes in the workplace," and nearly half had taken a class to improve their work skills during the last year.[50]

Which Jobs Will Likely Remain in the United States? It is difficult to predict which jobs will remain in the United States because even the Bureau of Labor Statistics often can't make accurate predictions. However, jobs that endure may share certain traits regardless of the industry they serve:[51]

- **Face-to-face.** Some jobs consist of *face-to-face contact*, such as a civil engineer who needs to scope a site.

- **Physical contact.** Other jobs require *physical contact*, such as those of dentists, plumbers, massage therapists, gardeners, and carpenters.

- **Complex patterns.** Other jobs rely on the human ability to *recognize complex patterns*, which is hard to automate, such as a physician's ability to diagnose an unusual disease (even if the X-rays are read by a radiologist overseas).

What Does the Future Look Like? Wage differences across countries are beginning to shrink, thanks in part to the United States' slow recovery from the 2008 recession and in part to the rising standard of living in many developing countries with educated, English-speaking workers who hold those outsourced jobs.[52] This means some service jobs, such as call-center workers, may come back to the United States if the savings from outsourcing are eliminated. It is too early to tell whether many U.S.

companies will take advantage of lower corporate tax rates and other possible incentives to bring jobs back to the United States or whether foreign companies will follow the lead of Japanese and German automakers to open production plants on U.S. shores. In the meantime, some workers may face a bigger threat from the increasing sophistication of robots and the use of artificial intelligence (AI) in the domestic workplace than from cheap labor oversees.

One fact remains clear, however: The more education you have, the more likely you are to keep your footing during times of economic change. For example, in November 2019 the unemployment rate for all U.S. workers was roughly 3.5%, but if you had a college degree, that number decreased to 2.0%. Chances are you'll make more money as well. The Bureau of Labor Statistics reported in 2018 that Americans with a bachelor's degree had median weekly earnings of $1,173 versus $712 for those with only a high school diploma.[53]

YOUR CALL

What kind of job or jobs are you interested in that would seem to provide you with some hope of steady employment in a fast-changing world?

TABLE 4.2

Top 10 Exporting Countries, 2019

| 1. China |
| 2. United States |
| 3. Germany |
| 4. Netherlands |
| 5. Japan |
| 6. France |
| 7. South Korea |
| 8. Hong Kong |
| 9. Italy |
| 10. United Kingdom |

Source: "Top 20 export countries worldwide in 2019," Statista, May 4, 2020, https://www.statista.com/statistics/264623/leading-export-countries-worldwide/.

When **exporting**, a company produces goods domestically and sells them outside the country. China was the world's top export country in 2019 and the United States was second (*see Table 4.2*). America's top exports include machinery and computers, mineral fuels, electrical machinery, aircraft, and vehicles.[54]

Sometimes other countries may wish to import U.S. goods but lack the currency to pay for them. In that case, the exporting U.S. company may resort to **countertrading**—that is, bartering goods for goods. When the Russian ruble plunged in value in 1998, some goods became a better medium of exchange than currency.

3. Licensing and Franchising   Licensing and franchising are two aspects of the same thing, although licensing is used by manufacturing companies and franchising is used more frequently by service companies.

In **licensing**, a company allows a foreign company to pay it a fee to make or distribute the first company's product or service. For example, the DuPont might license a company in Brazil to make Teflon, the nonstick substance that is found on some frying pans. Thus, DuPont, the licensor, can make money without having to invest large sums to conduct business directly in a foreign company. Moreover, the Brazilian firm, the licensee, knows the local market better than DuPont probably would.

Hotel franchises. A Marriott hotel in Dubai, United Arab Emirates. The hotel franchise is the third-largest in the world with approximately 6,000 properties. Artur Widak/Getty Images

Franchising is a form of licensing in which a company allows a foreign company to pay it a fee and a share of the profit in return for using the first company's brand name and a package of materials and services. For example, Burger King, Hertz, and Hilton Hotels, which are all well-known brands, might provide the use of their names plus their operating know-how (facility design, equipment, recipes, management systems) to companies in the Philippines in return for an up-front fee plus a percentage of the profits.

By now so-called U.S. stores are opening everywhere, and many franchise chains are experiencing the bulk of their growth overseas. McDonald's dominates the Franchise Direct 2019 report, followed by Burger King, Pizza Hut, Marriott, and Kentucky Fried Chicken.[55] We'll discuss franchising further when we cover entrepreneurship in Learning Module 2.

4. Joint Ventures   *Strategic allies* (described in Chapter 3) are two organizations that have joined forces to realize strategic advantages that neither would have if operating alone. A U.S. firm may form a **joint venture**, also known as a strategic alliance, with a foreign company to share the risks and rewards of starting a new enterprise together in a foreign country. For instance, in 2019 the U.S. Department of Transportation approved a joint venture between American Airlines and Qantas for new routes to foreign countries.[56] The Ford Motor Company and India-based Mahindra signed a joint venture agreement in October 2019 to "develop, market and distribute Ford brand vehicles in India and Ford brand and Mahindra brand vehicles in high-growth emerging markets around the world."[57]

Sometimes a joint venture is the only way a U.S. company can have a presence in a certain country, whose laws may forbid foreigners from ownership. For example, in China, this is the only way foreign cars may be sold in that country.

5. Wholly Owned Subsidiaries   A **wholly owned subsidiary** is a foreign subsidiary that is totally owned and controlled by an organization. The foreign subsidiary may be an existing company that is purchased outright. For example, Mastercard purchased Nets, a Denmark-based electronic payments platform, in 2019 for $3.19 billion.[58] A **greenfield venture** is a foreign subsidiary that the owning organization has built from scratch. ●

4.4 The World of Free Trade: Regional Economic Cooperation and Competition

THE BIG PICTURE

Barriers to free trade include tariffs, import quotas, and embargoes. Organizations promoting international trade are the World Trade Organization, the World Bank, and the International Monetary Fund. We discuss two major trading blocs, NAFTA (now USMCA) and the EU, as well as the Trans-Pacific Partnership. Major competitors with the United States are the "BRICS" countries—Brazil, Russia, India, China, and South Africa.

If you live in the United States, you see foreign products on a daily basis—cars, appliances, clothes, foods, beers, wines, and so on. Based on what you see every day, which countries would you think are our most important trading partners? China? Japan? Germany? United Kingdom? South Korea?

These five countries do indeed appear among the top leading U.S. trading partners. Interestingly, however, our foremost trading partners are our immediate neighbors—Canada and Mexico—whose products may not be quite so visible. *(See Table 4.3.)*

LO 4-4

Discuss barriers to free trade and ways companies try to overcome them.

TABLE 4.3 Top U.S. Trading Partners in Goods, September 2019

TOP 10 NATIONS THE U.S. EXPORTS TO	TOP 10 NATIONS THE U.S. IMPORTS FROM
1. Canada	1. China
2. Mexico	2. Mexico
3. China	3. Canada
4. United Kingdom	4. Japan
5. Japan	5. Germany
6. Germany	6. Vietnam
7. South Korea	7. South Korea
8. Netherlands	8. Ireland
9. Brazil	9. United Kingdom
10. Hong Kong	10. India

Source: U.S. Census Bureau, "Top Trading Partners—September 2019," https://www.census.gov/foreign-trade/statistics/highlights/top/top1909cm.html (accessed November 10, 2019).

Let's begin to consider free trade, the movement of goods and services among nations without political or economic obstruction.

Barriers to International Trade

Countries often use trade protectionism—the use of government regulations to limit the import of goods and services—to protect their domestic industries against foreign competition. The justification they often use is that this saves jobs. Actually, protectionism is not considered beneficial, mainly because of what it does to the overall trading atmosphere.

The devices by which countries try to exert protectionism consist of *tariffs*, *import quotas*, and *trade embargoes* and *sanctions*.

1. Tariffs A tariff is a trade barrier in the form of a customs duty, or tax, levied mainly on imports. At one time, for instance, to protect the American shoe industry, the United States imposed a tariff on Italian shoes. Actually, there are two types of tariffs: One, called a *revenue tariff*, is designed simply to raise money for the government, such as a tax on all oil imported into the United States. The other, which concerns us more, is a *protective tariff*, which is intended to raise the price of imported goods to make the prices of domestic products more competitive.

Between 2018 and 2019, the Trump administration imposed $550 billion worth of tariffs on Chinese goods, sparking what experts have called the "U.S.–China Trade War." These goods range from footwear to diapers to flat-screen televisions. In response, China retaliated with $185 billion worth of tariffs on American goods.[59]

2. Import Quotas An import quota is a trade barrier in the form of a limit on the numbers of a product that can be imported. Like a tariff, its intent is to protect domestic industry by restricting the availability of foreign products. Consumers in countries using tariffs and import quotas are likely to find price increases due to the reduction of imported products.[60] For example, China has an import quota on 17 categories of scrap metals.[61]

Quotas are designed to prevent dumping, the practice of a foreign company's exporting products abroad at a lower price than the price in the home market—or even below the costs of production—in order to drive down the price of the domestic product. In October 2019, the U.S. Commerce Department began an antidumping investigation into imports of glass containers from China. The department is trying to determine "whether certain glass containers from China are being dumped in the United States and to determine if producers from this country are receiving unfair subsidies."[62]

3. Sanctions and Embargoes A sanction is the trade prohibition on certain types of products, services, or technology to another country for specific reasons, including nuclear nonproliferation, terrorism, and humanitarian purposes. The key words here are *certain types*. For example, the U.S. broke diplomatic relations with Iran and levied its first round of sanctions against the country in 1980 after Iranian radicals captured 52 Americans at the U.S. Embassy in Tehran in November 1979 and held them hostage for 444 days. The Reagan administration declared Iran a state sponsor of terrorism in 1983, allowing for the implementation of broader sanctions. The White House has

The U.S. used import quotas against cars made in South Korea in the 1980s. Although these particular quotas are long gone, the U.S. has import quotas on many products including steel, beef, and dairy. Do you think the use of import quotas is a good thing over the long term? Monty Rakusen/Cultura/Getty Images

increased sanctions on Iran under most administrations since then, targeting the Middle Eastern nation's oil revenue and other vital exports.[63]

An **embargo** is a complete ban or prohibition of trade of one country with another so that no goods or services can be imported or exported from or to the embargoed nation. The key word here is *complete*, as in "complete ban." In response to North Korea's ramped-up testing of intercontinental ballistic missiles, for example, the Trump administration has pressured China to completely cut off its sale of oil and oil products to North Korea.[64] China is North Korea's chief trading partner.[65]

A sanction is different from an embargo. Sanctions may be considered "partial embargoes," since they restrict trade in certain areas.[66] For instance, the United States has trade sanctions with Iran that prohibit the export of any material that would help Iran in its nuclear program, but food and medicine are generally exempt from sanctions.[67]

Organizations Promoting International Trade

In the 1920s, the institution of tariff barriers did not so much protect jobs as depress the demand for goods and services, thereby leading to the loss of jobs anyway—and the massive unemployment of the Great Depression of the 1930s.[68] As a result of this lesson, after World War II the advanced nations of the world began to realize that if all countries could freely exchange the products that each could produce most efficiently, this would lead to lower prices all around. Thus began the removal of barriers to free trade.

The three principal organizations designed to facilitate international trade are the *World Trade Organization*, the *World Bank*, and the *International Monetary Fund*. Table 4.4 summarizes the background on each organization.

TABLE 4.4   Organizations Promoting International Trade

ORGANIZATIONS PROMOTING INTERNATIONAL TRADE				
PRINCIPAL ORGANIZATIONS	**PURPOSE**	**ESTABLISHED**	**MEMBER COUNTERS**	**IN THE NEWS**
World Trade Organization (WTO)	To monitor and enforce trade agreements	1995 in Geneva to replace the General Agreement on Tariffs and Trade	164	In 2019, the WTO launched the Osaka Declaration, which promotes the importance of data in a digital economy.*
World Bank	To provide low-interest loans to developing nations for improving transportation, education, health, and telecommunications	After WWII to help European countries rebuild	189	In November 2019, the World Bank launched a global learning target meant to cut the learning poverty rate by at least half by 2030. Currently, data shows that 53% of children in low- and middle-income countries suffer from learning poverty.**
International Monetary Fund (IMF)	Designed to assist in smoothing the flow of money between nations	1945	189	A 2019 IMF study found that the world needs a massive carbon tax in the next ten years to limit climate change. The tax would be $75 per ton by 2030.***

Sources:* "Azevêdo Joins Prime Minister Abe and Other Leaders to Launch 'Osaka Track' on the Digital Economy," WTO, June 28, 2019, https://www.wto.org/english/news_e/news19_e/dgra_28jun19_e.htm.

***"Ending Learning Poverty: A Target to Galvanize Action on Literacy," World Bank, November 8, 2019, https://www.worldbank.org/en/news/immersive-story/2019/11/06/a-learning-target-for-a-learning-revolution.

***C. Mooney and A. Freedman, "The World Needs a Massive Carbon Tax in Just 10 Years to Limit Climate Change, IMF Say," The Washington Post, October 10, 2019, https://www.washingtonpost.com/climate-environment/2019/10/10/world-needs-massive-carbon-tax-just-years-limit-climate-change-imf-says/.

Major Trading Blocs

A **trading bloc**, also known as an economic community, is a group of nations within a geographical region that have agreed to remove trade barriers with one another. The first trading blocs we'll consider are *NAFTA/USMCA* and the *European Union*. We'll then turn our focus to others.

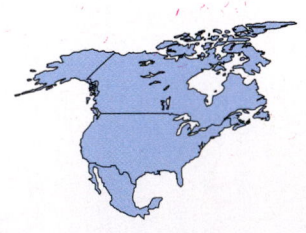

NAFTA & USMCA—Trade Across North America   Formed in 1994, the **North American Free Trade Agreement (NAFTA)** was a trading bloc consisting of the United States, Canada, and Mexico, encompassing **444 million people**. The agreement was supposed to eliminate 99% of the tariffs and quotas among these countries, allowing for freer flow of goods, services, and capital in North America. While many predicted the pact would cost the United States thousands of jobs, it seems to have both lost and created employment, while some of the benefits that Mexico would have enjoyed, as the NAFTA partner with the lowest labor costs, went to China instead when that country's low-wage economy began to boom. It is difficult to isolate all the real effects of the trade agreement, given the many other factors in each country's economy, but overall, the United States appears to have lost low-skilled manufacturing jobs and gained employment in autos and aerospace, according to the Economic Policy Institute.[69]

The United States, Mexico, and Canada renegotiated NAFTA in November 2018, drafting a new policy known as the United States–Mexico–Canada Agreement (USMCA). The new agreement includes new chapters covering digital trade, anti-corruption, and good regulatory practices. Congress approved the USMCA in January 2020, and it took effect later that year.[70]

The EU—The 27 Countries of the European Union
Formed in 1957, the European Union (EU) consists of 27 trading partners in Europe, covering nearly 500 million consumers.

Nearly all internal trade barriers have been eliminated (including movement of labor between countries), making the EU a union of borderless neighbors and one of the world's largest free markets. The EU had a gross domestic product of approximately $19.9 trillion in 2019.[71]

Recently, the influx of thousands of refugees pouring out of war-torn and poverty-stricken nations in the Middle East and Africa, including many middle-class Syrians, has put more pressure on the European Union, including calls to either reduce or severely limit free movement across Europe's borders. The EU also faces challenges to its founding principles from the apparent increase in populist and nationalist sentiments in some member countries. "We are seeing nationalism, populism and in a lot of countries a polarized atmosphere," said Germany's leader Angela Merkel in early 2018.[72] A 2019 study published by the European Central Bank suggests that protectionism, spurred by these populist and nationalist sentiments, may harm the trading bloc's growth.[73]

Table 4.5 describes four other trading blocs—APEC, ASEAN, Mercosur, and CAFTA.

TRADING BLOC	COUNTRIES	PURPOSES
Asia-Pacific Economic Cooperation (APEC)	21 Pacific Rim countries, most with a Pacific coastline, including the U.S., Canada, and China	To improve economic and political ties and to reduce tariffs and other trade barriers across the Asia-Pacific region
Association of Southeast Asian Nations (ASEAN)	10 countries in Asia, comprising a market of 610 million people: Brunei, Cambodia, Indonesia, Laos, Malaysia, Myanmar (Burma), the Philippines, Singapore, Thailand, and Vietnam	To reduce trade barriers among member countries. A China-ASEAN Free Trade Area was established in 2010, the largest free trade area in the world in terms of population.
Mercosur	Largest trade bloc in Latin America, with 5 core members—Argentina, Brazil, Paraguay, Uruguay, and Venezuela (currently suspended) — and 7 associate members: Bolivia, Chile, Colombia, Ecuador, Guyana, Peru, and Suriname	To reduce tariffs by 75% and achieve full economic integration. The alliance is also negotiating trade agreements with NAFTA, the EU, and Japan.
Central America Free Trade Agreement (CAFTA-DR)	Costa Rica, the Dominican Republic, El Salvador, Guatemala, Honduras, Nicaragua, and the U.S.	To reduce tariffs and other barriers to free trade

TABLE 4.5
Four Other Important Trading Blocs

Source: Brian Williams.

The Trans-Pacific Partnership—11 Pacific Rim Countries

Negotiated over seven years, the **Trans-Pacific Partnership (TPP)** is a trade agreement among **11 Pacific Rim countries**. It was signed on February 4, 2016. The United States, originally a party to the agreement, withdrew from the pact under the Trump administration; remaining members are Australia, Brunei, Canada, Chile, Japan, Malaysia, Mexico, New Zealand, Peru, Singapore, and Vietnam. The United States could rejoin the agreement in the future but is not currently expected to do so.[74]

Over time, the TPP will remove several additional barriers to trade, including most tariffs, and set commercial rules for everything from labor and environmental standards to drug patents. A World Bank study found that Japan, Vietnam, and Malaysia would get a big economic boost from the TPP (from increasing their exports), while North American countries would see much smaller gains.[75]

Show me the money! The United Nations recognizes 180 currencies that are used in 195 countries across the world.

Maria Toutoudaki/Getty Images

Most Favored Nation Trading Status

Besides joining together in trade blocs, countries will also extend special, "most favored nation" trading privileges to one another. **Most favored nation** trading status describes a condition in which a country grants other countries favorable trading treatment such as the reduction of import duties. The purpose is to promote stronger and more stable ties between companies in the two countries.

Exchange Rates

The **exchange rate** is the rate at which the currency of one area or country can be exchanged for the currency of another. Americans

Get out much? The number of U.S. passports issued each year has held steady over the past few years, reaching more than 20 million in 2019, according to the State Department. How does travel figure in your career plans?

gilaxia/iStock/Getty Images

deal in dollars with each other, but beyond the U.S. border we have to deal with pounds in England, euros in Europe, pesos in Mexico, and yuan in China. Because of changing economic conditions, the values of currencies fluctuate in relation to each other, so that sometimes a U.S. dollar, for example, will buy more goods and sometimes it will buy less.

EXAMPLE   Dealing with Currency Exchange—How Much Do Those Jeans *Really* Cost?

Assume that $1 trades equal to 1 British pound, symbolized by £1. Thus, an item that costs 3 pounds (£3) can be bought for $3. If the exchange rate changes so that $1 buys £1.5, then an item that costs £3 can be bought for $2 (the dollar is said to be "stronger" against the pound). If the rate changes so that $1 buys only £0.5, an item that costs £6 can be purchased for $9 (the dollar is "weaker").[76] In late 2019, the dollar was stronger, buying £.78, whereas back in 2014, it was weaker, averaging £.59. (Stated another way, £1 bought $1.68 in April 2014 and $1.28 in November 2019.)

How the Exchange Rate Matters. As this is written, the dollar is strong and the pound is weak, so that $1 will buy £.78. Thus, staying in London became less expensive for U.S. travelers.

A hotel room that rents for £100 cost a U.S. visitor $168 in 2014, but only $128 in 2019. Indeed, if during those years, 2014 to 2019, you were living in England working for a U.S. company and were paid in dollars, your standard of living went up.

The Varying Cost of Living for Different Cities. Prices also vary among countries and cities throughout the world, with the standard of living of London, say, being 20% more than that of Chicago.[77] Table 4.6 provides a sense of what a U.S. visitor's purchasing power is worth in London when $1 equals £.78 (or £1 equals $1.28)—the exchange rate in November 2019. Consider these prices for various goods in Chicago versus London (estimated in U.S. dollars, computed on *www.expatistan.com*):

TABLE 4.6   Comparison of Prices in Chicago and London

AVERAGE COSTS FOR:	CHICAGO[78]	LONDON[79]
2-liter Coke	$1.85	$2.42
Combo meal (Big Mac or similar)	$8.00	$8.00
Monthly rent, furnished studio (expensive area)	$2,158.00	$3,108.00
Monthly rent, furnished studio (average area)	$1,534.00	$2,543.00
Pair of designer jeans	$50.00	$99.00
Nike or similar sports shoes	$98.00	$96.00
1 liter (1/4 gallon) of gas	$0.85	$1.65
Two movie tickets	$24.00	$31.00

With this example, you can see why it's important to understand how exchange rates work and what value your U.S. dollars actually have.

YOUR CALL

Planning to visit any EU countries (e.g., Germany, France) that use the euro? Go online to *www.x-rates.com* and figure out the

exchange rate of the U.S. dollar and that country's currency. Then go to *www.expatistan.com* and figure out what things cost in that country's principal city versus a U.S. city near you. Could you afford to go?

The BRICS Countries: Important International Competitors

Coined by a financial analyst who saw the countries as promising markets for finance capital in the 21st century, the term *BRICS* stands for the five major emerging economies of Brazil, Russia, India, China, and South Africa.[80] *(See Table 4.7.)*

TABLE 4.7   BRICS Countries, 2018

	POPULATION	GDP IN US$ (millions)	GDP PER CAPITA (US$)	GROWTH RATE
China	1,395,380,000	$13,368,073M	$9,580	6.6%
India	1,352,617,328	2,718,732M	2,010	6.8
Brazil	209,469,333	1,867,818M	8,917	1.1
Russia	146,800,000	1,657,290M	11,289	2.3
South Africa	57,939,000	368,135M	6,354	0.8
For comparison, U.S.	327,200,000	20,500,000M	54,541	3.1

Sources: Country Economy, "BRICS 2019," https://countryeconomy.com/countries/groups/brics (accessed November 10, 2019); and Trading Economics, "United States GDP per Capita," https://tradingeconomics.com/united-states/gdp-per-capita (accessed November 10, 2019).

Though not a trading bloc as such, the BRICS are important because they hold 40% of the world's population. By comparison, the United States has just about 4.3% of the world's population.[81] Let's consider the largest of these countries in the order of their population size: China, India, and Brazil.

China   China's economy is now the second-largest in the world after that of the United States, and it may soon be the largest based on its strengths in manufacturing. The country's middle class has expanded significantly with more than 30% of its urban population considered middle class, compared to just 4% in 2000. A McKinsey & Company study predicts that 76% of China's urban population will enter the middle class by 2022.[82]

India   If China is well known for its manufacturing advantages, India's advantages have been its large English-speaking population, its technological and scientific expertise, and its reputation in services, such as "back office" accounting systems and software engineering. Services, and especially IT, make up almost two-thirds of India's GDP; its middle class now accounts for 8% percent of the world's total, up from 1% in the 1990s.[83] Unfortunately, India's economy has been struggling as of late because its middle class is spending less. This created a deceleration of one of the world's major fast-growing economies.[84]

Brazil   With the eighth-largest economy in the world,[85] benefiting from agriculture, mining, manufacturing, and services, Brazil experienced a decade of economic and social progress from 2003 to 2014, lifting 29 million people out of poverty.[86] In 2016, however, the country suffered a recession, the worst economic slump in 25 years, brought about by worldwide declines in commodity prices, a domestic political crisis, and rising inflation.[87] There is some hope though for South America's largest economy, based on recent financial reports. Its economic growth rate was positive in 2018 while inflation decreased from 8.7% to 3.6%.[88] ●

4.5 The Value of Understanding Cultural Differences

THE BIG PICTURE

Managers trying to understand other cultures need to understand the importance of national culture and cultural dimensions and basic cultural perceptions embodied in language, interpersonal space, communication, time orientation, religion, and law and political stability.

Whether you are abroad or at home, you are likely to find yourself working with people whose cultural norms and traditions are very different from your own. What time you arrive for a business meeting, where you sit in the room, how you introduce yourself or introduce people to each other, whether you tip in a restaurant and how much, and even what you eat and whether you share it with others at the table are just a few behaviors influenced by culture. One of your authors, Angelo Kinicki, encountered several of these scenarios during recent business trips to the United Arab Emirates. He was surprised to see men, who were very familiar with each other, touch noses when saying hello. He also realized that Arabs have a much different orientation toward time. It's much more fluid and flexible than in the United States. Angelo also had to adjust his style of introducing himself to women: no shaking hands unless a woman offered her hand. The start of business meetings is quite different than in the United States. Arabs like to spend more time engaging in pleasantries before getting down to business.

LO 4-5

Explain the value to managers of understanding cultural differences.

Cultural differences affect businesses in many ways. As one example, Western manufacturers of personal care products have faced an uphill battle to introduce deodorant products in China and other Asian countries, in part because people do not perceive sweating as embarrassing. Rather, it is seen as a normal aspect of human metabolism. "The traditional thinking [in China] is that sweating is good because it helps people detox," said Unilever's assistant manager for skin care. "There is a marketing barrier that is really hard to overcome." Unilever's cowboy- and boxer-themed ads also missed the mark for cultural reasons. "The series of advertisements we designed relied on the Western sense of humor," said the company's creative director. "Not many Chinese would understand this."[89]

Tipping point. The culture of tipping varies from country to country. In Europe, tips range from nothing (because a gratuity is already included in the total bill) to around 15% for exceptional service. In Eastern Asia, tipping can actually be considered offensive, while some Middle Eastern countries have laws mandating it. Jamie Grill/JGI/Blend Images LLC

The Importance of National Culture

A nation's culture is the shared set of beliefs, values, knowledge, and patterns of behavior common to a group of people. We begin learning our culture starting at an early age through everyday interaction with people around us. This is why, from the outside looking in, a nation's culture can seem so intangible and perplexing. As cultural anthropologist Edward T. Hall puts it, "Since much of culture operates outside our awareness, frequently we don't even know what we know. . . . We unconsciously learn what to notice and what not to notice, how to divide time and space, how to walk and talk and use our bodies, how to behave as men or women, how to relate to other people, how to handle responsibility. . . ."[90] Indeed, says Hall, what we think of as "mind" is really internalized culture.

Thus, because a culture is made up of so many nuances, visitors to a different and unfamiliar culture may experience feelings of discomfort and disorientation. These feelings are generally associated with "not understanding the verbal and nonverbal communication of the host culture" and the need for adaptability to accommodate "differences in lifestyles, living conditions and business practices in another cultural setting."[91]

Cultural Dimensions: The Hofstede and GLOBE Project Models

Misunderstandings and miscommunications often arise in international business relationships because people don't understand the expectations of the other side. A person from North America, Great Britain, Scandinavia, Germany, or Switzerland, for example, comes from a **low-context culture, in which shared meanings are primarily derived from written and spoken words.** Someone from China, Korea, Japan, Vietnam, Mexico, or many Arab cultures, on the other hand, comes from a **high-context culture, in which people rely heavily on situational cues for meaning when communicating with others,** relying on nonverbal cues as to another person's official position, status, or family connections.

One way to avoid cultural collisions is to have an understanding of various cultural dimensions, as expressed in the Hofstede model and the GLOBE project.[92]

Hofstede's Model of Four Cultural Dimensions   Thirty years ago, Dutch researcher and IBM psychologist Geert Hofstede collected data from 116,000 IBM employees in 53 countries and proposed his **Hofstede model of four cultural dimensions, which identified four dimensions along which national cultures can be placed: (1) individualism/collectivism, (2) power distance, (3) uncertainty avoidance, and (4) masculinity/femininity.**[93]

Individualism/collectivism indicates how much people prefer a loosely knit social framework in which people are expected to take care of themselves (as in the United States and Canada) or a tightly knit social framework in which people and organizations are expected to look after each other (as in Mexico and China). *Power distance* refers to the degree to which people accept inequality in social situations (high in Mexico and India, low in Sweden and Australia). *Uncertainty avoidance* expresses people's intolerance for uncertainty and risk (high in Japan, low in the United States). *Masculinity/femininity* expresses how much people value performance-oriented traits (masculinity: high in Mexico) or how much they embrace relationship-oriented traits (femininity: high in Norway). In general, the United States ranked very high on individualism, relatively low on power distance, low on uncertainty avoidance, and moderately high on masculinity.

Hofstede's work has attracted critics despite its groundbreaking contribution to understanding cultural differences. One criticism is that it views a country's population as a homogenous whole. However, most nations, such as the United States, France, and Germany, are groups of ethnic units not necessarily bounded by borders. Another criticism is that Hofstede based his work solely on IBM employees, which may not be the best indicator of the cultural system of a country.[94]

The GLOBE Project's Nine Cultural Dimensions   Started in 1993 by University of Pennsylvania professor Robert J. House, the **GLOBE project is a massive and ongoing cross-cultural investigation of nine cultural dimensions involved in leadership and organizational processes.**[95] (GLOBE stands for Global Leadership and Organizational Behavior Effectiveness.) GLOBE extends Hofstede's theory and results and evolved into a network of more than 150 scholars from 62 societies. Most of these researchers are native to the particular cultures being studied. The nine cultural dimensions are as follows:

- **Power distance—how much unequal distribution of power should there be in organizations and society?** *Power distance* expresses the degree to which a society's members expect power to be unequally shared.

- **Uncertainty avoidance—how much should people rely on social norms and rules to avoid uncertainty?** *Uncertainty avoidance* expresses the extent to which a society relies on social norms and procedures to alleviate the unpredictability of future events.

- **Institutional collectivism—how much should leaders encourage and reward loyalty to the social unit?** *Institutional collectivism* expresses the extent to which individuals are encouraged and rewarded for loyalty to the group as opposed to pursuing individual goals.

- **In-group collectivism—how much pride and loyalty should people have for their family or organization?** In contrast to individualism, *in-group collectivism* expresses the extent to which people should take pride in being members of their family, circle of close friends, and their work organization.[96]

- **Gender egalitarianism—how much should society maximize gender role differences?** *Gender egalitarianism* expresses the extent to which a society should minimize gender discrimination and role inequalities.

- **Assertiveness—how confrontational and dominant should individuals be in social relationships?** *Assertiveness* represents the extent to which a society expects people to be confrontational and competitive as opposed to tender and modest.

- **Future orientation—how much should people delay gratification by planning and saving for the future?** *Future orientation* expresses the extent to which a society encourages investment in the future, as by planning and saving.

- **Performance orientation—how much should individuals be rewarded for improvement and excellence?** *Performance orientation* expresses the extent to which society encourages and rewards its members for performance improvement and excellence.

- **Humane orientation—how much should society encourage and reward people for being kind, fair, friendly, and generous?** *Humane orientation* represents the degree to which individuals are encouraged to be altruistic, caring, kind, generous, and fair.

Data from 18,000 managers yielded the GLOBE country profiles shown in Table 4.8.

TABLE 4.8 Countries Ranking Highest and Lowest on the GLOBE Cultural Dimensions

DIMENSION	HIGHEST	LOWEST
Power distance	Morocco, Argentina, Thailand, Spain, Russia	Denmark, Netherlands, South Africa (black sample), Israel, Costa Rica
Uncertainty avoidance	Switzerland, Sweden, Germany (former West), Denmark, Austria	Russia, Hungary, Bolivia, Greece, Venezuela
Institutional collectivism	Sweden, South Korea, Japan, Singapore, Denmark	Greece, Hungary, Germany (former East), Argentina, Italy
In-group collectivism	Iran, India, Morocco, China, Egypt	Denmark, Sweden, New Zealand, Netherlands, Finland
Gender egalitarianism	Hungary, Poland, Slovenia, Denmark, Sweden	South Korea, Egypt, Morocco, India, China
Assertiveness	Germany (former East), Austria, Greece, United States, Spain	Sweden, New Zealand, Switzerland, Japan, Kuwait

(Continued)

TABLE 4.8   Countries Ranking Highest and Lowest on the GLOBE Cultural Dimensions (*Continued*)

DIMENSION	HIGHEST	LOWEST
Future orientation	Singapore, Switzerland, Netherlands, Canada (English speaking), Denmark	Russia, Argentina, Poland, Italy, Kuwait
Performance orientation	Singapore, Hong Kong, New Zealand, Taiwan, United States	Russia, Argentina, Greece, Venezuela, Italy
Humane orientation	Philippines, Ireland, Malaysia, Egypt, Indonesia	Germany (former West), Spain, France, Singapore, Brazil

Source: "*How Cultures Collide,*" Psychology Today, *July 1976, p. 69.*

Have you thought about how you stand in relation to various norms—in both your society and others? Would your views affect your success in taking an international job? The following self-assessment was created to provide feedback regarding these questions and to aid your awareness about your views of the GLOBE dimensions.

SELF-ASSESSMENT 4.2   CAREER READINESS

Assessing Your Standing on the GLOBE Dimensions

This survey is designed to assess your values in terms of the GLOBE dimensions. Please be prepared to answer these questions if your instructor has assigned Self-Assessment 4.2 in Connect.

1.   What are your three highest- and lowest-rated dimensions? How might these beliefs affect your ability to work with people from Europe, Asia, and South America?

2.   How do your dimensional scores compare to the norms for Americans shown in Table 4.8?

3.   What can you say during an interview to demonstrate that you possess the career readiness competency of cross-cultural awareness?

Recognizing Cultural Tendencies to Gain Competitive Advantage   The GLOBE dimensions show a great deal of cultural diversity around the world, but they also show how cultural patterns vary. For example, the U.S. managerial sample scored high on assertiveness and performance orientation—which is why Americans are widely perceived as being pushy and hardworking. Switzerland's high scores on uncertainty avoidance and future orientation help explain its centuries of political neutrality and world-renowned banking industry. Singapore is known as a great place to do business because it is clean and safe and its people are well educated and hardworking—no surprise, considering the country's high scores on social collectivism, future orientation, and performance orientation. By contrast, Russia's low scores on future orientation and performance orientation could foreshadow a slower-than-hoped-for transition from a centrally planned economy to free-enterprise capitalism.

Understanding these dimensions is important for managers, especially those who are working overseas. For example, research suggests that the way employees react to performance feedback and goal-setting is impacted by where they stand on the dimensions of collectivism and uncertainty avoidance.[97] Research also has shown that employee career proactivity varies based on where that person stands on the GLOBE's cultural dimensions.[98] The practical lesson to draw from all this: *Knowing the cultural tendencies of foreign business partners and competitors increases your career readiness and can give you a strategic competitive advantage.*[99]

Other Cultural Variations: Language, Interpersonal Space, Communication, Time Orientation, Religion, and Law and Political Stability

How do you go about bridging cross-cultural gaps? It begins with understanding. Let's consider variations in six basic culture areas: (1) *language,* (2) *interpersonal space,* (3) *communication,* (4) *time orientation,* (5) *religion,* and (6) *law and political stability.*

Note, however, that such cultural differences are to be viewed as *tendencies* rather than absolutes. We all need to be aware that the *individuals* we are dealing with may be exceptions to the cultural rules. After all, there *are* talkative and aggressive Japanese, just as there are quiet and deferential people in the United States, stereotypes notwithstanding.

1. Language   More than 7,100 different languages are spoken throughout the world, and it's indeed true that global business speaks English, although Mandarin Chinese and Spanish are spoken by more people globally.[100]

In communicating across cultures you have four options: (a) You can speak your own language. (b) You can use a translator. (Try to get one who will be loyal to you rather than to your overseas host.) (c) You can use a translation app, such as Google Translate, which turns a smartphone into an interpreter. (d) You can learn the local language—by far the best option.

It's possible to gain some language proficiency online. Several free apps, like Duolingo and Memrise, can provide instruction and practice in many widely spoken languages, including Spanish, Chinese, Russian, French, Italian, Arabic, German, and more. Most of these apps are easy to use and customizable; you can choose the level at which you want to begin (so you can brush up on the language you studied in high school, for instance, or start a brand new one), and you can test yourself with quizzes, flashcards, memory games, and more.[101]

2. Interpersonal Space   It is common for men to hold hands in friendship in the Middle East, and it does not carry any sexual connotation.

People of different cultures have different ideas about what is acceptable interpersonal space—that is, how close or far away one should be when communicating with another person. A global study of almost 9,000 people from 42 countries revealed some interesting patterns. (*See Figure 4.2.*) For instance, the people of North America and northern Europe tend to conduct business conversations at a range of 3.1 to 3.4 feet. For people in Asia, the range is about 3.6 to 4.2 feet. The average interpersonal space for social distance, personal distance, and intimate distance across the 42 countries was 4.43 feet, 3 feet, and 1 foot, respectively.[102]

Interestingly, there are times when the world develops a standard for interpersonal space. For example, during the COVID-19 pandemic many countries adopted a 6-foot social distancing standard to keep people from spreading the virus to each other.[103]

3. Communication   Research has found that cross-cultural communication competence plays a critical role for expatriates to communicate effectively.[104] Angelo has tried to deal with this issue by reading books targeted for specific countries. For example, Angelo read *Doing Business in the Middle East* [105] to prepare him for a consulting project in the United Arab Emirates (UAE). While he learned much from the book, a big takeaway was not to take everything at face value. For instance, it was suggested that females would not actively participate in classroom discussions and presenters should not try to encourage group discussion by randomly calling on people. He found that both of these recommendations did not fit for his managerial audience in Abu Dhabi. We consider communication matters in more detail in Chapter 15.

FIGURE 4.2

Comfortable Interpersonal Space for Different Countries

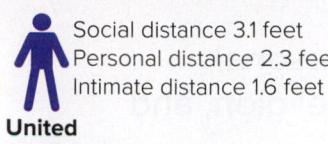
Social distance 3.1 feet
Personal distance 2.3 feet
Intimate distance 1.6 feet
United States

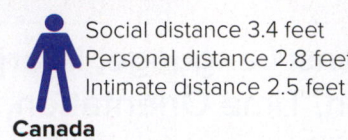
Social distance 3.4 feet
Personal distance 2.8 feet
Intimate distance 2.5 feet
Canada

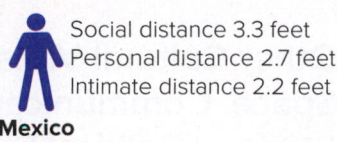
Social distance 3.3 feet
Personal distance 2.7 feet
Intimate distance 2.2 feet
Mexico

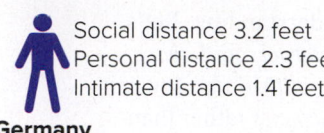
Social distance 3.2 feet
Personal distance 2.3 feet
Intimate distance 1.4 feet
Germany

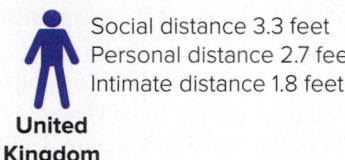
Social distance 3.3 feet
Personal distance 2.7 feet
Intimate distance 1.8 feet
United Kingdom

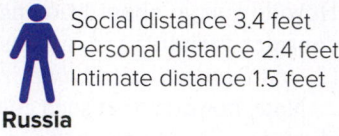
Social distance 3.4 feet
Personal distance 2.4 feet
Intimate distance 1.5 feet
Russia

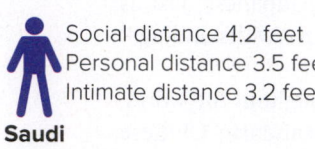
Social distance 4.2 feet
Personal distance 3.5 feet
Intimate distance 3.2 feet
Saudi Arabia

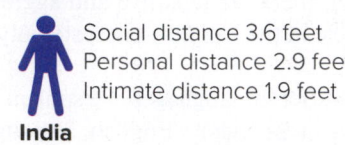
Social distance 3.6 feet
Personal distance 2.9 feet
Intimate distance 1.9 feet
India

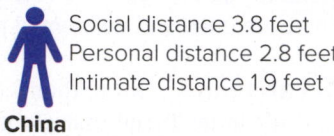
Social distance 3.8 feet
Personal distance 2.8 feet
Intimate distance 1.9 feet
China

Source: Data taken from A. Sorokowska, P. Sorokowski, P. Hilpert, K. Cantarero, T. Frackowiak, K. Ahmadi, et al, "Preferred Interpersonal Distances: A Global Comparison," Journal of Cross-Cultural Psychology, *March 2017, pp. 577–592.*

4. Time Orientation   Time orientation is different in many cultures. For example, Americans move at a different pace of business than people do in China. In the U.S., "time is money" and people are expected to be at meetings on time and meet deadlines. The Chinese, on the other hand, can be slower decision makers, preferring to build consensus and foster relationships before committing. During negotiations, Americans may find this different attitude toward punctuality frustrating and a waste of time, especially if they don't understand the underlying reason.[106]

Anthropologist Hall makes a useful distinction between *monochronic* time and *polychronic* time:

- **Monochronic time.** This kind of time is standard American business practice—at least until recently. That is, monochronic time is a preference for doing one thing at a time. In this perception, time is viewed as being limited, precisely segmented, and schedule driven. This perception of time prevails, for example, when you schedule a meeting with someone and then give the visitor your undivided attention during the allotted time.[107]

  Indeed, you probably practice monochronic time when you're in a job interview. You work hard at listening to what the interviewer says. You may well take careful notes. You certainly don't answer your cell phone or gaze repeatedly out the window.

- **Polychronic time.** This outlook on time is the kind that prevails in Mediterranean, Latin American, and especially Arab cultures. Polychronic time is a preference for doing more than one thing at a time. Here time is viewed as being flexible and multidimensional. This orientation can lead to work stress as people try to accomplish multiple things at once.[108] This perception of time prevails when you visit a Latin American client, find yourself sitting in the waiting room for 45 minutes, and then learn in the meeting that the client is dealing with three other people at the same time.

Research suggests that the distinction between monochronic and polychronic time is an important one, especially when it comes to work tasks. For example, when work tasks assume a polychronic view, but the workforce is monochronic, there will be conflict between the organization and the person. The end result is a stressful work environment.[109]

PRACTICAL ACTION   How to Run an International Meeting[110]

Meetings are a fact of life in most workplaces, and whether you are at home holding a virtual meeting or working abroad and dealing with people face to face, you'll want to employ your cultural awareness skills, along with your time management and people skills, to run effective gatherings. The standard meeting rules in U.S. culture, which advise having a clear goal, distributing an agenda, starting and ending on time, encouraging everyone to speak, and summing up to be sure everyone knows what follow-up actions are expected, may not apply everywhere or all the time. What will be different in an international setting, and how can you handle it successfully?

1. As in any setting where you will be speaking or making a presentation, know your audience. You can find out most of what you need to know by simply asking questions ahead of time. Does everyone have the background information they need to participate effectively in your meeting? Does anyone have a particular goal for the meeting or an item to add to the agenda? Are the participants decision makers, or will they need to defer to others and get back to you?

2. Be aware of participants' cultural norms for personal interactions. In some cultures, people bow when introduced; in others they shake hands. In Japan and China, they exchange business cards, handling the cards with both hands and reading them carefully. Some cultures use first names on short acquaintance, while in others it's considered disrespectful. Seating arrangements should consider cultural differences as well; some groups highly value status markers like a person's position at the table. It may make sense to set up individual, online meetings with team members across the globe to better understand their cultural norms before hosting a team meeting. This way, if something does come up, you don't risk making that person feel uncomfortable in a group setting.

3. Respect cultural differences in the perception of time in particular. In Sweden for instance, setting deadlines is acceptable and being on time is a sign of respect. In India time is measured in terms of what needs to be done, not in hours and minutes. In some Latin cultures, time is fluid and being late is not considered a problem. The same is true in parts of the Middle East. And speaking of time, don't forget time zones. Try and rotate your meeting times to accommodate team members across the globe if there isn't a convenient time for everyone.

4. Be ready to adapt. Some participants may arrive late or even early, some may bring guests, some may not consider it appropriate to speak up in front of others, or before others of higher rank have spoken, while others may interrupt. In some cultures, it's considered rude to get right down to business, as U.S. employees are trained to do, so participants may expect to socialize for a time before beginning. Some cultures may prefer not to have refreshments, while others may expect them and feel free to judge their quality.

5. Consider differences in decision-making styles. The British may sound like they're still open to discussion, but they are actually announcing their decision. The Chinese prefer long-term decisions to short-term choices. Business managers in Sweden prefer compromise to debate, and decisions can be long in the making in India because it's considered important to get everyone's input so the decision will last.

YOUR CALL

If you were holding a virtual meeting so you and your colleagues in the UK could present a sales proposal to a potential client in India, what questions would you want to ask participants ahead of time?

5. Religion   Trying to get wealthy Muslim investors in Dubai to buy some of your bank's financial products? Are you a Protestant doing business in a predominantly Catholic country? Or a Muslim in a Buddhist country? What are the most popular world religions, and how does religion influence the work-related values of the people we're dealing with? *(See Figure 4.3.)*

About 7 in 10 U.S. adults identify as Christians, but almost 23% say they have no religion, up from 18% in 2011. Slightly more than a quarter of them are atheists and agnostics; the others say they have no particular religion, though they may or may not believe in God.[111] Those who don't have a religious affiliation tend to be predominantly male and white or Asian.[112]

6. Law and Political Stability   Every firm contemplating establishing itself abroad must deal with other countries' laws and business practices, which frequently involves making calculations about political risk that might cause loss of a company's assets or

FIGURE 4.3

Current Followers of the Major World Religions

All population counts are estimated.

Sources: See "Major World Religions Populations Pie Chart Statistics List," http://www.age-of-the-sage.org/mysticism/world_religions_populations.htm, accessed June 8, 2018; https://www.israelnationalnews.com/News/News.aspx/221859; http://www.pewresearch.org/fact-tank/2017/04/07/why-people-with-no-religion-are-projected-todecline-as-a-share-of-the-worlds-population/.

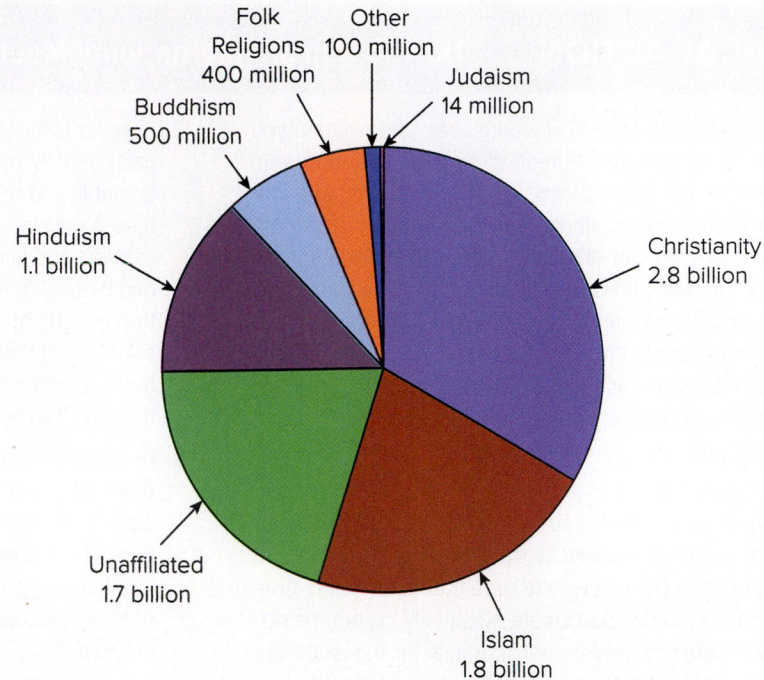

impair its foreign operations. Among the risks an organization might anticipate abroad are *instability, expropriation, corruption,* and *labor abuses.*

- **Instability.** Even in a developed country a company may be victimized by political instability, such as riots or civil disorders. This happened in 2019 in Hong Kong when Chinese authorities moved to limit the region's autonomy. In some developed nations, their very existence is threatened by separatist movements, with large sections clamoring to split off and become independent states—Quebec from Canada, Scotland from the United Kingdom, and Catalonia from Spain, for example—which could result in changes to the currency in use.

- **Expropriation.** **Expropriation** is defined as a government's seizure of a domestic or foreign company's assets. In 2019 Vancouver authorities recommended the expropriation of two rundown, downtown hotels for $1 each. The owners of the properties argued they had received offers in the tens of millions for each hotel but could not pursue them because of the city's expropriation process. The owners' arguments call into question the valuation methods and processes that different countries use for seizing a company's assets, which should be an important consideration for managers.[113]

- **Corruption.** Whether it's called *mordida* (Mexico), *huilu* (China), or *vzyatka* (Russia), it means the same thing: a bribe. Although the United States is relatively free of such corruption, it is an acceptable practice in other countries. Among the countries where corruption is most common are Venezuela, Afghanistan, South Sudan, North Korea, Yemen, Sudan, and Somalia.[114]

U.S. businesspeople are prevented from participating in overseas bribes under the 1978 **Foreign Corrupt Practices Act**, which makes it illegal for employees of U.S. companies to make "questionable" or "dubious" contributions to political decision makers in foreign nations. While this creates a

Many Muslims strive to pray five times a day, prostrating themselves on a prayer mat that faces the holy city of Mecca, located in Saudi Arabia. This religious practice may be difficult in a work setting in non-Muslim countries; however, some organizations provide a recommended prayer space as a way of promoting a culture of inclusion and openness.

Purestock/Getty Images

competitive disadvantage for those working in foreign countries in which government bribery may be the only way to obtain business, the United Nations Global Compact is attempting to level the playing field by promoting anti-corruption standards for business.

- **Labor abuses.** Overseas suppliers may offer low prices, but working conditions can be harsh, as has been the case for garment makers in Cambodia, Bangladesh, India, Myanmar, and Pakistan. Human Rights Watch reports that some common methods of getting workers to produce more include "restricting . . . toilet breaks; trimming their meal breaks; squeezing 'trainings' into lunch or other rest breaks so the 'production time' is not lost; disallowing drinking water breaks and other rest breaks."[115] Even worse, around 21 million people across the world are said to be forced to work with no pay.[116]

U.S. Managers on Foreign Assignments: Why Do They Fail?

The U.S. State Department estimated in 2018 that about 9 million U.S. citizens live abroad.[117] These individuals are called expatriates—people living or working in a foreign country. It can be very costly to support expatriates and their families. For example, living in cities such as Geneva, Brussels, Dubai, or Hong Kong can cost between $5,000 and $6,500 a month.[118] Are employers who are subsidizing these costs getting their money's worth? Not necessarily.

Expatriates often leave their foreign assignments early due to the challenges of adjusting to overseas assignments and embracing a different culture as part of everyday living. There are ways, however, to overcome these issues. For example, one study found that there is a significant relationship between demographics, such as gender and work experience, and the cultural acceptance of expatriates. This underscores how important it is important for organizations to create working environments that help expats adjust to different cultural values.[119] These might include offering seminars on cross-cultural differences, facilitating the establishment of social contacts, and other socialization activities. In addition, the sponsoring organization in the expat's home country should make sure the person is prepared for their foreign assignment by also providing training on what to expect abroad and lining up sponsors or mentors in the foreign office to ensure that the transition goes smoothly during the foreign assignment.

Unfortunately, problems may continue when expatriates return home. Research by EY (Ernst & Young) estimates that around 40% of expatriates leave their organization within two years of returning home.[120] Another study found that failure to effectively manage the return of expatriates reduced a company's return on investment.[121] These studies underscore the importance of managing the repatriation process.

Do you think you have what it takes to be an effective global manager? The following self-assessment can provide input to answering this question. It assesses your potential to be a successful global manager. ●

SELF-ASSESSMENT 4.3   CAREER READINESS

Assessing Your Global Manager Potential

This survey is designed to assess how well suited you are to becoming a global manager. Please be prepared to answer these questions if your instructor has assigned Self-Assessment 4.3 in Connect.

1. What is your reaction to the results?

2. Based on considering your five lowest-rated survey items, what can you do to improve your global manager potential?

3. How might you let a recruiter know that you are interested in working overseas and managing people from a different culture?

4.6 Career Corner: Managing Your Career Readiness

LO 4-6

Describe how to develop your cross-cultural competency.

You may think this chapter does not offer much when it comes to career readiness if you have no plans to work overseas. Don't make this assumption! In this 24/7 world, where we are always connected, cultural and national borders have all but disappeared, thanks to continuing advances in technology. Whether you work in the United States or abroad, workplace changes require us to understand, embrace, and use cultural awareness to enhance our personal and professional relationships.

Figure 4.4 shows the model of career readiness we discussed in Chapter 1. This chapter links with three of the KSAOs contained in this model. The most important one is the core competency of *cross-cultural competency*. The remaining two are the characteristics of *personal adaptability* and *self-awareness*. Personal adaptability is important because it helps when interacting with diverse people and when living or working in another country. Self-awareness is essential for becoming more culturally aware.

FIGURE 4.4

Career readiness competencies

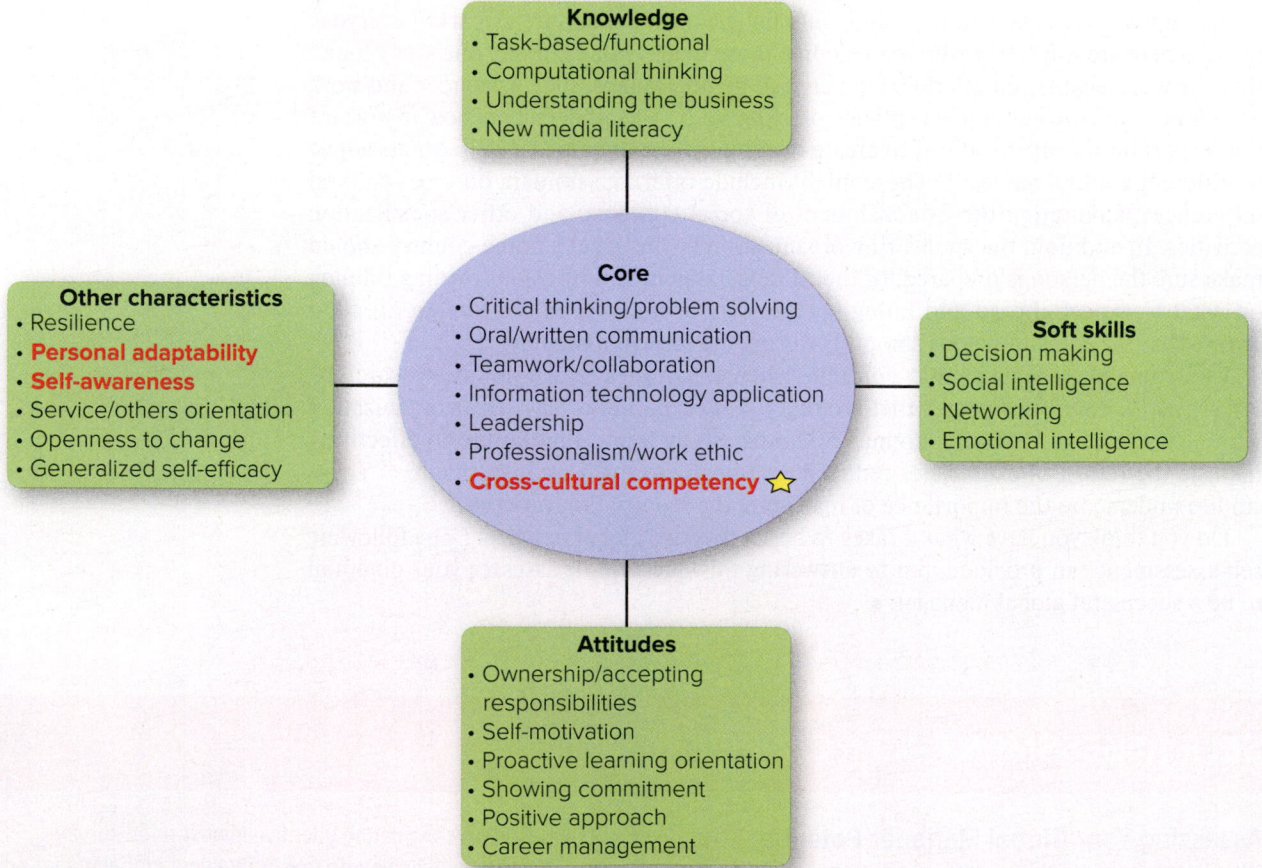

It may take a bit of effort to improve these competencies because they are firmly rooted in our experience and belief systems. A writer for *Fast Company* observed that "our cultural influences are so deeply embedded in who we are that it is difficult for most of us to recognize them in our own behavior. As a result, we don't think much about the cultural information expressed in many of the things we do or the fact that the vast majority of our behavior is shaped by our cultural surroundings. We just think of what we do as being natural."[122]

We recommend the following activities to enhance the core career readiness knowledge of cross-cultural competency:

1. Listen and Observe

Try to take the perspective of a native when interacting with others in a new cultural context. Listening and observing are the foundations of this kind of perspective taking. If a behavior or statement seems odd or confusing to you, look for the cultural logic or set of values that may explain it. For example, Angelo's international students rarely challenged him in the classroom. He felt they were not adequately contributing to classroom discussion due to a lack of confidence or inability to speak English. This assumption was wrong! Their behavior was caused by cultural values that grant tremendous respect and esteem to the role of professor. By understanding this cross-cultural perspective, Angelo was able to encourage his international students to take a more critical and participative perspective during classroom activities. Remember, it is generally good practice to check your understanding by first asking questions of someone familiar with the context at hand.

2. Become Aware of the Context

Context refers to the situational or environmental characteristics that influence our behavior.[123] Understanding context gives you insights that let you correctly interpret the "what" and "why" of someone's behavior. This in turn enables you to communicate more effectively with and influence others. You can develop awareness of context by "learning to read and adapt to the existing structure, rules, customs, and leaders in an unfamiliar situation," according to Bruce Tulgan, an expert on developing soft skills. Tulgan recommends answering four questions about structure, rules, customs, and leadership to increase your contextual awareness:

- "What do you know?
- What don't you know or understand?
- What do you need to know or understand better?
- How can you learn? What resources and support do you need?"[124]

Answering these questions increases your insights into the contextual effects of culture and enhances your ability to fit comfortably in a particular context.

3. Choose Something Basic

English is the generally accepted language of business. If you are a native speaker, it is still advisable to try to learn another language if you plan to work overseas or in a context where many people speak another language. Even a small effort shows respect and promotes cultural sensitivity.

A host of other activities can enhance your cross-cultural competency. Make it a goal to select several of them from the following list:[125]

- Study the principles or values of another religion.
- Observe people and interact with people from other cultures.
- Participate in a sporting event related to a different culture (cricket, karate, rugby, bocce, pétanque).
- Learn about traditions and celebratory days from other countries.

- Watch international films.
- Try the cuisine of other countries.
- Learn the history of dance forms in other countries.
- Attend seminars or speeches by culturally diverse speakers.
- Organize a diversity themed event or celebration.
- Follow world news on a regular basis.
- Take courses in black history, women's studies, Asian American studies, Chicano studies, and Native American studies.
- Take an anthropology class. ●

Key Terms Used in This Chapter

context 171
countertrading 152
cross-cultural awareness 146
culture 161
dumping 154
e-commerce 143
embargo 155
ethnocentric managers 148
European Union (EU) 157
exchange rate 158
expatriates 169
exporting 152
expropriation 168
Foreign Corrupt Practices Act 168
franchising 153
free trade 154
geocentric managers 148

global economy 144
globalization 142
global outsourcing 151
global village 143
GLOBE project 162
greenfield venture 153
high-context culture 162
Hofstede model of four cultural
  dimensions 162
import quota 154
importing 151
joint venture 153
licensing 152
low-context culture 162
maquiladoras 150
monochronic time 166
most favored nation 158

multinational corporation 146
multinational organization 146
North American Free Trade
  Agreement (NAFTA) 156
offshoring 151
outsourcing 151
parochialism 148
polycentric managers 148
polychronic time 166
sanction 154
tariff 154
trade protectionism 154
trading bloc 156
Trans-Pacific Partnership (TPP) 158
United States–Mexico–Canada
  Agreement (USMCA) 157
wholly owned subsidiary 153

Key Points

4.1 Globalization: The Collapse of Time and Distance

- Globalization is the trend of the world economy toward becoming more interdependent.
- The rise of the "global village" refers to the "shrinking" of time and space as air travel and electronic media have made global communications easier.
- The global economy is the increasing tendency of the economies of nations to interact with one another as one market.

4.2 You and International Management

- International management is management that oversees operations in or with organizations in foreign countries.
- The successful international manager is not ethnocentric or polycentric but geocentric.

4.3 Why and How Companies Expand Internationally

- Companies expand internationally for at least five reasons. They seek (1) cheaper or more plentiful supplies, (2) new markets, (3) lower labor costs, (4) access to finance capital, and (5) avoidance of tariffs on imported goods or import quotas.
- There are five ways in which companies expand internationally: (1) global outsourcing; (2) importing, exporting, and countertrading; (3) licensing and

franchising; (4) joint ventures; or (5) wholly owned subsidiaries.

4.4 The World of Free Trade: Regional Economic Cooperation and Competition

- Free trade is the movement of goods and services among nations without political or economic obstructions.
- Three barriers to free trade are tariffs, import quotas, and sanctions and embargoes.
- Three principal organizations exist that are designed to facilitate international trade: (1) the World Trade Organization, (2) the World Bank, and (3) the International Monetary Fund.
- A trading bloc is a group of nations within a geographical region that have agreed to remove trade barriers. Examples include (1) the North American Free Trade Agreement (NAFTA) and the United States–Mexico–Canada Agreement (USMCA) and (2) the European Union (EU).
- When doing overseas trading, managers must consider exchange rates, the rate at which the currency of one area or country can be exchanged for the currency of another's, such as American dollars in relation to Mexican pesos or European euros.
- The term BRICS stands for the five major emerging economies of Brazil, Russia, India, China, and South Africa.

4.5 The Value of Understanding Cultural Differences

- In low-context cultures, shared meanings are primarily derived from written and spoken words. In high-context cultures, people rely heavily on situational cues for meaning when communicating with others.

- Geert Hofstede proposed the Hofstede model of four cultural dimensions, which identified four dimensions along which national cultures can be placed: (1) individualism/collectivism, (2) power distance, (3) uncertainty avoidance, and (4) masculinity/femininity.

- Robert House and others created the GLOBE (for Global Leadership and Organizational Behavior Effectiveness) Project, a massive and ongoing cross-cultural investigation of nine cultural dimensions involved in leadership and organizational processes: (1) power distance, (2) uncertainty avoidance, (3) institutional collectivism, (4) in-group collectivism, (5) gender egalitarianism, (6) assertiveness, (7) future orientation, (8) performance orientation, and (9) humane orientation.

- A nation's culture is the shared set of beliefs, values, knowledge, and patterns of behavior common to a group of people. Visitors to another culture may experience culture shock—feelings of discomfort and disorientation. Managers trying to understand other cultures need to understand six basic cultural perceptions embodied in (1) language, (2) interpersonal space, (3) communication, (4) time orientation, (5) religion, and (6) law and political stability.

4.6 Career Corner: Managing Your Career Readiness

- You can develop your cross-cultural competency by engaging in three activities: (1) listen and observe, (2) become aware of the context, and (3) choose something basic.

Understanding the Chapter: What Do I Know?

1. What are three important developments in globalization?
2. What are some positives and negatives of globalization?
3. What are the principal reasons for learning about international management?
4. How do ethnocentric, polycentric, and geocentric managers differ?
5. What are five reasons companies expand internationally, and what are five ways they go about doing this expansion?
6. What are some barriers to international trade?
7. Name the three principal organizations designed to facilitate international trade and describe what they do.
8. What are the principal major trading blocs, and what are the BRICS countries?
9. Define what's meant by "culture" and describe some of the cultural dimensions studied by the Hofstede model and the GLOBE project.
10. Describe the six important cultural areas that international managers have to deal with in doing cross-border business.

Management in Action

Isolation of a Global Giant

Huawei was founded in 1987 as a Chinese provider of communications technology and smart devices. The company has approximately 194,000 employees and serves more than 3 billion people around the world. Huawei surpassed $100 billion in annual revenue in 2018, powered by its sales of more than 200 million smartphones that year. It holds the titles of the world's largest seller of telecommunications equipment and the second-largest smartphone maker.[126] The company also boasts that almost half of Fortune 100 companies have chosen Huawei "as their partner for digital transformation."[127]

Lately, however, Huawei is losing partners, entire countries in fact. In 2018 alone, the United States, United Kingdom, Australia, and New Zealand all banned the use of Huawei's 5G cellular technology. France and Germany were discussing similar bans, and authorities in Canada actually arrested Huawei's CFO on a U.S. warrant.[128] The U.S. also banned shipments of parts or components to Huawei in May 2019, resulting in the inability of companies like Qualcomm and Intel to export chips. Although this ban has been lifted, Huawei found other suppliers and no longer needs components from U.S. firms.[129] These setbacks have stunted Huawei's global expansion and isolated it to the Chinese market.

HUAWEI'S GLOBAL AMBITIONS

Huawei has had explosive growth in China. The company's revenue increased from around $20 billion in 2009 to over $100 billion in 2018, and it makes more phones than Apple. Huawei's growth "has come against the backdrop of China's continued rise . . . providing the firm with a huge base upon which to build its initial market," the BBC reported.[130] The Chinese market is quite saturated though, and if Huawei wants to grow, it needs to expand to new markets. According to one business analyst, Europe would be the place for Huawei to launch its new products.[131]

Huawei's international expansion has hit a snag. Critics accuse it of being too cozy with the Chinese government, which has caused a backlash against both its communications technology and smartphone business.[132]

A WORLD INCHING TOWARD 5G

At the heart of Huawei's international expansion woes is 5G technology. Let's first discuss this new wave of communications. Almost all cellular technology in the U.S. has been based on 4G technology (the "G" stands for generation) since 2010. Each cellular generation has introduced greater data transmission speed, with 5G being the fastest and most responsive currently in the market. Faster transmission and responsiveness allow you to stream Netflix movies more quickly, see high-resolution Ring doorbell surveillance videos, and even do virtual reality physical therapy. This technology also makes other innovations, such as driverless cars, possible. Major U.S. carriers introduced 5G in late 2018 and continue to expand it across the country, starting with highly populated cities.[133]

The speed and functionality of 5G technology also bring about security concerns in a globalized world. For example, critical functions and personal data can be hacked utilizing "backdoors" on a 5G platform. Some worry these backdoors may actually be exploited not just by private criminals, but also by hostile governments that control 5G developers.[134]

AN ARM OF THE CHINESE GOVERNMENT?

Huawei maintains it is a private company solely owned by its employees. In fact, the English version of the company's website specifically mentions: "No government agency or outside organization holds shares in Huawei."[135] Not so fast, say the United States and several other countries. They claim that vague Chinese intelligence laws could force Huawei to hand over data to the Chinese government, not only data from Chinese smartphone users, but also data from any Huawei product user in the world. Moreover, Chinese regulations require that private companies establish Chinese Communist Party branches within them and accept state-backed investment.[136] As a result, the U.S. government has said that Americans should not use imported Huawei phones, and federal government agencies are banned from buying them. Other countries, including the United Kingdom, New Zealand, and Australia, have barred the company's equipment from their 5G mobile networks.[137]

The United States and Canada have also gone after Huawei for other trade-related issues, including violations of sanctions against Iran. On December 1, 2018, Huawei's chief financial officer, Meng Wanzhou, was detained and charged in Canada by both American and Canadian authorities for allegedly covering up the organization's Iranian sanctions evasion scheme. The Chinese government calls the charges an attempt to stop Huawei's advancement across the globe.[138]

Not all countries have joined the anti-Huawei bandwagon. In 2019, China's fellow BRICS nation, Russia, agreed to incorporate Huawei equipment in its 5G telecommunications platform.[139] *Bloomberg* reports that Brazil is considering Huawei for its national telecommunications needs as well.[140] This essentially pits some of the largest emerging economies against North American and European nations. The Russians also are interested in a joint venture with Huawei to produce chips and software. The joint venture would include participation by the Russian government, which bolsters Western nations' claims that Huawei and its partners are government entities pretending to be commercial ones, according to *Forbes*.[141]

THE COST OF GLOBALIZATION

BRICS countries are not the only ones facilitating Huawei's international expansion. U.S. allies, such as France and Germany, have yet to ban Huawei's participation in 5G development, but the reason isn't trust in the company's independence. In fact, the European Union issued an advisory report in October 2019 warning of "uncontrolled software updates, manipulation of functionalities, inclusion of functions to bypass audit mechanisms, [and] backdoors" by companies such as Huawei. The hesitation seems to be related to globalization and the costs of moving away from Huawei's technology. For example, German telecommunications operators, such as Deutsche Telekom, have already invested heavily in Huawei's technology. Chinese technology is cheaper to secure, due to a globalized environment. What isn't cheap is divesting from this technology. In fact, the American Enterprise Institute estimates that it will cost billions for the Europeans to move away from Huawei.[142]

FOR DISCUSSION

Problem-Solving Perspective

1. What is the underlying problem in this case from the perspective of Huawei's CEO?

2. How can Huawei expand outside of China despite the obstacles it faces?

1. How is the global economy both helping and hurting Huawei?

2. If you were leading Huawei's expansion overseas, what type of international manager would you want to be—ethnocentric, polycentric, or geocentric? Explain your decision.

3. Based on Figure 4.1, which ways of expanding internationally has Huawei employed? Provide specific examples.

4. Huawei is based in China and looking to expand to Russia and Brazil. China, Russia, and Brazil are BRICS nations. Why is this significant?

5. Assume Huawei is allowed to enter the U.S. market. Based on GLOBE cultural dimensions, the United States scores lower than China on power distance, in-group collectivism, and uncertainty avoidance. With this in mind, how would you advise Huawei, a Chinese company, to modify its practices if it plans to enter the U.S. market?

Legal/Ethical Challenge

Should Qatar Be Hosting the 2022 World Cup?

In May 2015, seven Fédération Internationale de Football Association (FIFA) officials were arrested at the Hotel Baur au Lac in Zurich as they were preparing to attend the 65th FIFA Congress.[143] The arrests were tied to a multiyear investigation by the United States into collusion between FIFA officials and firms, including Al Jazeera (now beIN sport). The alleged collusion included the payment of at least $400 million in bribes by the firms in exchange for lucrative broadcasting and hosting rights for prestigious soccer tournaments. The Qatari government also offered FIFA an additional $480 million, according to *Sporting News Canada.*[144] More than 40 other officials, executives, and corporations around the world have since been charged. Many pleaded guilty and agreed to testify against others to secure leniency.[145]

This scandal has cast a spotlight on Qatar, the host of the 2022 soccer World Cup. Qatar's selection to host the world's most prestigious tournament has been tainted for a number of years by suspicions about the individuals who supported the bid of a rich nation that lacked facilities to host the event. The *Chicago Tribune* reported on an Argentine marketing executive who paid bribes for media rights and then made a deal with prosecutors to testify during the first trial of FIFA executives in a U.S. courthouse. The Argentinian did not provide bribes for the Qatari World Cup bid, but he was told of the Qatari bribes by FIFA members. This executive noted that one of the FIFA members sold his vote for Qatar for a paltry $1.5 million and then complained that another voting member got tens of millions more. Some voting members of FIFA have been charged as part of the corruption scandal but have yet to be extradited to the United States for trial. Another Argentine witness testified that a ledger of bribes, including payments of $750,000 and $500,000 to South American soccer federation presidents, was found.

Though these presidents did not have World Cup hosting votes, the payments were labeled "Q2022."[146]

Qataris' alleged bribing of FIFA officials could be cultural. Bribery in the Middle East continues to be more acceptable than in North America and Europe. For example, Transparency International states that in the Middle East, "most countries are failing in the fight against corruption."[147] The region has an average score of 39/100 on the organization's 2018 Corruption Perceptions Index. The United States scores 71/100 on the same index.[148]

Though the Middle East has a poor reputation when it comes to corruption, FIFA claims it has been unable to uncover evidence that would lead it to prevent Qatar from hosting the World Cup. Qatar also continues to deny it acted improperly or bought its right to host the tournament.

SOLVING THE CHALLENGE

What option would you choose if you were running FIFA?

1. Qatar should be stripped of its right to host the 2022 World Cup. There is obviously evidence of bribery and such an important tournament should not be tainted.

2. So far, prosecutors have not uncovered anything directly tying the Qataris to the corruption scandal. Stripping Qatar of its hosting privileges while it is building the infrastructure to host the tournament will lead to millions, or possibly billions, of dollars in losses and a significant number of lost jobs. Do nothing.

3. FIFA should have a third party open its own investigation of the events leading up to Qatar's being granted hosting privileges. The conclusion of this investigation should dictate what happens to the 2022 bid.

4. Suggest other options.

Learn more about Boeing's ethical responsibilities in a globalized world, and the impact its decisions had on various stakeholders, including those outside the U.S.

Assess your ability to apply concepts discussed in Chapters 3 and 4 to the case by going to Connect.

5

Planning

The Foundation of Successful Management

Kapook2981/iStock/Getty Images

After reading this chapter, you should be able to:

LO 5-1 Discuss the role of strategic management.

LO 5-2 Compare mission, vision, and value statements.

LO 5-3 Discuss the types and purposes of goals and plans.

LO 5-4 Describe SMART goals and their implementation.

LO 5-5 Outline the planning/control cycle.

LO 5-6 Describe how to develop the career readiness competency of *proactive learning orientation*.

FORECAST *What's Ahead in This Chapter*

We describe planning and its link to strategy. We define planning, strategy, and strategic management and state why they are important. We deal with the fundamentals of planning, including the mission, vision, and value statements, and the three types of planning—strategic, tactical, and operational. We consider goals, operating plans, and action plans; SMART goals, management by objectives, and cascading goals; and finally the planning/control cycle. We conclude with a Career Corner that focuses on how you can develop the career readiness competency of proactive learning orientation.

Start Your Career Off Right by Planning

The thought of starting a career (or switching to a new one) can be either intimidating or exciting. What's the difference? Having goals and a plan.

Setting Goals and Making a Plan

Here are some steps in the career-management process for you to consider as you start to build your career.[1]

1. Identify your options. Use the career readiness skill of self-awareness to write down your individual strengths, lifestyle preferences, passions, and work style. This should include an assessment of the career readiness competencies shown in Table 1.2—the functional, cross-cultural, computational, interpersonal, and other skills you can offer an employer. Then make a written list of the opportunities available to you through your networking, earlier work and volunteer experience, and other resources (don't forget the alumni and placement offices at your school). Now match up the two lists to discover where you should focus your career-building efforts.

2. Explore conditions in your target field. The career readiness skill of understanding the business will guide you to identify important factors like the demand for new hires in your chosen field or fields, the competencies expected of incoming employees, the likely salary range and opportunities for advancement, and any geographic limitations or requirements in the industry to be aware of. If your field or industry is concentrated in one or two parts of the country, for instance, be ready to move.

3. Create your action plan. Using what you learned from steps 1 and 2, write a list of actions you can take to achieve your goal of breaking into a new career. You are more likely to achieve your goals if they are "SMART"—specific, measurable against clear criteria to show progress, attainable with a chance of 50% or higher, relevant to you, and time bound with target dates for completion. We discuss the process of writing SMART goals in Section 5.4. Try to keep your steps or goals to a manageable number; somewhere between three and five is recommended. Prioritize and schedule them to create your plan, and if it helps you to give each one a name, by all means do so.

4. Track your progress. You'll see as you study this chapter that monitoring or controlling progress toward goals is an inherent part of the planning process. Each time you get a result from one of your efforts, whether it's positive or negative, that result constitutes feedback on how well you've selected your goals and how effective your plan is. If one step doesn't work out as planned, don't give up. Rely on your positive attitude and ability to adapt (more career readiness skills) and realize you have other opportunities to succeed. Try broadening your search and begin again.

Staying Resilient during the Process

Here are a few ideas about what else you can do to keep your hopes—and your finances—afloat during the career-building process.[2]

1. Know that it takes time to find a job, especially one that's a good fit for both you and the company that hires you. College graduates spend about five months, on average, landing their first job after graduation. If you are already working, even part-time, stay in the job while you pursue a new one. It's always easier to find a job if you have one. If you are not working, consider taking a part-time or seasonal job to generate some income because you'll want to avoid running up credit card debt.

2. Create a budget to be sure your income will cover your day-to-day expenses, such as a cell phone bill or car insurance. This is a lifelong habit that will serve you well.

3. Avoid making any major financial commitments until you've actually landed your target job and have a steady paycheck. You won't know how much you can afford to pay for a car until you know your salary, for example, and you may not want to be burdened by a new lease if your dream job requires you to relocate. As long as you have an appropriate interview outfit, even splurging on a professional wardrobe can wait until you know the dress code at your new employer.

For Discussion What fields or industries are interesting or appealing to you as places to work? What news and information about these areas can you start tracking now, and how will you will do that? Is there anyone in your network who can help you increase your understanding of the way this industry works? If not, how could you find someone?

5.1 Planning and Strategy

THE BIG PICTURE

The first of four functions in the management process is planning, which involves setting goals and deciding how to achieve them and which is linked to strategy. We define planning, strategy, and strategic management. We then describe three reasons strategic management and strategic planning are important.

LO 5-1

Discuss the role of strategic management.

The *management process,* as you'll recall (from Chapter 1), involves the four management functions of *planning, organizing, leading,* and *controlling,* which form four of the part divisions of this book. In this and the next two chapters, we discuss *planning* and *strategy.*

Planning, Strategy, and Strategic Management

"Move fast and break things."

Is that a plan or strategy? No, it's a slogan. In fact, it used to be Facebook's mantra to its software developers, suggesting that it's more important to release new products with bugs and to take care of problems as they occur. Facebook has dropped this mantra and now is creating plans with the help of others. CEO Mark Zuckerberg noted that ". . .We're going out and consulting with experts and trying to make sure that [we get things] right."[3]

Planning, which we discuss in this chapter, is used in conjunction with *strategy* and *strategic management,* as we describe in Chapter 6. Let's consider some definitions.

Planning: Coping with Uncertainty   As we've said (Chapter 1), **planning** is defined as setting goals and deciding how to achieve them. Another definition: planning is coping with uncertainty by formulating future courses of action to achieve specified

Navigating through uncertainty. Managing is not unlike driving during a thunderstorm. Drivers must deal with the uncertainties of the storm, while managers navigate their way through the uncertainty and ambiguity of market conditions, competitor actions, and supplier demands. ND700/Shutterstock

results.[4] A **plan** is a document that outlines how goals are going to be met. When you make a plan, you make a blueprint for action that describes what you need to do to realize your goals.

One important type of plan is a **business plan**, a document that outlines a firm's goals, the strategy for achieving them, and the standards for measuring success. Here you would describe the basic idea behind your business—the **business model**, which outlines the need the firm will fill, the operations of the business, its components and functions, as well as the expected revenues and expenses. It also describes the industry you're entering, how your product will be different, how you'll market to customers, how you're qualified to run the business, and how you will finance your business.

Strategy: Setting Long-Term Direction
A **strategy**, or strategic plan, sets the long-term goals and direction for an organization. It represents an "educated guess" about what long-term goals or direction to pursue for the survival or prosperity of the organization. We hear the word expressed in terms like "Apple's ultimate strategy . . ." or "Visa's overseas strategy . . ." or financial strategy, marketing strategy, and human resource strategy.

An example of a strategy is "Grow the business organically," which means "Increase revenue from existing and new customers rather than from acquiring other companies." However, strategy is not something that can be decided on just once. It generally is reconsidered every year because of ever-changing business conditions.

Strategic Management: Involving All Managers in Strategy
In the late 1940s, most large U.S. companies were organized around a single idea or product line. By the 1970s, Fortune 500 companies were operating in more than one industry and had expanded overseas. It became apparent that to stay focused and efficient, companies had to begin taking a strategic-management approach.

Strategic management is a process that involves managers from all parts of the organization in the formulation and the implementation of strategies and strategic goals. This definition doesn't mean that managers at the top dictate ideas to be followed by people lower in the organization. Indeed, precisely because middle managers in particular are the ones who will be asked to understand and implement the strategies, they should also help to formulate them.

As we will see, strategic management is a process that involves managers from all parts of the organization—top managers, middle managers, first-line managers, and team leaders—in the formulation, implementation, and execution of strategies and strategic goals to advance the purposes of the organization. Thus, planning covers not only strategic planning (done by top managers), but also tactical planning (done by middle managers) and operational planning (done by first-line managers and team leaders).

Planning and strategic management derive from an organization's mission and vision about itself, as we describe in the next section. *(See Figure 5.1.)*

FIGURE 5.1
Planning and strategic management
The details of planning and strategic management are explained in Chapters 5 and 6.

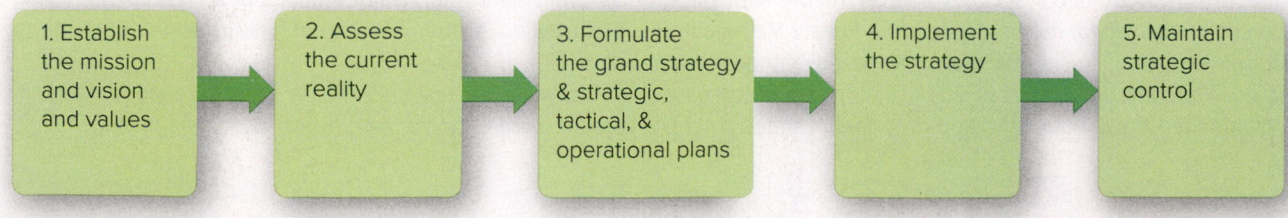

Why Planning and Strategic Management Are Important

An organization should adopt planning and strategic management for three reasons: They can (1) *provide direction and momentum*, (2) *encourage new ideas*, and above all (3) *develop a sustainable competitive advantage*.[5] Let's consider these three matters.

1. Providing Direction and Momentum   Some executives are unable even to articulate what their strategy is.[6] Others are so preoccupied with day-to-day pressures that their organizations can lose momentum. But planning and strategic management can help people focus on the most critical problems, choices, and opportunities. Burger King is a good example (see the nearby Example box).

If a broad group of employees is involved in the process, that can foster teamwork, promote learning, and build commitment across the organization. Indeed, as we describe in Chapter 8, strategy can determine the very structure of the organization—for example, a top-down hierarchy with lots of management levels, as might be appropriate for an electricity-and-gas power utility, versus a flat organization with few management levels and flexible roles, as might suit a fast-moving social media start-up.

Unless a plan is in place, managers may well focus on just whatever is in front of them, putting out fires—until they get an unpleasant jolt when a competitor moves out in front because it has been able to take a long-range view of things and act more quickly. In recent times, this surprise has been happening over and over as companies have been confronted by some digital or Internet trend that emerged as a threat—for example, as Amazon.com was to Borders bookstores; as Uber has been to taxi cabs; as Google News, blogs, and podcasts are to print newspapers.

Of course, a poor plan can send an organization in the wrong direction. Bad planning usually results from faulty assumptions about the future, poor assessment of an organization's capabilities, ineffective group dynamics, and failure to use management control as a feedback mechanism.[7] And it needs to be said that while a detailed plan may be comforting, it's not necessarily a strategy.[8]

EXAMPLE   The King of Turnarounds

Burger King is the second largest fast-food hamburger chain in the world, with more than 11 million guests visiting its restaurants each day.[9] For years, the restaurant chain averaged half the revenue of its biggest rival, McDonald's. McDonald's operates around 38,000 restaurants, more than double the number of Burger Kings across the globe.[10]

Lately, Burger King has grown tired of being second best. It needs a new direction, and Executive Chairman Daniel Schwartz is planning a collision course with McDonald's, leading to what some have called the "Burger Wars." In recent years, the restaurant chain has released humorous ads directed at McDonald's such as #NeverTrustAClown (McDonald's is known for its character clown, Ronald McDonald). Burger King also is using technology to its advantage. It offered Whoppers for 1 cent in 2018, as long as customers downloaded the Burger King app onto their phones. Then,

when customers went within 600 feet of a McDonald's, the deal would activate on their phone. The deal generated 1.5 million downloads of the Burger King app, making it the most downloaded app in the Apple Store for much of December 2018.[11]

Burger King isn't just being innovative with apps, it's also going in a different direction with burgers. The company started rolling out plant-based Impossible Whoppers in 2019. These meatless burgers are so similar to the real thing that a *Forbes* reporter couldn't tell the difference when trying both side-by-side. Impossible Whoppers will eventually be available at more than 7,000 U.S. Burger Kings, giving plant-based protein its biggest nationwide footprint to date.[12]

Schwartz understands that in order to build momentum around Burger King's plan, he needs middle-management's support. With this in mind, he's slashed overhead at the company's Miami headquarters, streamlined food preparation, and sold company-owned stores to franchisees. The savings were passed on to middle managers in the form of company stock, allowing them to feel the company's gains in their own wallets.[13]

Burger King's plan is showing some early success. In 2018, the restaurant chain opened up 1,000 restaurants around the globe, compared to McDonald's 600 stores. Burger King also increased its average volume per location by 30% while McDonald's gained only 20%.[14]

YOUR CALL

Do you believe Burger King's plan is sustainable? How can the restaurant chain involve first-line managers in the implementation of its new strategy?

2. Encouraging New Ideas   Some people object that planning can foster rigidity, that it creates blinders that block out peripheral vision and reduces creative thinking and action. "Setting oneself on a predetermined course in unknown waters," says one critic, "is the perfect way to sail straight into an iceberg."[15]

Actually, far from being a straitjacket for new ideas, strategic planning can help encourage them by stressing the importance of innovation in achieving long-range success. A recent research study of 227 technology-related businesses, for example, found that firms that supported and rewarded risk taking in their strategic planning achieved both high returns and a high level of innovative activity.[16] Along these lines, management scholar Gary Hamel says that companies such as Apple have been successful because they have been able to unleash the spirit of "strategy innovation." Strategy innovation, he says, is the ability to reinvent the basis of competition within existing industries—"bold new business models that put incumbents on the defensive."[17]

Some successful innovators are companies moving into new lines of business, particularly in entertainment. Mattel, maker of Barbie, Fisher-Price, and Hot Wheels, has seen a steady decline in sales, from $6 billion in 2014 to $4.5 billion in 2018. The company is now looking to develop movies based on its beloved brands and has eight film projects in the works with A-listers like Tom Hanks and Margot Robbie.[18] Red Bull is another well-known brand finding itself in the entertainment industry. The popular energy drink maker now has a media arm, Red Bull Media House, which produces both short programs and feature films.[19]

3. Developing a Sustainable Competitive Advantage   Strategic management can provide a sustainable *competitive advantage*, which, you'll recall (from Chapter 1), is the ability of an organization to produce goods or services more effectively than its competitors do, thereby outperforming them. We discuss the manner in which companies create competitive advantage more thoroughly in Chapter 6. You will learn that companies must have products or services that are valuable, rare, and difficult to imitate, and an organization poised to exploit its strengths. In today's global marketplace, competitive advantage can vary across countries. Uber is a good example.

Uber definitely had, and still has, competitive advantage when it comes to ride sharing in the United States. It's a different story when it comes to Africa. Bolt, previously known as Taxify, created its own competitive advantage by being the first company to offer motorbike-hailing. Motorbikes, which are called boda bodas, were a hit because they were more nimble when traveling through congested streets and communities. Bolt's success is clearly linked to its ability to localize product offerings more quickly than larger firms like Uber. It also gained competitive advantage by paying drivers with mobile money, "a technology popular in Uganda and other emerging economies because it allows people to receive and immediately store funds using a mobile phone."[20] •

5.2 Fundamentals of Planning

THE BIG PICTURE

Planning consists of translating an organization's mission and vision into objectives. The organization's purpose is expressed as a mission statement, and what it becomes is expressed as a vision statement; both should represent the organization's values, expressed in a values statement. From these are derived strategic planning, then tactical planning, then operational planning.

Are you hopeful? That's a good thing. Students who have more hope reportedly have higher grades and are more apt to finish college.

"Hope is the belief that the future will be better than the present," says columnist Elizabeth Bernstein, "and that you have some power to make it so." People who are hopeful "don't just have a goal or a wish, they have a strategy to achieve it and the motivation to implement their plan."[21]

First, however, you must determine your "goal or wish"—that is, your purpose. An organization must determine its purpose, too—what's known as its *mission*. And managers must have an idea of where they want the organization to go—the *vision*. Both mission and vision should express the organization's *values*. The approach to planning can be summarized in the diagram below, which shows how an organization's mission becomes translated into action plans. *(See Figure 5.2.)*

FIGURE 5.2

Making plans

An organization's reason for being is expressed in a *mission statement*. What the organization wishes to become is expressed in a *vision statement*. The values the organization wishes to emphasize are expressed in a *values statement*. From these are derived *strategic planning*, then *tactical planning*, and finally *operational planning*. The purpose of each kind of planning is to specify *goals* and *action plans* that ultimately pave the way toward achieving an organization's vision.

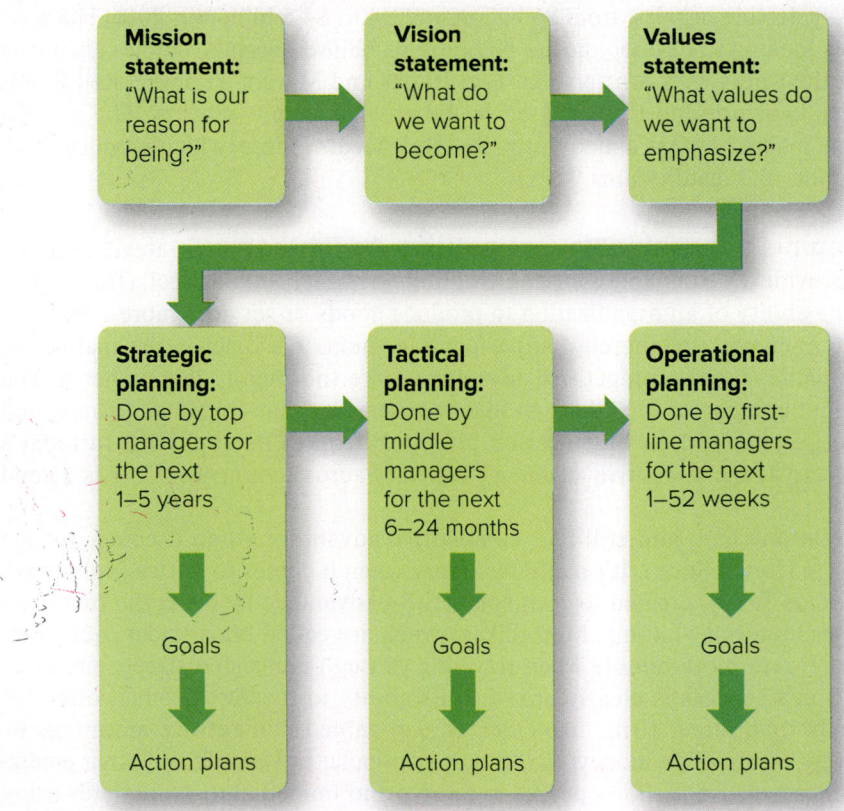

Mission statement: "What is our reason for being?"

Vision statement: "What do we want to become?"

Values statement: "What values do we want to emphasize?"

Strategic planning: Done by top managers for the next 1–5 years → Goals → Action plans

Tactical planning: Done by middle managers for the next 6–24 months → Goals → Action plans

Operational planning: Done by first-line managers for the next 1–52 weeks → Goals → Action plans

Mission, Vision, and Values Statements

The planning process begins with three attributes: a mission statement (which answers the question "What is our reason for being?"), a vision statement (which answers the question "What do we want to become?"), and a values statement (which answers the question "What values do we want to emphasize?"). *(See Table 5.1.)*

TABLE 5.1   Mission, Vision, and Values Statements

MISSION STATEMENTS: DOES YOUR COMPANY'S MISSION STATEMENT ANSWER THESE QUESTIONS?

1. Who are our customers?
2. What are our major products or services?
3. In what geographical areas do we compete?
4. What is our basic technology?
5. What is our commitment to economic objectives?
6. What are our basic beliefs, values, aspirations, and philosophical priorities?
7. What are our major strengths and competitive advantages?
8. What are our public responsibilities, and what image do we wish to project?
9. What is our attitude toward our employees?

VISION STATEMENTS: DOES YOUR COMPANY'S VISION STATEMENT ANSWER "YES" TO THESE QUESTIONS?

1. Is it appropriate for the organization and for the times?
2. Does it set standards of excellence and reflect high ideals?
3. Does it clarify purpose and direction?
4. Does it inspire enthusiasm and encourage commitment?
5. Is it well articulated and easily understood?
6. Does it reflect the uniqueness of the organization, its distinctive competence, what it stands for, what it's able to achieve?
7. Is it ambitious?

VALUES STATEMENTS: DOES YOUR COMPANY'S VALUES STATEMENT ANSWER "YES" TO THESE QUESTIONS?

1. Does it express the company's distinctiveness, its view of the world?
2. Is it intended to guide all the organization's actions, including how you treat employees, customers, etc.?
3. Is it tough, serving as the foundation on which difficult company decisions can be made?
4. Will it be unchanging, as valid 100 years from now as it is today?
5. Does it reflect the beliefs of those who truly care about the organization—the founders, CEO, and top executives—rather than represent a consensus of all employees?
6. Are the values expressed in the statement limited (five or so) and easy to remember, so that employees will have them top-of-mind when making decisions?
7. Would you want the organization to continue to hold these values, even if at some point they become a competitive disadvantage?

Sources: B. Nanus, Visionary Leadership: Creating a Compelling Sense of Direction for Your Organization *(San Francisco: Jossey-Bass, 1992), pp. 28–29;* "How to Write a Vision Statement," Cleverism, March 2, 2017, https://www.cleverism.com/write-vision-statement; P. M. Lencioni, "Make Your Values Mean Something," Harvard Business Review, *July 2002, pp. 113–117; and A Loehr,* "6 Steps to Defining Your Organizational Values," Rework, March 7, 2016, https://www.cornerstoneondemand.com/rework/6-steps-defining-your-organizational-values.

The Mission Statement—"What Is Our Reason for Being?"
An organization's **mission** is its purpose or reason for being. Determining the mission is the responsibility of top management and the board of directors. It is up to them to formulate a **mission statement**, which expresses the purpose of the organization.

"Only a clear definition of the mission and purpose of the organization makes possible clear and realistic . . . objectives," said Peter Drucker.[22] Whether the organization is for-profit or nonprofit, the mission statement identifies the goods or services the organization provides and will provide. Sometimes it also gives the reasons for providing them (to make a profit or to achieve humanitarian goals, for example).

The Vision Statement—"What Do We Want to Become?"
A **vision** is a long-term goal describing "what" an organization wants to become. It is a clear sense of the future and the actions needed to get there. "[A] vision should describe what's happening to the world you compete in and what you want to do about it," says one *Fortune* article. "It should guide decisions."[23]

Research has found that vision statements exhibiting the following characteristics are most effective:[24]

- **Clarity:** Employees understand the vision statement.
- **Future focus:** The vision statement describes the future, not the current state.
- **Abstractness and challenge:** The future is described as hypothetical and difficult, but achievable.
- **Idealism:** The future is portrayed as being highly desirable.

After formulating a mission statement, top managers need to develop a **vision statement**, which expresses what the organization should become, where it wants to go strategically.

EXAMPLE   Coca-Cola's Mission, Vision, and Values

The Coca-Cola Company is one of the world's largest beverage companies. It has more than 500 brands and nearly one out of four dollars spent on nonalcoholic drinks worldwide are spent on a Coca-Cola brand. Headquartered in Atlanta, the company is more than 130 years old. It employs about 700,000 people worldwide and had more than $31 billion in revenues in 2018. Some of its best-known brands include Coke, Coke Zero, Powerade, Schweppes, Dasani, Minute Maid, Fanta, Sprite, Honest Tea, and Smart Water. Many of its beverages are available in low-calorie or no-calorie versions.[25]

The company's website lists its mission, vision, and values as follows.

Our Mission[26]
Our mission is:

- To refresh the world in mind, body and spirit.
- To inspire moments of optimism and happiness through our brands and actions.
- To create value and make a difference.

Our Vision
To achieve our mission, we have developed a set of goals, which we will work with our bottlers to deliver:

People: Inspiring each other to be the best we can be by providing a great place to work.

Portfolio: Offering the world a portfolio of drink brands that anticipate and satisfy people's desires and needs.

Partners: Nurturing a winning network of partners and building mutual loyalty.

Planet: Being a responsible global citizen that makes a difference by helping to build and support sustainable communities.

Profit: Maximizing long-term return to shareholders, while being mindful of our overall responsibilities.

Productivity: Being a highly effective, lean and fast-moving organization.

Live Our Values

Our shared values guide our actions and describe how we behave in the world:

- **Leadership:** The courage to shape a better future
- **Collaboration:** Leverage collective genius
- **Integrity:** Be real
- **Accountability:** If it is to be, it's up to me
- **Passion:** Committed in heart and mind
- **Diversity:** As inclusive as our brands
- **Quality:** What we do, we do well

YOUR CALL

What do you think of Coca-Cola's mission, vision, and values? Are they explicit enough to guide employee behavior and company actions? Why or why not? Could any of them apply equally well to other businesses? Why or why not?

Heavy consumption. Coca-Cola has hundreds of brands, including Coca-Cola Classic, Sprite, and Fanta. Alignment among its mission, vision, and values isn't just important for employees as the company has millions of customers. Did you know that over 10,000 Coke-branded beverages are consumed every second of every day? Chones/Shutterstock

The concept of a vision statement also is important for individuals. Harvard professor Clayton Christensen believed that creating a personal life vision statement is akin to developing a strategy for your life. He found that people are happier and lead more meaningful lives when they are directed by personal vision statements.[27] For example, Angelo Kinicki, one of your authors, has a vision statement that says "to lead a life that influences the lives of others." Do you have a vision for your future career? Is it vague or specific? The following self-assessment was created to help you evaluate the quality of your career vision and plan. As you complete the self-assessment, think back to the Manage U at the beginning of the chapter and make modifications to your career plan as needed.

SELF-ASSESSMENT 5.1   CAREER READINESS

Assessing Career Behaviors and Future Career Identity

This self-assessment is designed to help you reflect on the vision of your career identity. Please be prepared to answer these questions if your instructor has assigned Self-Assessment 5.1 in Connect.

1. What did you learn about your future career identity? Are you surprised by the results?

2. Write a personal mission and vision statement using ideas discussed in this section. Share it with a friend for feedback.

3. Based on your results, what might you do to enhance your future career identity? Explain.

4. What things can you say during an interview to demonstrate that you possess the career-readiness competency of *career management*?

The Values Statement—"What Values Do We Want to Emphasize?" *Values,* we said in Chapter 3, are the relatively permanent and deeply held underlying beliefs and attitudes that help determine a person's behavior: integrity, dedication, teamwork, excellence, compassion, or whatever. Values reflect the qualities that represent an organization's deeply held beliefs, highest priorities, and core guiding principles.

After formulating a vision statement, then, top managers need to develop a **values statement**, also called a *core values statement*, which expresses what the company stands for, its core priorities, the values its employees embody, and what its products contribute to the world.[28] Values statements "become the deeply ingrained principle and fabric that guide employee behavior and company decisions and actions—the behaviors the company and employees expect of themselves," says former executive Eric Jacobsen. "Without a statement, the company will lack soul."[29]

SurveyMonkey, a publicly traded online survey development company, went about creating its values statement by doing what it does for its customers—creating surveys. The company surveyed its 700 employees throughout North America, Europe, and Asia on what they valued, resulting in a decision to endorse the following values:

- **Be Accountable**
- **Trust the Team**
- **Prioritize Health**
- **Listen to Customers**
- **Celebrate the Journey**

CEO Zander Lurie then ensured that these five values were aligned with the company's mission and vision. Soliciting employee feedback was important to SurveyMonkey because the company wanted to make sure its corporate values were aligned with employees' values: Research demonstrates that this consistency is important because it is associated with higher levels of employee motivation, job satisfaction, positive emotions, perceptions of being treated fairly by management, organizational citizenship behavior, employee engagement, and performance.[30] These findings support Lurie's conclusion that values need to be "more than just slogans we painted on the wall."[31]

A lighthouse is a great metaphor for strategic planning. A lighthouse provides a navigational aid and it warns boats about dangerous or hazardous areas. A strategic plan similarly provides direction to both employees and shareholders. It defines what an organization is trying to achieve and signifies what markets or opportunities are not going to be pursued.
George Diebold/Blend Images LLC

Three Types of Planning for Three Levels of Management: Strategic, Tactical, and Operational

Inspiring, clearly stated mission statements and vision statements provide the focal point of the entire planning process. Then three things happen:

- *Strategic planning by top management.* Using their mission and vision statements, top managers do **strategic planning**—they determine what the organization's long-term goals should be for the next one to five years with the resources they expect to have available. Effective strategic planning is integral to an organization's success because "[a] bad strategy will fail no matter how good your information is," says Microsoft co-founder Bill Gates.[32] Strategic plans communicate not only general goals about growth and profits, but also ways to achieve them. Today, because of the frequency with which world competition and information technology alter marketplace conditions, a company's strategic planning may have to be done closer to every one or two years than every five. Still, at a big company like Walmart, Ford, or Citibank, top executives cannot lose sight of long-range, multi-year planning.

EXAMPLE   Coca-Cola's Strategies

Coca-Cola recently announced several business and sustainability-related actions it took to revamp its corporate strategies. Five of them include:[53]

1. **More innovating, less sugar.** The company has launched nearly 600 new products, with a third of them having low or no sugar.

2. **Lifting, shifting, and scaling brands.** Coca-Cola utilized the strength of its global distribution system to expand 165 products into additional markets.

3. **Strategic investments for the future.** The company strengthened and expanded its portfolio through mergers and acquisitions, including the acquisition of coffee maker Costa Limited.

4. **Creating shared opportunity through growth.** Coca-Cola set out to show that it's committed to the planet. For example, the company announced its World Without Waste initiative, which is focused on collecting and recycling a bottle or can for each one they sell by 2030.

5. **Leveraging data.** The beverage maker developed a "data appendix" to share more details and metrics with various internal and external stakeholders so more informed decisions could be made across the company.

YOUR CALL

Coca-Cola recently decided to combine its business and sustainability reports into one strategic document. What message is it sending to stakeholders by doing this?

- *Tactical planning by middle management.* The strategic priorities and policies are then passed down to middle managers, who must do **tactical planning**—that is, they determine what contributions their departments or similar work units can make with their given resources during the next 6–24 months.

- *Operational planning by first-line management and team leaders.* Middle managers then pass these plans along to first-line managers and team leaders to do **operational planning**—that is, they determine how to accomplish specific tasks with available resources within the next 1–52 weeks.

The three kinds of managers are described further in Figure 5.3. ●

FIGURE 5.3

Three levels of management, three types of planning

Each type of planning has different time horizons, although the times overlap because the plans are somewhat elastic.

Top management chief executive officer, president, vice president, general managers, division heads	→	Strategic planning: 1–5 years	→	Make long-term decisions about overall direction of organization. Managers need to pay attention to environment outside the organization, be future oriented, deal with uncertain and highly competitive conditions.
Middle management functional managers, product-line managers, department managers	→	Tactical planning: 6–24 months	→	Implement policies and plans of top management, supervise and coordinate activities of first-line managers below, make decisions often without base of clearly defined information procedures.
First-line management and team leaders unit managers, first-line supervisors	→	Operational planning: 1–52 weeks	→	Direct daily tasks of nonmanagerial personnel; decisions often predictable, following well-defined set of routine procedures.

5.3 Goals and Plans

THE BIG PICTURE

The purpose of planning is to set a goal and then an action plan. There are two types of goals, short term and long term, and they are connected by a means-end chain. Finally, it's important to understand that the proper execution of a plan is just as important as properly developing it.

LO 5-3

Discuss the types and purposes of goals and plans.

Long-Term and Short-Term Goals

A **goal**, also known as an **objective**, is a specific commitment to achieve a measurable result within a stated period of time. Goals may be long term or short term.

Long-term goals are generally referred to as **strategic goals**. They tend to span one to five years and focus on achieving the strategies identified in a company's strategic plan. An example is to increase revenue from new customers by 10% over the next 12 months.

Short-term goals are sometimes referred to as **tactical** or **operational goals**, or just plain *goals*. They generally span 12 months and are connected to strategic goals in a hierarchy known as a means-end chain.

A **means-end chain** shows how goals are connected or linked across an organization. For example, a low-level goal such as responding to customer inquiries in less than 24 hours is the means to accomplishing a higher-level goal of achieving 90% customer satisfaction.

As we will see later in Section 5.4, goals should be SMART—specific, measurable, attainable, results-oriented, and with target dates.

The Operating Plan and Action Plan

Larry Bossidy, former CEO of both Honeywell International and Allied Signal, and global consultant Ram Charan define an **operating plan** as a plan that "breaks long-term output into short-term targets" or goals.[34] In other words, operating plans turn strategic plans into actionable short-term goals and action plans.

An **action plan** defines the course of action needed to achieve a stated goal. Whether the goal is long term or short term, action plans outline the tactics that will be used to achieve a goal. Each tactic also contains a projected date for completing the desired activities.

EXAMPLE   Southwest Airlines' Long- and Short-Term Goals

Southwest Airlines ranks #11 among *Fortune*'s 2020 Most Admired Companies, a list on which it has appeared for more than 25 years in a row. The Dallas-based carrier has continually achieved its strategic goals, and as of 2019 had been profitable for 47 consecutive years.[35]

Long-Term Strategic Goals.   Employee engagement, customer satisfaction, and profitability have been key strategic goals for Southwest since its inception. Employee engagement is created through the company's corporate culture, which focuses on employee satisfaction and well-being. The page of the company website announcing its vision and mission includes this central statement about its employees: "We are committed to provide our Employees a stable work environment with equal opportunity for learning and personal growth. Creativity and innovation are encouraged for improving the effectiveness of Southwest Airlines. Above all, Employees will be provided the same concern, respect, and caring attitude within the organization that they are expected to share externally with every Southwest Customer."[36] Employees were awarded a total of $667 million in 2019 as part of Southwest's profit-sharing program, which is in its 46th consecutive year.[37]

Lookalikes. Baggage handlers at Salt Lake City International Airport load a Southwest Airlines jet. One key to the airline's success is that all the planes in its fleet have been the same type, Boeing 737s, which saves on maintenance and training costs. Robert Alexander/Getty Images

The goal of Southwest's top managers is to ensure that the airline is highly profitable, and for years it has followed the general strategy of (1) keeping costs and fares down, to appeal to budget rather than business travelers; (2) offering a superior on-time arrival record and squeezing more flights per day from every plane; and (3) keeping passengers happy with its cheerful cabin crew and staff. One of the most important strategic decisions Southwest made was to fly just one type of airplane—Boeing 737s, 745 of them—to hold down training, maintenance, and operating expenses.[38] However, Southwest's decision to solely utilize this type of plane means that it is more vulnerable to technical problems, such as the recent grounding of all Boeing 737 MAX aircraft. (More information on the Boeing 737 MAX controversy is found in your continuing case, but

know that it caused Southwest's profits to decrease by $828 million in 2019.)[39] Southwest also competes head to head with legacy carriers when it comes to routes. The airline now flies to key airports of major cities—and even to some international destinations in Mexico, Costa Rica, and the Bahamas.

Short-Term Goals. Cutting costs and keeping fares low have traditionally been key operational goals for Southwest. To achieve its second operational goal, a superior on-time arrival record, the company did away with guaranteed seat reservations before ticketing so that no-shows wouldn't complicate (and therefore delay) the boarding process. To attract business travelers, Southwest changed the reservations policy slightly to ensure that passengers paying extra for "business select" fares would be placed at the front of the line. It also rewards "high-level" business travelers with what it calls the "A-List" designation. These individuals get automatic check-in and are guaranteed to board with the A-group or immediately before the B-group starts boarding. In addition, the airline tries to turn planes around in exactly 20 minutes so that on-time departures are more apt to produce on-time arrivals.

Southwest plans to improve pre-tax revenue by about $200 million thanks to a new reservation system and to continue reducing operating costs. The carrier also added Hawaii to its list of destinations in 2019.[40] According to CEO Gary C. Kelly, "Our operational and financial performances in 2019 were truly remarkable considering an estimated $828 million reduction in operating income and the significant reduction in planned flights due to the MAX groundings."[41]

YOUR CALL

Do you think the company will continue to achieve its strategic goals? Why or why not?

Plans Are Great, But . . .

Unless plans are effectively executed, they won't be worth more than the paper they are written on. "Strategy equals execution. All the great ideas and visions in the world are worthless if they can't be implemented rapidly and efficiently," said Colin Powell, former U.S. Secretary of State and Chairman of the Joint Chiefs of Staff.[42] Take for instance, Katerra, a technology-oriented construction start-up formed in 2015. The company's plan was to use automation to design and construct buildings for less cost and time than traditional builders. Unfortunately, Katerra's management failed to execute the plan. The company failed to complete around a dozen projects and could only name one project it actually delivered on time. The start-up ultimately lost many of its clients, closed its first factory, and laid off hundreds of employees.[43]

Conversely, a well-executed plan can spur growth and create a competitive advantage. Handshake, a career-services platform that connects students with employers is such an example. The company offers to partner with colleges and universities by storing student information, such as resumes, cover letters, and transcripts, all in one place. Handshake then provides over 420,000 employers with access to these materials so they can hire students for jobs and internships. After it accumulated partnerships with over 900 colleges and universities, Handshake rolled out the second stage of its plan, which allows any student with a ".edu" e-mail address to access its platform. This opportunity

Building an economy. Carpenters build a roof on a new home. Construction is a major contributor to America's economy. The industry has over 7 million employees and creates nearly $1.3 trillion worth of structures annually Huntstock/Getty Images

is available whether or not the student attends a partner institution. As a result of Handshake's ability to effectively execute its plan, it now has a dominant position in the career services market.[44] ●

5.4 Promoting Consistencies in Goals: SMART Goals, Management by Objectives, and Goal Cascading

THE BIG PICTURE

This section discusses SMART goals—goals that are specific, measurable, attainable, and results-oriented, and have target dates. It also briefly discusses a technique for setting goals, management by objectives (MBO), a four-step process for motivating employees. Finally, it introduces the concept of goal cascading, which attempts to ensure that higher-level goals are communicated and aligned with the goals at the next levels down in the organizational hierarchy.

LO 5-4

Describe SMART goals and their implementation.

Anyone can define goals. But as we mentioned earlier, the five characteristics of a good goal are represented by the acronym SMART.

SMART Goals

A **SMART goal** is one that is specific, measurable, attainable, and results-oriented, and has target dates.

Specific Goals should be stated in *specific* rather than vague terms. The goal "As many planes as possible should arrive on time" is too general. The goal that "Ninety percent of planes should arrive within 15 minutes of the scheduled arrival time" is specific.

Measurable Whenever possible, goals should be *measurable*, or quantifiable (as in "90% of planes should arrive within 15 minutes"). That is, there should be some way to measure the degree to which a goal has been reached.

Of course, some goals—such as those concerned with improving quality—are not precisely quantifiable. In that case, something on the order of "Improve the quality of customer relations by instituting 10 follow-up telephone calls every week" will do. You can certainly quantify how many follow-up phone calls were made.

Attainable   Goals should be challenging, of course, but above all, they should be realistic and *attainable*. It may be best to set goals that are quite ambitious so as to challenge people to meet high standards. Always, however, the goals should be achievable within the scope of the time, equipment, and financial support available. *(See Figure 5.4.)*

If too easy (as in "half the flights should arrive on time"), goals won't compel people to make much effort. If impossible ("all flights must arrive on time, regardless of weather"), employees won't even bother trying. Or they will try and continually fail, which will end up hurting morale. Finally, employees may resort to cheating. An example was the Department of Veterans Affairs' unrealistic goal of cutting wait times for appointments at VA hospitals by more than half. This was revealed in recent scandals in which VA administrators were found to have falsified statistics.[45]

Results-Oriented   Only a few goals should be chosen—say, five for any work unit. And they should be *results-oriented*—they should support the organization's vision.

In writing out the goals, start with the word "To" and follow it with action-oriented verbs—"complete," "acquire," "increase" ("to decrease by 10% the time to get passengers settled in their seats before departure").

Some verbs should not be used in your goal statement because they imply activities—the ways used to accomplish goals (such as having baggage handlers waiting). For example, you should not use "to develop," "to conduct," "to implement."

Target Dates   Goals should specify the *target dates* or deadline dates when they are to be attained. For example, it's unrealistic to expect an airline to improve its on-time arrivals by 10% in a short period of time. However, you could set a target date—three to six months away, say—by which this goal is to be achieved. That allows enough time for lower-level managers and employees to revamp their systems and work habits and gives them a clear time frame in which they know what they are expected to do.

Management by Objectives: The Four-Step Process for Motivating Employees

First suggested by Peter Drucker in 1954, *management by objectives* has spread largely because of the appeal of its emphasis on converting general objectives into specific ones for all members of an organization.[46]

Management by objectives (MBO) is a four-step process in which (1) managers and employees jointly set objectives for the employee, (2) managers develop action plans, (3) managers and employees periodically review the employee's performance, and (4) the manager makes a performance appraisal and rewards the employee according to results. The purpose of MBO is to *motivate* rather than to control subordinates.

Before we begin discussing these four steps, you may want to consider the quality of the goal-setting process in a current or former employer. Management by objectives and goal cascading will not work without an effective goal-setting process. The following self-assessment was developed to provide insight into the quality of goal setting within an organization.

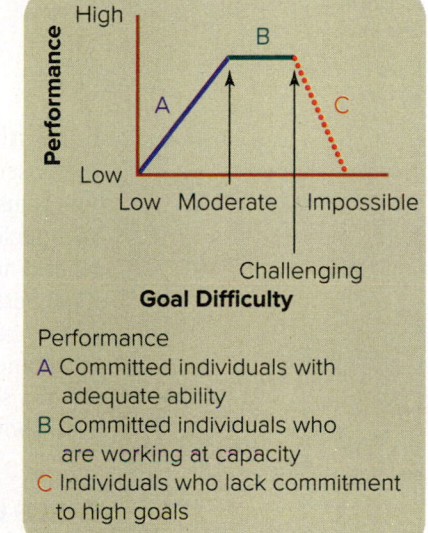

FIGURE 5.4

Relationship between goal difficulty and performance

Source: Adapted from E. A. Locke and G. P. Latham, A Theory of Goal Setting and Task Performance (Englewood Cliffs, NJ: Prentice Hall, 1990).

Performance
A Committed individuals with adequate ability
B Committed individuals who are working at capacity
C Individuals who lack commitment to high goals

What Is the Quality of Goal Setting within a Current or Past Employer?

This self-assessment is designed to assess the quality of goal setting in a company. Please be prepared to answer these questions if your instructor has assigned Self-Assessment 5.2 in Connect.

1. What are the strengths and weaknesses of goal setting in the company you selected?

2. Based on your results, what recommendations would you provide to senior management about improving the goal-setting process in this company? Explain.

3. What actions could you take to improve the goal-setting process in this company? Be specific.

1. Jointly Set Objectives You sit down with your manager and the two of you jointly set objectives for you to attain. Research shows that an assigned goal from your boss is just as effective as setting goals participatively. Moreover, people tend to set their own personal goals in response to receiving an assigned goal. A team of goal-setting experts noted that "the assignment of a goal encourages individuals to also set a personal performance goal, which in turn contributes to their performance."[47] It is important to remember what we learned about SMART goals. Managers garner greater acceptance to goal setting when employees believe the goal is attainable and they possess the skills and resources to achieve it.[48] Managers tend to set three types of objectives, shown in the following table. *(See Table 5.2.)*

TABLE 5.2 Three Types of Objectives Used in MBO: Performance, Behavioral, and Learning

PERFORMANCE OBJECTIVES
Express the objective as an outcome or end-result. Examples: "Increase small appliance sales by 10%." "Reduce turnover by 15%."

BEHAVIORAL OBJECTIVES
Express the objective as the behaviors needed to achieve an outcome. Examples: "Greet all potential automobile customers with a smile and offer to assist." "Ensure food is stored in seal-proof containers." "Attend five days of leadership training." "Learn basics of Microsoft Office software by June 1."

LEARNING OBJECTIVES
Express the objective in terms of acquiring knowledge or competencies. Examples: "Attend diversity training class." "Learn how the features in our sports utility vehicles compare to competitors."

Source: These descriptions were based on G. Latham, G. Seijts, and J. Slocum, "The Goal Setting and Goal Orientation Labyrinth: Effective Ways for Increasing Employee Performance," Organizational Dynamics, October–December 2016, pp. 271–277.

We want to briefly focus on the career readiness competency of *proactive learning orientation* because it fuels the achievement of learning objectives. Proactive learning orientation represents a desire to learn and improve one's knowledge, soft skills, and other characteristics in pursuit of personal development. Employers value this attitude because it helps drive the creativity and innovation needed in today's global economy. They also desire this competency because the "fast-paced business environment requires employees to refine and enhance their skills sets throughout their careers."[49] So where do you stand on this competency? Find out by taking the proactive learning orientation self-assessment.

2. Develop an Action Plan   Once objectives are set, employees are encouraged to prepare an action plan for attaining them. Action plans may be prepared for both individuals and work units, such as departments. It is important, however, for management to provide resources to support action plans. For example, North Carolina's Department of Health and Human Services provided $2 million in 2020 to support local health departments' action plans for fighting the state's opioid crisis.[50] Goals and plans that lack resources are likely to fail. Implementation of the plans can take between 6 and 18 months depending on the complexity of the goal.[51] Setting and using action plans also reduces procrastination. If this is sometimes a problem for you, break your goals into smaller and more specific subgoals.[52] This will get you going.

3. Periodically Review Performance   You and your manager should meet reasonably often—either informally as needed or formally every three months—to review progress, as should you and your subordinates. Indeed, frequent communication is necessary so that everyone will know how well he or she is doing in meeting the objectives.

During each meeting, managers should give employees feedback, and objectives should be updated or revised as necessary to reflect new realities. Feedback is essential for improving performance.[53] If you were managing a painting or landscaping business, for example, changes in the weather, loss of key employees, or a financial downturn affecting customer spending could force you to reconsider your objectives.

4. Give Performance Appraisal and Rewards, if Any   At the end of 6 or 12 months, you and your subordinate should meet to discuss results, comparing performance with initial objectives. *Deal with results*, not personalities, emotional issues, or excuses.

Because the purpose of MBO is to *motivate* employees, performance that meets the objectives should be rewarded—with compliments, raises, bonuses, promotions, or other suitable benefits. Failure can be addressed by redefining the objectives for the next 6- or 12-month period, or even by taking stronger measures, such as demotion. Basically, however, MBO is viewed as being a learning process. After step 4, the MBO cycle begins anew.

Cascading Goals: Making Lower-Level Goals Align with Top Goals

For goal setting to be successful, the following three things have to happen.

1. Top Management and Middle Management Must Be Committed
According to research, "When top management commitment [to MBO] was high, the average gain in productivity was 56%. When commitment was low, the average gain in productivity was only 6%."[54]

2. It is Best to Cascade Goals   The cascading process is most effective when goals are cascaded across the entire organization. According to a team of researchers, this broad-based approach is more likely to encourage collaboration and alignment across departments.[55]

3. Goals Must "Cascade"—Be Linked Consistently Down through the Organization   Cascading goals is the process of ensuring that the strategic goals set at the top level align, or "cascade," downward with more specific short-term goals at lower levels within an organization, including employees' objectives and activities. Top managers set *strategic goals*, which are translated into *divisional goals*, which are translated into *departmental goals*, which are translated into *individual goals*. The cascading process ends when all individuals have a set of goals that support the company's overall strategic goals. This process helps employees understand how their work contributes to overall corporate success.

Streaming goals. Onondaga Falls, at Ricketts Glen State Park, Pennsylvania. The downward flow of strategic goals to lower level ones re-sembles this type of cascading waterfall. Jon Bilous/Shutterstock

Example: The Vice President of the Claims Division of an automobile insurance company, which pays off requests (or claims) by customers seeking insurance payments to repair damage to their cars, may set the major goal (and SMART goal) of "increase customer satisfaction in Claims Division by 10%." In the cascading-goals process, the same goal would be embraced by the Assistant Vice President of Claims and the Recovery Director below the VP in the organizational hierarchy. Further down the hierarchy, the Recovery Unit Manager would reword the goal to be more specific to his or her department: "Decrease the number of customer complaints about claims by 10% over last year's average." For the individual Recovery Analyst at the lowest level, the goal could become: "Return all customer phone calls about claims within 24 hours."[56] Thus, all the subgoals in the organization are in alignment with the major goal specified by top management.

The Importance of Deadlines

There's no question that college is a pressure cooker for many students. The reason, of course, is the seemingly never-ending deadlines. But consider: Would you do all the course work you're doing—and realize the education you're getting—if you *didn't* have deadlines?

As we saw under the "T" (for "has target dates") in SMART goals, deadlines are as essential to goal setting in business as they are to your college career. Because the whole purpose of planning and setting goals is to deliver to a client specified results within a specified period of time, deadlines become a great motivator, both for you and for the people working for you.

It's possible, of course, to let deadlines mislead you into focusing too much on immediate results and thereby ignoring overall planning—just as students will focus too much on preparing for a test in one course while neglecting others. In general, however, deadlines can help you keep your eye on the "big picture" while simultaneously paying attention to the details that will help you realize the big picture. Deadlines can help concentrate the mind, so that you make quick decisions rather than put them off. Deadlines help you ignore extraneous matters (such as cleaning up a messy desk) in favor of focusing on what's important—realizing the goal's on time and on budget. Deadlines provide a mechanism for giving ourselves feedback. ●

PRACTICAL ACTION | Setting Goals for a Small Business

Goal setting can seem like an intimidating process, but it's both a necessary and a helpful one for the millions of small businesses (defined as having 500 or fewer employees) in the United States. In fact, a research study of 231 small businesses found that goal setting had a positive impact on the firm's performance.[57] These findings are important, particularly because small businesses account for 44% of U.S. economic activity and two-thirds of the nation's new jobs.[58]

The Great Lakes Brewing Company, Ohio's first craft brewery, is a good example of goal setting in small businesses.[59]

1. **Break large goals down into smaller ones:** Great Lakes developed a five-year strategic plan in 2013 and focused on three "bottom lines": social, economic, and environmental. We'll focus on the social bottom line, which the brewery breaks down into areas such as equitable compensation, safety, and employee wellness. Safety is then broken down into a measurable goal, which is to keep the number of safety-related incidents (recordable incident rate) at or below the industry average for any given year.

2. **Track progress toward goals:** Great Lakes has a safety committee that meets regularly to track the number of safety-related incidents at its factory. For example, in 2013 it was 3.05 and in 2018 it was 2.94. It then compares the incidents to that year's industry average (the industry average in 2018 was 3.1). The company knows it

is meeting its goal if its incident rate is below the industry average.

3. **Keep the goal in sight:** The brewery's management knows it must take action to ensure safety goals are met. For example, the company hired a full-time safety manager in 2015 to "give more attention to the development of safety programs and culture." The company also made some changes in 2017 to improve safety, such as changing its chemical storage policies and providing training and equipment for respiratory protection.

4. **Accept that setbacks will happen:** Just because the company strives to make improvements doesn't mean the number of safety-related incidents will always decrease. For example, Great Lakes' incident rate significantly increased from 0.48 in 2017 to 2.94 in 2018. Based on this setback, the company decided to change its safety manager in 2019 and re-evaluate its safety program.

5. **Celebrate success:** Great Lakes celebrated achieving 90% overall goal attainment in 2018. In recognition of this achievement, the company gave employees monetary bonuses.

YOUR CALL

What major goal of your own have you broken into smaller parts? If you have never done this, for what future goal do you think it would be an effective strategy for you?

5.5 The Planning/Control Cycle

THE BIG PICTURE

The four-step planning/control cycle helps you keep in control, to make sure you're headed in the right direction.

LO 5-5

Outline the planning/ control cycle.

Once you've made plans, how do you stay in control to make sure you're headed in the right direction? Actually, there is a continuous feedback loop known as the planning/control cycle. (The "organizing" and "leading" steps within the Planning–Organizing–Leading–Controlling sequence are implied here.) The ==planning/control cycle== has two planning steps (1 and 2) and two control steps (3 and 4), as follows: **(1) Make the plan. (2) Carry out the plan. (3) Control the direction by comparing results with the plan. (4) Control the direction by taking corrective action in two ways—namely, by (a) correcting deviations in the plan being carried out or (b) improving future plans.** *(See Figure 5.5.)* (We will see this model echoed later in Chapter 16 in the discussion of the Plan-Do-Check-Act cycle.)

FIGURE 5.5

The planning/control cycle

This describes a constant feedback loop designed to ensure plans stay headed in the right direction.

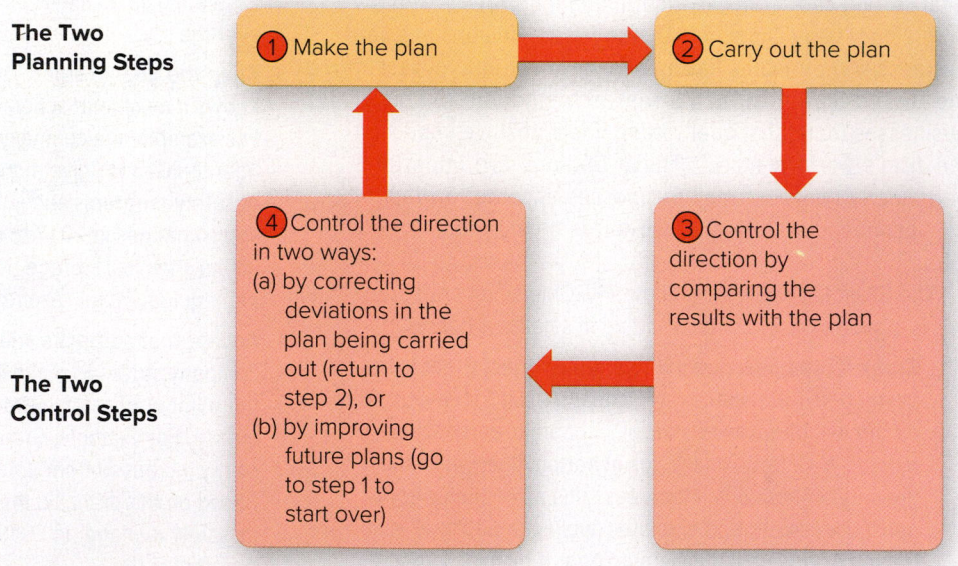

The Two Planning Steps

The Two Control Steps

1. Make the plan
2. Carry out the plan
3. Control the direction by comparing the results with the plan
4. Control the direction in two ways:
   (a) by correcting deviations in the plan being carried out (return to step 2), or
   (b) by improving future plans (go to step 1 to start over)

Source: Robert Kreitner, Management, *8th edition.*

The planning/control cycle loop exists for each level of planning—strategic, tactical, and operational. The corrective action in step 4 of the cycle (a) can get a project back on track before it's too late or (b) if it's too late, can provide data for improving future plans. ●

EXAMPLE   PG&E Fails to Manage Its Planning/Control Cycle

California suffered from the largest, most destructive, and deadliest wildfires ever recorded in the state between 2017 and 2019. During this time, more than 23 million acres burned, hundreds of lives were lost, and tens of billions of dollars' worth of damage occurred.[60] The state's investigators place the majority of the blame on Pacific Gas and Electric Company (PG&E), the utility that provides electric service to approximately 16 million Californians. In fact, PG&E's equipment started an average of more than one fire a day in California in recent years.[61]

Battling blazes. Firefighters battle the Kincade Fire in Healdsburg, California, in October 2019. The fire, caused by faulty PG&E equipment, was one of the many destructive wildfires that plagued the state between 2017 and 2019. Philip Pacheco/Getty Images

PG&E's woes started in 2010 when one of its pipelines exploded, killing eight people. State regulators started investigating the company and found that it spent millions of dollars less on maintenance than industry safety standards called for. At the same time, it collected more than $224 million more than it was authorized to collect in oil and gas revenues in the decade before the explosion. At PG&E, "There was very much a focus on the bottom line over everything: 'What are the earnings we can report this quarter?'" says Mike Florio, California's former utilities commissioner. PG&E still didn't have an effective plan in place to prevent more disasters, even after the 2010 pipeline explosion. In fact, state regulators found that the utility didn't even have a comprehensive safety plan and control process in place by 2017.[62]

PG&E finally filed a safety plan with state regulators in 2019, but it was too little, too late. The company admitted a year later that it had fallen short of meeting seven of its goals, including the need to clear trees away from power lines.[63] The cause was the company's failure to prioritize tree trimming in recent years, and now it can't find qualified workers to get the job done so it can meet its goals.[64]

PG&E's failure to effectively plan has had dire consequences for the company. It was forced to spend more than $20 billion to settle multiple lawsuits and pay government fines, which led to a claim of bankruptcy in 2019.[65] Even worse, the utility plead guilty to 84 criminal counts of involuntary manslaughter in 2020 for causing deadly fires.[66]

YOUR CALL

What could PG&E have done to avoid being in its current position?

5.6 Career Corner: Managing Your Career Readiness

Describe how to develop the career readiness competency of *proactive learning orientation*.

Planning is not one of the career readiness competencies associated with the model shown in Figure 5.6. The reason is not that employers don't value planning skills. Rather, it's the fact that other Career Readiness competencies are foundational to good planning. The soft skill of critical thinking/problem solving is a prime example.

The competency of *critical thinking/problem solving* is defined as sound reasoning to analyze situations, make decisions, and solve problems. These are all critical activities associated with planning and require the ability to obtain, interpret, and analyze both qualitative and quantitative information. In turn, this competency is driven by another career readiness competency: *proactive learning orientation*. Let's consider the link between planning, critical thinking, and proactive learning in more detail.

Critical thinkers don't make quick or rash decisions during the planning process. Instead, they consider alternative solutions to problems and remain open-minded. They remain open-minded by obtaining and considering a wide range of information before making a judgment. This is precisely what happens when someone has a proactive learning orientation. Proactive learners seek information and knowledge so that they expand their knowledge base, which makes them more effective planners. The point is that good planning requires critical thinking, which in turn requires a proactive learning orientation. This process ultimately results in expanding the career readiness competency of *task-based/functional* knowledge.

FIGURE 5.6

Career readiness competencies

Knowledge
- **Task-based/functional**
- Computational thinking
- **Understanding the business**
- New media literacy

Core
- **Critical thinking/problem solving**
- Oral/written communication
- Teamwork/collaboration
- Information technology application
- Leadership
- Professionalism/work ethic
- Cross-cultural competency

Other characteristics
- Resilience
- Personal adaptability
- Self-awareness
- Service/others orientation
- Openness to change
- Generalized self-efficacy

Soft skills
- Decision making
- Social intelligence
- **Networking**
- Emotional intelligence

Attitudes
- Ownership/accepting responsibilities
- Self-motivation
- **Proactive learning orientation** ☆
- Showing commitment
- Positive approach
- Career management

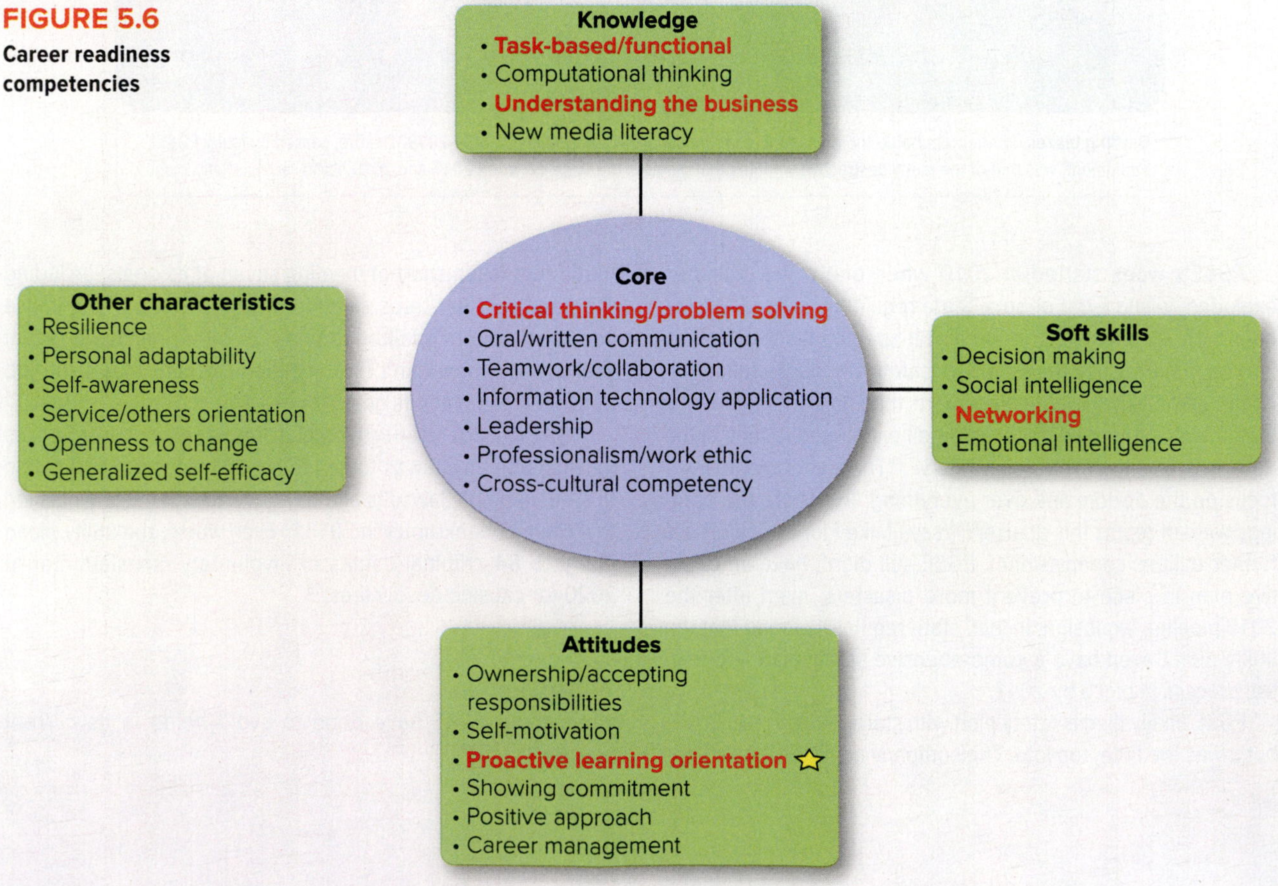

Effective planning requires you to be a proactive learner in areas beyond the technicalities of your profession. It also applies to two additional career readiness competencies: *understanding the business* and *networking*. Organizations want all of us to stay abreast of what is happening in the industries and markets in which we work. Doing so enables us to consider a wider bandwidth of information when planning. For example, staying current about trends in higher education enables us as authors to do a better job in planning the revisions of this product. We also find that many people fail to keep their social and professional networks up to date over time. This is a mistake! Failing to proactively maintain such networks means that we are losing contacts and valuable information that can aid the planning process and our career progression. As authors, for instance, we rely on our social networks to get feedback about what students and educational institutions are looking for in a textbook. As you can see, effective planning is grounded in information that comes from staying current about events within the industry in which we work and with people in our social networks.

The five competencies that we've introduced are highlighted in Figure 5.6. For the purposes of this section, we will focus more closely on the proactive learning orientation competency of career readiness.

Becoming More Proactive

Being "intentionally proactive" is the first step to becoming a proactive learner. "Being proactive means relying on your own choices instead of luck and circumstances. It's about controlling the situation rather than simply waiting for the outcomes," said one business writer.[67] Your proactivity may also lead others to be more proactive. To this point, self-made billionaire and Virgin Group founder, Sir Richard Branson says, "Simply put: positive, proactive behaviour spurs positive, proactive behaviour."[68] You can be more proactive by following four key recommendations:[69]

1. Focus on solutions rather than problems.
2. Take initiative and rely on yourself.
3. Set realistic goals and don't overpromise.
4. Participate and contribute to personal and professional conversations.

Keeping an Open Mind and Suspending Judgment

Keeping an open mind and suspending judgment are essential for developing a proactive learning orientation. This exercise was designed to assist you in this pursuit. Focus on your school work or a current job to practice the technique. You can repeat this process in the future whenever you desire to be open-minded.[70]

Step 1 Make a list of your current tasks, projects, or commitments at school or work.

Step 2 For each task listed in step one, identify the key moments it would be important to be open-minded and suspend judgment.

Step 3 For each of these moments, think of how you might apply the four key skills of being open minded:[71]

1. Question your beliefs. Many of us make decisions based on false beliefs and assumptions. You can check yourself by asking: What specific evidence supports my view? Is my knowledge based on facts or my experience? Why am I arguing with others who have more experience and knowledge? Am I offering an opinion or being opinionated? Based on answers to these questions, you can either proceed in the discussion or take a step back and allow your mind to take in new information.

2. **Pause and seek feedback.** Sometimes being open minded requires talking through a situation with someone else. Observe how others respond to your opinions and recommendations. Don't be married to a perspective, and admit it if you are wrong. If the goal of a discussion is to conduct better planning and make better decisions, then it does not matter whether people agree or disagree with your views. Your goal is to arrive at better decisions and help people to grow.

3. **Watch for communication blocks.** Be aware of words, concepts, or communication styles that elicit emotional responses from you and others. Train your brain to reframe negative thoughts and not jump to negative conclusions. Emotionality leads to defensiveness and the blocking of listening.

4. **Check the accuracy of your past judgments and predictions.** If your judgments and predictions have been wrong, consider the reasons and adjust in the future. ●

Key Points

5.1 Planning and Strategy

- Planning is defined as setting goals and deciding how to achieve them. It is also defined as coping with uncertainty by formulating future courses of action to achieve specified results.
- A plan is a document that outlines how goals are going to be met.
- A strategy, or strategic plan, sets the long-term goals and direction for an organization.
- Strategic management is a process that involves managers from all parts of the organization in the formulation and implementation of strategies and strategic goals.

5.2 Fundamentals of Planning

- An organization's reason for being is expressed in a mission statement.
- A vision is a long-term goal describing "what" an organization wants to become.
- Both mission and vision should express the organization's values. A values statement, or core values statement, expresses what the company stands for, its core priorities, the values its employees embody, and what its products contribute to the world.
- In strategic planning, managers determine what the organization's long-term goals should be for the next 1–5 years with the resources they expect to have available. In tactical planning, managers determine what contributions their work units can make with their given resources during the next 6–24 months. In operational planning, they determine how to accomplish specific tasks with available resources within the next 1–52 weeks.

5.3 Goals and Plans

- Long-term goals are generally referred to as strategic goals. They tend to span 1 to 5 years and focus on achieving the strategies identified in a company's strategic plan.
- Short-term goals are sometimes referred to as tactical goals, operational goals, or just plain goals. They generally span 12 months and are connected to strategic goals in a hierarchy known as a means-end chain.
- A means-end chain shows how goals are connected or linked across an organization. The accomplishment of low-level goals is the means leading to the accomplishment of high-level goals or ends.
- Strategic goals are set by and for top management and focus on objectives for the organization as a whole. Tactical goals are set by and for middle managers and focus on the actions needed to achieve strategic goals. Operational goals are set by first-line managers and team leaders and are concerned with short-term matters associated with realizing tactical goals.
- An operating plan is a plan that breaks long-term output into short-term targets or goals. Operational plans turn strategic plans into actionable short-term goals and action plans.
- An action plan defines the course of action needed to achieve the stated goal. Whether the goal is long term or short term, action plans outline the tactics that will be used to achieve the goal. Each tactic also contains a projected date for completing the desired activities.

5.4 Promoting Consistencies in Goals: SMART Goals, Management by Objectives, and Goal Cascading

- The five characteristics of a good goal are represented by the acronym SMART. A SMART goal is one that is specific, measurable, attainable, results-oriented, and has target dates.

- Management by objectives (MBO) is a four-step process in which (1) managers and employees jointly set objectives for the employee, (2) managers develop action plans, (3) managers and employees periodically review the employee's performance, and (4) the manager makes a performance appraisal and rewards the employee according to results. The purpose of MBO is to motivate rather than to control subordinates.

5.5 The Planning/Control Cycle

- Once plans are made, managers must stay in control using the planning/control cycle, which has two planning steps (1 and 2) and two control steps (3 and 4), as follows: (1) Make the plan. (2) Carry out the plan. (3) Control the direction by comparing results with the plan. (4) Control the direction by taking corrective action in two ways—namely, by (a) correcting deviations in the plan being carried out or (b) improving future plans.

5.6 Career Corner: Managing Your Career Readiness

- Planning requires the use of multiple career readiness competencies, including critical thinking/problem solving, proactive learning orientation, task-based/functional knowledge, understanding the business, and networking.
- You can increase the competency of proactive learning orientation by becoming more proactive and keeping an open mind and suspending judgment.

Understanding the Chapter: What Do I Know?

1. What are planning, strategy, and strategic management?
2. Why are they important?
3. What is the difference between a mission and a vision, a mission statement and a vision statement?
4. What are three types of planning?
5. What are two types of goals?
6. What are SMART goals?
7. What is management by objectives?
8. What three things have to happen for MBO to be successful?
9. Explain the planning/control cycle.

Management in Action

Amtrak Is on the Wrong Side of the Tracks

The National Railroad Passenger Corporation, better known as Amtrak, began operations in 1971. The railroad has more than 20,000 employees and serves more than 500 destinations in the United States and Canada on more than 21,400 miles of track. Amtrak customers took 32.5 million trips in 2019, setting a record year-over-year increase of 800,000 passengers.[72]

Congress created Amtrak because private railroads were failing. By the 1940s, rail travel became less popular as Americans chose buses, planes, and cars to get around the country. Eventually, the U.S. government consolidated the majority of passenger rail service under Amtrak's umbrella. The federal government is Amtrak's majority stockholder and guarantees its financial support, but the company is operated as a for-profit organization rather than a government entity.

Though it was created to save an unprofitable railroad system, Amtrak itself has never earned a profit since its inception. For example, the company lost $194 million and $170 million in 2017 and 2018, respectively.

Americans continue to choose other modes of transportation over Amtrak, and government subsidies are all that stand between the railroad and bankruptcy.[73]

Let's take a closer look at what's going on at America's only high-speed rail provider.

A LOSING MODEL

One of Amtrak's biggest problems is its price. For example, a four-hour Amtrak train from New York City to Boston is more expensive than hopping on a one-hour flight. Amtrak charges these high fares on popular Northeastern routes because its other routes across the country are either unprofitable or operating at a loss.[74] According to *Virginia Mercury,* ridership may be able to grow if Amtrak's prices were reduced.[75]

Amtrak's other challenge is America's sheer size. It is the fourth largest country in the world with 3.8 million square miles of land. Compare this with Japan's rail service, which has to cover an area smaller than the state of California. All of this rail needs maintenance and repair, which Amtrak can't afford. For example, simply bringing the rail tracks in the 453-mile Northeast Corridor to a state of good repair will cost $42 billion.[76]

To make matters worse, Amtrak's rails aren't the only asset in dire need of fixing. Its passenger cars have expected lifespans of 25 years, yet the average car in its fleet is well over 30 years old. And Amtrak's biggest investor, the federal government, which has spent more than $100 billion in taxpayer funds to keep the rail service operating, doesn't have the appetite to make large-scale investments in the railroad.[77]

LEADERSHIP HAS A NEW PLAN

Amtrak hired Richard Anderson as CEO in 2017 to chart a new strategy for the company. Anderson, formerly Delta Airlines' CEO, is changing the railroad's route system and the services it provides in the hopes of leading it to profitability for the first time in its 50-year history.

The first part of Anderson's plan includes breaking up long-distance train routes and substituting bus service. For example, he wants to change the Chicago to Los Angeles route and replace 500 miles of the trip with bus service. Anderson believes these types of routes don't meet the needs of today's commuters. "If we're going to deal with congestion, growing populations and the carbon footprint of automobiles, Amtrak is the best answer for intercity transportation in a 200- to 300-mile market," he says.[78] Reducing the number of unprofitable routes won't only help the carrier's bottom line, it will also reduce the costs associated with maintaining large swaths of railroad tracks.

The second part of Anderson's plan includes a reduction in some of the company's services. For example, Amtrak has decided to scrap its traditional dining car service. The reservation-based dining cars, staples of the U.S. railroad system, had shiny silverware and white linens. Fresh food, which could rival high-end restaurants, was provided by onboard kitchens. Now, Amtrak provides prepackaged meals and no longer has "white glove" service in most of its dining cars. The company estimates that this change will save around $2 million a year and attract a younger generation of new riders who are on the run, on their phones, and not looking to sit at a fancy, communal table. The change "is part of an evolution," says Peter Wilander, Amtrak's customer service chief.[79]

DERAILED PLANS?

Amtrak's strategic plan is showing some early success. The company posted a $29.8 million loss in 2019, its best operating performance ever.[80] And the company believes 2020 will be even better. "Our expectation is that in 2020, we will actually make money, we will have positive earnings for the first time in the company's history," says Amtrak Board Chairman Anthony Coscia.[81]

However, critics believe Anderson's pursuit of profitability has caused Amtrak's service to suffer. Jim Mathews, president and chief executive of the Rail Passengers Association, says train riders are lamenting the end of the dining car. "It is not just the food, it is the experience," he tells *The Washington Post*. Skeptical lawmakers, responsible for subsidizing the company, echo Mathews' concerns. "This is shortsighted and foolish," says Tennessee Congressman Steve Cohen. Representative Cohen feels Anderson is doing to rail service what he did to air service. Amtrak's decision is "like Delta Air Lines taking away amenities to passengers on their airplanes and making air traffic more like traveling on a bus," he says.[82]

Lawmakers, many from less populated states, have also taken aim at Anderson's plans to cut long-haul routes, which include stops in states like Kansas and New Mexico. "The idea that Amtrak would think about replacing passenger service with bus service for 400 miles and believe that we would still have a long-distance passenger train service is something I can't get over," said Kansas Senator Jerry Moran. Moran's criticism doesn't just put Amtrak's congressional budget allocation in jeopardy. The government also has broad discretion to direct the railroad to take or not take certain actions. In this case, the Senate ordered Amtrak to run its Southwest long-haul route as originally planned, shattering Anderson's strategy.[83]

Other lawmakers think the company's entire model should be re-evaluated. Oregon Congressman Peter DeFazio believes Anderson's profit-focused philosophy is inappropriate for a government-owned company like Amtrak. "I think part of the problem we're dealing with is the original mandate from Congress, which said that [Amtrak] is supposed to be run as a for-profit corporation," says DeFazio.[84]

Anderson's plans seem to be stalling as the company is on the verge of profitability.

FOR DISCUSSION

Problem-Solving Perspective

1. What is the underlying problem in this case from Amtrak CEO Richard Anderson's perspective?

2. What are some of the causes of this problem?

3. Do you believe Anderson's strategy and plans will turn the company around? Explain.

Application of Chapter Content

1. Using the steps in Figure 5.1, describe how Amtrak is making changes to become profitable.

2. How does congressional skepticism impact Amtrak's development of its mission and vision statements?

3. Define one specific strategic, tactical, and operational plan that Amtrak can utilize.

4. Develop a simple strategic goal, operational goal, and action plan for Amtrak: The goals need to be SMART. Then utilize a means-end chain to illustrate the relationship among the three.

5. Develop a planning/control cycle to make sure Amtrak is headed in the right direction.

Legal/Ethical Challenge

Are Profits More Important than Alzheimer's Patients?

Planning and strategy go together, and they flow from a company's mission and vision. Decisions made in the pursuit of corporate strategy are challenging because they ultimately involve choices about how to spend valuable resources. U.S. pharmaceutical giant Pfizer is a good illustration.

Pfizer decided in January 2018 to no longer pursue new research and development (R&D) in treatments for Alzheimer's disease, resulting in the loss of 300 jobs.[85] Worse yet, the approximately 5.5 million U.S. adults with this neurological disease no longer have one of the biggest pharmaceutical companies in their corner.[86] Pfizer made this challenging decision because of either low profitability or limited capacity, even though some of its Alzheimer's-related research showed potential.[87]

With respect to profitability, Alzheimer's research has proven to be costlier than most other R&D pursuits. A neuroscientist at Edinburgh University told *BBC Radio* that "More than 99% of trials for Alzheimer's drugs have failed in the past 15 years."[88] Investors thus are pressuring pharmaceutical companies to spend less on this research when they can pursue more profitable projects, such as treatments for anxiety disorders and erectile dysfunction.

Capacity becomes an issue in pharmaceutical research and development because it's difficult to run multiple large-scale R&D programs at the same time. This has led pharmaceutical companies to focus only on specific drugs. A former head of research and development at Pfizer told the *Financial Times*, "You can't run several programmes of that size, even with a budget like Pfizer's. . . . How many times can these companies take another shot when other parts of science like gene therapy are exploding, and when there's a desperate need for new drugs to replace opioids? There are many more areas where you can see the goal lines."[89] Pfizer's management team apparently agrees with this conclusion. The organization said in a statement that not pursuing Alzheimer's research "was an exercise to reallocate [spending] across our portfolio, to focus on those areas where our pipeline, and our scientific expertise, is strongest."[90]

Though Pfizer may be changing its strategy and its resource allocations, the company has kept its mission statement the same: "To be the premier, innovative biopharmaceutical company." Its values include "customer focus" and "integrity."[91] However, its latest decision is seen by some as contradictory to its mission and values. Alzheimer's Research UK says that companies should be encouraged to invest in research into neuroscience. For its part, the Alzheimer's Society called Pfizer's decision "disappointing" and a "heavy blow" to those living with dementia.[92]

Other big drug makers are not letting profit and limited capacity get in their way. A top scientist at Eli Lilly, one of Pfizer's competitors, told the *Financial Times*, "Taking care of Alzheimer's patients is a huge economic cost to society and now is not the time to give up." Eli Lilly's most advanced Alzheimer's drug failed in a large trial in 2016, but the company has vowed to continue Alzheimer's treatment R&D.[93] Another U.S. competitor, AstraZeneca, also remains committed to fighting the disease.

SOLVING THE CHALLENGE

What would you do if you were Pfizer's CEO?

1. Move on to other projects. Pfizer has an obligation to its shareholders not to throw money at projects that prove to be unsuccessful.

2. Continue funding Alzheimer's R&D. As a global leader in the pharmaceutical industry, Pfizer has an obligation to society to find treatments for diseases affecting millions of people. This would also be in line with its mission statement and values.

3. Contribute to agencies such as the National Institutes of Health so they can continue their studies of Alzheimer's.

4. Suggest other options.

6

Strategic Management

How Exceptional Managers Realize a Grand Design

Kapook2981/iStock/Getty Images

After reading this chapter, you should be able to:

LO 6-1 Identify the three principles underlying strategic positioning.

LO 6-2 Outline the five steps in the strategic-management process.

LO 6-3 Explain how an organization assesses the competitive landscape.

LO 6-4 Explain the three methods of corporate-level strategy.

LO 6-5 Discuss Porter's and Welch's techniques for formulating a business-level strategy.

LO 6-6 Describe how to create, execute, and control a functional-level strategy.

LO 6-7 Describe how to enhance your strategic thinking.

FORECAST   *What's Ahead in This Chapter*

We describe strategic positioning and three levels of strategy, and then consider the five steps in the strategic-management process. In assessing current reality, we describe the tools of SWOT analysis, VRIO, forecasting, and benchmarking. When discussing corporate-level strategy, we review three types of overall strategies, the BCG matrix, and diversification. In describing business-level strategy, we discuss Porter's five competitive forces and his four competitive strategies, as well as Welch's strategy formulation questions. When describing functional-level strategy, we discuss the importance of strategic implementation and control. We conclude with a Career Corner that focuses on how to develop your strategic thinking.

Your Personal Brand Requires a Strategy

As part of their overall competitive strategy, organizations create and build memorable brands for their products and services. Among the world's most valuable brands are Apple, Google, Microsoft, Coca-Cola, and Amazon, but brands don't have to be global to have value. For her blog about getting kids to eat vegetables, London mom Mandy Mazliah created a brand name, Sneaky Veg, and asked an artist to design a logo and distinctive graphics to help her creation stand out from the crowd.[1]

The term "branding" used to only be for businesses, but not anymore. Technological advancements, such as the advent of social media, mean individuals are in the public eye. In fact, 70% of employers use social media to screen candidates during the hiring process.[2] You'll need to build your own personal brand, if you are looking to gain employment upon graduation.

Why You Need a Personal Brand

Ceejay Dawkins, a tax manager at Deloitte, advises new college graduates thus:

> Build your brand. Whether it's being the first person at work in the morning or being the person that always asks intelligent questions—be known for something. Building that brand, building that solid reputation, will follow you through your career. People will notice that and will want you on their assignments.[3]

Quite simply, branding sells. Personal branding goes beyond having a resume or a Twitter, LinkedIn, or Instagram profile.[4] A strong personal brand lets potential employers learn about who you are, your passions, your areas of expertise, your relevant experience, and your aspirations. That's why it's a good idea for you to take control of the message you want to send employers about your career readiness and the information you want them to see on social media.

How to Create Your Brand

Your personal brand should have two components. The first reflects your unique identity and strengths (this is part of a SWOT analysis, which we will discuss in Section 6.3). The second conveys the fact that you are career ready. Developing this type of brand increases your chances of obtaining a desired job and a rewarding career.

Create and promote your personal brand with these steps:

1. Identify the core message of your brand. Consider any special training, education, talents, skills, family background, and special challenges overcome. Where do you see yourself in five years? Ten?

2. Write a personal branding statement. Your personal branding statement is a short paragraph describing who you are, what you stand for, and what you like to do. It emphasizes your unique knowledge and expertise as well as your personal life.[5]

3. Develop a social media strategy.[6] Choose the most appropriate platform for your message (Twitter and LinkedIn have very different audiences and purposes); polish your writing style; and make sure everything you share, whether in posts, comments, or a blog, is a good and truthful representation of your brand. Remember, everything an employer sees or reads about you tells a story about your brand. Ensure that your name, profile, picture, and imagery are the same, no matter what platform you are using. Keeping consistent profiles helps others find you easily and helps ingrain a picture of you in the minds of others.

4. Start networking. Don't wait until graduation to network; start now! Join groups and attend meetings for people in your field of interest. Meeting others in your industry, whether online or in person, can lead to great collaborative opportunities that will hone your teamwork skills.

For Discussion Do you have a personal brand? How would you shift your social media presence to make it more appealing to potential employers?

6.1 Strategic Positioning and Levels of Strategy

THE BIG PICTURE

Strategic positioning attempts to achieve sustainable competitive advantage by preserving what is distinctive about a company. It is based on the principles that strategy is the creation of a unique and valuable position, requires trade-offs in competing, and involves creating a "fit" among activities. There are three levels of strategy: corporate, business level, and functional.

LO 6-1

Identify the three principles underlying strategic positioning.

Harvard Business School professor Michael Porter is recognized as one of the most influential business school professors. *Fortune* writer Geoffrey Colvin described him "as the all-time greatest strategy guru."[7]

Is this high praise deserved? Certainly Porter's status as a leading authority on competitive strategy is unchallenged. The Strategic Management Society, for instance, voted Porter the most influential living strategist. We refer to him repeatedly in this chapter.

Strategic Positioning and Its Principles

According to Porter, **strategic positioning** attempts to achieve sustainable competitive advantage by preserving what is distinctive about a company. "It means," he says, "performing *different* activities from rivals, or performing *similar* activities in different ways."[8]

Three key principles underlie strategic positioning.[9]

1. Strategy Is the Creation of a Unique and Valuable Position

Strategic position emerges from three sources:[10]

- **Few needs, many customers.** Strategic position can be derived from serving the few needs of many customers. Example: Crocs sells only shoes, but it provides them to all kinds of people.

- **Broad needs, few customers.** A strategic position may be based on serving the broad needs of just a few customers. Example: Buy Buy Baby sells clothing, strollers, and other items for babies.

- **Broad needs, many customers.** Strategy may be oriented toward serving the broad needs of many customers. Example: Allegiant Airlines is a low-cost travel company that not only offers flights across the United States, but also owns budget-friendly hotels.

Strategy guru. Harvard Business School professor Michael Porter suggests that every company is subject to five forces: its current competitors, possible new competitors, the threat of substitutes for its products or services, the bargaining power of its suppliers, and the bargaining power of its customers. Tannen Maury/Shutterstock

2. Strategy Requires Trade-Offs in Competing

As a glance at the preceding choices shows, some strategies are incompatible. Thus, a company has to choose not only what strategy to follow but what strategy *not* to follow. Example: Neutrogena soap, points out Porter, is positioned more as a medicinal product than as a cleansing agent. In achieving this narrow positioning, the company gives up sales based on deodorizing; gives up large volume; and, accordingly, gives up some manufacturing efficiencies.

3. Strategy Involves Creating a "Fit" among Activities
"Fit" has to do with the ways a company's activities interact and reinforce one another. Example: A mutual fund company such as Vanguard Group follows a low-cost strategy and aligns all its activities accordingly, selling funds directly to consumers and minimizing portfolio turnover.

Research confirms that a misfit between a firm's activities can negatively affect its performance.[11] Take for example short-lived (1993–1995) Continental Lite, a low-cost spinoff of Continental Airlines. The airline tried to match some, but not all, of Southwest Airlines' activities. Continental Lite was not successful because all the pieces didn't fit, as they did at Southwest.

Levels of Strategy

Strategic management takes places at three levels, each supporting the other (*see Figure 6.1*). Though each level is distinct, there needs to be alignment across them. For instance, one study showed that organizations are more competitive when their corporate- and business-level strategies are aligned.[12]

FIGURE 6.1
Three levels of strategy

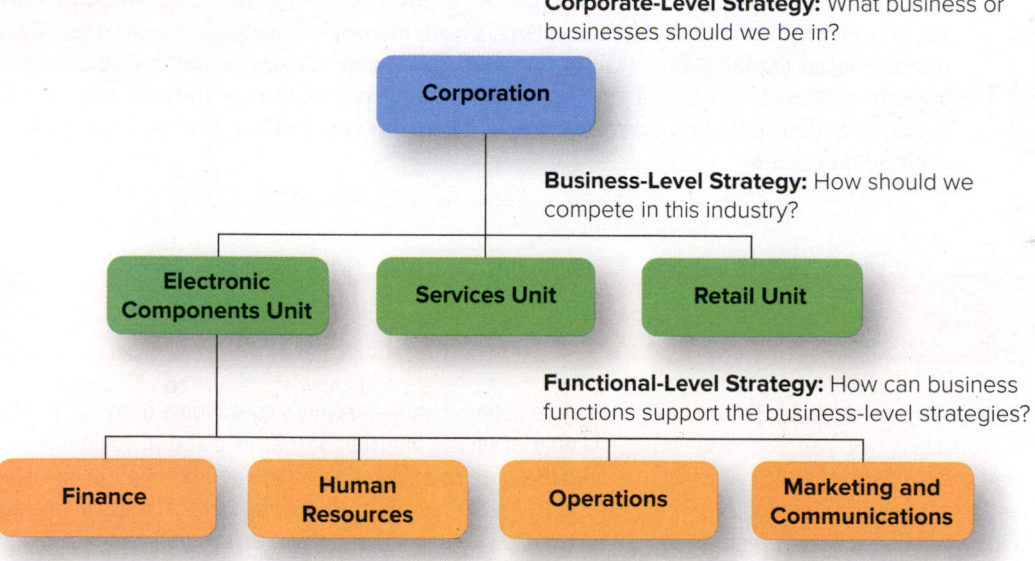

Level 1: Corporate-Level Strategy
Corporate-level strategy focuses on the organization as a whole. Executives at the most senior levels, generally referred to as the "C-Suite," typically conduct this type of strategic planning. This analysis answers questions such as "what business are we in?" and "what products and services shall we offer?" Strategic decisions at this level can involve acquisitions, such as Amazon's acquisition of Whole Foods. Joint ventures also are considered corporate-level strategies. For example, Fiat Chrysler and Taiwan's Foxconn are setting up a joint venture to build electric cars and Internet-connected vehicles in China.[13]

Level 2: Business-Level Strategy
Business-level strategy focuses on individual business units or product/service lines. Senior-level managers below the C-Suite typically are responsible for this level of strategy. Issues under consideration flow from decisions made at the corporate level and involve considerations such as how much to spend on marketing, new-product development, product expansion or contraction, facilities

expansion or reduction, equipment, pricing, and employee development. For example, Dunkin' teamed up with plant-based meat producer Beyond Meat to offer Beyond Sausage sandwiches at more than 9,000 of its locations in 2019. This strategy was aimed at appealing to changing consumer preferences.[14]

Level 3: Functional-Level Strategy   Functional-level strategy is a plan of action by each functional area of the organization to support higher level strategies. Functional managers lead planning discussions at this level, and the focus is on more tactical issues that support the execution of business-level strategies. For example, Dunkin's decision to offer Beyond Sausage sandwiches would require three related functional strategies. Marketing managers would first need to decide how to market the new sandwich. Store managers would then need to determine how best to make them with the existing equipment in the restaurant. Finally, operations managers would need to resolve the logistics for transporting the plant-based sausages to each location.

Does Strategic Management Work for Small as Well as Large Firms?

Evidence reveals that the use of strategic management techniques and processes is associated with increased small business performance.[15] Surprisingly, however, many small business owners do not engage in strategic planning.[16] A recent study of nine small- and medium-sized manufacturing, construction, and service businesses offers one potential explanation. Results revealed that these businesses had an operational and short-term focus based on "survival instinct" rather than a long-term strategic focus[17] The Example box describes how small businesses can use strategic planning to their advantage. ●

EXAMPLE   Strategic Planning Guides Growth and Organizational Change at Evernote and Groove

Evernote is a California-based company of about 325 people that makes apps and other products to help people collect and manage the information they need in their jobs and daily lives. The company recently found that it had been putting so much time and energy into creating a wide array of new features for its products that it risked losing sight of its core purpose. While most customers were happy with the small percentage of Evernote products they chose, it seemed that no one used the same products or had the same experience across products. So, perhaps by falling prey to the tech industry's pressure to innovate and constantly release new products, Evernote was expending a lot of its resources supporting features that each had only a very small user base. The goal of new CEO Ian Small is to better align Evernote's strategy with its core product by paring back some of its many other offerings and focusing on its foundations.[18]

Another firm that hopes to refocus on its core strategy is using a different path to get there. Groove, a start-up that develops help desk and online customer support software for small businesses, has fewer than 50 employees, all of whom work remotely. As the company's subscribers grew, so did the number of service interruptions, as its platform could not process the large amounts of data that were flowing through it. In response, CEO Alex Turnball decided in 2016 to completely rebuild the platform from scratch. The company, however, kept missing deadlines on the redesign. It didn't have the structure to scale up, the right people weren't in the right roles, and the discipline to execute quickly wasn't there. The organization, it seemed, couldn't go from start-up to scale up. With this in mind, Turnball made some key changes in 2018. He modified the organizational structure of Groove so that the right expert was in the right position, developed new routines and processes for product development, and brought in consultants to guide them along the way. Groove's platform relaunched later that year to rave reviews from customers.[19]

YOUR CALL

Why do you think Evernote and Groove temporarily lost sight of their strategic goals? Do you agree with their CEOs' plans for refocusing their respective companies? Why or why not?

6.2 The Strategic-Management Process

THE BIG PICTURE

The strategic-management process has five steps: Establish the mission, vision, and values statements; assess the current reality; formulate corporate, business, and functional strategies; strategic implementation; and maintain strategic control. All steps may be affected by feedback that enables the taking of constructive action.

When is a good time to begin the strategic-management process? There is not one correct answer. For instance, many organizations review their strategy every couple of years, but nowadays, that may not be frequent enough. This is especially true for organizations in fast-changing markets, such as technology and tourism.[20] In contrast, a crisis is often the catalyst for strategic planning. Toyota is a good example.

In 2020 the automaker encountered quality problems with its airbags, which may not inflate in a crash. The company was forced to recall 3.4 million vehicles globally and safety regulators are investigating whether the faulty airbags were responsible for eight deaths.[21] This is the second Toyota airbag recall in one year. At the same time, the automaker also recalled approximately 700,000 vehicles due to faulty fuel pumps, which could lead to engine failure while driving at high speeds.[22] The strategic-management process will surely assist CEO Akio Toyoda in determining how best to overcome these problems.

LO 6-2

Outline the five steps in the strategic-management process.

The Five Steps of the Strategic-Management Process

The strategic-management process has five steps, plus a feedback loop, as shown below. *(See Figure 6.2.)* Let's consider these five steps and bring them to life by examining how Microsoft is using them to revamp its corporate strategy.

FIGURE 6.2

The strategic-management process

The process has five steps.

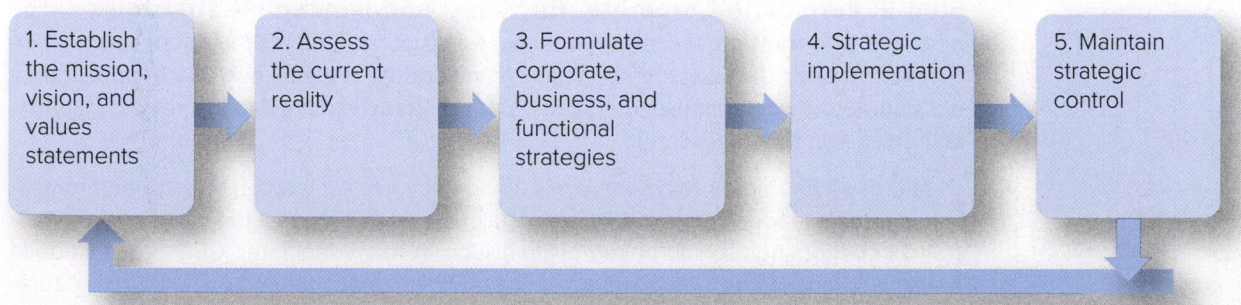

1. Establish the mission, vision, and values statements
2. Assess the current reality
3. Formulate corporate, business, and functional strategies
4. Strategic implementation
5. Maintain strategic control

Feedback: Revise actions, if necessary, based on feedback

Step 1: Establish the Mission, Vision, and Values Statements   We discussed mission, vision, and values statements in Chapter 5. The *mission statement*, you'll recall, expresses the organization's purpose or reason for being. A recent study found that almost a quarter of Fortune 100 companies have a faulty mission statement.[23] Employee involvement when developing mission statements may remedy these faults, as research indicates that the greater their involvement, the better the firm's financial performance.[24] The *vision statement* states what the organization wants to become, where it wants to go strategically. The *values statement* describes what the organization stands for, its core priorities, the values its employees embody, and what its products contribute to the world. Research has found that organizations that clearly articulate their values in their mission statement perform better.[25]

Microsoft Example: Microsoft has identified a number of core values that support its vision of helping "people and businesses throughout the world realize their full potential."[26] They include the need for innovation that "can and will contribute to a brighter world in big and small ways" and trustworthy computing that can "deliver secure, private, and reliable computing experiences based on sound business practices."[27]

Strategy HQ. Microsoft's corporate headquarters in Redmond, Washington, is where managers formulate the company's corporate, business, and functional strategies. With more and more companies communicating virtually, do you see strategy formulation continuing to happen at a central location? VDB Photos/Shutterstock

Step 2: Assess the Current Reality   The second step is to do a current reality assessment, or *organizational assessment*, to look at where the organization stands and see what is working and what could be different so as to maximize efficiency and effectiveness in achieving the organization's mission. Among the tools for assessing the current reality are SWOT analysis, VRIO analysis, forecasting, and benchmarking, all of which we discuss in Section 6.3.

Microsoft Example: Microsoft is a good example of a firm whose current reality has radically changed. The company, known for its Windows operating system and Office suite, earned around 80% of its revenue from desktop software sales in 2005. (Desktop software is stored on a computer.) By 2008, competitors such as Amazon introduced cloud-based software, which is software stored and run off the Internet. Cloud innovation left Microsoft scrambling as customers were looking for new ways to deliver software online. Microsoft needed to quickly leverage its resources and provide a solution for the market if it wanted to stay relevant.[28]

Step 3: Formulate Corporate, Business, and Functional Strategies   The next step is to translate the broad mission and vision statements into a corporate strategy, which, after the assessment of the current reality, explains how the organization's mission is to be accomplished. Three common grand strategies are growth, stability, and defensive, as we'll describe.

Microsoft Example: Microsoft knew it had to evolve if it wanted to grow and remain the market leader. Former CEO Steve Ballmer said in 2010 that the company was "all-in" in becoming a cloud-based organization. A few years later, CEO Satya Nadella formally introduced a mobile-first and cloud-first strategy for Microsoft utilizing Azure, the company's cloud-based platform.[29]

During the strategic-management process, strategy alternatives should be evaluated properly to select the best one to achieve strategic goals.[30] Strategy formulation is the process of choosing among different strategies and altering them to best fit the organization's needs. Formulating strategy is a time-consuming process both because it is important and because the strategy must be translated into more specific *strategic plans*, which determine what the organization's long-term goals should be for the next one to five years.

In Sections 6.4 and 6.5 we discuss the process by which managers create corporate-level strategy and business-level strategy, respectively.

Step 4: Strategic Implementation: Execute the Strategies

Putting strategic plans into effect is **strategy implementation**. Strategic planning isn't effective, of course, unless it can be translated into lower-level plans within the organization. This means that top managers need to check on possible roadblocks within the organization's structure and culture and see if the right people and control systems are available to execute the plans.[31] Strategic implementation is essential for success, requires significant involvement by leadership, and is considered to elicit the greatest challenge for managers.[32]

Microsoft Example: Microsoft has utilized its Azure platform as a foundation to execute new offerings, including software, gaming, and personal computing products. "Every one of our solutions is reinforcing our core intelligent cloud and intelligent edge platform," says CEO Nadella. The company reorganized its structure in order to further its ambitions in the fast-moving cloud market. For example, cloud-based artificial intelligence is now split between multiple executives, while Windows has been deprioritized. The company also acquired dozens of cloud start-ups since 2013 (almost double that of Amazon).[33]

Step 5: Maintain Strategic Control: The Feedback Loop

Strategic control consists of monitoring the execution of strategy and making adjustments, if necessary. To keep strategic plans on track, managers need control systems to monitor progress and take corrective action—early and rapidly—when things start to go awry. Corrective action constitutes a feedback loop in which a problem requires that managers return to an earlier step to rethink policies, redo budgets, or revise personnel arrangements.

Microsoft Example: Microsoft has a software error reporting system, which is designed to provide the company with real-time feedback when customers face issues with its Windows operating system. The system allows the company to quickly become aware of errors and push out solutions to users. Feedback also is used for future product development.[34]

All told, Microsoft's strategies are working. The company's revenue was up 14% between 2018 and 2019. The boost came from Microsoft's commercial cloud division, which increased revenues by 39%. CEO Nadella believes the company's cloud-based strategy is "resulting in larger, multi-year commercial cloud agreements and growing momentum across every layer of our technology."[35]

We discuss the details of the steps in the strategic-management process in the rest of this chapter.

SELF-ASSESSMENT 6.1

Assessing Strategic Thinking

This survey is designed to assess an organization's level of strategic thinking. Please be prepared to answer these questions if your instructor has assigned Self-Assessment 6.1 in Connect.

1. What is the level of strategic thinking? Are you surprised by the results?

2. If you were meeting with an executive from the company you evaluated, what advice would you provide based on the survey results and what you learned about assessing current reality?

6.3 Assessing the Current Reality

THE BIG PICTURE

To develop a grand strategy, you need to gather data and make projections, using tools such as SWOT analysis, VRIO analysis, forecasting, and benchmarking.

LO 6-3

Explain how an organization assesses the competitive landscape.

Figure 6.2 (and Chapter 5) demonstrate that the first step in the strategic-management process is to establish the organization's mission, vision, and values statements. The second step in the strategic-management process, *assess the current reality*, looks at where the organization stands internally and externally—to determine what's working and what's not, to see what can be changed to create sustainable competitive advantage: **Sustainable competitive advantage** exists when other companies cannot duplicate the value delivered to customers. An assessment helps to create an objective view of everything the organization does: its sources of revenue or funding, its work-flow processes, its organizational structure, client satisfaction, employee turnover, and other matters.

Among the tools for assessing the current reality are *SWOT analysis*, *VRIO analysis*, *forecasting*, and *benchmarking*.

SWOT Analysis

SWOT analysis is a good first step at gaining insight into whether or not a company has competitive advantage. **SWOT analysis** is a situational analysis in which a company assesses its strengths, weaknesses, opportunities, and threats. In Chapter 3 we introduced you to an organization's internal and external environments *(Figure 3.1)*. A SWOT analysis provides you with a realistic understanding of your organization in relation to its internal and external environments so you can better formulate strategy in pursuit of its mission. *(See Figure 6.3.)*

FIGURE 6.3

SWOT analysis

SWOT stands for strengths, weaknesses, opportunities, and threats.

INSIDE MATTERS—Analysis of Internal Strengths & Weaknesses

S—Strengths: internal environment
Strengths could be work processes, organization, culture, staff, product quality, production capacity, image, financial resources & requirements, service levels, other internal matters.

W—Weaknesses: internal environment
Weaknesses could be in the same categories as stated for Strengths: work processes, organization, culture, etc.

O—Opportunities: external environment
Opportunities could be market segment analysis, industry & competition analysis, impact of technology on organization, product analysis, governmental impacts, other external matters.

T—Threats: external environment
Threats could be in the same categories as stated for Opportunities: market segment analysis, etc.

OUTSIDE MATTERS—Analysis of External Opportunities & Threats

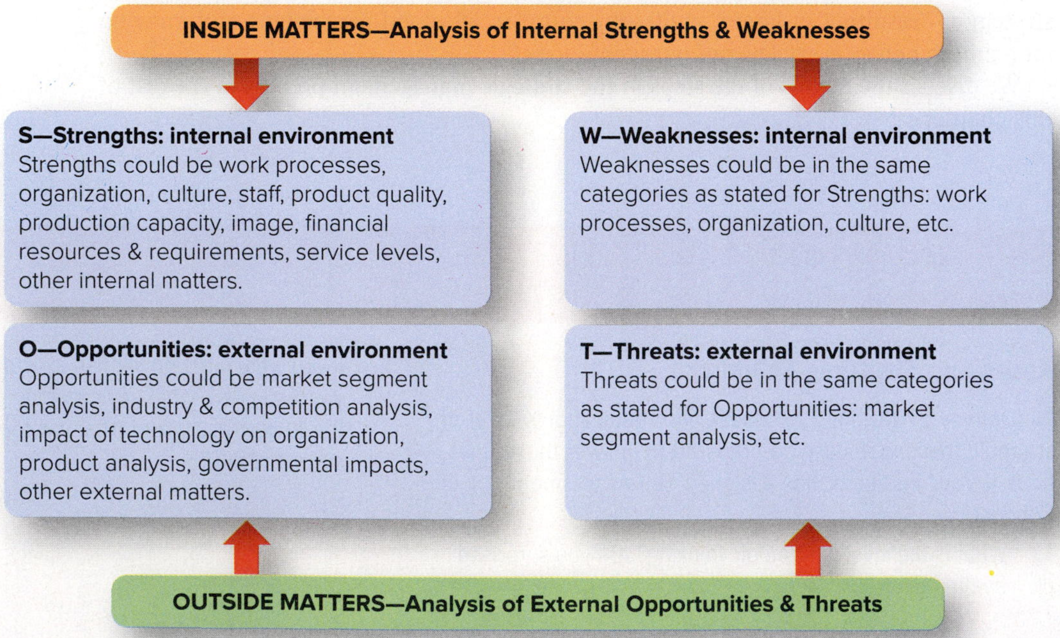

The SWOT analysis is divided into two parts: internal environment and external environment—that is, an analysis of *internal strengths and weaknesses* (internal environment) and an analysis of *external opportunities and threats* (external environment). How often should a SWOT analysis be conducted? The answer is: frequently in today's competitive environment. In fact, a recent study found that organizations need to compare their internal and external environments every 18 months or less.[36] The following table gives examples of SWOT characteristics that might apply to a college. *(See Table 6.1.)*

S—STRENGTHS (INTERNAL STRENGTHS)	W—WEAKNESSES (INTERNAL WEAKNESSES)
• Faculty teaching and research abilities • High-ability students • Loyal alumni • Strong interdisciplinary programs	• Limited programs in business • High teaching loads • Insufficient racial diversity • Lack of high-technology infrastructure
O—OPPORTUNITIES (EXTERNAL OPPORTUNITIES)	T—THREATS (EXTERNAL THREATS)
• Growth in many local skilled jobs • Many firms give equipment to college • Local minority population increasing • High school students take college classes	• Depressed state and national economy • High school enrollments in decline • Increased competition from other colleges • Funding from all sources at risk

TABLE 6.1 SWOT Characteristics That Might Apply to a College

Internal Environment: Analysis of Internal Strengths and Weaknesses   Does your organization have a skilled workforce? a superior reputation? strong financing? These are examples of organizational strengths—the skills and capabilities that give the organization special competencies and competitive advantages in executing strategies in pursuit of its vision.

Or does your organization have obsolete technology? outdated facilities? a shaky marketing operation? These are examples of organizational weaknesses—the drawbacks that hinder an organization in executing strategies in pursuit of its vision.

External Environment: Analysis of External Opportunities and Threats
Is your organization fortunate to have weak rivals? emerging markets? a booming economy? These are instances of organizational opportunities—environmental factors that the organization may exploit for competitive advantage.

Alternatively, is your organization having to deal with new regulations? a shortage of resources? substitute products? These are some possible organizational threats—environmental factors that hinder an organization's achieving a competitive advantage.

The following Example illustrates an application of SWOT analysis to Toyota, Japan's largest automaker.

EXAMPLE   SWOT Analysis: Analyzing Toyota Motor Corp.

Toyota has been making cars since 1937 and sells them in more than 170 countries. North America is one of its top two markets; the other is Japan, its corporate headquarters. Along with the luxury Lexus brand, Toyota markets the Corolla, Camry, Avalon, Sienna, RAV4, Highlander, and Prius, among other models. While the company plans big investments in automated driving and artificial intelligence and posted 2019 operating profits of $16.96 billion, it has seen its share of challenges associated with recalls and the COVID-19 outbreak in China.[37]

If you were a top Toyota manager, what strengths, weaknesses, opportunities, and threats would you identify in a SWOT analysis?

Internal Strengths The original "Toyota Way" stressed the values of continuous improvement and eliminating waste, from assembly line to boardroom. This innovative and much-copied philosophy helped Toyota develop a culture focused on planning, identifying rather than hiding problems, and prizing teamwork. The company's continued focus on quality and reliability, called the Toyota Production System, has enhanced its image as a strong brand.[38] Toyota models regularly make J.D. Power's rankings for performance; in 2019, the Camry and Yaris were among best performance cars.[39]

Toyota also is known for its strong research and development, with 20 R&D facilities in seven countries and research spending of nearly $10 billion in 2019. The company is outspent in R&D only by Volkswagen and Daimler.[40] Toyota's research has led to innovations like its best-selling hybrid vehicle, the RAV4. The company also has solid cash reserves,[41] and the enormous value of its brand is another strength.

Internal Weaknesses Beginning in 2000, Toyota suffered some widely publicized recalls, due to sticking accelerators (causing a U.S. criminal probe and $1.2 billion penalty) and an array of potential hazards including unstable steering columns and faulty airbags. Problems continued between 2016 and 2018 with the company again recalling millions of vehicles for faulty airbags.[42] As we mentioned earlier in the chapter, between 2019 and 2020 the automaker continued encountering quality problems with its airbags, with some defects possibly leading to deaths. The company was forced to recall 3.4 million vehicles during this time period alone.[43] Some analysts believe Toyota's design process is ineffective, which is leading to an increase in faulty parts.[44] These recalls are shattering consumer confidence and impacting the company's sales.

A Toyota Yaris hybrid.
Michele Eve Sandberg/Corbis Historical/Getty Images

External Opportunities It's anticipated that demand for hybrid vehicles will only increase, which will help Toyota profit from the investment it has made in such autos. At the same time, companies all over the world are exploring autonomous cars as the next big opportunity. Even Google has joined Ford, Tesla, and others in developing the required technology.[45] Toyota also believes it can develop self-driving cars over the next few decades, but like other car companies, it is taking a longer view on artificial intelligence and self-driving cars. "Right from the get-go, we figured it's going to be a time-consuming endeavor," says Toyota Executive Vice President Shigeki Tomoyama.[46]

Toyota is looking to expand into new markets as well. An opportunity to facilitate trade between African nations presented itself after more than 50 countries signed the African Continental Free Trade Agreement in 2018. Toyota invested $7.6 million into Sendy, a Kenyan logistics start-up, in 2020. Sendy provides technology that makes it easier to move goods through East African countries. "We have moved goods worth over 300 billion Kenyan shillings (~$1 billion) for businesses across East Africa with over 30,000 customers on our platform," says Sendy CEO Meshack Alloys.[47]

External Threats Fluctuations in currency exchange rates regularly threaten every global company, and Toyota is no exception. For example, the Toyota HiLux, Australia's top-selling automobile, may see a decrease in revenue due to the weakening of the Australian dollar compared to the Thai baht (Toyota builds the HiLux in Thailand).[48] Toyota also faces threats to its manufacturing plants. One such threat was the COVID-19 pandemic, which led to the temporary shutdown of 12 Toyota plants in China in 2020.[49]

YOUR CALL

Which internal strengths could Toyota make better use of in the future? Which internal weaknesses are most important for it to address? Is Toyota situated to take advantage of all its current external opportunities? Which external threats should it prioritize, and why?

Using VRIO to Assess Competitive Potential: Value, Rarity, Imitability, and Organization

How do managers determine if a company or its products possess a competitive advantage in the marketplace? Researchers have shown that an assessment of a company's resources and capabilities is essential to answering this question. A VRIO analysis is one such assessment and can help you better understand the collective resources needed to compete in a globalized and highly competitive market.[50]

VRIO (pronounced by its letters, "V-R-I-O") is a framework for analyzing a resource or capability to determine its competitive strategic potential by answering four questions about its value, rarity, imitability, and organization.[51] The questions are shown in Figure 6.4.

VRIO is a way to analyze a firm's competitive potential by asking four questions about value, rarity, imitability, and organization. A yes answer to each question means the resource or capability—that is, the business idea—has a competitive advantage (see Figure 6.4). Let's better understand each part of the VRIO framework by applying it to Toyota's investment in autonomous cars.

Value: Is the Resource or Capability Valuable?
Valuable means "Does the resource or capability allow your firm to exploit an opportunity or neutralize a threat?" If the answer is yes, the resource puts you in a competitive position. If no, then you're at a competitive disadvantage.

Toyota Example: Value is derived from market potential in this example. Industry experts estimate that the global market for autonomous vehicles will surpass $7 trillion by 2050, and that an estimated 300 million of these vehicles will be on the road at that time.[52] Indeed, the production of autonomous vehicles can provide value.

Rarity: Is the Resource or Capability Currently Controlled by Only a Few Firms or No Other Firms?
If the answer is yes, that status gives your firm at least some temporary competitive advantage. If the answer is no (because several competing firms exist), you're at least at equal competitive advantage, because you're no worse than the competition.

Toyota Example: More than 40 companies are currently developing autonomous cars. These companies include traditional automakers, technology brands, and telecommunications firms.[53] Toyota does not have competitive advantage based on this consideration.

Imitability: Is the Resource or Capability Costly for Other Firms to Imitate?
If the answer is yes, that gives you a definite competitive advantage. If no—because other firms can get into the market without much expense—that gives you only a temporary competitive advantage.

Toyota Example: Investing in autonomous driving technology takes billions. In fact, Volkswagen has spent $54.2 billion in driverless technology, making it the market leader. Toyota is #4, investing $4.32 billion.[54] Toyota's market share and cash provide it with some temporary competitive advantage.

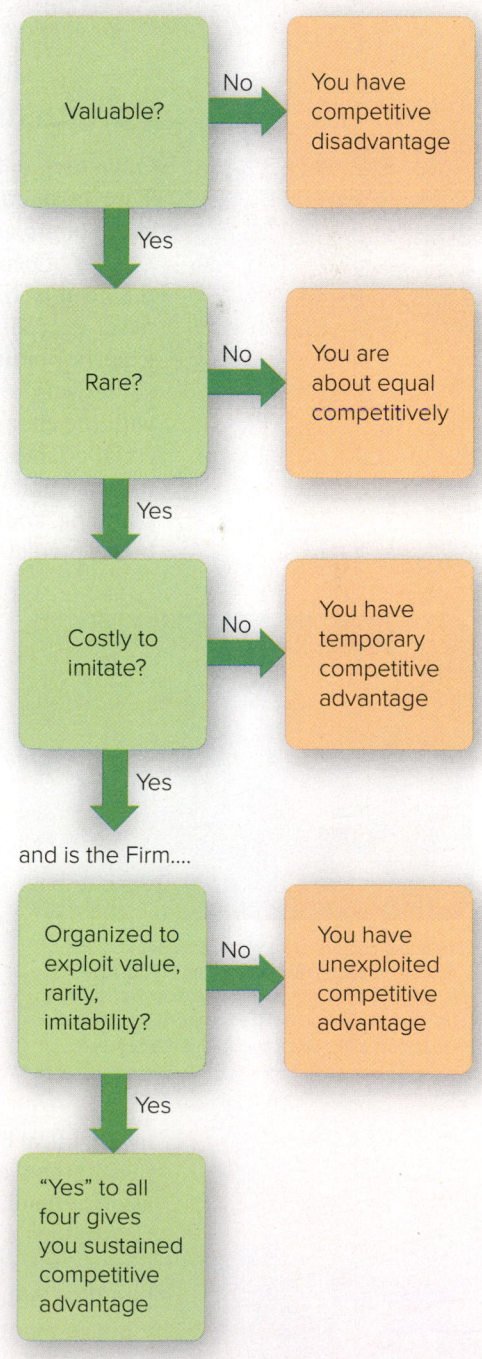

FIGURE 6.4

Is the resource or capability . . .

Source: Adapted from F. T. Rothaermel, Strategic Management: Concepts and Cases *(New York: McGraw-Hill Education, 2012), p. 91*

Is the resource or capability....

Valuable? — No → You have competitive disadvantage

Yes

Rare? — No → You are about equal competitively

Yes

Costly to imitate? — No → You have temporary competitive advantage

Yes

and is the Firm....

Organized to exploit value, rarity, imitability? — No → You have unexploited competitive advantage

Yes

"Yes" to all four gives you sustained competitive advantage

Organization: Is the Firm Organized to Exploit the Resource or Capability?

Research has found that organizational structure helps companies stretch and leverage their existing resources and capabilities.[55] If the firm has the necessary structure, culture, control systems, employee policies, and particularly financing—then, assuming yes answers on Value, Rarity, and Imitability, it would seem the firm has the competitive potential to go forward. If no, it may only have a temporary competitive advantage.

> **Toyota Example:** Toyota plans to introduce its first iteration of self-driving vehicles in the early 2020s, but still has a lot of work to do. Most importantly, they need to significantly increase the hiring of software engineers if they want to get past the research stage and on to production. This hiring will allow them to fully develop the needed hardware and software, as well as reduce the cost of technology. "If you think about building a research prototype, making a demonstration is pretty easy, but making a product is really hard," says James Kuffner, CEO of Toyota Research Institute Advanced Development Inc.[56] Toyota's organization does not seem to currently provide competitive advantage.

Forecasting: Predicting the Future

Once they've analyzed their organization's Strengths, Weaknesses, Opportunities, and Threats, planners need to do forecasting for making long-term strategy. A **forecast is a vision or projection of the future.**

Lots of people make predictions, of course—and often they are wrong.[57] In the 1950s, the head of IBM, Thomas J. Watson, estimated that the demand for computers would never exceed more than five for the entire world. In the late 1990s, many computer experts predicted power outages, water problems, transportation disruptions, bank shutdowns, and far worse because of computer glitches (the "Y2K bug") associated with the change from year 1999 to 2000.

Of course, the farther into the future one makes a prediction, the more difficult it is to be accurate, especially in matters of technology. Yet forecasting is a necessary part of planning, and research shows that managers who consider multiple points of view make better predictions than those who bet on one perspective.[58]

Trending doctors. Doctors Deborah Birx (left) and Anthony Fauci (right) describe their COVID-19 infection forecast at the White House in March 2020. Do you believe experts did an adequate job forecasting the impact of the virus? Mandel Ngan/Getty Images

Trend Analysis   A **trend analysis is a hypothetical extension of a past series of events into the future.** The basic assumption is that the picture of the present can be projected into the future. This is not a bad assumption, if you have enough historical data, but it is always subject to surprises. And if your data are unreliable, they will produce erroneous trend projections.

An example of trend analysis is a time-series forecast, which predicts future data based on patterns of historical data. Time-series forecasts are used to predict long-term trends, cyclic patterns (as in the up-and-down nature of the business cycle), and seasonal variations (as in holiday sales versus summer sales).

Contingency Planning: Predicting Alternative Futures   Companies are vulnerable to changes in their environment that may unexpectedly render their business strategy ineffective.[59] **Contingency planning**—also known as **scenario analysis**—is the creation of alternative hypothetical but equally likely future conditions. Managers apply the technique by making alternative plans for different scenarios and then using the one that best fits the situation at hand.

Apple is a good example of a company that experienced decreased financial performance by failing to conduct contingency planning. Apple did not create a plan for handling potential supply-chain problems in China despite the fact that it relies on China's manufacturers to assemble most of the products it sells worldwide.[60] When the COVID-19 pandemic hit in 2020, Apple could not get the assembly it needed in China, which resulted in the company missing its revenue projections. *The Wall Street Journal* concluded that these problems are "extending into supply chains around the world as assembly lines from Asia to Europe depend upon parts moving swiftly from China into their plants" and "the virus threatens to derail Apple's business just as the company was showing signs it had regained its momentum."[61] The point of this example is to reinforce that today's business environment is rapidly changing and more and more organizations are using scenario planning in response to environmental uncertainty.[62] The Example box illustrates how such planning is important for firms expanding abroad.

EXAMPLE   The Need for Contingency Planning when Expanding Overseas

India is one of the most coveted e-commerce markets in the world. There are 685 million people in the country who have yet to get online, and experts believe that e-commerce sales will grow to $200 billion by 2026.[63] Walmart, one of the world's largest retailers, took notice of these statistics and decided to purchase Flipkart for $16 billion in 2018.[64] Flipkart is India's leading e-commerce marketplace, selling over 80 million products across more than 80 categories including clothes, large appliances, and jewelry. The company launched in 2007 and boasts 100 million users.[65]

Walmart's plan to expand to a growing e-commerce market by purchasing a leading e-commerce marketplace sounded like a good one, until India changed its e-commerce regulations. A year after Walmart's purchase of Flipkart, Indian lawmakers devised a law that prohibits foreign companies from selling their own products online. The law is meant to level the playing field between small Indian companies and foreign multinational organizations such as Walmart and Amazon. There are around 12 million of these small "mom-and-pop" stores in India and they dominate 90% of the country's grocery retail sector.[66] The new law plunged foreign retailers' local operations into disarray. For example, Walmart was forced to pull thousands of products from its Flipkart marketplace. The new law has caused widespread disruptions on Flipkart's platform and dampened Walmart's projected revenue growth in India.[67]

Walmart's online inventory isn't the only part of its business strategy taking a hit; so is its image. The "motive of . . . Flipkart is not to do business, but to monopolise and control," say traders in the heart of Delhi's largest wholesale bazaar before chanting "Go back! Go back!" into the bazaar's microphones. These chants were part of approximately 700 December 2019 protests against firms like Walmart.[68]

Walmart's challenges in India may be insurmountable, according to Morgan Stanley. The brokerage firm released a report in February 2019 stating that the retailer's exit from Flipkart is not out of the question.[69]

YOUR CALL

How could Walmart have used contingency planning to better prepare for changes in India's e-commerce laws?

Benchmarking: Comparing with the Best

Benchmarking is a process by which a company compares its performance with that of high-performing organizations.[70] Consulting firm Bain & Company notes that "the objective of benchmarking is to find examples of superior performance and understand the processes and practices driving that performance. Companies then improve their performance by tailoring and incorporating these best practices into their own operations—not by imitating, but by innovating."[71] For example, drive-thru restaurant chains, such as McDonald's, Burger King, and Wendy's, are constantly watching and benchmarking against each other in order to maximize efficiency, cut costs, and increase profits. This has led to innovations in drive-thru configurations such as changing the number of windows, the menu, speaker boards and ordering approaches, all in the spirit of outperforming competitors.[72]

Aside from restaurants, research has found that benchmarking is a valuable tool to improve goal performance in a variety of industrial sectors.[73] These include investment firms, local governments, and airlines. For example, Charles Schwab may compare its rate of return on a certain stock portfolio against competitors.[74] Cities similarly benchmark

Driving comparisons. A Wendy's drive thru in Aurora, Colorado, during the lunch hour. Wendy's and Burger King customers wait in line at drive thrus for 3:50 and 3:55 minutes on average, respectively. McDonald's average wait time is 4:44 minutes, far behind competitors. Do you think this benchmark has the company's attention? Jim Lambert/Shutterstock

quality of life measures against other cities in the region, country, or world.[75]

The airline industry regularly uses benchmarks to measure success. For example, Southwest might compare its on-time departures and lost bag statistics against key competitors and the industry as a whole.

Figure 6.5 provides a 2019 comparison of nine U.S. airlines across benchmarks such as on-time arrivals, lost baggage complaints, and general complaints, as well as an overall ranking. Which airline do you think ranked the highest based on your own experience, or what you may have heard from family and friends?

The figure shows that Delta Airlines is ranked #1 overall in the United States, as well as being the most punctual carrier. American Airlines, the largest U.S. airline, came in last overall. The airline's senior vice president of operations blames its poor performance on a 2019 labor dispute with mechanics.[76] ●

FIGURE 6.5
Airline benchmarks, 2019

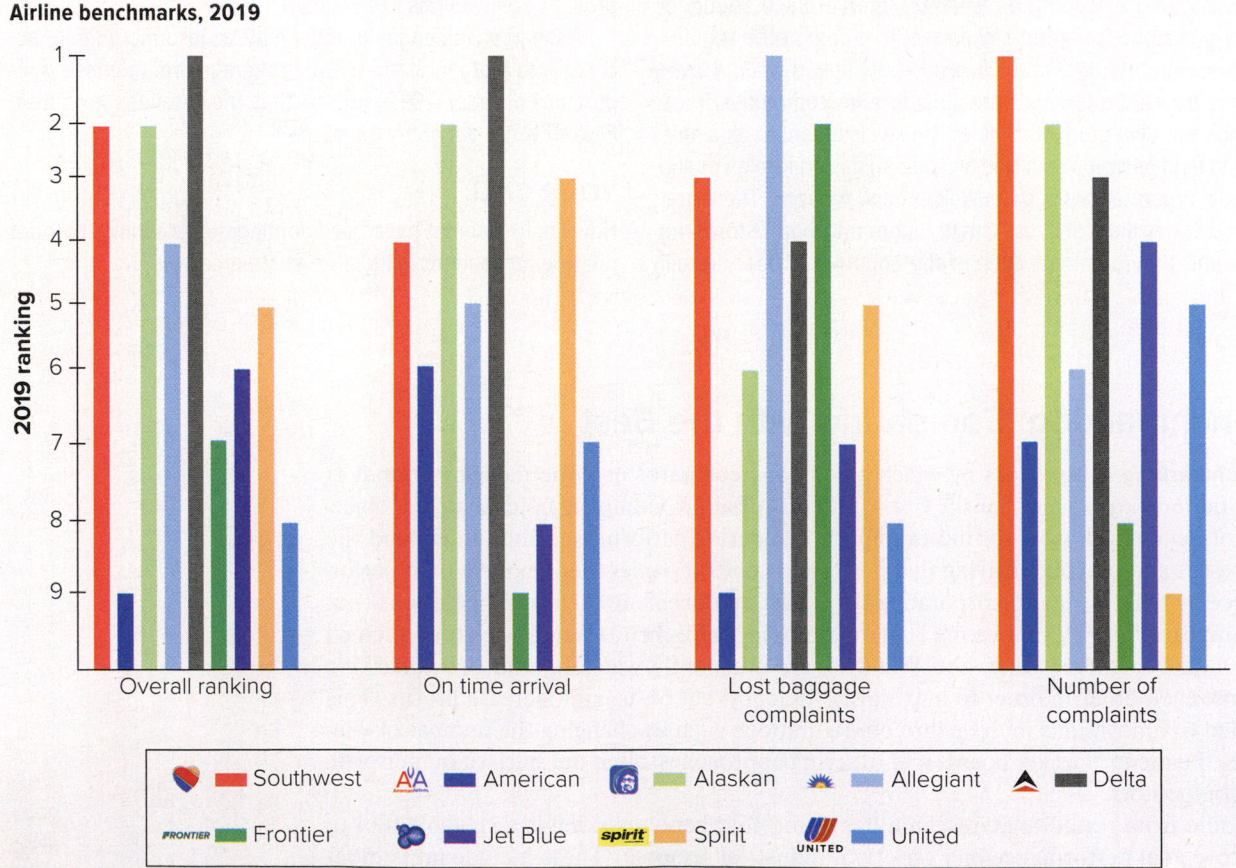

Source: Based on S. McCartney, "The Best and Worst U.S. Airlines of 2019," The Wall Street Journal, January 15, 2020, https://www.wsj.com/articles/the-best-and-worst-u-s-airlines-of-2019-11579097301?mod=searchresults&page=1&pos=3.

6.4 Establishing Corporate-Level Strategy

THE BIG PICTURE

Common corporate-level strategies are growth, stability, or defensive strategies. The Boston Consulting Group (BCG) matrix and diversification considerations are used to formulate corporate strategy.

After assessing the current reality (Step 2 in the strategic-management process), it's time to focus on corporate-level strategies. Three methods to understand corporate-level strategies are common grand strategies, the Boston Consulting Group (BCG) matrix, and diversification.

> **LO 6-4**
>
> Explain the three methods of corporate-level strategy.

Three Overall Types of Corporate Strategy

The three fundamental types of corporate strategies are *growth*, *stability*, and *defensive*.

1. The Growth Strategy A <mark>growth strategy</mark> is a grand strategy that involves expansion—as in sales revenues, market share, number of employees, or number of customers or (for nonprofits) clients served.

Often a growth strategy takes the form of an <mark>innovation strategy</mark>, growing market share or profits by innovating improvements in products or services (as in using an e-business approach in calculatedly disseminating information). We consider innovation further in Chapter 10.

Lululemon Example: Canadian apparel company Lululemon was established in 1998 as a yoga-inspired women's clothing line. Recently, the brand has been increasing sales by appealing to men as well. Lululemon claims it made the decision to expand to men's clothing based on "feedback from our guests, ambassadors and elite athletes."[77] The apparel maker's growth strategy has proven to be successful, with 20% of its 2018 sales ($3.3 billion) coming from men's clothing. Men's clothing sales continued to grow more than 30% in 2019, and the company is on target to double its men's business by the end of 2023. All of this growth led to Lululemon's stock price surging 91% in 2019.[78]

2. The Stability Strategy A <mark>stability strategy</mark> is a grand strategy that involves little or no significant change. McIlhenny Company, makers of Tabasco sauce, is a good example of a company using this strategy. Edmund McIlhenny produced the first Tabasco pepper sauce bottle in 1868 to give southern food "some flavor and excitement." Today, Tabasco sauce is labeled in 25 languages and dialects and sold in more than 180 countries. The company has added seven additional flavors to its offerings through the decades, but there hasn't been a significant change to the company's strategy.[79]

3. The Defensive Strategy A <mark>defensive strategy</mark>, or a *retrenchment strategy*, is a grand strategy that involves reduction in the organization's efforts. Canadian plane and

Hot strategy? Tabasco may be keen on adding some excitement to entrées, but it doesn't think its corporate strategy needs a kick. Do you think a company needs to make significant adjustments to its strategy if it seems to be working? Prachaya Roekdeethaweesab/Shutterstock

train manufacturer Bombardier adopted a defensive strategy by deciding to sell its business-jet division. The company is currently surviving on Canadian government loans and needs to reduce roughly $9 billion in debt it has accrued due to weak demand for business jets and manufacturing problems in its train division. "Can [Bombardier] survive with the three business units it has today? The answer is no," says Quebec Economy Minister Pierre Fitzgibbon.[80]

Variations of the three strategies are shown in Table 6.2.

TABLE 6.2 How Companies Implement Overall Corporate-Level Strategies

GROWTH STRATEGY

- It can improve an existing product or service to attract more buyers.
- It can increase its promotion and marketing efforts to try to expand its market share.
- It can expand its operations, as in taking over distribution or manufacturing previously handled by someone else.
- It can expand into new products or services.
- It can acquire similar or complementary businesses.
- It can merge with another company to form a larger company.

STABILITY STRATEGY

- It can go for a no-change strategy (if, for example, it has found that too-fast growth leads to foul-ups with orders and customer complaints).
- It can go for a little-change strategy (if, for example, the company has been growing at breakneck speed and feels it needs a period of consolidation).

DEFENSIVE STRATEGY

- It can reduce costs, as by freezing hiring or tightening expenses.
- It can sell off (liquidate) assets—land, buildings, inventories, and the like.
- It can gradually phase out product lines or services.
- It can divest part of its business, as in selling off entire divisions or subsidiaries.
- It can declare bankruptcy.
- It can attempt a turnaround—do some retrenching, with a view toward restoring profitability.

The BCG Matrix

Developed by the Boston Consulting Group, the **BCG matrix is a management strategy used by companies to evaluate their strategic business units on the basis of (1) their business growth rates and (2) their share of the market.** Business growth rate describes how quickly the entire industry is growing. Market share is the business unit's share of the market in relation to competitors. The purpose of evaluating each business unit in the company's portfolio is to identify the most effective way to direct the company's financial resources. In general, the BCG matrix suggests that an organization will do better in fast-growing markets in which it has high market share rather than in slow-growing markets in which it has low market share. These concepts are illustrated below. *(See Figure 6.6.)*[81]

A company should usually operate by investing profits from one or more successful but slow-growing units, called *cash cows*, into new products or services called *stars* that have demonstrated strong potential in growing markets and should be appropriately funded. Likewise, the BCG matrix will identify risky units with potential that may or may not produce revenue in the future and should be closely monitored. These are *question marks*. The final category, *dogs*, consists of units that are no longer succeeding and should be shut down or sold.

FIGURE 6.6

The BCG matrix

Market growth is divided into two categories, low and high. Market share also is divided into low and high. Thus, in this matrix, "stars" are business units that are highly desirable (high growth, high market share), compared to "dogs," which are not so desirable (low growth, low market share).

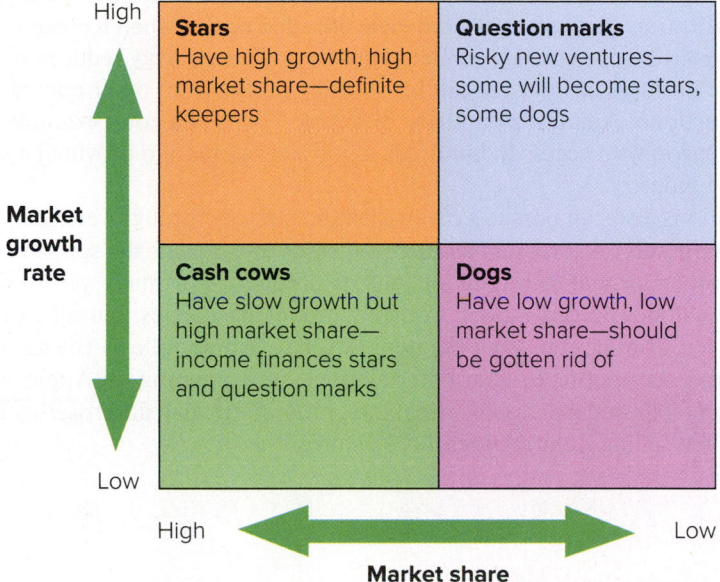

High

Market growth rate

Low

Stars
Have high growth, high market share—definite keepers

Question marks
Risky new ventures—some will become stars, some dogs

Cash cows
Have slow growth but high market share—income finances stars and question marks

Dogs
Have low growth, low market share—should be gotten rid of

High   **Low**

Market share

Let's use the BCG matrix to analyze Dell. The PC continues to be a cash cow for the computer maker, providing it with $2 billion in profit in 2018, despite slowing growth in the overall PC market. Dell has substantial market share here, which means it is still earning significant profits from its personal computer unit, which it can invest in its other products, particularly stars. Dell's innovative ultrathin monitors have undergone some design changes, which is expected to allow them to develop into stars with strong growth and high market share in a market that is still growing. The company's entry into cloud computing is seen as a question mark because it is a new venture in a market that is quickly filling up. Dell smart phones, on the other hand, were unable to compete against such titans as Apple; one analyst said the product did not meet customer needs and preferences. High investment combined with low return made this Dell product a dog.[82]

One drawback of the BCG matrix is that in practice it is fairly easy for managers to mischaracterize their business units, thereby erroneously drawing investment away from cash cows that still need it or writing off as dogs units or product lines that can yet flourish.

Now that you have learned about the tools companies use to create their grand strategies, what type of skills do you think managers need to use these tools? Do you think you possess those skills?

Diversification Strategy

The strategy of moving into new lines of business, such as Amazon purchasing Whole Foods or CVS buying Aetna, is called **diversification**. Other examples include JAB Holdings, a German investment firm, acquiring beverage brand Core Hydration. Core Hydration produces premium, nutrient-enhanced bottled water and organic fruit-infused beverages. The company had a close distribution relationship with JAB Holdings' Keurig Dr Pepper division, but as Core sales grew at an annual rate of around 115% from 2015 to 2018, JAB decided it was time for the beverage maker to join its portfolio.[83]

Companies generally diversify to either grow revenue or reduce risk. They grow revenue because the company now has new products and services to sell. **When a company purchases a new business that is related to the company's existing business portfolio, the organization is implementing related diversification.** Examples are Disney's purchase of 21st Century Fox and the combination of United Technologies and Rockwell Collins in the aviation industry. Companies sometimes attempt to reduce risk by using an unrelated diversification strategy. **Unrelated diversification occurs when a company acquires another company in a completely unrelated business.** This strategy reduces risk because losses in one business or industry can be offset by profits from other companies in the corporate portfolio. Amazon's purchase of Whole Foods is a good example. The deal provided Amazon with access to hundreds of physical stores and provided a solid entry into the food industry.[84]

Organizations also can pursue a diversification strategy through vertical integration. **In vertical integration, a firm expands into businesses that provide the supplies it needs to make its products or that distribute and sell its products.** For many years, Hollywood movie studios followed this model, not only producing movies, but also distributing them and even owning their own theaters.[85] Today, Apple follows the same path by producing and distributing its own entertainment programming on Apple TV+. Starbucks has long followed a plan of vertical integration by buying and roasting all its own coffee and then selling it through Starbucks stores.[86] ●

6.5 Establishing Business-Level Strategy

THE BIG PICTURE

Business-level strategy begins with an assessment of Porter's five competitive forces. Companies then are advised to select from one of four competitive strategies. We contrast this academic approach with a practical one proposed by Jack Welch, former CEO of General Electric. He recommended that leaders create business-level strategies by answering five key questions.

LO 6-5

Discuss Porter's and Welch's techniques for formulating a business-level strategy.

The creation of business-level strategy flows from the details contained in corporate strategies. The overall objective of strategy formulation at this level is to answer the question of how the company wants to compete in industries represented by the business units. Harvard professor Michael Porter is credited with devising the models and processes for establishing business-level strategies. We start by focusing on his analysis of his five competitive forces and then delve into a discussion of his four key competitive strategies. We end this section with a practical approach proposed by Jack Welch.

Porter's Five Competitive Forces

What determines competitiveness within a particular industry? After studying several kinds of businesses, strategic-management expert Michael Porter suggested, in his **Porter's model for industry analysis,** that business-level strategies originate in five primary competitive forces in the firm's environment: (1) threats of new entrants, (2) bargaining power of suppliers, (3) bargaining power of buyers, (4) threats of substitute products or services, and (5) rivalry among competitors.[87] Let's consider how Porter's model applies to streaming services we consume on a regular basis.

1. Threats of New Entrants New competitors can affect an industry almost overnight, taking away customers from existing organizations. For example, since Netflix found success by shifting its focus from in-store and mail-order DVD rentals to online streaming, traditional networks such as HBO, NBC, and CBS have started a streaming service as well. In addition, Amazon, Apple, and Disney have thrown their hats into the online streaming market, creating what many have called the "streaming wars."[88]

2. Bargaining Power of Suppliers Some companies are readily able to switch suppliers in order to get components or services, but others are not. Netflix needs to procure different movies and TV shows in order to keep its content diverse and fresh. This reliance may provide suppliers with higher power because there are limited companies producing media and entertainment content. As a result, Netflix has turned to producing its own original content. This content is showing signs of success, as it only accounts for 8% of Netflix's viewing options but dominates the subscriber most-watched list.[89]

3. Bargaining Power of Buyers Informed customers become better negotiators. For example, use of the Internet enabled one of your authors to get a higher trade-in on his current vehicle and a lower sales price on a new car. Netflix faces an uphill battle when it comes to customer switching costs. Subscribers don't have to worry about termination fees if they cancel their Netflix service and acquiring competitors' services is as easy as downloading an app.[90]

4. Threats of Substitute Products or Services Like all programming providers, Netflix must ensure that customers continue to prefer its offerings to the many other options available. This includes not only other streaming services, but also traditional cable providers and satellite television. Customers also may subscribe to discount Internet television service, such as Sling and YouTube TV.[91]

5. Rivalry among Competitors The preceding four forces influence the fifth force, rivalry among competitors. Think of the growing competition among online streaming networks engaged in the "streaming wars" and the number of services you can now utilize to watch your favorite shows. Once again, the Internet has intensified rivalries among all kinds of organizations.

Porter recommends that organizations conduct a good SWOT analysis that examines these five competitive forces. He believes that this enables companies to formulate effective strategy, using what he identified as four competitive strategies, as we discuss in the next section.

Streaming wars. Companies such as Netflix, Amazon, HBO, Hulu, and Disney are competing for your viewership. How do you feel about having so many options? Can too many be a bad thing? Ivan Marc/Shutterstock

Porter's Four Competitive Strategies

Porter's four competitive strategies (also called *four generic strategies*) are (1) cost-leadership, (2) differentiation, (3) cost-focus, and (4) focused-differentiation. The first two strategies focus on *wide* markets, the last two on *narrow* markets. WarnerMedia, which produces lots of media and publications, serves wide markets around the world. Your neighborhood video store (if one still exists) serves a narrow market of just local customers.

Let's look at these four strategies.

1. Cost-Leadership Strategy: Keeping Costs and Prices Low for a Wide Market
The cost-leadership strategy is to keep the costs, and hence prices, of a product or service below those of competitors and to target a wide market.

This puts the pressure on R&D managers to develop products or services that can be created cheaply, production managers to reduce production costs, and marketing managers to reach a wide variety of customers as inexpensively as possible.

Firms implementing the cost-leadership strategy include Timex, IKEA, computer maker Acer, retailers Walmart and Home Depot, and pen maker Bic.

2. Differentiation Strategy: Offering Unique and Superior Value for a Wide Market
The differentiation strategy is to offer products or services that are of unique and superior value compared with those of competitors but to target a wide market.

Because products are expensive, managers may have to spend more on R&D, marketing, and customer service. This is the strategy followed by Ritz-Carlton hotels and the maker of Lexus automobiles. Some studies have found that differentiation is important in uncertain environments, such as expanding overseas, where it can especially enhance performance.[92]

The differentiation strategy also is pursued by companies trying to create *brands* to differentiate themselves from competitors. Eyewear retailer Warby Parker invests in differentiation strategies for its glasses and contact lenses by making them "cool." Its stores feature a midcentury design with glowing shelves and associates in blue smocks hovering around low walnut tables. Warby's hip "eye exam suites" feel more like a vinyl-record listening room than a doctor's office.[93]

3. Cost-Focus Strategy: Keeping Costs and Prices Low for a Narrow Market
The cost-focus strategy is to keep the costs, and hence prices, of a product or service below those of competitors and to target a narrow market.

This is a strategy often executed with low-end products sold in discount stores, such as low-cost beer or cigarettes, or with regional gas stations, such as the Terrible Herbst, Rotten Robbie, and Maverik chains in parts of the western United States. Red Box, originally a kiosk-based video rental company, has added an on-demand streaming service with low costs. But, says one analyst, "The upside is similarly limited, since the appeal will mainly be to its existing kiosk customers."[94]

Needless to say, the pressure on managers to keep costs down is even more intense than it is with those in cost-leadership companies.

4. Focused-Differentiation Strategy: Offering Unique and Superior Value for a Narrow Market
The focused-differentiation strategy is to offer products or services that are of unique and superior value compared to those of competitors and to target a narrow market. Viking Cruises represents a good application of this strategy.

Viking Cruises, founded in 1997, is a river and ocean cruise provider based in Basel, Switzerland.[95] Its founder and chairman, Torstein Hagen, caters to wealthy, well-educated individuals who are over 55. "I can do my market research by looking in the mirror," the 77-year-old jokes. Viking's cruises start at $1,899, compared to typical competitors charging $399 a head. The Viking price includes Internet, alcohol with meals, and a daily shore excursion. Named the #1 Ocean Cruise Line by Travel + Leisure four years in a row, Viking's cruises often sell out a year in advance.[96]

Research shows that formal strategic planning helps organizations effectively react to challenging situations, make the right trade-off decisions, and develop a common team spirit and culture.[97] Self-Assessment 6.2 will help you better understand your own strategic planning skills.

SELF-ASSESSMENT 6.2   CAREER READINESS

Core Skills Required for Strategic Planning

This survey is designed to assess the skills needed in strategic planning. Please be prepared to answer these questions if your instructor has assigned Self-Assessment 6.2 in Connect.

1. Do you have what it takes? Are you surprised by the results?

2. Based on the results, what are your top two strengths and deficiencies when it comes to strategic planning?

3. What would you say during an interview to demonstrate that you possess the career readiness competencies associated with strategic thinking? Consider guidance found in the Career Corner.

An Executive's Approach toward Strategy Development

Jack Welch was one of the globe's most respected CEOs. During his 21 years as CEO, Welch transformed General Electric (GE) into the world's most admired and successful company with his innovative approach toward management. The company's revenue grew from $25 billion to $130 billion, and GE's market capitalization had a 30-fold increase of more than $400 billion under Welch's leadership.[98]

Welch's approach to strategy development was somewhat simplistic, but obviously effective. He believed that business strategy should be used to create a big "a-ha" for business—a smart, realistic, relatively fast way to gain sustainable competitive advantage. The former CEO created GE's business-level strategies by asking senior executives in the company's 10+ lines of business to answer the following five questions.[99]

What Does the Playing Field Look Like Now?   Managers need to understand who their competitors are, large and small. This includes veterans in the industry and potential new players. Each competitor's strengths and weaknesses should be analyzed (consider using a SWOT analysis, as we discussed in Section 6.3). Customers and buying habits should also be reviewed.

What Has the Competition Been Up To?   Strong competitors are always active. Managers need to understand what each competitor has done in the past year to change the playing field. Are there new products, technologies, or distribution channels that will change the market?

What Have You Been Up To?   In addition to an external analysis, managers also need to analyze what the company has done to change the competitive playing field. Has there been an acquisition, new product, or new technology that can be leveraged? Any lost competitive advantages, such as the departure of a key employee or proprietary technology, should be noted as well.

What's Around the Corner?   Managers need to identify what they fear the most in the year ahead. For example, what are some moves a competitor can make that can hurt the company? It's also important to keep an eye out for potential competitors merging or acquiring one another. From an internal perspective, managers need to ensure that top talent is being cared for with competitive pay and perks, as well as an inspiring organizational culture.

What's Your Winning Move?   The final question is based on what the manager wants to do going forward. This includes possible acquisitions, the launch of a new product, securing better talent, or taking advantage of globalization. In the end, managers need to ensure that customers stick with the company more than ever before and more than any other competitor. •

6.6 Strategic Implementation: Creating, Executing, and Controlling Functional-Level Strategies

THE BIG PICTURE

Strategic implementation involves executing and controlling functional-level strategies. A company's overall ability to deliver results is a function of effectively executing according to three processes: people, strategy, and operations. In order for execution to be successful, managers must overcome common roadblocks. Finally, strategic control is necessary to monitor results and make corrections, if necessary.

LO 6-6

Describe how to create, execute, and control a functional-level strategy.

Stage 1 of the strategic-management process establishes an organization's mission and its vision. Stage 2 assesses the organization's current reality. In stage 3 of the process, the organization formulates its corporate, business, and functional strategies. Now we come to the last two stages—stage 4, strategic implementation, and stage 5, strategic control.

We previously noted that strategic implementation entails the execution of strategic plans. To make this happen, managers need to create functional-level strategies, which outline the activities that must occur to achieve higher-order corporate and business-level strategies. We explain this process by first focusing on how managers execute strategy through the three core internal processes and then review obstacles to execution. We end with the role of strategic control.

Strategic Implementation: Creating, Executing, and Controlling Functional-Level Strategies

We earlier defined strategic implementation as the process of putting strategic plans into effect. Functional strategies are used to accomplish this task. A *functional strategy* is a plan of action by each functional area of the organization to support higher-level strategies. In other words, higher-level corporate- and business-level strategies flow down to the functional strategy. This is similar to goal cascading, which ensures that higher-level goals are communicated and aligned with the goals at the next levels down in the organizational hierarchy. (We discussed goal cascading in Chapter 5.) Typical functional areas include marketing, finance, human resources, operations, information technology, and distribution. Let's look at how supermarket giant Kroger might create functional strategies.

Kroger Example: Kroger is now automating two of its locations, revolutionizing the grocery store experience. The automated stores allow customers to create a shopping list on the Kroger app in advance. The app then guides shoppers to their selected products upon arrival into the store, lighting up product displays as customers approach them.[100] Kroger's decision to open two automated stores was a business-level strategy. Based on this business decision, its functional strategy might include training supermarket employees on this new automated system (operations function), ensuring word gets out about its innovative stores (marketing function), and ensuring that the mobile app is secure (information technology function).

Figure 6.7 portrays what Kroger's autonomous store strategy may look like across all three strategic levels.

Execution: Getting Things Done

Once management has formulated functional-level strategies, it's time to move forward and get things done. Larry Bossidy, former CEO of AlliedSignal (later Honeywell), and

FIGURE 6.7

An example of strategic implementation at Kroger

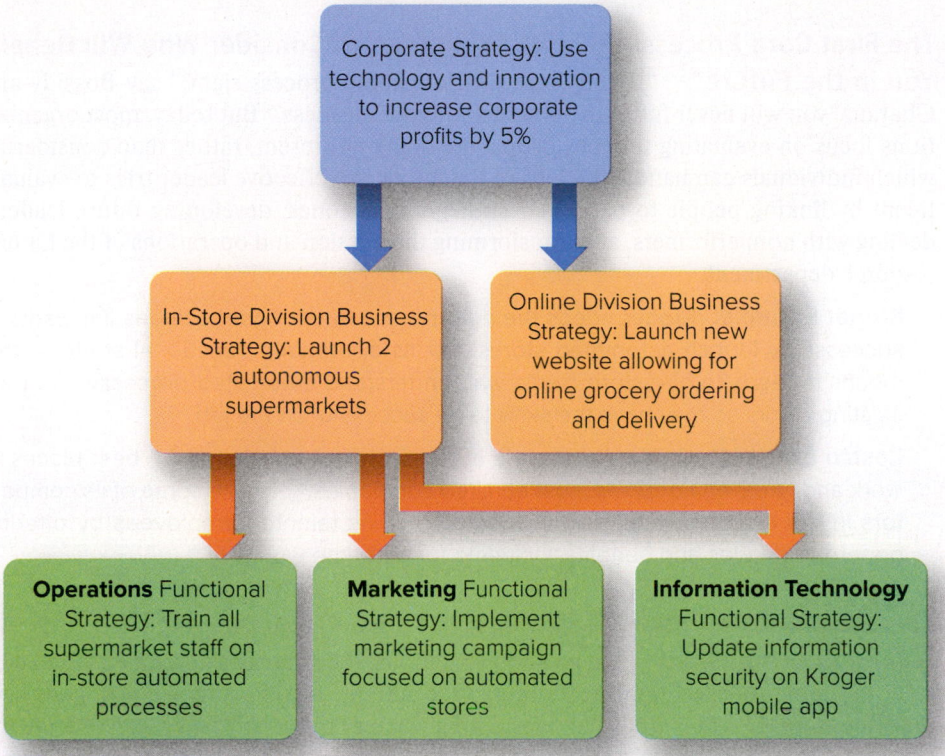

Ram Charan, a business adviser to senior executives, are authors of *Execution: The Discipline of Getting Things Done.*[101] **Execution, they say, is not simply tactics; it is a central part of any company's strategy.** It consists of using questioning, analysis, and follow-through to mesh strategy with reality, align people with goals, and achieve results promised.

How important is execution to organizational success in today's global economy? A survey of more than 400 global CEOs found that their number one challenge was executional excellence. Another study of 8,000 managers, in over 250 companies, found that respondents were three times as likely to miss performance commitments due to insufficient support from colleagues.[102]

A leader's inability to execute can mean their demise. Boeing fired CEO Dennis Muilenburg in 2019 because analysts claim he "made the mistake of consistently promising more than he could deliver." Muilenburg's inability to execute on Boeing's recovery strategy after a pair of 737 MAX fatal crashes led to Boeing's stock dropping 22%, and both airlines and suppliers suffering serious damage to their finances and reputations.[103]

Bossidy and Charan outline how organizations and managers can improve their ability to execute. Effective execution requires managers to build a foundation for execution within three core processes found in any business: people, strategy, and operations.[104]

The Three Core Processes of Business: People, Strategy, and Operations

A company's overall ability to execute is a function of effectively executing according to three processes: *people, strategy,* and *operations.* Because all work ultimately entails some human interaction, effort, or involvement, Bossidy and Charan believe that the *people* process is the most important. We'll discuss each of these three processes by first circling back to Kroger's plan for autonomous supermarkets. You'll also learn how a different type of storefront, Costco Wholesale, is utilizing each process.

The First Core Process—People: "You Need to Consider Who Will Benefit You in the Future"

"If you don't get the people process right," say Bossidy and Charan, "you will never fulfill the potential of your business." But today, most organizations focus on evaluating the jobs people are doing at present, rather than considering which individuals can handle the jobs of the future. An effective leader tries to evaluate talent by linking people to particular strategic milestones, developing future leaders, dealing with nonperformers, and transforming the mission and operations of the human resource department.

Kroger Example: Kroger needs the right people in the right positions if it wants to successfully launch automated stores. For its operational functional strategy, this means it needs to hire store clerks who understand automated processes, or train existing clerks so they have the skills to be successful on the job.

Costco Example: Costco Wholesale is No. 6 on *Indeed's* list of 50 best places to work and No. 9 on *Fortune's* most admired companies.[105] Unlike some of its competitors in the discount retail market, Costco recruits talented employees by offering generous salaries and benefits, including for part-time workers.[106]

The Second Core Process—Strategy: "You Need to Consider How Success Will Be Accomplished"

In most organizations, the strategies developed fail to consider the "how" of execution. According to the authors, a good strategic plan addresses nine questions. *(See Table 6.3.)* In considering whether the organization can execute the strategy, a leader must take a realistic and critical view of its capabilities and competencies. If it does not have the talent in finance, sales, and manufacturing to accomplish the vision, the chances of success are drastically reduced.

Kroger Example: Kroger will need to train its employees on automated processes, but before it can do that, it needs to train the trainers. For its marketing functional strategy, this includes training those who will later train marketing specialists on how to advertise these innovative stores on places such as social media.

Costco Example: One of Costco's most successful strategies is to promise—and deliver—the best deal on the brand-name and store-brand products it offers. It also makes shopping a fun experience by offering plenty of product samples and strategically placing merchandise to encourage customers to shop the entire store.[107]

TABLE 6.3   Necessary Answers: What Questions Should a Strong Strategic Plan Address?

Source: From Execution *by Larry Bossidy and Ram Charan, Crown Business, a division of Random House, Inc., 2002.*

1. What is the assessment of the external environment?
2. How well do you understand the existing customers and markets?
3. What is the best way to grow the business profitably, and what are the obstacles to growth?
4. Who is the competition?
5. Can the business execute the strategy?
6. Are the short term and long term balanced?
7. What are the important milestones for executing the plan?
8. What are the critical issues facing the business?
9. How will the business make money on a sustainable basis?

The Third Core Process—Operations: "You Need to Consider What Path Will Be Followed"

The strategy process defines where an organization wants to go, and the people process defines who's going to get it done. The third core process, operations, or the operating plan, provides the path for people to follow. The operating plan, as we described in Chapter 5, should address all the major activities in which the company will engage—marketing, production, sales, revenue, and so on—and then define short-term objectives for these activities to provide targets for people to aim at. We also discuss operations management in Chapter 16.

Kroger Example: Kroger needs to install the right technology and have proper technical support if it wants its automated stores to run smoothly. For its information technology functional strategy, this includes properly testing the new technology once installed and also making sure there is a support technician onsite in case customers or employees have trouble using the technology.

Costco Example: There's a reason Costco has nearly 100 million members. The wholesaler's membership model (in which customers pay a nominal annual fee for admission to the store), its unique shopping experience, and its carefully selected array of high-quality products at wholesale prices have allowed it to remain competitive even in an increasingly online retail world.[108]

By linking people, strategy, and operating plans, execution allows executives to direct and control the three core processes that will advance their strategic vision.

Execution Roadblocks

Execution doesn't always go smoothly and managers may face obstacles to strategic implementation for many different reasons. As you'll see, these roadblocks span all levels of an organization's hierarchy.

Overcoming Roadblocks in the C-Suite   Many executives appear to have an aversion to execution, which they associate with boring details—with the tedium of doing, as opposed to the excitement of visioning—and which they hand off to subordinates. Further, many organizational roadblocks are associated with organizational culture. Organizational culture is a system of shared beliefs and values within an organization that guides the behavior of its members. In this context, effective execution will not occur unless the culture supports and is aligned with the goal of getting quality work done in a timely manner.[109] (Chapter 8 presents 12 ways managers can attempt to create an execution-oriented culture.)[110]

Studies show that in addition to culture, leadership and organizational structure are key factors that impact strategy implementation.[111] The Practical Action box will provide you with advice on how to foster an execution-based environment in the workplace by focusing on leadership and culture.

PRACTICAL ACTION   Fueling Execution in the Workplace

The foundation of execution is based on alignment between leadership (as we discuss in Chapter 14) and organizational culture (discussed in Chapter 8). Specifically, research suggests that leaders need to be aware of deficiencies in their organization's culture that can lead to execution roadblocks and adjust their style accordingly.[112]

The *Harvard Business Review* (HBR) surveyed senior managers about the importance of various abilities, and execution ranked first among 16.[113] Bossidy and Charan suggest that there are seven essential types of leader behaviors that are needed to fuel the engine of execution. Managers are advised to engage in seven kinds of behaviors, as follows.

Know Your People and Your Business: "Engage Intensely with Your Employees" In companies that don't execute, leaders are usually out of touch with the day-to-day realities. Now that you are becoming familiar with the career readiness skills we've been describing in this book, including knowing the business, you won't be surprised that Bossidy and Charan insist leaders must engage intensely and personally with their organization's people and its businesses. They cannot rely on secondhand knowledge through other people's observations, assessments, and recommendations.

Insist on Realism: "Don't Let Others Avoid Reality" Many people want to avoid or shade reality, hiding mistakes or avoiding confrontations. Making realism a priority begins with the leaders being realistic themselves, and making sure realism is the goal of all dialogues in the organization. Being "clear and methodical" was one of the stand-out behaviors that improved execution in HBR's survey of thousands of performance reviews.[114]

Set Clear Priorities: "Focus on a Few Rather Than Many Goals" Leaders who execute focus on a very few clear priorities that everyone can grasp. It's also helpful for goals and plans to be simple; they should not have an overwhelming number of steps, nor be vague and lack appropriate details.[115]

Follow Through: "Establish Accountability and Check on Results" Failing to follow through is a major cause of poor execution. "How many meetings have you attended where people left without firm conclusions about who would do what and when?" Bossidy and Charan ask. Establishing accountability starts with aligning individual roles with the organization's strategy. Leadership needs to ensure that employees at all levels can articulate and evaluate their roles in strategic goals before they can be held accountable for achieving them.[116] Accountability and follow-up are important and reflect mastery of the career readiness skill of integrity.

Reward the Doers: "Show Top Performers That They Matter" What gets measured, gets done. What gets measured and rewarded, gets done faster.[117] If people are to produce specific results, they must be rewarded accordingly, making sure that top performers are rewarded far better than ordinary performers. To advocate for these team members, you'll rely on your career readiness skills of decision making and leadership.

Expand People's Capabilities: "Develop the Talent" Coaching is an important part of the executive's job, providing useful and specific feedback that can improve performance. HBR's survey of performance reviews found that "leaders who are great executors are skilled at giving feedback," especially positive feedback.[118]

Know Yourself: "Do the Hard Work of Understanding Who You Are" Leaders must develop "emotional fortitude" based on honest self-assessments. Four core qualities are authenticity, self-awareness, self-mastery, and humility. Self-awareness is another of the career readiness skills we discuss in this book, along with self-efficacy and openness to change.

YOUR CALL

Which behavior is probably the most difficult for you to adopt personally? Do you think your current or a past employer is or was good at execution? What obstacles may have impaired the company's ability to execute?

Overcoming Roadblocks Down the Hierarchy Putting strategic plans into effect often means dealing with other types of roadblocks, including resistance by people who feel the plans threaten their influence or livelihood. This is particularly the case when the plans must be implemented rapidly because delay is the easiest kind of resistance there is (all kinds of excuses are usually available to justify delays). Thus, top managers can't just announce the plans; they have to actively sell them to middle and supervisory managers. Research supports the conclusion that a person's beliefs are one of the key impediments to accepting change.[119]

Whether in the C-suite or in a specific department, research shows that if initial obstacles are not mitigated, they can bond together and create bigger challenges that are even more difficult to overcome.[120] Self-Assessment 6.3 assesses five common obstacles to strategic execution.

SELF-ASSESSMENT 6.3

Assessing the Obstacles to Strategic Execution

This survey is designed to assess the obstacles to strategic execution that may be impacting an organization's ability to execute. Please be prepared to answer these questions if your instructor has assigned Self-Assessment 6.3 in Connect.

1.　How does the company stand with respect to execution?

2.　Based on the results, what are the company's strengths and weaknesses when it comes to execution?

3.　What advice would you give to senior management about improving the company's ability to execute based on the results? Be specific.

Maintaining Strategic Control

The final stage in the strategic-management process is strategic control. *Strategic control* consists of monitoring the execution of strategy and taking corrective action, if necessary. To keep a strategic plan on track, suggests Bryan Barry, you need to do the following:[121]

- **Engage people.** You need to actively engage people in clarifying what your group hopes to accomplish and how you will accomplish it.
- **Keep it simple.** Keep your planning simple, unless there's a good reason to make it more complex.
- **Stay focused.** Stay focused on the important things.
- **Keep moving.** Keep moving toward your vision of the future, adjusting your plans as you learn what works.

Strategic control may take many forms, including budgets to monitor and control financial expenditures and total quality management. We discuss these and other control mechanisms in Chapter 16. ●

6.7 Career Corner: Managing Your Career Readiness

Strategic thinking is not one of the competencies in the career readiness model shown below. The reason is not that employers don't want you to have this skill. Rather, it's because other more specific competencies drive your ability to think strategically. Strategic thinking is defined as "envisioning what might happen in the future and then applying that to our current circumstances."[122] There are four career readiness competencies that drive your ability to think strategically: understanding the business, task-based functional knowledge, critical thinking/problem solving, and decision making.

LO 6-7

Describe how to enhance your strategic thinking.

Why Is Strategic Thinking Important to New Graduates?

Although you are unlikely to be hired as a strategic planner after graduation, don't be fooled into thinking that this skill is not important. A writer for *Harvard Business Review* noted that strategic thinking "can, and must, happen at every level of the organization; it's one of those unwritten parts of all job descriptions. Ignore this fact and you risk getting passed over for a promotion."[123] Employers still value this skill in new graduates for four reasons.[124]

1. Thinking strategically requires you to be forward-looking and alert for opportunities that may arise. Employers want people who are prepared to solve future problems that are difficult to predict.
2. The ability to see the big picture helps people connect the dots about what needs to get done in order to complete today's tasks and projects that support strategic goals.
3. Strategic thinkers pay attention to what is happening in business and society at large while understanding what may or not be credible information. This skill essentially makes you a more informed employee, and employers truly value such people.
4. Strategic thinkers are more likely to have a worldly perspective, an orientation that fits today's global economy.

Developing Strategic Thinking

There are four key activities for developing your ability to think more strategically: understanding the business, broadening your task and functional knowledge, decision making, and engaging in critical thinking and problem solving. (See *Figure 6.8*.) In this section, we focus on the career competencies of understanding the business and task and functional knowledge.

FIGURE 6.8

Career readiness competencies

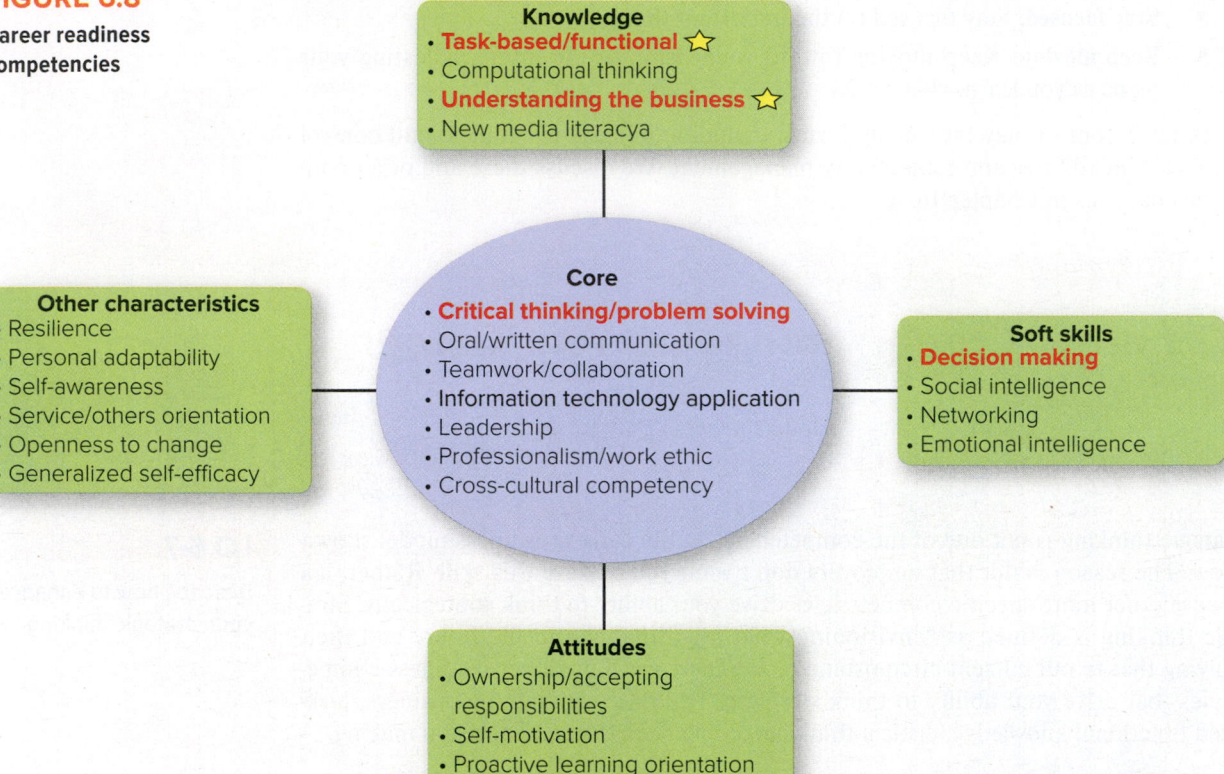

Knowledge
- **Task-based/functional** ⭐
- Computational thinking
- **Understanding the business** ⭐
- New media literacya

Core
- **Critical thinking/problem solving**
- Oral/written communication
- Teamwork/collaboration
- **Information technology application**
- Leadership
- Professionalism/work ethic
- Cross-cultural competency

Other characteristics
- Resilience
- Personal adaptability
- Self-awareness
- Service/others orientation
- Openness to change
- Generalized self-efficacy

Soft skills
- **Decision making**
- Social intelligence
- Networking
- Emotional intelligence

Attitudes
- Ownership/accepting responsibilities
- Self-motivation
- Proactive learning orientation
- Showing commitment
- Positive approach
- Career management

Understand the Business   This career readiness competency reflects the extent to which you understand a potential or current employer's business and strategies. This can be learned by studying a company's web page and annual report. You can look for any published SWOT analyses on a company or conduct one on your own.

Once you are hired, you also can extend your knowledge by networking with current employees, proactively seeking mentoring from experienced employees, attempting to participate in a job rotation program, and attending as many cross-functional or business meetings as possible.[125] The more you understand about the business, the more you'll be able to align what you are doing internally to changes in the external environment. In fact, research confirms that organizations employing continuous alignment can enjoy up to 15% annual growth, compared to competitors.[126] You also might consider joining industry groups or other professional associations affiliated with the type of work you are doing.[127]

Broaden Your Task and Functional Knowledge   Strategic thinking requires making connections between concepts, ideas, people, and events. The more ideas and experiences you have, the greater the ability to make connections. For example, international travel has enhanced our understanding about the nuances of cross-cultural behavior, which in turn has helped in writing about cross-cultural management. Make it a goal to try new things, visit new places, meet new people, and read about new topics. All of these activities will stimulate your mind and expand your base of knowledge.

Some experts suggest that strategic thinkers have a knowledge base that represents a "T." The top of the "T" reflects your breadth of knowledge and the stem reflects the depth of understanding about your primary area of expertise.[128] So in addition to trying and reading about new things, it would help to learn about the finer aspects of your employer's industry. Here again, it would be useful to attend industry or functional conferences. The goal of doing this is twofold: learn about the industry or work function and network. ●

Key Points

6.1 Strategic Positioning and Levels of Strategy

- Strategic positioning is based on the principles that strategy is the creation of a unique and valuable position, requires trade-offs in competing, and involves creating a "fit" among activities so that they interact and reinforce each other.
- The three levels of strategy are corporate, business, and functional.
- Strategic management works for both large and small firms.

6.2 The Strategic-Management Process

- The strategic-management process has five steps plus a feedback loop.
- Step 1 is to establish the mission, vision, and values statements. The mission statement expresses the organization's purpose or reason for being. The vision statement states what the organization wants to become and where it wants to go strategically. The values statement describes what the organization stands for, its core priorities, the values its employees embody, and what its products contribute to the world.
- Step 2 is to do a current reality assessment, to look at where the organization stands and see what is working and what could be different so as to maximize efficiency and effectiveness in achieving the organization's mission. Among the tools for assessing the current reality are SWOT analysis, VRIO analysis, forecasting, and benchmarking.
- Step 3 is to formulate corporate, business, and functional strategies. This means translating the company's broad mission and vision statements into a corporate strategy, which, after the assessment of the current reality, explains how the organization's

mission is to be accomplished. Three common grand strategies are growth, stability, and defensive.
- Step 4 is strategy execution—putting strategic plans into effect.
- Step 5 is strategic control, monitoring the execution of strategy and making adjustments.
- Corrective action constitutes a feedback loop in which a problem requires that managers return to an earlier step to rethink policies, budgets, or personnel arrangements.

6.3 Assessing the Current Reality

- Step 2 in the strategic-management process, assess the current reality, looks at where the organization stands internally and externally—to determine what's working and what's not, to see what can be changed so as to increase efficiency and effectiveness in achieving the organization's vision.
- Among the tools for assessing the current reality are SWOT analysis, VRIO analysis, forecasting, and benchmarking.
- In SWOT, organizational strengths are the skills and capabilities that give the organization special competencies and competitive advantages. Organizational weaknesses are the drawbacks that hinder an organization in executing strategies. Organizational opportunities are environmental factors that the organization may exploit for competitive advantage. Organizational threats are environmental factors that hinder an organization's achieving a competitive advantage.
- VRIO is a framework for analyzing a resource or capability to determine its competitive strategic potential by answering four questions about its value, rarity, imitability, and organization.

- Forecasting is another tool for assessing current reality. Two types of forecasting are (1) trend analysis, a hypothetical extension of a past series of events into the future, and (2) contingency planning, the creation of alternative hypothetical but equally likely future conditions.
- Benchmarking is a process by which a company compares its performance with that of high-performing organizations.

6.4 Establishing Corporate-Level Strategy

- Three common corporate-level strategies are (1) a growth strategy involving expansion—as in sales revenues or market share—and one form of growth strategy is an innovation strategy, growing market share or profits by innovating improvements in products or services; (2) a stability strategy, which involves little or no significant change; and (3) a defensive strategy, which involves reduction in the organization's efforts.
- The BCG matrix is a means of evaluating strategic business units on the basis of (1) their business growth rates and (2) their share of the market. In general, organizations do better in fast-growing markets in which they have a high market share rather than slow-growing markets in which they have low market shares.
- A diversification strategy pertains to deciding whether to expand or grow into other businesses. There are two types of diversification strategies: related and unrelated diversification.

6.5 Establishing Business-Level Strategy

- Formulating the business-level strategy makes use of Porter's five competitive forces and his four competitive strategies.
- Porter's model for industry analysis suggests that business-level strategies originate in five primary competitive forces in the firm's environment: (1) threats of new entrants, (2) bargaining power of suppliers, (3) bargaining power of buyers, (4) threats of substitute products or services, and (5) rivalry among competitors.
- Porter's four competitive strategies are as follows: (1) The cost-leadership strategy is to keep the costs,

and hence the prices, of a product or service below those of competitors and to target a wide market. (2) The differentiation strategy is to offer products or services that are of unique and superior value compared with those of competitors but to target a wide market. (3) The cost-focus strategy is to keep the costs and hence prices of a product or service below those of competitors and to target a narrow market. (4) The focused-differentiation strategy is to offer products or services that are of unique and superior value compared with those of competitors and to target a narrow market.
- Jack Welch's questions for developing business-level strategy include: (1) What does the playing field look like now? (2) What has the competition been up to? (3) What have you been up to? (4) What's around the corner? (5) What's your winning move?

6.6 Strategic Implementation: Creating, Executing, and Controlling Functional-Level Strategies

- Strategic implementation is the process of putting strategic plans into effect.
- A functional strategy is a plan of action by each functional area of the organization to support higher-level strategies.
- Execution is not simply tactics; it is a central part of any company's strategy. Execution consists of using questioning, analysis, and follow-through to mesh strategy with reality, align people with goals, and achieve results promised.
- Three core processes of execution are people, strategy, and operations.
- Execution roadblocks can occur in the C-suite and also down the organizational hierarchy.
- Strategic control consists of monitoring the execution of strategy and taking corrective action, if necessary.

6.7 Career Corner: Managing Your Career Readiness

- Four career readiness competencies—understanding the business, task-based functional knowledge, critical thinking/problem solving, and decision making—drive your ability to think strategically.

Understanding the Chapter: What Do I Know?

1. What is strategic positioning, and what are the three principles that underlie it?
2. What are the five steps in the strategic management process?
3. What are the tools that can help you assess a company's current reality?
4. Based on the SWOT of Toyota contained in this chapter, what advice would you give to CEO Akio Toyoda?
5. How is VRIO different from a SWOT analysis?
6. What are the three overall types of corporate strategy?

7. Describe how the BCG matrix and diversification are used to establish corporate-level strategy.

8. What are Porter's five competitive forces?

9. Explain Porter's four competitive strategies.

10. Describe Welch's questions for developing a business-level strategy.

11. In execution, what are the three core processes of business?

Management in Action

La Croix Is Losing the Sparkling Water Wars

European brands San Pellegrino and Perrier dominated the U.S. sparkling water market for decades until a little-known brewing company decided to venture outside beer-making. Heileman, a Wisconsin brewery, introduced LaCroix (pronounced "La-Croy") as a sparkling water addition to their beer lineup in 1981. LaCroix was a Midwest favorite until the National Beverage Corporation purchased the brand and distributed it nationwide in the 1990s.[129]

The U.S. sparkling water industry exploded in 2015. The industry grew 16.2% between 2015 and 2016, with LaCroix alone growing almost 73%.[130] As a result, the National Beverage Company's value went from $2 billion in 2016 to $4.1 billion in 2017.[131] It had the right product, at the right time, and there were talks of a lucrative acquisition by a big name brand.[132]

Then the bubble burst. After five years of steady growth, National Beverage's sales declined 14% between 2018 and 2019, with profits dipping 10%.[133] The beverage maker's stock also dropped 55%.[134] "The LaCroix brand has gone from bad, to worse, to disastrous in a relatively short period of time," says Laurent Grandet, a lead beverage analyst at Guggenheim Securities.[135]

Let's take a closer look at what's been plaguing LaCroix.

LACROIX'S UNEXPECTED POPULARITY

In order to better understand LaCroix's strategic decision making (or lack thereof), it's important to know how the brand became so popular in the first place.

The average person drank less than four gallons of bottled water a year in 1988.[136] Soda was king, with per capita consumption peaking at nearly 53 gallons in the 1990s. Then came the obesity crisis in the early 2000s, leading to increased skepticism of sugary, soft drinks. Consumers changed their behaviors and soda consumption plummeted.[137] Americans' craving for bottled water surged by 2015, with per capita consumption of 37 gallons per year.[138]

As consumers drank more water, they also looked for more variety to keep their increased H_2O habit from becoming dull. This is where LaCroix, with its 20 flavors, tried to create competitive advantage. The noncorporate, "underground" feel spoke to those who valued an authentic Midwestern beverage, instead of snobby European seltzer. These individuals are the types that are more prone to use social media and spread the word, meaning LaCroix had instant brand recognition through word-of-mouth.[139]

THE COMPETITION CATCHES UP

While LaCroix was able to become popular relatively fast, making carbonated water isn't a particularly difficult endeavor. It did not take much time for the world's largest carbonated beverage makers, Coca-Cola and PepsiCo, to come out with their own carbonated waters, challenging LaCroix for market control. Both organizations had the advantage of large distribution channels and marketing budgets, giving them an advantage over much smaller LaCroix.[140] PepsiCo launched its own line of flavored carbonated water, Bubly, in 2018. "So we see this brand as a brand of the future . . . you're going to see mini cans, you're going to see larger cans," says PepsiCo chairman and CEO Ramon Laguarta.[141] What should be alarming for LaCroix is that Bubly now owns over 6% of the U.S. sparkling water market.[142]

Coca-Cola also has developed AHA, its own sparkling water brand. The company is looking to utilize bold flavor infusions, such as Apple and Ginger, Strawberry and Cucumber, and Lime and Watermelon, as well as two caffeinated flavors.[143] Coca-Cola also acquired Topo Chico, a Mexican sparkling water brand, in 2017 for $220 million. Topo Chico is quite popular in the U.S. as well, specifically in Texas, where it dominates market share for imported sparkling water.[144] "Unsweetened flavored sparkling water is a dynamic and exciting category as we look at our long-term growth plans," says Brad Spickert, Coca-Cola North America's SVP of hydration.[145]

A BRAND GONE FLAT

Analysts believe PepsiCo and Coca-Cola, as well as other competitors such as Nestlé and Polar, are strategically outperforming a stagnant LaCroix. The company still sells in multipacks of six or 12 instead of varying their sizes as competitors have. They also don't have single-serve cans for easy placement in convenience stores. "If you look at the range of LaCroix four years ago, about 90% of it is exactly the same as what you can see in stores today. . . . They're not overly creative or aggressive in terms of trying new ways of growth in the segment," says Grandet. Customers have "discovered that other brands offer acceptable substitutes."[146]

LaCroix's distribution network also pales in comparison to competitors. It does not utilize a direct store delivery network for a majority of its retail channels, instead relying on warehouse distribution. PepsiCo, Nestle, and Polar all operate direct store delivery networks, which allow them to have dedicated display space in top retailers. PepsiCo, in particular, has used its established control over checkout line coolers to place Bubly alongside its popular core soft drinks brands. "[Pepsi has] added [Bubly] to all of those secondary locations, and they can do that because they're so powerful," according to Tom Dowdy, chief revenue officer for Hudson News Distributors, one of La Croix's distribution partners.[147] This may be one of the reasons analysts expect Bubly sales to surpass LaCroix by 2021.[148]

Industry experts don't have confidence that National Beverage CEO Nick Caporella has what it takes to bring back LaCroix's luster. Caporella does not believe LaCroix's woes are due to mismanagement. He actually blames "injustice" for the company's decline in sales and profits, rather than poor strategy. "Managing a brand is not so different from caring for someone who becomes handicapped," Caporella said in 2019. Analysts aren't pleased with Caporella's refusal to make strategic change. Along these lines, *CNBC*

declared, "LaCroix would be better served in the hands of an owner with strong brand-building capabilities, the financial resources to invest appropriately, and the willingness to do so."[149]

Will LaCroix be able to rebound?

FOR DISCUSSION

Problem-Solving Perspective

1. What is the underlying problem in this case from CEO Nick Caporella's perspective?

2. What are some of the causes of this problem?

3. What will it take for LaCroix to regain its momentum? Explain.

Application of Chapter Content

1. How can LaCroix create a "fit" among its activities?

2. Using the steps in Figure 6.2, describe how LaCroix should be transforming the way it does business.

3. Develop a SWOT analysis for LaCroix.

4. Do a VRIO assessment of LaCroix's sparkling water and recommend a solution based on this assessment.

5. Is La Croix employing a growth, stability, or defensive strategy? Explain.

6. Which of Michael Porter's four competitive strategies is LaCroix trying to follow? Explain.

7. What can LaCroix do to properly execute across the three core processes of business?

Legal/Ethical Challenge

Is Your School Selling Your Bank Accounts?

Colleges and universities typically earn revenue from tuition, state taxes, and donations. The contribution from state taxes has been decreasing, creating a funding problem for many colleges and universities. This challenge focuses on a new source of revenue for campuses around the United States: the selling of bank accounts to students. Wells Fargo, U.S. Bank, and other financial institutions have signed a number of deals with schools in order to promote their banking services. The strategy is for banks to come to campus and pitch their services to students, with schools receiving royalties from the banks based on the number of new accounts students open. These royalties can sometimes be as high as hundreds of thousands of dollars annually, according to *The Wall Street Journal*.[150] Do you think the schools are working on behalf of their students or the banks?

Banks may be eager to pay royalties to schools because they represent a lucrative target market—young

adults often strapped for cash. Students may not have enough in their accounts to cover nonacademic expenses like trips and off-campus meals. Banks often provide overdraft protection when student accounts are a bit short. This protection actually works like a high-cost loan, and banks can raise substantial revenue from the interest and fees they charge. In fact, the Consumer Financial Protection Bureau (CFPB) estimates that consumers pay $17 billion in overdraft fees annually.[151] The CFPB also found that the 482,000 college students at institutions with paid promotional agreements with banks paid more than three times the amount of fees, compared to the 839,000 students at colleges without such relationships. "Anyone that looks at this data and the extent to which large banks continue to team up with colleges and universities to gouge the student body with overdraft fees should be outraged," says a former CFPB student loan ombudsman.[152]

Students are receiving benefits for these fees. Many schools allow them to conveniently link their campus identification cards to banking services. Others actually allow a contracted bank to open a location on campus.

These strategic relationships also allow the banks to offer special accounts for students. For example, a U.S. Bank spokesperson said the bank wants to build long-term relationships with students "by providing them with the best student banking account in the marketplace."[153] The bank does offer a student checking account with no monthly fees, but students still incur overdraft charges and non-U.S. Bank ATM fees after the first four transactions.[154]

Banks claim that schools benefit from the arrangement just as their students do. "Schools are looking for funding," says the head of PNC's university banking program. Schools receive that funding in return for allowing banks to set up tables at campus events, advertise their products in mailings to students, and be known as the school's preferred banking option. *The Wall Street Journal* found that 112 U.S. colleges received nearly $18.7 million in 2017 for these types of activities. Much of it was in the form of royalties, but some schools even receive a cut of the banks' fees.[155]

Consumer watchdogs are concerned about schools receiving any sort of incentive from banks in return for promoting them. This concern is magnified by the troubled history of banks and universities. In the early 2000s, some financial aid offices were steering students toward loan packages that provided kickbacks to administrators. Other schools were suspected of pitching credit cards with deceptive offers or illegal incentives.[156] New laws were passed to address this bad behavior, but most do not extend to checking or debit accounts.[157]

SOLVING THE CHALLENGE

What would you do if you were a university president and a bank approached you?

1. Sign a contract that provides the university with an incentive for each account opened. Both the university and bank are providing students with special benefits. So it is all right if the school is compensated based on volume.

2. Sign a flat-fee contract only. Schools should not receive an incentive for each account opened, but they should be compensated for allowing the bank to have an increased presence on campus.

3. Refuse to sign a contract. Schools should be neutral parties and not be promoting banks.

4. Invent other options.

LEARNING MODULE 2

Entrepreneurship

After reading this learning module, you should be able to:

LM 2-1   Define *entrepreneurship* and discuss its importance across the world.

LM 2-2   Identify how entrepreneurs get started.

So You Want to Start a Business?

We would not be surprised if you answered yes, given the data shown in Figure LM 2.1. You can see that the number of start-ups has been growing since 2000, particularly in the last few years. Over 774,000 businesses were established in the United States in 2019, up approximately 38% from 2010.[1] Businesses have also been exiting, which occurs when an establishment goes from having one employee to having none, and the business remains closed for one year. All told, the growth of small businesses resulted in 1.8 million net new jobs for the U.S. economy, based on the Small Business Association's 2019 *Small Business Report*.[2]

Speaking from experience, we can tell you that owning your own business can be highly rewarding, but it's no picnic and requires perseverance and lots of hard work. As Biz Stone, co-founder of Twitter noted, "Timing, perseverance, and ten years of trying will eventually make you look like an overnight success."[3] Still interested in starting your own business?

Below are five issues to consider if you desire to start your own business.[4]

1. Identify your motives. Are you running away from something or running toward a goal? Either is okay, but it's important to understand your motives. If you are moving toward a goal, be specific

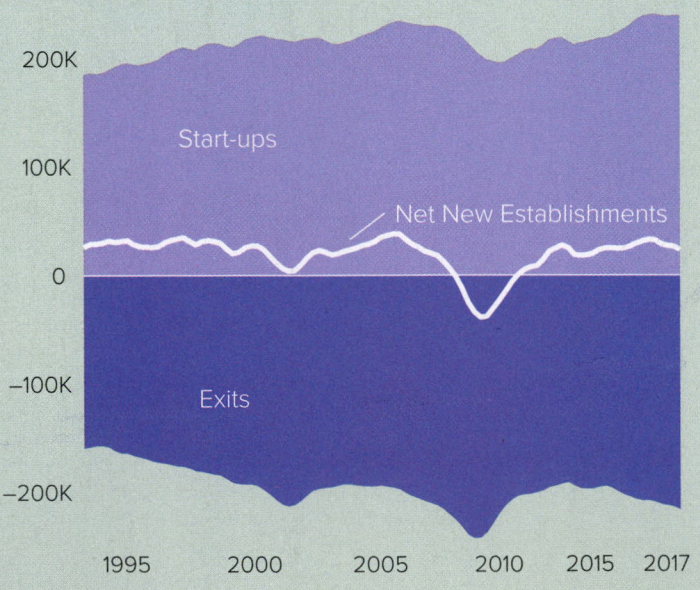

FIGURE LM 2.1   **Business start-ups and exits in the United States**

Source: "2019 Small Business Profile," U.S. Small Business Administration, Office of Advocacy, https://cdn.advocacy.sba.gov/wp-content/uploads/2019/04/23142610/2019-Small-Business-Profiles-States-Territories.pdf (accessed February 24, 2020).

about what you want and stay open to change. For example, when one of your authors, Angelo Kinicki, began his consulting activities, he started with the goal of running a sole proprietorship, and he kept his job at the university. This goal changed, as did the business decisions, when he and his wife Joyce decided to convert their business to a corporation. Joyce quit her job and served as president, running the company, and Angelo took a leave of absence from his university job. After growing the business to about nine employees and traveling around the world, they realized they were unhappy and needed a change. After discharging all but one employee, Angelo went back to the university and Joyce continued to run the business with only one additional employee. The business has continued to operate this way for many years, and everybody is happy.

2. **Build clients.** If you are currently working and have a business idea, we encourage you to find a market or clients before quitting your job. After all, your business idea won't work if you can't find people who want your product or service. Consider providing it free until you build up market interest. A friend of Angelo's is doing this as she attempts to market a new app. Her plan is to give it away, create demand, and then charge a nominal amount.

3. **Display humility.** Don't assume you have all the answers. Seek input from others who have started businesses, regardless of the industry. Studies show that humble leaders are more likely to establish profitable businesses.[5] Humble leaders also are more likely to recruit and promote capable innovators, empower entrepreneurship, and reward innovative contributions.[6]

4. **Surround yourself with the right people.** Consider what Steve Jobs, cofounder of Apple, had to say about hiring the right people. "When you're in a start-up, the first ten people will determine whether the company succeeds or not. Each is ten percent of the company. So why wouldn't you take as much time as necessary to find all A-players?" We couldn't agree more. Hire people who complement your skills and abilities by providing value differently than you do. Don't make the mistake of hiring only friends and family. Though these individuals may agree to work for less compensation and share your vision, you need to ensure you have people on the team who have the appropriate skill set, work ethic, and experience to make the venture a success.

5. **Learn the basics of accounting.** All owners need to understand financial statements. These tools are discussed in Chapter 16. For now, recognize the need to understand how to create and adhere to a budget and how to read a balance sheet and income statement. We also encourage you to hire a good accountant. And yes, those Introduction to Accounting courses are important!

For Discussion Have you ever thought about starting your own business? What excites you about the opportunity of starting a business, and what fears get in the way of your doing so? Explain.

FORECAST
What's Ahead in This Learning Module

This learning module considers entrepreneurship. We begin by exploring the foundation and importance of entrepreneurship and social entrepreneurship, with emphasis on the personal characteristics of entrepreneurs and explaining its importance around the world. We then explore the process of starting a novel business or franchise. We review the basics of writing a business plan, choosing an appropriate legal structure, obtaining financing, and creating the "right" type of organizational culture and design. We conclude by discussing some of the reasons businesses fail.

2.1 Entrepreneurship: Its Foundations and Importance

THE BIG PICTURE

Entrepreneurship, a necessary attribute of business, means the taking of risks to create a new enterprise. It can increase the standard of living around the world. Social entrepreneurship, in contrast, consists of improvising systems, devising new approaches, grasping opportunities others miss, and generating solutions to change society for the better. There are ten key characteristics of entrepreneurs that you should be familiar with.

LM 2-1

Define *entrepreneurship* and discuss its importance across the world.

Entrepreneurs drive innovation and growth around the world. According to *Startup Talky*, the most famous entrepreneurs of 2019 include Jeff Bezos, Bill Gates, Mark Zuckerberg, Sir Richard Branson, and Carlos Slim.[7] These individuals started with an idea or passion and turned it into great wealth via hard work and entrepreneurial thinking. Elon Musk is a great example.

Musk, born in South Africa in 1971, taught himself computer programming when he was 12. After receiving degrees in economics and physics, he pursued a doctoral degree in applied physics and material sciences at Stanford. He dropped out and started his foray into entrepreneurship. It began with co-founding Zip2, a software company he sold for $307 million. He then founded X.co, an online payment company that merged with Confinity, which turned into PayPal, which was purchased by eBay for $1.5 billion in 2002. Great start, but it was just the beginning.[8]

Musk used $6.3 million of his proceeds from these transactions to found Tesla Motors in 2004.[9] He also founded or co-founded other companies, such as SpaceX and The Boring Company. Like many entrepreneurs, he has a grand vision and goals. He has said that his goals "are to accelerate the world's transition to sustainable energy and to help make humanity a multi-planet civilization, a consequence of which will be the creating of hundreds of thousands of jobs and a more inspiring future for all."[10] Whether you agree with or admire Musk's ambitions, he exemplifies the characteristics of an entrepreneur.

Multiple entrepreneur. South African–born Elon Musk was a co-founder of PayPal, which provides payment processing for online vendors. He went on to shake up the auto business with Tesla Motors, which builds electric cars; develop SpaceX, a space exploration company; and retool the energy sector with SolarCity, a residential solar energy provider. He was said to be worth $35.4 billion in 2020. Nora Tam/Getty Images

This section defines entrepreneurship and explains how it is different from self-employment. We then discuss social entrepreneurship. Finally, we examine research on characteristics of entrepreneurs and conclude by exploring why entrepreneurship is important around the world.

Entrepreneurship: It's Not the Same as Self-Employment

Most small businesses originate with entrepreneurs, the people with the idea, the risk takers. The most successful entrepreneurs become wealthy and make the covers of business magazines: Oprah Winfrey (Harpo Productions); Fred Smith (Federal Express); Larry Page and Sergey Brin (Google). Failed entrepreneurs may benefit from the experience to return and fight another day—as did Henry Ford, twice bankrupt before achieving success with Ford Motor Co.

What Is Entrepreneurship? Although many definitions have been proposed, experts acknowledge three components of entrepreneurship. **Entrepreneurship** is a process of (a) recognizing opportunities for new venture creation or new value creation, (b) deciding to exploit these opportunities, and (c) "exploiting the opportunities by the way of new venture creation or new value creation . . . for realization of some desired value."[11] There are two types of entrepreneurs:

- An **entrepreneur** is someone who "organizes and operates a business or businesses, taking on greater than normal financial risks in order to do so."[12] Entrepreneurs start new businesses because they perceive an opportunity to introduce, change, or transform a product or service potentially desired by the market place. Steve Jobs, for example, invented the iPod and iPhone before there was any market demand.

- An **intrapreneur** is someone working inside an existing organization who sees an opportunity for a product or service and mobilizes the organization's resources to realize the idea. This person might be a researcher or a scientist but could also be a manager who sees an opportunity to create a new venture that might be profitable.

How Is Entrepreneurship Different from Self-Employment? Entrepreneurs and self-employed individuals share the commonality of owning a business, but they execute this role in very different ways. Let's explore these similarities and differences, starting with a definition of self-employment.

Self-employment is a way of working for yourself "as a freelancer or the owner of a business rather than for an employer."[13] As textbook writers, we are self-employed. We work for ourselves and hire contractors to help get things done. The same is true for many doctors, lawyers, accountants, insurance agents, electricians, and general contractors. Self-employed people are frequently experts in their fields and recognized members of their communities. In contrast, recall that entrepreneurs are motivated to introduce, change, or transform a product or service potentially desired by the marketplace. They are more interested in innovation and business growth than self-employed individuals. Let's consider five points of comparison:

1. Self-employed people work for themselves and sometimes hire others to assist in getting things done. The success of the business lies on the shoulders of the owner. When the owner retires or quits, the business generally closes. In contrast, entrepreneurs have people who *work with them.* Employees work together as a team to accomplish the entrepreneur's vision. Success at electric car company Tesla, for example, is dependent on everyone, not just Elon Musk. This is why a company outlives the participation or ownership of an entrepreneur. Tesla will continue with or without Musk at the helm.[14]

2. Self-employed people tend to stay in one geographic area, work virtually, and prefer to avoid taking risks. Entrepreneurs, on the other hand, are global thinkers who understand the need to take and manage risk. They won't grow the business without taking calculated risks.[15] Entrepreneurs are not afraid of failure or challenges. Musk's SpaceX program experienced quite a few failures and setbacks. For example, its Dragon spacecraft, designed to ferry NASA's astronauts to and from the International Space Station, exploded during a 2019 engine test.[16]

3. Self-employed owners and entrepreneurs have different mindsets. Self-employed people tend to do

Entrepreneurial rocket. Launch preparation for the SpaceX Dragon spacecraft at Cape Canaveral Air Force Station in Florida. Paul Hennessy/Alamy Stock Photo

much of the work themselves, partly because they are experts and want to save costs to maximize profits. Your authors certainly fall into that camp. Entrepreneurs like Elon Musk, however, realize "that they can't do everything so they delegate responsibilities to people they trust, who are smarter and more experienced than them in those areas, but still keep people accountable for their actions."[17]

4. There are a number of operational differences. Although both entrepreneurs and self-employed individuals are required to create a legally recognized organization, those who are self-employed can incorporate or file as sole proprietors. Entrepreneurs, in contrast, have a broader set of legal requirements and insurance and tax considerations.[18]

5. The final point of comparison involves scope of interests and influence. Entrepreneurs have broader aspirations aimed at influencing industries, markets, and greater numbers of people. Elon Musk, for example, wants to change the world. Self-employed individuals are more focused on operating a business in a specific geographic area and market. Their aspirations, interests, and scope of influence are much smaller.

Social Entrepreneurship

Social entrepreneurship consists of improvising systems, devising new approaches, grasping opportunities others miss and generating solutions to change society for the better.[19] It found its roots in the 1980s, when businesses began to realize that their customers cared about specific social issues. Businesses decided to support these issues, partly to increase customer loyalty and attract new customers. American Express is a good example of this practice. The company pledged in 1983 that for every new account opened and every purchase made with its card, it would donate to the Statue of Liberty restoration fund. The results were astonishing—new card applications increased by 45%, card usage increased 28% in the first month, and the company raised $1.75 million for the restoration fund in four months.

Many companies followed American Express's lead by marketing with a social cause closely aligned with their business offerings in health, education, and other areas.[20] Today, social entrepreneurship accounts for a third of startups, according to the Global Entrepreneurship Monitor.[21]

Why is this derivative of entrepreneurship becoming so popular? The answer may be related to corporate social responsibility (discussed in Chapter 3) and Porter's notion of *shared value* (discussed in Learning Module 1). As you may recall, shared value focuses on identifying and expanding the connections between societal and economic progress.[22] To Porter, the concept of shared value presents an opportunity for businesses to progress and meet the social needs of customers while generating revenue. Businesses that don't fulfill these needs risk being left behind.[23]

Though they typically make a profit, social entrepreneurs measure success not only by financial gains or customer satisfaction, but by the positive impact they have made in the community in the long run.[24] A recent study confirms that social entrepreneurship plays an especially important role in making today's world more equitable and sustainable.[25] The Example box profiles two social entrepreneurs who are reinvesting profits to maximize their social mission.

Restoring Lady Liberty. The Statue of Liberty on Liberty Island, New York City during restoration in 1985. Alfred Gescheidt/Getty Images

EXAMPLE   The Business of Curing Blindness

Bradford and Bryan Manning were diagnosed with Stargardt disease at the age of seven. Stargardt disease is a genetic eye disorder that causes blindness over time in children and young adults. The brothers had a desire to start a side project to expand awareness of visual impairment and allow them to raise money for eye disease research, but they didn't know how. As they were shopping for clothes one day, they realized that they selected clothing based on the softness of the fabric, not the style or size, because they couldn't see those things. "That day we discovered that we had both selected the same shirt based on its softness. So we thought, why not design clothing around its softness, its comfort and its fit?" says Bryan Manning.[26]

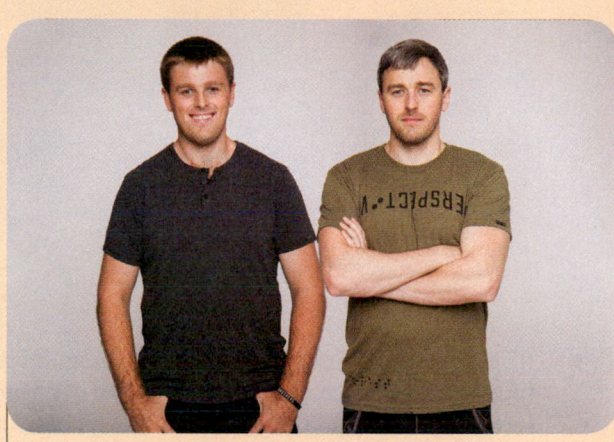

Manning Duo. Two Blind Brothers co-founders – Bryan (left) and Bradford (right). Courtesy of Two Blind Brothers

The brothers spent six months selecting soft fabric and designed versatile, chic, casual, or formal shirts they would want to wear themselves. They dubbed their company Two Blind Brothers and in 2017 put together a video on Facebook telling their story. The video exploded in popularity, the brothers were invited onto the Ellen DeGeneres show, and local news outlets picked up the story.[27] Two Blind Brothers was an instant hit.

The company offers Braille-enhanced t-shirts and henleys from $30 to $125, for men and women. All profits from sales go to the Foundation Fighting Blindness, an organization dedicated to funding support for vision-related research to provide preventions, treatments, and cures for eye disease. Two Blind Brothers has garnered Sir Richard Branson as a spokesperson, secured a pop-up at Macy's flagship Herald Square location in New York City, and raised more than $300,000 in the fight to find a cure for blindness.[28]

Bradford and Bryan attribute their success to the combination of "sharing our personal authentic story, tying it to a mission, [and] developing a product that someone loves."[29] Both brothers left their jobs in finance and are now focusing on fashion—and curing blindness—full time. Their future goals for Two Blind Brothers include product development to expand their offerings and securing some corporate partnerships in order to grow their sales channels.[30]

YOUR CALL

What other types of business do you think can make a profit while doing good at the same time? Do you see any drawbacks to social entrepreneurship ventures?

Characteristics of Entrepreneurs

Being an entrepreneur is what it takes to *start* a business; being a manager is what it takes to *grow or maintain* a business. As an entrepreneur or intrapreneur, you initiate new goods or services; as a manager you coordinate the resources to produce the goods or services—including, as we mentioned, the efforts of the intrapreneurs. Some of the examples of success we mentioned earlier—Oprah Winfrey (Harpo Productions) and Larry Page (Google)—are actually *both* entrepreneurs and effective managers. Other people, however, find they like the start-up part but dislike the management part. For example, Stephen Wozniak, entrepreneurial co-founder with Steve Jobs of Apple Computer, abandoned the computer industry completely and went back to college. Jobs, in contrast, went on to launch and manage another business, Pixar, which among other things, became the animation factory that made the movies *Toy Story* and *Finding Nemo*.

Do you think being an entrepreneur and being a manager require different skills? Researchers interested in this question typically compare personal characteristics of entrepreneurs with those of managers, and their answer is yes, the jobs require different traits and skills. Although a long list of potential characteristics of entrepreneurs exists, ten are believed to be most important (*see Figure LM 2.2*).[31]

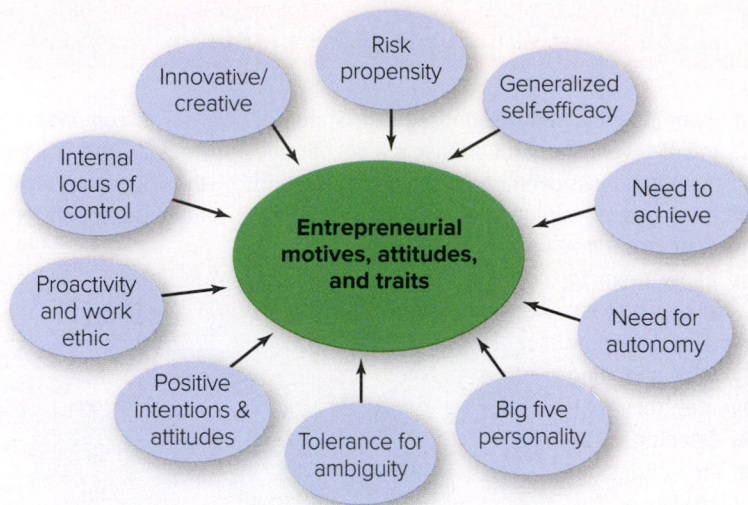

- **Risk propensity.** Research confirms that an increased ability to take risks distinguishes entrepreneurs from managers.[32] Managers must believe in themselves and be willing to make decisions; however, this statement applies even more to entrepreneurs. Precisely because they are willing to take risks in the pursuit of new opportunities—indeed, even to risk personal financial failure—entrepreneurs need the confidence to act decisively. As such, they prefer moderate levels of risk.

- **Generalized self-efficacy**. Generalized self-efficacy is a person's level of confidence about succeeding in different demanding situations. While managers and entrepreneurs both perform better when they have high self-efficacy, studies find that this characteristic is particularly important for entrepreneurs.[33] They need confidence to achieve goals in a broader set of activities such as attracting customers, handling technical problems, obtaining financial funding, and adhering to governmental rules and regulations. Studies also show that factors influencing self-efficacy differ between male and female entrepreneurs. Specifically, women have higher self-efficacy when they are mentored by female entrepreneurs, but the self-efficacy of men is not influenced by a mentor's gender.[34]

- **Need to achieve.** Both entrepreneurs and managers have a high need for achievement. However, entrepreneurs certainly seem to be motivated to pursue moderately difficult goals through their own efforts in order to realize their ideas and, they hope, financial rewards. Managers, by contrast, are more motivated by promotions and organizational rewards of power and perks.

- **Need for autonomy.** Although many of us prefer the freedom to act as opposed to being told what to do, entrepreneurs have a higher need for autonomy. They prefer to work for themselves, or with those they respect and admire, and studies show they have a strong preference for shaping their own destiny.[35] They are willing to forgo the security and comfort of working for an organization that provides stable salary and benefits. All told, entrepreneurs possess a greater need for autonomy than managers.

- **Big Five personality dimensions.** The Big Five are characteristics that psychologists have concluded define the core of our personality. They are discussed in detail in Chapter 11. The Big Five are *extroversion* (the quality of being outgoing, talkative, and sociable), *agreeableness* (being good-natured and cooperative), *conscientiousness* (being dependable, responsible, and persistent), *emotional stability* (being relaxed, secure, and even-keeled), and *openness to experience* (being imaginative, curious, and broadminded). Though entrepreneurs tend to be more extroverted, conscientious, and emotionally stable than managers, research suggests that openness to experience is the biggest differentiator between them.[36] Entrepreneurs also are less agreeable than managers.

- **Tolerance for ambiguity.** Every manager needs to be able to make decisions based on ambiguity—that is, unclear or incomplete—information. Recent research however finds that entrepreneurs generally have more tolerance for ambiguity.[37] This is most likely because they are trying to do things that haven't been done before.

- **Proactivity and work ethic**. Proactivity is a forward-looking perspective in which an individual is looking for opportunities to provide value beyond what others expect. This characteristic is desired by all organizations, but it is critical for entrepreneurs. You can't be entrepreneurial without being proactive.[38] One academic concluded that entrepreneurial proactivity consists of "introducing new products and services ahead of the competition and acting in anticipation of future demand to create change and shape environment, thereby creating a first move advantage *vis-a-vis competitors*."[39] Work ethic, which is an "other characteristic" of career readiness, also is a driver of entrepreneurship. It reflects the extent to which you accept accountability and display positive work habits such as punctuality, time management, sustained effort, and willingness to go beyond a job description or a boss's expectations (see again Table 1.2). Research demonstrates that strong work ethic is positively associated with entrepreneurial success.[40]

- **Internal locus of control**. If you believe "I am the captain of my fate, the master of my soul," you have what is known as an *internal locus of control*, the belief that you control your own destiny and that external forces will have little influence. (*External locus of control* means the opposite—you don't believe you control your destiny but that external forces do.) Although both entrepreneurs and managers like to think they have personal control over their lives, entrepreneurs were found to have higher levels of internal locus than managers.[41] A recent German study of 45 ultra-high net-worth individuals confirmed this finding, with 95% of participants describing themselves as someone who prefers to forge their own path.[42]

- **Innovative/creative ability.** *Innovation* leads to the creation of something new that makes money, while *creativity* produces new ideas about products, services, processes, and procedures. These definitions highlight that both innovation and creativity are fundamental to entrepreneurship. Entrepreneurs are generally more innovative and creative than others.[43]

- **Positive intentions and attitudes.** Researchers have long been interested in how our intentions affect our behavior. The question here is whether your intentions to engage in an entrepreneurial activity will result in your taking the risk to become an entrepreneur. The answer is yes. People become entrepreneurs when they form a personal intention to do so.[44] So where does the positive intention to become an entrepreneur come from? Researcher Icek Ajzen created the theory of planned behavior to answer that question.[45] This theory states that there are three general attitudes or beliefs that influence your intention to start a business. These include the attitude toward the behavior, subjective norm, and perceived behavioral control. For example, you may want to become an entrepreneur if you believe it is a valuable contribution to society (attitude toward behavior), if your parents and friends look highly upon the idea (subjective norm), and you have the resources to start a business (perceived control).

So where do you stand? Do you think you would like to be an entrepreneur? The following self-assessment was created to provide you with feedback about your entrepreneurial orientation, should your instructor assign it to you.

To What Extent Do You Possess an Entrepreneurial Spirit?

Please be prepared to answer these questions if your instructor has assigned Self-Assessment LM2.1 in Connect.

How motivated are you to be an entrepreneur, to start your own company? Do you have the aptitudes and attitudes possessed by entrepreneurs? This self-assessment allows you to compare your motivations, aptitudes, and attitudes with those found in a sample of entrepreneurs from a variety of industries. Go to connect.mheducation.com and take the self-assessment. When you're done, answer the following questions:

1. To what extent are your motives, aptitudes, and attitudes similar to those of entrepreneurs? Explain.

2. Based on your results, where are you most different from entrepreneurs in individual motives, aptitudes, and attitudes?

3. What do these gaps suggest about your entrepreneurial spirit? Discuss.

4. What things might you say during a job interview to demonstrate that you possess entrepreneurial characteristics? Explain.

Entrepreneurship Matters across the Globe

Entrepreneurship continues to be an economic generator across industries and countries around the world. The United States was recently ranked the best environment for cultivating entrepreneurship across 138 countries, according to the Global Entrepreneurship and Development Index.[46] In this section, we discuss the importance of entrepreneurship from the perspective of start-ups, innovation, job creation, and global experience.

Start-Ups Generate Wealth and Economic Development   Most of the get-rich stories we hear these days are about technology start-ups, such as Facebook, Yelp, Twitter, and Uber. A **start-up is a newly created company designed to grow fast.**[47] But all kinds of new endeavors are constantly being launched. Not all rely on technology, and not all are intended to quickly become big. What all new start-ups do have in common is that they are driven by an individual or group that relies on entrepreneurial thinking.

Vegetarian meat. A shopper chooses a package of Impossible Foods plant-based meat in a New York supermarket. Would you enjoy a "burger" made out of genetically modified soy instead of meat? rblfmr/Shutterstock

Here are some of *Forbes* best small business giants from 2019:[48] Advoco is an asset management company that keeps track of equipment for the likes of PepsiCo and Starbucks. The 67-employee company asks that every new hire sign a promise to be "courageous, driven, innovative, honest, confident and knowledgeable." Bruce Pomeroy and Andrew Skipper founded Evergreen, a real estate developer that allows its 54 employees to invest in each of its real estate projects. Finally, Life's Abundance, founded by Dennis and Carol Berardi, makes and sells healthy pet food. The company guarantees freshness and quality, touting the fact that it has never had a product recall.

While these businesses have so far remained small, others have experienced rapid growth. *Business Insider* identified 30 start-ups that began operating after 2009 and are now valued at over $1 billion each. They include plant-based food company Impossible Foods, food delivery service DoorDash, mattress and bedding company Casper, and Calm, a meditation app. Skilled entrepreneurship is driving the success of each firm.[49]

Entrepreneurship Drives Innovation   Innovation is the fuel for economic development, and it represents the foundation of entrepreneurial activities. Entrepreneurs and entrepreneurial firms propose and create new products and services sold around the world. Patents, licenses with which the government authorizes a person or company to exclude others from making using or selling an invention for a time, protect innovations. Small businesses, defined by the U.S. Small Business Administration (SBA) as those having fewer than 500 employees, are the form of business with which most entrepreneurs enter a market.[50] Small firms in turn are the primary source of patent creation in the United States. They generated 16.5 times as many patents as large firms in 2007, according to the SBA.[51] Studies also show that small and medium businesses that apply for patents are 21% more likely to experience a growth period after their application.[52] Table LM 2.1 reveals some interesting facts about small businesses in the United States.

Entrepreneurship Drives Job Creation   How often do we hear politicians run on a platform promising job creation? It's standard these days because job creation is good for citizens, communities, states, and countries. Historical figures show that small businesses employ over 47% of all private-sector employees. Moreover, from 2000 to 2018, small businesses created 9.6 million net new jobs while large businesses created 5.2 million.[53] This data confirms the importance of entrepreneurial firms.

Entrepreneurship Improves the World's Standard of Living   The standard of living is the level of "necessaries, comforts and luxuries which a person is accustomed to enjoy."[54] Clearly, entrepreneurial job creation improves standards of living around the world by transferring profits from the business to employees (in the form of pay) and thus to communities as employees are better able to make purchases that maintain or improve their material life. So what is the status of entrepreneurial activity around the globe? The annual Global Entrepreneurship Monitor (GEM) has been studying global

TABLE LM 2.1
Factoids about Small Businesses

- 36% of small businesses are female owned.
- 19% of small businesses are family owned.
- 50% of small businesses are home based.
- 22% of small businesses are financed by personal and family savings.
- 29% of small business owners have at least a bachelor's degree.
- 60% of people who start small businesses are between the ages of 40 and 60.
- 14% of small businesses are owned by immigrants.
- 62% of the U.S.'s 585 billionaires are self-made.
- 81% of small businesses don't have any staff.
- 99.9% of all firms in the U.S. are small businesses.
- 80% of firms survive one year; 50% survive five years; 33% survive ten years.
- 29% of small businesses are owned by minorities.

Sources: Data taken from "Frequently Asked Questions," Small Business Association, September 2019, https://cdn.advocacy.sba.gov/wp-content/uploads/2019/09/24153946/Frequently-Asked-Questions-Small-Business-2019-1.pdf; H. Kanapi, "Startup Statistics—The Numbers You Need to Know," Small Business Trends, March 28, 2019; https://smallbiztrends.com/2019/03/startup-statistics-small-business.html; D. Simovic, "39 Entrepreneur Statistics You Need to Know in 2020," Small Biz Genius, August 5, 2019, https://www.smallbizgenius.net/by-the-numbers/entrepreneur-statistics/.

entrepreneurship for 20 consecutive years. Its 2019 report is a summary of more than 164,000 interviews with people from 49 countries. The good news is that entrepreneurial activity is generally positively perceived and actively pursued around the world. For example, in most countries in Europe and North America, two-thirds to three-fourths of people believe successful entrepreneurs have high status. Most people around the world also believe that starting a business is a good career choice. These two statistics suggest that people around the world are interested in starting a business.[55]

2.2 Starting a Business

THE BIG PICTURE

Businesses start with an idea for a new product or service, or by licensing someone else's idea. Entrepreneurs then undertake a series of activities to build the foundation for getting the business off the ground. These activities include writing a business plan, choosing the company's legal structure, and arranging for financing. Once this foundation has been built, the job of building an organizational culture and design further helps the business take off. Finally, there are some common themes surrounding businesses that ultimately fail.

LM 2-2

Identify how entrepreneurs get started.

Have you ever had an idea for a product that did not exist? Many of us do in the course of life as we encounter situations in which some device would help us accomplish a task or make us happy. Lowell Wood is a good example. He became the most prolific inventor in U.S. history when he received his 1,085th patent from the U.S. Patent and Trademark Office in 2015.[56]

Wood is an astrophysicist, a self-taught paleontologist, and a computer scientist. He works hard at being creative. He told *Bloomberg Businessweek* that he "often failed or received the lowest score on the first exam given in a particular course and improved his marks through repetition and intense effort." He credits his ability to come up with new ideas and find creative solutions to problems to the amount of reading he does. He religiously reads three dozen academic journals from varying fields of study, a habit he learned from chemist and author Linus Pauling. Wood asked Pauling how he came up with all his great ideas. Pauling said, "There's really nothing to it all. You just read, and you remember what you read."[57] Wood is still making an impact today. His idea for a traveling wave reactor, which can provide "sustainable, scalable low-carbon energy for all the earth's inhabitants," is currently under production by Bill Gates's TerraPower company. The company is planning to release the first model in 2025.[58]

Lowell Wood Alex Wong/Getty Images

Businesses Start with an Idea

Some people might not be as creative as Lowell Wood, but we all have the potential to come up with a viable business idea. The following actions can assist any aspiring entrepreneur to uncover a business idea.

1. **Identify your passions, skills, and talents.** Your co-author Angelo Kinicki and his wife Joyce started a consulting business that built on their passions, skills, and experience. The idea was conceived from their love of teaching and helping others to learn and develop. Joyce had extensive experience and skills in human resource management, and Angelo was a proven academic who could easily explain complicated concepts to managers. They put their skills together to offer services targeted at assisting companies in developing and achieving strategic plans. They also engage in leadership development programs for

aspiring managers. The company has operated for more than 30 years. The takeaway is that your past experience and in-depth knowledge about an industry are great sources of new business ideas.[59]

2. **Identify a problem or frustration.** Chris Tidmarsh started Green Bridge Growers, "a commercial greenhouse in north central Indiana that provides herbs, lettuces and nasturtiums to local restaurants, and sunflowers and cosmos to florists," with his mother and co-founder Jan Pilarski. Tidmarsh has three college degrees from Hope College: chemistry, environmental studies, and French. He was diagnosed with autism during preschool and struggled to find meaningful employment after college. He started the company because his job as an environmental researcher ended due to his difficulty communicating with others, and he wanted to use his passion and knowledge about agriculture. The problem was finding an employer and work role that benefited from his background and interpersonal style. To make it work, Tidmarsh's mom does the administrative activities like accounting, marketing, and sales. "He perfects the spacing between rows of kale and spinach and keeps close tabs on water chemistry and soil acidity. He spends hours researching natural and effective pesticides to deal with aphids. The solution: 4,500 ladybugs."[60] Green Bridge Growers is known for actively blogging about its agricultural methods and the ways it is helping the planet. Its blogs also point to other start-ups that are doing ground-breaking work in the farming industry.[61]

3. **Identify an opportunity or need.** Do you see any opportunities associated with the billions of dollars people spend online? Brothers Patrick and John Collison did. They started Stripe Inc. in 2010 to help companies process their online transactions. The brothers built "software that businesses could plug into websites and apps to instantly connect with credit card and banking systems and receive payments. The product was a hit with Silicon Valley start-ups. Businesses such as Lyft, Facebook, DoorDash, and thousands that aspired to be like them turned Stripe into the financial backbone of their operations," according to *Bloomberg Businessweek*.[62] The company processes hundreds of billions of dollars a year for millions of businesses worldwide, charging a small fee for each one. Stripe continues to invest in new products, such as Stripe Capital, which provides businesses with fast, online access to the cash they need to grow. "We're investing now to build the infrastructure that'll power Internet commerce in 2030 and beyond. If we get it right, we can help the Internet fulfill its potential as an engine for global economic progress," says John Collison.[63]

Finding opportunities takes time, focus, and motivation. You first have to be looking for them. Jeff Bezos, who was a stock market researcher and hedge fund manager, followed Internet usage as part of his job. He decided to start Amazon when he realized that the surge in Internet usage provided an opportunity for online retailing. You also can find opportunities by considering markets that are not being served. Pay attention to current events and societal trends, then strike first so you can own the first-mover advantage.[64] For instance, the development of mobile devices triggered an opportunity for Uber's founders Garret Camp and Travis Kalanick. While searching for a cab in Paris, they realized the need to create an app that would hail a vehicle. The rest is history.

4. **Study customer complaints.** Customer complaints are a warning sign that something is wrong with a product or service. Thus they represent an opportunity to improve the offering. Consider Apple's response to the way iPhone batteries degraded as the product aged. To prolong the devices' lives, Apple used software controls to slow them down. Users were furious! The company decided to replace batteries in older phones for a reduced price instead and to provide more information about battery life within iOS.[65] Apple also was forced to pay up to $500 million in 2020 to settle a class action lawsuit stemming from its

Are you a glass half full or half empty kind of person? Entrepreneurs are more likely to see opportunity when others see challenges. Elenathewise/iStock/Getty Images

decision to slow down the devices.[66] We suspect this problem has made its way to the design engineers working on the issue of battery life. Perhaps it will lead to a breakthrough idea.

Franchising: Building on Someone Else's Idea

Most entrepreneurs come up with their own business ideas, but some leverage the proven ideas of others. Franchising, which we discussed in Chapter 4, is when a company (typically called the franchisor) allows another entity (typically called the franchisee) to pay it a fee and a share of the profits in return for using the company's brand name and a package of materials and services. In 2019, there were 773,603 franchised businesses in the United States, producing over $787 billion and employing more than 8.4 million people. McDonald's is the largest franchise with more than 38,000 restaurants in over 100 countries.[67] Other franchises include 7-11, The UPS Store, and Planet Fitness. Franchises have certain advantages and disadvantages, as well as special considerations for starting:

Footlong franchise. Subway employees topping sandwiches on the food preparation bar. Prachana Thong/Shutterstock

- **Advantages of franchising.** Opening a franchise instead of going it alone has its benefits. Franchise owners can take advantage of a proven brand instead of opening an unknown entity. There are volume discounts for ordering supplies from the franchise company's designated supplier, access to training and development for employees, and many franchise companies will offer loans to cover start-up costs.[68] Marketing and technology support is another advantage of owning a franchise. Take, for example, Subway, ranked #8 in *Franchise Direct's* top 2020 franchises. The company spent $468 million on nationwide advertising on behalf of its chain in 2018. Subway also redesigned its app so customers can order ahead of time and also utilize delivery.[69]

- **Disadvantages of franchising.** Opening a franchise also has its downsides. Just as the franchise company provides support and guidelines on how to operate its locations, there also are restrictions on what a franchisee can and cannot do, taking away entrepreneurial autonomy. This may include restrictions on modifying menu items or prices, changing suppliers, and even the way you decorate a location.[70] Another disadvantage is the extra fees, known as royalties, you need to pay the franchise company for using its brand and services. Subway franchise owners currently pay the company 12.5% of their weekly gross sales (4.5% goes toward advertising and 8% goes toward actual royalties). This is in addition to a $15,000 one-time franchise fee for opening a new Subway.[71]

- **Starting a franchise.** With these pros and cons of franchise ownership in mind, you should be aware of some important considerations prior to starting one. First, you'll need to budget extra money for the one-time franchise fee, which can be substantial for some franchises (e.g., McDonald's charges $45,000). You'll also need to do your research on the franchise you are interested in. What's the history of the franchise company and who is in charge? What does its finances look like? This research also should include a better understanding of the support the franchise company provides each location and the restrictions it has on franchise owner decision making. Finally, you should do your due diligence by speaking to current or former franchise owners to understand how their experience with the franchise company was. Is there anything they wish they knew prior to starting their franchise?[72]

Writing the Business Plan

A business plan is much more than a funding plan. It also answers critical questions such as, "What business are we in?" "What is our vision and where are we going?" and "What will we do to achieve our goals?" *Harvard Business Review* noted that "A plan helps detail how the opportunity is to be seized, what success looks like, and what resources are required, and it can be key to the investment decisions of angel investors, banks, and venture capitalists." A good plan also attracts high-quality talent.[73]

There are two camps regarding the value of creating a business plan. The first believes that entrepreneurs "learn by doing" and that planning is a waste of time because it takes effort away from doing, improvising, and pivoting. The idea is that the future is ever changing and unknown, and planning doesn't lead to more control. The other camp, in contrast, believes structured planning provides the foundation entrepreneurs need to launch a business, organize resources, hire employees, have accountability, and achieve results.[74] Which perspective sounds more reasonable to you?

Researchers have addressed this question. A recent six-year study of 1,000 would-be U.S. entrepreneurs compared planning practices and firm performance across one group that wrote formal plans and a second group that did not. The groups were balanced so that they were "statistical twins." Findings showed that entrepreneurs who planned were 16% more likely to survive than their identical nonplanning cohorts. Entrepreneurs tended to plan when the company was a high-growth–oriented start-up and when they were seeking funding.[75] All told, it pays to plan.

The components of a business plan vary, and people disagree about the level of detail to be included. Some suggest a one-page plan,[76] but the general sentiment is that a longer plan (15 to 25 pages)[77] is needed to cover the following areas:[78]

- **Executive summary.** This section is like a two-minute elevator pitch about the business. It provides conclusions and wraps up everything else in the plan. People generally write this section last so it can include important information from other sections.

- **Business description.** The business description helps people connect with your vision by outlining the business, its mission, vision, product or service, and the reason you started it. You also should conduct an analysis of your strengths, weaknesses, opportunities, and threats (SWOT analysis, discussed in Chapter 6). It's also recommended that you identify the principals in the business and the legal structure you will use.

- **Market analysis.** The market analysis reviews information about the market you are trying to enter, your competitors, where you fit in the market, how your product or service is unique, and the level of market share you expect to obtain. You also should analyze trends in your market area and industry and discuss profiles of "ideal" customers and any additional market research that supports the validity of your idea.

- **Organization and management.** This is where you show off the talent of the management team and any special employees, such as a well-known technical expert. Investors want to understand the talents of key team members and their previous successes. It's also useful to discuss the type of organizational culture and structure you think best positions the business for success.

- **Sales strategies.** The section on sales strategies reviews your ideas for marketing or promoting the product or service, your pricing strategy, your strategies for using the web and social media, and other activities for building brand awareness.

- **Funding requirements.** Now it's time to ask for the money you need to get this business running or to expand. Be realistic when you outline your funding requirements and set a range if you are unsure about exact future costs. Provide a timeline that links funding to expansion activities. You want to provide investors with realistic expectations.

■ **Financial projections.** Finally, develop revenue projections and conduct a cash flow statement. It's critical to identify your current financial needs and those expected in the future. Your revenue growth should be based on other information contained in the plan such as market trends, sales strategies, and human resource needs.

Choosing a Legal Structure

Your choice of a legal structure is one of the most important you will make as an entrepreneur. The reason is that this decision affects everything from the taxes you'll pay to your legal liability and control over the company. As we review the options, keep in mind that your choice depends on your personal and financial goals. Let's consider the four basic business entities: sole proprietorship, partnership, corporation, and limited liability (LLC).[79]

Sole Proprietorship   The Internal Revenue Service (IRS) defines a sole proprietor as "someone who owns an unincorporated business by himself or herself."[80] It's the simplest form of business structure. The sole proprietor gets to make all the decisions and has total control over the business. The key drawback, however, is that the owner has unlimited liability. If someone sues, the owner's personal and business assets are put at risk. Angelo Kinicki uncovered one key downside to this structure. It was hard to get financial backing for his consulting business when it operated as a sole proprietorship. Banks did not like the liability risk and would not lend him money to grow the business.

Partnership   The IRS defines a partnership as a relationship "between two or more persons who join to carry on a trade or business. Each person contributes money, labor or skill, and expects to share in the profits and losses of the business."[81] Partnerships generally begin with a common interest or experience. François Pelen is a good example. He left his position as a VP at Pfizer to start Groupe Point Vision with Patrice Pouts and Raphael Schnitzer, two fellow MBA students at HEC Paris. Groupe Point Vision now has 23 centers and has seen over 1.2 million patients.[82]

A partnership is an unincorporated business and there are two types: general and limited. In a *general partnership*, the partners equally share all profits and losses. In *limited partnerships*, "only one partner has control of its operation, while the other person or persons simply contribute to and receive only part of the profit."[83] This structure works well when you want to start a business with a family member or a friend. The drawbacks are the unlimited liability of the partners in general partnerships, and the risk of disagreements between them. Income and losses are "passed through" to the partners' individual taxable incomes.

Corporation   A corporation is an entity that is separate from its owners, meaning "it has its own legal rights, independent of its owners—it can sue, be sued, own and sell property, and sell the rights of ownership in the form of stocks."[84] There are two key types of corporations: C corporations and S corporations.

■ C corporations are owned by shareholders and are taxed as separate entities. The IRS states that this type of corporation "realizes net income or loss, pays taxes and distributes profits to shareholders. The profit of a corporation is taxed to the corporation when earned, and is taxed to the shareholders when distributed as dividends. This creates a double tax."[85] The benefit to the entrepreneur is that the legal entity and thus any liability exist separately from any individual owner of the business.

■ S corporations "are corporations that elect to pass corporate income, losses, deductions, and credits through to their shareholders for federal tax purposes. Shareholders of S corporations report the flow-through of income and losses on their personal tax returns and are assessed at their individual income tax rates.

This allows S corporations to avoid double taxation on the corporate income."[86] The benefit of an S corporation is that owners have limited liability and don't incur corporate tax. S-corps were the legal structure most frequently used by entrepreneurs in 2018, according to the National Small Business Association.[87]

Limited Liability Company (LLC)

A limited liability company (LLC) is a hybrid structure that combines elements of sole proprietor, partnership, and corporation. Each state may have different regulations regarding an LLC. "Limited liability means that its owners, also called members, are usually not personally responsible for the LLC's debts and lawsuits. . . . In the eyes of the IRS, LLC taxes usually resemble a sole proprietorship or partnership. The LLC does not pay income taxes itself: instead, the owners list business profits and losses on their personal tax returns."[88] Benefits of LLCs include fewer recordkeeping and reporting requirements than for corporations. LLCs were the second most frequently employed legal structure in 2018.[89]

Conclusions

You should not make a decision about the legal structure of a new business by yourself. The preceding information does not provide enough details for you to decide on your own. You want to obtain professional advice. The Kinickis, for instance, relied on the combined advice of their accountant and their attorney when deciding to transition their consulting company from a sole proprietorship to an S corporation. Our discussion here is not intended to provide all the information you need to start a business. We want to provide enough detail to enable you to ask good questions should you consider entrepreneurship.

Obtaining Financing

Whether they need equipment to start a small landscape business or a large investment to drive growth for a financial software firm like the Collison brothers' Stripe Inc., all entrepreneurs must eventually obtain financing. The amount depends on the nature of the business. The Small Business Administration, for example, put average start-up costs at less than $5,000, whereas the Kauffman Firm Survey suggests that $80,000 is a more accurate assessment.[90]

The availability of financing to start or grow a business can make the difference between pursuing an entrepreneurial dream and giving up. *Small Biz Genius*, for example, found that 27% of businesses aren't able to receive adequate financing to run.[91]

Below is a summary of financing options for start-ups:[92]

How much money do you think it takes to start a business? Census data show that 40% of new businesses were started with under $5,000.
Palto/Shutterstock

- **Personal funding.** A large percentage of entrepreneurs use their own savings or credit cards to initially fund a business. Banks like to see entrepreneurs invest in their own firms before they ask for a loan.

- **Family and friends (aka "love money").** Friends, parents, and other relatives are another common source of funding. You should expect to repay these loans as the business grows. Be careful when borrowing from or going into business with family and friends because people often have a hard time separating personal and business relationships.

- **Bank loans.** Bank loans were the most frequently used source of financing in 2017, according to the National Small Business Association, used by 64% of surveyed entrepreneurs. Banks generally want to see a good business plan and personal guarantees before they will lend. Entrepreneurs frequently use their homes as collateral for bank loans. The Small Business Association is another good source of loan financing. The mission of the SBA is to help "Americans start, build and grow businesses. Through an extensive network of field offices and partnerships with public and private organizations, SBA delivers its services to people throughout the United States, Puerto Rico, the U.S. Virgin Islands and Guam."[93] The SBA provides loans, "loan guarantees, contracts, counseling sessions and other forms of assistance to small businesses." It provides "an array of financing from the smallest needs in microlending—to substantial debt and equity investment capital (venture capital)."[94]

■ **Venture capital.** Venture capitalists (VCs) exchange funds for an ownership share in the company. They generally look for high-growth potential in industries like information technology, biotechnology, and communication and desire a high return on their investment. VCs essentially invest money for a share in controlling the company. This can include "the right to supervise the company's management practices" and "often involves a seat on the board of directors and assurance of transparency."[95]

Making a pitch to VCs is critical for those entrepreneurs needing a larger investment. The process begins with a business plan and a formal presentation. Lakshmi Balachandra worked at two VC firms and observed a number of these entrepreneurial presentations. She wondered why some proposals looked so good on paper and then turned into nonstarters based on presentations. She spent 10 years studying these dynamics.

Dr. Balachandra is now a professor at Babson College and is publishing insights from her research. They include the following:

1. Entrepreneurs are more successful getting financing when they laugh during pitches.

2. Entrepreneurs are more likely to get financing when they have friends or acquaintances in common with the VCs.

3. Judges prefer a calmer demeanor then over-the-top passion and excitement. People apparently equate calmness with effective leadership.

4. Interest in a start-up was due more to the entrepreneur's character and trustworthiness than to perceptions of competence.

5. Gender stereotypes play a role in investment decisions. People displaying stereotypically female behaviors such as warmth, sensitivity, and expressiveness were less likely than others to get funded.[96]

Let's focus a bit more on this last insight as research on gender bias during VC pitches has uncovered some problematic patterns. Multiple studies have shown that there is a strong gender bias against females in the pitch process. In one study, researchers concluded that "Investors prefer pitches presented by male entrepreneurs compared with pitches made by female entrepreneurs, even when the content of the pitch is the same."[97] Research also uncovered that the most deserving women entrepreneurs ironically faced the most resistance from venture capitalists.[98] A third study suggests that venture capitalists should stop this practice and embrace stereotypically female behavior as these traits can be advantageous. Researchers believe this would increase female entry into entrepreneurship and foster a more diverse and robust economy.[99]

■ **Angels.** Angel investors are wealthy individuals or retired executives who invest in small firms. "They are often leaders in their own field who do not only contribute their experience and network of contacts but also their technical and/or management knowledge. Angels usually finance the early stages of the business with investments in the order of $25,000 to $100,000."[100] They like to mentor would-be entrepreneurs and thus prefer those who are responsive to feedback.[101] Finally, Angels tend to finance companies in the software, mass market consumer goods, and equipment industries.[102]

■ **Crowd investing.** Crowd investing allows a group of people—the crowd—to invest in an entrepreneur or business online. The investors can take either an equity position in which they exchange money for stock or ownership in the company, or they can engage in debt investing by making a loan to the business.[103] GoFundMe, launched in 2010, is the world's largest, free social fundraising platform. The company has raised $9 billion from over 120 million donations for personal, business, and charitable causes.[104]

Creating the "Right" Organizational Culture and Design

At this stage in starting a business, the entrepreneur has a viable idea for a new or improved product and service, an established legal structure, a physical location in which to operate, and some level of financing. It's now time to decide on the type of organizational culture and design to adopt. These are important decisions because they affect employee behavior and performance across the individual, group, and organizational levels.

All entrepreneurs learn that they can't complete all tasks alone. They need people. At the early stages of a business, entrepreneurs tend to hire people they trust or who have values similar to their own. This group frequently includes family, friends, or experts in the industry. People generally get along and the excitement and interest in the new business drives motivation and performance. As the business grows, however, the founder or founders need to hire people with different skills, who may bring with them values and beliefs a little different from those of the current workforce. This is where organizational culture and design start to exert their influence on the business success.

Organizational culture, discussed in detail in Chapter 8, helps the business articulate its own values and beliefs, which generally flow from the founder's. There are different types of organizational culture, and a recent study confirms that the entrepreneur needs to identify the type that best fits the organization's vision and strategies, and his or her leadership style.[105] The business's evolving culture matters because it will influence employees' work attitudes and performance outcomes such as level of customer satisfaction, market share, operational efficiency, product/service quality, innovation, and financial performance.[106]

Organizational design, discussed in Chapter 8, is the process of designing the optimal structure of accountability and responsibility an organization will use to execute its strategies. In many small firms, the structure tends to form haphazardly and is rather simple. People pick up tasks as needed and there are no clear reporting relationships. This is feasible at first, but it quickly becomes dysfunctional as the business grows.

Growth brings the need for better organization and decision making. Like its culture, an organization's structure needs to fit the vision and strategies the business is pursuing. Chapter 8 discussed eight different organizational designs entrepreneurs might choose to organize the business. In the end, this decision can be difficult for entrepreneurs because they now must contend with sharing power, control, and decision making.

The Example box reviews the process Amanda Johnson used when transitioning from being an hourly employee to starting her own business. It illustrates many of the decisions entrepreneurs make as they start and grow a business.

EXAMPLE   Amanda Johnson Starts and Grows a Business

My dream was to be a big time writer, so I majored in journalism at Arizona State University. In preparation for my writing career, I had a part-time job and freelanced whenever possible. Then life happened.

I got married my last semester at school, purchased a home, and thought I'd settle into freelancing as the thing I'd be doing for the rest of my life. Then my husband was laid off and we found out we were expecting our first child. I felt the weight of growing bills and lack of health care. Did I want to give up

freelancing and my flexible schedule to try to find something more stable, only to have to take maternity leave? Would I be able to work *and* afford day care? Did I really want to go into a full-time career while my daughter was little? Should I give up on my dream of being independent?

I'd always been creative and used those skills while working in a flower shop during college. I now found myself wondering whether I could turn back to flowers and somehow turn that passion into viable source of income. We certainly needed the money.

Local shops were hiring but would only hire "designers" with years of experience. One shop admitted it was cautious about bringing me on as I'd be having a baby in the spring and might not be able to work during Valentine's Day! I started thinking about opening my own flower shop.

I knew what I loved about the flower shop I'd worked in during college: weddings, proms, and events. I loved the creative challenge and fun designs. I knew, too, what I didn't love: working holidays such as Valentine's and Mother's Day. Customers can be grouchy, and flowers have been getting more expensive. I also knew starting a flower shop involved a lot of overhead—renting a space, hiring employees—and I didn't have a lot of money to spend.

Frustrated after trying to find work in a shop and weighing the pros and cons of being away from home while caring for our daughter, I decided to start my own business. Strategically, I decided to focus only on wedding and event design. I kept the operation small by working with couples having small weddings so that I could easily design in the kitchen of my home. I invested in a small floral cooler. I named my company Butterfly Petals.

I'd always loved butterflies and, after an exhaustive search of available business names, I found "Petals" was the only floral-related word left! I started as a sole proprietorship. I didn't know the ins and outs of the business side at the time, and this was the fastest way to get up and running. I registered my business name and contacted floral suppliers to set up wholesale accounts. I took my own photos and put together a very basic website. Then I hustled. I brought arrangements to venues, dropped my cards in bridal salons.

There was a lot on the line since I was using my personal income to finance this new venture. I met clients at my dining room table or drove to various coffee shops to meet them during their lunch break. It took time and a few trusting clients, but I had my first bookings shortly after my daughter was born.

I realized I needed help managing taxes and other business issues, so I hired a professional bookkeeper. One of the recommendations was to switch from a sole proprietorship to an LLC in order to protect myself personally from the company's debts. The company grew over the next few years. I started creating events for clients with large wedding parties and higher table counts. The flowers and supplies took over, and I could no longer keep the work in my home. I had to decide whether I wanted the overhead of a studio space and employees to help with the demand. I was worried that my little company could not support me and the additional costs.

Amanda Johnson Courtesy of Amanda Johnson

On the other hand, I thought revenue would grow by bringing on extra team members because we could take on multiple weddings and events in a weekend. I also believed that moving the company out of my house would lead wedding and event professionals to take me seriously, creating a bigger pipeline of customers. I thus decided to take on my first studio, purchase additional inventory, and hire part-time employees. By this time, the business was able to support the costs and still provide me with income. After two years it was time to look for *another, larger* space!

By my 15th year, I was operating out of my third, and largest studio space. I had a massive rental inventory of vases, containers, and candle holders. We designed multiple events every weekend and had corporate clients and standing orders throughout the week. I learned to delegate and share my design knowledge with key members of my team so we could take on larger scale work and more events to keep the company afloat during the off-season.

I found out I was pregnant with my third child in fall of 2019 and realized my career had come full circle. The changing wedding industry brought more competition from new, talented designers with lower overhead and many millennial couples are changing the way they say "I Do." Many place emphasis on "experiences" for their guests such as destination weddings or fun dining experiences rather than investing in expensive wedding ceremonies and receptions. I decided it was time to focus on my family once again, only this time I cut back on the number of weddings. I only accepted smaller events for my spring 2020 season. I sold a lot of my inventory and moved back to a much smaller operation I could manage out of the house. It's strange and exciting to "retire" at the ripe old age of 38. Entrepreneurship was a constant challenge and learning experience and I'm grateful for the lessons learned and I look forward to what life has in store as I once again start over while becoming a new mom.

—Amanda Johnson

Why Entrepreneurial Ventures Fail

Earlier you learned that many new businesses fail. According to the Small Business Association, 70% of businesses survive their first two years, but that number falls to around 33% by year ten.[107] This means that the vast majority of new businesses will not live to see their 10th anniversary. Although there are many reasons why businesses fail, four common themes exist.[108]

- **Lack of effective planning.** Many businesses fail because they had an ineffective business plan, deviated from an effective one, or didn't even plan in the first place. As we noted earlier, businesses that effectively plan have a higher likelihood of success. Plans should be realistic and based on accurate, current information.

- **Insufficient capital.** A common mistake for new business owners is not understanding the need for sufficient capital for day-to-day operations. This can lead to the business closing before it has had a fair chance to succeed. In fact, cash-flow issues are the cause of 82% of small business closures. When determining how much money is required for your business, don't just think about start-up costs. Successful new businesses plan for the costs of staying in business, especially when they know they may not make a profit for a year or two.

- **Poor management.** As we noted in Section LM 2.1, not all entrepreneurs are effective managers. New business owners frequently lack relevant management expertise in areas such as finance, purchasing, hiring, and communications. Successful business owners educate themselves on the skills they lack, hire those with the required skills, or outsource work to competent professionals.

- **Lack of customer interest.** A new product or service needs to solve a problem or fulfill an existing need. Excellent management skills and access to plenty of capital won't make up for the fact that nobody wants what you are offering. In actuality, 42% of small businesses fail due to lack of customer interest. A good way to avoid this problem is to conduct effective market research as part of your business planning.

Key Terms Used in This Learning Module

Key Points

LM2.1 Entrepreneurship: Its Foundations and Importance

- Entrepreneurship, a necessary attribute of business, is the process of recognizing and exploiting opportunities.
- Two types of entrepreneurship are entrepreneurs and intrapreneurs.
- Entrepreneurship is different from self-employment.
- Social entrepreneurship consists of improvising systems, devising new approaches, grasping opportunities others miss, and generating solutions to change society for the better.
- Ten research-based characteristics of entrepreneurs are risk propensity, generalized self-efficacy, need to achieve, need for autonomy, Big Five personality, tolerance for ambiguity, proactivity and work ethic, internal locus of control, innovative/creative ability, and positive intentions and attitudes.
- Entrepreneurship matters around the globe because it (1) generates wealth and economic development, (2) drives innovation, (3) drives job creation, and (4) improves the world's standard of living.

LM2.2 Starting a Business

- All businesses start with an idea. Ideas come from four sources: (1) the entrepreneur's passions, skills, and talents; (2) a problem or frustration; (3) an opportunity or need; and (4) customer complaints.
- Franchising occurs when a company allows another entity (the franchisee) to pay it a fee and a share of the profits in return for using the company's brand name and a package of materials and services.
- Business plans help set the direction of a new business. They answer questions such as "What business are we in?"; "What is our vision and where are we going?"; and "What will we do to achieve our goals?"
- There are four fundamental legal structures entrepreneurs can use when starting a business: sole proprietorship, partnership, corporation, and limited liability company (LLC).
- There are a variety of funding sources entrepreneurs use to start and grow their new business. They include personal funding, loans from family and friends, bank loans, venture capital, angel investors, and crowd investing.
- Entrepreneurs need to establish an organizational culture and design that fit the vision and strategies being pursued by the new business.
- Common reasons why new businesses fail are lack of effective planning, insufficient capital, poor management, and lack of customer interest.

7

Individual and Group Decision Making
How Managers Make Things Happen

Kapook2981/iStock/Getty Images

After reading this chapter, you should be able to:

LO 7-1 Compare rational and nonrational decision making.

LO 7-2 Explain how managers can make decisions that are both legal and ethical.

LO 7-3 Describe how evidence-based management and data analytics contribute to decision making.

LO 7-4 Describe how artificial intelligence is used in decision making.

LO 7-5 Compare the four decision-making styles.

LO 7-6 Identify barriers to rational decision making and ways to overcome them.

LO 7-7 Outline the basics of group decision making.

LO 7-8 Describe how to develop the career readiness competencies of critical thinking/problem solving and decision making.

FORECAST   *What's Ahead in This Chapter*

We begin by distinguishing between rational and nonrational decision making and describe two nonrational models. We next discuss ethical decision making. The focus then turns to evidence-based decision making and the use of analytics and big data, which is followed by a related discussion of artificial intelligence and its impact on decision making. We then explore four general decision-making styles, describe 10 common decision-making biases, and review important aspects of group decision making and group problem-solving techniques. We conclude with a Career Corner that focuses on how you can develop the career readiness competencies of critical thinking/problem solving and decision making.

How to Make Good Decisions

"Every time you take on a challenge or make a decision, there's a chance you may come up short, and that's alright," says Aaron Meyers, President & COO of Hammer and Nails.[1] Making mistakes is always a possibility, but that can't stop you from making decisions. And you can learn from the result, which will help you hone your career readiness competencies of critical thinking/problem solving and decision making.[2] So how do you make good decisions? This chapter will discuss several kinds of decisions and different models for decision making. But here are a few general guidelines that apply to any formal or informal decision process.

Keep Your Mind Open

If you make prejudgments about a situation rather than keeping an open mind, you risk acting on your biases rather than on the facts. "Over the course of my career I've become increasingly open-minded, rather than becoming more set in my ways," says Cindy Hook, chief executive officer of Deloitte Asia Pacific.[3] To make good decisions you need to be ready to take in all valid information, even if it contradicts or questions your own beliefs and experience. (Just because you don't agree with something, that doesn't make it wrong.)

Use your communication skills to become a good and patient listener and, with your proactive learning orientation, load up on new facts and information. Don't decide the outcome ahead of time, either. It's sometimes easy to assume a decision will not turn out well, or a problem will remain unsolved. Taking a positive approach instead can only improve your decision making.[4] In summary, communication, proactive learning orientation, and a positive approach are career readiness competencies that contribute to your open-mindedness and can assist you in making better decisions.

Prioritize Your Decisions

Sometimes you may have to make multiple decisions, and all within a limited time. Some may be large and some small. How do you effectively manage this task? Here are four steps to help you prioritize decisions and get to the important ones first.[5]

1.   List the decisions you need to make over the relevant time period. Perhaps over the next six months you need to decide where and how to begin your job search, whether to buy a new car, and what to do with the belongings you left at home when you moved to your dorm or apartment. Make sure your list is complete and that you've identified the information you need to make each decision, such as the size of your budget for buying a car and the average price for the model you want.

2.   Characterize each decision according to its complexity and magnitude. Who or what is affected by each, and how much do you need in terms of tools and information to make your choice? The more ramifications and the more information needed, the larger and more complex the decision.

3.   Organize your decisions into three categories: Strategic decisions, like deciding how to frame your job search, will require the most time and attention, can affect the largest number of people, and probably also require you to gather the most information. Significant decisions demand less energy and information but are still important. Whether to buy a new car might fit into this category. Finally, quick decisions are the least complex you face, require the least input, and can often be resolved if you apply a simple rule. Deciding what old belongings to keep, throw out, or give away falls into this category.

4.   Note the timing for each decision. If you've done the first three steps, this one should be easy. For instance, you may need to complete (not just start) your job search before you can buy a car or even know whether you need one.

Move On from Your Mistakes

If a decision doesn't turn out as well as you'd hoped, start by forgiving yourself. Solving problems and making decisions are skills everyone can practice and get better at. Next, review the steps you took to arrive at your decision, and if it's not already clear what went wrong, try to identify the weak spot in your process.[6] Did you get too little information or fail to consider opposing viewpoints? Did you spend too much time on quick decisions and not enough on strategic or significant ones? If the problem is one you can remedy, congratulations. You've just learned something, and you've improved your career readiness skills too. Now move on!

Practice Mindfulness

We described mindfulness in Chapter 1 as awareness that comes from paying attention on purpose, in the present moment, and nonjudgmentally to the unfolding of experience in each moment.[7] Mindfulness improves your decision making because it reduces the amount of activation in your amygdala: The amygdala is like an alarm bell that engages your "fight-or-flight neural and hormonal systems."[8] Bottom line, a less active amygdala reduces emotionality and aggression while increasing self-control and thoughtfulness.[9] You can become more mindful by practicing meditation that focuses on your breath. Jon Kabat-Zinn, the father of mindful mediation, recommends that you stop, sit down, and "become aware of your breathing once in a while throughout the day." You can do this for seconds or minutes. The key is to "let go into full acceptance of the present moment, including how you are feeling and what you perceive to be happening. . . . just breathe and let go. Breathe and let be."[10] Research uncovered that mindfulness promotes innovativeness, self-determination, intrinsic motivation, positive interpersonal relationships, and the reduction of conflict.[11] Mindfulness also assists you in making more ethical decisions. This is evidenced by multiple studies finding a positive link between mindfulness and ethical decision making.[12] Angelo, one of your authors, started his classes with a 10-minute meditation to prepare his students for staying focused during classroom lectures and activities.

For Discussion Which of the above suggestions seem most practical? How might you implement them?

7.1 Two Kinds of Decision Making: Rational and Nonrational

THE BIG PICTURE

Decision making, the process of identifying and choosing alternative courses of action, may be rational, but it is often nonrational. Four steps in making a rational decision are (1) identify the problem or opportunity, (2) think up alternative solutions, (3) evaluate alternatives and select a solution, and (4) implement and evaluate the solution chosen. Two examples of nonrational models of decision making are (1) satisficing and (2) intuition.

LO 7-1

Compare rational and nonrational decision making.

Making good decisions is something you need to master now. Marcia Daszko, a writer for *Silicon Valley Business Journal*, believes that companies should not expect senior leaders to make all the decisions. She concluded that companies will be more effective if they involve employees in the decision-making process.[13] Will you be ready to make decisions when senior management comes to you with a problem?

This section will help you develop the career readiness competency of decision making. We'll first introduce the steps to making a rational decision. The focus then turns to nonrational decision making, which includes satisficing and intuition. Finally, we'll provide tips for improving your intuition.

A **decision** is a choice made from among available alternatives. **Decision making** is the process of identifying and choosing alternative courses of action.

If your company's product is in first place in its market and making a lot of money, is that a sign of great decision making? Consider the decisions that frame success at Starbucks.

EXAMPLE	Starbucks Uses Decision Making to Reclaim Its Soul

Starbucks' chairman emeritus, Howard Schultz, provides a good illustration of how effective strategic decision making can help a large organization find its way again.

Schultz joined the Seattle-based company as marketing director in 1982, when it was a small chain selling coffee equipment. Over nearly two decades, he gained control of the firm and, inspired by the coffee houses of Europe, transformed it into a comfortable "third place" between home and work, a place with a neighborhood feel selling fresh-brewed by-the-cup lattes and cappuccinos. Starbucks, named for the first mate of the whaling ship in Herman Melville's *Moby Dick*, had become the world's largest specialty coffee retailer by 2000.

Today, the company continues to dominate the market with more than $26 billion in revenue and 31,256 stores in 2019.[14]

A Crisis Brews Schultz stepped down as CEO in 2000 after serving 14 years as the coffee company's leader. For a while the business continued to thrive, but then two things happened that provoked a crisis. First, the company "lost a certain soul," says Schultz, as management became more concerned with profits than with store atmosphere and company values and extended existing product lines rather than creating new ones. Second, during the recession that began in 2007, tight-fisted consumers abandoned specialty coffees, causing the stock

A latte growth. A Starbucks storefront in Bangkok, Thailand. Asia accounted for almost half of the company's growth in 2019. i viewfinder/Shutterstock

price to nosedive. Schultz returned as CEO in January 2008, after an eight-year absence.

The Reinvention Begins "I didn't come back to save the company—I hate that description," Schultz told an interviewer. "I came back to rekindle the emotion that built it."[15] Among the risks he took to restore the company's luster was closing 800 U.S. stores, laying off 4,000 employees, and letting go most top executives. As a morale booster, he flew 10,000 store managers to New Orleans, recently destroyed by hurricane Katrina. Along with attending strategy sessions, they bonded in community-service activities, contributing thousands of volunteer hours to help restore parts of the city. "We wanted to give back to that community post-Katrina," says Schultz, "and remind and rekindle the organization with the values and guiding principles of our company before we did a stitch of business."

The Payoff After a couple of years, the company turned around, the result of better operations, modernized technology, a reinvigorated staff, and several innovations: It offered new coffee products, switched to a cold-brew process for iced coffee instead of simply brewing hot coffee and then chilling it, acquired (and then later closed) the La Boulange bakery chain, opened (and then closed) Teavana "tea bars," enabled customers to pay for coffee via a mobile-payment app, and even launched alcohol sales.[16] By early 2016, its revenues had risen 146% over the last decade, while earnings grew more than fivefold.[17]

Today's Challenges Schultz stepped down in April 2017 and was replaced by Kevin Johnson, the company's president and COO. Johnson is facing some challenges of his own. For example, the company decided in 2020 to temporarily close over half of its 4,300 China-based locations as the country battled the COVID-19 pandemic. This came at the same time that Chinese rival Luckin Coffee overtook Starbucks as the largest coffee chain in the country, mounting the greatest challenge Starbucks has faced in China. Johnson defended his decision to close stores saying it was done to protect the health and well-being of Starbucks employees.[18] The company also decided to phase out plastic straws from all of its locations by 2020. Though many supported the environmentally conscious decision, the company faced backlash from disability advocates who said disabled individuals would not be able to comfortably consume their beverages without the use of straws.[19]

YOUR CALL

As Starbucks faces new challenges, what can CEO Johnson learn from the company's past decisions in order to guide his decision-making process?

Rational Decision Making: Managers Should Make Logical and Optimal Decisions

The **rational model of decision making**, also called the classical model, explains how managers should make decisions. It assumes managers will make logical decisions that are the optimal means of furthering the organization's best interests.

Typically there are four stages associated with rational decision making. *(See Figure 7.1.)* These also are the steps in the standard model of problem solving. As stage 1 in the figure shows, for example, a decision is often an opportunity to solve a problem, which is a gap between an actual and a desired state.

FIGURE 7.1

The four stages in rational decision making

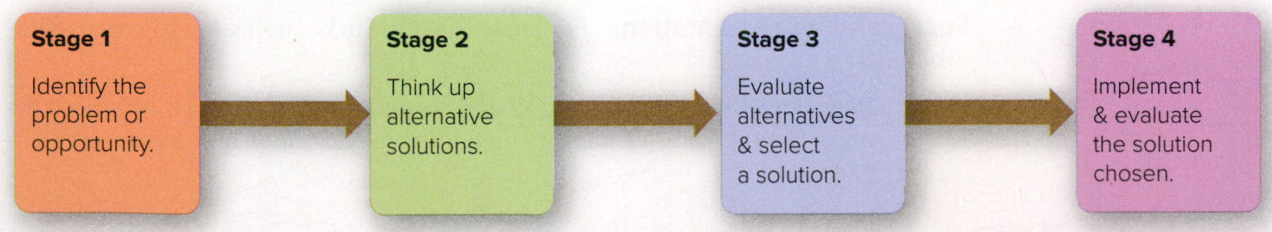

Stage 1	Stage 2	Stage 3	Stage 4
Identify the problem or opportunity.	Think up alternative solutions.	Evaluate alternatives & select a solution.	Implement & evaluate the solution chosen.

Stage 1: Identify the Problem or Opportunity— Determining the Actual versus the Desirable

As a manager, you'll probably find no shortage of **problems, or difficulties that inhibit the achievement of goals:** customer complaints, supplier breakdowns, staff turnover, sales shortfalls, competitor innovations, low employee motivation, and poor quality.

However, you also will often find **opportunities—situations that present possibilities for exceeding existing goals.** It's the farsighted manager, however, who can look past the steady stream of daily problems and seize the moment to actually do *better* than the goals he or she is expected to achieve. When a competitor's top salesperson unexpectedly quits, that creates an opportunity for your company to hire that person away to promote your product more vigorously in that sales territory.

Whether you're confronted with a problem or an opportunity, the decision you're called on to make is how to make *improvements*—how to change conditions from the present to the desirable. This is a matter of **diagnosis—analyzing the underlying causes.**

Stage 2: Think Up Alternative Solutions—Both the Obvious and the Creative

Employees burning with bright ideas are an employer's greatest competitive resource. "Creative thinking is a way of looking at problems from a fresh perspective with nontraditional solutions, according to *Forbes* writer Amanda Cotler. It's "the most important business strategy."[20]

After you've identified the problem or opportunity and diagnosed its causes, you need to come up with alternative solutions.

Stage 3: Evaluate Alternatives and Select a Solution— Ethics, Feasibility, and Effectiveness

In this stage, you need to evaluate each alternative not only according to cost and quality, but also according to the following questions: (1) Is it *ethical*? (If it isn't, don't give it a second look.) (2) Is it *feasible*? (If time is short, costs are high, technology unavailable, or customers resistant, for example, it is not.) (3) Is it ultimately *effective*? (If the decision is merely "good enough" but not optimal in the long run, you might reconsider.)

Today, the task of evaluating alternatives is facilitated by the use of *big data* (discussed in Section 7.3) and *artificial intelligence* (discussed in Section 7.4). In fact, recent research confirms that firms can make better decisions if they utilize these tools in the decision-making process.[21]

Stage 4: Implement and Evaluate the Solution Chosen

With some decisions, implementation is usually straightforward (though not necessarily easy—firing employees who steal may be an obvious decision, but it can still be emotionally draining). With other decisions, implementation can be quite difficult; when one company acquires another, for instance, it may take months to consolidate the departments, accounting systems, inventories, and so on.

Successful Implementation   For implementation to be successful, you need to do two things:

- **Plan carefully.** Especially if reversing an action will be difficult, you need to make careful plans for implementation. Some decisions may require written plans.

- **Be sensitive to those affected.** You need to consider how the people affected may feel about the change—inconvenienced, insecure, even fearful, all of which can trigger resistance. This is why it helps to give employees and customers latitude during a changeover in business practices or working arrangements.

Now that you understand the four stages of the rational model, to what extent do you think you use them when making decisions? Research shows that being responsible, diligent, humble, and open to new experiences increases your chances of rational decision making.[22] Would you like to improve the career readiness competency of *decision making*? If yes, then you will find the following self-assessment valuable as it assesses your problem-solving skills.

SELF-ASSESSMENT 7.1 CAREER READINESS

Assessing Your Problem-Solving Potential

This survey is designed to assess your approach to problem solving. Please be prepared to answer these questions if your instructor has assigned Self-Assessment 7.1 in Connect.

1. What is the status of your problem-solving skills? Are you surprised by the results?

2. Based on identifying the four lowest scored items on the assessment, what can you do to improve your problem-solving skills? Explain.

3. What things would you say during an interview to demonstrate that you possess this career readiness competency?

Evaluation One "law" in economics is the Law of Unintended Consequences—things happen that weren't foreseen. For this reason, you need to follow up and evaluate the results of any decision.

What should you do if the action is not working? Some possibilities:

- **Give it more time.** You need to make sure employees, customers, and so on have had enough time to get used to the new action.

- **Change it slightly.** Maybe the action was correct, but it just needs "tweaking"—a small change of some sort.

- **Try another alternative.** If Plan A doesn't seem to be working, maybe you want to scrap it for another alternative.

- **Start over.** If no alternative seems workable, you need to go back to the drawing board—to stage 1 of the decision-making process.

What's Wrong with the Rational Model?

The rational model is *prescriptive*, describing how managers ought to make decisions. It doesn't describe how managers *actually* make decisions. Indeed, the rational model makes some highly desirable assumptions—that managers have complete information, are able to make an unemotional analysis, and are able to make the best decision for the organization. *(See Table 7.1.)* We all know that these assumptions are unrealistic.

TABLE 7.1

Assumptions of the Rational Model

- **Complete information, no uncertainty:** You should obtain complete, error-free information about all alternative courses of action and the consequences that would follow from each choice.

- **Logical, unemotional analysis:** Having no prejudices or emotional blind spots, you are able to logically evaluate the alternatives, ranking them from best to worst according to your personal preferences.

- **Best decision for the organization:** Confident of the best future course of action, you coolly choose the alternative that you believe will most benefit the organization.

Nonrational Decision Making: Managers Find It Difficult to Make Optimal Decisions

<mark>Nonrational models of decision making</mark> explain how managers make decisions; they assume that decision making is nearly always uncertain and risky, making it difficult for managers to make optimal decisions. The nonrational models are *descriptive* rather than prescriptive: They describe how managers *actually* make decisions rather than how they should. Two nonrational models are (1) *satisficing* and (2) *intuition*.

1. Bounded Rationality, Hubris, and the Satisficing Model: "Satisfactory Is Good Enough"

During the 1950s, economist Herbert Simon—who later received the Nobel Prize—began to study how managers actually make decisions. From his research he proposed that managers could not act truly logically because their rationality was bounded by so many restrictions.[23] Called <mark>bounded rationality</mark>, the concept suggests that the ability of decision makers to be rational is limited by numerous constraints, such as complexity, time, money, and other resources, and their cognitive capacity, values, skills, habits, and unconscious reflexes. *(See Figure 7.2.)*

FIGURE 7.2   **Some hindrances to perfectly rational decision making**

- **Complexity:**
  The problems that need solving are often exceedingly complex, beyond understanding.

- **Time and money constraints:**
  There is not enough time or money to gather all relevant information.

- **Different cognitive capacity, values, skills, habits, and unconscious reflexes:**
  Managers aren't all built the same way, of course, and all have personal limitations and biases that affect their judgment.

- **Imperfect information:**
  Managers have imperfect, fragmentary information about the alternatives and their consequences.

- **Information overload:**
  There is too much information for one person to process.

- **Different priorities:**
  Some data are considered more important, so certain facts are ignored.

- **Conflicting goals:**
  Other managers, including colleagues, have conflicting goals.

Researchers also have uncovered another characteristic that can influence bounded rationality. This impediment to rational decision making is <mark>hubris</mark>, which we define as an extreme and inflated sense of pride, certainty, and confidence.[28] Carlos Ghosn, the former CEO of Renault-Nissan, is a good example of a leader who exhibited hubris. Ghosn took over Japanese automaker Nissan in 1999 and corporate performance exceeded everyone's expectations. The company's turnaround made him a celebrity and resulted in his feeling an extraordinary sense of self-importance, according to *The New York Times*. Ghosn demanded more pay than other Japanese chief executives, mandated that the company support him and his family with a private plane and other lavish perks, and enjoyed uncritical media attention to his decisions. Japanese authorities took notice of the French-Lebanese-Brazilian's flamboyant lifestyle in a country that frowns upon showing off. When prosecutors dug deeper into Ghosn's finances, they concluded he illegally lined his own pockets instead of working in the company's best interests.

Ghosn was arrested in 2018 but decided to flee Japan to Lebanon a year later instead of standing trial. His justification for illegally escaping prosecution was that he's a victim of bias and jealousy (he also compared his surprise arrest to the unexpected bombing of Pearl Harbor).[29] Studies show that Ghosn isn't the only hubris-prone leader with legal woes. Research demonstrates a positive relationship link between CEO hubris and unethical behavior, particularly in financial decision making.[30]

Because of impediments such as bounded rationality and hubris, managers don't always make an exhaustive search for the best alternative. Instead, they follow what Simon calls the ==satisficing model==—that is, managers seek **alternatives until they find one that is satisfactory, not optimal.**[31] Research shows that those who are more open to new experiences, responsible, and generally agreeable are less likely to satisfice.[32] Although "satisficing" might seem to be a weakness, it may well outweigh any advantages gained from delaying making a decision until all information is in and all alternatives weighed. As Hallmark found, however, making snap decisions that satisfice can backfire.

Hallmark Example: The Hallmark Channel aired a series of six ads for Zola, a wedding planning website, in December 2019. One of the ads featured a same-sex couple kissing, resulting in a complaint from an anti-LGBTQ hate group, which petitioned Hallmark to drop the ads. Hallmark executives swiftly removed the ads citing their content as "controversial." The move caused backlash from the LGBTQ community and its advocates. "The Hallmark Channel's decision to remove LGBTQ families in such a blatant way is discriminatory and especially hypocritical coming from a network that claims to present family programming," said The Gay & Lesbian Alliance Against Defamation. Hallmark reversed its decision a day after the ads were dropped but was forced to go into damage control mode. Mike Perry, the CEO of Hallmark Cards (which owns the Hallmark Channel), called the choice "wrong" and apologized for the "hurt and disappointment" it caused. Perry also fired Bill Abbott, who was in charge of the TV channel.[33]

Hubris on the run. Carlos Ghosn arrives at a Tokyo court before fleeing the country. Do you believe Ghosn is a criminal or victim? JiJi Press/Shutterstock

2. The Intuition Model: "It Just Feels Right"

Small entrepreneurs often can't afford in-depth marketing research and so they make decisions based on hunches—their subconscious, visceral feelings. For instance, Sharan Pasricha decided in 2012 to found Ennismore, a hospitality group. Pasricha had no hospitality experience when he decided to launch his business, instead going with his gut instinct. His empire now stretches from Paris to Portland and includes hotels, restaurants, and co-working spaces, among other ventures. Pasricha credits his success to *intuition*, saying you "have to feel things in the pit of your stomach—no spreadsheet can change that."[34]

"Going with your gut," or ==intuition==, **is making a choice without the use of conscious thought or logical inference.**[35] Intuition that stems from *expertise*—a person's explicit and tacit knowledge about a person, a situation, an object, or a decision opportunity—is known as a *holistic hunch*. Intuition based on feelings—the involuntary emotional response to those same matters—is known as *automated experience*.

Who is more likely to use intuition? Research finds that those who are high in self-esteem and risk propensity are more prone to use intuition.[36] Whether or not you have these personality traits, it is important to try to develop your intuitive skills because they are as important as, and sometimes superior to, rational analysis.[37] The Example box illustrates how Virgin CEO Richard Branson and others use intuition.

EXAMPLE   Harnessing the Power of Intuition

You might be wishing that you could make all difficult decisions not after a long consideration of data and consequences, but in an "aha!" moment in which you spontaneously recognize the answer to the problem. This recognition is called an *epiphany*—that instant when something clicks in the brain, a mental light bulb goes on, and the road ahead becomes crystal clear. Unfortunately, epiphanies are rare, but the intuition that often leads to them can be carefully honed.

Sir Richard Branson, the entrepreneurial founder of the Virgin Group, employs nearly 70,000 people across a variety of business lines, including a cruise line, airline, luxury game preserve, mobile phone company, and space-tourism group.[38] Branson relies on his instincts when calculating risks, putting trust in others, and making important business decisions. He appreciates advancements in technology and artificial intelligence but notes that "as we rely more and more on analytics to make our decisions, we're losing touch of our human instinct and we're taking human reasoning out of the equation." He believes this in turn makes people more risk-averse and conservative.[39] Recent research supports Branson's position, finding that although data is important, intuition is still a necessary part of decision making.[40]

Though he is a strong proponent of intuition, Branson understands that his gut isn't always right. For example, Virgin tried selling automobiles through the Internet in 2000. People didn't respond to that idea, and the company shut down the website in 2005. "Nobody gets everything right first time . . . [it's] how we learn from our mistakes that defines us," he says.[41] In the end, the innovative CEO believes you should "trust your intuition, stay curious and always put your people first if you want to thrive in the long-term."[42]

Branson is not alone in harnessing the power of intuitive ideas. A well-known story about the origins of Amazon credits founder Jeff Bezos's intuitive recognition that if, as he'd just read, the Internet was growing at 2,300% a year, it was worth quitting his job on Wall Street and starting an online bookstore to take advantage of that opportunity.[43] Steve Jobs, the late co-founder of Apple, believed "intuition is a very powerful thing, more powerful than intellect."[44] He also said, in a speech he made at Stanford University, "You have to trust in something, your gut, destiny, life, karma, whatever. This approach has never let me down, and it has made all the difference in my life."[45] And yet another genius, physicist Albert Einstein, once said, "All great achievements of science must start from intuitive knowledge. At times I feel certain I am right while not knowing the reason."[46]

YOUR CALL

Have you ever relied on your intuition to make an important decision or solve a big problem? How did your solution come to you, and how pleased were you with the result?

As a model for making decisions, intuition has at least two benefits. It can speed up decision making, which is useful when deadlines are tight.[47] It also helps managers when resources are limited. A drawback, however, is that it can be difficult to convince others that your hunch makes sense. In addition, intuition is subject to the same biases as those that affect rational decision making, as we discuss in Section 7.6.[48] Finally, research demonstrates that intuition is less effective when people face structured problems—those that can be broken down and approached sequentially.[49] Still, we believe that intuition and rationality are complementary and that managers should develop the courage to use intuition when making decisions.[50] Some suggestions for improving your intuitive skills are presented in the following Practical Action box. ●

PRACTICAL ACTION   How to Improve Your Intuition

How can you improve your intuition as Richard Branson recommends? (See the preceding Example box.) Here are some tips.[51]

1. **Don't rush to absorb information.** Many leaders rush to bad judgments because they don't fully absorb the information they receive. They filter out what they don't expect or want to hear, typically because of overconfidence in their own abilities (we discuss the *overconfidence bias*

in Section 7.6). To improve on this, you need to be aware of your own filters, defensiveness, or aggression that may discourage alternative arguments.

2. **Experience is relevant, but not absolute.** Experience provides context and allows us to identify potential solutions and anticipate challenges. Leaders can over-

come challenges that are similar to what they've seen in the past because they can make better decisions on where to focus their energy and resources. Familiarity with situations, however, is only beneficial if the experience isn't narrowly based. For example, if you are planning to enter the Vietnam market, would you utilize your own experience in launching a product in the United States, or would you rely on the experience of someone who has expanded into Asia? (The answer is relying on someone who has specific product experience in Asia.) You can improve in this area by relying on the right experience. This means you'll need to rely on others when appropriate.

3. **Temper your emotions.** Being passionate is a wonderful leadership quality and it can help inspire others. That said, unbridled passion may appear extreme and offensive. This is why you need some level of intellectual and emotional

detachment when making decisions. Detachment includes limiting cognitive biases that can negatively influence the decisions we make: We discuss cognitive biases in Section 7.6. For example, it is because of their ability to resist cognitive biases that we often see CFOs and lawyers become CEOs during periods of crisis. This does not suggest that you should avoid your emotions when making decisions, as studies show this can lead to its own problems.[52] You should, however, temper your emotions. Having processes in place to keep you aware of biases will help you detach.[53] One such process is having a devil's advocate, which we discuss in Section 7.7.

YOUR CALL

How can you use these three tips to improve your performance at school? Do you see any drawbacks to being more intuitive? Discuss.

Would you like to increase your level of intuition? It can be done, but first you need to know where you stand with respect to using intuition. Find out by taking Self-Assessment 7.2. •

SELF-ASSESSMENT 7.2   CAREER READINESS

Assessing Your Level of Intuition

This survey is designed to assess the extent you use intuition in your current job. Please be prepared to answer these questions if your instructor has assigned Self-Assessment 7.2 in Connect.

1.   Are you intuitive at work? Did the results surprise you?

2.   What can you do to increase the amount of intuition you use at work? Describe.

3.   What things might you say during a job interview to demonstrate that you possess the career readiness competency of critical thinking/problem solving?

7.2 Making Ethical Decisions

THE BIG PICTURE

A graph known as a decision tree can help one make ethical decisions.

The ethical behavior of businesspeople, as we discussed at length in Chapter 3, has become of increasing concern in recent years, brought about by a number of events.

LO 7-2

Explain how managers can make decisions that are both legal and ethical.

The Dismal Record of Business Ethics

According to a recent study from PwC (PricewaterhouseCoopers), the top reason for CEO departures among America's largest companies isn't poor financial performance, it's unethical behavior (*see Figure 7.3*). Figure 7.3 reveals that the number of CEOs fired

FIGURE 7.3

Reasons for CEO departures

Source: Data based on J. Green, "CEOs Fired for Ethical Lapses Hit New High as Complaints Soared," Bloomberg, May 15, 2019, https://www.bloomberg.com/news/articles/2019-05-15/ceos-fired-for-ethical-lapses-hit-new-high-as-complaints-soared.

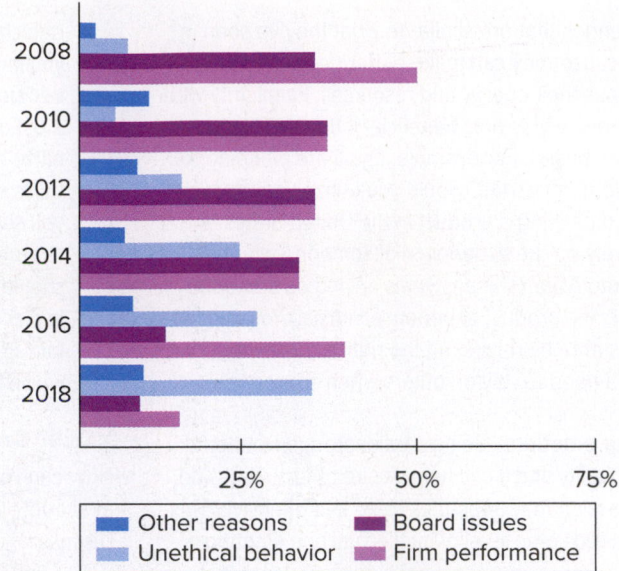

for ethical lapses quadrupled between 2008 and 2018. For example, the leaders of CBS, Barnes & Noble, Lululemon, and Intel were either fired or forced to resign in 2018 due to ethical lapses.[54]

The recent data on CEO departures is disturbing. Let's consider why this is happening before discussing a road map to ethical decision making.

What Is Causing the Growth in Ethical Lapses? *Harvard Business Review* suggests five reasons for the increase in CEO firings due to ethical lapses: (1) the public is "less forgiving" of poor behavior by executives, (2) regulations are more stringent, (3) companies are expanding operations into developing countries where ethical risks may be higher and laws less protective, (4) digital communications increase exposure to risk from both hackers and whistle-blowers, and (5) "the 24/7 news cycle and the proliferation of media in the 21st century publicizes and amplifies negative information in real time."[55]

Recent research sheds additional light on why unethical behavior occurs. One study demonstrated that unethical behavior is more apt to be tolerated when it comes from a high rather than a low performer.[56] Sadly, it seems that some organizations prefer performance over ethics. Other studies show that individual differences play a role in unethical behavior.[57] For example, compassionate people were found to engage in prosocial lying, such as to prevent others from feeling hurt or embarrassed or to help others financially. Prosocial lying helps others rather than yourself.[58] Moreover, those with excessive self-esteem were found to be more prone than others to engage in unethical decision making.[59]

Ethical decision making can be related to a host of issues, including how a company prices its products or how its employees behave in the workplace. Let's take a look at some examples.

Pricing Example: Pharmaceutical companies in particular have been singled out for the impact of their decisions. Take for example Alembic, the maker of blood pressure drugs. When Alembic's competitors were forced to recall their blood pressure–lowering medication due to contamination, the company saw an opportunity to increase its price by more than 320%. And Alembic wasn't alone. Pharmaceutical companies raised the prices of thousands of drugs in 2019, surpassing 2018 price increases by 17%. This includes around 40 drugs that saw triple-digit price increases, such as Alembic's blood pressure medication. "I don't believe any company that makes any drug, whether it is an innovative biotech cancer drug or a generic drug that's been around for 50 years, should take advantage of the marketplace to a degree that causes significant financial pain for patients," says Peter Pitts, president of the Center for Medicine in the Public Interest.[60]

Behavioral Examples: The #MeToo movement brought down prominent men in a wide range of industries over allegations of sexual misconduct, beginning with Harvey Weinstein, founder of a successful Hollywood film studio that bore his name, and going on to envelop dozens of politicians, business executives, sports figures, and popular and classical artists. Though Weinstein was later convicted of rape, other powerful CEOs were ousted for consensual relationships. This was the case for McDonald's CEO Steve Easterbrook. He was fired in 2019 for engaging in a relationship with a subordinate. Although the relationship was consensual, it violated McDonald's standards of conduct, which "prohibit employees with 'a direct or indirect reporting relationship' from 'dating or having a sexual relationship'" with superiors.[61] Publicly lying is another example of unethical behavior. A legislative aide to one of Florida's state representatives was quickly fired for falsely claiming that students who protested lax gun laws after 17 of their peers and teachers were killed in a high school shooting were paid actors.[62]

Positive Example: On the other side of the ledger, about 170 of the world's billionaires have pledged—

Some unethical behaviors like sexual harassment have morphed into their own logo. Ing. Andrej Kaprinay/Shutterstock

along with Microsoft co-founder Bill Gates, his wife Melinda, and mega-investor Warren Buffet—to give away more than half their money. The funds will go to charitable causes like "poverty alleviation, refugee aid, disaster relief, global health, education, women and girls' empowerment, medical research, arts and culture, criminal justice reform and environmental sustainability."[63] The Giving Pledge has been signed by billionaires from 23 countries in every age cohort from 30 to 90.[64]

How Are Companies Responding to Ethical Lapses?   Ethical concerns have forced the subject of right-minded decision making to the top of the agenda in many organizations. Indeed, many companies now have an ==ethics officer, someone trained about matters of ethics in the workplace, particularly about resolving ethical dilemmas.== More and more companies also are designing values statements to guide employees as to what constitutes day-to-day ethical behavior. These value statements influence areas such as hiring, evaluation, and compensation.[65] Studies confirm that having leaders coach and be role models for employees on these values will support ethical decision making across the company.[66] As a result of this raised consciousness on ethical decision making, managers must make sure their decisions are not just in compliance with laws and regulations but also ethical.[67]

Road Map to Ethical Decision Making: A Decision Tree

Undoubtedly, the greatest pressure on top executives is to maximize shareholder value, to deliver the greatest return on investment to the owners of their company. But is a decision that is beneficial to shareholders yet harmful to employees—such as forcing them to contribute more to their health benefits, as IBM has done—unethical? Harvard Business School professor Constance Bagley suggests that what is needed is a decision tree to help with ethical decisions.[68] A ==decision tree is a graph of decisions and their possible consequences; it is used to create a plan to reach a goal.== Decision trees are used to aid in making decisions, especially when there is uncertainty.[69] Bagley's ethical decision tree is shown in Figure 7.4.

FIGURE 7.4

The ethical decision tree: What's the right thing to do?

Source: Constance E. Bagley, "The Ethical Leader's Decision Tree," Harvard Business School Publishing Corporation, February 2003, https://hbr
.org/2003/02/the-ethical-leaders-decision-tree.

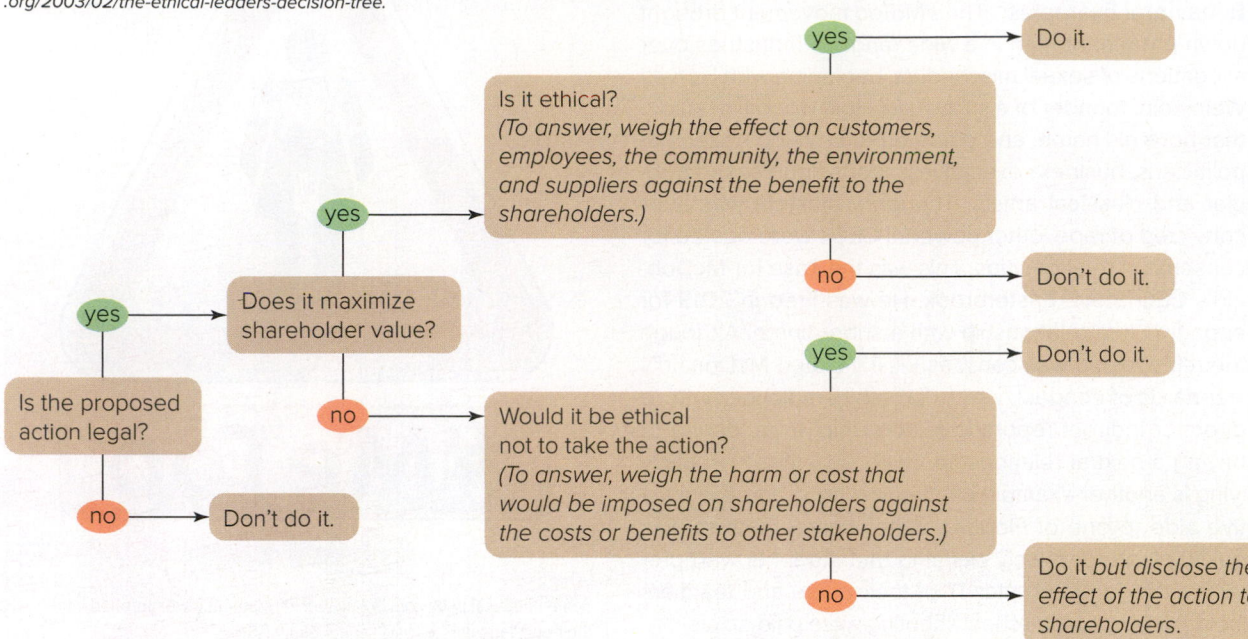

When confronted with any proposed action for which a decision is required, a manager works through the decision tree by asking the following questions.

1. **Is the proposed action legal?**   This may seem an obvious question. But, Bagley observes, "corporate shenanigans suggest that some managers need to be reminded: If the action isn't legal, don't do it."

2. **If "yes," does the proposed action maximize shareholder value?**   If the action is legal, one must next ask whether it will profit the shareholders. If the answer is "yes," should you do it? Not necessarily.

3. **If "yes," is the proposed action ethical?**   As Bagley points out, though directors and top managers may believe they are bound by corporate law to always maximize shareholder value, the courts and many state legislatures have held they are not. Rather, their main obligation is to manage "for the best interests of the corporation," which includes the interests of the larger community.

   Thus, says Bagley, building a profitable-but-polluting plant in a country overseas may benefit the shareholders but be bad for that country—and for the corporation's relations with that nation. Ethically, then, managers should add pollution-control equipment.

4. **If "no," would it be ethical *not* to take the proposed action?**   If the action would not directly benefit shareholders, might it still be ethical to go ahead with it?

   Not building the overseas plant might be harmful to other stakeholders, such as employees or customers. Thus, the ethical conclusion might be to build the plant with pollution-control equipment, but to disclose the effects of the decision to shareholders.

As a basic guideline to making good ethical decisions on behalf of a corporation, Bagley suggests that directors, managers, and employees need to follow their own individual ideas about right and wrong.[70] There is a lesson, she suggests, in the response of the pension fund manager who, when asked whether she would invest in a company doing business in a country that permits slavery, responded, "Do you mean me, personally, or as a fund manager?" When people feel entitled or compelled to compromise their own personal ethics to advance the interests of a business, "it is an invitation to mischief."[71]

To learn more about your own ethics, morality, and/or values (while contributing to scientific research), go to *www.yourmorals.org.*[72] ●

7.3 Evidence-Based Decision Making and Data Analytics

THE BIG PICTURE

This section describes seven principles for implementing evidence-based management. We also describe why it is hard to bring this approach to bear on one's decision making. Finally, we describe data analytics and big data and their use at all levels of an organization.

The World Health Organization (WHO) declared the COVID-19 outbreak a public health emergency of global concern. Thousands of individuals across all major continents contracted the disease, many of whom lost their lives. Multinational corporations, governments, and small businesses all made decisions they hoped would reduce the risk of spreading the virus, but not all of those tough calls were based on the latest health information. In other words, they weren't *evidence-based decisions.*[73]

As you learned in Chapter 1, there are 27 competencies that contribute to your career readiness. Four of these competencies relate to evidence-based decision making: *information technology application* (effectively using technology and learning new applications), *computational thinking* (using numbers to distill abstract concepts and conducting data-based reasoning), *critical thinking and problem solving* (analyzing situations, making decisions, and solving problems), and *decision making* (collecting, processing, and analyzing information in order to identify and choose from alternative solutions that lead to optimal outcomes). A common misconception is that using evidence in the decision-making process only requires hard skills, such as computational thinking. Yes, hard skills are important in today's data-driven environment,[74] but research shows that effective top managers also need strong soft skills. This is because senior-level managers need to utilize evidence to strategize, make decisions, communicate with stakeholders, and influence middle and lower-level managers to execute evidence-based decisions.[75]

In this section you'll learn about the basics of evidence-based decision making and how it can be implemented within organizations. We'll then discuss big data and data analytics, the backbone of today's evidence-based decisions. In Section 7.4, we take another step into the realm of technology-based decisions and discuss artificial intelligence.

LO 7-3

Describe how evidence-based management and data analytics contribute to decision making.

Evidence-Based Decision Making

"Too many companies and too many leaders are more interested in just copying others, doing what they've always done, and making decisions based on beliefs in what ought to work rather than what actually works," say Stanford professors Jeffrey Pfeffer and Robert Sutton. "They fail to face the hard facts and use the best evidence to help navigate the competitive environment."[76] In support of this conclusion, research revealed that half of organizational decisions failed to achieve their goals because leaders rushed to judgment, ignored alternatives, and imposed their preferred solutions, among a host of other reasons.[77] Companies that use *evidence-based management*—the translation of principles based on best evidence into organizational practice, bringing rationality to the decision-making process, as we defined it in Chapter 2—routinely trump the competition, Pfeffer and Sutton suggest.[78]

Seven Implementation Principles   Pfeffer and Sutton identify seven implementation principles to help companies that are committed to doing what it takes to profit from evidence-based management:[79]

1. **Treat your organization as an unfinished prototype.** Leaders need to think and act as if their organization were an unfinished prototype that won't be ruined by dangerous new ideas or impossible to change because of employee or management resistance.

   Danish Oil and Natural Gas Example: Danish Oil and Natural Gas, Denmark's largest energy company, faced doom when global overproduction sent gas prices plunging 90% in 2012. CEO Henrik Poulsen recognized the need to make a fundamental change. "We looked at the 12 different lines of business we were in and went through them asset by asset, to see where we saw competitive strength," says Poulsen. Offshore wind power, a small line of the company's business, came up as a potential route, but wind farm technology was still too expensive. Poulsen decided to rename the company Ørsted (after the legendary Danish scientist Hans Christian Ørsted, who discovered the principles of electromagnetism) and infused a cost-cutting goal into the workplace culture. Ørsted was able cut the cost of offshore wind power generation by 60%, producing billions in profits. Today, it's the world's largest offshore wind company with 30% market share.[80]

2. **No brag, just facts.** Leaders shouldn't make over-the-top assertions about forthcoming products, they should simply use available resources to make effective decisions.

   Casino Example: Lon O'Donnell is MGM Resorts' first-ever director of corporate slot analytics. O'Donnell's team uses data to find out what machines aren't being played and need to be replaced or relocated, what machines are most popular, and which areas of the casino pull in the most profits. Caesars Entertainment, one of MGM's biggest competitors, uses data to their advantage as well. The company studies player habits, as well as what hotel, spa, or restaurant amenities people enjoy the most.[81]

3. **See yourself and your organization as outsiders do.** Most managers are afflicted with "rampant optimism," with inflated views of their own talents and prospects for success, which causes them to downplay risks and continue on a path despite evidence that things are not working. "Having a blunt friend, mentor, or counselor," Pfeffer and Sutton suggest, "can help you see and act on better evidence."

4. **Evidence-based management is not just for senior executives.** The best organizations are those in which everyone, not just the top managers, are guided by the responsibility to gather and act on quantitative and qualitative data and share results with others.

5. **Like everything else, you still need to sell it.** "Unfortunately, new and exciting ideas grab attention even when they are vastly inferior to old ideas," the Stanford authors say. "Vivid, juicy stories and case studies sell

Data jackpot. A woman playing a slot machine in Las Vegas, Nevada. With close to 200,000 slot machines in Las Vegas, it's important for casinos to know which ones bring in the most revenue. Steve Allen/Brand X Pictures/Getty Images

better than detailed, rigorous, and admittedly dull data—no matter how wrong the stories or how right the data." To sell an evidence-based approach, you may have to identify a preferred practice based on solid if unexciting evidence, then use vivid stories to grab management's attention.

6. **If all else fails, slow the spread of bad practice.** Because many managers and employees face pressures to do things that are known to be ineffective, it may be necessary for you to practice "evidence-based misbehavior"—that is, ignore orders you know to be wrong or delay their implementation.

7. **The best diagnostic question: What happens when people fail?** "Failure hurts, it is embarrassing, and we would rather live without it," the authors write. "Yet there is no learning without failure. . . . If you look at how the most effective systems in the world are managed, a hallmark is that when something goes wrong, people face the hard facts, learn what happened and why, and keep using those facts to make the system better."[82] Take for example the U.S. civil aviation system, which rigorously examines airplane accidents, near misses, and equipment problems. Or mall owners who look for new uses for space, like co-working offices, as malls fall from favor and anchor stores like Sears and Macy's depart. In both these examples, evidence-based management makes the point that failure is a great teacher.[83] This means, however, that the organization must "forgive and remember" people who make mistakes, not be trapped by preconceived notions, and confront the best evidence and hard facts.

What Makes It Hard to Be Evidence Based   Despite your best intentions, it's hard to bring the best evidence to bear on your decisions. Among the reasons:[84] (1) There's too much evidence. (2) There's not enough *good* evidence. (3) The evidence doesn't quite apply. (4) People are trying to mislead you. (5) *You* are trying to mislead yourself. (6) The side effects outweigh the cure. (Example: Despite the belief that social promotion in school is a bad idea—that is, that schools shouldn't advance children to the next grade when they haven't mastered the material—the side effect is skyrocketing costs because it crowds schools with older, angrier students who demand more resources.) (7) Stories are more persuasive, anyway.

In Praise of Data Analytics

Perhaps the purest application of evidence-based management is the use of **data analytics**, which is the process of analyzing raw data sets in order to make conclusions about the information they contain.[85] Data analytics is increasingly done with specialized systems and software. One example is portfolio analysis, in which an investment adviser evaluates the risks of stocks using various data sources. Another example is the time-series forecast, which predicts future data based on patterns of historical data.

Some leaders and firms have become exceptional practitioners of data analytics. Netflix, for example, collects data from its 167 million subscribers in order to discover customer behavior and buying power. It then uses that information to recommend movies and TV shows based on subscriber preferences. The company says it earns over $1 billion in customer retention because the recommendation system accounts for over 80% of the content streamed on its platform. Netflix also uses analytics to conduct custom marketing and greenlight new original content.[86]

Data analytics also is expected to help the health care industry. Health care professionals can share electronic health records across all sectors of health care, which helps reduce medical errors and improve patient care. There also are cost advantages associated with the use of data analytics. For example, using data tools to drive health care efficiency and quality can cut overall health care costs by 12 to 17%, according to research from McKinsey & Company.[87]

Data has made its way into the sports world as well. The Example box illustrates how professional sports teams are taking advantage of data analytics.

EXAMPLE   Data Is the Champion of Sports

Baseball fans have been analyzing in-game stats for decades, in fact, this activity has its own name: sabermetrics, a term that acknowledges the work of the Society for American Baseball Research (SABR). Today's data analysis in sports is taking teams beyond these old-school stats and is making an impact in a variety of sports. As a result, the market for sports analytics is expected to reach top $5 billion by 2024.[88]

Better Indicators of Player Success The obsession with analytics in professional sports is the logical result of the *Moneyball* phenomenon. The Brad Pitt film of that name was adapted from a book by Michael Lewis called *Moneyball: The Art of Winning an Unfair Game*. The book described how the Oakland Athletics, then one of the poorest teams in Major League Baseball (with a payroll about a third the size of the New York Yankees), managed to go to the playoffs five times in seven years against better-financed contenders. The Athletics accomplished this by avoiding the use of traditional baseball statistics and finding better indicators of player success in data such as on-base percentage, slugging percentage, and the like. This creative use of analytics enabled the managers of the California club to concentrate their limited payroll resources on draft picks who were primarily talented college players rather than veteran professionals.[89] The team continues to rely on analytics to improve its odds, and the Houston Astros have taken the strategy to another level, hiring a NASA engineer to help them with data analysis.[90]

Analytics in Pro Sports Since then, analytic measures have been used to find better ways to value players and strategies in all major sports. In basketball, the application of data analytics reached its zenith with the Golden State Warriors, a frequent National Basketball Association champion. A group of data-loving Silicon Valley investors bought the floundering team a few years ago for $450 million (it's now worth $3.5 billion) and proceeded to fix it by asking the question, "What would happen if you built a basketball team by ignoring every orthodoxy of building a basketball team?" One unusual idea: Focus less on recruiting big men who could stuff the basket and more on players who could make three-point shots. This is because data shows that focusing on three-pointers increases a team's chances of winning.[91]

Delving into the statistics, the executives began to rebuild the team around star three-point shooters Stephen Curry and Klay Thompson and other players, which helped the Warriors make a higher percentage of three-pointers than any other team in the

Analytics slam dunk. Stephen Curry (#30) of the Golden State Warriors makes a three-point shot over OG Anunoby (#3) of the Toronto Raptors. Data shows that focusing on these shots are more advantageous for teams. Does this mean the end of the slam dunk? Ezra Shaw/Getty Images

league. "We're lightyears ahead of probably every other team in structure, in planning, in how we're going to go about things," says Golden State majority owner Joe Lacob. "We're going to be a handful for the rest of the NBA to deal with for a long time."[92] The Warriors made it to the NBA finals five years in a row (2015–2019), winning the championship in 2015, 2017, and 2018.[93]

Data drives the NFL as well. The New York Giants General Manager Dave Gettleman says he's hired "computer folks" to modernize the team's scouting department. Mike McCarthy, the former Green Bay Packers coach, spent last season at home planning for an entire football technology department. He's now going to use that department at his new team, the Dallas Cowboys. Finally, the Atlanta Falcons, not to be outdone by rivals, monitor their players' sleep habits and patterns, using an outside firm to collect data about how much sleep they get, and find ways for them to get more restorative rest. The Cleveland Browns head coach, Kevin Stefanski, summed up sports teams' new focus on analytics, saying, "Information is power."[94]

YOUR CALL

Executives and human resource professionals often make decisions as the old sports traditionalists did, relying on resume, degree, and years of experience when evaluating job applicants. What other more quantifiable measures might be used instead when hiring new college graduates?

Big Data: What It Is, How It's Used

"War is 90% information," according to French military leader Napoleon Bonaparte.[95] Experts say the store of the world's information will increase 61% each year, reaching 175 zettabytes in size by 2025.[96] (Just 1 zettabyte is equal to the contents of over 200 billion DVDs.)[97] This has led to a phenomenon known as **big data**, stores of data so vast that conventional database management systems cannot handle them, so very sophisticated analysis software and supercomputers are required.[98] Big data includes not only information in corporate databases, but also web-browsing data trails, social network communications, sensor data, and surveillance data.[99]

"Over the past five years companies have invested billions to get the most-talented data scientists to set up shop, amass zettabytes of material, and run it through their deduction machines to find signals in the unfathomable volume of noise," says data expert Scott Berinato. The concept of big data, he says, has changed our relationship with industries as different as translation services, retail, medicine, and sports.[100] In a 2018 survey of nearly 60 large firms in the financial, pharmaceutical, and other industries, 97% of respondents said they are currently investing in big data and artificial intelligence (AI) projects, and 73% said they have already seen measurable results from these efforts.[101] Big data analytics is the process of examining large amounts of data of a variety of types to uncover hidden patterns, unknown correlations, and other useful information. Research shows that big data analytics supports innovation, efficiencies, and firm performance in a wide variety of industries.[102] Let's consider five applications of big data.

Meeting Customer Needs

Companies must understand what customers need so they can meet market demands. Data can assist with this by providing a story about consumer behavior. Big data allows companies to spot trends, challenges, and opportunities. Take for instance Coca-Cola's "freestyle" fountain drink machines, located in many fast-food restaurants, cinemas, and amusement parks. There are more than 50,000 of these dispensers pouring 14 million drinks per day. The touch-screen freestyle machines allow customers to add flavors, such as lime or cherry, to their favorite drinks before dispensing (there are more than 100 combinations available).[103] The machines may provide customers with their favorite beverages, but they also provide Coca-Cola with valuable data. For example, the company analyzed its customers' preferences and found that more and more were adding cherry flavoring to their beverages. Based on this analysis, the beverage maker decided to introduce new Sprite Cherry and Sprite Cherry Zero products in retail stores.[104]

Coca-Cola's decision makers probably didn't sift through all their fountain drink machine numbers to discover that cherry was in demand. Instead, they heard from analysts who could interpret the data and present the lessons learned from reviewing the data. Those presenting the story don't need to be award-winning novelists; they do, however, need to close the communication gap between algorithms and executives by presenting the data in an understandable way so decisions can be made.[105] If properly presented, big data can help both online and brick-and-mortar businesses personalize shopping experiences, improve efficiencies, and reduce the costs of their supply chains, among other benefits.[106] Macy's is a good example of this. The retailer relies on data analytics to ensure merchandise efficiently gets from its warehouses to stores and meets demand during peak periods, such as back to school or the holiday season.[107]

Improving Human Resource Management Practices

Big data is impacting the HR functions of employee selection and retention. Historically, companies typically identified stars in their ranks based on evaluations from managers, which could often be subjective or prone to bias. Now, more and more organizations are using organizational network analysis to identify and promote talent. This analysis involves the use of data to measure an employee's influence across an organization. Some companies do this by assessing an employee's e-mail traffic, including whom they contact and how quickly they get a response. A principal at global consulting firm Deloitte calls this analysis an "X-ray view into the organization and the way work is truly getting done." Human resource software maker Workday has developed another data-driven tool to help identify talent. This feedback platform allows employees to thank their peers for assistance on a project or for helping them navigate a problem. The tool will help companies use the data to identify "knowledge brokers," those in the organization others turn to for guidance or insight.[108]

Companies also use big data in their efforts to retain employees. For example, Credit Suisse implemented a data collection and analysis system to discover why some high performers left the organization. The system stored the reasons employees gave during exit interviews and uncovered patterns so HR managers could prevent future departures. "We needed to look at why we don't have the compelling employee value proposition to keep that person here and look at who else is at risk," says William Wolf, the company's managing director and global head of talent.[109] The company has saved an estimated $70 million a year in HR costs as a result of this system.[110]

Enhancing Production Efficiency

Big data assists manufacturing efficiency. For example, Unilever, one of the world's biggest consumer goods companies, is using data from its sensor-equipped machines to create virtual models. These models can track physical conditions in a manufacturing facility and allow for testing of operational changes before actually implementing them. "We've got it in [plants that make] mayonnaise, soap, shampoos and conditioners, laundry detergents," says Dave Penrith, the company's chief engineer. Big data analytics also allow Unilever to make real-time changes, which optimize output, allow it to use materials more precisely, and limit waste from products that don't meet the company's standards.[111]

Advancing Health and Medicine

Big data is revolutionizing the health care industry. Predictive medicine, which is the practice of using genomic data to more accurately predict illnesses, is gaining traction because the cost of human-genome sequencing is falling. The reduced sequencing cost, from $100 million in 2009 to a couple thousand dollars in 2019, is growing the volume of genomics data. This data allows scientists to predict how illnesses like cancer will progress. For example, genetic data analytics organization NextBio is studying data related to medulloblastoma, the most common type of malignant brain tumor in children. The data allows NextBio to develop new targeted therapy approaches in order to increase patient survival rates.[112] Research supports the work of NextBio and other organizations, finding that efficient management, analysis, and interpretation of big data can revolutionize medical therapies and personalized medicine.[113]

Predicting repeat offenders. A handcuffed female inmate being escorted in a county jail. Would you be comfortable with an inmate being released based on big data predictions? David R. Frazier Photolibrary, Inc.

Aiding Public Policy

The majority of America's prison population has some sort of mental illness, but diagnosing and caring for prisoners effectively has been a challenge. That's where data-driven tools come in. Dallas-based technology and clinical services company HarrisLogic is pooling data from jails, police departments, emergency services, social services, and courts to identify mentally ill prisoners within 15 minutes of booking. This data is then shared with the prisoner's public defender and case provider, with the intention of getting the prisoner help. The software has saved Dallas County $30 million to date and is getting prisoners the help they need so they can stay out of trouble in the future. Stemming from this initiative, HarrisLogic is piloting a program that predicts the likelihood that a prisoner will commit a future offense. The company claims it can predict who will return to prison within six months with 72% accuracy, and who won't return with 99% certainty.[114]

Using Big Data Up and Down the Hierarchy   The five mentioned examples illustrate that big data is effectively being applied in various industries. That said, studies show that employees at all levels of the organization need to be trained to use big data tools for success to be sustained.[115] Table 7.2 describes applications of big data across organizational levels and highlights the career readiness competencies needed for effective implementation.

TABLE 7.2

The Use of Big Data at Different Levels of an Organization[116]

Managerial Level	Use of Big Data	Career Readiness Competencies
Lower	• Analyzing data • Project management • Safeguarding data • Presenting data to middle management	• Computational thinking • Information technology application • Critical thinking/problem solving • Teamwork/collaboration • Oral/written communication
Middle	• Deciding what data is necessary • Project management • Presenting data to executives	• Computational thinking • Decision making • Critical thinking/problem solving • Understanding the business • Oral/written communication
Top	• Making data-driven decisions and strategizing • Project management • Influencing others to support data-driven decisions	• Decision making • Critical thinking/problem solving • Oral/written communication • Leadership

Table 7.2 shows that soft skills are increasingly important as you move up the organizational hierarchy. Lower-level managers focus more on analyzing and safeguarding data. This includes the "hard" career readiness competencies of computational thinking and information technology application. You'll notice that more and more "soft" career readiness competencies present themselves as you progress up the management ladder. In fact, by the time you're a top manager, your focus will be on making decisions and influencing others. This will require mastering the career readiness competencies of decision making, critical thinking/problem solving, oral/written communication, and leadership — all soft skills.[117]

Managers at all levels of an organization can use big data to improve the company's bottom line, but data can do more than just boost profits. In Learning Module 1 we discussed how organizations can use their resources to support shared value and sustainable development. Do you think big data can be used to better society? The Example box profiles an organization doing just that. ●

EXAMPLE   Using Big Data for Sustainable Finance

Banco Bilbao Vizcaya Argentaria, S.A. (BBVA) is one of the largest financial institutions in the world with 7,744 branches across 30 countries. The Spanish bank has approximately 127,000 employees and over $750 billion in total assets.[118]

One of BBVA's biggest assets is the data it has on its 78 million customers. The bank established a Data & Analytics unit in 2014 and recognized data as a core competency by 2017. The unit's goal is to use data science to generate value for the bank

and society. "The [unit] was physically and structurally separated from the bank, which helped [it] . . . nurture and retain unique kinds of talent, initiate innovative data monetization projects and partnerships, and balance short-term and long-term BBVA demands," according to a report co-authored by the bank's former CEO and founder, Elena Alfaro.[119]

The bank's data-focused unit decided on using its resources for the good of society. It thus joined forces with the United

Nations (UN) in 2017 as part of the UN's Global Pulse initiative. This initiative was established "based on a recognition that digital data offer opportunities to gain a better understanding of changes in human well-being, and to get real-time feedback on how well policy responses are working."[120] Its mission is to use big data to achieve the UN's Sustainable Development Goals (SDGs) we discussed in Learning Module 1.

The collaboration between BBVA and the UN focused on SDGs in health, climate action, and infrastructure. (See Figure LM 1.2.) Specifically, BBVA analyzed customer credit card payments and ATM withdrawals before, during, and after natural disasters in order to develop resident activity models. These models can be used by disaster planners for future emergencies. Local governments, for instance, can use the information to plan for resources to be put in place to ease suffering and safeguard lives the next time a disaster strikes.[121]

One of the first disasters analyzed was Hurricane Odile, which struck Baja California, Mexico, in 2014. The hurricane was one of the worst to ever hit that region of the country. As part of the analysis, the UN Global Pulse first developed questions that needed to be answered with data. BBVA then analyzed the transactions of more than 100,000 anonymous Mexican customers to come up with metrics. One analysis related to what Baja California residents spent on the day before Odile made landfall. These results were separated by income levels so the UN could determine what the poorest residents needed. The spending was then compared to average spending habits in the region during normal times. "This type of real-time quantitative data on how people prepare for disaster could be used to inform proactive, targeted distribution of

Banking on data. Hurricane Odile caused significant damage to Los Cabos, Mexico in September 2014. The damage was devastating, but the situation also provided researchers with a treasure trove of data to help with future disasters. Victor R. Caivano/ AP Images

supplies or cash transfers to the most vulnerable, at risk populations," says Miguel Luengo-Oroz, chief data scientist at UN Global Pulse.[122]

BBVA's data-driven commitment to the SDGs has earned it praise around the world. The World Resources Institute, a global research company specializing in environmental studies and global development, recognized BBVA as one of the top five European banks for sustainable finance in 2019.[123]

YOUR CALL

In what other ways can organizations use big data for sustainable purposes? Do you see challenges associated with this practice?

7.4 Artificial Intelligence Is a Powerful Decision-Making Resource

THE BIG PICTURE

This section describes the three types of artificial intelligence (AI) and the pros and cons of their applications.

LO 7-4

Describe how artificial intelligence is used in decision making.

This section expands our discussion of data analytics by focusing on ground-breaking technology that allows machines to analyze data and make autonomous decisions with limited or no human contribution. These machines are called **autonomous devices** because they collect data from situations to make calculations, define probabilities, and make reason-based decisions according to programmed goals. Whether it be self-driving cars, machine learning in health care, space rovers, or advanced weapons, autonomous devices are making an impact in a variety of settings.[124]

Autonomous devices rely on ==artificial intelligence (AI),== **which is the ability of a computer system to perform tasks that normally require human intelligence.**[125] We share the view of computer scientist Yann LeCun, who says, "Our intelligence is what makes us human, and AI is an extension of that quality."[126] In this context, our intelligence refers to many of the career readiness competencies described in Chapter 1, including information technology application, computational thinking, critical thinking/problem solving, teamwork/collaboration, decision making, and personal adaptability (see Table 1.2).

This section reviews different types of AI as well as its benefits and challenges.

Types of AI

You may think of AI as being a 21st-century–based technology that is revolutionizing the way we do things, but the thinking behind AI goes back thousands of years. Around 350 BC, Aristotle proposed a formal, mechanical thought process known as *syllogism*, which uses deductive reasoning to form conclusions. For example, if all cats are animals, and all animals have four legs, then all cats have four legs. This example is an *algorithm*, which is a process or set of rules used by today's computers. More recently, British scientist Alan Turing invented an algorithm in 1950, before the advent of computers, to play chess with his friends—he lost that game.

The 1956 Dartmouth College Summer Research Project on artificial intelligence is considered to be the founding event of AI as a field of research. Many notable creations since then have paved the way for where we are today.[127] AI currently supports three important business needs: automating business processes, analyzing data, and engaging customers and employees.[128] Let's discuss each of these in more detail with a focus on The Home Depot, America's largest home improvement retailer.[129]

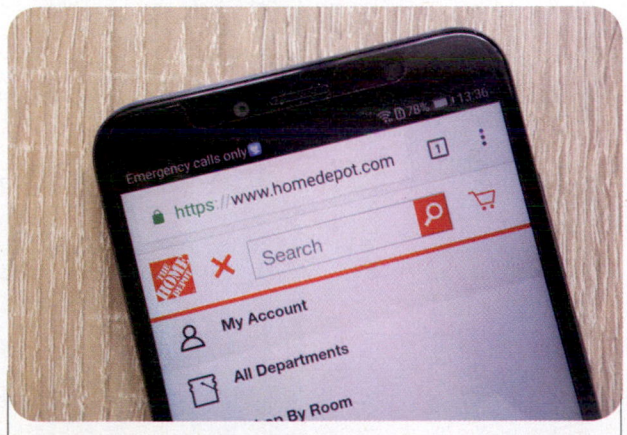

Just the nuts and bolts. The Home Depot has a simplified website for mobile devices. Piotr Swat/Shutterstock

- **Automated business processes.** The most common type of AI is the automation of digital and physical tasks. This is primarily achieved through ==robotic process automation (RPA),== **which is when robots act like a human inputing and extracting information.** These are not physical robots like you see in the movies; rather, they are code on a server that gives software commands. RPA is particularly useful for automating administrative and financial activities, such as transferring data from emails and call centers, updating company and customer records, and reconciling billing systems. The Home Depot app has voice technology, allowing customers to search through more than one million items online and in the company's more than 2,200 stores by just talking into their phone. The app is similar to Apple's Siri and can understand conversational questions and commands.

- **Data analysis.** AI can be used to detect patterns in vast volumes of data and interpret their meaning. ==Predictive analytics== **is a category of data analysis that makes "predictions about future outcomes based on historical data and analytics techniques."** This tool looks at past and current data to forecast trends and behaviors in real time, for tomorrow, or years into the future.[130] Organizations can use predictive analytics to see what a particular customer is likely to buy, identify fraud in real time, and even make medical diagnoses.[131] ==Machine learning== **is considered an extension of predictive analytics. It occurs when systems or algorithms automatically improve themselves based on data patterns, experiences, and observations.**[132] The Home Depot tracks data from all its in-store registers and online transactions to identify behavior anomalies based on past data. These anomalies may be from fraud, erroneous pricing, employee behavior, or something else.

- **Engaging customers and employees.** Companies can use AI to more closely engage employees and customers. This includes the use of chatbots and intelligent agents (programs designed to simulate conversation with human users and make decisions based on their environment) to provide 24/7 customer service, for tasks such as password reset requests, technical support questions, and product and service issues. Customer and employee engagement is the newest and least common type of AI, and it's still a work in progress. For example, Facebook found that its messenger chatbots couldn't answer 70% of user requests without employee intervention. The Home Depot has a 3D augmented reality tool that answers the question, "but how will this look in my home?" Customers can use their phones to take a picture of a room in their house and then virtually place a product, such as a refrigerator or chandelier, into the space using actual dimensions.

As you can see, The Home Depot is using all kinds of AI methods to develop a competitive advantage and earn accolades. The company's app earned the No. 1 spot on *Forrester's* 2019 mobile app rankings thanks to its functionality and strong user experience.[133] Table 7.3 highlights how other organizations are using AI to their advantage.

TABLE 7.3

Businesses Using AI to Enhance Performance[134]

TYPE OF AI	COMPANY EXAMPLES	TASKS
Automated business processes	Ford	Collaborative robots work alongside employees to sand the entire body surface of a Ford Fiesta in just 35 seconds.
	Liberty Mutual	Algorithms sift through large pools of applicants by scanning resumes.
Data analysis	Wells Fargo	AI screens customer transactions to detect suspicious purchases and fraud by detecting out-of-pattern behavior.
	IBM	The company's Watson technology can perform genomic big data analysis to determine cancer treatment options for people with tumors who are showing genetic abnormalities.
Customer and employee engagement	Morgan Stanley	Robo-advisors analyze client portfolios and provide customized investment strategies based on real-time market information.
	Amtrak	The company's chatbot, "Julie," has answered over 5 million customer questions and makes automated train bookings.

AI's Benefits

AI will transform the world as we know it. Humans could be relieved of some of the drudgery of work—and even some of the time commitment today's jobs often require. This is because more tasks could be safely assigned to AI applications or machine learning systems. Trying to skip the line to get into a sporting event or concert? AI-based facial recognition will allow you to redeem your ticket with a simple smile.[135] Finally, AI-assisted traffic lights that adjust to congested roads, bad weather, and accidents could make commuting in your self-driving car a breeze.

Organizations continue to use AI to develop competitive advantage. A survey of 1,100 U.S. companies from 10 industries revealed that firms predominately use AI to enhance current offerings, optimize internal processes, and make more effective decisions.[136] Figure 7.5 shows the full results of the survey.

Enhanced decision making is a thematic benefit of AI. Companies have to make strategic decisions on how to enhance current products, what new products to offer or markets to pursue, or how to optimize operations. Studies confirm that AI is significantly impacting these decisions' precision, speed, and credibility.[137] AI also helps organizations make better day-to-day decisions in order to save money. For example, Zest Automated Machine Learning (ZAML) is an AI-powered underwriting platform that helps lenders assess borrowers with little or no credit information or history using thousands of other data points. ZestFinance, the makers of ZAML, report that lenders using AI-based underwriting platforms cut financial losses by 23% annually.[138]

Facing AI. A facial recognition system identifies an official during a press conference in Japan. These systems will support the Tokyo 2020 Olympics to streamline admission into venues and ensure safety. Aflo/Shutterstock

AI's Drawbacks

AI has a unique set of challenges that must be overcome. The same leaders who were surveyed on the benefits of AI also were asked about its complications. Their top challenges included implementation, data issues, and cost. Let's explore these challenges further.

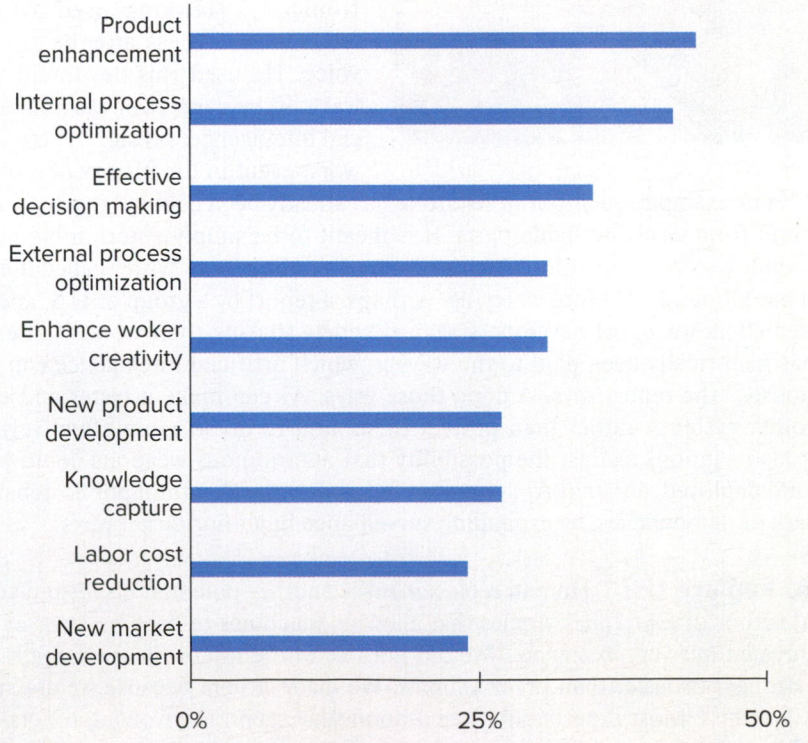

FIGURE 7.5

Benefits of AI

Source: Data based on J. Loucks, T. Davenport, and D. Schatsky, "State of AI in the Enterprise, 2nd Edition," Deloitte Insights, *October 22, 2018, https://www2.deloitte.com/us/en/insights/focus/cognitive-technologies/state-of-ai-and-intelligent-automation-in-business-survey.html.*

- **AI implementation.** The most cited challenge to AI is implementation. Experts believe this is due to the newness of the technology and the low levels of experience and on-the-job learning. Simply recruiting data scientists doesn't solve the implementation challenge. Companies need able domain experts to train AI systems.[139] For example, a data scientist can't train AI to sift through thousands of legal opinions in order to find patterns. A technology-oriented lawyer would need to assist with the training.

- **Data issues.** These challenges include access and integration. As we discussed in Section 7.3, it is important for companies to provide employees with access to credible, novel data. This is not an easy task. AI makes this challenge even more complex as there are times when data needs to be integrated across different systems. Take for example a virtual assistant that helps customers. Customer information may be in one system while financial data may reside in another system. The virtual assistant's training and configuration data may reside in yet a third system. All these systems may need to be integrated when they were never built to be integrated with other systems in the first place.[140]

- **Cost.** AI isn't cheap. In fact, companies pay between $6,000 and more than $300,000 for custom AI software, according to *WebFX*. Third-party AI software, such as a pre-built chatbot, may be more economical. Even these chatbots cost around $40,000 a year to operate. Cost depends on the type of AI, whether it is pre-built or customized, duration, and how the AI will be maintained.[141]

AI in the sky. A professional photography drone flies over the San Francisco piers. Are you comfortable knowing that such drones can be used for malicious purposes? Alex Yuzhakov/Shutterstock

Weaponizing AI   AI also has its fair share of critics because of the dangers it can pose to society. Among some of the most outspoken critics is Tesla's Elon Musk. Musk says AI is the "biggest risk we face as a civilization." The eminent late physicist, Stephen Hawking, was another critic. Hawking suffered from Lou Gehrig's disease, which gradually took away his ability to move or speak. Ironically, Hawking used AI-assisted technology to speak after he lost his own voice. He used this newfound voice to warn of the dangers of weaponized artificial intelligence, saying, "AI could be the worst event in the history of our civilization."[142] For example, an airborne AI drone has already been cobbled together, inexpensively and from easily available parts. It is meant to be simply entertaining but could conceivably become something much worse. A *New York Times* writer called it an "automated bloodhound."[143] More worrying, perhaps, a report by a group of U.S. and British AI researchers warns AI developers against widely sharing their work.[144] "Less attention has historically been paid to the ways in which artificial intelligence can be used maliciously," the report says. Among those ways: AI can make it faster and easier to hack other systems, rather than protect them, and to do so more effectively.[145] The report also cautions against the possibility that autonomous weapons could be developed and deployed, and that AI systems could undermine "truthful public debates," the hallmark of democracies, by expanding surveillance in authoritarian ways.

Will AI Replace Us?   Human replacement is another potential disadvantage. Bryan Walsh, author of *End Times*, argues that allowing machines to become smarter than us may threaten our very existence. "We did not rise to the top of the food chain because we're stronger or faster than other animals. We made it here because we are smarter," writes Walsh.[146] Most experts don't see a doomsday scenario involving robots, but the threat of them replacing humans in the workplace is a very real one. According to a 2019 Brookings Institution report, about 25% of the U.S. workforce (36 million jobs) may be replaced by AI in the next few decades.[147] Research supports the notion that replacing humans with machines is not the most effective way forward. A study of 1,500 companies found that firms see the most performance improvements when humans and machines work together. Through this collaboration, humans can leverage their leadership, teamwork, creativity, and social skills. Machines bring speed, scalability, and quantitative capabilities to the partnership.[148] The Practical Action box describes career readiness skills that will help you collaborate with machines rather than be replaced by them. ●

PRACTICAL ACTION   Career Readiness Skills Help You Collaborate with Robots

Robots are taking over tasks that can be automated, such as scheduling or credential validation. Humans, however, are necessary for the many things machines still can't do.[149] "AI will substitute for a set of tasks, but there's no reason it would have to be a total displacement," says economist Michael Webb. "The only thing you can say for sure is that the job will change."[150] Research shows that mastering the career readiness skills of *leadership, oral/written communication,* and *decision making* will allow you to partner with AI and increase your chances of success during this change.[151]

Adaptable, Visionary Leadership. AI will bring about intense disruption and rapid, ambiguous change. This will require leaders to use the career readiness competencies of personal adaptability and openness to change. Don't be afraid to change your mind if it improves decision making. You should commit to a new course of action when necessary and focus on learning rather than being right. Disruption also requires a clear vision from leadership because there is less clarity among followers about where one should go, what one should do, and why. As you may recall from Chapter 5, *vision* is a long-term goal describing "what" an organization wants to be. During times of ambiguous change, an effective vision will allow a leader to implement necessary organizational changes and give followers a clear path forward.[152] We further discuss effective leadership in Chapter 14.

Communicate Findings. As we discussed in Section 7.3, machines may be able to make complex calculations in a matter of nanoseconds, but humans still have to interpret their findings and use them to influence others. To this end, you'll need to develop communication skills that will allow you to inform and influence decision makers based on data. Your digital partner will take care of the calculations, you just need to sell the idea to management!

Ethical Decision Making. The ethical decision tree we introduced in Section 7.2 prescribes the steps in ethical decision making. These steps can easily be programmed into a machine, but what about weighing the ethical interests of multiple stakeholders in order to come to a decision? Experts say machines can't do that yet. Current AI technology struggles with ethical decision making because translating ethics into computer code is a challenging task and values differ across individuals and societies.[153] This means you need to step in and ensure two important principles. First, you need to review your digital partner's decisions for signs of behavior that may contradict ethical norms. This includes checking for biases, which we discuss in Section 7.6. Second, you'll need to ensure that the data you are feeding the machine is not producing skewed results. For now, your digital teammate is counting on you to keep it ethically in line!

7.5 Four General Decision-Making Styles

THE BIG PICTURE
Your decision-making style reflects how you perceive and respond to information. It could be directive, analytical, conceptual, or behavioral.

A **decision-making style** reflects the combination of how an individual perceives and responds to information. A team of researchers developed a model of decision-making styles based on the idea that styles vary along two different dimensions: value orientation and tolerance for ambiguity.[154]

LO 7-5

Compare the four decision-making styles.

Value Orientation and Tolerance for Ambiguity

Value orientation reflects the extent to which a person focuses on either task and technical concerns or people and social concerns when making decisions. Some people, for instance, are very task focused at work and do not pay much attention to people issues, whereas others are just the opposite.

The second dimension pertains to a person's *tolerance for ambiguity*. This individual difference indicates the extent to which a person has a high need for structure or control in his or her life. Some people desire a lot of structure in their lives (a low tolerance for ambiguity) and find ambiguous situations stressful and psychologically uncomfortable. In contrast, others do not have a high need for structure and can thrive in uncertain situations (a high tolerance for ambiguity). Ambiguous situations can energize people with a high tolerance for ambiguity.

When the dimensions of value orientation and tolerance for ambiguity are combined, they form four styles of decision making: *directive, analytical, conceptual,* and *behavioral. (See Figure 7.6.)*

FIGURE 7.6

Decision-making styles

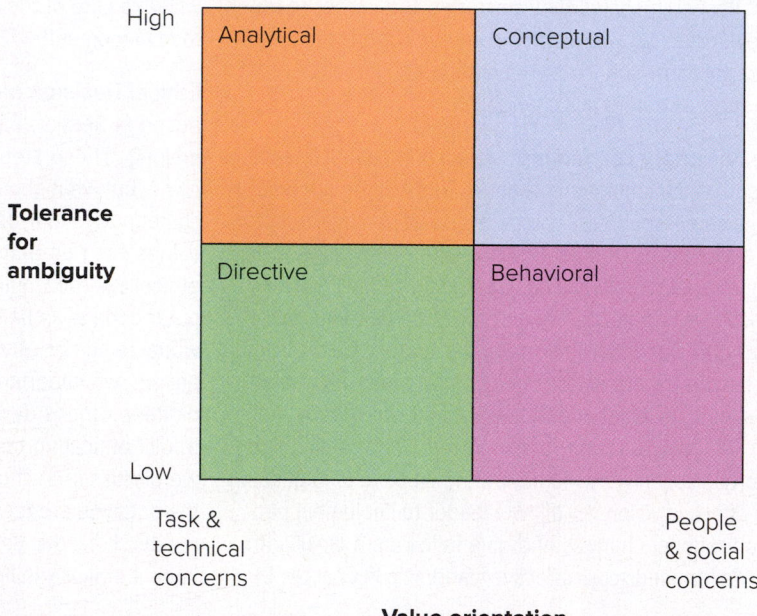

1. The Directive Style: Action-Oriented Decision Makers Who Focus on Facts

People with a directive style have a low tolerance for ambiguity and are oriented toward task and technical concerns in making decisions. They are efficient, logical, practical, and systematic in their approach to solving problems, and they are action oriented and decisive and like to focus on facts. Terry Jimenez, the chief executive of the *New York Daily News, Chicago Tribune,* and *Baltimore Sun* newspapers, fits this pattern. The move from print to digital media means newspapers need to make difficult cuts in order to stay alive, and Jimenez does not shy away from making difficult decisions. His newspapers cut half of their editorial staff in 2018 and Jimenez initiated additional cuts at the executive level in 2020.[155]

2. The Analytical Style: Careful Decision Makers Who Like Lots of Information and Alternative Choices

Managers with an analytical style have a much higher tolerance for ambiguity and respond well to new or uncertain situations. Ursula Burns had this style during her time as chief executive of Xerox. Burns was famous for asking subordinates to poke holes in her ideas and provide alternative choices. She also ensured her advisors came from diverse backgrounds so they could provide her with different perspectives.[156] Analytical managers like to consider more information and alternatives than those adopting the directive style. They are careful decision makers who take longer to make decisions, but they also tend to overanalyze a situation.

A successful analyzer. Ursula Burns speaks during the 2018 World Economic Forum in Davos, Switzerland. Denis Balibouse/Newscom

3. The Conceptual Style: Decision Makers Who Rely on Intuition and Have a Long-Term Perspective

People with a conceptual style have a high tolerance for ambiguity and tend to focus on the people or social aspects of a work situation. They take a broad perspective to problem solving and like to consider many options and future possibilities.

Conceptual types adopt a long-term perspective and rely on intuition and discussions with others to acquire information. They also are willing to take risks and are good at finding creative solutions to problems. Disney's former CEO, Bob Iger, fits this description. According to colleagues, Iger, who led the company from 2005 until February 2020, forged trust with business partners, even former adversaries. He was also known for taking risks in order to propel the company forward. These included Disney's purchase of the Star Wars franchise and 21st Century Fox, construction of additional theme parks in other countries, and launch of the Disney+ streaming service. Though conceptual types enjoy abstract challenges, research shows that they have particular difficulty with well-structured problems. These problems require specific facts and information, as well as a concrete methodology.[157]

4. The Behavioral Style: The Most People-Oriented Decision Makers

The behavioral style is the most people-oriented of the four styles. People with this style work well with others and enjoy social interactions in which opinions are openly exchanged. Behavioral types are supportive, are receptive to suggestions, show warmth, and prefer verbal to written information. Larry Sutton, CEO of RNR Tire Express, is a good example. Sutton believes that employees need to be fully served and valued so they in turn serve customers. He doesn't take himself too seriously, connects with his employees on a personal level, and will even clean his stores' bathrooms when needed.[158] Although they like to hold meetings, some people with this style have a tendency to avoid conflict and to be overly concerned about others. This can lead them to adopt a wishy-washy approach to decision making and to have a hard time saying no.

Which Style Do You Have?

Recent research shows that people typically utilize more than one decision-making style.[159] Most managers have characteristics that fall into two or three styles, and there isn't a best decision-making style that applies to all situations. Studies also reveal that decision-making styles affect our purchasing decisions and leadership style.[160] You can use knowledge of decision-making styles to increase your career readiness competencies in the following three ways.

Know Thyself   Awareness of your style assists you in identifying your strengths and weaknesses as a decision maker and facilitates the potential for self-improvement. As we mentioned earlier, studies confirm that personality dimensions also impact decision-making tendencies.[161] This means reflecting on your personality will help you gain additional insight into your decision-making style. (We cover personality in Chapter 11.)

Influence Others   You can increase your ability to influence others by being aware of decision-making styles. For example, if you are dealing with an analytical person, you should provide as much information as possible to support your ideas.

Deal with Conflict   Knowledge of styles gives you an awareness of how people can take the same information yet arrive at different decisions by using a variety of decision-making strategies. Different decision-making styles are one likely source of interpersonal conflict at work.

What style of decision making do you prefer? Would you like to learn how to use all of the styles more effectively? The following self-assessment can help. ●

SELF-ASSESSMENT 7.3   CAREER READINESS

What Is Your Decision-Making Style?

This survey is designed to assess your decision-making style. Please be prepared to answer these questions if your instructor has assigned Self-Assessment 7.3 in Connect.

1.   What is your dominant decision-making style?

2.   What are the pros and cons of your style?

3.   What might you say to a recruiter during a job interview to demonstrate your awareness regarding your decision-making style?

7.6 Decision-Making Biases

THE BIG PICTURE

Managers should be aware of ten common decision-making biases.

LO 7-6

Identify barriers to rational decision making and ways to overcome them.

If someone asked you to explain the basis on which you make decisions, could you even say? Perhaps, after some thought, you might come up with some "rules of thumb." Scholars call these **heuristics** (pronounced "hyur-ris-tiks")—strategies that simplify the process of making decisions. This section reviews these heuristics.

Ten Common Decision-Making Biases: Rules of Thumb, or "Heuristics"

Despite the fact that people use rules of thumb all the time when making decisions, that doesn't mean they're reliable. Indeed, some are real barriers to high-quality decision making. Among those that tend to bias how decision makers process information are (1) *availability*, (2) *representativeness*, (3) *confirmation*, (4) *sunk cost*, (5) *anchoring and adjustment*, (6) *overconfidence*, (7) *hindsight*, (8) *framing*, (9) *escalation of commitment*, and (10) *categorical thinking*.[162]

1. The Availability Bias: Using Only the Information Available   If you had a perfect on-time work attendance record for nine months but were late for work four days during the last two months because of traffic, shouldn't your boss take into account your entire attendance history when considering you for a raise? Yet managers tend to give more weight to more recent behavior. The reason is the availability bias—the use of information readily available from memory to make judgments.[163]

The bias, of course, is that readily available information may not present a complete picture of a situation. The availability bias may be stoked by the news media, which tend to favor news that is unusual or dramatic. Thus, for example, airplane crashes and terrorist attacks seem like they are happening in our backyards, which usually isn't the case. The odds that you'd be hurt walking down the street are actually higher than both.

Recent studies show that in the age of big data there is an increased chance of the availability bias. This occurs because big data contains a large amount of recent data. The recent data can overshadow smaller, more relevant data sets that may be important to a specific decision.[164] Thus, it is important to leave no stone uncovered when sifting through today's treasure trove of data so you can make the most informed decisions.

2. The Representativeness Bias: Faulty Generalizing from a Small Sample or a Single Event   As a form of financial planning, playing state lotteries leaves something to be desired. When, for instance, in 2019 the U.S. Powerball jackpot stood at $768 million, the third largest U.S. lottery prize in history, the odds of winning it were put at 1 in 292.2 million. (A person would have a far greater chance of being struck by an asteroid, with odds of 1 in only 1.9 million.)[165] Nevertheless, millions of people buy lottery tickets because they read or hear about a handful of fellow citizens who have been the fortunate recipients of enormous winnings. This is an example of the representativeness bias, the tendency to generalize from a small sample or a single event.

The bias here is that just because something happens once, that doesn't mean it is representative—that it will happen again or will happen to you. For example, the fact that you hired an extraordinary sales representative from a particular university doesn't mean the same university will provide an equally qualified candidate next time. Yet managers make this kind of biased hiring decision all the time.

3. The Confirmation Bias: Seeking Information to Support Your Point of View   The confirmation bias occurs when people seek information to support their point of view and discount data that does not support it. Though this bias is so obvious you may think it should be easy to avoid, we practice it all the time, listening to the information we want to hear and ignoring the rest, especially when we are highly committed to a point of view.[166] "We primarily rely on evidence that supports our opinions and beliefs, and disregard anything contrary to those beliefs," suggests psychologist John Grohol. We need to "seek out competing explanations and alternative viewpoints, and try and read them with an open mind."[167]

4. The Sunk-Cost Bias: Money Already Spent Seems to Justify Continuing

The sunk-cost bias, or sunk-cost fallacy, occurs when managers add up all the money they or others have already spent on a project and conclude it is too costly to simply abandon it, even when information exists supporting a change in course.[168] Research has found that this bias is more prevalent in moral judgments, because managers have a greater need to justify past decisions that may be seen as unethical.[169]

Most people have an aversion to "wasting" money. They may continue to push on with an iffy-looking project to justify the large sums of money already sunk into it. Imagine you spent $500 for front row seats to a popular Broadway musical. During the show, you quickly realize the acting is bad, the sets are not well done, and the tunes are giving you a headache. Would you go home during the intermission? Studies suggest most people will stay put, even though money previously spent should logically have no bearing on their decision.[170]

5. The Anchoring and Adjustment Bias: Being Influenced by an Initial Figure

Managers will often give their employees a standard percentage raise in salary, basing the decision on whatever the workers made the preceding year. They may do this even though the raise is completely out of alignment with what other companies are paying for the same skills. This is an instance of the anchoring and adjustment bias, the tendency to make decisions based on an initial figure.

The bias is that the initial figure may be irrelevant to market realities. This phenomenon is sometimes seen in used car sales where the dealer's initial price offered for the car sets the standard for negotiations. A negotiated price lower than the initial price may seem more reasonable to the buyer, though it may be higher than what the car is actually worth.[171] Interestingly, studies have uncovered that those who are more open to new experiences are more susceptible to this bias.[172]

6. The Overconfidence Bias: Blind to Our Own Blindness

The overconfidence bias is the bias in which people's subjective confidence in their decision making is greater than their objective accuracy. The overconfidence bias can lead to problematic decision making. In fact, recent studies found that those exhibiting this bias tend to make less profitable decisions, risk too much, and hurt their well-being.[173]

Overconfidence, it's suggested, promotes innovation, but is one of the primary reasons new businesses fail. Start-up founders are often overconfident when handling complex decisions or when failure is likely. Overconfidence bias also occurs when a founder is not especially skilled in a certain area. The best fix for this bias is to know your own limitations. "When you don't have the proper skills or knowledge yourself, find or hire someone who does," says angel investor Ron Flavin.[174]

7. The Hindsight Bias: The I-Knew-It-All-Along Effect

The hindsight bias is the tendency of people to view events as more predictable than they really are, as when at the end of watching a game we decide the outcome was obvious and predictable, even though in fact it was not. Sometimes called the "I-knew-it-all-along" effect, this occurs when we look back on a decision and try to reconstruct why we decided to do something. Recent research has found that as you age, the chances of hindsight bias increase, but the more autonomous you are, and the less you try to manage your impressions to others, the less susceptible you are to it.[175]

8. The Framing Bias: Shaping the Way a Problem Is Presented

The framing bias is the tendency of decision makers to be influenced by the way a situation or problem is presented to them. In general, people view choices more favorably when positively framed. For example, would you prefer to undergo a surgery if the "one-month survival rate is 90%" (positively framed) or if "there is a 10% chance of death in the first month" (negatively framed)? You'd be in line with research findings if you chose the first statement.[176] Overall, try framing your decision questions in alternate ways in order to avoid the framing bias.

9. The Escalation of Commitment Bias: Feeling Overly Invested in a Decision

If you really hate to admit you're wrong, you need to be aware of the **escalation of commitment bias**, whereby decision makers increase their commitment to a project despite negative information about it.

Take for example the Canadian Trans Mountain pipeline, which carries oil from Alberta to British Columbia. The Canadian government approved an approximately 600-mile extension in June 2019, at an estimated cost of between $5.4 and $7.4 billion. Less than a year later, the costs of the extension soared to $12.6 billion, but the project is still proceeding. "The Trans Mountain pipeline remains a project outside market forces. The arguments for it rest on misconceptions and propaganda," says Elizabeth May, a Canadian Member of Parliament opposed to the expansion.[177]

To reduce the escalation of commitment bias, researchers recommend that decision makers set minimum targets for performance and then compare their performance results with their targets. Managers also should be rotated in key positions during a project, and decision makers should be encouraged to become less ego-involved with the work. Finally, decision makers should be made aware of the costs of persistence, which in many cases requires more time, money, and effort than changing course.[178]

10. The Categorical Thinking Bias: Sorting Information into Buckets

Our mind is a categorization machine, taking in massive amounts of data and then simplifying and structuring it so we can make sense of the world. The **categorical thinking bias** is the tendency of decision makers to classify people or information based on observed or inferred characteristics. In its simplest form, categorical thinking can save us from danger, such as when it allows us to tell the difference between a stick and a snake.

However, this bias can lead to problematic decision making. Consider Facebook's practice of assigning political labels to its users based on their browsing history. Users are categorized as "moderate," "conservative," or "liberal," and this information is provided to advertisers. Advertisers may then mistakenly assume differences among these individuals are bigger than they really are and deliver a highly tailored message to each group. This, in turn, may widen differences and fuel divisiveness.[179] ●

7.7 Group Decision Making: How to Work with Others

THE BIG PICTURE

Group decision making has five potential advantages and four potential disadvantages. The disadvantage of groupthink merits focus because it leads to terrible decisions. It also is important to consider the characteristics of group decision making before allowing a group to make a decision. Finally, knowledge about group problem-solving techniques can enhance group decision-making effectiveness.

The movies celebrate the lone heroes who, like Charlize Theron or Liam Neeson, make their own moves and call their own shots. Most managers, however, work with groups and teams (as we discuss in Chapter 13). Research suggests that groups typically perform at the same level as the best individual decision makers and better than the median and worst comparison individuals.[180] Thus, to be an effective manager, you need to learn about decision making in groups.

LO 7-7

Outline the basics of group decision making.

Advantages and Disadvantages of Group Decision Making

Because you may often have a choice as to whether to make a decision by yourself or to consult with others, you need to understand the advantages and disadvantages of group-aided decision making.

Advantages　Using a group to make a decision offers five possible advantages.[181] For these benefits to happen, however, the group must be made up of diverse participants, not just people who all think the same way.

- **Greater pool of knowledge.** When several people are making the decision, there is a greater pool of information from which to draw. If one person doesn't have the pertinent knowledge and experience, someone else might.

- **Different perspectives.** Because different people have different perspectives—marketing, production, legal, and so on—they see the problem from different angles.

- **Intellectual stimulation.** A group of people can brainstorm or otherwise bring greater intellectual stimulation and creativity to the decision-making process than is usually possible with one person acting alone.

- **Better understanding of decision rationale.** If you participate in making a decision, you are more apt to understand the reasoning behind the decision, including the pros and cons leading up to the final step.

- **Deeper commitment to the decision.** If you've been part of the group that has bought into the final decision, you're more apt to be committed to seeing that the course of action is successfully implemented.

Disadvantages　The disadvantages of group-aided decision making spring from problems in how members interact.[182]

- **A few people dominate or intimidate.** Sometimes a handful of people will talk the longest and the loudest, and the rest of the group will simply give in. Or one individual, such as a strong leader, will exert disproportionate influence, sometimes by intimidation. Some leaders may even employ sham participation, which occurs when powerless, but useful individuals are selected by leaders to rubber stamp decisions and work hard to implement them.[183] These tactics reduce creativity.

- **Groupthink.** Groupthink occurs when group members strive to agree for the sake of unanimity and thus avoid accurately assessing the decision situation. Here the positive team spirit of the group actually works against sound judgment.[184] Groupthink is explored more thoroughly in the next section.

- **Satisficing.** Because most people would just as soon cut short a meeting, the tendency is to seek a decision that is "good enough" rather than to push on in pursuit of other possible solutions. Satisficing can occur because groups have limited time, lack the right kind of information, or are unable to handle large amounts of information.[185]

- **Goal displacement.** Although the primary task of the meeting may be to solve a particular problem, other considerations may rise to the fore, such as rivals trying to win an argument. Goal displacement occurs when the primary goal is subsumed by a secondary goal. A recent study found that strong group identification can lead to intergroup competition to the point that teams don't cooperate and their team goals displace the organization's.[186]

Groupthink

Cohesiveness isn't always good. When it results in groupthink, group or team members are friendly and tight-knit but unable to think "outside the box." Their "strivings for unanimity override their motivation to realistically appraise alternative courses of action," says Irwin Janis, author of *Groupthink*.[187]

The results of groupthink can include failure to consider new information and a loss of new ideas. Take for example Swissair, an airline that became so powerful that it earned the nickname "the Flying Bank." The company restructured its board to achieve a more ideologically and strategically "aligned" group. Due to the restructuring, the board lost most of its industrial expertise and opposing voices, and those who were left believed the company was invulnerable to bad decisions. The resulting groupthink led the airline to financial collapse and liquidation.[188]

Different perspectives or groupthink? A diversified team can offer differing points of view, as well as a greater pool of knowledge and intellectual stimulation. Or, it can offer groupthink and satisficing. What has been your experience when it comes to the value of decision making in the groups you've been in? Sam Edward/agefotostock

Symptoms of Groupthink   How do you know that you're in a group or team that is suffering from groupthink? Some symptoms include the following:[189]

- **Sense of invulnerability.** Group members have the illusion that nothing can go wrong, breeding excessive optimism and risk taking. They also may be so assured of the rightness of their actions that they ignore the ethical implications.

- **Rationalization.** Rationalizing protects the pet assumptions underlying the group's decisions from critical questions.

- **Dominant members.** Some members override others when they are trying to speak, are dismissive of ideas, ignore other members' points of view, or automatically adopt a negative stance toward conflicting opinions. Others may even turn to bullying those that don't agree with them, which research finds has negative effects on cohesiveness and group decision effectiveness.[190]

- **Illusion of unanimity and peer pressure.** The illusion of unanimity is another way of saying that a member's silence is interpreted as consent. If people do disagree, peer pressure leads other members to question the dissenters' loyalty.

- **"The wisdom of crowds."** Groupthink's pressure to conform often leads members with different ideas to censor themselves—the opposite of collective wisdom, says James Surowiecki, in which "each person in the group is offering his or her best independent forecast. It's not at all about compromise or consensus."[191]

No doubt you've felt yourself pulled into a "groupthink opinion" at some point. We all probably have. Self-Assessment 7.4 provides you with a way to evaluate the extent to which groupthink is affecting a team. Results provide insight into reducing this counterproductive group dynamic.

SELF-ASSESSMENT 7.4

Assessing Groupthink

The following survey was designed to assess groupthink. Please be prepared to answer these questions if your instructor has assigned Self-Assessment 7.4 in Connect.

1. Where does the team stand on the three aspects of groupthink?

2. Based on your survey scores, what would you do differently to reduce groupthink in the group you evaluated? Be specific.

Preventing Groupthink Janis believes it is easier to prevent groupthink than to cure it. As preventive measures, he and other writers suggest the following:[192]

- **Allow criticism.** Each member of a team or group should be told to be a critical evaluator, able to actively voice objections and doubts. Subgroups within the group should be allowed to discuss and debate ideas. Once a consensus has been reached, everyone should be encouraged to rethink his or her position to check for flaws. It is sometimes helpful for the group leader to withhold his or her opinion at first, to encourage others to speak up.

- **Allow other perspectives.** Outside experts should be used to introduce fresh perspectives. Different groups with different leaders should explore the same policy questions. Top-level executives should not use sham participation to rubber-stamp decisions that have already been made. When major alternatives are discussed, someone should be made devil's advocate to try to uncover all negative factors.

- **Reflect before entering a group discussion.** Individuals are more likely to gravitate toward the view that seems most popular if they do not reflect on their own opinions before a group discussion. One way to reflect is to write down your opinions before the start of a group meeting so you can circle back to them during the discussion.

Characteristics of Group Decision Making

If you're a manager deliberating whether to call a meeting for group input, there are four characteristics of groups to be aware of.

1. **They are less efficient.**   Groups take longer to make decisions. Thus, if time is of the essence, you may want to make the decision by yourself.[193] Faced with time pressures or the serious effect of a decision, groups use less information and fewer communication channels, which increases the probability of a bad decision.[194]

2. **Their size affects decision quality.**   The larger the group, the lower the quality of the decision.[195] Some research says that between 7 and 10 people is the optimal size.[196] Others suggest three is best.[197] (An odd number is considered best when the group uses majority rules.)

3. **They may be too confident.**   Groups are more confident about their judgments and choices than individuals are. This, of course, can be a liability because it can lead to groupthink and overconfidence bias.

4. **Knowledge counts.**   Decision-making accuracy is higher when group members know a good deal about the relevant issues.[198] It also is higher when a group leader has the ability to weigh members' opinions.[199] Depending on whether group members know or don't know one another, the kind of knowledge also counts. For example, people who are familiar with one another tend to make better decisions when members have a lot of unique information. However, people who aren't familiar with one another tend to make better decisions when the members have common knowledge.[200]

In general, group decision making is more effective when members feel that they can freely and safely disagree with each other. This belief is referred to as <mark>minority dissent</mark>, dissent that occurs when a minority in a group publicly opposes the beliefs, attitudes, ideas, procedures, or policies assumed by the majority of the group.[201] Minority dissent is associated with increased innovation within groups.[202] Do your teams at school or work allow minority dissent? If not, what can be done to increase its existence? Self-Assessment 7.5 can help answer these questions.

Toward consensus. Working to achieve cooperation in a group can tell you a lot about yourself. How well do you handle the negotiation process? What do you do when you're disappointed in a result achieved by consensus? Xavier Arnau/Getty Images

SELF-ASSESSMENT 7.5

Assessing Participation in Group Decision Making

The following survey measures minority dissent, participation in group decision making, and satisfaction with a group. Please be prepared to answer these questions if your instructor has assigned Self-Assessment 7.5 in Connect.

1. What is the level of minority dissent in the group, and to what extent are you satisfied with being a member of this group?

2. Use the three lowest items that measure minority dissent to answer the following question: What can you do to increase the level of minority dissent in this group? Be specific.

3. Why do you think many groups muzzle the level of minority dissent?

Group Problem-Solving Techniques: Reaching for Consensus

Using groups to make decisions generally requires that they reach a **consensus, which occurs when members are able to express their opinions and reach agreement to support the final decision.** More specifically, consensus is reached when "a group discusses and debates various courses of action, while taking care to address the concerns of each participant," says one expert in decision making. This is done "until every member can generally agree upon, or at least can live with, a way forward."[203] Consensus does not mean that group members agree with the decision, only that they are willing to work toward its success.

One management expert offers the following do's and don'ts for achieving consensus.[204]

- ▪ **Do's:** Use active listening skills. Involve as many members as possible. Seek out the reasons behind arguments. Dig for the facts.

- ▪ **Don'ts:** Avoid log rolling and horse trading ("I'll support your pet project if you'll support mine"). Avoid making an agreement simply to keep relations amicable and not rock the boat. Finally, don't try to achieve consensus by putting questions to a vote; this will only split the group into winners and losers, perhaps creating bad feelings among the latter.

More Group Problem-Solving Techniques

Decision-making experts have developed several group problem-solving techniques to aid in problem solving. Four we will discuss here are (1) *brainstorming*, (2) *devil's advocacy*, (3) the *dialectic method*, and (4) *post-mortems*.

1. Brainstorming: For Increasing Creativity

Brainstorming is a technique used to help groups generate multiple ideas and alternatives for solving problems.[205] Developed by advertising executive A. F. Osborn, the technique consists of having members of a group meet and review a problem to be solved. Individual members are then asked to silently generate ideas or solutions, which are then collected (preferably without identifying their contributors) and written on a board or flip chart. A second session is then used to critique and evaluate the alternatives. Research suggests that this session can be used to rank ideas based on creativity and social approval, which can ultimately assist decision makers.[206]

A modern-day variation of brainstorming is **electronic brainstorming, sometimes called brainwriting, in which members of a group come together over a computer network to generate ideas and alternatives.**[207] Research shows that electronic brainstorming can be advantageous because it allows for greater anonymity and an uninterrupted flow of ideas. It also limits the use of social cues, such as team member facial expressions and tone, which can impact the brainstorming process.[208]

Seven rules for brainstorming suggested by IDEO, a product design company, and others are shown below in Table 7.4.

TABLE 7.4 Seven Rules for Brainstorming[209]

1. **Defer judgment.** Don't criticize or allow pushback during the initial stage of idea generation. Phrases such as "we've never done it that way," "it won't work," "it's too expensive," and "our manager will never agree" should not be used.

2. **Build on the ideas of others.** Encourage participants to extend others' ideas by avoiding "buts" and using "ands."

3. **Encourage wild ideas.** Encourage out-of-the-box thinking. The wilder and more outrageous the ideas, the better.

4. **Go for quantity over quality.** Participants should try to generate and write down as many new ideas as possible because focusing on quantity encourages people to think beyond their favorite ideas. Studies show that the best ideas are generated within the first two minutes of brainstorming.

5. **Be visual.** Use different-colored pens (for example, red, purple, blue) to write on big sheets of flip-chart paper, whiteboards, or poster boards that are put on the wall.

6. **One conversation at a time.** The ground rules are that no one interrupts another person, no dismissing of someone's ideas, no disrespect, and no rudeness.

7. **Brainstorm questions.** Generate questions rather than answers, which makes it easier to push past biases.

Brainstorming is an effective technique for generating new ideas and alternatives. Moreover, research reveals that people can be trained to improve their brainstorming skills.[210]

2. Devil's Advocacy   Devil's advocacy gets its name from a traditional practice of the Roman Catholic Church. When someone's name comes before the College of Cardinals for elevation to sainthood, it is absolutely essential to ensure that the person had a spotless record. Consequently, one individual is assigned the role of *devil's advocate* to uncover and air all possible objections to the person's canonization. In today's organizations *devil's advocacy* assigns someone the role of critic. Figure 7.7 shows the steps in this approach. Note how devil's advocacy alters the usual decision-making process in steps 2 and 3 on the left-hand side of the figure.

3. The Dialectic Method   Like devil's advocacy, the dialectic method is a time-honored practice, going all the way back to ancient Greece. Plato and his followers attempted to identify a truth, called *thesis*, by exploring opposite positions, called *antitheses*. Court systems in the United States and elsewhere today rely on hearing directly opposing points of view to establish guilt or innocence. Accordingly, the dialectic method calls for managers to foster a structured dialogue or debate of opposing viewpoints prior to making a decision.[211] Steps 3 and 4 in the right-hand side of Figure 7.7 set the dialectic approach apart from common decision-making processes.

4. Project Post-Mortems   Said to have originated as a debriefing strategy used by the military, a project post-mortem is, as the name suggests, a review of recent decisions in order to identify possible future improvements. The idea is to carefully evaluate project

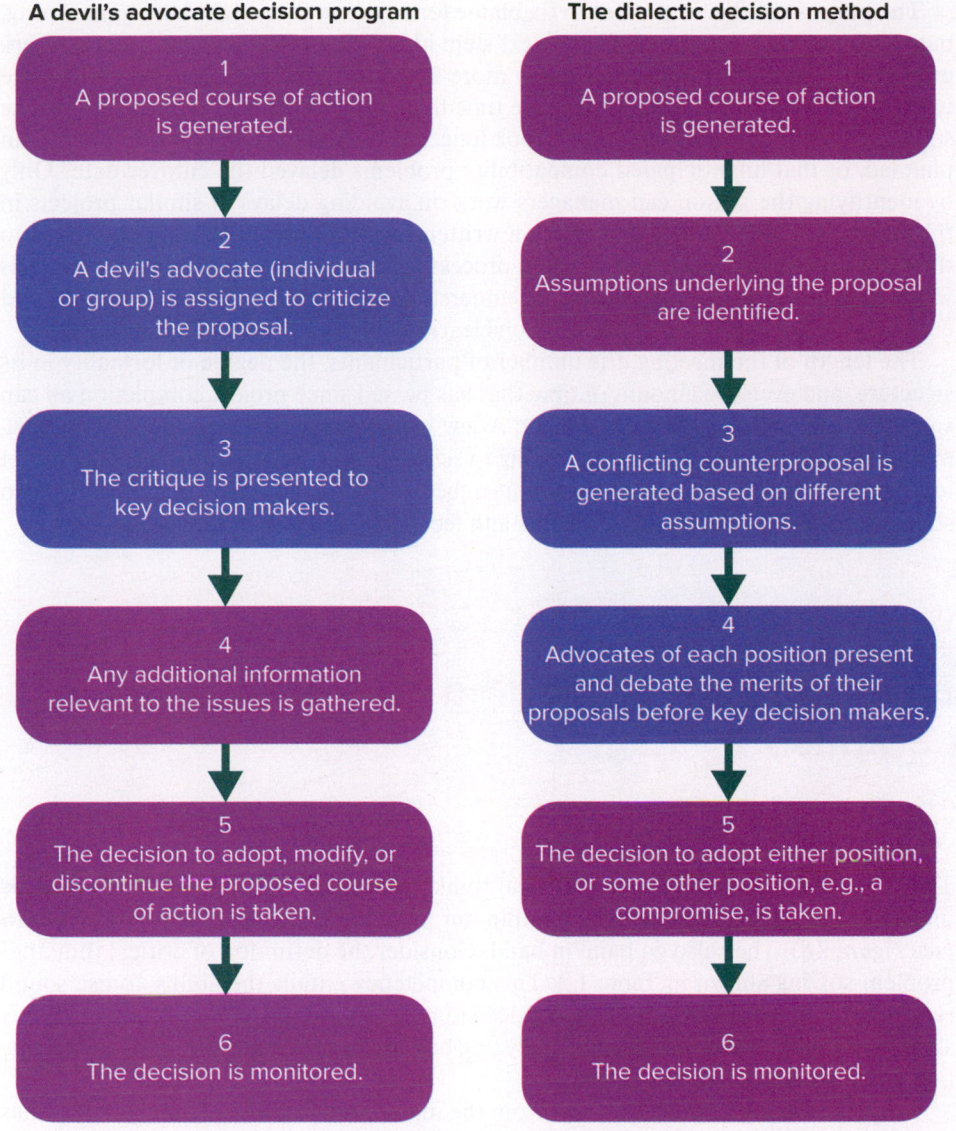

A devil's advocate decision program

1
A proposed course of action is generated.

2
A devil's advocate (individual or group) is assigned to criticize the proposal.

3
The critique is presented to key decision makers.

4
Any additional information relevant to the issues is gathered.

5
The decision to adopt, modify, or discontinue the proposed course of action is taken.

6
The decision is monitored.

The dialectic decision method

1
A proposed course of action is generated.

2
Assumptions underlying the proposal are identified.

3
A conflicting counterproposal is generated based on different assumptions.

4
Advocates of each position present and debate the merits of their proposals before key decision makers.

5
The decision to adopt either position, or some other position, e.g., a compromise, is taken.

6
The decision is monitored.

FIGURE 7.7

Techniques for stimulating functional conflict: Devil's advocacy and the dialectic method

Source: From R. A. Castler and R.C. Schwenk, "Agreement and Thinking Alike: Ingredients for Poor Decisions," Academy of Management Executive, February 1990, pp. 72–73.

results after the fact, noting what could be done differently and better, and then to record those insights to inform future decisions.[212] Benefits of post-mortems include:[213]

- **Process improvement.** Reviewing the project will help you identify areas for improvement for next time.

- **Boosting team cohesiveness.** Teams that are able to talk and listen to each other after the project is completed become closer and better understand each other's contributions.

- **Closure.** Holding a post-mortem is a collaborative way to end the project and give everyone a chance to have a final say.

- **Improving morale.** Celebrating successes will fire up the team. Teams that struggled can talk out project problems and iron out resentments.

The post-mortem usually takes place during a meeting of the project team and should begin with a thorough look at how the reality of the project differed from plans and expectations. For instance, did the upgrade of the company's computer system take more time or cost more money than budgeted? Were any steps in the process changed or eliminated as the project went along? How were unplanned contingencies handled? What went wrong, and what went right?

The purpose of this step is not to fix blame for anything that might have gone wrong, but rather to prepare the way for the next step: identifying ways in which recent experiences can help make future projects go more smoothly. For instance, if a project like upgrading a computer system took more time than anticipated, was the reason that the software vendor delivered late, that it took longer to train staff in the new program than planned, or that unanticipated compatibility problems delayed the cutover date? Only by identifying the reason can managers work on avoiding delays in similar projects in the future. The final step is to prepare a written report, which should be circulated to the team, to document the post-mortem process and findings. Research shows that this written report is instrumental in better understanding team member perspectives and encouraging the application of any lessons learned.[214]

The length of the meeting, the number of participants, the degree of formality in its structure, and even the amount of time that has passed since project completion all can vary with the complexity of the project. A few basic strategies for any successful post-mortem, however, are not to wait too long to schedule one, to prepare an agenda, to not let it get personal, and to encourage honest feedback from all participants, which also should include any customer comments and feedback received. ●

7.8 Career Corner: Managing Your Career Readiness

LO 7-8

Describe how to develop the career readiness competencies of critical thinking/problem solving and decision making.

The career readiness soft skills of critical thinking/problem solving and decision making are highly desired competencies within our model of career readiness shown below (*see Figure 7.8*). They also go hand in hand. Consider the definition of critical thinking/problem solving shown in Table 1.2. This competency entails the ability to use sound reasoning to analyze situations, make decisions, and solve problems. It also requires skills at obtaining, interpreting, and analyzing both qualitative and quantitative information while creatively solving problems.

Critical thinking is much different from the moment-to-moment thinking that guides our everyday activities. Moment-to-moment thinking is automatic and highly susceptible to the biases discussed in this chapter. In contrast, critical thinking requires more deliberate mental processes. We need to stop and consciously process information when trying to critically think about a problem.

This section provides suggestions for improving your decision making by engaging in critical thinking and problem solving. We then discuss how you can demonstrate these skills during an employment interview.

Improving Your Critical Thinking and Problem-Solving Skills

Good decision-making ability amounts to being able to understand the relationship between causes and outcomes. In other words, good decision makers can predict what will occur in a given situation. Reflecting on your past experiences and using a decision methodology are two ways to develop this skill.

Reflect on Past Decisions

Most problems you will encounter at work after graduation will not be new, but they may be unfamiliar to you.[215] This means there are ready-made solutions you can use. One

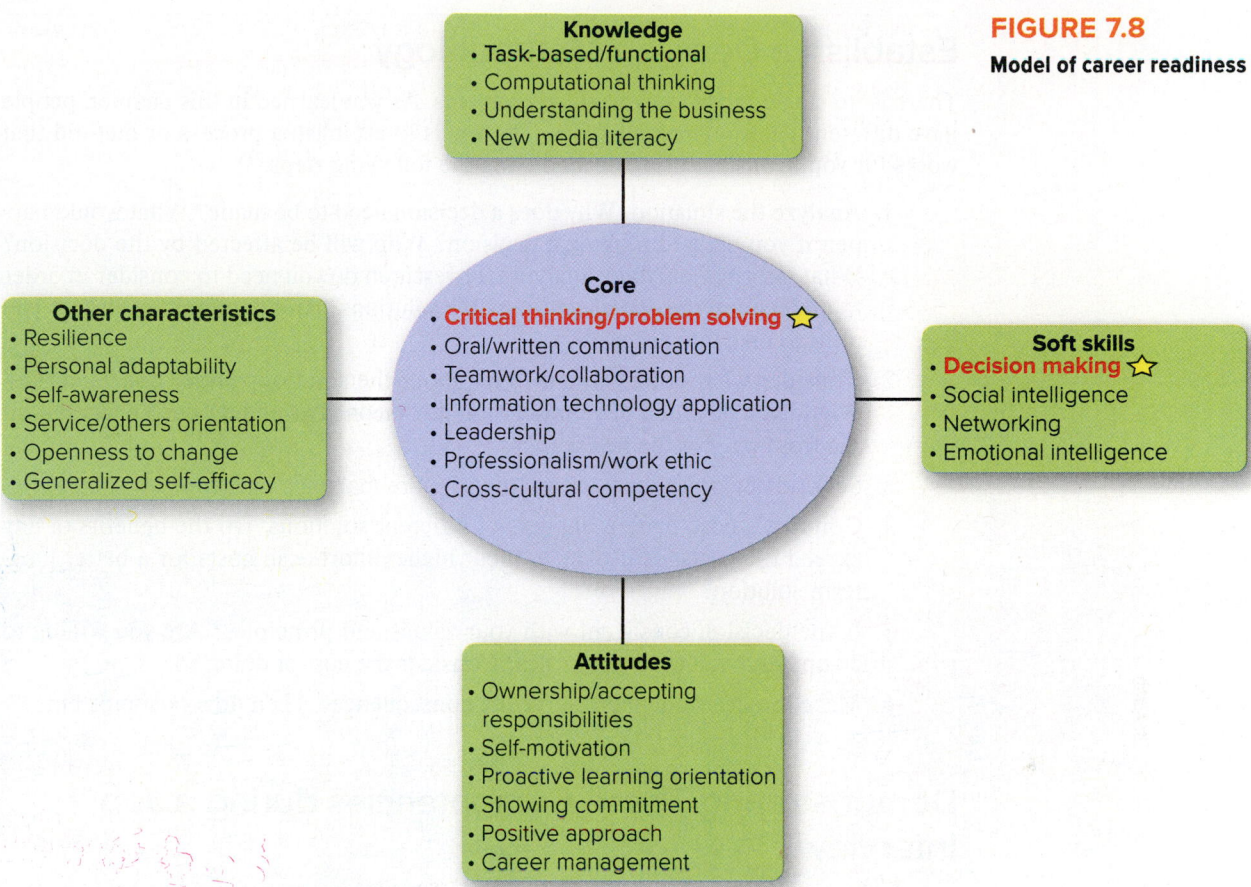

FIGURE 7.8
Model of career readiness

expert defined ready-made solutions as "best practices that have been captured and turned into standard operating procedures so that employees are better prepared to address regularly recurring problems."[216] By learning and applying these ready-made solutions, you can develop a larger set of options for solving problems, thereby improving your decision-making skills. This improvement will in turn assist you in resolving unanticipated problems. Use the following steps to increase your awareness of ready-made solutions.[217]

1. Think of a time in which you faced a problem either at work or in your personal life and you successfully resolved it. Now write down answers to the following questions:

   ■ What was the problem? Where did it occur and who was involved?

   ■ What was the solution?

   ■ Why did you select this solution?

   ■ What lessons can you derive from this experience that you can use when faced with similar problems?

2. Now think of a time you unsuccessfully solved a problem in your work or personal life. Write answers to the same questions listed above.

3. Think of someone you know who is very good at solving problems. Now focus on a specific problem you observed this person solving and write answers to the following questions:

   ■ What was the problem? Where did it occur and who was involved?

   ■ What was the solution?

   ■ What steps did the person follow in solving the problem?

   ■ What lessons can you learn from this and apply when faced with similar problems?

Establish a Decision Methodology

There is no single "right" way to solve problems. As you learned in this chapter, people have different decision-making styles. The key is to establish a process or method that works for you. Consider using or modifying the following steps:[218]

1. Analyze the situation. Why does a decision need to be made? What would happen if you delayed making a decision? Who will be affected by the decision? What information, data, analytics, or research do you need to consider in order to understand the causes and possible solutions? Are there political issues you need to take into account?

2. Consider what others would think about the solutions under consideration. Would you be proud of your decision if someone tweeted it out or printed it on the front page of the newspaper?

3. Seek advice or feedback from others before making a decision.

4. Conduct a cost–benefit analysis of different solutions. Do the benefits of any exceed the costs? Is it okay to incur higher short-term costs for a better long-term solution?

5. Is the decision consistent with your values and principles? Are you willing to co-opt your values or principles? Consider the cost of doing so.

6. Make the decision and observe the consequences. Then do a post-mortem.

Demonstrating These Competencies during a Job Interview

Being career ready means not only possessing career readiness competencies, but also being able to demonstrate them during a job interview. Assuming you possess some of these competencies, now it's time to make a plan for making a positive impression. We recommend that you start by preparing answers to the following behaviorally based questions:[219]

- Describe the process you use to make decisions. Provide a specific example in which this process resulted in a positive outcome.

- Tell me about a time in which you had to make a quick decision. How did you approach the situation and what obstacles did you face? How did you make this decision without having all the necessary information?

- Describe a time in which you used intuition to make a decision rather than relying on data or hard facts. What was the outcome of your decision, and what did you learn from the experience?

Key Terms Used in This Chapter

Key Points

7.1 Two Kinds of Decision Making: Rational and Nonrational

- A decision is a choice made from among available alternatives. Decision making is the process of identifying and choosing alternative courses of action. Two models managers follow in making decisions are rational and nonrational.

- In the rational model, there are four stages in making a decision: Stage 1 is identifying the problem or opportunity. A problem is a difficulty that inhibits the achievement of goals. An opportunity is a situation that presents possibilities for exceeding existing goals. This is a matter of diagnosis—analyzing the underlying causes. Stage 2 is thinking up alternative solutions. Stage 3 is evaluating the alternatives and selecting a solution. Alternatives should be evaluated according to cost, quality, ethics, feasibility, and effectiveness. Stage 4 is implementing and evaluating the solution chosen.

- Nonrational models of decision making assume that decision making is nearly always uncertain and risky, making it difficult for managers to make optimum decisions. Two nonrational models are satisficing and intuition.

7.2 Making Ethical Decisions

- Corporate corruption has made ethics in decision making once again important. Many companies have an ethics officer to resolve ethical dilemmas, and more companies are creating values statements to guide employees as to desirable business behavior.

- To help make ethical decisions, a decision tree—a graph of decisions and their possible consequences—may be helpful. Managers should ask whether a proposed action is legal and, if it is intended to maximize shareholder value, whether it is ethical—and whether it would be ethical not to take the proposed action.

7.3 Evidence-Based Decision Making and Data Analytics

- Evidence-based management means translating principles based on best evidence into organizational practice. It is intended to bring rationality to the decision-making process.

- Pfeffer and Sutton identify seven implementation principles to help companies that are committed to doing what it takes to profit from evidence-based management.

- Applying the best evidence to your decisions is difficult, for seven reasons: (1) There's too much evidence. (2) There's not enough good evidence. (3) The evidence doesn't quite apply. (4) People are trying to mislead you. (5) You are trying to mislead yourself. (6) The side effects outweigh the cure. (7) Stories are more persuasive, anyway.

- Big data requires handling by very sophisticated analysis software and supercomputers. Big data includes not only data in corporate databases, but also web-browsing data trails, social network communications, sensor data, and surveillance data.

- Big data analytics is the process of examining large amounts of data of a variety of types to uncover hidden patterns, unknown correlations, and other useful information. It can be used at all levels of an organization.

7.4 Artificial Intelligence Is a Powerful Decision-Making Resource

- Artificial intelligence (AI) is the ability of a computer system to perform tasks that normally require human intelligence.
- AI supports three important business needs: automating business processes, analyzing data, and engaging customers and employees.
- Firms predominately use AI to enhance current offerings, optimize internal processes, and make more effective decisions. The top challenges of AI include implementation, data issues, and cost.

7.5 Four General Decision-Making Styles

- A decision-making style reflects the combination of how an individual perceives and responds to information.
- Decision-making styles may tend to have a value orientation, which reflects the extent to which a person focuses on either task or technical concerns versus people and social concerns when making decisions. Decision-making styles also may reflect a person's tolerance for ambiguity, the extent to which a person has a high or low need for structure or control in his or her life.
- When the dimensions of value orientation and tolerance for ambiguity are combined, they form four styles of decision making: directive (action-oriented decision makers who focus on facts); analytical (careful decision makers who like lots of information and alternative choices); conceptual (decision makers who rely on intuition and have a long-term perspective); and behavioral (the most people-oriented decision makers).

7.6 Decision-Making Biases

- Ten common decision-making biases present real barriers to high-quality decision making. They are (1) availability, (2) representativeness, (3) confirmation, (4) sunk cost, (5) anchoring and adjustment, (6) overconfidence, (7) hindsight, (8) framing, (9) escalation of commitment, and (10) categorical thinking.

7.7 Group Decision Making: How to Work with Others

- Using a group to make a decision offers five possible advantages: (1) a greater pool of knowledge, (2) different perspectives, (3) intellectual stimulation, (4) better understanding of the reasoning behind the decision, and (5) deeper commitment to the decision.
- It also has four disadvantages: (1) a few people may dominate or intimidate; (2) it will produce groupthink, when group members strive for agreement among themselves for the sake of unanimity and so avoid accurately assessing the decision situation; (3) satisficing; and (4) goal displacement, when the primary goal is subsumed to a secondary goal.
- Some characteristics of groups to be aware of are (1) groups are less efficient, (2) their size affects decision quality, (3) they may be too confident, and (4) knowledge counts—decision-making accuracy is higher when group members know a lot about the issues.
- Using groups to make decisions generally requires that they reach a consensus, which occurs when members are able to express their opinions and reach agreement to support the final decision. Minority dissent should be allowed, so members can safely disagree with each other.
- Four techniques aid in problem solving. (1) Brainstorming helps groups generate multiple ideas and alternatives for solving problems. (2) Devil's advocacy assigns someone the role of critic. (3) The dialectic method calls for managers to foster a structured dialogue or debate of opposing viewpoints prior to making a decision. (4) A project post-mortem is a review of recent decisions in order to identify possible future improvements.

7.8 Career Corner: Managing Your Career Readiness

- The career readiness competencies of critical thinking/problem solving and decision making go hand in hand.
- Reflecting on your past experiences and using a decision methodology are two ways to improve critical thinking and problem solving.

Understanding the Chapter: What Do I Know?

1. What are the steps in rational decision making?

2. What are two models of nonrational decision making?

3. What are four ethical questions a manager should ask when evaluating a proposed action to make a decision?

4. What is big data?

5. What types of AI exist?

6. What are some of AI's benefits and drawbacks?

7. Describe the four general decision-making styles.

8. Can you name the 10 common decision-making biases?

9. What are the advantages and disadvantages of group decision making?

10. What are some symptoms of groupthink?

Juul Is Going Up in Smoke

Juul Labs is an American electronic cigarette company founded in 2017. The company manufacturers the Juul e-cigarette, which is an alternative to traditional, paper-based cigarettes. Juul's e-cigarettes became a hit in 2018, allowing the company to grow to 4,000 employees and a $38 billion valuation. Based on its initial success, Juul forecasted revenue of $3.4 billion in 2019, almost triple what it generated in 2018.[220]

The company's fortunes took a turn for the worse in 2019. A number of legal cases and regulatory action against the manufacturer halved its growth rate, resulting in layoffs and a 25% decrease in its stock price. Juul's valuation dropped to $12 billion by 2020, less than a third of what it was worth a year earlier.[221]

Let's take a closer look at Juul's troubles.

THE RISE OF VAPING

Robert Norris was the "Marlboro Man," a rugged, independent cowboy figure who was the face of Marlboro's campaign to attract men to cigarettes in the 1950s. The ad campaign helped Marlboro become the world's leading cigarette brand, a position it still holds. Norris, a nonsmoker himself, decided to abandon the campaign because of the example it was setting for children.[222] America followed Norris's lead. By 2018, just under 14% of adults smoked cigarettes, down from 42% in 1965.[223]

Juul entered the vaping market without a cowboy, but with a mission to "improve the lives of 1 billion adult smokers by eliminating cigarettes." The company's aversion to cigarettes is because they contain tobacco, a known carcinogen. Juul's battery-operated vaporizer works by converting liquid nicotine into a vapor that the user inhales, providing a similar experience to that of smoking regular cigarettes. Its USB-chargeable device (dubbed the "iPhone of cigarettes") is sleek and hardly noticeable, its snap-on cartridges cost less than cigarettes, and the whole vaping process leaves no lingering smell. Each 5% nicotine cartridge contains roughly the same addictive amount of nicotine as one pack of cigarettes. And though vapes don't contain tobacco, they may contain other chemicals such as benzene (a carcinogen) and acetamide (an industrial solvent). In fact, the CDC reports that vaping is the cause of more than 2,000 cases of severe lung disease, and there are investigations of over 127 cases of e-cigarette users experiencing seizures.[224]

The health concerns surrounding Juul are especially alarming because of its popularity among middle and high school students, a population that is prohibited by law from smoking. According to the *New England Journal of Medicine*, one in nine U.S. high school seniors say they vaped almost daily in 2019.[225] Experts believe Juul's popularity stems from its low price tag (a starter kit costs $50), ability to be discreet, and lack of odor. Its cartridges also come in many flavors. One Center for Disease Control (CDC) survey found that 31% of adolescents chose e-cigarettes because of "flavors such as mint, candy, fruit, or chocolate." The fact that almost one-fifth of middle and high school students have seen Juul used in school, or that millions have seen Juul's ads, does not help either.[226]

JUUL FACES SCRUTINY

The surging popularity of Juul among teenagers caught the attention of the Food and Drug Administration (FDA) in 2018. The regulatory agency conducted "a nationwide, undercover blitz" to investigate Juul, claiming the enforcement effort was the largest in its history. U.S. cities and entire countries, such as San Francisco, India, and Israel, also started to take notice of Juul's underage popularity, prompting them to ban flavored e-cigarettes. The Federal Trade Commission (FTC) joined the scrutiny over the e-cigarette maker in 2018, suspecting that Juul deliberately marketed its products to minors.[227]

Juul's CEO, K. C. Crosthwaite, responded to this increased scrutiny with a series of decisions. First, the company decided to stop selling many of its flavored e-cigarettes online and in stores. Juul also suspended all broadcast, print, and digital product advertising in the United States. "We must reset the vapor category by earning the trust of society and working cooperatively with regulators, policymakers, and stakeholders to combat underage use while providing an alternative to adult smokers," says CEO Crosthwaite.[228] The company vehemently denies marketing its products to youth, a claim that isn't resonating with many experts. For example, research by the Stanford University School of Medicine uncovered that "JUUL's mission statement . . . and their repeated assertion that their product is meant for 'adult smokers only' has not been congruent with its marketing practices over its first 3 years."[229] Others are more direct with their criticism. "We don't trust them," says Michael Green, the CEO of the Center for Environmental Health. "We think that their entire model is based on addicting a new generation of young people."[230]

Law enforcement and local governments aren't buying Juul's claims either. Federal prosecutors in California launched a criminal investigation of Juul in 2019.

Several school districts across the country also have filed suit against the company, claiming it has created a public nuisance, misrepresented its products, and endangered youth health.[231]

WHAT WILL THE FDA DECIDE?

Aside from the slew of investigations and lawsuits Juul is facing, the company also needs to submit an application to the FDA outlining why it should be allowed to continue selling its products in the United States. The application will need to prove that the benefit of helping adult cigarette smokers switch to a safer alternative outweighs the potential harm of getting teenagers addicted to nicotine. As part of this application process, Juul is doing the following:[232]

- **Cutting ties with the vapor technology association (VTA).** The company announced it wouldn't renew its membership with the VTA because it found itself disagreeing with the industry trade group on a number of issues. For example, Juul now supports banning flavored e-cigarettes, something the VTA is opposed to because of the impact on other e-cigarette retailers.

- **Relying on science and research.** Juul intends to send 250,000 pages of materials to the FDA, including more than 110 scientific studies supporting its products. The company's application is "designed to provide [the] FDA with the science and evidence needed to assess the role our products can play moving smokers away from cigarettes, while combating underage use," says a company spokesperson.

- **Using AI to modify its vaporizer.** What if your vaporizer could be trained to learn how often and how much you vape nicotine, then slowly substitute a non-nicotine product to taper you off the addictive chemical?

That's exactly what Juul is creating. Its new line of vaporizers would connect to a smartphone and apply machine learning to adjust delivery of nicotine and non-nicotine vaporizable material based on the smoker's behavior. The new vaporizers also would use enhanced technology to authenticate users to ensure they are over 21.

The FDA will release its decision in 2021, but some experts, including former FDA commissioner Scott Gottlieb, believe Juul's application is dead on arrival. "It's very clear that Juul can't keep their products out of the hands of kids. It could be that this product can't exist on the market anymore," says Gottlieb.[233]

FOR DISCUSSION

Problem-Solving Perspective

1. What is the underlying problem in this case from Juul CEO K. C. Crosthwaite's perspective?

2. What do you think about Juul's approach for solving the problem? Explain.

3. What do you think the FDA will decide? Why?

Application of Chapter Content

1. What are some barriers to Crosthwaite's ability to utilize rational decision making? Explain.

2. Is the VTA's support of flavored e-cigarettes ethical? Use Figure 7.4 in your response.

3. How is Juul utilizing evidence-based decision making? Explain.

4. How can Juul utilize big data to overcome the challenges it is facing?

5. Are regulatory and law enforcement agencies suffering from groupthink? Why or why not?

Legal/Ethical Challenge

Should Emotional Support Pets Be Treated the Same as Service Animals?

Emotional support dogs help people suffering from anxiety and other psychological disorders during airline travel. Airlines have responsively recognized this issue within the structure of federal guidelines, which have historically been vague on what constituted a service animal. For years, customers could bring their emotional support pets on board for free under certain conditions. First, airlines typically required customers to confirm that the animal had been trained to behave properly in public and to acknowledge their responsibility for the animal's conduct. Customers also needed to provide the airline with 48 hours' notice, a health

and vaccination form from a veterinarian, and a letter from a mental health professional stating the benefit received from the emotional support animal.[234] This policy caused a surge in emotional support animals on flights— from 481,000 in 2016 to 751,000 in 2017.[235]

The rise also contributed to a significant increase in onboard incidents. In fact, airlines reported receiving over 3,000 complaints about animals in 2018, up from 719 five years earlier.[236] The union representing United Airlines' flight attendants said many of these incidents included allergic reactions in other passengers and undesirable animal behaviors like aggressive behavior, biting, urination, and defecation.[237] This all contributed to the airline drawing the line when someone tried to bring a pet called Dexter on a flight leaving Newark in 2018. The airline refused not because Dexter was your typical four-legged emotional support animal, but because Dexter was a peacock—and quite a large one at that.[238]

Incidents such as the one involving Dexter resulted in the Department of Transportation drafting new rules. The rules now define a service animal as "a dog that is individually trained to do work or perform tasks for the benefit of a qualified individual with a disability, including a physical, sensory, psychiatric, intellectual, or other mental disability."[239] Animals that provide emotional support, comfort, and companionship are now treated as pets. The rule also cracks down on passengers' increasing attempts to fly with unusual animals such as ducks, pigs, iguanas, and yes, Dexter the peacock. This means these animals don't have to be allowed to fly inside the main cabin for free.[240]

The department's new rules have been welcomed by the airline industry. Others, however, have not been as supportive. "Emotional support animals provide emotional support and comfort to individuals with psychiatric disabilities and other mental impairments," says attorney Rebecca Wisch. Wisch contends that these animals are not specifically trained to perform tasks for a person who suffers from emotional disabilities, which is a requirement under the new rules. The number of people needing emotional support animals is not insignificant—statistics say that up to one in five Americans has a mental illness, according to *Forbes*. Those against this new policy say that these individuals need emotional support animals to help them get through our traumatic air travel system. Moreover, advocates point to the fact that emotional support animals are recognized as a "reasonable accommodation" for those with disabilities under the Federal Housing Act, so why not by the Department of Transportation?[241]

Service animals, unlike emotion support pets, are protected by the Americans with Disabilities Act (ADA) and can go wherever their owners go. Service dogs receive specific training in order to be certified as such. A seeing eye dog, for example, is a carefully trained dog that serves as a travel tool for persons who have severe visual impairments or are blind. Emotional support animals are not required to go through the same training and certifications, a loophole that *National Geographic* reports some pet owners have abused to avoid the airlines' surcharge of $125 or more for transporting regular pets.[242] A *CBS News* correspondent was actually able to purchase a support animal vest and accompanying mental health professional letter online without her cat even being evaluated. The registration took just five minutes and cost $150.[243]

SOLVING THE CHALLENGE

What would you do if you were an airline CEO?

1. Do not implement the new rules. The airline should allow emotional support pets to travel unrestricted, just as service dogs do. Airlines should not be in the business of categorizing passengers' pets.

2. Implement the new rules. Emotional support pets are not service dogs and should be treated differently. The airline needs to ensure the safety of employees, passengers, and other animals during flight.

3. Invent other options.

Boeing Continuing Case

Learn more about Boeing's planning, strategic, and decision making processes, and how they impacted the development of the 737 MAX.

Assess your ability to apply concepts discussed in Chapters 5 through 7 to the case by going to Connect.

8

Organizational Culture and Structure

Drivers of Strategic Implementation

Kapook2981/iStock/Getty Images

After reading this chapter, you should be able to:

LO 8-1 Explain why managers need to align organizational culture, structure, and HR practices to support strategy.

LO 8-2 Explain how to characterize an organization's culture.

LO 8-3 Describe the process of culture change in an organization.

LO 8-4 Identify the major features of an organization and explain how they are expressed in an organization chart.

LO 8-5 Describe the eight types of organizational structure.

LO 8-6 Explain how to use the career readiness competencies of understanding the business and personal adaptability to better understand and change your level of fit with an organization.

FORECAST   *What's Ahead in This Chapter*

We begin by discussing why organizational culture, organizational structure, and HR practices should be aligned to coordinate employees in the pursuit of an organization's strategic goals. We then describe levels of organizational culture, explain how culture is learned, and classify culture types. We also outline 12 mechanisms that can be used to change organizational culture. We then review seven features of organizations and show how they come together to form an organization chart. We next review eight types of organizational structure. We conclude with a Career Corner that focuses on how to use the career readiness competencies of understanding the business and personal adaptability to assess and better fit with organization's internal context.

How to Get Noticed in a New Job: Fitting into an Organization's Culture in the First 60 Days

If you want to make a great impression and get ahead at work, "you have to be sure to always overdeliver . . . with the emphasis being on *over*," says business columnist and former *Harvard Business Review* editor-in-chief Suzy Welch.[1]

Overdelivering means doing more than what is asked of you—not just doing the report your boss requests, for example, but doing the extra research to provide him or her with something truly impressive. Also, be sure your boss knows how hard you're working. "You want to get people's attention so they know you're great at your job," says one branding expert. "You also want to improve on yourself and continue to climb the corporate ladder."[2]

Among things you should do in the first 60 days are the following.

Be Aware of the Power of First Impressions

People form an opinion about where a relationship is headed within the first few minutes of an interaction.[3] Journalist and author Malcolm Gladwell concluded that "Snap judgments are, first of all, enormously quick: they rely on the thinnest slices of experience . . . they are also unconscious."[4] Counter the possibility of someone else's bias in such a quick judgment by using your career readiness skills of social and emotional intelligence to put your best foot forward.

See How People Behave by Arriving Early and Staying Late

"Many aspects of a company's culture can be subtle and easy to overlook," writes one expert. "Instead, observe everything." Try coming in 30 minutes early and staying a little late just to observe how people operate—where they take their meals, for example. If a meal was part of your interview, you've probably picked up some clues about whether they regularly eat out or are mostly brown-bagging it at their desks.[5]

Network with People and Ask Questions about How the Organization Works

Keep your networking skills at the ready; they represent a career readiness competency. During the first two weeks, get to know a few people and try to have lunch with them. Walk the halls and get to know receptionists, mail room clerks, and office managers, who can help you learn the ropes. Find out how the organization works, how people interact with the boss, and what the corporate culture encourages and discourages. You have a lot to learn, and research says that asking questions makes you appear *more* competent to others. It also improves your relationships and your performance.[6]

Seek Advice Instead of Feedback

Take advantage of opportunities to learn from others in the organization by asking for their advice rather than their feedback.[7] What's the difference? Recent research says people associate the word *feedback* with evaluations of the past, meaning that asking for feedback will get you opinions about how you've performed so far. But hearing the word "advice" makes people think of the future— and asking for it means you're more likely to get actionable tips on what you need to do to be more successful in the future. The career readiness competency of proactive learning orientation will help you here; don't be afraid to ask co-workers for advice as you start learning the job. At the end of 30 days, have a "How am I doing?" meeting with your boss.

Overdeliver

Because performance reviews for new hires generally take place at 60 to 90 days, you need to have accomplished enough—and preferably something big—to show your boss your potential. In other words, do as Welch suggests: overdeliver.

For Discussion How does the preceding advice square with your past experiences in starting a new job? Are there things you wish you could have done differently?

8.1 Aligning Culture, Structure, and Human Resource (HR) Practices to Support Strategy

THE BIG PICTURE

The study of organizing, the second of the four functions in the management process, begins with the study of organizational culture and structure, which managers use along with HR practices to implement strategy. Organizational culture consists of the set of shared, taken-for-granted implicit assumptions that a group holds in the workplace. Organizational structure describes who reports to whom and who does what.

LO 8-1

Explain why managers need to align organizational culture, structure, and HR practices to support strategy.

As you learned in Chapter 6, *strategy* consists of the large-scale action plans that reflect the organization's vision and are used to set the direction for the organization, and *strategic implementation* is all about executing strategy. In this section we explain why successful implementation of a firm's strategies is only possible when leaders align the right organizational culture, structure, and HR practices to support strategy.

How an Organization's Culture, Structure, and HR Practices Support Strategic Implementation

Strategic implementation is a difficult job. In fact, managers consistently rank the ability to successfully implement strategy as their number one concern, and the majority of strategic initiatives fail because of flawed execution.[8] Experts suggest the reason even the most well-crafted strategies break down is that they are not infused into organizations' daily activities. Leaders therefore need to configure their firms' operations and resources in ways that support firm strategies.[9]

Figure 8.1 shows that an organization's performance (i.e., its ability to execute strategy) depends on the extent to which three factors—organizational culture, organizational structure, and HR practices—work together to enable its strategy. Leaders are the main drivers of this alignment. Figure 8.1 also reveals that the alignment across these factors impacts group and social processes (discussed in Chapters 13 and 15), individual work attitudes and behaviors (discussed in Chapters 11 and 12), and finally overall organizational performance.[10]

Let's use the metaphor of a rope to visualize how culture, structure, and HR practices jointly enable strategy. A rope gets its strength from many small strands that are tightly woven together. When the strands unravel and separate from one another, the rope weakens significantly and is more likely to break. Organizations rely on closely entwined "strands" of culture, structure, and HR practices in order to achieve strategic objectives. Let's explore each of these elements in more detail.

Organizational Culture: The Shared Assumptions That Affect How Work Gets Done

We described the concept of *culture* in Chapter 4 on global management as "the shared set of beliefs, values, knowledge, and patterns of behavior common to a group of people." Here we are talking about a specific kind of culture called an *organizational culture*.

> You can think of an organization's culture, structure, and HR practices as three strands in a single rope. These strands must be tightly woven together to drive successful strategic execution. kyoshino/ Getty Images

According to organizational psychologist Edgar Schein, ==organizational culture==, sometimes called ==corporate culture==, **is defined as the set of shared, taken-for-granted implicit assumptions that a group holds and that determines how it perceives, thinks about, and reacts to its various environments.**[11] Organizational culture helps employees understand why the organization does what it does and how it intends to accomplish its long-term goals. In other words, culture is the "social glue" that binds members of the organization together through shared understanding. It is helpful to think of an organization's culture as its unique "personality" that manifests in a set of shared beliefs and values. Organizational culture is passed on to new employees by way of socialization and mentoring, and it significantly affects work outcomes at all levels.[12]

Organizational culture is one of the three factors shown in Figure 8.1 that influences a firm's performance.[13] It is important to remember that there is no universal "right" culture. Instead, the ideal culture for a particular organization is the one that best supports its chosen strategy.[14] Leaders are responsible for carefully crafting and managing their cultures to enable successful execution of their firms' strategies.[15] For example, Satya Nadella, Microsoft CEO, recently said, "What I realize more than ever is that my job is curation of our culture. If you don't focus on creating a culture that allows people to do their best work, then you've created nothing."[16]

Southwest Airlines is an example of a company with a culture that supports its strategy.

Southwest Example: The culture at Southwest Airlines is designed to support the airline's cost-leadership strategy. Southwest aims to be the most productive, reliable, and efficient airline in the world.[17] Employees at Southwest have total clarity about their roles—they know what is important in their jobs and what is not. Slogans, pictures, and repetitions of the company's vision, values, and mission adorn the physical environment, and many of these representations remind employees about what makes them and the airline special and unique. Workers also display a strong sense of ownership in and commitment to the company and its low-cost strategy. One Southwest employee recounted the story of being teased by coworkers during his first few months with the company because of his "reckless" use of paper clips and failure to print on both sides of a sheet of paper. He learned quickly that at Southwest, even an unnecessary paper clip is seen as something that prevents the company from keeping costs as low as possible, and employees hold each other accountable for doing their part to help the airline accomplish its strategy.[18]

We thoroughly discuss organizational culture in Sections 8.2 and 8.3.

FIGURE 8.1

How organizational culture, organizational structure, and human resource practices align to support strategic implementation

Source: Figure based in part on C. Ostroff, A. J. Kinicki, and R. S. Muhammad, "Organizational Culture and Climate," Handbook of Psychology, Volume 12: Industrial and Organizational Psychology, 2nd ed. (Hoboken, NJ: John Wiley & Sons, 2013), Chapter 24, pp. 643–676.

Corporate Strategy

Alignment

Organizational culture

Human resource practices

Organizational structure

Leadership

Group and social processes

Work attitudes and behaviors

Overall performance

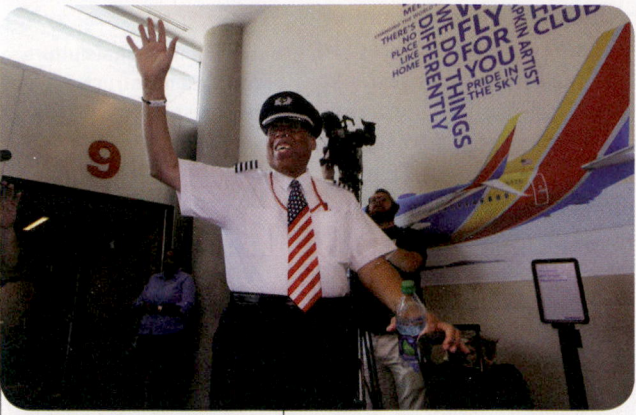

Southwest Airlines' employees find reminders of company culture all around them. These reminders include phrases painted on the company's walls, such as those visible in the background of this photo of Captain Louis Freeman boarding his last flight before retiring from a 36-year career as a pilot for the airline. LM Otero/AP Images

Organizational Structure: Who Reports to Whom and Who Does What

Organizational structure is a formal system of task and reporting relationships that coordinates and motivates an organization's members so that they can work together to achieve the organization's goals. As we describe in Section 8.5, organizational structure is concerned with who reports to whom and who specializes in what work.

Organizational structure is another factor that impacts a firm's ability to execute strategy.[19] Just as there is not one best organizational culture, there is no single organizational structure that is superior to others. Leaders are encouraged to structure their organizations in ways that are most conducive to accomplishing strategic goals.[20] A well-designed organizational structure encourages the relationships, attitudes, and behaviors needed to execute a particular strategy.[21]

Procter & Gamble (P&G) is an example of a company with a structure that supports its strategy.

P&G Example: P&G owns some of the most recognizable consumer product brands in the world, including Bounty, Pampers, Tide, and Crest. Part of P&G's purpose is to "provide branded products and services of superior quality and value that improve the lives of the world's consumers, now and for generations to come."[22] The company pursues growth through innovation and differentiation. Specifically, P&G continues to capture market share by providing innovative and superior quality products.[23] P&G is structured into six sector business units (SBUs): (1) fabric and home care, (2) baby and feminine care, (3) family care and new ventures, (4) grooming, (5) health care, and (6) beauty. The CEO of each unit has authority over both sales and products for the unit.[24] This structure empowers P&G's business units with the agility to innovate at speeds that are often impossible for large corporations.[25]

HR Practices: How the Organization Manages Its Talent

Human resource practices consist of all of the activities an organization uses to manage its human capital, including staffing, appraising, training and development, and compensation.

HR practices are the third key factor influencing a firm's ability to execute strategy. These practices focus on ensuring that employees have the necessary skills, motivation, and opportunities to contribute to the organization's unique strategic goals.[26]

HR practices at In-N-Out. CEO Lynsi Snyder hugs a long-time team member at the opening of one of In-N-Out Burger's new locations. Snyder was recently named one of the highest rated CEOs in the country, with employees sharing that they believe the senior leadership team genuinely cares about its people. Leonard Ortiz/ Getty Images

Different organizations take varied approaches to managing human capital, and leaders should deploy the HR practices that are most likely to facilitate the social processes, attitudes, and behaviors necessary for successful strategic implementation.[27] For example, a firm with an innovation strategy is likely to benefit from reward systems that incentivize risk taking and from selection systems that prioritize hiring outside candidates with new perspectives over promoting existing employees. But practices that reward efficiency and prioritize internal hiring and training would likely be a better fit for a firm pursuing low-cost leadership.[28]

In-N-Out Burger is an example of a company with HR practices that support its strategy.

In-N-Out Burger Example: At In-N-Out Burger, the mission is simple—"serve only the highest quality product, prepare it in a clean and sparkling environment, and serve it in a warm and friendly manner."[29] The restaurant has a small menu, uses farm fresh ingredients, maintains impeccably clean store locations, and has a "no-franchise" policy—all of which ensure that customers receive consistently high-quality food that looks good, tastes delicious, and is served in an enjoyable atmosphere.[30] The company is so serious about quality and customer satisfaction that when the sandwich buns delivered to its Texas-based stores were not up to par, it halted operations at all 37 locations in the state until the problem was fixed. The HR practices at In-N-Out are different than what one would expect in the fast-food industry, and they are a key tool the company uses to maintain its high standards. Restaurant managers' salaries can reach up to $160,000 a year, new associates start at $13.00 per hour, and employee benefits include flexible scheduling, 401(k) options, paid vacation time, free meals, and opportunities for extensive training.[31] These HR practices have translated into extremely low turnover rates in comparison to other industry players and a highly loyal and satisfied workforce.

Leadership Creates Alignment among Culture, Structure, and HR Practices

We have noted several times that an organization's culture, structure, and HR practices do not operate as isolated individual systems. Rather, these factors exert influence on one another, and leaders must align them so that they work in concert to support and reinforce firm strategy.[32] Good leaders are like orchestra conductors. Rather than integrating the sounds of many instruments into a meaningful whole, leaders understand how culture, structure, and HR practices operate and know how to leverage them to focus employees on the organization's broad strategic goals.[33] UPS is a good illustration of this perspective.

UPS Example: UPS clearly understood the importance of leadership when the company named its new CEO, Carol Tomé, in 2020. In her time as Home Depot's CFO, Tomé was credited with increasing shareholder value by 450% and making the company one of the highest-performing major retail organizations in the United States. Multiple UPS executives expressed their excitement with the choice because of Tomé's deep knowledge of the culture, structure, employees, and strategy at UPS. Former UPS CEO David Abney said, "I am extremely pleased for Carol and know she is the best choice to lead the company. She understands UPS's culture and values, is a strategic leader and possesses a customer-first mindset."[34] William Johnson, UPS lead independent director, said, "Carol is one of the most respected and talented leaders in corporate America and has a proven track record of driving growth at a global organization, maximizing shareholder value, developing talent and successfully executing against strategic priorities."[35]

Leading for alignment. UPS CEO Carol Tomé is known for her ability to align the key organizational elements that drive successful strategic implementation. Sally Montana/Redux Pictures

Leadership throughout the organization—not just in the C-suite—is key in aligning culture, structure, and HR practices.[36] Middle and first-line managers are critical in sustaining connections between culture, structure, and HR practices and connecting these factors to company strategy. This is because middle and first-line managers are on the ground and work face-to-face with employees on a regular basis. These managers can explain how workers' daily tasks link to broad organizational goals and can clarify the company's priorities and the logic behind its strategic choices.[37] Read the Example box to learn about a company that aligns its culture, structure, and HR practices to support its strategy. ●

Patagonia is a purpose-driven outdoor apparel company. Its mission statement is simple— "Patagonia is in business to save our home planet." The company has annual revenues of approximately $1 billion and has donated 1% of its sales to environmental causes since 1985. Ninety-one percent of its 3,000 employees describe it as a "great place to work," and corporate turnover is an astoundingly low 4%.[38]

Patagonia uses a growth strategy to create shared value through sustainable innovation. According to former CEO Rose Marcario, "I don't think it's a conflict of interest to say that you can make money, and have a prosperous and successful business, and you can also do good in the world."[39] Let's take a look at how Patagonia's strategy is supported by the alignment of its culture, structure, and HR practices.

Patagonia's Culture

Patagonia's culture is collaborative, socially conscious, and relaxed, and current and former employees describe it with words like "unique," "balance," "team," "care," and "environmental."[40]

Patagonia takes proactive measures to discourage hierarchy and the company encourages commitment, trust, and teamwork among employees. The office environment is completely open—even managers don't have their own offices. There also are outdoor workspaces, yoga studios, company bicycles, and common areas for groups to relax and collaborate.[41]

Patagonia's Structure

Patagonia has a flat organizational structure. According to Chief HR Officer Dean Carter, "There's just no reverence for reporting relationships or traditional hierarchies. As a matter of fact, we like breaking them because, often, the best ideas aren't from the manager; they're from the person whose hands are dirty doing the real work." The company hires people who are independent and expects all of its workers to speak up and be comfortable communicating directly with anyone else in the organization, including founder and chairman Yvon Chouinard.[42]

Alignment at Patagonia. Patagonia's culture, structure, and HR practices encourage employees to enjoy life and to take good care of themselves, their families, and each other. Philippe Petit/Getty Images

Patagonia's HR Practices

Dean Carter says, "At Patagonia, our view is that people are resources to steward, not resources for extraction and depletion. . . . So I'm stewarding the employee population as if I'm going to employ them for the next 100 years. I want to take good care of their children, because 100 years from now I might be employing their children or their grandchildren."[43]

Patagonia's employees receive:

- 2 paid months per year to intern with environmental groups.

- Family-focused support including on-site child care and paid parental leave.

- Bail money—for any employee who is arrested for a peaceful environmental protest.

- Flexibility in the form of 3-day weekends every other week and freedom to pursue their passions through the company's "Let My People Go Surfing Flex-time Policy."[44]

Patagonia also takes innovative approaches to hiring and performance management. Open positions often remain unfilled for up to a year as the company searches for the right person, and the company recently eliminated its traditional performance review system because it caused employees stress and took up unnecessary amounts of their time. Now, workers can opt-in to a developmental HR tool that is customized for the needs of individual workers and their managers. The updated system is based on regenerative agriculture principles that advocate for leaving soil in better shape after you harvest its crops, rather than depleting it and moving on to another plot of land.[45]

Patagonia's Leadership

Patagonia knows that simultaneously pursuing high financial performance and low environmental impact is not easy.[46] Leaders at all levels are actively involved in maintaining focus and aligning the company's resources to support its strategy:[47]

- At the top of the organization, Rose Marcario further amplified Patagonia's environmental and social commitments throughout the past decade. Marcario took more active political stances and announced that Patagonia would no longer create customized apparel for corporate clients whose businesses did not include sustainability as a core part of their mission.

- Board members and executives are responsible for "picking mountains." These broad strategic conversations are centered on whether and how initiatives align with the company's purpose, mission, and sustainable innovation strategy.

- Managers act as mentors, coaches, and supportive resources whose purpose is to align employees' work around points on these "mountains" and the company's strategic priorities.

YOUR CALL

What elements of structure, strategy, and culture do you see as the key drivers of Patagonia's successful strategic implementation?

8.2 What Kind of Organizational Culture Will You Be Operating In?

THE BIG PICTURE

Organizational culture appears in three levels: observable artifacts, espoused values, and basic assumptions. Culture is transmitted to employees through symbols, stories, heroes, rites and rituals, and organizational socialization. Cultures can be classified into four types: clan, adhocracy, market, and hierarchy.

"What was the last costume you wore?" the job interviewer asks you. "On a scale of 1 to 10, how weird are you?" "What would you do in the event of a zombie apocalypse?" "Would you rather be rich or would you rather be a king?"

These are the favorite interview questions of some of the world's most successful CEOs. For you as a job applicant, these questions might seem to have neither a connection with your performance in previous jobs, nor a "right" answer. But according to Harold Hughes, CEO of Bandwagon—a blockchain-based analytics company—"What's more important is the reasoning." The explanations you use to answer seemingly outlandish questions can tell a company a great deal about what you have experienced, who you are, and how you think.[48]

LO 8-2

Explain how to characterize an organization's culture.

Some organizational leaders use unique interview questions to assess potential person-organization fit. Bandwagon CEO Harold Hughes gets a strong sense of how interviewees think and what motivates them by listening to the reasoning behind their responses to these types of questions. BandwagonFanClub Inc.

Interviewers use questions like these to find out how well you will *fit in* with the organization. This is called <mark>person-organization (P–O) fit,</mark> and it reflects the extent to which your personality and values match the climate and culture in an organization.[49]

A big part of being successful in a particular job is learning to understand and fit in with the organization's culture.[50] The culture consists not only of the slightly quirky personalities you encounter but also all of an organization's normal way of doing business. After completing this section, you will be able to assess your level of fit with an organization.

The Three Levels of Organizational Culture

Organizational culture is present at three levels:[51]

1. Observable artifacts
2. Espoused values
3. Basic assumptions

Each level varies in terms of outward visibility and resistance to change (level 1 is most visible and least resistant to change, and level 3 is least visible and most resistant to change), and each level influences another level. Management scholars often use an iceberg to visualize organizational culture (*see Figure 8.2*). This is because the portion of an iceberg that we can easily see represents only a small portion of the whole thing. Most of an iceberg is under the water, just like a large part of an organization's culture lies beneath the surface. In order to understand an organization's culture, you need to "see" or understand the entire culture, not just the parts of it that you can immediately assess. Let's discuss each level of culture.

Gusto's observable artifacts. How many observable artifacts of Gusto's laid-back culture can you find in this photo? For starters, check out co-founder Josh Reeves' socks and the built-in employee shoe cubby beside him. What else do you see here that provides a glimpse into Gusto's culture? Ramin Rahimian/Redux Pictures

Level 1: Observable Artifacts—Physical Manifestations of Culture   We begin our discussion of organizational culture by looking at the top of the iceberg. Figure 8.2 shows that at the most visible level, organizational culture is expressed in *observable artifacts*—physical manifestations such as manner of dress, awards, myths and stories about the company, rituals and ceremonies, decorations, as well as visible behavior exhibited by managers and employees.

Gusto Example: Gusto provides cloud-based HR solutions for more than 100,000 companies in the United States and is on a mission to make work "meaningful for everyone, everywhere." Co-founders Josh Reeves, Edward Kim, and Tomer London want their offices to feel inviting and comfortable, so they have a "no shoes" policy and build walls of shoe cubbies into the entrances of each location. Employees are encouraged to wear fun socks, and the

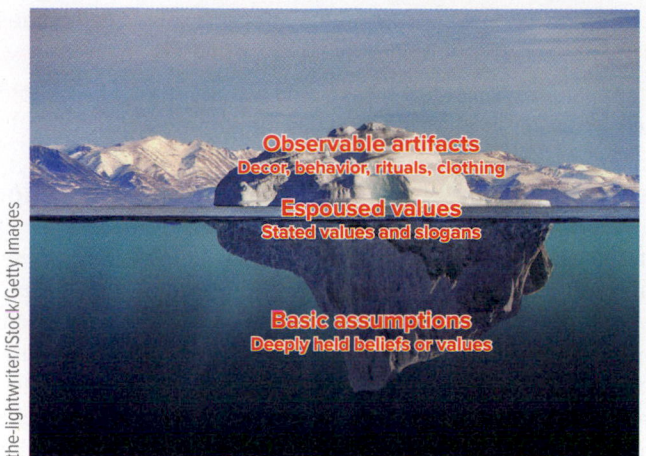

the-lightwriter/iStock/Getty Images

FIGURE 8.2
Levels of organizational culture

co-founders say the policy makes Gusto employees feel at home while they work. If you ever decide to visit a Gusto office, you'll have to remove your shoes, too! But don't worry—the company will provide funky Gusto socks and spa sandals to keep you cozy. [52]

Observable artifacts are the easiest element of culture to influence. Changing artifacts can start with something as simple as changing a dress code or replacing one wall decoration with another.

Level 2: Espoused Values—Explicitly Stated Values and Norms   As you can see in Figure 8.2, the second level of the iceberg is deeper and less visible than the first. This is where we find an organization's **espoused values—the explicitly stated values and norms preferred by an organization, as may be put forth by the firm's founders or top managers.** You can usually find evidence of an organization's espoused values by exploring its website for mission, vision, and values statements.

Goldman Sachs Example: Citing a lack of diversity on corporate boards of directors, Goldman Sachs—a leading global investment bank—recently announced that it would no longer underwrite IPOs for companies that don't have at least one "diverse" board member. The company offered to help connect firms with potential board candidates from underrepresented groups. This decision is in line with the company's core values of diversity, teamwork, and service excellence. According to CEO David Solomon, "This is an example of our saying, 'How can we do something that we think is right and helps moves the market forward?'"[53]

Although managers hope the values they espouse will directly influence employee behavior, employees don't always "walk the talk," and frequently they are influenced more by **enacted values—the values and norms actually exhibited in the organization.**[54] Consider the example of Comcast:

Comcast Example: Comcast has repeatedly landed on lists of America's most hated companies in recent years due to issues such as unauthorized charges on customers' bills and dismal customer care. There have even been instances of service representatives using profanity and behaving aggressively toward customers.[55] These experiences contradicted the company's espoused values of treating customers with integrity, fairness, and respect, and in 2015 Comcast got serious about overhauling its customer service to better align itself with the values it claimed to live by.[56] The company focused on decreasing the frequency of service calls and now handles almost 80% of customer issues through digital platforms that are faster and more efficient. Comcast also added options for customers to troubleshoot problems and schedule service visits through its app. These efforts drastically reduced the time it took for Comcast to connect with customers and resolve their issues, and by 2019 the company's name had fallen off of many "most hated" lists.[57]

It is more challenging to change espoused values than observable artifacts, but espoused values are easier to change than basic assumptions.

Level 3: Basic Assumptions—Core Values of the Organization

Figure 8.2 demonstrates that a substantial portion of an organization's culture exists at such a deep level that it is nearly impossible to grasp or articulate. *Basic assumptions* represent the unobservable yet core values of an organization's culture that are often taken for granted. The values at this level have a profound effect on employee behaviors because they have informed every decision in the organization's past and are thus entwined with its identity. For this same reason, basic assumptions are very difficult to change. Industry expert Karen Niovitch Davis warns that basic assumptions, left unchecked, can be a destructive force. According to Davis, "Old assumptions die hard if they're not examined and addressed. Try not to ignore the unwritten rules. It's terrible to find out about them after an employee crossed a line because they thought it was what you wanted."[58] Consider the example of Facebook and its struggle to change its culture.

Facebook Example: Facebook espouses five core values on its website: (1) be bold, (2) focus on impact, (3) move fast, (4) be open, and (5) build social value.[59] But according to Notre Dame ethics professor Joseph Holt, the company's deeply embedded basic assumptions are closer to (1) be reckless, (2) focus on making as much money as possible, (3) never let noneconomic concerns (like data privacy) get in the way of economic opportunities, (4) be no more open than required, and (5) accept bringing people closer together as merely a nice plus.[60] Facebook was once considered one of the best workplaces in the world, but former employees have begun to paint a picture of a culture that grew to actively discourage dissent, pressure workers to show unquestioning loyalty or risk permanent damage to their careers, and embrace the company culture above all else.[61] Many believe Facebook's underlying assumptions are the reason it ignored and even concealed serious concerns about data security and privacy.[62] Did you know that Facebook's original #3 core value was actually "move fast and break things"? It was this entrepreneurial spirit that drove the company's meteoric rise to the top. But a culture focused on growth at all costs without regard for the rules is no longer suitable for the company now that it is responsible for safeguarding the data of almost 2.5 billion users, and it seems Facebook continues to struggle to make any meaningful cultural improvements.[63]

How Employees Learn Culture: Symbols, Stories, Heroes, Rites and Rituals, and Organizational Socialization

Culture is transmitted to employees in several ways, most often through such means as (1) *symbols*, (2) *stories*, (3) *heroes*, (4) *rites and rituals*, and (5) *organizational socialization*.[64]

1. Symbols

A **symbol** is an object or action that represents an idea or quality. With respect to culture, symbols are artifacts used to convey an organization's most important values. Here are two examples of organizational culture symbols:

Nike Example: The Nike "swoosh" is designed to represent the wings of Nike—the Greek goddess of victory. It also resembles a check mark, a shape people naturally associate with positivity.

Intuit Example: The idea that led to Intuit started at married couple Scott Cook and Signe Ostby's kitchen table, where they sat and wondered if there might be a better way to balance their checkbook. Thirty-seven years later, that table is prominently displayed (and still used for brainstorming new ideas) at Intuit's California headquarters.[65]

2. Stories   A <mark>story</mark> is a narrative based on true events, which is repeated—and sometimes embellished upon—to emphasize a particular value. Stories are oral histories that are told and retold by members about incidents in the organization's history. Consider Lever.

Using stories to communicate culture. Leaders such as Lever CEO Sarah Nahm use stories as powerful tools for teaching new employees about an organization's culture. Sam Barnes/Getty Images

> **Lever Example:** Lever is a cloud-based recruiting software firm that helps companies like Mercedes-Benz, Netflix, Zoom, and Spotify to grow their workforces. CEO Sarah Nahm founded Lever in 2012 and spent the next two years as the only woman in the company. Now, 50% of Lever's 130+ employees are female, 40% are non-white, and the board has a fairly even gender distribution. Nahm recalls the difficulties she faced over the years as she worked to build an inclusive culture. Her experience growing the diversity of Lever's sales team taught her and others in the company about the power of stories for driving culture. She recalls, "There was one woman closing business as an account executive. We went to her and asked her what she would like to see done about that. She ultimately became an inspiring success. That experience taught us the power of storytelling to launch D&I [diversity and inclusion] initiatives. The first thing we did was tell her story. We published it to all of Lever's different channels. Organically, it became a powerful way for us to signal our intention to candidates we were talking to in our talent pool, women out there who didn't know about Lever and to our own employees." Lever has since been named one of *Fortune*'s top 50 best workplaces in technology.[66]

3. Heroes   A <mark>hero</mark> is a person whose accomplishments embody the values of the organization. Often, heroes are people who have endured great sacrifice for the organization's benefit. Heroes can emerge in single organizations or more broad social causes, as was the case when 16-year-old Greta Thunberg became the face of the global youth climate change movement.

> **Greta Thunberg Example:** Thunberg inspired a week-long school strike that brought together 6 million people around the world in a unified plea for climate change legislation. She has addressed numerous groups, including the U.N. Climate Action Summit and the U.S. Congress. In 2019 Thunberg became the youngest ever *Time Magazine* Person of the Year. "I'd like to tell my grandchildren that we did everything we could," she said in an interview for the magazine, adding "and we did it for them and for the generations to come."[67]

4. Rites and Rituals   <mark>Rites and rituals</mark> are the activities and ceremonies, planned and unplanned, that celebrate important occasions and accomplishments in the organization's life. Rituals transform ordinary movements into meaningful and symbolic practices. Their repetitive and predictable patterns comfort us and signal to us that we are a part of something bigger.[68] Military units and sports teams have long known the value of using ceremonies to hand out decorations and awards, but many companies have rites and rituals as well. Warby Parker and Starbucks are two examples.

> **Warby Parker Example:** Warby Parker gives every new employee two things: (1) a copy of the book *Dharma Bums,* because the company's name is derived from two of its characters, and (2) fresh pretzels from Martin's handmade pretzel company, a favorite of the company's founders that is located just a few blocks from Warby Parker's first offices.[69]

> **Starbucks Example:** Starbucks uses the psychology of rituals in its physical store layouts to keep customers coming back. Specifically, every Starbucks location has the same general flow and queueing pattern. The company also designs its digital platforms with repetitive principles. As you learned above, the familiarity and repetition you experience when you walk into a Starbucks café or open the app to order online might be the subconscious reason you decide to order Starbucks again a few days later.[70]

5. Organizational Socialization

Organizational socialization is defined as the process by which people learn the values, norms, and required behaviors that permit them to participate as members of an organization.[71] Converting from an outsider to an organizational insider may take weeks or even years, and employees form critical relationships and understandings about the organization during the process.[72] Organizational socialization occurs in three phases, researcher Daniel Feldman suggests—before you are hired, when you are first taken on, and when you have been employed a while and are adjusting to the job.[73]

The first phase *(anticipatory socialization phase)* occurs before you join the organization. In this phase you learn—from career advisors, web sources, or current employees—about the organization's needs and values and how your own needs, values, and skills might fit in. The second phase *(encounter phase)* takes place when you are first hired. In this phase you begin to learn what the organization is really like and how you might need to adjust your expectations. The company may help to advance this socialization process through various familiarization programs (known as "onboarding"). The third phase *(change and acquisition phase)* comes about once you have developed a strong sense of your work role. In this phase you begin to fine-tune necessary skills and tasks and better adjust to your work group's values and norms. The company may advance this phase of socialization through goal setting, incentives, employee feedback, continued support, and ceremonies (e.g., "graduation") that celebrate completion of the process.

NYU Example: New hires at New York University are partnered with a buddy during their first two months "to help welcome employees and reaffirm their decision to join NYU" as well as to provide a reliable contact for speedy answers on work practices and organizational culture. Among other characteristics, "the buddy should have a positive outlook on his/her work and use that perspective to help build self-confidence and loyalty in the new employee. The buddy should lead by example."[74]

Four Types of Organizational Culture: Clan, Adhocracy, Market, and Hierarchy

The *competing values framework* (CVF) provides a practical way for managers to understand, measure, and change organizational culture. The CVF, which has been validated by extensive research involving 1,100 companies, classifies organizational cultures into four types: (1) clan, (2) adhocracy, (3) market, and (4) hierarchy, as we'll explain.[75] *(See Figure 8.3.)*

Research leading to the development of the CVF found that organizational effectiveness varied along two dimensions:

- **The horizontal dimension—inward or outward focus?** This dimension expresses the extent to which an organization focuses its attention and efforts inward on internal dynamics and employees ("internal focus and integration") versus outward on its external environment and its customers and shareholders ("external focus and differentiation").

- **The vertical dimension—flexibility or stability?** This dimension expresses the extent to which an organization prefers decentralized decision making (flexibility and discretion) versus centralized authority (stability and control).

Combining these two dimensions creates the four types of organizational culture based on different core values—(1) clan culture, (2) adhocracy culture, (3) market culture, and (4) hierarchy culture.

Each culture type has different characteristics, and while one type tends to dominate in any given organization, it is the mix of types that creates competitive advantage. We begin our discussion of culture types in the upper-left quadrant of the CVF.

FIGURE 8.3

Competing values framework

Source: Adapted from K. S. Cameron, R. E. Quinn, J. Degraff, and A. V. Thakor, Competing Values Leadership *(Northampton, MA: Edward Elgar, 2006), p. 32.*

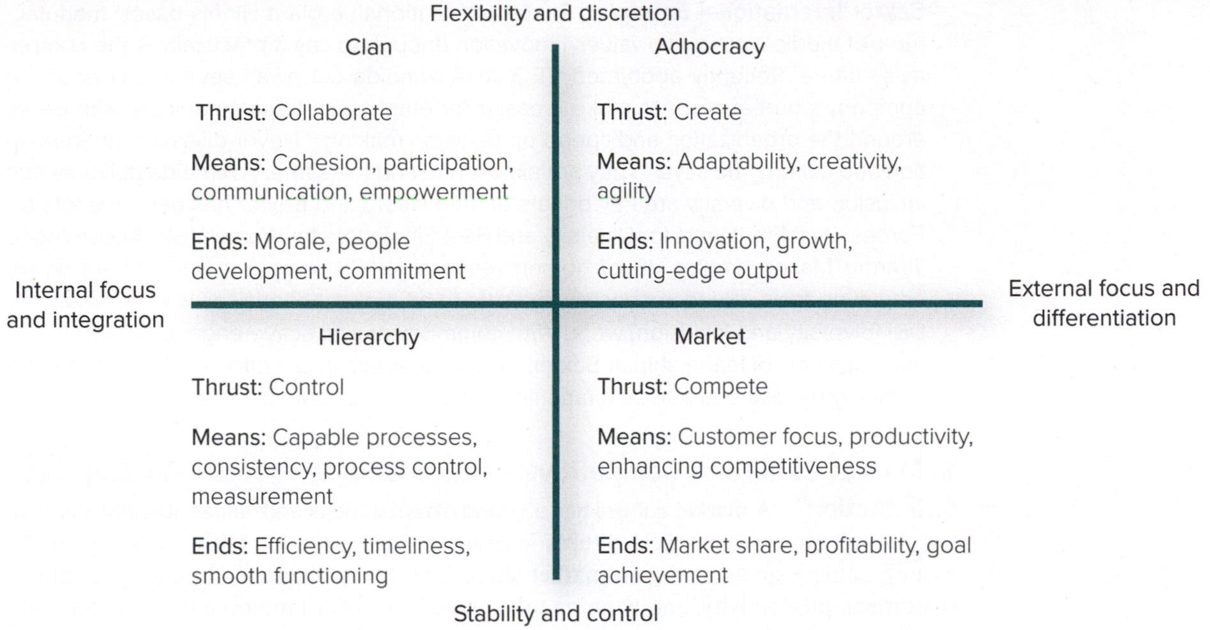

Flexibility and discretion

Clan   Adhocracy

Thrust: Collaborate   **Thrust:** Create

Means: Cohesion, participation,   **Means:** Adaptability, creativity,
communication, empowerment   agility

Ends: Morale, people   **Ends:** Innovation, growth,
development, commitment   cutting-edge output

Internal focus   External focus and
and integration   differentiation

Hierarchy   Market

Thrust: Control   **Thrust:** Compete

Means: Capable processes,   **Means:** Customer focus, productivity,
consistency, process control,   enhancing competitiveness
measurement

Ends: Efficiency, timeliness,   **Ends:** Market share, profitability, goal
smooth functioning   achievement

Stability and control

1. Clan Culture: An Employee-Focused Culture Valuing Flexibility, Not Stability

A **clan culture** has an internal focus and values flexibility rather than stability and control. You can see from Figure 8.3 that organizations with clan cultures want their employees to have a strong sense of identification with and commitment to the organization, as well as a feeling of "family." Clan cultures use collaboration to accomplish this goal. Companies with a clan culture are likely to devote considerable resources to training and developing their employees, and they view customers as collaborative partners. In clan cultures, employee behaviors are governed by strong norms rather than formal rules and authority figures.[76]

> **Wegmans Example:** Wegmans is a private, family-owned supermarket chain with approximately 50,000 employees. The company's values include the following statements:
>
> - We **care** about the well-being and success of every person.
> - We **respect** and listen to our people.
> - We **empower** our people to make decisions that improve their work and benefit our customers and our company.[77]
>
> Wegmans exhibits a clan culture. Former employees use language such as "the Wegmans family," and workers are known to spend entire careers working in Wegmans stores.[78] The company spends $50 million annually on employee training and development and its high levels of employee engagement are credited with driving its $9 billion+ annual revenues.[79] Wegmans has earned a spot on *Fortune*'s Best Companies to Work For list for 23 consecutive years, ranking #3 in 2020. "We are so grateful for our dedicated employees who have made us a part of this list . . ." said President and CEO Colleen Wegman, adding "Our people make shopping and working at Wegmans a truly special experience every day."[80]

2. Adhocracy Culture: A Risk-Taking Culture Valuing Flexibility

An **adhocracy culture** has an external focus and values flexibility. Creation of new and innovative products and services is the strategic thrust of this culture. Adhocracies are set up to encourage employees to be creative, adaptable, and quick to respond to changes. Employees in adhocracy cultures are encouraged to take risks and experiment with new ways of getting things done. Adhocracy cultures are well suited for start-up companies, firms in industries undergoing constant change, and firms in mature industries that are in need of innovation to enhance growth.

Baxter International Example: Baxter International, a giant Illinois-based manufacturer of medical products, values innovation enough to say it practically *is* the company's culture. Recently appointed CEO José Almeida cut away several layers of the company's bureaucracy to make it easier for employees to communicate with peers around the organization and speed up decision making. "Never disassociate innovation and culture," he says. "They are almost one and the same."[81] Almeida believes that inclusion and diversity are key drivers of innovation, and Baxter has earned spots on *Forbes*' Best Employers for Diversity and Best Employers for Women lists. According to Jeanne Mason, senior VP of human resources, "Creating a culture where every employee feels valued, respected and safe to be their authentic self is what drives our D&I [diversity and inclusion] work. With commitment and active engagement from the highest levels of leadership at Baxter, we are steadfast in our efforts to make our company a great place to pursue a meaningful career for people of all backgrounds."[82]

3. Market Culture: A Competitive Culture Valuing Profits over Employee Satisfaction   A market culture has a strong external focus and values stability and control. Companies with market cultures leverage employees' competitive drives to make money, achieve goals, and gain market share for the organization. In market cultures, customers, productivity, and winning take precedence over employee development and satisfaction. Employees in market cultures are expected to work hard, proactively react, and deliver quality work on time; those who deliver results are rewarded.

Tyson Foods Example: Tyson Foods is the world's second largest producer of chicken, beef, and pork, and it posted 2019 sales of $42.4 billion. Tyson Foods has a market culture focused on results, productivity, and profitability, and the company delivered shareholder returns of 695% between 2009 and 2019.[83] During a recent event at the New York Stock Exchange, Chairman John Tyson and CEO Noel White highlighted the company's expansion into new markets, strong diversified portfolio, and successful execution of long-term growth strategy.[84] Tyson Foods sold its 6.5% share in the plant-based protein company Beyond Meat in April 2019 and unveiled its own brand—Raised & Rooted—two months later. White explained, "We already had the infrastructure in place, so it's a fairly minimal investment on our behalf to be able to scale very quickly . . . so based on what the purchase price likely would have been, it was much more feasible for us to just develop all the further capabilities ourselves."[85] According to CFO Steward Glendinning, "We generate a lot of cash, and we focus on getting the highest returns on that money," adding, "We have a disciplined approach to mergers and acquisitions, and we're a team that's focused on returns greater than our cost of capital."[86]

4. Hierarchy Culture: A Structured Culture Valuing Stability and Effectiveness   A hierarchy culture has an internal focus and values stability and control over flexibility. Companies with this kind of culture implement various control mechanisms that help the company maintain a certain level of performance and efficiency according to a schedule. Hierarchical cultures are apt to have a formalized, structured work environment and a lot of rules. At the extreme, such cultures may seem like the company cares more about efficiency and standardization than it does its people.

McDonald's Example: McDonald's serves more than 70 million customers each day and operates in just about every country in the world. The company manages operations at this scale through routinization, standardization, division of labor, and formal accountability hierarchies.[87] McDonald's workers went on strike in November 2019, citing an imbalance of power and unfair treatment at the company. The workers called for a fair wage and basic dignity.[88] In a recent interview, McDonald's workers said anonymously what they wished they could say to their managers. They asked for better training, kinder treatment, and more support from management. Said one employee, "Treat employees like people, not numbers." Another worker said that hard work is recognized but being good at your job usually means you'll be expected to pick up others' slack in the interest of speed and efficiency.[89]

Are you curious about the type of culture that exists in a current or past employer? Do you wonder whether this culture is best suited to help the company achieve its strategic goals? The following self-assessment allows you to consider these questions.

SELF-ASSESSMENT 8.1

What Is the Organizational Culture at My Current Employer?

Please be prepared to answer these questions if your instructor has assigned Self-Assessment 8.1 in Connect.

1. How would you describe the organizational culture?
2. Do you think this type of culture is best suited to help the company achieve its strategic goals? Explain.

The Importance of Culture

Many people believe culture powerfully shapes an organization's long-term success by enhancing its systems (such as leadership and HR practices, discussed in Section 8.1) and influencing its important outcomes at various levels—and research supports this belief.[90] Recently, a team of scholars tested this hypothesis with a meta-analysis (a statistical procedure combining data from multiple studies) of more than 38,000 organizational units—either organizations as a whole or departments in different organizations—and 616,000 individuals.[91] The results are shown in Figure 8.4.

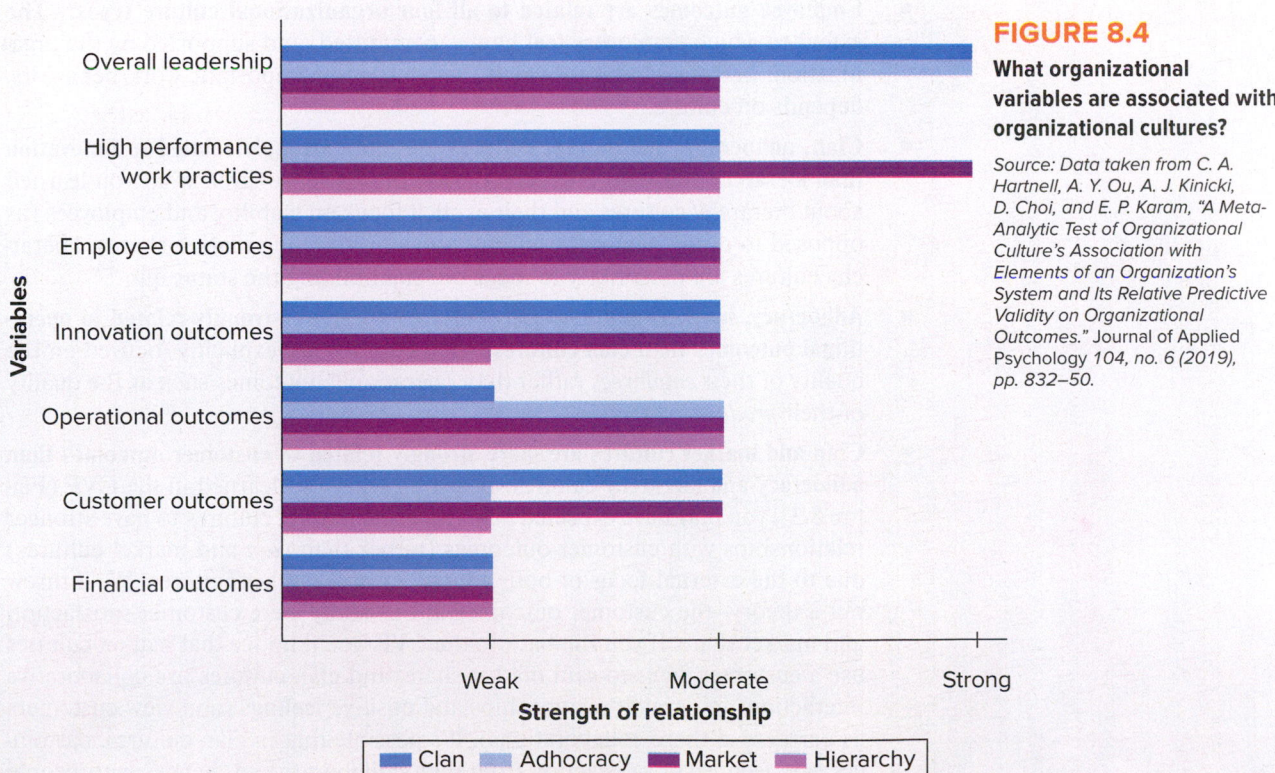

FIGURE 8.4

What organizational variables are associated with organizational cultures?

Source: Data taken from C. A. Hartnell, A. Y. Ou, A. J. Kinicki, D. Choi, and E. P. Karam, "A Meta-Analytic Test of Organizational Culture's Association with Elements of an Organization's System and Its Relative Predictive Validity on Organizational Outcomes." Journal of Applied Psychology *104, no. 6 (2019), pp. 832–50.*

Results revealed that culture is positively associated with a variety of factors and outcomes that are important to today's managers. Closer examination of Figure 8.4 leads to the following conclusions:

- **An organization's culture matters.** The type of organizational culture can be a source of competitive advantage. (See the remaining bullets for more specifics.)

- **Clan and adhocracy cultures are more strongly related to desirable leadership behaviors than market and hierarchy cultures.** But all four culture types are related to leadership in various ways. One explanation involves employee preferences for leadership that allows flexibility and discretion inherent in clan and adhocracy cultures as opposed to directive styles of leadership associated with fostering stability and control in hierarchy and market cultures.

- **Market cultures have the strongest relationship with high-performance work practices** (akin to the HR practices we discussed in Figure 8.1). But all four culture types are related to high-performance work practices (HPWPs) in various ways. High-performance work practices represent "bundles" of HR practices that are systematically grouped to enhance employee *abilities* (e.g., selection and training), *motivation* (e.g., compensation and career development), or *opportunities* (e.g., involvement and information sharing).

  We suggest that you pause here and take a few minutes to enjoy practicing your career readiness competency of critical thinking/problem solving with this fun exercise. First, sketch out the CVF and jot down the names and characteristics of the four culture types within the quadrants. Then, try and come up with some logical pairings between the culture types and the three HPWP bundles. (Here's one to get you started—we think that organizations with adhocracy cultures will be likely to use HPWPs focused on providing opportunities for employees. Why? Because adhocracy cultures want their employees to be innovative and creative, and increased opportunities to collaborate or gain new information should provide additional brain-fuel for innovation and creativity.) Your turn!

- **Employee outcomes are related to all four organizational culture types.** The extent to which employees feel happy, committed, and supported by the organization, and the extent to which they engage in important work behaviors, depends on culture.

- **Clan, adhocracy, and market cultures are more strongly related to innovation than hierarchy cultures.** This relationship makes sense given what you learned about hierarchy cultures and their explicit focus on stability and employees (as opposed to doing new and exciting things or grabbing market share). Hierarchy cultures are most likely to focus on "maintaining the status quo."

- **Adhocracy, market, and hierarchy cultures are more strongly related to operational outcomes than clan cultures.** Clan cultures are explicitly focused on the quality of their *employees* rather than operational outcomes such as the quality of their *products* or *services*.

- **Clan and market cultures are more strongly related to customer outcomes than adhocracy and hierarchy cultures.** Based on what you learned in the CVF (Figure 8.3), you may have expected *adhocracy* and market cultures to have stronger relationships with customer outcomes (rather than *clan* and market cultures) due to the external focus of both adhocracy and market cultures. We'll throw out a theory—the customer outcomes in this study were customer satisfaction and market share. If you flip back to the CVF, you'll notice that market cultures use a customer focus to gain market share, and clan cultures use collaborative interactions to develop relationships and positive feelings (and view customers as partners in these collaborations). It's possible that in clan cultures, customers gain feelings of satisfaction from their collaborative exchanges with people in the organization. It's also possible that employees working in adhocracy cultures are more focused on the fun, new, and innovative *thing* they're creating for the customer than they are on the *actual* customer.

- **There is a relationship between culture types and financial outcomes.** But it is weak across the board. This occurs because there are other organizational systems and processes that are stronger drivers of firm performance. HPWPs are one example according to the researchers who conducted this meta-analysis. Their results showed that financial outcomes were more strongly related to HPWPs than to culture. This would imply that investments in employees' career readiness competencies may pay dividends in the form of increased profits and revenues.

- **Companies with market cultures tend to have more positive organizational outcomes.** Managers are encouraged to make their cultures more market oriented.

As a final note, the results of the research presented in Figure 8.4 supported what we described in Figure 8.1. Specifically, the researchers found that organizational culture, organizational structure, and HR practices need to align in order to support strategic implementation.

Preparing to Assess P–O Fit before a Job Interview

So far you have learned quite a lot about organizational culture. You've discovered the three levels of culture, the five ways employees learn culture, the four culture types, and the research-backed reasons that culture is important in organizations. But how can you use this information to help determine your potential P–O fit with a company before you interview for a job? Here's a simple three-step process:[92]

1. Make a list of your personal values, strengths, and weaknesses—try to be honest, as this is the best way to accurately gauge fit.
2. Spend some time learning about the organization you plan to interview with by talking with current employees and researching the company online, then make a list of the organization's values, strengths, and weaknesses.
3. Compare your list of personal values, strengths, and weaknesses with those of the organization, then use the information to prepare questions for the interviewer about how well you might fit.

There are three reasons to estimate your fit with an organization before considering a job offer. First, better fit is associated with important outcomes, including more positive work attitudes, higher task performance, less work stress, and lower intention to quit (e.g., "I'm gonna tell em, 'they can take this job and . . .'").[93] Second, learning that there's a poor fit before you join an organization can potentially save you from wasting months or even years in a job that you don't enjoy. Finally, interviewers place a high priority on fit—84% of recruiters in a recent survey felt that culture fit was one of the most important predictors of a job offer, and 90% admitted to skipping over past applicants because they didn't seem to align well with the culture.[94] Here's an example of how this played out in real life for Tesla's general counsel:

Tesla Example: Dane Butswinkas left his job as Tesla's general counsel in February 2019 after spending only two months in the role. Butswinkas had worked for Tesla as outside counsel in the past, but he didn't realize how poorly he fit with the organization's culture until he started the full-time position in Palo Alto, CA. His departure wasn't a novel occurrence—more than 50 senior executives left their positions at Tesla between 2017 and 2019 as the company battled production, service, and reputational issues. Butswinkas rejoined the law firm of Williams & Connolly in Washington, D.C.—the organization with which he'd practiced for almost 30 years prior to taking the job at Tesla.[95] ●

8.3 The Process of Culture Change

THE BIG PICTURE

There are 12 ways a culture becomes established in an organization—and therefore 12 levers for culture change. These are (1) formal statements; (2) slogans and sayings; (3) rites and rituals; (4) stories, legends, and myths; (5) leader reactions to crises; (6) role modeling, training, and coaching; (7) physical design; (8) rewards, titles, promotions, and bonuses; (9) organizational goals and performance criteria; (10) measurable and controllable activities; (11) organizational structure; and (12) organizational systems and procedures.

LO 8-3

Describe the process of culture change in an organization.

Changing organizational culture is essentially a teaching process—that is, a process in which members instruct each other about the organization's preferred values, beliefs, expectations, and behaviors. Schein—the renowned organizational psychologist and culture expert introduced in Section 8.1—established 12 mechanisms for changing culture which we describe in this section.[96] The mechanisms represent levers that managers push and pull to create culture change. It's not an easy or fast process. If you plan to change an organization's culture, know that you will be pushing and pulling on multiple levers for an extended period of time until you've dusted the old culture out of every nook and cranny.

Creating culture change involves pushing and pulling change levers in a desired direction. It is very similar to pushing and pulling these levers on a control panel of a lifting mechanism. In both cases, individuals push levers in order to produce a desired outcome. Neramit Buakaew/Shutterstock

1. Formal Statements

One way to embed preferred culture is to create (or alter) existing formal statements of organizational philosophy, mission, vision, and values, as well as materials to use for recruiting, selecting, and socializing employees.

Hubspot Example: Hubspot creates inbound marketing, customer service, and sales software for more than 73,000 clients across 120+ countries.[97] Co-founder and CTO Dharmesh Shah says the company's Culture Code is a "perpetual 'work in progress'" that continues to evolve along with Hubspot. The company has updated the code—which it describes as the operating system that powers Hubspot—more than 25 times to date. Here are a few highlights from Hubspot's Culture Code:[98]

- Hubspot hires employees that have HEART. This stands for Humble, Empathetic, Adaptable, Remarkable, and Transparent.

- The code reminds that power is gained by sharing knowledge rather than hoarding it.

- A "no-door" policy gives everyone access to everyone at Hubspot, and your ability to influence should not depend on your position in the company hierarchy.

- The code proclaims, "We'd rather be failing frequently than never trying."

What strategy do you think Hubspot is pursuing? What type(s) of culture does Hubspot embody?

Culture Code. Leaders such as Hubspot co-founders Dharmesh Shah and Brian Halligan rely on the power of formal statements to communicate important elements of organizational culture. Hubspot's Culture Code is ever evolving and delivers a strong message about the company's values. Dina Rudick/Getty Images

2. Slogans and Sayings

Another way to create a more desirable corporate culture is to express it in company language, slogans, sayings, and acronyms.

Rebuilding trust after the financial crisis. Former CEO Beth Mooney used slogans and sayings on the Keycorp/Keybank website to communicate the company's core values and desired culture. Scott Eells/Getty Images

Keycorp Example: When Beth Mooney took the helm as CEO of Keycorp/Keybank—a Fortune 500 regional financial services institution based in Cleveland, OH—she knew her first priority had to be rebuilding the trust of the company's customers that had been damaged by the financial crisis. "Trust matters most in these industries," said Mooney, "because people are at their most vulnerable when it comes to their financial health and physical health. These are matters many feel the least equipped to understand. And if you're seriously ill, you're at the mercy of people who know how to make you well."[99] Mooney retired in 2020 after a nine-year tenure as CEO during which she transformed Key's culture and grew the company to be the 13th largest bank in the country.[100] According to Key's website, the company's core values "guide and inspire our company and employees every day as we work together for success."[101] The values spell TRAIL which stands for:

- Teamwork
- Respect
- Accountability
- Integrity
- Leadership

What strategy do you think Keycorp/Keybank is pursuing? What type(s) of culture does the company embody?

3. Rites and Rituals

As we mentioned earlier, rites and rituals represent the planned and unplanned activities and ceremonies that are used to celebrate important events or achievements.

Company Examples: Tech firms are known for their innovative rituals.[102] Here are a few examples to illustrate:

- LinkedIn encourages relationships with weekly gatherings called "Beers for My Peers" held at the speakeasy hidden inside its Empire State Building offices.
- Flipboard fosters innovation with a weekly Mock O'Clock get-together that gives employees the chance to introduce rough mockups of new ideas in a low-pressure environment complete with lots of snacks.
- Pinterest keeps its employees excited about both work and nonwork activities with its monthly Knit Con—a two-day project binge during which workers teach one another their hobbies and passions.

4. Stories, Legends, and Myths

A story is a narrative about an actual event that happened within the organization and that helps to symbolize its vision and values to employees. See the Example box to learn about how a story can be a powerful mechanism for changing a culture of silence into one where members are comfortable voicing their concerns.

EXAMPLE   Dr. Li Wenliang Dared to Tell His Story

On December 30, 2019, Dr. Li Wenliang—an ophthalmologist in Wuhan, China—learned of the emergence of a new strain of the virus responsible for the 2002 SARS outbreak. He sent a message to his colleagues, family, and friends to warn them: *"A new coronavirus infection has been confirmed and its type is being identified. Inform all family and relatives to be on guard."*

The police quickly silenced Dr. Wenliang by forcing him to sign a document admitting to lying and disrupting social order and promising to stop his "illegal" behavior. He was hospitalized with COVID-19 nine days later, and he broke his silence in a series of now famous social media posts and news interviews in which he shared his story from a hospital bed.

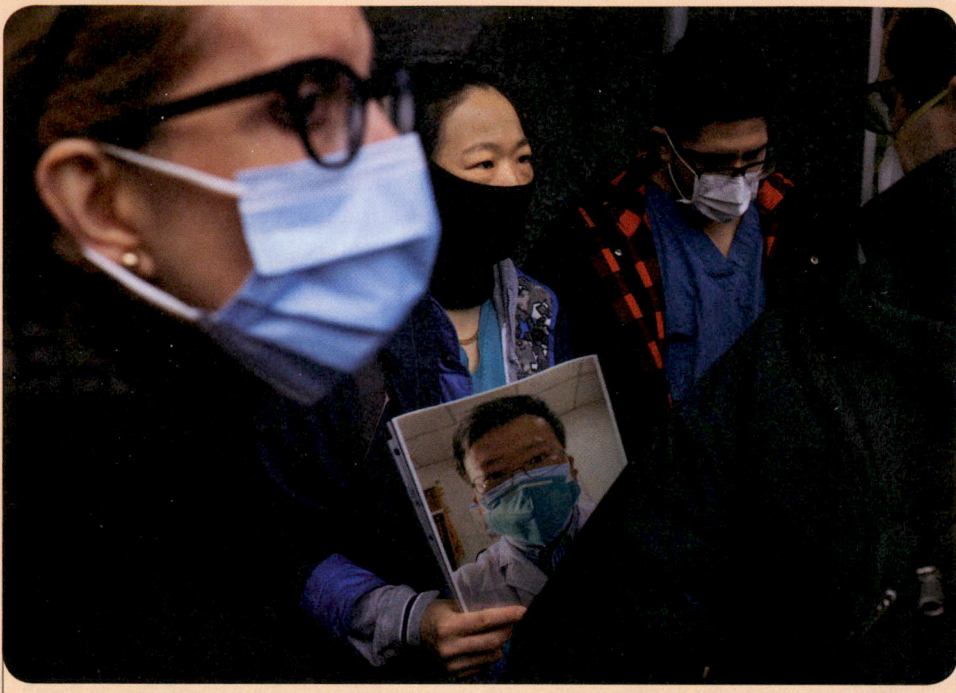

Dr. Wenliang's story lives on. Supporters all over the world praised Dr. Wenliang for his courage to speak up about COVID-19, and health care workers such as those pictured here used his image as they fought to procure adequate personal protective equipment (PPE) in their workplaces. Craig Ruttle/Redux Pictures

Dr. Wenliang told one reporter he decided to become a doctor because, "Lately, patient–doctor relationships have soured. I am happy as long as my patients are satisfied with their treatment." Dr. Wenliang felt the police had wronged him by accusing him of spreading rumors, adding, "Obviously I had been acting out of good will. I felt very sad seeing so many people losing their loved ones." He planned to spend 15 days in the hospital before joining with other medical professionals to fight the spread of the virus, adding, "That's where my responsibilities lie."[103]

Dr. Wenliang died in the hospital on February 7, 2020. Chinese citizens responded to the news of his passing with an unprecedented show of support on social media that some experts think will prove a historical turning point for the country. University of Hong Kong assistant professor of journalism and communication Fang Kecheng said, "[I]t's quite phenomenal because I think this is the first large-scale expression calling for free speech among netizens since Xi Jinping took power."[104]

Hundreds of mourners gathered in Wuhan to hold a vigil for Dr. Wenliang, in spite of Chinese laws against public assemblies. Around the world, similar events took place in honor of the doctor who is now credited with being the first medical professional to speak out publicly about the virus. Many people brought messages from friends and taped them around the gatherings.

"Goodbye Dr. Li," said one of the messages, "In the coming days, I will speak every bit of truth in respect of you."[105]

YOUR CALL

Do you think that Chinese citizens will continue to tell Dr. Wenliang's story? If so, how do you believe it will alter the country's culture?

5. Leader Reactions to Crises

How top managers respond to critical incidents and organizational crises sends a clear cultural message. When new leaders take over an organization, their responses to crises can indicate a desire to change the culture implemented by the previous leadership.

Boeing Example: Boeing struggled to repair its reputation after a series of safety incidents with its 737 MAX aircraft—including two fatal crashes that took the lives of 346 people. The aerospace company had been feverishly trying to keep up with its

A new leader's reaction to a crisis sends a message about culture change. In his new role as CEO, David Calhoun has promised to repair the elements of Boeing's culture that many believe resulted in two fatal 737 MAX crashes. Pictured here are workers clearing the wreckage from the Ethiopian Airlines crash that claimed the lives of 157 people aboard a Boeing 737 MAX airplane. Mulugeta Ayene/AP Images; Whitney Curtis/Redux Pictures

main rival, Airbus, and seemed to have sacrificed safety and quality for earnings. A former senior manager told reporters, "Something happened in the transition from, 'let's build a high-quality, safe product' to 'let's get it out done on time.'"[106] David Calhoun took over as CEO in January 2020 (after Boeing's board fired CEO Dennis Muilenburg) and made public statements criticizing the company for its decision making surrounding the 737 MAX. Calhoun told one reporter, "I'll never be able to judge what motivated Dennis, whether it was a stock price that was going to continue to go up and up, or whether it was just beating the other guy to the next rate increase."[107] He also said Boeing would need to "get rid of the culture of arrogance" that led employees to conceal design and safety problems from the Federal Aviation Administration in order to expedite production of the aircraft.[108]

*What strategy do you think Boeing is pursuing? What type(s) of culture does Boeing embody?

6. Role Modeling, Training, and Coaching

Many companies use structured training to deliver an in-depth introduction to their organizational values. Others use coaching or mentoring programs that provide employees with support and role models.

Estée Lauder Example: Estée Lauder was struggling to stay relevant to a new generation of consumers, so CEO Fabrizio Freda decided to implement a reverse-mentoring program. Younger workers created a knowledge-sharing portal called Dreamspace where they work with senior executives on topics like emerging technologies, social media influencers, and data security. The company then distributes a bi-monthly newsletter on key topics that emerge in those discussions.[109]

*What strategy do you think Estée Lauder is pursuing? What type(s) of culture does Estée Lauder embody?

7. Physical Design

Organizations experiment constantly to find the best office layouts that will encourage employee productivity. Physical design is an important change lever because it sends a strong and visible message about an organization's culture.

Tamara Mellon Example: Tamara Mellon co-founded the luxury footwear brand Jimmy Choo and went on to launch her own brand, Tamara Mellon, in 2016. One big change she made at her new company was to limit the number of physical barriers set up between employees. Mellon says she felt disconnected from her team at Jimmy Choo and didn't enjoy sitting in a corner office with two assistants essentially sitting guard outside. At Tamara Mellon offices, leaders sit with their teams, and everyone—including the executive team—works together out in the open. She said, "Perhaps the most significant result of having this open floor plan is the increased collaboration amongst teams. Ideas can bounce freely and be considered by people on various teams to hear and offer their opinion."[110]

What strategy do you think Tamara Mellon is pursuing? What type(s) of culture does Tamara Mellon embody?

8. Rewards, Titles, Promotions, and Bonuses

Rewards and status symbols are among the strongest levers an organization can use to embed or change its culture. This is because people have a strong desire to be rewarded, and incentives fulfill this need.

Company Examples: There is increasing pressure for businesses to lead the charge in sustainable stewardship of resources, as evidenced by the UN's Sustainable Development Goals (SDGs) and recent statements made by The Business Roundtable (both discussed in earlier chapters). This has resulted in firms changing their reward structures to incentivize creating shared value (CSV) and sustainable business initiatives. For example:

- Shell recently announced that it would begin linking executive compensation to short-term carbon emissions goals.
- Clorox wants to reduce plastic in its products, avoid animal testing, and lower its carbon emissions and recently implemented its IGNITE program that will tie executive compensation to achieving these goals.[111]

9. Organizational Goals and Performance Criteria

Many companies establish organizational goals and criteria for recruiting, selecting, developing, promoting, dismissing, and retiring people, all of which act as levers for communicating the desired organizational culture.

Netflix Example: Netflix has a corporate culture firmly focused on the expectation that employees are adults who can achieve their goals without complicated rules. Vacations are unlimited and the expense policy consists of just five words: "Act in Netflix's best interests." But former Chief Talent Officer Patty McCord, who helped build the company, says a great company needs to "eliminate the slackers, the laggards and the people who are just putting in his or her time."[112] Netflix managers are encouraged to think regularly about whether they would fight to keep each of their direct reports. This "keeper test" helps them determine which employees are star performers and which are ready to receive a generous severance package and move on to another organization.[113]

What strategy do you think Netflix is pursuing? What type(s) of culture does Netflix embody?

10. Measurable and Controllable Activities

An organization's leaders can pay attention to, measure, and control a number of activities, processes, or outcomes that can foster a certain culture. What leaders pay attention to acts as a powerful signal of company culture because it tells employees what aspects of their performance are most important to the company. Measurable and controllable activities also serve as an important lever for culture change.

Barclays Example: Barclays has a history of paying close attention to its employees' behaviors. In 2017 the company installed OccupEye devices—motion and heat sensors—to track the amount of time workers spent at their desks.[114] Then in 2020, the company partnered with Sapience software to implement people analytics technology that, according to the Sapience website, "provides real-time visibility into daily effort and capacity."[115] An anonymous source within the company said the system would alert employees to "avoid breaks" and added, "Employees are worried to step away from their desks, have full lunch breaks, take bathroom breaks or even get up for water, as we are not aware of the repercussions this might have on our statistics."[116]

What strategy do you think Barclays is pursuing? What type(s) of culture does Barclays embody?

Surveillance activities send a strong message to employees about company culture. How would you feel if your employer were tracking your internet use, the number of minutes spent at your workstation, or even the length of your bathroom breaks while at work? What kind of culture do you think this creates? Zenzen/Shutterstock

11. Organizational Structure

Recall from Figure 8.1 that organizational structure is one of the three key factors influencing an organization's ability to successfully implement its strategy. Leaders at Zappos are aware of this conclusion.

Zappos Example: In 2014, Zappos started a radical experiment in organizational structure called *holacracy* to encourage collaboration by eliminating workplace hierarchy—no titles and no bosses. Unfortunately, employees weren't sure how to get things done anymore, which resulted in such confusion that the company's 2015 turnover rate went from 20 to 30%.[117] The company remained committed to its newly flattened structure for several years but has started to back away from the approach. Each team at Zappos now operates as its own small business, and teams buy and sell their resources to one another to fund their operating budgets. The company says that this structure is "adapting our internal systems to more closely resemble real-world markets."[118]

What strategy do you think Zappos is pursuing? What type(s) of culture does Zappos embody?

12. Organizational Systems and Procedures

Organizational systems and procedures are levers for embedding and changing culture. For example, companies are increasingly modifying their work systems and procedures (for example, by implementing HPWPs) to make their cultures more collaborative and/or to improve innovation, quality, and efficiency.

Google Example: Google was built on a foundation of openness and transparency. In the company's early days, workers shared beers with founders Larry Page and Sergey Brin and could ask any questions they wanted. The company worked hard to maintain this culture as it grew by scaling its procedures for soliciting honest employee input. Google replaced these informal chats with something called TGIF, a weekly—then eventually, monthly—gathering of all Google employees where anyone in the company could ask questions of its leaders. CEO Sundar Pichai recently made a big change to TGIF when he announced that the meetings would be much more controlled and that discussions would only include "product and business strategy." According to Pichai, a major reason for the change was that he saw "a coordinated effort to share our conversations outside of the company after every TGIF" that "has affected our ability to use TGIF as a forum for candid conversations on important topics."[119]

What strategy do you think Google is pursuing? What type(s) of culture does Google embody?

Using Multiple Mechanisms to Drive Culture Change

As we mentioned in the introduction to this section, changing organizational culture isn't easy, and it certainly doesn't happen overnight. According to one HR news source, "Ignoring alignment of all culture drivers is why most culture change fails. Initiatives that change only some cultural aspects either have no impact or—worse—have a negative impact by adding conflicting messages. Executive teams must look at the culture holistically and address all primary drivers that need alignment."[120]

If you want to create lasting culture change you need to consider how all of the various levers work together, and how they can either support or work against each other. Read the Example box to learn about how one company approached culture change through multiple levers.

EXAMPLE   How Total Used Multiple Mechanisms to Improve Its Safety Culture

Safety is paramount in the oil and gas industry. A study that reviewed major oil drilling accidents found that an organization's "safety culture" was one of the most important factors that led to catastrophic safety failures.[121] When the French oil and gas company Total sought to transform its safety culture, Bernadette Spinoy—then SVP of Health, Safety, and Environment (HSE)—knew it would require the use of multiple change mechanisms.[122] Here are examples of the levers that Total used to change its culture:

- **Role modeling, training, and coaching.** Total wanted to embed safety in the organization by creating opportunities for employees to learn rather than by implementing punishments for violations. Although the company does penalize employees who clearly and/or repeatedly disregard safety standards, their focus is primarily on learning. For example, workers involved in safety incidents record videos discussing their experiences and how they learned from them and they share these videos with the rest of the company. Total also implemented a stronger employee training program that starts on day one and continues throughout employees' time with the company.

- **Rewards, titles, promotions, and bonuses.** The company implemented a reward system that emphasized positive reinforcement for employees doing a good job following safety standards. Now, any employee can nominate any other colleague for a safety award, and the company recognizes between 8 and 10 safety role models for every one safety sanction it hands down.

- **Measurable and controllable activities.** Total created an HSE team dedicated to evaluating safety incidents almost immediately after they occur. The team analyzes each incident for the specific factors that caused it. This helps the company gain a much better understanding of the reasons for safety failures, and, ultimately, the ways to prevent them in the future. (Research has demonstrated that discussions about how and why failures occurred are crucial for learning.)[123]

- **Organizational structure.** Total consolidated its HSE function by integrating HSE departments from various divisions across all of its business units. This restructuring allowed each branch to contribute its unique experiences and expertise. The company bases its organizationwide safety processes and procedures on the best practices identified through the collaboration of these groups.

- **Organizational systems and procedures.** the company implemented a system for making safety incidents visible at multiple levels. In the event of a safety incident, every senior leader receives a text describing the incident within hours. Then the company publishes the description of the incident on its intranet for all employees to see. In addition, the company publishes videos with overviews of accidents.

YOUR CALL

Do you think there are specific combinations of the 12 levers that are more important to pay attention to than others when attempting to change an organization's culture? Which ones, and why?

Don't Forget about Person–Organization Fit

Now that we have described the four key types of organizational culture and the levers managers can use to change culture, it's time to reflect on your person–organization (P–O) fit. Recall that P–O fit reflects the extent to which your personality and values match the climate and culture in an organization, and P–O fit is important because it can affect your work attitudes and performance.[124] While it is possible to change an organization's culture and thus create a better fit, many employees experiencing poor P–O fit end up searching for new jobs.[125] One way to prevent this is to assess your P–O fit before committing to a job, which can help you make more informed decisions about whether a particular company is one in which you'll be happy.

We have three activities for you to complete to measure your level of fit and see what you can do about it. The first is Self-Assessment 8.2, which measures your preference for the four types of culture in the CVF. The second is to answer the discussion questions associated with this assessment. You will be asked to conduct a gap analysis between the culture for a current or past employer and your preferred culture type. You can use this gap to make a plan of action for improving your P–O fit. The third is the two activities in the career readiness section at the end of this chapter, where we'll give you practical advice for questions you can ask to assess your level of fit. ●

SELF-ASSESSMENT 8.2

Assessing Your Preferred Type of Organizational Culture

This survey is designed to assess your preferred type of organizational culture. Please be prepared to answer these questions if your instructor has assigned Self-Assessment 8.2 in Connect.

1. In rank order, what are your preferred culture types? Are you surprised by the results?

2. Compute the gap between your preferred and actual culture types by subtracting your actual culture type score (Self-Assessment 8.1) from your preferred type score (Self-Assessment 8.2). Where are the largest gaps?

3. Make a plan to improve your person–organization fit. Focusing on your two largest culture types, identify what is causing the gaps. You will find it helpful to look at the survey items that measure these types.

4. Now use the 12 levers just discussed and suggest at least two things you can do to improve your level of fit.

8.4 The Major Features of an Organization

THE BIG PICTURE

Organizations are described according to seven major features. An organization chart is a visual representation of these features for a particular organization.

In Chapter 1, we defined an organization as a group of people who work together to achieve some specific purpose. But let's also consider Barnard's classic perspective, which views an **organization** as a system of consciously coordinated activities or forces of two or more people.[126] Taken together, these perspectives tell us that (1) an organization's managers make *intentional* choices about how to coordinate employees' work in order to achieve strategic goals and (2) these choices result in the organization's unique system of task and reporting relationships (i.e., the organization's structure). Managers

LO 8-4

Identify the major features of an organization and explain how they are expressed in an organization chart.

make choices about a variety of features when structuring their organizations, and we discuss each feature in detail in this section. But first, let's explain what we mean when we refer to the *features* of an organization.

If we asked you to describe your face to someone who wasn't able to see you, how would you do it? Chances are you would describe yourself according to your facial features, such your eye and eyebrow color, your skin tone, the prominence of your cheekbones, and the shape of your nose, lips, and overall face. In fact, this is a template that you can use to describe anyone's face, because all faces vary according to a small number of features.

Organizations, like faces, have common features. We can describe organizations by discussing how they vary along a set of seven features, much like we can describe unique faces according to the set of common features they share. Rawpixel Ltd/Getty Images

Now consider that all organizations, like faces, can be described according to a set of features. We discuss four features proposed by organizational psychologist Edgar Schein, and then present three others that most experts agree on.

Major Features of Organizations: Four Proposed by Edgar Schein

Schein proposed that all organizations can be described according to four features: (1) *common purpose*, (2) *coordinated effort*, (3) *division of labor*, and (4) *hierarchy of authority*.[127] Let's consider these.

1. Common Purpose: The Means for Unifying Members   An organization without purpose soon begins to drift and become disorganized. In order to remain "organized," there needs to be a reason for existing that all of the organization's members agree on. The common purpose unifies employees or members and gives everyone an understanding of the organization's reason for being. Every organization has its own purpose, just like all people have noses. But all noses are not alike, and organizations don't exist for the same purpose.

2. Coordinated Effort: Working Together for Common Purpose   The common purpose is realized through coordinated effort, the coordination of individual efforts into a group or organization-wide effort. Although it's true that individuals can make a difference, they cannot do everything by themselves. All organizations coordinate their employees' efforts, and we can describe organizations according to the different methods of coordination they choose.

Organizational culture is an important factor in choosing how to coordinate effort. For example, in clan cultures, coordination is best accomplished through interactions between people and teams, but in hierarchy cultures, coordination likely stems from rigid procedures and processes.

3. Division of Labor: Work Specialization for Greater Efficiency   Division of labor, also known as work specialization, is the arrangement of having discrete parts of a task done by different people. Even a two-person crew operating a fishing boat probably has some work specialization—one steers the boat and the other works the nets. With division of labor, an organization can parcel out the entire complex work effort to be performed by specialists, resulting in greater efficiency. One way to describe organizations is to discuss the specific ways they choose to divide their labor.

4. Hierarchy of Authority: The Chain of Command   The hierarchy of authority, or chain of command, is a control mechanism for making sure the right people do the right things at the right time. If coordinated effort is to be achieved, some people—namely, managers—need to have more authority, or the right to direct the work of others. Even in member-owned organizations, some people have more authority than others, although their peers may have granted it to them.

Authority is most effective when arranged in a hierarchy. Without tiers or ranks of authority, a lone manager would have to confer with everyone in her or his domain, making it difficult to get things done. Even in newer organizations that flatten the hierarchy, there still exists more than one level of management.[128] A flat organization is defined as one with an organizational structure with few or no levels of middle management between top managers and those reporting to them.

Finally, a principle stressed by early management scholars was that of unity of command, in which an employee should report to no more than one manager in order to avoid conflicting priorities and demands. Today, however, with advances in computer technology and networks, there are circumstances in which it makes sense for a person to communicate with more than one manager (as is true, for instance, with the organizational structure known as the matrix structure that we'll describe in the next section).

Hierarchy is another feature you can use to describe organizations. You can get a much better picture of an organization if you understand its unique hierarchy of authority.

Major Features of Organizations: Three More That Most Authorities Agree On

To Schein's four features we add three others that most authorities agree on: (5) *span of control;* (6) *authority, responsibility, and delegation;* and (7) *centralization versus decentralization of authority.*

5. Span of Control: Narrow (or Tall) versus Wide (or Flat)   The <mark>span of control</mark>, or span of management, refers to the number of people reporting directly to a given manager.[129] Span of control is another feature that can be used to describe organizations. There are two kinds of spans of control: narrow (or tall) and wide (or flat). (*See Figure 8.5.*)

FIGURE 8.5

Span of control organizational hierarchies

Source: "Organizational Hierarchies," Expert Program Management, 2017, https://expertprogrammanagement.com/2017/09/span-of-control/.

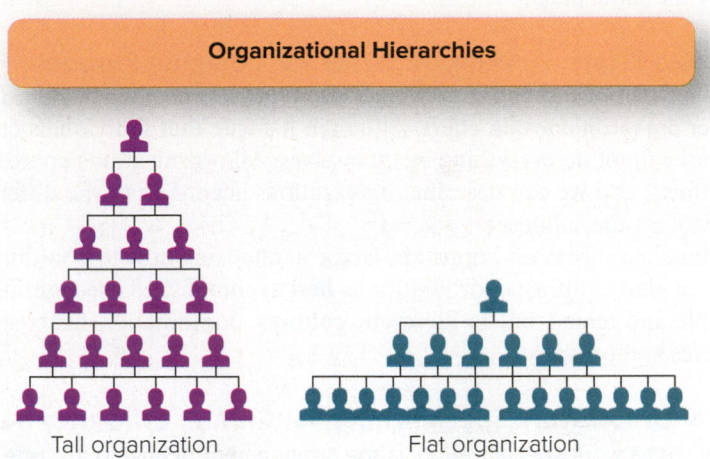

Organizational Hierarchies

Tall organization   Flat organization

Narrow Span of Control   This means a manager has a limited number of people reporting—three vice presidents reporting to a president, for example, instead of nine vice presidents. An organization is said to be *tall* when there are many levels with narrow spans of control. Refer to Figure 8.5 and you can see that in a tall organization with a narrow span of control, the number of workers reporting to a manager one level above them is relatively small.

Wide Span of Control   This means a manager has several people reporting—a first-line supervisor may have 40 or more subordinates, if little hands-on supervision is required, as is the case in some assembly-line workplaces. An organization is said to be *flat* when there are only a few levels with wide spans of control. You can see from Figure 8.5 that in a flat organization with a wide span of control, the number of workers reporting to a manager one level above them is much larger than in a tall organization.

Historically, spans of about 7 to 10 subordinates were considered best, but there is no consensus as to what is ideal. In general, when managers must be closely involved with their subordinates, as when the management duties are complex or when ethical concerns are high, they are advised to have a narrow span of control.[130] This is why presidents tend to have only a handful of vice presidents reporting to them. By contrast, first-line supervisors directing subordinates with similar work tasks may have a wide span of control. Today's emphasis on lean management staffs, increased efficiency, and greater worker autonomy means that many organizations try to make spans of control as wide as possible while still providing adequate supervision.

6. Authority—Accountability, Responsibility, and Delegation   In elephant families, authority over the herd rests with the oldest female, known as the matriarch. In human organizations, however, authority is related to management positions, and it is another feature we can use to describe organizations. <mark>Authority</mark> refers to the rights inherent in a managerial position to make decisions, give orders, and utilize resources. Disobeying orders may lead to consequences such as reprimand, demotion, or firing, and subordinates are expected to accept that a higher-level manager has a legitimate right to issue orders.

With authority goes *accountability, responsibility,* and the ability to *delegate* one's authority.

Accountability   Authority means <mark>accountability</mark>—managers must report and justify work results to the managers above them. Being accountable means you have the responsibility for performing assigned tasks.[131]

Responsibility   With more authority comes more responsibility. <mark>Responsibility</mark> is the obligation you have to perform the tasks assigned to you. A car assembly-line worker has less authority and responsibility than a manager of the assembly line. Whereas the line worker is generally responsible for one specific task, such as installing a windshield, the manager has much greater responsibilities.

Delegation   <mark>Delegation</mark> is the process of assigning managerial authority and responsibility to managers and employees lower in the hierarchy. To be more efficient, most managers are expected to delegate as much of their work as possible.[132] However, many bosses get hung up on perfection, failing to realize that delegation is not only a necessary part of managing, but one that impacts attitudes, productivity, and firm performance.[133]

Check out the Practical Action box for tips on delegating effectively.

PRACTICAL ACTION   How to Delegate Effectively

All managers must learn how to delegate—to assign management authority and responsibilities to people lower in the company hierarchy. Delegation also helps you avoid exhaustion from overwork. If, as a manager, you find yourself often behind, always taking work home, doing your subordinates' work for them, and constantly having employees seeking your approval before they can act, you're clearly not delegating well.[134] If you lack even the time to train someone to take over tasks for you, reprioritize some tasks and find the time.

How can you delegate more effectively? It's fine to start small. Here are some guidelines.[135]

Delegate Routine Tasks and Technical Matters   Always try to delegate routine tasks and routine paperwork, keeping only the tasks that call for your input. When there are technical matters, let the experts handle them.

Delegate Tasks That Help Your Subordinates Grow   Let your employees solve their own problems whenever possible. Let them try new things so they will grow in their jobs. Your success depends on theirs, so give them room to achieve.

Match Delegated Tasks to Your Subordinates' Skills and Abilities   While recognizing that delegation involves some risk, make your assignments appropriate to the training, talent, skills,

and motivation of your employees. Begin by asking your team members whether they can handle more work, and in what areas they would like to improve their skills or upgrade their responsibilities. Be sure you've given them the tools and clarity they need to get the job done, stay available for help and questions, but let your subordinates do what is now their job.

Delegating effectively is a skill that you can develop with time, experience, and practice. Good managers learn what and to whom to delegate, and they use delegation as a tool for improving both efficiency and effectiveness.
Shutterstock

Don't Delegate Confidential or Human Resource Matters   Tasks that are confidential or that involve the evaluation, discipline, or counseling of subordinates should never be handed off to someone else.

Don't Delegate Emergencies   By definition, an emergency is a crisis for which there is little time for solution and a high need for coordination within the organization. You should handle this yourself.

Don't Delegate Special Tasks That Your Boss Asked You to Do—Unless You Have His or Her Permission   If your supervisor entrusts you with a special assignment, such as attending a particular meeting, don't delegate it unless you have permission to do so.

YOUR CALL

Are any of these reasons that you might need to improve your delegating skills? What are some others?

7. Centralization versus Decentralization of Authority   Another feature we can use to describe organizations is the extent to which authority is centralized versus decentralized. This feature is concerned with who makes the important decisions in an organization.

Centralized Authority   With centralized authority, important decisions are made by higher-level managers. Very small companies tend to be the most centralized, although nearly all organizations have at least some authority concentrated at the top of the hierarchy. Walmart and McDonald's are examples of companies using this kind of authority. Two advantages of centralized authority are:

1. There is less duplication of work because fewer employees perform the same task; rather, the task is often performed by a department of specialists.

2. There are increased efficiencies because procedures are uniform and thus easier to control.[136]

Decentralized Authority   With decentralized authority, important decisions are made by middle-level and supervisory-level managers. Here, power has been delegated throughout the organization. Among the companies using decentralized authority are General Motors and Harley-Davidson. Two advantages of decentralized authority are:

1. Managers are encouraged to solve their own problems rather than escalate the decision to a higher level of management.

2. Decisions are made more quickly, which increases the organization's flexibility and efficiency.[137]

Thus far you've learned about seven different features used to describe organizations. Just as a police sketch artist uses descriptions of individual facial features (e.g., eye color, face shape, hair length and color, etc.) to build a complete drawing of a suspect's face, an organization's features combine into a visual depiction of its structure. This is known as the organization chart, discussed next.

The Organization Chart

Whatever the size or type of organization, its structure can be depicted in an organization chart. An organization chart is a box-and-lines illustration showing the formal lines of authority and the organization's official positions or work specializations. This is the family tree–like pattern of boxes and lines posted on workplace walls and given to new hires, such as for a hospital. *(See Figure 8.6.)*

At a very detailed level, organization charts provide information about an organization's features (e.g., its division of labor, chain of command, the extent to which it centralizes authority, etc.). More broadly, organization charts reveal information about two basic elements of organizational structure: (1) the *vertical hierarchy of authority*—who reports to whom—and (2) the *horizontal specialization*—who specializes in what work.

The Vertical Hierarchy of Authority: Who Reports to Whom   A glance up and down an organization chart shows the *vertical hierarchy*, the chain of command. A formal vertical hierarchy also shows the official communication network—who talks to whom. In a simple two-person organization, the owner might communicate with just an administrative assistant. In a complex organization, the president talks principally to the vice presidents, who in turn talk to the assistant vice presidents, and so on.

The Horizontal Specialization: Who Specializes in What Work   A glance to the left and right on the lines of an organization chart shows the *horizontal specialization*, the different jobs or work specialization. The husband-and-wife partners in a two-person digital graphics firm might agree that one is the "outside person," handling sales, client relations, and finances, and the other is the "inside person," handling

FIGURE 8.6
Organization chart
(example for a hospital)

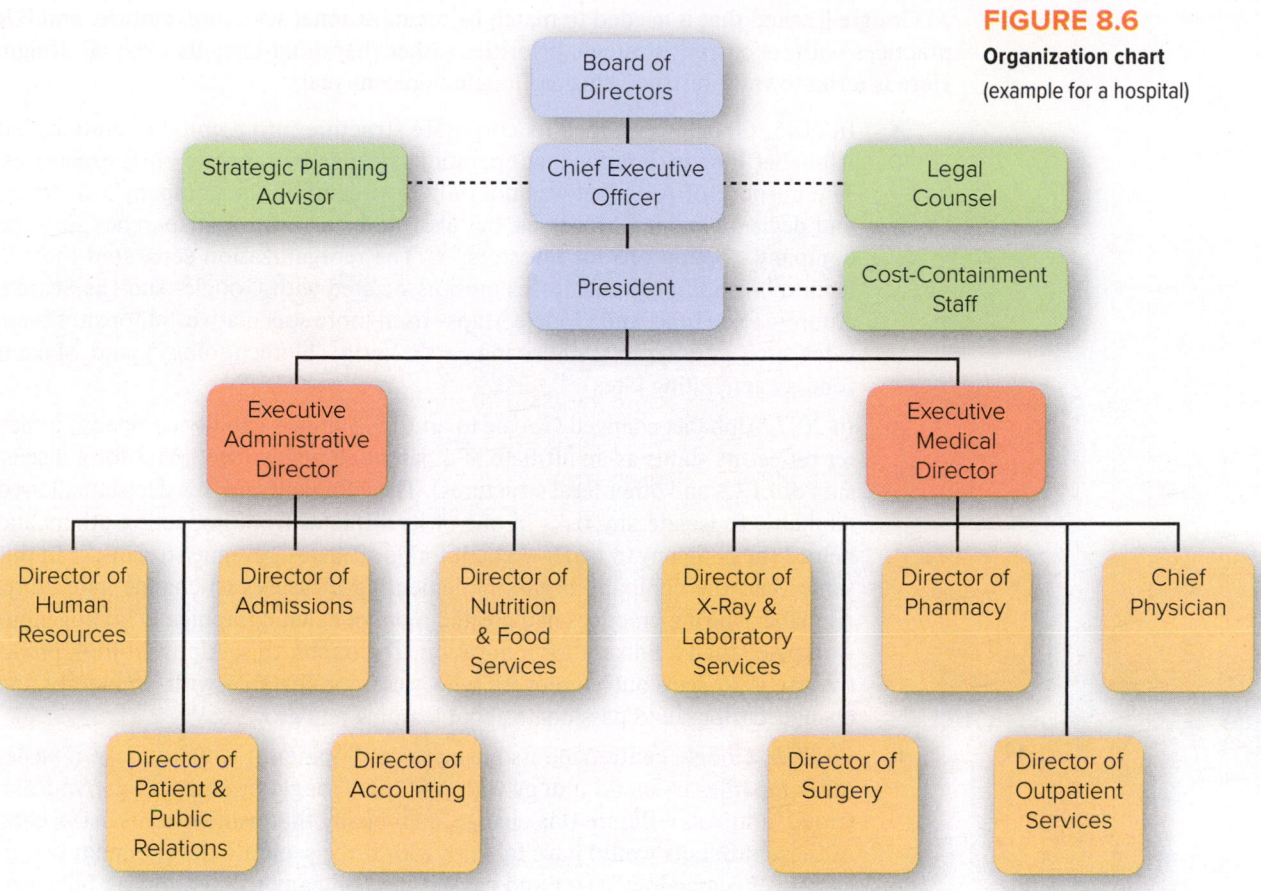

production and research. A large firm might have vice presidents for each task—marketing, finance, and so on.

In this section we described seven major features of an organization and how they come together in a visual representation known as an organization chart. In Section 8.5, we discuss how distinct combinations of these features form the basis of the eight types of organizational structure. ●

8.5 Eight Types of Organizational Structure

THE BIG PICTURE

The eight types of organizational structure are simple, functional, divisional, matrix, horizontal, hollow, modular, and virtual.

The right organizational structures help employees and organizations perform better, and the right structure for a particular organization can change as the organization evolves.[138]

Consider the example of Google, which, as mentioned previously, began as a freewheeling company with a strong culture of openness and innovation, but then grew. The problem, however, was that the company grew so quickly (it's now more than 100,000 people) that decision making became molasses-like. Said one report, "The unwieldy management and glacial pace of decision making were particularly noticeable in [Silicon Valley], where start-ups overtake behemoths in months."[139]

LO 8-5

Describe the eight types of organizational structure.

Google learned that it needed to match its organizational structure, culture, and HR practices with its current strategic priorities rather than hold onto its original design. Here is a rundown of restructuring at Google in recent years:

- In 2015, Google revamped its corporate structure into a conglomerate called Alphabet Inc., with individual operations headed by separate chief executives. The purpose of Alphabet was not only to streamline the company's structure and decision-making processes, but also "to bring more transparency into the company's operations for investors."[140] The reorganization separated the collection of traditional businesses most associated with Google—such as Search, Android, YouTube, and Google Maps—from more speculative "moonshot" ventures such as Waymo (self-driving cars), Verily (biotechnology), and Makani (energy generating kites).[141]

- In 2017, Alphabet changed Google to an LLC (limited liability company) to better reflect its status as an affiliate of a parent company (see LM 2 for a discussion of LLCs and other legal structures). The company said this decision allowed Alphabet to isolate any risks in one of its affiliates from impacting others and helped the company to better account for its affiliates' revenue streams.[142] In this same year, the company began implementing measures to change its culture. Alphabet's hiring practices had created more of a demographically homogenous workplace than a hotspot for innovation. To counter this, Alphabet took proactive steps to seek out employees who were comfortable with ambiguity and change, curious, and passionate about learning and growing.[143]

- In 2019, Google centralized its business development teams to make it easier for companies to spend money with multiple Google products (e.g., Android, Cloud, and Ads). Before this change, a company that wanted to invest in each of these products would have to work with three separate development teams, and this became inefficient and caused the company to miss out on business. Google's president of global partnerships and corporate development said that "The new structure will improve our ability to present a coordinated face to partners and allow us to contribute to business and product strategies that span across Google."[144]

Organizational design is concerned with designing the optimal structures of accountability and responsibility that an organization uses to execute its strategies. The eight organizational structures we discuss in this section can be grouped into three broad categories of organizational design:[145]

1. Traditional designs (simple, functional, divisional, and matrix structures).
2. Horizontal designs (horizontal structure).
3. Designs that open boundaries between organizations (hollow, modular, and virtual structures).

1. Traditional Designs: Simple, Functional, Divisional, and Matrix Structures

The traditional organizational design category includes the (1) simple, (2) functional, (3) divisional, and (4) matrix structures. The organizational structures that are considered traditional designs tend to rely on a vertical management hierarchy, with clear departmental boundaries and reporting arrangements, as follows.

The Simple Structure: For the Small Firm
The simple structure is often found in a firm's very early, entrepreneurial stages, when the organization is apt to reflect the desires and personality of the owner or founder. An organization with a **simple structure** has authority centralized in a single person, a flat hierarchy, few rules, and low work specialization. *(See Figure 8.7.)*

FIGURE 8.7

Simple structure: An example

There is only one hierarchical level of management beneath the owner.

Hundreds of thousands of organizations are arranged according to a simple structure—for instance, small mom-and-pop firms running landscaping, construction, insurance sales, and similar businesses. Examples: Both Hewlett-Packard and Apple Computer began as two-person garage start-ups that later became large.

The Functional Structure: Grouping by Similar Work Specialties   In the ==functional structure==, people with similar occupational specialties are put together in formal groups. This is a quite commonplace structure, seen in all kinds of organizations, both for-profit and nonprofit. *(See Figure 8.8.)*

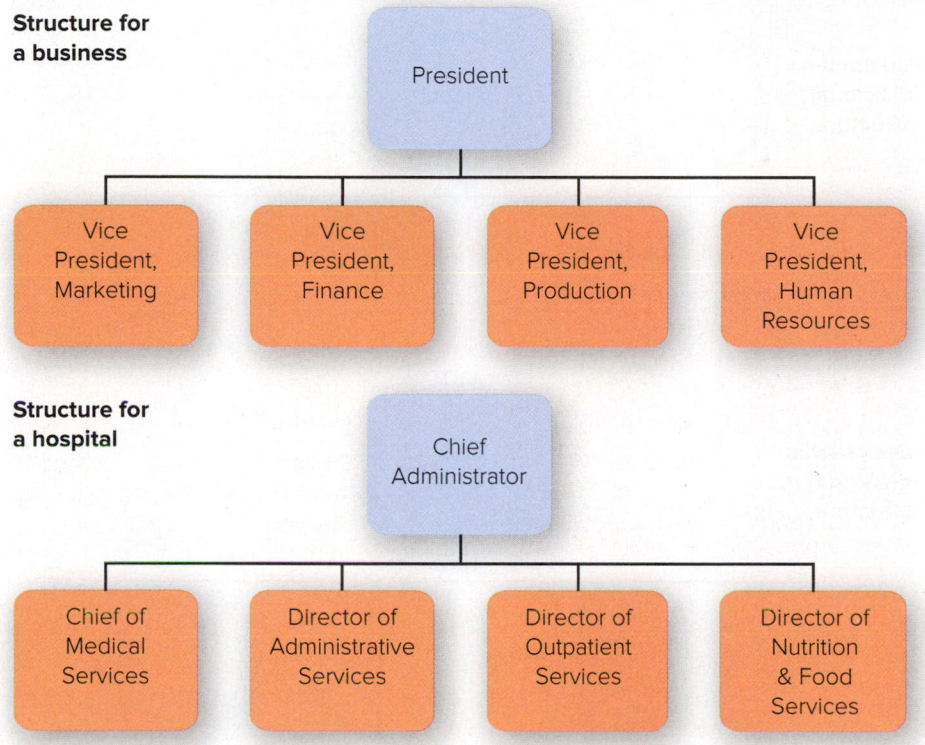

Structure for a business

President
- Vice President, Marketing
- Vice President, Finance
- Vice President, Production
- Vice President, Human Resources

Structure for a hospital

Chief Administrator
- Chief of Medical Services
- Director of Administrative Services
- Director of Outpatient Services
- Director of Nutrition & Food Services

FIGURE 8.8

Functional structure: Two examples

This shows the functional structure for a business and for a hospital.

Examples: A manufacturing firm will often group people with similar work skills in a Marketing Department, others in a Production Department, others in Finance, and so on. A nonprofit educational institution might group employees according to work specialty under Faculty, Admissions, Maintenance, and so forth.

The Divisional Structure: Grouping by Similarity of Purpose   In a ==divisional structure==, people with diverse occupational specialties are put together in formal groups by similar products or services, customers or clients, or geographic regions. *(See Figure 8.9.)*

- ==Product divisions== group activities around similar products or services. Example: ExxonMobil organizes its business into four product divisions: (1) Upstream (exploration activities), (2) Chemical (processing of butyl, polyethylene, etc.), (3) Downstream (distribution of crude oil), and (4) Natural Gas and Power Marketing (expanding markets for natural gas).

- ==Customer divisions== tend to group activities around common customers or clients. Examples: Ford Motor Co. has separate divisions for passenger-car dealers, for large trucking customers, and for farm products customers. A savings and loan

FIGURE 8.9

Divisional structure: Three examples

This shows product, customer, and geographic divisions.

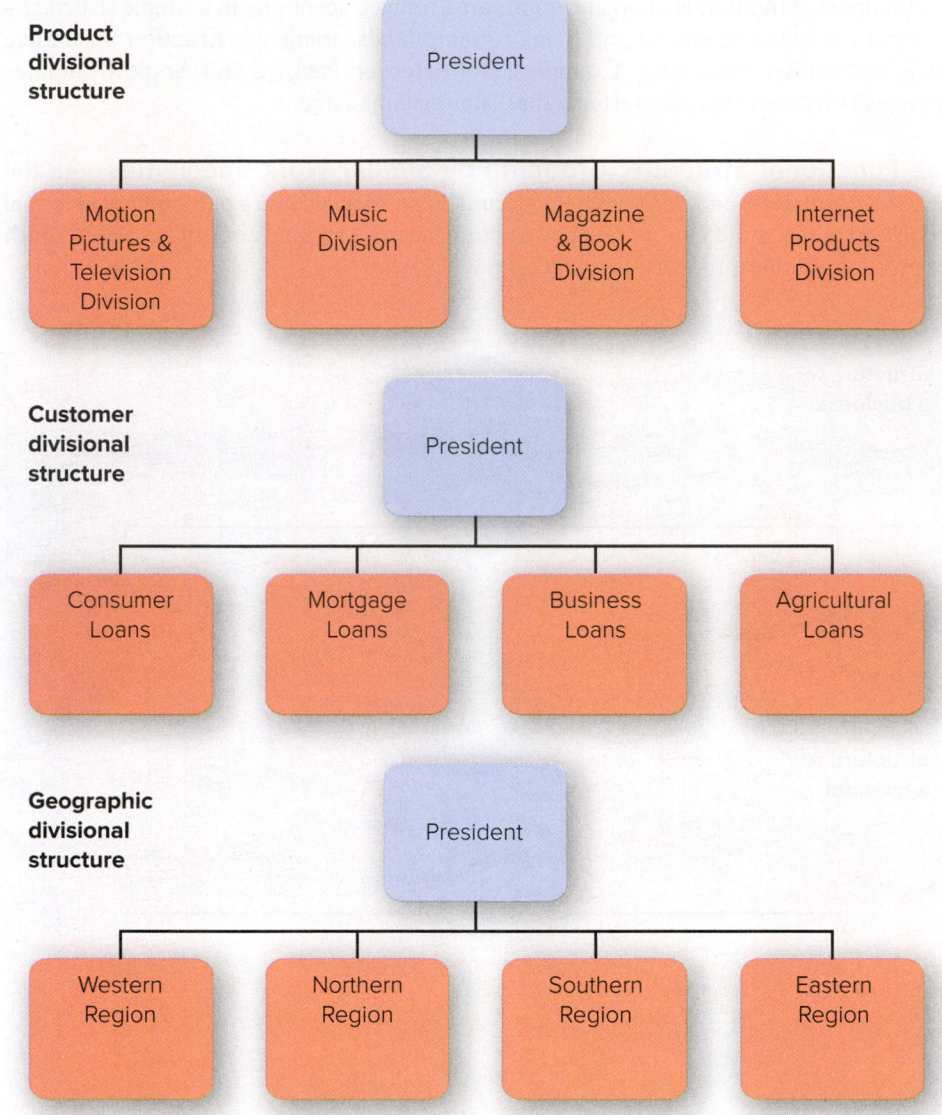

Product divisional structure

President

Motion Pictures & Television Division | Music Division | Magazine & Book Division | Internet Products Division

Customer divisional structure

President

Consumer Loans | Mortgage Loans | Business Loans | Agricultural Loans

Geographic divisional structure

President

Western Region | Northern Region | Southern Region | Eastern Region

company might be structured with divisions for making consumer loans, mortgage loans, business loans, and agricultural loans.

■ **Geographic divisions** group activities around defined regional locations. Example: This arrangement is frequently used by government agencies. The Federal Reserve Bank, for instance, has 12 separate districts around the United States. The Internal Revenue Service also has several districts.

The Matrix Structure: A Grid of Functional and Divisional for Two Chains of Command   In a **matrix structure**, an organization combines functional and divisional chains of command in a grid so that there are two command structures—vertical and horizontal. The functional structure usually doesn't change—it is the organization's normal departments or divisions, such as Finance, Marketing, Production, and Research & Development. The divisional structure may vary—as by product, brand, customer, or geographic region. *(See Figure 8.10.)*

A hypothetical example, using Ford Motor Co.: The functional structure might be the departments of Engineering, Finance, Production, and Marketing, each headed by a vice president. Thus, the reporting arrangement is vertical. The divisional structure

FIGURE 8.10

Matrix structure

An example of an arrangement that Ford might use.

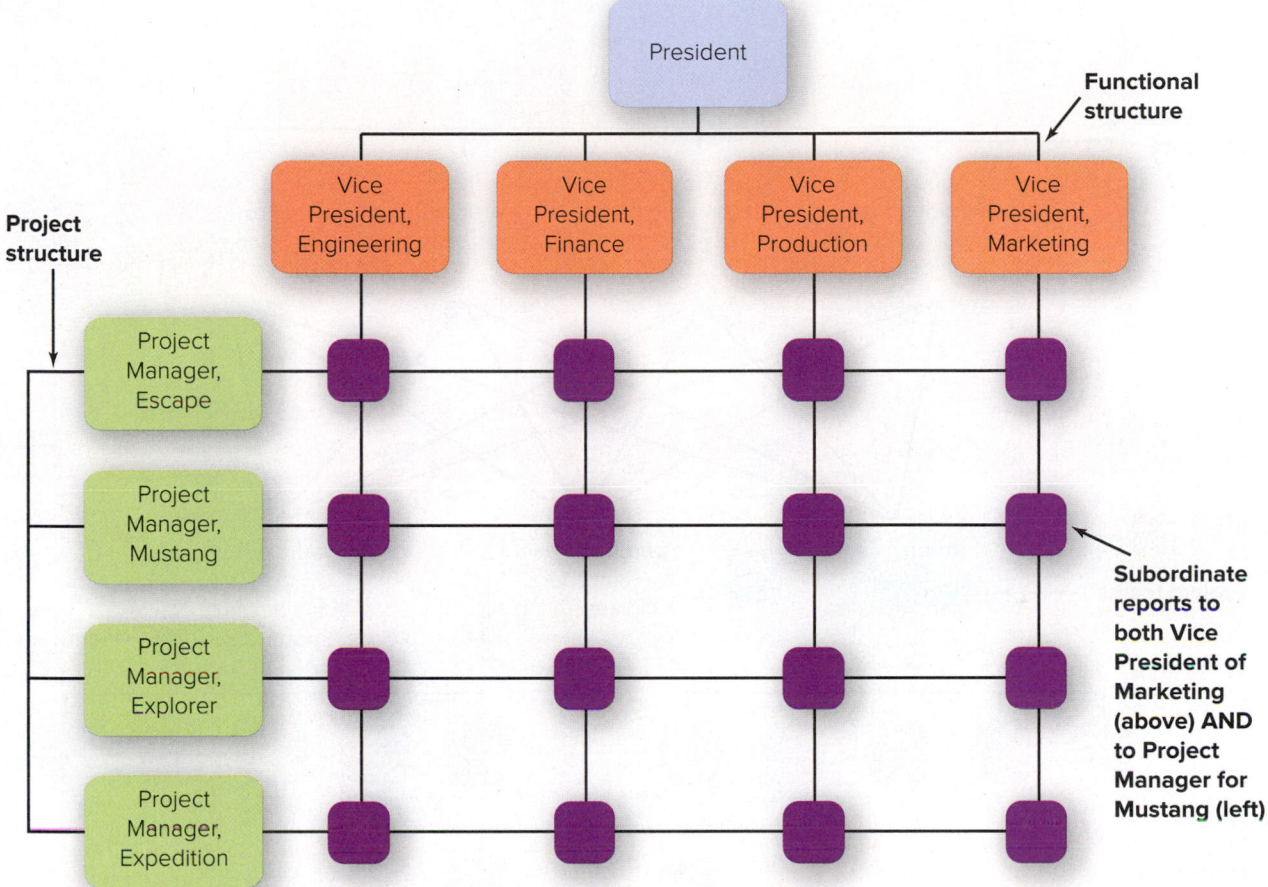

might be by product (the new models of Escape, Mustang, Explorer, and Expedition, for example), each headed by a project manager. This reporting arrangement is horizontal. Thus, a marketing person, say, would report to *both* the vice president of marketing *and* the project manager for the Ford Mustang. Indeed, Ford Motor Co. used the matrix approach to create the Fusion and a newer version of the Mustang.

2. The Horizontal Design: Eliminating Functional Barriers to Solve Problems

The horizontal design category includes the horizontal structure. In a ==horizontal structure==, also called a team-based design, teams or workgroups, either temporary or permanent, are used to improve collaboration and work on shared tasks by breaking down internal boundaries. For instance, when managers from different functional divisions are brought together in teams—known as cross-functional teams—to solve particular problems, the barriers between the divisions break down. The focus on narrow divisional interests yields to a common interest in solving the problems that brought them together. Yet team members still have their full-time functional work responsibilities and often still formally report to their own managers above them in the functional-division hierarchy. *(See Figure 8.11.)*

FIGURE 8.11

Horizontal design

This shows a mix of functional (vertical) and project-team (horizontal) arrangements.

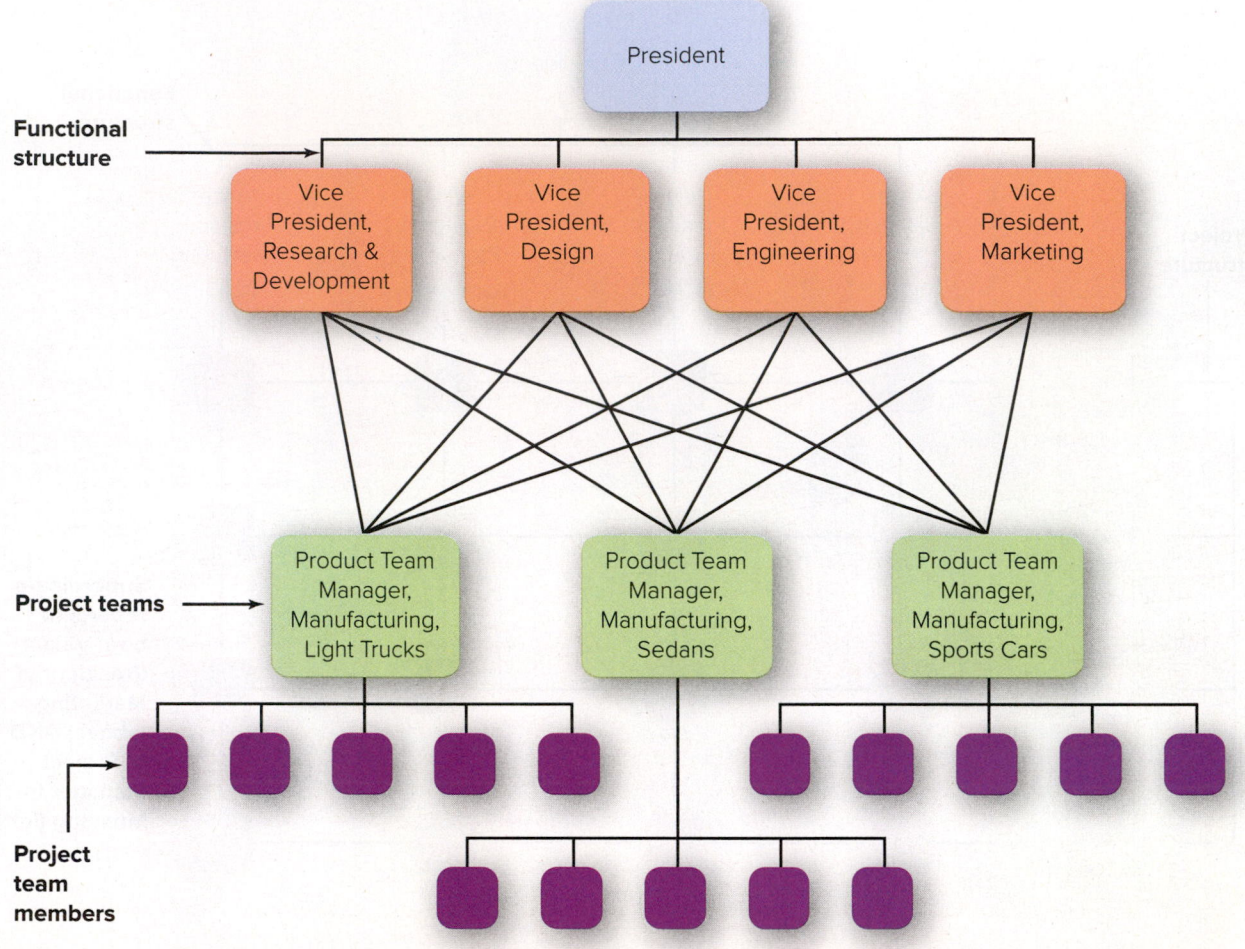

Upscale natural and organic-food grocery Whole Foods Market, now owned by Amazon, started out in 1980 as one store in Austin, Texas, and today has revenues of approximately $18 billion and 500 stores in North America and the United Kingdom.[146] The merger of Whole Foods and Amazon sent up red flags for many because the two companies had such radically different cultures. It was hard to imagine that there wouldn't be structural changes as Amazon's priorities made their way into Whole Foods stores.

Let's look at the organizational structure of Whole Foods before it was acquired by Amazon, and then explore structural changes since the acquisition.

Whole Foods, Pre-Amazon

Whole Foods' culture was built on cooperation, teamwork, and innovation. The company's management approach was based on autonomous profit centers of self-managed teams rather than hierarchy. In fact, one of Whole Foods' core operating principles was that all work was teamwork. These

characteristics were well-aligned with the organizational structure at Whole Foods, and they worked together to enable the execution of the company's differentiation strategy. Here were three of the key features of Whole Foods' structure:

- Each store was organized into roughly eight self-managed teams, each with a designated team leader. The leaders in each store also operated as a team, as did the store leaders in each region, and the directors of the company's 11 regions operated as a team.

- At the individual-store level, compensation was tied to team rather than individual performance, and performance measurements and individual pay schedules were open to all.

- Each team had the mission of improving the food for which it was responsible; was given wide flexibility in how it managed its responsibilities, hired and fired its members, and stocked its shelves; and was given a lot of power in how it responded to the changing tastes of local consumers.

Whole Foods' experienced big changes to its organizational structure and culture after merging with Amazon, and the two companies struggled to marry their very different approaches to doing business. A quick peek into a store such as the one pictured here demonstrates Amazon's strong physical presence in Whole Foods locations along with some of the elements of its culture. NYCStock/Shutterstock

delivery trucks. Their performance with this system is monitored via compliance scorecards. Workers who fail to comply have been reprimanded and even fired. Issues with poorly stocked shelves have been fairly common.

- Individual store personalities have been replaced with Amazon imagery throughout the stores, and employees are repeatedly reminded to place large signs over Prime deals and additional signs over samples and displays.

- Amazon has centralized marketing, purchasing, and procurement operations at the Austin, TX, Whole Foods headquarters.

- After implementing a $15 minimum wage for all Whole Foods workers, many

Whole Foods, Post-Amazon

Amazon's culture has been described as one where intense competition, physical exertion, and extreme monitoring and surveillance are the norm. This culture supports Amazon's cost leadership strategy, but it doesn't align well with the structure that was in place at Whole Foods prior to the acquisition. Here are some of the structural changes Amazon has made to Whole Foods stores:[147]

- A new order-to-shelf inventory system means employees often transfer inventory directly onto store shelves from

employees' schedules were cut by 3 to 5 hours, negating any increases from the raise.

YOUR CALL

Do you think Amazon's efforts to increase centralization in Whole Foods' structure will eventually pay off? Or do you think a horizontal design is better and should be left in place in a retail business such as a Whole Foods store?

3. Designs That Open Boundaries between Organizations: Hollow, Modular, and Virtual Structures

The opposite of a bureaucracy, with its numerous barriers and divisions, a **boundaryless organization** is a fluid, highly adaptive organization whose members, linked by information technology, come together to collaborate on common tasks. The collaborators may include not only co-workers but also suppliers, customers, and even competitors. This means that the form of the business is ever-changing, and business relationships are informal.[148]

The boundary-opening category of organizational design includes the *hollow, modular*, and *virtual* structures.

The Hollow Structure: Operating with a Central Core and Outsourcing Functions to Outside Vendors

In the **hollow structure**, often called the network structure, the organization has a central core of key functions and outsources other

FIGURE 8.12

Hollow structure

This is an example of a personal computer company that outsources noncore processes to vendors.

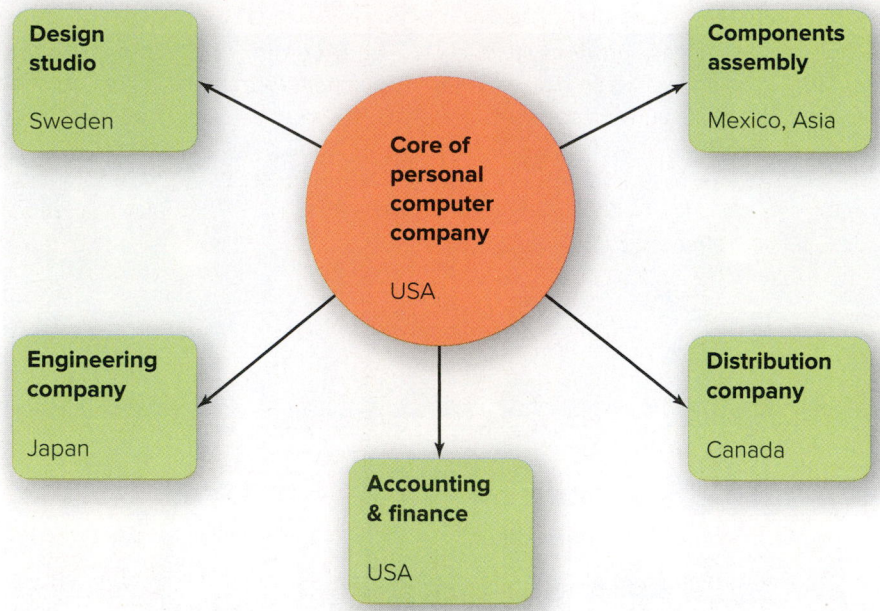

functions to vendors who can do them cheaper or faster. *(See Figure 8.12.)* A company with a hollow structure might retain such important core processes as design or marketing and outsource most other processes, such as human resources, warehousing, or distribution, thereby seeming to "hollow out" the organization.[149]

A firm with a hollow structure might operate with extensive, even worldwide operations, yet its basic core could remain small, thus keeping payrolls and overhead down. The glue that holds everything together is information technology, along with strategic alliances and contractual arrangements with supplier companies. 3M is an example of a company with a hollow structure. The company has outsourced multiple aspects of its business for years, including much of its manufacturing, reverse logistics, and e-catalog management.[150]

The Modular Structure: Outsourcing Pieces of a Product to Outside Firms

The modular structure differs from the hollow structure in that it is oriented around outsourcing certain *pieces of a product* rather than outsourcing certain *processes* (such as human resources or warehousing) of an organization. In a ==modular structure==, a firm assembles product chunks, or modules, provided by outside contractors. One article compares this form of organization to "a collection of Lego bricks that can snap together."

Apple Example: In manufacturing many of its devices, Apple procures component parts from a multitude of suppliers and then uses service vendors to assemble the components into a final Apple product. For example, touchscreen controllers come from a company in Norwood, MA; taptic engines (the technology that makes the "tapping" feeling happen when you execute some functions on your iPhone) come from Japan; and memory modules, phone casings, and ceramic capacitors come from China.[151] This example highlights a potential danger of using a modular structure. When COVID-19 took hold of China in early 2020, Apple's manufacturing and revenue took a major hit because so much of its supply chain was located there.[152]

The Virtual Structure: An Internet-Connected Partner for a Temporary Project

"There is fantastic talent out there to drive growing companies," says one industry observer, "but the best people are scattered everywhere and with full personal lives that prevent them from relocating to headquarters easily."[153] One consequence of this is the ==virtual structure==, an organization whose members are geographically apart, usually working with e-mail and other forms of information technology, yet which generally appears to customers as a single, unified organization with a real physical location.[154]

articulāte Example: articulāte is a fully remote e-learning company that is built on the values of autonomy, productivity, and respect. According to one of the company's engineers, "Autonomy doesn't mean 'work in a vacuum all by your lonesome.' In fact, we're very interdependent and collaborate a lot, so we do need to be available sometimes for our teammates. People on teams decide when they need each other and sync on schedules. A team's work hours are fluid, flexible, and determined by the people they impact." The company has provided e-learning software solutions to 98,000 organizations in 151 countries.[155] ●

8.6 Career Corner: Managing Your Career Readiness

Figure 8.13 shows the model of career readiness we introduced in Chapter 1. Organizational culture and structure are important aspects of an organization's internal context. Recall from Chapter 4 that an organization's internal context represents the situational or environmental characteristics that influence employees' behavior.[156]

If you want to know whether you fit in with an organization, you need to understand the organization's internal context. Knowing your level of fit is important because studies suggest that high levels of fit ultimately lead to higher job satisfaction, performance, and greater chances of being promoted.[157]

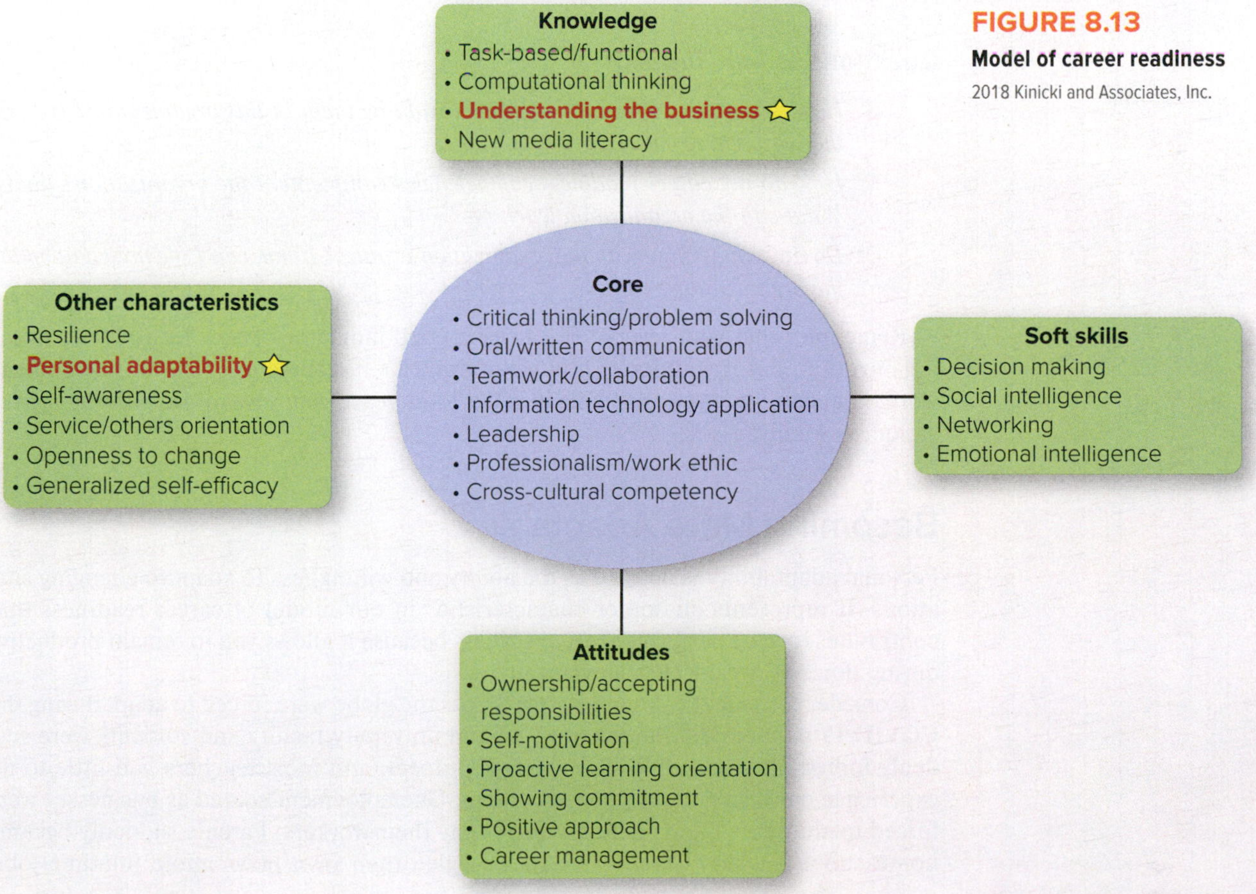

LO 8-6

Explain how to use the career readiness competencies of understanding the business and personal adaptability to better understand and change your level of fit with an organization.

FIGURE 8.13

Model of career readiness

2018 Kinicki and Associates, Inc.

Knowledge
- Task-based/functional
- Computational thinking
- **Understanding the business** ☆
- New media literacy

Other characteristics
- Resilience
- **Personal adaptability** ☆
- Self-awareness
- Service/others orientation
- Openness to change
- Generalized self-efficacy

Core
- Critical thinking/problem solving
- Oral/written communication
- Teamwork/collaboration
- Information technology application
- Leadership
- Professionalism/work ethic
- Cross-cultural competency

Soft skills
- Decision making
- Social intelligence
- Networking
- Emotional intelligence

Attitudes
- Ownership/accepting responsibilities
- Self-motivation
- Proactive learning orientation
- Showing commitment
- Positive approach
- Career management

Interestingly, adaptability—the ability to maintain fit when the organization's culture changes—seems to be equally or even more important in determining your performance. Recent research suggests that employees who adapt quickly to changing cultural norms have even better outcomes than employees who are a great fit with the organization when they are first hired.[158]

This section thus focuses on improving your career readiness competency of understanding the business by assessing an organization's internal context and improving your career readiness competency of personal adaptability so that you can adjust to changes in the organization's internal context.

Understanding the Business and Where You "Fit" In

We are focusing on understanding the business by assessing your level of fit with an organization. Experts suggest that knowing the answers to these questions about an organization will help you to make an assessment of fit.[159]

Questions to Ask of Your Prospective/New Colleagues

1. *What projects are you working on right now?*
2. *What do you hope to achieve here? What gets in your way?*
3. *What kinds of people succeed in this organization? What kinds of people don't succeed?*

Questions to Ask of Your Prospective/New Boss

1. *Would you tell me about someone you hired here who was very successful?*
2. *Would you tell me about someone you hired here who was not successful?*
3. *What do you want to be praising me for at my first performance review?*

Questions to Ask Yourself

1. *How do people respond to me when I walk by them in this organization? How do they respond to each other?*
2. *How do my career readiness competencies complement the organization's goals? What can the organization teach me?*
3. *Do my values align with the organization's values? If not, can I see myself adopting the organization's values?*

Remember that your level of fit can be a good indicator of how far you'll go in the organization, but if you don't fit in right away, it's not the end of the world. You can work on becoming more adaptable in order to increase your level of fit with the organization, as we discuss next.

Becoming More Adaptable

Personal adaptability is defined as the ability and willingness to adapt to changing situations. It represents an "other characteristic" in our model of career readiness that contributes to your performance and success because it allows you to remain productive during times of organizational change.[160]

Consider the extent to which people across the globe were forced to adapt during the COVID-19 pandemic. Millions of K–12 and university faculty and students were suddenly forced into an online learning environment, and most teachers had little to no experience delivering online course content. Unemployment soared as businesses were forced to shut down and could no longer pay their workers. Parents suddenly became homeschool teachers—often while they juggled their own now-remote full-time jobs.

Even the few businesses that were allowed to stay open (those classified as essential) had to make sweeping changes to their business models. Here are a few examples of businesses whose owners showed great personal adaptability during the quarantine:[161]

Horderly Example: Professional decluttering and organizing firm Horderly adapted to the COVID-19 pandemic by quickly shifting its in-home service to a fully online model. Within three days, the company had set up a virtual service and updated its website to direct visitors to information on how they could sign up.[162]

Glass Distillery Example: One of the first items to disappear from store shelves amid the initial COVID-19 panic was hand sanitizer, and bottles were selling for up to $100 a piece on some websites. Glass Distillery realized that it could use its supplies and equipment to produce hand sanitizer. The company offered free mini bottles to anyone who wanted to pick one up, and they kept an income stream by selling family-sized bottles for .39 cents per ounce. The Seattle police department ordered 5 gallons, and local grocers placed orders in bulk for their store workers.[163]

Try the following suggestions to increase your level of adaptability.

Adaptability during a pandemic. Ian MacNeil, founder of Glass Distillery, showed adaptability when he devised a creative solution to the COVID-19 induced hand sanitizer shortage. Courtesy of Glass Distillery

- **Focus on being optimistic.** Optimistic people see change as an opportunity. Because they therefore view work or career changes as challenges to be overcome, they have positive expectations about future events and confidence in their ability to adjust. Optimistic people tend not to whine. Rather, they attempt to change or influence a decision or they adapt and move on.[164]

- **Display a proactive learning orientation.** A proactive learning orientation reflects your desire to learn and improve other career readiness competencies. This attitude keeps you focused on learning and initiating the behavior desired by an organization during times of change.

- **Be more resourceful.** When faced with challenges, look for solutions not problems. Practice using project post-mortems, discussed in Chapter 7, to find creative ideas for improving results. It also helps to create contingency plans that identify what you can do if Plan A doesn't work.

- **Take ownership and accept responsibility.** This career readiness attitude is the willingness to accept responsibility for your actions. Adaptable people don't become "victim to external influences because they're proactive," according to a *Forbes* writer. He notes that, "To adapt to something new you must forego the old. Adaptable people don't hold grudges or eschew needlessly but instead absorb, understand and move on."[165] Indeed sound advice.

- **Expand your perspective by asking different questions.** Asking new or novel questions helps to broaden your perspective when faced with a challenge. Most of us tend to ask questions that are too narrow. Try something like: "What surprises me about this situation? What are impossible options in this situation? What data am I ignoring?"[166]

Key Terms Used in This Chapter

Key Points

8.1 Aligning Culture, Structure, and HR Practices to Support Strategy

- The challenge for top managers is to align the organization's culture, structure, and HR practices to support the execution of strategy.
- Organizational culture is defined as the set of shared, taken-for-granted implicit assumptions that a group holds and that determines how it perceives, thinks about, and reacts to its various environments.
- Organizational structure is a formal system of task and reporting relationships that coordinates and motivates an organization's members so that they can work together to achieve the organization's goals.

8.2 What Kind of Organizational Culture Will You Be Operating In?

- Organizational culture appears in three levels. Level 1 is observable artifacts. Level 2 is espoused values. Level 3 consists of basic assumptions.
- Culture is transmitted to employees in symbols, stories, heroes, rites and rituals, and organizational socialization.
- According to one common methodology known as the competing values framework, organizational cultures can be classified into four types: (1) clan, (2) adhocracy, (3) market, and (4) hierarchy.

8.3 The Process of Culture Change

- The 12 mechanisms/levers managers use to embed a culture in an organization are (1) formal statements; (2) slogans and sayings; (3) rites and rituals; (4) stories, legends, and myths; (5) leader reactions to crises; (6) role modeling, training, and coaching; (7) physical design; (8) rewards, titles, promotions, and bonuses; (9) organizational goals and performance criteria; (10) measurable and controllable activities; (11) organizational structure; and (12) organizational systems and procedures.
- Changing culture requires using multiple levers.

8.4 The Major Features of an Organization

- An organization is a system of consciously coordinated activities or forces of two or more people.
- Organizations vary according to seven features. Four proposed by Edgar Schein are (1) common purpose; (2) coordinated effort; (3) division of labor; and (4) hierarchy of authority, a control mechanism for making sure the right people do the right things at the right time.
- Three other common features are (5) span of control; (6) authority—accountability, responsibility, and delegation; and (7) centralization versus decentralization of authority.
- Whatever the size of an organization, it can be represented in an organization chart, a boxes-and-lines illustration showing the formal lines of authority and the organization's official positions or division of labor.

8.5 Eight Types of Organizational Structures

- Organizations may be arranged into eight types of structures: (1) simple, (2) functional, (3) divisional, (4) matrix, (5) horizontal, (6) hollow, (7) modular, and (8) virtual.

8.6 Career Corner: Managing Your Career Readiness

- You can use the career readiness competencies of understanding the business and personal adaptability to better understand and change your level of fit with an organization.

- You can ask questions of your colleagues, boss, and self to determine how you "fit" in a specific context.
- You can become more adaptable by being optimistic, displaying a proactive learning orientation, being more resourceful, taking ownership and accepting responsibility, and expanding your perspective by asking different questions.

Understanding the Chapter: What Do I Know?

1. To implement an organization's strategy, what are the important areas that managers must align?
2. Describe and explain the three levels of organizational culture.
3. What are five ways in which culture is transmitted to employees?
4. How would you describe the four types of organizational culture, according to the competing values framework?
5. Name 12 mechanisms/levers by which an organization's members teach each other preferred values, beliefs, expectations, and behaviors.
6. What are seven major features of organizations?
7. Describe the four organizational structures that represent traditional organizational designs.
8. Explain what is meant by horizontal organizational structure.
9. What are three organizational structures that open boundaries between organizations?

Management in Action

Wells Fargo's Sales Culture Fails the Company

How do you sell money? This is a fundamental challenge for retail banks, and Richard Kovacevich had a solution. He saw banks as stores, bankers as salespeople, and financial instruments as consumer products. Much like a deli worker asks if you'd like to upsize that combo or add dessert to your order, a banker should encourage you to add a credit card, savings account, or loan to your portfolio. Kovacevich called it "cross-selling," and he based it on the fact that customers with several accounts are much more profitable to a bank than customers with a single account. How many accounts should a customer have? Eight, according to the "Going for Gr-Eight" initiative he launched as CEO of Norwest in 1997. Why eight? Because, Kovacevich said, "It rhymes with GREAT!"[167]

SALES PRACTICES AT WELLS FARGO

Norwest merged with Wells Fargo in 1998; the bank retained the Wells Fargo name, and Kovacevich took the helm as president and CEO. He saw revenue growth as the bank's most important goal and cross-selling as the way to achieve it.[168] Bankers could earn between $500 and $2,000 in quarterly bonuses for hitting sales

targets, and district managers could increase their annual compensation by up to $20,000. According to former Wells Fargo worker Scott Trainor, "If you could sell, you had a job."[169]

The strong sales culture transformed Wells Fargo's bottom line, as evidenced by a 67% increase in the bank's stock from 2006 to 2015.[170] Unfortunately, the culture had a dark side. Steven Schrodt, who worked at a Wells Fargo branch in Lincoln, Nebraska, before resigning due to severe sales pressure in 2012, remembers managers encouraging those who hadn't reached sales goals to open accounts for their family members and friends. Other former employees describe searching for potential customers at retirement homes and local bus stops.[171]

Bankers who grew tired of asking friends, family, and strangers for business adopted more covert tactics. One former Wells Fargo employee recalls the day he discovered a high-performing co-worker's secret formula. A customer had applied for a home equity loan and somehow also ended up with a $20,000 personal line of credit. "So then I realized how he was doing all his loans, because he was basically tagging on other loan products in the same application so they wouldn't really notice when they signed the documents."[172]

Problems started to emerge in 2009. At this point, Richard Kovacevich was gone, John Stumpf was president and CEO, and Kovacevich's sales culture was deeply embedded. To investigate potential problems in retail sales practices (RSPs) in the bank's branches, Wells Fargo established an internal task force in 2012. The task force concluded that the unethical behavior was due to a small set of "rogue" individual branch workers.[173] Wells Fargo subsequently fired more than 5,000 "rogue" bankers between 2013 and 2016.[174]

WELLS FARGO ADMITS TO FRAUD: BLAMES PROBLEM ON WORKERS, NOT CULTURE

In September 2016, the Office of the Comptroller of the Currency (OCC), the Consumer Financial Protection Bureau (CFPB), and the Los Angeles City Attorney publicly fined Wells Fargo $185 million for opening millions of bank accounts without customers' knowledge.[175] The bank openly admitted to the fraud, but executives noted that Wells Fargo had official policies in place in their *Sales Quality Manual* requiring customers' consent "for each specific solution or service" and expressly prohibiting bankers from opening multiple accounts to increase incentive compensation.[176] In an interview with *The Wall Street Journal*, CEO Stumpf maintained, "there was no incentive to do bad things," adding, "the 1% that did it wrong, who we fired, terminated, in no way reflects our culture nor reflects the great work the other vast majority of the people do."[177] Former workers tell a different story.

Former employees who worked at Wells Fargo between 2004 and 2011 told *NPR* the fraud was pervasive and that managers were heavily involved. One former banker recalled sitting at a conference table with her managers in a windowless, locked room and receiving a "formal warning" to sign. Her managers told her that bankers who didn't meet sales goals were not team players, and poor team members would be fired and forced to carry the mark on their permanent records.[178] Employees who played by the rules and reported their concerns were fired from their jobs within weeks of reporting for things like "excessive tardiness."[179]

ANOTHER SCANDAL

Stumpf resigned from Wells Fargo in October 2016, and Timothy Sloan took over as CEO. Sloan immediately discontinued labeling branches "stores" and overhauled the bank's incentive compensation plan, shifting the focus to customer satisfaction and drastically reducing the emphasis on sales goals. He restructured the organization to fully centralize the bank's risk and HR functions, consolidating "much of the vast risk-control bureaucracy into a new office of ethics, oversight, and integrity, accountable to the board's risk committee."[180] In spite of Sloan's efforts, another scandal was brewing.

Earlier in 2016, executives at Wells Fargo had realized that hundreds of thousands of car loan customers had been charged for unnecessary auto insurance.[181] An internal report revealed that the costs of the gratuitous insurance resulted in auto loan defaults for more than 270,000 customers and the repossession of approximately 25,000 vehicles.[182] Federal probes into the insurance debacle shed light on yet another slew of internal issues with compliance, controls, and board oversight of operations at Wells Fargo.[183] In a report released in October 2017, OCC regulators slammed managers at Wells Fargo Dealer Services (the bank's auto loan unit) for ignoring customer complaints, failing to monitor contractors, and general laziness in responding to problems that had been unfolding since at least 2015.[184]

In July 2017, Wells Fargo publicly admitted it became aware of the auto insurance scandal a year prior. Interestingly, when the Senate Banking Committee asked, as part of the September 2016 hearings related to RSP fraud, if executives were "confident that this type of fraudulent activity does not exist" in other areas, the bank insisted problems were limited to individual employees in the community banking division.[185] Senator Sherrod Brown has since alleged that Wells Fargo "pure and simple lied to this committee—and lied to the public" in failing to disclose the auto insurance problems during the 2016 hearings.[186] Sloan has maintained there are fundamental differences between the RSP and auto insurance scandals, with only the former being fueled by sales incentives.[187]

AFTERMATH

In February 2018 the Federal Reserve capped Wells Fargo's growth and stated that the bank would not be allowed to accumulate any more assets until the Fed believed the bank had turned itself around.[188] Two months later, the CFPB handed down a record $1 billion fine related, in part, to the auto insurance scandal.[189] By early 2020 Wells Fargo agreed to a settlement with the DOJ, including a $3 billion fine related to the creation of three million fraudulent accounts between 2002 and 2016. The DOJ agreed to withhold criminal charges, provided that the bank continued to cooperate in investigations and comply with all relevant laws for three more years. As part of the settlement, Wells Fargo admitted to two criminal violations—identity theft and creating false bank records.[190]

By early 2020 the OCC had also fined eight of the bank's former executives a total of $59 million. Stumpf's $17.5 million portion of the total was the largest penalty the OCC had ever imposed on an individual. In addition, Stumpf received a lifetime ban from the banking industry.[191]

NEW LEADERSHIP, NEW STRUCTURE

The year 2019 brought a change in leadership when Sloan stepped down from his role as CEO. "It has become apparent to me that our ability to successfully move Wells Fargo forward from here will benefit from a new CEO and fresh perspectives," he said.[192] Charles Scharf, the former CEO of Visa and Bank of New York Mellon, took over as CEO, and he quickly announced a plan to radically restructure the bank as part of his effort to implement changes. Scharf's reorganization split the bank's structure into five lines of business, with each line overseen by its own CEO, and each CEO reporting directly to Scharf. He said, "These changes create the right structure to build our businesses over the long term and increase our ability to successfully execute on our top priority, which is the risk, regulatory and control work. I am confident that this organizational model and our strengthened risk and control foundation will bring greater focus and accountability to the company."[193]

Testifying before the House Financial Services Committee in March 2020, Scharf said, "I want to give you my personal assurance that we will do the work necessary to put Wells Fargo on sound footing with our customers, employees, regulators, shareholders, and the communities we serve," adding, "What we have done to date is not enough, and we will continue to drive progress."[194]

FOR DISCUSSION

Problem-Solving Perspective

1. What is the underlying problem in this case from the regulators' perspective?

2. What role do you believe Wells Fargo's executive leadership played in the RSP and auto insurance scandals?

3. What do you think regulators should have done to encourage permanent change in Wells Fargo's culture and prevent similar problems in the broader banking industry?

Application of Chapter Content

1. Using the competing values framework as a point of reference, how would you describe the organizational culture under CEO Kovacevich and under CEO Sloan? Provide examples to support your conclusions.

2. How do you think new branch employees learned the culture at Wells Fargo?

3. Describe how Wells Fargo's new CEO might use the 12 mechanisms/levers for culture change to improve the bank's culture.

4. Describe Wells Fargo's organizational structure before Scharf took over the bank. Then describe the structure after he became CEO. Explain the key differences, including what impact you think the changes will have.

5. What is the most important lesson from this case? Discuss.

Legal/Ethical Challenge

Should Socializing Outside Work Hours Be Mandatory?

Person–organization fit reflects the extent to which someone's personality and values match, or fit, with an organization's culture and climate. Good fit is important for both employees and organizations. This challenge involves the cultural considerations of asking employees to socialize outside work hours. If socializing outside work is an expectation of new hires, then it becomes something to consider when applying for jobs.

Why would companies ask employees to socialize outside of work hours? There are a number of good reasons: (1) fostering comfort and relaxation among employees, (2) helping people de-stress after a hard day, (3) learning more about one's colleagues, and (4) building teamwork and unity. All of these benefits should improve interpersonal relationships

and potentially boost productivity and customer service.

If such requests are voluntary, however, then it is likely that fewer people will show up, thereby reducing the benefits. People who show up are more likely to be like-minded and share a common race and gender, as well as hobbies. For example, one employee described the in-group at their company as the folks who hunted and fished together outside of work.[195] Voluntary requests can thus serve as a subtle way of promoting homogeneity rather than diversity.

Moreover, voluntary requests potentially set up a situation in which people develop unequal social networks. This can have unfair career advantages for those who attend because people discuss work-related issues at such gatherings. In an interview, advertising executive Ian Mirmelstein said his career has suffered since he stopped attending work happy hours.[196]

It thus makes some sense to make it mandatory to socialize outside of work. Some companies accept this conclusion. Zappos did in the past, and other companies continue the practice today. But some research says when employees feel forced to fake emotions—such as when they attend after-hours work events when they don't want to—they're more likely to engage in heavy drinking later on.[197]

One woman told a reporter that there was an unwritten requirement at her employer that "employees were expected to spend extra money and time on group lunches and twice-weekly drinks. This kind of socializing was necessary in order to get ahead." She was not told about the requirement during the hiring process, and she now feels a lack of fit. Her problem with the expectation is that she has two children to pick up from school and she tries to save money by taking her lunch to work. In a recent performance appraisal, she was told, "I needed to be more of a team player." Her feedback was partly based on her lack of socializing outside of work.[198]

SOLVING THE CHALLENGE

What are your thoughts about making it mandatory to socialize outside of work hours?

1. I think it's a good idea. The benefits exceed the costs, and I don't agree that it fails to appreciate diversity. The socializing activities can be varied to fit the values and needs of diverse employees, thereby supporting diversity.

2. I don't like it. What employees do after work hours is their business, and companies should not infringe on them. Socializing outside work hours should be voluntary.

3. I believe that employers have no business interfering with how employees spend time outside of work. This means that I don't want either voluntary or mandatory requests about socializing outside of work hours. If people want to socialize outside work, let them arrange it on their own.

4. Invent other options.

9

Human Resource Management

Getting the Right People for Managerial Success

Kapook2981/iStock/Getty Images

After reading this chapter, you should be able to:

LO 9-1 Discuss the importance of strategic human resource management.

LO 9-2 Discuss ways to recruit and hire the right people.

LO 9-3 Outline common forms of compensation.

LO 9-4 Describe the processes used for onboarding and learning and development.

LO 9-5 Discuss effective performance management and feedback techniques.

LO 9-6 List guidelines for handling promotions, transfers, discipline, and dismissals.

LO 9-7 Discuss legal considerations managers should be aware of.

LO 9-8 Describe labor–management issues and ways to work effectively with labor unions.

LO 9-9 Review the steps for becoming a better receiver of feedback.

FORECAST *What's Ahead in This Chapter*

This chapter considers human resource (HR) management—planning for, attracting, developing, and retaining an effective workforce. We consider how this subject fits in with the overall company strategy, culture, and structure; how to use HR practices for strategic advantage; and how to recruit and select qualified people. We describe the common forms of compensation, the processes used for onboarding and learning and development, and how to manage employee performance and give feedback. We discuss guidelines for handling promotions, discipline, and workplace performance problems. We go over basic legal requirements and consider the role of labor unions. We conclude with a Career Corner that focuses on how to become a better receiver of feedback.

How to Prepare for a Job Interview

Job candidates often make a few common mistakes in initial interviews. Here are some tips for using the career readiness competencies of career management, new media literacy, and communication skills to avoid them.

Ace Your Virtual Screening

According to one study by the Society for Human Resource Management, at least half of employers use video conferencing to screen candidates before scheduling in-person interviews.[1] These may not be as in-depth as face-to-face interviews, but they often are the first step to securing an invite to visit the company. There are several ways to prepare for virtual interviews. First, test your technology beforehand. Be sure you know how to work the meeting software and use this opportunity to iron out any issues that you may experience with it. Next, spend some time figuring out your best backdrop, lighting, and attire. Find a professional-looking, tidy spot in your home or office, take advantage of natural light, and wear something that will complement your appearance on camera. Finally, get rid of distractions. Open your computer settings and turn off pop-up notifications for e-mail, text messages, and other programs that will be noisy and bothersome to you and the interviewer.[2]

Be Prepared

Can you pronounce the names of the company and interviewer with which you're interviewing? Do you understand what the company makes or does, and the duties of the position for which you're interviewing? Do you know the company's competition? What new products or services are being offered? What are your greatest strengths and specific achievements? Your weaknesses? Research the company's website and any recent press about the firm. Check out the company's social media and see how they interact with followers. Identify strengths of yours that fit what the company does. When asked about your weaknesses, discuss how you recognized one, overcame a dilemma it posed, and were improved by it. Practice your answers, but not so much that you sound phony saying them.[3]

Dress Right and Be on Time

Dress neatly and professionally. Make sure you know the exact location of the interview, and if possible, do a test run a day or so before, at about the same time of day as your interview, so you know how long it will take to get there on time. When you arrive, be courteous to the receptionist and greet everyone who greets you. Silence your phone and don't take it out again until you've left the building. A recent study of 290 recruiters found that interviewers across industry segments agreed that (1) neat and professional appearance, (2) being on time, and (3) keeping your cell phone out of sight were among the most important factors in a job interview.[4]

Practice What to Say and What to Ask

Rehearse questions to ask the interviewer, such as the challenges for the position in the future and how success in the job will be defined. Don't make negative comments about your old company or boss. Rather, figure out the positives and convey what you gained from your experience.[5] If asked an inappropriate question (about age, marital status, whether you have children or plan to), politely say you don't believe the question is relevant to your qualifications.[6] Within 24 hours of the meeting, send an e-mail (with no misspellings or faulty grammar) thanking the interviewer and reiterating your interest in the position.[7] If you think you messed up part of the interview, use the e-mail to smooth over your mistakes.[8]

Know What You Will Be Asked

A recent survey found that up to 95% of employers use one or more background checks in the hiring process.[9] Some employers may ask for your GPA, especially if a job opening is highly competitive. If your grade point average is not as high as you would like, prepare an explanation.[10] Finally, be sure your social media profile is mostly private, and that whatever is public is limited, is not too personal, and would make your loved ones proud. At least 70% of employers scrutinize job seekers' social media profiles, sometimes in search of personal information they are not allowed to ask about, such as whether you are married.

Plan for a Strong Closing

Most interviews end with the recruiter asking something like "do you have any final questions for us?" You can make yourself more memorable if you prepare a strong response. Experts at the consulting firm Accenture recommend a couple of things. First, ask questions that are future-oriented and that emphasize your success. For example, "How do you envision this role expanding in the next five years, and how will you determine whether I've been successful on the job?" Finally—and most importantly, according to Accenture—is to close the interview by *asking for the job*. This expresses your sincere interest in the job and can lead to a discussion about next steps in the process.[11]

For Discussion What kind of advice do you see here that you wish you'd followed in the past? What will you do differently next time?

9.1 Strategic Human Resource Management

THE BIG PICTURE

Human resource management consists of the activities managers perform to plan for, attract, develop, and retain an effective workforce. Strategic human resource management consists of the process of designing and implementing systems of policies and practices that align an organization's human capital with its strategic objectives.

LO 9-1

Discuss the importance of strategic human resource management.

You learned in Chapter 8 that three key internal factors influence an organization's ability to successfully implement strategy. We discussed two of these factors—organizational culture and organizational structure—at length in Chapter 8. We now turn our attention to the third factor—the human resource (HR) practices organizations use to manage their most important assets—people. As previously defined, *HR practices* consist of all the activities organizations use to manage their human capital, including staffing, performance management, learning and development programs, and compensation.

The best companies know that how they manage their people is an important determinant of organizational success. For example, the top five workplaces for Millennials in 2020—Ultimate Software, Cisco, Edward Jones, Pinnacle Financial Partners, and Kimley-Horn—all make substantial investments in their people through unique and strategically aligned hiring, performance management, learning and development, and compensation practices.[12] Further, a recent study found that companies that place employees' experiences front and center outperform the S&P 500 stock market index by anywhere from 53 to 122 percentage points![13] Clearly, great human resources practices are a game changer.

In this section we explain how HR practices can generate superior firm performance and competitive advantages.

FIGURE 9.1

Human resource practices

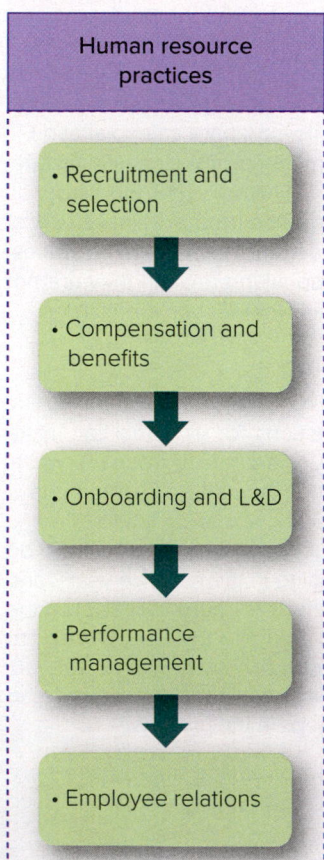

Human Resource Management: Managing an Organization's Most Important Resource

Human resource management (HRM) is the process of planning for, attracting, developing, and retaining an effective workforce. This process is made up of various HR practices including employee recruitment, compensation, onboarding, and performance management (*see Figure 9.1*).

Regardless of industry, all organizations use HR practices to some extent to manage their workers. For example, even the smallest mom-and-pop company with only two or three employees has to decide whom to hire (selection) and how much salary to pay (compensation). But according to a study of more than 12,000 companies across 34 countries, the organizations that grow the fastest, live the longest, and are the most profitable and productive are the ones that do the best job managing people.[14]

"If you're not thinking all the time about making every person valuable, you don't have a chance," according to former General Electric CEO Jack Welch. "What's the alternative? Wasted minds? Uninvolved people? A labor force that's angry or bored? That doesn't make sense!"[15] Indeed, companies ranked in the top 10 on *Fortune* magazine's 2020 Best Companies list—including Hilton, Ultimate Software, Wegmans Food Markets, Cisco, Workday, Salesforce, Edward Jones, Stryker, American Express, and Kimpton Hotels & Restaurants—have discovered that putting employees first is the foundation for success.[16] Here are a few ways these award-winning organizations are leading the pack in HRM:[17]

- Ultimate Software offers a whopping 45% match on employee 401K contributions (compared to the average employer match of 4.7%).

- Workday provides employees with backup child care options for days when parents' regular options fall through.

- Stryker extends health care benefits (medical, prescription, dental, vision), adoption assistance, and paid sick leave to both full-and-part-time employees.

Clearly, companies listed among the best places to work become famous by offering progressive and valued programs, policies, and procedures. Are you curious to see if a current or past employer is one of these progressive companies? You can find out by taking Self-Assessment 9.1.

SELF-ASSESSMENT 9.1

Assessing the Quality of HR Practices

This survey is designed to assess the quality of HR practices at your current place of employment. If you are not currently working, consider a previous job when completing the survey. Please be prepared to answer these questions if your instructor has assigned Self-Assessment 9.1 in Connect.

1. How did you rate the quality of the company's HR practices?

2. Based on your responses, what advice would you give the senior HR leader about how to improve its HR practices? Be specific. What are the consequences of having poor-quality HR practices? Explain.

Effective HRM means putting employees first, but successfully implementing corporate strategy takes more. Figure 9.2 outlines the process by which HR practices drive strategic implementation. Let's consider how this works.

Internal and External HR Fit Promote Strategic HR Management

Strategic human resource management is the process of designing and implementing systems of policies and practices that align an organization's human capital with its strategic objectives.[18] While HRM is about managing people, strategic HRM is about generating competitive advantages *through* people.[19] In other words, strategic HRM views people as valuable strategic assets of any organization.

A firm's approach to its human resources becomes strategic when it is integrated into the organization in ways that drive overall performance.[20] Specifically, as seen in Figure 9.2, HR systems drive strategic implementation when they foster two important types of "fit":[21]

1. *Internal fit* exists when all of the individual policies and practices within the HR system reinforce one another. For example, an organization that hires employees based on their performance potential rather than their previous experience needs to provide extensive opportunities for learning and development and should use a performance management system that rewards growth.

2. *External fit* exists when the HR system is aligned with the organization's culture and structure in support of firm-level strategy. For example, a firm that competes based on cost reductions and efficiency should reward objective job performance, provide targeted skills training, and define job performance clearly.

FIGURE 9.2
Strategic HRM: How HR practices support strategic implementation

Source: Figure based in part on: C. Ostroff, A. J. Kinicki, and R. S. Muhammad, "Organizational Culture and Climate," Handbook of Psychology: Volume 12, Industrial and Organizational Psychology, *2nd ed. (Hoboken, NJ: John Wiley & Sons, 2013), Chapter 24, pp. 643–676.*

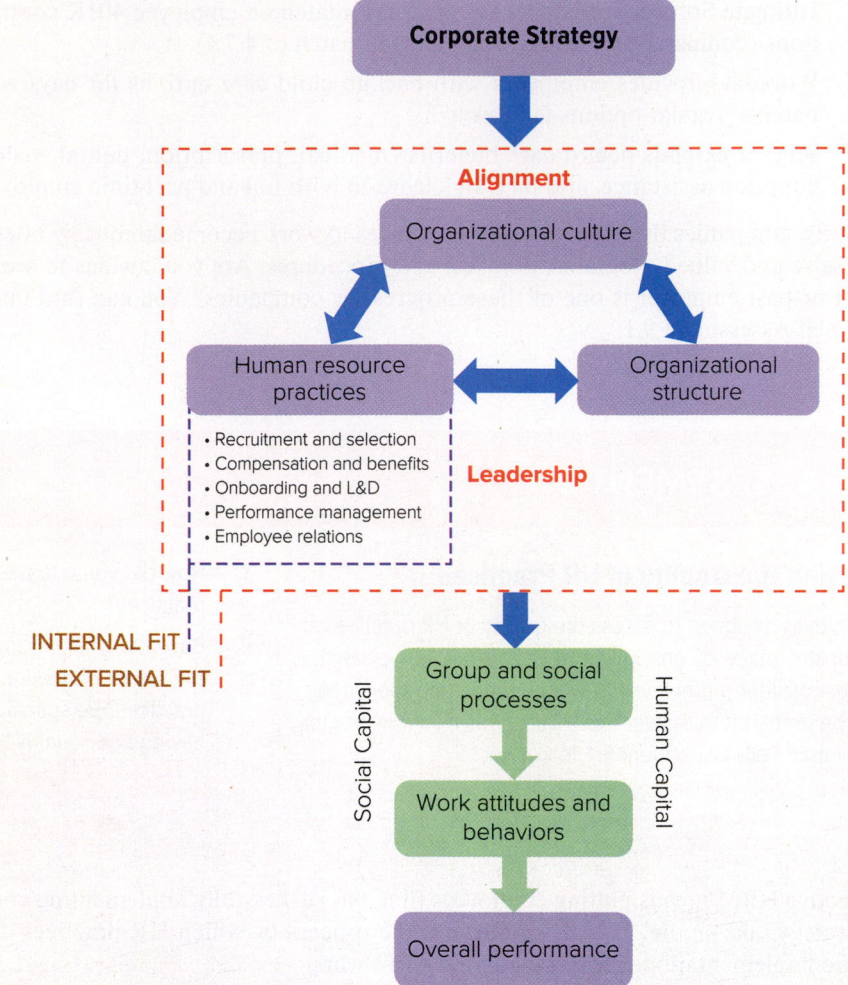

Research shows that organizations that achieve both internal and external HR fit have better outcomes, including employee satisfaction and firm performance.[22] One example is Airbnb.

Airbnb Example: Airbnb envisions a world where anyone can feel like they belong no matter where they go. Unfortunately, the company realized several years ago that it couldn't say the same for its employees. Airbnb created an "employee experience" department that was modeled after its "customer experience" department. New hires participate together in a week-long onboarding process, and this creates relationships that increase employees' sense of belonging in the company. Office spaces are designed to make employees feel like they are at home, and the company's "ground control" group is tasked with continually monitoring the environment to ensure employee experiences foster belonging.[23]

Strategic HRM enables the effective implementation of corporate strategies because it helps firms to generate and leverage two important, intangible resources: *human capital* and *social capital*.[24]

The Role of Human and Social Capital

Figure 9.2 shows that a combination of internal and external HR fit triggers the group and individual processes, attitudes, and behaviors needed for achieving organizational performance goals. Simply put, strategic HRM mobilizes necessary human capital and social capital.[25]

- **Human capital** is the economic or productive potential of employee knowledge, experience, and actions. Human capital stems from all of the employee competencies that are or could be valuable to the organization.

- **Social capital** is the economic or productive potential of strong, trusting, and cooperative relationships. Social capital stems from the reciprocity, knowledge, and capabilities that are embedded in both informal connections and close personal relationships.[26]

Strategic HRM gets the right people, competencies, and connections into the right places at the right time. Consider the following Example box about T-Mobile.

EXAMPLE | T-Mobile Applied Strategic HRM to Customer Service Employees

T-Mobile calls itself the "Un-carrier" because it strives to be different from all other telecom companies. Specifically, the company focuses on removing the typical customer "pain points" associated with mobile carriers. T-Mobile doesn't lock users into contracts, and it promises to provide an unparalleled customer service experience (a tall order when you consider that telecoms always manage to top annual lists of the "most hated companies." When Liz McAuliffe took over as T-Mobile's Chief HR Officer (CHRO) in 2016, she realized that HR needed to be reconfigured to achieve proper fit and better help the company execute its strategy.

At the time, T-Mobile was suffering from typical telecom industry ailments—unmotivated and disengaged employees who felt underutilized, restrained, and invisible. McAuliffe asked herself "How can we, as HR, best serve as advocates and stewards for every employee in their personal growth and career success?"

McAuliffe decentralized T-Mobile's HR structure and re-branded HR roles to "Employee Success Partners" (formerly HR business partners), "Talent Scouts" (formerly recruiters), and "Career Agents" (formerly L&D consultants). Customer service reps now receive enhanced training and coaching to build their competencies and broaden their career prospects. This has reduced annual turnover from 42% to 22% and decreased employee absenteeism by almost 25%. Customer service employees work in teams of people with complementary skills, and the company empowers teams to behave like small businesses and enact thoughtful, creative solutions to customer issues. By allowing reps to take the time to tailor service to individual customer needs, T-Mobile

T-Mobile president and CEO Mike Sievert is pictured here introducing Team of Experts at a company event. This initiative transformed the customer service experience by empowering small groups of employees to work together to solve customers' problems. Sean Rayford/AP Images

has removed pain points for employees as well as customers, drastically decreasing the incidence of misguided quick fixes.

Apology credits have dropped 37% because reps no longer feel pressured to generate quick (and often misguided) fixes. The number of service calls per customer account has decreased 21%, and T-Mobile has achieved its lowest cost-to-serve in company history. Additionally, customer retention levels reached an all-time high, and customer satisfaction and loyalty have skyrocketed.[27]

YOUR CALL

What specific changes at T-Mobile do you think improved internal and external fit the most?

What Is the Best Approach to Strategic Human Resource Management?

Figure 9.2 shows that when companies get strategic HRM "right" (i.e., when they achieve internal and external HR fit), they are more likely to generate the human and social capital necessary to successfully implement the firm's strategies. Recent research offers strong support for this idea, suggesting that the proper configurations of HR practices generate unique organizational capabilities that are difficult for competitors to understand and imitate.[28] In other words, HR practices can create competitive advantage. CarMax is one example.

> **Carmax Example:** CarMax is a regular on multiple "best companies" lists and has outperformed its industry sector in recent years.[29] One reason is the company's focus on its people as a strategic resource. The used auto seller continually updates its HR practices as its markets and strategic focus evolve and has shifted its sights to developing the cross-functional skills of its workforce. CarMax identifies employees for specialized management development programs that train them for flexible work assignments across the store. The company's internal website encourages employees to apply for lateral moves in order to build their skill sets. "We really want our folks to be thinking very broadly about where and how they can take their career," said Chief HR Officer Diane Long Cafritz.[30] One CarMax employee said "I am continually challenged in my job, which allows me to grow professionally," and another stated, "I get to help shape and reshape the business."[31]

But what does the right HR system look like? The answer is there is no "best" approach to strategic HRM. Rather, different firms will benefit from different approaches. As indicated by Figure 9.2, leadership plays a central role in this process.[32] Leaders must have a nuanced understanding of firm-level strategies, future performance goals and anticipated challenges, and how HR practices, structure, and culture fit together. They use this knowledge to answer three important questions:

1. What human and social capital does the firm have and how do we best leverage it?

2. What human and social capital does the firm need in order to get where it wants to go?

3. How does the firm acquire the human and social capital it lacks?

Every firm's configuration will look different, but at a broad level we can categorize strategic HRM approaches into one of two buckets: talent management and high-performance work systems. Let's discuss each of these in turn.

Talent Management   **Talent management** is an approach to strategic HRM that matches high-potential employees with an organization's most strategically valuable positions.[33] You can think of leaders who use talent management as Hollywood agents. Their job is to identify the people with the most potential to be stars—"the talent"— to polish and refine their skills, and to land them the roles where they will be most likely generate huge box office returns along with an Oscar nomination.[34] In addition to generating financial returns and competitive viability, the disproportionate investments leaders make in this elite group of employees are expected to impact them in three ways:[35]

- *Attitudes*—workers singled out as "stars" experience increased job satisfaction, engagement, and commitment to the organization.

- *Behaviors*—employees identified as high-potential respond with greater effort, better job performance, and lower turnover.

- *Cognitions*—workers respond to their organizations' elevated perceptions with higher self-efficacy and increased feelings of fulfillment.

Talent management is less about meeting short-term staffing needs and more about cultivating multiple, diverse talent pipelines that enable firms to plan for how they will continue to generate value and respond to changing markets over the long term.[36] Consider Zenefits.

Zenefits Example: The HR technology firm realized the value of its talent pipelines when several high-level industry executives were hospitalized with critical COVID-19 infections in early 2020. CEO Jay Fulcher called a meeting of the company's top 10 executives to ensure that their succession plans were ready to go in the event of sudden inability to work or death. Fulcher said it was "not a comfortable conversation" but that it was critical that the company had a plan to weather the effects of the pandemic.[37]

High-Performance Work Systems   The **high-performance work system (HPWS) approach to strategic HRM deploys bundles of internally consistent HR practices in order to improve employee ability, motivation, and opportunities across the entire organization.**[38] HPWSs impact overall organizational performance by systematically enhancing the individual performance of all of the organization's employees.[39] Research on this approach suggests that bundles of HR practices have stronger impacts on firm-level outcomes than individual HR practices.[40]

While talent management approaches are geared toward enhancing and leveraging the human and social capital of specific individuals, HPWSs focus on increasing organizations' collective levels of human and social capital. Let's consider how SAS uses a HPWS approach.

SAS Example: SAS has been voted one of *Fortune's* top 100 Best Companies for 23 consecutive years. Shannon Heath, corporate and executive communications leader at SAS, said, "SAS has always believed that if you treat people well, keep them challenged with interesting work, and respect them and their contributions, they will do their best work for you," adding, "Simply put—treat employees like they make a difference, and they will make a difference."[41] The company grew out of a software development project at NC State University and now occupies 900 acres of North Carolina woods. SAS offices are designed to feel like a college campus and feature biking and walking trails, a swimming pool, a large network of solar panels, and sports and fitness facilities. Employees at SAS receive challenging assignments and the autonomy to execute on projects as they see fit. This increases the sense of personal ownership workers have over projects and also allows for creativity and innovation.

Enhancing performance. At companies like SAS, swimming pools, fitness facilities, and outdoor activities are an important part of a broader HR system that focuses on respecting and valuing employees. UpperCut Images/SuperStock

Whether a company uses talent management, a HPWS, or some combination of the two, the ultimate goal is to maximize organizational performance. In the remainder of the chapter, we discuss each of these HR practices and how firms approach them to enable strategic implementation. ●

9.2 Recruitment and Selection: Putting the Right People into the Right Jobs

THE BIG PICTURE

Qualified applicants for jobs may be recruited from inside or outside the organization. The task of choosing the best person is enhanced by such tools as reviewing candidates' background information; conducting interviews; and screening with employment tests.

LO 9-2

Discuss ways to recruit and hire the right people.

The Society for Human Resource Management (SHRM) estimates that the recruitment and selection process for a single open position takes 36 days and costs $4,129 for the average organization.[42] Does this sound like a big investment to you? Then consider the fact that successfully recruiting and selecting qualified candidates has become increasingly difficult even for organizations willing to invest the time and money. Eighty-three percent of the HR professionals surveyed recently by SHRM said that they struggle to find qualified candidates to fill the increasing number of high-skilled jobs.[43] Moreover, experts expect this mismatch between the skills required by today's jobs and the skills available in the labor force will only worsen as technological advances will make many of today's job skills obsolete within two to five years. In fact, by the time you read this, 27% of available jobs will be for roles that didn't exist at the time of this writing.[44]

It shouldn't surprise you to learn then that today's CEOs are troubled more by their ability to find the right skills and talent for their organizations than virtually anything else.[45] Companies that want to find workers with the necessary skills need to do everything they can to get recruiting and selection right. Let's consider in more detail these important HR practices.

Recruitment: How to Attract Qualified Applicants

Recruiting is the process of locating and attracting qualified applicants for job openings. The word *qualified* is important: You want to find people whose skills, abilities, and characteristics are best suited to your organization's needs. In today's labor market, where the number of qualified job seekers is far lower than the number of available skilled jobs, firms need to be strategic in their approaches to generating applicants' interest. We discuss three recruiting approaches: *internal, external,* and *hybrid.*

1. Internal Recruiting: Hiring from the Inside   **Internal recruiting** means making people already employed by the organization aware of job openings. Many vacant positions in organizations are filled internally, and 70% of the talent professionals in a recent survey indicated that internal recruiting is becoming increasingly important in their organizations.[46] Companies use several techniques to identify potential applicants within their existing talent pools, including:

- *Internal job postings*—formal announcements about open positions circulated within the organization.

- *Informal nominations*—recommendations by managers who have direct experience observing and working with specific employees.

- *Employee profiles*—databases that house information on individual employee competencies and qualifications.

Internal recruiting may be a wise choice for companies that wish to boost retention by increasing employee commitment and engagement. It is also used by companies looking to close skills gaps. Consider the example of AT&T.

AT&T Example: AT&T uses two systems for internal recruiting. The first—Personal Learning Experience (PLE)—is an employee-facing system that catalogs workers' current competencies and allows them to search job openings within the company and assess the fit between their skills and those required by open positions. The PLE system also shows employees the training options available for acquiring particular job skills. The second—myCareer Profile (mCP)—is a management-facing system that the company uses to search for talent within its existing pool. Employees build profiles that include their qualifications, skills, work histories, and special training, and managers use the information to identify potential candidates for job openings.[47]

2. External Recruiting: Hiring from the Outside

External recruiting means **attracting job applicants from outside the organization.** In years past, notices of job vacancies were placed through newspapers, employment agencies, executive recruiting firms, union hiring halls, college job-placement offices, and word of mouth. Today more than 90% of U.S. organizations have taken at least some portion of their recruitment activities online.[48] Popular external recruitment sources include:

- *Social media*—approximately 80% of recruiters today use LinkedIn to locate potential talent, and at least 60% use Facebook. Instagram is gaining traction as a recruiting tool due to its popularity with Gen Z—25% of recruiters now reach job candidates on Instagram, and this number is significantly higher for Millennial recruiters (35%) and recruiters in tech firms (63%).[49] Research suggests that simply having a social media presence makes it far more likely that you will be invited for an interview.[50]

- *Online job postings*—companies advertise open positions on their own websites, on job search websites such as Indeed, CareerBuilder, and Glassdoor, and on university and union websites.

- *School partnerships*—recruiters identify talent through relationships with educational institutions, including universities, trade schools, and high schools.

Increased competition for qualified workers has caused companies to get creative with their external recruiting activities. McDonald's and Goldman Sachs are two examples.

Company Examples: McDonald's attempted to reach a wider audience of Gen Z applicants by embedding a special lens in its Snapchat ads. The lens showed users in a McDonald's uniform and gave them the option of sending a short video application—or, "Snaplication"—to their local store manager. Goldman Sachs recently kicked off a recruiting campaign that included posting job advertisements on Hulu, Spotify, and YouTube.[51]

3. Hybrid Approaches: Referrals and Boomerangs

You probably know people who have scored great jobs because they knew someone inside the organization. **Employee referrals** tap into existing employees' social networks to fill open positions with **outside applicants.** Referrals are popular among recruiters—they account for almost 50% of new hires in organizations.[52] According to experts, employee referrals work well because:[53]

- *Current employees are good judges of potential fit.* Referrers know what it takes to fit in with the organization's culture and to perform well in specific positions. This helps them to determine which members of their social networks would be a good fit for various jobs.

- *Referrers care about their reputations.* Current employees are careful about whom they recommend because their reputations in the organization may be enhanced or damaged by referred workers' job performance.

Another way that companies find qualified talent is from **boomerangs**—former **employees who return to the organization.** Boomerangs often are pulled away from their initial jobs by difficult life events or attractive opportunities to advance their skills and careers.[54] Boomerangs already understand the organization's culture and require little to no onboarding. Hiring them is cheaper and less time consuming. Modern organizations are increasingly open to the idea of "taking back" former employees.[55] Take the example of Kronos.

Kronos Example: Kronos is a workforce management software firm that has made *Fortune's* list of 100 Best Companies to work for multiple times. Kronos delivers cloud-based applications for improving employee engagement to companies across the globe. When Kronos was having trouble attracting top talent, CEO Aron Ain saw the need for a new approach to engaging the company's own workforce. One way that Kronos did this was by championing employees' careers, whether those happened inside or outside of the company. Said Ain, "We don't own our employees' careers. If they have a great offer, we support their decision to take it. Sure, we'd love to retain them and do everything in our power to do so, but if they choose to leave and they were a high-performer, we let them know that the door is open if they want to come back home." Ain sees boomerangs as a great source of talent for Kronos, in part because they are "more loyal than other employees—they have experienced other workplaces and appreciate what our company has to offer," adding that boomerang employees "bring new skills and experiences back to our company."[56]

Which Recruitment Approach Is Best?   There is no one best way to recruit potential applicants. Recall from Figure 9.2 (and what you learned in Chapter 8) that HR practices should be aligned with organizational culture and structure, and all of these elements should be carefully designed to support strategy. One company that does this particularly well is Costco.

Costco Example: Costco, the world's third-largest retailer, pursues cost leadership and differentiation strategies.[57] The company achieves high internal and external HR fit through its HR practices. Costco employees are cross-trained and empowered to make decisions, and they have some of the highest wages and benefits in the retail industry. Recently, the company even started offering paid parental leave for hourly workers.[58] Costco also recruits most of its talent from within, and this is a key driver of its under-10% employee turnover rate. Costco's turnover rate is astonishing compared to industry averages of 60 to 70%.[59] Said Costco co-founder Jim Sinegal, "People are happy with a job for more reasons than money," adding, "there's generally a pride in the organization . . . There's an attitude that there's security, that somebody does care about them . . . We're not offering jobs; we're offering careers."[60]

How Fit Figures into Recruitment   Recruiting is a lot like dating—both recruiters and job seekers want to know that the other party will be a good match before jumping into a serious commitment. In our discussion of organizational culture in Chapter 8 we described person–organization (P–O) fit as the extent to which a worker's personality and values match the organization's climate and culture. Here we look at another type of fit—**person–job (P–J) fit**—the extent to which a worker's competencies and needs match with a specific job. Research suggests that higher levels of P–J fit are associated with better job performance and increased job satisfaction, organizational commitment, and retention.[61] When there is poor P–J fit, both organizations and employees suffer.

Fit is important to our discussion because recruiters base their hiring recommendations in part on their assessments of job applicants' levels of P–O and P–J fit—with particular emphasis on the latter.[62]

How do you feel about the job you are in now, if you have one, or the last job you had? Do you feel like you are a "good fit" for the job? That is, do you like the work and does the work match your skills? Research shows that we are happier and more productive when our needs and skills fit the job requirements. If you would like to see whether or not you fit with your current (or last) job, complete Self-Assessment 9.2. You may find the results very interesting.

SELF-ASSESSMENT 9.2

Assessing Your Person–Job Fit

This survey is designed to assess your job fit. If you are not currently working, consider a previous job when completing the survey. Please be prepared to answer these questions if your instructor has assigned Self-Assessment 9.2 in Connect.

1. What is your level of fit?
2. Whether you have high or low fit, what are the main causes for your level of fit? Explain.
3. What questions might you ask a future recruiter to ensure a higher level of person–job fit? Be specific.

Selection: How to Choose the Best Person for the Job

Whether recruitment for a position results in a handful of applicants or a thousand, the hiring manager should use a systematic process to decide which applicant will receive a job offer. **Selection is the process of screening job applicants and choosing the best candidate for a position.** Essentially, selection is an exercise in *prediction*: How well will each candidate perform, to what degree will they fit, and for how long will they stay?

It has been said that selection decisions represent million-dollar decisions. Why? Because it is hard to fire someone once they are employed, and people with poor P–O or P–J fit can be costly in terms of lost productivity, poor employee attitudes, and turnover. This underscores the importance of selecting people who fit by using techniques that are reliable, valid, and legally defensible. Let's discuss these criteria in more detail.

What Are Legally Defensible Selection Tools?   **Legal defensibility is the extent to which the selection device measures job-related criteria in a way that is free from bias.** This means selection devices should only be used to measure factors that are directly related to job performance, and these devices should not discriminate based on non-job-relevant factors. (We discuss equal employment legislation in more detail in Section 9.7.) Establishing the reliability and validity of a selection technique is fundamental to legal defensibility.

- **Reliability represents the degree to which a test produces consistent scores.** When a test is reliable, an individual's score will remain about the same over time, assuming the characteristic being measured also remains the same. It would be similar to taking a midterm twice, two days apart. A reliable midterm would result in your scoring very similarly on both occasions.

- **Validity reflects the degree to which a test measures what it purports to measure**—nothing more and nothing less. If a test is supposed to predict performance, then candidates' actual performance should reflect their scores on the test. Using an invalid selection test can lead to poor selection decisions. It can also create legal problems if the test is ever challenged in a court of law. A valid midterm should measure content covered in the textbook and during lectures, and nothing else.

Three types of selection tools are *background information*, *interviews*, and *employment tests*.

Background Information: Application Forms, Resumes, and Background Checks   Application forms and resumes provide organizations with basic background information about job applicants, such as education, work history, certifications, and

citizenship. Unfortunately, a lot of background information consists of puffery and lies. Let's discuss three problems associated with background information in the selection process:

1. ***Application forms and resumes are susceptible to dishonesty***. A staggering 79% of job applicants lie on application forms and resumes (see the Example box).[63] One likely reason is that job seekers are trying to outsmart applicant tracking systems by doing whatever it takes to make sure key words in their resumes match the stated job requirements, whether they match the truth or not.[64] Other reasons include attempts to hide perceived deficiencies in technical or language skills, education, job history, or achievements.[65] Regardless of the reason for misstating or lying, be aware that you can be fired for lying on a job application or resume. We recommend honesty as the best policy.[66]

EXAMPLE   Lies Job Applicants Have Told

According to CareerBuilder CHRO Rosemary Haefner, some of the most frequent lies job applicants tell on their resumes are about their education, employment history, achievements, and criminal records. Here are a few real-world examples of what *not* to do.

Lies about Education   In 2018, Samsonite CEO Ramesh Tainwala resigned after reports surfaced that he had falsely claimed to have earned a doctorate in business administration on his resume. Investigations also revealed that Tainwala was referred to as "Dr." in at least two SEC filings. Tainwala later told reporters that he had enrolled in a PhD program in the 1990s but didn't finish his degree, saying that he "always felt embarrassed about it."[67]

Lies about Employment History   Australian officials sentenced Veronica Theriault to 25 months in jail after discovering that she had fabricated multiple items on her resume in order to secure a job as chief information officer for the Department of the Premier and Cabinet. Theriault had fabricated information about previous jobs and even impersonated someone named "Ms. Best"—whom she listed as a reference—on a phone call with the department.[68] As you might expect, people also embellish their salary histories, job titles, and achievements on projects.

Lies about Both   Largely due to unfilled openings at the U.S. Office of National Drug Control Policy, Taylor Weyeneth, then 23,

rose rapidly to the position of deputy chief of staff. However, almost as quickly he resigned, after an investigation by *The Washington Post* in early 2018 revealed that he had lied on three separate resumes about having a master's degree (which he had never completed) and about his work at a law office, where a supervisor said he had actually been let go for not showing up. Weyeneth in fact had no professional experience other than as a campaign volunteer and had even lied about being president of his fraternity.[69]

What to Do If You've Lied on Your Resume   Although the best choice is to tell the truth from the beginning, there are steps you can take to make things right if you've submitted embellished job application materials. Haefner suggests that you correct the dishonest portions of your application and resume and resubmit them. She says, "Tell the interviewer you noticed some errors on your original resume and have a revised copy," but cautions that, "unfortunately, there's no completely safe alternative other than withdrawing, because there's a chance they won't consider you for the job once they find out you lied. Bottom line: don't lie."[70]

YOUR CALL

Most employers compare resume data to cover letters, check references, call alma maters, do background checks, sleuth on Google, and administer skills tests.[71] Now that you know that, would you lie on your resume? Why or why not?

---

2. ***Application forms and resumes don't always provide useful information***. The types of education and experience that make an applicant qualified for a job today may be of little use in a few years due to rapid technological shifts, making information such as previous work history less relevant for hiring organizations. For these reasons, some experts are encouraging organizations to rely more on basic skills tests to assess candidates' competencies in the initial stages of the selection process.[72] Consider the following example of how companies are eliminating resumes in favor of a skills-based approach.

Pymetrics Example: Pymetrics is a hiring assessment firm that is helping companies replace resumes with skills assessments. In her years as a Harvard and MIT neuroscientist, co-founder and CEO Frida Polli learned that although there were accurate assessments available for certain skills and abilities, there wasn't a scalable or practical way for organizations to apply them. She and her team now develop assessment games that tell clients such as Tesla, Unilever, and Accenture the likelihood that a candidate will be successful in a particular role. Pymetrics also uses algorithms to continually check and adjust for biases. Polli says this has led to companies hiring more minorities and people who may have previously been passed over because they couldn't afford university tuition. She said, "A lot of our clients want to feel like they're tapping the broadest set of candidates out there and really finding the people that are best suited for them."[73]

The background information provided in application forms and resumes tells organizations about the educational and job opportunities candidates have had in the past. Pymetrics co-founder and CEO Frida Polli used neuroscience to develop a platform that instead measures candidates' natural aptitudes and their potential to excel in specific roles.
Steve Jennings/Getty Images

3. ***Background checks can lead to discrimination.*** Employers reach out to candidates' previous employers and references during the selection process to verify work history and get a better sense of whether applicants are likely to perform well. Issues can arise, however, when conversations conducted during background checks inadvertently reveal applicants' personal information. Although hiring companies are legally barred from basing hiring decisions on criteria such as age, disabilities, and marital status, knowledge of these and other related factors can lead to hiring discrimination. Some employers have enacted policies to limit what their managers can say about former employees; for instance, some allow the person serving as a reference only to confirm the former employee's job title and dates of employment.[74] Others allow references to state the reason for departure and whether the employee would be rehired.[75]

Interviews: Unstructured, Situational, and Behavioral-Description

The interview is the most commonly used employee-selection technique in organizations.[76] Interviews may take place face to face or virtually via phone or videoconference.

Interviewing takes three forms: *unstructured interviews* and the *two types of structured interviews—situational and behavioral-description.*[77]

- **Unstructured interviews** gather information about job candidates without the use of a fixed set of questions or a systematic scoring procedure. Unstructured interviews unfold like ordinary conversations, and proponents suggest that advantages include a more relaxed atmosphere and the freedom to explore certain topics in more depth.[78] However, decades of research have shown consistently that unstructured interviews have serious drawbacks, including low reliability, low validity, and high susceptibility to legal challenges.[79]

Despite robust evidence against unstructured interviews as selection devices, many companies still use them to their detriment. Consider the case of the Seasons 52 restaurant chain.

Seasons 52 Example: In 2018, Seasons 52 (a member of the Darden Restaurants family that also includes Olive Garden) agreed to pay $2.8 million to settle a federal lawsuit brought by applicants over 40 years of age who had experienced age discrimination during the hiring process at 35 of its restaurant locations. More than 100 rejected applicants testified that hiring managers had asked various discriminatory interview questions related to their birthdays, graduation dates, and ability to keep up with younger co-workers. Cheryl Machado said her interviewer told her the restaurant was interested in "'young,' 'fresh,' 'vibrant' and 'healthy' employees."

Machado added that "I was also shown a picture of young people in uniform and asked if I would be comfortable wearing a form-fitting, tight uniform."[80] George Simmons recalled that "My interview was going well until the interviewer asked me my age." When Simmons stated that he was 44, the interviewer told him "that the restaurant was looking for younger people."[81] The Darden Restaurants family had struggled to remain competitive in the restaurant industry in recent years and had set its sights on revamping its image to try to appeal to younger consumers. According to Equal Employment Opportunity Commission (EEOC) lawyer Daniel Seltzer, "A desire to appeal to younger customers bled into [the company concluding], 'Well, we'll appeal to younger customers by having younger workers.'"[82]

- The **structured interview** involves asking each applicant the same questions and comparing their responses to a standardized set of answers. Across multiple reviews of employment interview research spanning more than 60 years, one of the most consistent findings has been that structured interviews are far superior to unstructured interviews in their ability to predict applicants' future job performance.[83]

There are two types of structured interviews: situational interviews and behavioral-description interviews. Let's consider each one.

1. **Situational interviews** are structured interviews during which raters ask applicants how they would behave in hypothetical job situations. Example questions are: "What would you do if you saw two of your people arguing loudly in the work area?" and "How would you respond if your boss asked you to keep a secret from upper management?" The goal of situational interviews is to find out if the applicant can effectively handle various situations that may arise on the job.

2. **Behavioral-description interviews** are structured interviews during which raters explore applicants' job-related past behaviors. Example questions include: "Give me an example of a time when you needed to learn more about competitor organizations. What was the situation and what actions did you take?" and "Tell me about a time when you had to apply your understanding of cultural differences at work. What actions did you take as a result of your understanding?"[84]

Employment Tests: Ability, Performance, Personality, Integrity, and Others

The EEOC considers any employer-imposed employment requirement to be a test, including application forms, reference checks, and job interviews. Here we refer to a smaller subset of activities and define **employment tests** as the standardized devices organizations use to measure specific skills, abilities, traits, and other tendencies. Let's take a look at six employment tests in detail.

1. **Ability Tests** *Ability tests* measure job candidates' physical abilities, strength and stamina, mechanical ability, mental abilities, and clerical abilities.[85] Not all jobs require all of these abilities, and organizations should only test for the abilities that are directly related to job performance. For example, intelligence or cognitive ability tests are popular for predicting future executive performance, and perhaps with good reason. IBM's Supercomputer, Watson, recently analyzed the personality traits of leading CEOs in industries such as entertainment, finance, fashion, marketing, medicine, media, and politics and found that intellect was one of the top two traits necessary for success (altruism was the other).[86] Law enforcement agencies test for physical as well as reading and report-writing abilities.[87] Southern California Gas Company (SoCalGas) is an example of a company that uses an ability test.

SoCalGas Example: This utility company uses physical abilities testing and provides a test preparation booklet for potential applicants. The document clearly lists the components of the test [and how they are measured]—(1) upper arm strength [arm lift]; (2) abdominal strength and endurance [sit-ups test]; and (3) trunk strength [trunk pull test]—and explains why each is relevant to job performance. It also suggests that applicants build their strength over time as they prepare for the test, and it provides diagrams of each required exercise.[88]

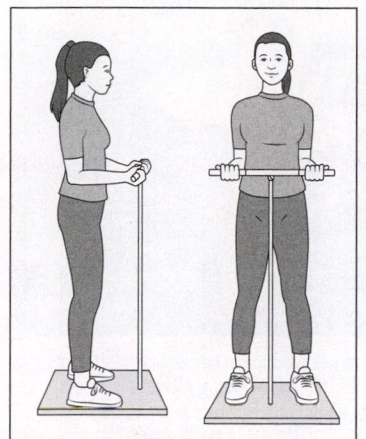  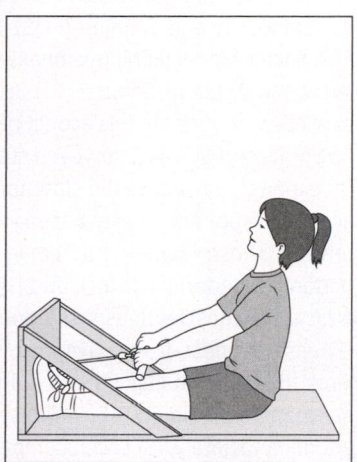

2. **Performance Tests**   *Performance tests,* or *skills tests,* measure performance on actual job tasks—so-called job tryouts—for example, when computer programmers take a test on a particular programming language or middle managers work on a small sample project.[89] Some companies use **assessment centers—selection devices in which management candidates participate in a series of interactive exercises over several days while being assessed by multiple evaluators.** Common assessment center activities include role plays, oral presentations, and in-basket exercises.[90] A team of researchers examined the relative accuracy by which ability tests and assessment center results predicted who would be successful on the job. Although both tests were effective, assessment center tests were more effective than ability tests.[91]

3. **Personality Tests**   *Personality tests* measure stable traits such as self-efficacy, self-esteem, locus of control, emotional stability, extroversion, agreeableness, conscientiousness, and openness to experience.[92] (We discuss these traits in detail in Chapter 11.) You'll notice that many of these traits represent competencies associated with career readiness, a topic of central importance for today's organizations. Experts estimate that at least 20% of organizations now incorporate personality testing into their hiring activities.[93] Check out the Example box for more on the pros and cons of personality testing in the selection process.

EXAMPLE   Personality Tests: Pros and Cons

Research tells us that skillfully administered personality tests can help organizations make better hiring decisions. This is especially true when the tests are combined with other selection measures. For example, recent studies suggest that a combination of (1) the Big Five personality dimensions, (2) a general ability test, and (3) an integrity test (discussed next) is a good predictor of future job performance.[94]

Despite the evidence supporting their validity, personality tests are still rife with potential for misinterpretation, misapplication, and employment discrimination. Organizations that are considering adopting personality testing should carefully weigh the following pros and cons:

Pros   Proponents of personality tests in hiring say that these devices:[95]

- Help to identify candidates who will fit well, be less likely to leave the organization, and exhibit superior performance.

(continued)

- Limit the influence of interviewers' unconscious biases on hiring decisions.
- Weed out those who may be prone to undesirable behaviors like dishonesty and deviance.

The California Commission on Peace Officer Standards and Training (POST) uses the Five Factor Model (FFM) personality test (discussed in detail in Chapter 11) in selecting new hires. To develop this aspect of its selection process, POST first surveyed subject matter experts from across the state to create an accurate list of personality-based job competencies. Those identified as being most important for performance included (1) integrity/ethics, (2) conscientiousness/dependability, (3) assertiveness/persuasiveness, (4) teamwork, (5) decision making and judgment, (6) adaptability/flexibility, (7) impulse control/attention to safety, (8) social competence, (9) emotional regulation and stress, (10) service orientation, and (11) tolerance. The commission defines each of these in detail and explains how each relates to both successful job performance, and dimensions of the FFM.[96]

The U.S. Military was one of the first U.S. organizations to use workplace personality testing. Its program began more than 100 years ago with inventories that attempted to measure soldiers' ability to withstand the sustained emotional traumas of combat during World War I. U.S. Air National Guard photo by Tech. Sgt. Ryan Campbell

Cons   Those who disagree with personality tests in hiring say that these devices are:[97]

- Subjective and open to interpretation by people who are not trained to evaluate results.
- Vulnerable to misuse by applicants who try to game the test.
- Potentially discriminatory because they raise the possibility of privacy violations when they inadvertently reveal information about personal characteristics such as mental health.

YOUR CALL

Would you be comfortable taking a personality test? Do you think it's better to answer the questions honestly or to choose responses that might make you appear better suited for the job? Explain.

4. **Integrity Tests**   *Integrity tests* "assess attitudes and experiences related to a person's honesty, dependability, trustworthiness, reliability, and pro-social behavior."[98] The rationale for these tests is that people who do poorly on them may have lower job performance and an increased tendency to engage in counterproductive work behaviors like theft, rule-breaking, and sabotage.[99] Overt integrity tests often ask specifically whether the applicant has ever engaged in illegal behavior. While integrity tests in general are easy to administer, it is also relatively easy for test takers to submit false responses.[100]

5. **Drug and Alcohol Tests**   Employers have a right to maintain drug-free and alcohol-free work environments, and we can say broadly that companies are permitted to test job applicants for drug and alcohol use. Some employers are covered by federal drug and alcohol testing laws, but many fall under state jurisdictions.[101] Organizations need to research the specific laws that apply to them before creating and implementing drug and alcohol testing policies. A few key points about drug and alcohol testing in the hiring process are:[102]

   - *Employers should not engage in selective testing.* Either every candidate in the pool gets tested or no one gets tested.

- *HR departments are struggling to keep up with marijuana laws.* Drug testing for marijuana use presents a complex problem for organizations. Laws are changing so rapidly that many companies are simply choosing to ignore the presence of THC on applicants' drug test results.

- *Employment drug and alcohol tests are on the decline.* Evolving legislation combined with a tight labor market puts pressure on companies to attract employees, and many are eliminating hurdles by scaling back on testing. Among companies that have reduced or eliminated drug testing are Goodwill, Target, and Kroger.

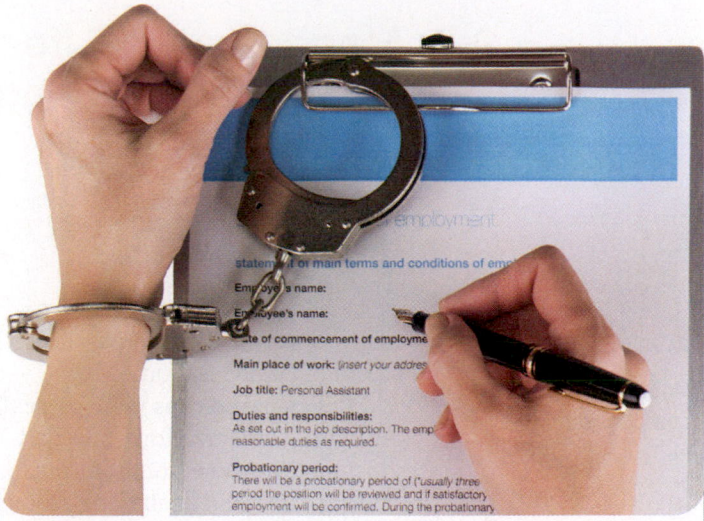

Do you believe organizations have a right to know about applicants' past criminal convictions? Would this information potentially bias your opinion of a qualified job candidate if you were a hiring manager? alexandre17/Getty Images

6. **Criminal and Financial Background Checks** Organizations that conduct *criminal and financial background checks* generally view negative marks on these records as indicators of low trustworthiness and/or poor character. Even when a past offense or financial issue is unrelated to the applicant's ability to perform the job safely and/or effectively, having a history of legal or financial troubles makes a candidate far less likely to receive a job offer.[103] The validity of criminal and financial background checks for predicting job-related outcomes is highly debated, and there is substantial evidence that these tests adversely impact applicants who belong to certain racial minority groups.[104] Here are the recent developments related to the use of criminal and financial background checks in the selection process:

- *"Ban the Box" is changing workplace procedures related to criminal background checks.* Approximately 20 years ago, a campaign to remove questions about applicants' criminal records from early stages of the hiring process—known as the "Ban the Box" movement—took shape. The movement began in response to the difficulties applicants with criminal backgrounds faced in finding employment and rebuilding their lives after criminal convictions.[105] Two decades later, at least 35 states and 150 cities and counties/parishes have enacted legislation to remove criminal background checkboxes from initial application forms.[106] Employers who operate under these laws are still allowed to perform criminal background checks later in the selection process, but proponents hope that employees will be more likely to hire people with criminal records if they are not aware of these records until after they make initial job offers.

- *Financial background/credit checks are losing popularity.* Many employers like to check applicants' credit histories and scores, although there is no evidence that credit scores predict qualifications, honesty, or job performance. However, in recent years, at least 11 states and 3 cities have passed laws to curb this practice while still allowing it in cases of security clearance or when it is required by law because of the position's financial responsibilities.[107] In early 2020 the U.S. House of Representatives passed the Comprehensive Credit Act of 2020, which aimed to reform credit reporting practices in part by heavily restricting the use of credit reports in hiring. As of this writing, the Senate had not yet voted on the bill.[108] ●

9.3 Managing an Effective Workforce: Compensation and Benefits

THE BIG PICTURE

Managers must manage for compensation—which includes wages or salaries, incentives, and benefits.

LO 9-3

Outline common forms of compensation.

Do we work only for a paycheck? Many people do, of course. But money is only one form of compensation.

Compensation has three parts: (1) wages or salaries, (2) incentives, and (3) benefits. In different organizations one part may take on more importance than another. For instance, in some nonprofit organizations (e.g., education, government), salaries may not be large, but health and retirement benefits may outweigh that fact. In a high-tech start-up, the salary and benefits may actually be somewhat humble, but the promise of a large payoff in incentives, such as stock options or bonuses, may be quite attractive.

These differences illustrate what you learned in Figure 9.2—namely, that compensation and benefits are one part of the strategic HRM process, and each firm should design their pay practices in the way that will attract, motivate, reward, and retain the specific kinds of employees and competencies needed to execute strategy. Compensation and benefits practices should have good internal fit such that they work in harmony with other HR practices such as recruiting, selection, and training. Compensation and benefits practices also need to have external fit such that they align with organizational culture and structure to jointly support broad strategic goals.[109]

Let's consider the three parts of compensation briefly. (We'll expand on them in Chapter 12 when we discuss ways to motivate employees.)

Wages or Salaries

Base pay consists of the basic wage or salary paid employees in exchange for doing their jobs. The basic compensation levels for particular jobs are determined by all kinds of economic factors: the prevailing pay levels in a particular industry and location, what competitors are paying, whether jobs are unionized, potential job hazards, and individual workers' experience and levels in the organization.

Incentives

To attract high-performing employees and to induce those already employed to be more productive, many organizations offer incentives, such as commissions, bonuses, profit-sharing plans, and stock options. Organization can use incentives to help to align workers with firm-level strategic objectives. We discuss incentives in detail in Chapter 12.

Benefits

Benefits, or **fringe benefits**, are additional nonmonetary forms of compensation designed to enrich the lives of all employees in the organization, which are paid all or in part by the organization. Examples include health insurance, dental insurance, life insurance, disability protection, retirement plans, holidays off, accumulated sick days and vacation days, recreation options, country club or health club memberships, family leave, discounts on company merchandise, counseling, credit unions, legal advice, and education reimbursement. For top executives, there may be "golden parachutes," generous severance pay for those who might be let go in the event the company is taken over by another company.

Benefits are no small part of an organization's costs. In December 2019, private industry spent an average of $34.72 per hour worked in employment compensation, of which wages and salaries accounted for 70.1% and benefits the remaining 29.9%.[110]

Managers should be aware that younger generations of workers regard workplace benefits differently than older generations.[111] In particular, data suggest that Millennial and Gen Z workers place high value on work–life balance and flexibility in their jobs and are willing to trade higher salary for more of these things. Recent research by PwC concluded that for younger generations, "work is a thing, not a place."[112]

We discuss benefits—including their motivating potential across different generations of workers—in more detail in Chapter 12 ●

9.4 Onboarding and Learning and Development

THE BIG PICTURE

Two ways organizations help newcomers to perform their jobs are through *onboarding* to fit them into the job and organization and through *learning and development* to upgrade their current skills and develop them for future opportunities.

We now turn our attention to the HR practices of onboarding and learning and development.

From a strategic HRM perspective, onboarding and learning and development (L&D) are HR practices that help an organization build the social and human capital necessary to accomplish its strategic objectives.[113]

Managers need to know that their approach to onboarding and L&D can make or break the organization's ability to retain top talent.[114] New employees who fail to establish relationships or who are unable to adapt to the organization's culture are likely to quit almost immediately.[115] Further, within six months, 90% of employees will decide whether to stay with the organization or seek opportunities elsewhere, and their experiences with onboarding and L&D play a big part in that decision.[116] Let's take a look at each of these important HR practices.

LO 9-4

Describe the processes used for onboarding and learning and development.

Onboarding: Helping Newcomers Learn the Ropes

Onboarding consists of the programs designed to integrate and transition employees into new jobs and organizations through familiarization with corporate policies, procedures, cultures, and politics, and clarification of work-role expectations and responsibilities. This process also is referred to as *employee socialization.*[117]

The Outcomes of Onboarding (and of Not Onboarding)   Effective onboarding programs generate a host of benefits. When companies invest the proper time and resources into creating a positive onboarding experience for employees, they are more likely to experience the positive outcomes listed in Table 9.1.[118] Alternatively, Table 9.1 also illustrates what happens when companies fail to invest properly in the employee onboarding experience.

Unfortunately, only about 12% of workers surveyed in a recent study strongly agreed that their organizations were doing a great job onboarding new employees.[119] According to talent management expert Amber Hyatt, organizations place themselves at a "significant disadvantage" when they neglect the onboarding process, adding that, "Employees who know what to expect from their company's culture and work environment make better decisions that are more aligned with the accepted practices of the company."[120]

TABLE 9.1

The Effects of Positive and Negative Onboarding Experiences

POSITIVE ONBOARDING EXPERIENCES GENERATE	NEGATIVE ONBOARDING EXPERIENCES GENERATE
• Increased commitment, job satisfaction, and productivity	• Decreased productivity and job satisfaction
• Higher customer satisfaction	• Lower customer satisfaction
• Lower turnover	• Higher costs and turnover

Source: Findings based on C. Caldwell and R. Peters, "New Employee Onboarding—Psychological Contracts and Ethical Perspectives," Journal of Management Development, 2018, pp. 27–39.

Onboarding Best Practices   Organizations take varied approaches to onboarding new employees. In a large organization, orientation may be a formal, established process. In a small organization, it may be so informal that employees find themselves having to make most of the effort themselves. At a minimum, research provides the following best practices for successful onboarding:

- *Involve leaders.* Onboarding works best when the people who will be supervising the new employee are involved. According to one study, a new employee is more than 3 times more likely to characterize onboarding as a success when their manager plays an active part throughout the process.[121] At Netflix, new employees get an orientation session with the company's executive management team. New employees also meet with the company's CEO by the time they finish their first quarter with the company.

- *Clarify expectations.* At minimum, the new employee needs to learn what is required in their new job, how the work will be evaluated, and who their immediate co-workers and managers are. Onboarding should clearly communicate role expectations and let the new employee know what "good" performance looks like in the organization and the job.[122] Netpeak, an Internet marketing agency, uses structured and automated onboarding "academies" to streamline and standardize onboarding. Tests and quizzes are built in at various steps in the process to ensure that new employees understand every aspect of their job-role requirements.[123]

- *Put the pieces together.* Most onboarding programs provide at least a basic description of the company, including its mission, vision, and history. But onboarding is a great time to have conversations with new employees about how their roles relate to the organization's larger purpose. Figure 9.2 is a helpful guide for these conversations, because onboarding naturally includes discussions of many of the elements (culture, structure, strategy) that are presented as reinforcing one another in that figure. The Predictive Index talent software company uses onboarding to help new hires understand how their everyday jobs connect to the firm's strategy. The company focuses its onboarding process on familiarizing new hires with the firm's structure, strategy, and approaches to talent management. New employees also have lunch with the firm's president and CEO on their first day of onboarding.[124]

- *Give it time.* Onboarding is sometimes confused with orientation (a one-time activity designed to "check all the boxes" for new employees—including completing paperwork, getting office keys, etc.). But onboarding is a process of integration that can last up to a year or more. Managers should remember that the onboarding process happens not just on the first day, or even in the first week. Don't try to squeeze everything in—there's plenty of time, and the focus should be on helping the new employee feel welcomed, not overwhelmed.[125] Google has formal onboarding activities built into new employees' jobs for at least six months. During that time, managers are supposed to have "check-in" meetings with their new employees at least once per month.[126]

Learning and Development: Helping People Perform Better

With traditional approaches to hiring, employers tried to recruit and select people whose qualifications matched the requirements of the job. Based on what you've learned thus far in the chapter, you know that hiring is no longer such a simple process. In today's workplace, what matters most is not so much what you know, but whether you are willing and able to learn.

The Learning and Development Process. The learning and development (L&D) process fills the gaps that exist between what employees currently know and what they need to know. The operative word here is *need,* because although it may be nice to learn a fun new skill at work every day, organizations operate under time and budget constraints. Managers need to determine the areas where L&D can make the biggest impact on successful implementation of the firm's strategy. The five-step process shown below is a simple tool for managers to use when making L&D decisions. *(See Figure 9.3.)* Keep in mind that L&D is an ongoing effort in organizations rather than a one-time event. Let's briefly discuss what managers do at each step.

- *Step 1: Assessment.* The first step in L&D is to figure out the organization's most pressing L&D needs. In organizations with a strategic HRM focus, this process is all about strategy—namely, managers need to ask, "What's holding us back from implementing strategy, and what can L&D help us to do better?"

- *Step 2: Objectives.* The second step in L&D is to set performance objectives. Here managers must determine what employees should be able to *do* after L&D that they could not do before, what skills should they have that they didn't have before, etc. Simply put, this step identifies the specific changes you hope to see after L&D.

- *Step 3: Selection.* The third step in L&D is to select the best method(s) for delivering L&D. Here you'll discuss, for example, whether L&D stays in house or gets outsourced; whether it takes place online, in a face-to-face setting, or in a blended format, etc.

- *Step 4: Implementation.* The fourth step in L&D is to go forward with L&D delivery.

- *Step 5: Evaluation.* The fifth step in L&D is determine whether the L&D has met/is meeting its objectives. If not, what needs to be adjusted?

FIGURE 9.3

Five steps in the learning and development process

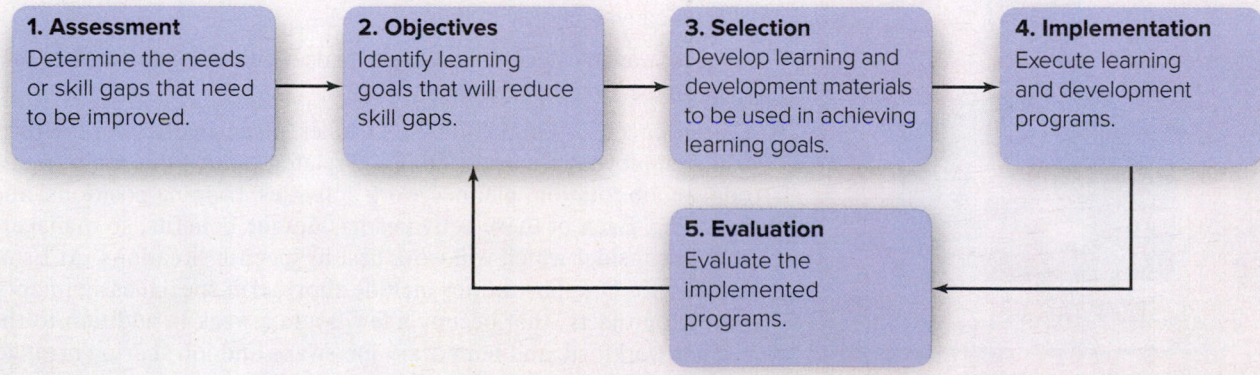

Many employees have to learn important skills on the job, and this often involves a great deal of trial-and-error. Technological advancements such as VR give employees the chance to practice and refine these skills in realistic, simulated environments before applying them at work.
Mark Nazh/Shutterstock

Different Types of Learning and Development There are all kinds of L&D methods. One way to distinguish them is according to whether they are helping employees to learn facts or skills.

- *L&D for facts.* If people are learning *facts*—such as work rules or legal matters—then online courses, shared documents, and e-books are effective. Bloomingdale's used Axonify's e-learning platform to deliver workplace safety-based L&D through <mark>microlearning</mark>—short bursts of content that employees can engage with for a few minutes at a time at their convenience (while sitting on the subway, waiting for an appointment, etc.). Bloomingdales' 10,000 employees now have access to standardized and convenient learning tools.[127]

- *L&D for skills.* If people are learning *skills*—such as the career readiness competencies of networking or decision making—then interactive techniques such as role-playing, case analysis, virtual reality (VR), and artificial intelligence (AI) work best. VR is an increasingly valuable L&D resource because it can simulate real situations and make learning more engaging, and this translates into better employee skills for retention and recall.

Hopefully you'll recall that one of the themes we've stressed throughout the text is the importance of developing your soft skills. According to the 2020 LinkedIn Workforce Learning Report (based on a survey of more than 6,600 professionals across 18 countries), soft skills are only getting more important. Hard skills lose their relevance after a few years, but soft skills such as the ones HR professionals ranked highest in the 2020 study—leadership, creative problem-solving, and communication—will never fall out of favor. Consider what the Best Western Hotel chain is doing to increase employees' soft skills.

Some organizations use animated coaching programs to deliver targeted L&D to their employees. Viktoria Kazakova/Shutterstock

Best Western Example: The company adopted Mursion virtual reality solutions to help its employees grow their soft skills, and employees have already benefited from increases in front desk employee satisfaction as well as better problem-solving skills.[128] Best Western's VR L&D targets the soft skills that are most strategically relevant for employees working in customer-oriented jobs, including positive attitude, handling conflict, and having difficult conversations.[129]

Another way to categorize L&D methods is according to whether they happen on-the-job or off-the-job.

- *On-the-job L&D.* On-the-job L&D takes place in the work setting while employees are performing job-related tasks. Four major methods are job rotation, planned work activities, training positions, and coaching. Each of these activities has unique benefits, so managers should consider which will work best in specific situations. At Estée Lauder, L&D opportunities include short-term special assignments, "stretch projects" that occupy a few hours a week in addition to the regular workload, and temporary job swaps and job-sharing arrangements so that employees can broaden their skills through new role experiences.[130] IBM uses AI to analyze employees' profiles, training progress, and desired career paths. The technology then targets L&D programs to individuals' specific needs, which can include animated simulations to provide coaching on desired behaviors.[131]

- *Off-the-job L&D.* Off-the-job L&D typically takes place in classrooms, at professional conferences, or through videoconferencing, games, simulations, and other e-learning platforms—all of which occur outside of your normal job duties. A requirement for off-the-job L&D is quite common across a variety of professions. For example, to maintain a professional certification with the Society for Human Resource Management (SHRM-CP or SHRM-SCP), HR professionals must earn at least 60 professional development credits (PDCs) every three years, and these should come from a mix of on-the-job and off-the-job activities. Off-the-job activities include participating in approved HR-related e-learning modules given by other experts, disseminating important HR knowledge through writing for a national or global audience, or attending local chapter meetings or state/national conferences. Walmart store employees engage with certain aspects of L&D through VR technology rather than on-the-job. This is because there are some facets of store associates' jobs that don't occur often enough for employees to get to practice (e.g., handling Black Friday crowds). There also are situations that associates would prefer to not have to mess up in person in order to improve their skills (e.g., responding to angry customers).[132]

See the Example box to learn about a company that is well known for its exceptional L&D.

<table>
<tr><td colspan="2" style="background:#e94e1b;color:white">EXAMPLE　　Keller Williams Realty: Learning for Earning</td></tr>
</table>

At Keller Williams, says realtor Cydne Seymour, "We don't believe in learning for knowing's sake, we believe in learning for earning's sake." Keller Williams Realty is a commission-based global real estate franchise company headquartered in Austin, Texas, with almost 180,000 agents in more than 1,000 regional offices around the world. Since 2014, it has been the largest such company in the world, with a strong commitment to educating, coaching, and developing its franchised associates. This drive to develop its agents is what the company believes not only sets it apart from competitors but also drives its steady growth and success.

In 2018, Keller Williams was promoted to top 10 hall of fame status by *Training* magazine (a professional development magazine for HR professionals). This honor is reserved for companies in any industry worldwide that have earned top spots on the magazine's annual training list for four years in a row. Among the criteria for leading the list each year are objective measures like the company's total budget for learning and development, that budget as a percentage of company payroll, the number of L&D hours per program and per employee, and

Your authors have conducted many educational classes off the job for executives. Do you think managers can readily apply this knowledge back at work? stevecoleimages/Getty Images

the results of several subjective measures and workplace surveys.

The company's learning and development tools and resources are available to agents at all levels of experience and are managed by the company's chief learning officer. The intention is to help all Keller Williams agents become experts in their particular markets, which can include luxury and commercial real estate and farm properties. The learning programs include Keller Williams University, which offers online multimedia training; skill building programs called MAPS Coaching; hundreds of onsite and virtual training classes; special events, including an annual "family reunion" (attended by 17,000 agents in 2019); and several others.

Keller Williams competes with an innovation strategy, and the company maintains its status as an industry superstar by continuing to invest aggressively in optimizing agents' and customers' experiences. Company co-founder, chair, and CEO Gary Keller says that it's important to "think about the market that I'm heading into and not the market that I'm in." In November 2019, he announced, "This quarter was the

(continued)

most impressive quarter we've experienced in our 36-year history of our company," adding, "we owe the entirety of our success to our agents. It's their expertise and their passion for the business that makes us the company we are . . . it's our agents that dictate where we're headed—especially in technology and education. Every day, we look to them and ask, 'How can we ensure the success you're having today continues?'"

The company's newest answer to that question is KW Command—an AI-enabled platform created to streamline the agent/buyer experience. This industry-leading technology was curated to provide effective solutions to the problems real estate agents face most often. Here are some of the problems, along with the solutions KWCommand offers:

- **PROBLEM: Rising tech costs** that make scalable and profitability difficult in the industry.

  ○ **SOLUTION: Free technology** for all company associates, including Command.

- **PROBLEM: Inaccurate conversion** because previous technology didn't differentiate adequately between clients at different stages in their home buying/selling journey.

  ○ **SOLUTION: Maximize priorities** with innovative AI analytics. Now when a client interacts with KWConnect, AI detects patterns and alerts the agent with a specific prediction about the client's stage in the buying process and a prompt that suggests an ideal time to connect with the client and schedule the next steps.

- **PROBLEM: Suboptimal groupings** of multiple key data points—including market data and property listings—because the traditional real estate system organizes by ZIP code, and buyers seek property according to neighborhood.

  ○ **SOLUTION: Change what no longer works** through new technology. In KWCommand, data is organized by community. This (1) improves agents' ability to serve clients' needs and (2) generates an advantage over competing firms.

YOUR CALL

Keller Williams employees and agents average 82 hours of formal learning a year, almost seven hours a month.[133] Do you think this is excessive? Can organizations spend too much on L&D? Explain.

Now that you have learned about the HR practices of recruitment, selection, compensation and benefits, onboarding, and learning and development, do careers in these fields interest you? Not everyone is suited for HR work, but it is very rewarding for some. The following self-assessment will help you decide whether or not a career in HR fits for you.

SELF-ASSESSMENT 9.3   CAREER READINESS

Is a Career in HR Right for You?

This survey is designed to assess your skills and interests and determine if a career in human resources is right for you. Please be prepared to answer these questions if your instructor has assigned Self-Assessment 9.3 in Connect.

1. Are you suited for a career in human resources? Which specific aspect of human resources do you prefer?

2. Look at the top two areas of HR for which you tested as being best suited. Look over the descriptions of these fields and then identify what skills you need to have to be successful.

3. Even if you do not pursue a career in HR, which skills do you feel you should continue to develop? Explain.

Learning and Development Is Worth the Investment   According to the LinkedIn 2020 Workforce Learning Report mentioned earlier, 94% of workers would be willing to stay with an organization longer if the organization were willing to provide them with continued learning opportunities that enhanced their careers.[134] This is good news because it means that employees are willing to learn. Said famous business theorist and Dutch executive Arie de Geus, "The ability to learn faster than your competitors may be the only sustainable competitive advantage."[135] We tend to agree with this statement and with experts who suggest companies need to build *learning cultures* where the desire and opportunity to learn is part of everyday organizational life.[136] ●

9.5 Performance Management

THE BIG PICTURE

Performance management is a set of processes and managerial behaviors that involve defining, monitoring, measuring, evaluating, and providing consequences for performance expectations. It is not a one-time event like a performance appraisal. Effective performance management can foster positive employee attitudes, higher performance, and better customer service.

LO 9-5

Discuss effective performance management and feedback techniques.

Want to know how well your managers think you're doing at work? Be prepared to be disappointed: 74% of employees say they don't get helpful feedback, according to recent Gallup research, and only 14.5% of managers strongly agree that they're effective at giving feedback.[137] Feedback about how you're doing in your job is part of performance management.

Performance Management in Human Resources

No doubt you've had the experience at some point of having a sit-down with a superior, a boss or a teacher, who told you how well or poorly you were doing—a *performance appraisal*. A performance appraisal is a single event, as we discuss later in this section. Performance management, by contrast, is a powerful ongoing activity that, when done well, can improve firm profitability as well as employee performance, productivity, motivation, and attitudes such as engagement.[138]

Performance management is defined as a set of processes and managerial behaviors that involve defining, monitoring, measuring, evaluating, and providing consequences for performance expectations.[139] It consists of four steps: (1) define performance, (2) monitor and evaluate performance, (3) review performance, and (4) provide consequences. *(See Figure 9.4.)*

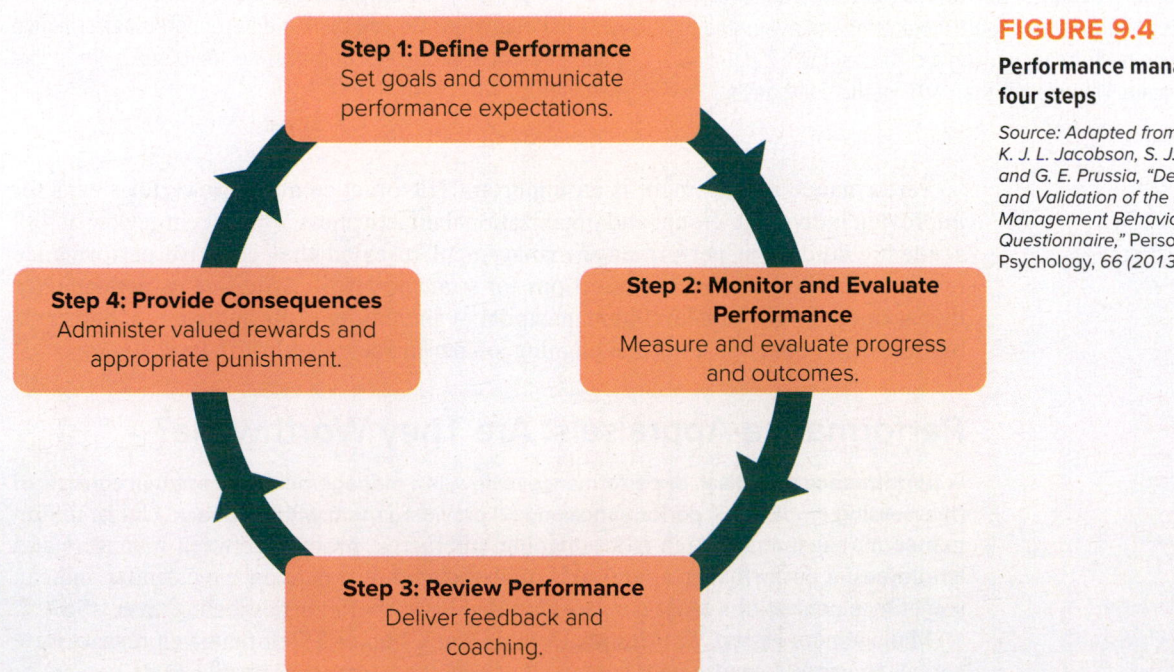

Step 1: Define Performance
Set goals and communicate performance expectations.

Step 2: Monitor and Evaluate Performance
Measure and evaluate progress and outcomes.

Step 3: Review Performance
Deliver feedback and coaching.

Step 4: Provide Consequences
Administer valued rewards and appropriate punishment.

FIGURE 9.4

Performance management: four steps

Source: Adapted from A. J. Kinicki, K. J. L. Jacobson, S. J. Peterson, and G. E. Prussia, "Development and Validation of the Performance Management Behavior Questionnaire," Personnel Psychology, *66 (2013), pp. 1–45.*

See the Example box to learn what the performance management process looks like at Regeneron.

EXAMPLE   Performance Management at Regeneron

Founded in 1988, New York–based Regeneron has more than 8,100 employees and ranks as one of the largest biotech companies in the world. Regeneron has won a number of awards as a best place to work, an innovation leader, a responsible workplace, and a top biotech firm. It was ranked by *Fortune* as one of the top 100 Best Places to Work in the United States in 2020.[140]

Performance management in biotech can be tricky, because the way managers need to evaluate and determine performance varies substantially across business units. For scientists developing new treatments, it can take years to determine whether a particular aspect of their performance has been successful. For employees in administrative and commercial roles, timelines are much shorter, and the process is more traditional.

A few years ago, Michelle Weitzman-Garcia, Regeneron's then executive director of workforce development, led the effort to redesign the company's performance management system to account for the company's unique needs. Here is a description of Regeneron's performance management process (as defined by Figure 9.4).

1. **Define performance.** Broadly, performance at Regeneron is defined along two axes: (1) results—what the employee needs to accomplish and (2) behaviors—how the employee needs to accomplish it. Managers define what those results and behaviors should be for employees in their unique departments.[141]

2. **Monitor and evaluate performance.** Before the overhaul, Regeneron's managers monitored and evaluated employee performance using a cumbersome 12-point rating scale. Now, fewer than 10% of the company's managers use ratings in the performance management process. Instead, managers use one of four forms tailored to track performance according to unique expectations for employees in (1) drug development, (2) product supply, (3) field sales, and (4) corporate functions.[142]

3. **Review performance.** The frequency and content of performance reviews at Regeneron varies for employees working in different units. For example, in some units, managers use a 30/30 review process that consists of 30 minutes of performance conversation with each employee they supervise every 30 days. In other units, performance reviews occur once or twice per year.[143]

4. **Provide consequences.** Regeneron uses a progressive discipline system to provide consequences for performance that falls below expectations.[144] With progressive discipline, managers work with employees using a series of graduated steps that aim to correct performance early, before it becomes problematic. Progressive discipline typically begins with informal conversation at the early stages and can result in serious action—including termination—in later stages. The company also offers employees the opportunity to earn above-market rewards for outstanding individual contributions, or when their work leads to exceptional firm performance.[145]

YOUR CALL

What do you think about the performance management process at Regeneron? Do you think a differentiated performance management approach is appropriate for biotech firms like Regeneron? Why or why not?

Performance management is an important HR practice and a powerful means for improving individual, group, and organizational effectiveness.[146] A recent review of 488 academic studies of performance management revealed that effective performance management has powerful implications for strategic HRM. Specifically, performance management builds unit-level human capital by increasing skills, motivation, and capabilities within business units and aligning job performance with firm-level strategy.[147]

Performance Appraisals: Are They Worthwhile?

A **performance appraisal**, or performance review, is a management process that consists of (1) assessing employees' performance and (2) providing them with feedback. Unlike performance management, which is an ongoing, interactive process between managers and employees, a performance appraisal is often dictated by a date on the calendar and can sometimes consist of a tense conversation that leaves both parties feeling unsatisfied.[148]

Management expert W. Edwards Deming (see Chapter 2) felt that such reviews were actually harmful because people remember only the negative parts.[149] Ninety percent of

HR professionals in one study declared they were dissatisfied with their performance review/management systems.[150] No wonder then that some companies began dropping the practice altogether, although they soon learned that putting nothing in its place left employees without needed and indeed desired feedback about how they were doing on the job. Some newer approaches to performance appraisal have emerged around two important research findings:

Frequent Feedback Is Best   Studies suggest that feedback is more accurate when given frequently.[151] Frequent feedback also allows managers and employees to reinforce key ideas about performance. Companies including Gap, Pfizer, Cigna, and Procter & Gamble have started to provide more frequent appraisals that let managers and employees make faster "course corrections" and prevent performance problems from piling up.[152] Consider Adobe's approach.

> **Adobe Example:** Adobe recently abandoned its use of traditional performance appraisals altogether—not because managing performance isn't worthwhile, but because the company's appraisal method wasn't doing anything to actually improve performance. Further, the company estimates that its old system burned through about 80,000 work hours. Adobe now uses "check-ins"—frequent, informal, engaging conversations between managers and employees aimed at motivating and improving performance. One benefit is that the process feels more egalitarian and less intimidating than a formal appraisal, and managers and employees are more truthful and direct in their conversations. Another benefit is that employees are no longer "ranked" next to their peers.[153] This decision echoes recent research that suggests ranking employees in relation to one another can destroy the cooperation and collaboration that today's innovative firms rely on.[154]

Feedback Should Be Future-Oriented   Good feedback should result in improved performance in the future. Of course, a performance appraisal has to include a discussion of past behavior, because past behavior is what is being appraised. But research suggests that the focus of the conversation should then switch to what can be done going forward.[155] Consider how Deloitte revamped its performance appraisal system.

> **Deloitte Example:** Deloitte, a global consulting firm, led the way in redesigning the performance review in 2015 after discovering, among other negatives, that the process in place was consuming nearly 2 million work hours a year, not nearly enough of which was spent in discussions of employees and their futures.[156] After much internal research, the company devised a streamlined system around three goals:
>
> 1. *Recognize performance*—appraisal data should provide information that can inform variable compensation and other decisions about employees.
>
> 2. *See performance clearly*—the system should produce accurate and non-biased "snapshots" of performance. This is achieved by having managers respond to four future-oriented statements about employees at the end of key projects, using a five-point scale (for example: "Given what I know of this person's performance, I would always want him or her on my team").
>
> 3. *Fuel performance*—with weekly "check-ins" between managers and team members. Weekly conversations center on performance, work priorities, and future opportunities for learning and development.[157]

Today, Deloitte continues to survey performance management and appraisal systems, and it reports that employees want regular feedback, likely influenced by the response mechanisms of social media, and that most companies are now able to obtain increasingly useful data for better HR decision making.[158] Let us look at performance appraisals in more detail, because they are still used by most organizations, albeit in some new and exciting forms.[159]

Two Kinds of Performance Appraisal: Objective and Subjective

There are two ways to evaluate an employee's performance—objectively and subjectively.

1. Objective Appraisals Objective appraisals, also called results appraisals, are based on facts and are often numerical. In these kinds of appraisals, you would keep track of such matters as the numbers of products the employee sold in a month, customer complaints filed against an employee, miles of freight hauled, and the like.

There are two good reasons for having objective appraisals:

- **They measure desired results.** Objectively measuring desired results enables managers to focus employees on the important or preferred outcomes. Examples would be the number of cars sold by salespeople, the number of journal publications for professors, and the number of defects for a manufacturing plant.

- **They are harder to challenge legally.** Not being as subject to personal bias, objective appraisals are harder for employees to challenge on legal grounds, such as for age, gender, or racial discrimination.

2. Subjective Appraisals Few employees can be adequately measured just by objective appraisals—hence the need for subjective appraisals, which are based on a manager's perceptions of an employee's (1) traits or (2) behaviors.

- **Trait appraisals.** *Trait appraisals* are ratings of such subjective attributes as "attitude," "initiative," and "leadership." Trait evaluations may be easy to create and use, but their validity is questionable because the evaluator's personal bias can affect the ratings.

- **Behavioral appraisals.** *Behavioral appraisals* measure specific, observable aspects of performance—being on time for work, for instance—although making the evaluation is still somewhat subjective. An example is the behaviorally anchored rating scale (BARS), which rates employee gradations in performance according to scales of specific behaviors. For example, a five-point BARS rating scale about attendance might go from "Always early for work and has equipment ready to fully assume duties" to "Frequently late and often does not have equipment ready for going to work," with gradations in between.

Who Should Make Performance Appraisals?

Most performance appraisals are done by managers; however, to add different perspectives, sometimes appraisal information is provided by other people who are knowledgeable about particular employees or jobs. Decisions about who appraises performance should be made in support of the company's strategic goals, as you will see in the examples we discuss.

Peers, Subordinates, Customers, and Self Among additional sources of performance information are co-workers and subordinates, customers and clients, and employees themselves.

- **Peers and subordinates.** Co-workers, colleagues, and subordinates may well see different aspects of your performance. Such information can be useful for development, although it probably shouldn't be used for evaluation. (Many managers will resist soliciting such information about themselves, of course, fearing negative appraisals.)

- **Customers and clients.** Some organizations, such as restaurants and hotels, ask customers and clients for their appraisals of employees. Publishers ask authors to judge how well they are doing in handling the editing, production, and marketing of their books. Automobile dealerships may send follow-up questionnaires to car buyers.

- **Self-appraisals.** How would you rate your own performance in a job, knowing that it would go into your personnel file? It's likely the bias would be toward rating yourself favorably. Nevertheless, *self-appraisals* help employees become involved in the whole evaluation process and may make them more receptive to feedback about areas needing improvement.

In terms of strategic HRM, managers should choose performance information sources based on whether the insights gleaned from them can improve performance in a way that improves strategic execution. If the firm can better deliver on its objectives when a source of performance information is included, then it may be worthwhile to include the source in the performance appraisal process. However, managers need to evaluate the relative validity of any additional source of information to determine how much weight it should carry. Consider the example of patient experience surveys in health care.

Patient Experience Surveys Example: Hospital reimbursements—the money hospitals ultimately receive (from health insurers, Medicare, etc.) for providing medical services—has become increasingly tied to patient satisfaction scores gathered from the Hospital Consumer Assessment of Healthcare Providers and Systems (HCAHPS) patient experience survey.[160] For many physicians and health care facilities, there is concern about whether patient reviews represent valid measures of quality of care. Some studies suggest, for example, that denying patients' requests for pain medications decreases patient satisfaction scores. The concern here is that if important outcomes are contingent upon these scores, some providers may be motivated to make decisions in the best interest of ratings, rather than patients' health.[161] Recently, a group of five major hospital associations published a list of recommendations for improving the validity of HCAHPS scores. Recommendations were related to, for example, improving response rates, refining survey items, and ensuring that the survey was understandable to people with varying levels of health literacy.[162]

360-Degree Assessment: Appraisal by Multiple Sources   We said that performance appraisals may be done by peers, subordinates, customers, and oneself. Sometimes all these may be used in a technique called a 360-degree assessment.

In a "theater in the round," the actors in a dramatic play are watched by an audience on all sides of them—360 degrees. Similarly, as a worker, you have many people watching you from all angles. With a **360-degree feedback appraisal**, or **360-degree assessment, employees are appraised not only by their managerial superiors but also by peers, subordinates, and sometimes clients,** thus providing several perspectives. Consider the following example of how Netflix uses 360-degree assessments as part of its performance appraisal process.

Netflix Example: Netflix is known for its hypercompetitive organizational culture, which company executives see as a primary source of competitive advantage.[163] The company's openly shared "culture deck" describes aspects of this culture with statements such as, "are extraordinarily candid with each other," and "keep only our highly effective people." Employees need to be able to "learn rapidly and eagerly," be "concise and articulate in speech and writing," and "thrive on change."[164] The company often uses "real-time 360" lunch and dinner meetings to appraise employee performance. In these meetings, anyone in attendance—from company executives to lower level support staff—is encouraged to share blunt and honest feedback with the employee being appraised.[165]

Typically, an employee chooses evaluators from 6 to 12 other people to make evaluations, who then fill out anonymous forms, the results of which are tabulated by computer. The employee then goes over the results with his or her manager and together they put into place a long-term plan for performance goals. The 360-degree appraisal is a popular tool—according to one report, more than 85% of *Fortune* 500 companies use this method.[166] When administered correctly, 360-degree appraisals are useful. For example, one recent study showed that this form of evaluation enhanced employees' innovative behaviors.[167] Here are a few best-practices presented in a recent review of research on 360-degree appraisals:[168]

1. *Keep it developmental*—the 360-degree appraisal is intended to be a source of developmental information, rather than a formal appraisal. Making raters aware that their feedback will be used for the former purpose increases the likelihood that they will provide constructive information.

2. *More isn't always better*—focus on choosing evaluators who can contribute unique and strategically valuable information about the employee's performance.

3. *Remember to reduce bias*—proponents of 360-degree appraisals often assume that this technique automatically reduces the likelihood that performance feedback will suffer from bias. Unfortunately, more raters often mean more opportunities for bias. Raters should be trained to recognize role-specific competencies as well as their own judgmental biases.

All told, collecting performance information from multiple sources can help the person being evaluated get a multi-dimensional view of their performance.

Forced Ranking: Grading on a Curve

To increase performance, a substantial number of *Fortune* 500 companies have some variant of performance review systems known as a forced ranking (or "rank and yank") system.[169] In **forced ranking performance review systems**, all employees within a business unit are ranked against one another and grades are distributed along some sort of bell curve—just like students being graded in a college course. Top performers (such as the top 20%) are rewarded with bonuses and promotions; the worst performers (such as the bottom 20%) are given warnings or dismissed.

Forced rankings rely on the theory that there is something inherently motivating about seeing how we stack up against others. This thinking underlies, for example, the "leaderboard" that Peloton users see when they take a virtual cycling class. The main idea is that we will be motivated to work harder and push ourselves further when we are in competition with others. Forced rankings were a cornerstone of many organizations for decades, but outlooks on their usefulness are shifting. Consider how GE's perspective on forced ranking has changed over time.

GE Example: In the 1980s, GE pioneered its famous "rank and yank" performance management system that required managers to rank their workforce according to performance ratings and "yank" (i.e., fire) the bottom 10%. The system persisted at GE for decades but has all but vanished in recent years.[170] The company's latest HR innovation is its PD@GE app.[171] This technology connects employees with both managers and peers and enables them to seek and give feedback in real time. Conversations are centered on performance improvement and can happen entirely through the app, although employees can request a face-to-face meeting with a supervisor at any time.[172]

This type of performance review system is rapidly losing favor. Here are key reasons:

1. *Forced rankings can eliminate good workers too.* Proponents of forced ranking say it encourages managers to identify and remove poor performers and structures a predetermined compensation curve, which enables them to reward top performers. However, opponents contend that the system eventually gets rid of talented as well as untalented people.[173] There may also be legal ramifications. A recent suit brought against Ford claimed the company used forced ranking to discriminate against older employees.[174]

2. *Forced rankings can negatively impact performance.* Numeric ratings, rankings, and formal evaluations without positive feedback may produce the opposite of their intended results—namely, create a culture of *reduced* performance, according to recent neurological and psychological research.[175] When Accenture eliminated its ranking system, its CEO said, "We're going to evaluate you in your role, not vis-à-vis someone else who might work in Washington, who might work in Bangalore. It's irrelevant. It should be about you."[176]

3. *Forced rankings are less applicable to modern work.* Forced ranking systems were originally conceived at the turn of the 20th century to measure the performance of manual laborers and factory workers. This seems inappropriate today, when more than 70% of workers are employed in service or knowledge-intensive jobs in which skills, attitudes, and abilities are hard to evaluate along a bell curve.

Effective Performance Feedback

As a manager, you may not feel comfortable about critiquing your employees' performance, especially when you have to convey criticism rather than praise. In fact, studies suggest that most managers unintentionally inflate their employees' performance ratings.[177] Nevertheless, giving performance feedback is one of the most important parts of the manager's job, and giving inaccurate or overly positive feedback is helpful to neither the employee nor the organization. Here are some research-backed suggestions for giving accurate, useful feedback:[178]

- *Take a problem-solving approach, avoid criticism, and treat employees with respect.* Recall the worst boss for whom you ever worked. How did you react to his or her method of giving feedback? Avoid giving criticism that might be taken personally.

  Example: Instead of saying, "You're picking up that bag of cement wrong" (which is both personal and also criticizes by using the word *wrong*), try, "Instead of bending at the waist, a good way to pick up something heavy is to bend your knees. That'll help save your back."

- *Be specific and direct in describing the employee's current performance and in identifying the improvement you desire.* Describe your subordinate's current performance in specific terms and concentrate on outcomes that are within his or her ability to improve.

  Example: Instead of saying, "You're always late turning in your sales reports." Try, "Instead of making calls on Thursday afternoon, why don't you take some of the time to do your sales reports so they'll be ready on Friday along with those of the other sales reps?"

- *Get the employee's input.* In determining causes of a problem, listen to the employee and get his or her help in crafting a solution. Be thoughtful and compassionate.

  Example: Instead of saying, "You've got to learn to get here by 9:00 a.m. every day." Say, "What changes do you think could be made so that your station is ready when people start calling at 9:00?"

- *Follow up.* Always check in with the employee later to be sure he or she has taken any corrective action you discussed and that you've made yourself available for any additional questions or input.

  Example: Instead of saying, "Why are you still turning in incomplete progress reports?" Try, "It's almost time for me to ask for your next progress report. Should we take a look at a draft of it together first?" ●

9.6 Managing Promotions, Transfers, Disciplining, and Dismissals

THE BIG PICTURE

As a manager, you'll have to manage employee replacement actions, as by promoting, transferring, demoting, laying off, or firing.

You will learn in Chapter 12 that employees' perceptions about being treated fairly are essential for their job satisfaction, engagement, productivity, and desire to remain at the company.[179] Have you ever been treated unfairly at work? Do you remember how you felt? Probably angry. The point here is that the issue of fair treatment is critical when managers consider who to promote, transfer, discipline, and fire. But you play a role in these decisions as well.

In terms of your own promotions, transfers, and other important career milestones, keep in mind that organizations expect you to take responsibility for yourself. As one expert put it, "We are now in the era of do-it-yourself career development."[180] Remember that career management is an important career-readiness competency, and consider the advice of Khadijah Sharif-Drinkard, senior vice president of business and legal at ViacomCBS and a Columbia University alum. Specifically—learn to advocate for yourself by highlighting your accomplishments and aspirations clearly to those above you. "You have to figure out ways that you get your own voice out there so that you can translate for people what you're really doing," says Sharif-Drinkard, adding, "because a lot of times people won't necessarily know."[181]

Let's consider some best practices for handling promotions, transfers, discipline, and dismissals.

Promotion: Moving Upward

Promotion—moving an employee to a higher-level position—is the most obvious way to recognize that person's superior performance (apart from giving raises and bonuses). There are three primary concerns with promotions: fairness, discrimination, and others' resentments. Let's look at each of these briefly:

Fairness It's important that promotion be *fair*. The step upward must be deserved. Managers should never promote employees for reasons of nepotism, cronyism, or other forms of favoritism.

Discrimination Promotion decisions cannot and should not discriminate on the basis of sexual orientation, ethnicity, gender, age, physical ability, or any other protected class. Further, decisions should not be made on the basis of any non-job-related factor (e.g., political affiliation) even if it isn't considered a legally protected factor, although recent evidence suggests this type of discrimination does occur.[182]

Others' Resentments If someone is promoted, someone else may be resentful about being passed over. As a manager, you may need to counsel the people left behind about their performance and their opportunities in the future. In fact, if you are passed over yourself, it is important not to let your anger build. Instead, gather your thoughts, then go in and talk to your boss and find out what qualities were lacking, suggests one report. As we said in the introduction to this section, you should take responsibility for your own career management by looking for ways to improve and showcase your knowledge, skills, and abilities. Above all, don't give up. It may be that this was not the right opportunity for you, and another will come when you least expect it.[183]

Transfer: Moving Sideways

Transfer is movement of an employee to a different job with similar responsibility. It may or may not mean a change in geographical location (which might be part of a promotion as well).

Employees might be transferred for four principal reasons:

1. To solve organizational problems by using their skills at another location
2. To broaden their experience in being assigned to a different position
3. To retain their interest and motivation by being presented with a new challenge
4. To solve some employee problems, such as personal differences with their bosses.

Remember that employees are hungry for opportunities to learn new skills and develop their competencies. Job transfers are one way that organizations can provide this kind of meaningful development for employees while simultaneously benefiting the firm.[184] Here are a few examples of how organizations use transfers:[185]

Company Examples: The National Football League (NFL) offers a "junior rotational program" that allows employees to rotate between departments including public affairs, finance, events, and marketing. Employees can spend anywhere from six to twelve months in each department. Each year, Emerson, a global manufacturing firm, gives between 8 and 18 employees the chance to spend one year in one of its U.S. offices and one year in one of its international offices through its "engineers in leadership" program. Procter & Gamble is known for rotating managers through different cities and jobs throughout their careers. Many employees come to expect that they and their families will be in a new home in a new town every three to five years. At P&G, it's "move up or move out."

Disciplining and Demotion: The Threat of Moving Downward

Poorly performing employees may be given a warning or a reprimand and then disciplined. That is, they may be temporarily removed from their jobs, as when a police officer is placed on suspension or administrative leave—removed from his or her regular job in the field and perhaps given a paperwork job or told to stay away from work.

Alternatively, an employee may be demoted—that is, have their current responsibilities, pay, and perquisites taken away, as when a middle manager is demoted to a first-line manager. (Sometimes this may occur when a company is downsized, resulting in fewer higher-level management positions.)

Demotions are uncomfortable for both managers and employees, and recent research suggests that more than 50% of employees who are demoted ultimately quit their jobs. But demotions don't necessarily mean the employee isn't a valuable asset to the company. In many cases, they are simply not a good fit for their current position and would be able to make valuable contributions elsewhere in the organization or after they've had more time in a lower-level position.[186] Here are a few tips for managing the demotion process:[187]

1. *Base demotion decisions on unbiased, well-documented evidence.* Demotions should be based on objective facts that have been documented by the organization.
2. *Communicate the organization's desire to retain the employee.* If you want to keep the employee and feel they will be a good fit in a different position, explain

this, and highlight the strengths that you feel make them the right person for the alternate job.

3. *Be honest about performance-related issues that led to the demotion.* Employees need honest and constructive feedback in order to learn and develop.

Dismissal: Moving Out of the Organization

Dismissals fall into three categories: layoffs, downsizings, and firings. We first discuss each type of dismissal. Then, we describe exit interviews, nondisparagement agreements, and employment at will, which often go along with dismissals.

Layoffs   The phrase being *laid off* tends to suggest that a person has been dismissed *temporarily*—as when a carmaker doesn't have enough orders to justify keeping its production employees—and may be recalled later when economic conditions improve. Many companies cite layoffs as necessary to improve profitability, although research suggests they do not, in fact, improve profits.[188] In some cases, there may be no other option, as companies such as Under Armour, Cheesecake Factory, Best Buy, and Disney found during the COVID-19 pandemic of 2020.[189]

Downsizings   A *downsizing* is a *permanent* dismissal; there is no rehiring later. An automaker discontinuing a line of cars or on the path to bankruptcy might permanently let go of its production employees. Recent research suggests that downsizing occurs more often due to pressure to meet investment analysts' earnings estimates rather than to correct for poor firm performance.[190]

Firings   The phrase *being fired*, with all its euphemisms and synonyms—being "terminated," "separated," "let go," "sacked," "axed," "canned"—tends to mean that a person was dismissed *permanently "for cause."* Firings occur due to, for example, absenteeism, sloppy work habits, failure to perform satisfactorily, or breaking the law. Interestingly, it's rare to hear news of a company firing the CEO. As one writer commented, the CEO "never gets fired," rather, he or she leaves "to pursue other opportunities" or "spend more time with the family."[191] But a recent study suggests that up to half of all CEOs that leave their jobs do so because they were fired.[192]

A few important points about firings are:

1. *Reasons for dismissals should be carefully documented.* Employers need to take steps to avoid employees suing for "wrongful termination."

2. *Remember those who stay.* Other employees may be affected by the firing of a supervisor, co-worker, or subordinate.[193]

3. *Dismissals are usually not a surprise.* Most bosses are conflict-averse, and you may see the handwriting on the wall when your own manager begins to interact with you less.[194]

4. *Firings are more common in some industries or job types than others.* For example, start-ups are quick to fire if new hires don't measure up quickly.[195]

Exit Interviews, Nondisparagement Agreements, and Employment at Will
An **exit interview** is a formal conversation between a representative from the organization and a departing employee to find out why he or she is leaving and to learn about potential problems in the organization. If you leave an organization, you can expect to have an exit interview—91% of Fortune 500 companies use exit interviews, along with 87% of mid-size firms. Unfortunately, research shows that even though many employees quit their

jobs because of poor relationships with their bosses, it's likely that employees will not share this information honestly in exit interviews, because they fear being retaliated against in ways that can damage their careers.[196]

A **nondisparagement agreement** is a contract between two parties that prohibits one party from criticizing the other; it is often used in severance agreements to prohibit former employees from criticizing their former employers. Employees who are laid off or whose jobs have been eliminated are often obliged to sign nondisparagement agreements in return for receiving severance pay—pay an employer may give a worker who leaves, such as the equivalent of two weeks of salary for each year he or she was employed. The #MeToo movement has reignited debates about nondisparagement agreements and the fact that they may prevent some victims of workplace harassment from speaking out. Some states have begun to update their laws to protect the rights of harassment victims.[197]

Employment at will is the governing principle of employment in the great majority of states, and it means that anyone can be dismissed at any time for any reason at all—or for no reason.[198] Exceptions are whistle-blowers and people with employment contracts. EEO laws also prohibit organizations' dismissing people for their membership in one or more protected classes.[199]

Managers should always work with HR to ensure they are being compliant with local, state, and federal law during dismissals. ●

9.7 The Legal Requirements of Human Resource Management

THE BIG PICTURE

Four areas of human resource law any manager needs to be aware of are labor relations, compensation and benefits, health and safety, and equal employment opportunity.

Laws underlie all aspects of the HR practices discussed so far. Whatever your organization's human resource strategy, in the United States (and in U.S. divisions overseas) it has to operate within the environment of the American legal system. In this section we discuss four areas you need to be aware of. Some important laws are summarized in Table 9.2.

LO 9-7

Discuss legal considerations managers should be aware of.

1. Labor Relations

The earliest laws affecting employee welfare had to do with unions, and they can still have important effects. Legislation passed in 1935 (the Wagner Act) resulted in the **National Labor Relations Board (NLRB)**, which enforces procedures whereby employees may vote to have a union and for collective bargaining. **Collective bargaining** consists of negotiations between management and employees about disputes over compensation, benefits, working conditions, and job security.

A 1947 law (the Taft-Hartley Act) allows the president of the United States to prevent or end a strike that threatens national security. (We discuss labor–management issues further in Section 9.8.)

TABLE 9.2   Some Important Recent U.S. Federal Laws and Regulations Protecting Employees

YEAR	LAW OR REGULATION	PROVISIONS
Labor Relations		
1974	Privacy Act	Gives employees legal right to examine letters of reference concerning them
1986	Immigration Reform & Control Act	Requires employers to verify the eligibility for employment of all their new hires (including U.S. citizens)
2003	Sarbanes-Oxley Act	Prohibits employers from demoting or firing employees who raise accusations of fraud to a federal agency
Compensation and Benefits		
1974	Employee Retirement Income Security Act (ERISA)	Sets rules for managing pension plans; provides federal insurance to cover bankrupt plans
1993	Family and Medical Leave Act	Requires employers to provide 12 weeks of unpaid leave for medical and family reasons, including for childbirth, adoption, or family emergency
1996	Health Insurance Portability and Accountability Act (HIPPA)	Allows employees to switch health insurance plans when changing jobs and receive new coverage regardless of preexisting health conditions; prohibits group plans from dropping ill employees
2007	Fair Minimum Wage Act	Increased federal minimum wage to $7.25 per hour on July 24, 2009
Health and Safety		
1970	Occupational Safety and Health Act (OSHA)	Establishes minimum health and safety standards in organizations
1985	Consolidated Omnibus Budget Reconciliation Act (COBRA)	Requires an extension of health insurance benefits after termination
2010	Patient Protection and Affordable Care Act	Employers with more than 50 employees must provide health insurance
Equal Employment Opportunity		
1963	Equal Pay Act	Requires men and women be paid equally for performing equal work
1964, amended 1972	Civil Rights Act, Title VII	Prohibits discrimination on basis of race, color, religion, national origin, sex, or sexual orientation
1967, amended 1978 and 1986	Age Discrimination in Employment Act (ADEA)	Prohibits discrimination in employees over 40 years old; restricts mandatory retirement
1990	Americans with Disabilities Act (ADA)	Prohibits discrimination against essentially qualified employees with physical or mental disabilities or chronic illness; requires "reasonable accommodation" be provided so they can perform duties
1991	Civil Rights Act	Amends and clarifies Title VII, ADA, and other laws; permits suits against employers for punitive damages in cases of intentional discrimination

2. Compensation and Benefits

The **Social Security Act of 1935** established the U.S. retirement system.

The passage of the **Fair Labor Standards Act of 1938 (FLSA)** established minimum living standards for workers engaged in interstate commerce, including provision of a federal minimum wage and a maximum workweek before overtime must be paid, along with banning child labor. A few important facts about the minimum wage:[200]

- *Federal minimum wage is $7.25 an hour.* It was raised to this level in 2009.
- *States have their own laws:*
  - 29 states and D.C. have minimum wages that are higher than the federal level.
  - 5 states do not have minimum wage levels.
  - When an employee is subject to both state and federal law, they earn the higher of the two rates (state or federal).
- *The federal minimum wage has never remained unchanged for this long.* As of 2019, the minimum wage had never stood unchanged for longer. In the 12+ years since the $7.25 per hour rate was set, inflation has increased 18%.

Proponents of a $15 minimum wage say it would help people pay their bills because existing minimum wages have not kept up with inflation, and it would create a fairer working environment because different states now pay wildly different minimums. Detractors say that the $15 figure is arbitrary and that a higher minimum would produce job losses, hurt low-skilled workers, have little effect on reducing poverty, and result in higher prices to consumers.[201]

Salaried executive, administrative, and professional employees are considered exempt from overtime rules—these are called white-collar exemptions. The remaining employees, called nonexempt, must be paid time and a half for any weekly hours in excess of 40. In 2020 the Department of Labor (DOL) updated the white-collar exemptions. Two key takeaways:[202]

- Workers must be paid overtime if they do not earn at least $35,568 per year (or $684 per week), regardless of white-collar job classification.
- Employers can satisfy up to 10% of standard salary level with nondiscretionary bonuses and incentive payments (to include commissions) that are paid annually or more frequently.

3. Health and Safety

From miners risking tunnel cave-ins to cotton mill workers breathing lint, industry has always had dirty, dangerous jobs. Beginning with the Occupational Safety and Health Act (OSH Act) of 1970, a body of law has grown that requires organizations to provide employees with nonhazardous working conditions (most recently augmented by an update to the Toxic Substances Control Act of 1976).[203] Later laws extended health coverage, including 2010 health care reform legislation, which requires employees with more than 50 employees to provide health insurance or pay a penalty.[204] (More than 20 million Americans have gained access to health insurance due to the passing of the Affordable Care Act.)[205]

4. Equal Employment Opportunity

The effort to reduce discrimination in employment based on racial, ethnic, and religious bigotry and gender stereotypes began with Title VII of the Civil Rights Act of 1964. This established the **Equal Employment Opportunity Commission (EEOC)**, whose job is to enforce antidiscrimination and other employment-related laws. Title VII applies to all organizations or their agents engaged in an industry affecting interstate commerce that employs 15 or more employees. Contractors who wish to do business with the U.S. government (such as most colleges and universities, which receive federal funds) must be in compliance with various executive orders issued by the president covering antidis-crimination. Later laws prevented discrimination against older workers and people with physical and mental disabilities. (We discuss these topics in detail in Chapter 11.)

Workplace Discrimination, Affirmative Action, Sexual Harassment, and Bullying

Three important concepts covered by equal employment opportunity (EEO) laws are *workplace discrimination*, *affirmative action*, and *sexual harassment*, which we discuss in this section. We also consider *bullying*, which is *not* covered by EEO laws.

Workplace Discrimination   **Workplace discrimination** occurs when employment decisions about people are made for reasons not relevant to the job, such as skin color, gender, religion, or age. Two fine points to be made here are that (1) although the law prohibits discrimination in all aspects of employment, it does not require an employer to extend *preferential treatment* because of these factors and (2) employment decisions must be made on the basis of job-related criteria.

There are two types of workplace discrimination:

- *Adverse impact.* **Adverse impact** occurs when an organization uses an employment practice or procedure that results in unfavorable outcomes to a protected class (such as workers over 40) over another group of people (such as workers under 40). For example, requiring workers to have "four to six years of experience" inadvertently creates adverse impact on older workers, because workers over 40 are likely to have more than six years of experience. This example would not be a problem, however, if work experience in this specific range were required to perform the job. Another example is basing a person's starting salary on what he or she earned at a previous job. This can discriminate against female applicants because they tend to make less money than males for performing the same job with the same level of experience and skills.

- *Disparate treatment.* **Disparate treatment** results when employees from protected groups (such as disabled individuals) are intentionally treated differently. An example would be making a decision to give all international assignments to people without disabilities because of the assumption that they won't need any special accommodations related to travel. Another example would be deciding to choose a male employee for a promotion over a female employee because of the assumption that the female employee—who happens to be pregnant—is going to give up her career soon anyway.[206]

When an organization is found to have been practicing discrimination, the people discriminated against may sue for back pay and punitive damages. In 2019, among complaints to the EEOC, the most frequently cited basis for charges of discrimination was retaliation (53.8%), followed by disability discrimination (33.4%); discrimination based on race (33%); sex discrimination, including sexual harassment and pregnancy discrimination (32.4%); and discrimination based on age (21.4%). These percentages are greater than 100% because some charges allege multiple types of discrimination.[207]

Discrimination can occur in HR practices even when managers are not consciously aware of it. Aware or not, the organization can be held liable. Organizations need to evaluate their selection devices on a regular basis to be sure they are not at risk of adversely impacting applicants who belong to underrepresented groups. Here's an example of one entrepreneur using AI to decrease discrimination in recruiting, hiring, and selection.

Blendoor Example: Stephanie Lampkin is the founder and CEO of Blendoor, a tech company that uses AI to remove discrimination from the hiring process. Unlike the applications of AI discussed earlier—that were biased by the data they were built from—Blendoor's algorithms are built on more comprehensive data sets. Said Lampkin, "Enterprises tend to hire people who look like people they have hired before and they use procedures that haven't changed. That's why Amazon's AI experiment didn't work. . . . You're baking in bias in the algorithm." The problem, says Lampkin, is that age-old hiring methods persist (for example, a bias toward hiring people from certain elite schools) even though they aren't linked to better firm performance. Blendoor works with companies to turn these biases on their heads. Blendoor's technology has helped some of its customers double the number of women they hire, and others have hired six times more underrepresented minorities.[208]

Blendoor founder and CEO Stephanie Lampkin—shown here speaking at the 2019 New York Times Annual Dealbook Conference—is changing the game with her company's comprehensive, data-driven application of AI that creates more accuracy and less bias in the hiring process.
Mike Cohen/Getty Images

Affirmative Action

==Affirmative action== focuses on achieving equality of opportunity within an organization. It aims to make up for past discrimination in employment by actively finding, hiring, and developing the talents of people from groups traditionally underrepresented due to discrimination. Steps include active recruitment, elimination of prejudicial questions in interviews, and establishment of minority hiring goals. It's important to note that EEO laws *do not* allow the use of hiring quotas.[209]

Affirmative action has created tremendous opportunities for women and minorities, but it has been resisted more by some who see it as working against their interests.[210] Consider what happened at Harvard.

Harvard Example: The issue of affirmative action made headlines when a group called the Students for Fair Admissions sued Harvard for its race-conscious admissions process. Specifically, the lawsuit alleged that Harvard had discriminated against Asian American applicants in its admissions process, unfairly holding them to a higher standard to gain admission. U.S. District Judge Allison Burroughs ruled that Harvard's admissions standards were constitutional, and said in her ruling, "It is this, at Harvard and elsewhere that will move us, one day, to the point where we see that race is a fact, but not the defining fact and not the fact that tells us what is important, but we are not there yet." She added, "Until we are, race-conscious admissions programs that survive strict scrutiny will have an important place in society and help ensure that colleges and universities can offer a diverse atmosphere that fosters learning, improves scholarship and encourages mutual respect and understanding."[211]

Sexual Harassment

==Sexual harassment== consists of unwanted sexual attention that creates an adverse work environment. This means obscene gestures, sex-stereotyped jokes, sexually oriented posters and graffiti, suggestive remarks, unwanted dating pressure, physical nonsexual contact, unwanted touching, sexual propositions, threatening punishment unless sexual favors are given, obscene phone calls, and similar verbal or physical actions of a sexual nature.[212] The harassment may be by a member of the opposite sex or a member of the same sex, by a manager, by a co-worker, or by an outsider. If the harasser is a manager or an agent of the organization, the organization itself can be sued, even if it had no knowledge of the situation.[213] Read the Example box for more information on sexual harassment at work.

EXAMPLE   Sexual Harassment at Work

Sexual harassment is never acceptable, but since 2017, it has become less hidden. Men in fields ranging from sports to entertainment to politics to media and the arts were accused of groping, making sexually inappropriate comments, and even rape by women who at last felt empowered, if not compelled, to speak out.

In what *The New York Times* called "a seismic shift in what behavior is tolerated in the workplace," personified in a movement called #MeToo, scores of men, often high-profile figures with years of professional achievement behind them, were fired, suspended, or forced to resign or step down based on once hushed-up behavior in the recent, or not-so-recent, past. Some have admitted guilt and apologized; others have denied it.[214] As of March 2020, estimates were that the movement had removed more than 200 powerful men from their positions. These include Larry Nassar (sentenced to up to 125 years in prison), Bill Cosby (sentenced to up to 10 years in prison), and Harvey Weinstein (sentenced to 23 years in prison for one case, awaiting trial on another).[215]

Sexual harassment is not a new behavior. It has occurred throughout history. Over the last two decades, psychologists attempted to understand its causes by studying men who harass or assault women. This research shows that male harassers "have different motivations yet typically share specific personality traits" that are amplified by having power, according to *The Wall Street Journal.* The two traits are *hostile masculinity* and *impersonal sexuality.* The *Journal* notes that "Men with 'hostile masculinity' find power over women to be a sexual turn-on. They feel anger at being rejected by a woman. . . . They justify their aggression and are often narcissists."[216] *Narcissism* consists of "an exaggerated—albeit fragile—sense of one's self-importance or influence, characterized by a persistent preoccupation with success, a need for authority, competitiveness, and pervasive patterns of grandiose thinking."[217] Individuals with this trait have inflated views of themselves, fantasize about being in control of everything, and like to attract the admiration of others. It's thus not surprising that narcissists tend to emerge as leaders.[218]

"Men with 'impersonal sexuality' prefer sex without intimacy or a close connection, which often leads them to seek promiscuous sex or multiple partners. Often, but not always, this type of person has had a difficult home environment as a child, with abuse or violence, or they had some anti-social tendencies as adolescents."[219]

What Organizations Are Doing to Combat Sexual Harassment
Organizations need to continue to improve their efforts to combat sexual harassment, because evidence suggests that typical

THE PURPLE CAMPAIGN

The Purple Campaign—founded by Ally Coll—wants to change the way organizations address and prevent sexual harassment. In order to earn the Purple Certification, a company must exemplify steadfast commitment both to preventing sexual harassment and to dealing with it properly if it happens. Courtesy of The Purple Campaign

methods—such as sexual harassment training seminars—aren't enough.[220] One nonprofit, called the Purple Campaign, is attempting something different. Ally Coll, the Purple Campaign's founder, believes that what's necessary is an "outside certification model" that holds organizations accountable to more rigorous, externally imposed standards.[221] To earn the Purple Campaign's certification, organizations need to meet six specific standards. According to the website, employers must:[222]

1. Establish a set of norms.
2. Ensure effective employee training.
3. Improve internal reporting systems.
4. Create fair investigation and adjudication procedures.
5. Measure success and make improvements.
6. Address the intersectionality of workplace harassment.

Uber, Amazon, Airbnb, and Expedia have agreed to participate in the Purple Campaign's pilot program.

YOUR CALL

Given that two personality traits are associated with sexual harassment, how can an organization stop it? Do you think tolerance for the covering up of sexual harassment and other inappropriate or illegal behavior seems to be evaporating? Will an outside certification help? Why or why not?

Two Types of Sexual Harassment   There are two types of sexual harassment, both of which violate Title VII of the 1964 Civil Rights Act.

1. *Quid pro quo harassment*—in this type, the person to whom the unwanted sexual attention is directed is put in the position of jeopardizing being hired for a job or obtaining job benefits or opportunities unless he or she implicitly or explicitly acquiesces.

2. *Hostile environment*—in this (more typical) type, the person being sexually harassed doesn't risk economic harm but experiences an offensive or intimidating work environment. Misogynistic remarks are particularly prevalent on social media.[223]

Table 9.3 presents some examples of sex-based behaviors that are unacceptable in the workplace. Managers should neither perpetrate these behaviors nor tolerate employees engaging in them.

TABLE 9.3   **Sexual Harassment: Examples of Unacceptable Workplace Behaviors**

- Offering sexual favors for rewards related to work or promotion.
- Uninvited touching, patting, or hugging of others' bodies.
- Sexually suggestive jokes, demeaning remarks, slurs, or obscene gestures or sounds.
- Sexual pictures or written notes of a sexual nature.
- Amusement at others' sexually harassing words or behaviors.

What Managers Can Do   Managers can take several actions to help prevent harassment from occurring in the workplace. These include:

- *Institute effective policy.* Managers should make sure their companies have an effective sexual harassment policy in place. The policy should be shown to all current and new employees, who should be made to understand that neither sexual harassment nor covering up for an offender will be tolerated under any circumstances.[224]

- *Establish a formal complaint procedure.* A formal complaint procedure should explain how charges will be investigated and resolved.

- *Train supervisors.* Supervisors should be trained in Title VII requirements and the proper procedures to follow when charges occur.

- *Investigate promptly and without bias.* If charges occur, they should be investigated promptly and objectively, and if substantiated, the offender should be disciplined at once—no matter his or her rank in the company.

Bullying   **Bullying** is repeated mistreatment of one or more persons by one or more perpetrators; it is abusive physical, psychological, verbal, or nonverbal behavior that is threatening, humiliating, or intimidating. It can happen at work just as easily and as often as in the schoolyard.

Indeed, new research suggests that between 75% and 90% of workers have experienced bullying on the job—either directly or as witnesses.[225] Bullying by supervisors typically takes the form of forcing long hours on workers or yelling and behaving in an intimidating or threatening way.[226]

Key facts about workplace bullying include:

- Men account for 70% of workplace bullies, and women are 65% of the targets. Women are the bullies only 30% of the time, but most of their targets (65%) are also women.[227]

A surprisingly common activity, bullying is apt to be verbal, involving shouting and name calling, or relational, including spreading malicious rumors and lies. Perhaps as many as half of all employees have experienced some sort of bullying on the job. Have you? Jetta Productions/The Image Bank/Getty Images

- Bullying can occur between colleagues, managers, and employees, but bosses are reported to be at least 51% of all workplace bullies.[228]

- In a recent survey, the most common types of bullying experienced were through aggressive e-mails (23.3%), co-worker gossip (22%), and yelling (17.8%).[229]

The Effects of Bullying   Research suggests that workplace bullying has numerous negative consequences. Here is a summary of what we know about the effects of being bullied at work:[230]

- *Mental health.* Almost 50% of workplace bullying victims say it has impacted their mental health. Bullying can cause anxiety, depression, and other mental health issues.

- *Physical health.* Almost 25% of workplace bullying victims say it has impacted their physical health. In a particularly alarming study of 80,000 employees across four years, researchers found that for those who had been bullied at work, the occurrence of cardiovascular health problems increased by 59%.

- *Work-related outcomes.* Almost 50% of workplace bullying victims say it has impacted their job performance. Bullying also affects job satisfaction, absenteeism, and intention to quit.

Table 9.4 presents some guidelines for combating bullying. ●

TABLE 9.4 Beating Back the Bully

- **Recognize the mistreatment as bullying:** Don't blame yourself, and don't wait to respond. Stand up for yourself from the start. (Yes, this is hard to do.)

- **Stay calm and confident:** Don't feed the bully's sense of power by showing fear.

- **Don't strike back:** It might get you fired. Ask to be treated with fairness and respect.

- **Avoid being alone with the bully:** Make sure someone can hear your interactions. Or record them on your smartphone.

- **Document what is happening:** Specifically describe to the bully the effect he or she is having on your work and state that you will no longer tolerate it. Also document in writing the date and details (make hard copies of any e-mails, texts, or other written communications), describe the effect on your work, and indicate whether any witnesses were present.

- **Know your next steps:** Get others on your side. Seek advice from your manager and HR manager and be ready to ask for a transfer or even seek a new job if all else fails.

Sources: K. Vasel, "Should You Secretly Tape Conversations with Your Boss?" CNN Business, September 30, 2018, https://www.cnn.com/2018/09/30/success/legal-to-record-conversations-boss-office/index.html; J. Miller, "Workplace Shaming: Why Some Employees Need a Time Out," LinkedIn, September 22, 2018, https://www.linkedin.com/pulse/workplace-shaming-why-some-employees-need-time-out-joshua-miller/; A. Morin, "How to Prevent a Workplace Bully from Taking Your Power," Inc., June 25, 2018, https://www.inc.com/amy-morin/how-to-prevent-a-workplace-bully-from-taking-your-power.html; R. Hosie, "What to Do If You're Being Bullied at Work," The Independent, March 9, 2018, https://www.independent.co.uk/life-style/workplace-bullying-what-to-do-definition-harassment-uk-by-boss-manager-a8247256.html.

9.8 Labor–Management Issues

THE BIG PICTURE

We describe the process by which workers get a labor union to represent them and how unions and management negotiate a contract. This section also discusses the types of union and nonunion workplaces and right-to-work laws. It covers issues unions and management negotiate, such as compensation, cost-of-living adjustments, two-tier wage systems, and givebacks. It concludes by describing mediation and arbitration.

Starting in 1943, James Smith worked his way up from washing dishes in the galley of a passenger train's dining car to waiter, earning tips on top of his wages of 36 cents an hour. The union job with the Brotherhood of Sleeping Car Porters, the first African American union, enabled him to go to college, and when he left the railroad he was hired as a civil engineer for the city of Los Angeles. "His story," says one report, "is emblematic of the role the railroads and a railroad union played in building a foundation for America's black middle class."[231] Unions also helped to grow the U.S. (and European) middle classes in general, bringing benefits to all, organized or not.

Labor unions are organizations of employees formed to protect and advance their members' interests by bargaining with management over job-related issues. The union movement is far less powerful that it was in the 1950s—indeed, its present membership has reached record lows—but it is still a force in many sectors of the economy. (*See Table 9.5.*) Despite declining membership, about 64% of U.S. adults hold a favorable view of unions today, the highest in almost two decades and up sharply from less than 50% in 2015.[232] Young adults hold more favorable views of unions (68%) than they do of business corporations (46%).[233]

LO 9-8

Describe labor–management issues and ways to work effectively with labor unions.

TABLE 9.5   **Snapshot of Today's U.S. Union Movement**

Who's in a union (2019)?
• 11.2% of full-time U.S. workers—down from a high of 35.5% in 1945 but also up about a quarter million workers since 2016
• 6.2% of private-sector workers (7.5 million)
• 33.6% of public-sector workers (7.1 million)
• Most members, public sector: local government (39.4%), including teachers, police officers, and firefighters
• Most members, private sector: utilities (23.4%), transportation and warehousing (16.1%), and telecommunications (14.1%)
• Union membership rate by gender: men (10.8%), women (9.7%)
• Union membership rate by race and ethnicity: Blacks (11.2%), Whites (10.3%), Asian Americans (8.8%), Hispanic Americans (8.9%)

Source: Bureau of Labor Statistics, "Union Members 2019," News Release, January 22, 2020, https://www.bls.gov/news.release/pdf/union2.pdf.

How Workers Organize

When workers in a particular organization decide to form a union, they first must get other workers to sign an *authorization card*, which designates a certain union as the workers' bargaining agent. When at least 30% of workers have signed cards, the union may ask the employer for official recognition.

Usually the employer refuses, at which point the union can petition the National Labor Relations Board (NLRB) to decide which union should become the *bargaining unit* that represents the workers, such as the Teamsters Union, United Auto Workers, American Federation of Teachers, or Service Employees International Union, as appropriate. (Some workers, however, are represented by unions you would never guess: Zookeepers, for instance, are represented by the Teamsters, which mainly organizes transportation workers. University of California, Berkeley, graduate student instructors are represented by the United Auto Workers.) An election is then held by the NLRB, and if 50% or more of the votes cast agree to unionization, the NLRB *certifies* the union as the workers' exclusive representative.

Labor agreements are formed through careful negotiations between union representatives, union members, and managers. Negotiating requires the career readiness competencies of critical thinking/problem solving and oral/written communication. What additional career readiness competencies do you think are especially important in negotiations?
Morsa Images/Getty Images

How Unions and Management Negotiate a Contract

Once a union is recognized as an official bargaining unit, its representatives can then meet with management's representatives to do collective bargaining—to negotiate pay and benefits and other work terms.

When agreement is reached with management, the union representatives take the collective bargaining results back to the members for *ratification*—they vote to accept or reject the contract negotiated by their leaders. If they vote yes, the union and management representatives sign a *negotiated labor-management contract*, which sets the general tone and terms under which labor and management agree to work together during the contract period.

The Issues Unions and Management Negotiate About

The key issues that labor and management negotiate are compensation, employee benefits, job security, work rules, hours, and safety matters. However, the first issue is usually the union security clause and management rights.

Union Security and Types of Workplaces

A key issue is: Who controls hiring policies and work assignments—labor or management? This involves the following matters:

- **The union security clause.** The basic underpinning of union security is the union security clause, the part of the labor–management agreement that states that employees who receive union benefits must join the union, or at least pay dues to it. In times past, a union would try to solidify the union security clause by getting management to agree to a *closed shop agreement*—which is illegal today—in which a company agreed it would hire only current union members for a given job.

- **Types of unionized and nonunionized workplaces.** The four basic kinds of workplaces are *closed shop*, *union shop*, *agency shop*, and *open shop. (See Table 9.6.)*

- **Right-to-work laws.** Individual states are allowed (under the 1947 Taft-Hartley Act) to pass legislation outlawing union and agency shops. As a result, 28 states have passed right-to-work laws, statutes that prohibit employees from being required to join a union as a condition of employment.

TABLE 9.6

Four Kinds of Workplace Labor Agreements

WORKPLACE	DEFINITION	STATUS
Closed shop	Employer may hire only workers for a job who are already in the union.	Illegal
Union shop	Workers aren't required to be union members when hired for a job but must join the union within a specified time.	Not allowed in 27 states (right-to-work states) Not allowed for public-sector employees
Agency shop	Workers must pay equivalent of union dues but aren't required to join the union.	Applies to public-sector teachers in some states, prohibited in others
Open shop	Workers may choose to join or not join a union.	Applies in 27 states (right-to-work states)

Business interests supporting such laws argue that forcing workers to join a union violates their rights and makes a state less attractive to businesses considering moving there. Union supporters say that states with such laws have overall lower wages and that all workers benefit from union gains, so everyone should be compelled to join.

The 27 work-to-right states are shown in dark blue in Figure 9.5.

FIGURE 9.5
States with right-to-work laws

What kind of state do you live in? (Alaska and Hawaii are non–right-to-work states.)

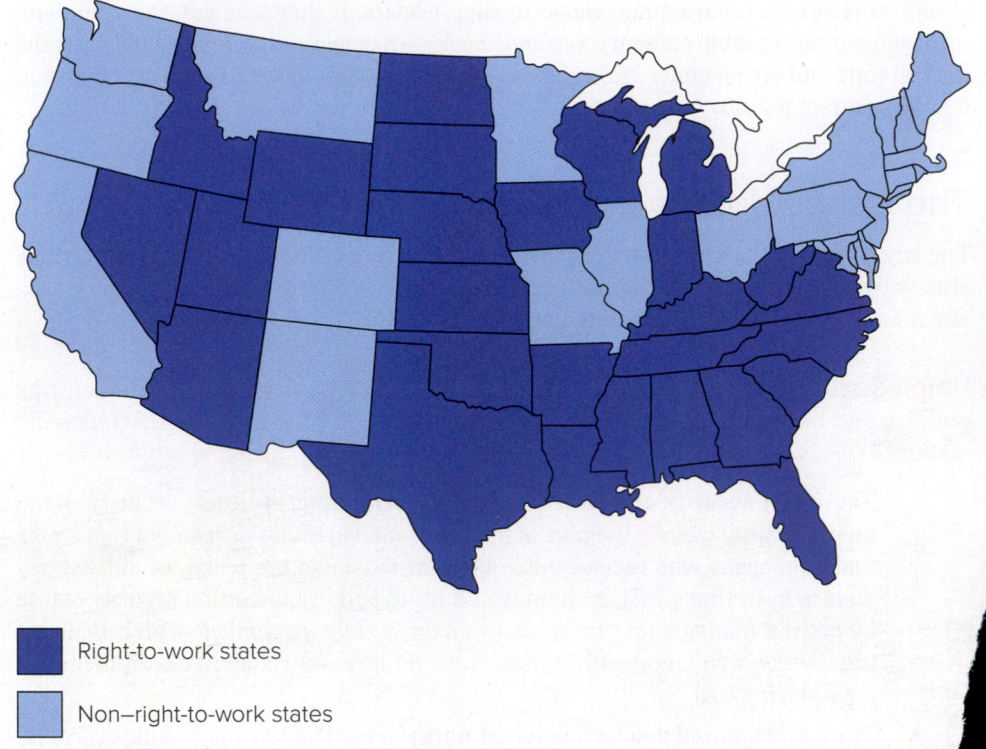

■ Right-to-work states

■ Non–right-to-work states

Compensation: Wage Rates, COLA Clauses, and Givebacks
Unions s
to negotiate the highest wage rates possible, or to trade off higher wages for some
else, such as better fringe benefits. Some issues involved with compensation a
follows:

- **Wage rates—same pay or different rates?** Wage rates subject to negotia
  include overtime pay, different wages for different shifts, and bonuses. In
  past, unions tried to negotiate similar wage rates for unionized employe
  working in similar jobs for similar companies or similar industries. Howeve
  the pressure of competition abroad and deregulation at home has forced many
  unions to negotiate <mark>two-tier wage contracts</mark>, in which new employees are paid
  less or receive fewer benefits than veteran employees have.

    In 2011, when automakers began to create new jobs, new union hires were
  offered about half the pay ($14 an hour) that autoworkers were getting before
  ($28). Such two-tier wage systems can be attractive to employers, who are able
  to hire new workers at reduced wages, and they also benefit veteran union
  members, who experience no wage reduction. However, among autoworkers, at
  least, such contracts may be on the way out.[234] Consider what happened
  recently at GM:

    GM Example: In fall 2019, 49,000 GM workers went on strike for 40 days to
  protest wages and other aspects of their employment contracts. One of the
  primary issues was the two-tier wage contracts that held many GM workers'
  salaries below $20 per hour. At the end of the strike, the workers emerged
  with, among other things, a deal to bring all of the company's lower-tier workers up to $32 per hour over the next four years.[235]

- **Cost-of-living adjustment.** Because the cost of living is always going up (at least
  so far), unions often try to negotiate a <mark>cost-of-living adjustment (COLA) clause</mark>,
  which during the period of the contract ties future wage increases to increases in

the cost of living, as measured by the U.S. Bureau of Labor Statistics' consumer price index (CPI). (An alternative is the *wage reopener clause*, which allows wage rates to be renegotiated at certain stated times during the life of the contract. Thus, a 10-year contract might be subject to renegotiation every two years.)

- **Givebacks.** During tough economic times, when a company (or, in the case of public employee unions, a municipality) is fighting for its very survival, management and labor may negotiate **givebacks**, in which the union agrees to give up previous wage or benefit gains in return for something else. Usually, the union seeks job security, as in a no-layoff policy.

Settling Labor–Management Disputes

Even when a collective-bargaining agreement and contract have been accepted by both sides, there may likely be ongoing differences that must be resolved. Sometimes differences lead to walkouts and strikes, or management may lock out employees. However, conflicts can be resolved through *grievance procedures*, *mediation,* or *arbitration.*

Grievance Procedures   A **grievance** is a complaint by an employee that management has violated the terms of the labor–management agreement. Example: An employee may feel he or she is being asked to work too much overtime, is not getting his or her fair share of overtime, or is being unfairly passed over for promotion.

Grievance procedures are often handled initially by the union's *shop steward*, an official elected by the union membership who works at the company and represents the interests of unionized employees on a daily basis to the employees' immediate supervisors. If this process is not successful, the grievance may be carried to the union's chief shop steward and then to the union's grievance committee, who deal with their counterparts higher up in management.

If the grievance procedure is not successful, the two sides may decide to try to resolve their differences by one of two ways—*mediation* or *arbitration*.

Mediation   **Mediation** is the process in which a neutral third party, a mediator, listens to both sides in a dispute, makes suggestions, and encourages them to agree on a solution. Mediators may be lawyers or retired judges or specialists in various fields, such as conflict resolution or labor matters.

Arbitration   **Arbitration** is the process in which a neutral third party, an arbitrator, listens to both parties in a dispute and makes a decision that the parties have agreed will be binding on them. Many corporations, new tech start-ups, and some for-profit colleges have vigorously embraced arbitration as a business tool with consumers and employees and students, forbidding them from resolving their complaints through class-action suits (when a large number of plaintiffs with similar complaints band together to sue a company).[236] Critics, however, contend that forcing consumers to sign agreements that require arbitration and prevent lawsuits has the effect of biasing resolutions in favor of business and constitutes a "privatization of the justice system."[237] Recent evidence suggests this may be changing:

Arbitration Claims Example: Attorney and Silicon Valley entrepreneur Ted Lidow was concerned when he realized that over the past several years, only about 30 out of 330 million Comcast and AT&T customers took the companies to arbitration (as mentioned in previous chapters, telecom companies have notoriously poor customer satisfaction ratings, making this figure especially unbelievable). He soon realized more than 1,000 people wanted to file arbitration claims (customers cannot bring class-action lawsuits against these companies because of the forced arbitration clauses they agree to in their contracts), but steep fees and other hurdles prevented them from starting the process. Lidow's idea was to use his start-up that helps people begin the arbitration process—FairShake—to help the thousands of customers file their arbitration claims all at once. Attorney Travis Lenkner did something similar when his law firm—Keller Lenkner—filed arbitration claims for 6,000 DoorDash employees in one summer. These attorneys believe that companies don't have even close to the amount of resources needed to deal with these claims at once, and they hope the overwhelming volume of arbitration claims will lead to changes in the way these disputes are resolved.[238]

What is your feeling about labor unions? Self-Assessment 9.4 enables you to answer this question by assessing your general attitudes toward unions. ●

SELF-ASSESSMENT 9.4

Assessing Your Attitudes toward Unions

This survey is designed to assess your attitude toward unions. Please be prepared to answer these questions if your instructor has assigned Self-Assessment 9.4 in Connect.

1. Where do you stand on your attitude toward unions—positive, neutral, or negative?

2. What experiences or events in your life have led to your attitude toward unions? Describe. What do you think lies in the future for labor unions?

3. Why has there been growing dislike for unions in the United States among some generations, and more acceptance and favoritism among other generations?

9.9 Career Corner: Managing Your Career Readiness

LO 9-9

Review the steps for becoming a better receiver of feedback.

"Feedback is the breakfast of champions," according to author, consultant, and management expert Dr. Ken Blanchard. Blanchard is telling us that feedback is essential for success at any endeavor. The problem, however, is that people are not very good at either giving or receiving feedback, even though we continuously engage in these activities. A team of researchers found, for example, that individual performance *decreased* by 13.3% after receiving feedback.[239] Further, performance decreased whether the feedback was positive or negative—but the drops were bigger for positive feedback! This may happen because our brains are wired to resist negative feedback, causing us to explain it away or outright reject it.[240] The brain identifies negative information faster than positive information and deems it more important in protecting us from harm.

Our focus here is to help you become a better receiver of feedback, because it is essential for developing career readiness. Regardless of how feedback is delivered, nothing happens unless the receiver accepts the feedback and decides to do something with it.[241]

Career Readiness Competencies

FIGURE 9.6
Model of career readiness
McGraw-Hill Education

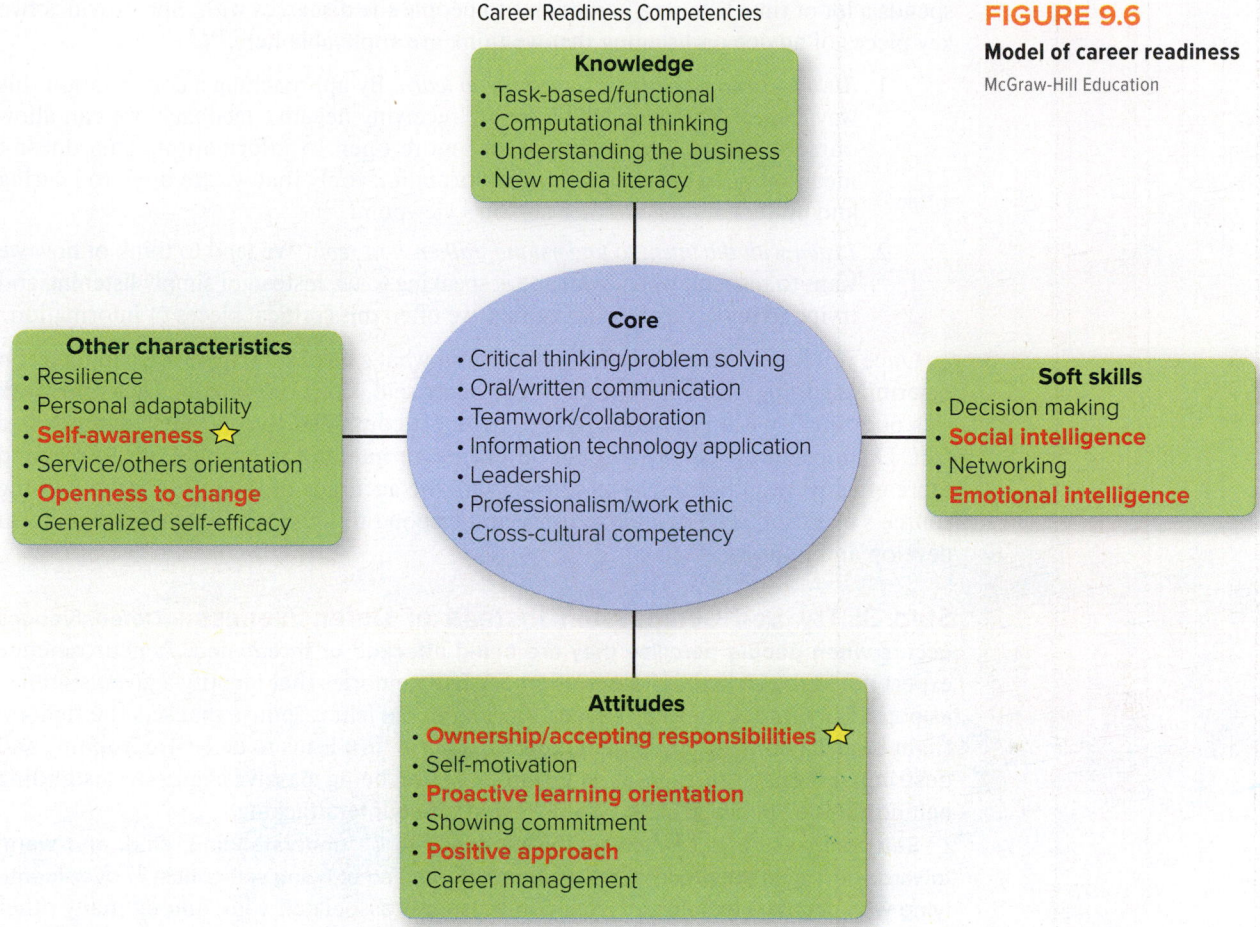

Knowledge
- Task-based/functional
- Computational thinking
- Understanding the business
- New media literacy

Core
- Critical thinking/problem solving
- Oral/written communication
- Teamwork/collaboration
- Information technology application
- Leadership
- Professionalism/work ethic
- Cross-cultural competency

Other characteristics
- Resilience
- Personal adaptability
- **Self-awareness** ⭐
- Service/others orientation
- **Openness to change**
- Generalized self-efficacy

Soft skills
- Decision making
- **Social intelligence**
- Networking
- **Emotional intelligence**

Attitudes
- **Ownership/accepting responsibilities** ⭐
- Self-motivation
- **Proactive learning orientation**
- Showing commitment
- **Positive approach**
- Career management

Becoming a Better Receiver

Becoming a better receiver takes some effort. Our model of career readiness reveals that you need to apply seven competencies: social intelligence, emotional intelligence, ownership/accepting responsibility, proactive learning orientation, positive approach, self-awareness, and openness to change *(see Figure 9.6)*. Use these competencies while putting the following steps into action:

Step 1: Identify Your Tendencies
You have received feedback many times during your life and most likely developed patterns of responding. Do you tend to argue? Do you defend yourself and dispute the facts? Do you create a diversion and blame someone else? Do you smile but hide your anger? Do you have a knee-jerk response to reject feedback but then consider its merits at a later point in time? The career readiness competency of taking ownership/accountability reminds us how important it is to take responsibility for our actions. This underscores the value of self-awareness, another career readiness competency, about our typical way of responding to negative feedback.[242]

Step 2: Learn How to Listen
Your brain's biology will jump into action upon receiving negative feedback. The amygdala, which acts like an alarm bell, suggests "threat," which in turn makes us hypervigilant to criticism and shuts down our ability to listen. This is unfortunate because it is essential to listen carefully and not interrupt when receiving negative feedback. Your goal during this process is to remain silent and strive to understand what is being communicated. NPR correspondent and seasoned journalist Celeste Headlee made her living interviewing people—meaning she

spends a lot of time listening, sometimes to people she disagrees with. She provides two key pieces of advice on listening that we think are applicable here:[243]

1. *Always assume you have something to learn.* By approaching a conversation this way, especially one in which we are receiving negative feedback, we can allow ourselves to be less defensive and more open to information. This doesn't mean we need to agree with the information—only that we are open to hearing and understanding another person's viewpoint.

2. *Listen with the intent to understand, rather than reply.* We tend to think of how we want to respond when someone is speaking to us, instead of simply listening and trying to understand. In doing this, we often miss critical pieces of information.

Once you have listened and fully understand what's been said, then you can focus on determining things such as whether what's being said is fact or opinion. That your work was poor quality is an opinion. That your report contained five misspelled words is a fact. Distinguishing facts from opinion during an interaction enables you to respond more effectively. Other things to consider are the accuracy of the information and the source's intention. The point is to listen and respond to those whose aim is to help you develop and improve.[244]

Step 3: Try Self-Compassion Instead of Defensiveness   ==Defensiveness== occurs when people perceive they are being attacked or threatened. A neuroscience expert noted the amygdala "accesses emotional memories that identify a given stimulus as potentially threatening and triggers the emotional fear response that sets the fight-or-flight biobehavioral response in motion."[245] This in turn leads to defensive listening and destructive behaviors such as shutting down or being passive-aggressive, standing behind rules or policies, creating a diversion, or counterattacking.

==Self-compassion== is defined as the tendency to be understanding, kind, and warm toward yourself in the process of pain or failure, instead of being self-critical or over-identifying with negative emotions.[246] Self-compassion is associated with, among many other positive outcomes, less defensiveness in the face of information that presents a threat to your self-concept. Recent studies suggest that self-compassion is also related to amygdala activity and developing more of it has important mental health benefits.

Remember to allow yourself to feel whatever it is you are feeling, while keeping in mind your sense of self-worth. When you are ready, it is usually helpful to ask questions such as, "I want to be sure I understand what you're saying. Do I have it right that you feel . . .?"[247] Asking questions quiets the amygdala and allows you to gain more insight about the threatening message.

Step 4: Ask for Feedback   Your emotional triggers are less likely to be activated if you seek feedback rather than wait for it to be delivered. Look for opportunities to ask for bite-sized pieces of information about your behavior or performance as you work. Smaller doses are less threatening. A simple way is to ask someone for one thing you did well on a project and one thing that could be improved. Remember that most of us don't receive all of the information we need to improve our performance, and one way to change this is to ask for feedback.[248] Engaging in this behavior is also likely to improve your image because research shows that explicitly seeking performance feedback results in higher performance ratings.[249]

Step 5: Practice Being Mindful   As defined in Chapter 7, mindfulness is "the awareness that emerges through paying attention on purpose, in the present moment, and nonjudgmentally to the unfolding of experience moment by moment."[250] Mindfulness builds ==psychological capital==—a positive state of psychological development that is characterized by high levels of hope, resiliency, optimism, and self-efficacy—and it can help you to be a better receiver of feedback.[251] Meditation is a great method for increasing your general level of mindfulness. (Refer to Chapter 7 for a refresher on how to practice mindfulness meditation.) ●

360-degree feedback appraisal 389
adverse impact 398
affirmative action 399
arbitration 407
assessment centers 375
base pay 378
behavioral-description interviews 374
behaviorally anchored rating scale (BARS) 388
benefits (or fringe benefits) 378
boomerangs 370
bullying 401
collective bargaining 395
compensation 378
cost-of-living adjustment (COLA) clause 406
defensiveness 410
disparate treatment 398
employee referrals 369
employment at will 395
employment tests 374
Equal Employment Opportunity Commission (EEOC) 397

exit interview 394
external recruiting 369
Fair Labor Standards Act of 1938 (FLSA) 397
forced ranking performance review systems 390
givebacks 407
grievance 407
high-performance work system (HPWS) 367
human capital 365
human resource management (HRM) 362
internal recruiting 368
labor unions 403
legal defensibility 371
mediation 407
microlearning 382
National Labor Relations Board (NLRB) 395
nondisparagement agreement 395
objective appraisals 388
onboarding 379
performance appraisal 386

performance management 385
person–job (P–J) fit 370
psychological capital 410
recruiting 368
reliability 371
right-to-work laws 405
selection 371
self-compassion 410
sexual harassment 399
situational interviews 374
social capital 365
Social Security Act of 1935 397
strategic human resource management 363
structured interview 374
subjective appraisals 388
talent management 366
transfer 393
two-tier wage contracts 406
union security clause 405
unstructured interviews 373
validity 371
workplace discrimination 398

Key Points

9.1 Strategic Human Resource Management

- Human resource (HR) management is the process of planning for, attracting, developing, and retaining an effective workforce.
- Strategic human resource management (HRM) is the process of designing and implementing systems of policies and practices that align an organization's human capital with its strategic objectives.
- Two concepts important to strategic HRM are (1) human capital and (2) social capital.
- Talent management and high performance work systems are two strategic HRM approaches.

9.2 Recruitment and Selection: Putting the Right People into the Right Jobs

- Recruiting is the process of locating and attracting qualified applicants for job openings. Recruiting is of three types: internal, external, and hybrid.
- The selection process is the screening of job applicants to hire the best candidates. Three types of selection tools are background information, interviewing, and employment tests.

- Background information is ascertained through application forms, resumes, and background checks.
- Interviewing takes three forms: (1) unstructured, (2) structured situational, and (3) structured behavioral-description.
- Employment tests are the standardized devices organizations use to measure specific skills, abilities, traits, and other tendencies.

9.3 Managing an Effective Workforce: Compensation and Benefits

- Compensation has three parts: wages or salaries, incentives, and benefits.
- In the category of wages or salaries, the concept of base pay consists of the basic wage or salary paid to employees in exchange for doing their jobs.
- Incentives include commissions, bonuses, profit-sharing plans, and stock options.
- Benefits are additional nonmonetary forms of compensation, such as health insurance, retirement plans, and family leave.

9.4 Onboarding and Learning and Development

- Companies often perform what is known as onboarding, a process designed to integrate and transition employees into new jobs and organizations through familiarization with corporate policies, procedures, cultures, and politics and clarification of work-role expectations and responsibilities.
- Learning and development entails a process for educating employees in the skills they need to do their jobs today and in the future.
- There are five steps in the learning and development process: (1) assessment, (2) objectives, (3) selection, (4) implementation, and (5) evaluation.

9.5 Performance Management

- Performance management consists of four steps: (1) define performance, (2) monitor and evaluate performance, (3) review performance, and (4) provide consequences.
- Performance appraisal consists of assessing an employee's performance and providing them with feedback. Appraisals are of two general types— objective and subjective.
- Performance feedback is one of the most important parts of the manager's job.

9.6 Managing Promotions, Transfers, Disciplining, and Dismissals

- Managers must manage promotions, transfers, disciplining, and dismissals, which often involve replacing an employee with a new employee.
- In considering promotions, managers must be concerned about fairness, nondiscrimination, and other employees' resentment.
- Transfers, or moving employees to a different job with similar responsibility, may take place in order to solve organizational problems, broaden managers' experience, retain managers' interest and motivation, and solve some employee problems.
- Poor-performing employees may need to be disciplined or demoted.
- Dismissals may consist of layoffs, downsizings, or firings.
- Exit interviews, nondisparagement agreements, and employment at will are three important parts of these processes.

9.7 The Legal Requirements of Human Resource Management

- Four areas of human resource law that any manager needs to be aware of are labor relations, compensation and benefits, health and safety, and equal employment opportunity.
- Labor relations are dictated in part by the National Labor Relations Board, which enforces procedures whereby employees may vote to have a union and for collective bargaining. Collective bargaining consists of negotiations between management and employees about disputes over compensation, benefits, working conditions, and job security.
- Compensation and benefits are covered by the Social Security Act of 1935 and the Fair Labor Standards Act, which established minimum wage and overtime pay regulations.
- Health and safety are covered by the Occupational Safety and Health Act of 1970, among other laws.

9.8 Labor–Management Issues

- Labor unions are organizations of employees formed to protect and advance their members' interests by bargaining with management over job-related issues.
- Among the issues unions negotiate are the union security clause, which states that workers must join the union or at least pay benefits to it.
- The four types of workplaces are closed shop (now illegal), union shop, agency shop, and open shop. Twenty-seven states have right-to-work laws that prohibit employees from being required to join a union as a condition of employment.

9.9 Career Corner: Managing Your Career Readiness

- Becoming a better receiver of feedback requires using seven career readiness competencies: social intelligence, emotional intelligence, ownership/ accepting responsibility, proactive learning orientation, positive approach, self-awareness, and openness to change.
- There are five steps to becoming a better receiver of feedback: (1) identify your tendencies, (2) learn how to listen, (3) try self-compassion instead of defensiveness, (4) ask for feedback, and (5) practice being mindful.

Understanding the Chapter: What Do I Know?

1. What is human resource management and its purpose, and what are the two types of fit important to it?
2. What is performance management, and what are the four steps in it?
3. Explain how strategic human resource management is related to organizational culture, structure, and strategy.
4. What are the three types of recruiting, and how do the three types of selection tools work?
5. Differentiate among the three types of compensation.
6. Describe onboarding, learning, and development.
7. Explain the difference between objective and subjective performance appraisals, and describe 360-degree feedback appraisal and forced ranking.
8. What are the four areas of human resource law a manager needs to be aware of?
9. Explain the concepts of discrimination, affirmative action, sexual harassment, and bullying.
10. What are the principal labor–management issues?

Difficulties Attracting and Retaining Human Capital in the Nursing Profession

Imagine a job that pays well above national averages and provides many opportunities for continuing education, specialization, and career advancement. It allows you to be active every day and to make a real difference in others' lives, along with the kind of scheduling flexibility some describe as "fantastic!"[252] Would you sign up? Strong salaries, lifelong learning opportunities, three-day workweeks, and meaningful work are common facets of a nursing career. And yet, hospitals consistently report nursing shortages stemming from both a lack of applicants and extremely high turnover rates. Turnover seems particularly high among newly minted registered nurses (RNs), with data suggesting approximately 17% of new nurses quit their first job within a year.[253] With all the positives associated with the career, why do hospitals have such a hard time attracting and retaining nurses?

COMPENSATION

Nursing is one of the college majors with the highest starting salaries, with new RNs earning an average of almost $71,000 annually.[254] This salary is competitive when compared to the $51,000 overall average starting salary for new college graduates and the U.S. median annual income of around $61,000.[255] RNs can earn six-figure annual incomes if they take night or overtime shifts or work as traveling nurses.[256]

But many RNs feel their salaries do not compensate them for the level of responsibility and the physical and emotional demands of the job.[257] One of the primary reasons cited for high nurse turnover, particularly in early careers, is that new nurses don't have a realistic understanding of job demands going in.[258] Many quickly recognize that good pay isn't enough to offset other job factors. As one nurse put it, "Nursing ain't for sissies, and if you choose nursing for the monetary benefits and not because you love the profession or love people, you will not stay."[259]

The gender pay gap is another compensation issue in the nursing profession. Although women account for 88% of nurses, female RNs earn around $6,000 less per year than their male colleagues.[260] Male RNs also enjoy significant career advancement and mobility advantages over female RNs, an effect described as a "glass escalator" that takes males in female-dominated professions "straight to the top" of the career ladder while their female counterparts spend their careers climbing lower rungs.[261]

INTERPERSONAL TREATMENT

It's not uncommon for nurses to experience verbal and physical abuse on the job. The mistreatment stems from three primary sources: doctors, other nurses, and patients.

The American Medical Association says doctors and nurses have an ethical obligation to work together and coordinate their efforts to ensure patients receive needed care.[262] In spite of this advice and the extensive training, skills, and knowledge nurses possess, they operate in an environment where doctors repeatedly question their competence. In a social media rant that went viral, Florida anesthesiologist Dr. David Glener said nurse practitioners were "useful but only as minions."[263]

Bullying is a problem among peers. Studies suggest that 40% of nurses have been bullied by other nurses. Nurse-on-nurse bullying isn't harmful just to the nurses who experience it—it's also detrimental to patient care.[264] As one chief nursing officer put it, "There's a direct link between bullying and poor patient outcomes," adding, "staff gets distracted by a strong personality or derailed by a bully, and it takes their focus away from providing quality care."[265]

Patients are a third source of nurse mistreatment. Nurse Suzanne Carroll said, "As nurses, I'm willing to bet that most of us have experienced sexual harassment at some point during our careers."[266] The reason? According to a nurse practitioner in a recent interview there's a persistent culture that allows patients to abuse nurses and pressures nurses to tolerate it. She said, "After a while, you learn to expect these things, but it is the repeated abuse that burns you out. You get so used to it that it becomes normal. The constant message of, 'the patient comes first,' I think, contributes to how we respond, or don't respond in these situations."[267] Abuse can also turn physical, with survey data suggesting that between one in four of nurses suffers violence from patients, their visitors, or their families.[268]

INJURIES ON THE JOB

Nurses experience frequent and serious work-related injuries. The Bureau of Labor Statistics (BLS) indicates that around 25,000 injuries are reported annually among nursing employees, with most stemming from the daily work of moving and lifting patients.[269] In spite of a long-held tradition of teaching safe lifting techniques to nursing students, decades of data now show there is no safe technique for manually lifting patients.[270]

Some hospitals have invested in nursing staff physical safety by purchasing specialized lifting equipment similar to that used to lift heavy parts in manufacturing facilities. Studies suggest that implementing these devices can reduce nurse low back pain by almost 50%.[271] In spite of data on the sheer volume of injuries and the methods that can substantially reduce injuries, says one article, "hospitals still are not employing enough assistive devices to help move patients, and that's a major reason why healthcare workers have one of the highest rates of occupational musculoskeletal injuries in the U.S."[272]

RESPONSES

Both patient outcomes and the bottom line suffer when nursing departments are understaffed.[273] Still, nurses continue to feel that hospital administrators undervalue their health and safety. Even so, their commitment and dedication to patient care persists, and this was never more evident than during the 2020 COVID-19 pandemic. Nurses around the country worked grueling hours in understaffed units, often without access to proper personal protective equipment, and put themselves and their families at risk every day.[274] Dr. Paul Dohrenwend, assistant chief of emergency medicine at Kaiser Permanente San Diego, said, "Nurses are the underappreciated heroes of this crisis." He added, "I thank everyone who's working to help get through this. I commend the scientists at big pharmaceutical companies who are developing better tests and vaccines. I thank the teachers setting up remote classes and the managers making tough business decisions. Everyone is playing a part—but none are more important than the nurses."[275]

FOR DISCUSSION

Problem-Solving Perspective

1. What is the underlying problem in this case from the perspective of a hospital administrator?

2. What role do you believe hospital administrators have played in contributing to nursing shortages and high nurse turnover?

3. What can hospitals do to increase nurse supply and retention rates?

Application of Chapter Content

1. What could hospitals do during recruitment and selection to help with nurse retention?

2. What type of learning or development might hospitals offer to help reduce nurse turnover?

3. What steps could hospitals take to ensure male and female nurses are given equal opportunities in compensation and promotion decisions?

4. Do hospitals have a legal and/or ethical responsibility to invest more money in equipment to prevent work-related nursing injuries? Why or why not?

5. What do you think are the primary reasons nurses experience so much mistreatment on the job, and what can hospitals and nurses do to decrease these incidents?

6. Why do you think so many nurses continue to work, despite the many challenges they face and the lack of safety on the job?

Legal/Ethical Challenge

Should Noncompete Agreements Be Legal?

This challenge considers the human resource policy of asking new hires to sign a noncompete agreement. Noncompete agreements (NCAs) are "employment provisions that ban workers at one company from going to work for, or starting, a competing business within a certain period of time after leaving a job."[276] In other words, the agreement prohibits the person signing it from working with another company that could be viewed as a competitor. The concept was born from the idea that when employees leave an organization, they might take trade secrets and other important information and use it to help a competitor gain a competitive advantage.[277]

Critical Intervention Services (CIS), a private security firm in Florida, sued Michael Kenny for violating a noncompete agreement after Kenny worked as a security guard for the company for 13 days. Shortly after starting the job, the veteran and single father was unable to find child care during his 7 p.m. to 7 a.m. shift. Kenny alleged that when he asked for a different shift, the company told him to either work his assigned shift or quit. CIS alleged that Kenny "went to work, not only for a direct competitor, but for an existing CIS client," and that he now had specialized security knowledge from the training he had participated in.[278]

Jessica Bell signed a noncompete agreement in a "stack of paperwork" she received when she joined Citrix software company in Raleigh, North Carolina. Bell got wind of potential layoffs at Citrix about two years into the job and began searching for employment with other companies. She took a position with Egnyte, a Silicon Valley–based tech firm that had recently opened a sales office in Raleigh. A few weeks into her new job, Bell and six other former Citrix employees working for Egnyte received letters from Citrix informing them that they were violating the noncompete clause. Egnyte filed suit against Citrix, asking that the court rule the noncompete agreements were overly broad and therefore unenforceable.

Citrix countersued Egnyte and the seven employees, stating that Egnyte had hired the former Citrix workers "in order to engage in unfair competition with Citrix." Egnyte vowed to foot the legal bill for all seven employees and maintained that it hired them on the basis of talent, not to steal Citrix's intellectual property or customers. Bell said, "I certainly didn't think this would have implications and that they would have any control or power over my ability to feed my family essentially after I left Citrix."[279] She noted an obvious misunderstanding about what she was agreeing to when she signed Citrix's noncompete clause.

The incidence of noncompete lawsuits has nearly tripled since 2000, and their legality varies by state.[280] About 20% of U.S. workers have signed such agreements. Noncompete clauses have even extended to lower-level jobs; approximately 14% of employees who make less than $40,000 a year are bound by them.[281]

SOLVING THE CHALLENGE

Should companies be allowed to force employees to sign noncompete agreements?

1. Of course. Every company needs to protect its proprietary and confidential information.

2. In moderation. I agree that it makes sense to protect proprietary information like formulas, equations, trade secrets, and intellectual property for certain occupations or industries. But this should not apply to all jobs, such as working in a sandwich shop.

3. No. They should be against the law because they prohibit people from finding employment.

4. Invent other options. Explain.

10

Organizational Change and Innovation
Lifelong Challenges for the Exceptional Manager

Kapook2981/iStock/Getty Images

After reading this chapter, you should be able to:

LO 10-1 Discuss what managers should know about organizational change.

LO 10-2 Discuss three forms of change, Lewin's change model, and the systems approach to change.

LO 10-3 Describe the purpose of organizational development.

LO 10-4 Describe the approaches toward innovation and components of an innovation system.

LO 10-5 Discuss ways managers can help employees overcome fear of change.

LO 10-6 Review the different ways to increase the career readiness competency of openness to change.

FORECAST   *What's Ahead in This Chapter*

In this chapter, we consider the nature of change in organizations, including the two types of change—reactive and proactive—and the forces for change originating outside and inside the organization. Next we explore forms and models of change. We then describe organizational development and discuss how you can manage employee fear and resistance to change. After discussing how to promote innovation within an organization, we conclude with a Career Corner that focuses on how to improve the career readiness competency of openness to change.

How Can I Be More Creative at Work?

Creativity is the process of generating novel ideas.[1] Do you think of yourself as creative? If you answered no, perhaps you thought the question was about whether you can draw, paint, compose music, design clothes, write poetry, or act in plays. But as creative and rewarding as those endeavors are, they are not the only ways in which your innate creativity can express itself. Neuroscience research shows that creative thought engages many different areas of the brain, and that the old right-brain/left-brain theory of the creative process has been a bit overrated.[2] That means that no matter how we think we're "wired," we all have the potential to be imaginative, innovative thinkers just by learning to look at things a little differently.

Creativity is a talent regularly sought by organizations. Indeed, a recent LinkedIn Learning report ranks creativity as the #1 most important soft skill demanded in today's workplace.[3] There are many fun and simple ways you can leverage your career readiness competencies of proactive learning, positive approach, problem solving, and self-motivation to continually stretch and develop your own creative ability over time. Try a few of the following to increase four career readiness competencies that drive your creativity:

Proactive Learning

Nothing fires up the imagination like curiosity. Use your proactive learning orientation to foster the habit of fearlessly asking questions about how everyday things work or where they come from and why.[4] Choose one or two questions at a time and look for answers in books, articles, nearby conferences or panel discussions, free or low-cost classes, podcasts, and TED Talks.[5] Your questions don't have to be about academic or work-related subjects, either. Learn a new sport. Take up a musical instrument. Join a chorus. As long as you're learning new things, you are keeping your creative muscle active. The Hope Lab, an organization dedicated to using technology to improve health outcomes for teens and young adults, has long maintained a culture of curiosity and innovation. One of the many ways it does so is by encouraging and helping pay for employees to take outside courses in everything from cooking to photography.[6]

Positive Approach

Positive feelings like gratitude, hope, joy, and empathy have been shown to build creative thinking.[7] You can actively cultivate these feelings with a little mindfulness. For instance, keep a "gratitude journal" by writing down one thing each day that you're grateful for, no matter how small. Elevate your capacity for joy by celebrating often, honoring even small events like a good grade on a test. Or, instead of wishing someone a happy birthday on social media and moving on, stop to make a phone call or take the person out for coffee or lunch. Reward yourself with a special meal if you've achieved a small milestone in your life. And don't sit still. Among its many benefits for physical health, exercise—even a simple bike ride or a walk outdoors—can also reinforce positive feelings.[8] Another aspect of positive approach is willingness to risk failure. "Studies show that you have a greater chance of success if you stick your neck out. Be a creative risk taker, step into the unfamiliar and unpredictable, and stretch beyond customary bounds," says a writer in *Psychology Today*, "Accept failure with open arms, learn from it, and take the perspective that failure happens *for* you, not *to* you."[9] Stretching outside your comfort zone is what creativity is all about.

Problem Solving

Hone your creative problem-solving skills by looking for challenges you can practice solving now. You don't have to wait for your boss or professor to give you a difficult assignment to start becoming better at this. Try learning to play chess, for instance. Its reliance on repeated patterns will strengthen your predictive abilities, and research has shown that chess players also demonstrate more than normal originality and flexibility of thought.[10] Not a fan of board games? Read detective novels by writers such as Agatha Christie or Sir Arthur Conan Doyle, still among the most widely read English-language writers of all time, or any of their more recent peers (search on Google or ask any librarian or bookseller). Or you can solve crosswords and other pencil-and-paper puzzles. All these activities will give your deductive and predictive powers a helpful workout.

Self-Motivation

Finally, setting creativity goals ignites the motivation to increase your level of creativity. A "personal creativity goal refers to the personal standard or aspiration that one's own job output should be creative," according to a team of creativity experts.[11] Setting a creativity goal will direct your attention and efforts at finding creative ways to perform your job. It will also impress your boss.

For Discussion Which of the above recommendations interest you? In what ways can you improve your creative skills, and what specific activities are you willing to commit to in order to increase your creativity?

10.1 The Nature of Change in Organizations

THE BIG PICTURE

Two types of change are reactive and proactive. Forces for change may consist of forces outside the organization—demographic characteristics; technological advancements; shareholder, customer, and broader stakeholder concerns; and social and political pressures. Or they may be forces inside the organization—human resource concerns and managers' behavior.

LO 10-1

Discuss what managers should know about organizational change.

"With so much technological advancement causing disruption in the market, there is much more desire for people who are strategic, innovative, customer-focused, and can adapt quickly," said Tom Giella, chair of health care for Korn Ferry.[12]

Change is truly all around us, and part of a manager's job is to identify the opportunities for change. Managers also need to understand the predominant forces driving change in today's organizations.

Fundamental Change: What Will You Be Called On to Deal With?

"It is hard to predict, especially the future," physicist Niels Bohr is supposed to have quipped.

But it is possible to identify and prepare for the future that has already happened, in the words of management theorist Peter Drucker.[13] Among the trends: Millennials will continue to be early adopters of new technology. Women will be a dominant force in the global marketplace. More people will move from rural to urban areas. Social networks will replace traditional institutions in driving change. Consumers will grow more informed, changing the power balance in the marketplace. A rising developing-world middle class will fuel global consumer spending. Spending on health and wellness will soar. Starting a new business will become easier. Niche markets will flourish. Cloud computing will do away with the brick-and-mortar office. Data will be critical for competitive advantage. Smart machines will get smarter.[14] There are also some supertrends specifically shaping the future of business:

1. The marketplace is becoming more segmented.
2. Competitors offering specialized solutions require us to get our products to market faster.
3. Some companies are unable to survive disruptive innovation.
4. Offshore suppliers are changing the way we work.
5. Knowledge, not information, is becoming the new competitive advantage.[15]

1. The Marketplace Is Becoming More Segmented and Moving toward More Niche Products   In the recent past, managers could think in terms of mass markets—mass communication, mass behavior, and mass values. Now we have "demassification," with customer groups becoming segmented into smaller and more specialized groups responding to more narrowly targeted commercial messages.

These marketing messages may even be shaped and personalized by artificial intelligence (AI) technology, allowing bots, for instance, to engage in conversations with individually targeted consumers or small groups of consumers. Some suggest that this kind of customer-centric marketng can help create relationships that result in loyal customers and repeat business.[16] The Configurator Database is a popular hub for consumers seeking customizable goods:

Configurator Database Example: The Configurator Database provides links to more than 1,300 configurators—companies that allow customers to design products according to their individual preferences and needs.[17] The brands range from mainstream to luxury in industries including food, pet supplies, and apparel. For example:

- *Rolex*—customers can select from a list of watch models, materials, dials, and bracelets to build a unique luxury timepiece.

- *Xbox Design Lab*—gamers can customize their controller's body, triggers, d-pad, ABXY buttons, and other options. There's even engraving available. In all, over 1 billion possible combinations exist.[18]

- *My Cereal Mix*—health-conscious consumers can build their own breakfast cereal by choosing from different bases, nuts, seeds, dried fruits, and extras like cacao nibs and coconut chips.

2. More Competitors Are Offering Targeted Products, Requiring Faster Speed-to-Market

Julie Bashkin, a McKinsey & Company senior external adviser, said many of the big, established companies McKinsey works with are experiencing a "head slap" moment because the start-ups that didn't concern them five years ago are now coming out in a "bee swarm." She added, "[T]hey seem to have come out of nowhere, and they seem to be moving fast with no resources. And they seem not to be weighed down by the baggage of their own success, like our big clients are."[19] Some of these competitors may be in and out of a market in a matter of days or months—like pop-up stores, "here today, gone tomorrow" retailers, such as those selling Halloween products. Consider how Hasbro has responded to this trend.

Hasbro Example: Hasbro established its "Quick Strike" team to develop toys and games in response to social media trends. In one instance, the team developed Hasbro's "Speak Out" game when Internet videos of people trying to pronounce words while wearing dental mouth guards went viral.[20] Speak Out went from concept to market in 11 weeks. "We've since expanded this approach to our broader organization," said president and COO John Frascotti, adding, "All of this is resulting in a faster, more nimble and more efficient product-to-market process."

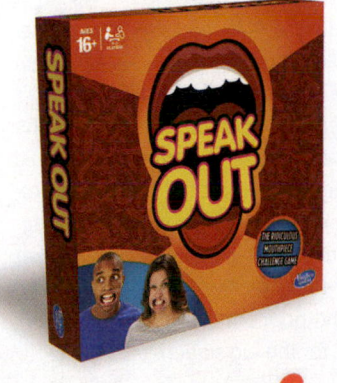

3. Some Traditional Companies May Not Survive Radical Change

In *The Innovator's Dilemma: When New Technologies Cause Great Firms to Fail,* Clayton M. Christensen, the late Harvard Business School professor, argued that when successful companies are confronted with a giant technological leap that transforms their markets, all choices are bad ones.

Hasbro developed Speak Out in response to a viral internet challenge. The game hit store shelves less than three months after the company's Quick Strike team first began working on the concept. Capitalizing on social media trends in this way requires a level of agility that established, market-leading firms often struggle to achieve. DreamToys/Shutterstock

Indeed, he thought, it's very difficult for an existing successful company to take full advantage of a technological breakthrough such as digitalization—what he called disruptive innovation.[21] Some companies that have the resources to survive disruption—to build "the next big thing"— fail to do so—while others are able to pivot successfully. The movie industry is currently experiencing the effects of this supertrend as described in the Example box.

EXAMPLE   Radical Change: Going to the Movies

The business model between movie studios and movie theaters has remained largely unchanged for over a century.[22] Studios produce films, then movie theaters get exclusive rights to show the films for some period of time (usually several months). Proceeds from ticket sales are split between the two entities in an arrangement that typically involves each party receiving between 40 and 60%.[23]

But in recent years people have begun to question whether this business model still makes sense. Streaming platforms like Netflix, Hulu, and Amazon are producing their own content, skipping theater releases altogether, and cinema visits have dipped to their lowest levels in two decades.[24]

Theaters' Attempts to Ward Off Changes   The big players in the theater business—AMC, Cinemark, and Regal—have invested heavily in customer amenities in an effort to retain and regain business. For example, moviegoers can now reserve seats in advance (no more being relegated to the dizzying front row if you arrive a few minutes late), and seats recline for a more comfortable movie-watching experience. In addition, many theaters have added full bars and restaurants, and loyalty programs have helped build repeat business.

These recent improvements have centered around research that suggests today's consumers are looking—and are willing to pay for—experiences.[25] According to AMC, investments in experiences have started to pay off—the chain reported a significant increase in ticket sales in the third quarter of 2019.[26] There's also plenty of anecdotal evidence to suggest that people who had given up on going to the movies have reconsidered. Said one *Wall Street Journal* reporter of his reluctant trip to see *Frozen 2* with his wife and five children, "We walked into an Emagine theater 10 miles from our house after dropping $10 a ticket ($9 for the kids) to reserve big cushy recliners with built-in heaters and ordering our pizzas and popcorn on an iPhone. It took that one visit to rekindle a love for the big screen."[27]

New Developments   But as theaters were investing millions in upgrades, studios were engaged in another conversation. Specifically, studios were questioning whether their businesses could be equally—or even more—viable, if they released films directly to consumers. Would a family of four, for example, be willing to spend $30 to $50 to watch a new release from the couch instead of spending up to twice that amount to see the movie in a theater?[28]

Indeed, movie studios could reduce their costs by up to 50% if they simply cut out theaters and adopted a direct-to-consumer model.[29] But the top players in the industry have been hesitant to test out the prospect. Then the COVID-19 pandemic caused a chain of events that some believe could permanently change the movie industry as we know it. In April 2020, Americans sat in their houses, movie theaters were shut down, and millions of kids were disappointed that they wouldn't get to see the new *Trolls* movie in the theater as planned. Universal used the opportunity to test the waters and released *Trolls World Tour* directly to streaming platforms as a 48-hour, $19.99 rental. After three weeks, the studio had made more money from the film than it had during the five months its original *Trolls* movie spent in movie theaters.

Universal CEO Jeff Shell said, "The results for 'Trolls World Tour' have exceeded our expectations and demonstrated the viability of PVOD [premium video on demand]. As soon as theatres reopen, we expect to release movies on both formats."[30] AMC president and CEO Adam Aron quickly responded that AMC would no longer show any Universal films in its theaters if Universal went through with the new arrangement. In a letter to the studio, Aron said "radical change by Universal to the business model that currently exists between our two companies represents nothing but downside for us and is categorically unacceptable to AMC Entertainment."[31]

What Happens Next?   Have we seen the end of the movie theater industry as we know it? According to one columnist, it's not a question of "if" movie theaters will become extinct, but "when."[32] Others are confident that multiple modes of movie watching can successfully co-exist and that there is still a massive contingent that will indeed continue to want to go to the movies.[33]

YOUR CALL

Do you think we are on the brink of a radical change in the movie industry? How should theaters respond if they want to continue to survive in an increasingly streaming world?

4. Offshore Suppliers Are Changing the Way We Work   As we said in Chapter 2, globalization and outsourcing are transforming whole industries and changing the way we work. China, India, Mexico, the Philippines, and other countries possess workers and even professionals willing to work twice as hard for half the pay, giving U.S. businesses substantial labor savings. While unquestionably some U.S. jobs have been lost, others have become more productive. Some engineers and salespeople, for example, have been liberated from routine tasks and can spend more time innovating and dealing with customers.

Uruguay Example: Did you know that Uruguay is one of the largest software exporters per-capita in the world? It has been called the "Silicon Valley of South America," and cities like Montevideo, Uruguay's capital, are brimming with IT entrepreneurs and tech start-ups. The right combination of talent, infrastructure, and incentives makes the country an ideal choice for companies looking to outsource IT functions. U.S. businesses also benefit from Uruguay's physical and time-zone proximity.[34]

But as some jobs have moved cross-border, dozens in aerospace, chemicals, and other industries are moving to the United States. Here are two examples:

Company Examples: German automaker Daimler AG (Mercedes) manufactures SUVs for both its global and domestic markets in Tuscaloosa County, Alabama. The company employs almost 4,000 people in the region directly, and more than 20,000 people indirectly.[35] Pietro Fiorentini, an Italian company, makes natural gas metering and pressure regulating equipment in West Virginia.[36]

5. Knowledge, Not Information, Is Becoming the New Competitive Advantage

In 2012, an Intel white paper predicted that "a technological change tsunami is rolling towards us that will wash away many previous perceptions of the world. The way we work will be swept into this new reality, and the knowledge worker is positioned to be the primary agent of change."[37] Was this prediction about the importance of knowledge workers accurate? Indeed, McKinsey research shows that knowledge jobs continue to grow in today's economy, and one analyst at Forrester recently suggested that jobs requiring empathy, intuition, and mental agility (all of these are components of the career readiness competencies shown in Table 1.2) will add approximately 300,000 jobs to the economy by 2030.[38] Two key points about knowledge work to consider:

- *The definition of knowledge work has changed*—As information technology does more of the work formerly done by humans, even in high-tech areas (such as sorting data for relevance), many low-level employees previously thought of as knowledge workers are now being recognized as "data workers," who contribute very little added value to the processing of information. Unlike routine information handling, knowledge work is analytic and consists of problem solving and abstract reasoning—exactly the kind of task required of skillful managers, professionals, salespeople, and financial analysts.

- *AI has not replaced knowledge workers*—The rise of knowledge workers is accelerating despite the proliferation of automation.[39] Indeed, the number of people in knowledge-work jobs—nonroutine cognitive occupations—now exceeds 1 billion across the globe.[40] According to one expert, rather than eliminate knowledge work, AI "empowers workers to do things that only humans can do."[41]

In industries where companies are struggling to compete with foreign manufacturers or bigger rivals that outsource their labor, AI could even save jobs by increasing knowledge workers' productivity and opportunities to make strategic contributions. Consider the example of a California-based furniture finishing company.

Professional Finishing Example: When Professional Finishing co-owner Dawn White announced plans to add a new robotic arm to the company's facility, one employee quickly piped in, "Hey let me know when the robot's up and running and I'll just quit." But the employee didn't lose his job, nor did anyone else. Instead, workers' productivity quadrupled, and many became robot operators and technicians. The robot took over some of the more physically demanding tasks common in furniture finishing and has allowed the human employees to focus on more delicate and intricate tasks.[42]

For companies like Professional Finishing, AI has enhanced rather than replaced, workers' jobs. Courtesy of Professional Finishing

Two Types of Change: Reactive and Proactive

Most CEOs, general managers, and senior public-sector leaders agree that incremental changes are no longer sufficient in a world that is operating in fundamentally different ways. Life in general, they say, is becoming more complex, and the firms that are able to manage that complexity are the ones that will survive in the long term.[43] Clearly, we are all in for an interesting ride.

As a manager, you will typically have to deal with two types of change: *reactive* and *proactive*.

1. Reactive Change: Responding to Unanticipated Problems and Opportunities

When managers talk about "putting out fires," they are talking about <mark>reactive change,</mark> making changes in response to problems or opportunities as they arise.

Reactive change can engender resistance, as was the case for some religious communities during the COVID-19 pandemic. Check out the Example box (we discuss resistance to change in detail in Section 10.5.)

EXAMPLE   Reactive Change: Religious Practices During COVID-19

Gathering as a community is a hallmark of many religious traditions. But when governors issued shelter-in-place orders for their states during COVID-19, faith communities quickly had to figure out new ways to connect with members, maintain important practices, and celebrate holidays while quarantined.

The timeframe of the pandemic presented a particularly difficult challenge because of the abundance of religious holy days it affected. The Jewish community was preparing to celebrate Purim, and, soon after, Passover; Hindus were gearing up for a month of Holi festivities; Christians were looking forward to Easter; and for Muslims, Ramadan—the most sacred month in the Islamic faith—was set to begin on April 23.

Brie Loskota, executive director for USC's Center for Religion and Civic Culture, said, "We're in like the religious sweeps week for the month of April," but added, "One thing that people often forget about religious life is it's actually remarkably adaptive."[44]

Reactive Changes   Here are a few examples of the ways religious communities adapted their traditions during the pandemic:

- For many members of the Muslim faith, adapting to the quarantine meant holding remote Iftar gatherings—breaking the daily Ramadan fast—with friends and family over Zoom.[45]

- Jewish faith leaders reminded their congregations that the expectation that observant members hear the Megillah—the Book of Esther—read aloud in person was not as important as preserving life. Many synagogues offered livestreams of their Purim services instead.[46]

- Some Hindus used the Likee video-sharing platform to participate in #HoliHai2020. The campaign gave Hindus the chance to "play Holi" and experience the colors of the festival through their phones while remaining safely quarantined.

Religious observances took on new forms in reaction to COVID-19. Communal traditions like Shabbat meals, Iftar dinners, and playing Holi went virtual as the world responded to concerns about virus transmission. What reactive changes did you experience in your own life as a result of the pandemic? What did you learn from those experiences?

vipman/Shutterstock, Fabian Strauch/Getty Images, powerofforever/Getty Images

Resistance to Change While the majority of religious communities adapted to the quarantine, some resisted. For example, pastor Tony Spell of the Life Tabernacle church in Central, Louisiana, refused to cooperate with Governor John Bel Edwards' statewide stay-at-home order and instead continued to hold services. Livestream video showed that most of his congregants were neither wearing face masks nor following social distancing protocol during these gatherings.[47] Police issued multiple citations and eventually arrested Spell for aggravated assault after he drove a bus toward one of the protestors standing outside of his church. They released him on bond and placed him under house arrest, but Spell continued to hold services at his church, even showing off his ankle monitor to church members.

YOUR CALL

How have you reacted to sudden changes in the past? Have you shown resistance? Adaptability? What do you think this means for your career readiness?

2. Proactive Change: Managing Anticipated Problems and Opportunities

In contrast to reactive change, proactive change, or planned change, involves making carefully thought-out changes in anticipation of possible or expected problems or opportunities.[48] The anticipation of increased automation has spurred proactive changes in the aerospace manufacturing industry. Consider the example of Airbus.

Airbus Example: The process for manufacturing passenger jets has changed very little over time. Much of the work is still done by hand, and rigorous safety standards and government certification requirements mean that precision, rather than efficiency, is paramount. But Airbus recently built a new facility for its A320 model that will help the company keep up with increasing demand while simultaneously readying itself for the future. Robots and remote-control-operated assembly platforms stand in the place of fixed cranes and assembly lines, and 20% fewer workers are needed to complete the job. Further, the open layout of the facility ensures maximum flexibility for any future changes to the manufacturing process. Experts believe that increases in automation across the industry will continue to unfold very slowly, and Airbus plans to be prepared. Said CEO Guillaume Faury, "This is one of the building blocks of our digital trajectory and robotization of our production."[49]

As we've stated, change can be hard, and the tools for survival are the career readiness competencies of personal adaptability and openness to change. We also know that organizations like to hire people who are adaptable and willing to accept change. How well do you think you fare in this regard? You can find out by taking Self-Assessment 10.1.

SELF-ASSESSMENT 10.1 CAREER READINESS

Assessing Your Openness to Change at Work

The following survey was designed to assess your attitudes toward change at work. Please be prepared to answer these questions if your instructor has assigned Self-Assessment 10.1 in Connect.

1. Where do you stand when it comes to your attitude toward change? Are you surprised by the results?

2. Based on your three lowest scoring survey items, how might you foster a more positive attitude toward change? Be specific.

3. What things might you say during an interview to demonstrate that you possess the career readiness competency of openness to change?

The Forces for Change Outside and Inside the Organization

How do managers know when their organizations need to change? The answers aren't clear-cut, but you can get clues by monitoring the forces for change—both outside and inside the organization. (*See Figure 10.1.*)

FIGURE 10.1   Forces for change outside and inside the organization

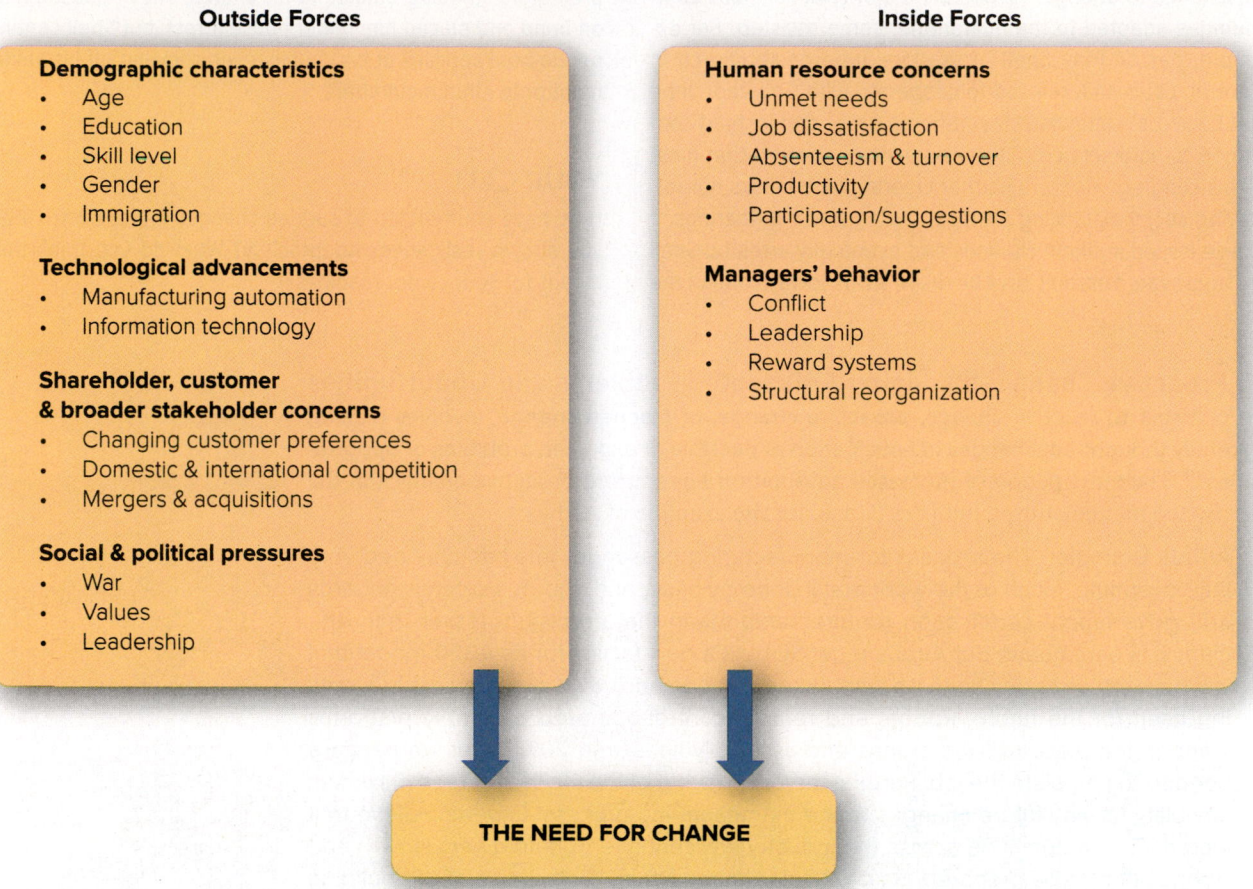

Outside Forces

Demographic characteristics
- Age
- Education
- Skill level
- Gender
- Immigration

Technological advancements
- Manufacturing automation
- Information technology

Shareholder, customer & broader stakeholder concerns
- Changing customer preferences
- Domestic & international competition
- Mergers & acquisitions

Social & political pressures
- War
- Values
- Leadership

Inside Forces

Human resource concerns
- Unmet needs
- Job dissatisfaction
- Absenteeism & turnover
- Productivity
- Participation/suggestions

Managers' behavior
- Conflict
- Leadership
- Reward systems
- Structural reorganization

THE NEED FOR CHANGE

Forces Originating Outside the Organization   External forces consist of four types, as follows.

1. Demographic Characteristics   Earlier we discussed the demographic changes occurring among U.S. workers, with the labor force becoming more diverse. Example: The number of young Americans aged 18 to 34 living with their parent(s) (rather than in a household shared with a spouse or partner) has increased by 1 million in the past two decades.[50] How might this affect their spending habits?

2. Technological Advancements   Technology is not just computer technology; it is any machine or process that enables an organization to gain a competitive advantage in changing materials used to produce a finished product. Ginni Rometty, former CEO of IBM, recently said, "We face an imminent and profound transformation of the workforce over the next five to 10 years as analytics and artificial intelligence change job roles at companies in all industries," adding that she expects AI will change "100 percent of jobs" in the coming decade.[51]

One industry in which technology has already led to widespread changes is winemaking. According to a recent article, "Artificial intelligence touches everything in winemaking from the soil analysis at the vineyards to how consumers select the right vintage to go with dinner."[52] Here are a few examples:

Winemaking Industry Example: Some winemakers now use drones equipped with infrared cameras to pinpoint irrigation needs, damage, and diseases in their vineyards. At Symington Family Estates in Portugal, a robot called VineScout paces up and down rows of grapevines recording key agricultural data. The French vineyard Château Mouton-Rothschild worked with Naio technologies to develop its robot—Ted—which it uses to weed and spray vines.[53] In terms of consumers, more than 25% rely on apps in making wine selections, and technology is playing an increasing role in predicting which wines will be pleasing to specific consumers.[54]

3. Shareholder, Customer, and Broader Stakeholder Concerns

A firm's shareholders, customers, and broader stakeholders can all exert significant pressure for change. As you learned in Learning Module 1, in recent years, much of this pressure has centered on shifting perspectives about the purpose of a corporation and whether a firm's obligations go beyond shareholder wealth creation to include shared value and sustainable development.[55]

- *Shareholders* have begun to be more active in pressing for organizational change. Some shareholders may form a **B corporation**, or **benefit corporation**, in which the company is legally required to adhere to socially beneficial practices, such as helping consumers, employees, or the environment. Among the leading B Corps in the United States are Patagonia, Eileen Fisher, Allbirds, Bombas, Ethique, and Uncommon Goods.[56] Shareholders in the oil and gas industry have recently called for their firms to do more to tackle climate change:

    Oil and Gas Example: Shareholders at major oil and gas companies have demanded more action on climate change at recent investor meetings. In 2019 over 99% of BP shareholders voted in favor of a proposal requiring the company to disclose more data on its carbon emissions and the alignment between its strategy and the goals of the Paris Climate Agreement.[57] Forty-one percent of shareholders at Exxon recently voted in favor of a similar proposal. Analysts believe that Exxon shareholders will increase these numbers to 50% within a matter of a few years.[58]

Drones, such as this one pictured over a vineyard, can gather agricultural information with incredible speed. This technological advancement has enabled some winemakers to visually inspect their vineyards for diseases and other issues at a rate of up to an acre per minute. How many human workers do you think it would take to perform the same task in the same amount of time? *freeprod/123RF*

- *Customers* are also becoming more demanding. As discussed in previous chapters, younger generations are more inclined to buy from a company if it is genuinely connected to a meaningful cause. Social impact consultant Meredith Ferguson said, "Young consumers today don't just want to just see brands take a stand on social issues, they want them to act on that stand—from the inside out."[59]

    Gen Z Example: Members of Gen Z may not have the buying power of Millennials or Gen Xers, but they have made it known that they are not afraid to use their voices to demand more from corporations. Research suggests that memes have become one of Gen Z's favorite modes of brand activism. Experts like the University of Maryland's Dr. Amna Kirmani suggest that this type of negative word of mouth is emerging as powerful form of consumer leverage.[60]

Gina Bulla—Senior Director of Brand Marketing and Insights for *The Atlantic*—educated Advertising Week Europe attendees in 2019 about responding to the unique demands of Gen Z consumers. *AWEurope/Shutterstock*

- *Broader stakeholders'* needs are becoming increasingly important for many corporations. The model of creating shared value (CSV) we presented in Learning Module 1 demonstrates how firms can simultaneously tackle global social issues and maximize shareholder wealth. Recent research suggests consumers may form deeper connections with brands that they perceive as creating shared value.[61]

To The Market Example: Jane Mosbacher Morris founded To The Market to connect corporations and consumers with more ethical and sustainable supply chains. Specifically, companies such as Target and Bloomingdale's partner with Mosbacher Morris' company to source accessories, home goods, and apparel made by members of vulnerable and underrepresented communities.[62] During the COVID-19 pandemic, the company called on its existing capabilities and relationships to fulfill orders for more than 2 million units of personal protective equipment (PPE).[63]

4. Social and Political Pressures   Social events can create great pressures. Consider the example of soda taxes.

Soda Taxes Example: Poor diet choices, such as reliance on sugary sodas, have led to more than 42% of U.S. adults and almost 20% of children from ages 2 to 19 being obese, which in turn has contributed to an epidemic of type 2 diabetes.[64] Several big U.S. cities, including Philadelphia, Boulder, San Francisco, Seattle, and Berkeley, have already passed special taxes on soda, often against well-funded opposition from soda companies.[65] Many are watching the UK with interest. Its two-tier soda tax, unlike others designed to raise revenue or discourage the purchase of soda, encourages soda makers to reduce the sugar content of their products to avoid the tax. It seems to be working, and proponents are now calling for a similar tax on baked goods like cakes and biscuits.[66]

Forces Originating Inside the Organization   Internal forces affecting organizations may be subtle, such as low job satisfaction, or more dramatic, such as constant labor–management conflict. Internal forces may be of the two following types: *human resource concerns* and *managers' behavior*.

1. Human Resource Concerns   Is there a gap between the employees' needs and desires and the organization's needs and desires? Job dissatisfaction—as expressed through high absenteeism and turnover—can be a major signal of the need for change. Recall from Chapter 9 that as the firm's strategy evolves, a strategic HRM perspective suggests the need to evaluate existing human and social capital and the HR practices being used to generate them. The right HR practices are the ones that generate the social processes and behaviors the organization needs to accomplish its goals.

Labor Strikes Example: One way employees express their dissatisfaction in order to effect change is through labor strikes. In 2018, approximately 485,000 workers went on strike—the highest number since the 1980s.[67] They included teachers, hotel workers, and auto workers. Some experts believe recent labor strikes are, in part, a reaction to the prevalence of the gig economy. Workers often maintain their income by jumping from one temporary job to another, but they are beginning to want options for a path to permanent, stable employment.[68]

2. Managers' Behavior   Excessive conflict between managers and employees or between a company and its customers is another indicator that change is needed. Perhaps there is a personality conflict, so that an employee transfer may be needed. Or perhaps some interpersonal training is required. Behavior issues often persist until stakeholders—be they customers, associates, or society at large—decide that enough is enough. Consider the example of Ken Fisher.

Ken Fisher Example: In late 2019, billionaire Ken Fisher, founder of Fisher Investments, made inappropriate remarks while addressing attendees at a money-management conference. Among other things, Fisher likened winning new clients to "trying to get into a girl's pants," and his comments quickly went viral on social media.

In an initial interview with Bloomberg, Fisher said his only regret was "I regret I accepted that speech invitation, because it was kind of a pain in the neck."[69] Later, after increased pressure, Fisher issued a statement saying, "Some of the words and phrases I used during a recent conference to make certain points were clearly wrong and I shouldn't have made them. I realize this kind of language has no place in our company or industry. I sincerely apologize."[70] ●

10.2 Forms and Models of Change

THE BIG PICTURE

This section discusses the three forms of change, from least threatening to most threatening: adaptive, innovative, and radically innovative. It also describes Lewin's three-stage change model: unfreezing, changing, and refreezing. Finally, it describes the systems approach to change: inputs, target elements of change, and outputs.

As we mentioned in Section 10.1, change may be forced upon an organization—reactive change, requiring you to make adjustments in response to problems or opportunities as they arise.

We are, however, in favor of proactive or planned change, which occurs when an organization tries to get out in front of impending demands. Being proactive involves making carefully thought-out changes in anticipation of possible problems or opportunities.

As a manager, particularly one working for an American organization, you may be pressured to provide short-term, quick-fix solutions. But when applied to organizational problems, this approach usually doesn't work: Quick-fix solutions have little staying power. Managers should rely on established science in order to effectively manage and implement proactive organizational change. This requires an understanding of the different forms of change, as well as two different models that can be applied systematically to the change process (all of which are discussed in this section).

> **LO 10-2**
>
> Discuss three forms of change, Lewin's change model, and the systems approach to change.

Three Forms of Change: From Least Threatening to Most Threatening

Whether organizational change is administrative or technological, it can be *adaptive*, *innovative*, or *radically innovative*, depending on (1) the degree of complexity, cost, and uncertainty and (2) its potential for generating employee resistance.[71]

Least Threatening: Adaptive Change—"We've Seen Stuff Like This Before"

Adaptive change is the reintroduction of a familiar practice—the implementation of a form of change that has already been experienced within the same organization. Of the three forms of change discussed in this section, adaptive change is the:

- *Easiest to implement successfully.* This form of change is lowest in complexity, cost, and uncertainty.

- *Least threatening to employees.* Because it is familiar, adaptive change is likely to create the least resistance.

Adaptive change is fairly common and often arises due to predictable, seasonal fluctuations in demand. Two hypothetical examples are:

Examples: During the annual Labor Day sale, a department store may ask its sales employees to work 12 hours a day instead of the usual 8. During tax-preparation time, a store's accounting department may require an increase in work hours.

Somewhat Threatening: Innovative Change—"This Is Something New for This Company"   <mark>Innovative change</mark> is the introduction of a practice that is new to the organization. Innovative change is:

- *Moderately difficult to implement.* This form of change is characterized by moderate complexity, cost, and uncertainty.

- *Somewhat threatening to employees.* Because it is less familiar than adaptive change, innovative change is apt to trigger some fear and resistance among employees.

Innovative changes may arise when an organization adopts a policy or practice that other organizations have embraced, but that is new for the firm.

Example: If a department store decides to adopt a new practice among its competitors by staying open 24 hours a day, requiring employees to work flexible schedules, it may be felt as moderately threatening.

Very Threatening: Radically Innovative Change—"This Is a Brand-New Thing in Our Industry"   <mark>Radically innovative change</mark> introduces a practice that is new to the industry. Radically innovative change is:

- *Very difficult to implement.* It is the most complex, costly, and uncertain form of change.

- *Highly threatening to employees.* It will be felt as extremely threatening to managers' confidence and employees' job security and may well tear at the fabric of the organization.[72]

   Example: Educators all over the world experienced radically innovative change when they suddenly were forced to deliver all of their course content remotely during the COVID-19 pandemic. While remote course delivery wasn't a new idea, most faculty had little to no experience with it. This was particularly true for K–12 educators who were steeped in a centuries-old tradition of teaching students face-to-face. Many educators found the possibility that their jobs could be permanently changed highly threatening.

Lewin's Change Model: Unfreezing, Changing, and Refreezing

Most theories of organizational change originated with the landmark work of social psychologist Kurt Lewin. Lewin developed a model with three stages—*unfreezing*, *changing*, and *refreezing*—to explain how to initiate, manage, and stabilize planned change.[73] *(See Figure 10.2.)* Throughout this section, we illustrate Lewin's model of change with the example of how Walmart successfully introduces robots into its stores.[74]

FIGURE 10.2

Lewin's model of change

1. "Unfreezing": Creating the Motivation to Change

In the unfreezing stage, managers try to instill in employees the motivation to change, encouraging them to let go of attitudes and behaviors that are resistant to innovation. For this "unfreezing" to take place, employees need to become dissatisfied with the old way of doing things. Managers also need to reduce the barriers to change during this stage.

Walmart Example: Bossa Nova inventory robots—autonomous devices that travel up and down retail store aisles checking inventory, identifying misplaced items, and discovering pricing issues—are currently at work in at least 1,000 Walmart stores. How does the company manage the unfreezing stage and convince store employees to adopt the change each time it introduces a robot in a new location? Bossa Nova co-founder and chief technology officer Sarjoun Skaff said, "In general terms, we position the robot as a productivity tool, the modern equivalent of a barcode scanning gun. We see the robot viewed as a tool or even as a part of the team."[75] Walmart's VP of Innovations, John Crecelius, said that the company has not had a hard time convincing employees that there is an "opportunity for the new technology to free them up from focusing on tasks that are repeatable, predictable and manual."[76]

Here, a Bossa Nova inventory robot roams the aisles of a Walmart store. Do you think you'd like to work alongside one of these robots?
Daniel Dorsa/Redux Pictures

2. "Changing": Learning New Ways of Doing Things

In the changing stage, employees need to be given the tools for change: new information, new perspectives, new models of behavior. Managers can help here by providing benchmarking results, role models, mentors, experts, and training. Change is more likely to be accepted if employees possess the career readiness competencies of proactive learning orientation and openness to change.[77]

Walmart Example: In the changing stage, Walmart invested heavily in training its employees to work alongside the robots. Accenture's managing director H. James Wilson said, "Walmart showed the importance of a 'getting to know you' period," adding, "A worker may feel it's an ethical violation if they don't get a proper introduction to their new AI colleague. Doing a week- or month-long demo helps workers understand how the AI works, which tasks it will handle, and so forth."[78]

3. "Refreezing": Making the New Ways Normal

In the refreezing stage, employees need to be helped to integrate the changed attitudes and behavior into their normal ways of doing things. Managers can assist by encouraging employees to exhibit the new change and then, through additional coaching and modeling, by reinforcing the employees in the desired change, as we'll discuss in Section 10.5.

Walmart Example: In the refreezing stage, Walmart employees who work with the robots have, according to one report from MIT, wholeheartedly embraced the chance.[79] Bossa Nova's chief business officer Martin Hitch said, "This boring, repetitive task of scanning the shelves—we have yet to meet someone who has liked to do that. Employees instantly become the advocates for the robot." Store employees have competitions to name their robots before giving each its own Walmart name tag. Finally, said Hitch, employees have taken to defending the robots by educating shoppers about their benefits.

FIGURE 10.3

Systems model of change

*Sources: Based on A. Kinicki,
Organizational Behavior: A
Practical, Problem-Solving
Approach (New York: McGraw-Hill
Education, 2021), Figure 16.6,
p. 648, which was adapted from
D. R. Fuqua and D. J. Kurpius,
"Conceptual Models in
Organizational Consultation,"
Journal of Counseling and
Development, July–August 1993,
pp. 602–618; D. A. Nadler and
M. L. Tushman, "Organizational
Frame Bending: Principles for
Managing Reorientation,"
Academy of Management
Executive, August 1989,
pp. 194–203.*

A Systems Approach to Change

Change creates additional change—that's the lesson of systems theory. Promoting someone from one group to another, for instance, may change the employee interactions in both (as from cordial to argumentative, or the reverse). Adopting a team-based structure may require changing the compensation system to pay bonuses based on team rather than individual performance. A *systems approach* to change presupposes that any change, no matter how small, has a rippling effect throughout an organization.[80]

- A *system*, you'll recall from Chapter 2, is a set of interrelated parts that operate together to achieve a common purpose. The systems approach can be used to diagnose what to change and determine the success of the change effort.

- The systems model of change consists of three parts: (1) *inputs*, (2) *target elements of change*, and (3) *outputs*. (See Figure 10.3.)

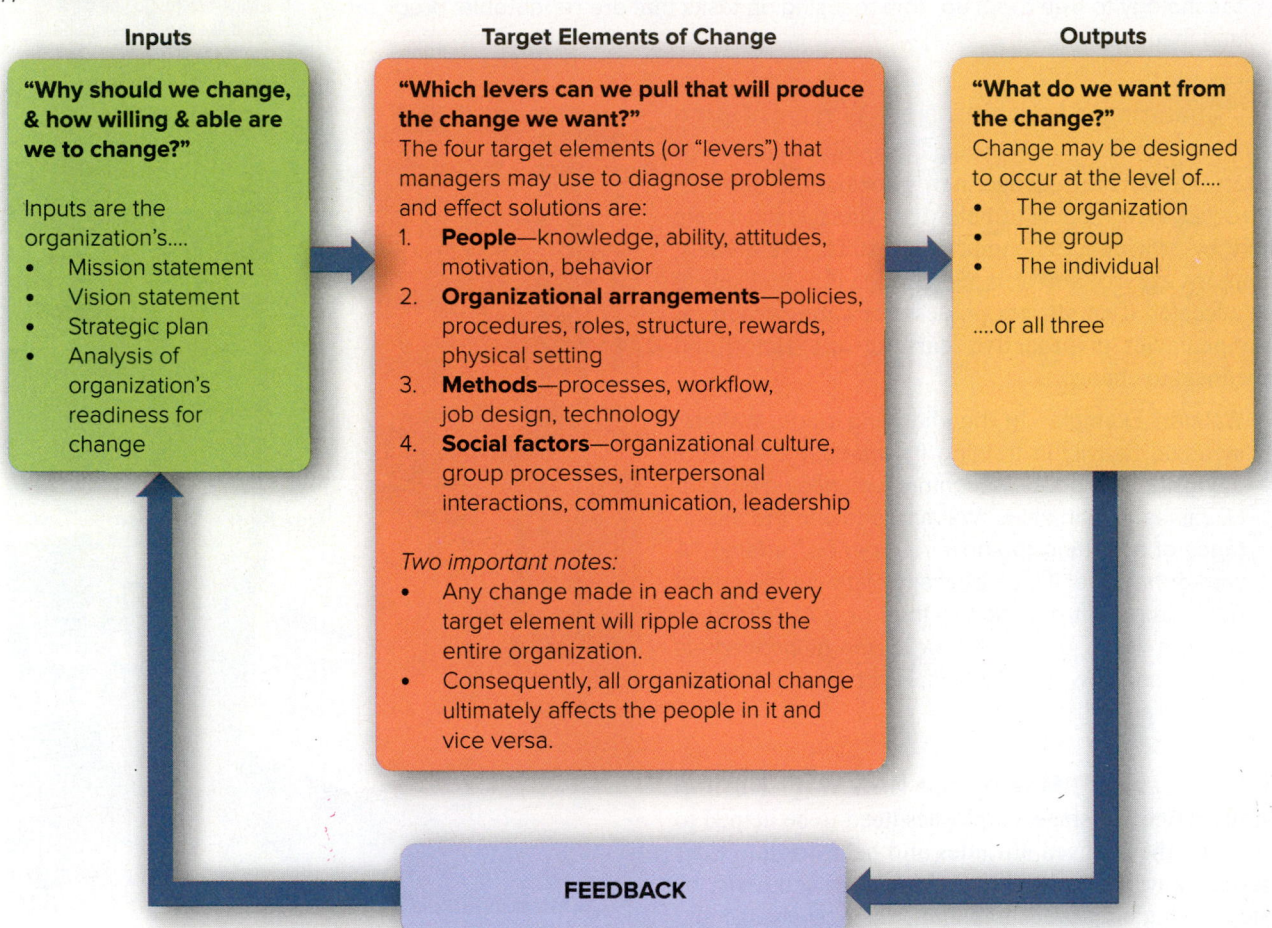

Inputs

"Why should we change, & how willing & able are we to change?"

Inputs are the organization's....
- Mission statement
- Vision statement
- Strategic plan
- Analysis of organization's readiness for change

Target Elements of Change

"Which levers can we pull that will produce the change we want?"
The four target elements (or "levers") that managers may use to diagnose problems and effect solutions are:
1. **People**—knowledge, ability, attitudes, motivation, behavior
2. **Organizational arrangements**—policies, procedures, roles, structure, rewards, physical setting
3. **Methods**—processes, workflow, job design, technology
4. **Social factors**—organizational culture, group processes, interpersonal interactions, communication, leadership

Two important notes:
- Any change made in each and every target element will ripple across the entire organization.
- Consequently, all organizational change ultimately affects the people in it and vice versa.

Outputs

"What do we want from the change?"
Change may be designed to occur at the level of....
- The organization
- The group
- The individual

....or all three

FEEDBACK

Inputs: "Why Should We Change, and How Willing and Able Are We to Change?"   "Why change?" A systems approach always begins with the question of why change is needed at all—what the problem is that needs to be solved. (Example: "Why change? Because our designers are giving us terrible products that we can't sell.")

Whatever the answer, the systems approach must make sure the desired changes align with the organization's *mission statement*, *vision statement*, and *strategic plan*—subjects we discussed in Chapter 5.[81]

A second question is "How willing and able are management and employees to make the necessary change?" **Readiness for change** is defined as the beliefs, attitudes, and intentions of the organization's staff regarding the extent of the changes needed and how willing and able they are to implement them.[82] Readiness has four components:

1. How strongly the company needs the proposed change.

2. How much the top managers support the change.

3. How capable employees are of handling the change.

4. How pessimistic or optimistic employees are about the consequences of the result.

Self-Assessment 10.2 will help you gauge your readiness for change. You can also use it to measure the readiness of an organization to which you belong.

SELF-ASSESSMENT 10.2   CAREER READINESS

What Is Your Readiness for Change?

If your instructor has assigned Self-Assessment 10.2 in Connect, think of a change at school, work, or another area of your life. Take Self-Assessment 10.2 to learn the extent of your readiness for change, or that of the organization in which the change needs to occur.

1.   Of the four components, which is the lowest?

2.   How do you think this result will affect the success of the particular change? Be specific.

3.   Who seems to be most ready, you (components 1 and 2) or the organization (components 3 and 4)?

4.   What things might you say during an interview to demonstrate that you possess the career readiness competency of personal adaptability?

Target Elements of Change: "Which Levers Can We Pull That Will Produce the Change We Want?"   The target elements of change represent four levers that managers may use to diagnose problems (such as "Our designers are too inbred and don't look outside the company for ideas") and identify solutions (such as "We need new managers and new blood in the Design Group").

As Figure 10.3 shows, the four target elements of change (the four levers) are

1. *People*—their knowledge, ability, attitudes, motivation, and behavior.

2. *Organizational arrangements*—such as policies and procedures, roles, structure, rewards, and physical setting.

3. *Methods*—processes, workflow, job design, and technology.

4. *Social factors*—culture, group processes, interpersonal interactions, communication, and leadership.

Two things are important to realize:

- **Any change made in each and every target element will ripple across the entire organization.** For example, if a manager changes a system of *rewards* (part of the organizational arrangements) to reinforce team rather than individual performance, that change is apt to affect *organizational culture* (one of the social factors).

- **All organizational change ultimately affects the people in it and vice versa.** Thus, organizational change is more likely to succeed when managers carefully consider the prospective impact of a proposed change on the employees.

Outputs: "What Results Do We Want from the Change?"   Outputs represent the desired goals of a change, which should be consistent with the organization's strategic plan. Results may occur at the organizational, group, or individual level (or all three) but will be most difficult to effect at the organizational level because changes will mostly likely affect a wide variety of target elements.

Feedback: "How Is the Change Working and What Alterations Need to Be Made?"   Not all changes work out well, of course, and organizations need to monitor their success. This is done by comparing the status of an output such as employee or customer satisfaction before the change to the same measurable output sometime after the change has been implemented.

Force-Field Analysis: "Which Forces Facilitate Change and Which Resist It?"
In most change situations being considered, there are forces acting for and against the change. **Force-field analysis** is a technique to determine which forces could facilitate a proposed change and which forces could act against it. Force-field analysis consists of two steps:

1. *Identify thrusters and counterthrusters.* The first step is to identify the positive forces (called thrusters) and the negative forces (called counterthrusters). We recommend brainstorming them separately, and then selecting the top three to five in each category.

2. *Remove the most important negative forces and increase positive forces.* The second step may sound simple, but it can be tricky to identify the forces at work.

Consider the Example box of how researchers used a force-field analysis to better understand whether change efforts would work in and around South Africa.

EXAMPLE   **Building "Sustainable, Drought-Resistant Communities" for the Basotho Population**

A recent academic study applied force-field analysis to the Basotho population in and around South Africa.[83] According to the researcher, over 80% of the Basotho depend on rain-fed agriculture to earn a living. Unfortunately, this area is extremely vulnerable to drought, and should one occur, the impacts would be absolutely devastating. The research asked whether a plan to build "sustainable, drought-resistant communities" by creating nonagricultural employment opportunities would be successful with this population.

Step One: Identify Thrusters and Counterthrusters   The study identified the forces that would both enable and hinder this effort:

- *Thrusters*
  - Current lack of rainfall
  - Land degradation
  - Soil erosion
  - High unemployment levels
  - Large households who would benefit from current/future employment opportunities

Researchers recently used force-field analysis to predict whether initiatives to encourage more nonagricultural ventures among the Basotho population in and around South Africa would be successful. Although the area is highly drought-prone, more than 75% of the Basotho population remains financially reliant on rainfed agriculture. Understanding the forces working for and against change is vital for change efforts of this scale.
Edwin Remsberg/Getty Images

- *Counterthrusters*
  - Low levels of education
  - Lack of interest in disaster and development causes

Step Two: Remove the Most Important Negative Forces and Increase Positive Forces The researchers provided several recommendations for moving the change in a positive direction, including:

1. *Education outreach*—beginning with members of the population who are aware of the importance of environmental issues.

2. *Community capacity-building projects*—leadership training, job and trade certifications, and other opportunities for competency development that involve all local institutions capable of teaching skills. These include driving schools, restaurants, and local educational institutions.

The researchers believed there would be tremendous positive ripple effects (what you might recognize as the creation of shared value) if these objectives were successfully implemented. For example, increased education and capacity-building could lower the population's currently high HIV/AIDS rates and reduce the use of misguided soil management techniques, reduce the deforestation caused by an overreliance on wood for energy in low socioeconomic status households, and encourage the development of significant infrastructure and industry for the Basotho population.

YOUR CALL

Have you ever faced a difficult change effort? How would a force-field analysis have helped you to better evaluate the situation and make important decisions?

Applying the Systems Model of Change There are two different ways to apply the systems model of change:

1. *As an aid during the strategic planning process.* Once a group of managers identifies the organization's vision and strategic goals, group members can consider the target elements of change when developing action plans to support the accomplishment of goals.

   Lego Example: Lego went from the brink of death in the early 2000s to being named the #1 toy brand in the world in 2019 and the world's most reputable company in 2020. The company's reinvention has been called "the greatest turnaround in corporate history."[84] After a string of failed attempts to overhaul its image and move away from the little plastic brick synonymous with the company's name, Lego's executives realized that removing the brick was not an option. Instead, they had to figure out how to innovate *around* their namesake product, and they ultimately did so by connecting their physical products with a limitless virtual universe.[85] Recent analyses credit the company's former CEO, Vig Knudstorp, with masterminding the reinvention. Examples of the target elements most critical to the transformation include:

   - *Organizational arrangements*—Knudstorp offloaded businesses in which the company had little expertise, including Legoland parks, and focused on building new digital content such as movies and TV shows.

   - *Methods*—Knudstorp switched to an outsourcing model for areas with high potential for value add from outside experts. Said one analyst, "What's made them successful over the past 10 years is their ability to create . . . by partnering with brilliant people. They've said: 'We might not make as much money if we outsource it, but the product will be better.'"[86]

   - *People*—Knudstorp leveraged people—both inside and outside the organization—to assist in the company's transformation. Dr. Anne Flemmert Jensen, former senior director of Lego's Global Insights group, said that her team helped Lego evolve by spending "all our time travelling around the world, talking to kids and their families and participating in their daily lives." Knudstorp also instituted crowdsourcing, and the company gives 1% of a product's net sales to the person who invented the idea for it. (We discuss crowdsourcing in more detail in Section 10.4.)

2. *As a diagnostic framework to identify the causes of an organizational problem and propose solutions.* We highlight this application by considering a consulting project conducted by one of your authors, Angelo Kinicki.

> **Example:** Dr. Kinicki was contacted by the CEO of a software company and asked to figure out why the presidents of three divisions were not collaborating with each other—the problem. It seemed two of the presidents had submitted the same proposal for a $4 million project to a potential customer. The software company did not get the work because the customer was appalled at having received two proposals from the same firm. Kinicki decided to interview employees by using a structured set of questions that pertained to each of the target elements of change. The interviews revealed that the lack of collaboration among division presidents was due to the reward system (an organizational arrangement), a competitive culture and poor communications (social factors), and poor workflow (a methods factor). Kinicki's recommendation was to change the reward system, restructure the organization, and redesign the workflow. ●

10.3 Organizational Development: What It Is, What It Can Do

THE BIG PICTURE

Organizational development (OD) is a set of techniques for implementing change, such as improving performance, revitalizing organizations, and adapting to mergers. OD has three steps: diagnosis, intervention, and evaluation. Four factors have been found to make OD programs effective.

LO 10-3

Describe the purpose of organizational development.

Organizational development (OD) is a set of techniques for implementing planned change to make people and organizations more effective. Note the inclusion of people in this definition. OD focuses specifically on people in the change process. (Some scholars apply the term "organizational development" to techniques designed to improve organizational effectiveness and the term "change management" to techniques designed to improve people effectiveness—techniques that will help them, in one definition, to adopt "new mindsets, policies, practices, and behaviors to deliver organizational results.")[87]

Often OD is put into practice by a person known as a **change agent**, a consultant with a background in behavioral sciences who can be a catalyst in helping organizations deal with old problems in new ways. Other organizations actually employ organizational development specialists who help the company to lead and manage change.

Whether they are change agents, OD specialists, or other types of experts, the people who help organizations implement change must work to understand both the interpersonal and situational factors that have shaped the organization and that continue to influence its decision makers.[88]

What Can OD Be Used For?

OD can be used to address the following three matters.

1. Improving Individual, Team, and Organizational Performance   Conflict is inherent in most organizations. Sometimes an OD expert, perhaps in the guise of an executive coach, can help advise on how to improve relationships or other issues within the organization.

Start-Up Example: Successful tech entrepreneur Jeff Wald said in a recent interview, "I've counted Fred Wilson as an investor, raised over $60 million in funding and sold my start-up WorkMarket to ADP. . . . But before all that, earlier on in my career, I had a start-up implode, leaving me bankrupt, depressed, and on the verge of moving back in with my parents."[89] Wald's first start-up, Spinback, was eventually acquired by Salesforce, but his memories of the company consist mostly of the constant conflict between two of his co-founders that eventually turned into a nasty legal battle. Wald later also experienced conflict with his WorkMarket co-founder and revealed that these types of interpersonal issues are incredibly common in the start-up community. Wald's board eventually forced him to hire a coach—an idea he first scoffed at, but that he now credits with helping him to move past his business failures and grow into a better leader and co-worker.

2. Revitalizing Organizations   Technology is changing so rapidly that nearly all modern organizations are having to adopt new ways of doing things in order to survive. OD can help by opening communication, fostering innovation, and dealing with stress.

Pacific Surf School Example: At Pacific Surf School in San Diego, instructors' ultra-chill attitudes were causing process issues and inefficiencies. The owners felt that surfing class time could be used more efficiently, and they hired the Lean Enterprise Institute (LEI) to teach instructors to apply lean principles (a set of five steps aimed at improving workforce efficiency and delivering value quickly) to their work. Within a short time, Pacific Surf School was able to increase class sizes by 50%, and students were spending more time on the water. Instructors also found more time to deal with issues like surfboard repairs.[90]

OD can help employees in all sorts of companies to adapt to changes and implement improved practices and techniques. OD for the instructors at Pacific Surf School translated into more surfers, more time catching waves, and more time to solve important problems. Matthew Micah Wright/ Getty Images

3. Adapting to Mergers   Mergers and acquisitions (M&A) are associated with increased anxiety, stress, absenteeism, turnover, and decreased productivity.[91] They're also quite common—in the United States alone, more than 12,000 M&A transactions occurred in 2019.[92] Imagine how employees at Sprint and T-Mobile must have felt as they waited two years for their firms to merge. It's likely employees at both firms encountered one or more of the multiple articles predicting "massive job cuts" as a result of the transaction.[93] OD experts are often called upon in such situations to help integrate two firms with varying cultures, products, and procedures.

How OD Works

Like physicians, OD managers and consultants follow a medical-like model. (Or to use our more current formulation, they follow the rules of evidence-based management.) They approach the organization as if it were a sick patient, using *diagnosis, intervention,* and *evaluation:*

- *Diagnosing* the organization's ills.
- *Prescribing* treatment or intervention.
- *Monitoring* or evaluating progress.

If the evaluation shows that the procedure is not working effectively, the conclusions drawn are then applied (via a feedback loop) to refining the diagnosis, and the process starts again. *(See Figure 10.4.)*

FIGURE 10.4

The OD process

Sources: Adapted from W. L. French and C. H. Bell Jr., Organization Development: Behavioral Interventions for Organizational Improvement (Englewood Cliffs, NJ: Prentice Hall. 1978); E. G Huse and T. G. Cummings, Organizational Development and Change, 3rd ed. (St. Paul: West, 1985).

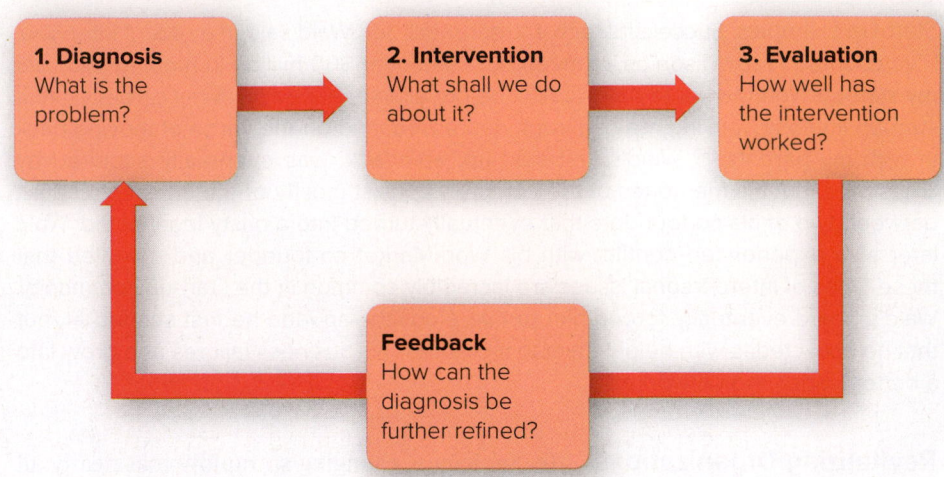

1. Diagnosis: What Is the Problem?

To carry out the diagnosis, OD consultants or managers use some combination of questionnaires, surveys, interviews, meetings, records, and direct observation to ascertain people's attitudes and to identify problem areas. A problem is defined as a gap between an outcome or result desired by managers and the actual status of the outcome or result. For example, if your goal was to lose 10 pounds over 6 months and you only lost five, your problem is to lose five more pounds.

2. Intervention: What Shall We Do about It?

"Treatment," or **intervention**, is the attempt to correct the diagnosed problems. Often this is done using the services of an OD consultant who works in conjunction with management teams. Some OD activities for implementing planned change include:

- Communicating survey results to employees to engage them in constructive problem solving.
- Observing employee communication patterns and teaching employees skills to improve them.
- Helping group members learn to function as a team.
- Stimulating better cohesiveness among several work groups.
- Improving work technology or organizational design.

Coaching is often employed to improve interpersonal relationships and leadership.[94] According to recent studies, between 21 and 40% of Fortune 500 companies currently use executive coaching, and U.S. companies alone spend around $166 billion each year on leadership development.[95] Studies suggest that executive coaching and leadership development programs positively impact leaders' self-efficacy beliefs, transformational leadership behaviors, and career satisfaction. Subordinates of executives who participate in these programs express lower turnover intentions and higher approval of their leaders.[96]

3. Evaluation: How Well Has the Intervention Worked?

An OD program needs objective evaluation to see if it has done any good. Answers may lie in hard data about absenteeism, turnover, grievances, and profitability, which should be compared with earlier statistics. The change agent can use questionnaires, surveys, interviews, and the like to assess changes in employee attitudes.

4. Feedback: How Can the Diagnosis and Intervention Be Further Refined?

If evaluation shows that the diagnosis was wrong or the intervention was not effective, the OD consultant or managers need to return to the beginning to rethink these two steps.

The Effectiveness of OD

Among organizations that have practiced organizational development are American Airlines, B.F. Goodrich, General Electric, Honeywell, ITT, Procter & Gamble, Prudential, Texas Instruments, and Westinghouse Canada—companies covering a variety of industries.

Research has found that OD is most apt to be successful under the following circumstances:

1. Multiple Interventions   OD success stories tend to use multiple interventions.[97] Goal setting, feedback, recognition and rewards, training, participation, and challenging job design have had good results in improving performance and satisfaction.[98]

2. Management Support   OD is more likely to succeed when top managers give the OD program their support and are truly committed to the change process and the desired goals of the change program.[99] Using employee feedback during the change process is one way to demonstrate this support.[100]

3. Goals Geared to Both Short- and Long-Term Results   Change programs are more successful when they are oriented toward achieving both short-term and long-term results. Managers should not engage in organizational change for the sake of change. Change efforts should produce positive results.[101]

By now you know that organizations are having trouble finding career-ready employees. Although new college graduates rate themselves as being proficient in a range of important career readiness competencies, employers indicate that the majority of new hires do not possess adequate levels of these competencies.[102] Recent research suggests that employers are particularly troubled by new hires' lack of soft skills, such as critical thinking/problem solving, teamwork, leadership, creativity, and adaptability.[103]

Let's consider the interventions organizations are using to solve this problem.

EXAMPLE   Career Readiness Interventions

Organizations are addressing career readiness gaps from multiple angles. These include:

- *In-house training*—more than one-third of the managers and executives surveyed in a recent study said their organizations have either already begun reskilling employees or are in the process of developing reskilling programs.[104]

  Example: In 2019, Salesforce launched a customizable version of its gamified training platform, myTrailhead. Organizations can purchase a license and configure the platform to their own training needs, and employees can earn badges and credentials for developing various soft skills.[105]

- *Certifications*—more than 26,000 employers in the United States have partnered with ACT WorkKeys to source applicants who have earned the organization's National Career Readiness Certificate (NCRC).[106]

Example: Glen Raven Custom Fabrics partnered with ACT WorkKeys to refine its hiring process and create a skilled talent pipeline. The company has filled 300 positions with employees who have earned, among other things, the NCRC.

- *Collaborations*—companies are increasingly likely to collaborate with colleges and universities in an effort to build a more career ready workforce. An important way that these collaborations can build important competencies is through internship programs that are designed specifically to address these skills gaps.[107]

  Example: Intel collaborates with faculty at several universities to develop open-source skill-development programs.[108]

YOUR CALL

Which of these important soft skills do you think is most important? How would you rate your level of this skill? What might you do to further develop your soft skills?

---

4. OD Is Affected by Culture   OD effectiveness is affected by cross-cultural considerations. Thus, an OD intervention that worked in one country should not be blindly applied to a similar situation in another country.[109]

10.4 Organizational Innovation

THE BIG PICTURE

Managers agree that the ability to innovate affects long-term success, and you will undoubtedly be asked to help your employer achieve this. This section provides insights into the ways organizations approach the goal of innovation. After discussing approaches toward innovation pursued by companies, we review the need to create an innovation system.

LO 10-4

Describe the approaches toward innovation and components of an innovation system.

| TRADITIONAL BUSINESS CASUAL | MODERN BUSINESS CASUAL |

AND

Do you have a need for work-appropriate clothing? How about pieces that you can wear to the gym? Perhaps a few additional items for going out on the town? What if a single outfit worked in all three of these settings? Clothing retailers have long relied on a consumer desire for occasion-specific clothing, but many of the clothing items that satisfy today's definition of business casual can take workers from a light morning workout to an afternoon board meeting to an evening social event. Can you see the need for innovation in this industry? Dean Drobot/Shutterstock, Djomas/Shutterstock, Pepsco Studio/Shutterstock, ASDF_MEDIA/Shutterstock

We live in a time of technological advancement that is creating transformative changes in the way we live, work, and play. Organizations are feeling both the opportunity and the pinch of this reality. Consider the situation faced by retail clothing companies now that Americans have gone from spending 5.9% of their income on clothing in 1987 to just 3.1% in recent years. Analyst Kayla Marci noted that "the lines between workwear and everyday apparel are becoming more blurred." Said Shawn Grain Carter, professor at the Fashion Institute of Technology, "Tea, the Saturday and Sunday Sabbath, a wedding, a funeral . . . What are you going to get dressed up for? Whereas baby boomers always had clothes for career, clothes for socializing and clothes for special occasions, I can wear my sneakers to every single event."[110]

Is the retail clothing industry an anomaly or is the need to innovate widespread? It's widespread! Results from a recent survey of 1,500 leaders showed that about 79% viewed innovation as key to their company's success.[111]

Innovation (as defined in Chapter 1) occurs when a new solution to an existing problem is valuable enough that consumers are willing to pay for it.[112] This definition underscores that innovations must be both novel and useful. We now take a closer look at innovation and the way organizations foster it. You will learn that innovation is more likely to occur when organizations create and support a system of innovation, which includes tailoring the characteristics of the physical environment to support innovation.

Approaches to Innovation

We can classify innovations by crossing their type with their focus, producing four distinct types. *(See Figure 10.5.)*

The Type of Innovation   Managers often need to improve a product or service they offer in response to competition or customer feedback. This response often amounts to a technological innovation. Or managers may need to improve the process by which a product is made or a service is offered. This need typically leads to a process improvement.

More specifically, a **product innovation** is a change in the appearance or functionality/performance of a product or a service or the creation of a new one. W. L. Gore recently looked to product innovation to jolt the company out of what its former CTO called "a stall point."[113]

FIGURE 10.5

Approaches toward
innovation

Focus of Innovation

		Improvement	New Directions
Type of Innovation	**Product**	**Apple iPhone** • Eleven generations/versions since first introduced in June 2007	**Driverless Cars** • Major automobile manufacturers and Waymo
	Process	**3-D Printing** • Alcoa's use of 3-D printing in its manufacturing process	**Home Construction** • Panelized homes

W. L. Gore Example: You may recognize W. L. Gore & Associates (Gore) as the company that manufactures Gore-Tex—the waterproof fabric used by companies like Patagonia, The North Face, and L.L.Bean. But the company's latest project is a far cry from outdoor apparel. Gore is currently working on developing a revolutionary type of corneal transplant with the same polymer it uses in surgical patches. The material has the right transparency, is flexible, and bends light just like human corneal tissue. The implant is revolutionary because (1) it is inert and therefore won't be rejected by the donor's body, and (2) it integrates itself into the donor's eyeball. The company hopes to bring the product to market by 2026.[114]

A **process innovation** is a change in the way a product or a service is conceived, manufactured, or distributed. McDonald's is experimenting with two process innovations:

McDonald's Example: Food delivery is expected to be a $76 billion business by 2022. McDonald's wants to ensure customers can experience their Big Mac meals and fries still piping hot by engaging drones to deliver its meals. The company is partnering with Uber Elevate (Uber's aerial division) and is hoping to gain FAA approval for broad implementation by 2023.[115] The chain is also experimenting with robotic fryers that it hopes will free up its workers to focus more on customer service.[116]

The Focus of the Innovation   The focus continuum measures the scope of the innovation.

Improvement innovations enhance or upgrade an existing product, service, or process. These types of innovations are often incremental and are less likely to generate significant amounts of new revenue at one point in time. Stitch Fix has used improvement innovation to remain competitive in recent years.

Stitch Fix Example: CEO Katrina Lake is capitalizing on her company's data analytics abilities to increase the personalization of customers' experiences. Now, instead of just receiving a box with five new items each month, customers can opt-in to the company's "Shop Your Looks" sub-service that periodically recommends an additional piece based on the items they already own. The service adds value by continuing to build customers' wardrobes around previous purchases, and the company will benefit from increased impulse purchases.[117]

In contrast, *new-direction innovations* take a totally new or different approach to a product, service, process, or industry. These innovations focus on creating new markets and customers and rely on developing breakthroughs and inventing things that didn't already exist. Orbital Insight is an example.

Product innovations in athletics are nothing new. Improvements in equipment have led to, for example, faster swimmers, longer golfers, and more accurate archers over the years. Still, governing bodies that preside over various sports often must determine whether their athletes are engaging in something called technology doping—using equipment that offers an unfair competitive advantage—as was the case with Nike's Vaporfly technology. At what point do you think innovation crosses a line in professional sports? Nattawit Khomsanit/Shutterstock

Orbital Insight Example: Orbital Insights uses satellite images to watch, capture, and analyze activity on Earth. It can, for example, tell you how many cars drove in and out of a particular shopping center parking lot over a busy weekend, or monitor production at a factory. Founder and CEO James Crawford said that his company's analyses provide more accurate data than traditional measures of economic activity. The technology is powered by AI, and Orbital recently launched a consumer version called Orbital Go that allows users to research answers to their own questions about what's happening on the planet.[118]

Can an Innovation Go Too Far?

Are all innovations good innovations, or is it possible for innovation to cross a line? This is a question that businesses will continue to confront as technology evolves and allows us to do things that were once not possible. This question arose recently when two runners shattered existing marathon records.

Nike Example: In fall of 2018, Eliud Kipchoge became the first person in history to run a marathon in less than 2 hours. One day later, Brigid Kosgei broke the women's world record to become the fastest woman in history. Both runners were wearing Nike shoes with the company's Vaporfly technology, which featured cutting-edge foam soles and embedded carbon fiber plates. According to Nike, the technology decreased a runners' effort by at least 4%. Track and field regulators grappled with the question of whether to allow this type of technology in official races going forward, and a 2020 World Athletics ruling ultimately limited both the thickness of foam soles and the number of embedded plates allowable in competition road shoes.[119]

An Innovation System: The Supporting Forces for Innovation

Innovation won't happen as a matter of course. It takes dedicated effort and resources, and the process must be nurtured and supported. Organizations do this best by developing an innovation system. An ==innovation system== is a set of mutually reinforcing structures, processes, and practices that drive an organization's choices around innovation and its ability to innovate successfully.[120]

Research and practice have identified seven components of an innovation system: innovation strategy; committed leadership; innovative culture and climate; required structure and processes; necessary human capital; human resource policies, practices, and procedures; and appropriate resources.[121] *(See Figure 10.6.)*

Do the components of an innovation system look familiar to you? If so, you're probably remembering our discussions in Chapters 8 and 9. Specifically, in these previous chapters, you learned that leadership is needed to align an organization's culture, structure, and HR practices so that they work together to support firm strategy. These important elements are also presented here as part of an organization's innovation system, and here too, they must be aligned and integrated for innovation to blossom, hence the dual-headed arrows in Figure 10.6.

Create an Innovation Strategy

Many companies fail in their improvement efforts because they lack an innovation strategy.[122] An ==innovation strategy==, which amounts to a plan for being more innovative, requires a company to integrate its

FIGURE 10.6

Components of an innovation system

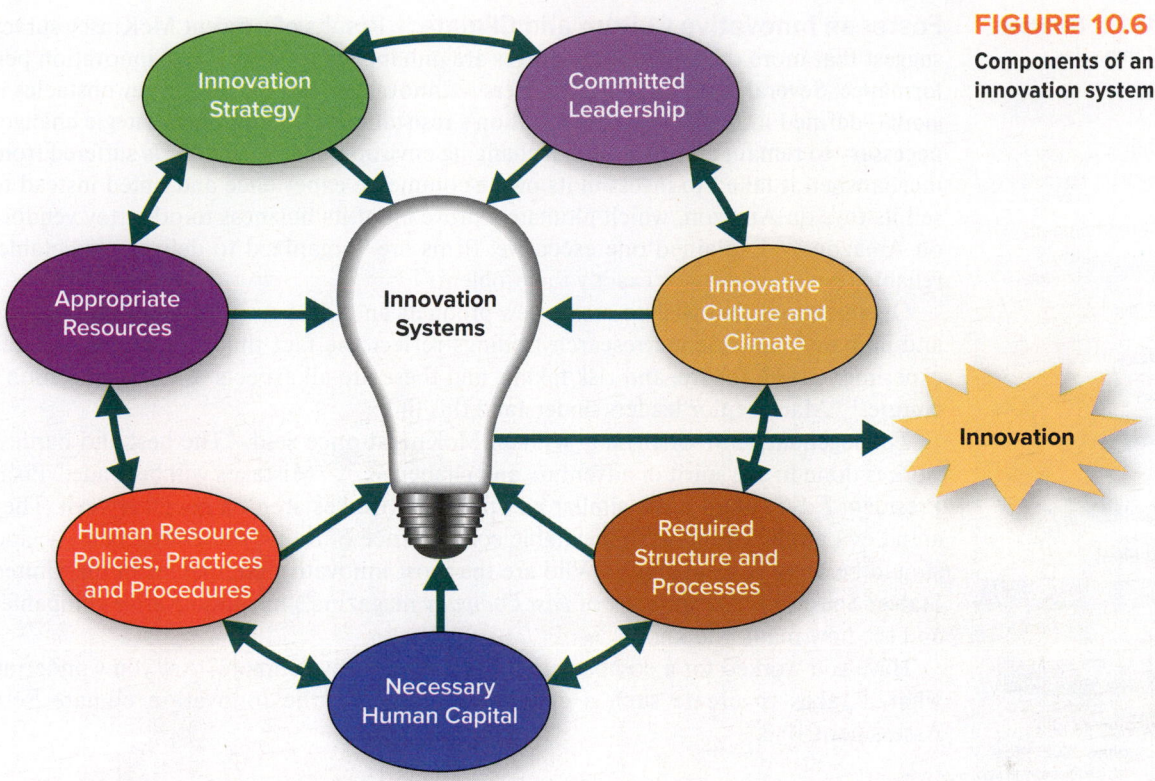

innovation activities into its business strategies. This integration encourages management to invest resources in innovation and generates employee commitment to innovation across the organization.

Consider the example of how Reckitt Benckiser innovates using a well-defined strategy.

Reckitt Benckiser Example: Reckitt Benckiser (RB) is the British company that owns brands such as Lysol, Woolite, and Clearasil. Its innovation strategy is characterized by small, incremental improvements. Specifically, rather than pursue massive innovations, RB focuses on taking its most successful products and tweaking them in modest ways that better solve consumers' problems. For example, the company's Finish dish detergent brand has gone from Finish 2-in-1, to Finish 3-in-1, to Finish All-in-1. With each iteration, RB made a small but valued improvement, and the company's sales and profits from the product have continued to increase.[123]

Commitment from Senior Leaders   One of the biggest lessons we have learned from our consulting experience is that the achievement of strategic goals is unlikely without real commitment from senior leaders.[124] Mars CEO Grant Reid is acutely aware of his role in supporting innovation.

Mars Example: "We've been in business for 107 years" said Mars CEO Grant Reid in a recent interview. "My job is to make sure that I'm setting us up for the next 100 years."[125] Innovation is essential for a company of this age to remain competitive, and Mars is committed to innovating in ways that create shared value for everyone in its supply chain. The company has pledged $1 billion toward achieving its sustainability goals.

TABLE 10.1   The Most Innovative Companies

| 1. Snap |
| 2. Microsoft |
| 3. Tesla |
| 4. Big Hit Entertainment |
| 5. HackerOne |
| 6. White Claw |
| 7. Shopify |
| 8. Canva |
| 9. Roblox |
| 10. Zipline |
| 11. Kaios Technologies |
| 12. Beyond Meat |
| 13. Bravado |
| 14. Meesho |
| 15. Spotify |

Source: "The World's 50 Most Innovative Companies 2020," Fast Company, https://www.fastcompany.com/most-innovative-companies/2020 (accessed May 8, 2020).

Foster an Innovative Culture and Climate   Results of a recent McKinsey survey suggest that more than 90% of executives are unhappy with their firms' innovation performance. Several factors serve as barriers to innovation, but one of the key obstacles is inertia—defined in LM 1 as an organization's resistance to making the strategic changes necessary to remain competitive in a changing environment.[126] Toys R Us suffered from inertia when it failed to invest in its own e-commerce experience and opted instead to sell its toys on Amazon, which ultimately drove all of its business to other toy vendors on Amazon.[127] Explained one executive, firms are "organized to deliver predictable, reliable results—and that's exactly the problem."[128]

Organizations that wish to create new products and ideas need an innovative culture and climate.[129] Academic research findings reflect the fact that innovation requires experimentation, failure, and risk taking, and these are all aspects of an organization's culture.[130] Many senior leaders understand this link.

The legendary 3M Chairman William McKnight once said, "The best and hardest work is done in the spirit of adventure and challenge. . . . Mistakes will be made." Pixar President Ed Catmull has a similar viewpoint: "Mistakes aren't a necessary evil. They aren't evil at all. They are an inevitable consequence of doing something new . . . and should be seen as valuable."[131] Who are the most innovative companies in the United States? See Table 10.1 for a list of *Fast Company* magazine's most innovative companies and see how many you know.

Have you worked for a company that has an innovative climate? Are you wondering what it takes to create such a climate? If yes, take the innovation climate Self-Assessment 10.3.

SELF-ASSESSMENT 10.3

How Innovative Is the Organizational Climate?

Please be prepared to answer these questions if your instructor has assigned Self-Assessment 10.3 in Connect.

1. What is the level of innovation? Are you surprised by the results? Explain.

2. Select the three lowest survey item scores. Use the content of these items to recommend what the company could do to become more innovative.

Required Structure and Processes   Organizational structure and internal processes can promote innovation if they foster collaboration, cross-functional communication, and agility. Flagship Pioneering is a good example.

Flagship Pioneering Example: Flagship Pioneering (FP) creates new ventures based on cutting-edge, or "pioneering," science. FP uses a formal process to evaluate opportunities for innovation. Exploration begins with the identification of a major social issue followed by a deep dive into the existing literature. Teams formulate hypotheses throughout this stage and work through them with a group of scientific advisers. The key rule at this stage is that every idea is entertained as long as its execution would create value. Later in the process, scientists run experiments designed to expose holes in the ideas, and employees are taught to respect what the data ultimately show.[132]

Organizational processes are an organization's capabilities in management, internal processes, and technology that turn inputs into outcomes. Processes play a critical role in innovation. The design and consulting firm IDEO, for example, employs a unique process when it helps companies to innovate (see the Example box).

Crowdsourcing, defined as the practice of obtaining needed services, ideas, or content by soliciting contributions from a large group of people typically via the Internet, is being used by more companies to help innovate.

Enable Makeathon Example: The Enable Makeathon is a contest sponsored by the Global Disability Innovation Hub. Its purpose is to accelerate the innovation of assistive technology for people with disabilities. The 2018 winning idea was Bleetech—a low-cost, digital encyclopedia for the hearing impaired. The platform allowed users to sign questions and receive answers back in sign language.[133]

EXAMPLE   IDEO's Approach to Innovation

IDEO (pronounced "EYE-dee-oh") is a unique, award-winning, and highly respected and influential global design firm. The company has more than 700 employees in nine offices, both in major U.S. cities and overseas in London, Munich, Shanghai, and Tokyo.[134] It is responsible for such innovative products as the first mouse for Apple, heart defibrillators that guide a user through the steps, and TiVo's "thumbs up–thumbs down" button. An intense focus on end-user behavior is the foundation of all the company does and is embedded in the three steps of its design thinking. The steps are inspiration, ideation, and implementation.[135]

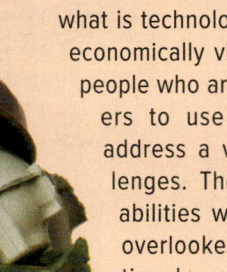

IDEO has successfully applied its design thinking innovation approach to a wide variety of problems, including reducing the enormous amount of food waste that occurs each year in the food industry. Ian Allenden/123RF

- **Inspiration.** As defined by David Kelley, IDEO's legendary founder, inspiration is the problem or opportunity that motivates the search for solutions.

- **Ideation.** Ideation is the process of generating, developing, and testing ideas.

- **Implementation.** The final step, implementation, links the problem's solution to people's lives.

Observing user behavior and working with prototypes are important aspects of each step. They help IDEO's diverse problem-solving teams both define client problems and gauge the effectiveness of their solutions.

Thinking Like a Designer   The company's consulting approach to products, services, processes, and strategy brings together what is desirable from a human point of view with what is technologically feasible and economically viable. It also allows people who are trained as designers to use creative tools to address a vast range of challenges. The goal: to tap into abilities we all have that are overlooked by more conventional problem-solving practices. Thinking like a designer relies on our ability "to be intuitive, to recognize patterns, to construct ideas that are emotionally meaningful as well as functional, and to express ourselves through means beyond words or symbols."[136]

Design Thinking Your Way to Innovative Solutions: Beyond Product Design   IDEO's design thinking has been so successful that many nonbusiness and nonproduct organizations are now engaging the company. For instance, IDEO recently partnered with the Rockefeller Foundation to help combat food waste. The goal of the project was to "help reduce the 1.3 billion tons of food wasted every year and equip food industry players with the design principles and support to cut waste further."[137] The collaboration generated multiple innovations, such as an online platform called the Food Waste Alliance where participants could continue to be engaged with the latest innovations in reducing food waste.

YOUR CALL

What is appealing to you about IDEO? To what extent does IDEO's approach to design force companies to use the seven components of an innovation system (see Figure 10.6)? Explain.

Develop the Necessary Human Capital   We defined human capital in Chapter 9 as the productive potential of an individual's knowledge and actions. Research has identified several employee characteristics that can help organizations innovate. For example, innovation has been positively associated with the individual characteristics associated with creativity, creative-thinking skills, intrinsic motivation, the quality of the relationship between managers and employees, and international work experience.[138]

> **Hackerone Example.** Companies like AT&T, Hyatt, Goldman Sachs, and Capital One hire HackerOne when they want to be sure their users' information is protected according to the highest security standards. This company doesn't build network security systems. Rather, HackerOne hires skilled hackers to test the vulnerability of its clients' existing systems. Organizations reward these benevolent hired hackers for finding security weaknesses before malicious hackers discover them.[139]

Human Resource Policies, Practices, and Procedures   Human resource (HR) policies, practices, and procedures need to be consistent with and reinforce the other six components of an innovation system. Here's what research tells us about the alignment of HR with the overall innovation system:

- *Alignment is related to valued outcomes.* Companies that align HR with the other components of the innovation system are more likely to be innovative and to have higher financial performance.[140]

- *Performance management and incentives are often not designed to foster innovation.* A company's performance management and incentive system are often at odds with an innovation culture and climate. Companies need to align their reward and recognition systems with innovation-related goals.[141]

Bringing people from different disciplines together to both brainstorm and train is a good way for a firm to foster the collaboration needed for innovation. Collaboration creates opportunities for communication and, thus, ideation, between unlikely parties. Collaboration also provides a safe space for risk taking. Economist John Galbraith once said, "In any great organization it is far, far safer to be wrong with the majority than to be right alone."[142] Galbraith is telling us that it takes courage and the "right" organizational culture to be innovative.

> **CarMax Example.** CarMax generates innovation through its cross-functional product teams. These teams consist of 7 to 9 members, and each must include at least one user-experience expert, one product manager, and one lead developer or engineer. The remaining members can come from any department. Teams work in short spurts and make short progress presentations every two weeks. This schedule encourages teams to take risks and learn from mistakes at a fairly quick pace.[143]

Appropriate Resources   Organizations need to put their money where their mouths are. If managers want innovation, they must dedicate resources to its development. Resources can include people, dollars, time, energy, knowledge, and focus.

> **Amazon Example:** Amazon recently pledged that it would invest $700 million to upskill its workforce by 2025. Machine Learning University is one of a list of possible initiatives that employees can participate in. It was designed to encourage innovation by giving employees the skills necessary to work with and create AI.[144] •

10.5 The Threat of Change: Managing Employee Fear and Resistance

THE BIG PICTURE

This section discusses the causes of resistance to change and the reasons employees fear change.

As we mentioned in Section 10.1, change may be forced upon an organization—*reactive* change, requiring you to make changes in response to problems or opportunities as they arise. Or an organization may try to get out in front of changes—*proactive* change, or planned change, which involves making carefully thought-out changes in anticipation of possible problems or opportunities.

What, then, are effective ways to manage organizational change and employees' fear and resistance to it? In this section, we discuss the following:

- The causes of resistance to change.
- Why employees resist change.

LO 10-5

Discuss ways managers can help employees overcome fear of change.

The Causes of Resistance to Change

Resistance to change is an emotional/behavioral response to real or imagined threats to an established work routine. Resistance can be as subtle as passive resignation and as overt as deliberate sabotage. As you will learn, change experts believe that resistance does not primarily reside within the individual but instead is a result of the context in which change occurs.[145]

Resistance can be considered to be the interaction of three causes. *(See Figure 10.7.)* They are

1. Employee characteristics.
2. Change agent characteristics.
3. The change agent–employee relationship.

For example, an employee's resistance is partly based on his or her perception of change, which is influenced by the attitudes and behaviors exhibited by the change agent and the level of trust between the change agent and the employee.[146]

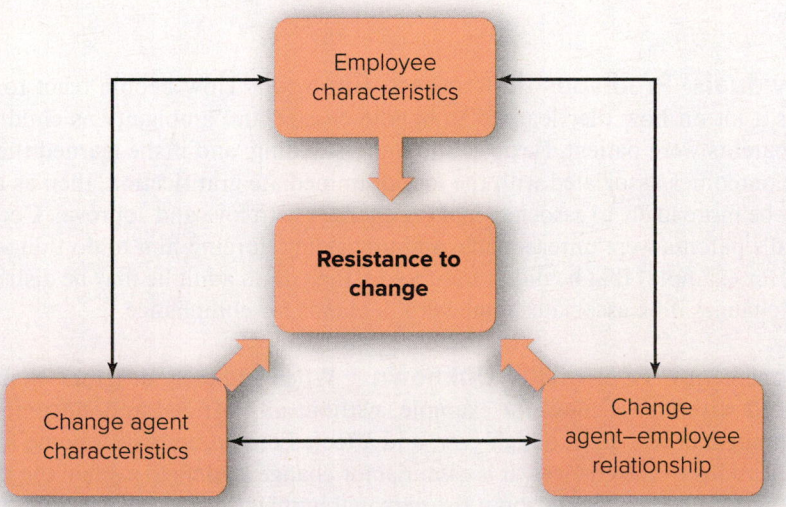

FIGURE 10.7

A model of resistance to change

Source: Adapted from R. Kreitner and A. Kinicki. Organizational Behavior, 9th ed. (Burr Ridge, IL: McGraw-Hill/Irwin, 2010), p. 549.

Let us consider these three sources of resistance.

1. Employee Characteristics   The characteristics of a given employee consist of his or her individual differences (discussed in Chapter 11), actions and inactions, and perceptions of change.[147] The next section discusses a variety of employee characteristics that relate to resistance to change. One of them involves personal adaptability, the career readiness competency that one columnist recently called an "underrated superpower in business."[148] How adaptable are you? You can find out by taking Self-Assessment 10.4.

SELF-ASSESSMENT 10.4   CAREER READINESS

How Adaptable Are You?

The following survey was designed to assess your level of adaptability. Please be prepared to answer these questions if your instructor has assigned Self-Assessment 10.4 in Connect.

1.   What is your level of adaptability? Are you surprised by the results?

2.   Based on your scores, identify three things you can do to increase your level of adaptability. Explain.

3.   What things might you say during an interview to demonstrate that you possess the career readiness competency of personal adaptability?

---

2. Change Agent Characteristics   The characteristics of the change agent—the individual who is a catalyst in helping organizations change—also consist of his or her individual differences, experiences, actions and inactions, and perceptions of change. Such characteristics that might contribute to employee resistance to change include leadership style, personality, tactfulness, sense of timing, awareness of cultural traditions or group relationships, and ability to empathize with the employee's perspective.[149]

3. Change Agent–Employee Relationship   As you might expect, resistance to change is reduced when change agents and employees have a trusting relationship—faith in each other's intentions. Mistrust, on the other hand, encourages secrecy, which begets deeper mistrust, and can doom an otherwise well-conceived change.[150]

Ten Reasons Employees Resist Change

Whether changes are adaptive, innovative, or radically innovative, employees may resist change for all kinds of reasons. Ten of the leading reasons for not accepting change are as follows.[151]

1. Individuals' Predisposition toward Change   How people react to change depends a lot on how they learned to handle change and ambiguity as children. If a child's parents were patient, flexible, and understanding, and if she learned there were positive outcomes associated with the loss of immediate gratification, then as an adult she may be more likely to associate making changes with love and approval. Conversely, if a child's parents were unreasonable and unyielding, forcing him to do things (piano lessons, for example) that he didn't want to do, then as an adult he may be distrustful of making changes if he associates them with demands for compliance.[152]

2. Surprise and Fear of the Unknown   When radically different changes are introduced without warning—for example, without any official announcements—the office rumor mill will go into high gear, and affected employees will become fearful of the implications of the changes. It is essential for change leaders to explain the rationale for change, to educate people about the personal implications of change, and to garner commitment to change.[153]

3. Climate of Mistrust   Trust involves reciprocal faith in others' intentions and behavior. Mistrust encourages secrecy, which causes deeper mistrust, putting even well-conceived changes at risk of failure. Managers who trust their employees make the change process an open, honest, and participative affair. All told, employees who feel fairly treated by managers during change are less likely to resist.[154]

4. Fear of Failure   Intimidating changes on the job can cause employees to doubt their capabilities. Self-doubt erodes self-confidence and cripples personal growth and development.

5. Loss of Status or Job Security   Administrative and technological changes that threaten to alter power bases or eliminate jobs—as often happens during corporate restructurings that threaten middle-management jobs—generally trigger strong resistance.

6. Peer Pressure   Even people who are not themselves directly affected by impending changes may actively resist in order to protect the interests of their friends and co-workers.

7. Disruption of Cultural Traditions or Group Relationships   Whenever individuals are transferred, promoted, or reassigned, it can disrupt existing cultural and group relationships.[155]

8. Personality Conflicts   Just as a friend can get away with telling us something we would resent hearing from an adversary, the personalities of change agents can breed resistance.

9. Lack of Tact or Poor Timing   Introducing changes in an insensitive manner or at an awkward time can create employee resistance. Employees are more apt to accept changes when managers effectively explain their value, as, for example, in demonstrating their strategic purpose to the organization.

10. Nonreinforcing Reward Systems   Employees are likely to resist when they can't see any positive rewards from proposed changes, as, for example, when one is asked to work longer hours without additional compensation.

   Where do you stand on change? Are you open to change and embrace it, or do you have tendencies to resist? The following self-assessment assesses the extent to which you resist change, which is the opposite of the career readiness competency of openness to change. Given that employers are looking for people who accept and embrace change, this assessment provides you good feedback about your attitudes toward change. If your scores indicate resistance, you should consider what can be done to move your attitudes in a more positive direction. ●

SELF-ASSESSMENT 10.5   CAREER READINESS

Assessing Your Resistance to Change

The following survey was designed to assess your resistance to change. Please be prepared to answer these questions if your instructor has assigned Self-Assessment 10.5 in Connect.

1.   Are you more or less willing to accept change? Discuss.

2.   Based on your scores, identify three things you can do to lower your resistance to change. These changes may involve new thoughts or beliefs or the display of new behaviors.

3.   What might you say during an interview to demonstrate that you possess the career readiness competency of openness to change?

10.6 Career Corner: Managing Your Career Readiness

Review the different ways to increase the career readiness competency of openness to change.

"Be open to change, and be willing to lean in and learn new skills," says Angelina Darrisaw, founder of the career coaching firm C-Suite Coach.[156] What do we know about the career readiness competency of openness to change (shown in Figure 10.8 below)?

- *It is an important career readiness competency.* Openness to change is the career readiness competency most related to the concepts discussed in this chapter. It is an "other characteristic" from the model shown below and was defined in Table 1.2 as "flexibility when confronted with change, ability to see change as a challenge, and willingness to apply new ideas, processes, or directives."

- *It is necessary for organizational change.* Employers desire this competency because of the constant need for organizations to adapt, change, and respond in novel or innovative ways to competitors.

- *It leads to positive work outcomes for you.* Openness to change supports employees' continuous learning and job satisfaction while reducing workplace annoyances and intentions to quit.[157] Openness to change is worth cultivating in yourself now and throughout your career.

So how can you become more open to change? What gets in your way? We answer these questions by first explaining the application of self-affirmation theory. We then review how self-compassion assists in promoting openness to change.

FIGURE 10.8

Model of career readiness

McGraw-Hill Education

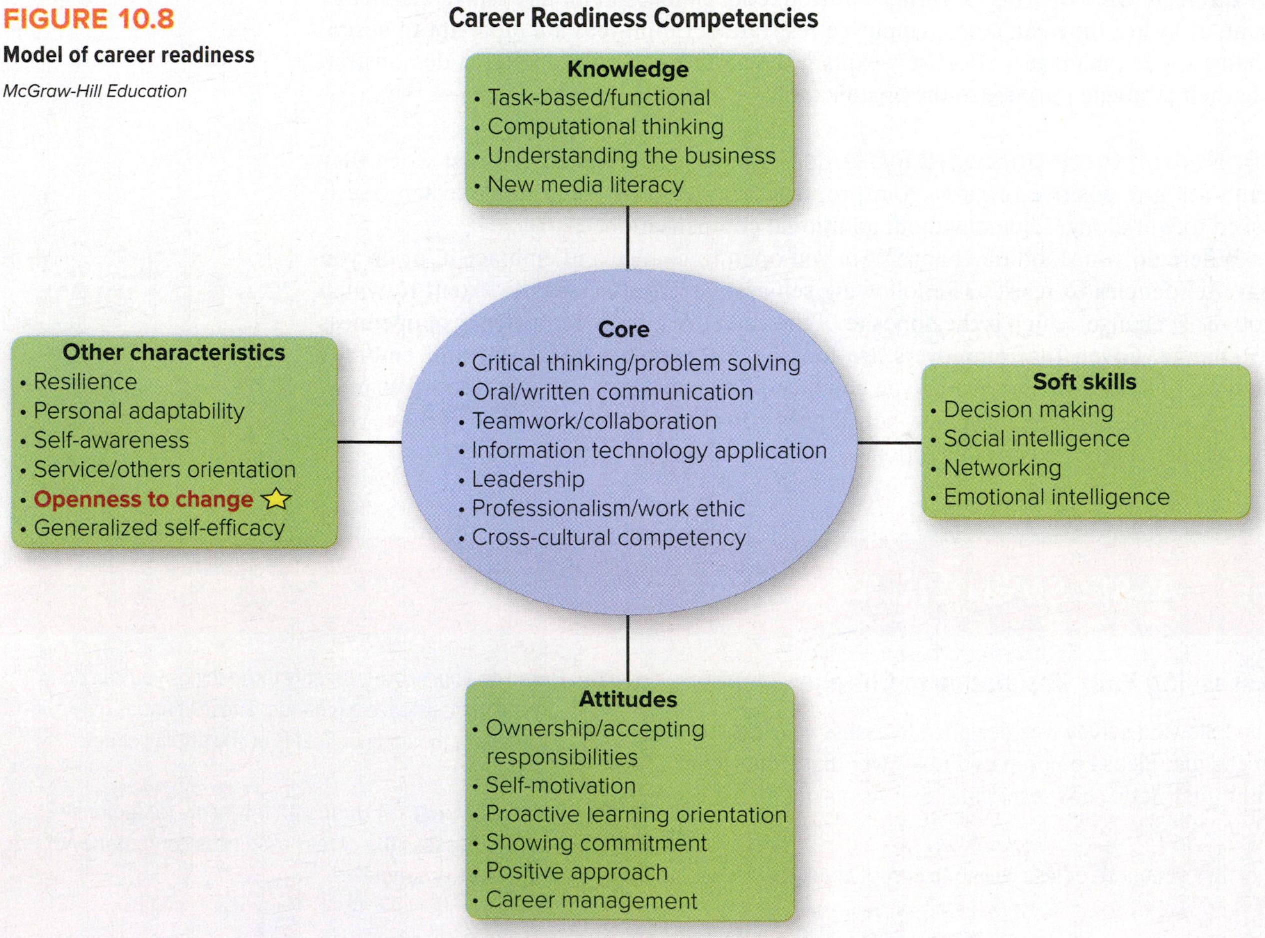

Career Readiness Competencies

Knowledge
- Task-based/functional
- Computational thinking
- Understanding the business
- New media literacy

Core
- Critical thinking/problem solving
- Oral/written communication
- Teamwork/collaboration
- Information technology application
- Leadership
- Professionalism/work ethic
- Cross-cultural competency

Other characteristics
- Resilience
- Personal adaptability
- Self-awareness
- Service/others orientation
- Openness to change ★
- Generalized self-efficacy

Soft skills
- Decision making
- Social intelligence
- Networking
- Emotional intelligence

Attitudes
- Ownership/accepting responsibilities
- Self-motivation
- Proactive learning orientation
- Showing commitment
- Positive approach
- Career management

Applying Self-Affirmation Theory

When we speak of not being open to change, we are concerned about more than just organizational change or feedback from a boss or colleague. Your openness to change affects your social interactions with friends, colleagues, loved ones, and even strangers during controversial conversations on topics like politics, the value of unions, immigration policy, the #MeToo movement, and sexual orientation.[158]

We explain self-affirmation theory in three parts:

1. **We have an innate need to maintain a positive overall self-view.** What causes us to be closed-minded about controversial topics or feedback about our behavior? According to self-affirmation theory, we all possess a strong desire to maintain a "global" or overall sense of self-integrity. In simpler terms, this means that as humans, we really want to see ourselves as generally good and virtuous people who behave in appropriate ways.[159]

2. **When our positive self-view is threatened, we switch to self-protective mode.** Two renowned psychologists note: "Much research suggests that people have a 'psychological immune system' that initiates protective adaptations when an actual or impending threat is perceived."[160] The goal of these mechanisms is to restore self-worth.

3. **We can maintain our self-view in two ways (and one is definitely the better choice).** When our self-view is threatened, we naturally attempt to protect it. Say, for example, that you get caught in a lie. Even though deep down you know you have behaved dishonestly, your psyche will do everything it can to keep on seeing itself as good and virtuous. The key message of self-affirmation theory is—don't fight the urge to affirm your self-view in this situation, but rather, work with it. Specifically, when you experience a threat to your self-view, remind yourself that you can *choose* to respond in one of two ways:

   ■ *Option 1: Maintain your self-view by denying any information that is related to the threat.*

     What would this look like? In the case of our example, probably an internal dialogue that includes phrases like "how dare they accuse me of lying," or "it wasn't really a lie; it was simply an omission of the whole truth," or "I didn't have a choice but to be dishonest." Notice here that you are still talking about the threat and are making statements that relate directly to it. Unfortunately, you are also taking a defensive and closed-off stance that is preventing you from learning and growing.

   ■ *Option 2: Maintain your self-view AND increase your openness to change by affirming facets of your self-view that are unrelated to the threat.*

     What would this look like? In the case of our example, you might choose an internal dialogue that goes something like "I am a loyal friend," or "I have compassion for others," or "I am a great teammate." Notice here that you are (1) making positive statements about yourself that you believe to be true and (2) avoiding the topic of the actual threat.

Which option do you think is the better choice? Research on this theory has firmly documented that while either of these options will help you to restore your self-view, the second option is better because it allows you to feel good about yourself while still remaining open to change and the possibility of personal growth and learning. This is because your use of these positive "self-affirmations" makes it easier for the two voices in your head to coexist—you can make a poor choice (i.e., tell a lie) and still remind yourself that you are good. One mistake doesn't have to define you![161]

Self-affirmations such as the ones listed above are defined as positive statements that impact your subconscious mind by drawing attention to your values and positive attributes and away from negative self-perceptions.[162] Self-affirmations flip our close-minded thoughts from negativity to positivity. Sample affirmations include:

- "My work does not define me; I'm a good person."
- "I learn from mistakes."
- "I can accomplish whatever I put my mind to."
- "I love my job and know that I am making a difference."
- "I'm not perfect, but I stick to my values."
- "I'm ethical."
- "I know I can do well, just like I did on the XYZ project."

If you want to increase your openness to either personal or work-related change, or to comments being made about a controversial subject such as immigration, try using self-affirmations when you feel threatened or get defensive. For example, if someone tells you that your views about immigration are naive, avoid the temptation to tell yourself, "I am not wrong about this because I am very well informed on the topic." Instead, try an affirmation that's not related to the immigration conversation—or to politics in general—at all. For example, "I am proud of my dedication to my physical health." And remember, being more open to change doesn't mean that you *have* to change your views—it simply means that you are always willing to consider views that are different from your own.

Practicing Self-Compassion

In Chapter 9 we defined self-compassion as the tendency to be understanding, warm, and kind to yourself when you experience pain or failure, rather than being self-critical or over-identifying with negative emotions. Dr. Christine Carter defines self-compassion as "gentleness with yourself." Here is what she had to say about using self-compassion to increase openness to self-development.

> We think that if we speak critically to ourselves, we will improve, but all the research shows with absolute certainty that self-criticism does not improve performance. It blocks your ability to learn from the situation and creates a stress response in which fight or flight are your only options. Personal growth is not on the menu when you are self-critical.[163]

When you are overly hard on yourself your body experiences distress—over time, you may experience symptoms such as anxiety, burnout, and depression.[164] When you have compassion for yourself, however, you let go of the need to be perfect, making it easier to increase your openness to change or your career readiness competency of positive approach. It allows us to "give ourselves the same kindness and care we'd give to a good friend," according to psychologist Kristen Neff.[165] Self-compassion protects self-identity by allowing you to appreciate the difference between being a bad person and making a bad decision. As noted in *Psychology Today*, "When you have self-compassion, you understand that your worth is unconditional."[166] This in turn makes it easier to accept feedback from others, to consider alternative viewpoints from your own, to own up to your mistakes, and to empathize with others.[167]

Try the following suggestions in pursuit of more self-compassion:

1. **Practice self-kindness.** Replace perfectionism and self-judgment with forgiveness and kindness. Accept your imperfections and talk to yourself as you would to a loved one.

2. **Remind yourself that you're not alone.** Psychotherapist Megan Bruneau reminds us that "to feel is to be human, and that whatever [we're] going through is also being experienced by millions of others. If we can recognize our shared humanity—that not one of us is perfect—we can begin to feel more connected to others, with a sense that we're all in this together."[168]

3. **Practice mindfulness meditation.** Mindfulness is a state of being present nonjudgmentally. Meditation can help you achieve this state and avoid the negative thoughts that inhibit openness to change.[169]

Key Terms Used in This Chapter

Key Points

10.1 The Nature of Change in Organizations

- Among supertrends shaping the future of business: (1) The marketplace is becoming more segmented and moving toward more niche products. (2) More competitors are offering targeted products, requiring faster speed-to-market. (3) Some traditional companies may not survive radical change. (4) China, India, and other offshore suppliers are changing the way we work. (5) Knowledge, not information, is becoming the new competitive advantage.

- Two types of change are reactive and proactive.

- Forces for change may consist of forces outside the organization (external forces) or inside it (internal forces).

10.2 Forms and Models of Change

- Organizational change can be adaptive, innovative, or radically innovative.

- Kurt Lewin's change model has three stages—unfreezing, changing, and refreezing—to explain how to initiate, manage, and stabilize planned change.

- A systems approach to change consists of three parts: inputs, target elements of change, and outputs, plus a feedback loop.

- Force-field analysis is a technique to determine which forces could facilitate a proposed change and which forces could act against it.

10.3 Organizational Development: What It Is, What It Can Do

- Organizational development (OD) is a set of techniques for implementing planned change to make people and organizations more effective.

- The OD process follows three-steps: (1) diagnosis, (2) intervention, and (3) evaluation.

- Four factors that make OD work successfully are (1) multiple interventions are used, (2) top

managers give the OD program their support, (3) goals are geared to both short- and long-term results, and (4) OD is affected by culture.

10.4 Organizational Innovation

- Innovation is the creation of something new and useful that gets commercialized.

- Crossing the types of innovation with the focus on the innovation results in four approaches to innovation.

- Innovation can produce new products or new processes and can vary in focus from improvement to new directions.

- An innovation system's seven components are (1) an innovation strategy; (2) commitment from senior leaders; (3) an innovative culture and climate; (4) required structure and processes; (5) necessary human capital; (6) appropriate resources; and (7) human resource policies, practices, and procedures.

10.5 The Threat of Change: Managing Employee Fear and Resistance

- Resistance to change is an emotional/behavioral response to real or imagined threats to an established work routine.

- Ten reasons employees resist change are as follows: (1) individuals' predisposition toward change, (2) surprise and fear of the unknown, (3) climate of mistrust, (4) fear of failure, (5) loss of status or job security, (6) peer pressure, (7) disruption of cultural traditions or group relationships, (8) personality conflicts, (9) lack of tact or poor timing, and (10) nonreinforcing reward systems.

10.6 Career Corner: Managing Your Career Readiness

- There are two key methods for improving your openness to change: self-affirmation theory and self-compassion.

1. What are the two principal types of change?

2. Describe the four external forces for change and two internal forces for change.

3. How does Kurt Lewin's model of change work?

4. What is the organizational development process?

5. What's the difference between a product innovation and a process innovation?

6. Explain four approaches to innovation.

7. What are four steps for fostering innovation?

8. Employee resistance can be considered to be the interaction of what three causes?

9. There are 10 reasons employees resist change. What are they?

10. How can you increase the career competency of openness to change?

Management in Action

Were Deadly COVID-19 Outbreaks aboard Carnival Cruise Ships the Result of Managers' Resistance to Change?

This case examines the COVID-19 outbreaks that occurred aboard Carnival cruise ships in the spring of 2020. By the end of April, the outbreaks had resulted in more than 1,500 positive cases of the virus and at least 39 deaths.[170] Let's begin by considering a timeline of events so that you can evaluate the behavior and decisions made by Carnival's leadership.

TIMELINE OF EVENTS

January 30: Carnival ship *Costa Smeralda* is docked near Rome. All 6,000 passengers and 1,000 crew members are quarantined after a woman and her partner became ill with symptoms that could be COVID-19.

February 1, 11:21 pm: The Carnival *Diamond Princess* is sailing around Asia when a representative from the company's sanitation vendor sends an e-mail to the chief administrative officer and a guest services account. The purpose of the e-mail is to alert the *Diamond Princess* crew that a woman in Hong Kong, who has recently been aboard the ship, had tested positive for COVID-19.

February 2, 11:33 am: Records show that Carnival's chief medical officer, Grant Tarling, sends an e-mail to Hong Kong health authorities with the subject line "Confirmed COVID-19 Case." In the e-mail, Tarling lists the infected passenger's name, age, and Princess Margaret Hospital room number.

February 2, 6:44 pm: According to statements from Carnival after-the-fact, this is when Tarling is actually made aware of the confirmed COVID-19 case.

February 3, 6:00 pm: *Diamond Princess* Captain Gennaro Arma announces to the ship's passengers that they may have been exposed to COVID-19. He adds that no one on board has reported illness but that they should avoid close contact with anyone showing respiratory distress, follow proper hand-washing protocol, and contact the ship's infirmary if they begin to feel symptoms. According to some of the ship's passengers, the crew continues to promote social activities, guests enjoy bars and buffets, people steam in saunas, and the evening's opera goes on as planned.

February 3: Evening: The *Diamond Princess* arrives in Yokohama. Japanese health workers immediately begin conducting medical screenings of the passengers.

February 3: Also on this day, news reports of countries denying entry to cruise ships around the world begin to surface.

February 4: Carnival spokesman says in statements after-the-fact that by this day the staff has discontinued "most" scheduled activities.

February 5: Japanese officials institute a ship-wide quarantine requiring passengers to stay in their cabins until further notice. According to Carnival CEO Arnold Donald, on this day he takes control of the company's response to the illness but had been made aware of it previously.

February 27: There are now 696 confirmed cases of COVID-19 aboard the *Diamond Princess*.

March 4: As the Carnival *Grand Princess* heads to Mexico, passengers receive a notification from the office of Grant Tarling under their cabin doors. The message says that the CDC is looking into a "small cluster" of COVID-19 cases in California that may be tied to the ship. The *Grand Princess* makes a U-turn and heads back toward California. Passengers notice that crew members are wearing gloves and setting out hand sanitizing stations. Events on the ship go on as planned, including swimming, card games, dance classes, concerts, and an evening show.

March 5: *Grand Princess* captain John Smith announces a quarantine over the ship's loudspeaker. All passengers must return to their cabins indefinitely. According to some passengers, many detour to the buffet before complying.

March 8: The CDC issues a public health advisory to warn U.S. citizens to avoid all cruise ship travel.

March 9: The *Grand Princess* docks in Oakland, California, and is immediately commandeered by the CDC. For the next 2 weeks, passengers shelter in place in their cabins and helicopters drop supplies and COVID-19 tests down to the ship's decks.

March 25: Of the 1,103 tests conducted, 103 have come back positive, 699 have come back negative, and the remaining are pending.[171] [After this date, no additional test results are publicized.]

EXECUTIVES' RESPONSES

Many have wondered why Carnival wasn't quicker and stricter with quarantines aboard its ships. After all, throughout the crisis, the CDC repeatedly warned that viral outbreaks would be particularly difficult to contain on cruises for several reasons (e.g., age and health of passengers, close physical proximity throughout the ship, shared staff quarters, etc.). CEO Arnold Donald maintained that the rate at which COVID-19 spread was the same in "an airport terminal, a subway station, a restaurant, a theater, a stadium," and that any evidence of a higher infection rate had "Nothing to do with cruise ships." At one point, Carnival's chief communications officer Roger Frizzell defended the company's position by passing around a Buzzfeed article that reported on multiple COVID-19 deaths having resulted after a family funeral service. (The CDC estimated infection rates aboard the affected ships at close to 20%, while the infection rate for the general population was closer to 3%.)

Carnival's executives maintained a sense of pride in their response to the viral outbreaks. Donald told reporters, "It wasn't like there were protocols, and that this was established. You're at sea, you're moving people around, and the rules are changing as you go." He added, "This is a generational global event—it's unprecedented. . . . Nothing's perfect, OK?"

Jan Swartz, president of Princess Cruises, thinks the company did everything it could have been expected to do. "It's very easy and Monday morning, you know, 20/20 hindsight, to say what's the view of what should have been occurring," said Swartz, adding "We did our best to take care of people." She believes the company's response may even have improved its reputation with some of its customers. "There are many loyal Princess guests who have told us that this has actually cemented Princess as their No.–1 vacation choice."

BACKLASH

John Padgett, Carnival's chief experience and innovation officer, told reporters that the company's executives were aware of the magnitude of the virus as far back as January 25. Padgett had been in contact with one of the company's manufacturers in Wuhan and had learned details about the virus that he discussed with the team, including Donald. "The biggest thing about that—it's a learning I don't think I'll ever forget, and we shared it with Arnold when we were talking—is that we actually had insight into the global situation much earlier than most."

If Carnival's executives had chosen to make different decisions during the outbreaks, it's possible that the lives and health of numerous passengers could have been spared. In addition, executives' decisions had wider-ranging impacts. Said Cindy Friedman, epidemiologist and head of the CDC cruise ship task force, "If these ships had stopped sailing, our large team could all be working on helping states and local public health authorities with their community outbreaks."

By July of 2020, Congress had opened an investigative probe to examine Carnival's response, the Australian police were conducting a criminal investigation to determine whether the company had purposefully lied to authorities about passengers' health in order to dock one of its ships in Sydney, and Carnival was facing multiple individual and class-action lawsuits.[172]

Arnold remained confident that consumer demand for cruises would bounce back after all the "negative noise" had a chance to die down.

FOR DISCUSSION

Problem-Solving Perspective

1. What is the underlying problem in this case from the CDC's perspective?
2. What are some of the causes of this problem?
3. Do you think Carnival CEO Arnold Donald should be held personally liable? Explain your rationale.

Application of Chapter Content

1. Using Figure 10.1, describe the forces for change both inside and outside Carnival during the outbreaks.
2. Does Carnival need adaptive, innovative, or radically innovative change? Explain.
3. Utilize Lewin's model of change (Figure 10.2) as a blueprint to describe how Carnival's executives might inspire change at Carnival.
4. Use a force-field analysis to explain the changes that did and did not occur at Carnival during the outbreaks.
5. Think about the outbreaks of COVID-19 aboard Carnival cruise ships and utilize the organizational development process (Figure 10.4) to remedy the issue.
6. What specific reasons can you see for Carnival executives' resistance to change? Explain.

Does Clearview Technology Violate Rights?

What if there were an easy way for police to locate suspects? Would law enforcement find this valuable? These are questions one company asked when they created an innovative solution for identifying people using AI.

Clearview AI has amassed a database of nearly 3 billion photographs from the Internet. The database is almost seven times bigger than that of the FBI, and Clearview's technology allows for almost instant identification of anyone in its database with just a simple face scan. The company says that all of its photos are obtained from sites where users have shared them publicly.

According to various sources, hundreds of companies, including 600 law enforcement agencies, are already using Clearview's face scanning app.[173] In Indiana, state police officers supposedly used Clearview to identify a shooter who had been captured on cell phone video within 20 minutes.[174] The Raleigh, North Carolina, police department allegedly paid $2,500 for a year-long subscription to the database.[175]

Others have expressed grave concern about the potential for Clearview's technology to violate civil rights. YouTube, LinkedIn, PayPal, Twitter, and Facebook have all sent cease-and-desist letters to prohibit the company from mining images from their sites. In Congress, Senator Ed Markey sent a letter to Clearview's founder to demand that the company release certain information. In the letter Markey noted, "The ways in which this technology could be weaponized are vast and disturbing. Using Clearview's technology, a criminal could easily find out where someone walking down the street lives or works. A foreign adversary could quickly gather information about targeted individuals for blackmail purposes."[176] Numerous studies have also demonstrated that AI facial recognition technology is significantly affected by racial bias.

Several groups have filed class action lawsuits against Clearview for violation of, for example, state biometrics and computer crimes laws.

SOLVING THE CHALLENGE

How would you rule if you were a judge deciding whether to continue to allow Clearview technology to remain on the market?

1. I would side with Clearview. If citizens choose to post photographs on the Internet without protecting their security, then Clearview has the right to find and save those photos.

2. I would side with the plaintiffs. Companies do not automatically have the right to obtain photographs from the Internet, and law enforcement agencies should not use technology that has proven bias issues.

3. I'm not sure who is right or wrong. I don't like the idea of wrongfully identifying and accusing people as criminals, but I also see the potential benefits of such a program for society.

4. Invent other options.

Boeing Continuing Case   McGraw Hill connect

In this part of the case you'll read about the impact of organizational change forces on Boeing. You'll also learn more about how the key drivers of strategic implementation impacted decision making at the company.

Go to Connect to assess your ability to apply the concepts discussed in Chapters 8, 9, and 10 to the Boeing case.

11

Managing Individual Differences and Behavior

Supervising People as People

Kapook2981/iStock/Getty Images

After reading this chapter, you should be able to:

LO 11-1 Describe the importance of personality and individual traits in the hiring process.

LO 11-2 Explain the effects of values and attitudes on employee behavior.

LO 11-3 Describe the way perception can cloud judgment.

LO 11-4 Explain how managers can deal with employee attitudes.

LO 11-5 Identify trends in workplace diversity that managers should be aware of.

LO 11-6 Discuss the sources of workplace stress and ways to reduce it.

LO 11-7 Describe how to develop the career readiness competencies of positive approach and emotional intelligence.

FORECAST *What's Ahead in This Chapter*

This first of five chapters on leadership discusses how to manage for individual differences and behaviors. We describe personality and individual behavior; values, attitudes, and behavior; and specific work-related attitudes and behaviors managers need to be aware of. We next discuss distortions in perception and consider what stress does to individuals. We conclude with a Career Corner that focuses on the career readiness competencies of a positive approach and emotional intelligence.

Making Positive First Impressions

The power of perception is so well known that we consciously try to manage other people's perceptions to ensure their first impression of us is a positive one. As we'll see below, some of the influences on others' perceptions of us that we can't control are unconscious biases about race, age, and gender; the weight of internal influences like the kind of day someone is having (called the fundamental attribution error); the inclination to be influenced by the most recent event or person encountered (the recency error); and the tendency to weigh early information most heavily (the primacy effect). And thanks to the confirmation bias, "people see what they expect to see."[1] But still, a great deal of someone's first impression of you is yours to control.

Creating positive first impressions is important in job or client interviews and other social situations. A writer for *The Wall Street Journal* noted, "[F]irst impressions are formed in milliseconds based on instinctive responses in the brain's emotion-processing center, the amygdala."[2] Studies say you have between 7 and 30 seconds to make a good impression.[3] The good news is that you can influence these perceptions by using the following suggestions and your career readiness skills of positive approach and self-awareness.

Be Prepared

Be ready to ask and answer questions in job interviews. This shows your eagerness to contribute as soon as possible.[4] When meeting new co-workers, subordinates, clients, or company executives, the same advice applies. You'll need to reflect on your strengths and weaknesses relative to the job you are seeking. This preparation is part of the career readiness competency of self-awareness. There's no substitute for the confidence you'll gain from having done your homework on both the company and yourself!

Stand (or Sit) Straight and Smile

Your body language conveys your confidence and invites others to feel confident in you as well. Lift your chin, straighten your back, and avoid crossing your arms or legs.[5] Dropping your shoulders and keeping them relaxed can improve the tone of your voice to further support the positive image you want to portray. Smiling suggests a friendly and open personality most people can readily warm to.

Look for Common Ground

It's only natural for us to like people who are similar to us in some way. Even a small link like a common interest in sports, music, or travel can help form a bond that will allow more positive associations to form as you communicate. You can indicate your interest in the other person by asking a few polite, open-ended questions to uncover such common ground.[6] "The better you make the other person feel, the more they'll be inclined to have a positive impression of you."[7]

Keep Up the Good Work

Once you've landed a job or a client account, continue solidifying the good impression you've made by being consistently reliable, prompt, humble, willing to learn, open to new experiences, and eager to be part of the team. These are all part of the career readiness competency of positive approach. Remember to ask for help when you need it and say thank you when it's given.[8]

If All Else Fails

Sometimes, despite our efforts, we fail to show our best selves. Perhaps we fumble the answer to an interview question, show up for a work event in the wrong clothes, or tell a crowd of new co-workers a joke that falls flat. An unqualified disaster? It doesn't have to be. Experts suggest giving yourself a little time to recover and then taking steps to remedy the negative impression by explaining what happened, presenting plenty of strong evidence in your favor, and asking for a second chance. Be prepared to spend time repairing the relationship, but don't give up.[9]

For Discussion What might you ask to create common ground with someone you are meeting for the first time? What can you say during a job interview to convey the impression that you are a positive and flexible person?

11.1 Personality and Individual Behavior

THE BIG PICTURE

Personality consists of stable psychological and behavioral attributes that give you your identity. We describe five personality dimensions and five personality traits that managers need to be aware of to understand workplace behavior.

LO 11-1

Describe the importance of personality and individual traits in the hiring process.

In this and the next four chapters we discuss the third management function (after planning and organizing)—namely, leading. *Leading,* as we said in Chapter 1, is defined as *motivating, directing, and otherwise influencing people to work hard to achieve the organization's goals.*

How would you describe yourself? Are you outgoing? aggressive? sociable? tense? passive? lazy? quiet? Whatever the combination of traits, which result from the interaction of your genes and your environment, they constitute your personality. More formally, **personality** consists of the stable psychological traits and behavioral attributes that give a person his or her identity.[10] As a manager, you need to understand personality attributes because they affect how people perceive and act within the organization.[11]

The Big Five Personality Dimensions

In recent years, the many personality dimensions have been distilled into a list of factors known as the Big Five.[12] The **Big Five personality dimensions** are (1) extroversion, (2) agreeableness, (3) conscientiousness, (4) emotional stability, and (5) openness to experience.

- **Extroversion:** How outgoing, talkative, sociable, and assertive a person is.
- **Agreeableness:** How trusting, good-natured, cooperative, and soft-hearted someone is.
- **Conscientiousness:** How dependable, responsible, achievement-oriented, and persistent someone is.
- **Emotional stability:** How relaxed, secure, and unworried a person is.
- **Openness to experience:** How intellectual, imaginative, curious, and broad-minded someone is.

Choose wisely. The most common form of personality testing is the self-report measure. This type of test relies on information provided by participants through multiple-choice questions.
SIAATH/Shutterstock

Pre-employment psychometric testing, which includes personality testing, has grown into an industry estimated to be worth $2 billion a year. This has been fueled by employers' increased desire to identify candidates in all fields with the career readiness skills they seek.[13] Companies are applying these assessments "not only to make more informed decisions when employing new people, but also to gauge existing employees' performance and ability as well as a tool for personal development and growth," says Joanne Bondin, director of MISCO, Malta's leading knowledge-based independent consulting firm.[14] Over 75% of Fortune 500 companies use these tests at different stages of the recruitment process, believing that hiring decisions will be more accurate and predictive of high performers.[15] But are they? Research finds the following:

- Conscientiousness has the most consistent relationships with important outcomes such as task performance, leadership behavior, supervisor-rated liking, resilience, and lower unemployment.[16]

- Highly conscientious individuals are more likely to be *perfectionists*—those striving for flawlessness. This can be a disadvantage, as perfectionism tends to have a negative impact on job performance.[17]

- Extroversion is closely related to higher levels of motivation, positivity, well-being, and interpersonal savviness, which lead to higher job performance.[18]

- Individuals high on conscientiousness, agreeableness, and emotional stability are less likely to engage in workplace deviance.[19]

Where do you think you stand in terms of the Big Five? You can find out by completing Self-Assessment 11.1.

SELF-ASSESSMENT 11.1   CAREER READINESS

Where Do You Stand on the Big Five Dimensions of Personality?

This survey is designed to assess your personality, using the Big Five index. Please be prepared to answer these questions if your instructor has assigned Self-Assessment 11.1 in Connect.

1. What is your personality profile, according to the Big Five?

2. Which of the Big Five is most likely going to help you achieve good grades in your classes and gain employment after graduation?

3. What things might you say during an interview to demonstrate that you have self-awareness regarding your personality?

Core Self-Evaluations

A core self-evaluation (CSE) represents a broad personality trait comprising four positive individual traits: (1) self-efficacy, (2) self-esteem, (3) locus of control, and (4) emotional stability. Managers need to be aware of these personality traits as they are related to employees' work attitudes, intrinsic motivation, creativity, ethical leadership, and performance.[20]

1. Self-Efficacy: "I Can/Can't Do This Task"   Self-efficacy is the belief in one's personal ability to do a task. This is about your personal belief that you have what it takes to successfully complete a specified task in a specific situation. This characteristic has been expanded into a broader motivational trait labeled generalized self-efficacy. Generalized self-efficacy represents the belief in one's general ability to perform across different situations."[21] It is a career readiness competency desired by employers.

Have you noticed that those who are confident about their ability tend to succeed, whereas those preoccupied with failure tend not to? Indeed, high expectations of self-efficacy have been linked to all kinds of positives, including academic performance, work performance, lower burnout, job satisfaction, and motivation.[22] One recent study of accounting students, for instance, found a significant positive association between self-efficacy and job performance.[23]

Among the implications for managers are the following:

- **Assign jobs accordingly.** Complex, challenging, and autonomous jobs tend to enhance people's perceptions of their self-efficacy. Boring, tedious jobs generally do the opposite.

- **Develop employees' self-efficacy and generalized self-efficacy.** Self-efficacy is a quality that can be nurtured. Employees with low self-efficacy need lots of constructive pointers and positive feedback.[24] Goal difficulty needs to match individuals' perceived self-efficacy, but goals can be made more challenging as performance improves.[25] Small successes need to be rewarded. Employees' expectations can be improved through guided experiences, mentoring, and role modeling.[26] It's also important to monitor employees' generalized self-efficacy because it impacts all aspects of our lives. For example, low generalized self-efficacy can foster **learned helplessness, the debilitating lack of faith in your ability to control your environment.**[27] High generalized self-efficacy, on the other hand, is positively linked to job performance and satisfaction.[28] This is particularly true for entrepreneurs and even athletes.[29]

Yes, I can! Believing you can succeed at something can assist you in actually performing well. Have there been times when you doubted your ability to perform a task? What was the end result?
Jacob Lund/Shutterstock

Would you like to enhance your generalized self-efficacy as way to improve your academic performance? If so, you can assess your generalized self-efficacy and learn about ways to apply the results by taking Self-Assessment 11.2. Results may enhance your confidence at achieving both your personal and work-related goals.

SELF-ASSESSMENT 11.2   CAREER READINESS

What Is Your Level of Generalized Self-Efficacy?

This survey is designed to assess your generalized self-efficacy. Please be prepared to answer these questions if your instructor has assigned Self-Assessment 11.2 in Connect.

1. What is your level of generalized self-efficacy?

2. Examine the three lowest item scores and determine the issues that are lowering your level of efficacy. What might

you do to improve your generalized self-efficacy based on this determination?

3. What things might you say during an interview to demonstrate that you possess the career readiness competency of generalized self-efficacy?

2. Self-Esteem: "I Like/Dislike Myself"   How worthwhile, capable, and acceptable do you think you are? The answer to this question is an indicator of your **self-esteem**, the extent to which people like or dislike themselves, their overall self-evaluation.[30] Research offers some interesting insights about how high or low self-esteem can affect people and organizations.

■ **People with high self-esteem.** Compared to people with low self-esteem, people with high self-esteem are more apt to handle failure better and to become leaders. They also are less likely to be depressed, experience employment gaps, and engage in counterproductive behavior at work.[31] However, when faced with pressure situations, people with high self-esteem have been found to become egotistical and boastful.[32]

■ **People with low self-esteem.** Conversely, low self-esteem people confronted with failure have been found to have focused on their weaknesses and to have had primarily negative thoughts.[33] Moreover, they are more dependent on others and are more apt to be influenced by them and to be less likely to take independent positions.

Can self-esteem be improved? According to one study, "low self-esteem can be raised more by having the person think of *desirable* characteristics *possessed* rather than of undesirable characteristics from which he or she is free."[34] Some ways in which managers can build employee self-esteem are shown below. *(See Table 11.1.)*

TABLE 11.1   **Some Ways That Managers Can Boost Employee Self-Esteem**

- Reinforce employees' positive attributes and skills.
- Provide positive feedback whenever possible.
- Break larger projects into smaller tasks and projects.
- Express confidence in employees' abilities to complete their tasks.
- Provide coaching whenever employees are seen to be struggling to complete tasks.

3. Locus of Control: "I Am/Am Not the Captain of My Fate"   As we discussed briefly in Chapter 1, **locus of control** indicates how much people believe they control their fate through their own efforts. If you have an *internal locus of control*, you believe you control your own destiny. If you have an *external locus of control*, you believe external forces control you.

Research shows internals and externals have important workplace differences. Internals exhibit less anxiety, greater work motivation, and stronger expectations that effort leads to performance. They also are better leaders and obtain higher salaries.[35] Most importantly, one's internal locus of control can be improved by managers providing more job autonomy to employees.[36]

These findings have two important implications for managers:

■ **Expect different degrees of structure and compliance for each type.** Employees with internal locus of control will probably resist close managerial supervision. Hence, they should probably be placed in jobs requiring high initiative and lower compliance. By contrast, employees with external locus of control might do better in highly structured jobs requiring greater compliance.

■ **Employ different reward systems for each type.** Since internals seem to have a greater belief that their actions have a direct effect on the consequences of that action, internals likely would prefer and respond more productively to incentives such as merit pay or sales commissions. (We discuss incentive compensation systems in Chapter 12.)

4. Emotional Stability: "I'm Fairly Secure/Insecure When Working under Pressure"   **Emotional stability** is the extent to which people feel secure and unworried and how likely they are to experience negative emotions under pressure. People with low levels of emotional stability are prone to anxiety and tend to view the world negatively, whereas people with high levels tend to show better job performance.

Emotional Intelligence: Understanding Your Emotions and the Emotions of Others

Emotional intelligence (EI) has been defined as "the ability to carry out accurate reasoning about emotions and the ability to use emotions and emotional knowledge to enhance thought."[37] Said another way, **emotional intelligence is the ability to monitor your and others' feelings and to use this information to guide your thinking and actions.**[38] It is a career readiness competency desired by employers and was first introduced in 1909. Since that time some claim EI to be the secret elixir to happiness and higher performance. In fact, *CareerBuilder* found that 71% of employers value an employee's emotional intelligence over their IQ.[39] Does research also hold emotional intelligence in such high regard?

What Do We Know about EI?   Recent research underscores the importance of developing higher EI, but it does not fully confirm its lofty expectations. EI was moderately associated with (1) better social relations and well-being, (2) job satisfaction, (3) better emotional control, (4) conscientiousness and self-efficacy, (5) organizational citizenship behavior, and (6) self-rated performance. Interestingly, EI was not found to be a driver of supervisory ratings of performance.[40] Daniel Goleman, a psychologist who popularized the trait of EI, concluded that it is composed of four key components: self-awareness, self-management, social awareness, and relationship management.[41] *(See Table 11.2.)*

TABLE 11.2   The Traits of Emotional Intelligence

TRAIT	DESCRIPTION	RELATED CAREER READINESS COMPETENCIES
Self-awareness	The most essential trait. This is the ability to read your own emotions and gauge your moods accurately, so you know how you're affecting others.	• Self-Awareness
Self-management	This is the ability to control your emotions and act with honesty and integrity in reliable and adaptable ways. You can leave occasional bad moods outside the office.	• Resilience • Personal Adaptability
Social awareness	This includes empathy, allowing you to show others that you care, and organizational intuition, so you keenly understand how your emotions and actions affect others.	• Cross-Cultural Competency • Social Intelligence
Relationship management	This is the ability to communicate clearly and convincingly, disarm conflicts, and build strong personal bonds.	• Oral/Written Communication • Teamwork/Collaboration • Networking • Showing Commitment • Service/Others Orientation

Can You Raise Your EI?   Table 11.2 shows that the underlying traits of EI are developed by focusing on the related career readiness competencies we introduced in Chapter 1. As you can see, the skills are interrelated. This means improving your EI requires you to master more than one career readiness competency.

Is there any way to raise your own emotional intelligence, to sharpen your career readiness? Although parts of EI represent stable traits that are not readily changed, other aspects, such as using empathy, can be developed.[42] Two suggestions for improvement are as follows:

- **Develop awareness of your EI level.** Becoming aware of your level of emotional intelligence is the first step. The self-assessment on the following page can be used for this purpose.

- **Learn about areas needing improvement.** The next step is to learn more about those EI aspects in which improvement is needed. For example, to improve your skills at using empathy, find articles on the topic and try to implement their recommendations. One such article suggests that empathy in communications is enhanced by (1) trying to understand how others feel about what they are communicating and (2) gaining appreciation of what people want from an exchange.[43] The Practical Action box illustrates how technology is used to develop empathy, a key component of EI. ●

PRACTICAL ACTION | Using Technology to Develop Empathy

Emotional intelligence is one of the most important skills a job candidate can have, and empathy is a key component of EI.[44] To empathize means to understand and even experience others' perspectives and feelings.[45] Empathy drives performance, increases engagement, helps us build relationships, decreases turnover, improves customer service, and fosters teamwork.[46]

Many experts believe we can develop our EI. But until recently, suggestions have consisted mostly of generic advice such as "develop an understanding of your own emotions"[47] or "put yourself in the other person's shoes."[48] Emerging technology is providing more immersive, and therefore realistic, methods for increasing EI. Let's look at two types.

Virtual Reality Based Empathy Training

Empathetic employees provide a higher level of customer service, are more collaborative, and produce more sales than less empathetic employees. Corporate training company Sweet-Rush developed a virtual hotel so corporate managers could experience what it felt like working in lower-level positions. The thought was that this experience would motivate managers to be more empathetic with colleagues working at the front desk or cleaning a guest room. "They don't understand what those people's jobs are like, yet they are making decisions for those people day in and day out," says John Carlos Lozano, chief creative officer at SweetRush.[49]

Relias, a health care talent company, also uses virtual reality to develop employee empathy. The company launched an empathy course for caregivers of dementia patients. The course allows caregivers to have a challenging, virtual experience with someone with limited cognitive ability. The program also imitates sound problems, replicating someone with hearing loss. Dana Thomas, vice president of content development at Relias, says the training is having a positive impact on both caregivers and their supervisors.[50]

App Based Empathy Training

The *Translator* app wants to help employees increase their "empathy muscle." Users provide personal information including gender, sexual orientation, and race to create an identity profile. The app then designs lessons—including audio exercises, simulations, and games—to teach users about other identities that are different from their own. For example, a white male worker might experience what it feels like to be a woman of color in a board meeting. This may include being called "honey" and having others ask her to get coffee because they assume she's a secretary. "It's amazing . . . how much people's attitude and behavior shifts," says Natalie Egan, Translator's CEO.[51]

Random App of Kindness (RAKi) is a free app that consists of nine minigames designed to improve specific aspects of users' empathy. These include emotion recognition, response inhibition, and caring for others' needs. The app takes interventions that have previously been used to increase empathy in face-to-face settings and translates them into easily accessible smartphone games.[52]

YOUR CALL

Do you believe that virtual reality, simulations, and games can help increase employees' empathy? What else can you do to develop this skill?

SELF-ASSESSMENT 11.3   CAREER READINESS

What Is Your Level of Emotional Intelligence?

The following survey is designed to assess your emotional intelligence. Please be prepared to answer these questions if your instructor has assigned Self-Assessment 11.3 in Connect.

1.   How do you stand on the five dimensions of emotional intelligence?

2.   Use the scores from the items to identify your strengths and liabilities.

3.   Identify two ways you can increase your emotional intelligence.

4.   What things might you say during an interview to demonstrate that you possess the career readiness competency of emotional intelligence?

11.2 Values, Attitudes, and Behavior

THE BIG PICTURE

Organizational behavior (OB) considers how to better understand and manage people at work. In this section, we discuss individual values and attitudes and how they affect people's actions and judgments.

LO 11.2

Explain the effects of values and attitudes on employee behavior.

FIGURE 11.1

Formal and informal aspects of an organization

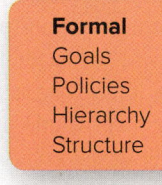

Formal
Goals
Policies
Hierarchy
Structure

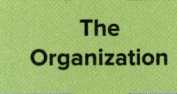

The
Organization

Informal
Values
Attitudes
Personalities
Perceptions
Conflicts
Culture

If you look at a company's annual report or at a brochure from its corporate communications department, you are apt to be given a picture of its *formal aspects*: Goals. Policies. Hierarchy. Structure.

Could you exert effective leadership if the formal aspects were all you knew about the company? What about the *informal aspects*? Values. Attitudes. Personalities. Perceptions. Conflicts. Culture. Clearly, you need to know about these hidden, "messy" characteristics as well. *(See Figure 11.1.)*

Organizational Behavior: Trying to Explain and Predict Workplace Behavior

The informal aspects are the focus of the interdisciplinary field known as ==organizational behavior (OB)==, which is dedicated to better understanding and managing people at work. In particular, OB tries to help managers not only *explain* workplace behavior but also *predict* it. This is so managers can better lead and motivate their employees to perform productively. OB looks at two areas:

- **Individual behavior.** This is the subject of this chapter. We discuss such individual attributes such as values, attitudes, personality, perception, and learning.

- **Group behavior.** This is the subject of later chapters, particularly Chapter 13, where we discuss norms, roles, and teams.

Let's begin by considering individual values, attitudes, and behavior.

Values: What Are Your Consistent Beliefs and Feelings about All Things?

==Values== are abstract ideals that guide one's thinking and behavior across all situations.[53] Lifelong behavior patterns are dictated by values that are fairly well set by the time people are in their early teens. After that, however, one's values can be reshaped by significant life-altering events. This includes having a child; undergoing a business failure; or surviving the death of a loved one, a war, or a serious health threat.

From a manager's point of view, it's helpful to know that values represent the ideals that underlie how we behave at work. Ideals such as concern for others, self-enhancement, independence, and security are common values in the workplace.[54] Managers who understand an employee's values are better suited to assign them to meaningful projects and to help avoid conflicts between work activities and personal values.[55]

Attitudes: What Are Your Consistent Beliefs and Feelings about Specific Things?

Values are abstract ideals—global beliefs and feelings—that are directed toward all objects, people, or events. Values tend to be consistent both over time and over related situations.

By contrast, attitudes are beliefs and feelings that are directed toward *specific* objects, people, or events. More formally, an <mark>attitude</mark> **is defined as a learned predisposition toward a given object**.[56] It is important for you to understand the components of attitudes because attitudes directly influence our behavior.[57]

It's not personal. Do you think managers should be giving employees personal advice? What would you do if someone at work asked for your thoughts on a personal problem they are having? Pressmaster/Shutterstock

Example: Job satisfaction is moderately associated with performance and strongly related to employee turnover.[58] Unhappy workers are less likely to demonstrate high performance, while happy workers are less likely to quit. This is why it is important for managers to track employees' attitudes and to understand their causes. For example, a survey conducted by 15Five, an employee performance management software maker, found that Gen Zers are looking for more than just a paycheck and vacation time to be happy on the job. These individuals want weekly meetings with conscientious managers who appreciate both their work and personal lives. In fact, 75% of Gen Zers have asked for personal advice during 1-on-1s with their managers. Employees without these scheduled weekly meetings experienced "a lack of trust, communication, and overall mental well-being."[59]

The Three Components of Attitudes: Affective, Cognitive, and Behavioral
Attitudes have three components—*affective, cognitive,* and *behavioral.*[60]

- **The affective component—"I feel."** The <mark>affective component of an attitude</mark> consists of the feelings or emotions one has about a situation. How do you *feel* about people who talk loudly on cell phones in restaurants? If you feel annoyed or angry, you're expressing negative emotions, or affect. (If you're indifferent, your attitude is neutral.)

- **The cognitive component—"I believe."** The <mark>cognitive component of an attitude</mark> consists of the beliefs and knowledge one has about a situation. What do you *think* about people in restaurants talking on cell phones? Is what they're doing inconsiderate, acceptable, even admirable (because it shows they're productive)? Your answer reflects your beliefs or ideas about the situation.

- **The behavioral component—"I intend."** The <mark>behavioral component of an attitude</mark>, also known as the intentional component, is how one intends or expects to behave toward a situation. What would you *intend to do* if a person talked loudly on a cell phone at the table next to you? Your action may reflect your negative or positive feelings (affective), your negative or positive beliefs (cognitive), and your intention or lack of intention to do anything (behavioral).

All three components are often manifested at any given time. For example, if you call a corporation and get one of those telephone-tree menus ("For customer service, press 1 . . .") that never seem to connect you to a human being, you might be so irritated that you would say

- "I hate being given the runaround." [*affective component—your feelings*]
- "That company doesn't know how to take care of customers." [*cognitive component—your perceptions*]
- "I'll never call them again." [*behavioral component—your intentions*]

A *positive approach* is one of the career readiness competencies desired by employers.[61] We defined this attitude in Chapter 1 as the "willingness to accept developmental feedback, to try and suggest new ideas, and to maintain a positive attitude at work." Research shows that positive supervisors are more likely to promote positive behaviors in employees.[62] This is important because those who are not positive at work or school are less likely to receive help from those around them. They also have lower levels of performance, citizenship behavior, and creativity.[63]

You can see why employers want to hire candidates with a positive attitude. Where do you think you stand on being positive at work? Find out by taking Self-Assessment 11.4.

SELF-ASSESSMENT 11.4   CAREER READINESS

Do You Have a Positive Approach at Work?

The following survey is designed to assess the extent you possess a positive approach or attitude at work. Please be prepared to answer these questions if your instructor has assigned Self-Assessment 11.4 in Connect.

1. How do you stand on the two dimensions underlying a positive approach?

2. Based on individual item scores, identify one strength and one weakness for the dimensions of positive attitude and feedback seeking and acceptance. Now discuss the actions you might take to improve your weaknesses.

3. What things might you say in an interview to demonstrate that you possess this career readiness competency?

When Attitudes and Reality Collide: Consistency and Cognitive Dissonance

One of the last things you want, probably, is to be accused of hypocrisy—to be criticized for saying one thing and doing another. Like most people, you no doubt want to maintain consistency between your attitudes and your behavior.

But what if a strongly held attitude bumps up against a harsh reality that contradicts it? Suppose you're extremely concerned about getting AIDS, which you believe you might get from contact with body fluids, including blood. Then you're in a life-threatening auto accident in a third-world country and require surgery and blood transfusions—including transfusions of blood from (possibly AIDS-infected) strangers in a blood bank. Do you reject the blood to remain consistent with your beliefs about getting AIDS?

In 1957, social psychologist Leon Festinger proposed the term <mark>cognitive dissonance</mark> to describe the psychological discomfort a person experiences between his or her cognitive attitude and incompatible behavior.[64] Because people are uncomfortable with inconsistency, Festinger theorized they will seek to reduce the "dissonance," or tension, of the inconsistency. How they deal with the discomfort, he suggested, depends on three factors:

- **Importance.** How important are the elements creating the dissonance? Most people can put up with some ambiguities in life. For example, many drivers don't think obeying speed limits is very important, even though they profess to be law-abiding citizens. People eat fried foods, even though they know that ultimately those foods may contribute to heart disease.

- **Control.** How much control does one have over the matters that create dissonance? A juror may not like the idea of voting for the death penalty but believe that he or she has no choice but to follow the law in the case. A taxpayer may object to their taxes being spent on, say, special-interest corporate welfare for a particular company but not feel that he can withhold taxes.

- **Rewards.** What rewards are at stake in the dissonance? You're apt to cling to old ideas in the face of new evidence if you have a lot invested emotionally or financially in those ideas. If you're a police officer who worked 20 years to prove a particular suspect guilty of murder, you're not apt to be very accepting of contradictory evidence after all that time.

The Practical Action box provides an example of three key methods Festinger suggested to reduce cognitive dissonance.

PRACTICAL ACTION | Reducing Cognitive Dissonance through Cognitive Reframing

College students feel a lot of pressure to be bright, intellectual, and capable of juggling all their newfound freedoms and responsibilities. But many also experience high levels of stress as they try to keep it all together. For those who struggle with additional, often invisible stressors such as anxiety, depression, and cognitive challenges and learning disabilities like dyslexia and attention deficit/hyperactivity disorder (ADHD), navigating the college experience can feel downright overwhelming.[65] The negative thoughts, feelings, and inner dialogue that often accompany these experiences can lead to further stress and can affect students' ability to succeed in college.[66]

How can you reduce the cognitive dissonance you experience as a result of high-performance expectations coupled with high stress in college? You can use a therapeutic technique called cognitive reframing (or cognitive restructuring) to identify, challenge, and modify negative thoughts.[67] Learning to reframe

Virgin Group CEO Richard Branson
Will Oliver/Shutterstock

destructive thoughts is a critical life skill that will help you lower your stress by promoting a greater sense of peace and control.[68] Cognitive reframing also fosters innovation.[69]

Give Yourself Some Advice

Virgin Group CEO Richard Branson struggled so much with dyslexia in high school that he dropped out. Now Branson is part of the global charity *Made By Dyslexia*, which aims to help people reframe dyslexia "as a positive influence in their lives." "My dyslexia has shaped Virgin right from the very beginning and imagination has been the key to many of our successes," says Branson.[70] The self-made billionaire suggests people struggling with cognitive differences write a letter to their younger selves explaining that the challenges they face are assets and unique capabilities rather than flaws. In Branson's letter to his teenage self, he says to "use your alternative ways of thinking to be creative and think bigger."[71]

Ask Yourself a Few Questions

Another useful technique for reframing your thoughts is called the ABCDEs of Cognitive Restructuring.[72] When you begin to feel like you aren't good enough, smart enough, or capable enough to succeed in college because of stress or invisible challenges, use this five-step process:

A. Name the event or problem. For example:

I have four exams in one week and my grades are important to me. I don't know how to tackle the challenge of studying in order to earn a high grade on all the exams.

B. List your beliefs about the event or problem.

I don't have enough time to study for all these exams. I will either need to focus on studying for one or two and accept poor performance on the others, or study just enough for each exam to get passing grades on all four.

C. Identify the consequences of your beliefs.

I won't earn the grades I want to earn in all four courses and my GPA will drop. This can reduce my ability to get a good job.

D. Formulate a counterargument to your initial thoughts and beliefs. Pessimistic thoughts are generally overreactions, so the first step is to correct inaccurate or distorted thoughts.

I have not considered creative methods for studying and performing well on all my exams. I may not be able to assemble thorough study guides for all four, but I know

others in my classes are in the same boat, and we may be able to combine our materials and work as a group to study for these exams. I also could ask my professors for advice on narrowing down the content for studying. The worst-case scenario is that I don't earn As on all four exams and I use this experience to learn to prepare earlier for future exams. One bad exam grade may not mean I am unable to earn a high final course grade or find a good job after graduation.

E. Describe how energized and empowered you feel at the moment.

I'm motivated to do as well as I can on these exams. I got into college and have made it this far. There is no reason I can't continue to be a successful student and go on to have a great career.

These questions will help you to identify destructive thought patterns, evaluate their merit, neutralize those that are unrealistic, and work to find solutions to the things causing your stress.

YOUR CALL

Do you struggle with high levels of stress because of your workload, responsibilities, a cognitive difference, or some other invisible challenge such as anxiety or depression that sometimes gets the better of your self-esteem? Which of the preceding suggestions would help you to reframe your experiences in a more positive light?

Behavior: How Values and Attitudes Affect People's Actions and Judgments

Values (global) and attitudes (specific) are generally in harmony, but not always. For example, a manager may put a positive *value* on helpful behavior (global) yet may have a negative *attitude* toward helping an unethical co-worker (specific). Together, however, values and attitudes influence people's workplace **behavior**—their actions and judgments. ●

11.3 Perception and Individual Behavior

THE BIG PICTURE

Perception, a four-step process, can be skewed by five types of distortion: stereotyping, implicit bias, the halo effect, the recency effect, and causal attribution. We also consider the self-fulfilling prophecy, which can affect our judgment as well.

LO 11.3

Describe the way perception can cloud judgment.

If you were a smoker, which warning on a cigarette pack would make you think more about quitting? "Smoking seriously harms you and others around you"? A blunt "Smoking kills"? Or a stark graphic image showing decaying teeth?

This is the kind of decision public health authorities in various countries are wrestling with. (One study found that highly graphic images about the negative effects of smoking had the greatest impact on smokers' intentions to quit.)[73] These officials, in other words, are trying to decide how *perception* might influence behavior.

The Four Steps in the Perceptual Process

Perception is the process of interpreting and understanding one's environment. The process of perception is complex, but it can be boiled down to four steps.[74] *(See Figure 11.2.)*

FIGURE 11.2 The four steps in the perceptual process

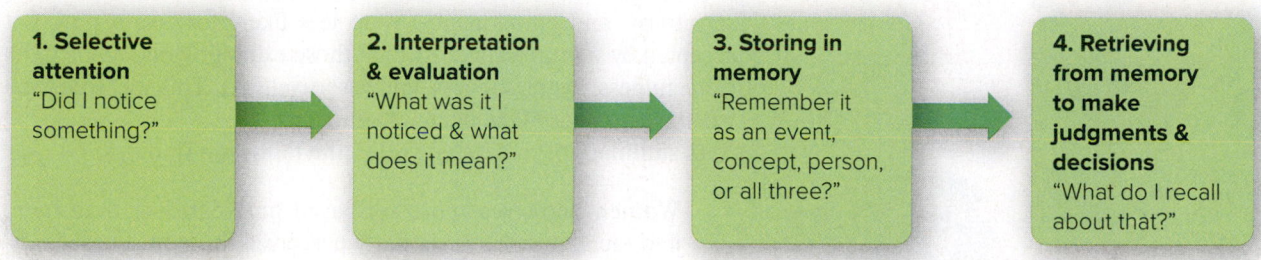

1. Selective attention	2. Interpretation & evaluation	3. Storing in memory	4. Retrieving from memory to make judgments & decisions
"Did I notice something?"	"What was it I noticed & what does it mean?"	"Remember it as an event, concept, person, or all three?"	"What do I recall about that?"

In this book we are less concerned about the theoretical steps in perception than in how perception is distorted, because this has considerable bearing on the manager's judgment and job. In any one of the four stages of the perception process, misunderstandings or errors in judgment can occur. Perceptual errors can lead to mistakes that can be damaging to yourself, other people, and your organization.

Five Distortions in Perception

Although there are other types of distortion in perception, we will describe the following: (1) *stereotyping*, (2) *implicit bias*, (3) the *halo effect*, (4) the *recency effect*, and (5) *causal attribution*.

1. Stereotyping: "Those Sorts of People Are Pretty Much the Same" If you're a tall African American man, do people make remarks about basketball players? If you're of Irish descent, do people believe you drink a lot? If you're Jewish, do people think you're money-oriented? If you're a woman, do people think you're automatically nurturing? All these are stereotypes. **Stereotyping** is the tendency to attribute to an individual the characteristics one believes are typical of the group to which that individual belongs.[75] Stereotyping doesn't have to be linked to only one group. Sometimes, we link multiple stereotypes together, causing the stereotype to get better or worse. For example, if someone negatively stereotypes African Americans and females, that person may attribute even worse characteristics to an African American female. On the other hand, linking can mitigate the negative effects of a stereotype. If someone for instance negatively stereotypes females, but positively stereotypes Asians, that person may not negatively perceive an Asian female.[76]

Principal areas of stereotyping that should be of concern to you as a manager are (1) *sex-role stereotypes*, (2) *age stereotypes*, and (3) *race/ethnicity stereotypes*. (People with disabilities, discussed in Section 11.5, also are apt to be stereotyped.)

Sex-Role Stereotypes A *sex-role stereotype* is the belief that differing traits and abilities make males and females particularly well suited to different roles. In the early days of the tech industry, for instance, computer programming was considered on par with secretarial work. This meant programmers were typically women. The need for higher-skilled and better-paid workers increased as the field became more complex. Guess what happened? Programming was upgraded to "men's work" as it was deemed too advanced for women. Some believe that the male-dominated tech industry today is the result of this stereotype.[77]

Certain personality traits also can be seen as positive for one gender, but negative for the other. Results from a recent Pew Research survey are a good example. Respondents viewed the term "powerful," an important leadership trait, as positive when describing a male and overwhelmingly negative when describing a female. On the flip side, "compassion" and "caring" were seen as positive traits for women, but more negatively for men.[78] Another recent study demonstrated that entrepreneurs displaying stereotypically female traits (warmth, sensitivity, and emotionality) were less likely to have a proposal accepted by venture capitalists than those exhibiting masculine traits (forcefulness, aggressiveness, and assertiveness). This was true even when the content of the pitch was the same.[79]

A summary of research revealed the following findings:

- Women perceived more sex-based mistreatment than men, and racial minorities similarly perceived more race-based mistreatment than whites. On the positive side, however, perceptions of sex and race differences have decreased over time.[80]

- Shareholders were more likely to criticize the actions of a woman CEO compared to her male counterparts regardless of the organization's performance. They also were more likely to tell a woman CEO how to manage the firm.[81]

- Male humor was perceived as more functional and less disruptive than humor expressed by females.[82]

- Women were less likely to be selected for promotions and prestigious positions even if their performance was the same as their male counterparts.[83]

- Less attractive female leaders were judged as being more truthful than attractive women. As a result, attractive women may find it more difficult to elicit high levels of loyalty, organization commitment, performance, and organizational citizenship behavior from their followers. Males generally did not face this issue regardless of their perceived attractiveness.[84]

Age Stereotypes Another example of an inaccurate stereotype is the belief that older workers can't master new skills, are not engaged, and don't have work–life balance. Recent studies refuted all these negative beliefs, but two-thirds of individuals age 45 to 74 still experience age-related discrimination.[85] This finding is problematic because 25% of all U.S. workers are predicted to be over the age of 55 by 2025, and the Transamerica Center for Retirement Studies found that more than half the nation's baby boomers plan to work beyond the age of 65.[86] Further, the labor force of workers aged 65 to 75 and up is expected to grow faster through 2024 than any other, between 4.5 and 6.4% per year, according to the U.S. Bureau of Labor Statistics.[87] Aptive Environmental, a pest solutions provider, is a good example of an organization that is ready for the boom in older workers.

Aptive Environmental Example: Aptive Environmental has locations in more than 3,700 cities nationwide. The company believes that "people make great companies, not the other way around." One of its core values is to "Elevate the Tribe," which means building a positive environment through kindness and loyalty. This extends to older employees as well. Reviewers on employment website *Monster* claim, "The respect for elders . . . is off the charts." Another employee mentioned, "It's awesome to learn from the older employees within the office. They really care about curating the next generations." Aptive Environmental is seeing results as part of their initiative to care for older workers. The company is the fastest-growing pest solutions provider in its industry and ranks #28 in *Entrepreneur's* "2019 Best Companies in America."[88]

Eliminating malaria. In addition to focusing on its employees, Aptive Environmental is also focusing on stopping the spread of malaria by mosquitoes. The company dedicates a portion of its profits to provide assistance to countries with the greatest need to combat the disease. welcomia/Shutterstock

Race/Ethnicity Stereotypes   Consider the stereotypes Dr. Sutton-Ramsey encountered while tending to an emergency room patient at Bellevue Hospital in Manhattan. When the doctor, who is African American, entered the patient's room, the patient's mother "demanded that a physician come in," according to *The Wall Street Journal.* "Well, you've got one, I'm here," said Dr. Sutton-Ramsey. The mother did not believe him and asked to see the physician in charge. The supervisor, who also was black, entered and asked how to be of assistance. "The patient ended up refusing medical care and left the emergency room."[89]

Studies of race-based stereotypes have demonstrated that people of color experience more perceived discrimination and less psychological support than whites.[90] Perceived racial discrimination also was associated with more negative work attitudes, physical health, psychological health, and organizational citizenship behavior.[91] Some of the experiences whites tend to take for granted at work that people of color may not experience include:[92]

- Being consistently in the racial majority.
- Having plenty of role models of their own race.
- Being heard in meetings without having to assert themselves.
- Making mistakes without other people offering race-related excuses for them.
- Succeeding without being hailed as an example of "progress."
- Not being asked to present the "white perspective" on a problem.
- Not having to worry about whether race will impede their career.

Not all race-based stereotypes are considered negative. For example, Asian Americans suffer from the *model minority* stereotype. This stereotype holds that Asian Americans are a "uniformly high achieving racial minority that has assimilated well into American society through hard work, obedience to social mores and academic achievement." As a consequence, many Asian Americans' suffering is "unseen, largely ignored, and overlooked," according to Vivian Tseng, senior vice president of the William T. Grant Foundation.[93]

Organizations have attempted to mitigate racial and ethnic stereotypes through diversity training, promoting positive diversity values, and reducing stereotypical cues in the workplace. Research points to another solution as well: Confront the perpetrator. One study showed that minorities who confronted prejudice in the workplace subsequently experienced more positive relationships with the perpetrator.[94]

2. Implicit Bias: "I Really Don't Think I'm Biased, but I Just Have a Feeling about Some People"   Consider the cause of the following research findings:[95]

- White applicants get around 50% more call-backs than black applicants with the same resume.

- College professors are 26% more likely to respond to a student e-mail when signed by Brad (typical white name) rather than Lamar (typical African American name).

- Physicians recommend less pain medications for black patients than whites when addressing the same injury.

Do you think these outcomes are the result of explicit or implicit bias? **Explicit bias refers to the attitudes or beliefs that affect our understanding, actions, and decisions in a conscious manner.**[96] "I don't let any teenage black men wearing hoodies come into my store; they might hold me up" is an example of explicit bias. Today, managers are unlikely to say white applicants should be chosen over black ones, and doctors don't claim that black patients feel less pain than white ones. What is happening is implicit rather than explicit.[97] **Implicit bias is defined as the attitudes or beliefs that affect our understanding, actions, and decisions in an unconscious manner.**[98] More than 85% of Americans consider themselves to be unprejudiced, but researchers conclude that most hold some degree of implicit racial bias.[99] Field experiments demonstrated that implicit bias affected employment decisions, courtroom decisions, and use of technology.

Judicial bias. Do you think judges are biased against black defendants? If so, how can this bias be eliminated? Renee Jones Schneider/Alamy Stock Photo

Implicit Bias in Employment Decisions   Implicit bias appears to affect employment-related decisions. A recent study showed that racism led to discriminatory decisions in hiring and performance evaluations. Ageism also was found to impact discriminatory hiring decisions.[100] Other studies have shown that supervisors are more likely to rely on gender, race, and other stereotypes when provided with ambiguous, open-ended performance evaluation questions.[101]

Implicit Bias in the Courtroom   The *Sarasota Herald-Tribune* reviewed 80 million electronic criminal records in multiple Florida databases in 2017. It found that judges across the state sentenced black defendants to far more time behind bars than white defendants. This was true even when the defendants committed the same crimes and had similar criminal histories. Some judges in the state were "incredulous and ashamed."[102]

Implicit Bias and Technology   Studies have found that people have implicit biases toward new information technology. Implicit biases about new information technology focus on abstract and unseen characteristics while biases about humans tend to be based on concrete and visible characteristics. Often times, managers believe that new technology is mysterious, nonhuman, and complex, which may erroneously lead them to believe it is superior to existing methods. This is an important implicit bias to be aware of as we are living in a society that is increasingly reliant on technology.[103] One way to reduce this bias is to master the career readiness competency of information technology application, which we introduced in Chapter 1. This will allow you to more effectively evaluate new information technology. (See Table 1.2.)

If changing explicit bias is difficult, taking steps to root out implicit bias is even harder. Nevertheless, police departments, in particular, are taking great steps forward, requiring intergroup contact, positive feedback, clear norms of behavior, and similar matters.[104]

3. The Halo Effect: "One Trait Tells Me All I Need to Know"   We often use faces as markers for gender, race, and age, but face and body characteristics can lead us to fall back on cultural stereotypes. For example, height has been associated with perceptions of prosperity—high income—and occupational success. Excess weight can be stereotypically associated with negative traits such as laziness, incompetence, and lack of discipline.[105] These examples illustrate the **halo effect, in which we form an impression of an individual based on a single trait.** (The phenomenon also is called the *horn-and-halo effect* because not only can a single positive trait be generalized into an array of positive traits, but the reverse also is true.)

As if we needed additional proof that life is unfair, it has been shown that attractive people generally are treated better than unattractive people. Studies show that attractive workers make about 12% more money than unattractive ones, good-looking real estate agents sell more houses, and attractive CEOs bring better stock returns for their companies. Attractive political candidates even win more elections.[106] Clearly, however, if a manager fails to look at *all* of an individual's traits, he or she has no right to complain if that employee doesn't work out.

EXAMPLE   The Halo Effect: Body Weight and Careers

Lulu Hunt Peters was an overweight child and, by early adulthood, weighed 200–220 pounds. She earned a medical degree from the University of California–Berkeley and dropped 70 pounds by adopting a strict low-calorie diet. Her book, *Diet & Health: With Key to the Calories*, sold millions of copies and became the first ever weight-loss book to make the best-seller list. All this happened before the year 1920.[107]

Peters' writings introduced a novel concept to a nation that had most recently been concerned that its citizens didn't have *enough* to eat during wartime. Her message was that being overweight was bad and resulted from individual choices to eat too much and exercise too little.[108] Peters saw obesity as shameful and believed dieting and remaining thin were signs of self-control. Her book even suggested that people who were unable to resist the temptations of food were likely to be immoral in their other behaviors as well.[109] Around this same time, in the early 20th century, Hollywood began to adopt similar ideals, and to this day the Western preference for thinness remains.

Does Higher Weight Equate to Lower Competence?   According to research, organizational decision makers use weight as a substitute for evaluating personal factors that predict work motivation, behavior, and ability. Specifically, there is a strong tendency to equate higher weight with laziness, sloppiness, unprofessionalism, and lower levels of intelligence, conscientiousness, self-discipline, productivity, and competence.[110] In short, organizations view overweight applicants and workers as less capable and less desirable.[111]

These generalizations about weight affect workers in virtually every aspect of organizational life. Almost half of employers say they are less inclined to hire obese candidates. Managers evaluate overweight workers more negatively than thin workers and judge them as less viable for supervisory and leadership roles. Workers who carry more weight typically have lower starting pay and also are more likely to experience bullying and harassment in the workplace.[112] Clearly, body weight activates a halo effect.

The Halo Misperception   Discrimination against overweight individuals stems largely from the misconception that body size is always the result of poor personal choices.[113] In truth, body size tells us very little in the absence of information about a person's genetics, general health profile, bone structure, and many other factors.

YOUR CALL

Do you allow weight to influence your judgments about others' abilities and characteristics? How can you suppress this bias in your role as a manager?

---

4. The Recency Effect: "The Most Recent Impressions Are the Ones That Count"   The **recency effect is the tendency to remember recent information better than earlier information,** perhaps because when you activate your recall, the later recollections are still present in working memory.[114] You see this misperception often operating among investors (even professionals), who are more likely to buy a stock if they see something about it in the news or if it has a high one-day return.[115]

5. Causal Attributions   Causal attribution is the activity of inferring causes for observed behavior. Rightly or wrongly, we constantly formulate cause-and-effect explanations for our own and others' behavior. Attributional statements such as the following are common: "Amir drinks too much because he has no willpower, but I need a few drinks after work because I'm under a lot of pressure."

Even though our causal attributions tend to be self-serving and are often invalid, it's important to understand how people formulate attributions because they profoundly affect organizational behavior. Take for instance a supervisor evaluating an employee with poor performance. The supervisor may reprimand the employee if they believe the poor performance is due to a lack of effort. Or training might be deemed necessary if the supervisor attributes the poor performance to a lack of ability. Finally, the supervisor may attribute the poor performance to bad luck, such as a natural disaster or a virus that has effectively shut down the country. This may lead to the poor performance being excused.[116]

As a manager, you need to be alert to two attributional tendencies that can distort one's interpretation of observed behavior—the *fundamental attribution bias* and the *self-serving bias*.

- **Fundamental attribution bias.** In the fundamental attribution bias, people attribute another person's behavior to his or her personal characteristics rather than to situational factors.

  Example: If someone cuts you off while driving, you are more likely to conclude that the driver is a jerk instead of considering the rationale for their reckless driving. It could be that the driver was rushing to get to the hospital.

- **Self-serving bias.** In the self-serving bias, people tend to take more personal responsibility for success than for failure. Research shows that employees tend to rely on this bias when performance results are public.[117]

  Examples: You get an A on an exam and conclude that it's due to your level of studying. Had you received a poor grade, you would more likely conclude that the professor wrote a poor exam or didn't effectively teach the subject matter. Another example occurs in car accidents, when both parties tend to blame the other driver.[118]

The Self-Fulfilling Prophecy, or Pygmalion Effect

The self-fulfilling prophecy, also known as the Pygmalion ("pig-mail-yun") effect, describes the phenomenon in which people's expectations of themselves or others lead them to behave in ways that make those expectations come true.

Expectations are important. An example is a waiter who expects some poorly dressed customers to be stingy tippers, who therefore gives them poor service and so gets the result he or she expected—a much lower tip than usual. Research has shown that by raising managers' expectations for individuals performing a wide variety of tasks, higher levels of achievement and productivity can be achieved.[119]

The lesson for you as a manager is that when you expect employees to perform badly, they probably will, and when you expect them to perform well, they probably will. (In the G. B. Shaw play *Pygmalion*, a speech coach bets he can get a lower-class girl to change her accent and her demeanor so that she can pass herself off as a duchess. In six months, she successfully "passes" in high society, having assumed the attributes of a woman of sensitivity and taste.)

Research shows that the effect of the self-fulfilling prophecy can be quite strong.[120] That is, managerial expectations powerfully influence employee behavior and performance. Among the things managers can do to create positive performance expectations: Recognize that everyone has the potential to increase his or her performance. Introduce new employees as if they have outstanding potential. Encourage employees to visualize the successful execution of tasks. Help them master key skills.[121] ●

EXAMPLE   "What's within You Is Stronger Than What's in Your Way"[122]

Erik Weihenmayer was diagnosed with an eye disease called juvenile retinoschisis at age 4 and was completely blind by his freshman year of high school. He recalls that, at the time, "I was afraid that I wasn't going to be able to participate in life."[123] But instead of shielding him from opportunities, his parents encouraged him to take up all the activities his peers were tackling.[124] Weihenmayer joined his high school wrestling team and went on to represent Connecticut in the National Junior Freestyle Wrestling Championships.[125] He also realized that the keen tactile senses he'd developed due to the loss of his sight made him especially suited for rock climbing, a hobby that eventually blossomed into a lifelong passion.

In 2001, Weihenmayer became the first blind person to summit Mount Everest.[126] Although Himalayan experts strongly discouraged him from attempting the climb because of his blindness, he persisted. He recalls, "They were judging me on the basis of one thing that they knew about me and that was being blind. But they didn't realize that there are a dozen other attributes that contribute to whether you're a good mountaineer or not."[127] Weihenmayer acknowledges that life isn't always easy but believes strongly that "People have the inner resources to become anything they want to be. Challenge just becomes the vehicle for tapping into those inner resources."[128] By 2008, he had earned the distinction of being one of only a few hundred people in history to complete the seven summits, meaning he has climbed to the top of the highest mountain on each of the seven continents.[129]

Weihenmayer is the co-founder of an organization called *No Barriers*, which aims to help those with challenges live rich and meaningful lives.[130] He believes that all of us should make the conscious decision to do the things that make us uncomfortable and live our most extraordinary lives, in spite of our fears or the beliefs we often allow to limit us.[131] He receives many letters from parents of children who are blind or have other disabilities, asking for guidance. His advice? "The key is to really

Erik Weihenmayer
Imke Lass/Redux Pictures

have tremendously high expectations and to teach kids how to be self-sufficient and confident and give them the skills that they need to succeed."[132]

YOUR CALL

Have you allowed yourself to be limited by certain expectations? What is something you've wanted to do but have been afraid to try because you don't believe you can?

11.4 Work-Related Attitudes and Behaviors Managers Need to Deal With

THE BIG PICTURE

Attitudes are important because they affect behavior. Managers need to be alert to the key work-related attitudes having to do with engagement, job satisfaction, and organizational commitment. Among the types of employee behavior they should attend to are their prosocial behaviors, on-the-job performance and productivity, and absenteeism and turnover.

LO 11-4

Explain how managers can deal with employee attitudes.

"Keep the employees happy," we often hear. It's true that attitudes are important, the reason being that *attitudes affect behavior.* But is keeping employees happy all that managers need to know to get results? We discuss motivation for performance in the next chapter. Here, let us consider what managers need to know about key work-related attitudes and behaviors.

Three types of attitudes managers are particularly interested in are (1) *employee engagement,* (2) *job satisfaction,* and (3) *organizational commitment.*

1. Employee Engagement: How Connected Are You to Your Work?

Research on job involvement has evolved into the study of an individual difference called <mark>employee engagement,</mark> defined as a "mental state in which a person performing a work activity is full immersed in the activity, feeling full of energy and enthusiasm for the work."[133] Employers, consultants, and academics have actively studied the causes and consequences of employee engagement given its potential for increasing individual, group, and organizational performance.[134] Let's consider what we've learned.

What Percentage of Employees Are Fully Engaged at Work? The ADP Research Institute attempted to answer this question by surveying over 19,000 employees around the world in 2015 and 2018. Results are shown in Figure 11.3.[135]

Results in Figure 11.3 reveal a high of 22% in India for 2018 in contrast to a low of 6% in China. The U.S. workforce had approximately 17% of employees fully engaged. The good news from this study is that employee engagement increased in most countries between 2015 and 2018. The bad news is that the global engagement average was only 15.9%. This means that roughly 84% of these employees were not fully engaged. What do you think is the impact of disengagement on important outcomes like performance, customer satisfaction, quality, or profits?

FIGURE 11.3

Fully engaged employees around the world

Source: Data obtained from M. Hayes, F. Chumney, C. Wright, and M. Buckingham, "The Global Study of Engagement Technical Report," ADP Research Institute, 2019.

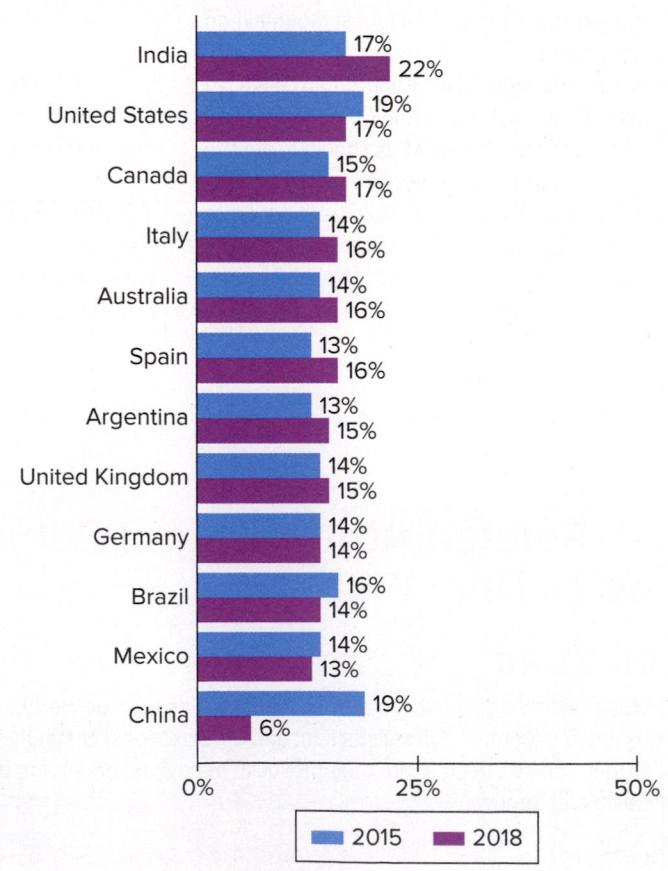

Outcomes Associated with Employee Engagement

Consulting firms such as Gallup, Hewitt Associates, and BlessingWhite have been in the forefront of collecting proprietary data supporting the practical value of employee engagement. For example, Gallup estimates that an organization whose employees are highly engaged can achieve 10% higher customer satisfaction/loyalty, 20% more productivity, and 21% greater profitability.[136] Other recent academic studies similarly showed a positive relationship between employee engagement, performance, and physical and psychological well-being and corporate-level financial performance, customer satisfaction, and control.[137] Waffle House, for example, is using the power of employee engagement.

Waffle House Example: The Waffle House, a 24-hour budget diner, has locations in 25 states, does not advertise, rarely changes its menu, and refused to take credit cards until 2006. What the Waffle House is known for is its robust employee support system. It provides managers bonuses for keeping turnover low and discourages them from overworking people. The restaurant's business model is based on cultivating regular diners. This means the company is looking for employees who smile and are ready to make easy conversation. "You will not be able to fake it," says Randy Coleman, a Waffle House restaurant manager. Waffle House is reaping the benefits of increased employee engagement as a result of its policies. Its employee-owned stock has increased 57 years in a row and the company is opening around 50 new restaurants a year.[138]

Engagement with a side of toast. A Waffle House employee serves diners in Nashville, Tennessee. As a diner, are you able to tell if restaurant staff are engaged? Nathan Morgan/Redux Pictures

How Can Managers Increase Employee Engagement?

There are four research-proven ways for managers to increase employee engagement. Let's explore them:

- **Design meaningful work.** People are engaged when their work contains variety and when they receive timely feedback about performance. Studies show that it is particularly important for employees to be assigned meaningful work that fully employs their skills.[139] For example, some law firms include pro bono time to serve those in poverty as part of each lawyer's job. Select financial brokerages follow the same practice, allowing brokers the opportunity to provide free or discounted advice to underprivileged parents who are sending their kids to college.[140]

- **Improve supervisor-employee relations.** People are more engaged when their manager is supportive and maintains a positive, trusting relationship with them.[141] A recent study found that managers who ignore negative employee emotions, such as anger, lose an opportunity to gain valuable feedback and reduce employee stress and frustration.[142] McDonald's is an example of a company that is taking these findings seriously. The restaurant chain has "stay" meetings, allowing supervisors to feel out employee pain points and build closer relationships with them. The company has found that stay meetings reduce the need for "exit meetings" or exit interviews.[143]

- **Provide learning and development opportunities.** A study by *Udemy for Business* found a strong connection between employee engagement and learning opportunities. The more employees were able to develop their technical and soft skills, the better they felt about their jobs. The study found that the optimal level of learning was between 31 to 50 hours per year, after which engagement decreased. This was most likely because employees still needed time to focus on their day jobs.[144] 1-800 GOT JUNK is a Canadian junk removal franchise that is known for its "A-Player Development Program." Employees are able to take classes on franchise development and strategic planning as part of the program.[145]

- **Reduce stressors.** ==Stressors== are environmental characteristics that cause stress. Studies show that engagement is lower and burnout is higher when employees are confronted with stressors they perceive are out of their control.[146] Take for instance the impact the COVID-19 pandemic had on doctors, nurses, and other hospital workers who could not access critical supplies such as face masks, gowns, and hand sanitizer as waves of infected patients came through their doors. These employees not only had to save the lives of their patients, but also keep themselves safe without proper gear. "Most physicians have never seen this level of angst and anxiety in their careers," said Dr. Stephen Anderson, a 35-year veteran of emergency rooms.[147]

Would you like to get better grades in your classes? One way to do that involves increasing your employee engagement. You can assess your level of engagement with your studies and consider methods to enhance it by taking Self-Assessment 11.5.

SELF-ASSESSMENT 11.5   CAREER READINESS

To What Extent Are You Engaged in Your Studies?

The following survey was designed to assess your level of engagement in your studies. Please be prepared to answer these questions if your instructor has assigned Self-Assessment 11.5 in Connect.

1.   What is your level of engagement?

2.   Find your three lowest-rated items. Based on the content of these items, what can you do to improve your level of engagement? Hint: Doing this requires you to identify the cause of the low ratings for each item.

3   What might you say during an interview to demonstrate that you possess the career readiness competency of self-motivation?

2. Job Satisfaction: How Much Do You Like or Dislike Your Job?

==Job satisfaction== is the extent to which you feel positive or negative about various aspects of your work. Most people don't like everything about their jobs. Their overall satisfaction depends on how they feel about several components, such as *work, pay, promotions, co-workers,* and *supervision.*[148] Among the key correlates of job satisfaction are stronger motivation, performance, job involvement, organizational commitment, and life satisfaction and less absenteeism, tardiness, turnover, and perceived stress.[149]

A recent study by CNBC/Survey Monkey indicates that an impressively high 85% of U.S. employees are somewhat or very satisfied with the jobs.[150] But what is the relationship between job satisfaction and job performance—does more satisfaction cause better performance, or does better performance cause more satisfaction? This is a subject of much debate among management scholars.[151] One comprehensive study found that (1) job satisfaction and performance are moderately related, meaning that employee job satisfaction is a key work attitude managers should consider when trying to increase performance, but (2) the relationship between satisfaction and performance is complex and it seems that both variables influence each other through a host of individual differences and work-environment characteristics.[152]

How satisfied are you with the job you are in now, if you have one, or the last job you had? You can find out by taking Self-Assessment 11.6.

SELF-ASSESSMENT 11.6

How Satisfied Are You with Your Present Job?

The following survey was designed to assess how satisfied you are with your current job, or a previous job, if you're not presently working. Please be prepared to answer these questions if your instructor has assigned Self-Assessment 11.6 in Connect.

1. What is your level of satisfaction with recognition, compensation, and supervision?

2. If you have low to medium satisfaction with any aspect of the job, identify what can be done to increase your job satisfaction. Be sure to consider what you can do, what your boss might do, or what the organization might do. Be specific.

3. Organizational Commitment: How Much Do You Identify with Your Organization?

Organizational commitment reflects the extent to which an employee identifies with an organization and is committed to its goals. It is important because research shows a significant positive relationship between organizational commitment and job satisfaction, performance, turnover, and organizational citizenship behavior—discussed in the next section.[153] Thus, if managers are able to increase job satisfaction, employees may show higher levels of commitment, which in turn can elicit higher performance and lower employee turnover.[154]

Important Workplace Behaviors

Why is it important for you to understand how to manage individual differences? Quite simply, so that you can influence others' behavior. Whether working on a student class project, or a project for your employer, your success partly depends on your ability to influence others' behavior.

One important classification of behavior is prosocial behavior (PSB), defined as voluntary behavior intended to benefit another, such as helping, donating, sharing, and comforting.[155] Do you engage in PSB? Whether or not you do, Figure 11.4 explains the driver of PSB and its consequences.

Figure 11.4 reveals that PSB is driven by the individual difference of prosocial motivation (PSM), which represents the desire to promote the well-being of others.[156] PSM explains why Microsoft founder Bill Gates is so committed to helping others through the Bill and Melinda Gates Foundation.

FIGURE 11.4

Model of prosocial behavior

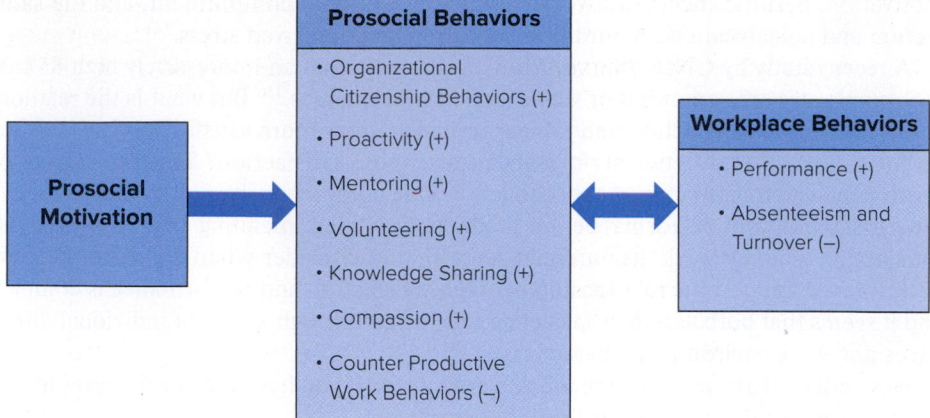

Prosocial Motivation → Prosocial Behaviors
- Organizational Citizenship Behaviors (+)
- Proactivity (+)
- Mentoring (+)
- Volunteering (+)
- Knowledge Sharing (+)
- Compassion (+)
- Counter Productive Work Behaviors (–)

↔ Workplace Behaviors
- Performance (+)
- Absenteeism and Turnover (–)

Bill Gates Example: Philanthropist Bill Gates and his wife Melinda Gates established the Bill and Melinda Gates Foundation in 2000. The organization is the largest private foundation in the world with over $46 billion in assets. The foundation helps people around the world lead healthy and productive lives by lifting communities out of hunger and extreme poverty.[157] Bill Gates accumulated his wealth as the co-founder, CEO, and president of Microsoft, where he was known to be a leader who inspired his followers.[158] He believes his time at Microsoft gathering teams of engineers and learning how they are inspired to be the reason he now has the "superpower" of transformational leadership. He is using this superpower to motivate those working on vaccines for diseases such as HIV and COVID-19.[159] Gates's success at Microsoft and at his foundation is largely attributed to his high level of conscientiousness, positivity, and empathy, according to *Business Insider.*[160]

Presidential achievement. Former President Barack Obama (right) awards the Presidential Medal of Freedom to Bill Gates (center) and his wife Melinda Gates (left) in 2016. The medal is the highest civilian award of the United States. Chip Somodevilla/Getty Images

Studies show that PSM may be the reason you help colleagues in the workplace, volunteer to do things that aren't part of your job responsibilities, and remain committed to your employer during hard times. Indeed, it is no surprise that organizations can benefit from boosting employees' PSM.[161]

Returning to Figure 11.4, researchers discovered that PSM leads to increased PSB. Although there are many forms of PSB, Figure 11.4 shows those that are particularly relevant for today's organizations. Research reveals that PSM was positively associated with organizational citizenship behaviors (discussed shortly), being proactive, mentoring others, volunteering, sharing knowledge with others, and being compassionate. What organization wouldn't want to see its employees display these positive behaviors? PSM also lead to a decrease in counter productive work behaviors (discussed shortly).[162] PSBs are most important to managers because they foster higher productivity and lower turnover (see Figure 11.4).

Notice the two-headed arrow between PSB and workplace behaviors. This illustrates the fact that PSBs not only lead to positive workplace behaviors, but positive workplace behaviors encourage people to engage in PSBs. For example, studies demonstrate that high performing work environments increase organizational citizenship behaviors.[163]

Sadly, PSM can sometimes be so strong that individuals engage in prosocial behaviors at personal cost.[164] Li Wenliang, a Wuhan doctor, is a good example of someone who demonstrated prosocial behaviors in the face of danger.

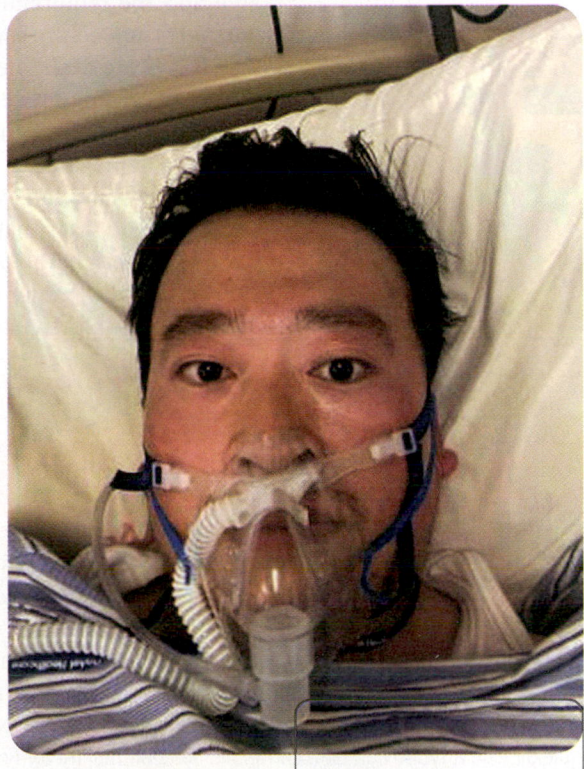

Dr. Li Wenliang
Li/Ropi/Newscom

Dr. Wenliang Example: Dr. Li Wenliang proactively tried to stop the spread of the COVID-19 pandemic in Wuhan, China, by warning others about the virus weeks before the government acknowledged it. After his messages went viral, Wenliang was reprimanded by Wuhan Police for his whistleblowing and threatened with jail time if he continued "rumor-mongering." The ophthalmologist returned to work at Wuhan Central Hospital after his encounter with police—putting his own safety at risk—with the hopes of saving others. Unfortunately, he died from the virus a few weeks later.[165]

We now focus on the two most frequently studied examples of PSB: organizational citizenship behaviors and counterproductive work behaviors. We'll then discuss the workplace behaviors of performance and turnover.

Organizational Citizenship Behaviors   One key outcome of increased PSM is increased **organizational citizenship behaviors (OCBs),** which are those employee behaviors that are not directly part of employees' job descriptions—that exceed their work-role requirements.[166] Examples include conscientiousness (working hard), sportsmanship (being positive during challenging times), civic virtue (working for the good of the organization), courtesy (respecting coworkers), and altruism (helping others).[167] Studies demonstrate a significant and moderately positive correlation between organizational citizenship behaviors and job satisfaction, productivity, efficiency, and customer satisfaction.[168] However, research also shows that although organizational citizenship behaviors should be promoted in the workplace, employees should not be pressured to engage in these behaviors. Pressuring employees is bad because it makes people believe they are being asked to perform more duties than expected, which makes them more reluctant to engage in them. Thus, providing employees with autonomy in determining whether, to whom, when, and how to help others is a simple way to encourage OCBs.[169]

Counterproductive Work Behaviors   Just as PSM increases OCBs, it also reduces counterproductive work behaviors (CWBs), which are types of behavior that harm employees and the organization as a whole.[170] Such behaviors may include absenteeism and tardiness, drug and alcohol abuse, and disciplinary problems but also extend to more serious acts such as accidents, sabotage, sexual harassment, violence, theft, and white-collar crime.[171] Some 98% of workers say they have witnessed or experienced uncivil behavior at their jobs.[172]

Clearly, if an employee engages in some kind of CWB, the organization needs to respond quickly and appropriately, defining the specific behaviors that are unacceptable and the requirements for acceptable behavior.[173] The problem, however, is that managers and co-workers do not have adequate opportunity to observe CWBs.[174] That's why it is more desirable to take preventive measures.[175] One way is to screen for CWB during the hiring process. For instance, it's been found that applicants scoring higher on cognitive ability (intelligence) tests are less likely to be involved in violence and property damage after they are hired.[176] Employees also are less likely to engage in CWB if they have satisfying jobs that offer autonomy, are treated fairly, aren't ostracized or asked to do tasks that fall outside their roles, and don't supervise too many people.[177] Finally, leader characteristics impact employee behavior too.[178] For example, a recent study found that leader narcissism contributed to employee CWBs.[179] The Example box discusses an unfortunate result of CWBs—a toxic workplace.

EXAMPLE   The Toxic Workplace: "Rudeness Is Like the Common Cold"[180]

Incivility. Rudeness. Jerks at work. They're all forms of counterproductive work behaviors or CWBs, and they're the bane of the office.

"Nothing is more costly to an organization's culture than a toxic employee," says management professor Christine Porath. "Rudeness is like the common cold—it's contagious, spreads quickly, and anyone can be a carrier."[181] Researcher Trevor Foulk concurs. "If someone is rude to me," he says, "it is likely that in my next interaction I will be rude to whomever I am talking to. You respond to their rudeness with your own rudeness."[182]

Sapping Energy and Productivity   Management professor Gretchen Spreitzer believes that difficult co-workers are "de-energizers" who spread their dispiriting attitude to others. "They leave you feeling depleted, fatigued, and exhausted."[183] A study supported this conclusion. People experiencing incivility from a co-worker ended up with fewer resources for controlling their own impulses later on. The more someone had to interact with a de-energizer, the more likely that person was rude to others.[184]

Examples of incivility include snippy remarks, interruptions, eye-rolling, and berating another employee for being late.[185] Toxic bosses may demoralize employees by such actions as "walking away from a conversation because they lose interest; answering calls in the middle of meetings without leaving the room; openly mocking people by pointing out their flaws or personality quirks in front of others," and similar incivilities, says Porath.[186]

Who's Most Likely to Be Uncivil?   Research has found that women tend to be the victims of incivility more than men. Men,

however, aren't usually the instigators. In fact, a recent study found that the perpetrators of incivility toward women tend to be other women.[187] Another study found that managers perceived victims of rudeness at work as having been the cause of incivility, even when they'd done nothing wrong. Even worse, this bias negatively impacted the manager's assessment of the victim's job performance. Victims, therefore, received less compensation and fewer promotions, adding insult to injury.[188]

The Price of Incivility   People who engage in negative and harmful behavior can hurt an organization's bottom line.[189] In fact, "avoiding a toxic employee can save a company more than twice as much as bringing on a star performer—specifically, avoiding a toxic worker was worth about $12,500 in turnover costs," says one writer.[190]

A study demonstrated that the costs of incivility are diminished well-being and job satisfaction, as well as increased job stress and withdrawal.[191] What's more, research suggests that it only takes *one* uncivil co-worker to cause feelings of isolation, job insecurity, and even health problems in others.[192] "The truth is that rude, abusive, harassing, and bullying behavior has been costing organizations big-time for decades," says Carrie Penman, chief compliance officer of NAVEX Global.[193]

YOUR CALL

If you were working in a toxic workplace and had to stay there for a while, what would you do to make things better?

In addition to the general positive effects of PSBs, managers are encouraged to foster PSBs because they are associated with increased performance and productivity, as well as decreased absenteeism and turnover.[194]

Performance and Productivity

Every job has certain expectations, but in some jobs performance and productivity are easier to define than in others. How many contacts should a telemarketing sales rep make in a day? How many sales should he or she close? Often a job of this nature will have a history of accomplishments (from what previous job holders have attained), so that it is possible to quantify performance behavior.

However, an ad agency account executive handling major clients such as a carmaker or a beverage manufacturer may go months before landing this kind of big account. Or a researcher in a pharmaceutical company may take years to develop a promising new prescription drug.

In short, the method of evaluating performance must match the job being done.

Absenteeism and Turnover

Should you be suspicious of every instance of absenteeism? Of course, some absences—illness, death in the family, or jury duty, for example—are legitimate. However, a lot of no-show behavior is related to job dissatisfaction.[195] One study of around 6,000 employees found that 40% called in sick simply because they didn't feel like going to work that day. The top three reasons for employees taking bogus sick days are for doing personal errands, catching up on sleep, and relaxing.[196]

Acting sick. A significant number of employees take bogus sick days because they don't feel like going to work. Do you believe companies should do more to validate if an employee is really sick? Dmytro Zinkevych/Shutterstock

Absenteeism may be a precursor to turnover, which, as we saw in Chapter 9, is when an employee abandons, resigns, retires, or is terminated from a job. Every organization experiences some turnover, as employees leave for reasons of family, better job prospects, or retirement. However, except in low-skill industries, a continual revolving door of new employees is usually not a good sign, because replacement and training are expensive. The Society for Human Resource Management estimated the average dollar cost of hiring a new employee to be $4,129 and put the time investment at 42 days.[197] That dollar amount may be a conservative estimate. Gallup suggests the cost of replacing a highly skilled employee can be as high as two times the employee's annual salary. As a consequence, voluntary turnover costs U.S. businesses $1 trillion a year.[198] The turnover challenge extends to losing temporary workers—individuals who sign contracts with predetermined end dates. In fact, research finds that temporary workers often develop organization-specific knowledge that is hard to replace.[199]

Experience demonstrates five practical ways to reduce turnover: (1) Base hiring decisions on the extent to which an applicant's values fit the organization's values. (2) Provide post-hiring support, which is referred to as onboarding. As we mentioned in Chapter 9, onboarding programs help employees to integrate and transition to new jobs by making them familiar with corporate policies, procedures, culture, and politics by clarifying work-role expectations and responsibilities.[200] (3) Focus on enhancing employee engagement and social networks.[201] (4) Incorporate realistic job previews (RJPs, discussed in Chapter 9) into the hiring process. (5) Offer employees benefits, such as flexible work hours (discussed in Chapter 12), that meet their needs and values.[202]

Increasing PSBs Managers can increase PSBs in their organizations by fostering PSM (*See Figure 11.4.*). This can be done by focusing on the drivers of PSM. Researchers believe there are two broad categories of drivers: dispositions and traits (internal to you) and situational and environmental factors (external to you).[203] We'll look at each individually and provide an example of how managers can strengthen each type of driver.

- Dispositions and traits include personality, values, self-esteem, empathic concern, positive emotions, feelings of competence, and humility. As a manager, one way you can improve this driver is by recruiting individuals with traits associated with PSM. Take for instance conscientiousness and agreeableness, which you learned about in Section 11.1. Research finds that high levels of these traits increase PSM.[204] Another way you can improve this driver is by providing opportunities for your employees to learn and develop some of these dispositions on and off-the-job, which we discussed in Chapter 9.

- Situational and environmental factors can foster PSM. For example, you will learn in Chapter 12 that jobs can be designed or structured in such a way that employees feel like they are doing meaningful work and that they are responsible for work outcomes. Both of these psychological states can fuel PSM.[205] Other situational and environmental factors include concepts we have discussed in the past, or will discuss in future chapters: organizational culture (Chapter 8), HR practices (Chapter 9) procedural justice (Chapter 12), norms (Chapter 13), servant leadership (Chapter 14), and transformational leadership (Chapter 14).

Putting it all together, the best companies understand that fostering PSM requires a two-pronged approach. First, organizations need to have HR practices in place that will lead to the recruitment or development of employees with traits and dispositions conducive to PSM. Second, companies need to develop jobs, policies, and an overall culture that lead to PSM. As a result, organizations will not only reap the performance-related benefits of PSB, but they will have employees who genuinely care about others. ●

11.5 The New Diversified Workforce

THE BIG PICTURE

One of today's most important management challenges is working with stakeholders of all sorts who vary widely in diversity—in age, gender, race, religion, ethnicity, sexual orientation, capabilities, and socioeconomic background. Managers also should be aware of the differences between internal and external dimensions of diversity and barriers to diversity.

LO 11-5

Identify trends in workplace diversity that managers should be aware of.

Might you hold a few preconceptions that are worth examining? Here's a reality check:

- **Assumption: Illegal immigrants dramatically affect the U.S. economy.** No, says the American Immigration Council. Undocumented immigrants represent less than 5% of the civilian workforce.[206]

- **Assumption: The racial wage gap has just about disappeared.** Unfortunately not, suggests a study of 1.8 million salaries of white men and men of color. African American men earn $0.87 for every dollar a white man earns. Hispanic or Latino workers earn $0.91 for every dollar earned by a white man.[207]

- **Assumption: Young workers earn less than they used to.** Yes, evidently. Federal Reserve data shows that Millennials earn 20% less today than 25–34-year-olds did in 1989. Another study found that the ability for children to earn more than their parents did has dropped by more than 40% since the 1940s.[208]

The United States is becoming more diverse in its ethnic, racial, gender, and age makeup. The trends that will shape the United States in the next few decades include (1) having more older people than children for the first time, (2) the current white majority becoming a minority, (3) there no longer being any single ethnic or racial majority, (4) millennials making up 75% of the workforce, (5) a rise in women participating in the workforce (particularly in senior leadership positions), (6) a drop in the share of middle-class households, and (7) a rise in the number of people who describe themselves as unaffiliated with any organized religion.[209]

Diversity enriches. A diverse population in a company can provide ideas, experience, and points of view that strengthen the business culture. What has been your experience, if any, with a diverse workplace?
Flamingo Images/Shutterstock

These upcoming trends require leaders to take a closer look at their current diversity practices so they remain competitive. "At Morgan Stanley, diversity is an opportunity—for clients, employees and the firm. By valuing diverse perspectives, we can better serve our clients while we help employees achieve their professional objectives," says James Gorman, the company's chairman and CEO.[210] Research finds that effective diversity practices are essential for an organization's success, yet many firms do not successfully manage them.[211] Let's explore this issue in more detail.

How to Think about Diversity: Which Differences Are Important?

Diversity represents all the ways people are unlike and alike—the differences and similarities in age, gender, race, religion, ethnicity, sexual orientation, capabilities, and socioeconomic background. Note here that diversity is not synonymous with differences. Rather, it encompasses both differences and similarities. Recent studies demonstrate that you should manage both simultaneously, with an understanding that diversity is complex and changes over time.[212]

To help distinguish the important ways in which people differ, diversity experts Lee Gardenswartz and Anita Rowe have identified a "diversity wheel" consisting of four layers of diversity: (1) *personality*, (2) *internal dimensions*, (3) *external dimensions*, and (4) *organizational dimensions. (See Figure 11.5.)*

Let's consider these four layers:

FIGURE 11.5

The diversity wheel

Four layers of diversity

Source: From Diverse Teams at Work *by Lee Gardenswartz and Anita Rowe. Copyright 2003, Society for Human Resource Management, Alexandria, VA.*

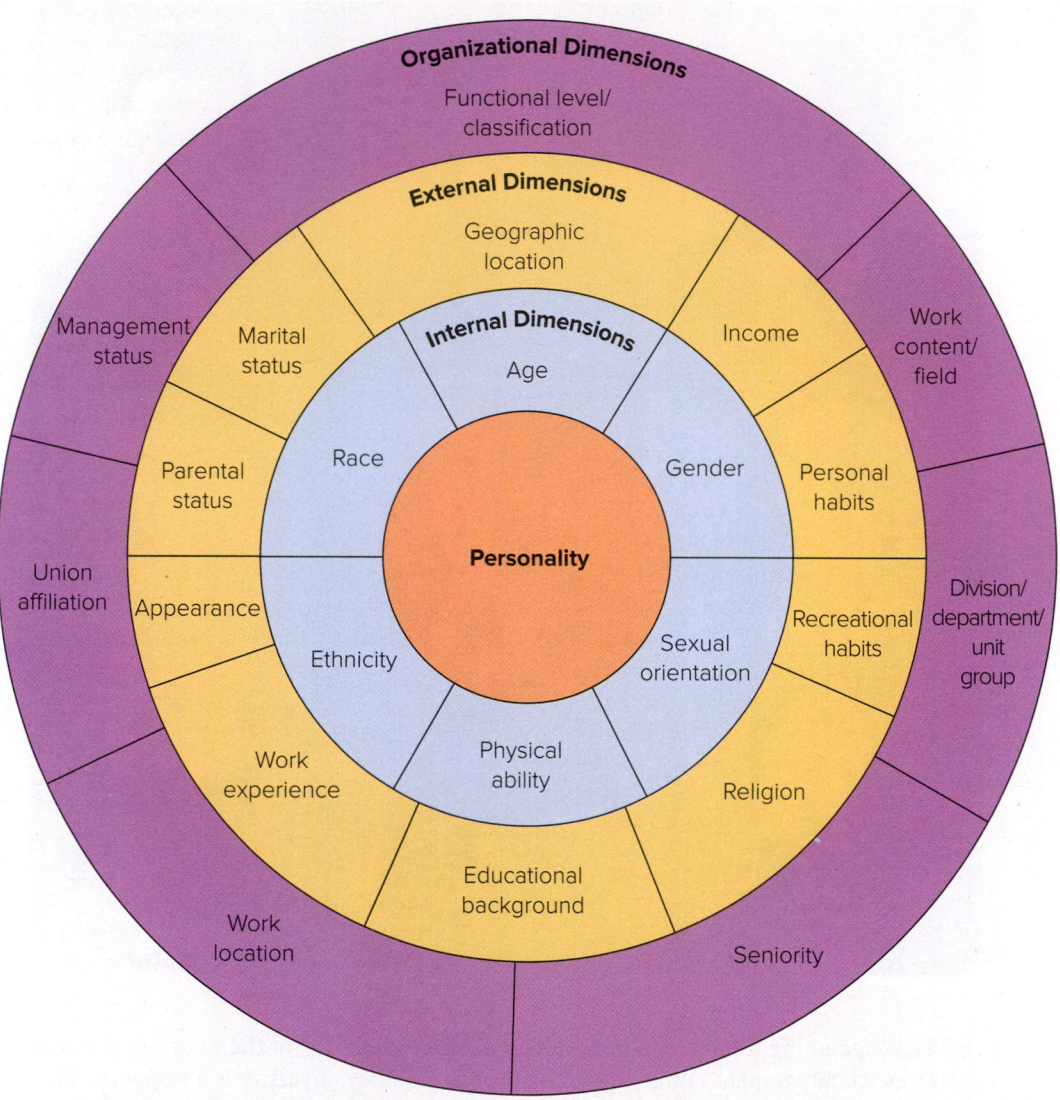

Personality   At the center of the diversity wheel is personality. It is at the center because, as we said in Section 11.1, *personality* is defined as the stable physical and mental characteristics responsible for a person's identity.

Internal Dimensions   Internal dimensions of diversity are those human differences that exert a powerful, sustained effect throughout every stage of our lives: gender, age, ethnicity, race, sexual orientation, and physical abilities.[213] These are referred to as the *primary* dimensions of diversity because they are not within our control, for the most part. Yet they strongly influence our attitudes, expectations, and assumptions about other people, which in turn influence our own behavior.

What characterizes internal dimensions of diversity is that they are visible and salient in people. And precisely because these characteristics are so visible, they may be associated with certain stereotypes—for instance, that certain ethnic groups carry viruses.

Viral Outbreak Example: The COVID-19 pandemic caused an outbreak of prejudice against East Asian communities (the first reported case of the virus was in Wuhan, China). "If you are seen to be Asian [even] if you are not coughing or displaying symptoms, people naturally walk away from you," according to Brian Wong, a Rhodes Scholar from Hong Kong. This denigration of certain populations is nothing new. Africans were targeted during the 2014 Ebola outbreak because the virus was first detected in Congo. Middle Easterners also faced discrimination in 2012 during the Middle East respiratory syndrome (MERS) outbreak. "Stigma, to be honest, is more dangerous than the virus itself," said WHO director-general Tedros Adhanom Ghebreyesus. The WHO now opts against denoting geographic locations when naming new viruses in order to reduce such stigma.[214]

Human targets. The first reported case of the COVID-19 pandemic was in China, which led to discrimination against East Asians around the world.
asiandelight/Shutterstock

External Dimensions

External dimensions of diversity include an element of choice; they consist of the personal characteristics that people acquire, discard, or modify throughout their lives: educational background, marital status, parental status, religion, income, geographic location, work experience, recreational habits, appearance, and personal habits. They are referred to as the *secondary* dimensions of diversity because we have a greater ability to influence or control them than we do internal dimensions.

Veterans Example: External dimensions exert a significant influence on our perceptions, behavior, and attitudes. Take for instance the roughly 245,000 U.S. veterans who leave the military annually. The transition to civilian life can be difficult due to the mental and physical toll war has taken on many of them. Moreover, many organizations see veterans as blindly having followed orders during their military service and not having leadership skills. This perception "couldn't be further from the truth," says Jim Farrell, senior vice president of operations at PepsiCo. Farrell, a former U.S. Army officer, believes veterans know how to think on their feet and balance the needs of teammates while accomplishing the mission. Toby Johnson, is a good example of how veterans can transition from military service to corporate America. Johnson was an Apache helicopter pilot during the early 2000 Iraqi invasion before returning to the United States and studying business. She landed her first job managing a Frito Lay factory in Pennsylvania and is now the company's vice president of sales operations.[215]

Organizational Dimensions

Organizational dimensions include management status, union affiliation, work location, seniority, work content, and division or department.

Trends in Workforce Diversity

How is the U.S. workforce apt to become more diverse in the 21st century? Let's examine five categories on the internal dimension—*age*, *gender*, *race/ethnicity*, *sexual orientation*, and *physical/mental abilities*—and one category on the external dimension, *educational level*.

Age: More Older People in the Workforce

Millennials have replaced baby boomers as the largest adult generation in the United States.[216] Yet they will find many older workers working alongside them. Over 20% of adults over 65 were either working or looking for work in 2019, compared to 10% in 1985. These older workers also were more educated—53% had at least a college degree, compared to 25% in 1985.[217]

Not only are older workers staying in the workforce longer, but a trend called "unretirement" also is becoming more common, say economists. Recent surveys have found that, thanks to longer life spans, employers' desire for experienced talent, and better

Age is just a number. An engineer (left) shows equipment to an apprentice (right). What benefits do you see to people of different generations working together?
Shutterstock

health, more than half of workers approaching retirement in the next five years expect they will return to work.[218] While income is sometimes the reason, an economist from Harvard Medical School found three other motivators in data from a national study: a sense of purpose, mental stimulation, and social engagement.[219]

Though many older workers either stay in the workforce or want to come back after retirement, they still face many challenges. For example, around 56% of workers over 50 are pushed out of jobs before they plan to retire. Older workers are going to great lengths to conceal their age as a result. Many shorten their work histories on social media and in conversations, others forgo displaying photographs of their grandchildren, and some even get cosmetic surgery. "There hasn't yet been a groundswell of consciousness-raising about age the way there is about gender, race and sexual preference," says Kathleen Christensen, director of the Alfred P. Sloan Foundation's working longer project. For instance, just 8% of CEOs said their diversity and inclusion strategies included a conversation about age, according to a PwC study.[220] These results are alarming in light of research that demonstrates age-inclusive firm strategies help older workers maintain or improve their well-being, engagement, and performance.[221]

Do you have much experience being around older people? How do you feel about the idea of working with them? To find out, try Self-Assessment 11.7.

SELF-ASSESSMENT 11.7   CAREER READINESS

What Are Your Attitudes about Working with Older Employees?

The following survey was designed to assess your attitudes about working with older employees. Please be prepared to answer these questions if your instructor has assigned Self-Assessment 11.7 in Connect.

1. What is the quality of your relationships with older employees? How about your satisfaction with working with older people?

2. How might the quality of relationships with older employees affect your performance and promotability?

3. What things might you say during an interview to demonstrate that you can work with people of all ages?

Gender: More Women Working   Women constituted the majority of the workforce (50.04%) at the start of 2020 for the first time in history. They also were awarded more college degrees than men, earning 57.3% of bachelor's, 59.4% of master's, and 53.3% of doctorate degrees.[222] Women also outnumbered men in medical school (50.5%) and law school (51.3%).[223] In addition, more businesses are now owned by women. They currently own more than 12 million businesses, which earn about $1.8 trillion annually.[224] Finally, women are gaining some ground in the top rungs of business. In 2020, women held 28 CEO positions in the Standard & Poor's 500 companies.[225]

Though these are uplifting statistics, the pay gap between men and women still exists. Specifically, women earned $0.81 cents for each dollar a man made in 2018.[226] This is particularly alarming because the percentage of families with children, who are headed by a single mother, nearly doubled between 1974 and 2015.[227] Factors contributing to the gap's persistence include education attainment, work experience, and gender discrimination. On this last point, around 42% of women say they have experienced gender discrimination at work, according to a Pew Research Center survey.[228]

Many countries have taken steps to fix the gender wage gap by implementing transparency laws. These laws require employers to disclose annual salaries, allowing women workers to see how much their male counterparts are making doing the same job. A recent study found that pay transparency laws did in fact reduce the gender pay gap, particularly in unionized workplaces that could quickly act on the information.[229]

The obstacles to women's progress are collectively known as the **glass ceiling**—the metaphor for an invisible barrier preventing women and minorities from being promoted to top executive jobs. Women are more likely than men to complete a college degree by the time they are 31,[230] so what factors are holding women back? Let's explore three.

- **Overwork**. One study found that the crushing culture of overwork disproportionately penalized women. This is because women are encouraged to take accommodations, such as going part-time or shifting to internally facing roles, when there are competing work–family demands.[231] Research suggests that companies find ways to keep employees involved with the organization when utilizing accommodations, such as letting mothers retain their laptops when on maternity leave.[232] This flexibility can increase female employee engagement and reduce stress.[233]

- **Stereotyping**. Experts believe that unconscious biases, often ingrained in corporate culture, put the brakes on the advancement of women.[234] These biases are implicit because they are unconscious, as we discussed earlier in the chapter. "If we want to change our behavior, we first need to understand the beliefs and assumptions in our company culture that underpin that behavior," says Caroline Gosling, an organizational change consultant.[235] Studies suggest three strategies, among many others, for changing this culture. First, companies need to ensure that senior leaders explicitly support gender balance. Second, organizations should seek out high performers (stars) who can provide effective mentoring for female leaders. Finally, there should be greater fairness and transparency regarding policies related to hiring and promotion.[236]

- **Flawed facts**. Only one in five women make it to the C-suite while research has found that men and women are very similar in confidence, appetite for risk, and negotiating skills.[237] This may be because men tend to sing their own praises more than women do. For example, one study found that men were 21% more likely to use stronger, more positive language about themselves than women.[238] And though men may

Female leadership. Marillyn Hewson, Chairman and Chief Executive Officer of the Lockheed Martin Corporation, during an Economic Club of Washington event. Hewson oversees a company with revenues exceeding $59 billion and over 100,000 employees. Kris Tripplaar/Newscom

praise themselves more, research does not support these praises. In fact, recent studies have found that peers, subordinates, and bosses believe women outperform men on key leadership competencies such as taking initiative, building relationships, collaboration and teamwork, and integrity and honesty.[239] Other studies have found that companies with more women executives have better financial performance, decision-making, and productivity.[240] One such study, by the Credit Suisse Research Institute, concluded that "the higher the percentage of women in top management, the greater the excess returns for shareholders."[241] We discuss women in leadership further in Chapter 14 and women and communication in Chapter 15.

Race and Ethnicity: More People of Color in the Workforce

The non-Hispanic white population in the United States is projected to decrease by 19 million people by 2060. In addition, whites are projected to change from 76.9% in 2016 to 68% in 2060; African Americans from 13.3% to 15%; Asians from 5.7% to 9.1%; Hispanics or Latinos from 17.8% to 27.5%; and American Indian/Alaskan Native from 1.3% to 1.4%.[242] People of color have hit the glass ceiling, with whites holding more of the managerial and professional jobs. In addition, two other trends show that U.S. businesses need to do a lot better by minority populations.

First, minorities tend to earn less than whites. Median household income in 2018 was $41,361 for African Americans and $51,450 for Hispanics. It was $70,642 for non-Hispanic whites. (Asians had the highest median income, at $87,194.)[243] A recent study uncovered why there may be such an income gap between African Americans and whites. The study found that employers are less likely to negotiate higher salaries with African American candidates, leading to significantly lower starting salaries than white job seekers.[244] Another trend supported by research is that minorities experienced more perceived discrimination, racism-related stress, and less psychological support than whites did.[245]

Some organizations have turned to *tokenism* to increase the visibility of minorities. **Tokenism is the practice of doing something symbolic to prevent criticism and give the appearance that people are being treated fairly.**[246] An organization may for instance recruit a small number of people from underrepresented groups in order to give the appearance of equality within a workforce. Studies show that tokenism has a negative impact on performance but may at times be unavoidable. In these cases, managers should ensure that all team members feel respected and included.[247]

Reversing these practices is important as effectively managing race and ethnic diversity in an organization increases its chances of success. For example, a study by McKinsey found that "companies in the top-quartile for ethnic and cultural diversity on their executive teams are 33 percent more likely to have industry-leading profitability."[248] Another study found that when workplace teams resemble their customers, the team is "more than twice as likely to innovate effectively for their end users."[249]

Sexual Orientation: LGBTQ People Become More Visible

It is difficult to accurately estimate the number of people in the United States who identify as part of the LGBTQ (lesbian, gay, bisexual, transgender, queer) community. A Gallup poll found 4.5% of the population so identified, or about 11 million people, up from 8.3 million in 2012.[250]

One likely reason it is difficult to estimate the LGBTQ population is that surveys on the topic have used different definitions of the terms and asked inconsistent questions.[251] Another is the possibility that negative attitudes about non-normative sexuality have made people reluctant to identify themselves as LGBTQ. In fact, a report by the Human Rights Campaign Foundation found that almost half of all LGBTQ Americans remain closeted in the workplace.[252] This is a concerning statistic as recent research shows that being your true self at work increases productivity, job satisfaction, work engagement, and well-being.[253]

Transgender is a term for people whose sense of their gender differs from what is expected based on the sex characteristics with which they are born.[254] That is, these are the estimated 1.3 million adults who feel their bodies and genders do not match, that the gender label they received at birth does not fit.[255] They may use labels such as *gender fluid* and *nonbinary*.

People in the United States have become more supportive of gay and lesbian rights over time, with 73% saying in 2019 that society should accept homosexuality, up from 56% 10 years before.[256] No doubt things will change further, since the U.S. Supreme Court made it clear in June 2015 that marriage is no longer *solely* a legal union between a man and a woman. "The right to marry is a fundamental right inherent in the liberty of the person," Justice Anthony Kennedy wrote (in *Obergefell v. Hodges*) in support of the majority ruling that states may not refuse to marry same-sex couples. "Under the Due Process and Equal Protection Clauses of the Fourteenth Amendment couples of the same sex may not be deprived of that right and that liberty."[257]

Meanwhile the pay gap that used to hold for gay and bisexual men has disappeared, and according to one report, gay men now earn on average 10% *more* than straight men in similar employment.[258] While studies are inconclusive, it appears that lesbian women have enjoyed a pay advantage over straight women (though not over men of any sexual orientation) and continue to do so, possibly because of career choices they make and the fact that women earn lower salaries overall.[259]

Provisions of the Affordable Care Act made it illegal for federally funded health care providers to discriminate against the LGBTQ community, but one-third of transgender people reported in a study that they had experienced at least one negative interaction with a health care provider. This ranged from denial of treatment to physical assault.[260] Another study found that 20% of LGBTQ adults have avoided seeking medical care out of fear of discrimination.[261] And, despite the changing social and legal landscape, "between 11 percent and 28 percent of LGBQ workers report losing a promotion simply because of their sexual orientation." Moreover, in a study of almost 28,000 transgender U.S. workers, 67 percent reported being fired, forced to resign, not hired, or denied a promotion in the past year.[262] Forty-two percent of LGBTQ people in a recent study reported using "vague language" to discuss their relationships, and 37% said they had hidden such a relationship to avoid being discriminated against. "When you're perceived as feminine— whether you're a woman or a gay man," said one gay man at a Fortune 500 company, "you get excluded from relationships that improve your career."[263]

People with Differing Physical and Mental Abilities

About 61 million people, or 25% of the U.S. population, have a disability that impacts major life activities, according to the Centers for Disease Control (CDC).[264] However, only about 30% of those between 16 and 64 are employed, and the unemployment rate for those with a disability is double that of those without.[265]

Since 1992 the **Americans with Disabilities Act (ADA)** has prohibited discrimination against people with disabilities and requires

Disability. Everyone recognizes the wheelchair as signifying that a person has a disability, but other disabilities are not easily identified—and may not invite understanding. Do you think that mental disabilities, for example, should be accommodated in employment? If you were subject to mood swings, do you think that would prevent you from doing your job effectively? Disability Images/Blend Images LLC

organizations to reasonably accommodate an individual's disabilities.[266] Research shows that the ADA has helped narrow the disability employment gap, but more work remains to be done.[267] In a recent survey of more than 3,000 supervisors by the nonprofit Kessler Foundation, only 28% of respondents said their organizations have disability hiring goals. One problem the supervisors reported was their perception that upper management was less committed to providing the training and accommodations that would be required for employees who required them.[268] Yet, according to Helena Berger, president of American Association of People with Disabilities, "having a disability may make you a better problem solver. You may be more innovative."[269]

Studies confirm that organizations can benefit from hiring those with disabilities. These benefits include increased profitability, innovation, and overall competitive advantage, as well as a more inclusive work culture.[270] Organizations can hire those with disabilities in greater numbers and take advantage of these benefits by (1) creating partnerships with organizations that work on behalf of those with disabilities, (2) highlighting stories of people with disabilities doing jobs that people assume they cannot do, and (3) collaborating with offices of disability services on college and university campuses to identify opportunities for graduating students with disabilities.[271]

Educational Levels: Mismatches between Education and Workforce Needs

Two important mismatches between education and workplace are these:

- **College graduates may be in jobs for which they are overqualified.** According to the Federal Reserve Bank of New York, about a third of all college graduates are overqualified for their jobs.[272] In other words, a great many college graduates are underemployed—working at jobs that require less education than they have. This number is higher than previous periods of similar economic growth, but experts believe the situation will be temporary for many. These individuals will see increased earnings as they gain more experience in their fields.[273]

- **High-school dropouts and others may not have the literacy skills needed for many jobs.** A recent study found that 5.4% of all people in the United States between the ages of 16 and 24 had dropped out of high school in 2017. Men have a higher dropout rate than women (6.4% versus 4.4%) and American Indian/ Alaska Native youth have the highest rate of any ethnicity.[274] If, as has been alleged, more than three-quarters of the American workforce reads below ninth-grade level, that is a problem for employers, because about 70% of the on-the-job reading materials are written at or above that level.[275]

Barriers to Diversity

Some barriers are erected by diverse people themselves. In the main, however, most barriers are put in their paths by organizations.[276] When we speak of "the organization's barriers," we are, of course, referring to the *people* in the organization—especially those who may have been there for a while—who are resistant to making it more diverse.

Resistance to change, which was discussed in Chapter 10, is an attitude that all managers come up against from time to time, and resistance to diversity is simply one variation. It may be expressed in the following six ways.

1. Stereotypes and Prejudices   Ethnocentrism is the belief that your native country, culture, language, abilities, or behavior is superior to those of another culture. When differences are viewed as being weaknesses—which is what many stereotypes and prejudices ultimately come down to—this may be expressed as a concern that diversity hiring will lead to a sacrifice in competence and quality.

2. Fear of Discrimination against Majority Group Members   Some employees are afraid that attempts to achieve greater diversity in their organization will result in bias against the majority group—that more black or Asian employees will be promoted to fire captain or police lieutenant, for example, over the heads of supposedly more qualified whites. Google recently fired an engineering employee for writing a long memo, which was soon made public, about why women (in his view) are not inherently suited for jobs in technology. The fired employee has sued Google, claiming the company discriminates against conservative white men.[277] A similar case happened with a white recruiter from YouTube. He claimed the company retaliated "against him after he complained that the video site discriminated against white and Asian male applicants in favor of hiring blacks, Hispanics and women." Alphabet Inc., parent company of Google and YouTube, told *The Wall Street Journal* that it would defend itself in both cases.[278]

3. Resistance to Diversity Program Priorities   Some companies, such as SAP, Procter & Gamble, and Levi Strauss & Co., have taken aggressive diversity approaches, such as offering special classes teaching tolerance for diversity and seminars in how to get along.[279] Some employees may see diversity programs as distracting them from the organization's "real work." In addition, they may be resentful of diversity-promoting policies that are reinforced through special criteria in the organization's performance appraisals and reward systems.

4. A Negative Diversity Climate   Diversity climate represents employees' perceptions about the extent to which an organization supports diversity.[280] Diversity climate is positive when employees view the organization as being fair to all types of employees, which promotes employee loyalty and overall firm performance.[281] It also enhances psychological safety. Psychological safety reflects the extent to which people feel free to express their ideas and beliefs without fear of negative consequences.[282] "Psychological safety isn't about being nice," says Amy Edmondson, who first coined the term. "It's about giving candid feedback, openly admitting mistakes, and learning from each other."[283] Research shows that psychological safety improves team and organizational performance, creativity, and organizational engagement.[284]

5. Lack of Support for Family Demands   In 2018, nearly 7 in 10 American children lived in families with two parents.[285] In 63% of such families, both parents worked; in 29.5%, only the father worked; and in 5%, only the mother worked.[286] Yet in a great many households, it is still women who primarily take care of children, as well as other domestic chores. When organizations aren't supportive in offering flexibility in hours and job responsibilities, these women may find it difficult to work evenings and weekends or to take overnight business trips. A few companies—such as Starbucks, McDonald's, IBM, AT&T, and Walmart—have begun offering or improving existing paid family leave policies, a benefit 94% of respondents recently told a Pew Center survey they thought would help families.[287] Congress recently passed the "Federal Employee Paid Leave Act," which grants federal employees up to 12 weeks of paid family leave for the birth, adoption, or foster of a new child.[288]

6. A Hostile Work Environment for Diverse Employees   Hostile work environments are characterized by sexual, racial, and age harassment and can be in violation of Equal Employment Opportunity law, such as Title VII of the Civil Rights Act.[289] Whether perpetrated against women, men, older individuals, or LGBTQ people, hostile environments are demeaning, unethical, and appropriately called "work environment pollution." A recent example involves Brinker Restaurant Corp, which owns Chili's and Maggiano's Little Italy restaurant chains. The company was sued by the Equal Opportunity Employment Commission (EOEC) in 2019 for subjecting female employees to "inappropriate touching, sexual gesturing and verbal harassment" and then retaliating against them if they complained. The company reached an agreement with the EOEC in 2020, agreeing to provide the women $150,000 and vowing to change employment practices that lead to a hostile work environment.[290] Data from the U.S. Equal Employment Opportunity Commission revealed that almost a third of the 72,675 complaints it received in 2019 involved sex.[291] You certainly won't get employees' best work if they believe the work environment is hostile toward them.

Ultimate Software is a good example of a company that has attempted to effectively manage diversity by overcoming these six barriers. ●

EXAMPLE   Ultimate Software's "People First" Culture

Ultimate Software is #2 on *Fortune* magazine's list of the *Best Places to Work* and has been included in the top 10 for four years in a row. The company specializes in cloud-based people management solutions and prides itself on putting "People First" in an inclusive environment that fosters respect for every employee.[292] "At Ultimate, it's the individual strengths, unique experiences, diverse views, and creative ideas of our people that make us who we are—working together and thriving as one team," says Vivian Maza, the company's chief people officer.[293] Here are some of the ways Ultimate is winning at diversity management.

Health and Family Benefits Ultimate pays 100% of its employees' health care premiums (medical, dental, vision), including coverage for costly fertility treatments. These benefits extend to families, including same-sex married couples. Employees enjoy paid maternity/paternity/adoption leave, and unlimited paid time off means they can worry less about taking time away from work to address personal or family needs.[294]

Communities of Interest The company prides itself on its five unique communities of interest: PRIDEUS (People Respecting Individual Differences Empower Ultimate Software), Women in Leadership, UltiVETS, UltiHOPE, and Women in Technology. These informal groups give employees opportunities for socializing, professional networking, and community service, and they provide professional development, diversity trainings (such as on transgender sensitivities), and peer-support groups for minorities in leadership positions.[295] All the communities are inclusive, meaning that anyone who considers him or herself an "ally" of the individuals represented in the groups is welcome to join.

Members also volunteer and raise money for nonprofit organizations and ally communities. For example, Ultimate's PRIDEUS group partnered with the Miami HEAT to sponsor the annual *Loud and Proud Dance Party* in South Florida, an event celebrating life and diversity for the LGBTQ+ community.[296] The *Women in Leadership* group sponsors the "Athena Scholarship," which gives two $20,000 college scholarships each year to daughters of Ultimate employees who are pursuing college careers in technology or who demonstrate superior leadership skills in their schools or communities.[297]

Technology Ultimate promotes diversity and fosters inclusion in its workplace through cutting-edge technology. Its main cloud-based offering, award-winning UltiPro, aims to help other companies do the same. UltiPro's advantage is that it integrates virtually all a company's HR needs into one seamless, inclusive platform that simplifies and elevates performance management using cutting-edge data capabilities. It provides managers with up-to-date, unbiased information needed for employment decisions, and it keeps employees on track toward their performance and career goals by recommending, and often providing, necessary trainings and professional development opportunities. The platform supports the unique cultural, fiscal, language, and legal/compliance needs for multiple users in multiple locations across the country or globe.[298]

Ultipro is designed to help companies clear many common diversity management hurdles. Its business intelligence tools can capture rich data across multiple levels to assess whether the organization is meeting strategic diversity goals.[299] Its intuitive design and cultural adaptability make it user-friendly for workers of all ages, digital competencies, and backgrounds. Its reliance on quantifiable metrics reduces the influence of unconscious biases in decision making.[300] The platform also overcomes social networking barriers separating diverse workers by identifying, recommending, and facilitating connections and mentorships between employees.[301] Finally, its UltiPro Perception tool helps mitigate one of the key diversity management issues in organizations by giving employees an accessible and anonymous way to voice needs, concerns, and opinions to upper management.[302]

YOUR CALL

Which of an organization's diversity management initiatives will be most important to you when you are interviewing for jobs? To what extent would Ultimate's diversity programs help recruit the best talent?

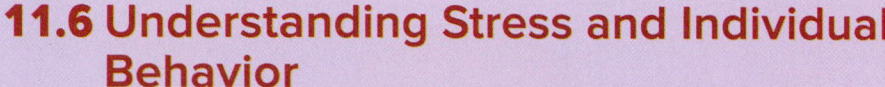

11.6 Understanding Stress and Individual Behavior

THE BIG PICTURE

Stress is what people feel when enduring extraordinary demands or opportunities and are not sure how to handle them. There are six sources of stress: individual differences, individual task, individual role, group, organizational, and nonwork demands. We describe some consequences of stress and discuss three methods organizations use to reduce it.

Stress is the tension people feel when they are facing or enduring extraordinary demands, constraints, or opportunities and are uncertain about their ability to handle them effectively.[303] Stress is the feeling of tension and pressure; the source of stress is called a *stressor*. Stress is generally caused by situations like overwork, unpredictable schedules and night shifts, unsafe workplaces, low wages, layoffs of colleagues, conflict at work, and family worries like the need to care for ill relatives while working.[304]

In this section we'll first consider what managers need to know about the sources and toll of job-related stress. The focus then turns to how organizations can reduce stressors. We'll conclude by discussing corporate wellness programs.

LO 11.6

Discuss the sources of workplace stress and ways to reduce it.

The Toll of Workplace Stress

Although stress, and our response to it, are highly personal events, here are some alarming statistics:[305]

- Around 83% of working U.S. adults suffer from work-related stress causing up to $300 billion in business losses, according to the American Institute of Stress.

- A 2019 Gallup poll found that Americans are "among the most stressed-out populations in the world" with over half of the population experiencing stress during the day.

- The U.S. Centers for Disease Control (CDC) report that stress is the leading workplace health problem.

- Around 62% of workers report that their work is the biggest stressor in their life.

- An estimated 1 million people are absent from the U.S. workplace each day due to stress-related factors.

Stress can cause conflicts and distraction at work; make you fatigued all the time; and generate problems like cardiovascular disease, chronic back pain, anxiety, and insomnia.[306]

From an organizational perspective, workplace stress diminishes positive emotions, job satisfaction, organizational commitment, and job performance and increases alcohol and illicit drug use, workplace deviance, and job turnover.[307] Indeed, historically researchers have generally believed that there is an *inverted U-shaped relationship* between stress and performance. *(See Figure 11.6.)* That is, low levels of stress lead to low performance (because people are not "charged up" to perform), but high levels of stress also lead to an energy-sapping fight-or-flight response that produces low performance. Optimal performance, according to this hypothesis, results when people experience moderate levels of stress.[308]

FIGURE 11.6

Stress and performance

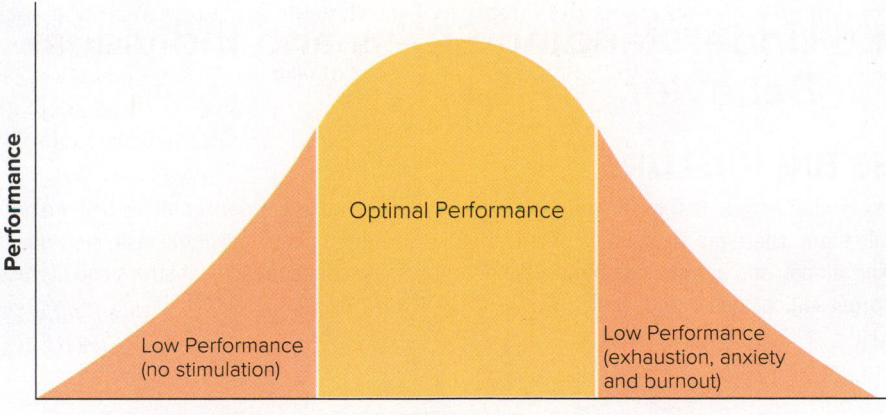

While a moderate amount of stress can have some health and behavioral benefits,[309] excess or negative stress reveals itself in three kinds of symptoms:

- **Physiological signs:** Lesser physiological signs are sweaty palms, restlessness, backaches, headaches, upset stomach, and nausea. More serious signs are hypertension and heart attacks.

- **Psychological signs:** Psychological symptoms include forgetfulness, boredom, irritability, nervousness, anger, anxiety, hostility, and depression. Research shows that 40% of Americans suffer from anxiety during the work day.[310]

- **Behavioral signs:** Behavioral symptoms include sleeplessness, changes in eating habits, and increased smoking/alcohol/drug abuse.[311] Studies show that when leaders don't get sleep they are more likely to be inpatient and abusive while also less charismatic.[312]

If stress is extreme, burnout can result. **Burnout is a state of emotional, mental, and even physical exhaustion,** expressed as listlessness, indifference, or frustration. Factors contributing to burnout include "always-on" work cultures, advanced technology, demanding bosses, difficult clients, and inefficient co-workers.[313] Clearly, the greatest consequence is reduced productivity. Research demonstrates that overstressed employees are apt to call in sick, get injured or have accidents, and have poor work performance.[314]

How Does Stress Work?

Stress has both physical and emotional components. Physically, according to Canadian researcher Hans Selye, considered the father of the modern concept of stress, stress is "the nonspecific response of the body to any demand made upon it."[315] Emotionally, stress has been defined as the feeling of being overwhelmed, "the perception that events or circumstances have challenged, or exceeded, a person's ability to cope."[316]

Stressors can be *hassles*, or simple irritants, such as misplacing or losing things, having concerns about one's physical appearance, and having too many things to do. For example, a frustrating morning commute was found to create stress and impair performance.[317] Stressors also can be *crises*, such as responding to a hurricane, global pandemic, stock market crash, or school shooting. These types of stress put your body and brain on red alert. "As our bodies get ready for responding to threat with a flight-or-flight response, that affects our cognition and perception," says psychologist Mauricio Delgado. "It narrows our attention and focus."[318] There also are *strong stressors*, which can dramatically strain a person's ability to adapt—for example, extreme physical discomfort, such as chronic severe back pain.

Stressors can be both *negative* and *positive*. That is, being fired or getting divorced can be a great source of stress, but so can being promoted or getting married. As Selye writes, "It is immaterial whether the agent or the situation we face is pleasant or unpleasant; all that counts is the intensity of the demand for adjustment and adaptation."[319] In addition, Selye distinguished between bad stress (what he called "distress"), in which the result of the stressor can be anxiety and illness, and good stress ("eustress," pronounced *yu stress*), which can stimulate a person to better coping and adaptation, such as performing well on a test.[320] In this discussion, however, we are mainly concerned with how stress negatively affects people and their performance.

The Sources of Job-Related Stress

There are six sources of stress on the job: (1) *demands created by individual differences*, (2) *individual task demands*, (3) *individual role demands*, (4) *work–life conflict*, (5) *group demands*, and (6) *organizational demands*.

1. Demands Created by Individual Differences: The Stress Created by Genetic or Personality Characteristics   Some people are born worriers, those with a gene mutation (known as BDNF) that Yale researchers identify with people who chronically obsess over negative thoughts.[321] Others are impatient, hurried, deadline-ridden, competitive types with the personality characteristic known as Type A behavior pattern, meaning they are involved in a chronic, determined struggle to accomplish more in less time.[322] Type A behavior has been associated with increased performance in the work of professors, students, and life insurance brokers.[323] However, it also has been associated with greater cardiovascular activity and higher blood pressure, as well as to heart disease, especially for individuals who showed strong feelings of anger, hostility, and aggression.[324]

2. Individual Task Demands: The Stress Created by the Job Itself   Some occupations are more stressful than others.[325] Being a retail store manager, for instance, can be quite stressful for some people.[326] But being a home-based blogger, paid on a piecework basis to generate news and comment, may mean working long hours to the point of exhaustion.[327] Jobs that require "emotional labor"—pretending to be cheerful or smiling all the time, no matter how you feel—can be particularly demanding.[328]

Low-level jobs can be more stressful than high-level jobs because employees often have less control over their lives and thus have less work satisfaction. Being a barista, day care teacher, hotel concierge, or purchasing agent, jobs that don't usually pay very well, can be quite stressful.[329]

3. Individual Role Demands: The Stress Created by Others' Expectations of You   Roles are sets of behaviors that people expect of occupants of a position. Stress may come about because of *role overload*, *role conflict*, and *role ambiguity*.[330]

- **Role overload:** Occurs when others' expectations exceed your ability. Example: If you as a student are carrying a full course load plus working two-thirds time plus trying to have a social life, you know what role overload is—and what stress is. Similar things happen to managers and workers.

- **Role conflict:** Occurs when someone feels torn by the different expectations of important people in one's life. Example: Your supervisor says the company needs you to stay late to meet an important deadline, but your family expects you to be home for your child's birthday party.

- **Role ambiguity:** Occurs when others' expectations are unknown. Example: You find your job description and the criteria for promotion vague, a complaint often voiced by newcomers to an organization.

Jobs with high task and role demands but low levels of personal control are particularly troublesome. In these cases, people are likely to find that their efforts to complete work activities are blocked, resulting in persistent stress, discomfort, and burnout. The

Have you ever felt like this person? Many jobs are stressful, some because people's lives are at stake (military personnel, firefighters, police officers), some because they are highly deadline-driven (event coordinators, public relations executives). What techniques do you use to manage stress? Do you ever just ignore it and plow through your daily activities?
Andrey_Popov/Shutterstock

problem is that individuals do not have the resources, power, or authority to influence the way the work gets done or the timelines for completion.[331] A seven-year study of people working in jobs with low control and high job demands experienced a "15.4% increase in the odds of death compared to low job demands. For those in high control jobs, high demands are associated with a 34% decrease in the odds of death compared to low job demands."[332]

4. Work–Family Conflict ==Work–family conflict== occurs when the demands or pressures from work and family domains are mutually incompatible.[333] Work and family can conflict in two ways: Work responsibilities can interfere with family life, and family demands can interfere with work responsibilities.[334]

For instance, an employee who is caring for an aging mother skips a department meeting to take his mother to a doctor's appointment (family interferes with work). Perhaps another day he works late to finish a report on time and has to reschedule his mother's follow-up appointment (work interferes with family).

Both these types of conflicts matter because their effects spill over both at home and at work causing a host of health issues.[335] Moreover, studies indicate that more than half of all employees believe that work–family balance is very important.[336] From a management perspective, we recommend that organizations strive to reduce stressors, increase employee engagement, and implement wellness programs to assist employees in balancing their work and family demands.[337] Wellness programs are discussed in the next section.

Recent research suggests that supervisors and senior executives should be cautious about work–life decisions that are only focused on their own ideologies (e.g., mothers should be primary caregivers to newborns) because preferences such as these can lead to negative outcomes.[338] For example, companies like American Express, Lululemon, Prudential, and Netflix have implemented gender-neutral parental-leave policies to help parents balance responsibilities associated with a newborn. Netflix, for instance, has raised the bar across the organization, allowing employees to take a full year of paid time off after the birth of a child.[339]

5. Group Demands: The Stress Created by Co-workers and Managers Even if you don't particularly care for the work you do but like the people you work with, that feeling can be a great source of satisfaction and prevent stress. When people don't get along, that can be a great stressor. Even if you have stress under control, a co-worker's stress might bother you, diminishing productivity.[340]

In addition, managers can create stress for employees. A boss who consistently engages in workplace behaviors like overt self-promotion, unwillingness to listen, a tendency to make unreasonable demands, lying, unfair decision making, and a general lack of ethics can become a source of stress.[341]

6. Organizational Demands: The Stress Created by the Environment and Culture The physical environments of some jobs are great sources of stress: poultry processing, asbestos removal, coal mining, firefighting, police work, ambulance driving, and so on. Even white-collar work can take place in a stressful environment, with poor lighting, too much noise, improper placement of furniture, and lack of privacy.

An organizational culture that puts high-pressure work demands on employees will fuel the stress response. One stressor that companies are beginning to recognize as a two-edged sword is the way in which communication technologies make it possible for even corporate employees to be on call around the clock, able or even encouraged to answer e-mails and other messages at night, on the weekend, and even on vacation.[342] To counter the stress-inducing effects of never getting away from the office, PwC uses a pop-up note to remind employees that they're checking their work e-mail on the weekend.[343] Health care consulting firm Vynamic discourages employees from both sending and responding to e-mails between 10 at night and 7 in the morning. "Stress was showing up as a challenge for our team—an area that we weren't really making improvements on," said CEO Dan Calista. "Through some conversations about the abundance of e-mail and the always-being-on nature of our jobs, we realized that this could be a great opportunity to create a structured way to disconnect on a regular basis, not just for vacations."[344]

European companies have taken stronger action. Volkswagen blocks after-hours e-mails to employees' phones, and Daimler deletes e-mails sent to employees who are on vacation.[345] Porsche is considering following their example by returning out-of-hours e-mails to the senders. Said one executive in favor of the change, "To read and reply to e-mails from the boss during the evenings is unpaid working time which increases stress—that's just not acceptable."[346] France has gone even further, effectively banning work e-mails during certain after-work hours for companies with more than 50 employees, adopting a new "right to disconnect" law similar to one already enacted in Germany in 2014.[347]

Reducing Stressors in the Organization

There are all kinds of **buffers**, or administrative changes, that managers can make to reduce stressors and improve employee well-being.[348] This section reviews six recommendations, starting with attempts to help people develop their resilience.

- **Build resilience.** *Resilience* represents the capacity to consistently bounce back from adversity and to sustain yourself when confronted with challenges.[349] It is a career readiness competency desired by employers. Do you think people are born resilient, or is it something that is learned over time? The consensus is that it represents a capacity that is developed over time.[350] Consider the example of inventor James Dyson. Dyson spent five years testing more than 5,000 versions of what he hoped would be a better vacuum cleaner that operated on the same principle as a cyclone. Today, his company, named after him, markets the Dual Cyclone bagless vacuum and almost 60 other products. His net value is over $13 billion.[351]

James Dyson with the Dyson Hot fan heater.
Dyson/Shutterstock

Resilience assists you in achieving goals by encouraging positive thinking in the face of setbacks and challenges. That is one reason it represents a career readiness competency desired by employers. To what extent do you possess the career readiness competency of resilience? Find out by taking Self-Assessment 11.8.

SELF-ASSESSMENT 11.8   CAREER READINESS

What Is Your Level of Resilience?

The following survey was designed to assess your level of resilience. Please be prepared to answer these questions if your instructor has assigned Self-Assessment 11.8 in Connect.

1.   What is your level of resilience?

2.   Looking at your item scores, identify the three areas where you scored lowest. Now, propose one idea for improving each these aspects of resilience. Be specific.

3.   What things might you say during an interview to demonstrate that you possess this career readiness competency?

Some strategies for building resilience are practicing mindfulness, which helps reduce stress, learning how to prioritize incoming information so you will process it more effectively and make better decisions, taking frequent short breaks from work to restore your focus, and mentally detaching from problems so you can respond to them rather than reacting emotionally.[352] Other recommendations include practicing optimism, using cognitive reframing when faced with challenges, remembering your comebacks from adversity, supporting others, and getting the proper amount of sleep.[353]

- **Roll out employee assistance programs.** Employee assistance programs (EAPs) include a host of programs aimed at helping employees to cope with stress, burnout, substance abuse, physical and mental health-related problems, family and marital issues, and any general problem that negatively influences job performance.[354] These assistance programs are especially important when it comes to employee mental health. Take for instance the percentage of workers reporting very good or excellent mental health, which differs across generations:

  - Gen Zers: 45%

  - Millennials: 56%

  - Gen Xers: 51%

  - Boomers: 70%

  The figures show that Gen Zers are the least likely to report a high level of mental health compared to other generations. This is a concern given the fact that Gen Zers, who started entering the workforce in 2019, are now the most populous generation.[355]

- **Recommend a holistic wellness approach.** A holistic wellness program focuses on self-responsibility, nutritional awareness, relaxation techniques, physical fitness, and environmental awareness. This approach goes beyond stress reduction by encouraging employees to try to balance physical, mental, and social well-being by accepting personal responsibility for developing and adhering to a health promotion program. Google's wellness program is discussed in the Example box.

EXAMPLE   Google's Wellness Initiatives

It's hard to find an article on successful corporate wellness programs that doesn't mention Google. The company's approach has become a gold standard against which other companies measure success in this arena.[356] Google clearly cares about its employees' well-being and quality of life. Here are some of the statements Google makes to its employees with its wellness initiatives.

We Want Employees to Feel Good Google offers a variety of onsite services to help employees feel better when they're not at their best, including physicians, physical therapists, and chiropractors.[357] Some managers reward employees with massage credits to cash in with one of the onsite masseurs, and the company encourages those in need of some extra zzz's to take a snooze in one of its nap pods.[358]

Google encourages employees to be proactive about their health with perks like reduced health insurance premiums for those who pursue fitness and a host of opportunities to do so during the workday. Googlers have access to free fitness centers, exercise classes, and bicycles and are encouraged to play intramural sports. Standing desks keep employees up and active, and workplace showers make workers feel more comfortable after riding bikes to work or breaking a sweat during workday exercise.[359]

We Want Employees to Eat Well Working at Google means having access to three healthy meals a day, plus healthy snacks, for free. The corporate office houses more than 30 eateries and cafés that serve a variety of entrees, juices, and snack options.[360] Color-coding nudges employees to make good choices; green or transparent containers hold healthier options like vegetables, and red or opaque ones hold options like croutons and cookies.[361] One employee said having the food options "saves me time and money, and helps me build relationships with my colleagues."[362] If free food wasn't enough, the company also offers its employees free cooking classes.[363]

We Want Employees to Have Fun and Learn New Things Google employees get to have fun at work. They have access to LEGO stations, ping-pong tables, bowling alleys, and

Googling food. Employees at Google headquarters in Mountain View, California can choose a free lunch from 15 different cafes on campus. What other company perks can help destress the workday? Erin Siegal/ Redux Pictures

arcade machines and can travel between floors using slides instead of elevators or stairs.[364]

We Want Employees to Stress Less Google does its part to ensure its employees are able to manage the stresses of daily life. There's a mindfulness meditation program for those who want to meditate and a concierge service that runs errands so employees have fewer demands to satisfy outside work.[365] Employees can even get free onsite haircuts.[366] Google tries to take care of life's bigger worries too. Surviving spouses receive 50% of their deceased loved one's salary for 10 years, and each child gets $1,000 per month until the age of 19.[367] Employees also have access to financial planning services and advisors to help them plan for the future.[368]

YOUR CALL

Which of Google's wellness perks are most appealing to you? How important will a corporate wellness program be for you when you are choosing an employer?

- **Create a supportive environment.** Job stress often results because employees work under poor supervision and lack freedom. Wherever possible, it's better to keep the organizational environment less formal, more personal, and more supportive of employees. Mentoring also can help reduce stress—for both mentors and mentees.[369] Some companies are helping employees relieve financial worries by paying them small amounts of money as an incentive to set cash aside in an emergency fund.[370]

- **Make jobs interesting.** Stress also results when jobs are routinized and boring. It's better to try to structure jobs so that they allow employees some freedom and variety.[371]

- **Make career counseling available.** Companies such as IBM make career planning available, which reduces the stress that comes when employees don't know what their career options are and where they're headed. •

11-7 Career Corner: Managing Your Career Readiness

Describe how to develop the career readiness competencies of positive approach and emotional intelligence.

This chapter has implications for developing at least six competencies associated with our model of career readiness *(see Figure 11.7)*: self-awareness, generalized self-efficacy, social intelligence, emotional intelligence, positive approach, and resilience. This section focuses on developing the attitude of positive approach and improving emotional intelligence.

FIGURE 11.7
Model of career readiness
©2022 Kinicki & Associates, Inc.

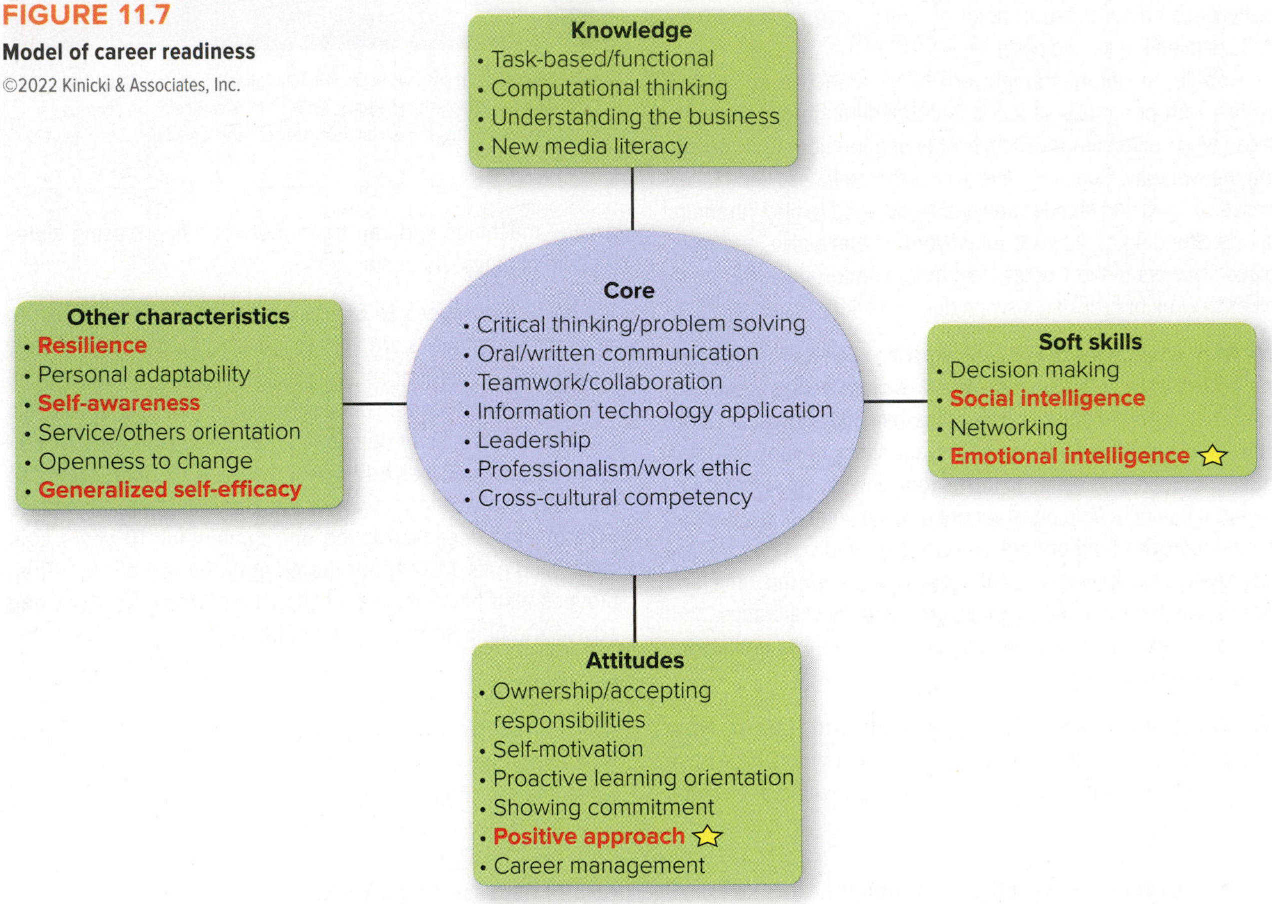

Knowledge
- Task-based/functional
- Computational thinking
- Understanding the business
- New media literacy

Core
- Critical thinking/problem solving
- Oral/written communication
- Teamwork/collaboration
- Information technology application
- Leadership
- Professionalism/work ethic
- Cross-cultural competency

Other characteristics
- **Resilience**
- Personal adaptability
- **Self-awareness**
- Service/others orientation
- Openness to change
- **Generalized self-efficacy**

Soft skills
- Decision making
- **Social intelligence**
- Networking
- **Emotional intelligence** ⭐

Attitudes
- Ownership/accepting responsibilities
- Self-motivation
- Proactive learning orientation
- Showing commitment
- **Positive approach** ⭐
- Career management

Fostering a Positive Approach

A *positive approach* represents a willingness to accept developmental feedback, to try and suggest new ideas, and to maintain a positive attitude at work. Maintaining a positive approach is hard given the hustle and bustle of life and employers' increased expectations for employees. We recommend a two-step approach for developing a positive approach.

Step 1: Identify Potentially Bad Attitudes
We all have bad days or stressful moments. The purpose of this step is to identify the types of negative behaviors that tend to crop up when you have a bad day or a stressful moment. This awareness can

help you replace potentially negative behaviors with positive ones. Answer the following questions.[372]

- Are you a *porcupine*? Porcupines send out verbal and nonverbal messages that say, "Stay away from me."

- Are you an *entangler*? Entanglers want to involve others in their interests. They push their concerns and want to be heard, noticed, and listened to.

- Are you a *debater*? Debaters like to argue even if there is no issue to debate.

- Are you a *complainer*? Complainers point out the problems in a situation but rarely provide solutions of their own.

- Are you a *blamer*? Blamers are like complainers but point out negatives aimed at a particular individual.

- Are you a *stink bomb thrower*? Stink bomb throwers like to make sarcastic or cynical remarks, use nonverbal gestures of disgust or annoyance, and sometimes yell or slam things.

Based on your answers, which bad behaviors do you tend to exhibit? Now consider how these behaviors may be perceived by others. It won't be positive. How can you catch yourself starting to behave in these negative ways? Finally, what can you do to replace these negative tendencies with positive ones? Be specific.

Step 2: Identify "Good Attitude" Behaviors   This step aims to assist you in breaking down the concept of "good attitudes" into specific behaviors. Once you identify the behaviors, your task is to focus on displaying them at work. Follow these recommendations:[373]

- Begin by defining what it means to have a good attitude. Think of people you know who display great attitudes. Next, generate a list of the characteristics they possess and the positive behaviors they exhibit at work.

- Take the first item on your list and break it down into smaller behavioral components. Describe it; then describe it some more. For example, if being "pleasant to others" is an example of a good attitude, describe what this looks like. A pleasant person says hello to all colleagues. Describing this further leads to, "She walks over to each person's desk in the morning and says, 'Hello, did you have a good evening?'" Describing it further shows that this person occasionally brings breakfast treats such as sweet rolls to share.

- Repeat the above step for each item on your "good attitude" list.

- Review the list of detailed behaviors and identify any themes. Are there any recurring behaviors, expressions, or gestures?

- Select a minimum of three behavioral themes or specific behaviors you want to focus on over the next two weeks. Consider situations in which these behaviors might be exhibited.

- Exhibit the targeted behaviors in the targeted situations. Observe how people react to you when you exhibit these positive behaviors. If the reaction is not positive, consider why.

- Repeat the last two steps for another set of behaviors.

Self-Managing Your Emotions

Self-management is a trait of emotional intelligence. It reflects the ability to control your emotions and act with honesty and integrity in reliable and adaptable ways. Here are some tips for enhancing this ability.[374]

- **Identify your emotional triggers and physiological responses.** What words, sayings, or situations cause your emotions to ramp up? Do you get nervous before a presentation or when meeting strangers? Keeping a journal is good way to identify your emotional triggers. Simply take a few minutes during the day to jot down your feelings and what caused them. For example, one of your authors knows that he tends to react emotionally when people use judgmental or derogatory words to describe other people or when someone is lying. His body lets him know because he feels flushed or his heart starts to beat faster. This awareness enables him to notice his "emotionality" and to focus on reducing it.

- **Engage in emotional regulation.** Pausing and reflecting is a good solution. When you sense heightened emotions, stop and take a couple of deep breaths. This will relax the emotional brain and engage the thinking brain, thereby allowing you to react in a less emotional manner.[375]

- **Channel your emotions.** Letting off steam is fine; just be sure to do it at the right place and time. Venting with a trusted friend is more effective than yelling at someone at work. Exercise is another way to fend off the potential stressors and emotions associated with being busy or overburdened.

- **Practice mindfulness.** Mindfulness encourages closer contact with life, allowing you to have greater awareness, understanding, acceptance of emotions, and ability to modify unpleasant moods. As such, research shows mindfulness improves well-being, performance, citizenship behavior, leadership, and teamwork. It also reduces stress.[376] As we discussed in Chapter 1, meditation is a great way to practice mindfulness. There also are mindfulness apps available, such as the VGZ Mindfulness Coach. Some companies, such as Aetna, offer workplace mindfulness training as well.[377] ●

affective component of
an attitude 465

Americans with Disabilities
Act (ADA) 491

attitude 465

behavior 468

behavioral component of an
attitude 466

Big Five personality
dimensions 458

buffers 499

burnout 496

causal attribution 474

cognitive component of an
attitude 465

cognitive dissonance 466

core self-evaluation (CSE) 459

counterproductive work behaviors
(CWBs) 482

diversity 485

diversity climate 493

emotional intelligence 462

emotional stability 462

employee assistance programs
(EAPs) 500

employee engagement 476

ethnocentrism 492

explicit bias 472

external dimensions of
diversity 487

fundamental attribution bias 474

generalized self-efficacy 459

glass ceiling 489

halo effect 473

holistic wellness program 500

implicit bias 472

internal dimensions of diversity 486

job satisfaction 478

learned helplessness 460

locus of control 461

organizational behavior (OB) 464

organizational citizenship behaviors
(OCBs) 481

organizational commitment 479

perception 469

personality 458

prosocial behavior (PSB) 479

prosocial motivation (PSM) 479

psychological safety 493

recency effect 473

roles 497

self-efficacy 459

self-esteem 461

self-fulfilling prophecy 474

self-serving bias 474

stereotyping 469

stress 495

stressors 478

tokenism 490

transgender 491

Type A behavior pattern 497

underemployed 492

values 464

work–family conflict 498

11.1 Personality and Individual Behavior

- Personality consists of the stable psychological traits and behavioral attributes that give a person his or her identity. There are five personality dimensions and five personality traits that managers need to be aware of to understand workplace behavior.

- The Big Five personality dimensions are extroversion, agreeableness, conscientiousness, emotional stability, and openness to experience.

- A core self-evaluation represents a broad personality trait comprising four positive individual traits: (1) Self-efficacy is the belief in one's personal ability to do a task. Low self-efficacy is associated with learned helplessness, the debilitating lack of faith in one's ability to control one's environment. (2) Self-esteem is the extent to which people like or dislike themselves. (3) Locus of control indicates how much people believe they control their fate through their own efforts. (4) Emotional stability is the extent to which people feel secure and unworried and how likely they are to experience negative emotions under pressure.

- Emotional intelligence is defined as the ability to monitor your and others' feelings and use this information to guide your thinking and actions.

11.2 Values, Attitudes, and Behavior

- Values must be distinguished from attitudes and from behavior. Values are abstract ideals that guide one's thinking and behavior across all situations.

- Attitudes are defined as learned predispositions toward a given object. Attitudes have three components. The affective component consists of the feelings or emotions one has about a situation. The cognitive component consists of the beliefs and knowledge one has about a situation. The behavioral component is how one intends or expects to behave toward a situation.

- When attitudes and reality collide, the result may be cognitive dissonance, the psychological discomfort a person experiences between his or her cognitive attitude and incompatible behavior.

11.3 Perception and Individual Behavior

- Perception is the process of interpreting and understanding one's environment. There are five distortions of perception. They are: (1) stereotyping, the tendency to attribute to an individual the characteristics one believes are typical of the group to which that individual belongs; (2) implicit bias, which refers to the attitudes or beliefs that affect our understanding, actions, and decisions in an unconscious manner; (3) the halo effect, the forming of an impression of an individual based on a single trait; (4) the recency effect, the tendency to remember recent information better than earlier information; and (5) causal attribution, the activity of inferring causes for observed behavior.

- The self-fulfilling prophecy (Pygmalion effect) describes the phenomenon in which people's expectations of themselves or others lead them to behave in ways that make those expectations come true.

11.4 Work-Related Attitudes and Behaviors Managers Need to Deal With

- Managers need to be alert to work-related attitudes having to do with (1) employee engagement, an individual's involvement, satisfaction, and enthusiasm for work; (2) job satisfaction, the extent to which you feel positive or negative about various aspects of your work; and (3) organizational commitment, reflecting the extent to which an employee identifies with an organization and is committed to its goals.

- Prosocial behavior is voluntary behavior intended to benefit another, such as helping, donating, sharing, and comforting. It is driven by the individual difference of prosocial motivation (PSM), defined as the drive to benefit others. Two behaviors related to prosocial behaviors are organizational citizenship behaviors and counterproductive citizenship behaviors. Prosocial behaviors impact an organizations performance, productivity, absenteeism, and turnover.

11.5 The New Diversified Workforce

- Diversity represents all the ways people are alike and unlike—the differences and similarities in age, gender, race, religion, ethnicity, sexual orientation, capabilities, and socioeconomic background.

- There are two dimensions of diversity: (1) Internal dimensions of diversity are those human differences that exert a powerful, sustained effect throughout every stage of our lives: gender, ethnicity, race, physical abilities, age, and sexual orientation. (2) External dimensions of diversity consist of the personal characteristics that people acquire, discard, or modify throughout their lives: personal habits, educational background, religion, income, marital status, and the like.

- By now the vocabulary surrounding LGBTQ issues has changed considerably. Transgender is an umbrella term for people whose sense of their gender differs from what is expected based on the sex characteristics with which they are born.

- There are six ways in which employees and managers may express resistance to diversity: (1) Some express stereotypes and prejudices based on ethnocentrism, the belief that one's native country, culture, language, abilities, or behavior is superior to that of another country. (2) Some employees are afraid of discrimination against majority group members. (3) Some employees see diversity programs as distracting them from the organization's supposed "real work." (4) There may be a negative diversity climate, defined as the employees' aggregate perceptions about the organization's diversity-related formal structure characteristics and informal values and their feelings of psychological safety, the extent to which they feel free to express ideas without negative consequences. (5) Organizations may not be supportive of flexible hours and other matters that can help employees cope with family demands. (6) Organizations may show lack of support for career-building steps for diverse employees.

11.6 Understanding Stress and Individual Behavior

- Stress is the tension people feel when they are facing or enduring extraordinary demands, constraints, or opportunities and are uncertain about their ability to handle them effectively. The source of stress is called a stressor.

- There are six sources of stress on the job: (1) Demands created by individual differences may arise from a Type A behavior pattern, meaning people have the personality characteristic that involves them in a chronic, determined struggle to accomplish more in less time. (2) Individual task demands are the stresses created by the job itself. (3) Individual role demands are the stresses created by other people's expectations of you. Roles are sets of behaviors that people expect of occupants of a position. Stress may come about because of role overload, role conflict, or role ambiguity. Work–life conflict falls in this category. (4) Group demands are the stresses created by co-workers and managers. (5) Organizational demands are the stresses created by the environment and culture of the organization. (6) Nonwork demands are the stresses created by forces outside the organization, such as money problems or divorce.

- Positive stress can be constructive. Negative stress can result in poor-quality work; such stress is revealed through physiological, psychological, or behavioral signs. One sign is burnout, a state of emotional, mental, and even physical exhaustion.

- There are buffers, or administrative changes, that managers can make to reduce the stressors that lead to employee burnout, such as adding extra staff or giving employees more power to make decisions. Some general organizational strategies for reducing unhealthy stressors are to roll out employee assistance programs, recommend a holistic wellness approach, create a supportive environment, make jobs interesting, and make career counseling available.

11.7 Career Corner: Managing Your Career Readiness

- A two-step approach is used to develop a positive approach at work. The first is to identify the types of negative behaviors that crop up during bad or stressful days. The second step is to identify and exhibit "good attitude" behaviors.

- You can increase your emotional intelligence by developing the ability to manage emotions. Four tips are: (1) identify your emotional triggers and physiological response, (2) engage in emotional regulation, (3) channel your emotions, and (4) practice mindfulness.

Understanding the Chapter: What Do I Know?

1. What are the Big Five personality dimensions?
2. What are four personality traits managers need to be aware of to understand workplace behavior?
3. How is emotional intelligence defined?
4. How do you distinguish values from attitudes and behavior?
5. What is the process of perception?
6. What are five types of distortion in perception, and what is the Pygmalion effect?
7. What are three work-related attitudes managers need to be conscious of?
8. How can managers increase prosocial behaviors?
9. Explain the two dimensions of diversity.
10. What are six sources of stress on the job?

Management in Action

Emotional Baggage at Away

Luggage designer, manufacturer, and retailer Away was founded in 2015 by Stephanie Korey and Jennifer Rubio. Their goal was to create stylish luggage that cost less than existing brands because it would be sold directly to consumers, eliminating the middleman. Its first product was a four-wheel, hard-shell bag that fit into an overhead compartment, came in 10 colors, and cost $225 (a similar item from Tumi cost $525).

The female-founded start-up was a hit and the company reached a valuation of $1.4 billion in 2019. Korey, who led the company as CEO, was featured on the cover of *Forbes*'s "30 under 30" issue and credited with designing a unique sales strategy. This strategy included 1,000 influencers pushing the brand on Instagram, keeping it top of mind for travelers.[378]

Korey soon became even more famous for her ambitious attitude, but not in a good way. A series of reports from former employees told a workplace horror story, uncovering a "cutthroat culture" where employees were regularly "brutally criticized." As a result, a negative light was shone on the online luggage retailer and Korey was forced to temporarily resign.[379]

Let's inspect Away's baggage.

ABUSIVE MANAGEMENT PRACTICES

Employees are attracted to Away's mission, which promises a lifestyle of inclusion and nice vacations.

"In my mind, it's a trivial product but the brand is more than just luggage. . . . It's about travel," says Avery, a former employee who blew the whistle on the company's toxic practices (her last name has not been published). Away's core values include being thoughtful, customer-obsessed, iterative, empowered, accessible and in it together. But Avery and other employees say the company's globally minded mission and values are just a smokescreen to get employees to work harder and cope with the resulting stress. They claim the following:

- *Empowered* means don't schedule time off, no matter how much you've been working.

- *Customer-obsessed* equals do whatever it takes to make the customer happy, even if it costs you your well-being.

- *In it together* means exploiting the fact that employees are close. For example, if one person is forced to work evenings, weekends, and holidays, the entire team does so in solidarity.[380]

Part of Away's *accessible* core value is to use Slack, an instant-messaging platform designed for workplaces. Slack users can utilize public or private channels of communication to discuss workplace issues and tasks that need to be completed. Away, though, has made it clear that privacy isn't an option. The company not only asks employees to refrain from private

Slack messages, it reportedly bans them from using e-mail to communicate with one another. The company calls it transparency; employees call it surveillance. And Away has done a good job of making its employees' point for them. Korey, for instance, fired several employees after reading their complaints about the company's diversity practices in a private LGBTQ channel they had started.[381]

Employee stress isn't just coming from the feeling of being watched. Former employees paint a picture of a company that demanded they work exceedingly long hours and limit time off for entire months at a time. For example, when Away introduced new luggage customization options, about 4,000 customer inquiries went unanswered, even as some Away employees logged 16-hour days. These types of situations happen "because senior leaders love coming up with ideas, but hate what happens to their profit margins when they hire more people," according to *Bloomberg*.[382] Overworked Away employees who couldn't keep up by answering messages immediately, even late at night or on weekends, would receive a public reprimand on Slack, worsening their mental state. It was "like having your pants pulled down in front of the company," a former employee told *Business Insider*.[383]

AWAY MAKES CHANGES . . . SORT OF

Away decided to act in response to the bad press it was getting. CEO Korey released an apology after viewing screenshots of her Slack messages, particularly one in which she called a manager "brain dead." "I can imagine how people felt reading those messages from the past, because I was appalled to read them myself. . . . I am sincerely sorry for what I said and how I said it. It was wrong, plain and simple." Away took it a step further, forcing Korey to resign and appointing Lululemon COO Stuart Haselden as the new CEO. A few days later, the company changed course. It attacked the media for its reporting on the toxic culture and announced that Korey would be staying on with Haselden as co-CEO.[384] Korey also is "exploring legal options" against *The Verge*, which was the first media outlet to publish former employee criticism. (She claims the outlet started a "social media mob.")[385]

IS THE COVERAGE FAIR?

Some experts agree with Away's reversal, calling the news coverage of Korey a "hit piece" and saying "people are getting soft."[386] In fact, Korey wasn't demanding of others what she did not demand of herself. The same former employees who complained to the press never denied their leader's work ethic. Korey was

always in the office, managed all the company's operations, and was regularly online past midnight. Moreover, she believed she was helping her employees' growth and development by providing clear and blunt feedback.[387]

Management expert and former Mozilla executive Melissa Nightingale points to the fact that most employee complaints came from Away's customer experience (CX) team. She believes CX is "the lifeblood of our orgs" but is often ignored by leaders like Korey and told to suck it up (because that's what Korey would do). "We burn them [CX] out and we totally know it," says Nightingale.[388]

Lambda School founder Austen Allred, a critic of how Korey is being treated, believes that the same issues could be uncovered at "something like 99%" of all high-growth start-ups, should a reporter go looking for it. It's true, Away's culture allowed it to grow at hyper speed, forming a cult-like following with celebrities and Millennials. Former employees say Away's growing pain is different though. They believe the company sold them a bill of goods, promising to disrupt the travel industry, but instead disrupted their family dinners and long-distance travel plans.[389]

Away, it seems, has become a brand consumers adore, instigates a culture people fear, and produces former employees who are burned out. Does its leader see a problem with this picture?

FOR DISCUSSION

Problem-Solving Perspective

1. What is the underlying problem in this case from co-CEO Haselden's point of view? Do you believe co-CEO Korey has a different point of view?

2. What do you think Away needs to do to reduce employee stress and burnout?

Application of Chapter Content

1. Use the Big Five personality dimensions to describe co-CEO Korey. Justify your description.

2. How would you characterize co-CEO Korey's emotional intelligence?

3. How does the company view employees who want to take time off or who do not immediately answer messages? Use attributional tendencies in your analysis.

4. What impact does Away's culture have on employee engagement, job satisfaction, and organizational commitment? Explain.

5. Which barriers to diversity is Away displaying?

6. What sources of job-related stress exist at Away? How can these be remedied?

Legal/Ethical Challenge

Should Airlines Accommodate Oversized People?

Traveling on an airplane can be extra difficult for overweight and tall people. The width of an average airplane seat has decreased from 18.5 inches in the early 2000s to around 17 inches.[390] Given individual differences in hip width, this can be a problem, particularly for women. The Civilian American and European Surface Anthropometry Resource Project (Caesar) investigated the issue, backed by funding from a consortium of scientific research organizations and engineering and aerospace companies.

The Caesar project measured more than 4,000 people from the United States and Europe and uncovered the following: "The hip breadth of men in the 95th percentile of the population, i.e., on the very big side, measures 17.6 inches." This means that 95% of all men can fit into a standard Airbus seat. In contrast, females face a different situation. According to Caesar's report, "the hip breadth of women in the 90th percentile is 19.2 inches, and those in the 95th percentile have hips measuring 22.4 inches."[391] The core skeletal system is the reason for the difference between men and women. Females simply have a larger pelvis than men.

Seat pitch, the distance between seat backs, also is decreasing. This makes for less leg room for all people. The typical seat pitch in economy class has narrowed from 35 to 31 inches, with some airlines offering as little as 28 inches of leg room.[392]

Do you think airlines should be bound by minimum seat size and leg room standards? The advocacy group Flyers Rights has campaigned for federally regulated seat sizes, citing concerns such as inability to quickly evacuate aircraft and health hazards like deep vein thrombosis.[393] Although there are currently no such regulations in the United States, federal judges recently ordered the Federal Aviation Administration (FAA) to review commercial airline seat sizes and pitch.[394] Some people believe that forcing airlines to establish bigger, standard seat sizes ultimately increases fares. Industry group Airlines for America opposes the idea, for instance. "The group notes that the FAA should regulate seat size for safety, but should not substitute its judgments for market forces on what people are willing to pay."[395] Others believe airlines should focus more on passenger comfort than profit. "There is an industry standard, and, within that standard, the obsession is profit," says Kimberly Dark, the author of *Fat, Pretty, and Soon to Be Old: A Makeover for Self and Society*.[396]

The trends are clear. In general, airlines are adding seats while decreasing seat width and pitch. These changes clearly affect taller, wider, and heavier individuals and may even pose health risks to passengers. "I don't think airlines are recognizing the size of Americans," a frequent flyer tells *The Wall Street Journal*.[397] Samoa Air is resolving this issue by charging fees based on passengers' weight. Does this seem ethical?

The question to consider is whether seat width and pitch should be regulated by law or determined by market forces.

SOLVING THE CHALLENGE

1. I recommend creating a national standard for airline seats based on the average passenger as opposed to using gender as part of the computation. I would standardize seat width based on passengers' average hip size. I also would standardize seat pitch so that it accommodates passengers' average height. Once this is done, I would charge passengers a special fee for more space.

2. Let market forces determine the design of airplanes and fares. The government should stay out of this issue. For example, Airbus's A220 expanded seat width to 18.5 inches and included 19 inches for the middle seat.[398]

3. Because women, on average, have larger hip breadth than men, it is not fair to base fees on the size of a seat. This would disadvantage women. I would standardize seat width based on the average size of women. People can pay extra fees if they want additional seat width or pitch.

4. Invent other options.

12

Motivating Employees

Achieving Superior Performance in the Workplace

Kapook2981/iStock/Getty Images

After reading this chapter, you should be able to:

LO 12-1 Explain the role of motivation in accomplishing goals.

LO 12-2 Identify the needs that motivate most employees.

LO 12-3 Discuss similarities and differences among three process theories.

LO 12-4 Compare different ways to design jobs.

LO 12-5 Discuss how to use four types of behavior modification.

LO 12-6 Discuss the role of compensation in motivating employees.

LO 12-7 Describe how to develop the career readiness competency of self-motivation.

FORECAST *What's Ahead in This Chapter*

This chapter discusses motivation from four perspectives: content (theories by Maslow, McClelland, Deci and Ryan, and Herzberg), process (equity, expectancy, and goal-setting theories), job design, and reinforcement. We then consider rewards for motivating performance and conclude with a Career Corner that focuses on how to enhance the career readiness competency of self-motivation.

Managing for Motivation: Building Your Own Motivation

Are you putting something off right now because you just haven't felt inspired to tackle it? Self-motivation is critical for work success because it drives performance, particularly in work situations where you're expected to apply good work habits and focus in order to be productive without constant supervision.[1] Consider that one study found organizations were 21% more profitable when their employees were self-motivated.[2] This finding supports employers' desire to hire people with the career readiness competency of self-motivation. You certainly want to possess this attitude.

Here are some suggestions for honing your self-motivation (and getting to that task you've been putting off).[3]

1. Reframe your reason. Perhaps you've having trouble accomplishing an objective because you haven't thought through why you're really aiming for it. A goal to look for a job in a particular field because one of your friends is or because someone said it was exciting may not be enough to ignite your inner drive. Try reframing the goal in terms that invoke your own values rather than someone else's: "I want to work at this company because I think it's a good match for my computational thinking, new media literacy, and written communication skills."[4]

2. Be realistic. Realistic goals aren't necessarily easy ones; the American Psychological Association reports that when we set goals that are challenging, we're 90 percent more likely to achieve them.[5] Realistic goals are specific. "I want to get a good job in an exciting field" is broad. "I want to get an entry-level job with a marketing research company" is specific and, therefore, realistic.

3. Set interim goals. At the same time, you shouldn't set yourself up to try accomplishing a big goal in one grand gesture. Break your big goal down into smaller ones, each with a date attached, to lay out a plan of smaller steps you can follow that all lead in the same direction. "I will draft my resume by the end of this month," and "During the two weeks after that, I will ask three people to critique and proofread it for me," are good interim goals toward your ultimate objective of finding an entry-level marketing job.

4. Celebrate ongoing achievements. Applaud yourself for reaching each of the milestones you've set. Few things are as motivating as rewards, and because each step you accomplish in your plan is bringing you closer to your big goal, each is worth a celebration. Treat yourself to something you've wanted or take time off to do something fun. You've earned it.

5. Hold yourself accountable. It's one thing to celebrate success, but if there are no consequences for failure, motivation can drag. A mentor who encourages you and checks in on your progress can give your forward momentum a regular boost. No mentor? Create your own by simply letting a friend know your goal and keeping that person up to date as you proceed through your plan. Dominican University psychology professor Dr. Gail Matthews recently studied 149 adults of all ages in businesses and other organizations in the United States and abroad. She found that well over 70% of those who used a weekly e-mail to report their goal achievement to a friend either completely accomplished their goal or got more than halfway there. Of those who didn't check in with anyone, only 35% achieved as much.[6]

6. Envision success. While you should anticipate setbacks (and forgive yourself for them), keeping the finish line in mind and regularly imagining yourself crossing it will soon become a mental habit that reinforces your positive approach and builds your professionalism and work ethic.

7. Create a "brag book." Start a journal that contains notes about your successes. This aids your recall of "rock star performance," which in turn fuels your self-confidence.[7] Self-confidence drives self-motivation and the associated desire to complete your short- and long-term projects. It also provides behavioral examples of your performance and career readiness competencies to discuss during job interviews.

For Discussion

Are you currently using any of these strategies? If not, which ones can you adopt now to achieve your most immediate goals?

12.1 Motivating for Performance

THE BIG PICTURE

Motivation is defined as the psychological processes that arouse and direct people's goal-directed behavior. There are four major perspectives that offer different explanations for how to motivate employees. They are content theories, process theories, job design, and reinforcement theory.

LO 12-1

Explain the role of motivation in accomplishing goals.

What would make you rise a half hour earlier than usual to ensure you got to work on time—and to perform your best once there? Among the possible inducements (such as those offered by SAS, Qualtrics, and HEB): free food, onsite laundry, four-day workweeks, child-care assistance, gym memberships, tuition reimbursement, and free transportation.[8]

How about repayment of your student loans—that's a big one! Currently, workers under age 40 carry almost 65% of the $1.5 trillion in outstanding student loan debt, and a recent study found that 86% of younger workers would stay with a company for at least five years if the firm provided help with loan repayment.[9] Madeline McIntosh, CEO of Penguin Random House, said that her company's decision to offer unique benefits like student loan repayment "helps turn entry-level hires into lifetime employees," and thinks this program has "outsized emotional or psychological benefits for employees."[10] Only 4 to 8% of companies currently offer this perk, but large employers like Fidelity Investments, Staples, PwC, and Aetna are joining them.[11]

How would you like for your employer to repay some of your student loan debt? More and more companies are offering this benefit to incentivize younger workers.
Brian A Jackson/Shutterstock

Whether employment rates are high or low, there are always companies, industries, and occupations in which employers feel they need to bend over backward to retain their human capital.

Motivation: What It Is, Why It's Important

Why do people do the things they do? The answer is this: They are mainly motivated to fulfill their wants and needs.

What Is Motivation and How Does It Work?   **Motivation** is defined as the psychological processes that arouse and direct goal-directed behavior.[12] Motivation is difficult to understand because you can't actually see it or know it in another person; it must be

inferred from one's behavior. Nevertheless, it's imperative that you as a manager understand the process of motivation if you are to guide employees in accomplishing your organization's objectives.

The way motivation works is complex because motivation is the result of multiple *personal and contextual factors. (See Figure 12.1.)*

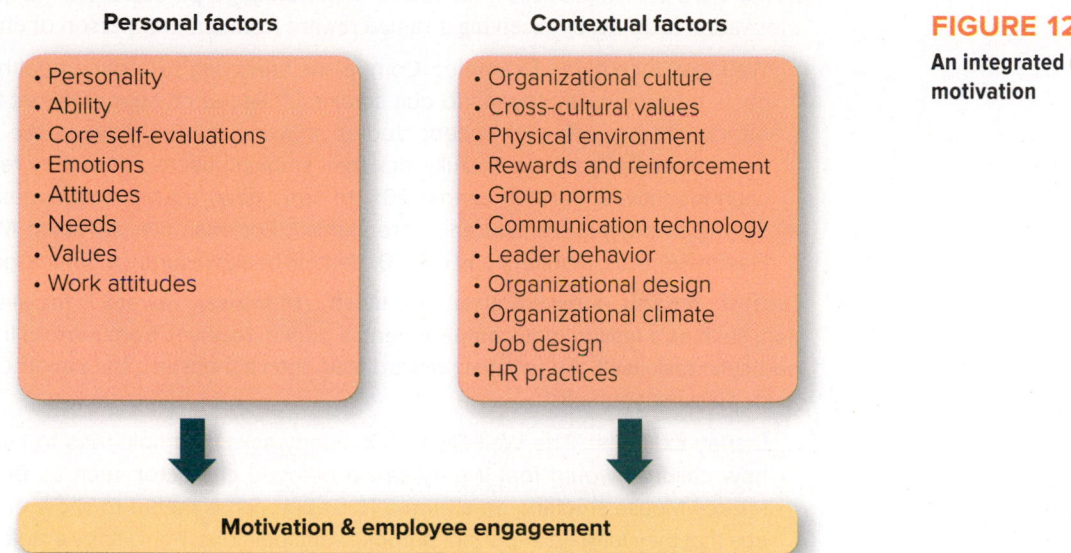

Personal factors

- Personality
- Ability
- Core self-evaluations
- Emotions
- Attitudes
- Needs
- Values
- Work attitudes

Contextual factors

- Organizational culture
- Cross-cultural values
- Physical environment
- Rewards and reinforcement
- Group norms
- Communication technology
- Leader behavior
- Organizational design
- Organizational climate
- Job design
- HR practices

Motivation & employee engagement

FIGURE 12.1

An integrated model of motivation

The individual personal factors that employees bring to the workplace range from personality to attitudes, many of which we described in Chapter 11. The contextual factors include organizational culture, structure, cross-cultural values, the physical environment, and other matters we discuss in this chapter and others throughout the text (e.g., Chapter 8–Figure 8.1; Chapter 9–Figure 9.2). Both categories of factors influence an employee's level of motivation and engagement at work.

However, motivation can also be expressed in a simple model—namely, that people have certain *needs* that *motivate* them to perform specific *behaviors* for which they receive *rewards* that *feed back* and satisfy the original need. *(See Figure 12.2.)*

FIGURE 12.2   A simple model of motivation

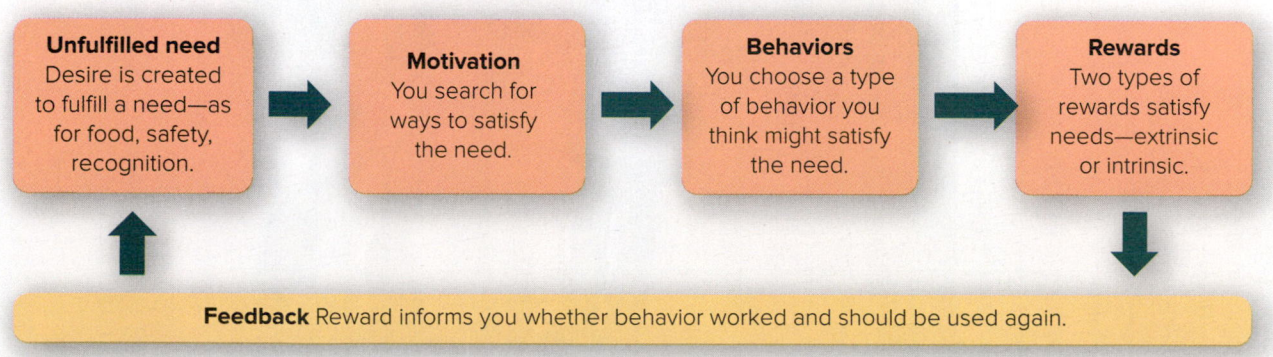

Unfulfilled need Desire is created to fulfill a need—as for food, safety, recognition.

Motivation You search for ways to satisfy the need.

Behaviors You choose a type of behavior you think might satisfy the need.

Rewards Two types of rewards satisfy needs—extrinsic or intrinsic.

Feedback Reward informs you whether behavior worked and should be used again.

For example, as an hourly worker you desire more money (need), which impels you (motivates you) to work more hours (behavior), which provides you with more money (reward) and informs you (feedback loop) that working more hours will fulfill your need for more money in the future.

Rewards (as well as motivation itself) are of two types—*extrinsic* and *intrinsic*.[13] Managers can use both to encourage better work performance. Let's discuss each of these and consider how employers use both extrinsic and intrinsic motivation to decrease employee tobacco use.

- **Extrinsic rewards—rewards given by others.** An ==extrinsic reward== is the payoff, such as money, a person receives from others for performing a particular task. Extrinsic motivation is driven by receiving a valued reward from another person or entity.[14]

    Wellness Incentives Example: Companies are trying to reduce health care costs by paying employees to quit smoking.[15] Research suggests that these efforts can pay off—with recent studies showing that employees are three times more likely to successfully kick their smoking habits when they receive cash incentives. Further, almost 20% of firms now require employees who smoke to pay higher insurance premiums.[16] For example, at Kitsap Mental Health Services, smokers pay a $100 monthly health insurance surcharge.

- **Intrinsic rewards—a reward given to yourself.** An ==intrinsic reward== is the satisfaction, such as a feeling of accomplishment, a person receives from performing the particular task itself. An intrinsic reward is an internal reward; the payoff comes from pleasing yourself.[17]

    Disney Example: The Walt Disney Company asks its employees to imagine how children would feel if they saw a beloved character such as Belle or Mickey Mouse smoking on a break. This approach is meant to show employees that they fulfill an important purpose with their jobs. For Disney employees, then, work has meaning, and they feel a sense of pride in themselves when they quit smoking and contribute to the greater good by setting a positive example for children.[18]

One of the intrinsic rewards that Disney employees—particularly those in character—experience is the sense of pride that comes with being a positive role model for so many admiring children. Jason Kempin/Getty Images

What types of rewards do you prefer to receive at work? Take Self-Assessment 12.1 to find out whether you are more motivated by extrinsic or intrinsic rewards.

SELF-ASSESSMENT 12.1   CAREER READINESS

Are You More Interested in Extrinsic or Intrinsic Rewards?

The following survey was designed to assess extrinsic and intrinsic motivation. Please be prepared to answer these questions if your instructor has assigned Self-Assessment 12.1 in Connect.

1. What is more important to you, extrinsic or intrinsic rewards? Are you surprised by the results?

2. How can you use the results to increase your motivation to obtain good grades in your classes?

3. What might you say during an interview to demonstrate your self-awareness regarding the rewards that motivate you?

We all are motivated by a combination of extrinsic and intrinsic rewards. Which type of reward is more valuable to you? Answering this question can help you generate self-motivation and higher performance while also increasing the career readiness competency of self-awareness.

Why Is Motivation Important?   It seems obvious that organizations would want to motivate their employees to be more productive. But motivation also plays a role in influencing a host of outcomes, including employee engagement, organizational citizenship, absenteeism, and service quality.[19] In order of importance, you as a manager want to motivate people to:

1. **Join your organization.** You need to instill in talented prospective workers the desire to come to work for you.

2. **Stay with your organization.** Whether you are in good economic times or bad, you always want to be able to retain good people.

3. **Show up for work at your organization.** In many organizations, absenteeism and lateness are tremendous problems.

4. **Be engaged while at your organization.** Engaged employees produce higher-quality work and better customer service.

5. **Do extra for your organization.** You hope your employees will perform extra tasks above and beyond the call of duty (be organizational "good citizens").

The Four Major Perspectives on Motivation: An Overview

There is no theory accepted by everyone as to what motivates people. In this chapter, therefore, we present the four principal perspectives. From these, you may be able to select what ideas seem most workable to you. The four perspectives on motivation are (1) *content*, (2) *process*, (3) *job design*, and (4) *reinforcement*, as described in the following four main sections.

The following is a quick overview of these four perspectives and the theories that utilize each.

1. *Content theories* emphasize needs as motivators.

    - *Maslow's hierarchy of needs* has five levels to be met in order.

    - *McClelland's acquired needs theory* posits three needs, for achievement, affiliation, and power.

    - *Deci and Ryan's self-determination theory* assumes people seek innate needs of competence, autonomy, and relatedness in order to grow.

    - *Herzberg's two-factor theory* differentiates hygiene factors and motivators that determine work satisfaction and dissatisfaction.

2. *Process theories* focus on the thoughts and perceptions that motivate behavior.

- *Equity/justice theory* proposes that people seek fairness and justice in their interactions and relationships.

- *Expectancy theory* says people are motivated by how much they want something and how likely they think it is they will get it.

- *Goal-setting theory* says goals that are specific, challenging, and achievable will motivate behavior.

3. *Job design theories* focus on designing jobs that lead to employee satisfaction and performance.

- *Scientific management theory* attempted to fit people to jobs by reducing the number of tasks workers had to perform to achieve a goal.

- *Job enlargement and job enrichment* are ways to fit jobs to people by offering more variety, challenges, and responsibility.

- *The job characteristics model* is an outgrowth of job enrichment that traces the effect of five job characteristics on employees' psychological states and work outcomes.

4. *Reinforcement theory* is based on the notion that motivation is a function of behavioral consequences and not unmet needs. ●

12.2 Content Perspectives on Employee Motivation

THE BIG PICTURE

Content perspectives are theories emphasizing the needs that motivate people. Needs are defined as physiological or psychological deficiencies that arouse behavior. The content perspective includes four theories: Maslow's hierarchy of needs, McClelland's acquired needs theory, Deci and Ryan's self-determination theory, and Herzberg's two-factor theory.

LO 12-2

Identify the needs that motivate most employees.

Content perspectives, also known as need-based perspectives, are theories that emphasize the needs that motivate people. Content theorists ask, "What kind of needs motivate employees in the workplace?" **Needs** are defined as physiological or psychological deficiencies that arouse behavior. They can be strong or weak, and because they are influenced by environmental factors, they can vary over time and from place to place.

In addition to McGregor's Theory X/Theory Y (see Chapter 2), content perspectives include four theories:

- Maslow's hierarchy of needs theory.
- McClelland's acquired needs theory.
- Deci and Ryan's self-determination theory.
- Herzberg's two-factor theory.

Maslow's Hierarchy of Needs Theory: Five Levels

In 1943, as one of the first researchers to study motivation, Abraham Maslow (mentioned previously in Chapter 2), put forth the **hierarchy of needs theory**, which proposes that people are motivated by five levels of needs: (1) physiological, (2) safety, (3) love, (4) esteem, and (5) self-actualization.[20] *(See Figure 12.3.)*

FIGURE 12.3
Maslow's hierarchy of needs

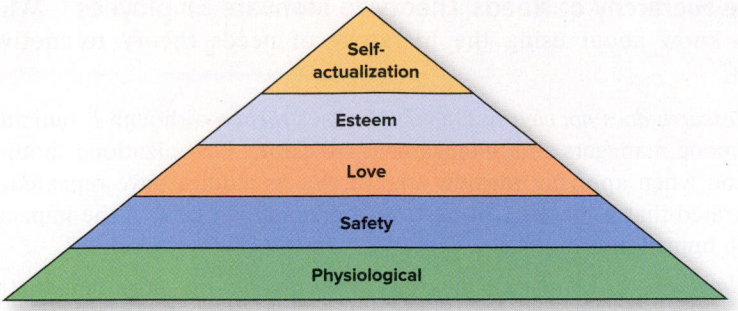

1. **Physiological need—the most basic human physical need:** Need for food, clothing, shelter, comfort, self-preservation. *Workplace example: these are covered by wages.*

2. **Safety need:** Need for physical safety, emotional security, avoidance of violence. *Workplace examples: health insurance, job security, work safety rules, pension plans satisfy this need.*

3. **Love need:** Need for love, friendship, affection. *Workplace examples: office parties, company softball teams, management retreats.*

4. **Esteem need:** Need for self-respect, status, reputation, recognition, self-confidence. *Workplace examples: bonuses, promotions, awards.*

5. **Self-actualization need—the highest level need:** Need for self-fulfillment: increasing competence, using abilities to the fullest. *Workplace example: sabbatical leave to further personal growth.*

The Five Levels of Needs   In proposing this hierarchy of five needs ranging from basic to highest level, Maslow suggested that needs are never completely satisfied. That is, our actions are aimed at fulfilling the "deprived" needs—those that remain unsatisfied at any point in time. Thus, for example, once you have achieved safety (security), which is the second most basic need, you will then seek to fulfill the third most basic need—love (belongingness).

To be successful, today's organizations must serve a much greater purpose than simply providing work for pay. Younger generations of workers are increasingly drawn to companies that provide opportunities for work–life balance, interpersonal relationships, and social activism. Which needs to do you hope to be able to meet through your work in an organization?
zeljkosantrac/E+/Getty Images

According to HR professional Ankita Poddar, modern organizations have to go beyond fulfilling Maslow's lower-level needs if they want to achieve competitive advantage. Said Poddar, "In a generation where benefits like working from home, free food and sleep pods are considered necessities, organizations have begun to realize that there lies a space unexplored; that when all basics are covered, employees are drawn to organizations that do good."[21] Indeed, the love, esteem, and self-actualization needs represented in Maslow's hierarchy inform many leading organizations' motivational toolkits. For example, employees at companies like IKEA, Danone (Dannon), Bosch, Natura, and Lavazza know that the work they do connects them to the greater social purpose of making the world a better and healthier place.[22]

Using the Hierarchy of Needs Theory to Motivate Employees   What should managers know about using the hierarchy of needs theory to motivate their employees?

1. *Research does not clearly support Maslow's theory*—although it remains popular among managers and management educators. Organizations should use caution when applying Maslow's hierarchy, as studies have repeatedly demonstrated that it presents, at best, an oversimplified view of the impact of needs on human motivation.[23]

2. *Maslow's work made an important contribution*—his work demonstrated that workers have needs beyond that of just earning a paycheck.

3. *Physiological and safety needs are still a necessary foundation*—to the extent the organization permits, managers should first try to meet employees' level 1 and level 2 needs, of course, so that employees won't be preoccupied with them. Says one HR expert, "You don't get productive employees if they can't afford to live."[24] This is why more companies now focus on paying a "livable wage" that is higher than the legally mandated minimum wage.[25]

McClelland's Acquired Needs Theory: Achievement, Affiliation, and Power

David McClelland, a well-known psychologist, proposed the ==acquired needs theory==, which states that three needs—achievement, affiliation, and power—are major motives determining people's behavior in the workplace.[26] Managers are encouraged to recognize three needs in themselves and others and to attempt to create work environments that are responsive to them.

FIGURE 12.4

McClelland's three needs

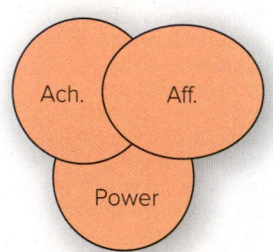

A "well-balanced" individual: achievement, affiliation, and power are of equal size.

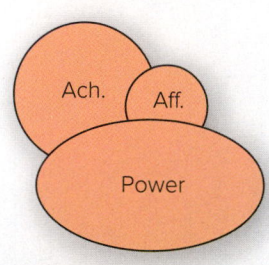

A "control freak" individual: achievement is normal, but affiliation is small and power is large.

The Three Needs   McClelland's theory makes two important assumptions about the needs for achievement, power, and affiliation:

1. *Needs are learned*—acquired needs theory suggests that we are not born with our needs; rather, we learn them from our culture and early life experiences.[27]

2. *One need often dominates*—the theory suggests that one of the three needs tends to be dominant in each of us, although some individuals have a more balanced set of needs. For example, some people have a higher need for power than for affiliation or achievement.[28] *(See Figure 12.4.)*

   ■ **Need for achievement—"I need to excel at tasks."** This is the desire to excel, to do something better or more efficiently, to solve problems, to achieve excellence in challenging tasks.[29]

   ■ **Need for affiliation—"I need close relationships."** This is the desire for friendly and warm relations with other people.[30]

   ■ **Need for power—"I need to control others."** This is the desire to be responsible for other people, to influence their behavior or to control them.[31]

McClelland identifies two forms of the need for power—personal and institutional.

1. *Personal power*—the negative kind is the need for *personal power*, as expressed in the desire to dominate others, and involves manipulating people for one's own gratification.

2. *Institutional power*—the positive kind, characteristic of top managers and leaders, is the desire for *institutional power*, as expressed in the need to solve problems that further organizational goals.

Where do you think you stand in terms of being motivated by these three needs? You can find out by completing Self-Assessment 12.2.

Assessing Your Acquired Needs

The following survey was designed to assess your motivation in terms of acquired needs. Please be prepared to answer these questions if your instructor has assigned Self-Assessment 12.2 in Connect.

1. What is the order of your most important needs? Are you surprised by this result?

2. Given that achievement and power needs are associated with career advancement, how might you increase these two need states?

3. What might you say during an interview to demonstrate that you have a high need for achievement?

Using Acquired Needs Theory to Motivate Employees   As a manager, you can apply acquired needs theory by appealing to the preferences associated with each need. Consider the following recommendations.

Need for Achievement   People motivated by the *need for achievement* prefer:[32]

- Working on challenging, but not impossible, tasks or projects.
- Situations in which good performance relies on effort and ability rather than luck.
- Being rewarded for their efforts.
- Receiving a fair and balanced amount of positive and negative feedback to improve their performance.

Need for Power   People who have a *high need for power* are more likely to enjoy:[33]

- Being in control of people and events and being recognized for this responsibility.
- Work that allows them to control or have an effect on people and be publicly recognized for their accomplishments.

Need for Affiliation   Those who tend to seek social approval and satisfying personal relationships may have a *high need for affiliation*. These individuals:[34]

- May not be the most efficient managers because at times they will have to make decisions that will make people resent them.
- Tend to prefer work, such as sales, that provides for personal relationships and social approval.

Deci and Ryan's Self-Determination Theory: Competence, Autonomy, and Relatedness

Developed by University of Rochester psychologists Edward Deci (pronounced "*Dee*-see") and Richard Ryan, **self-determination theory** assumes that people are driven to try to grow and attain fulfillment, with their behavior and well-being influenced by three innate needs: competence, autonomy, and relatedness.[35]

Focus on Intrinsic Motivation   Self-determination theory focuses primarily on intrinsic motivation and rewards (such as feeling independent) rather than on extrinsic motivation and rewards (such as money or fame). Intrinsic motivation is important because:[36]

- It is longer lasting than extrinsic motivation.
- It has a more positive impact on task performance than extrinsic motivation.

The Three Innate Needs   To achieve psychological growth, according to the theory, people need to satisfy the three innate (that is, inborn) needs of competence, autonomy, and relatedness:

1. **Competence—"I want to feel a sense of mastery."** People need to feel qualified, knowledgeable, and capable of completing a goal or task and to learn different skills.[37]

2. **Autonomy—"I want to feel independent and able to influence my environment."** People need to feel they have freedom and the discretion to determine what they want to do and how they want to do it.[38]

3. **Relatedness—"I want to feel connected to other people."** People need to feel a sense of belonging, of attachment to others.[39]

Using Self-Determination Theory to Motivate Employees   Managers can apply this theory by engaging in leader behavior that fosters the experience of competence, autonomy, and relatedness.[40] Following are some specific suggestions:

- **Competence.** Managers can provide tangible resources, time, contacts, and coaching to improve employee competence, making sure that employees have the knowledge and information they need to perform their jobs.

    Mascoma Bank Example: To increase competence, Mascoma Bank, headquartered in Lebanon, New Hampshire, partners with local universities to offer its employees learning opportunities that go beyond what the company itself can make available to them. Mascoma aims to pay employees back for the time and energy they put into their jobs with a mutual investment that includes both personal and professional development.[41]

- **Autonomy.** To enhance feelings of autonomy, managers can develop trust with their employees and empower them by delegating meaningful tasks to them. An example of this is an approach called a results-only work environment (ROWE). A ROWE focuses on results rather than on when or how work is done, which gives employees a great deal of freedom.

    Appriss Example: Louisville, KY–based Appriss software company tells employees in its benefits manual, "We won't micro manage you, we expect you to manage yourself." Under the company's ROWE, employees can work remotely and request unlimited time off, which the manual claims "respects our employees' needs to balance work with their other responsibilities and interests, while trusting them to be accountable for performance."[42]

- **Relatedness.** Many companies, such as Veterans United Home Loans, use camaraderie to foster relatedness.

    Veterans United Home Loans Example: Veterans United Home Loans (VUHL) is a certified "Great Place to Work" and was *Fortune's* #17 Best Company to Work For in 2020. When VUHL employees were surveyed about why they loved working for the company, the words most frequently repeated in their responses included "people," "family," "community," and "everyone." One way that managers build camaraderie at VUHL is by creating personalized 15-minute birthday celebrations for each employee throughout the year. Parties center on something about which employees are passionate. For example, for a comedy-club loving employee's birthday party, everyone in the office came up with an original joke.[43]

Are you feeling motivated in this course? To what extent does the instructor for this course satisfy your needs for competence, autonomy, and relatedness? You can find out by taking Self-Assessment 12.3.

Employees at Veterans United Home Loans are drawn to the sense of community and relatedness that the organization fosters. One type of activity that helps VUHL workers feel connected to others is volunteering. Here, VUHL employees are spending time assembling boxes of items for non-profit organizations on Martin Luther King Jr Day.
Courtesy of Veterans United Home Loans

SELF-ASSESSMENT 12.3   CAREER READINESS

Assessing Your Needs for Self-Determination

The following survey was designed to assess the extent to which an instructor is satisfying your needs for self-determination. Please be prepared to answer these questions if your instructor has assigned Self-Assessment 12.3 in Connect.

1. Are your needs being met? Do the results make sense in terms of your level of motivation in this course?

2. Based on the results, identify two things you might do to increase your motivation.

3. What might you say during an interview to demonstrate your self-awareness of your needs for competence, autonomy, and relatedness?

Herzberg's Two-Factor Theory: From Dissatisfying Factors to Satisfying Factors

Frederick Herzberg arrived at his needs-based theory as a result of a landmark study of 203 accountants and engineers who were interviewed to determine the factors responsible for job satisfaction and dissatisfaction.[44] Two key findings from Herzberg's study informed the two-factor theory:

1. Job satisfaction was more frequently associated with achievement, recognition, characteristics of the work, responsibility, and advancement.

2. Job dissatisfaction was more often associated with working conditions, pay and security, company policies, supervisors, and interpersonal relationships.

The result was Herzberg's **two-factor theory**, which proposed that work satisfaction and dissatisfaction arise from two different factors—work satisfaction from motivating factors and work dissatisfaction from hygiene factors.

Hygiene Factors versus Motivating Factors   In Herzberg's theory, the hygiene factors are the lower-level needs, and the motivating factors are the higher-level needs. The two areas are separated by a zone in which employees are neither satisfied nor dissatisfied. *(See Figure 12.5.)*

FIGURE 12.5

Herzberg's two-factor theory: satisfaction versus dissatisfaction

Motivating factors:
"What will make my people *satisfied*?"
Achievement
Recognition
The work itself
Responsibility
Advancement & growth

No satisfaction   Satisfaction

Neutral area: neither satisfied nor dissatisfied

Dissatisfaction   No dissatisfaction

Hygiene factors:
"What will make my people *dissatisfied*?"
Pay & security
Working conditions
Interpersonal relationships
Company policy
Supervisors

- **Hygiene factors—"Why are my people dissatisfied?"** The lower-level needs, <mark>hygiene factors,</mark> are factors associated with job dissatisfaction—such as salary, working conditions, interpersonal relationships, and company policy—all of which affect the job context in which people work.

According to Herzberg's two-factor theory, working conditions represent important hygiene factors—things that can lead to job dissatisfaction. Do you think that you would feel unhappy in your job if you had to work under these lighting conditions for 8 hours each day?
Gill Thompson/Shutterstock

According to the theory, hygiene factors don't make people happy, but they can drive considerable dissatisfaction when they are absent or problematic. For example, workers are not likely to be motivated to work harder because their office has great lighting, but poor lighting can make workers absolutely miserable.[45]

> **REI Example:** regularly rated as one of the top companies to work for by *Fortune* (No. 60 in 2020), REI is a good example. The company offers paid sabbaticals, paid sick days, and health insurance for both full- and part-timers.[46] The company's rate of part-time employee turnover, about 37%, is far lower than the industry average of 65%.[47]

- **Motivating factors—"What will make my people satisfied?"** The higher-level needs, <mark>motivating factors</mark>, or simply *motivators*, are factors associated with job satisfaction—such as achievement, recognition, responsibility, and advancement—all of which affect the job content or the rewards of work performance. Motivating factors—challenges, opportunities, recognition—must be instituted, Herzberg believed, to spur superior work performance. Southwest Airlines is a great example.

> **Southwest Airlines Example:** An example of a motivating factor would be to give workers more control over their work. When a Southwest flight was delayed for several hours recently, the gate agents decided to hold contests between the passengers, including a paper airplane contest and one for "worst driver's license photo."[48] The agents gave $25 airline vouchers and Southwest gear to the winners. When boarding finally began, the passengers applauded the employees. Southwest is known for empowering its employees to do whatever it takes to deliver unparalleled customer service, and it rewards them with a generous annual profit-sharing program. Said CEO Gary Kelly, "Our people are our greatest asset, and they deserve all the credit for our continued success," adding, "The vast majority of our employees describe their work as 'a calling,' and it's an honor to be able to recognize them for their passion, dedication, and their contributions."[49]

Using Two-Factor Theory to Motivate Employees   During the Great Recession, with fewer jobs available, many people felt they were stuck in jobs they disliked—only 39% said they were happy with their positions in 2009, according to a survey by the Conference Board.[50] In the midst of a strong economic recovery in 2019, in contrast, a survey of 9,000 workers found that 85% of U.S. employees were somewhat or very satisfied with their jobs; the contributing factor cited by the largest percentage of these survey respondents was "meaningfulness."[51] This finding supports the motivating factors component of Herzberg's theory.

Employee engagement is declining in developed countries, however, according to Gallup's State of the Global Workplace report. "Organizations and institutions have often been slow to adapt to the rapid changes produced by the spread of information technology, the globalization of markets for products and labor, the rise of the gig economy, and younger workers' unique expectations." Also according to the report, "Business and political leaders must recognize when traditional patterns in management practices, education or gender roles, for example, become roadblocks to workers' motivation and productivity and when selectively disrupting tradition will help clear a path to greater prosperity and transformed company cultures."[52]

There will always be some employees who dislike their jobs, but the basic lessons of Herzberg's research are that you should:

1. First eliminate dissatisfaction by making sure that hygiene factors such as working conditions, pay levels, and company policies are reasonable.

2. Next concentrate on spurring motivation by providing desired opportunities for achievement, recognition, responsibility, and personal growth (motivating factors).

Positive hygiene factors include allowing pets at work; offering video game arcades, fitness classes, and intramural sports (volleyball, soccer); and providing a library of free movies, books, and magazines.[53] Motivating factors include things like employee recognition, career counseling, and opportunities for growth, learning, and development.

Google Example: If you work at Google, you'll have paid maternity/paternity leave, on-site physicians, legal aid, and travel assistance—and if you die, the company will pay your family half your salary for a decade.[54] In addition to these hygiene factors, you'll also receive paid time off for volunteering and an abundance of opportunities to learn new skills and share your unique skills with your co-workers.[55]

The four needs theories are compared in Figure 12.6. Note how acquired needs theory (McClelland) and self-determination theory (Deci and Ryan) focus only on higher-level needs. ●

FIGURE 12.6

A comparison of needs and satisfaction theories: Maslow hierarchy of needs, McClelland acquired needs, Deci and Ryan self-determination, and Herzberg two-factor

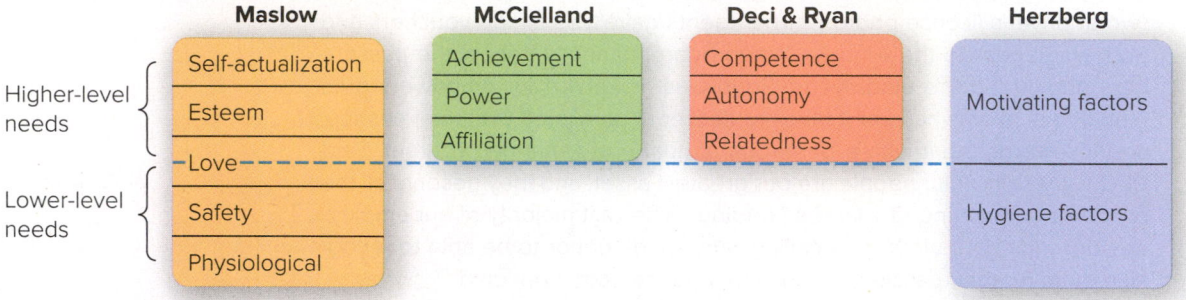

12.3 Process Perspectives on Employee Motivation

THE BIG PICTURE

Process perspectives, which are concerned with the thought processes by which people decide how to act, have three viewpoints: equity/justice theory, expectancy theory, and goal-setting theory.

Process perspectives are concerned with the thought processes by which people decide how to act—how employees choose behavior to meet their needs. Whereas need-based perspectives simply try to understand employee needs, process perspectives go further and try to understand why employees have different needs, what behaviors they select to satisfy them, and how they decide if their choices were successful.

In this section we discuss three process perspectives on motivation:

- Equity/justice theory.
- Expectancy theory.
- Goal-setting theory.

Equity/Justice Theory: How Fairly Do You Think You're Being Treated in Relation to Others?

Fairness—or, perhaps equally important, the *perception* of fairness—can be a big issue in organizations. For example, if, as a salesperson for Target, you received a 10% bonus for doubling your sales, would that be enough? What if other Target salespeople received 15%? And how about what the larger market is paying people with your competencies? "It tends to be whether you feel that you're being paid a fair market value," said Andrew Challenger, vice president at the oldest staffing firm in the country. Challenger added, "So if you have two master's degrees and you're a programmer and you have a really high value in the [labor] market and you're being paid $100,000 when you think you should be paid $120,000, you're not going to be particularly satisfied."[56] Equity/justice theory says you'll compare yourself, and your pay, to market data as well.

Equity theory is a model of motivation that explains how people strive for fairness and justice in social exchanges or give-and-take relationships. Pioneered by psychologist J. Stacey Adams, equity theory is based on the idea that employees are motivated to see fairness in the rewards they expect for task performance and are motivated to resolve feelings of injustice.[57] We will discuss Adams's ideas and their application, then discuss the extension of equity theory into what is called *justice theory*. We conclude by discussing how to motivate employees with both equity and justice theory.

Equity theory is based on *cognitive dissonance* (see Chapter 11), the psychological discomfort people experience between their cognitive attitude and incompatible behavior. According to equity theory:

- *Discomfort is motivating*— it's suggested that the discomfort caused by cognitive dissonance motivates us to take action to maintain consistency between our beliefs and our behavior. One expert noted, "People make work decisions based on what they're being paid and what others around them are being paid," adding, "If the person above me is making a lot more money than I am, but I feel like I could work harder and get promoted to get the same salary, I will be motivated to do that."[58]

- *We correct discomfort in one of several ways*—when we are victimized by unfair social exchanges ("I was *way* overcharged for that car repair!"), our resulting cognitive dissonance prompts us to correct the situation—whether it's slightly changing our attitude or behavior ("That shop is going to get my worst rating on Yelp") or, at the extreme, committing sabotage or workplace violence.[59]

Fairness matters to us, and we can see equity theory play out all around us. Consider the example of how Americans react to CEO pay.

CEO Compensation Example: The median compensation for a U.S. CEO is about $12.1 million, and most Americans (86%) believe CEOs are paid too much relative to the average worker.[60] How, then, might employees respond to knowing that the average pay for top CEOs in 2019 was around 278 times the average worker's pay?[61] Some experts suggest that such imbalances are partly responsible for employee dissatisfaction, theft, turnover, and lower firm performance.[62]

The Elements of Equity Theory: Comparing Your Inputs and Outputs with Those of Others The key elements in equity theory are *inputs*, *outputs (rewards)*, and *comparisons*. (See Figure 12.7.)

FIGURE 12.7   Equity theory

How people perceive they are being fairly or unfairly rewarded.

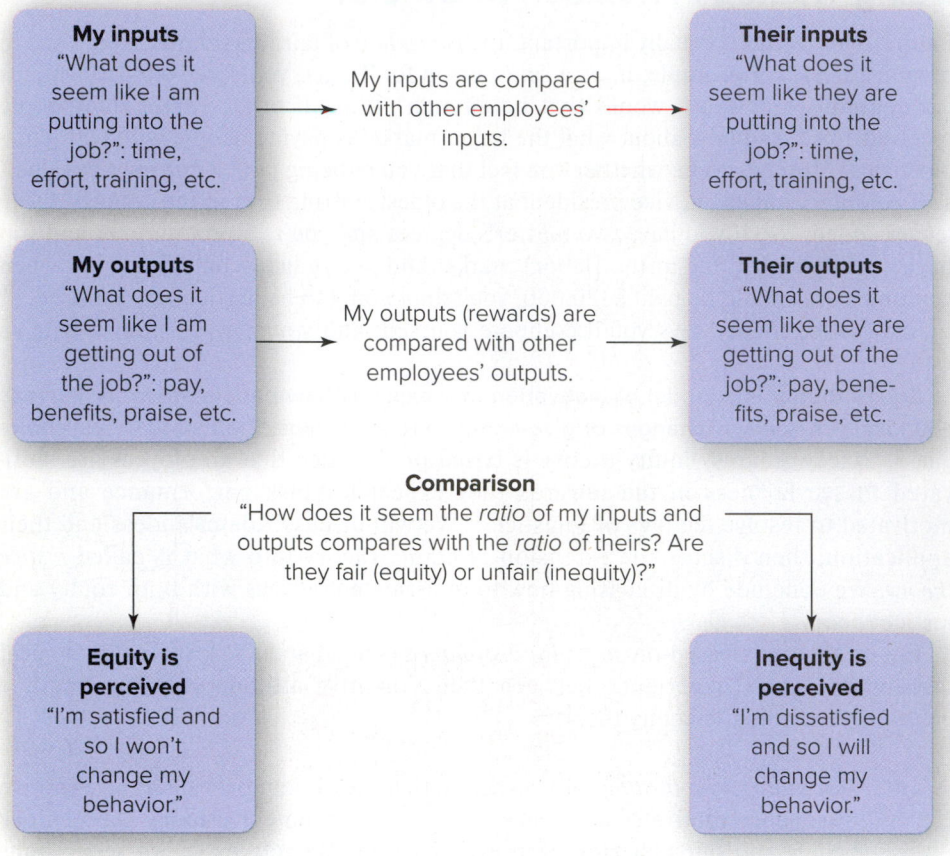

Inputs—"What do you think you're putting into the job?"   The inputs that people perceive they give to an organization include their

Time	Effort	Training	Experience	Education
Intelligence	Creativity	Seniority	Status	Social capital

Outputs or Rewards—"What do you think you're getting out of the job?"   Outputs are the rewards that people receive from an organization, and they include

Pay	Benefits	Praise and recognition
Bonuses	Promotions	Status perquisites

Comparison—"How do you think your ratio of inputs and rewards compares with those of others?"   Equity theory suggests that people compare the *ratio* of their own outcomes to inputs against the *ratio* of someone else's outcomes to inputs.[63]

- When employees compare the ratio of their inputs and outputs (rewards) with those of others—whether co-workers within the organization or even other people in similar jobs outside it—they follow the comparison with a judgment about fairness.

- When employees perceive there is *equity*, they are satisfied with the ratio and don't change their behavior.

- When employees perceive there is *inequity*, they feel resentful and act to change the inequity.

Using Equity Theory to Motivate Employees

Adams suggests that employees who feel they are being under-rewarded relative to their inputs will respond to the perceived inequity in one or more of the following negative ways:

- Reducing their inputs. ("I'm just going to do the minimum required.")
- Trying to change the outputs or rewards they receive. ("If they won't give me a raise, I'll just take stuff.")
- Distorting the inequity. ("They've never paid me what I'm worth.")
- Changing the object of comparison. ("They think I don't work as hard as Bob? He's a slacker compared to Sid.")
- Leaving the situation. ("I'm outta here!")

By contrast, employees who think they are treated fairly are:

- More likely to support organizational change.
- More apt to cooperate in group settings.
- Less apt to turn to arbitration and the courts to remedy real or imagined wrongs.

The Elements of Justice Theory: Distributive, Procedural, and Interactional

Beginning in the late 1970s, researchers in equity theory began to expand into an area called *organizational justice*, which is concerned with the extent to which people perceive they are treated fairly at work. Three different components of organizational justice have been identified: *distributive*, *procedural*, and *interactional*.[64]

- *Distributive justice*—"How fair are the rewards that are being given out? Distributive justice reflects the perceived fairness of the resources and rewards being distributed or allocated among employees. Employees perceive distributive justice when they believe that the organization has given them a fair share of rewards and resources.[65]

- *Procedural justice*—"How fair is the process for handing out rewards?" Procedural justice is defined as the perceived fairness of the process and procedures used to make allocation decisions. Employees have stronger feelings of procedural justice when they have a chance to voice their opinions about workplace procedures, and when those procedures are applied accurately and consistently.[66] Numerous studies have shown that procedural justice increases prosocial behaviors in organizations such as organizational citizenship behavior (discussed in Chapter 11).[67]

- *Interactional justice*—"How fair is the treatment I receive when rewards are given out?" Interactional justice relates to how organizational representatives treat employees in the process of implementing procedures and making decisions.[68] This form of justice is not about how decision making or procedures are perceived but rather whether people themselves believe they are being treated fairly when decisions are implemented. Employees that perceive low levels of interactional justice respond with decreased job performance and job satisfaction, and increased stress and destructive behaviors.[69] Fair interpersonal treatment necessitates that managers communicate truthfully and treat people with courtesy and respect.

Do you feel that your managers treat you fairly at your job? Take the following self-assessment to find out.

SELF-ASSESSMENT 12.4

Measuring Perceived Fair Interpersonal Treatment

The following survey was designed to assess the extent to which you are experiencing fair interpersonal treatment at work. Please be prepared to answer these questions if your instructor has assigned Self-Assessment 12.4 in Connect.

1. Are you being treated equitably?

2. Based on examining the three lowest scoring items, what could your manager do to improve your perceptions of equity?

3. What can you do to increase your perceptions of fair interpersonal treatment?

Using Equity and Justice Theories to Motivate Employees   It is important to remember that an individual's *perception* of justice becomes their *reality* when applying these theories. For example, one Gallup poll revealed that 40% of Americans felt they were underpaid.[70] Your understanding of equity and justice theories can enhance your effectiveness in the following ways:

- *Makes you a better manager.* Knowledge of equity and justice theories will allow you to hear out and better understand employee concerns. You also can communicate reasonable expectations and make sure objective measures for rewards are well understood.

- *Makes you a better co-worker.* As an employee yourself, you can motivate other workers by clearly understanding and communicating opportunities to improve their situations.

Here are five practical lessons to remember about equity and justice theories.

1. Employee Perceptions Are What Count   No matter how fair management thinks the organization's policies, procedures, and reward system are, each employee's perception of the equity of those factors is what counts.

   Meow Wolf Example: Two former employees of Meow Wolf—the immersive art installation phenomenon—sued the company for gender discrimination in 2019. In

Meow Wolf is known for providing eclectic, immersive, mind-bending experiences for visitors. Unfortunately, the company also recently became known for lawsuits filed by employees who perceived unfair treatment related to their gender. Mark Ralston/Getty Images

their lawsuit, the two women alleged that the company had displayed "a pattern and practice of subjecting female employees to different compensation, terms, conditions, and/or privileges of employment than their male colleagues." Both women also believed they had been terminated because they spoke up to supervisors about being underpaid and overscrutinized relative to male employees. In response to the filing, the company stated that "We are surprised and deeply saddened by these baseless allegations, which run completely counter to our culture, and will defend against them through the legal process."[71]

2. Employees Want a Voice in Decisions That Affect Them Managers benefit by allowing employees to participate in making decisions about important work outcomes. In general, employees' perceptions of procedural justice are enhanced when they have a voice in the decision-making process.[72] **Voice** is defined as employees' expression of work-related concerns, ideas, and/or constructive suggestions to managers.[73]

Managers are encouraged to seek employee input on organizational changes that are likely to affect the workforce. This conclusion was supported by the results of a recent study of 3,915 American workers. Results showed that the majority of workers feel strongly that they should have a voice in decisions regarding their work conditions, compensation, benefits, safety, and the products and services they work on. However, this study also revealed that today's workers have the least say when it comes to their compensation (59% reported having little to no say) and benefits (62% reported having little to no say).[74]

> **HSBC Example:** Senior executives at HSBC realized their company's culture had become overly hierarchical and had created an environment where decisions came from the top and employees didn't speak up. To encourage employee voice, the company instituted its Exchange, or, as it is more commonly referred to by employees, the "Shut Up and Listen" program. Through this program, managers and employees meet regularly to communicate according to three rules: (1) managers do not talk—they listen; (2) the meetings have no agenda; and (3) employees can bring up anything they choose. The company noticed that in earlier meetings, most of the topics involved issues with pay, co-workers, or other things in the work environment. But after employees grew accustomed to having a voice, the focus of the meetings shifted to topics such as how employees could better serve customers, improve products, or pursue career development opportunities.[75]

3. Employees Should Be Given an Appeals Process Giving employees the opportunity to appeal decisions that affect their welfare enhances their perceptions of distributive and procedural justice.

> **Student Example:** Did you know that as a student you likely have access to an appeals process? Most colleges and universities have processes in place that allow students to appeal course grades if they feel they have truly been treated unfairly. For example, at one university, students can appeal grades if they believe their instructor (1) made an error in calculating their grade or recording assignment submission dates, (2) failed to apply grading procedures in an equitable and unbiased way, or (3) did not assign grades according to the procedures set forth in the course syllabus.[76]

4. Leader Behavior Matters Employees' perceptions of justice are strongly influenced by the leadership behavior exhibited by their managers (leadership is discussed in Chapter 14). Thus, it is important for managers to consider the justice-related implications of their decisions, actions, and public communications.[77]

> **John Mackey Example:** John Mackey, CEO of Whole Foods, believes companies have a higher purpose. Said Mackey in a recent interview, "To engage in

conscious capitalism is to understand the purpose of business—beyond just making money."[78] As one sign of his commitment to fairness, Mackey has capped his own salary at $1 per year since 2007.[79] Compare this to the CEO pay cited earlier.

5. A Climate for Justice Makes a Difference   Managers need to pay attention to the organization's climate for justice. Justice climate relates to the shared sense of fairness felt by the entire workgroup. Research suggests that employees in organizations with strong justice climates exhibit:[80]

- Increased job satisfaction and organizational commitment.
- More helping behaviors.
- Enhanced job performance.

The discussion of equity/justice theory has important implications for your own career. For example, you could work to resolve negative inequity by asking for a raise or a promotion (raising your outputs) or by working fewer hours or exerting less effort (reducing inputs). You could also resolve the inequity cognitively, by adjusting your perceptions as to the value of your salary or other benefits (outcomes) or the value of the actual work done by you or your co-workers (inputs).

See the Example box to learn about how employees are speaking out against perceived justice violations.

EXAMPLE   Employee Activism

Voicing concerns can be a scary proposition because it exposes employees to increased risk. In fact, over 53.8% of the discrimination charges the EEOC received in 2019 were for retaliation, which occurs when employees are punished for asserting their and others' rights to fair treatment in the workplace.[81] But data suggest that, in spite of the risks, employees are becoming increasingly likely to speak up in response to concerns about their workplaces. In fact, employees are speaking up not only about things that directly affect them but also about how their company policies affect others outside of the organization, which is known as *employee activism*.

At Lush cosmetics, upper management regularly consults with employees to figure out which social issues are most important to them, and thus, which social issues the company should pursue at the corporate level. Here, climate activism is on full display in a Lush store window in the U.K. MediaWorldImages/Alamy Stock Photo

Younger Workers
One explanation for the increase in activism is that younger workers may be more comfortable speaking up when they are unhappy. Says one HR expert, "The floodgates for 'having your say' are open, particularly for younger employees coming into the workforce."[82] Indeed, many have attributed the rise in employee activism to generational differences, and the fact that Millennials and Gen Zs will make up more than 50% of the workforce by 2030 makes this issue especially important for organizations.[83]

Aversion to Hypocrisy
HR expert Peter Cappelli thinks another explanation for the increase in activism is equally likely. He believes that people—regardless of age—don't like hypocrisy and are inclined to call it out when they see it. Said Cappelli, "A great many—and perhaps most—companies have figured out that it helps their business to appear to be socially responsible. If you present yourself that way, if your motto is 'Don't be evil,'

for example, and then it turns out that you are doing something that isn't so easy to square with high moral values—such as doing business with unsavory clients or ducking sexual-harassment issues—then you look like a hypocrite." Cappelli added that "The complaints are at least in part because you told us you (and we) were doing good—that's partly why we came here and why we identify with you—and now you've sullied that, along with how I feel about myself working here."[84]

Activism in the News

Let's take a look at some examples of how companies have responded to employee activism in recent years.

Wayfair: Hundreds of employees at the e-commerce company walked off of the job in June 2019 after learning that their organization sold around $200,000 worth of furniture to a government contractor for use in child migrant detention facilities in Texas. In response, the company's founder donated $100,000 to the Red Cross for people in need of basic necessities at the border.[85]

Google: In November 2018, more than 20,000 Google employees participated in a walkout to call attention to the company's handling of sexual harassment complaints.[86] Among other things, the workers demanded that Google end its mandatory arbitration policy. A year later, the demands remained mostly unmet, but many credited the walkout for a wave of activism at Google and other large tech firms in the coming year.[87]

Lush: Lush Cosmetics consciously pursues employee activism through its "in-house activist," a position currently held by Carleen Pickard. Said Pickard in an interview, "We routinely pull staff in and ask them what should be the issue to work on."[88] Pickard's job is to gather workers' insights, formulate ideas for campaigns, and educate the company's workers about avenues it chooses to pursue.

Summary

Regardless of the reason, employees are speaking up more than ever before, and social media is making activism easier and more widespread. Some suggest employee activism may be a good wake-up call for organizations. Said one expert, "Employee voice is the cheapest smoke alarm you can buy."[89] When organizations' actions don't align with their values, they can expect employees to call them out.[90]

YOUR CALL

What do you think about the increase in employee activism? Have you ever spoken out against a company you worked for? Can you see yourself doing so in the future? Why or why not?

Expectancy Theory: How Much Do You Want and How Likely Are You to Get It?

Victor Vroom's **expectancy theory** boils down to deciding how much effort to exert in a specific task situation. This choice is based on a two-stage sequence of expectations—moving from effort to performance and then from performance to outcomes.[91]

The Three Elements: Expectancy, Instrumentality, and Valence   What determines how willing you (or an employee) are to work hard at tasks important to the success of the organization? The answer, says Vroom, is that you will do what you *can* do when you *want* to.

Your motivation, according to expectancy theory, involves the relationship between your *effort*, your *performance*, and the desirability of the *outcomes* (such as pay or recognition) you receive for your performance. These relationships, which are shown in the following illustration, are affected by the three elements of *expectancy*, *instrumentality*, and *valence*. (See Figure 12.8.)

1. Expectancy—"Will I Be Able to Perform at the Desired Level on a Task?" **Expectancy** is the belief that a particular level of effort will lead to a particular level of performance. This is called the *effort-to-performance expectancy*.

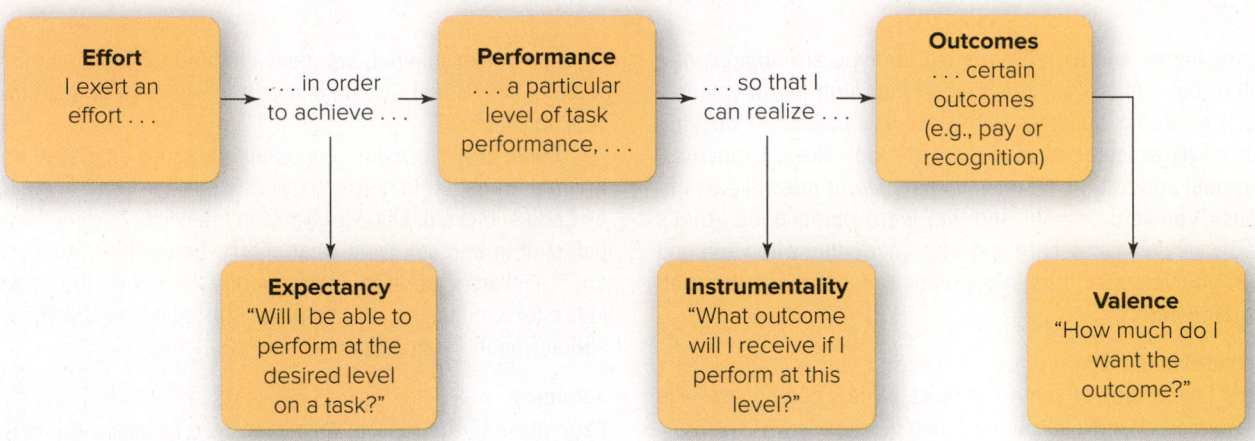

FIGURE 12.8
Expectancy theory: The major elements

- **High expectancy:** "The more hours I spend studying for this class, the higher my grade will be." This statement reflects high expectancy. That is, you believe your efforts matter in producing results.

- **Low expectancy:** "Regardless of how much I practice, I am never going to be able to dunk a basketball because I am 5'4"." This statement reflects low expectancy. That is, you do not see a link between your efforts and your ability to perform the task.

2. Instrumentality—"What Outcome Will I Receive if I Perform at This Level?"   Instrumentality is the expectation that successful performance of the task will lead to the outcome desired. This is called the *performance-to-reward expectancy.*

Some organizations motivate managers by tying executive compensation to measures of firm success. However, it can be difficult for managers to see a direct link between their work and their firms' overall performance. In other words, instrumentality may be low because even when executives feel they are doing a "good job," it may not show in their firms' broad performance data, and thus, they may not be rewarded. In addition, lower-level employees may see these arrangements as unfair, given that executives are often rewarded huge sums of money for gains that were produced by others. Some companies take specific measures to address these issues.

GE Example: GE linked its executives' annual bonuses to the firm's overall performance for 125 years. But in 2018, the company revamped the program to increase instrumentality and perceptions of fairness. GE executives' bonuses are now tied to the performance of their specific units, rather than overall firm performance.[92]

3. Valence—"How Much Do I Want the Outcome?"   Valence is value, the importance a worker assigns to the possible outcome or reward. Consider what motivates you to study for one of your courses. If you had a quiz tomorrow and it was worth 2 points (out of a possible 1000 total course points), would you exert as much effort studying as you would if the quiz were worth, say, 100 points? Probably not—because you likely don't care about 2 points nearly as much as you care about 100 points. Managers need to consider the valence of the rewards they offer for specific employees.

Worker Rewards Example: There are now five generations of workers in any given organization. Do you think they are all motivated by the same rewards? Evidence suggests that aside from salary (which seems to motivate most people to some degree) different generations of workers prefer different rewards. Among the more widely accepted ideas for the rewards preferred by each generation are:[93]

- *Traditionalists (1927–1945):* Prestigious job titles, praise for their loyalty, appreciation.

- *Baby Boomers (1946–1964):* Health insurance, working for someone they respect, authority, prestigious perks like parking spaces and posh offices, recognition.

- *Generation X (1965–1980):* Job security, challenge, mentoring, flexibility, opportunities for remote work, stock options.

- *Millennials (1981–1996):* Challenge, pursuing their passions, skills training (particularly new technology), feedback.

- *Generation Z (1997–):* Pursuing their passions, job security, flexible schedules, instant feedback.

For your motivation to be high, you must be high on all three elements—expectancy, instrumentality, and valence. If any element is low, your motivation goes down.

Using Expectancy Theory to Motivate Employees

The principal problem with expectancy theory is that it is complex. Even so, the underlying logic is understandable, and research supports its use as a motivational tool.[94]

When attempting to motivate employees, managers should ask the following questions:

- **What rewards do your employees value?** As a manager, you need to get to know your employees and determine what rewards (outcomes) they value, such as pay raises or recognition.

- **What are the job objectives and the performance level you desire?** You need to clearly define the performance objectives and determine what performance level or behavior you want so that you can tell your employees what they need to do to attain the rewards.

- **Are the rewards linked to performance?** You want to reward high performance, of course. Thus, employees must be aware that *X* level of performance within *Y* period of time will result in *Z* kinds of rewards. In a team context, however, research shows that it is best to use a combination of individual and team-based rewards.[95]

- **Do employees believe you will deliver the right rewards for the right performance?** Your credibility is on the line here. Your employees must believe that you have the power, the ability, and the will to give them the rewards you promise for the performance you are requesting.

Goal-Setting Theory: Objectives Should Be Specific and Challenging but Achievable

We have been considering the importance of goal setting since first introducing the topic in Chapter 5. **Goal-setting theory** suggests that employees can be motivated by goals that are specific and challenging but achievable. According to Edwin Locke and Gary Latham, the psychologists who developed the theory, it is natural for people to set and strive for goals; however, the goal-setting process is useful only if people *understand*, *accept*, and are *committed to* the goals.[96]

The Four Motivational Mechanisms of Goal-Setting Theory   Setting goals helps motivate because goals:[97]

1. **Direct attention:**   Goal setting directs your attention toward goal-relevant tasks and away from irrelevant ones.

2. **Regulate effort:**   The effort you expend is generally proportional to the goal's difficulty and time deadlines.

3. **Increase persistence:**   Goal setting makes obstacles become challenges to be overcome, not reasons to fail.

4. **Foster the use of strategies and action plans:**   The use of strategies and action plans make it more likely that you will realize success.

Stretch Goals   Companies committed to break-out growth sometimes adopt **stretch goals**, which are goals beyond what they actually expect to achieve. Rationales for stretching include:[98]

- Forcing people out of their comfort zones to achieve more.
- Building their confidence when they succeed.
- Insulating the company against future setbacks.
- Accepting the challenge of higher performance standards.

Companies like Google, Apple, Airbus, and 3M have all reported success with "wildly daring objectives."[99] Individuals, too, can benefit from setting stretch goals. Consider the young entrepreneur in the Example box the next time you think you can't do something difficult.

EXAMPLE   Dr. Anne-Marie Imafidon: From Child Prodigy to Stemette

As a 9-year-old student, Anne-Marie Imafidon was a challenge for her teachers. "I wasn't like a terror, I was just all over the place, a class clown," said Imafidon, adding, "I was kind of winding them up, because I don't sit still."[100] By the time she was 10, her school decided that she should sit for her GCSEs (British college entrance exams) in math and IT. She passed—becoming one of the youngest people ever to do so—and by 20 she had become one of the youngest people in history to receive a master's degree from the University of Oxford in mathematics and computer science (where she was one of only three women in a class of 70).[101]

Stemettes

Dr. Imafidon founded Stemettes in 2013. The organization exists to encourage girls between the ages of 5 and 22 to pursue careers in STEM (science, technology, engineering, and math) fields. Since 2013, nearly 45,000 young women have attended the organization's free workshops and events.[102] Now at 30 years old, Imafidon has one ultimate goal for Stemettes: one day it won't exist because it will no longer need to.[103] She sees a couple of things as especially important in accomplishing this goal:

- *Changing stereotypes.* Dr. Imafidon thinks that social expectations arising from stereotypes (such as the idea that "tech" people are nerdy white males like the characters in *The Big Bang Theory*) are one of the biggest barriers to young women entering STEM

Stemettes founder Dr. Anne-Marie Imafidon has a goal of encouraging so many women to pursue STEM careers that her organization will eventually be unnecessary. Shutterstock

fields. Said Imafidon, "Those kinds of things that we have, that then pervade into when decisions are being made by those young girls, so whether it's what their teachers say to them, what their parents might say to them, what their peers say to them . . . and there's nothing really that says the opposite."[104] Stemettes works to counter these stereotypes and show young women that they have just as much of a place in STEM as anyone else.

- *Telling true stories.* Dr. Imafidon acknowledges that *any* stories of smart women in pop culture are helpful;

she sees true stories as particularly important. She referenced the film *Hidden Figures* as an example, saying that while it's nice to see fictional examples of female scientists, "It's even cooler to know that your teacher's grandma probably helped stop the war by being a code-breaker at Bletchley."

YOUR CALL

Have you ever thought about trying to achieve something extraordinarily difficult? Did you pursue the goal, or did you shy away?

Other managers find, however, that this type of goal has drawbacks and should be used with care.[105] For example, stretch goals:

- Can demotivate employees because they set aims that seem unattainable.
- Can encourage unethical behavior as employees try to reach the goals in whatever way possible.
- Can lead companies to take unnecessary risks.

Many people believe that the use of stretch goals contributed to the emissions scandal at Volkswagen.[106] Recent research seems to confirm that stretch goals can have unintended negative consequences. According to the authors of one study, "when managers focus more on goal attainment than on how goals are attained, the resulting environment may facilitate unethical behavior to achieve those goals."[107]

Two Types of Goal Orientations   The concept of goal orientation proposes that we may have one of two reasons for trying to achieve a goal depending on our orientation. The **learning goal orientation** sees goals as a way of developing competence through the acquisition of new skills. Research on goal preferences suggests that people with a strong learning goal orientation

- Appreciate opportunities to enhance their skills, such as through training, performance feedback, and the assignment of challenging tasks.
- Are a great fit for jobs that call for creativity, willingness to embrace new ideas or adaptability to new environments, making effective use of performance feedback, and taking a proactive, problem-solving approach.

The **performance goal orientation** views goals as a way of demonstrating and validating a competence we already have by seeking the approval of others. Research suggests that those with a strong performance orientation may be less willing to take on new challenges for fear of failure and may set lower goals for themselves to avoid making themselves vulnerable to criticism. In a separate study the performance goal orientation was found to be "either unrelated or negatively related to performance" on the job.[108]

The possibility of failure is always present, but those with a strong performance orientation may find that it holds them back professionally because it lets them settle for achieving less. Among those who faced and overcame their fear of failure—and indeed the reality of failure—are:

- Beyoncé, who at age 9 lost a singing competition that would have brought her a recording contract.
- Thomas Edison, who famously said that failing thousands of times was simply a way of discovering what would not work.
- Fashion designer Donna Karan ("I failed draping!").
- Best-selling writer Stephen King, who from his teen years saved his rejection slips in order to motivate himself to keep trying.

Everyone deals with failure. Did you know that Beyoncé, along with the group Girls Tyme, lost to another group on *Star Search* in 1993? That didn't stop her from pursuing her passion, and she has 24 Grammy Awards (and 70 nominations) to show for it. In 2020, *Time* magazine named Beyoncé one of the 100 most influential women of the past century. Picturegroup/Shutterstock

Michael Jordan has said, "I've missed more than 9,000 shots in my career. I've lost almost 300 games. Twenty-six times I've been trusted to take the game winning shot and missed. I've failed over and over and over again in my life. And that is why I succeed." For those who fear failing lest they be judged, Theodore Roosevelt had this to say, "It is not the critic who counts," but rather the doer of deeds, "who at the best knows in the end the triumph of high achievement, and who at the worst, if he fails, at least fails while daring greatly, so that his place shall never be with those cold and timid souls who neither know victory nor defeat."[109]

You may recall that a proactive learning orientation is a career readiness competency desired by employers: It's the same type of attitude as a learning goal orientation. We provided Self-Assessment 5.3 to assess the extent to which you possess this competency.

Some Practical Results of Goal-Setting Theory   A *goal* is defined as an objective that a person is trying to accomplish through his or her efforts. Goal-setting experts Locke and Latham proposed the following recommendations when implementing a goal-setting program.[110] To result in high motivation and performance, according to recent research, goals must have a number of characteristics, as follows.

1. Goals Should Be Specific   Goals that are specific and difficult lead to higher performance than general goals like "Do your best" or "Improve performance." This is why it is essential to set specific, challenging goals.[111] Goals such as "Sell as many cars as you can" or "Be nicer to customers" are too vague. Instead, goals need to be specific—usually meaning *quantitative,* as in:

- "Boost your revenues 25%."
- "Cut absenteeism by 10%."

You can find examples of specific goals in most organizations. Consider Pacific Gas & Electric.

PG&E Example: Pacific Gas & Electric adhered to this recommendation in its updated wildfire prevention, safety, and public safety power shutoff (PSPE) programs. Specific goals for 2020 included: "Installing 592 automated sectionalizing devices on distribution lines with the aim of reducing the number of communities without power during a PSPS event," and "Adding 23 transmission switches capable of redirecting power and keeping substations and transmission lines energized in some areas during a PSPE event."[112]

2. Certain Conditions Are Necessary for Goal Setting to Work   In order for goal setting to be effective, people must:[113]

- Have the abilities and resources needed to achieve the goal.
- Be committed to the goal. Goal commitment can be fostered by allowing employees to participate in the process of establishing goals.

3. Goals Should Be Linked to Action Plans   An action plan outlines the activities or tasks that need to be accomplished in order to obtain a goal and reminds us of what we should be working on. Both individuals (such as college students) and organizations are more likely to achieve their goals when they develop detailed action plans.[114]

Calvary Public Hospital Example: Calvary Public Hospital in Bruce, Australia, has a strategic focus on palliative care. Health care workers in this field of medicine—one of the fastest-growing medical specialties—help people with terminal illnesses to have better quality of life, less stress, and less suffering. Included in the hospital's strategic action plan are both strategic goals and action plans. For example, one goal is "Be the thought leader in palliative and end of life care, influencing how the sector thinks about and approaches this." The corresponding action plan for this goal is "Continue to drive the palliative and end of life care strategy. Publicly promote Calvary's approach to end of life care."[115]

4. Performance Feedback and Participation in Deciding How to Achieve Goals Are Necessary but Not Sufficient for Goal Setting to Work Feedback and participation enhance performance only when they lead employees to set and commit to a specific, difficult goal.

Johnson & Johnson Example: In 2018, J&J set a goal to "help 100,000+ employees be at their personal best when it comes to their health and well-being by 2020."[116] The company engages several targeted mechanisms for gaining and maintaining employee commitment to health goals. Specifically, these are:

- *Culture.* At J&J, executives and managers work to infuse the culture with health and wellness.

- *Connection.* J&J uses a unique, confidential platform for engaging employees with information about health and wellness. The platform tracks, among other things, physical activity, which employees can cash in for things like additional fitness classes. Employees can see a variety of choices for pursuing wellness goals through the platform and can tailor their own experiences.

- *Communication.* The company communicates regularly with employees about the steps being taken to increase healthy eating and the progress being made toward wellness goals. There are also continued opportunities for employees to receive training and education about health initiatives.

Goals lead to higher performance when you use feedback and participation to stay focused and committed to a specific goal. Some of the preceding recommendations are embodied in the advice we presented in Chapter 5—namely, that goals should be SMART: specific, measurable, attainable, results-oriented, and have target dates. ●

12.4 Job Design Perspectives on Motivation

THE BIG PICTURE

Job design, the division of an organization's work among employees, applies motivational theories to jobs to increase performance and satisfaction. The traditional approach to job design is to fit people to jobs; the modern way is to fit jobs to the people, using job enrichment and approaches based on Herzberg's landmark two-factor theory, discussed earlier in this chapter. The job characteristics model offers five job attributes for better work outcomes.

According to one news source, between 43 and 53% of workers are bored with their jobs.[117] Have you ever been bored at work? Is there anything that can be done about this? **Job design** is (1) the division of an organization's work among its employees and (2) the application of motivational theories to jobs to increase satisfaction and performance. There are two different approaches to job design—one traditional, one modern—that can be taken in deciding how to design jobs. The traditional way is *fitting people to jobs*; the modern way is *fitting jobs to people*.[118]

LO 12-4

Compare different ways to design jobs.

Fitting People to Jobs

Fitting people to jobs is based on the assumption that people will gradually adapt to any work situation. Even so, jobs must still be tailored so that nearly anyone can do them. This is the approach often taken with assembly-line jobs and jobs involving routine tasks. For managers the main challenge becomes "How can we make the worker most compatible with the work?"

One technique is <mark>scientific management</mark>, **the process of reducing the number of tasks a worker performs.** When a job is stripped down to its simplest elements, it enables a worker to focus on doing more of the same task, thus increasing employee efficiency and productivity. This may be especially useful, for instance, in designing jobs for mentally disadvantaged workers, such as those jobs managed by Goodwill Industries. However, research shows that simplified, repetitive jobs lead to job dissatisfaction, poor mental health, and a low sense of accomplishment and personal growth.[119]

Fitting Jobs to People

Fitting jobs to people is based on the assumption that people are underutilized at work and that they want more variety, challenges, and responsibility. This philosophy, an outgrowth of Herzberg's theory, is one of the reasons for the popularity of work teams in the United States. The main challenge for managers is "How can we make the work most compatible with the worker so as to produce both high performance and high job satisfaction?"

Two techniques for this type of job design are (1) *job enlargement* and (2) *job enrichment*.

Job Enlargement: Putting More Variety into a Job   The opposite of scientific management, <mark>job enlargement</mark> **consists of increasing the number of tasks in a job to increase variety and motivation.** For instance, the job of installing flat screens in television sets could be enlarged to include installation of the circuit boards as well. Three important points about job enlargement:

- Proponents claim job enlargement can improve employee satisfaction, motivation, and quality of production.

- Research suggests job enlargement by itself won't have a significant and lasting positive effect on job performance. After all, working at two boring tasks instead of one doesn't add up to a challenging job.

- Job enlargement is just one tool of many that should be considered in job design.[120]

Job Enrichment: Putting More Responsibility and Other Motivating Factors into a Job   Job enrichment is the practical application of Herzberg's two-factor motivator-hygiene theory of job satisfaction.[121] Specifically, <mark>job enrichment</mark> consists of **building into a job such motivating factors as responsibility, achievement, recognition, stimulating work, and advancement.**

However, instead of the job-enlargement technique of simply giving employees additional tasks of similar difficulty (known as *horizontal loading*), with job enrichment employees are given more responsibility (known as *vertical loading*).[122]

3M Example: At 3M, managers know their job is to "hire good people, and leave them alone."[123] The company gives its employees the freedom to chase after crazy ideas—and fail at them—if learning is part of the process. In order to fuel this innovative spirit with employees at all levels, the company instituted its "dual ladder system" to give successful workers the choice of how to advance their careers. The system prevents employees from taking on management positions out of obligation and instead provides workers with the choice to pursue advanced and additional responsibilities in either a science/product development track or a management track.

The Job Characteristics Model: Five Job Attributes for Better Work Outcomes

Developed by researchers J. Richard Hackman and Greg Oldham, the job characteristics model of design is an outgrowth of job enrichment.[124] The **job characteristics model** **consists of**

- Five core job characteristics that affect
- Three critical psychological states of an employee, that in turn affect
- Work outcomes—the employee's motivation, performance, and satisfaction.

The model is illustrated in Figure 12.9.

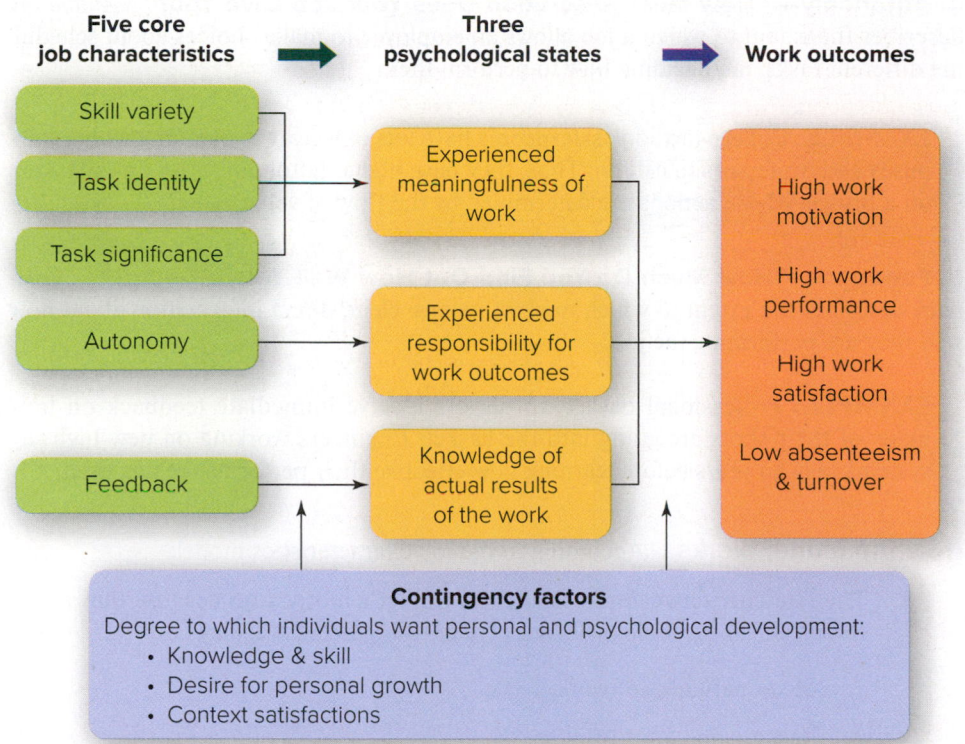

FIGURE 12.9

The job characteristics model

Source: From J. Richard Hackman and Greg R. Oldham, Work Redesign, *1e ©1980.*

Five Job Characteristics   The five core job characteristics are *skill variety*, *task identity*, *task significance*, *autonomy*, and *feedback*.

1. Skill Variety—"How Many Different Skills Does Your Job Require?"   *Skill variety* describes the extent to which a job requires a person to use a wide range of different skills and abilities.

EXAMPLE: The skill variety required by an executive chef is higher than that for a coffeehouse barista.

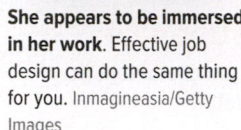

She appears to be immersed in her work. Effective job design can do the same thing for you. Inmagineasia/Getty Images

2. Task Identity—"How Many Different Tasks Are Required to Complete the Work?" *Task identity* describes the extent to which a job requires a worker to perform all the tasks needed to complete the job from beginning to end.

EXAMPLE: The task identity for a craftsperson who goes through all the steps to build a stained-glass window is higher than it is for an assembly-line worker who installs just the backup cameras on cars.

3. Task Significance—"How Many Other People Are Affected by Your Job?" *Task significance* describes the extent to which a job affects the lives of other people, whether inside or outside the organization.

EXAMPLE: A technician who was responsible for keeping a hospital's ventilator equipment working during the COVID-19 pandemic had higher task significance than a person unloading boxes of cereal in a grocery stockroom.

4. Autonomy— "How Much Discretion Does Your Job Give You?" *Autonomy* describes the extent to which a job allows an employee to make choices about scheduling different tasks and deciding how to perform them.

EXAMPLE: College-textbook salespeople have lots of leeway in planning which campuses and professors to call on. Thus, they have higher autonomy than do toll-takers on a bridge, whose actions are determined by the flow of vehicles.

5. Feedback—"How Much Do You Find Out How Well You're Doing?" *Feedback* describes the extent to which workers receive clear, direct information about how well they are performing the job.

EXAMPLE: Professional basketball players receive immediate feedback on how many of their shots are going into the basket. Engineers working on new highway systems may go years before learning how effective their performance has been.

How the Model Works   According to the job characteristics model:

- The five core characteristics affect a worker's motivation because they affect three critical psychological states (refer to Figure 12.9 again):

  1. Meaningfulness of work.

  2. Responsibility for results.

  3. Knowledge of results.

- In turn, these positive psychological states fuel important outcomes, including *high motivation*, *high performance*, *high satisfaction*, and *low absenteeism and turnover*.

Research shows that experienced meaningfulness is the most important psychological state.[125] Studies suggest that meaningfulness is so important, in fact, that 90% of workers would be willing to give up some of their pay if they were able to engage in more meaningful work.[126]

One other element—shown at the bottom of Figure 12.9—needs to be discussed: *contingency factors*. This refers to the degree to which a person wants personal and psychological development. Job design works when employees are motivated; to be so, they must have three attributes:

1. Necessary knowledge and skill.
2. Desire for personal growth.
3. Context satisfactions—that is, the right physical working conditions, pay, and supervision.

Job design works. But keep in mind that it is not for everyone. It is more likely to work when people have the required knowledge and skills, when they want to develop, and when they are satisfied with their jobs.[127]

Applying the Job Characteristics Model

There are three major steps to follow when applying the model.

- **Diagnose the work environment to see whether a problem exists.** This typically involves calculating a job's so-called motivating potential score (MPS)—the potential for a specific job to influence workers' motivation levels and job behaviors.[128]

- **Determine whether job redesign is appropriate.** If the MPS is low, an attempt should be made to determine which of the core job characteristics is causing the problem. You should next decide whether job redesign is appropriate. Job design is most likely to work in a participative environment in which employees have the necessary knowledge and skills.

- **Consider how to redesign the job.** Here you try to increase those core job characteristics that are problematic.

  Physicians Example: The combination of electronic health record (EHR) requirements and a ballooning doctor shortage have meant that primary care doctors are handling a rapidly growing volume of administrative tasks along with an increased patient load (sometimes seeing as many as one patient every 11 minutes). As a result, fewer than 50% of the 8,700 physicians surveyed in a recent study reported being happy in their jobs.[129] Physicians' #1 complaint was time-consuming record-keeping requirements, which 66% of respondents said have eaten away at the time they have available to spend with patients.

  In response to these problems, some physicians have taken to redesigning their own jobs. Specifically, many are adopting a "direct primary care" (DPC) model that cuts out insurance companies and, thus, much of the

The "direct primary care" model represents an attempt to drastically redesign primary care physicians' jobs. Which critical psychological states do you think are likely to increase in doctors who are able to spend significantly more time with their patients and significantly less time filling out paperwork? How might this impact patient outcomes?
Shutterstock

paperwork and regulation that can strip physicians of feelings of autonomy and task significance. According to the Direct Primary Care Coalition website, "It works. Since 2009, almost 1,200 new DPC practices have emerged and employers, unions, and even health plans now rely on DPC doctors to provide better care for their employees. Employers report their cost of providing health care goes down by as much as 20%. Patients love the care they get. Doctors love doing what they were trained to do instead of filling out insurance forms."[130] ●

12.5 Reinforcement Perspectives on Motivation

THE BIG PICTURE

Reinforcement theory suggests behavior will be repeated if it has positive consequences and won't be if it has negative consequences. This section also describes how to use four techniques—positive reinforcement, negative reinforcement, extinction, and punishment—to modify employee behavior.

LO 12-5

Discuss how to use four types of behavior modification.

When businesses were forced to abruptly shut their doors in mid-March of 2020, Chef-Stable, part owner of more than 20 restaurants, had to lay off around 700 workers. But as the group's restaurants adapted to a new delivery and curbside takeout model, a portion of their business returned, and they sought to rehire some of their workers. The problem was, many of their former employees were making more money from a combination of unemployment benefits and weekly $600 Federal Pandemic Unemployment Compensation checks than they had in their jobs—almost $400 more per week, to be precise. ChefStable would have had to offer a $25.40 hourly wage to its line cooks to match the temporary unemployment bonus. This story underscores the power of consequences in determining people's actions.[131]

The reinforcement perspective, which was pioneered by Edward L. Thorndike and B. F. Skinner, is concerned with how consequences affect behavior.[132] Two ideas form the foundation of the reinforcement perspective:

1. Skinner's concept of *operant conditioning*—the process of controlling behavior by manipulating its consequences, which is rooted in...

2. Thorndike's **law of effect**—which says behavior with favorable consequences tends to be repeated, while behavior with unfavorable consequences tends to disappear.[133]

From these underpinnings arose **reinforcement theory**, which attempts to explain behavior change by suggesting that behavior with positive consequences tends to be repeated, whereas behavior with negative consequences tends not to be repeated. The use of reinforcement theory to change human behavior is called *behavior modification.*

The Four Types of Behavior Modification: Positive Reinforcement, Negative Reinforcement, Extinction, and Punishment

Reinforcement is anything that strengthens the likelihood that a given behavior will be repeated in the future.

There are four types of behavior modification: (1) *positive reinforcement*, (2) *negative reinforcement*, (3) *extinction*, and (4) *punishment*. (See Figure 12.10.)

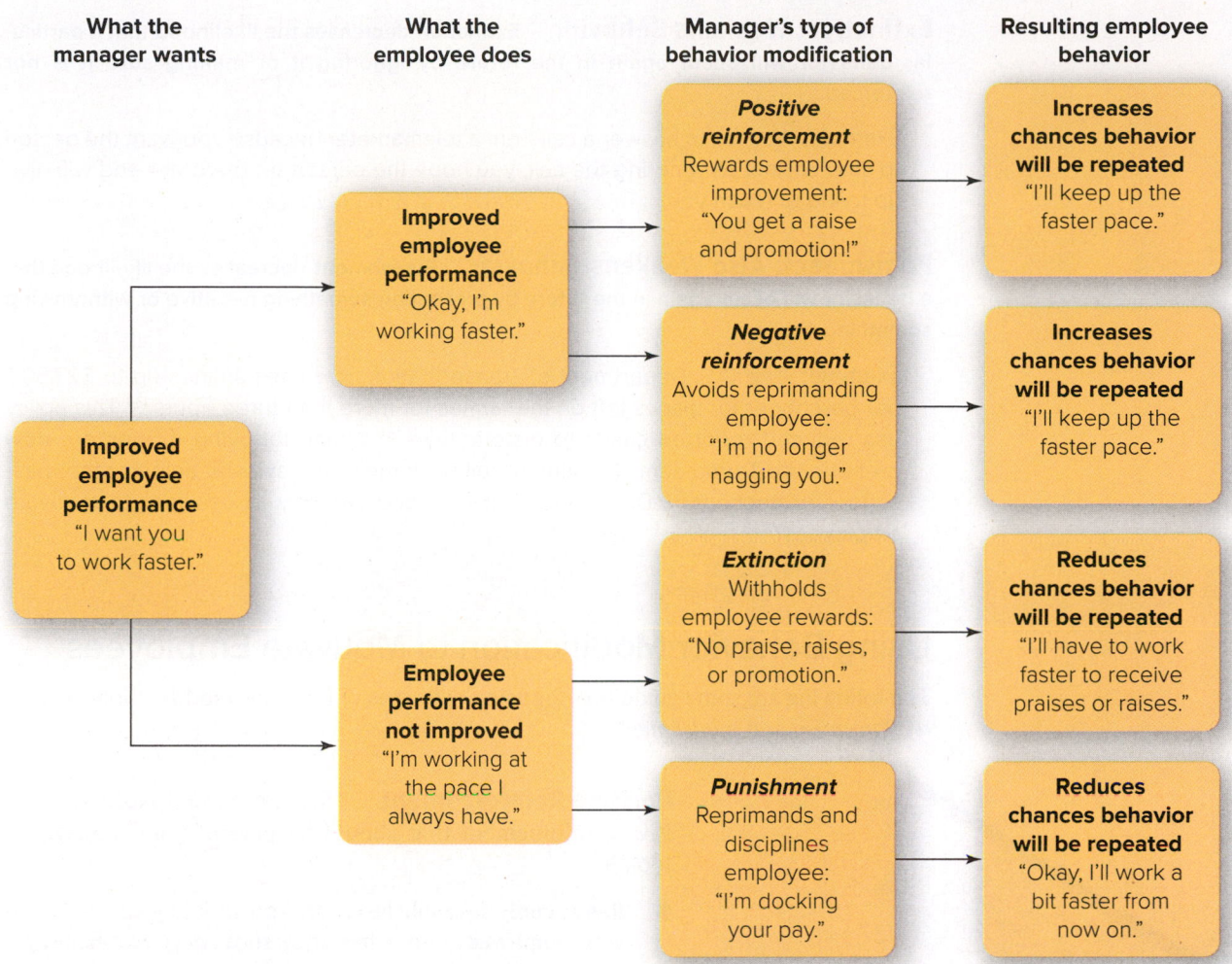

What the manager wants	What the employee does	Manager's type of behavior modification	Resulting employee behavior
Improved employee performance "I want you to work faster."	**Improved employee performance** "Okay, I'm working faster."	***Positive reinforcement*** Rewards employee improvement: "You get a raise and promotion!"	**Increases chances behavior will be repeated** "I'll keep up the faster pace."
		Negative reinforcement Avoids reprimanding employee: "I'm no longer nagging you."	**Increases chances behavior will be repeated** "I'll keep up the faster pace."
	Employee performance not improved "I'm working at the pace I always have."	***Extinction*** Withholds employee rewards: "No praise, raises, or promotion."	**Reduces chances behavior will be repeated** "I'll have to work faster to receive praises or raises."
		Punishment Reprimands and disciplines employee: "I'm docking your pay."	**Reduces chances behavior will be repeated** "Okay, I'll work a bit faster from now on."

FIGURE 12.10

Four types of behavior modification

These are different ways of changing employee behavior.

Positive Reinforcement: Strengthens Behavior   Positive reinforcement is the introduction of positive consequences to strengthen the likelihood that a particular behavior will occur again in the future.

> **Example:** A supervisor who has asked a salesperson to sell more policies might reward successful performance by saying, "It's great that you exceeded your sales quota, and you'll get a bonus for it. Maybe next time you'll sell even more and will become a member of the Circle of 100 Top Sellers and win a trip to Paris as well." Note the rewards: praise, more money, recognition, awards. Presumably this will *strengthen* the behavior and the sales rep will work even harder in the coming months.

Negative Reinforcement: Also Strengthens Behavior   Negative reinforcement is removal of a negative stimulus to strengthen the likelihood that a particular behavior will occur again in the future.

> **Example:** A supervisor who has been pestering a salesperson might say, "Now that you've exceeded your quota, I'll get off your case and stop the pestering." Note that the removal of the supervisor's negative statements is meant to increase the likelihood that the salesperson will continue to meet their quota.

Extinction: Weakens Behavior

Extinction decreases the likelihood that a particular behavior will occur again in the future by ignoring it or making sure it is not reinforced.

Example: You fail to answer a call from a telemarketer because you want the person to stop calling. By ignoring the call, you hope the person on the other end will give up trying to reach you.

Punishment: Also Weakens Behavior

Punishment decreases the likelihood that a behavior will occur again in the future by presenting something negative or withdrawing something positive.

Example: The U.S. Department of Transportation now fines airlines up to $27,500 per passenger for planes left on the tarmac for more than three hours.[134] This policy has reduced reported cases to historic lows.[135] Airline lobbying groups are now pressing the Trump administration to roll back the rule, however, among other passenger protections.[136] Do you think it's a good strategy to use fear to motivate employees?

Using Behavior Modification to Motivate Employees

The following are some guidelines for using two types of behavior modification—*positive reinforcement* and *punishment.*

The "carrot and stick" metaphor often is used to illustrate motivation through reward and punishment. Which do you think is the better motivator—the promise of reward (carrot) or the fear of punishment (stick)? Are there times when one may be more appropriate and/or effective than the other? Comstock Images/ Alamy Stock Photo

Positive Reinforcement There are several aspects of positive reinforcement that should be part of your managerial toolkit:

- **Reward only desirable behavior.** You should give rewards to your employees only when they show *desirable* behavior. Thus, for example, you should give praise to employees not for showing up for work on time (an expected part of any job) but for showing up early.

- **Give rewards as soon as possible.** You should give a reward as soon as possible after the desirable behavior appears. Thus, you should give praise to an early-arriving employee as soon as he or she arrives, not later in the week.

- **Be clear about what behavior is desired.** Clear communication is everything. You should tell employees exactly what kinds of work behaviors are desirable, and you should tell everyone exactly what he or she must do to earn rewards.

- **Have different rewards and recognize individual differences.** Recognizing that different people respond to different kinds of rewards, you should have different rewards available. Thus, you might give a word of praise verbally to one person, text or e-mail a line or two to another person, or send a hand-scrawled note to another.

Punishment Unquestionably there will be times when you'll need to threaten or administer an unpleasant consequence to stop an employee's undesirable behavior. Sometimes it's best to address a problem by combining punishment with positive reinforcement. Some suggestions for using punishment are as follows.

- **Punish only undesirable behavior.** You should give punishment only when employees show frequent *undesirable* behavior. Otherwise, employees may come to view you negatively, as a tyrannical boss. Thus, for example, you should reprimand employees who show up, say, a half hour late for work but not 5 or 10 minutes late.

- **Give reprimands or disciplinary actions as soon as possible.** You should mete out punishment as soon as possible after the undesirable behavior occurs. Thus, you should give a reprimand to a late-arriving employee as soon as he or she arrives.

- **Be clear about what behavior is undesirable.** Tell employees exactly what kinds of work behaviors are undesirable and make sure the severity of the disciplinary action or reprimand matches the severity of the behavior. A manager should not, for example, dock an hourly employee's pay if he or she is only 5 or 10 minutes late for work.

- **Administer punishment in private.** You would hate to have your boss chew you out in front of your subordinates, and the people who report to you also shouldn't be reprimanded in public, which would lead only to resentments that may have nothing to do with an employee's infractions.

- **Combine punishment and positive reinforcement.** If you're reprimanding an employee, be sure to also say what he or she is doing right and state what rewards the employee might be eligible for. For example, while reprimanding someone for being late, say that a perfect attendance record over the next few months will put that employee in line for a raise or promotion. ●

12.6 Using Compensation, Nonmonetary Incentives, and Other Rewards to Motivate: In Search of the Positive Work Environment

THE BIG PICTURE

Compensation, the main motivator of performance, includes pay for performance, bonuses, profit sharing, gainsharing, stock options, and pay for knowledge. Other, nonmonetary incentives address needs that aren't being met, such as work–life balance, growth in skills, positive work environment, and meaning in work.

In this section we consider the tools today's managers use to motivate superior employee performance. We begin by discussing the various monetary rewards that have dominated employee compensation models throughout recent history.

    We then turn our attention to nonmonetary incentives, because we know now that employees often choose jobs for reasons other than financial compensation. Numerous research studies support the notion that workers can be equally, and sometimes even more, motivated by:[137]

1. Work–life balance.
2. Personal growth.
3. A positive work environment.
4. Meaningful work.

LO 12-6

Discuss the role of compensation in motivating employees.

Is Money the Best Motivator?

Whatever happened to good old money as a motivator?

Many workers rate having a caring boss higher than monetary benefits.[138] For working parents, flexibility may be more important than salary.[139] A recent Gallup poll found that employees are 50% happier at work when they have close relationships with their co-workers.[140] Finally, a 2019 Jobvite survey of 1,500 Americans found that career growth opportunities were more important to job seekers than financial compensation, retirement benefits, or health care.[141] Clearly, then, motivating doesn't just involve money.

Motivation and Compensation

Most people are paid an hourly wage or a weekly or monthly salary. Both of these are easy for organizations to administer, of course. But by itself a wage or a salary gives an employee little incentive to work hard. Incentive compensation plans try to do so, although no single plan will boost the performance of all employees. (Indeed, a *Wall Street Journal* analysis found that the S&P 500 CEOs who earned the biggest pay increases in 2017 ran average-performing companies, and the CEOS of the top-performing companies earned average pay.)[142] What does this suggest to you about the link between pay and performance?

Characteristics of the Best Incentive Compensation Plans   In accordance with most of the theories of motivation we described earlier, for incentive plans to work, certain criteria are advisable, such as:

1. Rewards must be linked to performance and be measurable.
2. Rewards must satisfy individual needs.
3. Rewards must be agreed on by manager and employees.
4. Rewards must be believable and achievable by employees.

Popular Incentive Compensation Plans   In what way would you like to be rewarded for your efforts? Some of the most well-known incentive compensation plans are *pay for performance*, *bonuses*, *profit sharing*, *gainsharing*, *stock options*, and *pay for knowledge*.

Pay for Performance   Also known as *merit pay*, pay for performance bases pay on one's results. Thus, different salaried employees might get different pay raises and other rewards (such as promotions) depending on their overall job performance. Examples of pay-for-performance plans include:

- *Piece rate.* One standard pay-for-performance plan is payment according to a piece rate, in which employees are paid according to how much output they produce, as is often used with farm workers picking fruits or vegetables. Piece-rate employers must comply with state and federal minimum wage laws.[143]

- *Sales commission.* With a sales commission plan, sales representatives are paid a percentage of the earnings the company made from their sales, so that the more they sell, the more they are paid. The financial services company Edward Jones pays its employees a salary plus commissions on sales for the first four years and then commissions only, on a scale that increases from 9% to 40% over time.[144]

Bonuses   Bonuses are cash awards given to employees who achieve specific performance objectives. Signing bonuses are also a popular way to attract new employees, particularly in tight labor markets.

Company Examples: A recent review of available jobs showed that many organizations were offering bonuses to attract new employees. At Northwell Health, employees who successfully completed a three-month probationary period were offered a $10,000 bonus. Hyatt paid newly hired full-time room attendants a $1,000 bonus ($500 after a successful 90 days, and $500 after another three months).[145]

Profit Sharing   Profit sharing is the distribution to employees of a percentage of the company's profits.

Publix Example: Publix supermarket chain was founded in 1930. Founder George Jenkins wanted to build the company around employee ownership and profit sharing, but the Great Depression left workers with little to nothing to invest. Jenkins decided to give each employee a $2 per-week raise, then held the money back for stock shares. Publix continues its tradition of profit sharing to this day and is now the largest employee-owned supermarket company in the United States.[146]

Gainsharing   Gainsharing is the distribution of savings or "gains" to groups of employees who reduced costs and increased measurable productivity. Gainsharing has been applied in a variety of industries, from manufacturing to nonprofit, and is said to be used in more than a quarter of Fortune 1000 companies, as well as many small- to midsize businesses.[147] In one version (the so-called *Scanlon plan*), a portion of any cost savings, usually 75%, is distributed to employees.

Progressive Example: The Progressive Corporation, one of the nation's largest insurance providers, has adopted a performance-based gainsharing plan open to all officers and employees (except temporary workers). The plan calculates payments by multiplying paid earnings by a target percentage (a figure between 1% and 150% that varies by position) and by a performance factor.[148]

Stock Options   With stock options, certain employees are given the right to buy stock at a future date for a discounted price. The motivator here is that employees holding stock options will supposedly work hard to make the company's stock rise so that they can obtain it at a cheaper price.

Company Examples: U.S. companies that currently offer stock options include Nordstrom, WillowTree, Aflac, Real Self, Buffer, and Apple.[149]

Pay for Knowledge   Also known as *skill-based pay,* ==pay for knowledge== ties employee pay to the number of job-relevant skills or academic degrees they earn.[150]

> **Example:** The teaching profession is a time-honored instance of this incentive, in which elementary and secondary teachers are encouraged to increase their salaries by earning additional college credit. However, firms such as FedEx also have pay-for-knowledge plans.

Nonmonetary Ways of Motivating Employees

Employees who can behave autonomously, solve problems, and take initiative are apt to be the very ones who will leave if they find their own needs aren't being met—namely, employees crave (1) work–life balance, (2) personal growth, (3) a positive work environment, and (4) meaningful work.

The Need for Work–Life Balance

A recent article on the importance of work-life balance noted just how little of it workers currently have. "An executive at JPMorgan Chase & Co. gets unapologetic messages from colleagues on nights and weekends, including a notably demanding one on Easter Sunday. A web designer whose bedroom doubles as an office has to set an alarm to remind himself to eat during his non-stop workday. At Intel Corp., a vice president with four kids logs 13-hour days while attempting to juggle her parenting duties and her job." Indeed, nearly 40% of American professionals now work 11-hour days. In a study of thousands of workers, the biggest obstacles to work–life balance included unsupportive bosses and the pressure to be "always on" because of technology.[152]

Among the employer offerings designed to cater to the desire for work–life balance (at least for some employees) are *work–life benefits, flex-time,* and *vacation/sabbatical time.*

Work–Life Benefits   ==Work–life benefits== consist of initiatives and programs that employers implement in an effort to help employees balance the often competing needs of their work and home lives.[153] The purpose of such benefits is to remove barriers that make it hard for people to strike a balance between their work and personal lives, such as allowing parents time off to take care of sick children.

Work–life benefits include:

- Helping employees with day care costs or even establishing onsite centers.
- Access to mental health services.
- Offering domestic-partner benefits.
- Giving job-protected leave for new parents.
- Free or reduced gym memberships.
- Providing technology, such as mobile phones and laptops, to enable parents to work at home.[154] (Unfortunately, the workplace culture often tends to discourage paid leave for parents, particularly fathers.)[155]

How good are U.S. employers at making work–life benefits available? The United States actually ranks fairly low on this feature—27th out of 38 on a list of countries with the best work–life balance.[156]

Flex-Time   *Flex-time* is a characteristic of the flexible workplace—including part-time work, a compressed workweek, job sharing, and telecommuting. Among the top 10 companies offering flex-time arrangements in 2020 were XPLANE, Square Root, and Mindflash.[157]

The job performance of employees who were able to work from home improved by 13% in one nine-month flex-time experiment conducted by the National Bureau of Economic Research.[158] In another study, flexible work arrangements had a significant role in reducing chronic employee stress.[159]

Vacations and Sabbaticals   Some companies now offer unlimited paid vacation days to their employees, including Roku, Dropbox, and GE.[160] Sabbaticals—extended periods of paid time off that employees earn over several years—are another work–life benefit gaining in popularity. A few of the companies offering sabbaticals to U.S. employees are The Container Store, The Cheesecake Factory, REI, and Patagonia.[161]

The Need for Personal Growth   According to a recent survey, 94% of employees would stay with a company longer if they had opportunities for learning and development.[162] Young workers in particular, having watched their parents' layoffs and downsizing during the Great Recession, are apt to view a job as a way of gaining skills that will enable them to earn a decent living in the future. Employers have another point of view: They see it as developing *human capital*, which, as we saw in Chapter 9, is the economic or protective potential of employee knowledge, experience, and actions.

Learning opportunities can take three forms:

- **Studying co-workers.** Managers can see that workers are matched with co-workers from whom they can learn, allowing them, for instance, to "shadow" (watch and imitate) workers in other jobs or participate in interdepartmental task forces.

- **Tuition reimbursement.** Being reimbursed for partial or full tuition for part-time study at a college or university.

- **Learning and development.** According to *Training* magazine, U.S. companies spent $83 billion on employee learning and development in 2019.[163] Although instructor-led classrooms are still the dominant training method, 29.6% of learning hours were spent on online or other computer-based programs, including virtual classrooms and webcasts. Blended learning techniques accounted for about 28% of learning hours, and nearly 5% were conducted via mobile devices.

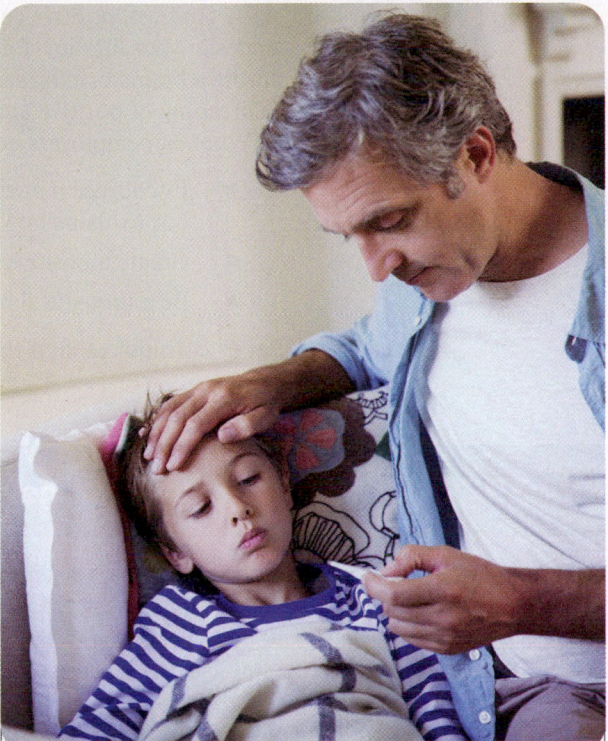

Balancing work with life. Work factors don't always allow for life factors—sick children, school appointments, family emergencies, problems with aging parents, medical appointments, and other personal matters. People around the world are urging employees to ease the single-minded focus on jobs by introducing more flexibility and balance into their lives—work–life balance. What are the top three nonwork concerns that you might have to deal with that you hope your employer might accommodate for you? Paul Bradbury/Getty Images

The Need for a Positive Work Environment   Wanting to work in a positive environment begins with the idea of well-being. ==Well-being== is the combined impact of five elements—positive emotions, engagement, relationships, meaning, and achievement (PERMA), according to renowned psychologist Martin Seligman.[164] There is one essential thing to remember about these elements: We must pursue them for their own sake, not as a means to obtain another outcome. In other words, well-being comes about by freely pursuing one or more of the five elements in PERMA.

==Flourishing== represents the extent to which our lives contain PERMA. When we flourish, our lives result in "goodness . . . growth, and resilience."[165]

- Flourishing is associated with positive outcomes like better job performance, increased organizational citizenship, lower turnover intentions, and positive mental health.[166]

- Unfortunately, many people are not flourishing. For example, according to the American Institute of Stress, workplace stress "has reached near-epidemic levels," and is contributing to increase reliance on caffeine, sugar, and anti-anxiety medication.[167] U.S. data further showed that only 11% of workplaces encourage employees to use mental health days.[168]

By contrast, positive emotions *broaden* your perspective about how to overcome challenges in your life—joy, for instance, is more likely to lead you to envision creative ideas during a brainstorming session. Positive emotions also *build* on themselves, resulting in a spreading of positive emotions within yourself and those around you.[169]

What can employers do to create a positive work environment?

- Encourage managers and co-workers to express gratitude (the Practical Action box explains how this can be done).
- Create a positive physical setting.
- Be a thoughtful boss.

Let us consider each of these suggestions.

PRACTICAL ACTION   How Managers Can Encourage Gratitude

Psychology professor and author Robert Emmons says that gratitude is a "basic human requirement."[170] People need to receive recognition and appreciation for the contributions they make.[171] Since we spend the majority of our waking hours at our jobs, this makes encouraging gratitude in the workplace vital, and studies suggest that gratitude increases job satisfaction, work productivity, and physical/mental health.[172] As one reporter put it, "Gratitude is the grease that makes working with others easier."[173] Here are some suggestions for encouraging gratitude with your friends and colleagues.

Be Specific One of the best ways to show others sincere appreciation is to give them praise that is specific and tied to how they have helped you or the organization achieve its goals.[174]

Lucid Software created a corporate gratitude flowchart to show gratitude to its employees. Rather than generic praise, the diagram contains a personalized message of gratitude for each employee written by the manager. Each note expresses specifically what the employee does to contribute to the company, and every employee receives a copy of the full flowchart at the end of the year.[175]

Use Gratitude to Build Relationships Gratitude not only bolsters individual employees' confidence, it also helps build partnerships across organizational boundaries.

The sales and service teams at Blinds.com came up with the "traveling department trophy" that it awards each month to the partner group that has made a noticeable impact. The trophy includes a "thank you breakfast" offering an opportunity for networking and relationship-building across divisions that may not otherwise interact.[176]

Do you like being appreciated for a job well done? We sure do—and so do most humans, according to experts in the field of psychology. Throughout your career, and especially as a manager, remember that a little gratitude goes a long way for employees. sirtravelalot/Shutterstock

Go Public Expressions of gratitude are particularly special when you give them to your co-workers.[177] Public accolades satisfy our social and esteem needs and serve as examples to others of the kinds of work behaviors the organization values. Furthermore, studies suggest that just witnessing expressions of gratitude, even if you are not the one being praised, is enough to generate positive benefits of gratefulness.[178] Clearly, public recognition can be a useful tool.

Encourage Peer-to-Peer Gratitude Some evidence suggests it may be more important for workers to be thanked by their peers than by their managers. Such praise may hold more weight because peers are highly familiar with what it takes to do the job well.[179]

Laszlo Bock, former senior VP of people operations at Google, created a digital tool called gThanks that Google employees could use to thank each other for their contributions to the company. Any worker could show gratitude to any other worker, and Bock often printed the messages of thanks and hung them outside his office.[180]

Make It Easy for Others to Practice Gratitude   Gratitude needs to be easy to practice if you want to inject it into your organization's culture. One company suggested keeping blank thank-you notes at the front desk that employees could grab whenever they wanted to send a note of thanks to another employee.[181]

Organizations can also make it easier for customers to show gratitude to employees. Disney introduced the hashtag #CastCompliment for visitors to use to recognize any outstanding experiences they've had with cast members (employees) while at the park. Employees' bosses then retweet the comments with the employees' photographs.[182]

Recognize the Power of Praise   Praise is a powerful tool no matter how you show it. Research suggests that it takes three positive comments to outweigh the impact of a single negative comment we receive.[183] Even if employees aren't performing as well as you'd like, it may be worthwhile to consider praising the things they *are* doing well instead of criticizing them for faults. We are more likely to repeat good behavior, and also be motivated to improve, when our efforts and contributions are recognized and appreciated.[184]

Southwest Airlines recognizes the power of praise. The company's CEO gives a weekly "shout out" to an employee who has done an outstanding job, and Southwest's magazine features a story about an exemplary employee each month.[185]

YOUR CALL

Can you recall a time when someone expressed sincere gratitude for your contributions to a project? How did this make you feel? What creative suggestions can you come up with to encourage more gratitude in your organization?

- **Positive physical settings.** The cubicle, according to new research, is stifling the creativity and morale of many workers, and the bias of modern-day office designers for open spaces and neutral colors is leading to employee complaints that their workplaces are too noisy or too bland. Some businesses, such as Hewlett-Packard and Cisco, have moved beyond cubicles to completely open offices while carefully controlling noise levels with soundscaping.[186]

- **Thoughtful bosses.** It's said that "people don't leave jobs, they leave managers."[187] In fact, one study found that 75% of American workers believe that their supervisor is the "most stressful part of their workday."[188] A Gallup study also found that about 50% of the 7,200 adults surveyed left a job "to get away from their manager."[189] Some of these employees were well paid, but is this enough?

The Need for Meaningful Work   Workers now want to be with an organization that allows them to feel they matter. One research study reported that workers would be willing to give up 23% of their lifetime future earnings for a job that would always be meaningful.[190] On a recent *Forbes* list of "the 25 most meaningful jobs that pay well," the top five were in the medical profession.[191] (See the Management in Action case at the end of the chapter for more about meaningful work in the medical profession.)

World War II concentration camp survivor Viktor Frankl, author of *Man's Search for Meaning*, strongly believed that "striving to find a meaning in one's life is the primary motivational force" for people.[192] In other words, it is the drive to find meaning in our lives that instills in us a sense of purpose and motivation to pursue goals. A legendary story is told of the cleaner at NASA who, when President Kennedy asked him what his job was, replied, "I'm helping to put a man on the moon."[193]

Meaningfulness, then, is characterized by a sense of being part of something you believe is bigger than yourself.[194] What follows are three suggestions for building meaning into your life.

1. **Identify activities you love doing.** Try to do more of these activities or find ways to build them into your work role, something Andrew Babish has done.

   Binging with Babish Example: Andrew Rea (a.k.a., Oliver Babish) is an American filmmaker and YouTube sensation. His cooking channel, Binging with Babish, has almost 7 million subscribers, and Rea credits it with pulling him out of a severe depression. The YouTube project allowed Rea to marry his love of filmmaking with his love of food. "Even if it hadn't become my career and completely changed my life, the late nights spent tinkering after work would've been worth it," Rea said. "I was cooking again, I was filming again, I was happy again."[195]

Binging with Babish YouTube Sensation Andrew Rea believes that the opportunity to engage with two of the things he loves most—cooking and film—has helped him to manage his depression.
Courtesy of Andrew Rea

2. **Find a way to build your natural strengths into your personal and work life.** Want to be more engaged with your school, work, and leisure activities? Take the time to list your highest strengths, your weaknesses, which strengths you use on a daily basis—and find what you can do to incorporate your strengths into your school, work, and leisure activities.

   Lloyds Banking Group Example: At London-based, multi-billion-dollar Lloyds Banking Group, selection decisions hinge in part on the extent to which job candidates are able to apply their natural gifts on the job. Specifically, the company uses virtual reality to place applicants into job situations and then evaluates their performance according to their strengths. According to the company's graduate and emerging-leadership development lead, Lisa Dell'Avvocato, "The more we allow candidates to reveal their natural strengths and behaviors, the more we can ensure that we align people to roles and teams where they will thrive."[196]

3. **Go out and help someone.** Research shows that people derive a sense of meaningfulness from helping others, that it creates an upward spiral of positivity.[197]

   Genentech Example: Employees at Genentech get a full week each year—Genentech Gives Back Week—to devote to volunteering. The company encourages its workers to give their time to local nonprofit organizations or to participate in company-sponsored charitable activities. Each year, the week is capped off with a concert (past performers include Justin Timberlake and Katy Perry).[198]

12.7 Career Corner: Managing Your Career Readiness

This chapter has clear implications for developing the career readiness attitude of self-motivation. It is an attitude within the career readiness model shown below. *(See Figure 12.11.)* The competency of self-motivation is defined as the ability to work productively without constant direction, instruction, and praise. It also includes the ability to establish and maintain good work habits and consistent focus on organizational goals and personal development. Practicing self-management is a great way to take a structured approach to increasing your self-motivation.

LO 12-7

Describe how to develop the career readiness competency of self-motivation.

FIGURE 12.11

Model of career readiness

©2018 Kinicki & Associates, Inc.

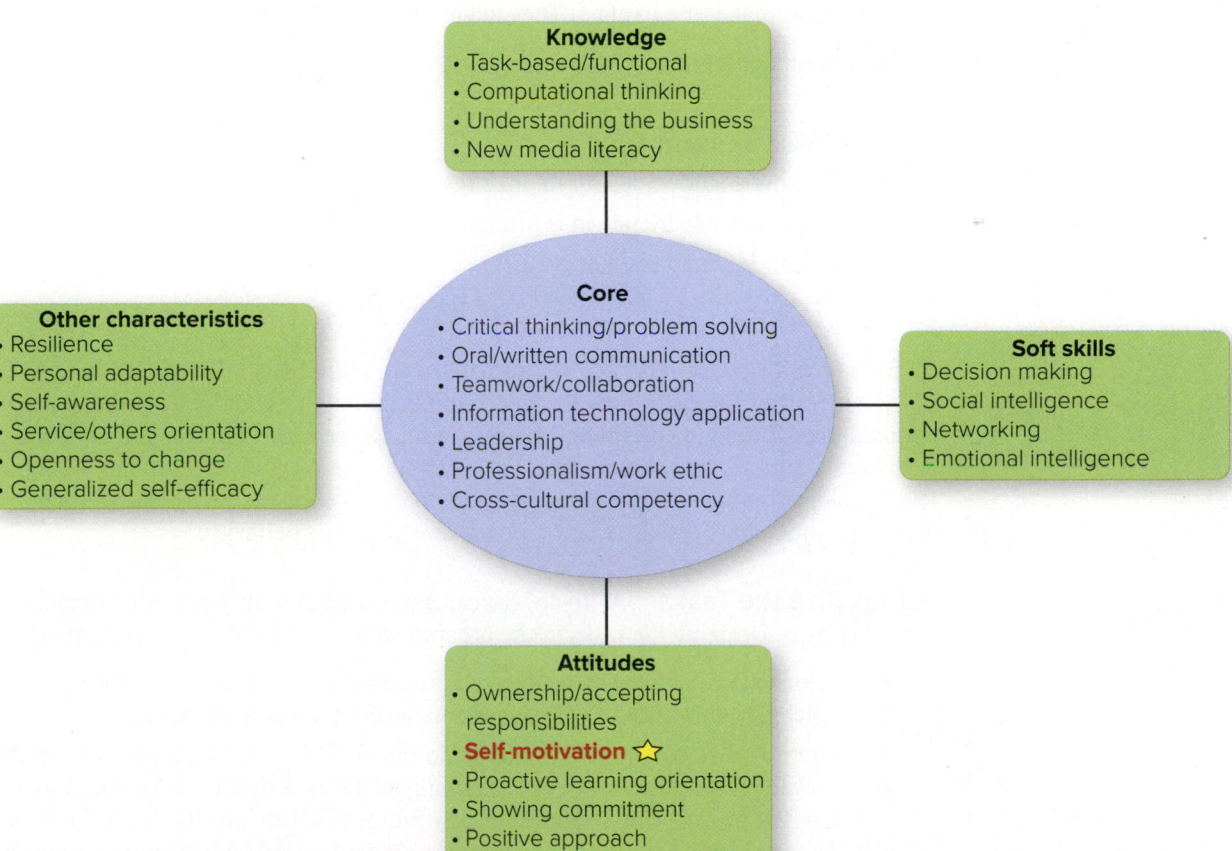

Self-management entails more than just controlling your emotions. Effective self-management requires making "a conscious choice to resist a preference or habit and instead demonstrate a more productive behavior."[199] The essence of self-management is understanding who you are, what you want in life, what you want to accomplish during your life-long journey, and then making it all happen. This pursuit of your dreams or goals is what drives the self-motivation employers are looking for.

In this section, we offer a six-step process to help you apply the principles of self-management on a daily basis. Then we offer tips on recharging to underscore the importance of balancing this intense self-effort with downtime and relaxation.

The Self-Management Process

1. Identify Your "Wildly Important" Long-Term Goal   Your goal can be as long term as a personal vision statement or as short term such as getting a job after graduation that fits your needs and values and pays a decent salary.

- The wildly important goal is your "north star" or guiding purpose.
- Writing it down is a reminder of how you should spend your time in both the short and long term.
- State your Wildly Important Goal in terms of the SMART framework we discussed in Chapter 5.

2. Break Your Wildly Important Goal into Short-Term Goals   Research tells us you are more likely to achieve your Wildly Important Goal if you break it down into smaller bite-size goals. For example, if your most important long-term goal is to get a good job after graduation, this step entails identifying the major milestones you must accomplish to make that happen. They might include outcomes like:

- Maintain a GPA of 3.0.
- Increase my career readiness.
- Obtain an internship.
- Become a student leader in one organization.
- Gain work experience in my functional field of study.
- Obtain funds to pay tuition.
- Network with professionals in my field of study.

3. Create a "To-Do" List for Accomplishing Your Short-Term Goals   A "to-do" list identifies the daily activities needed to achieve your short-term goals. It is your detailed plan for achieving them. You may want to use task management software to help create and organize your tasks. For example, one of your authors has a "higher-level" task list that spans outcomes he wants to achieve for the next year. He then creates more immediate task lists every month that guide his behavior.

4. Prioritize the Tasks   A "to-do" list can get overwhelming if you don't organize it. Organize by prioritizing the tasks in the order in which you need to complete them.

- Prioritizing in this way enables you to schedule your time to maximize your efficiency and smooth your achievement of interdependent tasks.
- There is one common error to avoid during this step. Research shows that people tend to work on "easy to complete" tasks rather than harder ones as a task list grows. This strategy actually makes you less productive because easier tasks are generally not as important as more difficult or time-consuming tasks.[200]
- One useful suggestion is to rank the tasks from (1) low importance to (5) high importance.

5. Create a Time Schedule   It's time to establish start and stop dates for each task once you have made your task list. Dates enable you to organize your schedule and monitor your progress. Here again you may find it useful to employ task management software.

6. Work the Plan, Reward Yourself, and Adjust as Needed   The best-laid plans generally have unforeseen inhibitors like illness, a car breakdown, or a crashed computer. Be flexible while working on your task plan. Finally, make the process fun by rewarding yourself for achieving various milestones. The reward should be something you value. One of your authors uses golf as his reward for completing his designated tasks.

Recharging

Self-motivation requires the ability to maintain consistent focus and self-direction toward accomplishing important goals. But it also requires that you practice self-care and allow yourself time to recharge and re-energize each day. Unfortunately, American workers tend to focus most of their energy on the former, and very little on the latter. A recent Gallup poll revealed that almost 25% of workers experience burnout either "often" or "always," and another 44% experience burnout some of the time.[201] We think it's essential that you include recharging as part of your self-motivation strategy. Here are a few tips:[202]

1. Figure Out What Recharging Means to You   When your smartphone or watch battery gets low, you have to put it on the charger and wait. There is no other solution—your devices have one and only one way to get their power back. But people are not devices, and the way we recharge is unique to us as individuals.

The trick is to figure out what recharging looks like for you. For example, for your author who happens to be an extravert, recharging means being social and interacting with people, whether by throwing a party for 30 friends, playing in a golf tournament, or taking a group Pilates class. For your other author who is decidedly introverted, recharging means being as far from most people as possible. She prefers having time at home in order to feel refreshed, and this might include a Netflix binge, an evening of food and drinks with immediate family or one or two close friends, or spending a weekend giving a closet the full KonMari treatment.

Don't feel guilty about doing what you need in order to recharge. Your iPhone doesn't apologize for needing to be plugged into the charger—and neither should you.

2. Include Mental and Physical Relaxation   Remember that recharging includes both mental and physical elements. Your body may be suffering the physical effects of stress even if you don't immediately feel it. One way to relax both your mind and body is through mindfulness meditation (discussed in several earlier chapters).

3. Accept Kindness   Often, we feel the need to prove to others that we can take care of everything on our own. Unfortunately, this can result in turning down offers of help and kindness. Maybe you have a friend who has offered to pet-sit for the weekend so that you can go on a camping trip. Or perhaps you know someone in massage therapy school who is looking for opportunities to practice their technique. Whatever they may be, remember to accept offers of kindness that will bring you joy and relaxation. Give yourself permission to be taken care of.

acquired needs theory 518
bonuses 547
content perspectives 516
distributive justice 527
equity theory 525
expectancy 531
expectancy theory 531
extinction 544
extrinsic reward 514
flourishing 549
gainsharing 547
goal-setting theory 533
hierarchy of needs theory 516
hygiene factors 522
instrumentality 532
interactional justice 527
intrinsic reward 514

job characteristics model 539
job design 537
job enlargement 538
job enrichment 538
justice climate 530
law of effect 542
learning goal orientation 535
meaningfulness 552
motivating factors 523
motivation 512
needs 516
negative reinforcement 543
pay for knowledge 548
pay for performance 547
performance goal orientation 535
piece rate 547
positive reinforcement 543

procedural justice 527
process perspectives 524
profit sharing 547
punishment 544
reinforcement 542
reinforcement theory 542
sales commission 547
scientific management 538
self-determination theory 519
stock options 547
stretch goals 534
two-factor theory 521
valence 532
voice 529
well-being 549
work–life benefits 548

Key Points

12.1 Motivating for Performance

- Motivation is defined as the psychological processes that arouse and direct goal-directed behavior.
- In a simple model of motivation, people have certain needs that motivate them to perform specific behaviors for which they receive rewards that feed back and satisfy the original need.
- Rewards are of two types: (1) extrinsic and (2) intrinsic.
- Four major perspectives on motivation are (1) content, (2) process, (3) job design, and (4) reinforcement.

12.2 Content Perspectives on Employee Motivation

- Content perspectives or need-based perspectives emphasize the needs that motivate people.
- Besides the McGregor Theory X/Theory Y (Chapter 2), need-based perspectives include (1) the hierarchy of needs theory, (2) the acquired needs theory, (3) the self-determination theory, and (4) the two-factor theory.
- The hierarchy of needs theory proposes that people are motivated by five levels of need.
- The acquired needs theory states that three needs are major motives determining people's behavior in the workplace.

- The self-determination theory assumes that people are driven to try to grow and attain fulfillment, with their behavior and well-being influenced by three innate needs.
- The two-factor theory proposes that work satisfaction and dissatisfaction arise from two different factors: work satisfaction from so-called motivating factors, and work dissatisfaction from so-called hygiene factors.

12.3 Process Perspectives on Employee Motivation

- Process perspectives are concerned with the thought processes by which people decide how to act. Three process perspectives on motivation are (1) equity theory, (2) expectancy theory, and (3) goal-setting theory.
- Equity theory focuses on employee perceptions as to how fairly they think they are being treated compared with others. The key elements in equity theory are inputs, outputs (rewards), and comparisons.
- Equity theory has expanded into an area called organizational justice, which is concerned with the extent to which people perceive they are treated fairly at work. Three different components of organizational justice have been identified: (1) distributive justice, (2) procedural justice, and (3) interactional justice.

- Expectancy theory is based on three concepts: expectancy, instrumentality, and valence of rewards.
- Goal-setting theory suggests that employees can be motivated by goals that are specific and challenging but achievable and linked to action plans.

12.4 Job Design Perspectives on Motivation

- Job design is, first, the division of an organization's work among its employees, and second, the application of motivational theories to jobs to increase satisfaction and performance.
- Two approaches to job design are fitting people to jobs (the traditional approach) and fitting jobs to people (the modern approach).
- Two techniques for fitting jobs to people include (1) job enlargement and (2) job enrichment.
- An outgrowth of job enrichment is the job characteristics model, which consists of (1) five core job characteristics that affect (2) three critical psychological states of an employee that in turn affect (3) work outcomes—the employee's motivation, performance, and satisfaction.
- The five core job characteristics are (1) skill variety, (2) task identity, (3) task significance, (4) autonomy, and (5) feedback.

12.5 Reinforcement Perspectives on Motivation

- Reinforcement theory attempts to explain behavior change by suggesting that behavior with positive consequences tends to be repeated, whereas behavior with negative consequences tends not to be repeated. Reinforcement is anything that causes a given behavior to be repeated.

- The use of reinforcement theory to change human behavior is called behavior modification.
- There are four types of behavior modification: (1) positive reinforcement, (2) negative reinforcement, (3) extinction, and (4) punishment.

12.6 Using Compensation, Nonmonetary Incentives, and Other Rewards to Motivate

- Compensation is one form of work motivator.
- Popular incentive compensation plans are (1) pay for performance, (2) bonuses, (3) profit sharing, (4) gainsharing, (5) stock options, and (6) pay for knowledge.
- There are also nonmonetary ways of compensating employees. Some employees will leave because they feel the need for work–life balance, the need to grow, the need for a positive work environment, and the need to matter. To retain such employees, nonmonetary incentives have been introduced, such as the flexible workplace.

12.7 Career Corner: Managing Your Career Readiness

- Self-motivation is increased by applying six steps of self-management.
- The six steps of self-management include the following: (1) Identify your wildly important long-term goal. (2) Break your wildly important goal into short-term goals. (3) Create a "to-do" list for accomplishing your short-term goals. (4) Prioritize the tasks you need to complete. (5) Create a time schedule for completing tasks. (6) Work the plan, reward yourself, and adjust as needed.
- Self-motivation also requires recharging.

Understanding the Chapter: What Do I Know?

1. What is motivation, and how does it work?
2. What are the four major perspectives on motivation?
3. Briefly describe the four content perspectives discussed in this chapter: hierarchy of needs theory, acquired needs theory, self-determination theory, and two-factor theory.
4. What are the principal elements of the three process perspectives: equity theory, expectancy theory, and goal-setting theory?
5. What is the definition of job design, and what are two techniques of job design?

6. Describe the five job attributes of the job characteristics model.
7. What are the four types of behavior modification?
8. What are six incentive compensation plans?
9. Discuss some nonmonetary ways of motivating employees.
10. Explain a process for using self-management to enhance the career readiness competency of self-motivation.

What Motivated Workers in the Face of a Pandemic?

Sometimes it's easy to figure out what's going to motivate workers. But at other times it's nearly impossible to know what would make someone want to persevere in a particular job. During the COVID-19 pandemic, health care workers across the globe stepped up and sacrificed themselves—in ways that the rest of us may never fully grasp—in order to take care of humanity. They exposed themselves and their families to the virus, they worked without proper personal protective equipment (PPE), and they kept at it during gruelingly long shifts, day after day. Reports estimated that health care workers' infection rates were somewhere between 10% and 20% of the total cases.[203] On the surface, it seemed there were no plausible explanations for why these workers continued to show up to their jobs throughout the crisis.

JUST HOW BAD WAS IT?

Health care jobs are some of the most stressful jobs in the world. Studies of occupational stress and burnout are often conducted using health care workers because as a professional group they are exposed to extreme stressors on a consistent basis in their jobs. In fact, pre-COVID-19, 63% of hospital nurses were already experiencing significant job burnout.[204] During the pandemic, things became much worse. Some ER nurses, who typically cared for 4 to 5 patients per shift, were suddenly responsible for 25+ patients, with more than one-third on ventilators requiring highly specialized care and attention.[205]

Health care workers realized quickly that they were at high risk of exposure to the virus. One nurse reported that managers gave him and his co-workers two N95 masks each week. Intended to be thrown away after each exposure to a dangerous pathogen, the masks became reusable, and nurses stored them in bags between shifts. "There's no way you're not getting it if you are working in the emergency room with the bare minimum protection," he said.[206]

Another nurse reported high levels of anxiety and worry surrounding health care workers' jobs. "I would say that there is 100 percent tension in the air, nurses and health care providers are scared," she said, adding, "They're scared to work and are mentally and physically being torn apart by this."[207]

INCENTIVES

As health care facilities became overcrowded and worker shortages became apparent, states began announcing incentives to attract more health care workers. For example, in Arkansas, Governor Asa Hutchinson announced

that nurses would receive a $1,000 monthly bonus payment during the pandemic, and that number would double to $2,000 if they worked in a facility with a confirmed case of COVID-19.[208] New York hospitals offered nurses upwards of $4,000 per week. Said one nurse who left her job in Detroit for a higher paying position in New York City, "When you're overworked and understaffed, you're going to go somewhere where they're going to be more appreciative of you," adding, "I felt like I was going to make a difference in New York."[209]

EXHAUSTION AND ILLNESS

No amount of money could have made up for the physical and mental toll that the pandemic took on health care workers. One ICU nurse experienced repeated bouts of respiratory symptoms, with COVID-19 testing coming up negative each time. She shared, "I realize that the mental anxiety that has been running through my veins for weeks on end since we've been talking about this is physically making me sick."[210]

Another nurse recalled passing out in her driveway after a 16-hour hospital shift in a COVID-19 unit. "I just closed my eyes for what I thought would be a minute and I woke up three hours later. I guess I was just that tired," she said.[211]

Due to the extreme precautions that health care facilities had to take in order to protect the population, most people who became gravely ill due to the virus had to face it alone, without the support of family or friends. For these people, physicians and nurses were their only connection, and for many, the last people they ever saw. Said one worker, "It's heartbreaking as a nurse to know that you are that person's everything and, sometimes, in their last moments . . . the weight of trying to fill the shoes of the people who can't be there is really heavy."[212]

PRESSING ON

Somehow, through all of this adversity, thousands of health care workers continued to show up for work ready to do everything they could to help the sick. Cardiac nurse Jeff Morawski said of his time in ICU during the pandemic, "You don't know what you're walking into, and you don't know if you'll be able to walk away without being sick, yourself," adding, "You walk in every day because you have a job to do."[213]

For many, shifts became focused on ways to keep themselves motivated, keep patients' spirits up, and care for one another. For example, nurses and physicians kept whiteboard tallies of COVID-19 patients who had successfully come off of ventilators and recovered as a way to remind themselves that there was hope amid all the despair they were witnessing. Critical care physician and medical director of care experience for the Henry Ford Health System Dr. Rana Awdish said that she started rituals in her clinic to check in on workers each day. She explained, "Not rounds on the patients, but rounds on the nurses and physicians, and just go to them and, you know, ask the open-ended questions of what concerns you most today, you know? Do you have what you need to take care of yourself? What are you worried about? Who's having the hardest time on your team? How can we support you?"[214] Another worker spent her time doing what she could to cheer up patients by drawing crowns, silly faces, and even *Tiger King* characters on her clear curved face shield before she entered their rooms (the shield had to be wiped clean with disinfectant after each visit, and each time, she drew something else for the next patient).

Crowds of people cheered on workers in cities like New York City each night, showing support with songs and applause. One nurse said that she had never felt more appreciated or supported than she did during the pandemic.[215]

THE LONG-TERM EFFECTS

In spite of the solidarity, positivity, and perseverance of health care workers amid the pandemic, real concerns exist about the long-term impacts that the crisis will have on their health. Said one expert, "A lot of people in the health care field have been struggling with burnout for a long period of time," adding, "If people don't have the ability to decompress or have that time to ground themselves, and care for themselves, go to the bathroom and eat good meals, see their families—especially if they're already dealing with that level of burnout—my concern is that that burnout is going to become

more severe."[216] Indeed, Dr. Awdish predicts that a surge of post-traumatic stress disorder is likely to ripple through the health care workforce as the chaos begins to calm down and health care workers have time to process the ethical dilemmas and heartbreaking situations they dealt with in their roles.[217]

FOR DISCUSSION

Problem-Solving Perspective

1. What is the underlying problem in this case from the perspective of hospital administrators?

2. What are the causes of this problem?

3. If you were a consultant to a hospital administrator, what recommendations would you make for fixing this problem?

Application of Chapter Content

1. What role did extrinsic and intrinsic motivation play in this case?

2. What were the major motivation issues at play in the health care industry according to the major needs-based theories of motivation (Maslow's hierarchy, McClelland's acquired needs, and Deci and Ryan's self-determination)?

3. What do you think were the major equity issues faced by health care workers during the pandemic?

4. How might the job characteristics model explain why health care workers were motivated to perform well?

5. Which types of nonmonetary compensation do you think played a part in this case?

6. Which elements of self-motivation were evident to you as you read the case?

Legal/Ethical Challenge

Are Workplace Wellness Programs Using Proper Motivational Tools?

Workplace wellness programs (WWPs) aim to motivate employees to live healthier lifestyles. Companies encourage participation by offering insurance premium discounts, cash prizes, health club memberships, and other rewards to employees who (1) participate in the programs and (2) reach certain health goals, including smoking cessation, weight loss, and blood glucose and blood pressure reduction.[218] More than two-thirds of U.S. employers currently offer wellness programs.[219] Proponents believe WWPs ultimately save companies money by making employees healthier, thereby reducing the likelihood that

employees will file costly medical claims.[220] This challenge looks at the use of health outcome–based rewards in voluntary WWPs.

Employees who choose to participate in voluntary WWPs provide personal medical data and undergo periodic health assessments to track their progress. One popular tool is the health risk appraisal, a questionnaire that gathers information about personal medical history, lifestyle choices, physiological metrics (weight, height), and family disease history, all of which are used to create a risk profile and plan of recommendations for the employees to address their health risks. Another commonly used tool, biometric screening, benchmarks and tracks employee data such as weight, body mass index (BMI), blood pressure, cardiovascular fitness, cholesterol, and blood glucose.[221]

One concern with WWPs is the risk of exposing workers' private medical data. Employers are typically prohibited from basing employment decisions on medical information. The Americans with Disabilities Act and the Genetic Information Nondiscrimination Act regulate how much personal medical data, if any, an employer is allowed to ask for, and the Health Insurance Portability and Accountability Act (HIPAA) sets strict standards for storage and access to individual health data. But wellness program vendors are often exempt from these provisions because many are not considered health care providers. Vendors may even sell health data to third parties and thus expose employees to the risk of unlawful disclosure and use of their data.[222]

Another concern is that WWPs tie employee rewards to metrics that can be (1) inaccurate and/or (2) uncontrollable. For example, many WWPs use fitness trackers to monitor employees' daily step counts and exercise frequency. But studies show that fitness trackers provide highly inaccurate and unreliable data.[223] Other popular incentives include weight loss and blood pressure/blood glucose reduction, but these metrics can fluctuate drastically in a single day and also depend on the reliability of the specific instruments used to measure them. Rewards tied to reductions in BMI are problematic because this measurement fails to account for factors such as muscle mass, body frame, and pregnancy, leaving otherwise highly fit employees at risk of being categorized as overweight or obese.[224]

The metrics used in WWPs also fail to account for factors that participants may have little to no control over. Eating healthier and exercising more are positive choices with health benefits for many people, but these practices aren't a surefire way to reduce weight and blood pressure/blood glucose in every participant. Certain medical conditions make meeting these goals extremely difficult, even with exemplary lifestyle choices.

The challenge is to decide whether organizations should tie employee rewards to employee health outcomes in voluntary WWPs.

SOLVING THE CHALLENGE

1. I am not in favor of tying employee rewards to health outcomes. Collecting and protecting employee medical information presents substantial risks including possible data breaches. Employees should have equal access to low-cost, quality health care, regardless of their personal health information, risk profiles, or health improvements. I would keep the programs voluntary and not administer rewards.

2. I think it's a good idea to tie rewards to employee health outcomes and to include waivers for employees to sign to authorize the release of their health information when they opt in to WWPs. Those who can improve their health-related outcomes should be rewarded for helping reduce the employer's health care costs.

3. I think it is a good idea to tie rewards to employee health outcomes, provided those outcomes can be measured reliably and accurately. Also, it is only fair to reward people for meeting goals they are actually able to control. Increasing stress-relieving practices such as meditation may be a more realistic goal for someone with hypertension than blood-pressure reduction. Employers should work with employees to come up with realistic, achievable, personalized goals.

4. Invent other options.

13

Groups and Teams
Increasing Cooperation, Reducing Conflict

Kapook2981/iStock/Getty Images

After reading this chapter, you should be able to:

LO 13-1 Identify the characteristics of groups and teams.

LO 13-2 Describe the development of groups and teams.

LO 13-3 Discuss ways managers can build effective teams.

LO 13-4 Describe ways managers can deal successfully with conflict.

LO 13-5 Describe how to develop the career readiness competency of teamwork/collaboration.

FORECAST   *What's Ahead in This Chapter*

In this chapter, we consider groups versus teams and discuss different kinds of teams. We describe how groups evolve into teams and discuss how managers can build effective teams. We also consider the nature of conflict, both good and bad. We conclude with a Career Corner that focuses on developing the career readiness competency of teamwork/collaboration.

Managing Team Conflict Like a Pro

Have you ever worked with a group or team that agreed about everything? Probably not. Everyone comes to a group project or assignment with different experiences, different ideas, and different expectations. Ideally, those differences bring out everyone's creative side and lead to a great conclusion, but often conflicts arise that take a little effort to overcome. Here are some suggestions for handling group conflict at school and at work that will help you hone your career readiness competencies of oral communication, teamwork/collaboration, leadership, and social intelligence.[1]

Acknowledge a Conflict Exists

Ignoring issues may help you avoid conflict in the short term but may lead to built-up resentment and future arguments. Face a conflict head-on by politely letting your teammates know you disagree with their position. Disagreements aren't always pleasant but airing them out helps head off bigger disputes in the future.

Ask a Lot of Questions

To resolve a conflict between group members, you first need to get an accurate idea of what the disagreement is about, find out what everyone thinks about it, and gather as many suggestions for resolving the conflict as you can. Before you decide that you have the one and only answer, individually ask team members what they think and what they want to achieve. Try to understand what is driving their behavior in the conflict.

Frame the Conflict around Behavior, Not Personalities

No one likes being attacked or criticized just because they disagree. Instead of saying, "You're holding everything up, Chris, because you're so stubborn," which is an attack on Chris's personality, try saying, "If you would please hear everyone out before you make up your mind, Chris, we'll be able to put more options on the table." This moves the focus to a behavior Chris can change and identifies the benefit to the group from doing so.

Remind Team Members about the Group Norms

Norms establish accepted ways of behaving, and they can make or break a group. We suggest you take the time to establish group norms shortly after forming. Remind everyone that your current project or assignment requires them to put forth their best and most cooperative efforts at working together in order to achieve your collective goal. This entails setting norms of taking responsibility for tasks, keeping on schedule, and not interrupting others in team meetings.

Choose Your Words with Care

Ever heard the phrase that you catch more bees with honey than vinegar? The point is that words matter when it comes to conflict. Saying, "Christa, this work stinks, I'd get better work from a high school student," is likely to create defensiveness and conflict. You want to stay away from an evaluative statement like this and replace it with specific, descriptive words. "Christa, your report had five computational errors, was two days late, and had five typos." Describe rather than evaluate.

You also want to avoid absolutes like always and never. "Jose, you never complete your team assignments on time," or "Rashad, you are always late to meetings." Absolutes are rarely true, and they foster defensiveness and conflict.

There is a big difference between saying, "You want to redraft the whole report *but* I want to stay on schedule," and saying, "You want to redraft the whole report *and* I want to stay on schedule." The first suggests your goals aren't compatible; the second says both sides have merit and compromise is possible.

Finally, don't give your teammates ultimatums or make rigid demands. Saying, "You all need to get me your parts of the project by tonight or else I will just do it myself," will make you look demanding, controlling, and difficult to work with. You can build more goodwill by working with your teammates on allocating tasks and setting deadlines instead of bossing people around.

Remember Conflict Can Be Productive

It's tempting to avoid or even fear conflict because open disagreement can be uncomfortable, but research shows that conflict isn't always bad. For example, teams that have a high level of disagreement in decision making, but good personal relationships, have more success.[2] With this in mind, look for the reasons behind the conflict. Is it about procedures or processes that can be adjusted, about personalities, which you can encourage people to work around in the short term, or about different ways of approaching the solution? The latter can be a gold mine of creativity for the group if you practice handling conflict effectively.

For Discussion Think back to a conflict that occurred in a group or team to which you belonged. What was the real cause of the disagreement, and how was it resolved? Would you do anything differently if you could?

13.1 Groups versus Teams

THE BIG PICTURE

Teamwork promises to be a cornerstone of future management. A team is different from a group. A group typically is management-directed, a team self-directed. Groups may be formal, created to do productive work, or informal, created for friendship. Work teams engage in collective work requiring coordinated effort. Types of teams are project teams, cross-functional teams, self-managed teams, and virtual teams.

LO 13-1

Identify the characteristics of groups and teams.

Serving the underserved. Tala CEO Shivani Siroya with her team. The company has locations in Kenya, Philippines, Mexico, and India. Ringo Chiu/ Alamy Stock Photo

Over a quarter century ago, management philosopher Peter Drucker predicted that future organizations would not only be flatter and information-based but also organized around teamwork—and that has certainly come to pass.[3]

In fact, your ability to work well as a team member is a career readiness competency desired by employers and it can affect your job opportunities and success, as well as influencing the kind of employers that might appeal to you. When applying for jobs, Gen Z employees are assessing not only their salary and benefits, but also the people they are going to be working with. A recent *Glassdoor* survey confirms this, finding that Gen Zers are more interested in the team they are going to work with than the work itself.[4] Organizations have found team building to be an important recruitment tool as a result of this culture shift. Take for instance Tala, a fintech company that provides financial services to underserved people and advertises its team-oriented environment to candidates. "We have team members from all walks of life, which brings in a diversity of opinions and experiences to meaningfully drive our innovation," says Gaurav Bhargava, Tala's vice president of credit.[5] Would you want to work on one of Tala's teams?

When you take a job in an organization, the chances are you won't be working alone. You'll be working with others in situations requiring teamwork. A survey of 1,300 companies found that people spend more than 50% of their time working in teams. Unfortunately, these same individuals reported that only 27% of their teams performed at high levels a majority of the time. Forty-three percent believed their teams performed optimally less than half the time.[6] Clearly, teamwork is essential for organizational success. Accounting software maker Xero is a good example of a company effectively managing teamwork.

Xero Example: Xero relies on an "inside-out" approach. This includes striving to attract the best people and creating a culture where everyone can do meaningful work. According to the company's website, "When we get this right, our people-focused culture resonates from the inside-out, ultimately delighting and delivering to our number one priority—our more than one million customers and partners across the world."[7]

How does the company's inside-out approach resonate at the team level? Xero's teams have autonomy over the products they build, and they even get to choose processes and metrics that suit their needs. The software maker wants everyone on the team to have a voice, appreciates diverse viewpoints, and encourages respectful disagreement. The company accomplishes this by offering leadership and communication training.[8]

Groups and Teams: How Do They Differ?

Aren't a group of people and a team of people the same thing? By and large, no. One is a collection of people, the other a powerful unit of collective performance. One is typically management directed, the other self-directed. Consider the differences, as follows.

What a Group Is: A Collection of People Performing as Individuals

A **group** is defined as (1) two or more freely interacting individuals who (2) share norms, (3) share goals, and (4) have a common identity.[9] A group is different from a crowd, a transitory collection of people who don't interact with one another, such as a crowd gathering on a sidewalk to watch a fire. And it is different from an organization, such as a labor union, which is so large that members also don't interact.

An example of a work group would be a collection of 10 employees meeting to exchange information about various company policies on wages and hours.

What a Team Is: A Collection of People with Common Commitment

McKinsey & Company management consultants Jon R. Katzenbach and Douglas K. Smith say it is a mistake to use the terms *group* and *team* interchangeably. Where groups have individual accountability, teams require both individual and mutual accountability in order to produce results. Thus, a **team** is defined as a small group of people working together with a common purpose, performance goals, and mutual accountability.[10] "Teams produce joint work product through the joint combinations of their members. This is what makes possible performance levels greater than the sum of all the individual bests of team members" says Katzenbach.[11]

H2M Example: H2M is a good example of a team. The company is an award-winning design, architecture, and engineering firm known for its team-oriented culture. The company has earned a teamwork score of 4.9/5 on online job review board *kununu* and includes teamwork as a core value. H2M also believes in promoting its team-based values to new graduates. To this end, CEO Rich Humann hosts a summer internship program that includes a focus on team building. The intent of the program is to develop teamwork and collaboration skills for the next generation of H2M employees.[12]

As you can see, teamwork is a soft skills career readiness competency desired by employers. It is defined as the ability to work effectively with and build collaborative relationships with diverse people, work within a team structure, and manage interpersonal conflict. How do you feel about working in teams? Would you prefer to work alone? You can examine your attitude toward teamwork by completing Self-Assessment 13.1.

SELF-ASSESSMENT 13.1   CAREER READINESS

Attitudes toward Teamwork

The following survey was designed to assess your attitude toward teamwork. Please be prepared to answer these questions if your instructor has assigned Self-Assessment 13.1 in Connect.

1. What is your attitude toward teamwork?

2. If you do not have a positive teamwork attitude, consider the reason and identify what you might do to foster a more positive attitude.

3. What might you say during an interview to demonstrate that you possess the competency of teamwork/ collaboration?

Formal versus Informal Groups

Groups can be either formal or informal.[13]

- Formal groups—created to accomplish specific goals. A **formal group** is a group assigned by organizations or its managers to accomplish specific goals. A formal group may be a division, a department, a work group, or a committee. It may be permanent or temporary. In general, people are assigned to them according to their skills and the organization's requirements.

- Informal groups—created for friendship. An **informal group** is a group formed by people whose overriding purpose is getting together for friendship or a common interest. An informal group may be simply a collection of friends who hang out with one another, such as those who take coffee breaks together. It also may be as organized as a prayer breakfast, a bowling team, a service club, a company "alumni group" (for example, former Apple employees), or a voluntary organization.

Informal influence. Employee happy hours are a good opportunity for colleagues to informally get together to discuss both work and non-work issues. Some of these discussions can influence formal work groups. Digital Vision/Getty Images

What's important for you as a manager to know is that informal groups can advance or undercut the plans of formal groups. The formal organization may make efforts, say, to speed up the plant assembly line or to institute workplace reforms. But members of informal groups who start to respect their own group over the formal organization can sabotage these efforts. This often happens over e-mails, lunch breaks, or informal gatherings, such as meeting after work for a beer.[14]

However, interestingly, informal groups also can be highly productive. "Research shows that appropriate connectivity in well-managed networks within organizations can have a substantial impact on performance, learning, and innovation," says Rob Cross, author of *A Practical Guide to Social Networks*.[15] A recent study of informal groups in the pharmaceutical industry confirms this, finding that informal groups had a positive effect on productivity and motivation. They also enhanced communication, autonomy, and process innovation.[16]

Types of Teams

Different types of teams have different characteristics. We can differentiate some typical teams according to their

1. Purpose.
2. Duration.
3. Level of member commitment.

Work Teams   A company's audit team and a professional sports team have several things in common. Like all work teams, they have a clear purpose that all members share. These teams are usually permanent, and members must give their complete commitment to the team's purpose in order for the team to succeed.

Project Teams   If you have ever completed a team project for a class, you have been part of a project team. Project teams at work are assembled to solve a particular problem or complete a specific task, such as brainstorming new marketing ideas for one of the company's products. Members can meet just once or work together for many years, depending on the nature of the assignment, and they may meet virtually or face to face. They can come from the same or different departments or functional areas, and while serving on the project team, they continue to fulfill their primary responsibilities.

Cross-Functional Teams   Cross-functional teams are designed to include members from different areas within an organization, such as finance, operations, and sales. Cross-functional teams can serve any purpose, they can be work teams or project teams, and their assignment can be long or short term. A recent study found that cross-functional teams improved organizational productivity and efficiency and also reduced costs.[17] T-Mobile is a good example of a company effectively using cross-functional teams to serve its customers. (See the nearby Example box.)

EXAMPLE   T-Mobile's Team of Experts

Turnover rates for customer service workers average 27% annually, which is among the highest in the business world. Departing employees cite a lack of challenging work, inadequate recognition, and too little flexibility as some of the reasons they've left their jobs. T-Mobile believes it has found a solution—cross-functional customer service teams. The company has revamped its customer call center to include teams of experts called TEX teams. TEX teams work in the same physical location but usually serve a dedicated geographic region hundreds of miles away. For example, a team in Charleston serves around 120,000 customers in Philadelphia.[18]

Employee-Run Mini-Businesses   Each 40-person TEX team resembles a mini-business and includes customer service representatives, tech specialists, coaches, a team lead, and a resource manager responsible for scheduling and management. The team is expected to manage its own profit and loss statements and team leaders are involved in quarterly business reviews with senior managers. "Our team leads used to look at things like handle time and schedule adherence. Now they look at their P&L—are they keeping and growing customer business? Are they reducing calls per account and cost to serve? They're like mini-CEOs running their own businesses," says Callie Field, the company's executive vice president of customer care.[19]

Learning and development are also an important part of the cross-functional team experience. It starts with TEX team coaches who mentor reps on the business impact of their individual decisions. For example, did a rep's decision for a given customer positively impact the customer's loyalty and the team's financial performance? Reps also are able to develop their technical skills by working collaboratively with skilled tech specialists. These specialists allow reps to stay on the line when a customer is having a complex hardware or software issue resolved, which allows the rep to learn how to handle these types of issues on future calls.[20]

A Team-Based Payoff   Research finds that service organizations achieve 50% more success when they encourage reps to tap into one another's expertise.[21] T-Mobile's cross-functional team model is no exception. Annual turnover has been reduced by 48%, while rep engagement has hit an all-time high. The company boasts some of the highest employee satisfaction rates and their customer call centers earned 24 "Best Place to Work" awards in 2019 alone.[22]

Employees aren't the only ones thrilled about T-Mobile's TEX teams. Customers are excited about being able to speak to a team of humans instead of robots or automated phone menus. They also don't have to worry about being transferred from rep to rep, or being put on hold, because they have a dedicated team of experts available at the same time.[23] Nielsen honored T-Mobile's transformation of its customer service experience by awarding it the top customer service spot in the wireless industry for two years in a row.[24] The wireless carrier also snagged the industry's highest customer service score from J.D. Power in 2020, the 19th time the company has ranked highest among its competitors.[25]

YOUR CALL

Customers who call T-Mobile more than once for support may not always receive the same team member and may speak to another member of the team who is not as familiar with their account. How can the company ensure each 40-person TEX team is sharing information on the roughly 120,000 customers they are serving?

Self-Managed Teams   **Self-managed teams** are defined as groups of workers who are given administrative oversight for their task domains. It's estimated that around 80% of the Fortune 1000 and 81% of manufacturing firms use self-managed teams.[26] Experts believe these teams increase productivity between 15 and 20% and that the autonomy they provide can lead to increased innovation.[27]

The most common chores of today's self-managed teams are work scheduling and customer interaction, and the least common are hiring and firing. Most self-managed teams also are found at the shop-floor level in factory settings, although some experts predict growth of the practice in service operations and even management ranks. Self-managed teams have been found to have a positive effect on productivity and attitudes of self-responsibility and control, although there is no significant effect on job satisfaction and organizational commitment.[28]

Research provides three takeaways for creating self-managed teams:[29]

- Ensure a leader quickly emerges.
- Select the right individuals to join the team.
- Provide proper training for team members.

Although these conclusions don't qualify as a sweeping endorsement of self-managed teams, experts expect a trend toward such teams in North America because of a strong cultural bias in favor of direct participation.

Virtual Teams   **Virtual teams** work together over time and distance via electronic media to combine effort and achieve common goals. Given technological advances, they are growing in popularity. There was a 159% increase in remote work between 2005 and 2017. Most recently, the number of U.S. employees working remotely grew from 3.9 million in 2015 to 4.7 million in 2020.[30] But is remote work good for business? A 2019 International Workplace Group survey of more than 15,000 businesspeople across more than 100 countries found the following:[31]

- 85% of businesses reported that productivity had increased in their company because of the flexibility provided by remote work.
- 80% of employees said that when choosing between two similar employment offers, they would select the one that offered flexible working hours.
- 50% of workers worked outside of their main office headquarters for at least 2.5 days a week.
- 65% of businesses said flexible workspaces reduced both capital and operational expenditures.

Advocates say virtual teams are very flexible and efficient because they are driven by information and skills, not by time and location. People with needed information and/or skills can be team members, regardless of where or when they actually do their work.[32] Nevertheless, virtual teams have pros and cons like every other type of team.

Virtual teams and distributed workers present many potential benefits: ability to leverage diverse knowledge, skills, and experience across geography and time (you don't have to have an SAP expert in every office); ability to share knowledge of diverse markets; and reduced commuting and travel expenses.[33] There are real estate cost savings of around $2,000 per employee as well because remote employees require limited or no office space.[34] The flexibility often afforded by virtual teams also can reduce work–life conflicts for employees, which some employers contend makes it easier for them to attract and retain talent.[35]

Online collaboration. Technology not only allows people to communicate where, when, and with whom they wish, but it also allows many people and organizations to work without offices. What are the advantages and disadvantages for you personally of telecommuting and virtual work? Rido/Shutterstock

Virtual teams have challenges, too. It is more difficult for them than for face-to-face teams to establish team cohesion, work satisfaction, trust, cooperative behavior, and commitment to team goals.[36] Thus, virtual teams should be used with caution. It should be no surprise that building team relationships is more difficult when members are geographically distributed. Nearly 50% of companies using virtual teams said this hurdle and time zone differences are significant challenges. Members of virtual teams also reported being unable to observe the nonverbal cues of other members and experiencing a lack of collegiality. These challenges apply to virtual teams more generally, as does the difficulty of leading such teams. When virtual teams cross country borders, cultural differences, holidays, time zones, and local laws and customs also can cause problems.[37] The Practical Action box provides advice for overcoming virtual team challenges.

PRACTICAL ACTION | High-Performing Virtual Teams

We put together a collection of nine practices to help focus your efforts and accelerate your success as a member or leader of a virtual team.

1. **Adapt your communications.** Learn how the various remote workers function, including their preferences for e-mail, texts, and phone calls. Then make sure you have reliable tools to accommodate those preferences. It often is advisable to have regularly scheduled contact using technology such as telepresence robots, chat apps, and videoconferencing (such as Skype).[38] Be strategic and talk to the right people at the right times about the right topics. Don't just blanket everybody via e-mail—focus your message.

2. **Have fun.** Use technology to keep distributed workers connected. Acknowledging birthdays and recognizing accomplishments are especially important for those who are not regularly in the office. Software developer Clevertech allows remote employees to spend some time during the day playing video games with each other. CEO Kuty Shalev believes games like Fortnite encourage employees to band together and solve problems, building interpersonal and work relationships within the company.[39]

3. **Build trust.** Building trust takes effort; it doesn't happen magically. It is fostered by having face-to-face meetings at least once a year and by getting to know each other. Team-building activities can be built into the annual meeting agenda. Sharing personal information (hobbies, family information) and displaying flexibility in dealing with technological or geographic challenges can engender trust.[40]

4. **Be a good partner.** Often, members of virtual teams are not direct employees of your employer but are independent contractors. Nevertheless, your success and that of your team depend on them. *Treat them like true partners*

and not hired help. You need them, and presumably they need you.

5. **Encourage feedback and communication.** Effective virtual teams don't hoard information. Resources and information should flow freely, routine feedback should be provided, and communication should be transparent. Shared file sites on the cloud (on Google Docs, Dropbox, and other platforms) can serve as information hubs for all team members.[41]

6. **Document the work.** If team members work in different time zones, some projects can receive attention around the clock as they are handed off from one zone to the next. Doing this effectively requires that both senders and receivers clearly specify what they have completed and what they need in each transfer.

7. **Select individuals who can thrive.** Successful remote workers tend to be organized, self-disciplined, intrinsically motivated, and independent, according to *Thrive Global*.[42] Consider bringing on potential hires as freelancers before extending an offer for long-term employment. This approach helps ensure they develop rapport with colleagues and succeed in a nontraditional work environment.[43]

8. **Use your communication skills.** Because so much communication is written, virtual team members should write in easy-to-understand and to-the-point language. Responsiveness also is key in order to maintain trust, even if that response is as simple as replying "Thanks" to confirm you've received an e-mail.[44]

9. **Develop a team charter**. Many of the virtual practices mentioned here can be incorporated into a written team charter, which is an outline of how a team will manage teamwork activities. We further discuss team charters in Section 13.3 but know that they are especially important in virtual teams because these units require more structure.

Researchers and consultants agree about one aspect of virtual teams—*there is no substitute for face-to-face contact*. Meeting in person is especially beneficial early in virtual team development, and team leaders are encouraged to meet even more frequently with key members.[45] In-person meetings also are important when there is a need to re-organize or re-strategize. Face-to-face interactions can be as simple as lunch, water-cooler conversations, social events, or periodic meetings. Whatever the case, such interactions enable people to get familiar with each other and build credibility, trust, and understanding. This reduces misunderstandings and makes subsequent virtual interactions more efficient and effective. It also increases job performance and reduces conflict and intentions to quit.[46]

Face-to-face interactions enable people to get real-time feedback, forge meaningful and real connections, and get a better sense of what others actually think and feel.[47] Moreover, virtual teams cannot succeed without some additional and old-fashioned factors, such as team commitment, good communication, clear objectives, effective leadership, and a results-driven culture.[48] Underlying many of these, research finds, is one of the truly essential elements to effective teams of all types—trust.[49] ●

13.2 Stages of Group and Team Development

THE BIG PICTURE

Groups can evolve into teams by going through five stages of development: forming, storming, norming, performing, and adjourning. They also can develop if they are forced to change in response to a crisis. We'll look at both these processes.

LO 13-2

Describe the development of groups and teams.

Tuckman's Five-Stage Model

Managers often talk of products and organizations going through stages of development, from birth to maturity to decline. Groups and teams go through the same thing. One theory proposes five stages of development: *forming, storming, norming, performing,* and *adjourning*.[50] *(See Figure 13.1.)*

These stages are meant to represent the process by which new or start-up teams evolve into completing tasks. Keep the following two things in mind as you study these stages:

- These stages often aren't of the same duration or intensity or even necessarily always in this sequence.[51]

- When you join an existing team, which is likely to occur when you obtain your first job after graduation, the team is most likely operating in the performing stage. Adding a new member like yourself suggests that the team needs to revisit some of the earlier stages of group development.

Let's consider the five stages of group development.

Stage 1: Forming—"Why Are We Here?"   The first stage, forming, is the process of getting oriented and getting acquainted. This stage is characterized by a high degree of uncertainty as members try to break the ice and figure out who is in charge and what the group's goals are.[52] For example, if you were to become part of a team that is to work on a class project, the question for you as an individual would be "How do I fit in here?" For the group, the question is "Why are we here?"[53]

At this point, mutual trust is low, and there is a good deal of holding back to see who takes charge and how. Conflict at this stage may actually be beneficial, leading to increased creativity.[54] Of course the group needs leadership and direction at this juncture. If a formal leader (e.g., the class instructor or a supervisor) does not exist or fails to assert his or her authority, an emergent leader will eventually step in to fill this need.[55] During this stage leaders should allow time for people to become acquainted and to socialize. As mentioned earlier, there are times when a new member joins a team that has completed the forming stage. The team leader, or a designated mentor, needs to ensure this person catches up to and is aligned with the rest of the team. This may require temporarily returning to the forming stage to discuss goals, build trust, and socialize.[56] Much of this can be accomplished through onboarding programs, which we discussed in Chapter 9.

Stage 2: Storming—"Why Are We Fighting over Who's in Charge and Who Does What?"
The second stage, storming, is characterized by the emergence of individual personalities and roles and conflicts within the group. For you as an individual, the question is "What's my role here?" For the group, the issue is "Why are we fighting over who's in charge and who does what?" This stage may be of short duration or painfully long, depending on the goal clarity and the commitment and maturity of the members.

This is a time of testing. Individuals test the leader's policies and assumptions as they try to determine how they fit into the power structure. Subgroups take shape, and subtle forms of rebellion, such as procrastination, occur. Many groups stall in stage 2 because power politics may erupt into open rebellion.

In this stage, the leader should encourage members to suggest ideas, voice disagreements, and work through their conflicts about tasks and goals.

Stage 3: Norming—"Can We Agree on Roles and Work as a Team?"
In the third stage, norming, conflicts are resolved, close relationships develop, and unity and harmony emerge. For individuals, the main issue is "What do the others expect me to do?" For the group, the issue is "Can we agree on roles and work as a team?" Note, then, that the *group* may now evolve into a *team*.

Teams set guidelines related to what members will do together and how they will do it.[57] The teams consider such matters as attendance at meetings, being late, use of cell phones and laptops during meetings, and what to do when someone misses a team assignment.

Groups that make it through stage 2 generally do so because a respected member other than the leader challenges the group to resolve its power struggles so something can be accomplished. Questions about authority are resolved through unemotional, matter-of-fact group discussion. A feeling of team spirit is experienced because members believe they have found their proper roles. Group cohesiveness, a "we feeling" binding group members together, is the principal by-product of stage 3.[58]

This stage generally does not last long. Here the leader should emphasize unity and help identify team goals and values.

Stage 4: Performing—"Can We Do the Job Properly?"
In performing, members concentrate on solving problems and completing the assigned task. For individuals, the question here is "How can I best perform my role?" For the group/team, the issue is "Can we do the job properly?" During this stage, the leader should allow members the empowerment they need to work on tasks.

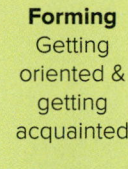

FIGURE 13.1

Five stages of group and team development

Forming
Getting oriented & getting acquainted

Storming
Individual personalities & roles emerge

Norming
Conflicts resolved, relationships develop, unity emerges

Performing
Solving problems & completing the assigned task

Adjourning
Preparing for disbandment

Turning teamwork into action. This group clearly is in the performing stage of group development. Does it appear that all participants are equally engaged in dealing with the task at hand? If you were a member of this group, what would you do to motivate all members to actively participate in completing the task? Syda Productions/Shutterstock

Stage 5: Adjourning—"Can We Help Members Transition Out?" Some teams make it to the final stage of adjourning, in which members prepare for disbandment. Having worked so hard to get along and get something done, many members feel a compelling sense of loss. For the individual, the question now is "What's next?" For the team, the issue is "Can we help members transition out?"

The leader can help ease the transition by rituals celebrating "the end" and "new beginnings." Parties, award ceremonies, graduations, or mock funerals can provide the needed punctuation at the end of a significant teamwork project. The leader can emphasize valuable lessons learned in group dynamics to prepare everyone for future group and team efforts.

Is Tuckman's Model Accurate? Although research does not support the notion that groups can't perform until the performing stage, both academics and practitioners agree that groups have a life cycle.[59] Research also shows us that high-performing teams successfully navigating the process of group or team development tend to display productive energy toward getting things done.[60] Do your current teams at work or school display this productive energy? You can find out by completing Self-Assessment 13.2.

SELF-ASSESSMENT 13.2

Assessing Your Team's Productive Energy

The following survey was designed to assess your team's productive energy. Please be prepared to answer these questions if your instructor has assigned Self-Assessment 13.2 in Connect.

1. To what extent does the team display productive energy? Are you surprised by the results?

2. Based on your survey scores, what can be done to improve the level of energy being displayed by the team? Be specific.

3. What would the survey suggest that you should do next time you are the leader of a work or school project team?

Punctuated Equilibrium

Groups don't always follow the distinct stages of Tuckman's model. In another type of group development, called <mark>punctuated equilibrium</mark>, they establish periods of stable functioning until an event causes a dramatic change in norms, roles, and/or objectives. The group then establishes and maintains new norms of functioning, returning to equilibrium. *(See Figure 13.2.)* Punctuated equilibrium often occurs in the wake of unexpected change.[61] The United Kingdom's departure from the European Union, known as "Brexit," is a good example of punctuated equilibrium.

Brexit Example: The United Kingdom (UK) joined the European Union (EU) in 1973 and experienced over four decades of relative equilibrium. The country voted 52% to 48% in June 2016 to leave the 28-member alliance, sparking a political earthquake (abrupt change #1). Both the UK and the EU spent roughly a year after the vote preparing for exit negotiations. Then former UK Prime Minister Theresa May triggered "Article 50"—the EU's official mechanism for a member-state's exit— on March 29, 2017 (abrupt change #2). The UK and EU negotiated the terms of Brexit for more than two years. During that time, they discussed a post–Brexit world, including future trade and immigration policies. Both parties approved the exit deal on January 29, 2020, and the UK officially left the EU on January 31, 2020 (abrupt change #3). The UK and EU will observe an 11-month transition phase until January 2021, when a post–Brexit Europe will re-emerge.[62] ●

Leave the EU! Pro-Brexit demonstrators protest outside the Houses of Parliament on November 23, 2016, in London, England. Jack Taylor/ Getty Images

FIGURE 13.2

Punctuated equilibrium

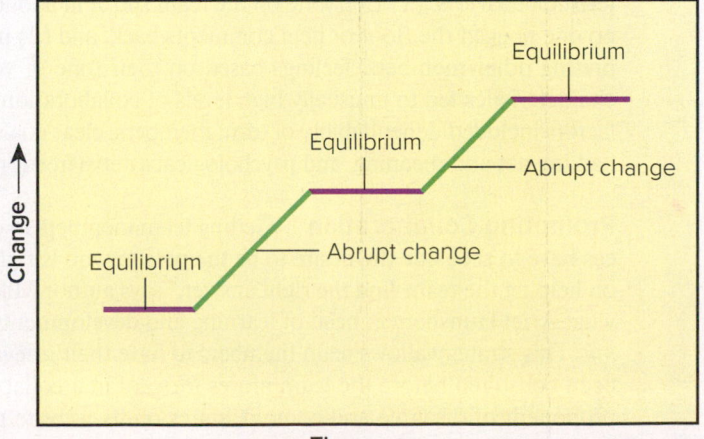

13.3 Building Effective Teams

THE BIG PICTURE

To build a group into a high-performance team, managers must consider matters of collaboration, trust, performance goals and feedback, motivation through mutual accountability and interdependence, team composition, roles, norms, and team processes.

LO 13-3

Discuss ways managers can build effective teams.

"What is a high-performance team?" Current research and practice suggest eight attributes: participative leadership, shared accountability, sense of common purpose, trust and open communication, clear role expectations, early conflict resolution, collaboration, and effective team processes.[63] Thus, as a future manager, the first thing you have to realize is that building a high-performance team is going to require some work. But the payoff will be a stronger, better-performing work unit.[64]

The most essential considerations in building a group into an effective team are (1) *collaboration*, (2) *trust*, (3) *performance goals and feedback*, (4) *motivation through mutual accountability and interdependency*, (5) *composition*, (6) *roles*, (7) *norms*, and (8) *effective team processes*.

---

1. Collaboration—the Foundation of Teamwork

==Collaboration== is the act of sharing information and coordinating efforts to achieve a collective outcome. As you might expect, teams are more effective when members collaborate.[65] Collaboration is the secret sauce enabling teams to produce more than the sum of their parts.[66] Unfortunately, an organization's reward systems can undermine employees' motivation to collaborate.[67] For example, in a recent *Harvard Business Review Analytics Services* survey of 1,185 health care executives, 63 percent of respondents blamed competing incentives as a key barrier to collaboration.[68]

Some organizations are addressing the challenges around reward systems in order to promote greater collaboration among their ranks. Take for instance BubbleBum, an Irish manufacturer of booster seats that are sold in 27 countries. The company reinforces teamwork in its team-based structure by focusing rewards on team rather than individual performance. "If you do not achieve your priorities, you are letting your team down," says founder Grainne Kelly.[69]

What Do Highly Collaborative Teams Have in Common?   An exhaustive survey by Google was aimed at discovering what made the best of its hundreds of work teams successful. The researchers found that the company's highest-performing teams shared two characteristic behaviors: (1) Everyone on the team spoke in about equal proportion, meaning that no one hogged the floor or held comments back, and (2) members were very good at interpreting other members' feelings based on their tone of voice and nonverbal cues. These characteristics led to unusually high levels of collaboration and success.[70] Other influential factors included dependability of team members, clear goals, structure and clarity, work that had impact and meaning, and psychological safety (freedom from judgment).[71]

Promoting Collaboration   Getting team members to collaborate is not easy. "Employees have to set aside the desire to be the person who is right in every discussion, and focus on helping the team find the right answer," says author Mike Steib.[72] This includes utilizing what Ariel Hunsberger, head of learning and development at Slack, calls *disagree and commit*. This strategy allows team members to have their grievances heard and feel like they've been consulted before the team moves forward in a collaborative way.[73] Amazon, another proponent of disagree and commit, states on its website that its leaders are "obligated to respectfully challenge decisions when they disagree. . . . They do not compromise for the

Delivering collaboration. Amazon employees at its Hyderabad, India, location discussing a project. Do you agree with the company's "disagree and commit" approach? Dhiraj Singh/Getty Images

sake of social cohesion. Once a decision is determined, they commit wholly."[74] Team leaders and managers can reinforce this behavior by structuring team communication and decision making in a way that promotes dissent. Two specific methods for achieving this are devil's advocacy and the dialectic method, which we discussed in Chapter 7. (See Figure 7.7.)

Recent research suggests two additional ways to promote collaboration in the workplace. First, team members should learn to listen more than they talk. We often don't listen because we're worried about our own performance or believe our ideas are better than others', or both. As a consequence, we get into avoidable conflicts, miss opportunities, alienate others, and diminish team effectiveness. One way to keep a conversation alive is by asking open-ended questions that start with "what" and "how" because they prompt others to provide more information about the issue at hand. Second, team members are encouraged to practice empathy. The use of empathy requires effective listening, which demonstrates that we care about what someone else is saying. This is why empathy allows individuals to understand why others may have differing perspectives and gives way to curiosity and constructive conversations instead of judgment.[75]

2. Trust: "We Need to Have Reciprocal Faith in Each Other"

Trust is defined as reciprocal faith in others' intentions and behaviors. The word *reciprocal* emphasizes the give-and-take aspect of trust—that is, we tend to give what we get: Trust begets trust, distrust begets distrust. Trust is based on *credibility*—how believable you are based on your past acts of integrity and follow-through on your promises.[76] Four decades of research supports a positive relationship between team members' trust and team performance.[77] Moreover, a recent study found that mutual trust between team leads and team members led to more effective communication and increased organizational citizenship behaviors.[78]

Researchers believe trust has three core drivers known as the "Trust Triangle"—authenticity, logic, and empathy. If trust breaks down, you can often trace it back to one of these drivers. Let's look at each driver.[79]

- **Authenticity.** "I'm seeing the real you." People tend to trust you if they believe you're being your genuine self.

- **Logic.** "Your reasoning and judgment make sense." You stand a better chance of having people trust you if they have faith in your judgment and competence.

- **Empathy.** "You care about me and my success." People will trust you if they believe you really care about them.

The Example box discusses how leaders can build trust with others.

Building a culture of trust starts with the leader of the team or work unit. For the company as a whole, that leader is the CEO. As you learned from our discussion of the trust triangle, authenticity and empathy are two of the simplest ways to foster trust.[80] Consider the case of Marriott CEO Arne Sorenson, the leader of the world's largest hotel company. Sorenson was candid, empathetic, and vulnerable during a March 2020 video to employees outlining the devastating effects the COVID-19 pandemic had on the company's operations. As a result, Marriott was forced to furlough tens of thousands of employees. "I can tell you that I have never had a more difficult moment than this one. There is simply nothing worse than telling highly valued associates—people who are the very heart of this company—that their roles are being impacted by events completely outside of their control," said Sorenson.[81]

Arne M. Sorenson, President and Chief Executive Officer, Marriott International, Inc., attends a White House meeting to discuss the response to the COVID-19 pandemic.
Shutterstock

operator of link-building company Loganix. "I like to set a standard by using our own company blog to discuss the times I've messed up big time but, more importantly, what I've learned from them." [84]

Ask for Help Some leaders view asking for help from employees as a weakness, but it is actually a strength that can enhance the *logic* driver of the trust triangle. This is because competent leaders know when they need the help of others in order for the company to be successful. Trust is then recognized as a two-way street, allowing employees to communicate more openly with their leaders and teammates.[85] "Asking for help from others can rally your team around shared goals, and it breeds an environment that's conducive to productive collaboration," says Carey Rome, CEO of Cypress Resources. Leaders also are demonstrating their trust in an employee's abilities when they seek his or her particular expertise. That trust can then become a great motivator and push the employee to excel even further.[86] Research has shown that asking for help also increases trust and cooperation in teams because it stimulates oxytocin production.[87] Oxytocin, known as the "trust molecule," is that warm and fuzzy feeling you get when you feel really good about someone.[88]

Take Responsibility for Your Mistakes   When leaders admit to making mistakes, they are creating an opportunity to be genuine and earn respect, strengthen their teams, grow as a leader, and lead by example. This ultimately builds a culture of trust.[82] Karl Kangur, founder and CEO of content marketing solution MRR Media, is not afraid to admit his errors and even views them as learning opportunities. "I'm very open with the team about times that I've made mistakes. This helps me avoid making the same mistakes and shows the rest of the team that we're all equal," says Kangur.[83] "You have to be forgiving of mistakes and ready to transition each one into a learning experience," agrees Adam Steele, owner and

YOUR CALL

Do you see showing vulnerability as a strength or weakness? Are there times when you feel your feelings of vulnerability should be hidden? Why or why not?

---

3. Performance Goals and Feedback

As an individual you no doubt prefer to have measurable goals and to have feedback about your performance. The same is true with teams. Teams are not just collections of individuals. They are individuals organized for a collective purpose. That purpose needs to be defined in terms of specific, measurable performance goals with continual feedback to tell team members how well they are doing.[89]

An obvious example is the teams you see on television at Indianapolis or Daytona Beach during automobile racing. When the driver guides the race car off the track to make a pit stop, a team of people quickly jack up the car to change tires, refuel the tank, and clean the windshield—all in a matter of seconds. The performance goal is to have the car back on the track as quickly as possible. The number of seconds of elapsed time—and the driver's place among competitors once back in the race—tells the team how well they are doing.

4. Motivation through Mutual Accountability and Interdependence

Do you work harder when you're alone or when you're in a group? When clear performance goals exist, when the work is considered meaningful, when members believe their efforts matter, and when they don't feel they are being exploited by others—this kind of culture supports teamwork.[90] Being mutually accountable to other members of the team rather than to a supervisor makes members feel mutual trust and commitment—a key part in motivating members for team effort. Mutual accountability is fostered by having team "members share accountability for the work, authority over how goals are met, discretion over resource use, and ownership of information and knowledge related to the work."[91]

Do you like it when your performance is contingent on someone else's efforts? Your answer reflects your experience with team member interdependence. ==Team member interdependence== reveals the extent to which team members rely on common task-related team inputs, such as resources, information, goals, and rewards, and the amount of interpersonal interactions needed to complete the work.[92] A study of more than 7,000 teams showed that interdependence affects team functioning, which in turn influences team performance.[93] Another study of insurance sales teams found that team interdependence optimized sales performance.[94] The key takeaway from research is the need for team leaders to monitor the quality of team member interdependence.[95]

Cooperation and collaboration. A crew swarms over a car driven by A. J. Allmendinger during a pit stop in the NASCAR 2014 Sprint Cup All-Star Race at Watkins Glen, New York. Cereal maker General Mills was able to cut the time workers changed a production line for a Betty Crocker product from 4.5 hours to just 12 minutes by adapting ideas in efficiency and high performance from a NASCAR pit crew working at blinding speed. Jerry Markland/Stringer/Getty Images

5. Team Composition

==Team composition== reflects the collection of jobs, personalities, values, knowledge, experience, and skills of team members. The concept is related to our discussion of workforce diversity in Chapter 11, where you learned that diversity is good for business and that it must be effectively managed.[96]

For example, a study examining the characteristics of effective teams at Cisco found that one of the top three such qualities was members' conviction that their values were shared.[97] This is a feeling you've probably experienced as a member of a team or club built around common interests.

The most important idea to remember is that team member composition should fit the responsibilities of the team. Fit enhances effectiveness and misfit impedes it.[98] Here are four conclusions derived from research on team composition:

- Consider having a higher tolerance for uncertainty during the early stages of team development (forming and storming). This same suggestion applies to self-managed and virtual teams due to their relative lack of imposed direction and face-to-face communication.[99]

- Utilize greater diversity in the way you solve problems. Teams that do this have an edge over teams with a uniform or consistent problem-solving approach.[100]

- Try to avoid assigning employees to multiple teams. Organizations guilty of this tend to see a decrease in overall performance. Performance becomes even worse when the organization is handling complex tasks.[101]

- Utilize public performance feedback in mixed-gender groups. It leads to the emergence of capable leaders and positive group outcomes.[102]

6. Roles: How Team Members Are Expected to Behave

==Roles== are socially determined expectations of how individuals should behave in a specific position. As a team member, your role is to play a part in helping the team reach its goals. Members develop their roles based on the expectations of the team, of the organization, and of themselves, and they may do different things.

Two types of team roles are task and maintenance. *(See Table 13.1.)*

TABLE 13.1   **Task and Maintenance Roles**

TASK ROLES	DESCRIPTION
Initiator	Suggests new goals or ideas
Information seeker/giver	Clarifies key issues
Opinion seeker/giver	Clarifies pertinent values
Elaborator	Promotes greater understanding through examples or exploration of implications
Coordinator	Pulls together ideas and suggestions
Orienter	Keeps group headed toward its stated goal(s)
Evaluator	Tests group's accomplishments with various criteria such as logic and practicality
Energizer	Prods group to move along or to accomplish more
Procedural technician	Performs routine duties (handing out materials or rearranging seats)
Recorder	Performs a "group memory" function by documenting discussion and outcomes
MAINTENANCE ROLES	**DESCRIPTION**
Encourager	Fosters group solidarity by accepting and praising various points of view
Harmonizer	Mediates conflict through reconciliation or humor
Compromiser	Helps resolve conflict by meeting others halfway
Gatekeeper	Encourages all group members to participate
Standard setter	Evaluates the quality of group processes
Commentator	Records and comments on group processes/dynamics
Follower	Serves as a passive audience

Source: Adapted from discussion in K. D. Bonno and P. Shoats, "Functional Roles of Group Members," *Journal of Social Issues, Spring 1948, pp. 41–49.*

Task Roles: Getting the Work Done   A ==task role==, or task-oriented role, consists of behavior that concentrates on getting the team's tasks done. Task roles keep the team on track and get the work done. If you stand up in a team meeting and say, "What is the real issue here? We don't seem to be getting anywhere," you are performing a task role.

Examples include coordinators, who pull together ideas and suggestions; orienters, who keep teams headed toward their stated goals; initiators, who suggest new goals or ideas; and energizers, who prod people to move along or accomplish more are all playing task roles.

Maintenance Roles: Keeping the Team Together

A **maintenance role**, or relationship-oriented role, consists of behavior that fosters constructive relationships among team members. Maintenance roles foster positive working relationships among team members. If someone at a team meeting says, "Let's hear from those who oppose this plan," they are playing a maintenance role.

Examples are encouragers, who foster group solidarity by praising various viewpoints; standard setters, who evaluate the quality of group processes; harmonizers, who mediate conflict through reconciliation or humor; and compromisers, who help resolve conflict by meeting others "halfway."

---

7. Norms: Unwritten Rules for Team Members

Norms are more encompassing than roles. **Norms** are general guidelines or rules of behavior that most group or team members follow.[103] Norms point out the boundaries between acceptable and unacceptable behavior.[104] Although some norms can be made explicit, typically they are unwritten and seldom discussed openly. Nevertheless, research shows that they have a powerful influence on group and organizational behavior.[105]

Why Norms Are Enforced: Four Reasons

Norms tend to be enforced by group or team members for four reasons:[106]

- **To help the group survive—"Don't do anything that will hurt us."** Norms are enforced to help the group, team, or organization survive.

  Example: The manager of your team or group might compliment you because you've made sure the team has the right emergency equipment.

- **To clarify role expectations—"You have to go along to get along."** Norms also are enforced to help clarify or simplify role expectations.

  Example: At one time, new members of Congress wanting to buck the system by which important committee appointments were given to those with the most seniority were advised to "go along to get along"—go along with the rules in order to get along in their congressional careers.

- **To help individuals avoid embarrassing situations—"Don't call attention to yourself."** Norms are enforced to help group or team members avoid embarrassing themselves.

  Examples: You might be ridiculed by fellow team members for dominating the discussion during a report to top management ("Be a team player, not a show-off"). Or you might be told not to discuss religion or politics with customers, whose views might differ from yours.

- **To emphasize the group's important values and identity—"We're known for being special."** Finally, norms are enforced to emphasize the group's, team's, or organization's central values or to enhance its unique identity.

  Examples: Nordstrom's department store chain emphasizes the great lengths to which it goes to provide exceptional customer service. Some colleges give an annual award to the instructor whom students vote best teacher.

Indeed, team norms are incredibly important. The Practical Action box details how team members can build effective norms. Keep these in mind for your current and future teams at school.

High-performing teams use the power of team norms to overcome challenges and obstacles.[107] Team norms allow a team to increase collective performance through healthy debate and clarity of purpose and roles, which in turn lead to high performance.[108] The following suggestions can help any team to build effective team norms.

Look to the Past for What Worked Effective norms propel a team toward effective group dynamics and performance, whereas ineffective ones become an anchor. Studies show that identifying earlier team practices that worked is a good way to establish preferred norms.[109] Simply think about great teams you were part of and consider the various norms that guided their efforts. What made that team so great? Do the same for an ineffective team on which you worked. This exercise provides you with a list of practices that did and did not work. You can then rank them by their significance to the current tasks at hand. For example, Missouri's Department of Elementary and Secondary Education encourages school district teams to rank effective past practices by importance when deciding which ones to use on new teams.[110]

Break Down Norms into Behaviors Once you have a list of norms, convert them to measurable behaviors. For example, the norm of encouraging equal participation in meetings results in the behavior of soliciting input from everyone when making a team decision.[111] Part of this norm can be first soliciting input from those who've spoken the least. This will provide them with a voice in case your team has members that dominate meeting discussions.[112]

Accountability Is Key Accountability plays a key role in setting normative expectations. Creating a system to police behavior can actually be fun! Imagine serving on a team that has restricted the use of phones during meetings. How might this be enforced? One team observed by *Harvard Business Review* mandated a $5 penalty for each time someone got distracted by his or her phone. The $5 was put in a "norm bucket." The team used some of the resulting funds to go out for drinks at the end of the year and donated the remainder to charity.[113] One way to promote accountability is to formalize team norms: This can be done by developing a team charter, which is discussed shortly.[114]

YOUR CALL

How well do you think an organization could incorporate all the suggestions listed here for creating effective team norms? What other strategies do you think contribute to the adoption of effective norms?

8. Effective Team Processes

Teams, like individuals, get things done by turning inputs into desired outputs. Studies show that high-performing teams accomplish this task by using effective team processes.[115] ==Team processes== are team members' interdependent acts that transform inputs to outcomes through activities directed toward organizing taskwork to achieve collective goals. These activities can be cognitive, verbal, and behavioral.[116] There are three additional activities teams can use to improve team processes, beyond the seven just discussed.

Team charters should be written. This provides teams with written documentation regarding norms and other operational agreements. BestPix/Shutterstock

- **Create a team charter.** A ==team charter== outlines how a team will manage teamwork activities. It "represents an agreement among members as to how the team will work as an empowered partnership in making binding decisions and sharing accountability for delivering quality products/services that meet user/customer needs in a timely and cost-efficient way."[117] One of your authors, Angelo Kinicki, requires teams in his classes to create charters. He does this because research shows team charters are associated with higher, sustained performance, particularly for teams that are low on team conscientiousness.[118]

- **Engage in team reflexivity.** ==Team reflexivity== is a collective process by which members reflect on the team's objectives, strategies, methods, and processes and adapt accordingly.[119] Research shows that team reflexivity can help improve team performance, trust, and creativity.[120] It also reduces team members' burnout because it provides them a sense of control and support.[121] One way to engage in team reflexivity is to conduct project post-mortems, which we defined in Chapter 7 as a review of recent decisions to identify possible future improvements. Post-mortems are an effective way to improve team processes, boost team cohesiveness, provide closure, and improve morale.[122] Moreover, teams can prepare a written report documenting the post-mortem process and findings. This document can effectively serve as a basis for future team charters and norms.[123]

- **Give team members a voice.** <mark>Team voice</mark> reflects the extent to which team members feel free to express opinions, concerns, proposals, or thoughts about work-related issues.[124] Experts suggest that simple acts, such as asking others what they think during conversations, or providing dedicated speaking time to each member during a meeting, can increase team voice.[125] Research confirms this, finding that inclusive leadership promotes team voice and facilitates innovation, which leads to increased team performance. The caveat is that team voice should be decentralized and a select few should not dominate discussions.[126]

Putting It All Together

Thus far in this chapter we have considered the things that make groups and teams both effective and ineffective. We hope you understand that creating and leading a high-performance team takes planning and skill. The first step in improving a team's performance, however, involves an assessment of its effectiveness.

So how can you determine whether a team is effective? A group's output surely is one indicator, but there are others that are more "team process oriented." You can get an idea of these process-oriented indicators by taking Self-Assessment 13.3. ●

SELF-ASSESSMENT 13.3

Assessing Team Effectiveness

The following survey was designed to assess the overall effectiveness of a team's internal processes. Please be prepared to answer these questions if your instructor has assigned Self-Assessment 13.3 in Connect.

1. How effective is the team?
2. What aspects of the team's internal processes are most in need of positive development?
3. Based on your survey scores, what are three recommendations for improving the team's internal processes? Be specific.

13.4 Managing Conflict

THE BIG PICTURE

Conflict, an enduring feature of the workplace, is a process in which one party perceives that its interests are being opposed or negatively affected by another party. Conflict can be negative (bad) or functional (good). Indeed, either too much or too little conflict can affect performance. This section identifies four sources of conflict in organizations and describes four ways to stimulate constructive conflict.

Mistakes, pressure-cooker deadlines, differing personalities, increased workloads, demands for higher productivity, and stress—all contribute to on-the-job conflict.[127] Most people envision *conflict* as meaning shouting and fighting, but as a manager you will encounter more subtle, nonviolent forms: opposition, criticism, arguments. Thus, a definition of conflict seems fairly mild: <mark>Conflict</mark> is a process in which one party perceives that its interests are being opposed or negatively affected by another party.[128]

Conflict is a natural aspect of life. A place to begin our discussion of conflict is to consider the two types of conflict—dysfunctional and functional.

LO 13-4

Describe ways managers can deal successfully with conflict.

The Nature of Conflict: Disagreement Is Normal

Conflict is simply disagreement, a perfectly normal state of affairs. Conflicts may take many forms: between individuals, between an individual and a group, between groups, within a group, and between an organization and its environment.

Although all of us might wish to live lives free of conflict, it is now recognized that certain kinds of conflict can actually be beneficial. Let us therefore distinguish between *dysfunctional conflict* (bad) and *functional conflict* (good).

- **Dysfunctional conflict—bad for organizations.** From the standpoint of the organization, **dysfunctional conflict** is conflict that hinders the organization's performance or threatens its interests. For example, Hans Berglund, vice CEO of fertilizer company AgroPlasma, created dysfunctional conflict by using a racial slur against an African American Uber driver. Berglund's behavior damaged AgroPlasma's reputation and led to employees not wanting to work under his leadership.[129] As a manager, you need to do what you can to remove dysfunctional conflict, sometimes called negative conflict. In the case of Berglund, the company fired him and released a statement saying they do not share his values and ethics.[130]

- **Functional conflict—good for organizations.** The good kind of conflict is **functional conflict**, which benefits the main purposes of the organization and serves its interests.[131] This type of conflict is also called productive conflict and occurs "when team members openly discuss disagreements and divergent perspectives without fear, anxiety, or perceived threat."[132] Studies show that functional conflict can lead to superior team problem solving and decision making,

Mark Zuckerberg, co-founder and CEO of Facebook, testifies in 2018 before a joint meeting of the US Senate Committee on the Judiciary and the US Senate Committee on Commerce, Science, and Transportation.
Shutterstock

and greater organizational effectiveness.[133] For instance, Facebook's acknowledgment that the personal data of 87 million users was improperly accessed by marketing and political consulting firms raised multiple questions for the company. Public anger and mistrust brought founder and CEO Mark Zuckerberg before a wary Congress to testify about the company's security procedures and transparency. The result was revamped internal policies, and possibly new government regulations, that will make the company a more trusted platform for its more than 2.5 billion active users worldwide.[134]

The ability to effectively work with others is a career readiness competency desired by employees. Do you see yourself as easy to get along with and relatively conflict free? Self-Assessment 13.4 was designed to answer this question. It assesses the extent to which your work relationships contain dysfunctional or functional conflict.

SELF-ASSESSMENT 13.4

Interpersonal Conflict Tendencies

If your instructor has assigned Self-Assessment 13.4 in Connect, you will learn how well you get along with others at work and/or school.

1.　Does your score match your perception of yourself?

2.　The assessment measures how well you get along with others and how they treat you; both are sources of conflict. If you were to improve the measure, what other factors do you think should be included?

Can Too Little or Too Much Conflict Affect Performance?

It's tempting to think that a conflict-free work group is a happy work group, as indeed it may be. But is it a productive group? In the 1970s, social scientists specializing in organizational behavior introduced the revolutionary idea that organizations could suffer from *too little* as well as *too much* conflict. Neither scenario is good.

- **Too little conflict—inactivity.** Work groups, departments, or organizations that experience too little conflict tend to be plagued by apathy, lack of creativity, indecision, and missed deadlines. The result is that organizational performance suffers.

- **Too much conflict—warfare.** Excessive conflict, on the other hand, can erode organizational performance because of political infighting, dissatisfaction, lack of teamwork, and turnover. Workplace aggression and violence are manifestations of excessive conflict.[135]

Thus, it seems that a moderate level of conflict can induce creativity and initiative,[136] thereby raising performance, as shown in the diagram in Figure 13.3. As you might expect, however, what constitutes "moderate" will vary among managers.

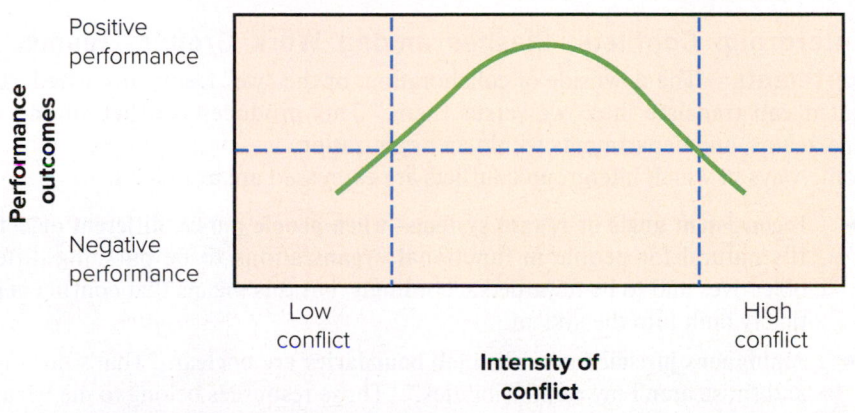

FIGURE 13.3

The relationship between intensity of conflict and performance outcomes

Too little conflict or too much conflict causes performance to suffer.

Sources: Derived from L. D. Brown, Managing Conflict at Organizational Interfaces (Englewood Cliffs, NJ: Prentice-Hall, 1983).

Four Kinds of Conflict: Personality, Envy, Intergroup, and Cross-Cultural

There are a variety of sources of conflict—so-called *conflict triggers*. Four of the principal ones are based on (1) *personality*, (2) *envy,* (3) *intergroup dynamics,* and (4) *cultural differences*. By understanding these, you'll be better able to take charge and manage the conflicts rather than letting the conflicts take you by surprise and manage you.

1. Personality Conflicts: Clashes Because of Personal Dislikes or Disagreements   We've all had confrontations, weak or strong, with people because we disagreed with them or disliked their personalities, such as their opinions, their behavior, their looks, whatever. Personality conflict is defined as interpersonal opposition based on personal dislike or disagreement. Such conflicts often begin with instances of *workplace incivility*, or employees' lack of regard for each other, which, if not curtailed, can diminish job satisfaction and well-being, while increasing stress, turnover, and withdrawal.[137]

2. Envy-Based Conflicts: Clashes Because of What Others Have   Envy is as an unpleasant feeling of inferiority and resentment caused by comparing yourself with a person or group who possesses something you desire.[138] It is a source of conflict because it can threaten self-esteem and promotes the attitude of injustice. This motivates people to restore equity by tearing others down or elevating self-perceptions.[139] Research has found that higher feelings of competitiveness are positively correlated with workplace envy.[140] Take for example the case of Jussie Smollett, an actor famous for his role in the Fox series *Empire*.

Jussie Smollett Example: Smollett, a gay African American actor, alleged in January 2019 that he was attacked on his way to a Chicago Subway store by two white men yelling racial and homophobic slurs. After an outpouring of support for the actor from celebrities and the NAACP, police learned from the perpetrators of the attack that Smollett himself had orchestrated the whole thing. The reason? Chicago Police allege that Smollett was "dissatisfied with his salary" compared to his co-stars and wanted to draw attention to himself. He "took advantage of the pain and anger of racism to promote his career," alleged Chicago police superintendent Eddie Johnson shortly after Smollett was arrested for making a false police report.[141]

As the Smollett example shows, envious employees are more likely to have low levels of organizational citizenship behaviors and high levels of counterproductive work behaviors.[142] In contrast, some research demonstrates that envy at work is not always poisonous.[143] For example, a recent study found that a moderate level of envy between employees is a "good driver for success" and promotes "healthy competition."[144] Managers can limit the negatives associated with envy by eliminating preferential treatment of employees, explaining why some employees are rewarded and celebrated, and providing mentoring programs.[145]

3. Intergroup Conflicts: Clashes among Work Groups, Teams, and Departments

The downside of collaboration, or the "we" feeling discussed earlier, is that it can translate into "we versus them." This produces conflict among work groups, teams, and departments within an organization.

Some ways in which intergroup conflicts are expressed are as follows:

- **Inconsistent goals or reward systems—when people pursue different objectives.** It's natural for people in functional organizations to be pursuing different objectives and to be rewarded accordingly, but this means that conflict is practically built into the system.

- **Ambiguous jurisdictions—when job boundaries are unclear.** "That's not my job and those aren't my responsibilities." "Those resources belong to me because I need them as part of my job." Unclear task responsibilities can often lead to conflict. Take for instance the case of two state troopers ticketing a woman who was driving around her neighborhood in April 2020. The troopers alleged that the driver was violating a social distancing order associated with the COVID-19 outbreak by leaving her house for a nonessential reason. The state social distancing order was meant to keep people at a distance from each other so they could not spread the virus, but the woman was driving alone. A reason for this incident occurring could be that police officers were placed in a tough spot in interpreting ambiguous, medically related guidelines.[146]

- **Status differences—when there are inconsistencies in power and influence.** It can happen that people who are lower in status according to the organization chart actually have disproportionate power over those theoretically above them, which can lead to conflicts.

4. Cross-Cultural Conflicts: Clashes between Cultures

With cross-border mergers, joint ventures, and international alliances being common features of the global economy, there are frequent opportunities for clashes between cultures. Often success or failure, when business is being conducted across cultures, arises from dealing with differing assumptions about how to think and act.

Developing the career readiness competency of cross-cultural awareness and having an open mind will allow you to minimize multicultural conflicts. Cross-cultural awareness was defined in Chapter 4 as the ability to operate in different cultural settings. We know for example that culture impacts the way individuals react to performance feedback.[147] (See Table 4.8.) This reaction can be the cause of conflict if you don't have cultural awareness and an open mind to different cultural views. Research confirms this, demonstrating that open-minded individuals are better prepared to work in cross-cultural situations than those who are not.[148]

How to Stimulate Constructive Conflict

As a manager you are being paid not just to manage conflict but even to create some, where it's constructive and appropriate, in order to stimulate performance. Constructive conflict, if carefully monitored, can be very productive under a number of circumstances: when your work group seems afflicted with inertia and apathy, resulting in low performance; when there's a lack of new ideas and resistance to change; when there seem to be a lot of yes-people (expressing groupthink) in the work unit; when there's high employee turnover; or when managers seem unduly concerned with peace, cooperation, compromise, consensus, and their own popularity rather than in achieving work objectives.[149]

The following four strategies are used to stimulate constructive conflict.

1. Spur Competition among Employees
Competition is, of course, a form of conflict, but competition is often healthy in spurring people to produce higher results as long as it does not lead to extreme envy. Thus, a company will often put its salespeople in competition with one another by offering bonuses and awards for achievement—a trip to a Caribbean resort, say, for the top performer of the year.

2. Change the Organization's Culture and Procedures
Competition also may be established by making deliberate and highly publicized moves to change the corporate culture—by announcing to employees that the organization is now going to be more innovative and reward original thinking and unorthodox ideas. Procedures, such as paperwork sign-off processes, also can be revamped. Results can be reinforced in visible ways through announcements of bonuses, raises, and promotions.

3. Bring in Outsiders for New Perspectives
Without "new blood," organizations can become stagnant and resistant to change. This is why managers often bring in outsiders—people from a different unit of the organization, new hires from competing companies, or consultants. With their different backgrounds, attitudes, or management styles, these outsiders can bring a new perspective and can shake things up.

4. Use Programmed Conflict: Devil's Advocacy and the Dialectic Method
==Programmed conflict== is designed to elicit different opinions without inciting people's personal feelings. Sometimes decision-making groups become so bogged down in details and procedures that nothing of substance gets done. The idea here is to get people, through role-playing, to defend or criticize ideas based on relevant facts rather than on personal feelings and preferences.

The method for getting people to engage in this debate of ideas is to do disciplined role-playing, for which we discussed two proven methods in Chapter 7: *devil's advocacy* and the *dialectic method*. These two methods work as follows:

- **Devil's advocacy—role-playing criticism to test whether a proposal is workable.** ==Devil's advocacy== is the process of assigning someone to play the role of critic.

    Periodically role-playing devil's advocate has a beneficial side effect in that it is great training

Top employee. Companies frequently stimulate constructive competition among employees to produce better performance. Top salespeople, for instance, may be rewarded with a trip to a resort. Do you think you would do well in a company that makes you compete with others to produce higher results? wavebreakmedia/Shutterstock

for developing analytical and communicative skills. However, it's a good idea to rotate the job so no one person develops a negative reputation. The Practical Action box provides some tips on playing the devil's advocate.

- **The dialectic method—role-playing two sides of a proposal to test whether it is workable.** Requiring a bit more skill training than devil's advocacy does, the <mark>dialectic method</mark> is the process of having two people or groups play opposing roles in a debate in order to better understand a proposal. After the structured debate, managers are more equipped to make an intelligent decision.[150]

PRACTICAL ACTION   Playing the Devil's Advocate

Research shows that teams effectively utilizing devil's advocates perform better than those who don't.[151] What happens when you are chosen as the team's opposing viewpoint? How can you be critical of the team's ideas without upsetting your colleagues? Here are four tips for successfully playing this important role.

1. **Listen closely.** You need to actively listen to someone's idea before potentially disagreeing with it. That means paying attention and making sure the idea-sharer knows you are listening.[152] For example, repeat the idea you just heard in your own words before providing your opposing viewpoint. This is called paraphrasing. Colleagues are more receptive to feedback when they believe you are truly hearing them.[153]

2. **It's not a game of gotcha.** Devil's advocacy should be framed as a way to stimulate constructive conflict, not generate resentment. The goal is not to be an adversary. Rather, it is to reduce uncertainty and inspire learning.[154] The airing of differing opinions should be heard by the rest of the team as a nonthreatening, alternate way to evaluate solutions to an issue.[155] The devil's advocate helps bring up issues that might otherwise be ignored. Sometimes that leads to discrediting an idea, which is fine.[156]

3. **Stay positive.** Research reveals that teams perform worse when an opposing opinion is seen as confrontational. Divergent opinions should be presented in a constructive way so they will not be taken personally or emotionally.[157] For example, try to find something meaningful about an idea and comment on that before you introduce your opposing viewpoint. Colleagues are more receptive to your point of view if they believe you've listened to them with an open mind.[158]

4. **Don't beat a dead horse.** Your goal is not to win a debate, so don't dwell once you've made your point. If the team is not convinced by your argument the first two times, repeating your point again probably won't change things.[159] What it may do is cause frustration and dysfunctional conflict with your colleagues. Let it go!

Career Readiness Competencies to Help You to Better Handle Conflict

Whatever kind of organization you work for, you'll always benefit from knowing how to manage conflict. There are five career readiness competencies that enable you to work on disagreements and keep them from flaring into out-of-control personality conflicts: *teamwork/collaboration*, *social intelligence*, *openness to change*, *emotional intelligence*, and *oral/written communication*.[160] (See Table 1.2.) Let's consider how to use them in the context of a student project team. Assume that your team is composed of four people and you are behind schedule in completing your final team project.

1. Teamwork/Collaboration   Establishing common ground or sharing a common goal are great ways to promote teamwork/collaboration. Given that your team is behind schedule on the project, contact your teammates and discuss what still needs to be done to get back on track. Remind them of the project deadline and see what obstacles stand between them and making the due date. By inviting others to collaborate you are offering an olive branch. This shows you're open to their needs, willing to listen, and that you understand conflict is a two-way street.

2. Social Intelligence   Social intelligence is the ability to connect with others in a meaningful way, to recognize and understand another person's feelings and thoughts, and to use this information to stimulate positive relationships and beneficial interactions. One of the best ways to exercise social intelligence is to show empathy toward others. As we mentioned earlier, the use of empathy requires effective listening, which demonstrates that we care about what someone else is saying. If someone on your project team isn't accepting of feedback, try to figure out the source of their frustration. Recognize it aloud so you validate what they're feeling. You can show you are truly listening by using expressions such as, "Mario, I suspect you are disappointed in . . ."

3. Openness to Change   Openness to change includes being flexible when confronted with change, seeing change as a challenge, and being willing to apply new ideas, processes, or directives. Are you for instance using a method of communication that doesn't work well for others and is slowing the project team down? Offer an example of something you'd like to do differently in the future: "Team, I know I prefer to text message instead of e-mail, but this method isn't providing the level of detail we need in our communications. I'll use e-mail so we are more efficient." This creates an atmosphere for others on the team to evaluate their own ways as well.

4. Emotional Intelligence   Emotional intelligence is the ability to monitor your emotions and those of others, to discriminate among them, and to use this information to guide your thinking and behavior. For example, be aware of your own temper before meeting with someone on your project team who is not meeting deadlines. We're humans and we can be imperfect and irrational at times. You can reflect by yourself, but it may not be a bad idea to talk with a friend or classmate who is not on the team. Taking a step back and reflecting allows a calmer you to enter the conversation, which will reduce the chances of further conflict.

5. Oral/Written Communication   Don't tell the person what they said, how they felt, or what they did. Using language like "I felt" instead of "you said" removes blame from the conversation and does not make assumptions about the other person's intentions. For example, instead of saying, "Brittany, you did not let others on the team speak so they couldn't complain about your work quality," say, "Brittany, when the conversation ended, I felt like our classmates didn't have a chance to express their opinions of what we've completed thus far. This could have been a learning opportunity for us."

Dealing with Disagreements: Five Conflict-Handling Styles

Even if you're at the top of your game as a manager, working with groups and teams of people will now and then put you in the middle of disagreements, sometimes even destructive conflict. There are five conflict-handling styles, or techniques, you can use for handling disagreements with individuals: *avoiding, obliging, dominating, compromising,* and *integrating.*[161] Figure 13.4 shows how each of the styles can be distinguished from the others by the parties' relative concern for others (on the y-axis) and for themselves (on the x-axis).

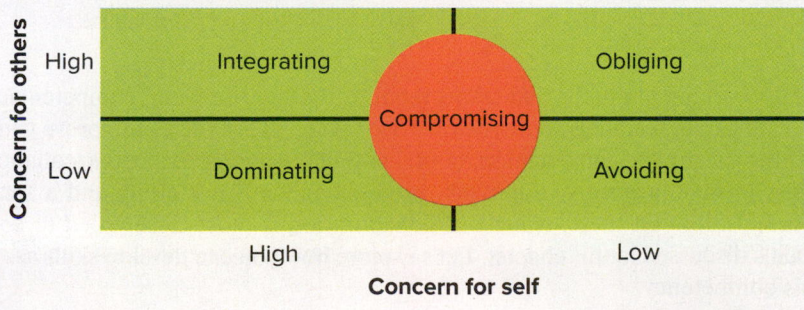

FIGURE 13.4

Five common conflict-handling styles

Source: From M. A. Rahim, "A Strategy for Managing Conflict in Complex Organizations," Human Relations, 1985, p. 84.

Avoiding—*Avoiding* is ignoring or suppressing a conflict. It is appropriate for trivial issues, when emotions are high and a cooling-off period is needed, or when the cost of confrontation outweighs the benefits of resolving the conflict.

Obliging—An obliging or accommodating manager allows the desires of the other party to prevail. This style may be appropriate when it's possible to eventually get something in return or when the issue isn't important to you.

Dominating—Also known as "forcing," *dominating* is simply ordering an outcome, when a manager relies on their formal authority and power to resolve a conflict. It is appropriate when an unpopular solution must be implemented and when it's not important that others commit to your viewpoint.

Compromising—In *compromising*, both parties give up something to gain something. It is appropriate when both sides have opposite goals or possess equal power.

Integrating—In this collaborative style, the manager strives to confront the issue and cooperatively identify the problem, generating and weighing alternatives and selecting a solution. It is appropriate for complex issues plagued by misunderstanding.

Research demonstrates that when companies focus on training their employees on these conflict-handling styles, they tend to see an increase in innovativeness and productivity.[162] What type of conflict-handling style do you think you have? How can you improve your ability to resolve conflict? Self-Assessment 13.5 can help answer these questions. ●

SELF-ASSESSMENT 13.5   CAREER READINESS

What Is Your Conflict-Management Style?

The following exercise is designed to determine your conflict-handling style. Please be prepared to answer these questions if your instructor has assigned Self-Assessment 13.5 in Connect.

1. Were you surprised by the results? Why or why not? Explain.

2. Were the scores for your primary and backup conflict-handling styles relatively similar, or was there a large gap? What does this imply? Discuss.

3. Is your conflict-handling style one that can be used in many different conflict scenarios? Explain.

4. What things might you say during an interview to demonstrate that you possess the ability to manage conflict?

13.5 Career Corner: Managing Your Career Readiness

Effectively working in groups and teams requires the use of several competencies from the model of career readiness shown below. (See Figure 13.5.) You can improve your teamwork skills by using the competencies of oral communications, teamwork/collaboration, social intelligence, a positive approach, professionalism/work ethic, and a service to others orientation. Of these, teamwork/collaboration is most closely tied to concepts and models discussed in this chapter. Let's explore how you can develop skills associated with this competency.

FIGURE 13.5

Model of career readiness
McGraw-Hill Education

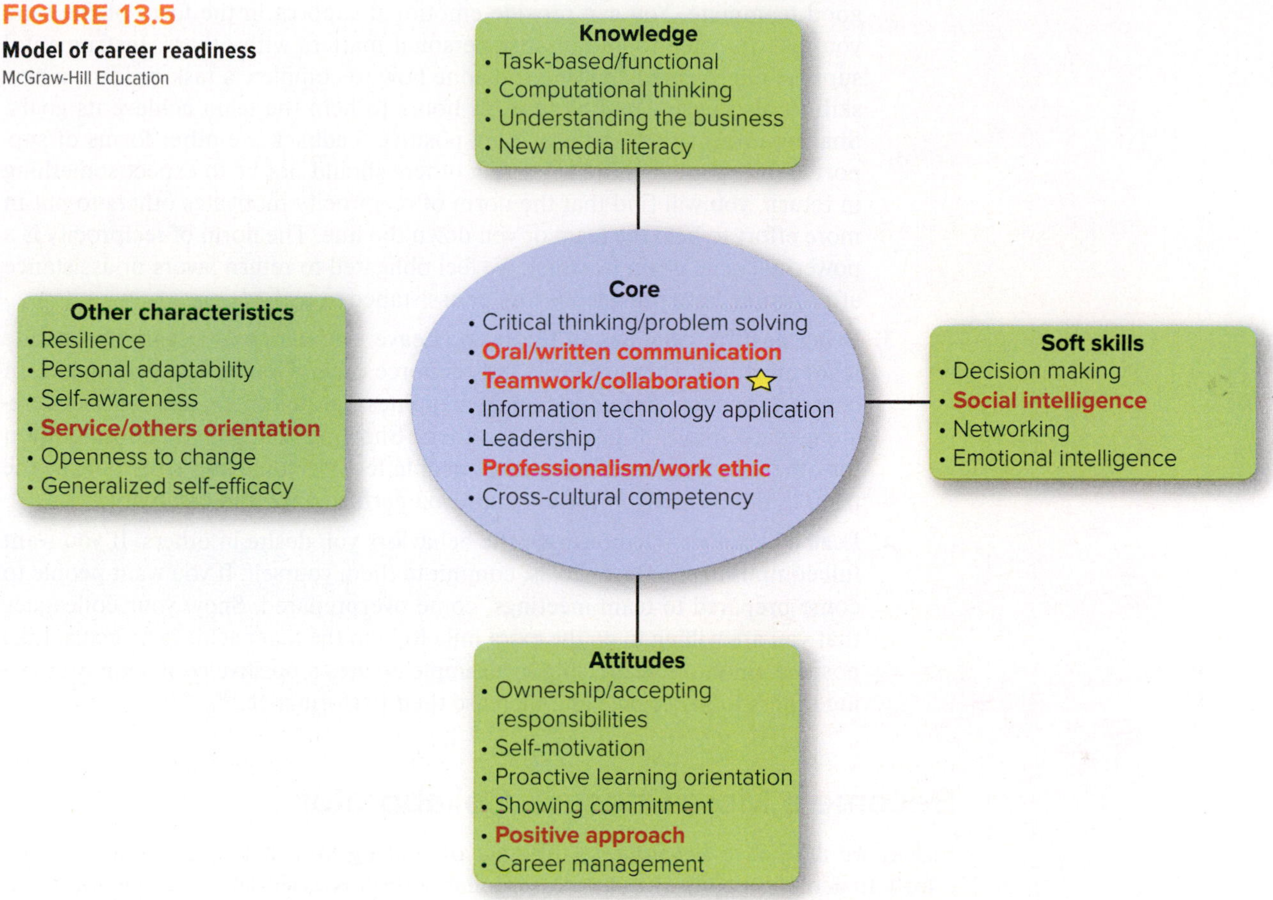

Knowledge
- Task-based/functional
- Computational thinking
- Understanding the business
- New media literacy

Other characteristics
- Resilience
- Personal adaptability
- Self-awareness
- **Service/others orientation**
- Openness to change
- Generalized self-efficacy

Core
- Critical thinking/problem solving
- **Oral/written communication**
- **Teamwork/collaboration** ⭐
- Information technology application
- Leadership
- **Professionalism/work ethic**
- Cross-cultural competency

Soft skills
- Decision making
- **Social intelligence**
- Networking
- Emotional intelligence

Attitudes
- Ownership/accepting responsibilities
- Self-motivation
- Proactive learning orientation
- Showing commitment
- **Positive approach**
- Career management

Become a More Effective Team Member

Teamwork requires a group of people to integrate their efforts in the pursuit of achieving a common goal. Below are four actions you can employ to become a better team member.

1. **Commit to the team.** "The best teams win together, learn together, adapt together, lose together, and grow together," says executive coach Shawn Murphy. Vince Lombardi, considered one of the all-time best coaches in professional football, lived this philosophy. He said, "Individual commitment to a group effort—that is what makes a team work, a company work, a society work, a civilization work." We all know that one player cannot do it all in team sports. Great players, such as NBA superstar LeBron James, are strategic in their approach toward teamwork. They realize that their job is to help team members raise their level of play while also inspiring and motivating them to achieve specific goals. It's the same at school and work. Consider your school project teams as an opportunity to apply your best talents toward the goal of increasing the team's overall grade. Commitment to a team comes down to your willingness to put the needs of others over self-interests. Yes, you may sacrifice some individual recognition in this process, but the team benefits. The key action here is the willingness to focus on the greater good of the team.[163]

2. **Support team members.** Actor Will Smith states, "If you're not making someone else's life better, then you're wasting your time. Your life will become better by making other lives better." This sentiment is precisely what it means to be a

LO 13.5

Describe how to develop the career readiness competency of teamwork/collaboration.

good teammate. You can provide emotional support in the form of the time you take to listen to and discuss personal matters with others. Instrumental support might entail showing someone how to complete a task or learn a new skill. It also means putting in extra hours to help the team achieve its goals. Sharing information and providing positive feedback are other forms of support. While your goal in supporting others should not be to expect something in return, you will find that the norm of reciprocity motivates others to put in more effort to help the team or you down the line. The norm of reciprocity is a powerful social norm by which we feel obligated to return favors or assistance after people have provided favors or assistance to us.[164]

3. **Bring positive emotions to the team.** Leave criticism and negativity outside team meetings. They are toxic and reinforce others' tendency to complain. In contrast, positive emotions such as happiness, gratefulness, and kindness create upward spirals of positivity in others. Showing concern and consideration for others in team meetings makes people feel welcome and truly part of the team. Studies show this fosters improved performance and creativity.[165]

4. **Lead by example.** Demonstrate the behaviors you desire in others. If you want full commitment to team goals, commit to them yourself. If you want people to come prepared to team meetings, come overprepared. Show your colleagues that you are willing to go the extra mile to help the team achieve its goals. Like positive emotions, leadership by example creates a positive contagion motivating others to participate and increase their performance.[166]

Become a More Effective Collaborator

Earlier we defined *collaboration* as the act of sharing information and coordinating efforts to achieve a collective outcome. Collaboration is essential for teamwork, but it isn't the same thing as teamwork. Teamwork requires some formal structure such as a team leader, agendas for meetings, and organization. Collaboration is more spontaneous, less structured, and less hierarchical. You don't need an agenda item that says "collaborate." Here are some tips for becoming a more effective collaborator.

1. **Listen and learn.** Author Ken Blanchard said it well: "None of us is as smart as all of us." You can't get the best from people if you don't encourage them to share their ideas, opinions, and beliefs. You may not agree with them, but people need to be heard. Remember that sharing different perspectives is essential for collaboration.[167] Listening is the flip side of talking. Active listening requires effort and motivation. You can improve your listening by withholding judgment, asking questions, showing respect, keeping your concentration and focus in the present moment, and remaining quiet.[168]

2. **Be open-minded.** It's difficult to collaborate if you aren't open to others' ideas.[169] You won't get the benefit of your teammates' experience and knowledge if you fail to consider their input. Being open also requires you to stop trying to impress others by having the best or brightest ideas. Just contribute what you can and let the team decide what ideas work best.[170] ●

Key Terms Used in This Chapter

adjourning 572

collaboration 574

conflict 581

cross-functional teams 567

devil's advocacy 585

dialectic method 586

dysfunctional conflict 582

formal group 566

forming 570

functional conflict 582

group 565

group cohesiveness 571

informal group 566

maintenance role 579

norming 571

norms 579

performing 571

personality conflict 583

programmed conflict 585

punctuated equilibrium 573

roles 577

self-managed teams 568

storming 571

task role 578

team 565

team charter 580

team composition 577

team member interdependence 577

team processes 580

team reflexivity 580

team voice 581

trust 575

virtual teams 568

Key Points

13.1 Groups versus Teams

- Groups and teams are different—a group is typically management-directed, a team self-directed. A group is defined as two or more freely interacting individuals who share collective norms, share collective goals, and have a common identity. A team is defined as two or more individuals committed to a common purpose, performance goals, and approach for which they hold themselves mutually accountable.

- Groups may be either formal, established to do something productive for the organization and headed by a leader, or informal, formed by people seeking friendship with no officially appointed leader.

- Teams are of various types, including work, project, cross-functional, self-managed, and virtual.

13.2 Stages of Group and Team Development

- A group may evolve into a team through five stages. (1) Forming is the process of getting oriented and getting acquainted. (2) Storming is characterized by the emergence of individual personalities and roles and conflicts within the group. (3) In norming, conflicts are resolved, close relationships develop, and unity and harmony emerge. (4) Performing is characterized by members concentrating on solving problems and completing the assigned task. (5) In adjourning, members prepare for disbandment.

- A group also can develop by means of punctuated equilibrium, in which it establishes periods of stable functioning until an event causes a dramatic change in norms, roles, and/or objectives. The group then establishes and maintains new norms of functioning, returning to equilibrium.

13.3 Building Effective Teams

- There are eight considerations managers must take into account in building a group into an effective team. (1) They must ensure individuals are collaborating. (2) They must establish a climate of trust. (3) They must establish measurable performance goals and have feedback about members' performance. (4) They must motivate members by making them mutually accountable to one another. (5) They must consider team composition. (6) They must consider the role each team member must play. (7) They must consider team norms. (8) They must have effective team processes.

13.4 Managing Conflict

- Conflict is a process in which one party perceives that its interests are being opposed or negatively affected by another party. Conflict can be dysfunctional, or negative. However, constructive, or functional, conflict benefits the main purposes of the organization and serves its interests. Too little conflict can lead to inactivity; too much conflict can lead to warfare.

- Four devices for stimulating constructive conflict are (1) spurring competition among employees, (2) changing the organization's culture and procedures, (3) bringing in outsiders for new perspectives, and (4) using programmed conflict to elicit different opinions without inciting people's personal feelings.

- Four kinds of conflict are personality, envy, intergroup, and cross-cultural.

- There are five conflict-handling styles: avoiding, obliging, dominating, compromising, and integrating.

- Working in groups requires the use of several career readiness competencies, including oral communications, teamwork/collaboration, social intelligence, a positive approach, professionalism/work ethic, and service to others.

- You can become a better team member by committing to the team, supporting team members, bringing positive emotions to the team, and leading by example.
- You can become a better collaborator by listening and learning and being open-minded.

Understanding the Chapter: What Do I Know?

1. How do groups and teams differ?
2. What's the difference between formal groups and informal groups?
3. Describe the five types of teams.
4. What are the stages of group and team development?
5. Explain the eight most essential considerations in building a group into an effective team.

6. How do functional and dysfunctional conflict differ?
7. How would you go about stimulating constructive conflict?
8. What are devil's advocacy and the dialectic method?
9. What five career readiness competencies can help you better handle conflict?
10. How can I become a better team member?

Management in Action

Must-See Quarantine TV

Late-night TV has been a mainstay of network television for generations. Johnny Carson entertained audiences for a few decades starting in the 1960s before being replaced by the likes of David Letterman and Jay Leno in the 1980s and 1990s.[171] Today, the three most watched hosts, Stephen Colbert, Jimmy Fallon, and Jimmy Kimmel, each bring in tens of millions of viewers and more than $400 million in ad revenue per year.[172]

Late-night TV shows may have different hosts, but their live studio-audience format is largely similar. They typically start with a monologue poking fun at the day's news and prerecorded or live skits. This is followed by celebrity interviews and musical performances. Most shows have an announcer, house band, and dozens of stage crew, writers, producers, and others that make it all happen. It takes a high-performing team to deliver a high-quality show. But what happens when a pandemic leaves studios empty, prohibits famous guests from traveling, and restricts hosts to their houses? That's exactly what happened during the COVID-19 outbreak.[173]

Let's shine a spotlight on what many called "Quarantine TV."

IN-HOUSE PRODUCTION, LITERALLY

Samantha Bee, host of the Emmy Award-winning late-night show *Full Frontal with Samantha Bee*, was filming a segment for her show when she encountered an issue she had never dealt with before. "There was literally a screeching hawk, circling up in the sky," she recalled. Bee wasn't filming at some exotic location overseas, she was actually on set—at her house. She asked her new makeshift production crew, her husband and three children, to please hold shooting for hawk sounds. "You have to be OK with whatever nature provides. This is really uncharted territory for any of us," she said.[174]

Bee wasn't alone in a new world of late-night TV production due to the COVID-19 pandemic. Social-distancing and self-quarantining guidelines meant hosts had to work virtually with limited resources. Molly McNearney, the co-head writer and a producer of ABC's *Jimmy Kimmel Live*, said it took three hours to shoot a six-minute monologue with host Jimmy Kimmel. "He's used to having a teleprompter guy and a team of 140 people helping him there," she said.[175] Instead, Kimmel and other hosts used iPhones and videoconferencing tools to record segments and celebrity interviews.

COLLABORATING TO SERVE AN AUDIENCE IN SHOCK

Hosts may be the face of a show, but there are dozens—if not hundreds—of individuals on these late-night teams making sure it all goes as smoothly as possible. Late-night show content typically reflects daily events and what society is thinking, which writers quickly incorporate into the show's monologue, skits, and questions for celebrity guests. This requires efficient and collaborative processes. First, producers source the most interesting and important material. After the material has been developed, writers script it in a way that draws laughs. Then different crews, such as video, audio, and makeup, act to meet taping deadlines. After all of this has been completed, editors enter the process to make sure the show meets broadcast standards.

The COVID-19 pandemic interrupted this interconnected system by shutting down lavish Hollywood and New York studios. Production crews scrambled from their homes, trying to connect virtually to meet deadlines. *The Tonight Show* showrunner Gavin Purcell needed to change his team's processes in order to ensure the show could keep airing and entertaining the millions who were quarantined at home. Purcell developed new virtual norms with an understanding that the same on-set resources everyone was used to weren't going to be there. "We're now trying to create a normalcy, in a world where nothing is normal right now, but we're trying to make it so that the actual production of it is a little bit more simplified and put systems in place."[176]

These production systems were incredibly important in a world that was reeling from a pandemic and looking for some late-night TV stress relief before bed. "We are a staff of planners, and even though this is something you could never plan for, those skills are coming in handy," said *Late Night with Seth Meyers* showrunner Mike Shoemaker. Shoemaker, whose show was being filmed in host Meyers' attic crawl space, needed to guide a team that was highly performing, but regressed to its more primitive days due to inexperience with virtual technology and the need for new roles. "Every day a new problem arises that literally never existed before and we problem-solve the solution for next time. Then something completely different goes wrong."[177]

Working in a virtual environment was particularly difficult for writers whose creativity is predicated on timing, banter, and constant collaboration with teammates. "If I had a joke idea or could punch up somebody else's joke, I would just walk over to their office, say it to them, and walk back. It's done in about 12 seconds," said *The Tonight Show* writer Gerard Bradford. "Now it takes maybe five minutes, because you have to

e-mail or text that person and wait for them to reply." Virtual shows also meant no studio audiences, so writers couldn't gauge how their jokes landed in real time. "You forget how important nonverbal communication is," said *Late Night* writer Alex Baze. Writers are typically able to get performance feedback from a studio audience's laughter, raised eyebrows, shifting in seats, etc. Without an audience, that feedback is missing, making it harder for changes to the next day's show. "Even when it's done, you're like, 'Well, I don't know if that was good,'" said Baze.[178]

All in all, production teams were able to adapt to a new way of producing content for millions of viewers. Experts, however, believe audiences were more forgiving in their content and quality critiques because it was the first time in modern history that a pandemic had made such a drastic impact on people's daily lives.[179] Viewers may not be as understanding the next time. For example, Jimmy Fallon's creative use of his daughters to help him with skits or Samantha Bee chopping wood in her backyard will only go so far on shows that need fresh content every night.[180] Content that doesn't intrigue viewers will lead to decreased viewership, which means less ad revenue for the network.[181] With this in mind, late-night TV teams will need to be better prepared in case they find themselves in this situation again. Will they be?

FOR DISCUSSION

Problem-Solving Perspective

1. What is the underlying problem in this case from the perspective of late-night showrunners?
2. What are the causes of this problem?

Application of Chapter Content

1. What are some virtual best practices late-night production managers could have employed for their remote teams? Explain.
2. Use Tuckman's Five-Stage Model to describe how the change in producing late-night TV could have caused teams to devolve.
3. Describe the disruption of late-night TV production using the concept of punctuated equilibrium (Figure 13.2).
4. How did the COVID-19 pandemic impact late-night TV production groups' ability to function as effective teams? Explain using the eight considerations of effective teams.
5. What types of conflict could stem from changes in the way production teams did their jobs? How could you effectively manage this conflict?

Recreational Marijuana Use: A Manager's Quandary

This challenge examines issues that may arise when co-workers smoke marijuana together outside work. We first provide background on the legalities of using marijuana before reviewing the case.

Legalities of Using Marijuana

Eleven states and the District of Columbia have legalized recreational marijuana use as of 2020: Alaska, California, Colorado, Illinois, Maine, Massachusetts, Michigan, Nevada, Oregon, Vermont, and Washington. Another 33 allow for medical marijuana use. Both recreational and medical marijuana use are still deemed illegal by the federal government, however.[182] As a result, some employers screen employees for marijuana use, even in states where it is permissible. This is particularly true for employers that contract with the federal government and certain positions deemed "safety-sensitive," such as commercial drivers and heavy equipment operators. Some states that allow for marijuana use have pushed back. For example, Nevada enacted a law in 2020 protecting employees from discrimination solely on the basis of marijuana use.[183]

The Case

You work in a state where it is illegal to use marijuana recreationally, and your employer has a zero-tolerance policy regarding the use of drugs. You also are a supervisor at a telephone call center and have very positive relationships with members of your work team and your manager. Blake is a member of your work team.

Blake invited you to his birthday party at his home, and you happily agreed to attend. During the party, you walked out to the backyard to get some fresh air and noticed that Blake and several other employees of your company were smoking marijuana. None of these individuals have prescriptions for medical marijuana. You have been told on several occasions by members of your own work team that these same individuals have used marijuana at other social events.

Although Blake is a member of your work team, the other smokers are not. You don't really feel any need to tell management about these people smoking pot because you have never noticed their being impaired at work. At the same time, you feel conflicted because your employer takes a hard stand against the use of any drugs. If the company found out that you knew about their smoking, it could adversely affect your career. The company expects managers to act with honesty and integrity and to be forthright with senior management.

The following week you receive an e-mail from the vice president of human resources to evaluate Blake for a promotion to a supervisory position. Blake is one of three people being considered. You have a great relationship with the VP, but you know he takes a hard line on drug use. At the same time, you believe Blake is a good employee, but you wonder whether his smoking marijuana shows bad judgment for someone being considered for a managerial position at the company. As you close the VP's e-mail, you begin to consider how to respond.

SOLVING THE CHALLENGE

As Blake's supervisor, what would you do?

1. I would not tell the vice president of human resources about Blake's drug use. He's doing a good job and I have not seen any impairment.

2. I would tell the vice president of human resources about the incident in which I observed Blake smoking marijuana, but I also would reinforce that he is a good performer. My gut feeling is that I need to honor the company's zero-tolerance policy on drug use.

3. I would talk to Blake. I would explain my predicament and then ask him about the frequency of his drug use. If Blake promised to stop smoking marijuana, I would not tell the vice president of human resources about the incident.

4. Invent other options. Discuss.

14

Power, Influence, and Leadership

From Becoming a Manager to Becoming a Leader

Kapook2981/iStock/Getty Images

After reading this chapter, you should be able to:

LO 14-1 Describe managers' appropriate use of power and influence.

LO 14-2 Identify traits and characteristics of successful leaders.

LO 14-3 Identify behaviors of successful leaders.

LO 14-4 Discuss situational leadership.

LO 14-5 Describe transactional and transformational leadership.

LO 14-6 Describe contemporary leadership perspectives and concepts.

LO 14-7 Explain how to develop the career readiness competency of self-awareness.

FORECAST   *What's Ahead in This Chapter*

How do leaders use their power and influence to get results? This chapter considers this question. We discuss the sources of a leader's power and how leaders use persuasion to influence people. We then consider the following approaches to leadership: trait, behavioral, situational, full range, and contemporary perspectives. We conclude with a Career Corner that focuses on developing the career readiness competency of self-awareness.

Improving Your Leadership Skills

According to one company's chief research executive writing in *Inc.* magazine, "Leadership is the art of execution. It's the art of getting things done."[1] This chapter introduces you to a number of insightful theories about leadership. For now, "getting things done" by leading others is a good place to begin thinking about what kind of leader you are and might become.

Here are some suggestions for improving your career readiness competency of leadership.

1. Discover your leadership style. We all develop a style of leading that is based on personal characteristics, traits, gender, interpersonal skills, and utilization of power and influence skills.[2] Identifying your leadership style is thus an ongoing process that evolves as you acquire more experience and responsibility in the workplace. You can think of this process as simply discovering what your strengths are over time and developing some flexible ways to use them in helping others achieve goals.[3] We include seven self-assessments in this chapter to help you gain an understanding about your leadership style.

2. Adopt a proactive learning orientation. This suggestion follows naturally from the first one. Becoming a leader is a process that never actually ends, which means you need to keep learning about your industry, yourself, your skills, and your strengths and weaknesses as you move through your career.[4] Take classes or courses online, network with peers and mentors, ask questions, stay open-minded, seek challenging opportunities, and look outside your industry occasionally for ideas and practices you can adapt to your own leadership toolkit. A proactive learning orientation is a career readiness competency desired by employers.

3. Recognize that there is no single best way to lead. As motivational speaker and writer Jack Canfield says, "True leaders understand that they have the opportunity and ability to respond differently to every situation. When events arise, whether they're good or bad, leaders see these events as neutral. But they see their response to these events as crucial."[5] You will need to adapt your leadership strategy to each situation that calls for it, or, as Tesla's CEO Elon Musk says, "I move myself to where the biggest problem is."[6]

4. Show your followers that you value them. Delegate responsibility to those you lead and earn their respect by modeling ethical behavior. Always give credit where it is due, praise in public and criticize in private, and ask for help when you need it. Don't be stingy with compliments and encouragement.[7] Work on building trust with your team, too, by communicating with honesty and truth, being an attentive listener and a positive thinker, and accepting the responsibility that comes with being the leader.[8]

5. Practice mindfulness. You can reduce stress and worry, sharpen your focus, and make more thoughtful decisions by adopting the habit of mindfulness, which means focusing your awareness on the present and accepting your feelings and thoughts.[9] Mindfulness becomes easier through meditation, which you can practice with simple techniques for as little as 5 or 10 minutes a day.[10] Mindfulness also helps you lead others through tough times and crises by enabling you to communicate calm, purposefulness, and positivity. (See Chapter 7 for more on mindfulness meditation.)

For Discussion One business writer suggests it's time for business leaders to abandon an old "rule" of leadership that says "great leaders work alone."[11] Do you agree that effective leadership should include motivating, developing, and encouraging others? Why or why not?

14.1 The Nature of Leadership: The Role of Power and Influence

THE BIG PICTURE

Leadership skills are needed to create and communicate a company's vision, strategies, and goals as well as to execute on these plans and goals. This section highlights the way successful managers use power and influence to achieve these ends and describes six sources of power and nine influence tactics they use to lead others. Leaders use the power of persuasion to get others to follow them. Five approaches to leadership are described in the next five sections.

LO 14.1

Describe managers' appropriate use of power and influence.

Leadership. What is it? Is it a skill anyone can develop? How important is it to organizational success?

==Leadership== is the ability to influence employees to voluntarily pursue organizational goals.[12] "Leadership" is a broad term, as this definition implies. It can describe a formal position in an organization, which usually carries a title like CEO or CFO, or an informal role, such as that played by an expert whose opinion we value in some area.

Although not everyone is suited to being a good leader, evidence shows that people can be trained to be more effective leaders.[13] In response, more companies are using management development programs to build a pipeline of leadership talent. They also provide leadership coaching to targeted employees. ==Leadership coaching== is the process of enhancing the skills and abilities that a leader needs in order to help the organization achieve its goals, according to one expert.[14] It is estimated that U.S. companies spent over $15 billion on coaching in 2019.[15]

Effective leadership matters! A recent study spanning 60 years and more than 18,000 firm-years showed that CEO behavior significantly impacted organizational performance.[16] Don't take this study to mean effective leadership only matters at the top. Other research reinforces the value of fostering effective leadership at all levels of an organization.

Let's begin our study of leadership by considering the difference between leading and managing and the role of power and influence skills.

What Is the Difference between Leading and Managing?

Bernard Bass, a leadership expert, concluded that "leaders manage and managers lead, but the two activities are not synonymous."[17] Broadly speaking:

- *Leaders* inspire others, provide emotional support, and try to get employees to rally around a common goal. Leaders also play a key role in *creating* a vision and strategic plan for an organization.

- *Managers* typically perform functions associated with planning, investigating, organizing, and control, and leaders focus on influencing others. Managers, in turn, are charged with *implementing* the vision and plan. We can draw several conclusions from this division of labor.

Good leaders are not necessarily good managers, and good managers are not necessarily good leaders. Further, effective leadership requires effective managerial skills at some level. Consider these contrasting examples:

Laurent Potdevin Example: Laurent Potdevin resigned from his position as Lululemon's CEO in 2018 due to managerial deficiencies that produced culture issues and

HR concerns.[18] Company insiders revealed that Potdevin exhibited unprofessional behavior on a regular basis and made managerial decisions based on favoritism and personal relationships with employees as opposed to qualifications. A company spokesperson said that Potdevin "fell short of our standards of conduct" in a press release following his resignation.[19]

Pamela Nicholson Example: Pamela Nicholson served as CEO of Enterprise from 2013 to 2019. In the 32 years before she assumed the top spot, Nicholson amassed an impressive resume of management and leadership experience with the company. She was named one of *Fortune* magazine's "most powerful women in business" for 13 years in a row and was voted one of Glassdoor's highest-rated CEOs. Executive Chairman Andrew Taylor said, "She joined our company fresh out of college and rose from a management trainee behind the rental counter to our top leadership team through a combination of great management skills, keen business instincts and just plain hard work."[20]

Great leaders have strong managerial skills. Pamela Nicholson spent decades sharpening her managerial skills at Enterprise before ultimately leading the company as CEO. Tom Gannam/AP Images

Managers conduct planning, organizing, directing, and control. Leaders inspire, encourage, and rally others to achieve great goals. Managers implement a company's vision and strategic plan. Leaders create and articulate that vision and plan. Table 14.1 summarizes the key characteristics of managers and leaders.

TABLE 14.1

Characteristics of Managers and Leaders

BEING A MANAGER MEANS . . .	BEING A LEADER MEANS . . .
Planning, organizing, directing, controlling	Being visionary
Executing plans and delivering goods and services	Being inspiring, setting the tone, and articulating the vision
Managing resources	Managing people
Being conscientious	Being inspirational (charismatic)
Acting responsibly	Acting decisively
Putting customers first—responding to and acting for customers	Putting people first—responding to and acting for followers
Mistakes can happen when managers don't appreciate people are the key resource, underlead by treating people like other resources, or fail to be held accountable	Mistakes can happen when leaders choose the wrong goal, direction, or inspiration; overlead; or fail to implement the vision
Coping with complexity—complex organizations are chaotic without good management	Coping with change—organizations need leadership to direct the constant change necessary for survival in today's dynamic business landscape

Sources: Adapted from the following sources: P. Lorenzi, "Managing for the Common Good: Prosocial Leadership," Organizational Dynamics, Vol. 33, No. 3 (2004), p. 286; J. P. Kotter, "What Leaders Really Do," Harvard Business Review, December 2001, pp. 85–96; the role of leadership within organizational change is discussed in J. P. Kotter, Leading Change (Boston: Harvard Business School Press, 1996); managing in the world of complexity is discussed in G. Sargut and R. G. McGrath, "Learning to Live with Complexity," Harvard Business Review, September 2011, pp. 68–76; M. J. Mauboussin, "Embracing Complexity," Harvard Business Review, September 2011, pp. 88–92.

Do you want to lead others or understand what makes a leader tick? Then take the following self-assessment. It provides feedback on your readiness to assume a leadership role and can help you consider how to prepare for a formal leadership position.

Managerial Leadership: Can You Be *Both* a Manager and a Leader?

Absolutely. The latest thinking is that individuals are able to exhibit a broad array of the contrasting behaviors shown in Table 14.1 (a concept called *behavioral complexity*).[21] Thus, in the workplace, many people are capable of engaging in **managerial leadership, which involves both influencing followers to internalize and commit to a set of shared goals, and facilitating the group and individual work that is needed to accomplish those goals.**[22] Here, the "influencing" part is leadership and the "facilitating" part is management.

Managerial leadership may be demonstrated not only by managers appointed to their positions, but also by those who exercise leadership on a daily basis but don't carry formal management titles (such as certain co-workers on a team).

Six Sources of Power

Power is the ability to marshal human, informational, and other resources to get something done. Defined this way, power is all about influencing others. The more influence you have, the more powerful you are, and vice versa.

To really understand leadership, we need to understand the concept of power and authority. *Authority* is the right to perform or command; it comes with the job. In contrast, *power* is the extent to which a person is able to influence others so they respond to requests.

People who pursue **personalized power—power directed at helping oneself**—as a way of enhancing their own selfish ends may give the word power a bad name. However, there is another kind of power, **socialized power—power directed at helping others.** Both of your authors are high on socialized power. We are motivated to write this textbook because our goal is to help you be the best you can be at work and in your personal life.

Within organizations there are typically six sources of power leaders may draw on: *legitimate, reward, coercive, expert, referent,* and *informational.*[23]

1. Legitimate Power: Influencing Behavior Because of One's Formal Position   **Legitimate power, which all managers have, is power that results from managers' formal positions within the organization.** All managers have legitimate power over their employees, deriving from their position, whether it's a construction boss, ad account supervisor, sales manager, or CEO. This power may be exerted both positively or negatively—as praise or as criticism, for example.

Police Department Example: All managers possess legitimate authority, but in organizations that have more rigid hierarchical structures, this authority is easier to see. Police departments tend to have clearly defined lines of authority indicating exactly which positions have authority over other positions.

The villain/superhero dichotomy often depicted in pop culture is one way to think about power. Both villains and superheroes are characterized as having extraordinary ability to influence others. Villains use this power to further their own selfish causes (personalized power), often harming others in the process. Superheroes use this power to further the greater good (socialized power), improving the world as they go. How will you use your power?
yarruta/123RF

2. Reward Power: Influencing Behavior by Promising or Giving Rewards

Reward power, which all managers have, is power that results from managers' authority to reward their subordinates. Rewards can range from praise to pay raises, from recognition to promotions.

Tallgrass Freight Company Example: Tallgrass Freight brokerage company rewards its tops sales employees and a plus-one with a trip to Las Vegas for its Club 200 celebration. To be awarded, employees must generate at least $200,000 in gross profits in a year. Said COO David Barnes, "We want to incentivize our agents for the right sort of performance," adding "to be at this level of gross profit generation . . . means this is a truly elite group of freight agents."[24]

3. Coercive Power: Influencing Behavior by Threatening or Giving Punishment

Coercive power, which all managers have, results from managers' authority to punish their subordinates. Punishment can range from verbal or written reprimands to demotions to terminations. In some lines of work, fines and suspensions may be used. Boards of directors also have this type of power—they can fire the company's CEO with a vote. Coercive power has to be used judiciously, of course, since a manager who is seen as being constantly negative will produce a lot of resentment among employees.

Tapestry Example: Tapestry is a luxury fashion company that owns the Coach, Kate Spade, and Stuart Weitzman brands. In 2019 the company's board of directors fired CEO Victor Luis and replaced him with board chairperson Jide Zeitlin. Said Zeitlin in an e-mail to the company's employees, "Given we have not delivered on our potential, the Board decided it was time to make a change at the top and asked me to step in as CEO."[25]

4. Expert Power: Influencing Behavior Because of One's Expertise

Expert power is power resulting from one's specialized information or expertise. Expertise, or special knowledge, can be mundane, such as knowing the work schedules and assignments of the people who report to you. Or it can be sophisticated, such as having computer or medical knowledge. Administrative assistants may have expert power because, for example, they have been in a job a long time and know all the necessary contacts. CEOs may have expert power because they have knowledge not shared with many others.

Dr. Anthony Fauci Example: During the COVID-19 pandemic, Dr. Anthony Fauci emerged as one of the most trusted sources of medical information in America.[26] Dr. Fauci graduated first in his class from Cornell University Medical College and has served as the director of the National Institute of Allergy and Infectious Diseases (NIAID) for more than 30 years. A *Business Insider* poll found that Dr. Fauci was the most trusted leader in the country during the crisis.[27]

Expert power (such as that exhibited by Dr. Anthony Fauci during COVID-19) is especially important in times of crisis, because this is when we must rely on those with highly specialized knowledge to guide critical decisions. Oliver Contreras/Alamy Stock Photo

5. Referent Power: Influencing Behavior Because of One's Personal Attraction

Referent power is power deriving from one's personal attraction. As we will see later in this chapter (under the discussion of transformational leadership, Section 14.5), this kind of power characterizes strong, visionary leaders who are able to persuade their followers through their charisma. Referent power may be associated with managers, but it is more likely to be characteristic of leaders.

Angela Ahrendts Example: Angela Ahrendts—former head of online retail and physical stores for Apple—has an impressive career history. In recent years, she went from being Burberry's CEO to Apple's highest-paid executive. Ahrendts was credited with turning Burberry around at a time when the brand was on the heels of failure. Apple hired Ahrendts in large part because of her charisma, energy, and ability to motivate people—all of which it saw as key leadership skills.[28]

6. Informational Power: Influencing Behavior Because of the Logical and/or Valuable Information One Communicates

==Informational power== is power deriving from one's access to information. Although not included as a separate source of power in the original research on power bases in organizations, later research added informational power to the typology.[29] People who are "in the know" in organizations may be seen as having informational power. People with access to information may also withhold it or release it selectively in order to demonstrate their power.[30] This latter use of informational power can be toxic, and some companies take proactive measures to avoid it.

Bridgewater Associates Example: At Bridgewater Associates—the world's largest hedge fund—communication revolves around transparency. The company records all of its meetings and managers are punished for withholding information. Managers at the fund will not hire a new stock analyst if interview questions reveal that the candidate is likely to hide information to use as an advantage over colleagues.[31]

Now that you've learned about the six bases of power, complete Self-Assessment 14.2 to identify which bases you prefer to use. Answering the associated questions will help you understand how the various forms of power can both help and hurt you when trying to influence others.

SELF-ASSESSMENT 14.2   CAREER READINESS

What Kind of Power Do I Prefer?

If your instructor has assigned Self-Assessment 14.2 in Connect, you will learn which bases of power you prefer to use.

1. Which of the six bases of power do you prefer to use?
2. Describe how this form of power helps you at school, at work, and in social situations.
3. Which of the six bases is your least preferred? What are the implications for you at school, at work, and in social situations?
4. What things might you say during an interview to demonstrate that you understand how to use power when influencing others?

Common Influence Tactics

An author for *Harvard Business Review* recently posed two questions: "Why are self-confident blowhards so often believed? Why are experts so often ignored?"[32] The answer, according to numerous experts, lies in the ability to use specific tactics in order to influence others.[33] ==Influence tactics== are conscious efforts to affect and change behaviors in others. Influence tactics can be used for good (e.g., persuading co-workers to pitch in their time for a community volunteer effort) or for bad (e.g., pressuring a subordinate into keeping a boss's unethical behavior a secret).

We previously defined leadership as "the ability to influence employees to voluntarily pursue organizational goals." This definition reinforces the importance of developing good influence skills and the fact that employers see this as a key career readiness competency. The nine most common ways people try to get their bosses, co-workers, and subordinates to do what they want are listed in Table 14.2, beginning with the most frequently used.

TABLE 14.2 **Nine Common Influence Tactics**

INFLUENCE TACTIC	DESCRIPTION	EXAMPLE
1. Rational persuasion	Trying to convince someone with reason, logic, or facts	As CEO of ACORD, Bill Pieroni helps insurance and financial services companies to make strategic choices and outperform competitors. He encourages firms to use data to develop the most successful marketing campaigns, saying "Marketing is data, is grids, is information ... Start with facts and then justify."[34]
2. Inspirational appeals Brian Ach/Getty Images	Trying to build enthusiasm by appealing to others' emotions, ideals, or values	When Indya Moore's *Elle* magazine cover photo won the Cover of the Year award at New York Fashion Week, she used the opportunity and her acceptance speech to inspire others to be more accepting of others. Moore (pictured at left) wore earrings made of photo frames—8 frames hanging from each ear—to represent the 16 black transgender women who had been murdered in 2019. She said, "This year, sixteen known women were taken from us," adding, "On this day that I'm celebrated and awarded for being visible, I decided to bring them with me."[35]
3. Consultation Scott Taetsch/Getty Images	Getting others to participate in planning, decision making, and changes	"Prioritize people over tasks," said WNBA commissioner and former Deloitte CEO Cathy Engelbert (pictured at left). Known for her collaborative style, Engelbert attributed her success to factors such as "building a team that brings you solutions instead of challenges, listening to and collaborating with them."[36]
4. Ingratiation	Getting someone in a good mood prior to making a request	A recent article referred to Boeing as "one of the biggest players in the Washington influence game."[37] Said another, "For decades, Boeing has worked to ingratiate itself with both Democrats and Republicans in Washington."[38] The company is known for spending millions on lobbying aimed at influencing federal aviation policy and defense contracts. Said one expert, "This is a blue chip company that lots of government officials have long been proud to be associated with."[39]
5. Personal appeals	Referring to friendship and loyalty when making a request or asking a friend to do a favor	Mallun Yen, founder of Operator Collective and former Cisco VP, recommends calling on your network of close relationships to succeed at work. She suggests encouraging this behavior in others by asking a friend, "tell me two specific things I can do to help you" and following through on your commitment.[40]
6. Exchange	Making explicit or implied promises and trading favors	This type of exchange is sometimes called a quid pro quo ("this for that"). Exchanges can be a useful tool for building employee loyalty. For example, during the COVID-19 pandemic, after more than 3.3 million Americans filed for unemployment by March 21, 2020, some CEOs made public commitments to suspend layoffs at their companies. These included Morgan Stanley, Visa, and Citigroup.[41]
7. Coalition tactics	Getting others to support your efforts to persuade someone	Many organizations partner with celebrities in order to build successful campaigns. This is an example of a coalition. In the closing moments of the musical *Hamilton,* Elizabeth Schuyler Hamilton sings that she is proudest of her role in founding the first private orphanage in New York City. That same charity— called Graham Windham—is still in operation and serves 4,500 children each year. The organization credited the cast's ongoing support with reinvigorating interest in and donations toward its services.[42]

(Continued)

TABLE 14.2 *Continued*

INFLUENCE TACTIC	DESCRIPTION	EXAMPLE
8. Pressure	Demanding compliance or using intimidation or threats	CEO activism—corporate leaders taking public stands on social and political issues—is on the rise. Said Salesforce CEO Marc Benioff, "Today CEOs need to stand up not just for their shareholders, but their employees, their customers, their partners, the community, the environment, schools, everybody."[43] In 2019 Benioff exerted pressure by announcing that Salesforce would cease to do business with companies that used its software to sell semi-automatic weapons.[44]
9. Legitimating tactics	Basing a request on authority or right, organizational rules or policies, or explicit/implied support from superiors	Researchers at the University of Queensland recently studied 385 occupational health and safety (OHS) professionals to determine the influence tactics that were most effective to use when convincing organizational leaders about matters that impacted worker safety. The study found that leaders were especially resistant when OHS professionals used legitimating tactics to justify their requests by calling on law and policy.[45]

Sources: Descriptions of these influence tactics are based on D. Kipnis, S. Schmidt, and I. Wilkinson, "Intraorganizational Influence Tactics: Exploration in Getting One's Way," Journal of Applied Psychology, August 1980, pp. 440–452; Table 1 in G. Yukl, C. M. Falbe, and J. Y. Youn, "Patterns of Influence Behavior for Managers," Group & Organization Management, March 1993, pp. 5–28.

Which Influence Tactics Do You Prefer? When you read the list of tactics, each probably meant something to you. Which do you most commonly use? Knowing the answer can help you better choose the appropriate tactic for any given situation and thus increase the chance of achieving your desired outcome. You can enhance your self-awareness about the career readiness competency of leadership by completing Self-Assessment 14.3.

SELF-ASSESSMENT 14.3 CAREER READINESS

Which Influence Tactics Do I Use?

If your instructor has assigned Self-Assessment 14.3 in Connect, you will learn which of the nine influence tactics you use and in what order of frequency.

1. Is your rational persuasion score the highest? Regardless, give some specific examples of ways you use this tactic.

2. Which tactic is your least preferred (lowest score)? Provide examples of situations when and how you may use this tactic.

3. What might you say during an interview to demonstrate that you understand how to use these nine tactics to influence others?

How to Use the Tactics to Influence Outcomes

Research and practice provide some useful lessons about the relative effectiveness of influence tactics.

- **Rely on the core.** *Core influence tactics*—rational persuasion, consultation, collaboration, and inspirational appeals—are most effective at building commitment.
- **Be authentic.** Don't try to be someone else. Be authentic to your values and beliefs.
- **Consult rather than legitimate.** Some employees are more apt to accept change when managers rely on a consultative strategy and are more likely to resist change when managers use a legitimating tactic.

- **"Ingratiation" is not a good long-term strategy.** Ingratiation improved short-term sales goal achievement but reduced it in the long term in a study of salespeople. Glad handing may help today's sales but not tomorrow's.

- **Be subtle.** Subtle flattery and agreement with the other person's opinion (both forms of ingratiation) were shown to increase the likelihood that executives would win recommendation to sit on boards of directors.

- **Learn to influence.** Research with corporate managers of a supermarket chain showed that influence tactics can be taught and learned. Managers who received 360-degree feedback on two occasions regarding their influence tactics showed an increased use of core influence tactics.

You'll need to understand *and* effectively apply a range of influence tactics to be effective. But you can learn and improve influence tactics to move resisters to compliance and move those who are compliant to commitment. ●

14.2 Trait Approaches: Do Leaders Have Distinctive Traits and Personal Characteristics?

THE BIG PICTURE

Trait approaches attempt to identify distinctive characteristics that account for the effectiveness of leaders. We describe (1) positive task-oriented traits and positive/negative interpersonal attributes (narcissism, Machiavellianism, psychopathy) and (2) some results of gender studies.

Consider a leader called one of the "most powerful women in business" by *Fortune* magazine, a former CIA operations officer, graduate of University of Pennsylvania's Wharton School, and one-time official in the White House Office of Management and Budget and later the Pentagon, who has led one of the world's largest defense contractors since 2013. "Performance speaks for itself," she says, adding, "absent performance, you really don't have anything to say . . . Results are, at the end of the day, all that really do matter."[46] That leader is Phebe Novakovic, CEO of General Dynamics. She seems to embody the traits of (1) dominance, (2) intelligence, (3) self-confidence, (4) high energy, and (5) task-relevant knowledge. General Dynamics stock has returned an average of 16% annually since Novakovic took the lead as CEO in 2013.[47]

These are the five traits that researcher Ralph Stogdill in 1948 concluded were typical of successful leaders.[48] Stogdill is one of many contributors to **trait approaches to leadership**, which attempt to identify distinctive characteristics that account for the effectiveness of leaders.[49]

LO 14-2

Identify traits and characteristics of successful leaders.

Positive Task-Oriented Traits and Positive/Negative Interpersonal Attributes

Traits play a central role in how we perceive leaders, and they ultimately affect leadership effectiveness.[50] This is why researchers have attempted to identify a more complete list of traits that differentiate leaders from followers. Table 14.3 shows an expanded list of both positive *and* negative interpersonal attributes often found in leaders.[51] Notice the inclusion of the Big Five traits we discussed in Chapter 11 as positive attributes.

General Dynamics CEO Phebe Novakovic displays dominance, intelligence, self-confidence, high energy, and task-relevant knowledge—five traits that researchers suggest are common among highly successful leaders. Brian Snyder/Newscom

TABLE 14.3   Key Task-Oriented Traits and Interpersonal Attributes

POSITIVE TASK-ORIENTED TRAITS	POSITIVE INTERPERSONAL ATTRIBUTES	NEGATIVE INTERPERSONAL ATTRIBUTES
• Intelligence	• Extraversion	• Narcissism
• Conscientiousness	• Agreeableness	• Machiavellianism
• Open to experience	• Emotional intelligence	• Psychopathy
• Emotional stability		
• Positive affect		

We have discussed most positive interpersonal attributes elsewhere, but we need to describe the negative, or "dark side," traits of some leaders. Known collectively as the "dark triad," these traits are narcissism, Machiavellianism, and psychopathy.[52] Leaders who display these negative traits have a strong negative impact on employees' job satisfaction, well-being, and mental health.[53]

- **Narcissism.** Narcissism is defined as "a self-centered perspective, feelings of superiority, and a drive for personal power and glory."[54] Narcissists have inflated views of themselves, seek to attract the admiration of others, and fantasize about being in control of everything. Although passionate and charismatic, narcissistic leaders may provoke counterproductive work behaviors in others, such as strong resentments and resistance.[55] They also tend to act more narcissistically when they perceive that someone has treated them unfairly.[56]

- **Machiavellianism.** Inspired by the pessimistic beliefs of Niccolò Machiavelli, a philosopher and writer (*The Prince*) in the Italian Renaissance, Machiavellianism (pronounced "mah-kyah-*vel*-yahn-izm") displays a cynical view of human nature and condones opportunistic and unethical ways of manipulating people, putting results over principles. This view is manifested in such expressions as "All people lie to get what they want" and "You have to cheat to get ahead." Like narcissism, Machiavellianism is also associated with counterproductive work behaviors, especially as people begin to understand that they are being coldly manipulated.[57]

- **Psychopathy.** Psychopathy ("sigh-*kop*-a-thee") is characterized by lack of concern for others, impulsive behavior, and a dearth of remorse when the psychopath's actions harm others. Not surprisingly, a person with a psychopathic personality can be a truly toxic influence in the workplace.[58]

If you have a propensity for any of these, you need to know that the expression of "dark side" traits tends to result in career derailment—being demoted or fired.[59]

What Do We Know about Gender and Leadership?

The increase in the number of women in the workforce has generated much interest in understanding the similarities and differences between female and male leaders.

Are Women Represented in Leadership Positions?   Women make up more than half the workforce and more than half of all college students in the United States, but they are still fighting to achieve gender parity in leadership.[60] Women are making gains at the top but are still highly underrepresented. There were 38 women CEOs leading Fortune 500 companies in 2020, a tiny number, but more than ever before.[61] Lisa Su is one example:

Lisa Su Example: Advanced Micro Devices' (AMD) stock was near an all-time low when Lisa Su stepped in as CEO in 2014. Since then, the company's stock price has increased by more than 1,300% and AMD hit a record high share price in 2020.[62] Su credits her parents with providing important life lessons that she has carried into her career, including hard work, patience, and continuous learning. "My key trait is determination," said Su, adding, "meaning there's no problem that can't be solved if you really put your mind to it." On the company's future, Su said, "What I like to always say is that the best is yet to come."[63]

Do Men and Women Vary in Terms of Leadership? Researchers have studied gender and leadership in terms of whether women and men are equally likely to emerge as leaders, whether they engage in different leader behaviors or use different styles of leadership, and whether they vary in terms of their effectiveness as leaders.[64] In general, results are mixed—some favor female leaders and others favor male leaders—and any gender differences in these variables tend to be small. In other words, the ability to lead effectively doesn't hinge on gender, and there is no reason to believe that the gender imbalance present in corporate leadership roles stems from one gender being "better" at leadership than another. Here is a summary of what we know:[65]

- **Leader emergence:**
  - According to a recent review of historical leadership research, women are still less likely to emerge as leaders in organizations than men. This highlights the importance of increased mentoring, leadership development, and other programs aimed at the inclusion of more women in organizations' leadership pipelines.[66]

- **Leader behavior:**
  - A meta-analysis of 45 different studies found that female leaders used more transformational leadership behaviors than male leaders.
  - A meta-analysis of 112 different studies of abusive supervision (a type of destructive leadership discussed later in the chapter) found that male leaders exhibited more abusive behaviors than female leaders.

- **Leader style:**
  - Women are more likely to use a democratic or participative style than men, and men are more likely to use an autocratic and directive style.

- **Leader effectiveness:**
  - Women and men are similarly effective as leaders.
  - When there are more men than women in the organization and when the setting is more masculine, men tend to be rated slightly higher than women on leadership effectiveness.
  - It's not clear whether and how leader gender impacts firm performance. The popular press has promoted the idea that companies have significantly higher financial performance when females are members of the upper echelon—the CEO and the top management team (TMT).[67] But research results on TMT gender diversity and firm performance are mixed. A recent academic meta-analysis of 146 studies from 33 different countries found that "there are small but dependably positive associations of female representation in CEO positions and TMTs with long-term value creation."[68]

See the Example box for evidence of gender differences in leadership during a global crisis.

EXAMPLE   Gender and Leadership During a Crisis

Less than 7% of world countries were led by women in 2020.[69] But when COVID-19 took hold in the early part of the year, it became clear that there was something unique about them: Countries with female leaders seemed to be faring much better in dealing with the pandemic than those led by men. While it's not possible to draw firm conclusions from such a small sample, scholars and other experts quickly took note of the trend.[70] Let's take a look at some of these leaders' responses.

Mary Long/Shutterstock

Prime Minister Silveria Jacobs (Sint Maarten) Prime Minister Silveria Jacobs was praised for her "straight to the point messaging" and direct, no-nonsense communication with the residents of Sint Maarten, the Dutch side of Saint Martin, an island in the Caribbean.[71] In a video address that went viral, Jacobs told the people of Sint Maarten, "Simply. Stop. Moving," adding, "If you do not have the type of bread you like in your house, eat crackers. If you do not have bread, eat cereal, eat oats, sardines."[72] In a separate address the prime minister said, "Together we can do this . . . Each and every one of us. These regulations are not put in place to test your faith or to push you to your limits. It is a matter of protecting your life and to get our livelihood safe, so that we can continue and return to proper economic development so that we can all thrive."[73]

Prime Minister Jacinda Ardern (New Zealand) In mid-May of 2020, when much of the world was still under lockdown, New Zealand declared that it had "virtually eliminated" the virus after going several days without a new positive diagnosis. The country instituted a nationwide lockdown early in the pandemic that included firm restrictions on travel and the suspension of all businesses except for groceries, gas stations, hospitals, and pharmacies. Said one media outlet, "The Prime Minister of New Zealand made clear, concise statements about the situation to the nation, and was bolstered by a team of scientists and health professionals to help stop any confusion or panic about the sudden austerity." By May, the nation of 4.8 million people had seen only 21 deaths from the virus.[74]

President Tsai Ing-wen (Taiwan) According to Johns Hopkins University data, Taiwan—with a population of 23 million—had only 7 COVID-related deaths by mid-May of 2020.[75] President Tsai Ing-wen was credited for her "calm, steady, and competent"

response.[76] Said one reporter, "Tsai has demonstrated grit in leading Taiwan's response to the COVID-19 pandemic. She has relied on science, preparedness, clear and consistent communication with the public, a strong health system, and technocratic competence to shield Taiwan from the worst effects of the virus."[77]

Prime Minister Katrín Jakobsdóttir (Iceland) Iceland's government—led by Prime Minister Katrin Jakobsdóttir—collaborated with deCODE biotech company to offer free COVID-19 testing to all of its citizens, regardless of whether they had symptoms. The country also used a rigorous contact-tracing program to locate and isolate those with potential exposure. Because of these early and widespread efforts, Iceland avoided many of the strict lockdown measures and business closures instituted by other countries.[78]

The "Why" Experts speculated on the reasons that female-led countries fared better amid the pandemic. One reason may be that these leaders felt less restricted by expectations of "how a leader should behave" because they likely had to fight especially hard and take nontraditional paths to get to where they are.[79] Another possibility—perhaps these leaders were more open to collaboration and outside expertise. Said University of Edinburgh Medical School Chair of Global Health Dr. Devi Sridhar, "The only way to avoid 'groupthink' and blind spots is to ensure representatives with diverse backgrounds and expertise are at the table when major decisions are made."[80] A third reason may be that these responses were not due strictly to leader gender, but rather, reflected the larger societal norms and attitudes of countries that were willing to elect female leaders. Said two female scholars, "Greater involvement of women results in a broader perspective on the crisis, and paves the way for the deployment of richer and more complete solutions than if they had been imagined by a homogeneous group."[81]

YOUR CALL

Based on this example, how might increased inclusion of women in firm leadership positions benefit organizations?

Are There Social Forces Working against Women Leaders? Women's representation in leadership is increasing, but nowhere do their numbers approach their proportion in the overall population. As we stated above, women are less likely to emerge as organizational leaders than men, and this stems in large part from the fact that firms often fail to include women in their leadership pipelines.[82] Women managers also are less likely to get plum assignments or international experience.[83] Why do these differences in leadership opportunities persist? The social forces at play include:

- *Failure to recognize gender discrimination.* A recent Pew Research study revealed disparities in the extent to which women and men recognize the existence of gender discrimination in leadership.[84] For example:

    o   Approximately 70% of women believed there were too few women in top executive and political leadership positions; only about 50% of men agreed.

    o   Approximately 70% of women believed that women have to work harder to prove themselves as worthy for leadership positions due to structural barriers and heightened expectations; only about 50% of men agreed.

    o   Approximately 60% of women believed that gender discrimination presented a major barrier to female leadership; only about 44% of men agreed.

- *Persistence of sexist attitudes throughout women's lives.* Gender norms are internalized in us at a very young age, and research suggests our attitudes about gender are very difficult to change. A recent study for the National Bureau of Economic Research found that the strength of sexist attitudes in a woman's state of birth continues to influence her career outcomes throughout her life, regardless of whether she moves to a state with more egalitarian attitudes about gender.[85]

- *Existence of increased obstacles once women reach leadership positions.* A primary obstacle is that women tend to receive more scrutiny in leadership roles than men do.

    o   One recent study found that people responded more negatively to ethical scandals when organizations had female leaders.[86]

    o   Other studies have shown that women are less likely to speak up in meetings due to this increased scrutiny, although onlookers often incorrectly attribute it to a lack of confidence.[87]

    o   Results from a study using an 18-year dataset of activist investors showed that "female CEOs are more likely than male CEOs to come under threat from activist investors, and also are more likely to have simultaneous threats from multiple activist investors."[88] An activist investor is a shareholder who owns more than 5% of a public company's voting stock and desires to change management practices.

Are Knowledge and Skills Important?

Knowledge and skills are extremely important! A team of researchers identified four basic skills leaders need. *(See Table 14.4.)*

TABLE 14.4   Four Basic Skills for Leaders

WHAT LEADERS NEED	AND WHY
Cognitive abilities to identify problems and their causes in rapidly changing situations	Leaders must sometimes devise effective solutions in short time spans with limited information, and this requires strong cognitive abilities. Google CEO Sundar Pichai's former professors remember him as a "shy, quiet, but extremely intelligent" student.[89] Pichai earned a Master's in engineering from Stanford and an MBA from the University of Pennsylvania's Wharton School of Business.
Interpersonal skills to influence and persuade others	Leaders need to work well with diverse people. Zoom has become known for its company culture focused on happiness, and many have praised CEO Eric Yuan for his role in building and maintaining this positivity. Said one reporter, Yuan "is probably one of the most likeable people you will meet in the Valley. It is no surprise that Zoom's culture is so highly recognized these days."[90]
Business skills to maximize the use of organizational assets	Leaders increasingly need business skills as they advance up through an organization. One valuable but often-overlooked skill that most people can develop with a little effort is curiosity.[91] Ulta CEO Mary Dillon is known for exhibiting curiosity by asking questions and listening intently. Dillon makes frequent store visits to learn from associates, and she has been praised her for the way she communicates with everyone from executives to store employees. Said Tara Simon, SVP of Merchandising for the company, "I was here when Mary arrived . . . and from the moment she walked in the door, it was like she was a breath of fresh air because she's so curious."[92]

(Continued)

TABLE 14.4 *Continued*

WHAT LEADERS NEED	AND WHY
Conceptual skills to draft an organization's mission, vision, strategies, and implementation plans	Conceptual skills matter most for individuals in the top ranks in an organization. Entrepreneurs may have their conceptual skills tested on a regular basis. Now-billionaire CEO Sara Blakely's father regularly asked her, "What have you failed at this week?" After repeated setbacks, she eventually came up with the line of slimming intimate wear she called Spanx.[93]

Source: Adapted from T. V. Mumford, M. A. Campion, and F. P. Morgeson, "Leadership Skills Strataplex: Leadership Skill Requirements across Organizational Levels," Leadership Quarterly, 2007, pp. 154–166.

So What Do We Know about Leadership Traits?

Trait theory offers us four conclusions.

1. **We cannot ignore the implications of leadership traits.** Traits play a central role in the way we perceive leaders, and they do ultimately affect leadership effectiveness.[94] For instance, focus, confidence, transparency, and integrity were among the top traits listed in a survey of current business leaders, along with patience, openness, and generosity.[95] More specifically, many companies attempt to define leadership traits important for their context.

   BNSF Railway Example: BNSF Railway Company recognizes the importance of leadership traits. According to the company's website, "While many different railroads combined to form BNSF, the people who worked at those railroads shared many traits. The people who built BNSF were—and continue to be—a unique breed, blending the forward-thinking of dreamers with the pragmatism of results-oriented business leaders."[96]

2. **The positive and "dark triad" traits suggest the qualities that are conducive and detrimental to success in leadership roles.** According to expert scholars, narcissistic leaders often have groundbreaking ideas but fail to execute them successfully. Such execution requires the collaboration of an entire team, and narcissists' need to control even small details can make followers miserable and unwilling to work together to achieve goals.[97]

   Travis Kalanick Example: Insiders have described former Uber CEO Travis Kalanick as a micromanager and control freak.[98] He also was known to be combative and unwilling to listen to others' ideas in board meetings. Kalanick was eventually ousted from his role after a series of scandals and a whistleblower took the company from being "the world's most valuable" to "the world's most dysfunctional" start-up.[99]

   Personality tests and other trait assessments can help evaluate your strengths and weaknesses on these traits. Connect ™ contains a host of tests you can take for this purpose.

3. **Organizations may want to include personality and trait assessments in their selection and evaluation processes.** Among the growing number of companies using psychometric testing are Citigroup, ExxonMobil, Ford Motor Company, Procter & Gamble, Hewlett-Packard (HP), and JPMorgan Chase.[100]

   Petra Coach Example: Tennessee-based executive coaching firm Petra Coach recommends that firms use personality testing to facilitate teamwork. Said CEO Andy Bailey, "Knowing how each individual on a team prefers to communicate is a huge asset in business and can help individuals overcome any challenge or personal conflict."[101]

   Recall from our discussion in Chapter 9 that there are legitimate concerns about bias and accuracy associated with workplace personality testing. Organizations should stick with validated, job-related personality assessments and should use them for development purposes rather than employment decisions.[102]

4. **Cross-cultural competency is an increasingly valued task-oriented trait.** It's also a career readiness competency. As more companies expand their international operations and hire more culturally diverse individuals for domestic operations in the United States, they want to enhance employees' global mind-set.[103] A **global mindset is your belief in your ability to influence dissimilar others in a global context.**

Coca-Cola EXAMPLE: The Coca-Cola Company sees the value of cross-cultural competency. The company tests every participant in its "high potential leader" program for cross-cultural intelligence.[104] ●

14.3 Behavioral Approaches: Do Leaders Show Distinctive Patterns of Behavior?

THE BIG PICTURE

Behavioral leadership approaches try to determine unique behaviors displayed by effective leaders. These approaches can be divided into two categories: (1) task-oriented behavior and (2) relationship-oriented behavior.

A leader's traits, gender, and skills directly affect their choice of behavior. The focus of those interested in **behavioral leadership approaches is to determine the key behaviors displayed by effective leaders.** These approaches identified two categories of leader behavior:

LO 14.3

Identify behaviors of successful leaders.

- Task-oriented behavior.
- Relationship-oriented behavior.

Much of what we know about task-oriented and relationship-oriented leader behaviors is based on research done at The Ohio State University and University of Michigan. Both studies found that leader behaviors tend to focus on tasks and/or relationships:

	THE OHIO STATE UNIVERSITY	UNIVERSITY OF MICHIGAN
Task-oriented leader behavior	Initiating structure	Production-centered
Relationship-oriented leader behavior	Consideration	Employee-centered

Task-Oriented Leader Behaviors

The primary purpose of **task-oriented leadership behaviors is to ensure that human, physical, and other resources are deployed efficiently and effectively to accomplish the group's or organization's goals.**[105] Examples of task-oriented behaviors include planning, clarifying, monitoring, and problem solving. As mentioned in the introduction at the beginning of this section, task-oriented leadership behaviors may be referred to as initiating-structure or production-centered behaviors.

The Focus of Task-Oriented Leadership: "Here's What We Do to Get the Job Done"

Initiating-structure leadership is leader behavior that organizes and defines—that is, "initiates the structure for"—what employees should be doing to maximize output. Production-centered leader behaviors emphasize the technical or task-related aspects of employees' roles. Clearly, these are very task-oriented approaches.

- **Sonia Syngal Example:** Gap, Inc., is relying on its new CEO—Sonia Syngal—to display task-oriented leadership. Said board chair and interim CEO Bob Fisher, "Sonia has all of the characteristics and experiences needed to effectively execute against the work ahead. She is an excellent operator who drives innovation and decisive action."[106]

Task-oriented leader behaviors are positively related to measures of leadership effectiveness, according to research.[107]

Relationship-Oriented Leader Behavior

Relationship-oriented leadership is primarily concerned with the leader's interactions with his or her people. The emphasis is on enhancing employees' skills and creating positive work relationships among co-workers and between the leader and the led. Such leaders often act as mentors, providing career advice, giving employees assignments that will broaden their skills, and empowering them to make their own decisions.[108] One of the simplest and best ways to engage relationship-leadership is to ask open questions and listen attentively.[109]

The Focus of Relationship-Oriented Leadership: "The Concerns and Needs of My Employees Are Highly Important"

TIAA CEO Roger Ferguson has expressed admiration for leaders who possess not only high levels of task knowledge, but also the ability to empathize and see the humanity in their followers. To what degree do you value relationship-oriented behaviors? Monica Schipper/ Getty Images

Consideration is leader behavior that is concerned with group members' needs and desires and directed at creating mutual respect or trust. **Employee-centered leader behaviors** emphasize relationships with subordinates and attention to their individual needs. These are important behaviors to use in addition to task leadership because they promote social interactions and identification with the team and leader.

Roger Ferguson, Jr. Example: TIAA CEO Roger Ferguson, Jr., believes in relationship-oriented leadership. In a recent speech, Ferguson said "Leaders who want to have a great impact also have to have empathy," adding, "I don't think you can inspire a follower if you don't understand that they have human needs and you're trying to bring them along on this journey."[110]

Relationship-oriented leader behaviors are positively related to measures of leadership effectiveness, according to research.[111]

The most effective leaders use different blends of task-oriented and relationship-oriented behaviors when interacting with others. To what extent do you think you do this when interacting with school or work colleagues? You can answer this question by taking Self-Assessment 14.4.

SELF-ASSESSMENT 14.4 CAREER READINESS

Assessing Your Task- and Relationship-Oriented Leader Behavior

The following survey was designed to evaluate your own leader behavior. Please be prepared to answer these questions if your instructor has assigned Self-Assessment 14.4 in Connect.

1. Do you prefer to use task or relationship leadership? Why do you think this is the case?

2. Look at the items for the two lowest scored items for initiating structure and consideration and then identify how you can increase the extent to which you display both types of leadership.

3. What things might you say during an interview to demonstrate that you can be both task- and relationship-oriented in your approach toward leading others?

So What Do We Know about the Behavioral Approaches?

Two key conclusions we may take away from the behavioral approaches are the following:

1. **A leader's behavior is more important than his or her traits.** It is important to train managers on the various forms of task and relationship leadership.
2. **There is no type of leader behavior that is best suited for all situations.** Effective leaders learn how to match their behavior to the situation at hand. We discuss how to do this in the next section. ●

14.4 Situational Approaches: Does Leadership Vary with the Situation?

THE BIG PICTURE

Effective leadership behavior depends on the situation at hand, say believers in two contingency approaches: Fiedler's contingency leadership model and House's path–goal leadership model.

Perhaps leadership is not characterized by universally important traits or behaviors. There is likely no one best style that will work in all situations. This is the point of view of proponents of the ==situational approach== (or contingency approach) to leadership, who believe that effective leadership behavior depends on the situation at hand. That is, as situations change, different leader styles become appropriate.

Let's consider two situational approaches: (1) Fiedler's *contingency leadership model* and (2) House's *path–goal leadership model.*

LO 14.4

Discuss situational leadership.

1. The Contingency Leadership Model: Fiedler's Approach

The oldest contingency model of leadership was developed by Fred Fiedler and his associates beginning in 1954.[112] The ==contingency leadership model== determines if a leader's style is (1) task-oriented or (2) relationship-oriented and whether that style is effective for the situation at hand.

Two Leadership Orientations: Tasks versus Relationships

Fiedler's contingency model requires that leaders identify their leadership style.

- *There are two leadership styles in Fiedler's model:* The two leadership styles in Fiedler's contingency model are (1) task-oriented and (2) relationship-oriented.[113] Which do you think is your style? That is, as a leader, are you more concerned with task accomplishment or with people?

- *Your leadership style is determined by your LPC score:* To find out your leadership style, you would fill out a questionnaire (known as the least preferred co-worker, or LPC, scale), in which you think of the co-worker you least enjoyed working with and rate him or her according to an eight-point scale of 16 pairs of opposite characteristics (such as friendly/unfriendly, tense/relaxed,

At the heart of situational leadership is the phrase "It Depends." More specifically, this approach says the best style of leadership *depends* on the situation. What works in one situation doesn't necessarily work in another. KlaraDo/Shutterstock

efficient/inefficient). The higher the score, the more the relationship-oriented the respondent; the lower the score, the more task-oriented.[114]

Three Dimensions of Situational Control   Once a leader identifies their leadership style, they should next evaluate the context to determine their level of *situational control*—how much control and influence they have in their immediate work environment.

There are three dimensions of situational control: *leader-member relations, task structure,* and *position power.*

- **Leader-member relations—"Do my subordinates accept me as a leader?"** This dimension, the most important component of situational control, reflects the extent to which a leader has or doesn't have the support, loyalty, and trust of the work group.

- **Task structure—"Do my subordinates perform unambiguous, easily understood tasks?"** This dimension refers to the extent to which tasks are routine, unambiguous, and easily understood. The more structured the jobs, the more influence a leader has.

- **Position power—"Do I have power to reward and punish?"** This dimension refers to how much power a leader has to make work assignments and reward and punish. More power equals more control and influence.

For each dimension, the amount of control can be *high,* in which case the leader's decisions will produce predictable results because he or she has the ability to influence work outcomes. Or it can be *low,* in which case the leader doesn't have that kind of predictability or influence. By combining the three different dimensions with different high/low ratings, we have eight different leadership situations. These are represented in Figure 14.1.

FIGURE 14.1   **Representation of Fiedler's contingency model**

Source: Adapted from F. E. Fiedler, "Situational Control and a Dynamic Theory of Leadership," in B. King, S. Streufert, and F. E. Fiedler (eds.), Managerial Control and Organizational Democracy (New York: John Wiley & Sons, 1978), p. 114.

Situational Control	High-Control Situations			Moderate-Control Situations				Low-Control Situations
Leader-member relations	Good	Good	Good	Good	Poor	Poor	Poor	Poor
Task structure	High	High	Low	Low	High	High	Low	Low
Position power	Strong	Weak	Strong	Weak	Strong	Weak	Strong	Weak
Situation	1	11	111	1V	V	V1	V11	V111

Optimal Leadership Style	Task-Oriented Leadership	Relationship-Oriented Leadership	Task-Oriented Leadership

Which Style Is Most Effective?   Neither leadership style is effective all the time, Fiedler's research concludes; rather, each is better suited for certain situations.

- **When is a task-oriented style best?** The task-oriented style works best in either *high-control* or *low-control* situations.

  High-control situation—leaders' decisions produce predictable results because they can influence work outcomes.

  Low-control situation—leaders' decisions can't produce predictable results because they can't really influence outcomes.

- **When is a relationship-oriented style best?** The relationship-oriented style works best in situations of *moderate control*.

What do you do if your leadership style does not match the situation? According to Fiedler's model it's better to try to match leaders with suitable situations rather than try to alter their leadership styles to better fit the situations.[115] Fiedler did not believe that people could change their basic leadership style.

2. The Path–Goal Leadership Model: House's Approach

A second situational approach, advanced by Robert House beginning in the 1970s, is the **path–goal leadership model,** which holds that the effective leader makes available to followers desirable rewards in the workplace and increases their motivation by clarifying the paths, or behaviors, that will help them achieve those goals and providing them with support. A successful leader thus "clears the path" and helps followers by tying meaningful rewards to goal accomplishment, reducing barriers, and providing support, so as to increase "the number and kinds of personal payoffs to subordinates for work-goal attainment."[116]

Numerous studies testing various predictions from House's original path–goal theory provided mixed results.[117] As a consequence, he proposed a new model, a graphical version of which is shown in Figure 14.2.

FIGURE 14.2   General representation of House's revised path–goal theory

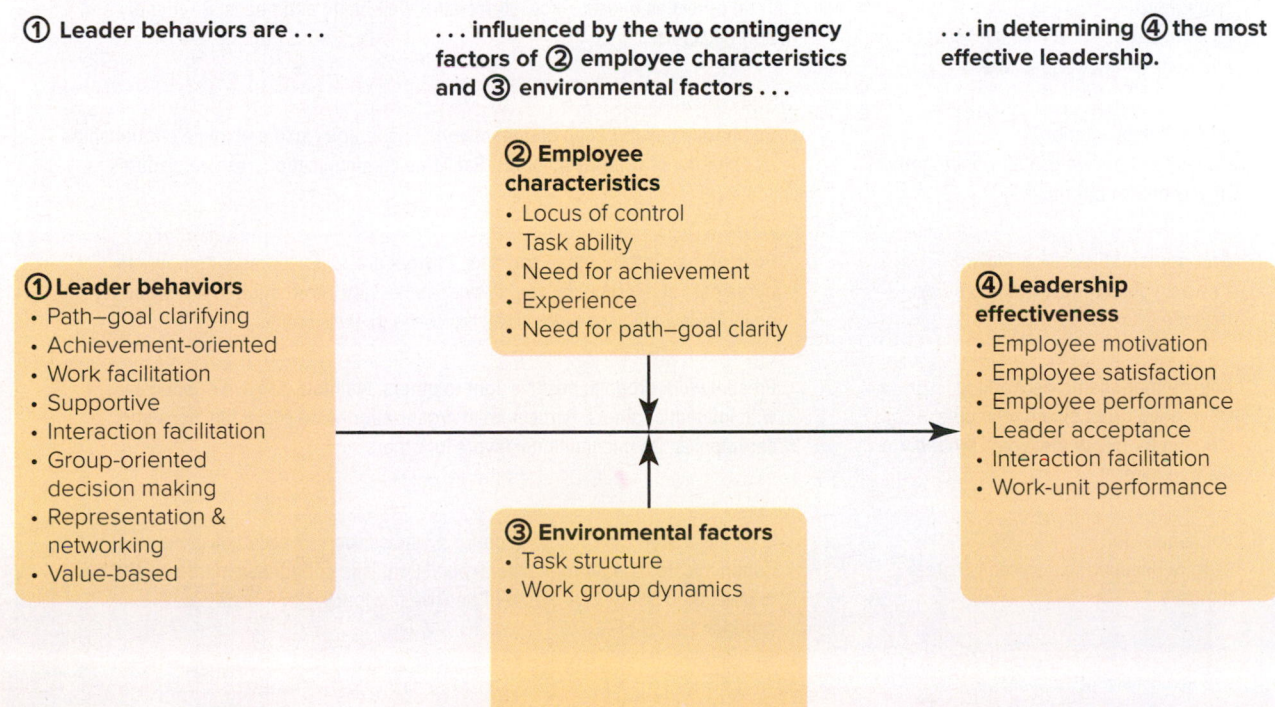

What Determines Leadership Effectiveness: Employee Characteristics and Environmental Factors Affect Leader Behavior

Two contingency factors, or variables—*employee characteristics* and *environmental factors*—cause some *leadership behaviors* to be more effective than others.

- **Employee characteristics:** Five employee characteristics are locus of control (described in Chapter 11), task ability, need for achievement, experience, and need for path–goal clarity.

- **Environmental factors:** Two environmental factors are task structure (independent versus interdependent tasks) and work group dynamics.

Originally, House proposed that there were four leader behaviors, or leadership styles. The revised theory expands the number of leader behaviors from four to eight. (*See Table 14.5.*)

TABLE 14.5   Eight Leadership Styles of the Revised Path–Goal Theory

STYLE OF LEADER BEHAVIORS	DESCRIPTION OF BEHAVIOR TOWARD EMPLOYEES
1. Path–goal clarifying ("Here's what's expected of you and here's how to do it.")	Clarify performance goals. Provide guidance on how employees can complete tasks. Clarify performance standards and expectations. Use positive and negative rewards contingent on performance.
2. Achievement-oriented ("I'm confident you can accomplish the following great things.")	Set challenging goals. Emphasize excellence. Demonstrate confidence in employee abilities.
3. Work facilitation ("Here's the goal, and here's what I can do to help you achieve it.")	Plan, schedule, organize, and coordinate work. Provide mentoring, coaching, counseling, and feedback to assist employees in developing their skills. Eliminate roadblocks. Provide resources. Empower employees to take actions and make decisions.
4. Supportive ("I want things to be pleasant, since everyone's about equal here.")	Treat others as equals. Show concern for well-being and needs. Be friendly and approachable.
5. Interaction facilitation ("Let's see how we can all work together to accomplish our goals.")	Emphasize collaboration and teamwork. Encourage close employee relationships and sharing of minority opinions. Facilitate communication; resolve disputes.
6. Group-oriented decision making ("I want your suggestions in order to help me make decisions.")	Pose problems rather than solutions to work group. Encourage members to participate in decision making. Provide necessary information to the group for analysis. Involve knowledgeable employees in decision making.
7. Representation and networking ("I've got a great bunch of people working for me, whom you'll probably want to meet.")	Present work group in positive light to others. Maintain positive relationships with influential others. Participate in organization-wide social functions and ceremonies. Do unconditional favors for others.
8. Value-based ("We're destined to accomplish great things.")	Establish a vision, display passion for it, and support its accomplishment. Communicate high performance expectations and confidence in others' abilities to meet their goals. Give frequent positive feedback. Demonstrate self-confidence.

What Does Path–Goal Look Like in Practice? In contrast to Fiedler's contingency model, House's path–goal model assumes that a leader's style is flexible. In other words, as a leader, you should figure out the style that will work best for your particular employees and environment, and then use that style. Here are two hypothetical examples:

- Employees with an internal locus of control are more likely to prefer achievement-oriented leadership or group-oriented decision-making leadership because they believe they have control over the work environment. The same is true for employees with high task ability and experience.

- Employees with an external locus of control, however, tend to view the environment as uncontrollable, so they prefer the structure provided by supportive or path–goal clarifying leadership. The same is probably true of inexperienced employees.

What does adapting one's leadership style to followers' needs and the environment look like in real-life? Consider the following example.

Andrew Cuomo Example: New York Governor Andrew Cuomo is known for his aggressive and, at times, combative leadership style. Cuomo once explained his approach to leading by saying, "There is no governor . . . no executive . . . no mayor who can succeed in this position without being strong-willed. It does not work." He added, "You can't be a pushover, easy-go-lucky, everybody's-best-friend politician and be a successful executive. You can't be both . . . I'm a chief executive who has to get stuff done. It's what it takes to do the job."[118] But amid the COVID-19 pandemic, Cuomo rose to national fame not because of his trademark toughness, but rather, because he displayed an uncharacteristically soft and empathetic side. Said former campaign worker Lis Smith, "Cuomo really understands what people want and need to hear right now . . . he understands there is a very human element to this crisis." She added, "Andrew is showing a side of him that has always been there, but not necessarily in a public way, and that a lot of people really need right now. Yeah, they need an effective leader. But they also need Mr. #$%&! Rogers."[119]

Governor Andrew Cuomo, known as a no-nonsense and often rough leader, exemplified the idea of adapting one's style to the situation in several uncommonly delicate speeches and appearances during the COVID-19 pandemic. Lev Radin/Shutterstock

During one particularly inspiring press briefing Cuomo said, "New York loves all of you. Black and white and brown and Asian and short and tall and gay and straight. New York loves everyone. That's why I love New York. It always has, it always will. And at the end of the day, my friends, even if it is a long day, and this is a long day, love wins. Always. And it will win again through this virus."[120]

So What Do We Know about the Situational Approaches?

There have not been enough direct tests of House's revised path–goal theory using appropriate research methods and statistical procedures to draw overall conclusions.[121] Research on transformational leadership, however, which is discussed in Section 14.5, is supportive of the revised model.[122]

Applying situational leadership theory is not easy. In any leadership role, you will encounter many different situations, and there is no one best style for managing all of them. In addition, we all tend to rely on behaviors that have worked for us in the past even if the situation we face suggests we should change. We justify our actions by reasoning that we are doing what we are good at, but in fact we are vulnerable to our own biases about what we think works and what doesn't.

Although further research is needed on the new model, we can offer several important implications for managers:[123]

- **Use more than one leadership style.** Effective leaders possess and use more than one style of leadership. Thus, you are encouraged to study the eight styles offered in path-goal theory so that you can try new leader behaviors when a situation calls for them.

- **Help employees achieve their goals.** Leaders should guide and coach employees in achieving their goals by clarifying the path and removing obstacles to accomplishing them. Effective coaching was found to increase employees' performance.[124]

- **Alter your leadership behavior for each situation.** A small set of employee characteristics (ability, experience, and need for independence) and environmental factors (task characteristics of autonomy, variety, and significance) are relevant contingency factors, and managers should modify their leadership style to fit them. The career readiness competencies of emotional and social intelligence are helpful tools for doing so.

- **Provide what people and teams need to succeed.** View your role as providing others with whatever they need to achieve their goals. For some it could be encouragement, and for others it could be direction and coaching. ●

PRACTICAL ACTION   Applying Situational Theories

How can you make situational theories work for you? A team of researchers proposed a general strategy that managers can use across a variety of situations. It has five steps.[125] We explain how to implement the steps by using the examples of a head coach of a sports team and a sales manager.

- **Step 1: Identify important outcomes.** Managers must first identify the goals they want to achieve. For example, the head coach may have a goal of winning a certain number of games or avoiding injuries to key players, whereas a sales manager's goal might be to increase sales by 10% or reduce customers' complaints by half.

- **Step 2: Identify relevant leadership behaviors.** Next managers need to identify the specific types of behaviors that may be appropriate for the situation at hand. The list in Table 14.5 is a good starting point. A head coach in a championship game, for instance, might focus on achievement-oriented and work-facilitation behaviors. In contrast, a sales manager might find path–goal clarifying, work facilitation, and supportive behaviors more relevant for the sales team. Don't try to use all available leadership behaviors. Rather, select the one or two that appear most helpful.

- **Step 3: Identify situational conditions.** Fiedler and House both identify a set of potential contingency factors to consider, but there may be other practical considerations. For example, a star quarterback on a football team may be injured, which might require the team to adopt a different

strategy for winning the game. Similarly, the need to manage a virtual sales team with members from around the world will affect the types of leadership most effective in this context.

- **Step 4: Match leadership to the conditions at hand.** There are too many possible situational conditions for us to provide specific advice. This means you should use your knowledge about management and employee behavior to find the best match between your leadership styles and behaviors and the situation at hand. The coach whose star quarterback is injured might use supportive and values-based behaviors to instill confidence that the team can win with a different quarterback. Our sales manager also might find it useful to use the empowering leadership associated with work-facilitation behaviors and avoid directive leadership.

- **Step 5: Decide how to make the match.** Managers can use guidelines from either contingency theory or path–goal theory: change the person in the leadership role or change his or her behavior. It is not possible to change the head coach in a championship game. This means the head coach needs to change his or her style or behavior to meet the specific challenge. In contrast, the organization employing the sales manager might move him or her to another position because the individual is too directive and does not like to empower others. Or the sales manager could change his or her behavior, if possible.

14.5 The Full-Range Model: Using Transactional and Transformational Leadership

THE BIG PICTURE

The full-range model of leadership describes leadership along a range of behaviors, with the most effective being transactional and transformational. Transformational leadership impacts followers in four important ways.

We have considered the major traditional approaches to understanding leadership—the trait, behavioral, and situational approaches. But newer approaches offer something more by trying to determine what factors inspire and motivate people to perform beyond their normal levels.

One recent approach proposed by Bernard Bass and Bruce Avolio, known as ==full-range leadership==, suggests that leadership behavior varies along a full range of leadership styles, from passive (laissez-faire) "leadership" at one extreme, through transactional leadership, to transformational leadership at the other extreme.[126] Passive leadership is not leadership, but transactional and transformational leadership behaviors are both necessary and positive aspects of being a good leader.[127]

LO 14.5

Describe transactional and transformational leadership.

Transactional and Transformational Leadership

Transactional Leadership   As a manager, your power stems from your ability to provide rewards (and threaten reprimands) in exchange for your subordinates doing the work. When you do this, you are performing ==transactional leadership==, focusing on clarifying employees' roles and task requirements and providing rewards and punishments contingent on performance. Like task-oriented leadership, transactional leadership also encompasses setting goals and monitoring progress.[128] Melanie Perkins understands this perspective.

> **Melanie Perkins Example:** Melanie Perkins is the co-founder and CEO of the online graphic design platform Canva. Perkins understands that transactional behaviors are a necessary foundation for effective leadership. In a recent interview, she said "One of the most important things is to be able to set big goals that inspire and motivate your team. I think it's easier to attract great people when you set out to achieve something that's crazy huge, because great people like great challenges. It's also essential to set a clear direction for the company and frequently talk about the future. If everyone knows where you are trying to get to, I think there's less debate about the small things that don't matter."[129]

Canva CEO Melanie Perkins knows the value of transactional leadership—including setting clear goals and paying close attention to progress—in achieving an organization's bigger goals. Eóin Noonan/Getty Images

Transactional leadership has a positive association with leader effectiveness and group performance.[130]

Transformational Leadership   ==Transformational leadership== transforms employees to pursue organizational goals over self-interests. Transformational leaders, in one description, "engender trust, seek to develop leadership in others, exhibit self-sacrifice, and serve as moral agents, focusing themselves and followers on objectives that transcend the more immediate needs of the work group."[131] Whereas transactional leadership gets people to do *necessary* things, transformational leadership engenders *exceptional* things—significantly higher levels of intrinsic motivation, trust, commitment, and loyalty—that can produce significant organizational change and results.[132] Michael Dowling is a good example of a transformational leader.

Michael Dowling Example: Northwell Health CEO Michael Dowling was recently ranked as one of the most beloved CEOs in the country according to employee ratings on Glassdoor.[133] Dowling exhibits transformational leadership in the way he inspires employees to work toward something bigger. Dowling begins developing personal relationships with followers from their very first day with the company. Said one worker about her experience at new-employee orientation, "I immediately felt connected to the organization . . . He described how each and every single job plays a major role in patient experience and the overall success of the organization. This was truly remarkable."[134] Dowling has said of his leadership approach: "People want to belong to something and they want to identify with something and as a leader they want to believe in what you believe in . . . They have to believe in you and believe in what the purpose is that you're trying to promote . . . and you can only do that by personal contacts. That's why I met with employees all the time. To me it is absolutely key. Be a regular human being."[135]

Transformational leadership is influenced by two factors:

1. **Individual characteristics:** The personalities of such leaders tend to be more extroverted, agreeable, proactive, and open to change than nontransformational leaders. (Female leaders tend to use transformational leadership more than male leaders do.)[136]

2. **Organizational culture:** Adaptive, flexible organizational cultures are more likely than rigid, bureaucratic cultures to foster transformational leadership.

The Best Leaders Are Both Transactional and Transformational

It's important to note that transactional leadership is an essential *prerequisite* to effective leadership, and the best leaders learn to display both transactional and transformational styles of leadership to some degree. Indeed, research suggests that transformational leadership leads to superior performance when it "augments," or adds to, transactional leadership.[137] See the Example box to learn about a leader who exhibits both transactional and transformational leadership.

EXAMPLE	The Superior Performance of a Leader Who Is Both Transactional and Transformational: Home Depot's Ann-Marie Campbell

Ann-Marie Campbell ranked number 20 on *Fortune*'s 2019 most powerful women list.[138] She began her career with Home Depot more than 30 years ago as a cashier and now oversees 2,000+ stores and 400,000+ employees as executive vice president of U.S. stores.[139] She has been instrumental in Home Depot meeting its goal to increase annual revenues from $88 billion to $100 billion.[140]

Let's look at how Campbell uses a mix of transactional and transformational leadership.

Transactional Campbell's years of experience in a variety of roles at Home Depot—including store manager and regional vice president—give her unique insight into what it takes for employees and the company to be successful. She uses transactional leadership to maximize employee productivity and engagement and drive overall firm performance. For example, she went against industry norms and converted full-time store associates from variable work schedules to more desirable fixed schedules. She also led the company's $11 billion plan to improve both associates' and customers' experiences, focusing on initiatives including new order management software for workers and on-line pickup lockers in stores.[141]

On how she approaches getting employees to perform in their roles, she said, "People want to be successful, so it is important to clearly communicate what success is."[142]

Transformational Campbell's leadership goes beyond transactional behaviors. Said one Home Depot district manager, "She finds a way to inspire people, to rise to the occasion and (help others) reach their goals that they didn't think they could reach—through courageous leadership, the ability to provide clear direction and by simplifying a message."[143] Of her path to executive leadership,

Campbell said, "As you grow with any organization . . . it is no longer about you. It's about how do you inspire and motivate others to be the best they can be, and how do you harness the collective value of your team to make it the best team." She added, "That's what I've learned as I've moved up through different roles, is think about the bigger organization, the broader purpose of the organization, the broader things that you're trying to get accomplished, and focus on that and not just on individual performance.[144]

YOUR CALL

What unique individual characteristics are displayed by Campbell? What other types of leader behavior has she exhibited?

Four Key Behaviors of Transformational Leaders

Whereas transactional leadership behaviors—though important—can feel dispassionate, transformational leadership behaviors excite passion, inspiring and empowering people to look beyond their own interests to the interests of the organization. Leaders who are transformational appeal to their followers' self-concepts—their values and personal identity—to create changes in their goals, values, needs, beliefs, and aspirations.

Transformational leaders use four key kinds of behavior that affect followers.[145]

1. Inspirational Motivation: "Let Me Share a Vision That Transcends Us All" Transformational leadership motivates followers by inspiring them. This inspiration requires that leaders:

Have charisma—a form of interpersonal attraction that inspires acceptance and support. At one time, charismatic leadership—which was assumed to be an individual inspirational and motivational characteristic of particular leaders, much like other trait-theory characteristics—was viewed as a category of its own, but now it is considered part of transformational leadership.[146] Someone with charisma, then, is more able to persuade and influence people and to make others feel comfortable and at ease than someone without charisma.[147]

Communicate a vision—a transformational leader inspires motivation by offering an agenda, a grand design, an ultimate goal—in short, a *vision*, "a realistic, credible, attractive future" for the organization, as leadership expert Burt Nanus calls it.[148] John Hennessy, former president of Stanford University and current chair of Google's parent company Alphabet, believes that inspirational motivation is a critical skill for effective leadership. He concluded, "The ability to tell appropriate, compelling and inspiring stories is essential. Describing work as a journey shared among colleagues helps bring employees together in a common cause."[149]

Martin Luther King Jr. Civil rights leader Martin Luther King was an inspiration to millions of people. Here he is addressing people during the March on Washington at the Lincoln Memorial. This is where he gave his famous "I Have a Dream" speech. Do you think charismatic business leaders like King are able to be more successful than more conventional and conservative managers? Agence France Presse/Central Press/Getty Images

Examples: Civil rights leader Martin Luther King Jr. had a vision—a "dream," as he put it—of racial equality. Candy Lightner, founder of Mothers Against Drunk Driving, had a vision of getting rid of alcohol-related car crashes. Apple Computer's Steve Jobs had a vision of developing an "insanely great" desktop computer. To recruit John Scully, who was CEO of Pepsi at the time, Jobs asked, "Do you want to sell sugared water the rest of your life, or do you want a chance to change the world?"[150]

2. Idealized Influence: "We Are Here to Do the Right Thing"

Transformational leadership inspires trust in followers. Transformational leaders:

- *Express integrity* by being consistent, single-minded, and persistent in pursuit of their goal.
  - *Display high ethical standards* and act as models of desirable values.
  - *Make sacrifices* for the greater good.

University of Virginia men's basketball coach Tony Bennett is known for behaving with integrity and for his willingness to sacrifice personally for the good of his players and institution. These are important elements of idealized influence. Rich Barnes/Getty Images

Coach Tony Bennett Example: The University of Virginia offered head men's basketball coach Tony Bennett a handsome raise after his team won the 2019 national championship. But Bennett turned down the offer and asked that the money go instead to his staff. In addition, Bennett and his wife Laurel gave $500,000 to a career-development program for current and former members of the team. In a statement to the press, Bennett said, "I have more than enough, and if there are ways that this can help out the athletic department, the other programs, and coaches, by not tying up so much [in men's basketball], that's my desire."[151]

3. Individualized Consideration: "You Have the Opportunity Here to Grow and Excel"

Transformational leaders don't just express concern for subordinates' well-being. They actively encourage them to grow and excel by giving them challenging work, more responsibility, empowerment, and one-on-one mentoring.

Steve Beauchamp Example: Paylocity CEO Steve Beauchamp has a reputation for the individualized consideration that he gives to employees. Said one account manager, "Leadership is approachable and appreciative . . . makes you feel like a person and less of a number. While working one day, our CEO walked around expressed his appreciation, personally thanked everyone for working for him."[152] Said another employee, "the CEO is always approachable and you do feel like he has the best interests of the company and his staff in mind."[153]

4. Intellectual Stimulation: "Let Me Describe the Great Challenges We Can Conquer Together"

Transformational leaders are gifted at communicating the organization's strengths, weaknesses, opportunities, and threats so that subordinates develop a new sense of purpose. Employees become less apt to view problems as insurmountable or "that's not my department." Instead they learn to view them as personal challenges that they are responsible for overcoming, to question the status quo, and to seek creative solutions.

Girls Who Code founder Reshma Saujani has displayed intellectual stimulation by showing thousands of young women that they can not only break into computer science fields, but also completely rewrite the landscape for future women in technology. Will Glaser/The New York Times

Reshma Saujani Example: Reshma Saujani is on a mission to close the persistent gender gap in the technology sector. The Harvard and Yale graduate and former corporate lawyer founded Girls Who Code not only to teach young women coding skills (which the organization has done for nearly 100,000 girls so far), but more broadly, to fundamentally alter their belief that they need to be perfect in order to be successful. Says friend Trina DasGupta, "It's not overstating it to say [Saujani] started a movement."[154]

Have you worked for a transformational leader? The following self-assessment measures the extent to which a current or former manager used transformational leadership. Taking the assessment provides a good idea about the specific behaviors you need to exhibit if you want to lead in a transformational manner.

So What Do We Know about Transformational Leadership?

It works! Research shows that transformational leadership is associated with many positive outcomes such as increased organizational, team, and individual performance; job satisfaction; employee identification with their leaders and with their immediate work groups; employee engagement; and intrinsic motivation.[155]

There are three practical applications of transformational leadership.

1. It Can Be Used to Train Employees at Any Level   Not just top managers but employees at any level can be trained to be more transformational.[156] It is best to couple this training with developmental coaching and job challenges.[157]

2. You Can Prepare and Practice Being Transformational   The simplest way to practice is to write down ideas for exhibiting the four key behaviors of transformational leadership—inspirational motivation, idealized influence, individualized consideration, and intellectual stimulation—the next time you attend a team meeting at school or work.

- You might inspire your teammates by highlighting the benefits of doing a good job, by building the team's confidence in their ability to complete the assignment, and by telling the team you believe in them.

- You can drive idealized influence by explaining your role or commitment to working on the assignment and modeling high-performance behaviors.

- Show individualized consideration by describing the resources and support available to the team, by demonstrating a supportive attitude to everyone, and by recognizing people for their accomplishments.

- Foster intellectual stimulation by describing the team's challenges, explaining the tasks or goals everyone needs to achieve, and highlighting why successfully completing the assignment will help the team.

3. It Should be Used for Ethical Reasons   While ethical transformational leaders enable employees to enhance their self-concepts, unethical ones select or produce obedient, dependent, and compliant followers. Without honesty and trust, even transformational leaders lose credibility—not only with employees but also with investors, customers, and the public. ●

14.6 Contemporary Perspectives and Concepts

THE BIG PICTURE

Contemporary leadership perspectives explore relationships between leaders and followers and consider changing views about leaders' roles. Contemporary concepts in leadership include humility, empowerment, ethics, followership, and abusive supervision.

LO 14.6

Describe contemporary leadership perspectives and concepts.

Here we turn our attention to contemporary leadership perspectives and concepts. Contemporary perspectives include (1) the *leader-member exchange (LMX) model of leadership* and (2) *servant leadership*. Contemporary concepts of study include (1) *leading with humility*, (2) *empowering leadership*, (3) *ethical leadership*, (4) *the role of followers*, and (5) *abusive supervision*.

Leader–Member Exchange Leadership: Having Different Relationships with Different Subordinates

Proposed by George Graen and Fred Dansereau, the **leader–member exchange (LMX) model of leadership** emphasizes that leaders have different sorts of relationships with different subordinates.[158] Two ways that LMX differs from other models of leadership are:

1. *LMX focuses on relational quality in leader-follower dyads.* Unlike other models we've described, which focus on the behaviors or traits of leaders or followers, the LMX model looks at the *quality* of relationships between managers and subordinates.[159]

2. *LMX assumes that leaders have distinctive relationships with each follower.* Unlike other models, which presuppose stable relationships between leaders and followers, the LMX model assumes each manager–subordinate relationship is unique.[160]

This model is one of the most researched approaches to studying leadership, and it has significant practical implications for managers and employees.

In-Group Exchange versus Out-Group Exchange   The unique relationship, which supposedly results from the leader's attempt to delegate and assign work roles, can produce two types of leader–member exchange interactions.[161]

- **In-group exchange: trust and respect.** In the *in-group exchange*, the relationship between leader and follower becomes a partnership characterized by mutual trust, respect and liking, and a sense of common fates. Subordinates may receive special assignments and special privileges.

- **Out-group exchange: lack of trust and respect.** In the *out-group exchange*, leaders are characterized as overseers who fail to create a sense of mutual trust, respect, or common fate. Subordinates receive less of the manager's time and attention than those in the in-group exchange relationships.

What type of exchange do you have with your manager? The quality of the relationship between you and your boss matters. Not only does it predict your job satisfaction and happiness, but it also is related to turnover. You can assess the quality of the relationship with a current or former boss by completing Self-Assessment 14.6.

Assessing Your Leader–Member Exchange

The following survey was designed to assess the quality of your leader–member exchange. Please be prepared to answer these questions if your instructor has assigned Self-Assessment 14.6 in Connect.

1. Where do you stand on the different dimensions underlying leader–member exchange? Are you surprised by the results?

2. Do you think the quality of your leader–member exchange is impacting your job satisfaction or performance? Explain.

3. Based on your survey scores, how might you improve the quality of your relationship with your boss? Be specific.

Is the LMX Model Useful? Yes! Consider that:

- *High-quality LMX relationships engender positive outcomes.* High LMX is associated with individual-level behavioral outcomes like task performance, turnover, organizational citizenship, counterproductive behavior, and attitudinal outcomes such as organizational commitment, job satisfaction, and justice.[162]

- *Other types of leadership encourage high-quality LMX relationships.* A recent study showed that task, relationship, and transformational leadership all have their positive effects on employees via their immediate impact on the quality of an LMX. This is important because it tells us that "the effectiveness of any given leadership behavior is likely to be influenced by the followers' perceptions of their relationship with their leader, such that followers with good relationships with their leader will respond more positively in terms of performance to a given leadership behavior, compared to followers with poor relationship with their leader."[163]

The key takeaway for you is to take ownership of bad relationships with bosses. One expert suggested two generic practices: First, "It pays to figure out what motivates your boss . . . find ways to help her talk about her successes." Second, for bosses who like control, give "lots of information about what you're doing and offer choices about next steps so he can make the decision."[164]

Servant Leadership

Servant Leadership: "I Want to Serve Others and the Organization, Not Myself" The term *servant leadership*, coined by Robert Greenleaf in 1970, reflects not only his one-time background as a management researcher for AT&T but also his views as a lifelong philosopher and devout Quaker.[165] **Servant leadership** focuses on providing increased service to others—meeting the goals of both followers and the organization—rather than to yourself. Sylvia Metayer is a good example.

Sylvia Metayer Example: Ms. Metayer is Chief Growth Officer for Sodexo, a global company with more than 470,000 workers. The company provides a wide range of integrated services, including food and

Servant leaders see leadership as an act of service. The focus of servant leadership, then, is to help others—both followers and organizations—to achieve goals.
Sergey Tinyakov/123RF

reception, cleaning, energy management, grounds maintenance, and building maintenance and security. She believes strongly that a leader's purpose is to serve others. In one interview, Metayer said, "I'm learning that to be a CEO is to be a servant. My main job is to support our employees and be a support to our clients and to our consumers." Said Metayer, "I think the most important thing . . . is how do you make people's work easier?" adding, "The world is changing very fast, so we have to create career paths, and we have to support the training of our people so that they're ready for change."[166]

Servant leadership is not a quick-fix approach to leadership. Rather, it is a long-term approach to life and work.[167] Leaders should try to adopt the ten characteristics and behaviors of servant leaders shown in Table 14.6.

TABLE 14.6   Ten Characteristics and Behaviors of Servant Leaders

1. Focus on listening
2. Ability to empathize with others' feelings
3. Focus on healing suffering
4. Self-awareness of strengths and weaknesses
5. Use of persuasion rather than positional authority to influence others
6. Broad-based conceptual thinking
7. Ability to foresee future outcomes
8. Believe they are stewards of their employees and resources
9. Commitment to the growth of people
10. Drive to build community within and outside the organization

Source: From L. C. Spears, "Introduction: Servant-Leadership and the Greenleaf Legacy," in L. C. Spears (ed.), Reflections on Leadership: How Robert K. Greenleaf's Theory of Servant-Leadership Influenced Today's Top Management (New York: John Wiley & Sons, 1995), pp. 1–14.

Employees whose manager displays the characteristics shown in Table 14.6 are likely to be happier, more productive, more creative, and more willing to go above and beyond their customary duties.[168] The following self-assessment measures the extent to which you possess a servant orientation. Results from the assessment will enhance your understanding of what it takes to really be a servant leader, and they provide insight into the career readiness competency of service/others orientation.

SELF-ASSESSMENT 14.7   CAREER READINESS

Assessing Your Servant Orientation

The following survey is designed to assess the extent to which you possess a servant orientation. Please be prepared to answer these questions if your instructor has assigned Self-Assessment 14.7 in Connect.

1. To what extent do you possess a servant orientation? Are you surprised by the results?

2. How might you demonstrate more servant leadership in your teams at work or school? Be specific.

3. What things might you say during an interview to demonstrate that you possess the career readiness competency of service/others orientation?

The Power of Humility

Humility is a relatively stable trait grounded in the belief that "something greater than the self exists."[169] Although some think it is a sign of weakness or low self-esteem, nothing could be further from the truth.

Satya Nadella. The Microsoft CEO was one of *Harvard Business Review*'s top 10 best performing CEOs of 2019.[170] But he told Microsoft's outgoing CEO Steve Ballmer that he would accept the top position "only if you want me to."[171] When a journalist asked Nadella's friends to describe him in one word, responses included "humble," "empathetic," "listener," and "empowering."[172] When Nadella built his senior leadership team, he looked specifically for people who would be empathetic, respectful of all employees regardless of their level in the company, and willing to learn from others.[173] Chesnot/ Getty Images News/Getty Images

Humble leaders tend to display five key qualities that employees value:[174]

1. High self-awareness.
2. Openness to feedback.
3. Appreciation of others.
4. Low self-focus.
5. Appreciation of the greater good.

An essential element of leader humility is willingness to learn. Humble leaders surround themselves with people who can help them grow.[175] Consider the following example.

Kara Goldin Example: Kara Goldin, founder and CEO of the $100 million-dollar beverage company Hint, sees intellectual humility as central to leading a successful organization. Goldin said, "I've always tried to be humble about what I don't know and surround myself with people who are more knowledgeable than I am." She also said that humility is one of the traits she's looking for when she hires new team members. "I never hire the candidate who comes off as the 'smartest person in the room,'" said Goldin, adding, "because someone who lacks interest in spending time around people who are more intelligent than them won't help to make them (or their team) better at their jobs."[176]

The scientific study of humility is relatively new, but studies suggest that this trait is associated with many positive outcomes, including:[177]

- Follower humility.
- Follower self-efficacy.
- Follower performance.
- Team creativity.

What can we conclude about humility in the context of managing others? We suggest that managers:

1. *Shift the focus.* Try to be more humble by changing the focus of your accomplishments from "me" to "we." Share credit with others, but by all means be authentic. Don't try to fake humility.[178]
2. *Ask, don't tell.* Try to spend more time asking questions and less time talking about yourself or telling people what to do.[179]

3. *Build humility into the culture.* An organization's culture can promote humility. Research suggests that this type of culture focuses on employee development, transparency, and tolerance for mistakes.[180]

Empowering Leadership

Empowering Leadership: "I Want My Employees to Feel They Have Control over Their Work" Empowering leadership represents the extent to which a leader creates perceptions of psychological empowerment in others. Psychological empowerment is employees' belief that they have control over their work. Empowering leadership was found to have positive effects on performance, organizational citizenship behavior, and creativity for individuals and teams.[181] Let's see how this process works.

Increasing employee psychological empowerment requires four kinds of behaviors—leading for (1) meaningfulness, (2) self-determination, (3) competence, and (4) progress. Let's consider how the late Bernard Tyson, CEO of Kaiser Permanente from 2013 until he passed away in 2019, exhibited these behaviors.

- **Leading for meaningfulness: inspiring and modeling desirable behaviors.** Managers lead for meaningfulness by *inspiring* their employees and *modeling* desired behaviors. Example: Employees may be helped to identify their passions at work by the leader's creating an exciting organizational vision that employees can connect with emotionally.

  Said a friend of Tyson, "The son of a minister and a homemaker, Bernard never forgot where he came from and always stayed true to his values," adding, "He embraced his opportunity to be a change maker, and he leaves behind a staggering legacy of accomplishments."[182]

Kaiser Permanente's former CEO Bernard Tyson speaking about the company's fight to end homelessness at the annual Afrotech conference on November 9, 2019. Tyson passed away unexpectedly only hours later and left a huge void in the hearts of those he inspired with his leadership. One of the many things Tyson was known and respected for was his empowering leadership style. Robin L Marshall/Getty Images

- **Leading for self-determination: delegating meaningful tasks.** Managers can lead for employee self-determination by *delegating* meaningful tasks to them. Delegation is most effective when managers can truly let go.

  "In the past, power was centralized in the hands of the few people who had access to information," said Tyson in an interview. "Now that information is available everywhere, the leader's critical question is, 'How do I charge up the organization so that we're maximizing the intellect of all of our people?'"[183]

- **Leading for competence: supporting and coaching employees.** It goes without saying that employees need to have the necessary knowledge to perform their jobs. Accomplishing this goal involves managers' *supporting* and *coaching* their employees.

  Tyson mentored up-and-coming health care executives as part of his membership in the National Association of Health Services Executives. Said one writer who had observed Tyson in action, "Bernard thoughtfully put this executive through the paces before offering his support—creating an invaluable first-hand learning experience for the up-and-coming health care leader. Through education and mentoring, helping with early-career development, and providing real-world experiences, Bernard helped shape the future of health care by supporting its next generation of leaders."[184]

- **Leading for progress: monitoring and rewarding employees.** Managers lead for progress by *monitoring* and *rewarding* others. We discussed how to do this in Chapter 12.

  When asked about his approach to leading an organization like Kaiser Permanente, Tyson said, "The days of a hierarchical leader being the know-all, the understand-all, and the be-all individual makes no sense in today's environment. You have an organization made up of people with skills, talent, and intelligence." He added, "The challenge is no longer how to instruct people in what to do. It is to set the direction and performance expectations, and then to inspire and motivate people. . . . In a complex organization like Kaiser Permanente, you manage the organized chaos with clarity about the mission, the value proposition, and the end game . . . All the incentives and resources need to be aligned to that."[185]

Ethical Leadership

Ethical Leadership: "I Am Ready to Do the Right Thing"

==Ethical leadership== represents normatively appropriate behavior that focuses on being a moral role model. Society has become increasingly cynical of CEO behavior over the past 20 years. With each corporate scandal—from Enron to Arthur Andersen and Worldcom to #MeToo—the number of CEOs forced out of their roles each year due to ethical failures has grown. A recent study by PwC consulting firm found that in 2018, ethical lapses were—for the first time—the #1 reason for CEO departures from the 2,500 largest companies across the globe, with 39% of successions occurring for this reason.[186] Ethical leadership includes communicating ethical values to others, rewarding ethical behavior, and treating followers with care and concern.[187]

Amy Fuller Example: Amy Fuller, Chief Marketing and Communications Officer for Accenture, the global management consulting firm, described the importance of ethical leadership in a story about a former telecommunications industry client. Said Fuller, "His company went through month after month of difficult times as the market moved from analogue to digital systems . . . Their revenues were plummeting." In order to try to save his company, she said, "the business owner tried to keep the problems a secret and took loans against every personal asset he could to keep making payroll." Fuller encouraged the client to be honest with his employees. "They cried, hugged him, shared in his challenge, and all agreed to a reduction in pay," said Fuller, adding that they "all pulled together to ride the storm and turn the company around—and they did."[188]

Here is what research tells us about ethical leadership:[189]

- Ethical leadership is clearly driven by personal factors related to our beliefs and values.
- It also has a reciprocal relationship with an organization's culture and climate. In other words, an ethical culture and climate promote ethical leadership, and ethical leadership in turn promotes an ethical culture and climate.
- Such leadership is positively related to employee job satisfaction, organizational commitment, organizational citizenship behavior, motivation, and task performance.
- It also is negatively associated with job stress, counterproductive work behavior, and intentions to quit.

Check out the Example box about a leader who uses both empowering and ethical leadership.

EXAMPLE   Lauren Bush Lauren's Empowering, Values-Driven Leadership at FEED

Lauren Bush Lauren, or "LBL," witnessed devastating poverty during her travels as an undergraduate student spokesperson for the United Nations World Food Program and decided to make it her life's work to end world hunger.[190] She cofounded FEED to focus on food-deprived, school-aged children across the globe.[191] The company sells bags, T-shirts, and towels, and each item features a stenciled number to indicate how many meals it provides. For example, a consumer's purchase of FEED's original and most popular product, the burlap FEED 1 bag, feeds one school child for one year.[192]

Here are the ways LBL empowers others to accomplish FEED's mission:

1. Empowering teammates. LBL credits much of FEED's success to the people on her team. She believes the best way to do business is to find talented people and get out of their way. She says, "The most important thing you can do when starting a business is surround yourself with smart people who know a lot more than you do in certain realms."[193] In FEED's early days, LBL realized the company was on the verge of

Lauren Bush Lauren, founder of FEED. Eamonn McCormack/WireImage/ Getty Images

bankruptcy due to shipping costs. She met with an accountant at UPS and quickly learned she knew nothing about supply chain management—so she hired the accountant to manage FEED's supply chain.[194]

2. Empowering consumers. LBL knows that ending world hunger requires large-scale participation. FEED empowers consumers to be part of the solution by attaching tangible donations to each product they purchase. LBL designed FEED to appeal to Millennials' desire to be involved in meaningful endeavors, saying, "What FEED does is give individuals a way to participate in very big, overwhelming world issues in a way that's fun, creative, accessible and easy."[195]

3. Empowering those in need. FEED's business model strives to empower everyone in its supply chain, including its manufacturers. The company makes all its products under fair-labor conditions and partners with artisans in food-insecure countries so people in need can earn a living manufacturing FEED's items.[196] FEED also aims to empower the children it serves. LBL describes meeting a little girl in Rwanda who was receiving a free daily meal through FEED. The girl told LBL she wanted to be the first female president of Rwanda.[197] As the company website states, "When a child is given a free, nutritious school lunch, it can break the cycle of poverty she was born into and empower her to change her own life."[198]

LBL believes the best way to succeed in a socially focused enterprise is to combine your passion with a cause you truly care about. She created FEED by blending her love of fashion and design with her passion for ending world hunger.[199] She also notes the importance of choosing partners who share your organization's values; she has turned down opportunities to sell FEED's products in stores whose values didn't align with her own.[200]

FEED has donated more than 100 million meals to date. Says LBL, "I have learned so much about being a leader over the last ten years of starting and growing FEED. I have made many mistakes along the way, but each has been an incredible learning opportunity. And every day, I try to lead from a place where the mission and founding intention behind FEED is my driving force and north star."[201]

YOUR CALL

How is LBL's leadership both ethical and empowering? How do ethics and empowerment combine to make FEED so successful in accomplishing its mission?

Followers: What Do They Want, How Can They Help?

Leadership is a two-way street. That is, the quality of leadership depends on the qualities of the followers being led.[202] Leaders and followers need each other, and the quality of the relationship determines how followers respond and behave.[203]

What Do Followers Want in Their Leaders?
Research shows that followers seek and admire leaders who create feelings of

- **Significance.** Such leaders make followers feel that what they do at work is important and meaningful.
- **Community.** These leaders create a sense of unity that encourages followers to treat others with respect and to work together in pursuit of organizational goals.
- **Excitement.** The leaders make people feel energetic and engaged at work.[204]

What Do Leaders Want in Their Followers?
Followers vary, of course, in their level of compliance with a leader, with *helpers* (most compliant) showing deference to their leaders, *independents* (less compliant) distancing themselves, and *rebels* (least compliant) showing divergence.[205]

Leaders clearly benefit from having helpers (and, to some extent, independents). They want followers who are productive, reliable, honest, cooperative, proactive, and flexible. They do not want followers who are reluctant to take the lead on projects, fail to generate ideas, are unwilling to collaborate, withhold information, provide inaccurate feedback, or hide the truth.[206]

We give some suggestions on how to be a better follower—and enhance your own career prospects—in the following Practical Action box.

PRACTICAL ACTION　How to Be a Good Leader by Being a Good Follower

Changing business culture and the increasing power of technology have shifted the relationship between leaders and followers. Good followers today don't simply follow. They are empowered to let leaders know when things are going in the wrong direction.

Here's how you can become an intelligent follower. These same skills can make you a good leader, too.[207]

1. See yourself as a leader in training. Leaders know what the people on their team are doing and they see how the various pieces fit together to help the organization accomplish overarching goals. Learn about what co-workers, customers, and bosses are doing, what they want, and what drives them to do their best work (or to prevent others from working well). The better you understand the people around you, the better you will be able to work with them in the present to accomplish goals, and the better you will be able to lead them in the future.

2. Choose your battles. You can't win at everything, but you can choose where to invest your time and energy. Learn how to get along with co-workers, subordinates, and bosses who are similar to you as well as with those who are different.

3. Be brave. Don't be afraid to tell your boss—diplomatically—when you think he or she may be wrong and to offer intelligent alternatives. Helpful feedback is always valuable. Remember, also, to be supportive when things are going well.

4. Work collaboratively. Being a good team player, meeting your goals, and letting the team take credit when appropriate can go a long way toward bringing out the best in others, including your boss when you are in a follower role. Also keep your boss informed; no one likes being caught by surprise.

5. Think critically. Develop your ability to ask the right questions, raise intelligent challenges, and maintain your own competence and motivation.

YOUR CALL

Although it's always in your and the leader's best interest if you become a good follower, sometimes the two of you may differ so completely in habits, dislikes, and so on that you may simply have to look for opportunities outside your present work situation. Do you think you've been a good follower in past jobs?

Abusive Supervision

The concepts of humility, empowerment, and ethical leadership discussed above are positive aspects of leadership. In contrast, research has also sought to better understand the impacts of destructive leader behaviors on followers and organizations. As you learned in Chapter 3, abusive supervision occurs when supervisors repeatedly display verbal and nonverbal hostility toward their subordinates.[208] Abusive supervision does not include physical contact between supervisors and subordinates; rather, it focuses on behaviors such as public humiliation, insults, shouting, and ignoring subordinates.[209]

What Causes Supervisors to Be Abusive?　Research has identified several factors that prompt abusive supervision.[210] They include:

- *Organizational culture:* Factors in a supervisor's environment may make abusive supervision more likely. These factors include aggressive organizational norms and abusive role models.

- *Individual differences:* Researchers have found significant correlations between supervisors' individual differences and the propensity to behavior abusively toward subordinates. These factors include psychological entitlement (a

Have you experienced or witnessed a supervisor who repeatedly treats subordinates with hostility? A boss who screams, mocks, or perhaps ignores employees on a regular basis? If so, try thinking about the abusive behavior as good lesson on what not to do as a leader. Pavlo Syvak/123RF

person's general belief that they deserve more than others) and Machiavellianism.

- *Early life experiences:* Supervisors' early life experiences impact the likelihood that they will abuse subordinates. Research has found that supervisors who witnessed aggression between their parents and those who were the targets of parental aggression are more likely to engage in abusive supervision.

What Do We Know about How Abusive Supervision Affects Employees?   Scholars have studied the negative outcomes of abusive supervision for more than 20 years. Key findings from more than 200 studies tell us the following:[211]

- *Abusive supervision increases negative outcomes:* Subordinates of abusive supervisors are more likely to engage in deviant and counterproductive behaviors at work and are more likely to experience depression and emotional exhaustion.

- *Abusive supervision decreases positive outcomes:* Subordinates of abusive supervisors experience decreased job satisfaction and job performance and are less likely to engage in organizational citizenship behaviors.

What Should Organizations Do to Deal with and Prevent Abusive Supervision?   Abusive supervision consists of behaviors that are unacceptable and inappropriate, but unfortunately, not usually considered illegal on their own. Still, these behaviors clearly are damaging to employees and organizations. According to SHRM, firms should take the following steps to reduce both the occurrence and impact of abusive supervision:[212]

- Implement strong and clear policies about supervisory behavior—including the types of behavior that are and are not acceptable in the organization.

- Provide training to supervisors and employees on appropriate behaviors and on how to recognize abusive supervisory behaviors.

- Establish fair processes for dealing with complaints about abusive supervision, including safe reporting channels and protections from retaliation for employees who report it.

- Use regular employee attitude surveys to help uncover unreported cases of abusive supervision and potential patterns of abuse.

In conclusion, we strongly suggest that you, as a manager, avoid behaviors that are considered abusive toward subordinates. Instead, focus on developing your ability to be humble, empowering, and ethical in your leadership. ●

14.7 Career Corner: Managing Your Career Readiness

LO 14-7

Explain how to develop the career readiness competency of self-awareness.

This chapter demonstrated that leadership is a concept with much breadth and depth. You learned that it affects all aspects of organizational effectiveness, thus requiring the combined use of 14 career readiness competencies from the model shown below: understanding the business, critical thinking/problem solving, oral/written communication, leadership, social intelligence, networking, emotional intelligence, self-motivation, professionalism/work ethic, personal adaptability, self-awareness, service/others orientation, openness to change, and generalized self-efficacy. (See Figure 14.3.)

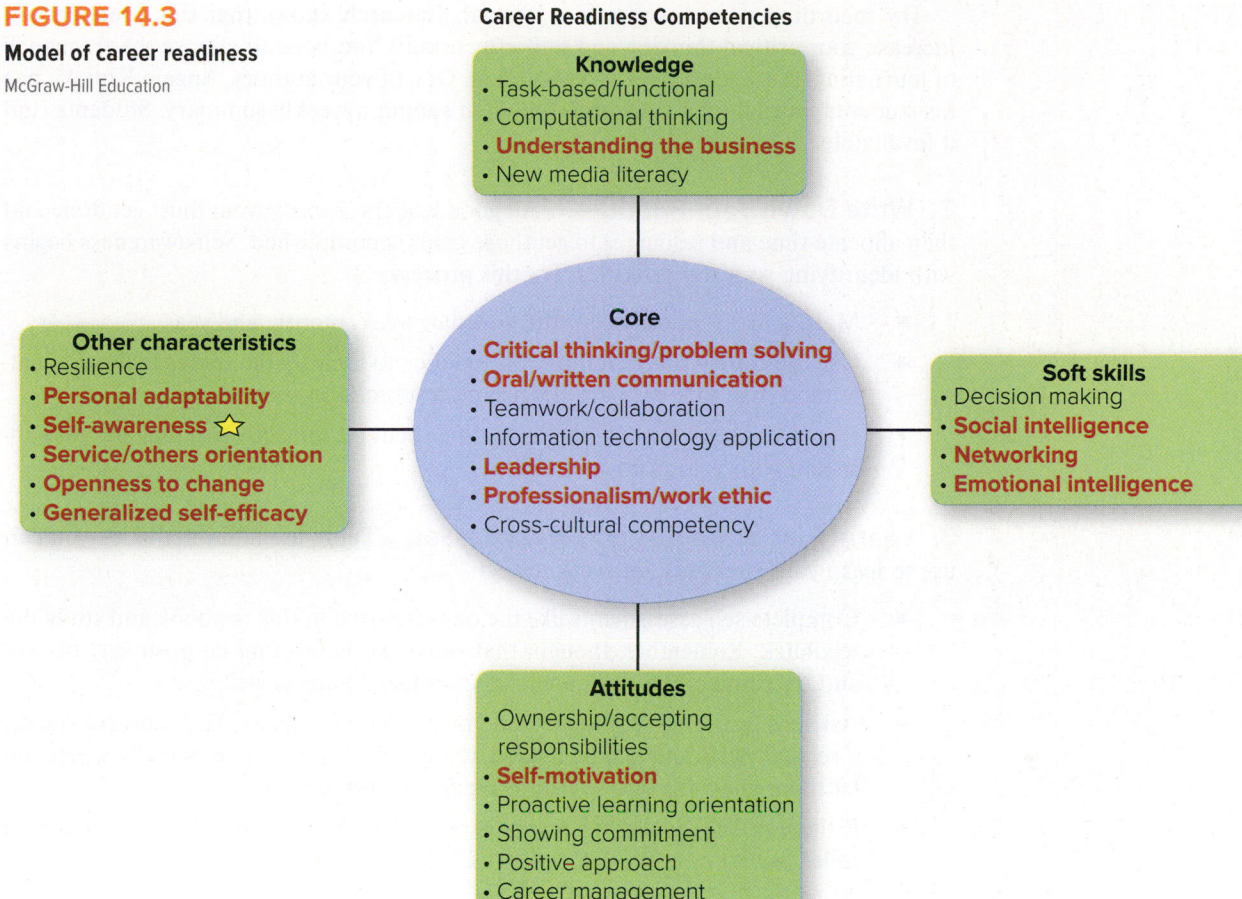

FIGURE 14.3

Model of career readiness

McGraw-Hill Education

Career Readiness Competencies

Knowledge
- Task-based/functional
- Computational thinking
- **Understanding the business**
- New media literacy

Other characteristics
- Resilience
- **Personal adaptability**
- **Self-awareness** ⭐
- **Service/others orientation**
- **Openness to change**
- **Generalized self-efficacy**

Core
- **Critical thinking/problem solving**
- **Oral/written communication**
- Teamwork/collaboration
- Information technology application
- **Leadership**
- **Professionalism/work ethic**
- Cross-cultural competency

Soft skills
- Decision making
- **Social intelligence**
- **Networking**
- **Emotional intelligence**

Attitudes
- Ownership/accepting responsibilities
- **Self-motivation**
- Proactive learning orientation
- Showing commitment
- Positive approach
- Career management

We obviously can't discuss here how to develop all these competencies. To make this section more manageable, we focus on the critically important competency of *self-awareness*.

Becoming More Self-Aware

"Self-awareness seems to have become the latest management buzzword — and for good reason," said one management expert in a recent article.[213] According to research, self-awareness increases creativity, decision quality, leadership effectiveness, and job satisfaction. Developing self-awareness is not just an intellectual exercise. It entails understanding who you are and what you stand for. It requires thinking about your life vision, values, personality, needs, behavioral tendencies, and social skills. You can become more self-aware by taking the following actions:

1. Take the Time to Reflect Most of us are so busy accomplishing our daily activities or short-term goals that we leave ourselves no time to reflect and learn.[214] This pattern gets tasks done but can prevent our learning the new skills needed for more difficult assignments or promotions. You can build intentional reflection into your life by considering the following questions on a regular basis:

- What happened?
- What did I learn in general?
- What did I learn about me?
- What will I do to improve in the future?[215]

Try recording your answers in a journal. Research shows that this practice will increase your critical thinking and self-reflection.[216] You need to choose the frequency of journaling, but once a week is a minimum. One of your authors, Angelo Kinicki, has his students journal on a daily basis and then submit a weekly summary. Students find it invaluable.

2. Write Down Your Priorities

All good leaders identify what must get done and then allocate time and resources to get those goals accomplished. Self-awareness begins with identifying your top priorities. Try this process:

- Make a list of priorities for the next day, week, month, and year.

- Use the clarity you gain from this practice to identify the things that truly matter and plan to focus your efforts and resources on these things.

- Figure out how you can minimize time spent on the activities that are not consistent with your primary interests.[217]

3. Learn Your Strengths and Weaknesses

There are a few activities you can use to learn your strengths and weaknesses:

- Complete self-assessments like the ones featured in this textbook and study the feedback. Remember, though, that self-assessments can be positively biased, and try some of the additional activities listed here as well.

- Ask family, friends, colleagues, and mentors for feedback. They observe you on a regular basis and can be a good source of information, especially when you let them know it's safe to give you really honest feedback.

- If there is a particular behavior you really want to change, ask a trusted person to let you know every time you exhibit it.

4. Avoid the Dunning-Kruger Effect

Consider the following statements: "If I was just intelligent, I'd be okay. But I am fiercely intelligent, which most people find very threatening" (actress Sharon Stone). "People the world over recognize me as a great spiritual leader" (actor Steven Seagal). Most overly gifted people do not go around boasting like this. Albert Einstein, for example, never told people that he was "fiercely intelligent."

Developed by two psychology professors—Dr. David Dunning and Dr. Justin Kruger—the **Dunning-Kruger effect** is "a cognitive bias whereby people who are incompetent at something are unable to recognize their own incompetence. And not only do they fail to recognize their incompetence, they're also likely to feel confident that they actually are competent."[218] Consider this effect in light of results from an online quiz asking 10,000 people how they react to constructive criticism. Only 39% said they deal with constructive criticism by considering the cause of that feedback.[219] It's possible that the other 61% are caught up in the Dunning-Kruger effect.

The point is that this bias will detract from your ability to recognize your own weaknesses, which then prevents you from correcting them. Seeking regular feedback and focusing on a proactive learning orientation are two ways to overcome the Dunning-Kruger effect.[220] ●

behavioral leadership
approaches 611

charisma 621

charismatic leadership 621

coercive power 601

consideration 612

contingency leadership
model 613

Dunning-Kruger effect 634

employee-centered leader
behaviors 612

empowering leadership 628

ethical leadership 629

expert power 601

full-range leadership 619

global mind-set 611

influence tactics 602

informational power 602

initiating-structure leadership 611

leader–member exchange (LMX)
model of leadership 624

leadership 598

leadership coaching 598

legitimate power 600

Machiavellianism 606

managerial leadership 600

narcissism 606

path–goal leadership model 615

personalized power 600

power 600

production-centered leader
behaviors 611

psychological empowerment 628

psychopathy 606

referent power 601

relationship-oriented
leadership 612

reward power 601

servant leadership 625

situational approach 613

socialized power 600

task-oriented leadership
behaviors 611

trait approaches to leadership 605

transactional leadership 619

transformational leadership 619

Key Points

14.1 The Nature of Leadership: The Role of Power and Influence

- Leadership is the ability to influence employees to voluntarily pursue organizational goals. Power is the ability to marshal human, informational, and other resources to get something done.
- Within an organization there are typically six sources of power leaders may draw on: (1) legitimate power, (2) reward power, (3) coercive power, (4) expert power, (5) referent power, and (6) informational power.
- There are nine influence tactics for trying to get others to do something you want, ranging from most used to least used tactics as follows: rational persuasion, inspirational appeals, consultation, ingratiating tactics, personal appeals, exchange tactics, coalition tactics, pressure tactics, and legitimating tactics.

14.2 Trait Approaches: Do Leaders Have Distinctive Traits and Personal Characteristics?

- Trait approaches to leadership attempt to identify distinctive characteristics that account for the effectiveness of leaders.
- Five positive task-oriented traits are (1) intelligence, (2) consciousness, (3) openness to experience, (4) emotional stability, and (5) positive affect. Among the positive attributes are extraversion, agreeableness, and emotional intelligence. Among the negative attributes are narcissism, Machiavellianism, and psychopathy.
- Women occupy a growing but still very small number of CEO and top-management positions in the United States.

14.3 Behavioral Approaches: Do Leaders Show Distinctive Patterns of Behavior?

- Behavioral leadership approaches try to determine the unique behaviors displayed by effective leaders. Two categories are task-oriented behavior and relationship-oriented behavior.
- Task-oriented behaviors are those that ensure that people, equipment, and other resources are used in an efficient way to accomplish the mission of a group or organization.
- Relationship-oriented leadership is primarily concerned with the leader's interaction with his or her people.
- Four basic skills for leaders are (1) cognitive abilities, (2) interpersonal skills, (3) business skills, and (4) conceptual skills.

14.4 Situational Approaches: Does Leadership Vary with the Situation?

- Proponents of the situational approach (or contingency approach) to leadership believe that effective leadership behavior depends on the situation at hand—that as situations change, different styles become effective. Two contingency approaches are the Fiedler contingency leadership model and House's path–goal leadership model.
- The Fiedler contingency leadership model determines if a leader's style is task-oriented or relationship-oriented and if that style is effective for the situation at hand.

- The House path–goal leadership model, in its revised form, holds that the effective leader clarifies paths through which subordinates can achieve goals and provides them with support. Two variables, employee characteristics and environmental factors, cause one or more leadership behaviors to be more effective than others.

14.5 The Full-Range Model: Using Transactional and Transformational Leadership

- Full-range leadership describes leadership along a range of styles (from passive to transactional to transformational), with the most effective being transactional/transformational leaders.
- Transformational leadership encourages employees to pursue organizational goals over self-interests and is influenced by leaders' individual characteristics and an organization's culture.
- Four key behaviors of transformational leaders in affecting employees are they inspire motivation, inspire trust, encourage excellence, and stimulate employees intellectually.

14.6 Contemporary Perspectives and Concepts

- The leader–member exchange (LMX) model of leadership emphasizes that leaders have different sorts of relationships with different subordinates.

- Servant leadership focuses on providing increased service to others—meeting the goals of both followers and the organization—rather than the goals of oneself.
- Humble leaders tend to display five key qualities valued by employees: high self-awareness, openness to feedback, appreciation of others, low self-focus, and appreciation of the greater good.
- Empowering leadership represents the extent to which a leader creates perceptions of psychological empowerment in others.
- Ethical leadership represents normatively appropriate behavior that focuses on being a moral role model.
- Leaders want followers who are productive, reliable, honest, cooperative, proactive, and flexible.
- Abusive supervision represents supervisors' sustained verbal and non-verbal hostility toward subordinates.

14.7 Career Corner: Managing Your Career Readiness

- Becoming a more effective leader requires the application of 14 career readiness competencies.
- You can become more self-aware by taking the following four actions: (1) Take the time to reflect. (2) Write down your priorities. (3) Learn your strengths and weaknesses. (4) Avoid the Dunning-Kruger effect.

Understand the Chapter: What Do I Know?

1. What is the difference between being a manager and being a leader?
2. What are six sources of power?
3. In brief, what are five approaches to leadership described in this chapter?
4. What are some positive task-oriented traits and positive/negative interpersonal attributes related to leadership?
5. Explain the difference between task-oriented and relationship-oriented leader behavior.
6. Briefly discuss the two types of situational leadership approaches.
7. What are key aspects of transformational leadership?
8. Explain the leader–member exchange (LMX) and servant leadership models.
9. Describe contemporary leadership concepts.
10. Explain how you can become more self-aware.

Management In Action

Adam Neumann's Rise and Fall at WeWork

In 2001, 22-year-old Adam Neumann moved to the United States from Israel. He attended Baruch College in New York City but dropped out when he was four credits shy of a diploma, trying his hand instead at being an entrepreneur. After two failed ventures, Neumann and friend Miguel McKelvey started a business called Green Desk, renting out desks in co-working spaces for people and companies that weren't ready to invest in their own offices. By 2010, their company WeWork was born.[221]

How, exactly, did WeWork work? Essentially, the company leased office spaces in metropolitan areas like New York City and San Francisco—where flexible working space was in high demand—then split them into tiny 64 square foot sections. WeWork then sublet the sections to professionals, providing amenities such as restaurants, office equipment like copy machines, and camaraderie. Neumann sold investors on his business model by positioning WeWork as a tech and lifestyle company, but critics say it was never anything more than a glorified subleasing firm.[222] How is it possible, then, that by 2019, WeWork had more than 520 locations across the globe and a valuation of almost $50 billion (compared to its biggest competitor's $3.7 billion valuation)?

INSPIRING LEADERSHIP

Neumann "led with unusual exuberance and excess," said one reporter, adding that it was the CEO's "combination of entrepreneurial vision, personal charisma and brash risk-taking" that made WeWork the most valuable start-up in the country at one point.[223] The CEO often had outlandish goals, including an idea to create shared office spaces on Mars and to give the world's 150 million orphans a family in WeWork.[224]

Neumann seemed to believe that he had extraordinary abilities to accomplish the impossible. For example, he invested in Life Biosciences, a life-extension start-up company, because he wanted to live forever.[225] As another example, according to one insider, Neumann once said, "when countries are shooting at each other, I want them to come to me."[226] A source close to the company described Neumann as "an intense person who thinks he is a Jesus figure," but added that "he's also very good at what he does . . . He was almost like a televangelist."[227] Neumann's ability to motivate was acknowledged even by former company executives who strongly disliked him.

TROUBLE IN THE WORKS

Still, those who spent enough time with Neumann eventually saw holes in his visionary and charismatic façade. Said one real-estate executive who dealt with WeWork, "He clearly is very smart and ambitious . . . but he starts talking about some of the more germane aspects of the city's land-use process . . . and he has no idea what he's talking about. Your bulls–t meter just goes off with him." The executive added that Neumann was "the quintessential person who doesn't know what they don't know."[228]

Others have expressed disappointment with the lack of alignment between the vision that Neumann pitched and the reality inside the company. "From the outside," said one former employee, "a lot of the pitch to the public and employees is all about this 'we' thing, but the closer you get to the core of the company, the less it exists. It's all about 'me' and 'I.'"[229]

Ultimately, it was WeWork's S-1 filing—the registration form that companies use when they are planning an initial public offering (IPO)—that alerted investors to the company's and CEO's troubles. For example, as a managing member of the separate private company "We Holdings, LLC" Neumann trademarked the right to the word "We." He then reorganized WeWork under the umbrella "The We Company" and charged it—his own company—$5.9 million for the rights to use the word.[230] Neumann was also taking near zero-interest loans from WeWork, using the money to buy office buildings, then renting the spaces back to WeWork.[231]

Former Twitter CEO Dick Costolo said of Neumann, "this is not the way everybody behaves." Costolo characterized "the degree of self-dealing" inside WeWork as "egregious."[232] But former employees said that it was nearly impossible to talk Neumann down from anything, no matter how absurd it seemed. One insider told a reporter, "one time, we asked one of the top execs . . . 'can you bring him back to reality?' And she said, 'when Adam comes in and wants to do this or that, even if it's a really bad idea, we will figure out how to do it.'"[233]

NEUMANN'S OUSTER

Experts have speculated that the qualities in Neumann that fueled the company's meteoric rise proved to also be huge liabilities for WeWork.[234] Investors rejected WeWork's IPO and cut the company's valuation by 75%.[235] The company ousted Neumann from his role and by the end of 2019 had cut its workforce by 20% while continuing to open new co-working spaces.[236] In April 2020, Japanese multinational conglomerate SoftBank pulled out of its offer to buy a controlling share in the struggling company.[237] As a minority shareholder, Neumann stood to gain approximately $975 million from the deal. In May 2020, Neumann announced that he was suing SoftBank, saying that the conglomerate was "secretly taking actions to undermine" WeWork.[238]

FOR DISCUSSION

Problem-Solving Perspective

1. What is the underlying problem in this case from the investors' perspective?

2. What are the causes of this problem?

3. What recommendations would you make to investors for fixing this problem?

Application of Chapter Content

1. From which sources did Neumann draw power? Which influence tactics did he use to gain followers' and investors' support?

2. From the perspective of trait theories, how would you evaluate Neumann? Which traits did he possess? Which traits was he lacking?

3. Evaluate Neumann according to the full-range leadership model. Which behaviors did he exhibit? Which behaviors did he fail to exhibit?

4. Consider Neumann in light of contemporary leadership approaches and concepts. Specifically, how

would you rate Neumann in terms of his humility, ethics, and followers' behaviors?

5. Do you see issues with Neumann's self-awareness? Would you suggest that he suffered from the Dunning-Kruger effect? Explain your answers.

Legal/Ethical Challenge

Should Starbucks have a Corporate Loitering Policy?

Starbucks launched a multimillion-dollar global brand campaign in 2014 called "Meet Me at Starbucks." The ad focused not on coffee, but instead on the idea that Starbucks stores were a great place to socialize, whether to catch up with friends, conduct business, or hold a group meeting.[239] But in some Starbucks locations, it was only OK to hang out if you were buying something.

Up until mid-2018, Starbucks didn't have a corporate policy on loitering. Instead, individual stores were expected to set their own rules about whether people could sit inside or use the restroom for free; at some locations, the answer was yes, but at others, it was no.[240] This was the case at a Philadelphia Starbucks where two black men were arrested for trespassing and disturbance. Business partners Donte Robinson and Rashon Nelson were waiting to meet with an associate when one of them asked to use the restroom. They hadn't purchased anything, and the store manager called the police after the men refused to leave. A video of Robinson and Nelson being taken away in handcuffs went viral and sparked public outrage and accusations of racial profiling.[241]

Starbucks CEO Kevin Johnson apologized publicly for the incident and flew to Philadelphia to meet with Robinson and Nelson in person.[242] The men settled with Starbucks for an undisclosed amount plus an offer of a free college education through the company's partnership with Arizona State University. They also settled with the city of Philadelphia for a symbolic $1 each and a promise that the city would start a $200,000 entrepreneurship program for its public high school students.[243]

The Philadelphia location did have a no-loitering policy, but the guidelines for whether police should be engaged to enforce rules varied by region and may have been difficult for managers to interpret. Johnson said that threats and serious disturbances may warrant law enforcement, but that the Philadelphia manager's decision to call the police in this situation was "completely inappropriate."[244] A corporate spokesperson said the manager was no longer employed by Starbucks as part of a "mutual decision."[245] The company closed more than 8,000 of its U.S. locations for an entire day soon after the event to conduct training on racial and other unconscious biases.[246]

Starbucks eventually announced that it was changing its corporate policy (or lack thereof) on loitering. In a statement, the company said, "any person who enters our spaces, including patios, cafes and restrooms, regardless of whether they make a purchase, is considered a customer."[247] Some praised the company's decision, but others questioned whether the decision made good business sense.

SOLVING THE CHALLENGE
What would you have done if you were CEO of Starbucks?

1. I would not have instituted a corporate loitering policy. Decisions on how to manage customers and when to involve police should be made by store-level leadership, not corporate executives. Some locations are busier than others and should be able to decide whether nonpaying customers are taking up space that would otherwise go to paying customers. Managers should also have the discretion to call the police when they feel it's appropriate. A single bad decision by one store manager shouldn't represent the entire company, and most managers know how to apply these types of policies in a fair and nondiscriminatory fashion. The additional bias training will help prevent similar incidents from occurring in the future.

2. I think the new corporate loitering policy is a good idea. This type of leadership should come from the top of the organization and set the tone for what's important to the company. A corporate policy would provide clearer guidance to store managers on how to handle nonpaying customers and would also protect the company from liability due to store managers making bad decisions. Starbucks should also provide clear and consistent guidelines for managers on when it's appropriate to call law enforcement.

3. I think that corporate loitering policies might be a good idea, provided they do not lead to excessive lost business for particular stores. For example, a good policy might state that loitering is welcomed as long as there are no paying customers waiting for a seat. If paying customers don't have anywhere to sit, then nonpaying customers should leave to make room for them. I think all employees should participate in unconscious-bias training to ensure the policy is applied fairly and consistently.

4. Invent other options.

15

Interpersonal and Organizational Communication

Mastering the Exchange of Information

Kapook2981/iStock/Getty Images

After reading this chapter, you should be able to:

LO 15-1 Describe the communication process.

LO 15-2 Compare communication channels and appropriate ways for managers to use them.

LO 15-3 Identify barriers to communication and ways managers can overcome them.

LO 15-4 Discuss how managers can successfully use social media to communicate.

LO 15-5 Identify ways for managers to improve their listening, writing, and speaking skills.

LO 15-6 Review the techniques for improving the career readiness competency of networking.

FORECAST *What's Ahead in This Chapter*

This chapter describes the process of transferring information and understanding between individuals and groups. It shows how you can use different channels and patterns of communication, both formal and informal, to your advantage. We also describe several communication barriers—physical, personal, cross-cultural, nonverbal, and gender differences—and we discuss how managers use social media to communicate more effectively. We also provide recommendations for becoming a better listener, writer, and speaker. We conclude with a Career Corner that focuses on developing the career readiness competency of networking.

Improving Your Use of Empathy

Why should you care about using empathy? Because it can be a differentiator in finding and holding a meaningful job after graduation. Mark Lobosco, vice president of talent solutions at LinkedIn, concluded that "as we enter the 2020s, empathy will reshape the way employers hire and retain talent." He proposed that "instead of putting shareholder value over all . . . a company's purpose now includes investing in employees. Companies are becoming more empathetic not only to attract candidates, but also to retain their workforce amid increasing expectations of what employers owe to their people."[1]

Lobosco is telling us that empathy, which reflects the ability to feel, understand, and act on another person's feelings and emotions,[2] is a key component of effective communication for both individuals and organizations. It's part of the career readiness skill of emotional intelligence and represents a natural human ability everyone has, and one that you can learn and actively develop.[3]

Empathy will help you gain a better and more accurate understanding of what's really going on when you communicate with others at work—what they need, what they're feeling, why they're saying what they're saying, and even what they aren't saying. That, in turn, will help shape your response and make you a better communicator with stronger work and personal relationships. In support of these conclusions, research revealed that empathy was related with more positive perceptions of justice (recall our discussion in Chapter 12), greater task performance, better communication competence, and greater prosocial behaviors (recall our discussion in Chapter 11).[4]

Empathy also improves your leadership skills and your ability to defuse conflict.[5] It should be easy to see that someone who conveys empathy and understanding toward others will more easily earn their respect and thus be better able to lead and direct them. And your ability to resolve conflict ultimately depends on your being able to see what matters to all the parties and what each side hopes to achieve.

Empathy can even improve your performance in job interviews by helping you understand what the interviewer needs in a new hire. In this way, you can show why you're the right one for the job.

Here are some suggestions for developing empathy and strengthening your emotional intelligence in the process.

Practice Your Best Listening Skills

Interrupting others, or even thinking about how you're going to respond instead of actually listening to what's being said, prevents you from focusing on the other person and their message. Checking your phone during in-person conversations also limits your ability to focus on what is being said.

Be Mindful

You can't use empathy if you aren't mindful. Mindfulness enables you to ignore the negative, insecure, or irrelevant thoughts that pop into your head and distract you from listening to what someone is saying.[6] How else can you accurately assess what someone is feeling or thinking? Mindfulness can foster personal success above and beyond its influence on using empathy. Georgina Miranda, chief visionary officer for She Ventures, notes that mindfulness helped her successfully climb Mt. Everest twice. "If you can learn to tame your mind, you can learn to live fully in the present moment. And then you will have the most successful life," said Georgina.[7]

Observe Nonverbal Cues and Be Mindful of Your Own

Pay attention to the speaker's body language, facial expression, and tone of voice. Are these giving a message that contradicts the words being spoken? Try to find out why. Watch your own nonverbal behavior, too. For instance, maintain comfortable eye contact while listening and speaking. It's also important to be aware of any facial expressions such as frowning or body language like crossing your arms that may convey a lack of interest or frustration.[8]

Practice Perspective Taking

Perspective taking amounts to taking another person's point of view when communicating with them.[9] For example, if someone was walking toward you on the street and asked for directions to the nearest restaurant, would you give the directions from your perspective facing the person, or from the person's perspective facing you? You should take her perspective. If the person were from out of town, as opposed to being a local, would you provide more detailed instructions? The answer is yes if you were taking this person's perspective. If you're having trouble understanding where someone is coming from, try asking yourself what you would do if the situation were reversed and you were in that person's shoes. This imagined swap is the essence of empathy because it lets you perceive and feel what the other person is seeing, hearing, and feeling. Research demonstrated that perspective taking enhances our ability to understand others' internal thoughts and feelings.[10]

Know Your Audience

Whether you're making a presentation to a group or speaking one-on-one, be sure you understand how much your audience already knows about the topic on which you're speaking. Use that knowledge to avoid overexplaining or leaving people in the dark.

Show Genuine Interest and Be Curious

It's hard to be empathetic if you are only concerned about yourself or what you want in a situation. Caring about others' welfare will go a long way to improving your empathy. Connecting with someone's thoughts and feelings also is facilitated by curiosity. For example, if a classmate comes up to you during finals week and says, "I am exhausted," you could reply, "so am I, finals are tough. I know how you feel." But there is a more powerful response and it involves curiosity. It begins by recognizing that you really don't know what is making your fellow student exhausted. It could be that he is working two jobs to pay the rent and is tending to sick parents. Alternatively, it could simply be the fact the person is studying for five final exams. It would be better to allow your curiosity to ask questions, listen, and learn before trying to be empathetic.[11]

For Discussion One way to put these suggestions into practice is to challenge yourself to have a substantive conversation in which you really connect with someone you consider difficult to communicate with or with whom you frequently disagree. Can you make a plan to try this? Which tips will be most helpful to you?

15.1 The Communication Process: What It Is, How It Works

THE BIG PICTURE

Communication is the transfer of information and understanding from one person to another. The process involves sender, message, and receiver; encoding and decoding; the medium; feedback; and "noise," or interference. Managers need to tailor their communication to the appropriate medium (rich or lean) for the appropriate situation.

LO 15-1

Describe the communication process.

Our goal in this chapter is to increase your understanding about being an effective communicator. You will learn that effective communication involves more than having good verbal or written skills, and it represents an important career readiness competency desired by employers.[12] To that end, one expert concluded that "developing effective professional communication takes time, needs practice and is a lifelong personal development exercise.[13] We begin your communication journey by defining communication and reviewing the communication process. We then discuss a contingency approach for selecting the appropriate communication medium.

Communication Defined: The Transfer of Information and Understanding

Researchers have begun to examine communication as a form of social information processing, in which receivers interpret messages by cognitively processing them. This work has led to the development of a perceptual model of communication that depicts it as a process in which receivers create meaning in their own minds.[14]

Communication—the transfer of information and understanding from one person to another—is an activity that you as a manager will have to do a lot. The fact that we communicate all the time is a problem because it leads to the assumption that we are good at it. How good a communicator do you think you are? A survey of 200 U.S. employers and 4,200 graduating seniors revealed that while nearly 80% of the college students in the survey believed they were competent in both oral and written communication, only 42% of employers thought students were correct about their oral skills, and only 56% said students had good writing skills.[15] It's results like these that reinforce the conclusion that your communication skills represent an important career readiness competency desired by employers.

You don't have to shout to communicate. Comstock Images/Alamy Stock Photo

You are an *efficient communicator* when you can transmit your message accurately in the least amount of time. You are an *effective communicator* when your intended message is accurately understood by the other person. Are efficiency and effectiveness equally important? The answer will become clearer as you read this section. Let's focus on the effectiveness aspect of communication by discussing the basics of the communication process.

How the Communication Process Works

Communication has been said to be a process consisting of "a sender transmitting a message through media to a receiver who responds."[16] A diagram of this communication process is shown below. *(See Figure 15.1.)* Let's take a look at its different parts.

Sender, Message, and Receiver   The **sender** is the person wanting to share information—called a message—and the **receiver** is the person for whom the message is intended, as follows.

Sender → Message → Receiver

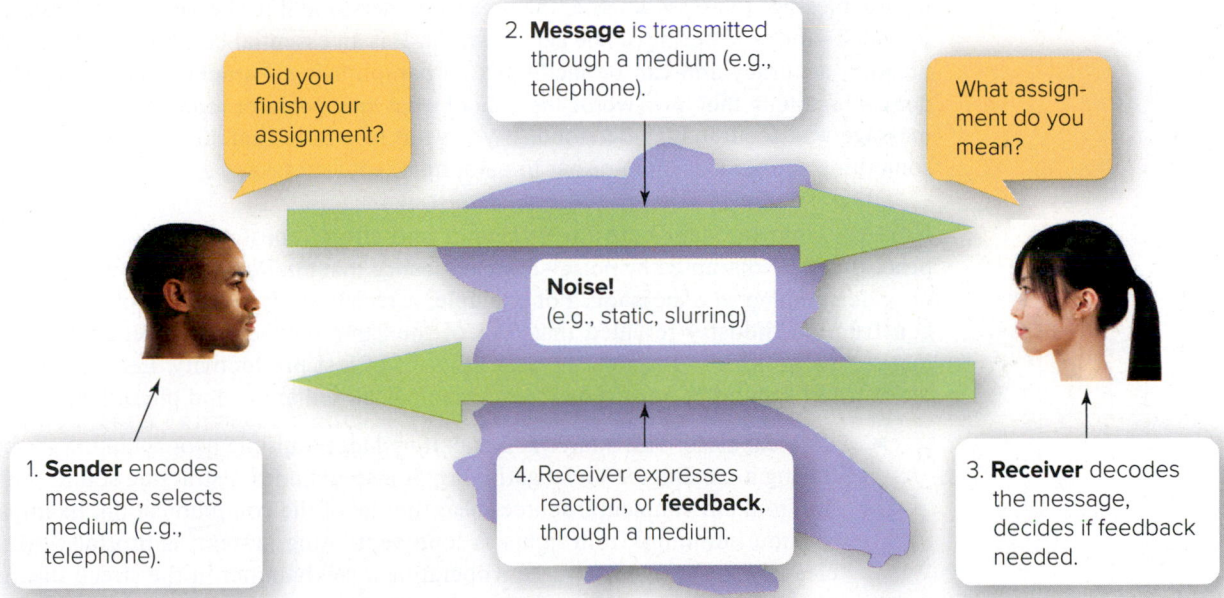

FIGURE 15.1   The communication process
"Noise" is not just noise or loud background sounds but any disturbance that interferes with transmission—static, fadeout, distracting facial expressions, an uncomfortable meeting site, competing voices, and so on.

(male): Wolf/Fuse/Getty Images; (female): Takayuki/Shutterstock

Encoding and Decoding   Of course, the process isn't as simple as just sender/message/receiver. If you were an old-fashioned telegraph operator using Morse code to send a message over a telegraph line, you would first have to encode the message, and the receiver would have to decode it. But the same is true when you are sending the message by voice to another person in the same room and have to decide what language to speak in and what terms to use, and when you are texting a friend and can choose your words, your abbreviations and even an emoji or two.

   Encoding is translating a message into understandable symbols or language. **Decoding** is interpreting and trying to make sense of the message. Thus, the communication process is now

Sender **[Encoding]** → Message → **[Decoding]** Receiver

The Medium   The means by which you as a communicator send a message is important, whether it is typing a text or an e-mail, hand-scrawling a note, or communicating by voice in person or by phone or videoconference. The means is the <mark>medium</mark>, the **pathway by which a message travels:**

Sender [Encoding] → Message **[Medium]** Message → [Decoding] Receiver

Feedback   "Flight 123, do you copy?" In the movies, that's what you hear the flight controller say when radioing the pilot of a troubled aircraft to see whether he or she received ("copied") the previous message. And the pilot may radio back, "Roger, Houston, I copy." This acknowledgment is an example of <mark>feedback</mark>, **whereby the receiver expresses his or her reaction to the sender's message.**

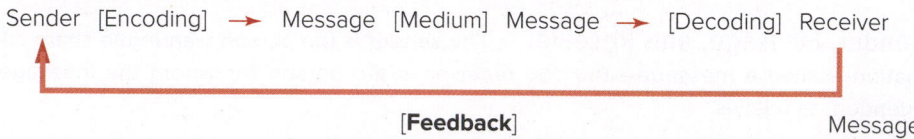

Feedback is essential for *effective* communication because it enables the person sending the message to assess whether the receiver understood it in the same way the sender intended—and whether he or she agrees with it. It is an essential component of communication accuracy and can be facilitated by paraphrasing. <mark>Paraphrasing</mark> **occurs when people restate in their own words the crux of what they heard or read.** It clarifies that a message was accurately understood. If you want to ensure that someone understands something you said, ask him or her to paraphrase your message.

Noise   Unfortunately, both the efficiency and effectiveness of the communication process can be disrupted by <mark>noise</mark>—**any disturbance that interferes with the transmission or understanding of a message.** For example, a recent study of 517 employees in the construction industry revealed that 65% of the sample experienced reduced performance due to noise.[17] Imagine the cost in terms of lost productivity. Let's investigate the four key sources of noise: physical, psychological, semantic, and physiological.[18]

- **Physical noise.** This source is literal. It includes multiple people talking at once during a meeting or social gathering. It also includes distracting sounds coming from environmental sources near the site of the communication. Examples include humming from lights; a loud ventilating system; janitorial workers cleaning; construction workers operating a jackhammer in the street; disorganized PowerPoint slides; phones ringing; and people talking in offices, cubicles, or on their phones. If you ever worked in an open office environment, you know what we mean. Open office designs have been found to contain more noise than traditional office environments where people work in separate spaces.[19]

- **Psychological noise.** This source pertains to individual differences such as personality, attitudes, emotions, beliefs, or thoughts, which impact our ability to encode and decode messages. Introverts, for example, were found to be more negatively affected by noise than extroverts.[20] Strong emotions, such as fear, sadness, or jubilance also can interfere with your ability to process information. Our beliefs represent another interesting source of noise. We tend to "tune out" when a speaker espouses something we disagree with. Consider your belief about writing lecture notes on paper versus recording them on laptops. Could you be inadvertently adding noise to your learning experience because of this belief? Although there are pros and cons to both approaches, the consensus is that it is better to write notes in a notebook.[21]

- **Semantic noise.** This source is caused by the words used when communicating. Noise can occur during encoding or decoding, for example, when people from different cultures stumble over each other's languages. One of your authors—Angelo Kinicki—was consulting in Asia and found, for instance, that his suggestion that Asian managers "touch base" (a baseball reference) with their colleagues drew blank looks. We discuss cross-cultural barriers to communication later in the chapter. The COVID-19 outbreak at the Smithfield Foods meat plant in Sioux Falls, South Dakota, is a great, but sad, example of semantic noise.

Smithfield Foods Example: The Smithfield Foods pork processing plant is the ninth largest hog-processing plant in the United States. The plant employees about 3,700 workers who are mainly immigrants and refugees from Myanmar, Ethiopia, Nepal, the Congo, and El Salvador. There are roughly 40 different languages spoken at the plant. Although English is among the top 10 languages used by employees, others are Spanish, Kunama, Swahili, Nepali, Tigrinya, Amharic, French, Oromo, and Vietnamese. Language barriers were a key factor in the spread of COVID-19 among 783 workers, resulting in two deaths. Federal investigators noted that "workers who showed symptoms were sent home with informational packets that were written only in English."[22] Julia, the adult daughter of two plant workers, told a reporter that "my parents don't know English. They can't advocate for themselves."[23] The Centers for Disease Control (CDC) also stated that language barriers impaired their ability to help.[24]

Jargon is another source of semantic noise.[25] **Jargon is terminology specific to a particular profession or group.** (Example: "The HR VP wants the RFP to go out ASAP." Translation: "The vice president of human resources wants the request for proposal to go out as soon as possible.") *Buzzwords* are designed to impress rather than inform. (Example: "Could our teams interface on the ad campaign that went viral, and then circle back with the boss?")[26] Noise also occurs in *nonverbal communication* (discussed later in this chapter), when our physical movements and our words send different messages.

■ **Physiological noise.** Have you ever attended a lecture when you had a bad cold and headache? If yes, you understand the impact of physiological noise. This form of noise reflects our physical symptoms at a point in time as well as any physical impairments. For example, your authors know that their ability to process a case analysis in class is impaired when we are sick. Being sick makes it very difficult to stay focused and actively listen to all the students' comments.

This student struggles to pay attention during class due to physiological noise. Steve Hix/Getty Images

Selecting the Right Medium for Effective Communication

All kinds of communication tools are available to managers, ranging from one-to-one face-to-face conversation all the way to use of the mass media. However, managers need to know when and how to use the right tool for the right situation—when to use e-mail or when to meet face-to-face, for example. Selecting the wrong medium, regardless of the message, can be costly to one's career. Consider the example of Capt. Brett Crozier.

Capt. Brett Crozier Example: Captain Crozier was the commander of the USS Theodore Roosevelt when an outbreak of the COVID-19 pandemic occurred aboard his ship. Crozier wrote a four-page letter to military officials about the outbreak and his displeasure with how it was being handled by the Navy. He communicated that "we are not at

Captain Crozier speaking to the sailors on the deck of their vessel. U.S. Navy photo by Mass Communication Specialist Seaman Alexander Williams

war. Sailors do not need to die. If we do not act now, we are failing to properly take care of our most trusted asset—our Sailors."[27] His letter was ultimately leaked to the mainstream media.

Crozier was relieved of his duty by then-acting Secretary of the Navy, Thomas Modly. Modly told reporters, "While I do take issue with the validity of some of the points in Captain Crozer's letter, he was absolutely correct in raising them. It was the way in which he did it . . . that was unacceptable to me."[28] Modly and others see Crozier's actions as disobeying the chain of command. Although many people believe that Crozier did the right thing to protect his sailors, his actions apparently violated communication norms within the military. As of our writing, we do not know who leaked the Captain's letter.[29]

All media have their own advantages and disadvantages, and there are a few different criteria to consider when choosing the right medium.[30] For instance, texts and tweets require the writer to be brief and precise, and like e-mails (which generally are brief), they provide a record of the communication that in-person and phone communication don't. They can also be sent almost without regard to time-zone differences. But unlike voice, video call, and in-person messages, written communications often fail to convey nuances of meaning through tone of voice and body language, and thus they can more easily be misinterpreted. Many a manager has discovered that a simple phone call can cut through layers of misinterpreted e-mails.

We can generally categorize differences between communication media in terms of whether a given medium is *rich* or *lean*. What does this mean?

Is a Medium Rich or Lean in Information?   Media richness indicates how well a particular medium conveys information and promotes learning. That is, the "richer" a medium is, the better it is at conveying information.[31] The term *media richness* was proposed by respected organizational theorists Richard Daft and Robert Lengel as part of their contingency model for media selection.[32]

Types of media can be positioned along a continuum ranging from high to low media richness, as shown in Figure 15.2.

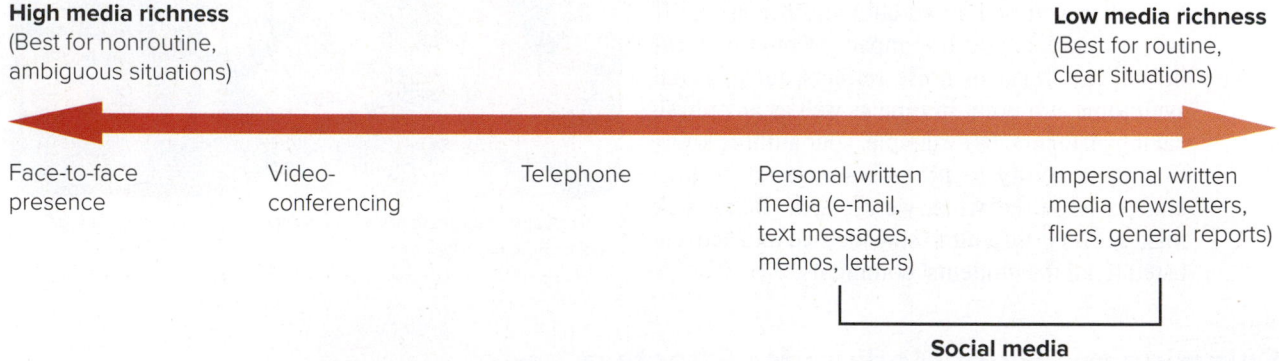

High media richness
(Best for nonroutine, ambiguous situations)

Low media richness
(Best for routine, clear situations)

Face-to-face presence

Video-conferencing

Telephone

Personal written media (e-mail, text messages, memos, letters)

Impersonal written media (newsletters, fliers, general reports)

Social media

FIGURE 15.2   Contingency model of media selection

Face-to-face communication, also the most personal form of communication, is the richest. It allows the receiver of the message to observe multiple cues, such as body language and tone of voice. It allows the sender to get immediate feedback, to see how well the receiver comprehended the message. At the other end of the media richness scale, impersonal written media are just the reverse—only one cue and no feedback—making them low in richness.

As you might expect, people have preferences for the type of medium they like to use, and they have different perceptions of the richness of the same medium.[33] Males and people with extroverted and agreeable personality characteristics tend to use media high in richness. Contrary to stereotypes, age has no impact on media richness preference.[34] What are your preferences?

Matching the Appropriate Medium to the Appropriate Situation
In general, the following guidelines are useful.[35]

Rich Medium: Best for Nonroutine Situations and to Avoid Oversimplification
A *rich* medium is more effective with nonroutine situations. Examples: In what way would you like your boss to inform you of a nonroutine change, like the introduction of a new employee benefit? Via a memo tacked on the bulletin board (a lean medium)? Or via a face-to-face meeting or phone call (a rich medium)?

The danger of using a rich medium for routine matters (such as monthly sales reports) is that it results in *information overload*—the delivery of more information than necessary.

Lean Medium: Best for Routine Situations and to Avoid Overloading
A *lean* medium is more effective in routine situations. Examples: In what manner would you as a sales manager like to get routine monthly sales reports from your 50 sales reps? Via time-consuming phone calls (a somewhat rich medium)? Or via e-mails or text messages (a somewhat lean medium)? The danger of using a lean medium for nonroutine matters (such as an announcement of a company reorganization) is that it results in information *oversimplification*—it doesn't provide enough of the information the receiver needs and wants.

E-mail and social media like Facebook, LinkedIn, and Twitter vary in media richness, being leaner if they impersonally blanket a large audience and are anonymous (or posted under a screen name), and richer if they mix personal textual and video information that prompts quick conversational feedback.[36] We discuss social media in Section 15.4.

The Example box illustrates how two hospitals incorporated a contingency approach when communicating with their stakeholders during the COVID-19 pandemic. ●

EXAMPLE — Two Health Systems Use a Contingency Approach to Communication During the COVID-19 Pandemic

Orest Holubec, senior vice president/chief communication officer at Providence St. Joseph Health System, in Renton, Washington, and Catherine Harrell, chief marketing officer for Franciscan Missionaries of Our Lady Health System in Baton Rouge, Louisiana, discussed with a reporter how their hospitals communicated during the pandemic.

Holubec: Providence St. Joseph Health relied upon multiple media channels when communicating with various stakeholders. The first decision was to use cable news to communicate with external stakeholders. The organization did this because it had identified the first U.S. case of the COVID-19 pandemic and it wanted to quickly reach the largest audience it could with reliable information. The hospital also employed social media to communicate with the public due to its large number of followers on this medium.

The health system expended additional effort communicating with external stakeholders. This consisted of personal appearances by the CEO on CNN and other national news channels as well as regular podcasts from the CEO.

Providence St. Joseph used a different communication strategy with its employees. It began with daily operational meetings that included internal staff from the clinical, communications, and operations side of the business. They also instituted a daily 7:30 a.m. call with about 300 employees across the seven states in which the hospital operates to obtain reliable information about what was happening in each of its hospitals. This was followed by a daily huddle meeting with 50 to 60 members of the communications team to determine how and when to communicate what was learned from these meetings to the 120,000 caregivers employed by the organization.

E-mail, SharePoint, and an app employees had on their smartphones were used to provide employees with timely and relevant information. Social media also was populated with information because many of the employees were followers.

Harrell: Franciscan Missionaries of Our Lady Health System employed a very proactive and open approach toward communication. Communication with external stakeholders focused on local market media outlets at the beginning of the pandemic because of the hospital's great working relationships with them. Physicians, for example, made daily appearances on TV stations to answer viewer-submitted questions. Social media, including blogs and infographics, also were used to answer the public's most frequently asked questions.

Internal communications with employees were proactive and transparent. Harrel noted that the communication goal was to "provide information to the organization before they have questions and certainly to update information in this quickly changing environment." The chief medical officer distributed a daily e-mail update with pertinent information, including "the latest number of cases in both Louisiana and Mississippi, any procedural changes such as PPE (personal protective equipment) conservation efforts, supply chain updates, mission and HR with an emphasis on resources and resilience."[37] The intranet was used to publicize hospital resources and to answer employees' questions. Daily "town halls" were used to provide live dial-in opportunities for employees to communicate with management.

Finally, the CEO relied on daily operational meetings with executives and a weekly phone call for all leaders to enhance the richness of his communications. He also conducted podcasts in order to reach all employees.[38]

YOUR CALL

To what extent did these two health organizations adhere to the recommendations about matching the communication medium to the situation at hand?

15.2 How Managers Fit into the Communication Process

THE BIG PICTURE

Formal communication channels follow the chain of command, which consists of three types—vertical, horizontal, and external. Informal communication channels develop outside the organization's formal structure. One example is the grapevine. Another, face-to-face communication, builds trust and depends heavily on managers' effective listening skills.

LO 15-2

Compare communication channels and appropriate ways for managers to use them.

If you've ever had a low-level job in nearly any kind of organization, you know that there is generally a hierarchy of management between you and the organization's president, director, or CEO. If you had a suggestion that you wanted him or her to hear, you certainly had to go up through management channels. That's formal communication. However, you may have run into that top manager in the elevator. Or in the restroom. Or in a line at the movie theatre. You could have voiced your suggestion casually then. That's informal communication.

Formal Communication Channels: Up, Down, Sideways, and Outward

Formal communication channels are recognized as official. The organization chart we described in Chapter 8 indicates how official communications—memos, letters, reports, announcements—are supposed to be routed.

Formal communication is of three types: (1) *vertical*—meaning upward and downward, (2) *horizontal*—meaning laterally (sideways), and (3) *external*—meaning outside the organization.

1. Vertical Communication: Up and Down the Chain of Command
Vertical communication is the flow of messages up and down the hierarchy within the organization: bosses communicating with subordinates, subordinates communicating with

bosses. As you might expect, the more management levels through which a message passes, the more it is prone to some distortion.

- **Downward communication—from top to bottom. Downward communication** flows from a higher level to a lower level (or levels). In small organizations, top-down communication may be delivered face-to-face. In larger organizations, it's delivered via meetings, e-mail, official memos, company publications, and town hall meetings. Downward communication became quite difficult during the COVID-19 pandemic due to the closure of offices and the fears associated with the pandemic. Fran Caradonna, CEO of the Saint Louis Brewery, which produces Schlafly beer, used companywide e-mails with the subject line "Be Well" to communicate about the state of the business and to show compassion. Cisco Systems' CEO Chuck Robbins similarly comforted his employees through the use of weekly all-company videoconference calls.[39]

Upward bound. How do you communicate with a manager two or three levels above you in the organization's hierarchy? You can send a memo through channels. Or you can watch for informal opportunities like this when a manager heads for a cup of coffee. Jacobs Stock Photography/Getty Images

- **Upward communication—from bottom to top. Upward communication** flows from a lower level to a higher level(s). Often, this type of communication is from a subordinate to his or her immediate manager, who in turn will relay it up to the next level, if necessary. It is very important to share updates via e-mail, phone, or videoconferencing with your boss if you work virtually. That said, whether or not you work virtually or physically near your boss, we recommend asking your manager how they would like to stay in touch. Some managers prefer seeing you rather than receiving an e-mail.[40] All told, effective upward communication depends on an atmosphere of trust and psychological safety.[41] Employees are less likely to pass on bad news when they don't trust the boss.

Types of downward and upward communication are shown below. *(See Table 15.1.)*

TABLE 15.1   Types of Downward and Upward Communication

Downward Communication

Most downward communication involves one of the following kinds of information:

- Instructions related to particular job tasks. Example (supervisor to subordinate): "The store will close Monday for inventory. All employees are expected to participate."
- Explanations about the relationship between two or more tasks. Example: A manager may request an employee to complete a task ahead of schedule because another department needs the output before it can begin working on a critical task.
- Explanations of the organization's policies, practices, and procedures. Example: "The human resources department sends an e-mail blast about new benefits or procedures for taking vacations."
- A manager's feedback about a subordinate's performance. Example: "You missed the project deadline by two days, which impacted the team's ability to meet the customer's needs. Let's discuss the reason for this."
- Attempts to encourage a sense of mission and dedication to the organization's goals. Example: "Manager calls team meeting to discuss how the team is contributing to company's strategic goals."

Upward Communication

Most upward communication involves the following kinds of information:

- Reports of progress on current projects. Example: "We are three hours behind in taking inventory. What can we do to catch up?"
- Reports of unsolved problems requiring help from people higher up in the organization. Example: "We can't complete our tasks because we need input from another department."
- New developments affecting the work unit. Example: "Two employees want to take vacation the same week. How would you like to handle this?"
- Suggestions for improvements. Example: "Can you help me interpret results on this spreadsheet?"
- Reports on employee attitudes and efficiency. Example: "Our customer satisfaction scores have gone down over the last year. Let's schedule a department meeting to create a plan of action."

Sources: Adapted from D. Katz and R. Kahn, The Social Psychology of Organizations *(New York: Wiley, 1966); and E. Planty and W. Machaver, "Upward Communications: A Project in Executive Development,"* Personnel *Vol. 28 (1952), pp. 304–318.*

2. Horizontal Communication: Within and between Work Units   ==Horizontal communication== flows within and between work units; its main purpose is coordination. As a manager, you will spend perhaps as much as a third of your time in this form of communication—consulting with colleagues and co-workers at the same level as you within the organization. In this kind of sideways communication, you will be sharing information, coordinating tasks, solving problems, resolving conflicts, and getting the support of your peers. Horizontal communication is encouraged through the use of meetings, committees, task forces, and matrix structures.

This form of communication is particularly important because it is essential for innovation.[42] Unfortunately, horizontal communication is impeded by four causes:

1. Specialization that makes people focus on only their jobs rather than on collaboration.

2. Competition or rivalry between workers or work units can prevent sharing of information.

3. An organizational culture that does not encourage collaboration, cooperation, or innovation.

4. Incentive systems that reward individual behavior over collaboration detract from sharing information or resources.

3. External Communication: Outside the Organization   ==External communication== flows between people inside and outside the organization. This form of communication is increasingly important because organizations desire to communicate with other stakeholders—customers, suppliers, shareholders, or other owners—in pursuit of their strategic goals. Small business owners in particular rely on external communication to help grow their businesses. This was particularly important for Jennifer Hyman, CEO and co-founder of Rent the Runway.

Jennifer Hyman observing operations in the Rent the Runway warehouse. George Etheredge/The New York Times/Redux Pictures

Rent the Runway Example: Rent the Runway, located in New York, is an online service providing designer dresses and accessories for rent. The company has about 1,150 employees and $44 million in revenue. Hyman took special effort to communicate with customers and other external stakeholders during the COVID-19 pandemic to promote business. You can imagine customers' reluctance to rent a dress during the pandemic given that the garment was recently worn by someone else. Clearly, this crisis could be deadly for this company. Hyman recognized the problem and decided to reassure customers about the safety procedures being used to clean the clothing. She relied on social media to get the message out to current and potential customers that the cleaning processes being used were based on scientific research conducted by the CDC.[43]

Informal Communication Channels

==Informal communication channels== develop outside the formal structure and do not follow the chain of command—they are more spontaneous, can skip management levels, and can cut across lines of authority.

Two types of informal channels are (1) the *grapevine* and (2) *face-to-face communication.*

The Grapevine   The ==grapevine== is the unofficial communication system of the informal organization, a network of in-person and online gossip and rumor. Workplace gossip can be positive or negative, and it serves important functions.[44] For example, research shows that the grapevine delivers as much as 70% of all organizational communication, although only a little more than half of executives understand that the rumor mill is more active when official communication is lacking. In a recent series of interviews with 800 employees in a range of industries, 47% said that when a speech from a company leader

conflicts with the grapevine, they are more likely to believe the grapevine. Written or online company communications, such as e-mails and newsletters, edged out the grapevine, but only slightly; 51% of those interviewed said they trusted a newsletter more than rumor.[45]

Managers can reduce the negative effects of the grapevine by following these four suggestions:[46]

1. **Rely on an open-door policy.** Employees are less like to gossip when they have direct and easy access to management.

2. **Provide fast and transparent information.** This recommendation is important during a crisis, such as dealing with COVID-19 or during organizational change.

3. **Quickly respond to gossip.** Gossip is like a wildfire. Left untreated, it spreads fast and wide. Managers are encouraged to use both rich and lean communication media to correct erroneous gossip.

4. **Be a role model.** Don't let employees see or hear you gossiping. It's better to demonstrate integrity while proactively communicating with others.

Face-to-Face Communication   Despite the entrenched use of quick and efficient electronic communication in our lives, face-to-face conversation is still justifiably a major part of most people's workday. Employees value authentic human contact with the boss and welcome the implication that their manager cares about them. Face time builds relationships and trust, shows respect for employees as individuals, and thus is highly motivating. Netflix CEO Reed Hastings doesn't have an office at all. "I just had no need for it," he says. "It is better for me to be meeting people all around the building."[47]

Some basic principles apply to making the most of face-to-face communication in the work environment.

1. **Make time for face-to-face.** Rather than hoping to catch people at random, schedule time with individual employees, and make sure you'll both be free of distractions (including cell phones) for the few minutes your interaction will take. This is not the moment to multi-task.

2. **Listen more and talk less.** Listen not just to the words the other person is saying, but also to the emotional content behind the words. Make eye contact and observe body language. This will help you be empathetic, a topic discussed in the last section of this chapter. When it's your turn to speak, be brief. If your message is specific or factual, prepare your facts and outline your thoughts ahead of time. Expect questions and be prepared with answers.

3. **Be mindful and show interest.** We have mentioned several times in this textbook how important it is to be mindful and stay in the moment. This is extremely important in face-to-face conversations because it enhances your listening skills while demonstrating interest. Asking questions and using nonverbal cues like nodding are good ways to stay mindful and show interest.

4. **Hold employee town hall meetings.** For in-person meetings with groups of employees, "town hall" meetings, often held monthly or quarterly, usually consist of a presentation by managers and an open question-and-answer session. Town hall meetings also can be held virtually. Apple CEO Tim Cook, for example, held a virtual town hall meeting in 2020 to allow employees to pose questions about the effects of the pandemic on the company. Cook told participants, "If we stay focused on doing what we do best, if we keep investing, if we manage the business wisely and make decisions collaboratively, if we take care of our teams, if our teams take care of their work, I don't see any reason to be anything but optimistic."[48]

Meetings are probably the most frequently used mechanism for communicating formally or informally with a group of people. They can be held virtually or face-to-face, and we're sure you have attended them in the past. How many of them produced useful results or conclusions? Probably not too many if you believe a report in *Inc.* magazine.

Experts estimated that bad meetings cost $399 billion in the U.S. and $58 billion in the UK in 2019.[49] Let's consider how you can improve these stats when you next attend or lead a meeting (see the Practical Action box). ●

PRACTICAL ACTION   Tips for Improving Meetings

So what makes for a good meeting? One expert suggested that effective meetings should "feel like five friends having a conversation over coffee."[50] We're not sure about this description. Another proposed that they should produce results by having "high participation, good energy, constructive collaboration, and meaningful conversations."[51] Now we can get behind this description. Here are some tips for making this happen.

What to Do as a Meeting Leader[52]

1. **It all starts with a purpose.** Before you call a meeting, ask yourself what specific task or tasks you want the meeting to accomplish. Write these down in the form of an agenda with time limits for each point, leaving brief time slots for attendees' input and discussion. Creating an agenda does more than keep you on track; it helps others know what they should prepare for the meeting, saving valuable time.

2. **Invite the appropriate people.** The list of attendees needs to fit the task at hand. Participants should be there for a clear purpose and should possess the necessary knowledge or expertise to participate. Don't fall prey to inviting everybody and their sister to the meeting.

3. **Pick a good day and time to meet.** Surveys reveal that Mondays and Fridays are the least favorite days to meet while Tuesday and Wednesday are most preferred. Results also suggest that people prefer to meet in the morning or right before lunch. Very few like evening meetings.[53] Don't assume these findings fit your situation. The point is to ask participants for their preferences and select the best day and time.

4. **Start the meeting effectively.** This can be done by:
   - Provide a brief opening welcome.
   - State the purpose and goals for the meeting.
   - Motivate participation by noting that participants were selected because you or the organization needs their input and wisdom to achieve the goal.
   - Take time for introductions if everyone does not know each other.
   - Introduce ground rules or meeting norms if this is a new group.
   - Review the agenda.

5. **Start and end on time.** Respect other people's time commitments. Be the first in the meeting room and start when you said you would. Stick to the time limits you've allowed for each agenda item and keep your eye on the clock. Learn how to gently but firmly cut off unproductive discussion. ("Thanks for your contribution, Jay. Let's quickly hear from one more person before we move on to the next point.")

6. **Put extraneous issues in a parking lot.** Meetings often lead to conversations about important issues that go beyond the purpose of the meetings. Rather than being distracted by them during your meeting, put them in the metaphorical parking lot. The parking lot is a recording of these issues on a white board, flip chart, or digital notes. It is a good idea to discuss next steps for items in the parking lot at the end of your meeting.

7. **Follow up.** Within 24 hours of the meeting, clarify results and expectations by sending attendees a summary of decisions made, tasks to be performed, and who is to perform them and when.

What to Do as a Meeting Participant

1. **Prepare but stay flexible.** Respond promptly to the meeting invitation. Read the agenda (ask for one if you don't receive it ahead of time) and be prepared with any facts or data you may be called upon to present. You should also prepare to be flexible because meetings don't always go as planned. For example, if you have 15 minutes scheduled to present, prepare both a full presentation and a shortened one in case your time is limited.

2. **Be on time.** Showing up late is disrespectful and disruptive. It can also make the meeting run over time if the leader decides to wait for you.

3. **Participate intelligently.** Expect to contribute to the meeting, but make sure your contributions are brief, professional, and on point. Ask questions that start with "how" and "what" rather than "why." These types of questions don't put people on the defensive or delve into fact finding. Instead, they encourage colleagues to open up and think expansively.[54]

4. **Follow up.** If you came away from the meeting with a to-do list, be sure you act on it in a timely way so the goals of the meeting can be achieved. You may even be able to avoid having to attend another meeting to go over the same agenda all over again.

YOUR CALL

To what extent have you used these suggestions in past meetings? Do you see any problems in following these suggestions?

15.3 Barriers to Communication

THE BIG PICTURE

We describe several barriers to communication. Physical barriers include sound, time, and space. Personal barriers include variations in communication skills, processing and interpreting information, trustworthiness and credibility, attentional issues, and generational considerations. Cross-cultural barriers are a greater challenge as more jobs include interactions with others around the globe. Nonverbal communication can present a barrier if it conflicts with the spoken message. Finally, gender differences can present barriers but can be overcome.

If you have ever been served the wrong drink because the server couldn't hear you in a loud restaurant, clicked on a broken web link, missed your boarding call because the airport's public address system was full of static, or taken offense at a text you later found you misinterpreted, you've experienced a barrier to communication. Communication barriers produce noise (discussed in Section 15.1) that interferes with how messages are transmitted or understood, and barriers can occur within any step of the communication process, as shown in Table 15.2.

LO 15-3

Identify barriers to communication and ways managers can overcome them.

TABLE 15.2 **How Barriers Happen in Various Steps of the Communication Process**

All it takes is one blocked step in the communication process for communication to fail. Consider the following.

- **Sender barrier—no message gets sent.** Example: If a manager has an idea but is afraid to voice it because he or she fears criticism, then obviously no message gets sent.

- **Encoding barrier—the message is not expressed correctly.** Example: If people have a different first language, the meaning of words can be misinterpreted.

- **Medium barrier—the communication channel is blocked.** Example: When a computer network is down, the network is an example of a blocked medium.

- **Decoding barrier—the recipient doesn't understand the message.** Example: You pulled an all-nighter traveling back from spring break and today your brain is fuzzy and unfocused during class lectures.

- **Receiver barrier—no message gets received.** Example: Because you were texting during a class lecture, you weren't listening when the professor announced a new assignment due to tomorrow.

- **Feedback barrier—the recipient doesn't respond enough.** Example: You give someone driving directions, but since they only nod their heads and don't repeat the directions back to you, you don't really know whether you were understood.

Consider the idea of fake news—a concept we discuss in detail in Section 15.4—and how biases related to it can surface at multiple steps of the communication process:

- Encoding—sender purposefully distorts the information that is communicated.
- Medium—news outlets fail to report important information.
- Receiver—various groups interpret the information according to personal biases rather than making an assessment of whether the information is factual.

Have you ever tried to communicate only to wind up feeling like the people in this photo? If so, you are not alone. Common communication barriers can make even the simplest exchanges difficult. pathdoc/Shutterstock

- Feedback—receiver fails to comment on an issue because they know you have a different perspective.

In this section we'll look at several types of communication barriers—physical, personal, cross-cultural, nonverbal, and gender differences.

1. Physical Barriers: Sound, Time, Space

Try shouting at someone over the roar of a crowd at a concert and you know what physical communication barriers are. Physical communication barriers consist of things in your physical environment that prevent effective communication. They include:

- *Technology issues* such as crashed laptops or phone reception problems.
- *Noise* such as others talking over you or construction sounds.
- *Physical distance* which presents a barrier when there is either too much of it or not enough of it for the people involved in the communication.

   Too much physical distance might present a communication barrier. For example, for people who prefer to work in an office and spend face-to-face time with colleagues, working from home and communicating over Zoom or other meeting platforms can make communication difficult.

   Not enough physical distance might present a communication barrier. For example, for people who have trouble concentrating, open plan offices can be challenging. These floor plans can provide workspaces that are well-lit and airy, are cheap to construct, and make it easier to include others in impromptu meetings and discussions. But they can be noisy and full of distractions, and people may feel unable to escape being "on" all day because they have less privacy than they would like.[55] (Refer back to the Example box in Chapter 2 for more on what the data say about the effectiveness of open offices.)

Imagine yourself working in each of these environments. How do you think the physical barriers that accompany working from home would affect your ability to communicate with coworkers? How about the physical barriers that arise in open plan offices? Which of these work environments would present more physical barriers for you, personally? Rawpixel.com/Shutterstock; Cathy Yeulet/123RF

2. Personal Barriers: Individual Attributes That Hinder Communication

"Is it them or is it me?" How often have you wondered, when someone has shown a surprising response to something you said, how the miscommunication happened? Let's examine five personal barriers that contribute to miscommunication.

Variable Skills in Communicating Effectively Merriam-Webster recently added the abbreviation "TL;DR" to its dictionary. It stands for "too long; didn't read," and its popularity highlights our increased desire for efficient communication. Chances are you have worked with people who are great at communicating effectively and efficiently and with people who are not so great at these things. Two important points about variable communication skills are:

- **Some people are simply better communicators than others.** They have the vocabulary, the writing ability, the speaking skills, the facial expressions, the eye contact, the dramatic ability, and the social skills to express themselves in a superior way. Some managers can communicate a project update in a three-sentence e-mail, while others write three paragraphs.

- **Better communication skills can be learned.**[56] The final section in this chapter discusses a variety of ways you can improve your communication effectiveness.

Variations in the Way We Process and Interpret Information Because communication is a perceptual process in which people use different frames of reference and experiences to interpret the world around them, they are selective about which things have meaning to them and which do not. These frames of references are associated with individual differences such as age, political affiliation, religious affiliation, values, beliefs, and education. These differences affect what information we attend to and how we interpret it, what we think we hear, and how we respond. The point is that we all have a natural tendency, according to psychologist Carl Rogers, to judge others' statements from our own point of view (especially if we have strong feelings about the issue).[57]

Let's consider what you can do to reduce distortions in information processing:

- **Senders can avoid misinterpretation by communicating clearly.** What differentiates effective communicators, according to HR and management consultant Susan Heathfield, is their understanding that ensuring the receiver's correct interpretation of the intended message is in large part up to the sender. "The sender must present the message clearly and with enough detail so that the receiver shares meaning with the sender during and following the communication."[58]

- **Receivers can avoid misinterpretation by paraphrasing.** Communication barriers can occur when receivers incorrectly decode messages. One way for receivers to avoid this is to use paraphrasing—discussed in Section 15.1—to succinctly restate the sender's message to ensure they have properly interpreted the meaning of the message. As a bonus, the act of paraphrasing requires you to use critical thinking—an indispensable career readiness competency.

Variations in Trustworthiness and Credibility Without trust between you and the other person, communication is apt to be flawed. Instead of communicating, both of you will be concentrating on defensive tactics, not the meaning of the message being exchanged. Consider the impact of these issues on employees and organizations and how you can use trust to improve communications:

- **Low trust damages communication.** Which in turn reduces outcomes like job satisfaction, openness to change, engagement, citizenship behavior, and performance.[59]

- **Focus on building a trusting foundation.** The solution, says leadership development expert Joseph Folkman, is to build trust first. "Trust is a critical element in effective communications. Often when leaders need to make an important presentation, they will spend a great deal of time and effort working on their delivery and making sure they have the right content," Folkman said. He added, ". . . research reveals that they also ought to spend time on ensuring that they have . . . high levels of trust."[60]

Does this photo look familiar to you? For many of us, working on multiple devices at once and juggling several tasks simultaneously have become the norm. When was the last time you worked, mindfully, on just one thing at a time? JGI/Tom Grill/Getty Images

Attentional Issues   Do you find your mind wandering over the course of a day? Do you forget people's names shortly after meeting them? These are signs of mindlessness. <mark>Mindlessness</mark> is a state of reduced attention. It is expressed in behavior that seems rigid or thoughtless.[61]

Many of us are in a constant state of cognitive overload. Life's dynamics put all of us into occasional states of mindlessness. Our brains simply can't keep up with all the stimuli we receive, according to clinical psychologist Vincent Greenwood. "While we've never had more tools for productivity, creativity and problem-solving, we've never been so overwhelmed—constantly bombarded by alerts, messages and the demand to master the next new technological breakthroughs," said Greenwood. He said our constant state of cognitive overload results in a "neural buzz experience of trying to walk up a downward moving escalator, which leaves one feeling frustrated, disempowered and worn out."[62]

Here are two things you can do to reduce the impact of attentional issues on communications:

- **Try focusing on one thing at a time.** One way many of us deal with modern life is by multitasking. But, warns neuroscientist Dr. Michael J. Levitin, doing so lowers the quality of each task we complete. Our brains aren't wired to pay close attention to multiple tasks at once, and the more tasks we try to juggle, the more mindless we become.

- **Take a (digital) break.** Another barrier to listening, ironically, is cell phones. If we're looking at our screens all the time, how can we really be listening to those who are right before us?[63] One way that we can safeguard our cognitive resources and ability to be mindful in communication is to take periodic breaks not only from our endless tasks, but also from our cell phones, even when we are not in direct communication with others. A recent study of 414 people found that those who took a break from tasks but remained on their phones performed worse on subsequent tasks than those who took any other type of break. "Cell phone breaks resulted in the same levels of cognitive depletion as not taking any break at all," according to the study researchers.[64]

Generational Differences   If you've tried to teach an older relative how to text or use Instagram Stories, you may have some appreciation for how difficult it can be for older generations to adapt to new technologies. On the other hand, U.S. Senator Bernie Sanders, age 79, maintains an active Twitter feed with more than 9 million followers.[65] Here are some key points about generational communication differences in the modern workplace:

- **Younger generations are growing less likely to use e-mail.** With office norms generally becoming less formal and younger generations of workers moving into the workplace, a preference has grown for platforms like Slack and Microsoft Teams over traditional e-mail. Many members of older generations still prefer to use e-mail.[66]

- **Oldest and youngest employees are most open to embracing new technology.** A recent survey of over 3,000 workers in seven countries found that while, as expected, 18- to 24-year-old workers were most receptive to adopting new technologies at work, 55- to 74-year-old workers ranked second-highest in terms of this "digital dexterity." Interestingly, middle-aged workers were least open to using new technologies.[67]

- **Organizations should provide training and support.** Regardless of whether they are dealing with new technology or new employees who need to learn existing technology, organizations should provide plenty of support and training for workers to help keep them up to date on using these communication tools.

3. Cross-Cultural Barriers

As we discussed in Chapter 2, culture refers to the shared practices, values, ideas, and objects that bind a collective—such as a society—and that foster a sense of order and stability in members' lives and interactions.[68]

Culture naturally affects the way we communicate with those who share our culture and those who don't because the norms and beliefs of our cultures are so deeply ingrained in our thoughts and behaviors. Language and style differences are two ways that culture can become a communication barrier:

- **Language differences.** One obvious reason is that language differences often exist. For example, jokes and humor are very much linked to culture.[69] One of your authors found that good American jokes don't necessarily get laughs in Europe, Asia, and Scandinavia. Even the United States and Great Britain, whose cultures share many elements, are often said to be "two countries divided by a common language" (an ironic observation often attributed to the British playwright George Bernard Shaw). For example, if a British supervisor tells you that your work is "quite good," for example, don't get too excited—it means your work is average, at best.[70]

- **Style differences.** Communication styles can vary widely by culture and knowing what to expect gives workers a great advantage. Preparation is the key, as evidenced by the following example.

  Dutch Training Example: A U.S. executive for a coffee company recently received 50 hours of language training for an assignment in the Netherlands, even though English is widely spoken there. The payoff? "I do not take the [Dutch] cultural norm of the direct and very honest communication style personally," the executive said. "Therefore, I do not overreact to questions or communications that others may find offensive or confrontational. This has helped me build very positive relationships, as I assume positive intent regarding the content of the communication, and never get side-tracked based on the style of communication."[71]

See the Practical Action box for tips on improving your cross-cultural communication.

PRACTICAL ACTION | Improving Your Cross-Cultural Communication Fluency

Dr. Elizabeth Tuleja—professor of intercultural communication and global leadership at the University of Notre Dame—said, "You can know all the functional aspects of international business. But if you don't know how to develop relationships and understand people based upon their norms and behavior and what they expect from you, then you're not going to be as successful."[72] This lesson is valuable whether you are working in a foreign country or domestically, because the American workforce is more culturally diverse than ever.

It's natural for cultural differences to make us feel somewhat uncomfortable at first. But Dr. Tuleja suggests we view them as the chance to grow both ourselves and our organizations, saying, "we must be able to embrace such differences and acknowledge them as opportunities for learning and enrichment rather than forces for confusion and trouble."

Here are suggestions for improving your cross-cultural communication abilities:[73]

Prepare Yourself Ahead of Time There are plenty of resources available to help you get better at communicating across cultures. For example, you can find podcasts, articles, books, and online learning programs on this topic. You can also talk with friends and family members who have experience with cross-cultural communication. Learn everything you can on your own, first.

Observe One of the best ways to learn something is to simply watch others. If you want to know how to communicate with someone from a particular culture, pay attention when two or more people from that culture communicate with one another. Observe body language; notice how close they stand to each other while communicating; and listen for things like tone, specific words, and the pace of the conversation.

Be Genuinely Curious Have you ever avoided interacting with someone from a different culture because you were afraid of making a mistake and offending them? This is natural, but unfortunately, it causes many of us to miss out on opportunities for understanding, productive working relationships, and friendships. You should know that if you ask questions about another person's culture with a genuine sense of curiosity and an authentic desire to learn more about them, most people will be happy to help you understand their culture better. Said communication skills expert Pellegrino Riccardi, "If someone's genuinely curious about you, it creates a human bond, a human connection." He added, "You can't build trust without people being brave enough and honest enough and tuned into each other . . . cultural fluency is showing genuine interest in other people who have a different story . . . it's no more advanced than that."[74]

Know That You Will Make (Lots of) Mistakes The way that we communicate is deeply ingrained, and you should expect that no matter how much cultural communication training you participate in or expertise you build, you are going to continue to make mistakes. One of your authors—Denise Breaux Soignet—knows this first hand. Denise teaches both students and organizations about workplace religious inclusion and accommodation, yet when a local Imam—whom she had not yet met—walked into her classroom to spend the day talking with her students about Islam, Denise instinctively and enthusiastically stuck out her hand for a handshake as she introduced herself. The Imam graciously bowed and explained that he did not shake hands with women other than his family members and his wife. It turned out to be a great learning opportunity for the students—Denise and the Imam talked about it with the class for several minutes to explain the *why* behind the communication difference (because the Imam saw it as a sign of respect for women) and to demonstrate that it's ok to make mistakes in cross-cultural communication, no matter how much knowledge and experience you have.

YOUR CALL

How can you do a better job of improving your cross-cultural communication?

4. Nonverbal Communication: How Unwritten and Unspoken Messages May Mislead

==Nonverbal communication== consists of messages sent outside of the written or spoken word. We primarily express nonverbal communication through (1) *eye contact*, (2) *facial expressions*, (3) *body movements and gestures*, and (4) *touch*.[75] Some research suggests that about half of what we communicate is transmitted nonverbally.[76]

1. Eye Contact
Westerners use eye contact to signal the beginning and end of a conversation, to reflect interest and attention, and to convey both honesty and respect.[77] Most people from Western cultures tend to avoid eye contact when conveying bad news or negative feedback. In many Eastern cultures, however, lowering one's eyes is a sign of respect.[78] Incorrectly interpreting these nonverbal communications as evasive behavior could lead to unfortunate misunderstandings.

2. Facial Expressions
A search of Reddit forums on how to identify someone as an American is likely to return one answer over and over—they're smiling.[79] You're probably used to thinking that smiling represents warmth, happiness, or friendship, whereas frowning represents dissatisfaction or anger. But people in some cultures are less openly demonstrative than people in the United States.[80] One study showed photographs of facial expressions to thousands of people in 44 countries. Among the findings were that, in cultures with low uncertainty avoidance (see Chapter 4), people judged smiling faces as indicating untrustworthiness and possibly even lower intelligence. One U.S. novelist reported in *The New York Times* that when she smiled too much during a visit to Hong Kong, the woman she was speaking to stepped away from her in alarm.[81]

Russia Example: In Russia, smiling for no reason isn't common. Russian film director Yulia Melamed said she was once stopped by police because she was smiling while walking around. She added, "It's strange for a person to walk down the street and smile. It looks alien and suspicious." This is why, ahead of the 2018 World Cup, Russian organizations including FIFA, Russian Railways, and Moscow Metro conducted smiling training for employees so that they would seem more welcoming to foreign visitors.[82]

If you were raised in the U.S. then you've probably internalized the belief that smiling at others is expected as part of polite communication. But did you know that in many places across the globe, people find smiling odd, distracting, and even suspicious? Max Bukovski/Shutterstock

3. Body Movements and Gestures   Open body positions, such as leaning slightly backward, express openness, warmth, closeness, and availability for communication. Closed body positions, such as folded arms or crossed legs, can signal defensiveness. Angling your body away from the other person generally makes you look uninterested.[83] You can use these conclusions to improve communications with others.

4. Touch   Norms for touching vary significantly. For example, kissing on the cheek, patting on the shoulder, and hugging may seem appropriate in business for some people, but others find these actions offensive in a professional context. Said behavioral psychologist Denise Dudley, "I don't want to live in a world where we outlaw hugging in the workplace . . . But we also need a world where we all feel comfortable."[84] As with physical touch in other realms of life, there should always be mutual consent for physical affection at work. Beyond this important rule, a few general guidelines are:[85]

- **Observe how others behave.** Take the time to learn the norms in your workplace.

- **Be mindful of power dynamics.** If you have power over an employee and you ask them for permission to hug or kiss on the cheek, they may feel pressured to oblige even if they are uncomfortable. A good rule is to limit this kind of affection to colleagues on the same level.

- **Set your own boundaries and respect those of others.** Practice how you will communicate your comfort level with physical affection. For example, "I'm so glad to see you, and I'm not a hugger," or "thank you, but I'd prefer an elbow bump to a kiss on the cheek," work just fine. Remember to be respectful of the physical boundaries that others set for themselves, too.

5. Gender Differences

According to scientific evidence, we can make two general statements about gender and communication differences: (1) there are some observable differences in communication across the gender spectrum and (2) most of these differences likely are the result of socialization rather than biology.[86] In other words, people of different genders do tend to have different communication styles and make different communication choices, and they do this because they've been conditioned to do so.

What does this mean for managers? Broadly, managers should be aware that communication choices may reflect gender norms and should use this understanding to enhance and improve communications in their workplaces. Table 15.3 presents a comparison of masculine and feminine communication norms. These represent the social expectations for gendered communication that are prevalent in the United States.

Exchange of views? Men and women have different communication styles. How effective do you think you are at communicating with the opposite sex? Shutterstock

TABLE 15.3   Gender and Communication: Masculine and Feminine Social Norms

COMMUNICATION CHARACTERISTIC	MASCULINE NORMS	FEMININE NORMS
Taking credit	Using "I" statements (e.g., "I did this" and "I did that"); boasting about achievements	Using "We" statements, (e.g., "We did this" and "We did that"); refraining from boasting about achievements
Displaying confidence	Hiding uncertainty about an issue	Revealing a lack of certainty about an issue
Talking patterns	Interrupting and talking over others	Waiting to speak until others are finished
Listening	Listening silently and without the need for positive overlaps such as "I agree" or "that's right" to demonstrate listening	Using positive overlaps such as "I agree" or "That's right" to demonstrate listening while another is speaking
Focus of talk	Reporting. Demonstrating expertise.	Building relationships. Sharing.
Making requests	Directing, such as "this needs to be done by the end of the day."	Asking, such as "would you do this by the end of the day?"

Sources: Derived from A. Nelson and C. D. Brown, The Gender Communication Handbook *(San Francisco: Pfeiffer, 2012); D. Tannen,* You Just Don't Understand: Women and Men in Conversation *(New York: Ballantine Books, 1990); R. Bucher,* Diversity Consciousness: Opening Our Minds to People, Cultures, and Opportunities, *4th ed. (Boston: Pearson, 2015), p. 130.*

Dr. Deborah Tannen, a renowned Georgetown University Linguistics professor, recommends that everyone become aware of how differing linguistic styles affect our perceptions and judgments. A **linguistic style** is a person's characteristic speaking patterns—pacing, pausing, directness, word choice, and use of questions, jokes, stories, apologies, and similar devices. For example, in a meeting, regardless of gender, "those who are comfortable speaking up in groups, who need little or no silence before raising their hands, or who speak out easily without waiting to be recognized are more apt to be heard," she says. "Those who refrain from talking until it's clear that the previous speaker is finished, who wait to be recognized, and who are inclined to link their comments to those of others will do fine at a meeting where everyone else is following the same rules but will have a hard time getting heard in a meeting with people whose styles are more like the first pattern."[87] ●

15.4 Social Media and Management

THE BIG PICTURE

We discuss social media and their use by employees and managers. We then turn our attention to the impact of social media on managers' and organizations' effectiveness, including applications to recruiting, productivity, sales, innovation, and reputation management. We also consider the costs of social media use, such as the effects of cyberloafing, as well as growing concerns about security, privacy, and false information. Finally, we discuss the importance of setting effective social media policies.

LO 15-4

Discuss how managers can successfully use social media to communicate.

Social media, which use web-based and mobile technologies to generate interactive dialogue with members of a network, are woven into every aspect of our lives. We begin our exploration of these technologies by documenting their general use. We then examine the effects of social media on managerial and organizational effectiveness, review the downside of social media, discuss the key impacts of texting on management and organizational behavior, and discuss the need for organizations to develop effective social media policies.

The Use of Social Media Has Changed the Fabric of Our Lives

The widespread use of social media is changing our personal lives, the very nature of how businesses operate, and the principles of management. Consider these three statistics:[88]

- More than half of the world's population, or nearly 3.8 billion people, used social media in 2020. That's an increase of 9.2% from 2019.

- A survey of 529 small business owners found that 3 out of 4 invested in social media advertising in 2019. Overall, businesses spent more than $89 billion on social media advertising in 2019.

- Over 50% of new brands are discovered through public social media feeds.

These figures show the power of social media in today's digital world, but what do you think research has to say about this phenomenon? You may not be surprised to learn that recent studies link a company's effective use of social media to an increase in brand awareness, brand loyalty, and sales.[89] Nike is an example of an organization that has embraced social media.

Nike Example: Oregon-based Nike is one of the most well-known sports apparel and equipment manufacturers in the world. The 73,000-employee company has demonstrated in recent years that it knows how to garner attention through social media. For example, Nike organized a team of three elite runners to try to break a world record by running a marathon in under two hours. The entire race, dubbed #Breaking2, was livestreamed on Facebook and Twitter, putting the brand and its Zoom Superfly Elite shoes in front of fans worldwide. Nobody was able to break the two-hour mark, but #Breaking2 "brought [the Nike] brand back to the heart of what achievement means in sport. It is not about overpaid athletes, Instagram or fashion—it's about pushing the body to its limits," said Ben Davis, an editor at Econsultancy.[90]

Besides the business application of social media, they affect our lives in countless other ways. Consider, for example, the 2019 and ongoing Hong Kong protests over Chinese interference in the semi-autonomous region. Clashes between police and pro-democracy activists became increasingly violent, limiting the press's ability at times to cover potential police brutality. Instead, many Hong Kong college students braved tear gas and water cannons to tweet, livestream, and send updates from the front lines of the demonstrations. Social media became an important tool in both rallying supporters to the fight and also holding police accountable for how they treated protesters.[91]

Social media also can be used to keep people connected across continents and time zones, as well as when they are close by, but conditions make physical interaction dangerous. One such time was during the COVID-19 pandemic when many states limited social events to no more than 10 people. Digital Memorial is an example of an organization that used the power of social media to keep people in touch.

Digital Memorial Example: Digital Memorial operates 14 funeral homes in Kentucky and Indiana. The firm broadcasts funerals on Facebook Live using an iPad so that family and friends can mourn the loss of a loved one virtually. This service became increasingly important when the COVID-19 pandemic hit Kentucky and limitations on social gatherings were implemented. Mourners—many of whom were just down the street—were able to use Digital Memorial's service to watch funerals in real time while adhering to social distancing rules. "With the limited number of folks that we're allowed to gather, it just gives a way of being a participant in the service and paying respects to a loved one," said Digital Memorial's Kent Johnson.[92]

What does data suggest about the use of social media? Figure 15.3 shows the usage of various social networks across different age groups. Those between the ages of 18 and 29 use social media more than any other group, and those over 64 the least. All told, however, it appears all age groups use these platforms, underscoring the need for businesses to use social media tools to engage with stakeholders of all ages. It's no wonder, then, that the communications capabilities of social media continue to grow and expand and that managers need to keep up with their increasing potential.

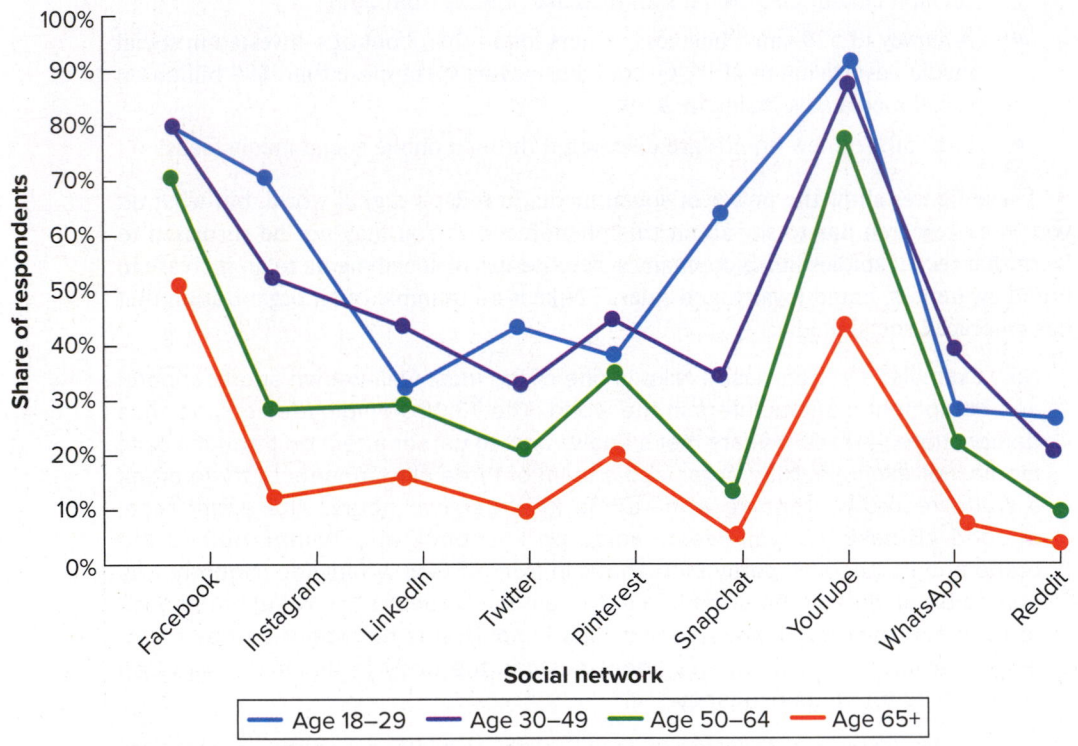

FIGURE 15.3

Age distribution at the top social networks

Source: Data obtained from "Social Media Fact Sheet," Pew Research Center, Internet and Technology, https://www.pewresearch.org/internet/fact-sheet/social-media/ (accessed May 18, 2020).

Moreover, global businesses are using social medial platforms to reach audiences in developing countries around the world. And it's not just a matter of mastering Facebook and Twitter. This is because some governments, including China, actively block their citizens' access to these Western platforms. Instead, global companies need to know which social networks are most popular in different countries and adapt to those. Here is a sampling of popular social media platforms across the world:[93]

- WeChat is China's largest social media platform with over 1 billion monthly active users.
- Facebook lookalike VR is Russia's most popular site with around 100 million monthly active users.
- Latin America favors WhatsApp, which has approximately 415 million users split across 33 countries, including Mexico, Brazil, and Argentina.

Social Media and Managerial and Organizational Effectiveness

With their ease of use, speed, and potential to draw huge audiences, social media have increasing applications for managers' and organizations' effectiveness. We will look at social media use in employment recruiting, employee and employer productivity, innovation, sales, and corporate reputation.

Employment Recruiting   Social media are widely used for recruiting employees. There are four considerations we want you to be aware of with respect to this issue: networks used, research as a job applicant, screening, and legal implications. Let's take a closer look at each of these topics.

- **Networks used:** More than 90% of companies today use social media for recruiting,[94] especially for recruiting "passive" job candidates—that is, those who aren't actively looking for a new job. Although Facebook and LinkedIn have 2.6 billion and 675 million users, respectively, recruiters prefer LinkedIn. A national survey of recruiters revealed that 91% used LinkedIn versus 74% for Facebook.[95] One reason many employers prefer LinkedIn, for instance, is that the platform allows them to filter for specific skill sets that candidates may have.[96] In addition, job applicants and recruiters both like to use text messaging for recruiting purposes.[97]

- **Research as a job applicant:** Investigating companies is part of your preparation for finding a job after graduation. How do you plan to do this? Social media networks are one key source of information you should utilize. For example, anecdotal evidence reveals that a majority of job applicants use social media to conduct research on companies of interest and would consider a new job opportunity if they heard about it through their online network.[98] Many applicants also check industry-specific hosting and social networking platforms. These include:[99]

  GitHub: Online community of more than 50 million software developers. Microsoft purchased GitHub for $7.5 billion in 2018, reflecting the growing importance of industry-specific social media platforms.

  Dribbble: Tens of millions of web designers visit Dribbble to showcase projects, boost their portfolios, and share designs.

  Mediabistro: Provides a platform for media and content professionals to not only find jobs and network but also to learn new skills and develop expertise.

- **Screening:** Many companies use social media for more than just scouting new employees. Studies show that an increasing number of hiring managers are turning to social media to screen applicants and verify the information they provide.[100] According to a CareerBuilder survey of 1,000 hiring managers, 70% of companies checked out potential hires' social media pages, including their sometimes unguarded profiles on Facebook and LinkedIn. Fifty-seven percent of the employers who checked a candidate's social media page decided not to hire the applicant based on what they saw.[101] Indeed, your social media profile can make or break your ability to land your dream job. The Practical Action box provides some tips for managing your online presence so you don't get stuck on the wrong end of a hiring decision.

What you post on your social media pages may be visible to the entire world. Is there anything there you wouldn't want a prospective employer to see? Barcin/Getty Images

PRACTICAL ACTION   Building a Personal Social Media Brand

As you've learned, employers are increasingly relying on social media to hire new talent. How can you stand out in the crowd in a good way? You may want to start by referring back to Chapter 6's Manage U feature, where we discussed the development of an effective social media strategy. Here are some additional tips for managing your online brand.

1. **Optimize your profile's "curb appeal."** Make sure you list timely, accurate information about your current and recent jobs on LinkedIn or other industry-specific networking sites. It's also important to demonstrate your increasing level of experience or broadening set of skills in your job descriptions. Remember to fill out every section of your profile with key words important to recruiters in your industry and to provide a unique headline that briefly describes what makes you so special. Finally, try and stick with layman's terms as much as possible. For example, don't assume that recruiters know what "KPIs" or "schema markups" are.[102]

2. **Participate in industry-related chat rooms and discussion groups.** It is worth the effort to positively contribute to ongoing online conversations because it raises your profile and introduces your name to new connections. You can even consider starting an industry-specific blog, if you're really an expert. Don't feel intimidated if you are still a novice. Asking intelligent questions can help your networking efforts, even if you're still learning the ropes.

3. **Keep a positive online presence.** Your overall presence on Facebook, Instagram, Twitter, LinkedIn, and other sites should not harm your professional image. "First impressions happen in the blink of an eye, and many are now taking place on social media, before you even step foot inside an interview," says Blair Decembrele, a career expert at LinkedIn. With this in mind, delete any embarrassing old photos, tweets, or other postings.[103] When deciding what to keep and what to delete, always think, "Would I want this to appear on the evening news?"

4. **Be authentic and personable.** Sometimes going overboard with positivity makes you come off looking fake and unrelatable. Companies aren't searching for perfection. They want to know the real you—your struggles and your successes. Be personal so your online community, including potential employers, become attached to you and your brand.[104] For example, if your background is in engineering, you may consider posting a "behind-the-scenes" video to Instagram showing how you approach solving a complex mechanical problem.

YOUR CALL

Think of 8 to 10 companies in an industry you'd like to work in. What kind of online brand do you think recruiters at those companies are looking for?

- **Legal implications:** It's important to note that social media can lead to hiring discrimination, which we discussed in Chapter 9. Social media, for instance, can reveal an applicant's religious affiliation, age, family composition, or sexual orientation—factors recruiters should not consider for employment purposes. "Screening social media allows employers to look inside a person's head to see who a candidate really is," said Les Rosen, CEO of Employment Screening Resources. "But if you use it incorrectly, there's a world of privacy and discrimination problems that could arise."[105]

Employee Productivity   While overuse of and even addiction to social media exist and can cause serious problems,[106] there seems little doubt that social media tools at work, used appropriately, can make communication by and among employees more productive. In fact, recent studies show that productivity is a driving force behind the use of all forms of technology at work, including social media. The key for employees, managers, and employers is to harness the speed and reach of social media to enhance individual performance.[107]

Research finds that social media can lead to higher performance, increased job satisfaction, and greater creativity and collaboration.[108] Employees who work remotely can especially benefit from social media's capabilities. Here are two specific benefits for remote workers:

- **Promoting Productivity from Afar:** Customized scheduling, organizing, networking, document sharing, messaging, and other digital communication options help relieve remote workers of the need to commute, attend routine meetings, and be distracted by colleagues.[109]

- **Staying Organized Virtually:** Digital productivity tools that control e-mail, organize links and contacts, prioritize tasks, and even edit prose can help remote workers stay focused and organized so they can meet deadlines and enjoy work–life balance.[110]

At the same time, managers need to remember that employees don't have to be in touch all the time, no matter how easy it is. There is plenty of evidence that everyone should unplug from e-mail and social media on a regular basis, if not during every evening, weekend, vacation, and holiday.[111] UK credit-card processing price comparison website Cardswitcher is a good example of an organization dedicated to making sure their employees unplug.

Cardswitcher Example: Stephen Hart, CEO of Cardswitcher, was concerned that his employees' extended use of technology after hours was leading to burnout and a lack of work–life balance. With this in mind, Cardswitcher decided in 2018 to prevent e-mails from being sent by employees after work hours. "We've noticed a marked improvement in productivity, attendance and well-being in our workplace," said Hart a year after implementing the restrictions. Hart also is "pretty convinced that the change has benefited our business in other, less obvious, ways."[112]

How often do you use social media while at work? Do you think it is helping or hindering your performance? You can find out by completing Self-Assessment 15.1.

SELF-ASSESSMENT 15.1   CAREER READINESS

To What Extent Are You Effectively Using Online Social Networking at Work?

The following survey was designed to assess how well you are using social networking in your job. Please be prepared to answer these questions if your instructor has assigned Self-Assessment 15.1 in Connect.

1. To what extent are social media helping or hurting your performance at work?

2. Based on your survey scores, what can you do to more effectively use social media at work? Be specific.

3. What things might you say during an interview to demonstrate that you possess the career readiness competency of *new media* literacy?

Employer Productivity   Companies of all sizes and in all industries believe in the benefits of social media, including their ability to keep employees engaged and satisfied, and therefore productive. Swiss pharmaceutical giant Novartis, for example, uses social media games to teach employees about its products, reaching 600 workers around the world and logging a 12% jump in employee satisfaction as a result. French personal care company L'Oréal is another example of a company harnessing the power of social media.[113]

L'Oréal Example: L'Oréal had a recruiting problem. The world's largest cosmetic company attempted to use employee testimonials shared on social media to attract new talent, but their strategy didn't work because trust in their brand was falling. People didn't want to hear about how great L'Oréal was from strangers. What the company discovered was that people using social media to identify great places to work would trust the recommendations of friends and family. With this in mind, the company created two Instagram hashtags. The first, #LifeatLoreal, was meant for corporate communications so both current and prospective employees could find out what was happening across the organization. These included fun events and a showcasing of the company's culture. The second hashtag was #LorealCommunity. This focused on employees sharing how they interacted with colleagues inside and outside of work. Between the two hashtags, L'Oréal was able to show off what a great place it was to work and gathered the interest of 200,000 viewers, who then shared these hashtags with family and friends.

The essence of social media is *connectivity*. If used effectively, social media enable businesses to:

- **Connect with key stakeholders.** The use of social media allows you to connect in real time and over distances with many customers, suppliers, employees, potential talent, and other key stakeholders.

- **Connect with varied sources of expertise inside the organization.** We've seen such connectivity demonstrated in virtual teams, redefining conventional organizational boundaries and drawing on different sources of talent, knowledge, and experience throughout the organization.

- **Connect with varied sources of expertise outside the organization.** Social media can cross organizational boundaries and connect with outsiders to help in problem solving. An example is *crowdsourcing*, as we'll see below. A variant is *crowdfunding*, raising money via online sources.

On the other hand, if not managed effectively, social media can create many legal, financial, and human resource risks.[114] For instance, almost 97% of fantasy football players spend time on their fantasy football team during the workday, to the tune of 7 hours a week. That's almost the equivalent of losing an entire workday![115] In fact, the price tag for productivity lost to fantasy football was $9 billion in 2019.[116]

Innovation in Social Media: Crowdsourcing   If you are looking for an innovative solution to a problem, you might conclude that the more people you have thinking about the problem, the more potential ideas will be generated. That's the idea behind **crowdsourcing**, using the Internet and social media to enlist a group outside the organization for help solving a problem. The strategy has drawn a lot of attention, especially for its use in fundraising (crowdfunding) on such sites as Kickstarter, but it has a mixed record of success.[117]

Some crowdsourcing efforts are organized as competitions, with individuals volunteering to solve a problem by a certain deadline to win a prize. The LEGO Ideas platform is a good example.

LEGO Example: LEGO is famous for its interlocking plastic bricks, but did you know that the Danish company was a first mover in the crowdsourcing space? The toymaker introduced the LEGO Ideas platform in 2008 as a way for users to come up with new ideas for LEGO sets. Consumers take pictures of an innovative LEGO set and send it in. Any idea that receives over 10,000 votes from other LEGO users is reviewed by LEGO. If LEGO accepts the idea, the user gets to work with the company to make their idea a reality and also receives 1% of the model's sales. More consumer-submitted LEGO ideas passed the 10,000-vote threshold than ever before in 2020, providing the company with 26 models to consider. Keep in mind that there's more to the LEGO Ideas platform than new idea generation—it provides an opportunity for the company to validate demand for ideas before moving forward with mass production.[118]

Innovative rock stars. The popular Beatles "Yellow Submarine" Lego model originated from the Lego Ideas platform. Splash News/Newscom

Researchers have studied crowdsourcing and found that it can boost product quality, speed up processes, and increase creativity, but it isn't suitable for all situations. One such situation is when a firm is working on a proprietary or secretive project that should not be revealed to the public.[119] Here is some additional research-based advice for developing effective crowdsourcing programs:[120]

- Link crowdsourcing efforts to incentives in order to motivate participants. (Think back to LEGO's offer to provide winners with royalties on sales of their models.)

- Promote your own ideas first and invite public comment. This opens the conversation and gives potential collaborators needed insight into the organization and its needs.

- Publicly respond to contributors so that their ideas are validated. This also encourages others to come forward because they feel confident their ideas will be heard.

Sales and Brand Recognition   Is it logical to expect that an "effective" social media presence generates customers and brand recognition? Yes, for the following reasons:

1. Social media can increase product/service awareness and generate customer inquiries.
2. Social media can enhance relationships with customers.
3. Social media can increase the ability to reach customers on a global scale.
4. For small or local businesses, social media can foster co-promotion of local businesses and the image of small businesses in the area.[121]
5. Social media can foster consumers' conversations about brands.[122]

Dove's "Project #ShowUs" is a good example of an effective, consumer-led social media campaign.

Dove Example: Personal care company Dove wanted to improve its brand awareness by shattering beauty stereotypes. The company's 2019 #ShowUs campaign included over 5,000 images created by women and nonbinary individuals (those who do not exclusively identify as male or female) from over 39 countries. The pictures included no enhancements or modifications, in line with a public rebellion against fake images, anorexic-looking models, and airbrushed celebrities. Women

The true you. Have you ever felt intimidated by online pictures of celebrities? These images are often enhanced or modified. Dove's #ShowUs campaign highlighted the beauty of just being you. The campaign also kept the company's name within view. Nicky J Sims/Getty Images

were able to become part of the collection by sharing their images through the #ShowUs hashtag, and the Dove logo was conspicuously placed to keep the organization at the top of consumers' minds.[123]

Don't assume that the mere use of social media automatically results in more sales and brand recognition. Research suggests that social media won't create positive outcomes unless two conditions are present.[124] First, the company must possess both competence in social media skills and technology and commitment in the form of dedicated resources. Second, a successful social media strategy requires consumers or customers with social media skills. A PR specialist writing in *Forbes* suggests companies should also make sure their messages are relevant, timely, and surprising, and marketers should track their results to learn what works.[125] GoPro is an example of an organization with a strong social media strategy.

GoPro Example: GoPro manufacturers the world's most versatile camera, yet its social media strategy may be equally adaptable. The company has a presence on Facebook (10.7 million followers), Instagram (16.2 million followers), and Twitter (2.23 million followers), but it doesn't post the same content across all its social media accounts. Instead, the camera maker has identified what each platform is most effective for and tailored a strategy to enhance their presence on each. Facebook is used to promote the GoPro brand, connect with new customers, and enhance GoPro's relationship with existing ones. The company showcases the quality of their cameras on Instagram by promoting user-generated posts and holding contests. Twitter, on the other hand, is primarily used for product announcements. GoPro's diversified social media strategy allows it to create value, promote products, and interact with its customers.[126]

Corporate Reputation   Some companies have been very successful at using social media to build and protect their reputations online. Research suggests that this is an effective strategy.[127] For example, recent studies showed that the effective use of social media wasn't just beneficial for increasing brand awareness, it also was vital for restoring a company's reputation after a crisis. A case in point involves an African American guest staying at a Portland Hilton-branded hotel in 2018. The guest was wrongly accused of trespassing by hotel security and removed from the property. The guest posted the entire incident online and it quickly went viral, causing an uproar over racial bias at hotels. Hilton quickly responded on Twitter by apologizing to the guest and letting him—and the world—know that the employees involved had been fired.[128]

As the Hilton example shows, one of the biggest dangers that managers face is negative comments about the organization posted by disgruntled customers or even employees. Some tips for defusing these and limiting the harm they can do are:

1. **Create and enforce a social media policy for employees.** We'll discuss social media policies in more detail shortly. At a minimum, your policy should limit what employees can say on the organization's web pages and ensure that all posted content meets the highest ethical standards.[129]

2. **Appoint experienced managers to monitor your social media presence and respond quickly and appropriately to negative posts.** A great deal of damage can occur online in a short time, and all of it in the public eye. Take for instance Dolce & Gabbana's recent rollout of its fall sneakers. The Italian luxury fashion house's first mistake was posting the new shoes on Instagram with the statement "I'm thin & gorgeous." Instagrammers took offense and complained that the post shamed people for not having an ideal body type. Co-founder Stefano Gabbana decided to address the matter by calling customers who complained "fat and ugly." As you might expect, the company's decision not to have an experienced social media manager handle the situation made things much worse.[130]

3. **Acknowledge there is a problem.** Gracefully accepting that someone has a genuine issue with the organization, its product or service, or its posts—even if the problem is a misunderstanding on his or her part—can go a long way toward

defusing bad feelings. If the organization is in error, the appropriate manager should say so and apologize.[131]

4. **Don't delete the comment (with exceptions).** You won't make a problem go away by deleting a negative post; in fact, you may make things worse. If the person who left the original post, or another viewer, figures out you deleted it, they may get even more upset, repost the comment, and call you out for deleting it. Deleting comments also can make you look careless or guilty. An exception might entail deleting a post if it contains threatening or profane language, or if the person is harassing or spamming your page.[132]

5. **Take the conversation offline if necessary.** If a customer refuses to be satisfied, take the conversation to a private sphere such as phone or e-mail. Not only will this keep it out of the public eye and prevent further damage to the brand, but the individualized attention may also reduce the customer's ire.[133]

A company's reputation is affected by posts made by current and former employees. Sites like Glassdoor.com, for instance, allow people to publicly (and anonymously) rate their employers on criteria like salary, benefits, work–life balance, career advancement possibilities, and even the quality of the employment interview. Firms that are confident they have happy employees can encourage them to spread the buzz about office parties, outings, and incentives and rewards on corporate websites, social media, and blogs, building the company's image as a good place to work. This recommendation was confirmed by findings from a study of 2,300 employees in 15 different countries. Over a third of surveyed employees indicated they were sharing praise or positive comments about their employer on social media.[134]

Downsides of Social Media

It's fair to say the digital age and rise of social media have introduced almost as many difficulties as efficiencies into people's lives. Some of these problems relate to cyberloafing, microaggressions, security breaches, privacy concerns, and false information.

Cyberloafing   Lost productivity due to **cyberloafing**—using the Internet at work for personal use—is a primary concern for employers in their adoption of social media. Studies have found that employees cyberloaf for many reasons including boredom, habits or addiction, and social norms.[135] Here are some eye-opening facts about this phenomenon:[136]

- Experts suggest cyberloafing costs businesses up to $85 billion per year in lost productivity.
- A recent study of over more than 1,000 U.S. office workers found that almost 60% of them couldn't make it through the day without checking social media.
- In a survey of almost 200 professionals, 97% of males and 85% of females felt as if cyberloafing was acceptable in the workplace.

Indeed, cyberloafing can have terrible consequences for businesses. Many firms have developed social media policies to address this, which we'll discuss in the next section. Here are some other ways in which businesses have been able to reduce cyberloafing:[137]

- **Group social media breaks:** Groups that take designated social media breaks know when their time starts and ends. Kliff Kingsbury, the coach of the NFL's Arizona Cardinals, is a believer in these breaks. He provides his team with breaks dedicated to checking cell phone messages and social media every 30 minutes or so. Afterwards, Kingsbury continues his meetings and drills with the team fresh and refocused.
- **Monitoring software:** Some companies install programs that either limit employees' online access or monitor what they're doing. One such example is Keylogger, which can record an employee's every keystroke as well as take note

of every website visited and e-mail sent. Though studies have found monitoring software to be generally effective at controlling cyberloafing, it can also lead to a decrease in employee loyalty.[138]

- **Meaningful work:** Often times, cyberloafing is an employee's way of saying they aren't engaged in their job. You may recall that we discussed in Chapter 11 how meaningful work increases employee engagement and productivity.[139] With this in mind, managers may need to turn their attention from cyberloafing to the work itself. "People who find their work engaging are more diligent and productive," says Dr. Carolyn Goerner, founder of consulting firm Practical Paradigms. "So perhaps the best way to combat cyberloafing is to make sure employees' jobs are motivating."[140]

Phubbing and FOMO

Microaggressions, or acts of unconscious bias, include a number of seemingly tiny but repeated actions, like interrupting others, mispronouncing or mistaking someone's name, and avoiding eye contact.[141] One particular form of microaggression is called *phubbing*, for phone snubbing or ignoring those present in order to pay attention to a mobile phone. A study by professors at Baylor University found that employees who were phubbed by their manager felt they could no longer trust that manager to keep promises or treat them fairly. This led to negative effects on their psychological preparedness to work, job satisfaction, and job performance.[142] The Baylor study shows how damaging phubbing can be in the workplace, which means it's important for you to understand what leads to it. Here are some research-based findings:

- Low levels of self-esteem and satisfaction with life can lead to phubbing.[143]
- Phubbing tends to be more common among younger people, who are more intimately connected to their phones, and among men, who view interruptions as less onerous than women.[144]
- Even if unused, a cell phone on the table can make people feel less connected to those they are with.[145]

Phubbing doesn't have to recur, however. The phubbed should calmly explain how they feel, and phubbers should use empathy to understand the harm their microaggression is doing to their communications and their relationships.[146]

Researchers have found that the urge to phub others springs from the fear of missing out—**FOMO**—or of being out of touch with something happening in our social network.[147] FOMO is exacerbated by our habits, such as paying attention to our phones during sleep hours. One study, for example, found that 40% of students reported waking at night to answer phone calls, and 47% woke to answer text messages. Psychologists demonstrated that "people of all generations seem to have succumbed to the phenomenon."[148]

Among the many consequences of FOMO are fatigue, stress, and anxiety.[149] A study on college students who had their cell phones taken away is a good example of the anxiety brought about by FOMO.

FOMO Example: Researchers examined 163 college students' anxiety levels after giving up their phones for one hour. Light users of smartphones experienced no increases in anxiety, while moderate users showed signs of increased anxiety after 25 minutes without a phone. These levels of anxiety stayed steady for the remaining time of the hour-long study. Heavy users, in contrast, revealed heightened anxiety after 10 phone-free minutes, and their level of anxiety increased over time.[150]

Psychologist Adam Alter offers some advice for those suffering from FOMO. He notes that "there is no silver bullet solution, and going cold turkey is nearly impossible. It's really about sustainable use. The best thing we can do is to section off parts of our lives from technology to keep them sacred and tech-free."[151] An example is leaving your phone outside your bedroom at night or turning it off when eating with others.

Security: Guarding against Cyberthreats

Security is defined as a system of safeguards for protecting information technology against disasters, system failures, and unauthorized access that result in damage or loss. Security is a continuing challenge, with computer and cell-phone users constantly having to deal with threats ranging from malicious software (malware) that tries to trick people into yielding passwords and personal information to viruses that can destroy or corrupt data.[152] Here are some key statistics on cyberthreats:[153]

- Cybercriminals steal around $1.5 trillion a year.

- Hackers target someone every 39 seconds, with seniors over age 60 as their preferred targets.

- Between 45 and 50% of stolen personal information can be traced back to social media hacks.

- More than four in five consumers believe cybercrime is, in fact, a crime and should be prosecuted as such. However, 42% find it acceptable to commit "morally questionable online behaviors in certain circumstances,"[154] which may help explain why employees are often called the weakest link in a company's defense against a security threat.

Citing cyberattacks on major companies like Equifax, Verizon, and Target, *Harvard Business Review* noted that "attackers didn't need to break down a wall of ones and zeros, or sabotage a piece of sophisticated hardware; instead they simply needed to take advantage of predictably poor user behavior."[155] Password recklessness is an example of such behavior. In fact, more than three-quarters of Millennials, for example, use the same password in more than 50 different places.[156] A motivating strategy called "social proof" can help nudge employees toward safer online behavior at work by showing or informing them of how others act in the same circumstances and then giving them the tools and education they need to follow suit.[157]

The key to protecting digital communication systems against fraud, hackers, identity theft, and other threats is prevention. Table 15.4 presents some ways to protect yourself.[158]

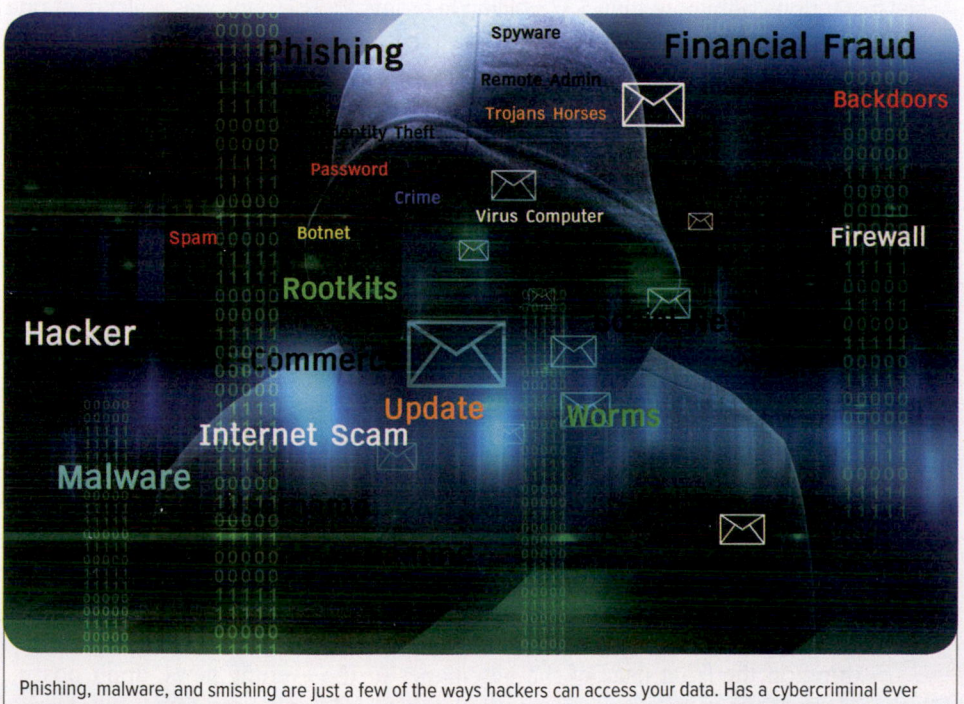

Phishing, malware, and smishing are just a few of the ways hackers can access your data. Has a cybercriminal ever attempted to steal your information? Joe Prachatree/Shutterstock

TABLE 15.4

Protecting against Security and Privacy Breaches on the Internet

- **Don't use passwords that can be easily guessed.** Use weird combinations of letters, numbers, and punctuation, and mix uppercase and lowercase, along with special characters such as !, #, and %.

- **Don't use the same password for multiple sites.** Avoid using the same password at different sites, because if hackers or scammers obtain one account, they potentially have your entire online life.

- **Don't reveal sensitive information on social networking sites.** Even people who set their profiles to Facebook's strictest privacy settings may find sensitive information leaked all over the web.

- **Consider moving sensitive information to a cloud server.** The odds are pretty good that a major cloud provider, such as Google or Microsoft, will do a better job than you at securing your information against various risks.

- **Make sure to encrypt.** Encryption is a process that encodes a message or file so it can only be read by those with a key to decrypt the information.[159] There are many free tools to do this including LastPass and VeraCrypt. Some Windows and Mac operating systems also have built-in encryption.[160]

- **Keep antivirus software updated.** The antivirus software on your computer won't protect you forever. Visit the antivirus software maker's website and enable the automatic update features.

Privacy: Keeping Things to Yourself

Privacy is the right of people not to reveal information about themselves. Threats to privacy can range from name migration, as when a company sells its customer list to another company, to online snooping, to government prying and spying. The results of a 2019 Pew survey demonstrate how concerning this issue is. The survey found that over 80% of Americans feel as if they have little control over their data.[161] And they have every right to be worried as a privacy breach can be disastrous. Take for instance a potentially devastating violation of privacy, **identity theft, in which thieves hijack your name and identity and use your good credit rating to get cash or buy things.** A data breach at Capital One Bank is a good example of how devastating this issue can be.

Capital One Bank Example: Capital One Bank is one of the top-10 largest U.S. financial institutions with more than $373 billion in assets.[162] The bank was a victim of one of the worse hacks of 2019 when intruders stole the personal information of over 100 million account holders in the United States and Canada. Hackers were able to secure all the ingredients necessary for identity theft, including customer social security numbers, birth dates, and account numbers, as well as other personal information. Although the FBI was able to apprehend the perpetrators, the damage to the bank's credibility was already done. "Capital One, once a 'darling' of digital transformation for its innovation in financial services, must now go about the long road to regain customers' trust—all thanks to a breach, which in large part, was certainly avoidable," said Hims Pawar, a principal solutions architect at database management firm Delphix.[163]

You can bolster your privacy by being aware of three issues: the role of users, privacy at work, and the responsibility of websites. Let's take a closer look.

- **The role of users:** The recent misuse of Facebook users' personal data indicates nothing posted online is ever truly private.[164] In some cases, Internet users are their own worst enemies, posting compromising images and information about themselves on social networking sites that may be available to, say, potential employers. Others, like the co-founder of Dolce & Gabbana mentioned previously whose critical remarks to a customer went viral, disastrously fail to think before they post. It has wisely been said that if you wouldn't want to see something on the front page of the newspaper or the evening news, don't post it. Many of the cautions we discussed in Table 15.4 apply here, too.

- **Privacy at work:** As for privacy at work, "Generally in the workplace, there isn't a right to privacy," according to Melissa Ventrone, a privacy attorney.[165] Monitoring of electronic communications is widespread. In most circumstances, employers are permitted to monitor—that is, read—their employees' e-mail and track their Internet use, and a majority of employers in a recent Gartner survey said they did so.[166] An employee's inappropriate use of the Internet can be devastating. A recent CareerBuilder survey of more than 1,000 HR professionals, for instance, found that a third of employers "have found content online that caused them to reprimand or fire an employee."[167]

- **Responsibility of websites:** Social media sites have a role to play in protecting our privacy. *The New York Times* recently analyzed 150 privacy policies from popular websites, such as Facebook and Google, and found them to be an "incomprehensible disaster."[168] Experts believe these sites should be communicating their privacy policies to users in a plain, straightforward way. Research supports this, finding that when sites develop simple privacy statements, users are more prone to trust them with their data.[169]

False Information: What's the Story with Fake News?

The widespread use of social media has led to an increase of false information being spread about individuals and businesses. Let's consider the two types of false information: *misinformation* and *disinformation*. Misinformation is information that is "false but not created with the intention of causing harm." This may be an honest mistake, such as mistyping a figure in a news article and later updating the report with the correct information. On the other hand, disinformation is information that is false and deliberately misleading.[170] An important type of disinformation is *fake news*, or false information intentionally published under the guise of being authentic news.[171] Let's discuss the history of fake news, its impact, and what can be done about it.

History of Fake News Contrary to popular belief, fake news is not a new term coined by Donald Trump. It actually dates back to the 16th century. Back then, it was referred to as false news and described newspapers that didn't print the truth. The term evolved into fake news and was used more generally by the 19th century.[172] The 2016 presidential election brought fake news to center stage when Donald Trump used the term to describe what he said were false news reports adverse to his campaign.[173]

The Impact of Fake News Today, many individuals see fake news as a threat to democracy, free debate, and the entire Western order, largely because it's accelerated by social media.[174] In fact, a recent survey of 803 social media users found that 86% saw fake news stories on their social media newsfeeds.[175] A father whose son was murdered is a heartbreaking example of the devastating effects of fake news.

David Wheeler Example: David Wheeler lost his 6-year-old son in the 2012 Sandy Hook massacre. Since then many conspiracy theorists have wrongly accused Wheeler of falsifying his child's murder as part of a political campaign. Not only has he had to deal with the grief of losing his son, he also has received death threats due to the false information that has spread about him on social media. "It has been incredibly painful to have to live through this, to have to face this kind of thing for the offense of speaking publicly," said Wheeler.[176]

Fake news, however, isn't just political and has crossed into the commercial space, putting companies on edge. A survey of 588 large companies across 13 countries, for instance, found that 84% felt threatened by false rumors started on social media.[177] Metro Bank serves as a good example of the devastating effects of fake news.

Metro Bank Example: Metro Bank has more than 70 locations in the United Kingdom and around 2,700 employees. The bank became a victim of false rumors in 2019 when news spread on Twitter and WhatsApp saying that the bank was on the verge of collapse. In fact, Metro Bank was not in bad shape and was forced to take to social media to reassure customers of its financial health. The damage, however, was already done. Many of the bank's customers started emptying their accounts, and its shares dropped 11%.[178]

Fake news! How can you tell fact from fiction in a digital world?
Georgejmclittle/Shutterstock

Another recent study shows how quickly commercially oriented fake news can spread. The study examined 126,000 Twitter stories tweeted by 3 million people. It found that false news reached more people than the truth—and it reached them six times faster. Researchers believe the creativity of the rumors, and the emotional reactions of recipients, had a lot to do with the results.[179] "Fake news today is like a modern-day tech suicide bomber in the worlds of communication, reputation and branding. It only takes one well-planned success to hurt a lot of people or an organization," said Mike Paul, president of public relations firm Reputation Doctor.[180]

What Can Be Done about Fake News Many tech companies have banded together to push back against fake news, especially during times of crisis. Facebook, Twitter, and Google are examples of organizations that fought fake news during the COVID-19 pandemic.

COVID-19 Fake News Example: Fake news was spreading faster than COVID-19 when the pandemic hit in 2020. Some sites advertised fake treatments for the virus, for instance, while others posted misinformation about death counts. Companies like Facebook, Twitter, and Google banded together in response and targeted myths, falsehoods, and scams on their platforms. "We're helping millions of people stay connected while also jointly combating fraud and misinformation about the virus, elevating authoritative content on our platforms, and sharing critical updates in coordination with government health care agencies around the world," the group said in a rare joint statement.[181]

You, too, can join the ranks of companies pushing back against fake news by better discerning online fact from fiction. The Practical Action box provides you with some guidance.

PRACTICAL ACTION   Defending Against Fake News

Fake news, as we've discussed, can be devastating for both people and organizations. You need to ensure you are able to steer clear of disinformation not just for political reasons, but so you make the right decisions about everything. Here are six tips to assist you.[182]

1. **Don't Fall for the Algorithm:** Twitter, Facebook, Reddit, and other social media companies use algorithms to post customized advertisements for users. Many of these are actually fake news meant to hold users' attention by providing biased information. If you do decide to click on these advertisements, make sure you verify the

material provided by checking another well-known source.

2. **Visit Trusted Sources, but Still Double Check:** It's important to visit trusted news apps and websites directly, but what can be trusted nowadays? Keep in mind that what you believe is a trusted site may at times be biased. For example, someone who gets their news from *Fox News* may believe a person who prefers *MSNBC* is consuming biased news, and vice versa. Although trusted sources may be in the eye of the beholder, we encourage you to find multiple sources

to confirm something that your preferred news outlet reports.

3. **Beware of Non-Political Biases:** Not all fake news takes advantage of political biases; some focus on the decision-making biases we discussed in Chapter 7. For example, fake news sites are known to take advantage of the confirmation bias, which we defined as the tendency to seek information that supports our point of view while also discounting any disconfirming information. Research has found that these sites use short, simple statements that lack evidence, but lend credence to what some users are thinking. Fake news sites also benefit from the ==illusory truth effect==, which is when our brain equates repetition with trust. For example, many politicians repeat slogans as a way to make something that sounds familiar seem true. This tactic isn't new. It was used by Adolf Hitler in his political manifesto, *Mein Kampf,* in 1925, saying, "Slogans should be persistently repeated until the very last individual has come to grasp the idea."[183]

4. **Check the Math:** Untrustworthy websites often times use erroneous statistics to make bogus claims. Take for example a website that says a certain ethnic population is responsible for thousands of murders in the United States. A simple check of a trusted government site, such as an FBI database, will help you make sure the murder rates match up and whether they make sense. We encourage you to use trusted sites to verify the figures presented by those you are not familiar with.

5. **Use Your Contacts:** Check in with someone who is more knowledgeable about a subject if you come across information on the Internet you aren't sure about. This includes medical advice, legal questions, and a whole host of other issues. Social media is a great place to find tips and tricks for many things, but if you need to make an important decision, consult an expert.

6. **Know the Difference between Opinions and Facts:** You can be very passionate about your opinions, but that doesn't mean they are facts. *Facts* can either be proven or disproven by objective evidence such as research. On the other hand, someone is stating an *opinion* when expressing their own belief or values. If you sometimes have trouble discerning between the two, you aren't alone. A recent Pew Research Center survey of 5,035 U.S. adults provided respondents with 10 statements—five factual and five opinion-based. The survey results demonstrated that 40% of the respondents could not correctly identify which were facts and which were opinions.[184] With this in mind, it's important to vet the information that is put in front of you and make sure it has been objectively verified.

YOUR CALL

Think back to the career readiness competencies we discussed in Chapter 1. (See Table 1.2.) Can any of them assist you in defending against fake news? Explain.

Managerial Considerations in Creating Social Media Policies

The purpose of a social media policy at work is not to completely close off employees' access to personal e-mails and texts or even shopping websites. Many employees already feel guilty if they need to deal with personal messages at work but say they would quit their job if their ability to do at least some personal tasks during the workday were restricted.[185] And while as much as half of social media use during work hours may be taking place for nonwork reasons, research finds that many employees do use social media for constructive work purposes. This includes making and nurturing professional connections and seeking solutions to problems from those both inside and outside the organization.[186]

Social Media Policy   A ==social media policy== describes the who, how, when, and for what purposes of social media use, and the consequences for noncompliance. Research demonstrates that such a policy can not only clarify expectations and relieve guilt, but also prevent impulsive or abusive posts and messages that can damage an organization's or an individual's reputation.[187] The essential elements of an effective social media policy are outlined in Table 15.5.

TABLE 15.5   Seven Elements of an Effective Social Media Policy

Applies the same standards across all posts and platforms. Employees should understand that they represent their company wherever they post, not only on professional networks like LinkedIn but also on sites more generally used for personal expression such as Twitter and Instagram. The same standards should thus apply everywhere.

Identifies sites employees may use at work. Depending on the company's goals, it may want to limit employees' social media use during the workday to specific sites.

Informs employees of terms of use and conditions of the platforms they'll be using. Violations of terms can limit the employee's future access to the site.

Identifies who may speak for the company and for what purpose. If the employer maintains a corporate Facebook page or Twitter feed, for example, only specified employees should be empowered to post there.

Clarifies the distinction between personal and work-related posts. Remind employees that their personal posts can affect their professional life.

Requires professional behavior online. Managers and employees alike should be cautioned against cyberbullying and the unfair or discriminatory use of any information about others they may find online.

Upholds confidentiality. Internal complaints and conflicts should never be aired online where partners, clients, and competitors can read about them. Proprietary information should never be disclosed in any forum, including on the internet. Employees who are in doubt about whether a post violates confidentiality should contact the company's social media team before posting.

Discourages anonymous posts. If the content of a post or message meets the highest standards of professionalism and respect for others, it should not need to be anonymous. At the same time, employees should be encouraged to clarify when they are speaking on behalf of the company and when they are not.

Specifies the consequences of violations. Employees should understand what is at risk if they violate the company's social media policy and whether they will be disciplined, receive training, or even be dismissed.

Sources: D. Ku, "5 Terrific Examples of Company Social Media Policies for Employees," Post Beyond, January 2, 2020, https://www.postbeyond.com/blog/5-terrific-examples-of-company-social-media-policies-for-employees/; J. Bouman, "Need Social Media Policy Examples? Here Are 7 Terrific Social Policies to Inspire Yours," Everyone Social, March 15, 2019, https://everyonesocial.com/blog/need-sample-social-media-policies-here-are-7-to-inspire-yours/; K. Keeler, "10 Must-Haves for an Effective Government Social Media Policy," Government Social Media Organization, May 8, 2017, https://gsmo.org/10-must-haves-for-an-effective-government-social-media-policy/.

The Example box describes selected elements of several companies' current social media policies.

EXAMPLE   **A Variety of Social Media Policies**

Here are selected provisions from some prominent companies' social media policies.[188]

At IBM, employees may say in their posts that they work for the company, but they must make it clear they speak for themselves and not the organization. They are also not permitted to use IBM logos or trademarks unless authorized by the company.[189] IBM does not state what disciplinary action may result as a consequence of violating its social media policy.

Best Buy's policy can be summed up with the phrase, "Protect the brand. Protect yourself." The company's guidelines are split into two sections: "What You Should Do" and "What You Should Never Disclose." Best Buy also believes that an employee's responsibility to the organization doesn't end when their shift ends. For this reason, its policy "applies to both company-sponsored social media and personal use as it relates to Best Buy."[190] Violating the electronic retailer's social media policy can lead to termination.[191]

Intel believes its employees should be respectful toward both the company and its competitors. "Play nice. Anything you publish [about competitors] must be true and not misleading, and all claims must be substantiated and approved."[192]

Walmart asks its associates to "consider using company established channels for job-specific issues."[193] The world's largest private employer[194] encourages team members to utilize Walmart's "Open Door Process" or WalmartOne.com instead of posting anything on Facebook or Instagram. Walmart also asks employees not to respond to customer inquiries or comments directed at the company on social media without explicit approval.[195]

The Washington Post wants its employees to remember that "*Washington Post* journalists are always *Washington Post* journalists.*" They are advised to refrain from "writing, tweeting or posting anything—including photographs or video—that could objectively be perceived as reflecting political, racial, sexist, religious or other bias or favoritism."[196] The *Post* extended its social media policy in 2017 to prohibit employees from "disparaging the products and services of the *Post*'s advertisers, subscribers, competitors, business partners or vendors." Editorial employees, however, are exempt from this prohibition in order to safeguard their independence.[197]

Clothing retailer GAP strikes a conversational tone about the serious issue of privacy. "Don't even think about it . . . Talking about financial information, sales trends, strategies, forecasts, legal issues, future promotional activities. Giving out personal information about customers or employees. Posting confidential or non-public information . . . There's no winner in that game."[198]

YOUR CALL

Best Buy, *Washington Post*, and other organizations believe that what employees post on their personal social media accounts can expose them to disciplinary action. Do you agree with this position? Why or why not?

Assessing an Organization's Social Media Readiness Consider the social media readiness of an organization to which you belong. Self-Assessment 15.2 helps you assess leadership's attitude toward social media, such as

- How supportive management is of creating communities.
- How well the culture fosters collaboration and knowledge sharing.
- How widely social media is used to collaborate.

With this knowledge you can determine how well your own attitudes fit with those of the organization, and it may even unveil opportunities for you to improve the organization's readiness. ●

SELF-ASSESSMENT 15.2

Assessing Social Media Readiness

Please be prepared to answer these questions if your instructor has assigned Self-Assessment 15.2 in Connect.

1. To what extent is the organization ready for capitalizing on social media?

2. Based on the results, what recommendations would you make to management about improving the value of social media within the company? Be specific.

15.5 Improving Communication Effectiveness

THE BIG PICTURE

We describe how you can be a more effective listener, as in communicating nondefensively, employing empathy, and engaging in active listening. We offer tips for becoming a more effective writer. Finally, we discuss how to be an effective speaker through three steps.

LO 15-5

Identify ways for managers to improve their listening, writing, and speaking skills.

Recent research suggests managers spend almost all of their time communicating and that poor communication likely costs organizations more than $30 billion annually.[199] It's no surprise, then, that written and verbal communications skills are among the top career readiness competencies desired by employers.[200]

How would you assess your communication skills? Do you think you are better than most? Do you know when it's time to stop talking during a job interview? An applicant for the job of vice president at water utility Aqua America did not, and spent 25 minutes answering the CEO's first interview question. The CEO told *The Wall Street Journal*, "I felt like I was being filibustered. . . . There should be no need for verbal diarrhea."[201] The candidate wasn't hired. You can check out your communication skills by completing the following self-assessment. If your score is lower than you prefer, seek out ideas for improving your skills.

SELF-ASSESSMENT 15.3   CAREER READINESS

Assessing My Communication Competence

This scale measures your communication competence. Please be prepared to answer these questions if your instructor has assigned Self-Assessment 15.3 in Connect.

1. Are you surprised by the results? Explain.

2. Based on your scores, what are your top three strengths and your three biggest weaknesses?

3. How might you use your strengths more effectively in your role as a student?

4. What might you say or do during an interview to demonstrate that you possess the career readiness competency of oral/written communication?

Let's see how you can be more effective at the essential communication skills.

Nondefensive Communication

Using evaluative or judgmental comments such as "Your work is terrible" or "You're always late for meetings" spurs defensiveness, and once defensiveness enters the conversation, constructive communication shuts down.[202] **Defensive communication** can include either aggressive, attacking, angry communication or passive, withdrawing communication. Abusive supervision, which was discussed in Chapter 14, is likely to foster defensiveness among employees. The better alternative is **nondefensive communication**—communication that is assertive, direct, and powerful. Let's discuss three ways that you can avoid defensive communication and foster nondefensive communication:

- **Avoid defensiveness triggers.** You may be surprised to learn that defensiveness is often triggered by nothing more than a poor choice of words or nonverbal posture during interactions. In the language of behavior modification, these triggers are *antecedents* of defensiveness. For example, using absolutes like "always" or "never" is very likely to create a defensive response. Try to avoid using absolutes because they are rarely true. You can instead increase your communication competence by avoiding defensive antecedents and employing the positive antecedents of nondefensive communication shown in Table 15.6.

TABLE 15.6   Antecedents of Defensive and Nondefensive Communication

TOWARD DEFENSIVENESS		TOWARD NONDEFENSIVENESS	
STYLE	EXAMPLE	STYLE	EXAMPLE
Evaluative	"Your work is sloppy."	Descriptive	"Your work was two days late."
Controlling	"You need to . . ."	Problem solving	"What do you think are the causes of the missed deadline?"
Strategizing	"I'd like you to agree with me during the meeting so that we can overcome any challenges."	Straightforward	"Vote your conscience at the meeting. You can agree or disagree with my proposal."
Neutral	"Don't worry about missing the deadline, it's no big deal."	Empathetic	"I sense you are disappointed about missing the deadline. Let's figure out how we can get back on schedule."
Superior	"Listen to me, I've worked here 20 years."	Equal	"Let's figure out the causes of the missed deadline together."
Certain	"We tried this idea in the past. It just doesn't work."	Honest and open	Using I-messages: "I am angry about the way you spoke to the customer because our department looked unresponsive."

Sources: Based on J. R. Gibb, "Defensive Communication," Journal of Communication, 1961, pp. 141–148; and "Reach Out: Effective Communication," Sunday Business Post, April 14, 2013.

- **Allow emotions to settle.** Communicating nondefensively begins with making sure your emotions are in check. Don't have important conversations when you are emotional.
- **Manage your intentions.** Other actions include framing your message into terms that acknowledge the receiver's point of view, freeing yourself of prejudice and bias, asking good questions and actively listening to responses, and being honest about your intentions. Your communications will be more effective and nondefensive when you communicate with the intention of helping others.[203]

Given that we want you to learn how to promote nondefensive communication, we encourage you to complete Self-Assessment 15.4. It assesses whether a current or past work environment is supportive of nondefensive communication.

SELF-ASSESSMENT 15.4

Does Your Organization Have a Supportive or Defensive Communication Climate?

The following survey was designed to assess the supportive and defensive communication climate of your organization. Please be prepared to answer these questions if your instructor has assigned Self-Assessment 15.4 in Connect.

1.   Where does the work environment stand in terms of having a supportive or defensive communication climate?

2.   Based on your survey scores, what advice would you give to management in order to promote a more supportive communication climate? Be specific.

3.   Considering your project teams at school, what can you do to create a more supportive communication climate in these teams?

Students at Maury Elementary School in Washington, D.C., participating in an empathy-building program. Throughout the course of a school year, students develop empathy by observing a baby's growth and development and learning to recognize and identify its feelings. Sarah L. Voisin/Getty Images

Using Empathy

Although researchers propose multiple types of empathy, the general consensus is that, as described in the Manage U feature at the start of the chapter, **empathy is the ability to recognize and understand another person's feelings and thoughts.**[204] It is a reflective technique that fosters open communication. Empathy is beneficial throughout our lives, not only in our professional careers.

Example: In Danish schools, students spend one hour per week on "Klassens tid," or time with their classes, which centers on learning empathy. During this hour, students come together and discuss problems they are facing in life, and the other students and teacher work to listen attentively, understand others' perspectives, and devise thoughtful solutions. The focus of the lessons is not to excel above other students, but rather, to help the students see how they can help one another.[205]

Empathy works for managers because it is not the same thing as uncritically accepting others' words and behavior; rather, it relies on a conscious effort to understand the emotional impact of our own words and behavior on others.[206]

Psychologist Paul Ekman's research shows that your ability to be empathetic depends on using three distinct types of empathy: cognitive empathy, emotional empathy, and compassionate empathy.

- **Cognitive empathy.** Having cognitive empathy means you can "identify how another person feels and consider what they may be thinking."

- **Emotional empathy.** Emotional empathy is the ability to "physically feel what another feels."

- **Compassionate empathy.** With compassionate empathy we "not only grasp a person's predicament and feel their feelings, but we're moved to help in some way." Ekman says this form of empathy is dependent on first mastering your cognitive and emotional empathy.[207]

Research shows that mindfulness, the ability to stay in the moment in a nonjudgmental way, is positively associated with empathy.[208] If you want to be more empathetic, then strive to be mindful when communicating with others. Medical students, for example, are being trained to do this. Medical students in the United States are increasingly being trained to use empathy when talking with patients, and the admissions test for medical school will now include questions designed to test applicants' existing understanding of psychology and human behavior. "Empathy is a cognitive attribute" rather than a trait, according to Dr. Mohammadreza Hojat, a research professor of psychiatry at Jefferson Medical College.[209] This means that empathy is something that we can learn to do better.[210]

Being an Effective Listener

"The greatest communication secret is listening. It may sound counterintuitive, but in order to lead, one must listen first," says best-selling author Jean Ginzburg.[211] Sir Richard Branson, entrepreneurial founder of the Virgin Group, agrees. The lesson he learned from his father was "Listen more than you speak. Nobody learned anything by hearing themselves speak."[212]

Actively listening, truly listening, requires more than just hearing, which is merely the physical component. **Active listening is the process of actively decoding and interpreting verbal messages.** Active listening requires full attention and processing of information, which hearing does not. We think that three points about active listening are worth noting here:

- **Listening is an important communication skill.** There is general consensus that listening is a cornerstone skill of communication competence. In studies that support this conclusion, active listening made receivers feel more understood. It also led people to conclude that their conversations were more helpful, sensitive, and supportive.[213] Clearly, active listening yields positive outcomes.

- **Most of us don't listen as well as we think we do.** Unfortunately, many of us think we are good listeners when evidence suggests just the opposite. Said Cornell professor Judi Brownell, "most managers certainly believe they listen more effectively than they do."[214] It takes effort to actively listen, and you won't be a better listener unless you are motivated to become one.

- **You can learn to be a better listener.** The good news is, if you are motivated to do so, you can become a better listener.[215] Said writer Kate Murphy, "Like a sport or playing a musical instrument—the more you do it the better you get at it."[216]

We studied the advice of radio journalists and podcasters—professionals who make a living by listening and having conversations with others—to devise recommendations for becoming a better listener. Don't worry—you won't read any of the old "make eye contact, nod your head, and smile" advice here. Said award-winning journalist Celeste Headlee—whose TED talk "10 ways to have a better conversation" has over 18 million views, "There is no reason to learn how to show you're paying attention if you are in fact paying attention."[217] We focus instead on changing your mindset and using conversational skills that will actually make your conversations more interesting, and therefore, increase the likelihood that you will *want* to listen. Here are five recommendations for improving your listening skills.

1. Focus on the Other Person

In order to truly listen to another person and ensure that they feel heard, you should focus on them instead of yourself. This is easier said than done, as so often we listen with the intent to respond rather than with the intent to hear. We also tend to want to relate others' stories to our own (e.g., saying "I know exactly how you feel because that happened to me, too" and then proceeding to tell our own story).

Said Emmy-winning journalist Faith Salie, "We think we're building a bridge of sharing . . . but most of the time, we're really putting up scaffolding over someone else's story and clambering all over it."[218] During the COVID-19 pandemic, Salie said one of the most important things she learned from watching her child's Zoom class was, "When in doubt, mute yourself."[219]

2. Ask Open-Ended Questions

The quality of a conversation often boils down to the quality of the questions being asked. And while asking questions isn't exactly *listening,* you will be much more engaged in a conversation—and therefore much more apt to listen intently—if you ask good questions. Journalists, whether they are writing for a newspaper or speaking into a microphone, begin questions with "who," "what," "when," "where," "why," or "how."

Peppers Pizzeria Example: At Peppers Pizzeria in Thibodaux, LA, owner Grady Verrett trains staff to use open-ended questions. Specifically, servers aren't allowed to ask customers "was everything ok?" when they bring out the check at the end of the meal. This, according to Verrett, is likely to generate a one-word polite response that provides no valuable information for improving the business. Instead, servers are trained to ask things like "what's one thing about your meal that could have been better," or "tell me what you thought of the amount of pepperoni on your pizza" in order to generate useful feedback for the restaurant and show customers that their opinions matter. (How do we know all of this? Because one of your authors—Denise Breaux Soignet— was a server at Peppers during graduate school!)

An important part of being a good listener is asking questions that generate rich, interesting, and useful responses. Peppers Pizzeria continues to thrive and improve because servers are taught to ask the kinds of questions that get customers talking openly and honestly about their dining experiences. Courtesy of Peppers Pizzerial

These types of questions elicit information beyond "yes" or "no" and help get to the most important information contained in a story.[220] Here are examples of closed-ended and open-ended questions:

- **Closed-ended questions:** "Are you having trouble with this task?" and "Can I trust you to be kinder to your employees?"

- **Open-ended questions:** "What do you think would be the best way for you to improve your skills at this task?" and "When do you feel most frustrated with your employees?"

3. Approach Conversations with Curiosity

According to Amanda Ripley, seasoned journalist for *The Washington Post* and *The Atlantic,* approaching conversations with genuine curiosity, rather than with the intent of getting others to believe what we believe, makes others feel truly heard. This, in turn, leads to richer, more meaningful, and more trusting conversations. Said Ripley, "Listening allows people to coexist. People will put up with a lot of difference if they feel heard." She added, "People will open up to different ideas and opinions . . . people need to feel heard or else everything goes to hell, one way or another, because people pull to extremes—they stop listening, they demonize each other, they can't see any shared humanity."

Here are examples of noncurious and curious questions:[221]

- **Noncurious questions:** "Did you miss the project deadline because you prioritized the wrong things?" and "What's your preferred way to communicate with your teammates, because clearly what we're using isn't working."

- **Curious questions:** "Would you describe the absolute biggest roadblock during this project and why it was such a game-changer for you?" and "If you could build your perfect team-communication tool, what would it look like?"

4. Avoid the Tendency to Judge

One reason listening is so difficult is that when another person speaks, particularly on something about which we feel passionate, we become emotionally invested in our own strong views on the subject and want to compartmentalize what they are saying as either "right" or "wrong." If you've ever had a conversation with a polarizing relative at the Thanksgiving dinner table, you've likely experienced this first hand. One way that you can help yourself to listen more openly and be less judgmental is to ask nonjudgmental questions. The language of nonjudgmental questions—words like "curious," "opinion," "thoughts," and "feelings"—helps you to understand someone's point of view better while avoiding the need to protect something you believe. The language of judgmental questions—words like "good," "bad," "right," and "wrong,"—sets you up for defensiveness, and thus, poor listening. Here are examples of judgmental and nonjudgmental questions:[222]

- **Judgmental questions:** "What do you have against participative management?" and "Why is it so bad for me to ask you to be on time?"

- **Nonjudgmental questions:** "How has your management style changed and evolved over time as you've worked with different people?" and "How do you feel about how time-oriented we are here?"

5. Be Mindful and Fully Present

This advice may seem obvious but given the pace of our modern work lives and our tendency to multitask, we think it bears repeating. With every distraction you add to the mix, your ability to listen decreases.[223] As we said at different points earlier in the chapter, communication requires trust and a feeling of being heard, and we can't accomplish either of these things if we are looking at our phone or typing an e-mail while someone is talking to us.

Do you think you are an effective listener? Effective listening is an essential skill associated with the career readiness competencies of social and emotional intelligence. If you want to increase these

Try focusing on the other person, asking open-ended questions, being curious, avoiding judgment, and being mindful in conversations with others. This will make you more involved and interested in the subject matter. Image Source/Stockbyte/Getty Images

competencies, feedback regarding your listening habits will be valuable. You can get this feedback by completing Self-Assessment 15.5.

SELF-ASSESSMENT 15.5   CAREER READINESS

Assessing Your Listening Style

The following survey was designed to assess the overall strength of your listening skills. Please be prepared to answer these questions if your instructor has assigned Self-Assessment 15.5 in Connect.

1.   Is your listening style detached, passive, or involved? Based on your survey scores, what can you do to become more of an involved listener? Be specific.

2.   Think of two ways you can practice better listening in your teams at work or school. Be specific.

3.   What can you say or do during an interview to display your listening skills?

Being an Effective Writer

Writing is an essential career readiness and management skill, all the more so because messaging platforms have replaced the telephone in so much of business communication. Taking a business writing class can be a major advantage. (Indeed, as a manager, you may have to identify employees who need writing training.) Following are some tips for writing business communications more effectively.

Start with Your Purpose   Rather than building up to the point, if you are delivering routine or positive news you should start by telling your purpose and stating what you expect of the reader. Along the same lines, when e-mailing, make sure the subject line clearly expresses your reason for writing. For instance, "Who is available Thursday afternoon?" does not inform the reader of your topic as well as "Davis project meeting moved to Thursday 3 p.m." does.

Write Simply, Concisely, and Directly   Short and sweet is the key.[224] Keep your words simple and use short words, sentences, and phrases. Be direct instead of vague and use active rather than passive voice. (Directness, active voice: "Please call a meeting for Wednesday." Vagueness, passive voice: "It is suggested that a meeting be called for Wednesday.")

Know Your Audience   Send your message to all who need the information it contains, but *only* to those people. Resist the urge to include everyone, and be especially careful, in responding to messages, to think before you click "Reply All." If you are feeling emotional as you write, don't click "Send" at all but instead save your draft, take a break of at least a few hours, and go back to it later. Your feelings may have changed and your communication, and your relationships, will likely be better for it.

Don't Show Ignorance of the Basics   Texting has made many people more relaxed about spelling and grammar rules. Although this is fine among friends, as a manager you'll need to create a more favorable impression in your writing. Besides using spelling and grammar checkers, proofread your writing before sending it on. Check people's names and titles in particular and be especially aware that auto-correct features can make incorrect assumptions about what you meant to say.

Being an Effective Speaker

The ability to talk to a room full of people—to make an oral presentation—is one of the greatest skills you can have. And in case you think you won't ever have this skill, "Public speaking is a skill anyone can build," according to communications expert Carmine Gallo. "I've interviewed young business professionals in their 20s and 30s whose careers are soaring and who get promoted much faster than their peers largely because of their ability to deliver presentations more effectively," said Gallo, adding, "Here's the key. They work at it."[225]

Would you prefer to give a public speech or be chased by a zombie? If you're like many of the people who responded to a recent survey, then you're probably more comfortable with the living dead. Fear of public speaking is no joke—but you can increase your level of comfort and skill by following the four suggestions we present. You can do this! Daniel Villeneuve/123RF; sararoom/123RF

Still, we acknowledge that public speaking can be scary. More than 31% of Americans are either "afraid" or "very afraid" of public speaking, according to the 2019 Chapman University survey of American fears (for comparison, this fear ranked higher than being murdered, inability to pay off college debt, snakes, spiders, zombies, and clowns).[226] But 70% of more than 2,000 working U.S. professionals in a recent survey agreed that the ability to make a skillful presentation was "critical" to their careers. And even more said they would like to be better at it.[227]

However you feel or think you feel about public speaking, there is no doubt you'll have to call upon your presentation skills during your career. Here are four broad suggestions for improving your speaking skills:

1. **Check out the TED model.** You can find some good models in the many TED talks available online.[228] These resources provide ideas for how to conceptualize and structure your presentation based on the outcome(s) you'd like to achieve with it.

2. **Ask questions to help yourself prepare.** You can do away with a great deal of anxiety about speaking in public by knowing what and how to prepare. For instance, ask ahead of time:

   - Who will the audience be?
   - How much time will you be allowed?
   - What technology might be available for incorporating audio or visual material?
   - Who else may be speaking?
   - Will there be a question-and-answer session afterward?

3. **Arrive early and check the room to be sure promised equipment is in place and working.**

4. **Follow Dale Carnegie's classic advice about structuring your presentation:** (1) Tell them what you're going to say. (2) Say it. (3) Tell them what you said.[229]

   ■ **Tell them what you're going to say.** The introduction should take 5 to 15% of your speaking time, and it should prepare the audience for the rest of the presentation. Avoid jokes and such tired phrases as "I'm honored to be with you here today. . . ." Because everything in your speech should be relevant, be bold and go right to the point with a "grabber" such as a personal story that attracts listeners' attention and prepares them to follow you closely.[230] The art of storytelling has become recognized as a key skill for modern leaders because it is an authentic way to strengthen connections.[231] By sharing a story first, you let the audience know that you are human, and this builds trust and reciprocity between you.[232] For example:

     "Good afternoon. You may not have thought much about identity theft, and neither did I until my identity was stolen—twice. Today I'll describe how our supposedly private credit, health, employment, and other records are vulnerable to theft and how you can protect yourself."

   ■ **Say it.** The main body of the speech takes up 75 to 95% of your time. The most important thing to realize is that your audience won't remember more than a few points anyway. Choose them carefully and cover them as succinctly as possible. Here are two more suggestions:

     ■ *Do your homework.* Speak about what you know best, understand your audience's point of view and preconceptions, and check and recheck your facts. These preparatory steps enhance your confidence and ensure you have credibility with your listeners.

     ■ *Pay attention to transitions.* When you practice this part of your presentation, be particularly attentive to transitions during the main body of the speech. Listening differs from reading in that the listener has only one chance to get your meaning. Thus, be sure you constantly provide your listeners with guidelines and transitional phrases so they can see where you're going. Example:

       "There are five ways the security of your supposedly private files can be compromised. The first way is . . . The second way happens when . . ."

   ■ **Tell them what you said.** The end might take 5 to 10% of your time. Many professional speakers consider the conclusion to be as important as the introduction, so don't drop the ball here. You need a solid, strong, persuasive wrap-up.

     Use some sort of signal phrase that cues your listeners that you are heading into your wind-up. Examples:

     "Let's review the main points . . ."
     "In conclusion, what CAN you do to protect against unauthorized invasion of your private files? I point out five main steps. One . . ."

     Give some thought to the last thing you will say. It should be strongly upbeat, a call to action, a thought for the day, a little story, a quotation. Examples:

     "I want to leave you with one last thought . . ."
     "Finally, let me close by sharing something that happened to me . . ."

     Then say, "Thank you," and stop. ●

Predictor for success. Enjoying public speaking and being good at it are the top predictors of success and upward mobility. How might you develop these skills? Hill Street Studios/Blend Images/Alamy Stock Photo

15.6 Career Corner: Managing Your Career Readiness

LO 15-6

Review the techniques for improving the career readiness competency of networking.

Communication is a career readiness competency that requires the application of 12 competencies from the model of career readiness shown below (*see Figure 15.4*). You can improve your communication skills by recognizing the need to also develop the following competencies: new media literacy, oral/written communication, teamwork/collaboration, leadership, social intelligence, networking, emotional intelligence, self-motivation, positive approach, career management, self-awareness, and generalized self-efficacy.

FIGURE 15.4

Model of career readiness

McGraw-Hill Education

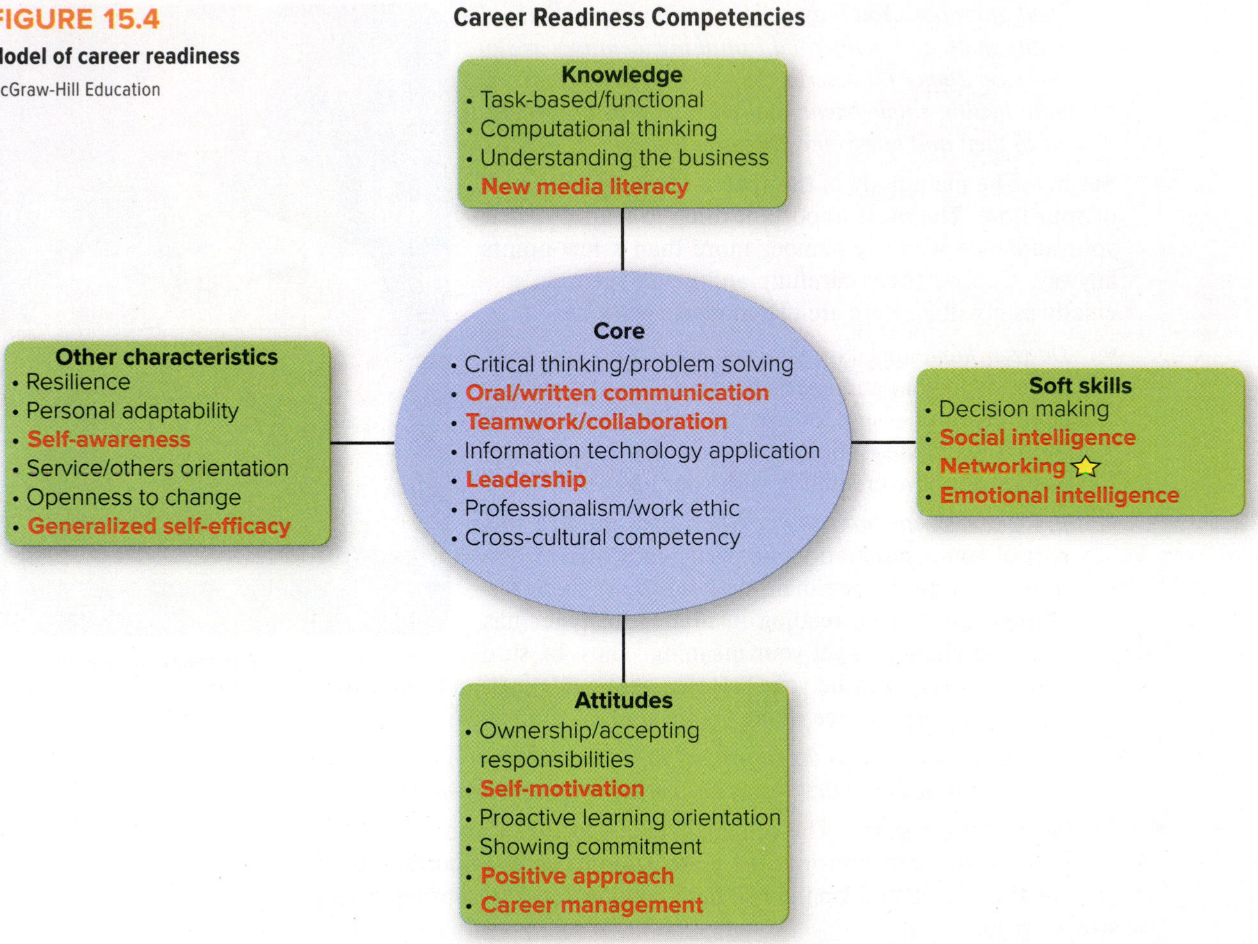

Career Readiness Competencies

Knowledge
- Task-based/functional
- Computational thinking
- Understanding the business
- **New media literacy**

Core
- Critical thinking/problem solving
- **Oral/written communication**
- **Teamwork/collaboration**
- Information technology application
- **Leadership**
- Professionalism/work ethic
- Cross-cultural competency

Other characteristics
- Resilience
- Personal adaptability
- **Self-awareness**
- Service/others orientation
- Openness to change
- **Generalized self-efficacy**

Soft skills
- Decision making
- **Social intelligence**
- **Networking** ☆
- **Emotional intelligence**

Attitudes
- Ownership/accepting responsibilities
- **Self-motivation**
- Proactive learning orientation
- Showing commitment
- **Positive approach**
- **Career management**

We are going to focus on the competency of networking because it plays a key role in getting a job after graduation and requires good communication skills.[233] Networking is the ability to build and maintain a strong, broad professional network of relationships. It typically requires developing and using contacts from one context in another.

Improve Your Face-to-Face Networking Skills

We're sure you've heard the phrase, "It's not what you know, it's who you know." A recent survey of 1,535 U.S. adults partially supported this conclusion. Results showed that 31%, 11%, and 23% found their jobs via networking, online job boards, and other ways such as applying in person, respectively.[234] Unfortunately, many of us dislike networking and even view it as "insincere and manipulative, even slightly unethical," according to *The Wall Street Journal*.[235] Networking is not meant to be manipulative, nor is it all about you. Two writers for the *HelpGuide* summed it up nicely. They noted:

> Networking is also about helping others. As human beings, we are wired to connect with others. Without these connections, you can become isolated and experience loneliness and even depression. So the real goal of networking should be to re-invigorate your existing relationships and develop new ones.[236]

We'd like to assist you in developing the career readiness competency of networking by providing the following recommendations. Put them to work now as opposed to waiting until you are in the job market.

Create a Positive Mindset

A negative attitude about networking is a roadblock to developing this competency. Pursue a more positive attitude by eliminating the thought that networking is a game. Networking is more enjoyable when it is driven by your authentic intention to develop genuine relationships, rather than by your desire to land a job. Strive to view networking as a vehicle to make more friends and connect with people with similar interests. This mindset is more likely to take you further with the relationship because it creates shared bonding rather than the pursuit of self-interests.[237]

Identify Your Career Goals

Before doing any networking, you need to be clear about your goals and plans. Establish a 5- to 10-year career goal and then develop a high-level action plan for accomplishing it. Say, for example, that your 5-year goal is to be employed in a job in which you supervise at least five employees and make $150,000. Now write down what goals you need to meet in years 1–4 to meet this overall goal. Try to identify a few people who can kickstart or accelerate the achievement of this goal. They can be people you know or second-degree acquaintances of people you know. These individuals should become targets of your networking. If you don't know anyone, then your task is to find social outlets where you can meet these types of people.

Network with a Purpose

Have a purpose for attending networking events. Do you want to reconnect with friends and acquaintances, or do you want to meet new people? What type of people do you want to meet? We encourage you to look for people with common interests who can help you and people whom you can help.[238] Research shows that networkers tend to spend the majority of their time with people they already know, so we encourage you to avoid putting pressure on yourself to meet strangers. In support of this conclusion, *The Wall Street Journal* reported that "a wealth of research suggests that your less-cultivated business acquaintances, or 'weak ties,' have more information, opportunities and potential introductions to share with you than either your close contacts or total strangers."[239]

Build Personal Connections

The key is to draw people into meaningful conversations. People will remember more about you if the conversation is meaningful and has some degree of emotionality. For example, you probably won't be remembered if you lead with: So where do you work? Where are you from? Do live nearby? You'll get a more positive response by asking insightful or interesting questions. One consultant suggested using questions such as, "Have you been working on anything exciting recently?" or "Any exciting plans this summer?"[240] To create emotionality in the conversation, you might ask, "What was the highlight of your day?" or "What's keeping you awake at night?"[241] By asking good questions you not only create a positive first impression, but you might cause the other person to learn something that helps them grow.

Be Mindful   It's worth emphasizing the need to be mindful when communicating with others. For example, you might think it's fine to interrupt a conversation with someone to answer your phone, but others might think differently. Try your best to avoid phubbing and FOMO. Maintain eye contact with those with whom you are conversing and avoid the tendency to let wandering eyes survey the room for the next person you want to meet. That's an easy way to send the message that the person in front of you is not important.

Follow Up   Be sure to follow up with those individuals you found particularly interesting or would like to see again. Use whatever medium of communication you deem relevant. While texting and e-mail are fast, we have had very positive experiences when we've written a handwritten note of appreciation.[242] ●

Key Terms Used in This Chapter

Key Points

15.1 The Communication Process: What It Is, How It Works

- Communication is the transfer of information and understanding from one person to another. The process involves sender, message, and receiver; encoding and decoding; the medium; feedback; and dealing with "noise."
- The sender is the person wanting to share information. The information is called a message. The receiver is the person for whom the message is intended. Encoding is translating a message into understandable symbols or language. Decoding is interpreting and trying to make sense of the message. The medium is the pathway by which a message travels. Feedback is the process in which a receiver expresses his or her reaction to the sender's message.
- The entire communication process can be disrupted at any point by noise, defined as any disturbance that interferes with the transmission or understanding of a message. The four key sources of noise are physical, psychological, semantic, and physiological.
- For effective communication, a manager must select the right medium. This choice is based on matching media richness with the situation at hand.

15.2 How Managers Fit into the Communication Process

- Communication channels may be formal or informal.
- Formal communication channels follow the chain of command and are recognized as official. Formal communication is of three types: (1) Vertical communication is the flow of messages up and down the organizational hierarchy. (2) Horizontal communication flows within and between work units; its main purpose is coordination. (3) External communication flows between people inside and outside the organization.
- Informal communication channels develop outside the formal structure and do not follow the chain of command. Two aspects of informal channels are the grapevine and face-to-face communication. The grapevine is the unofficial communication system of the informal organization.

15.3 Barriers to Communication

- Barriers to communication are of five types: (1) physical barriers, (2) personal barriers, (3) cross-cultural barriers, (4) nonverbal barriers, and (5) gender differences.
- Five personal barriers are (1) variable skills in communicating effectively, (2) information processing and interpretation, (3) variations in trustworthiness and credibility, (4) attentional issues, and (5) generational considerations.
- Cross-cultural, nonverbal, and gender barriers also impact communication.

15.4 Social Media and Management

- Social media contribute heavily to employee and employer productivity. They are widely used in employment recruiting and have applications in employee and employer productivity, organizational innovation (via crowdsourcing), in sales, and in reputation management.
- Social media have costs as well. These include cyberloafing, phubbing and FOMO, security

threats, privacy issues, and the spread of false information.

- One type of false information is fake news, or false information intentionally published under the guise of being authentic news.
- Managers should engage employees in the creation of fair and effective social media policy to ensure social media tools are consistently put to constructive work purposes.

15.5 Improving Communication Effectiveness

- Nondefensive communication is essential for effective communication.
- Three types of empathy are cognitive, emotional, and compassionate.
- You can improve active listening by (1) focusing on the other person, (2) asking open-ended questions, (3) approaching conversations with curiosity, (4) avoiding the tendency to judge, and (5) being fully present.
- To become an effective writer, start with your purpose. Write simply, concisely, and directly. Know your audience and follow basic spelling and

grammar rules for appropriately formal communication.

- To become an effective speaker, study successful models, know your subject, and prepare and rehearse ahead of time. For the presentation itself, follow three simple rules. Tell people what you're going to say. Say it. Tell them what you said.

15.6 Career Corner: Managing Your Career Readiness

- Becoming a more effective communicator requires the application of 12 career readiness competencies. They are new media literacy, oral/written communication, teamwork/collaboration, leadership, social intelligence, networking, emotional intelligence, self-motivation, positive approach, career management, self-awareness, and generalized self-efficacy.
- You can develop your networking competency by following six recommendations: (1) Create a positive mindset. (2) Identify your career goals. (3) Network with a purpose. (4) Build personal connections. (5) Be mindful. (6) Follow up.

Understanding the Chapter: What Do I Know?

1. Explain the communications process.
2. What are some common sources of noise in communication?
3. Explain the differences between formal and informal communication channels.
4. What are the five types of barriers to communication and examples of each?
5. Explain how social media can contribute to employee productivity.
6. How does social media make employers more productive?
7. What are some of the costs of social media in organizations?
8. What should managers know about creating a social media policy?
9. How can I become a more effective listener?
10. How can I use networking to improve my job prospects?

Management in Action

Fyre and Fury

Imagine "a world of surreal experiences and inspired curiosity that touches the sweet spot between imagination and possibility . . . a place where the tropical sun shines all day, and our celebrations ignite the night."[243] This is a snippet from the marketing campaign for Fyre Fest, a luxury concert event that 20-something socialite/entrepreneur Billy McFarland and rapper Ja Rule conceptualized when they discovered the beautiful Bahamas' Exuma Islands in October 2016. McFarland had no experience producing live music festivals, but he had plenty of connections, knew how to raise money, and understood the power of messaging.[244]

Fyre Festival took off on social media less than two months later when Kendall Jenner, Bella Hadid, Emily Ratajkowski, and other influencers simultaneously Instagrammed the event's first advertisement. The video featured crystal-blue waters, yachts, and supermodels "frolicking and dancing on a beach."[245] Ticket packages ranged from $1,500 to $400,000 and included promises of luxury beach villas, treasure hunts, white-glove concierge services, and the finest gourmet food and drinks from famed restaurateur Stephen Starr—all on the private Exuma island of Fyre Cay that once belonged to the late drug lord Pablo Escobar. The social media campaign was a massive success, and thousands of adventurous concertgoers quickly cashed in on the chance to be part of the extravaganza. What they got was anything but.[246]

FYRE FESTIVAL GOES DOWN IN FLAMES

On Thursday, April 27, 2017, throngs of excited festivalgoers began arriving in the Exumas. Organizers had arranged first-class transportation between the airport and the festival and a white-glove service to deliver attendees' luggage straight to their reserved luxury villas. Instead, attendees rode on packed school buses to an unfinished, gravel-covered development plot speckled with emergency-relief tents. There was nary a villa, concierge, shower, or gourmet meal in sight.[247] There were no celebrity sightings and no musicians because McFarland and his team, seeing disaster ahead, had already secretly alerted them to stay away. McFarland had sent no such messages to the rest of the attendees, who arrived to dashed dreams.[248]

Event staff told attendees, "It's every man for himself," as they rushed to grab tents in a free-for-all.[249] "They had no way to communicate with anybody," said one attendee, who remembers McFarland standing atop a table frantically yelling instructions at the crowd.[250] Another recalls "everyone you spoke to had a different answer and no one knew who was in charge . . . there were no [phone] chargers or electricity outlets . . . and there was barely service."[251] Attendees who weren't lucky enough to find hotel rooms on the island or transportation back to the airport slept on soaking wet mattresses and dined on sliced bread and cheese. They found their luggage piled inside a giant shipping container and searched for their bags in the darkness with cell phone lights. The event was a complete and utter disaster.

Thousands of ticketholders eventually made their way off the island in a mass exodus marked by hunger, exhaustion, bewilderment, and anger. The only direct communication they received from the organizers was a single e-mail saying, "The festival is being postponed until we can further assess if and when we are able to create the high-quality experience we envisioned."[252] Fyre organizers took to social media in the days that followed, blaming the weather and the Exumas' poor infrastructure for the fiasco.[253] In reality, McFarland had tried to plan an unprecedented event on an undeveloped construction lot. He failed his team, vendors, attendees, and the people of the Bahamas.

WHERE DID THINGS GO WRONG?

A big event starts with a big idea—a concept for a theme, audience, and experience. A fairly standard process is then used to plan the event. Organizers first calculate a realistic idea of their financial resources, aligning all subsequent decisions with this budget. Second comes logistics, which include searching for a venue; ensuring that the venue provides a safe and suitable infrastructure; securing any necessary additions, upgrades, and permits; contracting with vendors (caterers, service staff, security, sanitation companies); and booking talent (musicians, performers). Third, and only after logistics are in place, organizers develop and distribute marketing materials and use those to sell admission. The process requires experience, expertise, and a constant flow of communication among various stakeholders.[254] McFarland did things his own way. He began by paying models and influencers hundreds of thousands of dollars to advertise a fantasy; sold tickets to said fantasy; and repeatedly ignored information indicating that he didn't have the time, money, or expertise to pull it off.

The island of Fyre Cay didn't exist, nor did the lavish villas people had booked through the festival's website, and McFarland had repeatedly failed to find production firms that would execute the event on his terms. One executive recalls a familiar scene: "They [production companies] would say 'It's going to cost, like, $5 million to stage this thing,' and the Fyre guys would say, 'No, it'll cost $300,000.' There was a complete detachment from reality."[255] Six weeks before the event, "Nothing had been done. . . . Festival vendors weren't in place, no stage had been rented, transportation had not been arranged," according to former Fyre talent producer Chloe Gordon. Planners warned McFarland and his team that they didn't have the money to put on the event they had advertised and should instead roll tickets over to a 2018 event and begin planning it immediately. Gordon recalls a Fyre executive responding, "Let's just do it and be legends, man." She quit a week later.[256]

Rumors began to circulate among entertainment industry professionals in the weeks before the festival, and on April 2, *The Wall Street Journal* reported growing concerns about the event. Vendors, contractors, and artists were severing ties when they didn't receive payment, and ticketholders were still in the dark about logistics.[257] Maude Etkin, an interior designer and ticketholder from Manhattan, says Fyre hadn't responded to e-mails for weeks.[258] Through it all, McFarland continued to promote Fyre Festival as a top-notch experience through his website and social media platforms, hanging onto his fantasy until the bitter end.

TRIAL BY FYRE

Class-action lawsuits against McFarland and the Fyre organization quickly surfaced, with vendors, employees, and attendees citing fraud, breach of contract, and negligent misrepresentation. McFarland took a plea deal in March 2018, admitting to two counts of wire fraud and forfeiting $27 million. He was sentenced to six years in federal prison and has since been ordered to pay millions to compensate unpaid lenders and slighted festivalgoers.[259] Fyre media is, in turn, seeking to recoup damages through at least 14 lawsuits of its own against performers who failed to show up for the event and influencers who the organization alleges provided misleading information to ticketholders through social media.[260] In May 2020, Kendall Jenner—one of the aforementioned influencers—agreed to pay $90,000 for, among other things, leading followers to believe that Kanye West was performing at the festival.

FOR DISCUSSION

Problem-Solving Perspective

1. What is the underlying problem in this case from an event-planning perspective?

2. What were the causes of this problem?

3. What recommendations would you make to someone trying to execute a similar idea in the future?

Application of Chapter Content

1. What kinds of vertical and horizontal communication errors did McFarland make while attempting to plan the festival?

2. What do you see as the biggest barriers to communication in this situation?

3. How did McFarland's background and lack of experience affect the way he processed the messages he received during planning?

4. Would you say McFarland was ultimately effective or ineffective at using social media? Explain.

5. Do you think McFarland could have successfully executed this event if he had been a better communicator? What, specifically, would have to change?

Legal/Ethical Challenge

The Cost of Speaking Out against Your Employer

The COVID-19 pandemic put immense stress on the U.S. health care system. Some of America's largest cities, such as New York, Chicago, and New Orleans, were hardest hit and faced a lack of supplies and personnel. Kenia Barkai worked at Detroit Medical Center's Sinai-Grace Hospital as a nurse. She first mentioned to hospital management in February 2020 that there was a lack of staffing and protective equipment at the hospital, putting workers and patients at risk.[261] Barkai also told her boss that she was tasked with treating both COVID-19 and non-COVID-19 patients. This meant she may inadvertently have spread the virus. Barkai's complaints, however, fell on deaf ears.[262]

Sinai-Grace saw a surge of COVID-19 patients in March 2020, leading to worsening conditions. Barkai continued her complaints, this time telling management she was going to report her work conditions to state regulators. A few days later, the 11-year veteran posted a seven-second video to Facebook. The video showed Barkai putting on gear and saying, "I have my gloves, my hair covering, my mask, my gown and I'm ready to rock and roll. I'm going in," before treating a COVID-19 patient.[263] Barkai's post was picked up by local Detroit news and broadcast. The hospital fired her a few days later, citing a violation of their social media policy.[264]

Barkai's firing led Sinai-Grace nurses to organize a sit-in and motivated others to speak up. Physicians and nurses told news outlets horrifying stories of a hospital that looked like a "third world country in a war zone."[265] "We've had patients die in hallway beds because the nurse didn't find they didn't have a pulse until it was too late," said one physician. "Each nurse has so many patients that by the time they come to check on their next one, there is a chance that patient may not have a pulse anymore." Two ER workers said that another patient's breathing tube disconnected from a ventilator and hospital staff were so busy that the patient died before anyone could reconnect it.[266]

A vindicated Barkai filed a whistleblower lawsuit against Sinai-Grace Hospital alleging the hospital retaliated against her for speaking up. "[The hospital] can't retaliate against a nurse whose sole goal was to advise the authorities of inappropriate actions that were jeopardizing patient care," said Jim Rasor, Barkai's attorney.[267] On the other hand, the hospital's social media policy bans posts that interfere with work or "create potential harm to others," such as patients and staff. Posts that release confidential information also are banned.[268]

SOLVING THE CHALLENGE

Assume you were an administrator at Sinai-Grace Hospital when Barkai's video went live. Would you have fired her?

1. No. Barkai did not reveal any confidential information in her video and stated her opinion about the hospital's working conditions on her own personal Facebook feed. She should be reinstated and compensated for wrongful termination.

2. Yes. Barkai's video caused additional harm to a hospital in the middle of a devastating pandemic. She should have followed protocol by placing a complaint with regulators instead of going public.

3. Invent other options.

In this part of the case you'll learn more about key communication issues at Boeing. You'll also explore factors related to individual differences, motivation, groups and teams, and leadership at the company.

Go to Connect to assess your ability to apply the concepts discussed in Chapters 11, 12, 13, 14, and 15 to the Boeing case.

16

Control Systems and Quality Management

Techniques for Enhancing Organizational Effectiveness

Kapook2981/iStock/Getty Images

After reading this chapter, you should be able to:

LO 16-1 Describe control as a managerial function.

LO 16-2 Describe the steps in the control process and types of control.

LO 16-3 Discuss ways that managers can control an organization.

LO 16-4 Explain the total quality management process.

LO 16-5 Discuss contemporary control issues.

LO 16-6 Discuss the process for managing career readiness and review six tips for managing your career.

FORECAST *What's Ahead in This Chapter*

The final management function, control, is monitoring performance, comparing it with goals, and taking corrective action as needed. We identify six reasons for the need of management control, explain the steps in the control process, and describe three types of control managers use. Next, we discuss ways that managers can control an organization using the balanced scorecard. We then turn our focus to total quality management (TQM). Finally, we explain two contemporary control tools before concluding with a Career Corner that focuses on the career readiness competency of career management.

Mentors Can Help You Control Your Career

Mentoring is the process of forming and maintaining intensive and lasting developmental relationships between a variety of developers (people who provide career and psychosocial support) and a junior person (the protege).[1] Mentors are experienced, knowledgeable, and trusted people willing to coach you throughout the passages of your career. You may find your mentor through networking or a personal introduction. This person will usually be someone active in your field or industry and familiar with the issues professionals in it face.

Having a mentor is a uniquely valuable career development opportunity, but it also offers a way for you to benchmark, or compare, yourself to someone more experienced and discover the skills or topics you need to work on in order to measure up. As this chapter shows, organizations frequently use benchmarking strategies to make course corrections to their own performance and to develop their employees.

Because of their status in the organization or industry, mentors are, by definition, busy people. You may meet with your mentor regularly or only a few times, but you want to be both respectful and get the most from the opportunity. Here are a few strategies for making the collaboration successful for both of you.[2]

Set Goals

Identify specific goals you want to achieve in the relationship—and in each meeting or conversation—and let your mentor know what they are so you can work toward them together. You've learned in this course that goals are motivating; they also give you a way to measure your progress and correct course as needed. Being a protege is an active process and your mentor is not going to do your work for you. You need to take charge of your learning.

Come Prepared

Do your homework before meeting with your mentor and come to the meeting with an agenda in hand. This makes it more likely you will stay on task and optimize your time together. If you want advice on writing a report, send a draft beforehand and be ready to discuss it. If your mentor recommends an action, take that step before checking in to discuss what happened as a result. Ask lots of questions, but first make sure you truly can't answer or research them on your own and that they draw on your mentor's unique knowledge and experience.

Stay Open-Minded

You can feel free to disagree with your mentor but bring solid information and good ideas to any debate and respectfully evaluate your mentor's input. Be ready to accept your mentor's feedback even if it's sometimes critical. Such individual coaching can be the most valuable part of your experience as a protege because it gives you the tools you need to grow. Finally, remember to fight off the Dunning-Kruger effect we discussed in Chapter 14.

Respect Your Mentor's Time

Commit to the relationship, because it's up to you, not your mentor, to make it work. Show up for all meetings and start and end on time to avoid taking advantage of your mentor's generosity. Limit contacts between sessions for the same reason. Ask what's acceptable if, for instance, you want to e-mail a brief question for a quick yes–no answer. Always say thank you.

Know When It's Not Working

Sometimes a mentoring relationship doesn't work out because the mentor can't provide the right kind of help or doesn't have the time to commit. If that's the case, and if you're sure you've done all you could to make the collaboration succeed, it's time to gracefully let your mentor know you are ready to step out on your own. Don't forget, however, to show gratitude for all that they have offered you. Later, analyze what you believe you really need in a mentor and try looking for a closer match.

For Discussion A mentoring relationship is a two-way street. When you reach out to a potential mentor, what can you offer in return for the coaching and expertise? Make a list of ideas, considering what your age, cultural background, goals, and outside interests might contribute to the collaboration.

16.1 Control: When Managers Monitor Performance

THE BIG PICTURE

Controlling is monitoring performance, comparing it with goals, and taking corrective action. This section describes six reasons control is needed.

LO 16-1

Describe control as a managerial function.

Control is making something happen the way it was planned to happen. **Controlling is defined as monitoring performance, comparing it with goals, and taking corrective action as needed.** Controlling is the fourth management function, along with planning, organizing, and leading, and its purpose is plain: to make sure that performance meets objectives.

- **Planning** is setting goals and deciding how to achieve them.
- **Organizing** is arranging tasks, people, and other resources to accomplish the work.
- **Leading** is motivating people to work hard to achieve the organization's goals.
- **Controlling** is concerned with seeing that the right things happen at the right time in the right way.

All these functions affect one another and in turn affect an organization's performance and productivity. *(See Figure 16.1.)*

FIGURE 16.1   **Controlling for effective performance**

What you as a manager do to get things done, with controlling shown in relation to the three other management functions. (These are not lockstep; all four functions happen concurrently.)

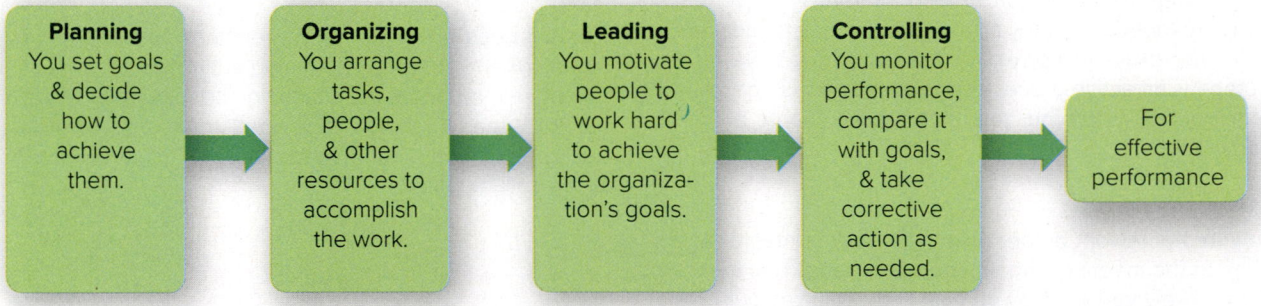

Planning
You set goals & decide how to achieve them.

Organizing
You arrange tasks, people, & other resources to accomplish the work.

Leading
You motivate people to work hard to achieve the organization's goals.

Controlling
You monitor performance, compare it with goals, & take corrective action as needed.

For effective performance

Lack of control mechanisms can lead to problems for both managers and companies, especially during already challenging times. For example, in the wake of the COVID-19 pandemic, businesses started losing revenue and shedding millions of jobs. This led to what the chairman of the Federal Reserve called the worst economy in history.[3] More importantly, the virus killed hundreds of thousands of people around the world. Could greater control have helped avoid or reduce the consequences of COVID-19? Of course. Control can save lives!

There are six reasons control is needed. Let's examine each using the COVID-19 pandemic as an example.

1. **To adapt to change and uncertainty.** Markets shift. Consumer tastes change. New competitors appear. Technologies are reborn. New materials are invented. Government regulations are altered. All organizations must deal with these kinds of environmental changes and uncertainties. Control systems can help managers anticipate, monitor, and react to these changes.

    Virtual learning. Millions of Americans are pursuing an online education. Do you believe online classes provide an equivalent experience to in-person? Rido/Shutterstock

    Higher Education Example: Around one-third of college students were enrolled in online classes in early 2020 before the COVID-19 pandemic hit the United States. In a matter of weeks, almost all college campuses went virtual, leading to the biggest mass migration to online education in history.[4] Colleges, many of which were gradually building their online programs for years, were—for the most part—able to quickly adapt. According to experts, most institutions had at least one person in the administration who had planned for online education as a way to keep things going in case of a fire or other natural disaster.[5] "[Coronavirus] is online education's moment," said Chip Paucek, the CEO of 2U Inc., an online education company.[6]

2. **To discover irregularities and errors.** Small problems can mushroom into big ones. Cost overruns, manufacturing defects, employee turnover, bookkeeping errors, and customer dissatisfaction are all matters that may be tolerable in the short run. But in the long run, they can bring about even the downfall of an organization.

    Death Count Example: Pennsylvania's COVID-19 related death count almost doubled over a span of two days because the state began adding "probable deaths" to its count. These deaths were presumed to be caused by COVID-19 but weren't confirmed with a test. A few days later, the state abruptly changed course and removed hundreds of deaths from its official count because it did not have enough information on them. These errors in the state's counting methodology led to mass confusion among coroners. "There's a discrepancy in the numbers . . . accuracy is important," said Charles Kiessling Jr., president of the Pennsylvania Coroners Association.[7] Without accurate numbers, the state risked a miscount of deaths, a misunderstanding of how the virus was spreading, and overburdening hospital staff.[8]

3. **To reduce costs, increase productivity, or add value.** Control systems can reduce labor costs, eliminate waste, increase output, and increase product delivery cycles. In addition, controls can help add value to a product so that customers will be more inclined to choose them over rival products.

    Meeting the challenge. A Ford Motor Company assemblyman puts together a ventilator at the automaker's Rawsonville plant in Michigan. The plant was converted into a ventilator factory as hospitals faced shortages of these life-saving devices. Carlos Osorio/AP Images

    Ford and General Electric Example: The Ford Motor Company made B-24 bombers in 1941 during World War II—and in 2020 the company declared war on COVID-19. Ford teamed up with General Electric (GE) to expand production of desperately needed ventilators to keep ailing COVID-19 patients alive. The

automaker was able to produce 50,000 ventilators within 100 days by using GE's expertise and opening its automobile production line to ventilator production. "Our deep understanding of the health care industry with Ford's supply chain and production expertise will help meet the unprecedented demand for medical equipment," said GE Healthcare President and CEO Kieran Murphy.[9]

4. **To detect opportunities and increase innovation.**   Hot-selling products. Competitive prices on materials. Changing population trends. New overseas markets. Controls can help alert managers to innovative opportunities that might have otherwise gone unnoticed.[10]

> **Amazon Example:** The COVID-19 pandemic provided an opportunity for organizations like Amazon to further their use of robots on manufacturing floors. The online retailer utilized more than 200,000 mobile robots to deliver shelves of products to workers packing items for shipment. The robots eliminated the need for Amazon workers to walk among rows of shelves to find products, keeping them safe during a time when social distancing was important.[11]

5. **To provide performance feedback.**   Can you improve without feedback? When a company becomes larger or when it merges with another company, it may find it has several product lines, materials-purchasing policies, customer bases, and worker needs that conflict with each other. Controls help managers coordinate these various elements by providing feedback.[12] Research demonstrates that feedback also has a control function for individuals and teams, and the quality of this feedback affects employee attitudes and performance.[13]

> **Performance Feedback Example:** As more and more employees were forced to work from home due to self-quarantine orders, companies needed to find a way to effectively provide performance feedback. For example, the CEO of a 1,000-person tech company messaged or called his direct reports at least once a day in order to keep the lines of communication open. A simple "Checking to see if you need anything from me" went a long way in making sure the CEO had a finger on the pulse of his team. Other managers had 15-minute morning check-ins to regroup on overnight developments and plan the day. Unsurprisingly, a recent study found that these behaviors made employees feel better connected and engaged.[14]

6. **To decentralize decision making and facilitate teamwork.**   Controls allow top management to decentralize decision making at lower levels within the organization and to encourage employees to work together in teams. Studies have found that organizations who effectively utilized control enjoyed greater creativity, responsiveness, and performance.[15]

> **Health Care Example:** The COVID-19 pandemic unleashed a never-before-seen global health crisis requiring hospitals to provide team-based care. "This is not like anything anybody in health care has experienced ever . . . teamwork, being able to innovate, problem solve and move forward, are more critical in this moment than they've ever been," said Dr. Jessica Dudley, the chief clinical officer at Press Ganey. Doctors, nurses, advance practice providers, and others used technology such as virtual web chats or Zoom calls to break down silos, quickly hold critical thinking sessions, and diagnose patients. Hospitals also utilized health information exchanges so that doctors could safely and efficiently access patient health care records no matter where the patient came from.[16]

The six reasons control is needed are summarized below. *(See Figure 16.2.)* •

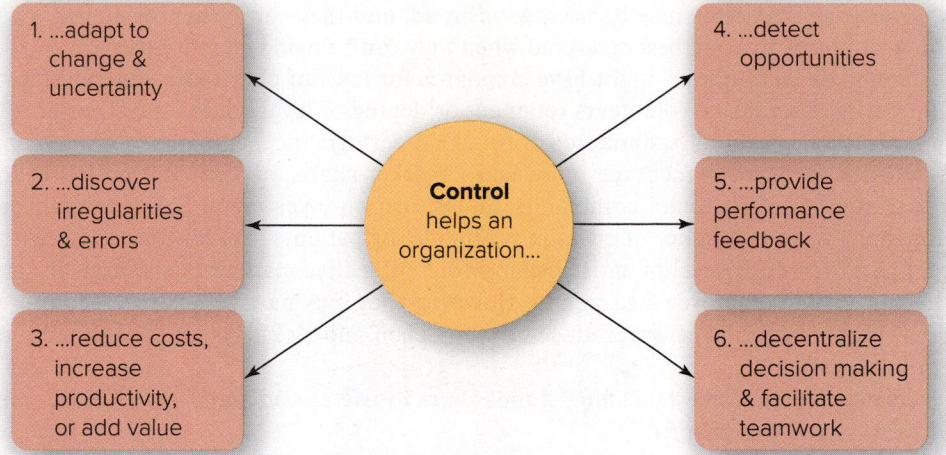

FIGURE 16.2
Six reasons control is needed

16.2 The Control Process and Types of Control

THE BIG PICTURE

This section describes the four steps in the control process and three types of controls.

Control systems ensure that different business activities are furthering the achievement of company goals. Following the steps in the control process assists managers in determining whether an organization's current course of action is working or whether a change in plans or activities is needed. This section reviews the steps in the control process and discusses three different types of controls.

LO 16-2

Describe the steps in the control process and types of control.

Steps in the Control Process

Control systems may be altered to fit specific situations, but generally they follow the same steps. The four ==control process steps== are (1) establish standards; (2) measure performance; (3) compare performance to standards; and (4) take corrective action, if necessary. *(See Figure 16.3.)*

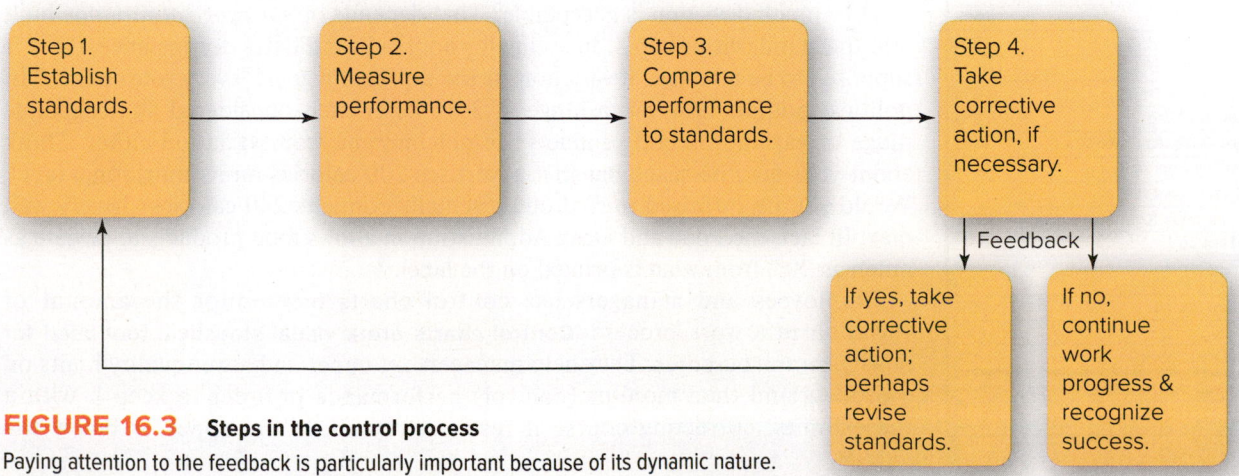

FIGURE 16.3   **Steps in the control process**
Paying attention to the feedback is particularly important because of its dynamic nature.

1. Establish Standards: "What Is the Outcome We Want?"   A ==control standard==, or performance standard or simply standard, is the desired performance level for a given goal. Standards may be narrow or broad, and they can be set for almost anything, although they are best measured when they can be made quantifiable.

Nonprofit institutions might have standards for level of charitable contributions, number of students or volunteers retained, or degree of legal compliance. For-profit organizations might have standards of financial performance, employee hiring, manufacturing defects, percentage increase in market share, percentage reduction in costs, number of customer complaints, and return on investment. Service organizations may look at number of customers, clients, or patients served; time spent with each; and resulting level of satisfaction. More subjective standards also can be set, such as level of employee satisfaction. However, they may have to be expressed more quantifiably in terms of, say, reduced absenteeism and sick days and increased job applications.

One technique for establishing standards is to use *the balanced scorecard*, as we explain later in this chapter.

2. Measure Performance: "What Is the Actual Outcome We Got?"   The second step in the control process is to measure performance, such as by number of products sold, units produced, time to completion, profit margin, or cost per item sold.[17]

This is harder than you think. Consider the example of measuring the length of a marathon. Kimberly Nickel thought she ran a personal best of 4 hours 37 minutes in the PNC Milwaukee Marathon. She proudly posted a selfie on Facebook showing the medal she received. Later that day, however, she received a note from race organizers indicating that "the 26.2 mile course had been laid out incorrectly, making it about 0.8 miles too short and disqualifying the race as an official or certified marathon."[18] Nickel sadly took down the posted photos.

Performance data are usually obtained from five sources: (1) employee behavior and deliverables, (2) peer input or observations, (3) customer feedback, (4) managerial evaluations, and (5) output from a production process.

3. Compare Performance to Standards: "How Do the Desired and Actual Outcomes Differ?"   The third step in the control process is to compare measured performance against the standards established. Most managers are delighted with performance that exceeds standards, which becomes an occasion for handing out bonuses, promotions, and perhaps offices with a view. For performance that is below standards, they need to ask: Is the deviation from performance significant? The greater the difference between desired and actual performance, the greater the need for action.

How much deviation is acceptable? That depends on *the range of variation* built into the standards in step 1. In voting for political candidates, for instance, there is supposed to be no range of variation; as the expression goes, "every vote counts." In political polling, however, a range of 3 to 4% error is considered an acceptable range of variation. Food products are not immune from variation either. Think about your favorite snack bar that advertises 200 calories on its nutritional label. Would you be surprised to find out it actually contains 240 calories? It very well may! In fact, the Food and Drug Administration allows food products to deviate as much as 20% from what is printed on the label.[19]

Employees and managers use control charts to monitor the amount of variation in a work process. ==Control charts== are a visual statistical tool used for quality control purposes. They help managers set upper and lower quality limits on a process and then monitor (control) performance in order to keep it within these limits, correcting course if results stray above the upper or below the

What's in my food? A typical nutrition facts label includes servings and nutritional content such as calories, fat, and other information. How closely do you read these labels as you browse the grocery store? Food and Drug Administration

Nutrition Facts

8 servings per container
Serving size   2/3 cup (55g)

Amount per serving
Calories   230

	% Daily Value*
Total Fat 8g	**10%**
Saturated Fat 1g	**5%**
Trans Fat 0g	
Cholesterol 0mg	**0%**
Sodium 160mg	**7%**
Total Carbohydrate 37g	**13%**
Dietary Fiber 4g	**14%**
Total Sugars 12g	
Includes 10g Added Sugars	**20%**
Protein 3g	
Vitamin D 2mcg	10%
Calcium 260mg	20%
Iron 8mg	45%
Potassium 235mg	6%

* The % Daily Value (DV) tells you how much a nutrient in a serving of food contributes to a daily diet. 2,000 calories a day is used for general nutrition advice.

lower limit over time.[20] Let's examine the steps in developing and using a control chart:

1. Managers construct control charts by first looking at historical data for the process they want to measure. Examples include the number of tax returns completed by a CPA firm per week, tons of steel produced by a manufacturer per day, or dollar volume of charitable contributions solicited by a nonprofit during a month-long fund drive.

2. Historical information is then used to establish the normal or desired performance and its allowable upper and lower limits. *(See Figure 16.4.)* Each of these flows has a separate horizontal line on the chart, which also functions as a timeline.[21] Some managers may even group multiple streams of data into one control chart instead of having different ones — this is called a *group* control chart.[22]

3. When a process goes "out of control"—that is, when it exceeds either the upper or the lower limit—management takes note and investigates. Some variations may be routine or expected, such as a rise in the volume of toy orders before the holiday shopping season or an uptick in charitable donations following a natural disaster. But other variations, such as a sudden drop in production because a machine has broken down or a large number of employees are out ill, will show up on a control chart as deviations and indicate an "out of control" situation that requires attention.

- **Applying control charts to studying:** Let's assume that your experience reveals that in order to complete the assigned reading for all your courses before finals, you need to read 55 pages a night for the next two weeks. Fifty-five pages a night is your desired performance, and depending on how efficiently you can make up for lost time, you might set 35 pages as your acceptable lower limit and 75 as your upper limit. We created the control chart by drawing three horizontal lines with your upper limit on top, your lower limit on the bottom, and your desired rate of 55 pages a night in the middle (see Figure 16.4). The timeline of two weeks is shown at the bottom of the chart. To put it to use, simply mark the number of

FIGURE 16.4 Sample control chart for completing assigned readings

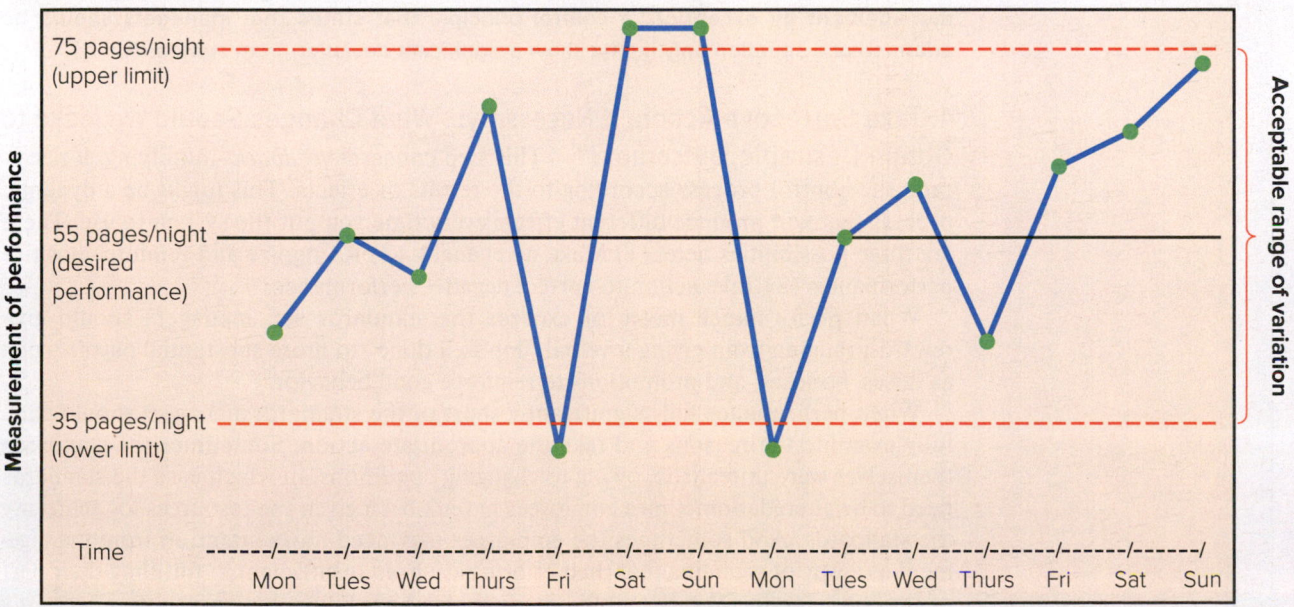

Control and space flight. The Juno space probe was built by Lockheed Martin and is operated by NASA. Courtesy NASA/JPL-Caltech

pages you read each night as a point on the chart, and then connect the dots. Looking at Figure 16.4, you can see that the student exhibited acceptable performance from Monday through Thursday of the first week. Friday's reading was below acceptable limits, which the student made up for by exceeding the upper limit of 75 pages a day on Saturday and Sunday. This was followed by a substandard performance on Monday and then reading levels within acceptable limits the rest of the week.

The range of variation is often incorporated into computer systems to assist with ==management by exception==, a control principle that states that managers should be informed of a situation only if data show a significant deviation from standards.

4. Take Corrective Action, If Necessary: "What Changes Should We Make to Obtain Desirable Outcomes?"   This step concerns *feedback*—modifying, if necessary, the control process according to the results or effects. This might be a dynamic process that will produce different effects every time you put the system to use. There are three possibilities here: (1) Make no changes. (2) Recognize and reinforce positive performance. (3) Take action to correct negative performance.

When performance meets or exceeds the standards set, managers should give rewards, ranging from giving a verbal "Job well done" to more substantial payoffs such as raises, bonuses, and promotions to reinforce good behavior.

When performance falls significantly short of the standard, managers should carefully examine the reasons and take the appropriate action. Sometimes the standards themselves were unrealistic, owing to changing conditions, in which case the standards need to be altered. Sometimes employees haven't been given the resources for achieving the standards. And sometimes the employees may need more attention from management as a way of signaling that their efforts have been insufficient in fulfilling their part of the job bargain. The Example box discusses how UPS uses control to ensure it's operating effectively.

EXAMPLE   UPS Uses the Control Process to Ensure Success

Helping younger drivers train for successful careers has been a priority for UPS. The carrier is the biggest shipping company on the planet with more than 129,000 delivery drivers around the world.[23] UPS designed a high-tech training center called Integrad around research showing how people learn from video games and smartphones.[24]

Integrad's curriculum consists of a five- to nine-day experiential learning course enhanced by virtual-reality simulations so drivers can practice delivery methods without ever leaving the building. UPS says, "The intent of the simulations [is] to help students identify potential hazards by visualizing other vehicles, pedestrians, traffic signs and signals, the basis of what a driver needs to drive defensively." Drivers also have an opportunity to practice delivery methods in a realistic setting on an outside course called "Clarkville, USA." The course mimics a small town "arrayed with small houses, street signs and even a dog bowl to alert drivers of the presence of a dog."[25]

Integrad operates 12 sites in 10 different U.S. states, in addition to locations in Germany and the United Kingdom. The program has so far trained more than 12,000 drivers in "safe work methods, safe driving methods, customer service methods, training in using the handheld computer (DIAD—acronym for Delivery Information Acquisition Device) for recording delivery information, proper package selection, and UPS history."[26]

UPS utilizes the control process after drivers have completed the Integrad program to ensure the program's learning objectives continue to be met. The company establishes standards for routine tasks, such as number of pickups and deliveries in an hour. It then measures drivers' performance and compares it with the standards, taking corrective action, if

A UPS driver in Washington, DC inventories and organizes packages in the back of his delivery truck. Paul J. Richards/Getty Images

necessary. Consider this example from its Louisville, Kentucky, operations.

Establishing Standards UPS establishes standards for its drivers that project the number of miles driven, deliveries, and pickups. A typical day for a UPS driver might include driving 60 miles to make 120 or more deliveries.[27]

Measuring Performance UPS managers get a constant stream of feedback about drivers' performance from the DIAD device and from two on-board computer systems. On-Road Integrated Optimization and Navigation (ORION) optimizes the drivers' routes, and telematics relay information about how often drivers back up and whether they are wearing seat belts. "Everything the driver does is being measured," says the company's business manager in Louisville.[28]

Comparing Performance to Standards UPS managers compare a driver's performance (miles driven and number of pick-ups and deliveries) with the standards that were set for his or her particular route. A range of variation may be allowed to take into account issues like winter or summer driving, or traffic conditions that slow productivity.

Taking Corrective Action If a driver fails to perform to the standards set, UPS can take corrective actions ranging from mentoring and development to termination.[29]

YOUR CALL

The UPS controls were devised by industrial engineers based on experience. Do you think the same kinds of controls could be established for, say, filling out tax forms for H&R Block?

Types of Controls

There are three types of control: feedforward, concurrent, and feedback. You'll notice that the major difference between each is timing. Let's consider how they work and their association with the steps in the control process.

Feedforward Control   Feedforward control focuses on preventing future problems.
It does this by first collecting information about past performance in order to establish new standards. Plans are then made to avoid pitfalls or roadblocks prior to starting a

task or project. This practice essentially helps people learn from mistakes and make better decisions.[30] A recent study confirmed the benefits of effective feedforward control, showing it improved organizational performance and maximized profits.[31] Southwest Airlines is an example of a company that believes in the power of feedforward control. The airlines' top two HR executives told a radio host that employees at the company who make a mistake on the customer's behalf are coached or retrained instead of being punished.[32]

Concurrent Control   Concurrent control entails collecting performance information in real time. This enables managers to measure performance and determine if employee behavior and organizational processes conform to regulations and standards. Corrective action can then be taken immediately when performance is not meeting expectations. For instance, trucking companies use GPS tracking to track their fleet's location and speed, as well as to receive safety alerts. The real-time information gathered also can be used to optimize future routes and reduce fuel consumption.[33]

Technology is typically used for concurrent control. Word-processing software is a good example. It immediately lets us know when we misspell words or use incorrect grammar. Corporate online monitoring of our e-mail and Internet use is another example of concurrent control.

Where's my truck? GPS technology allows organizations to receive real time details on the status of their fleet.
Alexander Kirch/Shutterstock

Feedback Control   This form of control is extensively used by supervisors and managers. Feedback control amounts to collecting performance information after a task or project is done. This information then is used to correct or improve future performance. Classic examples include receiving test scores a week after taking a test, receiving customer feedback after purchasing a product, receiving student ratings of teaching performance weeks after teaching a class, rating the quality of a movie after watching it, and participating in a performance review at work.

The problem with feedback control is that it often occurs too late. For instance, if an instructor is doing a bad job in the classroom, he or she needs to make changes right away. Learning 10 weeks later that his or her performance was ineffective does not help current students. The same is true when it comes to customer satisfaction and quality. On the positive side, many people want feedback, and late is better than never.

Health insurer Cigna recognized the limitations of providing feedback in annual performance reviews. The company now focuses on "frequent, simpler, and less time intensive" performance reviews that can be done at any time of the year. The new system also allows for feedback from the entire team, not just supervisors.[34] ●

16.3 What Should Managers Control?

THE BIG PICTURE

Managers are encouraged to control four different aspects of organizational effectiveness: financial performance, customer consideration, internal business processes, and employee outcomes associated with innovation and learning. These aspects of organizational performance are captured in the balanced scorecard. A strategy map is a visual representation of the relationship among the four key components of organizational performance.

By now you know that managers are responsible for delivering results associated with organizational effectiveness or performance. Their jobs depend on it! But how do managers know what results to focus on given the many different activities, projects, and goals that are pursued on an ongoing basis? It's not an easy decision and the consequences of controlling the wrong outcomes can be very costly. Consider the following examples involving Walmart and United Airlines.

LO 16-3

Discuss ways that managers can control an organization.

Walmart and United Airlines Examples: Walmart's biggest expense is its labor costs, which made it an easy target for managers to cut when the retailer tried to increase profits in 2018. While this decision seemed reasonable given market conditions, the results of this decision paint a different picture. A recent congressional study found that Walmart's sole focus on cutting costs had significant negative implications for taxpayers who had to pay for more government-funded, low-income support programs to subsidize Walmart employees who lost their jobs or had their hours reduced. Unfortunately, the decision also reduced Walmart's resilience in the long term, which hurt shareholder value.[35] United Airlines had to cancel thousands of flights due to the COVID-19 pandemic but was unable to provide excellent customer service by refunding passengers who were impacted by the canceled flights. Instead of refunding billions in airfare, which United officials claimed would have plunged the company into bankruptcy, the airline issued "electronic travel certificates," or gift certificates, for future travel. This caused an uproar among United's passengers and led to the Department of Transportation threatening regulatory action against the airline.[36]

These examples bring us back to the major question addressed in this section: What should managers control? Answering this question requires planning, strategic thinking, and effective control mechanisms. It also entails careful consideration of an organization's stakeholders, which we discussed in Chapter 3 and Learning Module 1. We answer the question of "what should managers control" by discussing a framework called the balanced scorecard.

The balanced scorecard is based on an approach to organizational effectiveness that requires organizational leaders to balance the interests of shareholders, customers, society/environment, and employees.[37] Let's take a look at the logic and structure of the balanced scorecard and how its application results in creating a strategy map.

The Balanced Scorecard: A Comprehensive Approach to Managerial Control

As we learned from Walmart and United Airlines, simply measuring and controlling financial performance, such as sales figures and labor costs, or operational matters, such as customer satisfaction, is not enough.[38] Successful companies go beyond these traditional measures and seek an integrated approach to control that answers these four questions:

1. What does success look like to our shareholders?
2. How do we appear to our customers?

3. What must we do extremely well?

4. Are we equipped for continued value and improvement?

Harvard professors Robert Kaplan and David Norton sought to answer these questions by developing the balanced scorecard. Kaplan and Norton's **balanced scorecard** provides top managers a fast but comprehensive view of the organization via four indicators: (1) financial metrics, (2) customer metrics, (3) internal-business process metrics, and (4) metrics associated with innovation and learning.

"Think of the balanced scorecard as the dials and indicators in an airplane cockpit," write Kaplan and Norton. For a pilot, "reliance on one instrument can be fatal. Similarly, the complexity of managing an organization today requires that managers be able to view performance in several areas simultaneously."[39] It is not enough, say Kaplan and Norton, to simply measure financial performance, such as sales figures and return on investment. Operational matters, such as customer satisfaction, are equally important.[40]

The balanced scorecard establishes *goals* and *performance measures* according to four "perspectives," or areas—*financial, customer, internal-business processes,* and *innovation and learning. (See Figure 16.5.)*

FIGURE 16.5 The balanced scorecard: Four perspectives

Source: Adapted from R. S. Kaplan and D. P. Norton, "The Balanced Scorecard—Measures That Drive Performance," Harvard Business Review, January–February 1992, pp. 71–79.

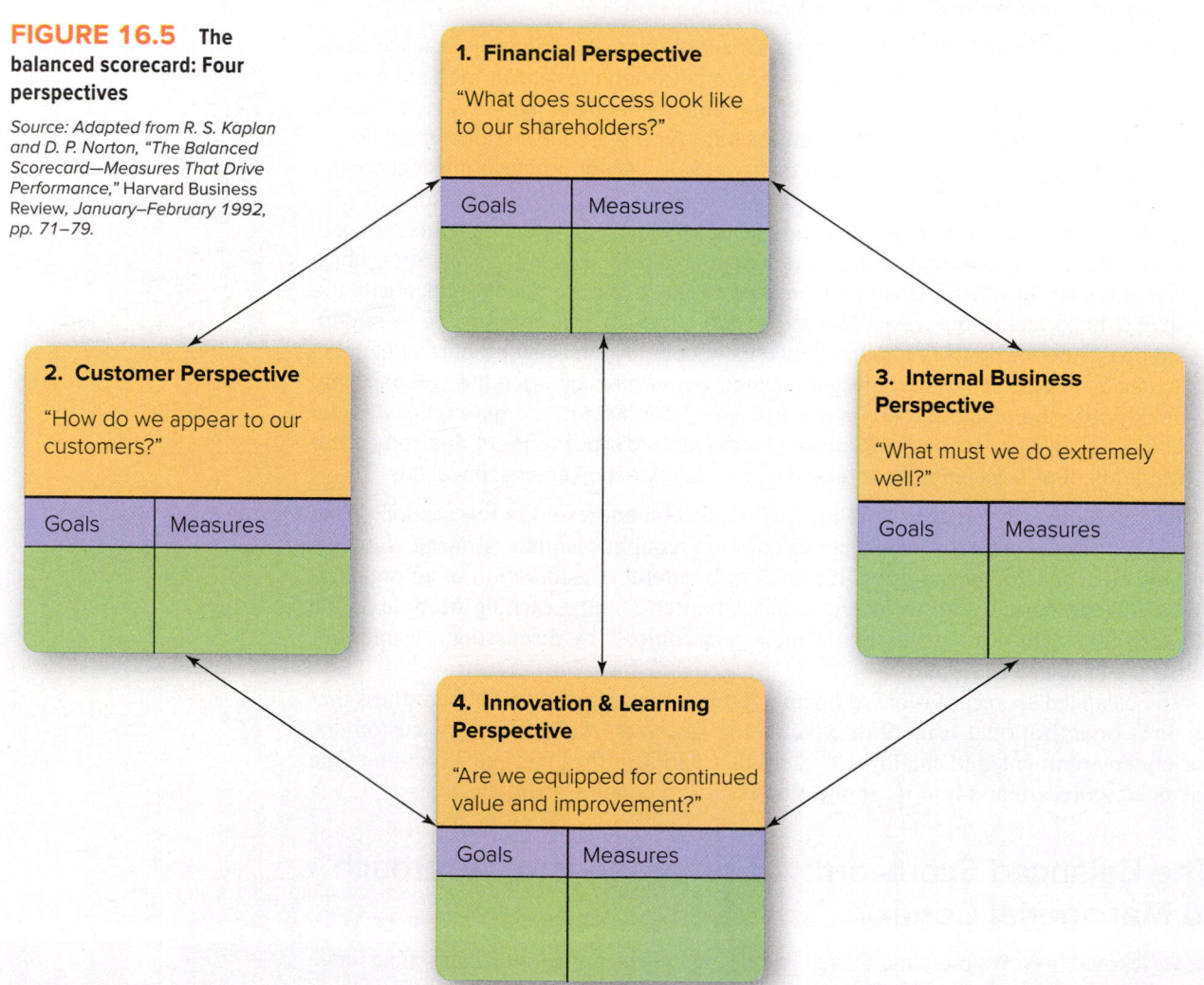

The balanced scorecard is rooted in the saying, "What you measure is what you get." Kaplan and Norton thus recommended that companies should establish, measure, and control quantifiable goals for each perspective that support the organization's vision and strategies. Research confirms the power of the balanced scorecard, demonstrating that businesses that utilize it are more likely to be innovative, gain competitive advantage, and perform better.[41] Let's now consider each of the scorecard's four perspectives.

Financial Perspective: "What Does Success Look Like to Our Shareholders?"

Corporate financial strategies and goals generally fall into two buckets: revenue growth and productivity growth. Revenue growth goals might focus on increasing revenue from both new and existing customers. Game publisher Electronic Arts (EA), for instance, used to rely on one-time sales of video games. The company is now adding additional streams of revenue by offering in-game purchases of items that enhance player performance and personalize game play. Today, 35% of players in EA's two most valuable franchises, Madden and FIFA, spend money on in-game purchases.[42]

Productivity metrics like revenue per employee or total output produced divided by number of employees are common organization-level goals. We also can measure productivity in terms of costs. For example, Macy's is closing 125 underperforming stores in an attempt to decrease costs and improve profitability. "We will focus our resources on the healthy parts of our business, directly address the unhealthy parts of the business and explore new revenue streams," said Jeff Gennette, the company's chairman and COO.[43]

There are many elements associated with the financial perspective. We will focus on three: budgets, financial statements, and financial ratios.

Budgets   A **budget** is a formal financial projection. It states an organization's planned activities for a given period of time in quantitative terms, such as dollars, hours, or number of products. Budgets are prepared not only for the organization as a whole but also for the divisions and departments within it. Most organizations use budgets to provide a yardstick against which managers can judge how well they are controlling monetary expenditures. Some firms also use budgets to signal company priorities and changing trends.[44] Various software tools and apps are available to help you manage personal or freelance budgeting, such as Quicken, Mint, and CountAbout.[45]

There are many different kinds of budgets, but we will focus on incremental budgeting as it's the most widely used type.[46] **Incremental budgeting** allocates increased or decreased funds to a department by using the last budget period as a reference point; only incremental changes in the budget request are reviewed. One difficulty is that incremental budgets tend to lock departments into stable spending arrangements; they are not flexible in meeting environmental demands. Another difficulty is that a department may engage in many activities—some more important than others—but it's not easy to sort out how well managers performed at the various activities. Thus, the department activities and the yearly budget increases take on lives of their own.

In general, we can identify two types of incremental budgets: *fixed* and *variable*.

Hail to the spreadsheet. Professionals often use software, such as Microsoft Excel, to perform budgeting activities. Rawpixel.com/Shutterstock

- **Fixed budgets:** Also known as a *static budget*, a **fixed budget** allocates resources on the basis of a single estimate of costs. That is, there is only one set of expenses; the budget does not allow for adjustment over time. For example, you might have a budget of $50,000 for buying equipment in a given year—no matter how much you may need equipment exceeding that amount.

- **Variable budgets:** Also known as a *flexible budget*, a **variable budget** allows the allocation of resources to vary in proportion with various levels of activity. That is, the budget can be adjusted over time to accommodate pertinent changes in the environment. For example, you might have a budget that allows you to hire temporary workers or lease temporary equipment if production exceeds certain levels. As a freelancer, you might set up your budget to allow for the unexpected, like the purchase of a second monitor for your laptop if you accept an assignment that requires it.

Financial Statements

A **financial statement** is a summary of some aspect of an organization's financial status. Research demonstrates that the information contained in such a statement is essential in helping managers maintain financial control over the organization.[47]

There are three basic types of financial statements: *the balance sheet, income statement*, and *statement of cash flows*. We'll look at each statement individually.

- **The balance sheet:** A **balance sheet** summarizes an organization's overall financial worth—that is, assets and liabilities—at a specific point in time.

    Assets are the resources that an organization controls; they consist of current assets and fixed assets. *Current assets* are cash and other assets that are readily convertible to cash within one year's time. Examples are inventory, sales for which payment has not been received (accounts receivable), and U.S. Treasury bills or money market mutual funds. *Fixed assets* are property, buildings, equipment, and the like that have a useful life that exceeds one year but that are usually harder to convert to cash. *Liabilities* are claims, or debts, by suppliers, lenders, and other nonowners of the organization against a company's assets. ExxonMobil is a good example of an organization that keeps a close eye on its assets and liabilities.

    ExxonMobil Example: Oil giant ExxonMobil spent decades ensuring it had a healthy balance sheet in case of a catastrophe. That catastrophe came in 2020 when oil prices plummeted due to a combination of COVID-19 and oversupply. The company's previous focus on balancing its assets and liabilities paid off during a time of uncertainty, allowing it to continue investing in strategic projects and paying shareholders. "Exxon remains committed to satisfying the needs of its large retail investor base in paying dividends, and it won't shy away from tapping its balance sheet to come up with cash if needed in the short term," said CEO Darren Woods.[48]

- **The income statement:** The balance sheet depicts the organization's overall financial worth at a specific point in time. By contrast, the **income statement** summarizes an organization's financial results—revenues and expenses—over a specified period of time, such as a quarter or a year.

    You will need to understand an income statement if you end up self-employed or start a business. We created a sample profit and loss statement for a two-person operation consisting of an owner and one employee *(see Table 16.1)*. The company is doing quite well with $196,776.21 of net income, computed by subtracting total expenses from gross profit. You also can see the types of expenses that confront any small business. You have expenses for insurance, payroll and payroll taxes, accounting, auto, rent, supplies, and other expenses.

- **The statement of cash flows:** The **statement of cash flows** reports the cash generated and used over a specific period of time. Generally, this period of time matches the company's income statement.[49]

Have you ever heard the saying "cash is king"? Stakeholders are often interested in how much actual cash an organization is generating because it shows how solvent the company is. This is what differentiates the statement of cash flows from an income

TABLE 16.1

Sample Profit and Loss
Statements

LACI, THE COMPUTER DOCTOR
PROFIT & LOSS
JANUARY 1 THROUGH DECEMBER 31, 2021

Income:		Jan 1–Dec 31, 2021
Sales		520,615.00
Services Income		32,320.00
Total Income:		552,935.00
Parts and Materials	54,218.00	
Gross Profit		498,717.00
Expenses:		
Bank Service Charges		180.00
Charitable Donations		2,300.00
Dues and Subscriptions		1,750.35
Insurance:		
General Liability Insurance	2,035.00	
Workman's Compensation Insurance	1,018.00	
Total Insurance Expense		3,053.00
Payroll Taxes:		
Payroll 941	14,826.22	
Federal Unemployment Tax	215.00	
State Unemployment Tax	312.00	
Total Payroll Taxes		15,353.22
Payroll:		
Officer Wages	190,000.00	
Salary and Wages	52,329.21	
Total Payroll:		242,329.21
Accounting and Legal		1,803.50
Automobile Expenses:		
Maintenance	323.00	
Gas	1,318.49	
License	782.20	
Total Automobile Expenses:		2,423.69
Office Rent		24,000.00
Office supplies		2,016.48
Repairs and Maintenance		218.60
Telephone and Internet		2,472.18
Utilities		3,040.56
TOTAL EXPENSE		300,940.79
NET INCOME		197,776.21

A J. Crew factory store at the Arundel Mills Outlet Mall in Maryland. melissamn/Shutterstock

statement—the latter often includes noncash revenues or expenses, which can be misleading. For example, a firm that has significant revenue, but does not actually receive the revenue in time to pay its expenses, will face problems.[50] Because companies generate and use cash in different ways, the statement of cash flows is separated into three sections: *operating activities* (cash generated from a company's core business as opposed to investments and borrowing), *investment activities* (cash generated from investments), and *financing activities* (cash generated from owners or debtors). J. Crew is a good example of what happens when a firm runs out of cash.

J. Crew Example: Department stores were already experiencing a shortage of cash and taking on debt due to decreasing revenues before the COVID-19 pandemic hit in 2020. J. Crew, which brought its preppy style to U.S. malls in the 1990s, was no exception. The company closed around 500 stores in March 2020 as shopping malls shut down due to the COVID-19 pandemic. This meant the already cash-strapped company didn't have the funds to pay its loan payments, rent, or employee payroll, forcing it into bankruptcy in May 2020. Raya Sokolyanska, a vice president at Moody's, believes the COVID-19's disruption of the retail sector was particularly hard felt because of the need for retailers to unload unsold inventory to raise cash. "J. Crew's bankruptcy will be the first in a wave of defaults among retailers" with weak financials, said Sokolyanska.[51]

Financial Ratios   Financial statements provide data on a firm, but often times managers need a simple way to measure progress against internal goals, competitors, or the overall industry. This can be done with ==financial ratios==, which are indicators determined from a company's financial information and used for comparison purposes.[52] Some of the most common ratios measure a company's *liquidity*, *turnover*, and *profitability*. Table 16.2 lists an example of a ratio for each of these categories, what the ratio measures, and how to calculate it.

TABLE 16.2   **Popular Financial Ratios**

RATIO	CATEGORY	WHAT IS MEASURED	FORMULA
Current Ratio	Liquidity	A company's ability to pay short term obligations due within a year.	$\dfrac{\text{Current Assets}}{\text{Current Liabilities}}$
Asset Turnover Ratio	Turnover	The efficiency in which a company uses assets to generate revenue.	$\dfrac{\text{Sales}}{\text{Average Total Assets}}$
Return on Investment Ratio	Profitability	The amount of return on a particular investment relative to its cost.	$\dfrac{\text{Net Income}}{\text{Cost of Investment}}$

Sources: W. Kenton, "Current Ratio," Investopedia, *April 28, 2020*, https://www.investopedia.com/terms/c/currentratio.asp; A. Hayes, "Asset Turnover Ratio," Investopedia, *April 28, 2020*, https://www.investopedia.com/terms/a/assetturnover.asp; J. Chen, "Return on Investment (ROI)," Investopedia, *April 27, 2020*, https://www.investopedia.com/terms/r/returnoninvestment.asp.

Customer Perspective: "How Do We Appear to Our Customers?"

Many companies rightfully view customers as one of their most important stakeholders—why wouldn't they? After all, customers generate the revenue needed to achieve financial performance. A company without any customers has no income. The balanced scorecard translates this belief into measures such as customer satisfaction/loyalty and retention. Let's examine each in a bit more detail.

Customer Satisfaction   Companies would not exist without satisfied customers. ==Customer satisfaction== is the measure of how products or services provided by a firm meet customer expectations. As you might expect, losing a dissatisfied customer means losing revenue, but did you know that replacing that customer is an even greater challenge? In fact, studies show that it is six to seven times more expensive to acquire a new customer than it is to keep a current one.[53] Being creative is one research-proven way to keep customers satisfied. A study of airline customer service agents, for instance, found that employees who energetically and creatively tried to solve passenger problems increased customer satisfaction—even when the solution wasn't what the passenger wanted.[54] Alaska Airlines is a good example of an airline promoting creative problem solving. The airline empowers its customer service agents to offer refunds, rewards, and even cash, to make things right for customers instead of escalating the problem to management.[55]

Customer Retention   Whereas customer satisfaction measures how customers are feeling, <mark>customer retention</mark> refers to the actions companies take to reduce customer defections. In other words, the goal of customer retention programs is to keep customers loyal because loyal customers tend to be repeat buyers and they tell others good things about a company's products and services.[56] Effective customer retention programs focus on three techniques. Let's explore each using the Ritz-Carlton hotel chain as an example.[57]

- **Set customer expectations:** Organizations should set customer expectations early and a bit lower than what they can actually provide. This eliminates uncertainty about the level of expected service and ensures they will always meet commitments.

  Example: The Ritz-Carlton lists its "Gold Standards" on its website so guests are aware of its pledge to "provide the finest personal service and facilities for guests who will always enjoy a warm, relaxed, yet refined ambiance."

Impeccable service. Doormen at the Ritz-Carlton Hotel in New York open doors for a guest. Keith Bedford/Redux Pictures

- **Go the extra mile:** Going above and beyond customer expectations helps companies build strong relationships and long-term loyalty. In fact, 60% of customers are willing to pay more for a better experience, showing it's well worth it to go that extra mile.[58]

  Example: Ritz-Carlton employees, from housekeeping to management, can spend up to $2,000 per guest, per day, to resolve problems without asking their supervisor for permission.

- **Make it personal:** Personalized service improves the customer experience and strengthens an organization's bond with its clientele. An Access Development survey, for instance, found that 70% of businesses created a more personalized experience in order to improve client retention in 2018.[59]

  Example: Ritz-Carlton employees give guests a warm, sincere greeting using their name; fulfill their needs; and provide a fond farewell, again addressing guests by their name.

Internal Business Perspective: "What Must We Do Extremely Well?"

Whereas the customer perspective represents the revenue side of the financial equation, the internal business perspective portrays the cost side. This perspective captures critical organizational activities that allow organizations to effectively meet their financial objectives and customers' expectations while creating value for society and the communities that they serve.[60] The balanced scorecard measures these activities by looking at metrics such as productivity, efficiency, quality, and safety.

Productivity   Productivity can be applied at any level, whether for you as an individual, for the work unit you're managing, or for the organization you work for. Productivity is defined by the formula of *outputs divided by inputs* for a specified period of time. Outputs are all the goods and services produced. Inputs are not only labor but also capital, materials, and energy. That is,

$$\text{Productivity} = \frac{\text{Outputs}}{\text{Inputs}} \quad \text{or} \quad \frac{\text{Goods} + \text{Services}}{\text{Labour} + \text{Capital} + \text{Materials} + \text{Energy}}$$

There are two tools managers can use to set standards or goals for productivity.

- **Benchmarking:** A process by which a company compares its performance with others, as we discussed in Chapter 6. Companies use internal benchmarks to set performance standards, competitive benchmarking to assess themselves against their competitors, and strategic benchmarking when they are ready to look outside their industry. The J.D. Powers Company is a good example of a company that assists the automotive industry and its customers with benchmarking. The firm provides data on how well competing automobiles satisfy buyers in several areas including initial quality, dependability, overall performance and appeal, and sales and service.[61]

- **Best practices:** Best practices refers to "a set of guidelines, ethics or ideas that have been shown to produce optimal results."[62] Companies often develop best practices internally through managers' and employees' positive experiences on the job, and they sometimes adopt the strategies with which other companies have succeeded in similar situations. For example, teams were found to have higher performance levels when they established a process of regularly meeting to discuss work processes or best practices.[63]

Efficiency As we discussed in Chapter 1, efficiency means to use resources—people, money, raw materials, and the like—wisely and cost effectively. Good managers aren't only concerned with efficiency though; they also need to ensure they are being effective. This means managers achieve results by making the right decisions and successfully carrying them out (think back to the definition of *management*: the pursuit of organizational goals efficiently and effectively). The National Marrow Donor Program is a good example of an organization that is focused on improving both its efficiency and effectiveness.

National Marrow Donor Program Example: Seven in 10 people in the United States who need a life-saving bone marrow or cord blood transplant do not have a suitable donor within their families. That's where the "Be the Match Registry," run by the nonprofit National Marrow Donor Program (NMDP) comes into play, with more than 16 million registered potential donors. When NMDP recently resolved to double its annual transplant rate, its managers realized the organization needed a new strategic plan. After consulting with other nonprofits and health care organizations, it chose the balanced scorecard approach for its ability to incorporate powerful quality management strategies as well improve internal processes. Improvements that have already been made at NMDP include reduced time to find matches, increased global brand awareness and donor recruitment, earlier referrals from physicians, and lower medical costs for patients and families.[64]

Quality High-quality products and services are vital to an organization's success. This is especially true in crowded markets such as technology. Quality is one reason Apple, for instance, can price its iPhone higher than any other mobile device in the industry. This is because the company has established a history of delivering market-leading products.[65] In fact, a 2019 survey of more than 2,000 smartphone customers found that over 90% of iPhone users intended to buy another one when the time came for an upgrade.[66]

In Section 16.4, we'll discuss how organizations can use total quality management techniques to ensure they are effectively managing the quality of their products and services. For now, it's important to know that quality contributes to increasing customer loyalty, building a strong reputation, and managing costs.[67]

Safety As we discussed in Learning Module 1, organizations have a responsibility for the safety of the communities in which they serve.[68] Part of this responsibility is related to not harming the community (i.e., making sure your factory does not poison a town's drinking water), which is a direct measure of community safety. Other times, the impact is indirect, such as making sure your employees, many of whom come from local communities, are safe. Phoenix Sintered Metals is a good example of an organization committed to its employees' safety.

Phoenix Sintered Metals Example: Family-owned Phoenix Sintered Metals is a Pennsylvania manufacturer of metal parts. The company is "committed to continuous improvement" in its occupational health and safety policies and procedures. To this end, Terry Fustine, Phoenix's safety coordinator, took advantage of a program offered by Pennsylvania's Occupational Health and Safety Administration (PA OSHA). The program provides for free occupational safety and health consultation services, including a walkthrough of facilities. During the initial walkthrough, PA OSHA consultants identi-

Safety first. The Phoenix Sintered Metals Safety Committee at the company's headquarters in Brockway, Pennsylvania. Courtesy of Phoenix Sintered Metals

fied issues associated with housekeeping, labeling, machine guarding, electrical, safety orientation, and other hazards. The company corrected these issues, explained the safety concerns to employees, and enhanced their safety training and departmental audits. Phoenix also improved its written safety and health program policy manual. The company's focus on safety contributed to a 66% drop in recordable injuries and led to its acceptance into Pennsylvania's "Safety and Health Achievement Recognition Program," singling Phoenix Sintered Metals out among its peers as a model for workplace safety. And for those in the company worried about the bottom line—all of the changes were made at minimal cost.[69]

Innovation and Learning Perspective: "Are We Equipped for Continued Value and Improvement?"

Learning and development of employees are the foundation for all other goals in the balanced scorecard. The idea here is that capable and motivated employees, who possess the resources and motivation needed to get the job done, will provide higher-quality products and services in a more efficient manner. Making this happen requires a commitment to invest in progressive human resource practices (recall our discussion in Chapter 9) and technology. Typical metrics in this perspective are employee attitudes (Chapter 11), turnover (Chapter 11), organizational culture (Chapter 8), and resource capabilities. Let's consider each of these measures.

Employee Attitudes   As we discussed in Chapter 11, employee attitudes are incredibly important and influence workers' behavior. Successful managers aren't satisfied with just "happy" employees, they strive to increase employee engagement, job satisfaction, and commitment. As we discussed many times in this textbook, there is an abundance of research demonstrating that these attitudes can increase performance and customer outcomes while reducing turnover and absenteeism.[70]

Employee Turnover   Every organization experiences some turnover, which, as we saw in Chapter 9, is when an employee abandons, resigns, retires, or is terminated from a job. Recent studies demonstrate that job satisfaction and organizational commitment are the strongest predictors of turnover.[71] There is, however, a difference between functional and dysfunctional turnover. Let's dig a bit deeper into the differences.[72]

- **Functional turnover:** This turnover occurs when underperformers leave a firm. Functional turnover is common in large accounting, consulting, and laws firms employing an "up or out" philosophy. Those who are unable to progress are in effect let go. Take for example tenure at universities. Professors who are trying to obtain tenure ("tenure-line faculty") have a certain number of years to do so based on their research, teaching, and service to the institution. Those who are not able to achieve tenure are eventually let go.

- **Dysfunctional turnover:** This is the opposite of functional turnover and occurs when a company's best performers leave. A variety of reasons can contribute to dysfunctional turnover, but a common cause is low potential for advancement. For example, if a company is in the habit of filling its management positions with external candidates instead of looking at high-performing internal ones, employees are likely to seek opportunities for advancement at other firms.

Successful companies don't just measure an overall turnover rate. They need to figure out if the employees they couldn't retain were high or low performers. This will determine if the turnover was functional or dysfunctional.[73] Let's think of an employee named Ava and assume she just resigned from her sales manager position. HR may take a look at Ava's personnel file and examine her last performance appraisal. If Ava earned high marks, the turnover is most likely dysfunctional. Another way to make this determination is to ask Ava's manager if they would rehire her. If the answer is yes, you have dysfunctional turnover.

Exit interviews also can assist in better understanding the reasons for turnover. These are formal conversations that take place between a departing employee and HR, or another manager, to determine the reason why the person is leaving.[74] Let's return to our example of Ava. HR can utilize an exit interview to determine if she left because she was dissatisfied, or because her spouse got a job in another state and they needed to move.

Resource Capabilities   Managers need to ensure employees have the resources they need to be successful. This includes investing in employee learning and development and in technology that supports achievement of the organization's goals. Let's look at how a dairy farm used Slack to keep their employees connected and safe during the COVID-19 pandemic.

Wickstrom Dairies Example: California-based Wickstrom Dairies has 28 employees and 2,500 cows that need 200,000 pounds of feed a day. Wickstrom employees typically have in-person pre-shift meetings to find out what their assignments are, what happened overnight with sick animals, and the status of any equipment repairs. All this changed when COVID-19 hit. The cows weren't worried, but Wickstrom's employees needed to stay connected. The company facilitated this by investing in Slack, an online office communications tool. Employees utilized Slack to keep each other informed about what needed to be done around the farm and also posted updates on animals and equipment—all while keeping social distancing in place. "Slack has made everybody's job easier. And safer. Our cows are vitally important, but our people rank higher," said Aaron Wickstrom, the dairy company's co-owner.[75]

Organizational Culture   We discussed organizational culture in Chapter 8, but here we want to specifically reiterate the importance of people-focused cultures. As you may recall from Chapter 2, people-focused organizations are guided by the Theory Y view that people are essentially good, trustworthy, and productive, and that they flourish when they are empowered to act independently in an atmosphere that respects their diversity and values their well-being. CarMax, the nation's largest used car retailer, is a good example of a company with a people-focused culture.

CarMax Example: CarMax operates more than 200 stores in 41 states. The company focuses on increasing collaboration as well as respect and support for its employees. "Our associates' dedication and drive to not only support the customer, but also each other, is what makes CarMax a great place to work," said Diane Cafritz, the company's chief human resources officer. Employees are encouraged to cross-train and explore opportunities outside their own departments in order to better their skills and abilities. CarMax employees also are encouraged to share their time, talents, and resources to volunteer in the local communities they serve in order to increase their own well-being. CarMax has earned top accolades for its people-focused approach, including 15 years as one of *Fortune*'s "100 Best Companies to Work For."[76]

A Carmax associate at the company's Plano, Texas location talks with a customer about the value of his used truck. LM Otero/AP Images

To what extent is/was your current or past employer committed to the people, technology, and organizational culture needed to support its strategy? You can find out by completing Self-Assessment 16.1.

SELF-ASSESSMENT 16.1

Assessing the Innovation and Learning Perspective of the Balanced Scorecard

The survey was designed to assess the innovation and learning perspective of the balanced scorecard. Please be prepared to answer these questions if your instructor has assigned Self-Assessment 16.1 in Connect.

1. Where does the company stand in terms of commitment to innovation and learning? Are you surprised by the results?

2. Use the three highest and lowest scores to identify the strengths and weaknesses of this company's commitment to innovation and learning.

3. Based on your answer to question 2, provide three suggestions for what management could do to improve its commitment to innovation and learning.

Strategy Mapping: Visual Representation of the Path to Organizational Effectiveness

Have you ever worked for a company that failed to effectively communicate its vision and strategic plan? If yes, then you know how it feels to be disengaged because you don't know how your work contributes to organizational effectiveness. Kaplan and Norton recognized this common problem and developed a tool called a strategy map.

A **strategy map** is a "visual representation of a company's critical objectives and the crucial relationships among them that drive organizational performance." Maps show relationships among a company's strategic goals. This helps employees understand how their work contributes to their employer's overall success.[77] They also provide insight into how an organization creates value for its key constituents. For example, a map informs others about the knowledge, skills, and systems that employees should possess (innovation and learning perspective) to innovate and build internal capabilities (internal business perspective) that deliver value to customers (customer perspective), which eventually creates higher shareholder value (financial perspective). Research confirms the value of strategy mapping, demonstrating that its effective use substantially improves the implementation success of balanced scorecards. These maps also have been found to facilitate strategy formation, performance measurement system development, and strategy evaluation and communication.[78]

We created an illustrative strategy map in Figure 16.6. Starting with learning and growth, the arrows in the diagram show the logic that connects goals to internal processes, to customers, to financial goals, and finally to the long-term goal of providing shareholder value. For example, you can see that organizational culture affects the internal process goals related to innovation, operational improvements, and good corporate citizenship. This causal structure provides a strategic road map of how the company plans to achieve organizational effectiveness.

FIGURE 16.6   Sample strategy map for Keurig Dr. Pepper

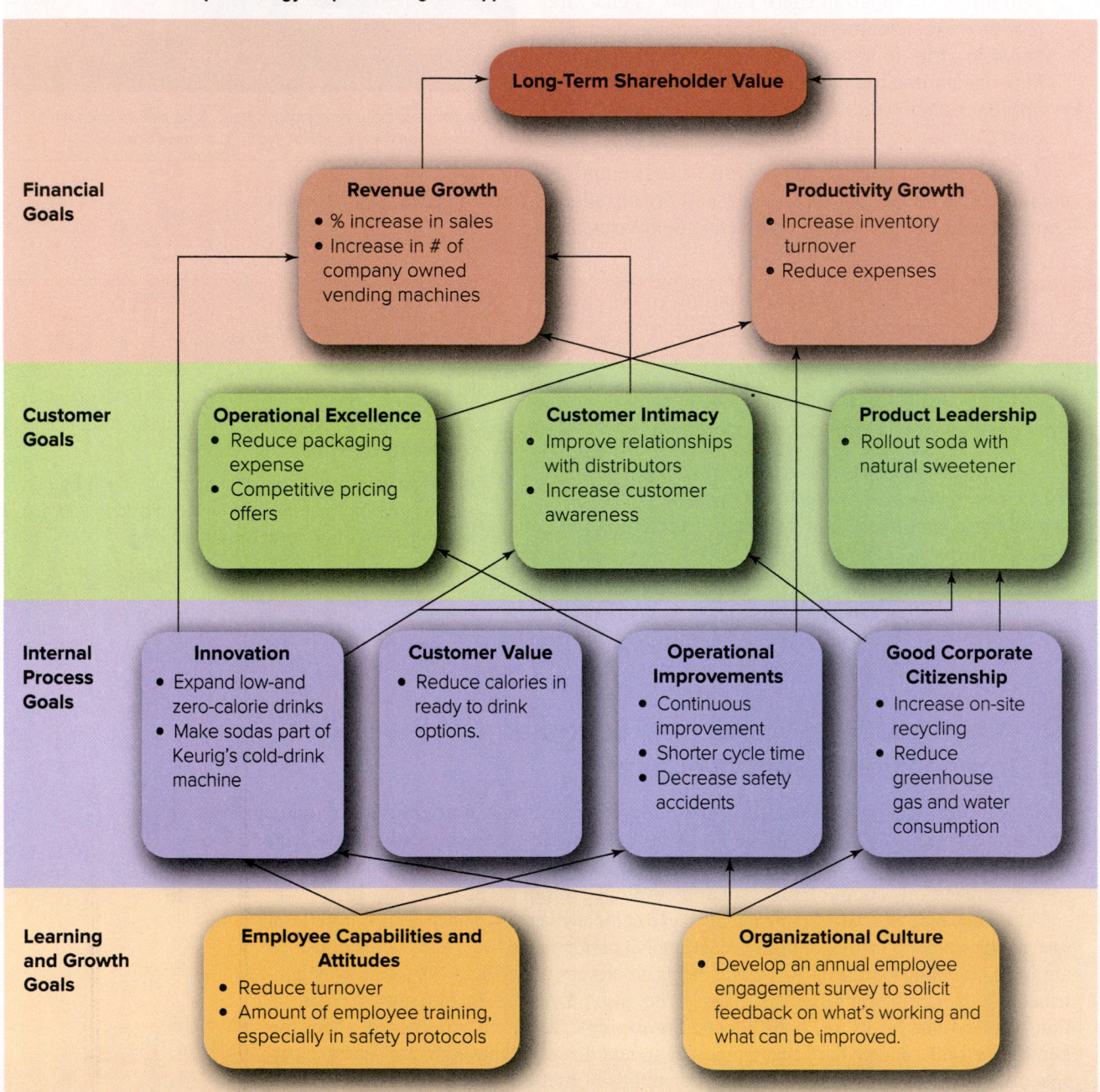

Sources: This map was based on information in "Corporate Social Responsibility," Dr. Pepper Snapple Group, https://www.drpeppersnapplegroup.com/company/environmental-sustainability (accessed May 21, 2020); J. Natsu, "Keurig Dr Pepper Plans to 'Drink Well, Do Good' with Major New Commitments," Environmental Leader, June 6, 2019, https://www.environmentalleader.com/2019/06/180124/; "Corporate Responsibility Report 2018, Keurig Dr Pepper, 2018, https://www.keurigdrpepper.com/content/dam/keurig-brand-sites/kdp/files/KDP-CR-Report-2018.pdf; "Keurig Dr Pepper Reports Strong 4th Quarter and Full Year 2018 Results," Keurig Dr Pepper, February, 28, 2019, https://investors.keurigdrpepper.com/2019-02-28-Keurig-Dr-Pepper-Reports-Strong-4th-Quarter-and-Full-Year-2018-Results.

You can also detect which of the four perspectives is most important by counting the number of goals in each perspective. For this sample map, there are four, five, eight, and four goals for the financial, customer, internal processes, and learning and growth perspectives, respectively. You also can see that internal process goals affect eight other goals—count the number of arrows coming from internal process goals. All told, the beauty of a strategy map is that it enables leaders to present a strategic road map to employees on one page. It also provides a clear statement about the criteria used to assess organizational effectiveness.

There is one final benefit to strategy maps. They serve as the starting point for any organization that wants to implement goal cascading or management by objectives. For example, one of your authors, Angelo Kinicki, has worked with several organizations that cascaded a top-level strategy map like the one shown in Figure 16.6 down three to four organizational levels.[79] •

16.4 Total Quality Management

THE BIG PICTURE

Total quality management (TQM) is dedicated to continuous quality improvement, training, and customer satisfaction. Two core principles are people orientation and improvement orientation. Some techniques for improving quality are employee involvement, benchmarking, outsourcing, reduced cycle time, and statistical process control.

LO 16-4

Explain the total quality management process.

Adventist Health White Memorial (AHWM), a 353-bed, nonprofit, faith-based teaching hospital in Los Angeles was one of six 2019 winners of the coveted Malcolm Baldrige National Quality Award.[80] This award is "given by the President of the United States to businesses and to education, health care, and nonprofit organizations that apply and are judged to be outstanding in seven areas of performance excellence." The seven areas are leadership; strategy; customers; measurement, analysis, and knowledge management; workforce; operations; and results.[81]

AHWM counts reliability as a key goal and more than meets it. The hospital has sustained near or perfect performance when it comes to treating heart attack patients since 2013. It also has had zero emergency department returns after outpatient surgery since 2014, placing it in the top national decile. AHWM doesn't rest on its stellar performance and continuously studies the changing market to determine what patients may need in the future. To this end, the hospital uses surveys, focus groups of key stakeholders, and other mechanisms to identify the types of services that provide value and differentiate it from competitors.[82]

Another source of pride for AHWM is its process efficiency and effectiveness. For example, the hospital has reduced its emergency department length of stay from over 250 minutes in 2015 to around 150 minutes in 2018, a level very close to the national top quartile. AHWM was able to accomplish this by using a real-time electronic dashboard that monitors each phase of a patient's stay in the emergency department. This allows caregivers to deliver timely, patient-centered care.[83]

How can organizations be more like AHWM? This is what we'll be discussing in this section. We'll start with an overview of what we mean by quality before discussing total quality management and its core principles. The focus will then turn to tools, techniques, and standards that organizations can utilize to uphold a high standard of quality.

Quality Control and Quality Assurance

Quality refers to the total ability of a product or service to meet customer needs. Quality is seen as one of the most important ways of adding value to products and services, thereby distinguishing them from those of competitors. Two traditional strategies for ensuring quality are quality control and quality assurance.

Quality Control   Quality control is defined as the strategy for minimizing errors by managing each stage of production. Quality control techniques were developed in the 1930s at Bell Telephone Labs by Walter Shewhart, who used statistical sampling to locate errors by testing just some (rather than all) of the items in a particular production run.

Quality Assurance   Developed in the 1960s, quality assurance focuses on the performance of workers, urging employees to strive for "zero defects." Quality assurance has been less successful because often employees have no control over the design of the work process.

Deming Management: The Contributions of W. Edwards Deming to Improved Quality

Now that you have a better understanding of quality, let's see how we got to the standards we have today. In the early 20th century, Frederick Taylor's scientific management philosophy, designed to maximize worker productivity, had been widely instituted. But by the 1950s, scientific management had led to organizations that were rigid and unresponsive to both employees and customers. W. Edwards Deming's challenge, known as Deming management, proposed ideas for making organizations more responsive, more democratic, and less wasteful. These included the following principles.

1. Quality Should Be Aimed at the Needs of the Consumer   "The consumer is the most important part of the production line," Deming wrote.[84] Thus, the efforts of individual workers in providing the product or service should be directed toward meeting the needs and expectations of the ultimate user.

2. Companies Should Aim at Improving the System, Not Blaming Workers Deming suggested that U.S. managers were more concerned with blaming problems on individual workers rather than on the organization's structure, culture, technology, work rules, and management—that is, "the system." By treating employees well, listening to their views and suggestions, Deming felt managers could bring about improvements in products and services.

3. Improved Quality Leads to Increased Market Share, Increased Company Prospects, and Increased Employment   When companies work to improve the quality of goods and services, they produce less waste, experience fewer delays, and are more efficient. Lower prices and superior quality lead to greater market share, which in turn leads to improved business prospects and consequently increased employment.

4. Quality Can Be Improved on the Basis of Hard Data, Using the PDCA Cycle   Deming suggested that quality could be improved by acting on the basis of hard data. The process for doing this came to be known as the PDCA cycle, a Plan-Do-Check-Act cycle using observed data for continuous improvement of operations.

(See Figure 16.7.) Like the steps in the control process in Figure 16.3, step 3 ("Check") is a *feedback* step, in which performance is compared to goals. Feedback is instrumental to control.

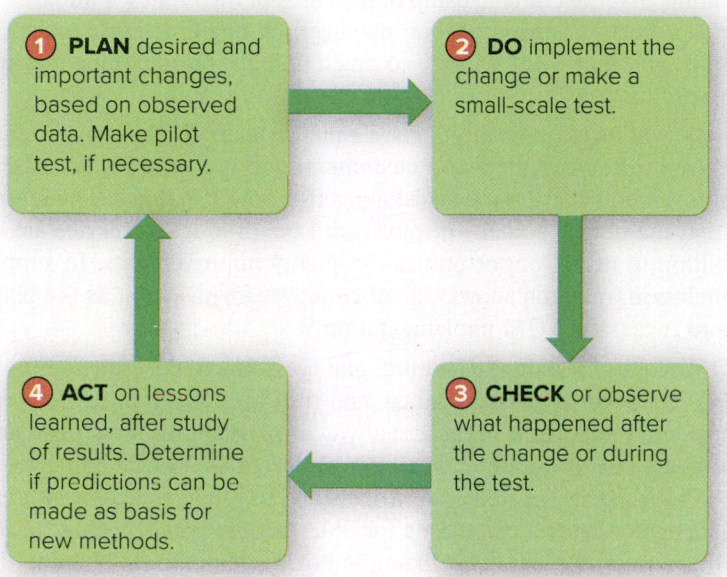

FIGURE 16.7

The PDCA cycle: Plan-Do-Check-Act

The four steps continuously follow each other, resulting in continuous improvement.

Source: From W. Edwards Deming, Out of the Crisis, Plan Do Study Act Cycle, Massachusetts Institute of Technology, 2000, p. 88.

Core TQM Principles: Deliver Customer Value and Strive for Continuous Improvement

Total quality management (TQM) is defined as a comprehensive approach—led by top management and supported throughout the organization—dedicated to continuous quality improvement, training, and customer satisfaction. There are four components to TQM:

1. Make continuous improvement a priority.
2. Get every employee involved.
3. Listen to and learn from customers and employees.
4. Use accurate standards to identify and eliminate problems.

These may be summarized as **two core principles of TQM**—namely, (1) people orientation—everyone involved with the organization should focus on delivering value to customers—and (2) improvement orientation—everyone should work on continuously improving the work processes.[85] Let's look at these further.

1. People Orientation—Focusing Everyone on Delivering Customer Value
Organizations adopting TQM value people as their most important resource—both those who create a product or service and those who receive it. Thus, not only are employees given more decision-making power, so are suppliers and customers.

This people orientation operates under the following assumptions.

- **Delivering customer value is most important.** The purpose of TQM is to focus people, resources, and work processes to deliver products or services that create value for customers. Toyota is a long-time practitioner of TQM. The company's Lexus plant in Georgetown, Kentucky, its largest vehicle

Toyota's manufacturing plant in Georgetown, Kentucky. John Sommers II/Getty Images

manufacturing plant worldwide, produces more than half a million cars a year and more than 600,000 engines.[86] The 750 employees who worked on the first Lexus line to be built in the United States received more than 150,000 hours of special sensory training so they could "rely on sight, sound and touch to know that the craftsmanship of the car is of the highest standard," said Mike Bridge, Lexus assistant general manager. "A machine can't make those judgments, and that's why we take so much time to train before a new model goes into production."[87]

- **People will focus on quality if given empowerment.** TQM assumes that employees (and often suppliers and customers) will concentrate on making quality improvements if given the decision-making power to do so. The reasoning here is that the people actually involved with the product or service are in the best position to detect opportunities for quality improvements. In support of this conclusion, research shows lack of employee involvement as the biggest obstacle to successful TQM implementation.[88]

- **TQM requires training, teamwork, and cross-functional efforts.** Employees and suppliers need to be well trained, and they must work in teams. Teamwork is considered important because many quality problems are spread across functional areas. For example, if cell phone design specialists conferred with marketing specialists (as well as customers and suppliers), they would find that the challenge of using a cell phone for older people is pushing 11 tiny buttons to call a phone number. The Example box discusses how Hyundai is utilizing TQM to compete in the luxury car market.

EXAMPLE   Hyundai's Genesis Takes on the Luxury Car Market

The Hyundai Motor Co. is well known for its economical automobiles, but it took the luxury car market by storm when it introduced its Genesis brand in 2016. The South Korean carmaker's luxury line of vehicles supplanted Audi, BMW, Lexus, and Mercedes-Benz to top *Consumer Reports'* 2020 annual ranking of automotive brands.[89] How did a company that manufactures no-frills compact vehicles outdo established German and Japanese luxury brands? The answer lies in Hyundai's ability to create a high-quality vehicle that earns high marks from its owners.[90]

Things weren't always smooth sailing for the Genesis. It was first introduced to the market under the Hyundai label in 2008. Poor quality resulted in sales dropping from 264,000 to 90,000 vehicles two years later.[91] These results caught the attention of Hyundai's chairman, Chung Mong Koo. Mong Koo is known for demanding unwavering obedience from his employees. "His orders and initiatives are carried out swiftly, meticulously and without question," according to *Fortune*.[92] Mong Koo sent a memo telling factory managers that poor quality would no longer be tolerated and reinforced this directive by visiting factories himself, looking for quality-control problems. For example, he asked a factory worker to open an engine hood during one of these visits and quickly saw that all the bolts inside were different colors. After the factory manager was publicly reprimanded, all the bolts were properly painted black.[93]

Mong Koo also increased the size of Hyundai's quality-control department from 100 to 1,000 people. He asked this expanded team to thoroughly inspect each and every vehicle, down to the bolts. This was not their only mandate, however. Quality-control engineers were expected to solicit feedback from employees on how to improve quality.[94] A leader who demanded obedience from all had made an important exception—quality issues can and should be questioned by everyone in the organization.[95]

Hyundai's change in quality-control protocol seems to be producing results. Genesis was rated the most dependable brand in the 2020 J.D. Power Vehicle Dependability Study. The study is based on responses from nearly 37,000 purchasers and ranks brands by the number of problems found by original owners of the cars in 2019. Genesis received the lowest number of 89 problems per 100 vehicles, compared to the industry average of 134. Lexus took second place with a score of 100.[96]

YOUR CALL

Genesis and South Korean automaker Kia are part of the same manufacturing group, but Kia came in second to Genesis in the J.D. Power Initial Quality Study. What can Kia do to catch up? Is it a coincidence that South Korean automakers have topped the quality rankings?

2. Improvement Orientation—Focusing Everyone on Continuously Improving Work Processes

Although big schemes, grand designs, and crash programs have their place, the lesson of the quality movement from overseas is that the way to success is through continuous, small improvements. **Continuous improvement** is defined as ongoing, small, incremental improvements in all parts of an organization—all products, services, functional areas, and work processes. Kia Motors, the Korean car maker that has sold autos in the United States for about 20 years, has worked hard to establish a reputation for quality. Its Global Command and Control Center monitors live feeds from all its assembly plants in real time from South Korea, and production is limited to 7 million cars a year to ensure that quality remains high. Said one industry analyst about Kia's parent firm Hyundai, "All the people I meet at Hyundai are hell-bent on making sure quality is getting better all the time. This special mind-set . . . says that 'we will be best at what we do, wherever we go and whatever it takes.'"[97]

This improvement orientation focuses on increasing operational performance and makes the following assumptions.[98]

- **It's less expensive to do it right the first time.** TQM assumes that it's better to do things right the first time than to do costly reworking. To be sure, creating high-quality products and services requires a costly investment in training, equipment, and tools, for example. But it is less expensive than dealing with poor quality and the poor customer relationships that result.

- **It's better to make small improvements all the time.** This is the assumption that continuous improvement must be an everyday matter, that no improvement is too small, and that there must be an ongoing effort to make things better a little bit at a time all the time. For example, BMW relies on data-driven improvements to help reduce lead times and lower costs. The automaker links the large quantity of sensor and process data from production and logistics to quickly and easily make even the smallest of changes. "Smart Data Analytics is setting new standards for our production system" and "speeds up continuous improvement," said Christian Patron, head of BMW's Innovation and Digitalization in Production System.[99]

- **Accurate standards must be followed to eliminate small variations.** TQM emphasizes the collection of accurate data throughout every stage of the work process. It

A modern Kia car factory production line in Slovakia.
Shutterstock

also stresses the use of accurate standards (such as benchmarking) to evaluate progress and eliminate small variations, which are the source of many quality defects.

- **There must be strong commitment from top management.** Employees and suppliers won't focus on making small, incremental improvements unless managers go beyond lip service to support high-quality work, as do the top managers at Ritz-Carlton, Amazon, and Ace Hardware.

Kaizen is a Japanese philosophy of small continuous improvement that seeks to involve everyone at every level of the organization in the process of identifying opportunities and implementing and testing solutions.[100] It offers advantages for large and small companies alike, whether manufacturers or service firms, as the Example box shows.

EXAMPLE   Kaizen in Action

Mitsubishi Heavy Industries Group used to tailor-make each piece of its equipment for use in chemical and environmental plants. Today, the company's use of Kaizen methods has led to the development of a standardized product that fulfills the needs of all its clients. This standardized product means a reduction in engineering and design costs, a decrease in design errors, and a reduction in cost to the customer of 5 to 10%.[101]

Wagamama, a trendy UK restaurant chain with locations in the United States, saw early adoption of technology as the improvement identified by Kaizen principles. The company was years ahead of its competition in building customer-focused digital solutions. For example, its Wagamamago app (described as "Uber for diners") allows customers to walk in, order, eat, and simply go. The app is estimated to save guests an average of 12 minutes at every meal and is the first of its kind in the industry.[102]

Boeing utilizes Kaizen principles in the building of its 737 aircraft at its Renton production facility near Seattle, Washington.[103] The company solicits feedback from its assembly workers on ways to improve efficiency during repeated Kaizen meetings. These meetings also address environmental considerations, such as the reduction of greenhouse gases during aircraft production.[104] Kaizen principles have greatly improved Boeing's aircraft production speed, which is important since it fiercely competes on this dimension with rival Airbus.

YOUR CALL

Some recommended tips for implementing Kaizen methods include actively looking for unconventional ideas, thinking about how to do something instead of why it can't be done, and avoiding both excuses and perfection.[105] Do you think this is good advice for Mitsubishi, Wagamama, and Boeing? Why or why not?

Applying TQM to Services

Manufacturing industries provide tangible products (think jars of baby food); service industries provide intangible products (think child care services). Manufactured products can be stored (such as dental floss in a warehouse); services generally need to be consumed immediately (such as dental hygiene services). Services tend to require a good deal of people effort (although some services can be provided by machines, such as vending machines and ATMs). Finally, services are generally provided at locations and times convenient for customers; that is, customers are much more involved in the delivery of services than they are in the delivery of manufactured products.

One clear prerequisite for providing excellent service is effective training. Supermarket industry leader Publix, for instance, provides training in three venues: on-the-job from experts or managers, through in-store computers, and via offsite peer-led workshops. Publix's training program covers the basics, such as how to use a particular knife to cut meat, to food safety and first aid, to more abstract skills such as a course in "Exploring Leadership Styles."[106] The Example box describes how Nordstrom and Trader Joe's are striving for service excellence.

EXAMPLE   Service Excellence

A customer experience study conducted in 2019 found that 72% of consumers are willing to switch companies due to just one bad experience.[107] So how can companies keep a loyal customer following? Consider the practices used by two companies known for providing great customer service: Nordstrom and Trader Joe's.

NORDSTROM

Nordstrom operates more than 100 stores in the United States and Canada.[108] Nordstrom's "superior customer service is . . . [a] factor that positions it more defensively against competition at the mall and online," according to *Yahoo Finance*.[109]

Nordstrom's competitive advantage starts with using employee empowerment to elicit employees' creativity. The entirety of the department store's employee handbook fits on a single 5 × 8 card and has one rule: "Use best judgement in all situations." This idea makes it clear that empowerment is not just a benefit of working at Nordstrom, *it's your job*. With this in mind, the company asks its employees to come up with creative solutions to issues that couldn't be fully covered by a predetermined set of policies. For example, a Nordstrom employee found that a customer had left her luggage and flight itinerary in the parking lot of a Connecticut store. The employee hopped in his car, drove her luggage to JFK, and reached her before her flight. There is no rule that can foresee that kind of issue.[110]

Nordstrom also uses its newly enhanced supply chain management to deliver quality customer experiences. The company's re-imagined supply chain puts customers at the center, allowing them to get exactly what they need, when they need it. To accomplish this the retailer connected its inventory across stores and facilities within a market so customers had easy access to a larger selection of products. Nordstrom also is using robotics and automation to house aisles worth of products in a compact space, allowing for quick retrieval. The company hopes that its new technology "will continue to get our customers the right product at the right place at the right time as well as reduce out of stocks, extended fulfillment and shipping delays."[111]

TRADER JOE'S

Trader Joe's operates more than 500 grocery stores nationwide and made a name for itself selling hipster-yuppie snacks like

A Trader Joe's cashier assisting a customer. Dorothy Alexander/Alamy Stock Photo

wild salmon jerky and $2 wines.[112] The chain was ranked first in the supermarket category of the 2019 American Customer Satisfaction Index (ACSI) Retail Report and stays competitive by quickly reacting to its customers' needs.[113] Managers are called captains (employees are the crew) and spend most of their days on the retail floor, wearing Hawaiian shirts and interacting with customers. If a customer asks about a product, the captain or crew member instantly brings the product, opens it, and indulges in a taste test with the customer to see whether they like it. Trader Joe's also refunds the price of any product customers are not satisfied with, even if it has been opened.[114]

Allowing captains to spend their time on the retail floor also allows them to learn about customer needs and quickly react to them instead of asking customers to send their feedback to a call center. For example, a Trader Joe's in Nevada decided to stock up on a customer's favorite soy ice-cream cookie. Another location in Phoenix decided to open earlier than the company standard hour of 9 am so its local community could shop at a time that was convenient for them.[115]

YOUR CALL

Do you think Nordstrom's and Trader Joe's approaches to customer service can compete with online shopping? Why or why not?

Perhaps you're beginning to see how judging the quality of services is a different animal from judging the quality of manufactured goods, because it comes down to meeting the customer's *satisfaction*, which may be a matter of *perception*. (After all, some hotel guests, restaurant diners, and supermarket patrons, for example, are more easily satisfied than others.)

Some people view college students as customers. Do you? For those schools that care about the quality of what they offer, it is important to assess student satisfaction with the college or university as a whole. If you are curious about your level of satisfaction with your college or university, then complete Self-Assessment 16.3.

Assessing Your Satisfaction with Your College or University Experience

The following survey was designed to assess the extent to which you are satisfied with your college experience. Please be prepared to answer these questions if your instructor has assigned Self-Assessment 16.3 in Connect.

1. What is your level of satisfaction? Are you surprised by the results?

2. Based on your scores, identify three things that your college or university might do to improve student satisfaction. Be specific.

3. Are students really customers? Explain your rationale.

Some TQM Tools, Techniques, and Standards

Several tools and techniques are available for improving quality. We described benchmarking in Chapter 10. Here we describe *outsourcing, reduced cycle time, statistical process control, Six Sigma,* and *quality standards ISO 9000* and *ISO 14000.*

Outsourcing: Let Outsiders Handle It   ==Outsourcing== (discussed in detail in Chapter 4) **is the subcontracting of services and operations to an outside vendor.** Usually, this is done to reduce costs or increase productivity.[116] For example, outsourcing short-term and project work to freelance or contract workers in the so-called gig economy saves companies many employee-related expenses. Research has some key findings on outsourcing:[117]

- Outsourcing generally enhances firm performance.
- Most outsourcing is of IT-related functions.
- The number of tasks outsourced depends on what an organization is trying to accomplish. Companies seeking access to expertise typically outsource a limited number of tasks whereas companies seeking operational efficiency outsource more tasks.

Outsourcing also is being done by many state and local governments, which, under the banner known as privatization, have subcontracted traditional government services such as fire protection, correctional services, and medical services. Overall, around 300,000 U.S. jobs get outsourced each year.[118]

Reduced Cycle Time: Increasing the Speed of Work Processes   Another TQM technique is the emphasis on increasing the speed with which an organization's operations and processes can be performed. This is known as ==reduced cycle time, or reduction in steps in a work process,== such as fewer authorization steps required to grant a contract to a supplier. The point is to improve the organization's performance by eliminating wasteful motions, barriers between departments, unnecessary procedural steps, and the like.[119]

Microsoft Example: Microsoft's finance group was able to consolidate and simplify various reports, tools, and content into an automated, role-based personalized report. The group also was able to use bots in finance operations, credit and collections, management reporting, and taxes. Microsoft reduced the time spent compiling and validating data by 20% as a result of these actions, saving over 150,000 hours of work each quarter.[120]

Statistical Process Control: Taking Periodic Random Samples   As the pages of this book were being printed, instruments called densitometers and colorimeters were used to measure ink density and trueness of color, taking samples of printed pages at fixed intervals. This is an ongoing check for quality control.

All kinds of products require periodic inspection during their manufacture: hamburger meat, breakfast cereal, flashlight batteries, wine, and so on. The tool often used for this is **statistical process control**, a statistical technique that uses periodic random samples from production runs to see if quality is being maintained within a standard range of acceptability. If quality is not acceptable, production is stopped to allow corrective measures.[121]

Statistical process control is the technique that McDonald's uses, for example, to make sure that the quality of its burgers is always the same, no matter where in the world they are served. Companies such as Intel and Motorola use statistical process control to ensure the reliability and quality of their products. Not all organizations are users of statistical process control. A recent study, for example, found that almost 30% of organizations did not use this technique because of a lack of resources or simply because they didn't understand it.[122]

Six Sigma and Lean Six Sigma: Data-Driven Ways to Eliminate Defects   *Sigma* is the Greek letter statisticians use to define a standard deviation. In the quality-improvement process known as Six Sigma, the higher the sigma, the fewer the deviations from the norm—that is, the fewer the defects. Developed by Motorola in 1985, Six Sigma has since been embraced by Citibank, the U.S. Army, Dow Chemical, and other organizations.[123] There are two variations, *Six Sigma* and *Lean Six Sigma*.

- **Six Sigma** **Six Sigma** is a rigorous statistical analysis process that reduces defects in manufacturing and service-related processes. By testing thousands of variables and eliminating guesswork, a company using the technique attempts to improve quality and reduce waste to the point where errors nearly vanish. In everything from product design to manufacturing to billing, the attainment of Six Sigma means there are no more than 3.4 defects per million products or procedures.[124]

  Six Sigma also may be thought of as a philosophy to reduce variation in your company's business and make customer-focused, data-driven decisions. The method preaches the use of Define, Measure, Analyze, Improve, and Control (DMAIC). Team leaders may be awarded a Six Sigma "black belt" for applying DMAIC.

- **Lean Six Sigma** More recently, companies are using an approach known as **Lean Six Sigma**, which focuses on problem solving and performance improvement—speed with excellence—of a well-defined project.[125] Data sharing company Convergency is a good example of an organization harnessing the power of Lean Six Sigma.

  Convergency Example: Convergency is a cloud-based system provider for pharmaceutical companies. The company's business intelligence portal has been used for instant data sharing from clinical trials on the COVID-19 pandemic. Part of what Convergency offers is a team of Lean Six Sigma experts who help labs and other health care operations accelerate data processing by up to 70% to save time and expense. One of the company's clients in Japan, for instance, reported cutting costs by more than 50%.[126]

Six Sigma and Lean Six Sigma may not be perfect because they cannot compensate for human error or control events outside a company.[127] Still, they let managers approach problems with the assumption that there's a data-oriented, tangible way to approach problem solving.

ISO 9000 and ISO 14000: Meeting Standards of Independent Auditors   If you're a sales representative for Du Pont, a U.S. chemical company, how will your overseas clients know your products have the quality they are expecting? If you're a purchasing agent for an Ohio-based tire company, how can you tell whether the synthetic rubber you're buying overseas is adequate?

At one time, buyers and sellers simply had to rely on a supplier's past reputation or personal assurances. In 1987, the International Organization for Standardization (ISO), based in Geneva, Switzerland, created a set of quality-focused procedures and standards. Let's focus on two: ISO 9000 and ISO 14000. There are two such standards:

- **ISO 9000** The ==ISO 9000 series== consists of quality-control procedures companies must install—from purchasing to manufacturing to inventory to shipping—that can be audited by independent quality-control experts, or "registrars." The goal is to reduce flaws in manufacturing and improve productivity by adopting eight "big picture" quality management principles:

  Customer focus.

  Leadership.

  Involvement of people.

  Process approach.

  System approach to management.

  Continual improvement.

  Factual approach to decision making.

  Mutually beneficial supplier relationships.[128]

  Companies must document their ISO 9000 procedures and train their employees to use them. The ISO 9000 series of standards was expanded to include ISO 9001:2015. "ISO 9001 is the only standard within the ISO 9000 family that an organization can become certified against, because it is the standard that defines the requirements of having a Quality Management System."[129] Member organizations in 170 countries contribute to the development of ISO standards.[130]

- **ISO 14000** The ==ISO 14000 series== extends the concept, identifying standards for environmental performance. ISO 14000 dictates standards for documenting a company's management of pollution, efficient use of raw materials, and reduction of the firm's impact on the environment. An organization can earn ISO 14001:2015 certification, which means it has an environmental management system that meets stringent ISO standards.[131]

Takeaways from TQM Research

TQM principles have been used by thousands of organizations through the years. Although companies do not always use the tools, techniques, and processes as suggested by experts, a team of researchers concluded that the vast majority of TQM adopters follow its general principles, which in turn fosters improved operational performance.[132] Researchers also identified four key inhibitors to successfully implementing TQM: (1) the failure to provide evidence supporting previous improvement activities, (2) the lack of a champion who is responsible for leading the implementation, (3) the inability to measure or track results of the program, and (4) the failure to develop a culture of quality or continuous learning.[133] Managers need to overcome these roadblocks for TQM to deliver its intended benefits. ●

SELF-ASSESSMENT 16.3

To What Extent Is Your Organization Committed to Total Quality Management?

This self-assessment is designed to gauge the extent to which the organization you have in mind is committed to total quality management (TQM).

Please be prepared to answer these questions if your instructor has assigned Self-Assessment 16.4 in Connect.

1. Which of the five dimensions is most and least important to the organization? Are you surprised by this conclusion? Explain.

2. Based on the three lowest-rated items in the survey, what advice would you give to senior leaders in the company?

3. Considering all of the questions in the survey, which three do you think are most important in terms of fostering TQM in a company? Why?

16.5 Contemporary Control Issues

THE BIG PICTURE

This section describes two contemporary control issues: artificial intelligence and employee tracking and monitoring.

At this juncture in your learning experience regarding principles of management you know that every function of management has been influenced by technology. As such, you shouldn't be surprised to find out that the control function is similarly impacted.

In this section we discuss two important technological advancements that have made an impact on how managers control organizations. We'll start with a focus on the rise of artificial intelligence (AI) as part of the control function by analyzing three areas in which AI is having its greatest impact. Then, we'll turn our attention to how technology is assisting organizations to track and monitor their workforce.

LO 16-5

Discuss contemporary control issues.

Using Artificial Intelligence to Control

In Chapter 7 we discussed the many ways in which AI can benefit organizations. One of these ways is enhancing control functions. With this in mind, let's go back to our discussion of the Deloitte Insights survey of AI in Chapter 7. The survey of 1,100 companies showed that 44% of firms use AI for product enhancement; 42% use it for internal process automation; and 24% use it for labor cost reduction. (See again Figure 7.5.) You'll recall from our discussion of the balanced scorecard in Section 16.3 that there is a link between these findings and the scorecard's internal business perspective. The survey shows that companies are engaging in three AI-powered activities related to internal business control: *reducing errors and defects, increasing productivity,* and *enhancing supply chain management.* Let's examine each more closely.

Reducing Errors and Defects   From exploding phones, to faulty automobile airbags, to arthritis drug recalls, product recalls in the first two decades of the 2000s have cost over $50 billion, according to a study by Allianz.[134] Even worse, many production errors have proven to be deadly. Take, for instance, officials acknowledging in April 2020 that "sloppy laboratory practices" at the Centers for Disease Control and Prevention (CDC) led to contamination that rendered the nation's first COVID-19 tests useless. "C.D.C. did not manufacture its test consistent with its own protocol," said a spokeswoman for the Food and Drug Administration.[135]

AI can be used to minimize these sorts of mishaps. Companies like GE, Intel, Bosch, and Microsoft are focusing on so-called "smart manufacturing," which can reduce product defects, shorten unplanned downtimes, and improve manufacturing transition times. German conglomerate Siemens is a good example of an organization using smart manufacturing.

A Siemens employee works on a turbine at a company factory.
Ulrich Baumgarten/Getty Images

Siemens Example: Industrial manufacturer Siemens has around 385,000 employees worldwide and needs effective control practices to ensure it continues to generate profit like it did in 2019 when the company made more than $6 billion in profit.[136] To this end, the company aims to monitor, record, and analyze all aspects of manufacturing, from design to delivery, to find problems and solutions they did not even know existed. The German government has dubbed these collective practices "Industry 4.0." Siemens' ability to improve its gas turbines emissions is a good example of Industry 4.0 practices. The company's latest gas turbines have over 500 sensors that continuously monitor temperature, pressure, stress, and other variables. All this information is fed into their AI system that is learning how to continuously adjust fuel valves to create optimal conditions for combustion (more combustion results in less unwanted emissions). "Even after experts had done their best to optimize the turbine's nitrous oxide emissions," said Dr. Norbert Gaus, Head of Research in Digitalization and Automation at Siemens Corporate Technology, "our AI system was able to reduce emissions by an additional ten to fifteen percent."[137]

Increasing Productivity

We previously noted that productivity is an important metric of an organization's internal business processes. Today, AI practices are enhancing productivity metrics in a wide variety of industries. Take, for instance, a recent PwC survey of 500 executives finding that 54% believe AI solutions implemented in their businesses have already increased productivity.[138] Accenture believes AI has even more in store for us, projecting that by 2035 it will increase productivity by more than 40%. Experts believe AI can improve productivity in two key ways. Let's look at each using Italian train operator Trenitalia's innovative maintenance practices—which have saved the company around $140 million annually—as an example.[139]

- **Make decisions faster and with more confidence:** AI can automate and prioritize routine decision-making processes, leading to more efficient and effective decisions. Trenitalia wanted to minimize unnecessary downtime for repairs that hurt productivity and wasted resources on maintenance costs. "Every year we spend €330 million [$362 million] on parts and on repairing parts which are subject to continual wear and tear," said Enrico Grigliatti, the company's chief financial officer. Trenitalia utilized AI to perform all required preventive maintenance interventions at exactly the right time, ensuring optimal asset utilization and minimal unplanned downtime.

- **Access real-time, actionable insights from data:** AI can understand patterns in big data that humans cannot. It can then predict future opportunities and recommend actions to capitalize on these opportunities. Trenitalia owns and operates around 2,000 electro-trains, 2,000 locomotives, and 30,000 coaches and wagons. Around 40% of the maintenance needs of this fleet is corrective, meaning the issues are unforeseen. This can cause expenditures and delays that infuriate executives and passengers alike. Trenitalia remedied this by installing 6 million sensors on its trains to gather information on operating performance. The train operator uses predictive AI to extrapolate and analyze this large amount of data to make operations and maintenance decisions to maximize efficiency and increase safety.

Enhancing Supply Chain Management

The **supply chain** is the sequence of suppliers that contribute to creating and delivering a product, from raw materials to production to final buyers. Supply chains are a major cost center for most companies, and the way firms structure the distribution of their products can have enormous financial impact. Companies are therefore paying closer attention to the sourcing, shipping, and warehousing of their products and the ingredients and component parts they require. AI has the ability to significantly increase efficiency all over the supply chain. McKinsey estimates that firms could save between $1.3 to $2 trillion a year using AI in supply chain and manufacturing. Let's focus on how AI can optimize different areas of the supply chain using two examples.[140]

Lineage Logistics Example: Lineage Logistics transports and cold stores 20 to 30 billion pounds of food for grocery stores and restaurants. The company's clientele includes Walmart, Tyson, and McDonald's. Lineage developed an AI algorithm to optimize its pallet transportation practices. The algorithm forecasts when orders arrive and leave its warehouse, allowing employees to put the right pallets in the right position. Items that stay in the warehouse longer are put in

Thawing the supply chain.
Frozen food stored at a Lineage Logistics facility in Heywood, United Kingdom.
Molly Darlington/Newscom

the back, while items that move more quickly are placed toward the front. Instead of moving pallets around like a game of Tetris, AI shows the company how to be smarter about where items are placed. As a result, Lineage has increasing its efficiency by 20%.

Infinera Example: Telecom manufacturer Infinera uses machine learning to analyze production times and assist sales associates by providing more accurate delivery dates. The company's AI system doesn't just look at traditional manufacturing and shipping schedules to estimate when products will arrive. It integrates historical delivery information with customer feedback, weather reports, and logistics. This allows it to accurately predict the entire production process, from the moment a product starts on the production line to the time it is delivered to a customer's doorstep.

Employee Tracking and Monitoring

Another way technology is helping managers control organizations is through tracking and monitoring employees. Measuring employee performance with surveillance is not new. For example, since 2017 U.S. companies have been required by law to monitor their long-haul drivers with electronic logging devices (ELDs). These ELDs evaluate a truck driver's location and speed to track how they space sleeping and driving.[141]

Trucking companies aren't the only industry monitoring employees. Gartner surveyed 239 large corporations and found that about half use some type of monitoring techniques to keep an eye on their workforce. These include analyzing texts of e-mails and social media messages, as well as gathering biometric data. Moreover, Gartner projects that by 2021 over 80% of companies will use some sort of employee monitoring technology.[142] Some of these technologies, however, are helping companies monitor workers in controversial ways. Let's examine the advantages and disadvantages of employee tracking and monitoring.

Advantages of Employee Tracking and Monitoring   There are numerous benefits to monitoring and tracking employees. Monitoring can help uncover problems such as harassment or employee theft; reduce incidents of employees wasting company time; and highlight bottlenecks where employees spend more time than expected in their work processes. Moreover, employee monitoring and tracking can make sure that safety practices are being followed, which is one of the reasons why trucking companies use those ELDs we discussed earlier.[143] The Example box profiles a company effectively using tracking technology in the workplace.

EXAMPLE   **Microchipping Employees**

Wisconsin-based Three Square Market provides self-service mini-markets to hospitals, hotels, and company breakrooms. These mini-markets are essentially unattended retail environments where employees can purchase products from open shelves, coolers, or freezers, using a self-checkout kiosk. Three Square Market boasts that employers who install their markets into breakrooms will enjoy increased employee satisfaction, productivity, and retention.[144]

YOUR BADGE IS INSIDE YOU

As interesting as Three Square Market's self-service mini-markets may be, their practice of microchipping their employees at their corporate offices may be even more intriguing. Fifty of the company's then 80 corporate employees volunteered in 2017 to have a chip—the size of a large grain of rice—injected into their hand. The chips allow employees to access company

Chipped up. Three Square Market CEO Todd Westby using his hand, which has a chip inside it, to access the office. Would you agree to have your employer insert a chip inside your body? MEGA/Newscom

offices and computers with a simple wave of their hand, as well as buy food and drinks in the company cafeteria without exchanging money. The encrypted chip also stores personal and health information in case an emergency occurs at work. Some company employees actually use their chips 10 to 15 time a day, saving them at least 20 minutes.[145]

THE CHIP ISN'T JUST FOR EMPLOYEE CONVENIENCE

Three Square Market's employees may benefit from the convenience provided by the chip, but it also has practical uses for the company. For example, managers can track who has access to secure areas of the office without being worried that someone may lose their badge. The company foots the $300 bill to have the chip inserted due to all the benefits provided to both employer and employees.[146] Employees can of course have them removed when they end their employment with Three Square Market. Today, an additional 30 employees have gotten the chip, meaning 80 of around 250 employees, or nearly a third, are taking advantage of this technology. "You get used to it; it's easy," said Patrick McMullan, the company's president. As far as McMullan knows, only two of his employees have ever had their chips removed—and that was when they left the company.[147]

YOUR CALL

Three Square Market claims it does not use its chip to monitor employees, but do you see privacy issues associated with being able to track your employees all the time—including when they are not at work? Why or why not?

Disadvantages of Employee Tracking and Monitoring   As you can imagine, employee tracking and monitoring programs have created concerns about employee privacy. Some employers believe that these types of programs may make it difficult to retain employees because they create an intrusive environment that signals a lack of trust. Moreover, the additional data generated by tracking and monitoring devices means more information can be misused if it lands in the wrong hands.[148]

Though the very concept of employee monitoring and tracking may have negative connotations, research shows that these programs may be acceptable to employees and bring about positive outcomes if properly implemented.[149] Here are two recommendations to ensure tracking and monitoring programs work out in everyone's favor:[150]

- **Communicate employee expectations:** Autonomy is a valued workplace commodity, but that does not mean that managers cannot set and enforce acceptable uses for their employees' technology and time. These expectations should be communicated clearly and consistently.

- **Apply tracking and monitoring appropriately:** Programs should be designated as technology meant to support and protect employees, not oversee them. For example, in a large call center where hundreds of employees are on the receiving end of thousands of calls, user activity monitoring can assist in making sure employees have the resources they need and are not feeling overwhelmed. With this in mind, companies should ensure that workforce monitoring software is visible and transparent, so employees understand that it's for their benefit.

A Gartner survey has some good news for employers considering the use of workplace tracking and monitoring programs. The 2018 survey found that 30% of employees were comfortable with their employer monitoring their e-mail, compared to only 10% in 2015. Even more important, when an employer explained the reasons for the monitoring, the percentage of employees reporting comfort with it increased to 50%.[151] PwC is an example of an organization that is planning to use workplace tracking and monitoring in a way that may give employees comfort when returning to work after the COVID-19 pandemic.

Retracing your steps. More and more firms are engaging in contact tracing in an effort to contain COVID-19. Are you able to recall every person you came into contact with in the past week? Redkey USB/Shutterstock

PwC Example: Accounting and consulting firm PwC has developed an app that tracks how close employees get to each other by monitoring their smartphones' Bluetooth and wi-fi signals. The app allows the firm to do contact tracing—the process of identifying people who may have been exposed to the virus. For example, if an employee tests positive for COVID-19, HR can identify employees whose phones came close to the infected person's phone in prior weeks. Those who may have been exposed to the virus are then contacted and asked to stay home. David Sapin, a principal at PwC who developed the app, says those worried about privacy can rest assured that it only monitors people when they are on company property.[152] ●

16.6 Career Corner: Managing Your Career Readiness

We've all heard stories of successful people who did not follow a structured or intentional path to their careers, but they are the exception, not the rule. Most successful people do not sit back and wait for opportunities to present themselves. They are more likely to pursue a proactive approach to career management.

Control plays a critical role in the career readiness competency of career management, which represents the proactive management of your career and the seeking of opportunities for professional development. We look at Figure 16.8 to discuss this relationship. You will learn that managing your career entails using many of the ideas discussed in previous Career Corner features.

LO 16-6

Discuss the process for managing career readiness and review six tips for managing your career.

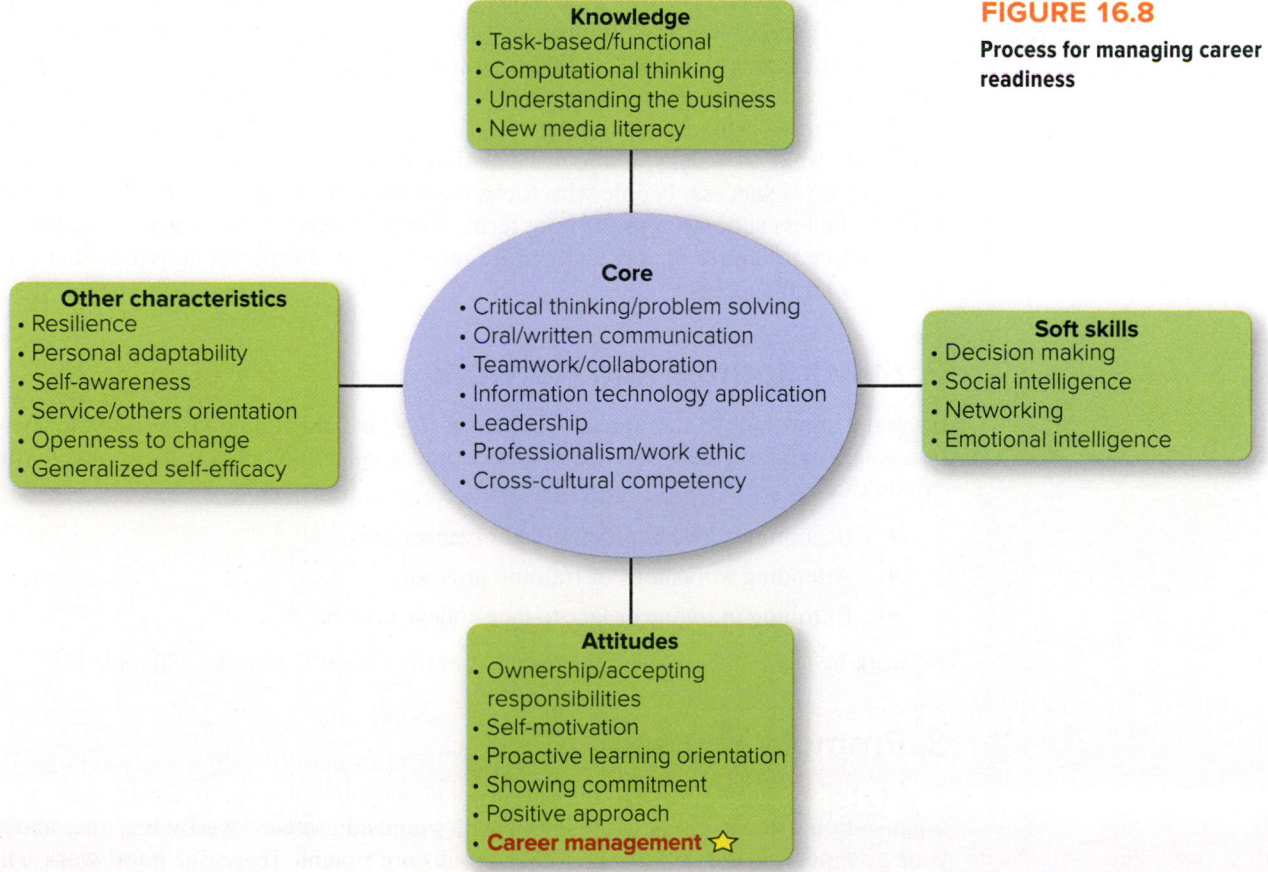

FIGURE 16.8

Process for managing career readiness

Both the control process and the process for managing career readiness begin with identifying what you want to accomplish. In so doing, recognize that a job and a career are not the same thing. Jobs are something we do to earn money, they tend to be temporary, and they are in service of someone or something else. Some people are perfectly happy with a job. In contrast, your career belongs to you and lasts a lifetime. You own it, manage it, nurture it, and create it to fit your values and needs.[153] Careers are what we do in pursuit of our own needs and fulfillment rather than someone else's. This distinction underscores the importance of using the career readiness competencies of ownership/accepting responsibility, self-motivation, self-awareness, and openness to change to manage your career.

Many college students do not have a clear vision for their career. They are more focused on getting a decent job after graduation. If this is true for you, then we suggest starting the career management process by focusing on finding a job that fits your values, needs, and financial objectives. Regardless of whether you are pursuing your dream job or not, you still need to be concerned about your career readiness because employers want people with these skills. So how do you proceed?

Using the process shown in Figure 16.8, start by identifying a small set of career readiness competencies from the categories of core, knowledge, soft skills, attitudes, and other characteristics shown in Table 1.2 and discussed throughout this textbook. This decision gets you started on creating a development plan. Next, consult the Career Corner sections in this textbook to design small developmental experiments. Finally, engage the control process by monitoring, evaluating, and rewarding your progress.

Here are six more generic tips for managing your career. They go far beyond having a good resume.[154]

1. Make Every Day Count

Every action you display at work is a paint stroke on the canvas of your brand. If you want people to perceive you as a motivated, skilled, passionate, and career-ready employee, then act that way. Improving your self-management skills, which were discussed in the Career Corner for Chapter 12, is a good starting point. We then recommend that you brush up on your time management skills. They are essential for handling the workload and competing priorities you will experience in your first job.[155] We want to warn you about a one-time management mistake that can affect your long-term success. People who focus on completing easy, short-term tasks were found to be less successful in the long term. The short-term sense of accomplishment leads people to ignore the critically more important and difficult activities that produce long-term success.[156]

2. Stay Informed and Network

It's really important to stay abreast of changes in your field and industry. Look for new trends, changing regulations, best practices, and applications of new technology. You can do this by:

- Becoming active in professional organizations.
- Attending workshops or training programs.
- Enrolling in online or face-to-face college classes.[157]

Network by using the suggestions presented in the Career Corner for Chapter 15.

3. Promote Yourself

The goal of self-promotion is to inform others about your value and potential impact on organizational goals. Don't confuse this with grandstanding or overtly boasting about your greatness. Use humility. You also should not assume that your good work will always be recognized and publicized, or you'll be disappointed. Here are some suggestions for effective self-promotion:[158]

- Discuss your accomplishments and the specific actions you took to make them happen. Focus on facts and figures rather than personality to avoid a perception of self-interest.

- Discuss the benefits your actions had on your team, department, or division. This forces you to take a "big picture" perspective, which also minimizes the impression of self-interest.

- Discuss how others contributed to the accomplishments. Using "we" instead of "I" is a good way of sharing the limelight. This reinforces that you are a team player, which is another career readiness competency.

4. Roll with Change and Disruption

Careers rarely follow an organized trajectory. It's more likely your career will have tributaries, roundabouts, and personal diversions. Data from a 2019 Bureau of Labor Statistics survey suggests that on average people change jobs 12 times during their careers.[159] These changes are either voluntary, such as moving on for a better opportunity, or involuntary, such as being fired or laid off. If you move voluntarily, congratulations! You now have the opportunity to reinvent yourself. If the departure is not by choice, you'll likely feel disappointed, angry, or humiliated. Give yourself time to recover as research shows that job loss is one of the most stressful life events we experience.[160] It's essential to learn from the situation and put bitterness behind you. No recruiter wants to hear job applicants bad-mouth previous employers.

5. Small Things Matter during Interviews

The best resume, experience, and career readiness will not withstand interpersonal blunders that occur during the recruitment process. CareerBuilder's national survey of 2,600 recruiters identified the following deal-breakers:

- Don't lie. Period. Two-thirds of recruiters will disqualify you from contention if you do.

- Be a team player and go into your interview with confidence, not arrogance. Almost 60% of recruiters viewed arrogance in a negative light. Why would they want to hire you if you already think you're too good for the job?

- Dress professionally by knowing what is appropriate for the environment you'll be working in. Dressing too casually for an interview can be a deal-breaker for nearly half of recruiters.[161]

6. Use Technology for Self-Development and Creating Good Habits

Our careers aren't only based on what we do while working but also can be impacted by what we do with our time outside the workplace. Nowadays, technology plays a critical role in our personal lives and can lead to some bad habits. Take for instance the amount of time we spend on our phones instead of doing other tasks. American adults spent around 3.5 hours a day on their smartphone in 2019, which was an increase of 20 minutes from the year before.[162] Not all uses of technology are problematic though. There are ways that you can use it to positively impact your self-development and create good habits. Here are a few:[163]

- **Listen to podcasts:** These are an excellent way for those seeking advice on self-improvement, but who don't enjoy reading or have the time, to get some great tips. Podcasts have become popular lately because they are accessible from anywhere, on any device, and many are free. Your authors, for example, recorded free podcasts for professors seeking to improve their students' classroom experience.

- **Utilize productivity apps:** Time-tracking apps help you find your work habits and patterns so you can improve them. Apps like Toggl, Hours, and Qbserve also include task management tools. These allow you to keep to-do lists, share tasks with others, and even stay off sites that will distract you.

- **Master new skills:** The Internet provides us with many opportunities for personal development. One website, Skillshare, provides different classes to help you master new skills. Whether you are trying to learn a new language, how to make sound financial investments, or photography, Skillshare has free lessons that are utilized by thousands of users.

- **Exercise:** Keeping your physical health in shape is an important part of self-development. Exercising improves your memory, concentration, self-esteem, and helps you keep that positive attitude. There are hundreds of fitness apps available, many for free, that are designed for those with a tight schedule and limited time to exercise. One example is the Johnson & Johnson Official 7-Minute Workout. The app has a seven-minute workout that you can do anywhere, shows you how to do each move, and counts down from 30 seconds as you do them.[164]

Epilogue: Suggestions for Future Success and Happiness

THE BIG PICTURE

As we end the book, this section describes some life lessons to take away.

We have come to the end of the book, our last chance to offer some suggestions to take with you that we hope will benefit you in the coming years. Following are some life lessons pulled from various sources that can make you a "keeper" in an organization and help you be successful.

- **Adopt a proactive approach to life-long learning.** Life in general is not going to become less complex. This requires all of us to continue to grow and develop if we want to be active, positive contributors to our families, work environments, communities, and society at large. Keep challenging yourself and don't accept mediocrity.

- **Find your passion and follow it.** Laura Green worked as a marketing manager for a rapidly growing company and then worked at her father's firm, LendingOne. Green eventually concluded that none of what she did really made her happy. Her father told her to follow her passion in order to feel fulfilled. "Well, I've always loved dogs," she replied. "I want to do something with animals." Green ended up creating Hound & Co., a marketplace for dog products. Today, this is her full-time job.[165] Find something that inspires you, that you love to do, and do it vigorously.

- **Encourage self-discovery, and be realistic.** To stay ahead of the pack, you need to develop self-awareness, have an active mind, and be willing to grow and change. Legendary designer Diane von Furstenberg recalls the lesson she learned from early mistakes that reduced her control over her business and diluted her brand: "Your worst moments are your best souvenirs."[166]

- **Every situation is different, so be flexible.** No principle, no theory will apply under all circumstances. Industries, cultures, supervisors, employees, and customers will vary. It's not a sign of weakness to be willing to change something that isn't working or to try something new.[167] The COVID-19 pandemic, for instance, taught us a lot about trying new things. "It's a fantastic [post-COVID-19] world that we are going to have the opportunity to change. This is a new beginning for so many things that we can do moving forward . . . you never know where the exact great idea is going to come from. . . . And that is exciting," says Joele Frank, managing partner of public relations firm Joele Frank Wilkinson Brimmer Katcher.[168]

- **Focus on career readiness.** Today we live and work in a team universe. Try getting feedback on your interpersonal skills from friends, colleagues, and team members, and develop a plan for improvement. Even nonverbal communication is a people skill. Ryan Chan, CEO of UpKeep Maintenance Management, is always on the prowl to add unique talent his fast-moving technology startup. "I strive to hire gritty, resourceful people who are willing to go the extra mile to stand out from the crowd," says Chan.[169]

- **Learn how to develop leadership skills.** Every company should invest in the leadership development of its managers if it is to improve the quality of its future leaders. But you also can work to develop your own leadership skills. For instance, offer to help others, take the initiative when action is needed (sometimes called being a self-starter), and don't be afraid to ask for more responsibility to demonstrate what you're capable of.[170] Another life lesson: If you set the bar high, even if you don't reach it, you end up in a pretty good place—that is, achieving a pretty high mark.

- **Treat people as if they matter, because they do.** If you treat employees, colleagues, and customers with dignity, they respond accordingly. Brian Mitchell played in the National Football League for 14 years. He was extremely aggressive on the football field, but a different man in his career as a television and radio host. "Always remember the Golden Rule and treat people the way you want to be treated," says Mitchell. He believes that if you treat people with respect and courtesy when they want something from you, they are more likely to treat you in the same manner when you ask for something from them.[171]

- **Draw employees and peers into your management process.** The old top-down, command-and-control model of organization is moving toward a flattened, networked kind of structure. Managers now work more often with peers, where lines of authority aren't always clear or don't exist, so that one's persuasive powers become key. Power has devolved to front-line employees who are closest to the customer and to small, focused, self-managed teams that have latitude to pursue new ideas. Ask them what they think are the best ways to get things done.[172]

- **Keep your cool, and take yourself lightly.** The more unflappable you appear in difficult circumstances, the more you'll be admired by your bosses and co-workers. Having a sense of humor helps. The renowned British physicist and author Stephen Hawking spent his career looking for the answers to impenetrable questions like, "Where did the universe come from?" and "How will it end?" Yet he was famously witty and relished the opportunity to appear as himself on popular TV shows like *The Simpsons*, *Star Trek: The Next Generation*, and *The Big Bang Theory*, appearances that he said made him more famous than his complex theories about the universe.[173]

- **Go with the flow, and stay positive.** Life has its ebbs and flows. You'll have good times and bad. During this journey, don't focus too heavily on negative events and thoughts. Negative thoughts rob you of positive energy and your ability to perform at your best. In contrast, a positive approach toward life is more likely to help you flourish.[174]

We wish you the very best of luck. Follow your dreams and enjoy the journey!

Angelo Kinicki   *Denise Breaux Soignet*

balance sheet 708

balanced scorecard 706

best practices 712

budget 707

concurrent control 704

continuous improvement 721

control chart 700

control process steps 699

control standard 700

controlling 696

customer retention 711

customer satisfaction 710

Deming management 718

feedback control 704

feedforward control 703

financial ratios 710

financial statement 708

fixed budget 707

income statement 708

incremental budgeting 707

ISO 9000 series 726

ISO 14000 series 726

Kaizen 722

Lean Six Sigma 725

management by exception 702

outsourcing 724

PDCA cycle 719

quality 718

quality assurance 718

quality control 718

reduced cycle time 724

Six Sigma 725

statement of cash flows 708

statistical process control 725

strategy map 715

supply chain 728

total quality management (TQM) 719

two core principles of TQM 719

variable budget 708

Key Points

16.1 Control: When Managers Monitor Performance

- Controlling is defined as monitoring performance, comparing it with goals, and taking corrective action as needed.
- There are six reasons that control is needed: (1) to adapt to change and uncertainty; (2) to discover irregularities and errors; (3) to reduce costs, increase productivity, or add value; (4) to detect opportunities and increase innovation; (5) to provide performance feedback; and (6) to decentralize decision making and facilitate teamwork.

16.2 The Control Process and Types of Control

- There are four control process steps. (1) The first step is to set standards. A control standard is the desired performance level for a given goal. (2) The second step is to measure performance, based on written reports, oral reports, and personal observation. (3) The third step is to compare measured performance against the standards established. (4) The fourth step is to take corrective action, if necessary, if there is negative performance.
- There are three types of control: feedforward, concurrent, and feedback.

16.3 What Should Managers Control?

- Kaplan and Norton's balanced scorecard provides top managers a fast but comprehensive view of the organization via four perspectives: (1) financial, (2) customer, (3) internal-business process, and (4) innovation and learning.
- The financial perspective includes budgets, financial statements, and financial ratios.

- The customer perspective includes customer satisfaction and retention.
- The internal-business perspective considers productivity, efficiency, quality, and safety.
- The innovation and learning perspective looks at employee attitudes, turnover, resource capabilities, and organizational culture.
- The strategy map, a visual representation of the four perspectives of the balanced scorecard, enables managers to communicate their goals so that everyone in the company can understand how their jobs are linked to the overall objectives of the organization.

16.4 Total Quality Management

- Quality refers to the total ability of a product or service to meet customer needs.
- Among the principles of Deming management are (1) quality should be aimed at the needs of the consumer; (2) companies should aim at improving the system, not blaming workers; (3) improved quality leads to increased market share, increased company prospects, and increased employment; and (4) quality can be improved on the basis of hard data, using the PDCA, or Plan-Do-Check-Act, cycle.
- Total quality management (TQM) is defined as a comprehensive approach—led by top management and supported throughout the organization—dedicated to continuous quality improvement (such as through Kaizen), training, and customer satisfaction. The two core principles of TQM are people orientation and improvement orientation.
- In the people orientation, everyone involved with the organization is asked to focus on delivering value to customers, focusing on quality. TQM requires training, teamwork, and cross-functional efforts.

- Several techniques are available for improving quality. (1) Outsourcing is the subcontracting of services and operations to an outside vendor. (2) Reduced cycle time consists of reducing the number of steps in a work process. (3) Statistical process control is a statistical technique that uses periodic random samples from production runs to see if quality is being maintained within a standard range of acceptability. (4) Six Sigma is a rigorous statistical analysis process that reduces defects in manufacturing and service-related processes. (5) ISO 9000 consists of quality-control procedures companies must install—from purchasing to manufacturing to inventory to shipping—that can be audited by independent quality-control experts, or "registrars." ISO 14000 extends the concept to environmental performance.

16.5 Contemporary Control Issues

- Two contemporary control issues include artificial Intelligence (AI) and employee tracking and monitoring.

- AI can be used to reduce errors and defects, increase productivity, and enhance supply chain management.
- Employee tracking and monitoring has both advantages and disadvantages. Advantages include uncovering problems, reducing instances of employees wasting time, highlighting bottlenecks, and enforcing safety practices. Disadvantages include privacy concerns, employee retainment issues, and data vulnerability.

16.6 Career Corner: Managing Your Career Readiness

- Developing the competency of career management requires the application of four additional career readiness competencies: ownership/accepting responsibility, self-motivation, self-awareness, and openness to change.
- Six generic tips help you manage your career: (1) Make every day count. (2) Stay informed and network. (3) Promote yourself. (4) Roll with change and disruption. (5) Small things matter during interviews. (6) Use technology for self-development and creating good habits.

Understanding the Chapter: What Do I Know?

1. What is control and what are six reasons control is needed?
2. Explain the steps in the control process.
3. Describe the three types of control.
4. Explain the four perspectives of the balanced scorecard.
5. What is a strategy map?
6. Discuss total quality management and its two core principles.
7. Explain the following TQM tools and techniques: outsourcing, reduced cycle time, the ISO 9000 series, the ISO 14000 series, statistical process control, and Six Sigma and Lean Six Sigma.
8. How can artificial intelligence enhance the control process?
9. What are the advantages and disadvantages to employee tracking and monitoring?
10. What are some ways you can manage your career?

Management in Action

The U.S. Shale Boom . . . and Bust

Who produces most of the world's oil? Your first guess may be somewhere in the Middle East. Indeed, that area of the planet has long been the center of the global oil market and derives much of its revenue from the export of crude oil.[175] Pointing to Saudi Arabia, Iraq, or Iran would therefore be a good guess, but you would be wrong. The United States is now the world's largest crude-oil producer, beating out Saudi Arabia, Russia, and other countries. This is in large part due to U.S. shale's boom in crude oil production since 2014. Shale drove American daily oil output from 8.8 million bar-rels in 2014 to a record 12.2 million barrels in 2019. As a result, the United States is now king of "black gold."[176]

Things are not well in the kingdom though. Fuel demand in 2020 plunged by 30%, or 30 million barrels a day, as the COVID-19 pandemic grounded air travel, decreased vehicle usage, and led to a worldwide recession. As a result, oil fields from Texas to North Dakota had to shut off their drills, causing tens of thousands of U.S. oil workers to lose their livelihood. The future of the U.S. oil industry looks grim with experts predicting over a thousand bankruptcies by the end of 2021.[177] Will U.S. shale survive the great oil crash of 2020?

WHAT IS SHALE OIL ANYWAY?

Before we continue any further, it's important to gain a better understanding of shale oil, which is crude oil that lies between layers of shale rock. It's produced by drilling into the shale rock and pumping water, sand, and chemicals into it—a process known as "fracking." The oil is located thousands of feet deep into the rock, making it quite labor intensive and costly to get to. In fact, some experts put the cost of the entire process at around $60 a barrel. This means that when oil prices dip below $60, many shale oil companies lose money if they continue to operate.[178]

On the other hand, conventional oil is quite cheap to produce because it is closer to the earth's surface and does not require complex fracking techniques. This is the primary way in which the world's other top producers get to their oil. Saudi Arabia, for instance, is able to produce conventional oil for under $10 a barrel, making it more resilient during price slumps.[179]

A FRACTURED CONTROL SYSTEM

The formula for success in the U.S. shale industry was simple. First, as long as oil prices remained high, there was enough profit to keep shale exploration and production going. This was the case between 2011 and 2014 when oil prices averaged $90 a barrel. Second, smaller shale companies needed low-interest bank financing in order to stay afloat. And the banks delivered to the tune of almost $250 billion in 2014 alone.[180]

Things started to change in 2016 as there was an oversupply of oil in the world markets, decreasing the price of oil to around $26 a barrel. The Federal Reserve also increased interest rates that same year, which meant banks were unwilling to lend to shale companies at the same low rates. This one-two punch resulted in shale companies having negative income statements and balance sheets filled with debt. Dozens of companies declared bankruptcy in 2016, but those that were able to withstand the storm saw light at the end of the tunnel when oil prices went back up between 2017 and 2019.[181]

The lesson from the 2016 crisis was that shale companies couldn't simply rely on market supply and demand to stay afloat. They needed to find ways to reduce their break-even point in order to stay competitive. Companies such as Occidental Petroleum Corp. and CrownQuest Operating were able to reduce their costs to around $30 a barrel, but that meant they didn't have enough cash to pay shareholders. And even $30 a barrel wasn't enough when the COVID-19 pandemic hit. The virus sent oil prices to below $0 a barrel because there was such oversupply of the commodity in the market that producers couldn't afford to store it.[182] U.S. shale seemed to hit a wall—fluctuating oil prices were causing havoc on operations while costs couldn't be reduced any further.

DRILLING FOR DATA

Advancements in technology may provide hope for an industry on life support. Keep in mind that oil companies haven't typically shied away from technology. French and Italian oil companies Total and Eni, for instance, are owners of some of the "Top 500 most powerful supercomputers of 2019."[183] The problem is that much of the industry's data are never used. "A lot of data are collected, but a lot of it is very isolated," said Binu Mathew, head of product management at Baker Hughes. "Only a small percentage of it is actually being analysed."[184]

If oil companies could do a better job controlling their operations in real time they could have competitive advantage, especially during challenging times. This is where AI and data analytics come into the picture. According to Mark Mills, a senior fellow at the Manhattan Institute, "Bringing analytics to bear on the complexities of shale geology, geophysics, stimulation, and operations to optimize the production process would potentially double the number of effective stages, thereby doubling output per well and cutting the cost of oil in half." Oil companies can use AI and analytics to find the best drilling locations, optimize how and where they steer their drill bits, find the best ways to rupture the shale, and ensure efficient truck and rail logistics.[185]

Shell is a good example of a company using AI and data analytics to its advantage. The company partnered with Hewlett-Packard to develop fiber optic cables that provide sensors throughout the ground. The data from these sensors is then transferred to Amazon Web Services cloud-based servers for its AI to extract and analyze. The results provide engineers with a more accurate idea of what lies below the ground. This is important because drilling in the wrong place can cost companies upwards of $100 million. Another oil giant, Chevron, is such a believer in the power of AI and data analytics that it is installing around 1 million sensors in a new oilfield it is launching in Kazakhstan in 2022. Experts believe that Shell and Chevron's digital practices can help improve their oil production costs by 6 to 8%.[186]

Machines are another important part of the equation. Drilling is a continuous process and machines are subject to working long hours under severe temperatures and conditions. AI can help ensure that these machines are working efficiently. For example, some companies fit their machines with sensors that collect performance data. AI then compares the data to aggregated data, ensuring that parts are replaced on time and unplanned disruptions are minimized.[187]

An Accenture and Microsoft survey of oil companies found that 86 to 90% believed "an increase in their analytic capabilities . . . would increase the value of their business." The companies surveyed also expected to increase their investment in AI and data analytics an average of 8.5% in the next few years.[188] Technology-based control practices show that there may be hope yet for U.S. shale.

Problem-Solving Perspective

1. What is the underlying problem in this case from the perspective of U.S. shale companies?

2. What are the causes of the problem?

3. How can effective control practices assist in solving the problem?

Application of Chapter Content

1. Why is control necessary for U.S. shale companies? Explain.

2. Utilize the steps in the control process to show how shale companies can ensure that their business activities are leading to goal achievement.

3. Would implementing analytics and cloud-based control mechanisms allow for feedforward, concurrent, or feedback control? Explain.

4. Create a balanced scorecard to give a view of U.S. shale. Utilize all four perspectives.

5. How can U.S. shale exhibit the two core principles of total quality management? Explain.

6. What are some disadvantages to U.S. shale's use of AI? Discuss.

Legal/Ethical Challenge

Using GPS to Track Employees

More companies are using GPS apps to track the whereabouts of their employees for productivity and safety-related reasons. A 2019 study of 1,585 employees showed that nearly a third of them were tracked via GPS by their employers.[189]

Employee tracking is growing in both the commercial and government sectors. For example, the city of Park Hills, Missouri, installed GPS devices in 2018 on city-owned vehicles, including some police cruisers. The city administrator believed the tracking devices would lead to "better-spent drive time, improvement of the safety of city employees, improvement of job performance, [and] improvement of services provided to the community." The system is not very expensive. The GPS devices were provided for free with the city signing a two-year contract and paying a $200 monthly subscription fee.[190]

GPS tracking can apply after an employee's shift is over. If a worker takes an employer-owned vehicle home at night or over the weekend, it might continue sending its location. Tracking devices on mobile phones also may continue broadcasting an employee's location during time off.[191] One in 10 employees responded to a QuickBooks survey saying that they were, in fact, being tracked 24 hours a day, confirming concerns of around-the-clock tracking.[192]

Employees out in the field may not be the only ones being tracked in the future. Amazon was granted patents for the design of warehouse tracking wristbands in 2018. The company currently has its warehouse "pickers" stand in front of shelves and move items into bins, tracking each product with a handheld barcode scanner. Amazon says the wristbands will speed up the fulfillment process by freeing up employees' hands from scanners and their eyes from computer screens. This isn't the only information the company can track

though. Any wearable can collect personal information about an employee, even unintentionally.[193] Convergys, a customer call center in North Carolina, reportedly lectures employees on "how using the bathroom too often is the same thing as stealing from the company." The company clocks its employees' bathroom visits—from the moment they leave their cubicles to the time they return—and sends this information to their supervisors for approval.[194]

The legal landscape around tracking employees is "very vague," said Lew Maltby, the president of the National Workrights Institute. Federal privacy laws do not explicitly bar businesses from using GPS to track their employees. With this in mind, an employee's chances of success in court will depend on different factors, including whether or not consent was given to be tracked and whether the device being tracked belongs to them or the company. "It's essentially whatever shocks the judge," said Maltby.[195]

SOLVING THE CHALLENGE

What would you do if you were the CEO of a company and your managers proposed an employee GPS tracking system?

1. The company needs to use all means to ensure employee productivity and safety. Employees need to provide consent, as a condition of employment, to being tracked when using company vehicles and/or electronic devices at any time of the day. If you are in possession of company property, the company needs to know what you are up to. Let's implement the tracking system.

2. The company should not be tracking employees, on or off the clock, as this is an invasion of privacy. The last thing we need to do is play "Big Brother" and demoralize our workforce. Let's find other ways to ensure productivity and safety.

3. Employee productivity and safety is important but needs to be balanced with privacy concerns. Employees should consent to being tracked while on the clock, but once they've clocked out the tracking system should be disabled. Let's implement a limited tracking system.

4. Invent other options.

Learn more about managerial control at Boeing and how it may have contributed to the 737 MAX disaster.

Assess your ability to apply concepts discussed in Chapter 16 to the case by going to Connect

The Project Planner's Toolkit

Flowcharts, Gantt Charts, and Break-Even Analysis

THE BIG PICTURE

Three tools used in project planning, which was covered in Chapter 5, are flowcharts, Gantt charts, and break-even analysis.

Project planning may begin (in the definition stage) as a back-of-the-envelope kind of process, but the client will expect a good deal more for the time and money being invested. Fortunately, there are various planning and monitoring tools that give the planning and execution of projects more precision. Three tools in the planner's toolkit are (1) flowcharts, (2) Gantt charts, and (3) break-even analysis.

Tool #1: Flowcharts—for Showing Event Sequences and Alternate Decision Scenarios

A *flowchart* **is a useful graphical tool for representing the sequence of events required to complete a project and for laying out "what-if" scenarios.** Flowcharts have been used for decades by computer programmers and systems analysts to make a graphical "road map," as it were, of the flow of tasks required. These professionals use their own special symbols (indicating "input/output," "magnetic disk," and the like), but there is no need for you to make the process complicated. Generally, only three symbols are needed: (1) an oval for the "beginning" and "end," (2) a box for a major activity, and (3) a diamond for a "yes or no" decision. *(See Figure A.1, next page.)*

Computer programs such as iGrafx's ABC FlowCharter are available for constructing flowcharts. You can also use the drawing program in word processing programs such as Microsoft Word.

Benefits   Flowcharts have two benefits:

- **Planning straightforward activities.** A flowchart can be quite helpful for planning ordinary activities—figuring out the best way to buy textbooks or a car, for example. It is also a straightforward way of indicating the sequence of events in, say, thinking out a new enterprise that you would then turn into a business plan.

- **Depicting alternate scenarios.** A flowchart is also useful for laying out "what-if" scenarios—as in if you answer "yes" to a decision question you should follow Plan A, if you answer "no" you should follow Plan B.

Limitations   Flowcharts have two limitations:

- **No time indication.** They don't show the amounts of time required to accomplish the various activities in a project. In building a house, the foundation might take only a couple of days, but the rough carpentry might take weeks. These time differences can't be represented graphically on a flowchart (although you could make a notation).

FIGURE A.1   Flowchart: website, print, or television?

Example of a flowchart for improving a company's advertising.

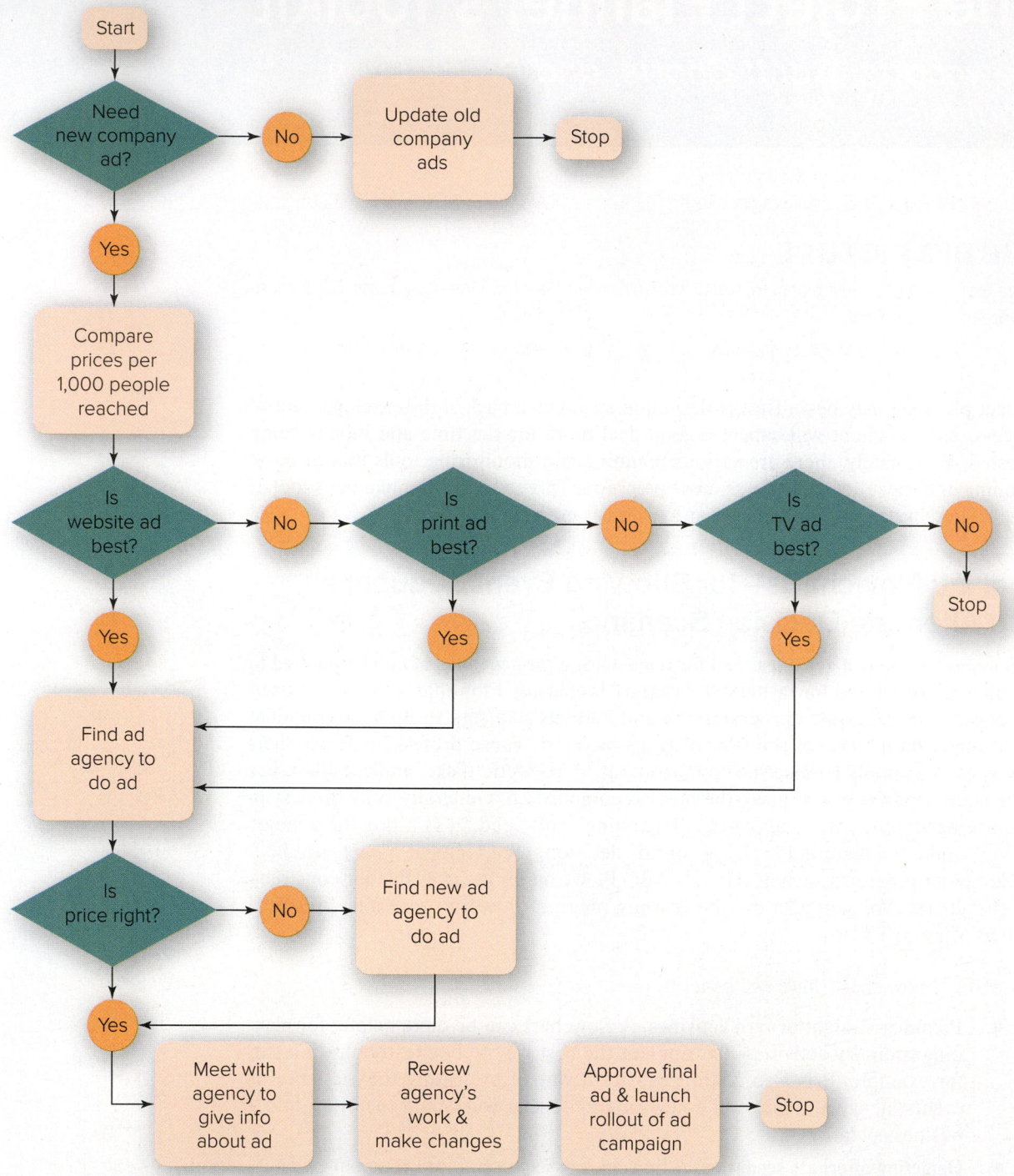

- **Not good for complex projects.** They aren't useful for showing projects consisting of several activities that must all be worked on at the same time. An example would be getting ready for football season's opening game, by which time the players have to be trained, the field readied, the programs printed, the band rehearsed, the ticket sellers recruited, and so on. These separate activities might each be represented on their own flowcharts, of course. But to try to express them all together all at once would produce a flowchart that would be unwieldy, even unworkable.

Tool #2: Gantt Charts—Visual Time Schedules for Work Tasks

We have mentioned how important deadlines are to making a project happen. Unlike a flowchart, a Gantt chart can graphically indicate deadlines.

The Gantt chart was developed by **Henry L. Gantt,** a member of the school of scientific management (discussed in Chapter 2). **A *Gantt chart* is a kind of time schedule—a specialized bar chart that shows the relationship between the kind of work tasks planned and their scheduled completion dates.** *(See Figure A.2.)*

A number of software packages can help you create and modify Gantt charts on your computer. Examples are CA-SuperProject, Microsoft Project, Primavera SureTrak Project Manager, and TurboProject Professional.

Benefits   There are three benefits to using a Gantt chart:

- **Express time lines visually.** Unlike flowcharts, Gantt charts allow you to indicate visually the time to be spent on each activity.

- **Compare proposed and actual progress.** A Gantt chart may be used to compare planned time to complete a task with actual time taken to complete it, so that you can see how far ahead or behind schedule you are for the entire project. This enables you to make adjustments so as to hold to the final target dates.

- **Simplicity.** There is nothing difficult about creating a Gantt chart. You express the time across the top and the tasks down along the left side. As Figure A.2 shows, you can make use of this device while still in college to help schedule and monitor the work you need to do to meet course requirements and deadlines (for papers, projects, tests).

Limitations   Gantt charts have two limitations:

- **Not useful for large, complex projects.** Although a Gantt chart can express the interrelations among the activities of relatively small projects, it becomes cumbersome and unwieldy when used for large, complex projects. More sophisticated management planning tools may be needed, such as PERT networks.

FIGURE A.2   **Gantt chart for designing a website**

This shows the tasks accomplished and the time planned for remaining tasks to build a company website.

Accomplished: |||||||||
Planned: \\\\\\\

Stage of development	Week 1	Week 2	Week 3	Week 4	Week 5
1. Examine competitors' websites	||||||||||||||| \\\\\\\\\\	\\\\\\\\\\			
2. Get information for your website	||||||||||||||| \\\\\\\\\\	||||||||||||||| \\\\\\\\\			
3. Learn Web-authoring software		||||||||||||||| \\\\\\\\\\	||||||||||||||| \\\\\\\\\		
4. Create (design) your website			\\\\\\\\\\	||||||||||||||| \\	\\\\\\
5. "Publish" (put) website online					\\\\\\\\\\\\

- **Time assumptions are subjective.** The time assumptions expressed may be purely subjective; there is no range between "optimistic" and "pessimistic" of the time needed to accomplish a given task.

Tool #3: Break-Even Analysis—How Many Items Must You Sell to Turn a Profit?

Break-even analysis **is a way of identifying how much revenue is needed to cover the total costs of developing and selling a product.** Let's walk through the computation of a break-even analysis, referring to the illustration. *(See Figure A.3.)* We assume you are an apparel manufacturer making shirts or blouses. Start in the lower-right corner of the diagram on the following page and follow the circled numbers as you read the descriptions below.

① *Fixed costs (green area):* Once you start up a business, whether you sell anything or not, you'll have expenses that won't vary much, such as rent, insurance, taxes, and perhaps salaries. These are called **fixed costs, expenses that don't change regardless of your sales or output.** Fixed costs are a function of time—they are expenses you have to pay out on a regular basis, such as weekly, monthly, or yearly. Here the chart shows the fixed costs (green area) are $600,000 per year no matter how many sales units (of shirts or blouses) you sell.

② *Variable costs (blue area):* Now suppose you start producing and selling a product, such as blouses or shirts. At this point you'll be paying for materials, supplies, labor, sales commissions, and delivery expenses. These are called **variable costs, expenses that vary directly depending on the numbers of the product that you produce and sell.** (After all, making more shirts will cost you more in cloth, for example.) Variable costs, then, are a function of volume—they go up and down depending on the number of products you make or sell. Here the variable costs (blue area) are relatively small if you sell only a few thousand shirts but they go up tremendously if you sell, say, 70,000 shirts.

③ *Total costs (first right upward-sloping line—green plus blue area added together):* The sum of the fixed costs and the variable costs equals the total costs (the green and blue areas together). This is indicated by the line that slopes upward to the right from $600,000 to $3,000,000.

④ *Total sales revenue (second right upward-sloping line):* This is the total dollars received from the sale of however many units you sell. The sales revenue varies depending on the number of units you sell. Thus, for example, if you sell 30,000 shirts, you'll receive $1,800,000 in revenue. If you sell 40,000 shirts, you'll receive somewhat more than $2,400,000 in revenue.

⑤ *Break-even point (intersection of dashed lines):* Finding this point is the purpose of this whole exercise. **The break-even point is the amount of sales revenue at which there is no profit but also no loss to your company.** On the graph, this occurs where the "Total sales revenues" line crosses the "Total costs" line, as we've indicated here where the dashed lines meet. This means that you must sell 30,000 shirts and receive $1,800,000 in revenue in order to recoup your total costs (fixed plus variable). Important note: Here is where pricing the shirts becomes important. If you raise the price per shirt, you may be able to make the same amount of money (hit your break-even point) by selling fewer of them—but that may be harder to do because customers may resist buying at the higher price.

⑥ *Loss (red area):* If you fail to sell enough shirts at the right price (the break-even point), you will suffer a loss. **Loss means your total costs exceed your total sales revenue.** As the chart shows, here you are literally "in the red"—you've lost money.

⑦ *Profit (black area):* Here you are literally "in the black"—you've made money. All the shirts you sell beyond the break-even point constitute a profit. **Profit is the amount by which total revenue exceeds total costs.** The more shirts you sell, of course, the greater the profit.

   The kind of break-even analysis demonstrated here is known as the *graphic method.* The same thing can also be done algebraically.

FIGURE A.3 **Break-even analysis**

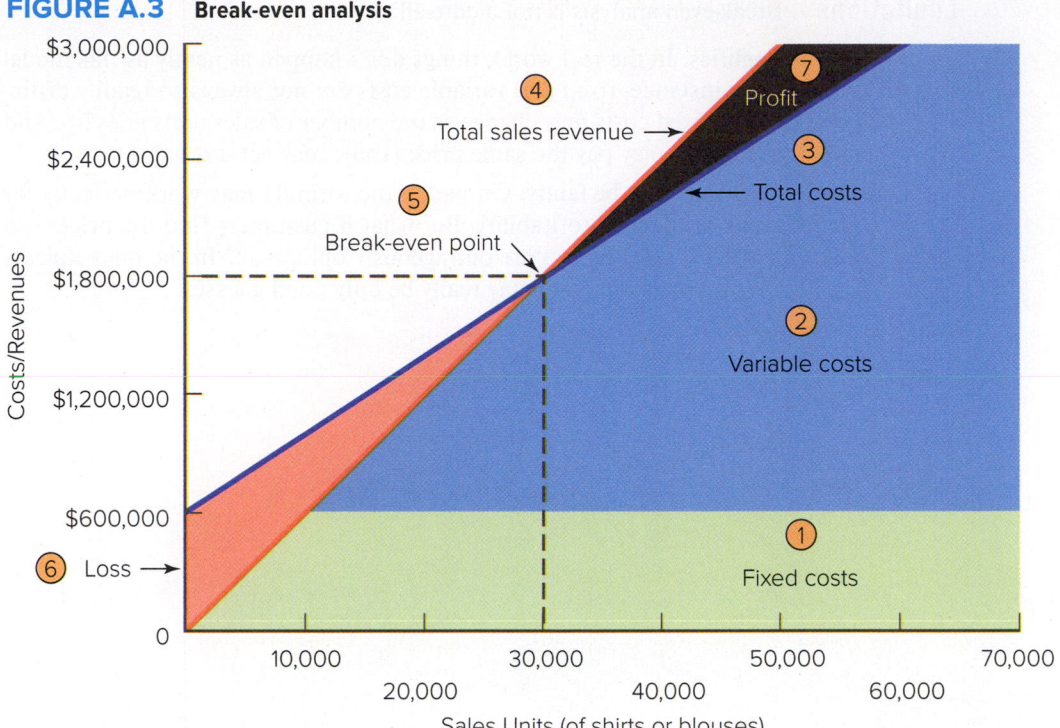

Benefits Break-even analysis has two benefits:

- **For doing future "what-if" alternate scenarios of costs, prices, and sales.** This tool allows you to vary the different possible costs, prices, and sales quantities to do rough "what-if" scenarios to determine possible pricing and sales goals. Since the numbers are interrelated, if you change one, the others will change also.

- **For analyzing the profitability of past projects.** While break-even analysis is usually used as a tool for future projects, it can also be used retroactively to find out whether the goal of profitability was really achieved, since costs may well have changed during the course of the project. In addition, you can use it to determine the impact of cutting costs once profits flow.

EXAMPLE **Break-Even Analysis: Why Do Airfares Vary So Much?**

Why do some airlines charge four times more than others for a flight of the same distance?

There are several reasons, but break-even analysis enters into it.

United Airlines's average cost for flying a passenger 1 mile in a recent year was 11.7 cents, whereas Southwest's was 7.7 cents. Those are the break-even costs. What they charged beyond that was their profit.

Why the difference? One reason, according to a study by the U.S. Department of Transportation, is that Southwest's expenses are lower. United flies more long routes than short ones, so its costs are stretched out over more

miles, making its costs for flying shorter routes higher than Southwest's.

Another factor affecting airfares is the type of passengers flying a particular route—whether they are high-fare-paying business travelers or more price-conscious leisure travelers. Business travelers often don't mind paying a lot (they are reimbursed by their companies), and those routes (such as Chicago to Cincinnati) tend to have more first-class seats, which drives up the average price. Flights to vacation spots (such as Las Vegas) usually have more low-price seats because people aren't willing to pay a lot for pleasure travel. Also, nonstop flight fares often cost more than flights with connections.

Limitations   Break-even analysis is not a cure-all.

- **It oversimplifies.** In the real world, things don't happen as neatly as this model implies. For instance, fixed and variable costs are not always so readily distinguishable. Or fixed costs may change as the number of sales units goes up. And not all customers may pay the same price (some may get discounts).

- **The assumptions may be faulty.** On paper, the formula may work perfectly for identifying a product's profitability. But what if customers find the prices too high? Or what if sales figures are outrageously optimistic? In the marketplace, your price and sales forecasts may really be only good guesses.

CHAPTER 1

1. NACE Staff, "Employers Rate Career Competencies, New Hire Proficiency," December 11, 2017, www.naceweb.org/career-readiness/competencies/employers-rate-career-competencies-new-hire-proficiency. Also see M. Tarpey, "The Skills You Need for the Jobs of the Future," February 16, 2017, www.careerbuilder.com/advice/the-skills-you-need-for-the-jobs-of-the-future.

2. K. Armstrong, "At Keller Demo Day, Six Student Teams Pitch Their Companies," *New Jersey Tech Weekly*, August 24, 2017, http://njtechweekly.com/art/3393-at-keller-demo-day-six-student-teams-pitch-their-companies/.

3. P. Ingrassia, "How GM's Mary Barra Does It," *Fortune,* September 9, 2016, http://fortune.com/mary-barra-general-motors-essay/.

4. B. Vlasi, "G.M. Chief Mary Barra Is Named Chairwoman, Affirming Her Leadership," *The New York Times,* January 5, 2016, p. B3.

5. A. Hartmans, "The Fabulous Life of Amazon CEO Jeff Bezos, the Second Richest Person in the World," *BusinessInsider.com,* May 15, 2017, http://www.businessinsider.com/amazon-founder-ceo-jeff-bezos-early-life-2017-5.

6. R. Barker, "No, Management Is *Not* a Profession," *Harvard Business Review,* July–August 2010, pp. 52–60.

7. M. P. Follett, quoted in J. F. Stoner and R. E. Freeman, *Management,* 5th ed. (Englewood Cliffs, NJ: Prentice Hall, 1992), p. 6.

8. S. McChrystal, *Team of Teams* (New York: Penguin Publishing Group, 2015).

9. D. Ewing-Chow, "Is Cultured Meat the Answer to the World's Meat Problem?" *Forbes,* June 20, 2019, https://www.forbes.com/sites/daphneewingchow/2019/06/20/is-cultured-meat-the-answer-to-the-worlds-meat-problem/#5aaf518c4468.

10. G. Schaefer, "Lab-Grown Meat: Beef for Dinner—Without Killing Animals or the Environment," *Scientific American,* September 14, 2018, https://www.scientificamerican.com/article/lab-grown-meat/.

11. D. Ewing-Chow, "Is Cultured Meat the Answer to the World's Meat Problem?" *Forbes,* June 20, 2019, https://www.forbes.com/sites/daphneewingchow/2019/06/20/is-cultured-meat-the-answer-to-the-worlds-meat-problem/#5aaf518c4468.

12. G. Schaefer, "Lab-Grown Meat: Beef for Dinner—Without Killing Animals or the Environment," *Scientific American,* September 14, 2018, https://www.scientificamerican.com/article/lab-grown-meat/.

13. J. Bunge, "Tyson Takes Stake in Cultured Meat Startup: U.S. Meat Processor Places a Bet on Meat Grown from Animal Cells," *The Wall Street Journal,* January 29, 2018, https://www.wsj.com/articles/tyson-takes-stake-in-cultured-meat-startup-1517244019.

14. E. Newburger, "As the Lab-Grown Meat Industry Grows, Scientists Debate if It Could Exacerbate Climate Change," *CNBC,* October 19, 2019, https://www.cnbc.com/2019/10/19/lab-grown-meat-could-exacerbate-climate-change-scientists-say.html.

15. P. Paramasivam, "Lab-Grown Meat Producer Memphis Meats Raises $161 Million in Funding Led by SoftBank," *Reuters,* January 22, 2020, https://www.reuters.com/article/us-memphis-meats-funding/lab-grown-meat-producer-memphis-meats-raises-161-million-in-funding-led-by-softbank-idUSKBN1ZL2O0.

16. E. Newburger, "As the Lab-Grown Meat Industry Grows, Scientists Debate if It Could Exacerbate Climate Change," *CNBC,* October 19, 2019, https://www.cnbc.com/2019/10/19/lab-grown-meat-could-exacerbate-climate-change-scientists-say.html.

17. D. Ewing-Chow, "Is Cultured Meat the Answer to the World's Meat Problem?" *Forbes,* June 20, 2019, https://www.forbes.com/sites/daphneewingchow/2019/06/20/is-cultured-meat-the-answer-to-the-worlds-meat-problem/#5aaf518c4468.

18. J. Bunge, "Startup Serves Up Chicken Produced from Cells in Lab," *The Wall Street Journal,* March 15, 2017, https://www.wsj.com/articles/startup-to-serve-up-chicken-strips-cultivated-from-cells-in-lab-1489570202.

19. D. Ewing-Chow, "Is Cultured Meat the Answer to the World's Meat Problem?" *Forbes*, June 20, 2019, https://www.forbes.com/sites/daphneewingchow/2019/06/20/is-cultured-meat-the-answer-to-the-worlds-meat-problem/#5aaf518c4468.

20. D. Ewing-Chow, "Is Cultured Meat the Answer to the World's Meat Problem?" *Forbes*, June 20, 2019, https://www.forbes.com/sites/daphneewingchow/2019/06/20/is-cultured-meat-the-answer-to-the-worlds-meat-problem/#5aaf518c4468.

21. D. Ewing-Chow, "Is Cultured Meat the Answer to the World's Meat Problem?" *Forbes*, June 20, 2019, https://www.forbes.com/sites/daphneewingchow/2019/06/20/is-cultured-meat-the-answer-to-the-worlds-meat-problem/#5aaf518c4468. Also see E. Newburger, "As the Lab-Grown Meat Industry Grows, Scientists Debate if It Could Exacerbate Climate Change," *CNBC,* October 19, 2019, https://www.cnbc.com/2019/10/19/lab-grown-meat-could-exacerbate-climate-change-scientists-say.html.

22. E. Newburger, "As the Lab-Grown Meat Industry Grows, Scientists Debate if It Could Exacerbate Climate Change," *CNBC,* October 19, 2019, https://www.cnbc.com/2019/10/19/lab-grown-meat-could-exacerbate-climate-change-scientists-say.html.

23. G. Schaefer, "Lab-Grown Meat: Beef for Dinner—Without Killing Animals or the Environment," *Scientific American,* September 14, 2018, https://www.scientificamerican.com/article/lab-grown-meat/.

24. A. Lucas, "Lab-Grown Meat Start-Up Raises $14 Million to Build Production Plant," *CNBC,* October 10, 2019, https://www.cnbc.com/2019/10/10/future-meat-technologies-a-lab-grown-meat-start-up-raises-14-million-dollars.html.

25. D. Ewing-Chow, "Is Cultured Meat the Answer to the World's Meat Problem?" *Forbes,* June 20, 2019, https://www.forbes.com/sites/daphneewingchow/2019/06/20/is-cultured-meat-the-answer-to-the-worlds-meat-problem/#5aaf518c4468.

26. "Entry Level Management Salaries," *Glassdoor,* https://www.glassdoor.com/Salaries/entry-level-management-salary-SRCH_KO0,22.htm (accessed December 20, 2019). Also see "Middle Management Salaries," *Glassdoor,* https://www.glassdoor.com/Salaries/middle-management-salary-SRCH_KO0,17.htm (accessed December 20, 2019).

27. B. Schwartz, "Rethinking Work," *The New York Times,* August 30, 2015, pp. SR-1, SR-4. Schwartz is the author of *Why We Work* (New York: Simon & Schuster, 2015).

28. A. Rapp, "Be One, Get One: The Importance of Mentorship," *Forbes,* October 2, 2018, https://www.forbes.com/sites/yec/2018/10/02/be-one-get-one-the-importance-of-mentorship/#4a5ac5f97434.

29. P. Drucker, reported in R. L. Knowdell, "A Model for Managers in the Future Workplace: Symphony Conductor," *The Futurist,* June–July 1998.

30. M. Haas and M. Mortensen, "The Secrets of Great Teamwork*," Harvard Business Review*, June 2016, https://hbr.org/2016/06/the-secrets-of-great-teamwork.

31. Susan L. Solomon, interviewed by A. Wolfe, "Susan L. Solomon," *The Wall Street Journal,* February 6–7, 2016, p. C11. Also see "Susan L. Solomon," New York Stem Cell Foundation, http://nyscf.org/about-us/boards-councils/board-of-directors/item/228-susan-l-solomon-chief-executive-officer (accessed February 3, 2020).

32. Editorial Board, "Where Have All the Public Companies Gone?" *Bloomberg Opinion,* April 9, 2018, https://www.bloomberg.com/opinion/articles/2018-04-09/where-have-all-the-u-s-public-companies-gone.

33. M. Wursthorn and G. Zuckerman, "Fewer Listed Companies: Is That Good or Bad for Stock Markets?" *The Wall Street Journal (Online)*, January 4, 2018. https://search.proquest.com/docview/1984379501?accountid=8361

34. M. Hrywna, "80% of Nonprofits' Revenue Is from Government, Fee for Service," *TheNonProfitTimes,* September 19, 2019, https://www.thenonprofittimes.com/news/80-of-nonprofits-revenue-is-from-government-fee-for-service/.

35. "Directory of Charities and Nonprofit Organizations," *Guidestar*, https://www.guidestar.org/nonprofit-directory/public-societal-benefit/mutualmembership-benefit-organizations/1.aspx (accessed January 24, 2020).

36. H. Mintzberg, *The Nature of Managerial Work* (New York: Harper & Row, 1973).

37. H. Mintzberg, *The Nature of Managerial Work* (New York: Harper & Row, 1973).

38. M. Porter and N. Nohria, "How CEOs Manage Time," *Harvard Business Review,* Vol. 96, No. 4 (July–August 2018), pp. 42–51.

39. H. Mintzberg, *The Nature of Managerial Work* (New York: Harper & Row, 1973).

40. Ed Reilly, quoted in W. J. Holstein, "Attention-Juggling in the High-Tech Office," *The New York Times,* June 4, 2006, sec. 3, p. 9.

41. H. Mintzberg, *The Nature of Managerial Work* (New York: Harper & Row, 1973).

42. N. Bowles, "Concept of Work/Life Balance on Its Way to Being Obsolete," *San Francisco Chronicle,* November 2, 2013, pp. D1, D3. Also see H. L. Gray, "7 Tips for Work-Life Balance as an Entrepreneur," February 11, 2016, www.huffingtonpost.com/haley-lynn-gray/7-tips-for-work-life-balance-as-an-entrepreneur_b_9206250.html.

43. J. Kabat-Zinn, "Mindfulness-Based Interventions in Context: Past, Present, and Future," *Clinical Psychology: Science and Practice,* Summer 2003, p. 145.

44. "Multitasking: Switching Costs," American Psychological Association, http://www.apa.org/research/action/multitask.aspx.

45. E. Halliwell, "When the Mind Goes Dark," *Mindful,* February 2018, pp. 40–49. Also see U. R. Hülsheger, J. W. B. Lang, F. Depenbrock, C. Fehmann, F. R. H. Zilstra, and H. J. E. M. Alberts, "The Power of Presence: The Role of Mindfulness at Work for Daily Levels and Change Trajectories of Psychological Detachment and Sleep Quality," *Journal of Applied Psychology,* November 2014, pp. 1113–1128.

46. C. Comaford, "Why Mindfulness and Meditation Matter in Leadership," *Forbes,* March 13, 2016, https://www.forbes.com/sites/christinecomaford/2016/03/13/why-mindfulness-and-meditation-matter-in-leadership/2/#53707eb54e6b.

47. M. Tabaka, "9 Unusual Ways to Improve Your Short-Term Memory, Ranked by Weirdness," *Inc.,* June 26, 2017, https://www.inc.com/marla-tabaka/forgetfulness-is-just-annoying-9-unusual-ways-to-improve-your-memory.html.

48. N. Klemp, "5 Reasons Your Company Should be Invested in Mindfulness Training," *Inc.,* October 17, 2019, https://www.inc.com/nate-klemp/5-reasons-your-company-should-be-investing-in-mindfulness-training.html; M. Levin, "Why Google, Nike, and Apple Love Mindfulness Training, and How You Can Easily Love It Too," *Inc.,* June 12, 2017, https://www.inc.com/marissa-levin/why-google-nike-and-apple-love-mindfulness-training-and-how-you-can-easily-love-.html; "Mindfulness for Managers: Feeling Good Is Good for Business," *TOPMBA,* November 14, 2016, https://www.topmba.com/jobs/career-trends/mindfulness-managers-feeling-good-good-business.

49. "Mindfulness for Managers: Feeling Good Is Good for Business," *TOPMBA,* November 14, 2016, https://www.topmba.com/jobs/career-trends/mindfulness-managers-feeling-good-good-business.

50. "Mindfulness for Managers: Feeling Good Is Good for Business," *TOPMBA,* November 14, 2016, https://www.topmba.com/jobs/career-trends/mindfulness-managers-feeling-good-good-business.

51. C. Comaford, "Why Mindfulness and Meditation Matter in Leadership," *Forbes,* March 13, 2016, https://www.forbes.com/sites/christinecomaford/2016/03/13/why-mindfulness-and-meditation-matter-in-leadership/2/#53707eb54e6b.

52. K. Swisher, "Google CEO Sundar Pichai Canceled an All-hands Meeting about Gender Controversy Due to Employee Worries of Online Harassment," *Recode,* August 10, 2017, https://www.recode.net/2017/8/10/16128380/google-cancels-all-hands-meeting-controversy-memo.

53. R. L. Zweigenhaft and G. W. Domhoff, *The New CEOs: Women, African American, Latino, and Asian American Leaders of Fortune 500 Companies* (Lanham, MD: Rowman & Littlefield, 2011).

54. "Women CEOs Speak," Korn Ferry Institute, November 2017, https://engage.kornferry.com/Global/fileLib/Women_CEOs_speak/KF-Rockefeller-Women-CEOs-Speak-Nov_2017.

55. R. L. Katz, "Skills of an Effective Administrator," *Harvard Business Review,* September–October, 1974, p. 94. Also see M. K. De Vries, "Decoding the Team Conundrum: The Eight Roles Executives Play," *Organizational Dynamics,* Vol. 36, No. 1 (2007), pp. 28–44.

56. B. Vlasic, "New GM Chief Is Company Woman, Born to It," *The New York Times,* December 11, 2013, pp. A1, A3.

57. Dan Akerson, quoted in R. Wright and H. Foy, "GM Beats Rivals to Put Woman in Driving Seat," *Financial Times,* December 11, 2013, p. 1.

58. B. Vlasic, "New GM Chief Is Company Woman, Born to It," *New York Times,* December 10, 2013, https://www.nytimes.com/2013/12/11/business/gm-names-first-female-chief-executive.html.

59. Gary Cowger, who mentored Barra, quoted in D. A. Durbin and T. Krishner, "Mary Barra, a Child of GM, Prepares to Lead It," *AP,* December 24, 2013, http://bigstory.ap.org/article/mary-barra-child-gm-prepares-lead-it (accessed February 27, 2016).

60. Mary Barra, quoted in B. Vlasic, "New GM Chief Is Company Woman, Born to It," *New York Times,* December 10, 2013, https://www.nytimes.com/2013/12/11/business/gm-names-first-female-chief-executive.html.

61. J. Bennett and S. Murray, "Longtime Insider Is GM's First Female CEO," *The Wall Street Journal,* December 11, 2013, pp. A1, A10.

62. M. Spector and C. M. Matthews, "GM Admits to Criminal Wrongdoing," *The Wall Street Journal,* September 18, 2015, pp. B1, B2. Also see M. Spector, "GM Does a U-Turn in Ignition-Switch Case Motion," *The New York Times,* October 7, 2015, p. B4. Also see G. Nagesh and J. S. Lublin, "Investors Yet to Value GM Changes," *The Wall Street Journal,* February 1, 2016, www.wsj.com/articles/investors-yet-to-value-gm-changes-1454371679.

63. G. Nagesh, "GM's Long-Haul Plan," *The Wall Street Journal,* October 26, 2015, p. R2. Also see G. Nagesh and J. Lublin, "Investors Yet to Value GM Changes," *The Wall Street Journal,* February 1, 2016. Also see B. Vlasic, "Buoyed by North America, GM Posts $9.7 Billion Profit for 2015," *The New York Times,* February 4, 2016, p. B2.

64. Dan Akerson, quoted in B. Vlasic, "New GM Chief Is Company Woman, Born to It," *New York Times,* December 10, 2013, https://www.nytimes.com/2013/12/11/business/gm-names-first-female-chief-executive.html.

65. B. Vlasic, "New GM Chief Is Company Woman, Born to It," *New York Times,* December 10, 2013, https://www.nytimes.com/2013/12/11/business/gm-names-first-female-chief-executive.html.

66. Durbin and Krishner, "Mary Barra, a Child of GM, Prepares to Lead It," *The Dallas Morning News,* December 28, 2013, https://www.dallasnews.com/business/autos/2013/12/29/mary-barra-a-child-of-gm-prepares-to-lead-it/.

67. "2019 Global Talent Trends," *Linkedin Talent Solutions,* 2019, https://business.linkedin.com/talent-solutions/recruiting-tips/global-talent-trends-2019?trk=bl-po.

68. "Five Fifty," *McKinsey Quarterly,* https://www.mckinsey.com/featured-insights/future-of-work/five-fifty-soft-skills-for-a-hard-world?cid=fivefifty-eml-alt-mkq-mck&hlkid=c63e6da84c4b499f8b0cb2e4a7b32f41&hctky=1758915&hdpid=f980f771-2f72-4126-94c5ba868b14bec4 (accessed February 6, 2020).

69. M. Eggleston, " Millennials Need Soft Skills Training," *Training Industry,* July 21, 2014, https://www.trainingindustry.com/blog/performance-management/millennials-need-soft-skills-training/.

70. T. Elmore, "The Seven Top Skills Google Now Looks for in Graduates," *Psychology Today,* July 19, 2018, https://www.psychologytoday.com/us/blog/artificial-maturity/201807/the-seven-top-skills-google-now-looks-in-graduates.

71. "Measuring the ROI of Soft Skills," *EBSCO for Corporate,* August 29, 2018. https://www.ebsco.com/blog-corporate/article/measuring-the-roi-of-soft-skills.

72. "Interpersonal Skills for Managers," American Management Association, http://www.amanet.org/training/seminars/interpersonal-skills-for-managers.aspx#how_will_you_benefit.

73. A. Kalish, "11 Cheap Online Classes You Can Take to Improve Your Interpersonal Skills," *The Muse,* https://www.themuse.com/advice/11-cheap-online-classes-you-can-take-to-improve-your-interpersonal-skills.

74. CEO recruiter, quoted in Colvin, "Catch a Rising Star," *CNN Money,* January 30, 2006, https://money.cnn.com/magazines/fortune/fortune_archive/2006/02/06/8367928/index.htm.

75. CEO recruiter, quoted in Colvin, "Catch a Rising Star," *CNN Money,* January 30, 2006, https://money.cnn.com/magazines/fortune/fortune_archive/2006/02/06/8367928/index.htm.

76. M. Csikszentmihalyi, *Flow: The Psychology of Optimal Experience* (New York: Harper Collins, 1990); *Beyond Boredom and Anxiety* (San Francisco: Jossey-Bass, 1975). Also see *Creativity: Flow and the Psychology of Discovery and Invention* (New York: Harper Perennial, 1996).

77. K. Schwab, "The Fourth Industrial Revolution: What It Means, How to Respond," *World Economic Forum,* January 14, 2016, https://www.weforum.org/agenda/2016/01/the-fourth-industrial-revolution-what-it-means-and-how-to-respond/.

78. A. Lipsman, "US Ecommerce 2019: Mobile and Social Commerce Fuel Ongoing Ecommerce Channel Shift," *eMarketer,* June 27, 2019, https://www.emarketer.com/content/us-ecommerce-2019.

79. Forrester Research, "112 Results for 'Disruption' in Everything," https://www.forrester.com/search?range=504001&N=204=0%200&tmtxt=+disruption&page=1 (accessed February 10, 2016).

80. K. Kirkham, "How Big Is the Digital Universe?" *100Tb,* June 28, 2019, https://blog.100tb.com/how-big-is-the-digital-universe.

81. B. Carson and K. Chaykowski, "Live Long and Prosper: How Anne Wojcicki's 23andMe Will Mine Its Giant DNA Database for Health and Wealth Biz," *Forbes,* June 6, 2019, https://www.forbes.com/sites/bizcarson/2019/06/06/23andme-dna-test-anne-wojcicki-prevention-plans-drug-development/#54c47db2494d.

82. B. Carson and K. Chaykowski, "Live Long and Prosper: How Anne Wojcicki's 23andMe Will Mine Its Giant DNA Database for Health and Wealth Biz," *Forbes,* June 6, 2019, https://www.forbes.com/sites/bizcarson/2019/06/06/23andme-dna-test-anne-wojcicki-prevention-plans-drug-development/#54c47db2494d.

83. B. Carson and K. Chaykowski, "Live Long and Prosper: How Anne Wojcicki's 23andMe Will Mine Its Giant DNA Database for Health and Wealth Biz," *Forbes,* June 6, 2019, https://www.forbes.com/sites/bizcarson/2019/06/06/23andme-dna-test-anne-wojcicki-prevention-plans-drug-development/#54c47db2494d.

84. E. Brodwin, "Genetic Testing Is the Future of Healthcare, But Many Experts Say Companies Like 23andMe Are Doing More Harm than Good," *Business Insider,* January 12, 2019, https://www.businessinsider.com/future-healthcare-dna-genetic-testing-23andme-2018-12.

85. B. Carson and K. Chaykowski, "Live Long and Prosper: How Anne Wojcicki's 23andMe Will Mine Its Giant DNA Database for Health and Wealth Biz," *Forbes,* June 6, 2019, https://www.forbes.com/sites/bizcarson/2019/06/06/23andme-dna-test-anne-wojcicki-prevention-plans-drug-development/#54c47db2494d.

86. B. Ross, "23andMe CEO Goes Beyond 'Wall of a White Coat,'" *Bio IT World,* January 15, 2018, http://www.bio-itworld.com/2018/01/15/23andme-ceo-goes-beyond-wall-of-a-white-coat.aspx.

87. B. Carson and K. Chaykowski, "Live Long and Prosper: How Anne Wojcicki's 23andMe Will Mine Its Giant DNA Database For Health and Wealth Biz," *Forbes,* June 6, 2019, https://www.forbes.com/sites/bizcarson/2019/06/06/23andme-dna-test-anne-wojcicki-prevention-plans-drug-development/#54c47db2494d.

88. E. Brodwin, "Genetic Testing Is the Future of Healthcare, But Many Experts Say Companies Like 23andMe Are Doing More Harm than Good," *Business Insider,* January 12, 2019, https://www.businessinsider.com/future-healthcare-dna-genetic-testing-23andme-2018-12.

89. B. Carson and K. Chaykowski, "Live Long and Prosper: How Anne Wojcicki's 23andMe Will Mine Its Giant DNA Database for Health and Wealth Biz," *Forbes,* June 6, 2019, https://www.forbes.com/sites/bizcarson/2019/06/06/23andme-dna-test-anne-wojcicki-prevention-plans-drug-development/#54c47db2494d.

90. A. Regalado, "23andMe Pulls Off Massive Crowdsourced Depression Study," *MIT Technology Review,* August 1, 2016, https://www.technologyreview.com/s/602052/23andme-pulls-off-massive-crowdsourced-depression-study/.

91. M. Herper, "23andMe Gets $300 Million Boost from GlaxoSmithKline to Develop New Drugs," *Forbes,* July 25, 2018, https://www.forbes.com/sites/matthewherper/2018/07/25/23andme-gets-300-million-boost-from-glaxo-to-develop-new-drugs/#2aab70f13213.

92. M. Baram, "The FTC Is Investigating DNA Firms Like 23andMe and Ancestry over Privacy," *Fast Company,* June 5, 2018, https://www.fastcompany.com/40580364/the-ftc-is-investigating-dna-firms-like-23andme-and-ancestry-over-privacy.

93. E. Brodwin, "Genetic Testing Is the Future of Healthcare, But Many Experts Say Companies Like 23andMe Are Doing More Harm than Good," *Business Insider,* January 12, 2019, https://www.businessinsider.com/future-healthcare-dna-genetic-testing-23andme-2018-12.

94. J. McLaughlin and Z. Dorfman, "Exclusive: Pentagon Warns Military Members DNA Kits Pose 'Personal and Operational Risks,'" *Yahoo News,* December 23, 2019, https://www.yahoo.com/news/pentagon-warns-military-members-dna-kits-pose-personal-and-operational-risks-173304318.html.

95. B. Ross, "23andMe CEO Goes Beyond 'Wall of a White Coat,'" *Bio IT World,* January 15, 2018, http://www.bio-itworld.com/2018/01/15/23andme-ceo-goes-beyond-wall-of-a-white-coat.aspx.

96. C. Farr, "Consumer DNA Testing Has Hit a Lull— Here's How It Could Capture the Next Wave of Users," *CNBC,* August 25, 2019, https://www.cnbc.com/2019/08/25/dna-tests-from-companies-like-23andme-ancestry-see-sales-slowdown.html.

97. B. Carson and K. Chaykowski, "Live Long and Prosper: How Anne Wojcicki's 23andMe Will Mine Its Giant DNA Database for Health and Wealth Biz," *Forbes,* June 6, 2019, https://www.forbes.com/sites/bizcarson/2019/06/06/23andme-dna-test-anne-wojcicki-prevention-plans-drug-development/#54c47db2494d.

98. A. Gaffney, "Can Tech Companies Disrupt Healthcare? Many Consumers Think So," *PWC,* January 16, 2019, https://www.pwc.com/us/en/industries/health-industries/library/tech-companies-disrupt-healthcare-2018.html.

99. A. Williams, "Will Robots Take Our Children's Jobs?" *The New York Times,* December 11, 2017, https://www.nytimes.com/2017/12/11/style/robots-jobs-children.html. Also see C. C. Miller, "Evidence That Robots Are Winning the Race for American Jobs," *The UpShot,* March 28, 2017, https://www.nytimes.com/2017/03/28/upshot/evidence-that-robots-are-winning-the-race-for-american-jobs.html.

100. S. Lohr, "Robots Will Take Jobs, but Not as Fast as Some Fear, New Report Says," *The New York Times,* January 12, 2017, https://www.nytimes.com/2017/01/12/technology/robots-will-take-jobs-but-not-as-fast-as-some-fear-new-report-says.html.

101. "US Foreign-Born Gains Are Smallest in a Decade, Except in Trump States," *Brookings,* October 2, 2019, https://www.brookings.edu/blog/the-avenue/2019/10/01/us-foreign-born-gains-are-smallest-in-a-decade-except-in-trump-states/.

102. United States Census Bureau, "2017 National Population Projections Tables," https://www.census.gov/data/tables/2017/demo/popproj/2017-summary-tables.html.

103. United States Census Bureau, "2017 National Population Projections Tables," https://www.census.gov/data/tables/2017/demo/popproj/2017-summary-tables.html.

104. United States Census Bureau, "2017 National Population Projections Tables," https://www.census.gov/data/tables/2017/demo/popproj/2017-summary-tables.html.

105. A. Simone, "The 'How Are You?' Culture Clash," *The New York Times,* January 20, 2014, p. A15.

106. A. Simone, "The 'How Are You?' Culture Clash," *The New York Times,* January 20, 2014, p. A15.

107. N. Saval, "Globalisation: The Rise and Fall of an Idea That Swept the World," *The Guardian,* July 14, 2017, https://www.theguardian.com/world/2017/jul/14/globalisation-the-rise-and-fall-of-an-idea-that-swept-the-world.

108. P. Wiseman, and M. Crutsinger, "IMF, World Bank Push Back against Globalization's Detractors," *Business Insider,* October 14, 2017, http://www.businessinsider.com/ap-imf-world-bank-push-back-against-globalizations-detractors-2017-10.

109. N. Bloom and J. Van Reenan, "Why Do Management Practices Differ across Firms and Countries?" *Journal of Economic Perspectives,* Vol. 24, No. 1 (2010), pp. 203–224.

110. A. Einstein, "Former Audi Boss Charged in the VW Diesel Scandal That Won't Die," *CNBC,* July 21, 2019, https://www.cnbc.com/2019/07/31/former-audi-boss-charged-in-the-vw-diesel-scandal-that-wont-die.html.

111. D. Rushe, "Oliver Schmidt Jailed for Seven Years for Volkswagen Emissions Scam," *The Guardian,* December 17, 2017, https://www.theguardian.com/business/2017/dec/06/oliver-schmidt-jailed-volkswagen-emissions-scam-seven-years.

112. M. Kennedy, "Houston Astros Dismiss Team Manager, General Manager over Sign-Stealing Scandal," *NPR,* January 13, 2020, https://www.npr.org/2020/01/13/795959620/houston-astros-dismiss-team-manager-general-manager-over-sign-stealing-scandal.

113. M. Kouchaki and I. H. Smith, "The Morning Morality Effect: The Influence of Time of Day on Unethical Behavior," *Psychological Science,* January 2014, pp. 95–102.

114. J. Roberts and D. Wasieleski, "Moral Reasoning in Computer-Based Task Environments: Exploring the Interplay between Cognitive and Technological Factors on Individuals' Propensity to Break Rules," *Journal of Business Ethics,* October 2012, pp. 355–376.

115. D. Schaffhauser, "9 in 10 Students Admit to Cheating in College, Suspect Faculty Do the Same," *Campus Technology,* February 23, 2017, https://campustechnology.com/articles/2017/02/23/9-in-10-students-admit-to-cheating-in-college-suspect-faculty-do-the-same.aspx.

116. "Ethics Pays," *EthicalSystems.org,* http://ethicalsystems.org/content/ethics-pays (accessed February 21, 2016).

117. A. Tugend, "In Life and Business, Learning to Be Ethical," *The New York Times,* January 11, 2014, p. B5.

118. A. E. Tenbrunsel, University of Notre Dame, quoted in A. Tugend, "In Life and Business, Learning to Be Ethical," *The New York Times,* January 11, 2014, p. B5.

119. "The 2019 US Cities Sustainable Development Report," *Sustainable Development Solutions Network,* July 8, 2019, https://www.sustainabledevelopment.report/reports/2019-us-cities-sustainable-development-report/.

120. C. L. Dubois and D. A. Dubois, "Expanding the Vision of Industrial-Organizational Psychology Contributions to Environmental Sustainability, *Industrial and Organizational Psychology,* Vol. 5, No. 4, pp. 480–483.

121. J. Hackenberg, "The UN's Sustainable Development Goals Aren't Just Doing Good, They're Good Business," *Forbes,* August 29, 2019, https://www.forbes.com/sites/jonquilhackenberg/2019/08/29/the-uns-sustainable-development-goals-arent-just-doing-good-theyre-good-business/#24edf12f53d9.

122. I. Embree, "How 17 Companies Are Tackling Sustainable Development Goals (and Your Company Can, Too)," *HuffPost,* September 13, 2016, https://www.huffpost.com/entry/how-17-companies-are-tack_b_11991808.

123. "Business Roundtable Redefines the Purpose of a Corporation to Promote 'An Economy That Serves All Americans,'" *Business Roundtable,* August 19, 2019, https://www.businessroundtable.org/business-roundtable-redefines-the-purpose-of-a-corporation-to-promote-an-economy-that-serves-all-americans.

124. "The 2019 US Cities Sustainable Development Report," *Sustainable Development Solutions Network,* July 8, 2019, https://www.sustainabledevelopment.report/reports/2019-us-cities-sustainable-development-report/.

125. J. Aaker, Stanford Graduate School of Business, quoted in C. B. Parker, "Stanford Research: The Meaningful Life Is a Road Worth Traveling," *Stanford Report,* January 1, 2014, http://news.stanford.edu/news/2014/january/meaningful-happy-life-010114.html. The study is R. F. Baumeister, K. D. Vohs, J. L. Aaker, and E. N. Garbinsky, "Some Key Differences between a Happy Life and a Meaningful Life," *Journal of Positive Psychology,* Vol. 8, No. 6 (2013), pp. 505–516.

126. M. Seligman, *Flourish* (New York: Free Press, 2011), p. 17.

127. M. Seligman, *Flourish* (New York: Free Press, 2011).

128. R. Levering, "The 100 Best Companies to Work for 2016," *Fortune,* March 15, 2016, pp. 143–165.

129. M. Seligman, *Flourish* (New York: Free Press, 2011).

130. "100 Best Companies to Work For," *Fortune,* 2019, https://fortune.com/best-companies/2019/.

131. M. C. Bush and S. Lewis-Kulin, "100 Best Companies to Work for 2017," *Fortune,* March 15, 2017, p. 86.

132. J. Shanker, "The Most Attractive Employers in 2019, According to Current College Students," *Yahoo Finance,* June 9, 2019, https://finance.yahoo.com/news/best-employers-business-2019-175454210.html.

133. Nace Staff, "Are College Graduates 'Career Ready'?" *National Association of Colleges and Employers,* February 19, 2018, Job Outlook 2018 survey, https://www.naceweb.org/career-readiness/competencies/are-college-graduates-career-ready/.

134. Nace Staff, "Are College Graduates 'Career Ready'?" *National Association of Colleges and Employers,* February 19, 2018, Job Outlook 2018 survey, https://www.naceweb.org/career-readiness/competencies/are-college-graduates-career-ready/. Also see M. Elliott, "Watch The Skills Gap," 2016, http://www.adeccousa.com/employers/resources/skills-gap-in-the-american-workforce; M. Elliott, "5 Skills College Grads Need to Get a Job," *USA Today,* 2015, http://www.usatoday.com/story/money/personalfinance/2015/05/03/cheat-sheet-skills-college-grads-job/26574631.

135. T. D. Fishman and L. Sledge, "Reimagining Higher Education: How Colleges, Universities, Businesses, and Governments Can Prepare for a New Age of Lifelong Learning," *Deloitte,* May 22, 2014, https://www2.deloitte.com/us/en/insights/industry/public-sector/reimagining-higher-education.html.

136. "Future Work Skills 2020," Institute for the Future for the University of Phoenix Research Institute, 2011, p. 13, http://www.iftf.org/uploads/media/SR-1382A_UPRI_future_work_skills_sm.pdf.

137. Nace Staff, "Are College Graduates 'Career Ready'?" *National Association of Colleges and Employers,* February 19, 2018, Job Outlook 2018 survey, https://www.naceweb.org/career-readiness/competencies/are-college-graduates-career-ready/. Also see https://www.education.ne.gov/nce/ne-career-readiness-standards/; https://www.forbes.com/sites/nicholaswyman/2018/08/03/hiring-is-on-the-rise-but-are-college-grads-prepared-for-the-world-of-work/#793195644e7e.

138. J. Bughin, E. Hazan, S. Leund, P. Dahlström, A. Wiesinger, and A. Subramaniam, "Skill Shift: Automation and the Future of the Workforce," McKinsey Global Institute. Division Paper. May 2018.

139. K. Davidson, "Employers Find 'Soft Skills' Like Critical Thinking in Short Supply," *The Wall Street Journal,* August 30, 2016, https://www.wsj.com/articles/employers-find-soft-skills-like-critical-thinking-in-short-supply-1472549400.

140. L. Pinto and D. Ramalheira, "Perceived Employability of Business Graduates: The Effect of Academic Performance and Extracurricular Activities," *Journal of Vocational Behavior,* 2017, pp. 165–178.

141. "2019 Global Talent Trends," *Linkedin Talent Solutions,* 2019, https://business.linkedin.com/talent-solutions/recruiting-tips/global-talent-trends-2019?trk=bl-po.

142. S. Dawkins, A. W. Tian, A. Newman, and A. Martin, "Psychological Ownership: A Review and Research Agenda," *Journal of Organizational Behavior,* 2017, pp. 163–183.

143. T. Williams, "7 Core Competencies Shape Career Readiness for College Graduates," January 12, 2016, https://www.goodcall.com/news/7-core-competencies-shape-career-readiness-for-college-graduates-03909.

144. M. Jay, "The Secrets of Resilience," *The Wall Street Journal,* November 11-12, 2017, pp. C1–C2.

145. R. Dellenger, "Joe Burrow's Remarkable Rise Has Been Beyond Even His Wildest Dreams," *Sports Illustrated,* November 26, 2019, https://www.si.com/college/2019/11/26/joe-burrow-lsu-tigers-nfl.

146. P. Thamel, "The Legend of Joe Burrow: From Overlooked at Ohio State to Heisman Frontrunner at LSU," *Yahoo Sports,* November 6, 2019, https://sports.yahoo.com/the-legend-of-joe-burrow-from-being-mocked-at-ohio-state-to-heisman-frontrunner-at-lsu-234857735.html?guccounter=1&guce_referrer=aHR0cHM6Ly93d3cuZ29vZ2xlLmNvbvbS8&guce_referrer_sig=AQAAAFr4rbmVDFABIXochjLm_cL_rUcolBqVuRuXTx8ETjMT-XE8y9SkM8IoraWI-28x0CfpN_2L5ueay0wjn9t9w3Q6dsaO4NPALTMb_F8BvBg7xdWErZphrNWOS4BsdFJYO91vNuo6PLrsKQUShvDcoU1TT_FqLTjHZU3lyFttt93O.

147. M. Jay, *Supernormal: The Untold Story of Adversity and Resilience* (New York: Hachette Book Group, 2017).

148. B. Tulgan, *Bridging the Soft Skills Gap* (Hoboken, NJ: John Wiley, 2015). Also see L. Gillin, *10 Soft Skills You Need* (Dover, DE: Global Courseware, 2015).

149. S. Bates and S. Miller, "The Class of 2017: Ready to Work," *HR Magazine,* August 2017, p. 8. Also see "The Difference Between an Internship & a Co-Op," October 29, 2017, https://www.thebalance.com/whats-the-difference-between-an-internship-and-a-coop-1987135.

150. Additional insights can be found in W. Enelow, "Charting Your Course," *HR Magazine,* September 2017, pp. 20–21. Also see S. Shellenbarger, "Don't Feel Stuck: It's Time to Update Your Career Blueprint," *The Wall Street Journal,* February 15, 2017, p. A9.

151. B. J. Fogg, "On the Journey to New Habits, Take Tiny Steps," *The Wall Street Journal,* January 5, 2020, https://www.wsj.com/articles/on-the-journey-to-new-habits-take-tiny-steps-11577985523. Also see L. MacLellan, "A Stanford University Behavior Scientist's Elegant Three-Step Method for Creating New Habits," *Quartz,* January 4, 2017, https://qz.com/877795/how-to-create-new-good-habits-according-to-stanford-psychologist-b-j-fogg/.

152. K. Wang and I. Kim, "At Its Peak, Forever 21 Made $4.4 Billion in Revenue. Here's What Led to the Brand's Downfall and Bankruptcy," *Business Insider*, September 30, 2019, https://www.businessinsider.com/forever-21-bankruptcy-rise-fall-retail-apocalypse-fast-fashion-2019-9.

153. S. Berfield, E. Ronalds-Hannon, and L. Coleman-Lochner, "The Failure of the Forever 21 Empire," *Bloomberg,* January 17, 2020, https://www.bloomberg.com/news/features/2020-01-17/the-failure-of-the-fast-fashion-forever-21-empire.

154. S. Berfield, E. Ronalds-Hannon, and L. Coleman-Lochner, "The Failure of the Forever 21 Empire," *Bloomberg,* January 17, 2020, https://www.bloomberg.com/news/features/2020-01-17/the-failure-of-the-fast-fashion-forever-21-empire.

155. K. Wang and I. Kim, "At Its Peak, Forever 21 Made $4.4 Billion in Revenue. Here's What Led to the Brand's Downfall and Bankruptcy," *Business Insider*, September 30, 2019, https://www.businessinsider.com/forever-21-bankruptcy-rise-fall-retail-apocalypse-fast-fashion-2019-9.

156. S. Berfield, E. Ronalds-Hannon, and L. Coleman-Lochner, "The Failure of the Forever 21 Empire," *Bloomberg,* January 17, 2020, https://www.bloomberg.com/news/features/2020-01-17/the-failure-of-the-fast-fashion-forever-21-empire.

157. S. Berfield, E. Ronalds-Hannon, and L. Coleman-Lochner, "The Failure of the Forever 21 Empire," *Bloomberg,* January 17, 2020, https://www.bloomberg.com/news/features/2020-01-17/the-failure-of-the-fast-fashion-forever-21-empire.

158. S. Berfield, E. Ronalds-Hannon, and L. Coleman-Lochner, "The Failure of the Forever 21 Empire," *Bloomberg,* January 17, 2020, https://www.bloomberg.com/news/features/2020-01-17/the-failure-of-the-fast-fashion-forever-21-empire.

159. S. Berfield, E. Ronalds-Hannon, and L. Coleman-Lochner, "The Failure of the Forever 21 Empire," *Bloomberg,* January 17, 2020, https://www.bloomberg.com/news/features/2020-01-17/the-failure-of-the-fast-fashion-forever-21-empire.

160. S. Berfield, E. Ronalds-Hannon, and L. Coleman-Lochner, "The Failure of the Forever 21 Empire," *Bloomberg,* January 17, 2020, https://www.bloomberg.com/news/features/2020-01-17/the-failure-of-the-fast-fashion-forever-21-empire.

161. K. Wang and I. Kim, "At its Peak, Forever 21 Made $4.4 Billion in Revenue. Here's What Led to the Brand's Downfall and Bankruptcy," *Business Insider*, September 30, 2019, https://www.businessinsider.com/forever-21-bankruptcy-rise-fall-retail-apocalypse-fast-fashion-2019-9.

162. K. Wang and I. Kim, "At its Peak, Forever 21 Made $4.4 Billion in Revenue. Here's What Led to the Brand's Downfall and Bankruptcy," *Business Insider*, September 30, 2019, https://www.businessinsider.com/forever-21-bankruptcy-rise-fall-retail-apocalypse-fast-fashion-2019-9.

163. J. McCarthy, "Forever 21 Has Aged: Now It's Outflanked on Sustainability, Fast Fashion and Relevance," *The Drum,* October 1, 2019, https://www.thedrum.com/news/2019/10/01/forever-21-has-aged-now-its-outflanked-sustainability-fast-fashion-and-relevance.

164. K. Wang and I. Kim, "At Its Peak, Forever 21 Made $4.4 Billion in Revenue. Here's What Led to the Brand's Downfall and Bankruptcy," *Business Insider*, September 30, 2019, https://www.businessinsider.com/forever-21-bankruptcy-rise-fall-retail-apocalypse-fast-fashion-2019-9.

165. S. V. Smith and C. Garcia, "Forever 21 Reveals the Flaws of Fast Fashion," *NPR,* October 18, 2019, https://www.npr.org/2019/10/18/771219861/forever-21-reveals-the-flaws-of-fast-fashion.

166. S. Maheshwari, "One Family Built Forever 21, and Fueled Its Collapse," *Chattanooga Times Free Press,* October 25, 2019, https://www.timesfreepress.com/news/business/national/story/2019/oct/25/one-family-built-forever-21-and-fueled-its-co/506509/.

167. K. Wang and I. Kim, "At Its Peak, Forever 21 Made $4.4 Billion in Revenue. Here's What Led to the Brand's Downfall and Bankruptcy," *Business Insider*, September 30, 2019, https://www.businessinsider.com/forever-21-bankruptcy-rise-fall-retail-apocalypse-fast-fashion-2019-9.

168. S. Berfield, E. Ronalds-Hannon, and L. Coleman-Lochner, "The Failure of the Forever 21 Empire," *Bloomberg,* January 17, 2020, https://www.bloomberg.com/news/features/2020-01-17/the-failure-of-the-fast-fashion-forever-21-empire.

169. J. McCarthy, "Forever 21 Has Aged: Now It's Outflanked on Sustainability, Fast Fashion and Relevance," *The Drum,* October 1, 2019, https://www.thedrum.com/news/2019/10/01/forever-21-has-aged-now-its-outflanked-sustainability-fast-fashion-and-relevance.

170. S. Berfield, E. Ronalds-Hannon, and L. Coleman-Lochner, "The Failure of the Forever 21 Empire," *Bloomberg,* January 17, 2020, https://www.bloomberg.com/news/features/2020-01-17/the-failure-of-the-fast-fashion-forever-21-empire.

171. N. Sachmechi, "Former Forever 21 Billionaire Couple Slated to Sell Troubled Retailer for Just $81 Million," *Forbes,* February 3, 2020, https://www.forbes.com/sites/nataliesachmechi/2020/02/03/former-forever-21-billionaire-couple-slated-to-sell-troubled-retailer-for-just-81-million/#48f9f04b68ae.

172. E. Chochrek, "Forever 21 Bankruptcy Case Headed Toward Liquidation or Dismissal, Says US Trustee," *Footwear News,* May 12, 2020, https://footwearnews.com/2020/business/legal-news/forever-21-bankruptcy-case-dismissed-liquidation-1202984461/.

173. J. McCarthy, "Forever 21 Has Aged: Now It's Outflanked on Sustainability, Fast Fashion and Relevance," *The Drum,* October 1, 2019, https://www.thedrum.com/news/2019/10/01/forever-21-has-aged-now-its-outflanked-sustainability-fast-fashion-and-relevance.

CHAPTER 2

1. "Learn about Gen Z (aka Generation Z) on GEN HQ," The Center for Generational Kinetics, https://genhq.com/igen-gen-z-generation-z-centennials-info/ (accessed December 9, 2019).

2. R. Glazer, "Want to Understand Gen Z? Check Out These 5 Experts," *Forbes*, June 26, 2019, https://www.forbes.com/sites/robert-glazer/2019/06/26/want-to-understand-gen-z-check-out-these-5-experts/#ca97fa6b4a00.

3. I. Leung, "The Tech Industry Is Getting Very People and Culture Focused, Here's Why," *Forbes*, August 5, 2017, https://www.forbes.com/sites/irisleung/2017/08/05/the-tech-industry-is-getting-very-people-and-culture-focused-heres-why/#9db558e57b84.

4. I. Leung, "The Tech Industry Is Getting Very People and Culture Focused, Here's Why," *Forbes*, August 5, 2017, https://www.forbes.com/sites/irisleung/2017/08/05/the-tech-industry-is-getting-very-people-and-culture-focused-heres-why/#9db558e57b84.

5. M. St. Amour, "Most College Students Work, and That's Both Good and Bad," *Inside Higher Ed*, November 18, 2019, https://www.insidehighered.com/news/2019/11/18/most-college-students-work-and-thats-both-good-and-bad.

6. M. Biro, "#WorkTrends: Building a People-Focused Culture." *TalentCulture*, April 19, 2019, https://talentculture.com/worktrends-building-a-people-focused-culture/.

7. Tom Peters, quoted in J. A. Byrne, "The Man Who Invented Management," *BusinessWeek*, November 28, 2005.

8. M. Alderton, "How to Apply Peter Drucker's Management Theory," *business.com*, October 11, 2019, https://www.business.com/articles/management-theory-of-peter-drucker/.

9. "Store Locator," *Wegmans*, https://www.wegmans.com/stores/store-locator.html (accessed December 10, 2019); "Here's Why Wegmans Employees Love What They Do," *Wegmans Food Markets*, https://jobs.wegmans.com/employee-satisfaction-at-wegmans (accessed December 10, 2019).

10. "Here's Why Wegmans Employees Love What They Do," *Wegmans Food Markets*, https://jobs.wegmans.com/employee-satisfaction-at-wegmans (accessed December 10, 2019).

11. J. Natale, "Wegmans Ranked #1 on List of the 2019 Best Workplaces in Retail by Great Place to Work and Fortune," *Wegmans*, November 7, 2019, https://www.wegmans.com/news-media/press-releases/2019/test-2/wegmans-ranked-1-on-list-of-the-2019-best-workplaces-in-retail-by-great-place-to-work-and-fortune.html.

12. J. Natale, "Wegmans Ranks #1 for Best Customer Experience According to 2018 Temkin Experience Ratings," *Wegmans*, April 10, 2018, https://www.wegmans.com/news-media/press-releases/2018/wegmans-ranks--1-for-best-customer-experience-according-to-2018-.html.

13. C. M. Christensen and M. E. Raynor, "Why Hard-Nosed Executives Should Care about Management Theory," *Harvard Business Review*, September 2003, pp. 67–74.

14. C. M. Christensen and M. E. Raynor, "Why Hard-Nosed Executives Should Care about Management Theory," *Harvard Business Review*, September 2003, p. 68.

15. S. L. Montgomery and D. Chirot, quoted in F. Zakaria, "Something in the Air," *The New York Times Book Review*, August 23, 2015, pp. 14–15. Montgomery and Chirot are authors of *The Shape of the New: Four Big Ideas and How They Made the Modern World* (Princeton, NJ: Princeton University Press, 2015).

16. G. D. Babcock and R. Trautschold, *The Taylor System in Franklin Management*, 2nd ed. (New York: Engineering Magazine Co., 1917).

17. L. Held, "Profile—Lillian Gilbreth," *Psychology's Feminist Voices*, http://www.feministvoices.com/lillian-gilbreth/ (accessed December 11, 2019).

18. L. Koppes, "Biography of Lilian Evelyn Moller Gilbreth," *Society for the Psychology of Women*, https://www.apadivisions.org/division-35/about/heritage/lilian-gilbreth-biography (accessed December 11, 2019).

19. S. Caramela, "The Management Theory of Frank and Lillian Gilbreth," *business.com*, February 23, 2018, https://www.business.com/articles/management-theory-of-frank-and-lillian-gilbreth/.

20. L. C. Prieto and T. A. Phipps, "Re-Discovering Charles Clinton Spaulding's 'The Administration of Big Business,'" *Journal of Management History*, 2016, pp. 73–90.

21. L. C. Prieto and T. A. Phipps, "Re-Discovering Charles Clinton Spaulding's 'The Administration of Big Business,'" *Journal of Management History*, 2016, p. 82.

22. N. Bloom, R. Sadun, and J. Van Reenen, "Does Management Really Work?" *Harvard Business Review*, November 2012, pp. 76–82.

23. B. Rice, "The Hawthorne Defect: Persistence of a Flawed Theory," *Psychology Today*, February 1982, pp. 70–74.

24. A. Maslow, "A Theory of Human Motivation," *Psychological Review*, July 1943, pp. 370–396.

25. K. Cherry, "How Maslow's Famous Hierarchy of Needs Explains Human Motivation." *Verywell Mind*, December 3, 2019, https://www.verywellmind.com/what-is-maslows-hierarchy-of-needs-4136760.

26. D. McGregor, *The Human Side of Enterprise* (New York: McGraw-Hill, 1960).

27. T. Agovino, "Fine-Tuning the Open Office," *SHRM*, June 7, 2019, https://www.shrm.org/hr-today/news/all-things-work/pages/open-offices.aspx.

28. The history of the office workplace is described in N. Saval, *Cubed: A Secret History of the Workplace* (New York: Doubleday, 2014).

29. M. Konnikova, "The Open Office Trap," *The New Yorker*, January 7, 2014, www.newyorker.com/business/currency/the-open-office-trap.

30. K. Sehgal, "It's Time to Bring Back the Office Cubicle," *Fortune*, January 18, 2017, http://fortune.com/2017/01/18/i-hate-open-offices/.

31. A. Tank, "Why It's Time to Ditch Open Office Plans," *Entrepreneur*, February 7, 2019, https://www.entrepreneur.com/article/327142.

32. S. Shellenbarger, "Why You Can't Concentrate at Work," *The Wall Street Journal*, May 9, 2017, https://www.wsj.com/articles/why-you-cant-concentrate-at-work-1494342840.

33. G. James, "Open-Plan Offices Kill Productivity, According to Science," *Inc.*, May 18, 2017, https://www.inc.com/geoffrey-james/science-just-proved-that-open-plan-offices-destroy-productivity.html.

34. P. Singh, "Why Open Plan Offices Are Bad News for Employees." *Entrepreneur*, January 8, 2019. https://www.entrepreneur.com/article/325959.

35. J. Corsello and D. Minor, "Want to be More Productive? Sit Next to Someone Who Is," *Harvard Business Review*, February 14, 2017, https://hbr.org/2017/02/want-to-be-more-productive-sit-next-to-someone-who-is.

36. K. Rempfer, "Army's New Chicago Team Will Use 'Big Data' to Recruit Gen Z," *Army Times*, August 23, 2019, https://www.armytimes.com/news/your-army/2019/08/23/armys-new-chicago-team-will-use-big-data-to-recruit-gen-z/.

37. A. Ricky, "How Data Analysis in Sports Is Changing the Game," *Forbes*, January 31, 2019, https://www.forbes.com/sites/forbestechcouncil/2019/01/31/how-data-analysis-in-sports-is-changing-the-game/#3622f0773f7b.

38. B. Cohen, J. Diamond, and A. Beaton, "The Decade When Numbers Broke Sports," *The Wall Street Journal*, December 19, 2019, https://www.wsj.com/articles/2010s-decade-when-numbers-broke-sports-11576710216.

39. A. Ricky, "How Data Analysis in Sports Is Changing the Game," *Forbes*, January 31, 2019, https://www.forbes.com/sites/forbestechcouncil/2019/01/31/how-data-analysis-in-sports-is-changing-the-game/#3622f0773f7b.

40. J. Pfeffer and R. I. Sutton, "Profiting from Evidence-Based Management," *Strategy & Leadership*, Vol. 34, No. 2 (2006), pp. 35–42. Also see J. Pfeffer and R. I. Sutton, "Evidence-Based Management," *Harvard Business Review*, January 2006, pp. 63–74.

41. R. Kulkarni, "Big Data Goes Big," *Forbes*, February 7, 2019, https://www.forbes.com/sites/rkulkarni/2019/02/07/big-data-goes-big/#65f5855f20d7.

42. J. Kent, "Kaiser Permanente to Use Real-Time SDOH Data to End Homelessness," *HealthITAnalytics*, March 13, 2019, https://healthitanalytics.com/news/kaiser-permanente-to-use-real-time-sdoh-data-to-end-homelessness; "How Airlines Are (Finally) Stepping Up Their Loyalty Programs with Big Data," *Skift*, September 18, 2019, https://skift.com/2019/09/18/how-airlines-are-improving-their-loyalty-programs-with-big-data/.

43. N. Martin, "How Healthcare Is Using Big Data and AI To Cure Disease," *Forbes*, August 30, 2019, https://www.forbes.com/sites/nicolemartin1/2019/08/30/how-healthcare-is-using-big-data-and-ai-to-cure-disease/#22e9030c45cf.

44. "7 Ways Big Data Could Revolutionize Our Lives by 2020," *Datafloq*, https://datafloq.com/read/7-ways-big-data-revolutionize-lives-2020/321 (accessed December 12, 2019).

45. "5 Applications of Big Data in Government," *Datafloq*, https://datafloq.com/read/5-applications-big-data-in-government/65 (accessed December 12, 2019).

46. B. Marr, "3 Massive Big Data Problems Everyone Should Know About," *Forbes*, June 15, 2017, https://www.forbes.com/sites/bernardmarr/2017/06/15/3-massive-big-data-problems-everyone-should-know-about/#286d2cdf6186.

47. B. Tita and K. Maher, "U.S. Steel, the Company That Built America, Faces Its Age," *The Wall Street Journal*, December 15, 2019, https://www.wsj.com/articles/u-s-steel-the-company-that-built-america-faces-its-age-11576443004?mod=searchresults&page=1&pos=2.

48. A. Barman, "U.S. Steel Imports Down YTD: Are Tariffs Really Helping?" *Yahoo Finance*, December 3, 2019, https://finance.yahoo.com/news/u-steel-imports-down-ytd-125712110.html.

49. "US Steel to Pay $8.5 Million to Settle Air Pollution Lawsuit," *WTAE*, December 13, 2019, https://www.wtae.com/article/us-steel-air-pollution-lawsuit-settlement-clairton-coke-works/30226709.

50. B. Tita and K. Maher. "U.S. Steel, the Company That Built America, Faces Its Age," *The Wall Street Journal*, December 15, 2019, https://www.wsj.com/articles/u-s-steel-the-company-that-built-america-faces-its-age-11576443004?mod=searchresults&page=1&pos=2.

51. A. Sisk, "U.S. Steel: $1B in Upgrades to Plants near Pittsburgh Will Help with Air Pollution, Efficiency," *NPR*, May 2, 2019, https://stateimpact.npr.org/pennsylvania/2019/05/02/u-s-steel-1b-in-upgrades-to-plants-near-pittsburgh-will-help-with-air-pollution-efficiency/.

52. G. Bradt, "Why HSBC CEO John Flint Got Fired: Poor Future Fit with His New Boss," *Forbes*, August 5, 2019, https://www.forbes.com/sites/georgebradt/2019/08/05/why-hsbc-ceo-john-flint-got-fired-poor-future-fit-with-his-new-boss/#7259cdd37e11.

53. "About the Manufacturing Sector," *U.S. Bureau of Labor Statistics*, https://www.bls.gov/iag/tgs/iag31-33.htm#iag31-33emp1.f.p (accessed December 13, 2019).

54. C. Kapitan, "Why Manufacturing Is Not Cool," *Industry Week*, February 28, 2019, https://www.industryweek.com/leadership/article/22027236/why-manufacturings-not-cool; "Marketing Strategies to Help Manufacturers Recruit Skilled Employees," *The Whole Brain Group*, November 19, 2017, https://blog.thewholebraingroup.com/marketing_strategies_help_manufacturers_recruit_skilled_employees.

55. R. Cohn, "Hiring Hard-to-Find Manufacturing Talent in a Competitive Market," *Automation.com*, October 18, 2018, https://www.automation.com/automation-news/article/hiring-hard-to-find-manufacturing-talent-in-a-competitive-market.

56. A. Mitchell, "Michelin Finds Newest Recruits in High School," *Greenville News*, March 9, 2019, https://www.greenvilleonline.com/story/money/2018/03/09/michelin-launches-first-its-kind-high-school-apprentice-program-greenville/410980002/; J. Levitz, "To Recruit Workers, Manufacturers Go to Parents' Nights," *The Wall Street Journal*, December 17, 2017, https://www.wsj.com/articles/to-recruit-workers-manufacturers-go-to-parents-nights-1513425600?mod=searchresults&page=1&pos=9.

57. W. Johnson, "Your Organization Needs a Learning Ecosystem," *Harvard Business Review*, July 22, 2019, https://hbr.org/2019/07/your-organization-needs-a-learning-ecosystem.

58. L. Searing, "The Big Number: Millennials to Overtake Baby Boomers in 2019 as Largest Population Group," *The Washington Post*, January 27, 2019, https://www.washingtonpost.com/national/health-science/the-big-number-millennials-to-overtake-boomers-in-2019-as-largest-us-population-group/2019/01/25/a566e636-1f4f11e9-8e21-59a09ff1e2a1_story.html; D. Jones, "5 Tips for Building a Learning Culture in Your Workplace," *The Balance*, January 17, 2018, https://www.thebalance.com/building-learning-culture-3878190.

59. A. Garvin, "Building a Learning Organization," *Harvard Business Review*, July/August 1993, pp. 78–91; and T. Kelly, "Measuring Informal Learning: Encourage a Learning Culture and Track It!" Training Industry, March 21, 2014, www.trainingindustry.com/professional-education/articles/measuring-informal-learning.aspx.

60. J. Miller, "Why a Culture of Learning Should Be Built from the Top Down," *Inc.*, October 17, 2017, https://www.inc.com/jeff-miller/68-percent-of-employees-want-to-learn-from-their-ceos-which-means-its-time-to-teach.html.

61. P. Sisson, "Why Walmart Is Turning Its New Headquarters into a Walkable Town Square." *Curbed*, November 19, 2019, https://www.curbed.com/2019/11/19/20970158/walmart-home-office-urbanism-corporate-hq-retail.

62. S. M. Heathfield, "4 Tips to Make Training and Development Work," *The Balance*, November 7, 2016, https://www.thebalance.com/employee-training-transfer-tips-1919302.

63. D. Jones, "5 Tips for Building a Learning Culture in Your Workplace," *The Balance*, January 17, 2018, https://www.thebalance.com/building-learning-culture-3878190.

64. J. Pfeffer, and P. Jeffrey, *The Human Equation: Building Profits by Putting People First* (Boston: Harvard Business Press, 1998); J. C. Collins and J. I. Porras, *Built to Last: Successful Habits of Visionary Companies* (New York: Harper Business, 2002).

65. R. A. Posthuma, M. C. Campion, M. Masimova, and M. A. Campion, "A High Performance Work Practices Taxonomy," *Journal of Management*, Vol. 39, No. 5 (2013), pp. 1184–1220.

66. "High-Performance Work Practices in CLABSI Prevention Interventions," *AHRQ*, https://www.ahrq.gov/hai/cusp/clabsi-hpwpreport/clabsi-hpwpap.html (accessed December 24, 2019).

67. R. Kehoe and P. Wright, "The Impact of High-Performance Human Resource Practices on Employees' Attitudes and Behaviors," *Journal of Management*, 2013, pp. 366–391; J. Delaney and M. Huselid, "The Impact of Human Resource Management Practices on Perceptions of Organizational Performance," *Academy of Management Journal*, 1996, pp. 949–969.

68. R. Kehoe and P. Wright, "The Impact of High-Performance Human Resource Practices on Employees' Attitudes and Behaviors," *Journal of Management*, 2013, pp. 366–391; J. Delaney and M. Huselid, "The Impact of Human Resource Management Practices on Perceptions of Organizational Performance," *Academy of Management Journal*, 1996, pp. 949–969; M. J. Mazzei, C. B. Flynn, and J. J. Haynie, "Moving Beyond Initial Success: Promoting Innovation in Small Businesses through High-Performance Work Practices," *Business Horizons*, 2016, pp. 51–60; J. Combs, Y. Liu, A. Hall, and D. Ketchen, "How Much Do High-Performance Work Practices Matter? A Meta-Analysis of Their Effects on Organizational Performance," *Personnel Psychology*, 2006, pp. 501–528.

69. C. Caldwell and L. Floyd, "High Performance Work Systems," *Graziadio Business Review*, https://gbr.pepperdine.edu/2014/12/high-performance-work-systems/ (accessed January 2, 2020); K. Hu, "Whole Foods to Bring Back Employee Stock Option Program after Calls to Unionize," *Yahoo Finance*, September 12, 2018, https://finance.yahoo.com/news/whole-foods-bring-back-employee-stock-option-program-calls-unionize-182009491.html.

70. "The Ritz-Carlton Factsheet and Gold Standards," https://www.ritzcarlton.com/en/about/gold-standards (accessed January 2, 2020).

71. W. Bauck, "2019 Was the Year Sustainability Finally Burst into the Fashion Mainstream," *Fashionista*, December 12, 2019, https://fashionista.com/2019/12/fashion-sustainability-movement-mainstream-2019.

72. D. Stofleth, "A Short History of Sustainable Development," *Rethinking Prosperity*, May 20, 2015, http://rethinkingprosperity.org/a-short-history-of-sustainable-development/; "About Us," Club of Rome, https://www.cluborome.org/about-us/ (accessed December 15, 2019).

73. "What Is Sustainability?" *UCLA Sustainability*, https://www.sustain.ucla.edu/about-us/what-is-sustainability/ (accessed December 24, 2019).

74. M. Porter and C. van der Linde, "Green and Competitive: Ending the Stalemate," *Harvard Business Review*, 1995, https://hbr.org/1995/09/green-and-competitive-ending-the-stalemate.

75. C. B. Bhattacharya, "Do Sustainability Efforts Make Companies Attractive to Everyone?" *The Quint*, December 14, 2019, https://www.thequint.com/lifestyle/books/business-sustainability-market-shareholders-sales.

76. "What Is Sustainable Management?" University of Wisconsin, https://sustain.wisconsin.edu/sustainability/sustainable-management/ (accessed December 15, 2019).

77. "What Is Sustainable Management?" University of Wisconsin, https://sustain.wisconsin.edu/sustainability/sustainable-management/ (accessed December 15, 2019).

78. "Driving Sustainability through Business and in Our Operations," JPMorgan Chase & Co., https://www.jpmorganchase.com/corporate/Corporate-Responsibility/environment.htm (accessed December 15, 2019).

79. "Integrate the Principles for Responsible Management Education," *UN Global Compact*, https://www.unglobalcompact.org/take-action/action/management-education (accessed December 15, 2019).

80. "The Sustainable Development Goals," *Principles for Responsible Management Education*, https://www.unprme.org/resource-docs/SDGGuideforManagementEducationweb.pdf (accessed December 15, 2019).

81. "Integrate the Principles for Responsible Management Education," *UN Global Compact*, https://www.unglobalcompact.org/take-action/action/management-education (accessed December 15, 2019).

82. "Partners and Sponsors," PRME, https://www.unprme.org/about-prme/partners-and-sponsors/ (accessed December 15, 2019).

83. A. L. Kristof-Brown, R. D. Zimmerman, and E. C. Johnson, "Consequences of Individuals' Fit at Work: A Meta-Analysis of Person-Job, Person-Organization, Person-Group, and Person-Supervisor Fit," *Personnel Psychology*, Summer 2005, pp. 281–342.

84. Good.Co Team, "Job Seekers: Stop Creeping on Your Ex Online and Start Doing This Instead," February 19, 2014, https://good.co/blog/job-seekers-digital-research.

85. This list was partially based on M. Yate, "Interview Strategies for Recent Graduates," *HR Magazine*, Spring 2019; H. Huhman, "7 Things to Research Before Any Job Interview," August 29, 2014, https://www.glassdoor.com/blog/7-research-job-interview; Good.Co Team, "20 Things Recruiters Want, But Won't Tell You (HR Insider)," July 28, 2014, https://good.co/blog/things-recruiters-want-from-candidates-interview.

86. N. Parletta, "From Recycled Plastic to 3D Printing: More Creative Sustainable Fashion Solutions," *Forbes*, November 30, 2019, https://www.forbes.com/sites/natalieparletta/2019/11/30/from-recycled-plastic-to-3d-printing-more-creative-solutions-for-sustainable-fashion/#18ad134d1fc4.

87. "Why Sustainable Fashion Matters," *Forbes*, October 7, 2019, https://www.forbes.com/sites/ellevate/2019/10/07/why-sustainable-fashion-matters/#431e8b4f71b8.

88. R. Suhrawardi, "The Big Issues Facing Fashion in 2019," *Forbes*, January 16, 2019, https://www.forbes.com/sites/rebeccasuhrawardi/2019/01/16/the-big-issues-facing-fashion-in-2019/#7aa7cd0923a9.

89. N. Parletta, "From Recycled Plastic To 3D Printing: More Creative Sustainable Fashion Solutions," *Forbes*, November 30, 2019, https://www.forbes.com/sites/natalieparletta/2019/11/30/from-recycled-plastic-to-3d-printing-more-creative-solutions-for-sustainable-fashion/#18ad134d1fc4.

90. C. Voinov, "FAQ: Leather Sustainability," *Suston Magazine*, June 16, 2019, http://sustonmagazine.com/2019/06/16/faq-sustainable-leather/.

91. "India: The Toxic Price of Leather," Pulitzer Center, February 4, 2014, https://pulitzercenter.org/reporting/india-toxic-price-leather-0.

92. C. Voinov, "FAQ: Leather Sustainability," *Suston Magazine*, June 16, 2019, http://sustonmagazine.com/2019/06/16/faq-sustainable-leather/.

93. C. Sitzer, "What Is Vegan Leather, Anyway?!," *Green Matters*, May 20, 2019, https://www.greenmatters.com/p/what-is-vegan-leather.

94. D. Tsekova, "What Is Vegan Leather, and Should You Be Wearing It?" *Bloomberg Businessweek*, August 22, 2019, https://www.bloomberg.com/news/articles/2019-08-23/what-is-vegan-leather-and-should-you-be-wearing-it-quicktake.

95. "About Stella—Stella McCartney Brand History," *Stella McCartney*, https://www.stellamccartney.com/experience/us/about-stella/ (accessed December 18, 2019).

96. B. Deitz, "Should Your Next Handbag Be Vegan Leather?" *Coveteur*, August 31, 2019, https://coveteur.com/2019/08/31/vegan-leather-really-better-environment/.

97. R. Sibley, Rebecca, "The Ethical Dilemma of Vegan Leather," *Redbrick*, December 4, 2019, https://www.redbrick.me/vegan-leather-ethical-dilemma/.

98. O. Petter, "Why 'Vegan Leather' Is Not as Environmentally Friendly as You Think," *The Independent*, November 1, 2019, https://www.independent.co.uk/life-style/fashion/vegan-leather-real-fake-pvc-sustainable-sustainability-fashion-ethics-a9060911.html.

99. R. Sibley, "The Ethical Dilemma of Vegan Leather," *Redbrick*, December 4, 2019, https://www.redbrick.me/vegan-leather-ethical-dilemma/.

100. H. Horton, "Faux Leather Promoted by 'Ethical Designers' like Stella McCartney Is Polluting the Oceans with Plastic, BBC Expert Says," *The Telegraph*, October 11, 2018, https://www.telegraph.co.uk/news/2018/10/11/faux-leather-promoted-ethical-designers-like-stella-mccartney/.

101. O. Petter, "Why 'Vegan Leather' Is Not as Environmentally Friendly as You Think," *The Independent*, November 1, 2019, https://www.independent.co.uk/life-style/fashion/vegan-leather-real-fake-pvc-sustainable-sustainability-fashion-ethics-a9060911.html.

102. "Our Technology," *Modern Meadow*, http://www.modernmeadow.com/our-technology/ (accessed December 18, 2019).

103. S. Spellings, "How Guilty Should You Feel about Wearing Leather?" *The Cut*, March 1, 2019, https://www.thecut.com/2019/03/is-wearing-real-leather-or-faux-leather-sustainable.html.

104. N. Axworthy, "Stella McCartney Unveils Vegan Faux Fur Made with Plants Not Plastic," *VegNews*, October 9, 2019, https://vegnews.com/2019/10/stella-mccartney-unveils-vegan-faux-fur-made-with-plants-not-plastic.

CHAPTER 3

1. "Employee Experience Survey Findings," *HR Acuity*, October 15, 2019, https://www.hracuity.com/benchmark-studies/employee-experience-survey-findings.

2. J. Bouilloud, G. Deslandes, and G. Mercier, "The Leader as Chief Truth Officer: The Ethical Responsibility of 'Managing the Truth' in Organizations," *Journal of Business Ethics*, Vol. 157 (2019), pp. 1–13. Also see R. Csernyik, "Why Is 'Courage' Suddenly Such a Popular Job Requirement?" *Quartz at Work*, August 20, 2019, https://qz.com/work/1686328/does-courage-belong-in-entry-level-jobs/; Indeed Job Postings Search, https://www.indeed.com/jobs?q=courage&l&advn=3144953596781994&vjk=1864d30f06f0da55 (accessed January 30, 2020).

3. R. M. Kidder, *Moral Courage*, (New York: HarperCollins, 2005), p. 74. Also see M. Howard and J. Cogswell, "The Left Side of Courage: Three Exploratory Studies on the Antecedents of Social Courage," *The Journal of Positive Psychology*, January 2018, pp. 1–17; M. Howard, J. Farr, A. Grandey, and M. Gutworth, "The Creation of the Workplace Social Courage Scale (WCS): An Investigation of Internal Consistency, Psychometric Properties, Validity, and Utility," *Journal of Business and Psychology*, 2016, pp. 1–18.

4. P. Bregman, "To Develop Leadership Skills, Practice in a Low-Risk Environment," *Harvard Business Review*, April 5, 2019.

5. R. M. Kidder, *Moral Courage*, (New York: HarperCollins, 2005), p. 74.

6. D. Comer and L. Sekerka, "Keep Calm and Carry On (Ethically): Durable Moral Courage in the Workplace," *Human Resource Management Review*, Vol. 29 (2018), pp. 116–130.

7. W. Tate and L. Bals, "Achieving Shared Triple Bottom Line (TBL) Value Creation: Toward a Social Resource-Based View (SRBV) of the Firm," *Journal of Business Ethics*, Vol. 152 (2018), pp. 803–826.

8. K. Halvorsen, "The Good Bowl Donates More than $30,000 to Charity in Its First Year of Business," *UpNorthLive*, July 2, 2019, https://upnorthlive.com/news/local/the-good-bowl-donates-more-than-30000-to-charity-in-its-first-year-of-business. Also see "Mission," *The Good Bowl*, https://www.goodbowleatery.com/mission/ (accessed February 16, 2020).

9. "Story," *Nurdle in the Rough,* https://www.nurdleintherough.com/about-2 (accessed February 16, 2020).

10. P. Renjen, "Right Here, Right Now: Taking Action on Financial Crime," *Forbes,* February 6, 2020, https://www.forbes.com/sites/deloitte/2020/02/06/right-here-right-now-taking-action-on-financial-crime/#4dd59ae64f36.

11. E. Gillespie, "Patagonia Donates Entire Trump Tax Cut to Environmental Groups, *Fortune,* November 29, 2018, https://fortune.com/2018/11/29/patagonia-to-donate-entire-trump-administration-corporate-tax-cut-to-environmental-groups-ceo-calls-tax-cut-irresponsible/.

12. R. Michalak, reported in D. Gelles, "Gobble Up, but Still Doing Good for the World," *The New York Times,* August 23, 2015, p. BU-3.

13. C. Troitino, "The New Ben & Jerry's CEO Driving Unilever's Responsible Food Future," *Forbes,* August 17, 2018, https://www.forbes.com/sites/christinatroitino/2018/08/17/the-new-ben-jerrys-ceo-driving-unilevers-responsible-food-future/#71d15a55471a.

14. "Generation Z: Latest Characteristics, Research, and Facts," *Business Insider,* https://www.businessinsider.com/generation-z (accessed February 12, 2020).

15. K. Gilchrist, "How Millennials and Gen Z Are Reshaping the Future of the Workforce," *CNBC,* March 5, 2019, https://www.cnbc.com/2019/03/05/how-millennials-and-gen-z-are-reshaping-the-future-of-the-workforce.html.

16. E. Best and N. Mitchell, "Millennials, Gen Z, and the Future of Sustainability," *BSR,* October 24, 2018, https://www.bsr.org/en/our-insights/blog-view/millennials-generation-z-future-of-sustainable-business.

17. "The Deloitte Global Millennial Survey 2019," *Deloitte,* https://www2.deloitte.com/global/en/pages/about-deloitte/articles/millennial-survey.html (accessed February 10, 2020).

18. J. Fromm, "How Modern Consumers Are Redefining the Hospitality Industry," *Forbes,* February 6, 2020, https://www.forbes.com/sites/jeff-fromm/2020/02/06/how-modern-consumers-are-redefining-the-hospitality-industry/#2640705c7745.

19. M. Maloni, M. S. Hiatt, and S. Campbell, "Understanding the Work Values of Gen Z Business Students," *The International Journal of Management Education,* 2019, pp. 1–13. Also see C. Miller and S. Yar, "Young People Are Going to Save Us All from Office Life," *The New York Times,* September 20, 2019, https://www.nytimes.com/2019/09/17/style/generation-z-millennials-work-life-balance.html.

20. P. Charan Shubham and L. Murty, "Secondary Stakeholder Pressures and Organizational Adoption of Sustainable Operations Practices: The Mediating Role of Primary Stakeholders," *Business Strategy and the Environment,* Vol. 27 (2018), pp. 910–923.

21. A. Scott, "Hilton Named the #1 Company to Work For in the U.S.," Hilton, February 14, 2019, https://newsroom.hilton.com/corporate/news/employees-rank-hilton-the-best-place-to-work-in-the-us.

22. "2020 100 Best Companies to Work For: Hilton," *Fortune,* https://fortune.com/best-companies/hilton-worldwide-holdings/ (accessed February 22, 2020).

23. C. Tkaczyk and M. Schuyler, "Why Hilton Is the Best Company to Work For in America," *Great Place to Work,* https://www.greatplacetowork.com/resources/podcast/why-hilton-is-the-best-company-to-work-for-in-america (accessed February 22, 2020).

24. "What Is a Sole Proprietorship?" *Business Dictionary,* http://www.businessdictionary.com/article/42/what-is-a-sole-proprietorship/ (accessed February, 9, 2020).

25. Associated Press, "Barrio Brewing Owners Bestow Company to Their Employees," *U.S. News,* December 17, 2019, https://www.usnews.com/news/best-states/arizona/articles/2019-12-17/barrio-brewing-owners-bestow-company-to-their-employees. Also see R. Boren, "Alton Steel Sold; Converted to Employee Stock Ownership Plan," *St. Louis Post-Dispatch,* August 17, 2019, https://www.stltoday.com/business/local/alton-steel-sold-converted-to-employee-stock-ownership-plan/article_b0f0c0fe-5944-5822-b948-6bf0eb320d39.html.

26. "Governance Documents," *Facebook Investor Relations,* https://investor.fb.com/corporate-governance/default.aspx (accessed February 9, 2020).

27. P Houdek, "Rewards for Falling Off a Horse: Bad Corporate Governance Is Enabling Managers to Receive Pay for Luck," *Organizational Dynamics,* July–September 2017, pp. 189–194.

28. I. Javaid, "CS Gender 3000 Report Shows One-Fifth of Board Positions Globally Now Held by Women," *Credit Suisse,* October 10, 2019, https://www.credit-suisse.com/about-us-news/en/articles/media-releases/cs-gender-3000-report-shows-one-fifth-of-board-positions-globall-201910.html.

29. A. Wahid, "The Effects and the Mechanisms of Board Gender Diversity: Evidence from Financial Manipulation," *Journal of Business Ethics,* Vol. 159 (2019), pp. 705–725.

30. J. Green, "Women Exceed 25% of Board Seats on S&P 500 for the First Time," *Bloomberg,* October 23, 2019, https://www.bloomberg.com/news/articles/2019-10-23/women-exceed-25-of-board-seats-on-s-p-500-for-the-first-time.

31. M. Sauter and G. Suneson, "America's Most Hated Companies," *24/7 WallSt,* January 28, 2020, https://247wallst.com/special-report/2020/01/29/americas-most-hated-companies-7/4/.

32. A. Levy, "Amazon's Doubling Down on Grocery Delivery," *The Motley Fool,* November 1, 2019, https://www.fool.com/investing/2019/11/01/amazons-doubling-down-on-grocery-delivery.aspx.

33. M. Cerullo, "Amazon Plans to Open Cashierless Supermarkets, Report Says," *CBS News,* November 20, 2019, https://www.cbsnews.com/news/amazon-go-grocery-store-ecommerce-giant-reportedly-plans-to-open-bigger-cashierless-supermarkets-by-2020/. Also see M. Boyle, "Robots in Aisle Two: Supermarket Survival Means Matching Amazon," *Bloomberg,* December 3, 2019, https://www.bloomberg.com/features/2019-automated-grocery-stores/.

34. J. Li, J. Xia, and E. Zajac, "On the Duality of Political and Economic Stakeholder Influence on Firm Innovation Performance: Theory and Evidence from Chinese Firms," *Strategic Management Journal,* Vol. 39 (2018), pp. 193–216.

35. "Kayak Paddle Achieves Sought-After Aesthetics Using Carbon Fiber Recycled from Aircraft Production," *RTP Company,* https://www.rtp-company.com/kayak-paddle/ (accessed February 6, 2018).

36. R. Drewniak and R. Karaszewski, "Diffusion of Knowledge in Strategic Alliance: Empirical Evidence," *International Entrepreurship and Management Journal,* Vol. 16, No. 2 (2019), pp. 387–416.

37. D. Blevins and R. Ragozzino, "An Examination of the Effects of Venture Capitalists on the Alliance Formation Activity of Entrepreneurial Firms," *Strategic Management Journal,* Vol. 39 (2018), pp. 2075–2091.

38. A. Frangoul, "AES and Google in 10-Year Tie Up to Push Expansion of Clean Energy," *CNBC,* November 7, 2019, https://www.cnbc.com/2019/11/06/aes-and-google-in-10-year-tie-up-to-push-expansion-of-clean-energy.html.

39. "AES and Google Create Strategic Alliance to Accelerate the Future of Energy," *Business Wire,* November 6, 2019, https://www.businesswire.com/news/home/20191106005447/en/AES-Google-Create-Strategic-Alliance-Accelerate-Future.

40. Bureau of Labor Statistics, "Union Members—2019," January 22, 2020, https://www.bls.gov/news.release/pdf/union2.pdf; D. Desilver, "10 Facts about American Workers," *Pew Research Center,* August 29, 2019, https://www.pewresearch.org/fact-tank/2019/08/29/facts-about-american-workers/.

41. "Worker-Participation EU," https://worker-participation.edu/National-Industrial-Relations/Across-Europe/Trade-Unions2 (accessed February 17, 2020).

42. A. Davila, C. Rodriguez-Lluesma, and M. Elvira, "Engaging Stakeholders in Emerging Economies: The Case of Multilatinas," *Journal of Business Ethics,* Vol. 152 (2018), pp. 949–964.

43. J. MacKinnon, "Cleveland Clinic Is Ohio's Largest Employer; Amazon Rising on the List," *Akron Beacon Journal,* June 18, 2019, https://www.beaconjournal.com/news/20190618/cleveland-clinic-is-ohios-largest-employer-amazon-rising-on-list.

44. "Amazon Announces Plans to Expand in Ohio; Two New Amazon Robotics Fulfillment Centers Will Create More Than 2,500 Full-Time Jobs," *Business Wire,* July 22, 2019, https://www.businesswire.com/

news/home/20190722005134/en/Amazon-Announces-Plans-Expand-Ohio-New-Amazon. Also see Associated Press, "Amazon Building Two More Distribution Centers in Ohio," *WOSU Radio,* July 22, 2019, https://radio.wosu.org/post/amazon-building-two-more-distribution-centers-ohio#stream/0.

45. J. MacKinnon, "Ohio Fulfills Amazon Tax Credits for New Facilities," *Beacon Journal,* July 22, 2019, https://www.beaconjournal.com/news/20190722/ohio-fulfills-amazon-with-tax-credits-for-new-facilities.

46. L. Finaldi, "Amazon, Now Headed to Venice, Known for Pursuing Tax Breaks, *Herald Tribune,* January 27, 2020, https://www.heraldtribune.com/business/20200127/amazon-now-headed-to-venice-known-for-pursuing-tax-breaks.

47. L. Finaldi, "Amazon, Now Headed to Venice, Known for Pursuing Tax Breaks, *Herald Tribune,* January 27, 2020, https://www.heraldtribune.com/business/20200127/amazon-now-headed-to-venice-known-for-pursuing-tax-breaks.

48. J. MacKinnon, "Ohio Fulfills Amazon Tax Credits for New Facilities," *Beacon Journal,* July 22, 2019, https://www.beaconjournal.com/news/20190722/ohio-fulfills-amazon-with-tax-credits-for-new-facilities.

49. "Amazon to Open 500-Job Fulfillment Center Near Chicago," *NBC Chicago,* October 11, 2019, https://www.ecommercebytes.com/2019/10/11/amazon-to-open-another-fulfillment-center-in-illinois/.

50. L. Zumbach, "Tax Incentives Are Good For Amazon. What About the Local Economy?" *Chicago Tribune,* March 8, 2018, https://www.chicagotribune.com/business/ct-biz-amazon-warehouse-jobs-0311-story.html.

51. J. Passy, "This Is What Amazon's 'HQ2' Was Going to Cost New York Taxpayers," *MarketWatch,* November 14, 2018, https://www.marketwatch.com/story/what-amazons-hq2-means-for-taxpayers-in-new-york-and-virginia-2018-11-14.

52. I. Ivanova, "After Amazon's HQ2 Hunt, Some States Target Corporate Tax Breaks," *CBS News,* Feb 18, 2019, https://www.cbsnews.com/news/after-amazons-hq2-hunt-some-states-target-corporate-tax-breaks/.

53. B. Casselman, "Promising Billions to Amazon: Is It a Good Deal for Cities?" *The New York Times,* January 26, 2018, https://www.nytimes.com/2018/01/26/business/economy/amazon-finalists-incentives.html.

54. J. Garsd, "This City Told Amazon and Google: No Incentives for You," *NPR,* February 15, 2019, https://www.npr.org/2019/02/15/695156096/this-city-told-amazon-and-google-no-incentives-for-you.

55. A. Glazer, "Everything You Think You Know about Corporate Tax Incentives Is Wrong," *Fast Company,* February 25, 2019, https://www.fastcompany.com/90310500/everything-you-think-you-know-about-corporate-tax-incentives-is-wrong.

56. "UAS By the Numbers," *Federal Aviation Administration,* https://www.faa.gov/uas/resources/by_the_numbers/ (accessed February 8, 2020).

57. E. Morris, "New FAA Regulations for Drones: What You Need to Know," *Sheffield,* May 20, 2019, https://www.sheffield.com/2019/new-faa-regulations-drones.html. Also see A. Shapiro and T. Rule, "A Look at the FAA's Proposed Drone Regulations," *NPR,* December 27, 2019, https://www.npr.org/2019/12/27/791918147/a-look-at-the-faas-proposed-drone-regulations.

58. C. Rodriguez, "Biggest-Ever Climate Protest in Photos: Greta Thunberg and the World's Youth Demand Action," *Forbes,* September 21, 2019, https://www.forbes.com/sites/ceciliarodriguez/2019/09/21/biggest-ever-climate-protest-in-photos-greta-thunberg-and-the-worlds-youth-demand-action/#701c6328ab4d.

59. "Armed U.S. Gun Rights Activists Rally Against Proposed Virginia Gun Laws," *CNBC,* January 20, 2020, https://www.cnbc.com/2020/01/20/thousands-of-armed-activists-gather-at-virginias-pro-gun-rally.html.

60. P. Cohen, "Hiring Slowed in September as Unemployment Rate Fell to a 50-Year Low," *The New York Times,* October 4, 2019, https://www.nytimes.com/2019/10/04/business/economy/jobs-report.html. Also see G. Iacurci, "Unemployment Is Nearing Great Depression Levels. Here's How the Eras Are Similar—And Different," *CNBC,* May 19,

2020, https://www.cnbc.com/2020/05/19/unemployment-today-vs-the-great-depression-how-do-the-eras-compare.html.

61. M. Fitzgerald, "Here's a List of Recession Signals That Are Flashing Red," *CNBC,* September 2, 2019, https://www.cnbc.com/2019/09/02/heres-a-list-of-recession-signals-that-are-flashing-red.html. Also see R. Arora, "Interest Rate Cuts Are Good for Small Business," *Forbes,* September 25, 2019, https://www.forbes.com/sites/rohitarora/2019/09/25/interest-rate-cuts-are-good-for-small-business/#78be3b21244e.

62. W. Kenton, "Balance of Trade (BOT)" *Investopedia,* May 17, 2019, http://www.businessdictionary.com/article/42/what-is-a-sole-proprietorship/.

63. J. Tankersley, "Trump Hates the Trade Deficit. Most Economists Don't," *The New York Times,* March 5, 2018.

64. N. Hiller, R. Piccolo, and S. Zaccaro, "Economic Assumptions and Economic Context: Implications for the Study of Leadership," *The Leadership Quarterly* (in press).

65. J. Cox, "That 50-Year Low in Unemployment Isn't Helping Worker Paychecks," *CNBC,* October 7, 2019, https://www.cnbc.com/2019/10/07/that-50-year-low-in-unemployment-isnt-helping-worker-paychecks.html.

66. M. Haenlein and A. Kaplan, "A Brief History of Artificial Intelligence: On the Past, Present, and Future of Artificial Intelligence," *California Management Review,* 2019, pp. 5–14.

67. P. Economy, "The (Millennial) Workplace of the Future Is Almost Here—These 3 Things Are about to Change Big Time," *Inc.,* January 15, 2019, https://www.inc.com/peter-economy/the-millennial-workplace-of-future-is-almost-here-these-3-things-are-about-to-change-big-time.html.

68. P. Economy, "The (Millennial) Workplace of the Future Is Almost Here—These 3 Things Are about to Change Big Time," *Inc.,* January 15, 2019, https://www.inc.com/peter-economy/the-millennial-workplace-of-future-is-almost-here-these-3-things-are-about-to-change-big-time.html.

69. R. Jenkins, "4 Ways Technology Is Changing the Way You Work," *Inc.,* May 13, 2019, https://www.inc.com/ryan-jenkins/4-ways-technology-is-changing-way-you-work.html.

70. J. Bughin, E. Hazan, S. Leund, P. Dahlström, A. Wiesinger, and A. Subramaniam, "Skill Shift: Automation and the Future of the Workforce," McKinsey Global Institute, Division Paper, May 2018.

71. Statista Research Department, "Internet of Things (IoT) Connected Devices Installed Base Worldwide from 2015–2025," *Statista,* November 14, 2019, https://www.statista.com/statistics/471264/iot-number-of-connected-devices-worldwide/.

72. P. Austin, "What Will Smart Homes Look Like 10 Years from Now?" *Time,* July 25, 2019, https://time.com/5634791/smart-homes-future/.

73. F. Dahlqvist and M. Patel, "Growing Opportunities in the Internet of Things," *McKinsey,* July 2019, https://www.mckinsey.com/industries/private-equity-and-principal-investors/our-insights/growing-opportunities-in-the-internet-of-things.

74. C. Towers-Clark, "IoT Security Must Evolve to Survive," *Forbes,* June 14, 2019, https://www.forbes.com/sites/charlestowersclark/2019/06/14/iot-security-must-evolve-to-survive/#4dbc8be735c1.

75. S. Sheth, "Diabetes Management: Glucose Monitors That Connect to your Smartphone," *Dlife,* June 5, 2018, https://dlife.com/diabetes-management-glucose-monitors-that-connect-to-your-smart-phone/.

76. Insider Intelligence, "The Security and Privacy Issues That Come with the Internet of Things," *Business Insider,* January 6, 2020, https://www.businessinsider.com/iot-security-privacy.

77. C. Towers-Clark, "IoT Security Must Evolve to Survive," *Forbes,* June 14, 2019, https://www.forbes.com/sites/charlestowersclark/2019/06/14/iot-security-must-evolve-to-survive/#4dbc8be735c1.

78. A. Ng, "More Than 1,000 Android Apps Harvest Data Even After You Deny Permissions," *CNET,* July 8, 2019, https://www.cnet.com/news/more-than-1000-android-apps-harvest-your-data-even-after-you-deny-permissions/.

79. Insider Intelligence, "The Security and Privacy Issues that Come with the Internet of Things," *Business Insider,* January 6, 2020, https://www.businessinsider.com/iot-security-privacy.

80. A. Derrick, "What Is the Ring Doorbell and How Does It Work?" *Lifewire*, December 13, 2019, https://www.lifewire.com/how-ring-doorbell-works-4583925.

81. C. Weinschenk, "Report: Blockchain Could Improve Smart Home IoT Security—And Customer Perception," *Telecompetitor*, October 31, 2018, https://www.telecompetitor.com/report-blockchain-could-improve-smart-home-iot-security-and-customer-perception/.

82. L. Eliot, "The Reasons Why Millennials Aren't as Car Crazed as Baby Boomers, and How Self-Driving Cars Fit In," *Forbes*, August 4, 2019, https://www.forbes.com/sites/lanceeliot/2019/08/04/the-reasons-why-millennials-arent-as-car-crazed-as-baby-boomers-and-how-self-driving-cars-fit-in/#196b3c7663fc

83. D. Kiley, "BMW, Daimler Join Forces in $1.1 Billion Ride-Hailing, Car-Sharing Deal," *Forbes*, February 25, 2019, https://www.forbes.com/sites/davidkiley5/2019/02/25/bmw-daimler-team-up-in-1-1-billion-ride-hailing-car-sharing-deal/#155d4e0e171b.

84. A. Fetters, "Why Ecotourism Is Booming," *U.S. News*, November 16, 2017, https://travel.usnews.com/features/why-ecotourism-is-booming.

85. K. Lopez, "Millennials and Generation Z Travel Trends in 2020," *The Fox Magazine*, November 21, 2019, https://thefoxmagazine.com/travel/millennials-and-generation-z-travel-trends-in-2020/.

86. J. Fromm, "Millennials Shaking Up the Wedding Industry," *Forbes*, August 15, 2018, https://www.forbes.com/sites/jefffromm/2018/08/15/millennials-shaking-up-the-wedding-industry/#5c643bbd20e0.

87. A. Daniller, "Two-Thirds of Americans Support Marijuana Legalization," *Pew Research Center*, November 14, 2019, https://www.pewresearch.org/fact-tank/2019/11/14/americans-support-marijuana-legalization/.

88. J. Ortiz, "Anti-Vaxxers Open Door for Measles, Mumps, Other Old-Time Diseases Back from Near Extinction," *USA Today*, March 28, 2019, https://www.usatoday.com/story/news/health/2019/03/28/anti-vaxxers-open-door-measles-mumps-old-time-diseases/3295390002/.

89. J. Garrison, "Nearly Half U.S. Residents to Be 'Obese' in 2030, 1 in 4 to Have 'Severe Obesity,' Study Says," *USA Today*, December 19, 2019, https://www.usatoday.com/story/news/nation/2019/12/19/nearly-half-u-s-residents-obese-2030-harvard-study-finds/2699318001/.

90. "Disability and Obesity," Centers for Disease Control and Prevention, https://www.cdc.gov/ncbddd/disabilityandhealth/obesity.html (accessed February 13, 2020).

91. A. Geiger and G. Livingston, "8 Facts about Love and Marriage in America," Pew Research Center, February 13, 2019, https://www.pewresearch.org/fact-tank/2019/02/13/8-facts-about-love-and-marriage/. Also see L. Carroll, "Birth Rate in U.S. Falls to Lowest Level in 32 Years, CDC Says," *NBC News*, May 15, 2019, https://www.nbcnews.com/health/womens-health/birth-rate-u-s-falls-lowest-level-32-years-cdc-n1005696; J. Wood, "The United States Divorce Rate Is Dropping, Thanks to Millennials," *World Economic Forum*, October 5, 2018, https://www.weforum.org/agenda/2018/10/divorce-united-states-dropping-because-millennials/; K. Turner, "Secularism Is on the Rise, but Americans Are Still Finding Community and Purpose in Spirituality, *Vox*, June 11, 2019, https://www.vox.com/first-person/2019/6/4/18644764/church-religion-atheism-secularism.

92. A. Geiger and G. Livingston, "8 Facts about Love and Marriage in America," *Pew Research Center*, February 13, 2019, https://www.pewresearch.org/fact-tank/2019/02/13/8-facts-about-love-and-marriage/.

93. W. Shi, S. Pathak, L. Song, and R. Hoskisson, "The Adoption of Chief Diversity Officers among S&P 500 Firms: Institutional, Resource Dependence, and Upper Echelons Accounts," *Human Resource Management*, Vol. 57 (2018), pp. 83–96.

94. D. Criss, "The Definition of a Nationalist," *CNN*, October 23, 2018, https://www.cnn.com/2018/10/23/politics/nationalism-explainer-trnd/index.html.

95. T. Young, "Judge Rules Trump Administration Can't Expand Coal Leasing on Public Lands without Analyzing Environmental and Economic Costs to the Public," *Sierra Club*, April 22, 2019, https://www.sierraclub.org/press-releases/2019/04/judge-rules-trump-administration-can-t-expand-coal-leasing-public-lands.

96. C. Day and T. Parti, "Democrats Propose Trillions in Spending on Climate-Focused Plans to Restructure Economy," *The Wall Street Journal*, September 4, 2019, https://www.wsj.com/articles/democrats-propose-trillions-in-spending-on-climate-focused-plans-to-restructure-economy-11567591200.

97. "The Most Litigious Countries in the World," *Clements Worldwide*, https://www.clements.com/sites/default/files/resources/The-Most-Litigious-Countries-in-the-World.pdf. (accessed October 2, 2018).

98. R. Plummer, "Ride-Sharing War Looms as Ola Enters London Market," *BBC*, February 10, 2020, https://www.bbc.com/news/business-51443419.

99. C. Riley and S. Prokupecz, "U.N. Calls for Investigation after Saudi Crown Prince Implicated in Hack of Jeff Bezos' Phone," *CNN*, January 23, 2020, https://www.cnn.com/2020/01/22/tech/jeff-bezos-mbs-phone-hack/index.html.

100. J. Scheck, "Saudi Prince Courted Amazon's Bezos before Bitter Split; Pair Worked Cordially to Try to Establish an Amazon Presence in Kingdom before Rift over Alleged Phone Hacking," *The Wall Street Journal (Online)*, January 27, 2020.

101. D. Mulkeen, "Bribery and International Business: What Role Does Culture Play?" *Communicaid*, January 3, 2016, https://www.communicaid.com/cross-cultural-training/blog/bribery-international-business-what-role-does-culture-play/. Also see K. Gerasimova, "The Critical Role of Ethics and Culture in Business Globalization," *GothamCulture*, September 29, 2016, https://gothamculture.com/2016/09/29/critical-role-ethics-culture-business-globalization/.

102. L. T. Hosmer, *The Ethics of Management* (Homewood, IL: Irwin, 1987). Also see Y. Paik, J. Lee, and Y. Pak, "Convergence in International Business Ethics? A Comparative Study of Ethical Philosophies, Thinking Style, and Ethical Decision-Making between U.S. and Korean Managers," *Journal of Business Ethics*, Vol. 156 (2019), pp. 839–855.

103. N. DeCosta-Klipa, "MIT Reveals How Much Money They Got from Jeffrey Epstein, and Pledges to Donate It to Charity," *Boston.com*, August 23, 2019, https://www.boston.com/news/education/2019/08/23/mit-epstein-money. Also see J. Bacon, C. McCoy, and J. Ortiz, "Billionaire Jeffrey Epstein Pleads Not Guilty to Sex-Trafficking Claims That 'Shock the Conscience,'" *USA Today*, July 10, 2019, https://www.usatoday.com/story/news/nation/2019/07/08/jeffrey-epstein-court-sex-trafficking-charges/1671254001/.

104. C. Atiyeh, "Everything You Need to Know about the VW Diesel-Emissions Scandal," *Car and Driver*, October 24, 2017, https://blog.caranddriver.com/everything-you-need-to-know-about-the-vw-diesel-emissions-scandal/.

105. B. Zycher, "The Volkswagen Emissions Scandal and the Bureaucratic Pursuit of Power," *Investors Business Daily*, October 18, 2017, https://www.investors.com/politics/commentary/the-volkswagen-emissions-scandal-and-the-bureaucratic-pursuit-of-power/.

106. E. D. Lawrence, "VW Executive Pleads Guilty in Emissions Scandal," *USA Today*, August 4, 2017, https://www.usatoday.com/story/money/cars/2017/08/04/vw-executive-pleads-guilty-emissions-scandal/539754001/.

107. Associated Press, "Volkswagen Executives Charged in Admissions Scandal," *Marketwatch*, September 24, 2019, https://www.marketwatch.com/story/volkswagen-executives-charged-in-emissions-scandal-2019-09-24.

108. C. Riley, "Germany Fines Volkswagen $1.2 Billion over Diesel Scandal," *CNN Money*, June 13, 2018, https://money.cnn.com/2018/06/13/investing/volkswagen-fine-germany/index.html.

109. Associated Press, "Volkswagen Executives Charged in Admissions Scandal," *Marketwatch*, September 24, 2019, https://www.marketwatch.com/story/volkswagen-executives-charged-in-emissions-scandal-2019-09-24.

110. C. Ruawald and K. Mutassek, "German Prosecutors Charge More VW Employees in Diesel Probe," *Bloomberg*, January 14, 2020, https://www.bloomberg.com/news/articles/2020-01-14/german-prosecutors-charge-more-vw-employees-in-diesel-probe.

111. D. Shepardson, "Canadian Prosecutors Propose $196.5 Million Fine against Volkswagen for Diesel Violations," *CNBC,* January 22, 2020, https://www.cnbc.com/2020/01/22/reuters-america-canadian-prosecutors-propose-196-point-5-million-fine-against-volkswagen-for-diesel-violations.html.

112. "Fulfilling the American Dream: Liberal Education and the Future of Work," *Association of American Colleges and Universities*, July 2018, https://www.aacu.org/sites/default/files/files/LEAP/2018EmployerResearchReport.pdf.

113. "The State of Ethics and Compliance in the Workplace," *Ethics and Compliance Initiative,* March, 2018, http://www.boeingsuppliers.com/GBES2018-Final.pdf.

114. "Workplace Misconduct and Reporting: A Global Look," *Ethics and Compliance Initiative,* 2019, https://43wli92bfqd835mbif2ms9qz-wpengine.netdna-ssl.com/wp-content/uploads/Global-Business-Ethics-Survey-2019-Third-Report-1.pdf.

115. "Conflicts of Interest," *Ethics and Compliance Initiative,* 2016, https://www.ethics.org/knowledge-center/conflicts-of-interest-report/download-conflicts-of-interest-report/.

116. T. Dyson, "Study: Drug Company Payments to Doctors May Increase Opioid Prescribing," *UPI,* January 22, 2019, https://www.upi.com/Health_News/2019/01/22/Study-Drug-company-payments-to-doctors-may-increase-opioid-prescribing/4201548163107/.

117. C. Ornstein, T. Weber, and R. Jones, "We Found over 700 Doctors Who Were Paid More Than a Million Dollars by Drug and Medical Device Companies," *ProPublica,* October 17, 2019, https://www.propublica.org/article/we-found-over-700-doctors-who-were-paid-more-than-a-million-dollars-by-drug-and-medical-device-companies.

118. B. Tepper, "Consequences of Abusive Supervision," *Academy of Management Journal,* Vol. 43, No. 2 (2000), pp. 178–190.

119. M. Gonzalez-Morales, M. Kernan, T. Becker, and R. Eisenberger, "Defeating Abusive Supervision: Training Supervisors to Support Subordinates," *Journal of Occupational Health Psychology*, Vol. 23, No. 2 (2018), p. 151.

120. B. J. Tepper, "Consequences of Abusive Supervision," *Academy of Management Journal,* Vol. 43, No. 2 (April 2000), p. 178.

121. R. Vogel, and M. Mitchell, "The Motivational Effects of Diminished Self-Esteem for Employees Who Experience Abusive Supervision," *Journal of Management,* September 2017, pp. 2218–2251. Also see J. Mackey, R. Frieder, J. Brees, and M. Martinko, "Abusive Supervision: A Meta-Analysis and Empirical Review," *Journal of Management,* July 2017, pp. 1940–1965; Y. Zhang, X. Liu, S. Xu, L. Yang, and T. Bednall, "Why Abusive Supervision Impacts Employee OCB and CWB: A Meta-Analytic Review of Competing Mediating Mechanisms," *Journal of Management,* Vol. 45, No. 6 (July 2019), pp. 2474–2497.

122. Y. Zhang and T. C. Bednall, "Antecedents of Abusive Supervision: A Meta-Analytic Review," *Journal of Business Ethics,* December 2016, pp. 455–471.

123. M. Price and T. Williams, "When Doing Wrong Feels So Right: Normalization of Deviance," *Journal of Patient Satisfaction,* Vol. 14, No. 1 (March 2018), pp. 1–2.

124. "Trampoline Parks Exploding in Popularity, But Expert Warns of 'Catastrophic Injuries'," *CBS News,* March 20, 2019, https://www.cbsnews.com/news/trampoline-parks-rising-in-popularity-expert-warns-of-catastrophic-injuries/.

125. Quote taken from J. Meigs, "Blame BP for Deepwater Horizon. But Direct Your Outrage to the Actual Mistake," *Slate,* September 30, 2016, https://slate.com/technology/2016/09/bp-is-to-blame-for-deep-water-horizon-but-its-mistake-was-actually-years-of-small-mistakes.html. Also see J. Blum, "Two Years after Five Killed in Oklahoma Well Explosion, Few Changes in Safety Rules," *Houston Chronicle,* January 22, 2020, https://www.houstonchronicle.com/business/energy/article/Two-years-after-five-killed-Oklahoma-well-14993451.php.

126. R. Venkatesan and L. Benton, "How Companies Can Take a Stand Against Bribery," *Harvard Business Review,* September 17, 2018.

127. "Ethisphere Recognizes 128 World's Most Ethical Companies for 2019," *Ethisphere,* February 26, 2019, https://ethisphere.com/128-worlds-most-ethical-companies-for-2019/.

128. M. Jameel and J. Yerardi, "Workplace Discrimination Is Illegal. But Our Data Shows It's Still a Huge Problem," *Vox,* February 28, 2019, https://www.vox.com/policy-and-politics/2019/2/28/18241973/workplace-discrimination-cpi-investigation-eeoc.

129. M. Freedman-Weiss, A. Chiu, D. Heller, A. Cutler, W. Longo, N. Ahuja, and P. Yoo, "Understanding the Barriers to Reporting Sexual Harassment in Surgical Training," *Annals of Surgery,* April 2, 2019. Also see C. Hart, "The Penalties for Self-Reporting Sexual Harassment," *Gender & Society,* May 1, 2019.

130. H. Bourne, M. Jenkins, and E. Parry, "Mapping Espoused Organizational Values," *Journal of Business Ethics,* Vol. 159 (2019), pp. 133–148.

131. B. Kabanoff, "Equity, Equality, Power, and Conflict," *Academy of Management Review,* April 1991, pp. 416–441.

132. Example given by accounting professor D. Jordan Lowe, in "Making Ethical Decisions: Mood Matters," November 13, 2015, W. P. Carey School of Business, Arizona State University, http://research.wpcarey.asu.edu/accounting/making-ethical-decisions-mood-matters.

133. P. Mudrack and E. Mason, "Utilitarian Traits and the Janus-Headed Model: Origins, Meaning, and Interpretation," *Journal of Business Ethics,* Vol. 156 (2019), pp. 227–240.

134. J. Robbins, "How Long before These Salmon Are Gone? 'Maybe 20 Years'," *The New York Times (Online),* September 16, 2019. Also see Duke University, "California Salmon Could Be Harmed by More Dams," September 27, 2007.

135. S. Krouse, "The New Ways Your Boss Is Spying on You: It's Not Just Your Email," *The Wall Street Journal,* July 20, 2019, p. B1.

136. B. Van Voris, "SAC's Mathew Martoma Seeks Freedom in Appeals Court Bid," *Bloomberg Businessweek,* October 28, 2015, www.bloomberg.com/news/articles/2015-10-28/sac-s-mathew-martoma-seeks-freedom-in-appeals-court-bid.

137. K. Leswing, "Former Apple Lawyer in Charge of Preventing Insider Trading Is Indicted on Insider Trading Charges," *CNBC,* October 24, 2019, https://www.cnbc.com/2019/10/24/apple-lawyer-indicted-for-insider-trading.html.

138. J. Eaton, "How a Drugmaker Bribed Doctors and Helped Fuel the Opioid Epidemic," *AARP,* January 24, 2020, https://www.aarp.org/health/drugs-supplements/info-2019/insys-opioid-bribery-case.html. Also see E. Taguchi, J. Lefferman, E. McNiff, S. Sergi, and L. Effron, "Insys Founder John Kapoor Sentenced for Role in Fraud, Bribery Scheme That Contributed to Opioid Crisis," January 23, 2020, https://abcnews.go.com/Business/authorities-drugmaker-paid-off-doctors-lied-insurance-companies/story?id=61488372.

139. F. Norris, "Goodbye to Reforms of 2002," *The New York Times,* November 6, 2009, pp. B1, B6.

140. "Has Sarbanes-Oxley Failed?" *The New York Times,* July 24, 2012, www.nytimes.com/roomfordebate/2012/07/24/has-sarbanes-oxley-failed?action=click&module=Search&region=searchResults%230&version=&url=http%3A%2F%2Fquery.nytimes.com%2Fsearch%2Fsitesearch%2F%23%2FSarbOx%2F (accessed March 31, 2016).

141. "SEC Charges Comscore Inc. and Former CEO with Accounting and Disclosure Fraud," *U.S. Securities and Exchange Commission*, 2019, https://www.sec.gov/news/press-release/2019-186.

142. F. J. Evans, quoted in C. S. Stewart, "A Question of Ethics: How to Teach Them?" *The New York Times,* March 21, 2004, sec. 3, p. 11.

143. "IBIS Initiatives: Giving Voice to Values," *University of Virginia Darden School of Business*, https://www.darden.virginia.edu/ibis/initiatives/gvv (accessed February 14, 2020).

144. W. Hason, J. Moore, C. Bachleda, A. Canterbury, C. Franco Jr., A. Marion, and C. Schreiber, "Theory of Moral Development of Business Students: Case Studies in Brazil, North America, and Morocco," *Academy of Management Learning & Education,* September 2017, pp. 393–414.

145. M. Mitchell, M. Baer, M. Ambrose, R. Folger, and N. Palmer, "Cheating under Pressure: A Self-Protection Model of Workplace Cheating Behavior," *Journal of Applied Psychology,* January 2018, p. 54.

146. See "8 Astonishing Stats on Academic Cheating," *Open Education Database,* http://oedb.org/ilibrarian/8-astonishing-stats-on-academic-cheating. (accessed January 30, 2018).

147. D. Newton, "Looking the Other Way on Cheating in College," *Forbes,* August 31, 2019, https://www.forbes.com/sites/dereknewton/2019/08/31/looking-the-other-way-on-cheating-in-college/#27a03fb392b6. Also see K. Weiss, "Focus on Ethics Can Curb Cheating, Colleges Find," *Los Angeles Times,* February 15, 2000, https://www.latimes.com/archives/la-xpm-2000-feb-15-mn-64455-story.html.

148. M. Mitchell, M. Baer, M. Ambrose, R. Folger, and N. Palmer, "Cheating under Pressure: A Self-Protection Model of Workplace Cheating Behavior," *Journal of Applied Psychology,* January 2018, pp. 54–73.

149. J. Culver, "'A Punch in the Gut': Georgia State Patrol Troopers Fired after Investigation into Cheating Allegations," *USA Today,* January 29, 2020, https://www.usatoday.com/story/news/nation/2020/01/29/30-georgia-state-patrol-troopers-fired-amid-cheating-scandal/4615213002/.

150. L. Kohlberg, "Moral Stages and Moralization: The Cognitive Developmental Approach," in T. Lickona, ed., *Moral Development and Behavior: Theory, Research, and Social Issues* (New York: Holt, Rinehart and Winston, 1976), pp. 31–53. Also see J. W. Graham, "Leadership, Moral Development and Citizenship Behavior," *Business Ethics Quarterly,* January 1995, pp. 43–54.

151. Adapted in part from W. E. Stead, D. L. Worrell, and J. Garner Stead, "An Integrative Model for Understanding and Managing Ethical Behavior in Business Organizations," *Journal of Business Ethics,* March 1990, pp. 233–242. Also see D. Lange, "A Multidimensional Conceptualization of Organizational Corruption Control," *Academy of Management Review,* July 2008, pp. 710–729; M. J. Pearsall and A. P. J. Ellis, "Thick as Thieves: The Effects of Ethical Orientation and Psychological Safety on Unethical Team Behavior," *Journal of Applied Psychology, Vol.* 96 (2011), pp. 401–411.

152. M. Kuenzi, D. Mayer, and R. Greenbaum, "Creating an Ethical Organizational Environment: The Relationship between Ethical Leadership, Ethical Organizational Climate, and Unethical Behavior," *Personnel Psychology,* Vol. 73 (2020), pp. 43–71.

153. M. Gorsira, L. Steg, A. Denkers, and W. Huisman, "Corruption in Organizations: Ethical Climate and Individual Motives," *Administrative Sciences,* Vol. 8, No. 4 (February 19, 2018), pp. 1–19.

154. B. Dattner, T. Chamorro-Premuzic, R. Buchband, and L. Schettler, "The Legal and Ethical Implications of Using AI in Hiring," *Harvard Business Review,* April 25, 2019. Also see L. May, "Addressing the Biases Plaguing Algorithms," *Harvard Business Review,* May 13, 2019.

155. S. Valentine, S. Hanson, and G. Fleischman, "The Presence of Ethics Codes and Employees' Internal Locus of Control, Social Aversion/Malevolence, and Ethical Judgment of Incivility: A Study of Smaller Organizations," *Journal of Business Ethics,* Vol. 160 (2019), pp. 657–674.

156. D. Meinert, "Creating an Ethical Workplace," *Society for Human Resource Management,* April 1, 2014, https://www.shrm.org/hr-today/news/hr-magazine/pages/0414-ethical-workplace-culture.aspx.

157. J. Cheng, H. Bai, and X. Yang, "Ethical Leadership and Internal Whistleblowing: A Mediated Moderation Model," *Journal of Business Ethics,* Vol. 155 (2019), pp. 115–130.

158. "Whistle-Blower Law Protects Outside Consults, Too," *San Francisco Chronicle,* March 5, 2014, p. A6.

159. "How to File a Safety and Health Complaint," Occupational Safety and Health Administration, https://www.osha.gov/workers/file_complaint.html (accessed February 7, 2018).

160. "Whistleblower-Informant Award," Internal Revenue Service, https://www.irs.gov/compliance/whistleblower-informant-award (accessed February 15, 2020).

161. "2019 Annual Report to Congress: Whistleblower Program," U.S. Securities and Exchange Commission, 2019, https://www.sec.gov/files/sec-2019-annual-report-whistleblower-program.pdf.

162. D. Boyle and D. Gaydon, "SEC Whistleblower Program Expands," *Strategic Finance,* Vol. 101, No. 5 (November, 2019), pp. 38–45.

163. K. Kellehner, "How Whistleblowers Have Taken Down the Titans of American Business," *Fortune,* September 27, 2019, https://fortune.com/2019/09/27/what-is-a-whistleblower-famous-examples-business/?showAdminBar=true.

164. D. Arnold, R. Bernardi, P. Niedermeyer, and J. Schmee, "The Effect of Country and Culture on Perceptions of Appropriate Ethical Actions Prescribed by Codes of Conduct: A Western European Perspective among Accountants," *Journal of Business Ethics,* Vol. 70, No. 4 (2007), pp. 327–340. Also see C. Moore, J. Detert, L. Treviño, V. Baker, and D. Mayer, "Why Employees Do Bad Things: Moral Disengagement and Unethical Organizational Behavior, *Personnel Psychology,* Vol. 65 (2012), pp. 1–48; K. Niven and C. Healy, "Susceptibility to the 'Dark Side' of Goal-Setting: Does Moral Justification Influence the Effect of Goals on Unethical Behavior?" *Journal of Business Ethics,* Vol. 137, No. 1 (2016), pp. 115–127; R. Zeal, R. Jeurissen, and E. Groenland, "Organizational Architecture, Ethical Culture, and Perceived Unethical Behavior Towards Customers: Evidence from Wholesale Banking," *Journal of Business Ethics,* Vol. 158, No. 3 (September 2019), pp. 825–848.

165. S. Berger, "Daymond John–Backed Start-Up Bombas Is Reinventing the Sock—and It's Bringing in $100 Million a Year," *CNBC,* April 16, 2019, https://www.cnbc.com/2019/04/16/daymond-john-backed-sock-start-up-bombas-is-bringing-in-millions.html.

166. A. Garcia, "Bombas Founders Wanted to Help the Homeless—by Giving Them Socks," *CNN,* November 12, 2018, https://www.cnn.com/2018/11/12/success/bombas-socks-fresh-money/index.html.

167. N. Taylor, "What Is Corporate Social Responsibility?" *Business News Daily,* June 19, 2015, www.businessnewsdaily.com/4679-corporate-social-responsibility.html.

168. A. Carroll, "Managing Ethically with Global Stakeholders: A Present and Future Challenge," *Academy of Management Executive,* May 2004, pp. 118. Also see A. Carroll, "Corporate Social Responsibility: The Centerpiece of Competing and Complementary Frameworks," *Organizational Dynamics,* April–June 2015, pp. 87–96.

169. P. Bhardwaj, P. Chatterjee, K. Demir, and O. Turut, "When and How Is Corporate Social Responsibility Profitable?" *Journal of Business Research,* Vol. 84 (2018), pp. 206–219. Also see A. M. Anderson, "Do Ethics Really Matter to Today's Consumers?" *Forbes,* August 20, 2019, https://www.forbes.com/sites/theyec/2019/08/20/do-ethics-really-matter-to-todays-consumers/#6e73c0f12d0e.

170. M. Friedman, *Capitalism and Freedom* (Chicago: University of Chicago Press, 1962). Also see S. Gallagher, "A Strategic Response to Friedman's Critique of Business Ethics," *Journal of Business Strategy,* January 2005, pp. 55–60.

171. P. Samuelson, "Love That Corporation," *Mountain Bell Magazine,* Spring 1971.

172. K. Kim, M. Kim, and C. Qian, "Effects of Corporate Social Responsibility on Corporate Financial Performance: A Competitive-Action Perspective," *Journal of Management,* Vol. 44, No. 3 (March, 2018), pp. 1097–1118. Also see T. Lys, J. Naughton, S. Chopra, D. Minor, A. Chernev, S. Schuyler, and M. Kashner, "Take 5: How Companies Benefit from Corporate Social Responsibility," *Kellogg Insight,* March 1, 2018, https://insight.kellogg.northwestern.edu/article/benefits-of-corporate-social-responsibility; O. Petrenko, F. Aime, J. Ridge, and A. Hill, "Corporate Social Responsibility or CEO Narcissism? CSR Motivations and Organizational Performance," *Strategic Management Journal,* Vol. 37 (2016), pp. 262–279.

173. D. Pontefract, "Salesforce CEO Marc Benioff Says the Business of Business Is Improving the State of the World," *Forbes,* January 7, 2017, https://www.forbes.com/sites/danpontefract/2017/01/07/salesforce-ceo-marc-benioff-says-the-business-of-business-is-improving-the-state-of-the-world/#3b4190ee7eb0.

174. B. Komar and E. Barela, "Announcing the Salesforce.org Social Impact Report 2019," *Salesforce.org,* September 23, 2019, https://www.salesforce.org/announcing-the-salesforce-org-social-impact-report-2019/.

175. S. Kunthara, "Salesforce Foundation Announces $18 Million Donation to Bay Area Causes," *San Francisco Chronicle,* https://www.sfchronicle.com/business/article/Salesforce-foundation-announces-18M-donation-to-13254359.php (accessed February 22, 2020).

176. "Annual Report 2018–2019," *SPARK SF Public Schools*, https://www.sparksfpublicschools.org/annual-report. (accessed February 22, 2020).

177. "Salesforce Announces Largest Renewable Energy Agreement to Date, on Path to Achieving 100 Percent Renewable Energy," *Salesforce.com*, August 30, 2018, https://www.salesforce.com/company/news-press/press-releases/2018/08/180830/. Also see P. Flynn, "Salesforce's Journey to Net-Zero Greenhouse Gas Emissions," *Salesforce.com*, April 13, 2017, https://www.salesforce.com/blog/2017/04/salesforce-net-zero-greenhouse-gas.html.

178. D. Gallagher, "Making It Rain at Salesforce.com," *The Wall Street Journal*, February 26, 2015, p. C8.

179. D. Brownlee, "How The 'Best Companies to Work For' Engage Employees and Retain Top Talent," *Forbes*, September 4, 2019, https://www.forbes.com/sites/danabrownlee/2019/09/04/how-the-best-companies-to-work-for-engage-employees-and-retain-top-talent/#79dc656c1eca.

180. L. Saad, "Americans as Concerned as Ever about Global Warming," *Gallup*, March 25, 2019, https://news.gallup.com/poll/248027/americans-concerned-ever-global-warming.aspx.

181. M. McGrath, "Climate Change: 'Clear and Unequivocal' Emergency, Say Scientists," *BBC*, November 6, 2019, https://www.bbc.com/news/science-environment-50302392.

182. Definitions adapted from U.S. Environmental Protection Agency, "Climate Change: Basic Information," February 23, 2016, https://www3.epa.gov/climatechange/basics/.

183. C. L. Dubois and D. A. Dubois, "Expanding the Vision of Industrial-Organizational Psychology Contributions to Environmental Sustainability," *Industrial and Organizational Psychology*, Vol. 5, No. 4 (December 2012), pp. 480–483.

184. See G. Enderle, "How Can Business Ethics Strengthen the Social Cohesion of a Society?" *Journal of Business Ethics*, Vol. 150 (2018), pp. 619–629. Also see "Natural Capital Accounting: Connecting the Pillars of Sustainability," *System of Environmental Economic Accounting*, https://seea.un.org/events/natural-capital-accounting-connecting-pillars-sustainability (accessed February 8, 2020).

185. H. Hoffower and T. Rogers, "Bill Gates Is Once Again the Richest Person in the World," *Business Insider*, November 19, 2019, https://www.businessinsider.com/billionaire-bill-gates-net-worth-spending-2018-8.

186. C. Clifford, "These 14 Billionaires Just Promised to Give Away More than Half of their Money Like Bill Gates and Warren Buffett," *CNBC*, May 31, 2017, https://www.cnbc.com/2017/05/31/14-billionaires-signed-bill-gates-and-warren-buffetts-giving-pledge.html.

187. "Bill & Melinda Gates Foundation Dedicates Additional Funding to the Novel Coronavirus Response," *The Bill and Melinda Gates Foundation*, February 5, 2020, https://www.gatesfoundation.org/Media-Center/Press-Releases/2020/02/Bill-and-Melinda-Gates-Foundation-Dedicates-Additional-Funding-to-the-Novel-Coronavirus-Response.

188. H. Syse of the Peace Research Institute, Oslo, Norway, quoted in "Special Report on Business Ethics: Enhancing Corporate Governance," press release, *Knowledge@Wharton*, February 25, 2016, http://knowledge.wharton.upenn.edu/special-report/special-report-on-business-ethics-enhancing-corporate-governance/?utm_source=kw_newsletter&utm_medium=email&utm_campaign=2016-02-25. The report is "Special Report on Business Ethics: Enhancing Corporate Governance," February 2016, *Knowledge@Wharton* and AKO Foundation, http://d1c25a6gwz7q5e.cloudfront.net/reports/2016-02-25-Enhancing-Corporate-Governance.pdf.

189. S. Berger, "Top Reason CEOs Were Ousted in 2018 was Because of Scandal," *CNBC*, May 15, 2019, https://www.cnbc.com/2019/05/15/pwc-strategy-report-top-reason-ceos-were-ousted-in-2018-was-scandals.html.

190. L. Baselga-Pascual, A. Trujillo-Ponce, E. Vähämaa, and S. Vähämaa, "Ethical Reputation of Financial Institutions: Do Board Characteristics Matter?" *Journal of Business Ethics*, Vol. 148, No. 3 (2018), pp. 489–510.

191. L. Paine and S. Srinivasan, "A Guide to the Big Ideas and Debates in Corporate Governance," *Harvard Business Review*, October 14, 2019.

192. A. Merendino and R. Melville, "The Board of Directors and Firm Performance: Empirical Evidence from Listed Companies," *Corporate Governance*, Vol. 19, No. 3 (2019), pp. 508–551.

193. W. Oh, Y. Chang, and T. Kim, "Complementary or Substitutive Effects? Corporate Governance Mechanisms and Corporate Social Responsibility," *Journal of Management*, Vol. 44, No. 7 (September 2018), pp. 2716–2739.

194. See L. Paine and S. Srinivasan, "A Guide to the Big Ideas and Debates in Corporate Governance, *Harvard Business Review*, October 14, 2019. Also see N. Hussain, U. Rigoni, and R. Orij, "Corporate Governance and Sustainability Performance: Analysis of Triple Bottom Line Performance," *Journal of Business Ethics*, Vol. 149 (2018), pp. 411–432.

195. C. Flammer, B. Hong, and D. Minor, "Corporate Governance and the Rise of Integrating Corporate Social Responsibility Criteria in Executive Compensation: Effectiveness and Implications for Firm Outcomes," *Strategic Management Journal*, March 26, 2019.

196. C. Flammer, B. Hong, and D. Minor, "Corporate Governance and the Rise of Integrating Corporate Social Responsibility Criteria in Executive Compensation: Effectiveness and Implications for Firm Outcomes," *Strategic Management Journal*, March 26, 2019.

197. C. Roper, "This Woman Invented a Way to Run 30 Lab Tests on Only One Drop of Blood," *Wired*, February 18, 2014, https://www.wired.com/2014/02/elizabeth-holmes-theranos/. Also see S. Waikar, "What Can We Learn from the Downfall of Theranos?" *Insights by Stanford Business*, December 17, 2018, https://www.gsb.stanford.edu/insights/what-can-we-learn-downfall-theranos.

198. C. Weaver, "Agony, Alarm and Anger for People Hurt by Theranos's Botched Blood Tests; They Led to Changes in Medical Treatment and a Scramble for Answers; Some Patients Weren't Told for Months about Unreliable Results," *The Wall Street Journal (Online)*, October 20, 2016. Also see A. Hartmans and P. Leskin, "The Rise and Fall of Elizabeth Holmes, Who Started Theranos When She Was 19 and Is Now Facing Federal Charges of 'Massive Fraud,'" *Business Insider*, February 11, 2020, https://www.businessinsider.com/theranos-founder-ceo-elizabeth-holmes-life-story-bio-2018-4#as-theranos-started-to-rake-in-millions-of-funding-holmes-became-the-subject-of-media-attention-and-acclaim-in-the-tech-world-she-graced-the-covers-of-fortune-and-forbes-gave-a-ted-talk-and-spoke-on-panels-with-bill-clinton-and-alibabas-jack-ma-24.

199. N. Statt, "Walgreens Brought Theranos to Its Stores without Even Testing the Technology," *The Verge*, May 25, 2016, https://www.theverge.com/2016/5/25/11776018/theranos-walgreens-blood-testing-partnership-validation. Also see A. Hartmans and P. Leskin, "The Rise and Fall of Elizabeth Holmes, Who Started Theranos When She Was 19 and Is Now Facing Federal Charges of 'Massive Fraud,'" *Business Insider*, February 11, 2020, https://www.businessinsider.com/theranos-founder-ceo-elizabeth-holmes-life-story-bio-2018-4#as-theranos-started-to-rake-in-millions-of-funding-holmes-became-the-subject-of-media-attention-and-acclaim-in-the-tech-world-she-graced-the-covers-of-fortune-and-forbes-gave-a-ted-talk-and-spoke-on-panels-with-bill-clinton-and-alibabas-jack-ma-24.

200. C. Weaver, "Agony, Alarm and Anger for People Hurt by Theranos's Botched Blood Tests; They Led to Changes in Medical Treatment and a Scramble for Answers; Some Patients Weren't Told for Months about Unreliable Results," *The Wall Street Journal (Online)*, October 20, 2016.

201. A. Garcia, "Theranos Founder Elizabeth Holmes' Trial set for Summer 2020," *CNN*, June 29, 2019, https://www.cnn.com/2019/06/28/tech/theranos-elizabeth-holmes-trial-date/index.html.

202. S. Waikar, "What Can We Learn from the Downfall of Theranos?" *Insights by Stanford Business*, December 17, 2018, https://www.gsb.stanford.edu/insights/what-can-we-learn-downfall-theranos.

203. J. Reingold, "Theranos' Board: Plenty of Political Connections, Little Relevant Expertise," *Fortune,* October 15, 2015, https://fortune.com/2015/10/15/theranos-board-leadership/.

204. S. Waikar, "What Can We Learn from the Downfall of Theranos?" *Insights by Stanford Business,* December 17, 2018, https://www.gsb.stanford.edu/insights/what-can-we-learn-downfall-theranos.

205. M. Say and P. Wasley, "The Theranos Crisis: Where Was the Board?" *Forbes,* April 27, 2016, https://www.forbes.com/sites/groupthink/2016/04/27/the-theranos-crisis-where-was-the-board/#3ff998fdc58e.

206. T. Dunn, V. Thompson, and R. Jarvis, "Ex-Theranos Employees Describe Culture of Secrecy at Elizabeth Holmes' Startup: 'The Dropout' Podcast Ep. 1," *ABC News,* March 12, 2019, https://abcnews.go.com/Business/theranos-employees-describe-culture-secrecy-elizabeth-holmes-startup/story?id=60544673.

207. These suggestions were partly based on K. Quindlen, "19 Easy and Immediate Ways You Can Live a More Ethical Life," *Thought Catalog,* August 18, 2015, https://thoughtcatalog.com/kim-quindlen/2015/08/19-easy-and-immediate-ways-you-can-live-a-more-ethical-life. Also see I. Ivanova, "Trying to Reduce Your Carbon Footprint? Don't Fall for These Myths," *CBS News,* April 22, 2019, https://www.cbsnews.com/news/trying-to-reduce-your-carbon-footprint-dont-fall-for-these-myths/; A. Packham, "How to Reduce Your Carbon Footprint, Buy Less Junk in 2020," *MSN,* December 28, 2019, https://www.msn.com/en-ph/lifestyle/lifestyle-buzz/how-to-reduce-your-carbon-footprint-buy-less-junk-in-2020/ar-BBYrPmU.

208. A. Gabriel, J. Koopman, C. Rosen, J. Arnold, and W. Hochwarter, "Are Coworkers Getting into the Act? An Examination of Emotion Regulation in Coworker Exchanges," *Journal of Applied Psychology,* published online December 2, 2019.

209. B. L. Fredrickson, *Positivity* (New York: Three Rivers Press, 2009), p. 70.

210. B. Fredrickson and T. Joiner, "Perspectives on Psychological Science. Reflections on Positive Emotions and Upward Spirals," Vol. 13, No. 2 (2018), pp. 194–199.

211. "5 'Life Hacks' to Live More Ethically in 2017," *The Ethics Centre,* January 11, 2017, http://www.ethics.org.au/on-ethics/blog/january-2017/5-life-hacks-to-live-more-ethically-in-2017.

212. B. Gunia, "The Sleep Trap: Do Sleep Problems Prompt Entrepreneurial Motives but Undermine Entrepreneurial Means?" *Academy of Management Perspectives,* Vol. 32, No. 2 (2018), pp. 228–242.

213. "5 'Life Hacks' to Live More Ethically in 2017," *The Ethics Centre,* January 11, 2017, http://www.ethics.org.au/on-ethics/blog/january-2017/5-life-hacks-to-live-more-ethically-in-2017.

214. K. Quindlen, "19 Easy and Immediate Ways You Can Live a More Ethical Life," *Thought Catalog,* August 18, 2015, https://thoughtcatalog.com/kim-quindlen/2015/08/19-easy-and-immediate-ways-you-can-live-a-more-ethical-life.

215. The last two suggestions were taken from R. Amster, "9 Tips to Help You Strengthen Your Integrity," *Success,* August 16, 2017, https://www.success.com/article/9-tips-to-help-you-strengthen-your-integrity/.

216. S. Kim, C. Colicchia, and D. Menachof, "Ethical Sourcing: An Analysis of the Literature and Implications for Future Research," *Journal of Business Ethics,* Vol. 152 (2018), pp. 1033–1052.

217. K. Quindlen, "19 Easy and Immediate Ways You Can Live a More Ethical Life," *Thought Catalog,* August 18, 2015, https://thoughtcatalog.com/kim-quindlen/2015/08/19-easy-and-immediate-ways-you-can-live-a-more-ethical-life.

218. H. Chavez, "10 Ways to Become a More Ethical Consumer," *Life Hack,* http://www.lifehack.org/414951/10-ways-to-become-a-more-ethical-consumer (accessed October 3, 2018).

219. T. Winter, P. Williams, J. Ainsley, and R. Schapiro, "Lori Loughlin, Felicity Huffman among 50 Charged in College Admissions Scheme," *NBC News,* March 12, 2019, https://www.nbcnews.com/news/us-news/feds-uncover-massive-college-entrance-exam-cheating-plot-n982136.

220. Associated Press, "Feds: Charity Funneled Millions in College Bribery Scam," *WTTW,* March 15, 2019, https://news.wttw.com/2019/03/15/feds-charity-funneled-millions-college-bribery-scam.

221. L. Camera, "The Price of an Unfair Advantage," *U.S. News,* March 15, 2019, https://www.usnews.com/news/the-report/articles/2019-03-15/a-victim-in-the-college-admissions-scandal-students-with-disabilities.

222. S. Jaschik, "New Details on Test Fraud in Admissions Scandal," *Inside Higher Ed,* April 15, 2019, https://www.insidehighered.com/quicktakes/2019/04/15/new-details-test-fraud-admissions-scandal.

223. T. Winter, P. Williams, J. Ainsley, and R. Schapiro, "Lori Loughlin, Felicity Huffman among 50 Charged in College Admissions Scheme," *NBC News,* March 12, 2019, https://www.nbcnews.com/us-news/feds-uncover-massive-college-entrance-exam-cheating-plot-n982136.

224. E. Levenson, "The Mastermind. The Brains. The Coach. Meet the Cooperating Witnesses in the College Admissions Scam," *CNN,* March 13, 2019, https://www.cnn.com/2019/03/13/us/cooperating-witnesses-college-admissions-scheme/index.html.

225. T. Winter, P. Williams, J. Ainsley, and R. Schapiro, "Lori Loughlin, Felicity Huffman among 50 Charged in College Admissions Scheme," *NBC News,* March 12, 2019, https://www.nbcnews.com/news/us-news/feds-uncover-massive-college-entrance-exam-cheating-plot-n982136.

226. T. Winter, P. Williams, J. Ainsley, and R. Schapiro, "Lori Loughlin, Felicity Huffman among 50 Charged in College Admissions Scheme," *NBC News,* March 12, 2019, https://www.nbcnews.com/news/us-news/feds-uncover-massive-college-entrance-exam-cheating-plot-n982136.

227. K. McLaughlin and M. DeGuerin, "Here's Everyone Who Has Been Sentenced in the College Admissions Scandal So Far," *Insider,* February 7, 2020, https://www.insider.com/college-admissions-scandal-full-list-people-sentenced-2019-9#felicity-huffman-was-sentenced-to-14-days-in-jail-2.

228. R. Frehse, "The Longest Prison Sentence So Far in the College Admissions Scandal Has Just Been Handed Down: 6 Months," *CNN,* November 13, 2019, https://www.cnn.com/2019/11/13/us/toby-macfarlane-sentence-college-admissions-scandal/index.html.

229. E. Kadvany, "Pressure over College Admissions 'Out of Control,'" *Palo Alto Online,* March 14, 2019, https://www.paloaltoonline.com/news/2019/03/14/pressure-over-college-admissions-out-of-control.

230. P. Gray, "Kindergarten Teachers Are Quitting, and Here Is Why," *Psychology Today,* December 20, 2019, https://www.psychologytoday.com/us/blog/freedom-learn/201912/kindergarten-teachers-are-quitting-and-here-is-why.

231. J. England, "The Mess That Is Elite College Admissions, Explained by a Former Dean," *Vox,* May 8, 2019, https://www.vox.com/the-highlight/2019/5/1/18311548/college-admissions-secrets-myths.

232. "What Students Are Saying about the College Admissions Cheating Scandal: Current Events Conversation," *New York Times (Online),* March 21, 2019.

233. A. Kamenetz, "A New Look at the Lasting Consequences of Student Debt," *NPR,* April 4, 2017, www.npr.org/sections/ed/2017/04/04/522456671/a-new-look-at-the-lasting-consequences-of-student-debt.

234. J. Mitchell, "How to Apply for Student-Debt Forgiveness for Victims of School Fraud," *Wall Street Journal* (Online), January 20, 2016, http://blogs.wsj.com/briefly/2016/01/20/student-debt-forgiveness-for-victims-of-school-fraud-at-a-glance/.

235. P. Fain, "Feds' New Methodology for Borrower Defense," *Inside Higher Ed,* December 11, 2019, https://www.insidehighered.com/quicktakes/2019/12/11/feds-new-methodology-borrower-defense.

236. A. Nova, "Around 15,000 Former Students Will Have Their Loans Canceled," *CNBC,* December 14, 2018, https://www.cnbc.com/2018/12/14/education-department-cancels-150-million-in-student-loans.html.

237. S. Cowley, "DeVos Toughens Rules for Student Borrowers Bilked by Colleges," *The New York Times (Online),* August 30, 2019.

LEARNING MODULE 1

1. "The Lazy Person's Guide to Saving the World," *United Nations: Sustainable Development Goals,* https://www.un.org/sustainabledevelopment/takeaction/ (accessed February 24, 2020).

2. A. Mull, "The Murky Ethics of the Ugly-Produce Business," *The Atlantic,* January 25, 2019, https://www.theatlantic.com/health/archive/2019/01/ugly-produce-startups-food-waste/581182/.

3. S. Meier and L. Cassar, "Stop Talking about How CSR Helps Your Bottom Line," *Harvard Business Review,* January 31, 2018, https://hbr.org/2018/01/stop-talking-about-how-csr-helps-your-bottom-line.

4. I. Hengst, P. Jarzabkowski, M. Hoegl, and M. Muethel, "Toward a Process Theory of Making Sustainability Strategies Legitimate in Action," *Academy of Management Journal,* Vol. 63, No. 1 (2020), pp. 246–271.

5. P. Nigam, "Can Occidental Petroleum Achieve Carbon Neutrality?" *Yahoo Finance,* April 2, 2019, https://finance.yahoo.com/news/occidental-petroleum-achieve-carbon-neutrality-190356292.html.

6. S. Gharib, "Occidental Petroleum Wants to Be 'Part of the Solution' on Climate Change," *Yahoo Finance,* June 12, 2017, https://finance.yahoo.com/news/occidental-petroleum-wants-apos-part-161532635.html.

7. "Improving Plastics Management," Organisation for Economic Cooperation and Development, 2018, https://www.oecd.org/environment/waste/policy-highlights-improving-plastics-management.pdf.

8. S. Gibbens, "A Brief History of How Plastic Straws Took over the World," *National Geographic,* July 9, 2018, https://www.nationalgeographic.com/environment/2018/07/news-plastic-drinking-straw-history-ban/.

9. E. Peker, "Companies Go to New Depths for Ocean Plastic in Recycling Push; Multinationals like Coca-Cola, Adidas and HP Reuse Trash Fished from Seas or Collected on Coastlines," *The Wall Street Journal,* November 4, 2019, https://www.wsj.com/articles/companies-go-to-new-depths-for-ocean-plastic-in-recycling-push-11572875512.

10. R. Eccles and S. Klimenko, "The Investor Revolution: Shareholders Are Getting Serious about Sustainability," *Harvard Business Review,* May-June (2019), pp. 107–116. Also see M. Porter and M. Kramer, "Creating Shared Value: How to Reinvent Capitalism—and Unleash a Wave of Innovation and Growth," *Harvard Business Review,* January–February (2011), pp. 1–17.

11. "5 Businesses That Are Creating Value for Society," *Driving Innovation,* https://drivinginnovation.ie.edu/5-businesses-that-are-creating-value-for-society/ (accessed March 7, 2020).

12. HT Correspondent, "Reliance Jio Q4 2019-20 Results: Gross Addition of 24 Million New Subscribers," *Hindustan Times,* May 1, 2020, https://tech.hindustantimes.com/tech/news/reliance-jio-q4-2019-20-results-24-million-new-subscribers-added-story-MKDv1IenSWrl3Qqck9f5dN.html.

13. A. Pressman, "How Reliance Jio Became India's Wireless Wonder," *Fortune,* August 25, 2019, https://fortune.com/2019/08/25/reliance-jio-india-mobile-wireless-service/. Also see J. Waring, "Reliance Jio Widens Lead as Profit Soars," *Mobile World Live,* January 20, 2020, https://www.mobileworldlive.com/asia/asia-news/reliance-jio-widens-lead-as-profit-soars/.

14. M. Porter and M. Kramer, "Creating Shared Value: How to Reinvent Capitalism—and Unleash a Wave of Innovation and Growth," *Harvard Business Review,* January–February 2011, pp. 1–17. Also see M. Porter and M. Kramer, "Strategy & Society: The Link between Competitive Advantage and Corporate Social Responsibility," *Harvard Business Review,* Vol. 84, No. 12 (2006), pp. 78–92.

15. M. Porter and M. Kramer, "Creating Shared Value: How to Reinvent Capitalism—and Unleash a Wave of Innovation and Growth," *Harvard Business Review,* January–February 2011, pp. 1–17.

16. D. Matten and J. Moon, "Reflections on the 2018 Decade Award: The Meaning and Dynamics of Corporate Social Responsibility," *Academy of Management Review,* Vol. 45, No. 1, pp. 7–28.

17. M. Kramer, R. Agarwal, and A. Srinivas, "Business as Usual Will Not Save the Planet," *Harvard Business Review,* June 12, 2019, pp. 2–6.

18. "What Happens When CSR Is Tied to Your Business Goals?" *Blackbaud,* https://foundations.blackbaud.com/blog/what-happens-when-csr-is-tied-to-your-business-goals. Also see "CDW Honored for Strength of Strategy and Inclusiveness," *CDW Newsroom,* December 19, 2019, https://www.cdw.com/content/cdw/en/newsroom/articles/awards/2019/12/19/cdw-honored-for-strength-of-strategy-and-inclusiveness.html.

19. M. Kramer, R. Agarwal, and A. Srinivas, "Business as Usual Will Not Save the Planet," *Harvard Business Review,* June 12, 2019, pp. 2–6.

20. Fortune Editors, "Change the World 2019: Where Business Creates Virtuous Circles," *Fortune,* August 19, 2019, https://fortune.com/2019/08/19/change-the-world-circular-economy/.

21. "Pioneering Business Approach Expands Healthcare in Indian Villages," *Novartis,* December 8, 2017, https://www.novartis.com/stories/access-healthcare/pioneering-business-approach-expands-healthcare-indian-villages.

22. "How to Create a Supply Chain Competitive Advantage," *Blume Global,* https://www.blumeglobal.com/learning/supply-chain-competitive-advantage/ (accessed March 4, 2020).

23. Y. Slenk, "How Williams-Sonoma, Inc. Is Furnishing a Better Planet," *Forbes,* March 13, 2019, https://www.forbes.com/sites/edfenergyexchange/2019/03/13/how-williams-sonoma-inc-is-furnishing-a-better-planet/#46085bbd60ce.

24. "Williams-Sonoma, Inc. Shares Progress Toward a More Sustainable Future with Release of 2018 Corporate Responsibility Scorecard," *Business Wire,* October 7, 2019, https://www.businesswire.com/news/home/20191007005234/en/WILLIAMS-SONOMA-SHARES-PROGRESS-SUSTAINABLE-FUTURE-RELEASE-2018.

25. I. De Wit, "How Can Business Clusters Drive Success," *World Economic Forum,* July 30, 2015, https://www.weforum.org/agenda/2015/07/how-can-business-clusters-drive-success/.

26. M. Porter and M. Kramer, "Creating Shared Value: How to Reinvent Capitalism—and Unleash a Wave of Innovation and Growth," *Harvard Business Review,* January–February 2011, pp. 1–17.

27. T. Noland, "Creating Magic through Shared Value," *Triple Pundit,* June 13, 2013, https://www.triplepundit.com/story/2013/creating-magic-through-shared-value/50961.

28. "Business at Its Best: Driving Sustainable Value Creation," *Accenture,* http://cecp.co/wp-content/uploads/2016/12/Business_at_its_best.pdf (accessed March 3, 2020).

29. M. Kramer, R. Agarwal, and A. Srinivas, "Business as Usual Will Not Save the Planet," *Harvard Business Review,* June 12, 2019, pp. 2–6.

30. M. Porter and M. Kramer, "Creating Shared Value: How to Reinvent Capitalism—and Unleash a Wave of Innovation and Growth," *Harvard Business Review,* January–February 2011, pp. 1–17. Also see C. Redfield, "To Better Showcase Our Quality Produce, We're Refreshing Our Shopping Experience," https://corporate.walmart.com/newsroom/2019/11/20/to-better-showcase-our-quality-produce-were-refreshing-our-shopping-experience (accessed March 3, 2020).

31. M. Pfitzer, V. Bockstette, and M. Stamp, "Innovating for Shared Value," *Harvard Business Review.* Vol. 91, No. 9 (2013), pp. 100–107.

32. M. Arumugam, "Campbell Soup Increases Sodium as New Studies Vindicate Salt," *Forbes,* July 18, 2011, https://www.forbes.com/sites/nadiaarumugam/2011/07/18/campbell-soup-increases-sodium-as-new-studies-vindicate-salt/#1ba95e3e77a5.

33. M. Maltenfort, "Building Resiliency in Campbell Soup's Agricultural Supply Chain," *Net Impact,* July 17, 2019, https://www.netimpact.org/node/80282.

34. C. Luetge and B. von Liel, "Why CSV Makes Sense for Business Schools," *Financial Times,* June 10, 2014, https://www.ft.com/content/f47575be-e280-11e3-a829-00144feabdc0.

35. "The Sustainable Development Goals Report 2019," *United Nations,* https://unstats.un.org/sdgs/report/2019/The-Sustainable-Development-Goals-Report-2019.pdf

36. G. T. Lumpkin and S. Bacq, "Civic Wealth Creation: A New View of Stakeholder Engagement and Societal Impact," *Academy of Management Perspectives,* Vol. 33, No. 4 (2019), pp. 383–404.

37. "The 2019 US Cities Sustainable Development Report," *Sustainable Development Solutions Network,* July 8, 2019, https://www.sustainabledevelopment.report/reports/2019-us-cities-sustainable-development-report/.

38. J. Hackenberg, "The UN's Sustainable Development Goals Aren't Just Doing Good, They're Good Business," *Forbes,* August 29, 2019, https://www.forbes.com/sites/jonquilhackenberg/2019/08/29/the-uns-sustainable-development-goals-arent-just-doing-good-theyre-good-business/#24edf12f53d9.

39. M. Hoek, "CSV and the SDGs—Creating Shared Value Meets the Sustainable Development Goals," *HuffPost,* April 10, 2017, https://www.huffpost.com/entry/csv-and-the-sdgs-creating-shared-value-meets-the_b_58eb9ceae4b0acd784ca5a63.

40. "Contributing to the Global Goals," *Nestlé,* https://www.nestle.com/csv/what-is-csv/contribution-global-goals (accessed March 8, 2020).

41. "BD: Healthcare Worker Safety," *Shared Value Initiative,* December, 2013, https://www.sharedvalue.org/sites/default/files/resource-files/SharedValueinAction_BD_12-2013_0.pdf.

42. "Sustainability at BD," *BD,* https://www.bd.com/en-us/company/sustainability-at-bd (accessed March 6, 2020). Also see M. Hoek, "CSV and the SDGs—Creating Shared Value Meets the Sustainable Development Goals," *HuffPost,* April 10, 2017, https://www.huffpost.com/entry/csv-and-the-sdgs-creating-shared-value-meets-the_b_58eb9ceae4b0acd784ca5a63.

43. M. Kramer, R. Agarwal, and A. Srinivas, "Business as Usual Will Not Save the Planet," *Harvard Business Review,* June 12, 2019, pp. 2–6.

44. M. Kramer, R. Agarwal, and A. Srinivas, "Business as Usual Will Not Save the Planet," *Harvard Business Review,* June 12, 2019, pp. 2–6.

45. "Progress Toward Sustainable Development Is Seriously Off-Track," *UN News,* November 6, 2019, https://news.un.org/en/story/2019/11/1050831.

46. D. Matthews, "The Surprising Strategy behind the Gates Foundation's Success," *Vox,* February 11, 2020, https://www.vox.com/future-perfect/2020/2/11/21133298/bill-gates-melinda-gates-money-foundation.

47. J. da Costa, "The Sustainable Development Goals: What They Are and Why You Should Care," *Forbes,* November 14, 2019, https://www.forbes.com/sites/forbesnonprofitcouncil/2019/11/14/an-improvement-science-approach-to-goal-setting/#3ef605d9542e.

48. "The New Role for Government & NGOs," Harvard Business School Institute for Strategy & Competitiveness, https://www.isc.hbs.edu/creating-shared-value/csv-explained/pages/new-role-for-government-and-ngo.aspx (accessed March 16, 2020).

49. R. Koch, L. Roa, J. Pyda, M. Kerrigan, E. Barthélemy, and J. G. Meara, "The Bill & Melinda Gates Foundation: An Opportunity to Lead Innovation in Global Surgery," *Surgery,* Vol. 165, No. 2 (February 2019).

50. "Frequently Asked Questions," Gates Foundation–India Office, https://www.gatesfoundation.org/Where-We-Work/India-Office/Frequently-Asked-Questions (accessed March 16, 2020).

51. "Partnering with China for Global Development: Private Sector Engagement," Bill & Melinda Gates Foundation, https://www.gatesfoundation.org/Where-We-Work/China-Office/Supporting-Global-Development/Private-Sector-Engagement (accessed March 16, 2020).

52. T. Haselton and J. Novet, "Bill Gates Leaves Microsoft Board," *CNBC,* March 13, 2020, https://www.cnbc.com/2020/03/13/bill-gates-leaves-microsoft-board.html.

53. G. Avery, "Top Leaders Shift Their Thinking on Corporate Social Responsibility," *Strategy & Leadership,* Vol. 45, No. 3 (2017), pp. 45–46.

54. J. Harrison, R. Phillips, and R. Freeman, "On the 2019 Business Roundtable 'Statement on the Purpose of a Corporation,'" *Journal of Management,* Vol. 46, No. 7 (2020), pp. 1223–1237.

55. R. Kaplan, G. Serafem, and E. Tugendhat, "Inclusive Growth: Profitable Strategies for Tackling Poverty and Inequality," *Harvard Business Review,* January-February 2018, pp. 126–133.

56. M. Kramer, R. Agarwal, and A. Srinivas, "Business as Usual Will Not Save the Planet," *Harvard Business Review,* June 12, 2019, pp. 2–6.

57. J. Maltha, "Philips Ranks #1 on Fortune's Change the World Sustainability All Stars List," *Philips News Center,* August 21, 2019, https://www.philips.com/a-w/about/news/archive/standard/news/articles/2019/20190821-philips-ranks-1-on-fortunes-change-the-world-sustainability-all-stars-list.html.

58. R. Kanani, "How Philips Innovates for Sustainability," *Thomson Reuters Foundation News,* August 20, 2014, https://news.trust.org/item/20140820014651-4t7fm/. Also see E. Specchia and K. Gonciarenko, "Philips Re-aligns Its 'Lives Improved' Target with the UN 2030 Sustainable Development Agenda Following the Completion of Its Portfolio Transformation," *Philips News Center,* March 28, 2019, https://www.usa.philips.com/a-w/about/news/archive/standard/news/press/2019/20190328-philips-re-aligns-its-lives-improved-target-with-the-un-2030-sustainable-development-agenda.html.

59. "Mastercard Receives 2017 Global Shared Value Award," Global Action Summit, November 7, 2017, https://www.prnewswire.com/news-releases/mastercard-receives-2017-global-shared-value-award-300551061.html. Also see "The Private Sector Is Becoming a Major Catalyst for Sustainability," Center for Inclusive Growth, August 22, 2018, https://www.mastercardcenter.org/insights/private-sector-becoming-major-catalyst-sustainability; "Mastercard Partners with USADF and CIAT to Open Up New Opportunities for Smallholder Farmers across Africa," *Mastercard Newsroom,* July 10, 2019, https://newsroom.mastercard.com/mea/press-releases/mastercard-partners-with-usadf-and-ciat-to-open-up-new-opportunities-for-smallholder-farmers-across-africa/.

60. A. Ignatius, "Businesses Exist to Deliver Value to Society," *Harvard Business Review,* Vol. 96, No. 2 (March–April 2018), pp. 82–87.

61. A. Ignatius, "Businesses Exist to Deliver Value to Society," *Harvard Business Review,* Vol. 96, No. 2 (March–April 2018), pp. 82–87.

62. Sustainable Development Goals, "'World's Most Powerful Job Creators,' Small Enterprises Vital to Achieving Global Goals—UN Official," *United Nations,* May 11, 2017, https://www.un.org/sustainabledevelopment/blog/2017/05/worlds-most-powerful-job-creators-small-enterprises-vital-to-achieving-global-goals-un-official/.

63. C. Charpentier, R. Landveld, and N. Shahiar, "Role of MSMEs and Entrepreneurship in Achieving the SDGs," *ICSB Gazette,* Issue 3 (September 9, 2019). Also see "Small and Medium Enterprises (SMEs) Finance," World Bank, https://www.worldbank.org/en/topic/smefinance (accessed February 26, 2020).

64. *Fortune* Editors, "Change the World 2019: Where Business Creates Virtuous Circles," *Fortune,* August 19, 2019, https://fortune.com/2019/08/19/change-the-world-circular-economy/.

65. F. Burton, "Novo Holdings Invests $72 Million in Sustainable Products Leader LanzaTech," *LanzaTech,* August 6, 2019, https://www.lanzatech.com/2019/08/06/novo-holdings-invests-72-million-in-sustainable-products-leader-lanzatech/.

66. M. Heimer and E. Fry, "*Fortune*'s 2019 Change the World List: Companies to Watch," *Fortune,* August 19, 2019, https://fortune.com/2019/08/19/change-the-world-2019-companies-to-watch/.

67. H. Menear, "English Tea Shop: Creating Shared Value, the Right Way," *Supply Chain Digital,* June 8, 2019, https://www.supplychaindigital.com/scm/english-tea-shop-creating-shared-value-right-way. Also see "Why Companies Should Make 2018 the Year of Creating Shared Value," *English Tea Shop,* March 14, 2018, https://www.edie.net/blog/Why-companies-should-make-2018-the-year-of-Creating-Shared-Value/6098479.

68. G. T. Lumpkin and S. Bacq, "Civic Wealth Creation: A New View of Stakeholder Engagement and Societal Impact," *Academy of Management Perspectives,* Vol. 33, No. 4 (2019), pp. 383–404.

69. T. Malmqvist, "Are We Actually Making Progress on the SDGs?" *GreenBiz,* May 16, 2019, https://www.greenbiz.com/article/are-we-actually-making-progress-sdgs.

70. S. Sarasvathy and A. Rameshi, "An Effectual Model of Collective Action for Addressing Sustainability Challenges," *Academy of Management Perspectives,* Vol. 33, No. 4 (2019), pp. 405–424.

71. J. Horne, M. Recher, I. Michelfelder, J. Jay, and J. Kratzer, "Exploring Entrepreneurship Related to the Sustainable Development Goals—Mapping New Venture Activities with Semi-Automated Content Analysis," *Journal of Cleaner Production,* Vol. 242 (January 1, 2020), pp. 1–10. Also see S. Sarasvathy and A. Rameshi, "An Effectual Model of Collective Action for Addressing Sustainability Challenges," *Academy of Management Perspectives,* Vol. 33, No. 4 (2019), pp. 405–424.

72. M. Granryd, "More Than Just a Phone: Mobile's Impact on Sustainable Development," *World Economic Forum,* September 20, 2018, https://www.weforum.org/agenda/2018/09/more-than-just-a-phone-mobile-s-impact-on-sustainable-development/.

73. T. Myers, "The U.N.'s Sustainable Development Goals? There's an App for That," *The Washington Examiner,* August 30, 2018, https://www.washingtonexaminer.com/weekly-standard/the-united-stations-sustainable-development-goals-are-being-met-with-smartphone-technology-and-entrepreneurship.

74. Z. Winn, "Platform Helps Farmers Out of Extreme Poverty," *MIT News,* November 14, 2018, news.mit.edu/2018/ricult-thailand-pakistan-farmers-1115.

75. E. Best, "Millennials, Gen Z, and the Future of Sustainability," *BSR,* October 24, 2018, https://www.bsr.org/en/our-insights/blog-view/millennials-generation-z-future-of-sustainable-business.

76. D. Holger, "Financial Advisers Turn to ESG, Warily," *The Wall Street Journal,* March 16, 2020, https://www.wsj.com/articles/financial-advisers-turn-to-esg-warily-11584217002.

77. "Rising Leaders on the Sustainable Development Goals," *Yale Center for Business and the Environment,* https://cbey.yale.edu/programs/rising-leaders-on-the-sustainable-development-goals (accessed February 26, 2020).

78. L. Henderson, A. Wersun, J. Wilson, S. Yeung, and K. Zhang, "Principles for Responsible Management Education in 2068," *Futures,* Vol. 111 (August 2019), pp. 81–89.

79. P. Thomas, "Harvard Gets Requests as It Searches for Business School Dean," *The Wall Street Journal,* March 13, 2020, https://www.wsj.com/articles/harvard-gets-requests-as-it-searches-for-business-school-dean-11584095644?mod=searchresults&page=1&pos=3.

80. G. Weybrecht, "Moving Forward: Sustainable Development Goals and Business Schools," *AACSB,* April 22, 2019, https://www.aacsb.edu/blog/2019/april/moving-forward-sustainable-development-goals-and-business-schools.

81. "Course Syllabus: KPPI-917-5: Corporate Social Innovation, Spring 2019," *Northwestern University Kellogg School of Management,* https://www4.kellogg.northwestern.edu/syllabus/syllabus_files/KPPI-917-5-41_Spring2019.pdf (accessed February 28, 2020).

82. "Course Syllabus: Sustainable Business & The New Economy," *NYU Leonard N. Stern School of Business,* 2017, http://w4.stern.nyu.edu/bspa/docs/syllabi/Spring%202017/hollender_syllabus_spring2017.pdf.

83. B. Thompson, "Students Apply Sustainable Business Concepts to Uplift Challenged Community," *Georgia Tech Scheller College of Business,* August 14, 2019, https://www.scheller.gatech.edu/centers-initiatives/ray-c-anderson-center-for-sustainable-business/news/articles/students-apply-sustainable-business-concepts-to-uplift-challenged-community.html.

84. "Minor in Sustainable Business," *University of Miami 2019-2020 Academic Bulletin,* http://bulletin.miami.edu/undergraduate-academic-programs/business/economics/sustainable-business-minor/. Also see "Minor in Sustainable Business," *University of Oregon,* https://business.uoregon.edu/ug/minors/sustainable-business (accessed March 2, 2020).

85. M. Porter and M. Kramer, "The Lesson Behind *Fortune*'s 'Change the World' List," *Fortune,* August 18, 2016, https://fortune.com/2016/08/18/change-the-world-essay/.

86. M. Barnett, I. Henriquez, and B. Husted, "Beyond Good Intentions: Designing CSR Initiatives for Greater Social Impact," *Journal of Management,* Vol. 46, No. 6 (2020), pp. 937–964.

87. M. Kramer, R. Agarwal, and A. Srinivas, "Business as Usual Will Not Save the Planet," *Harvard Business Review,* June 12, 2019, pp. 2–6.

88. L. Scott and A. McGill, "SDG Challenge 2019," *PWC,* https://www.pwc.com/gx/en/sustainability/SDG/sdg-2019.pdf.

89. R. Kaplan, G. Serafem, and E. Tugendhat, "Inclusive Growth: Profitable Strategies for Tackling Poverty and Inequality," *Harvard Business Review,* January-February 2018, pp. 126–133.

90. L. Scott and A. McGill, "SDG Challenge 2019," *PWC,* https://www.pwc.com/gx/en/sustainability/SDG/sdg-2019.pdf.

91. D. Buss, "P&G CEO Taylor Embraces Sustainability Thinking in C-Suite and Beyond, *Chief Executive,* June 21, 2019, https://chiefexecutive.net/procter-gamble-ceo-taylor-embraces-sustainability/.

92. G. De Clercq, "France's Engie to Exit 20 Countries, Wary of Big M&A," *Reuters,* February 28, 2019, https://www.reuters.com/article/us-engie-results-strategy/frances-engie-to-exit-20-countries-wary-of-big-ma-idUSKCN1QH110. See also E. Wenzel, "20 C-Suite Sustainability Champions for 2020," *Green Biz,* January 6, 2020, https://www.greenbiz.com/article/20-c-suite-sustainability-champions-2020.

93. H. Clancy, "Engie's Renewables Chief on Scaling Corporate Contracts, Hydrogen Hopes and Offshore Wind," *Green Biz,* November 4, 2019, https://www.greenbiz.com/article/engies-renewables-chief-scaling-corporate-contracts-hydrogen-hopes-and-offshore-wind.

94. "Sustainable Development Goal 3," *UN Sustainable Development Goals Knowledge Platform,* https://sustainabledevelopment.un.org/sdg3 (accessed March 12, 2020).

95. "Sustainable Development Goal 5," *UN Sustainable Development Goals Knowledge Platform,* https://sustainabledevelopment.un.org/sdg5 (accessed March 12, 2020). Also see L. Zhou, "A Historic New Congress Will Be Sworn in Today," *Vox,* January 3, 2019, https://www.vox.com/2018/12/6/18119733/congress-diversity-women-election-good-news.

96. "Sustainable Development Goal 8," *UN Sustainable Development Goals Knowledge Platform,* https://sustainabledevelopment.un.org/sdg8 (accessed March 12, 2020).

97. T. Malmqvist, "Are We Actually Making Progress on the SDGs?" *GreenBiz,* May 16, 2019, https://www.greenbiz.com/article/are-we-actually-making-progress-sdgs.

98. N. Aizenman, "Gates Foundation Says World Not on Track to Meet Goal of Ending Poverty by 2030," *NPR,* September 17, 2019, https://www.npr.org/sections/goatsandsoda/2019/09/17/761548939/gates-foundation-says-world-not-on-track-to-meet-goal-of-ending-poverty-by-2030.

99. M. Kramer, R. Agarwal, and A. Srinivas, "Business as Usual Will Not Save the Planet," *Harvard Business Review,* June 12, 2019, pp. 2–6.

100. L. Scott and A. McGill, "SDG Challenge 2019," *PWC,* https://www.pwc.com/gx/en/sustainability/SDG/sdg-2019.pdf.

101. M. Kramer, R. Agarwal, and A. Srinivas, "Business as Usual Will Not Save the Planet," *Harvard Business Review,* June 12, 2019, pp. 2–6.

102. L. Scott and A. McGill, "SDG Challenge 2018—From Promise to Reality: Does Business Really Care about the SDGs?" *PWC,* https://www.pwc.com/gx/en/sustainability/SDG/sdg-reporting-2018.pdf.

103. I. Hengst, P. Jarzabkowski, M. Hoegl, and M. Muethel, "Toward a Process Theory of Making Sustainability Strategies Legitimate in Action," *Academy of Management Journal,* Vol. 63, No. 1 (2020), pp. 246–271.

104. "Connecting Our World: 2017 Corporate Responsibility Report," *TE Connectivity,* https://www.te.com/content/dam/te-com/documents/about-te/corporate-responsibility/global/TEConnectivityCorporateResponsibilityReport2017.pdf. Also see "Change the World," *Fortune,* 2019, https://fortune.com/change-the-world/2019/te-connectivity/.

105. P. Preston, "Overcoming Design Challenges in Creating Shared Value," *Phil Preston,* November 20, 2018, https://philpreston.com.au/design-challenges-shared-value-strategies/.

106. A. Kim, P. Bansal, and H. Haugh, "No Time Like the Present: How a Present Time Perspective Can Foster Sustainable Development," *Academy of Management Journal,* Vol. 62, No. 2 (2019), pp. 607–634.

107. M. Kramer and M. Pfitzer, "The Ecosystem of Shared Value," *Harvard Business Review,* Vol. 94, No. 10 (2016), pp. 80–89.

108. N. Christiansen, "6 Steps to Create Shared Value in Your Company," *GreenBiz*, June 20, 2014, https://www.greenbiz.com/blog/2014/06/20/6-steps-implement-csv-your-company.

109. P. Martorana and C. Smith, "Cultivating the Sage's Creative Vision Insights from Perennial Wisdom on Approaching Organizational Change and Sustainability," *The Journal of Corporate Citizenship*, No. 62 (June 2016), pp. 76–90.

110. Z. Wood. "Unilever Warns It Will Sell Off Brands That Hurt the Planet or Society," *The Guardian*, July 25, 2019, https://www.theguardian.com/business/2019/jul/25/unilever-warns-it-will-sell-off-brands-that-hurt-the-planet-or-society.

111. G. T. Lumpkin and S. Bacq, "Civic Wealth Creation: A New View of Stakeholder Engagement and Societal Impact," *Academy of Management Perspectives*, Vol. 33, No. 4 (2019), pp. 383–404. Also see J. Howard-Grenville, G. Davis, T. Dyllick, C. Miller, S. Thau, and A. Tsui, "Sustainable Development for a Better World: Contributions of Leadership, Management, and Organizations," *Academy of Management Discoveries*, Vol. 5, No. 4 (2019), pp. 355–366.

112. M. Kramer, R. Agarwal, and A. Srinivas, "Business as Usual Will Not Save the Planet," *Harvard Business Review*, June 12, 2019, pp. 2–6.

113. D. Matten and J. Moon, "Reflections on the 2018 Decade Award: The Meaning and Dynamics of Corporate Social Responsibility," *Academy of Management Review*, Vol. 45, No. 1, pp. 7–28.

114. D. Buss, "Revolution Foods Co-Founders Trying to Turn School Meals Upside-Down," *Chief Executive*, December 12, 2019, https://chiefexecutive.net/revolution-foods-co-founders-trying-to-turn-school-meals-upside-down/. Also see J. Pothering, "How Revolution Foods Made a Business of Healthy Food for Healthier Students," *Entrepreneur*, October 14, 2014, https://www.entrepreneur.com/article/238277.

115. M. Porter and M. Kramer, "Creating Shared Value: How to Reinvent Capitalism—and Unleash a Wave of Innovation and Growth," *Harvard Business Review*, January-February (2011), pp. 1–17.

116. M. Hoek, "CSV and the SDGs—Creating Shared Value Meets the Sustainable Development Goals," *HuffPost*, April 10, 2017, https://www.huffpost.com/entry/csv-and-the-sdgs-creating-shared-value-meets-the_b_58eb9ceae4b0acd784ca5a63.

CHAPTER 4

1. C. Stokes, "The Cross-Cultural Competence Challenge," *Global Connection*, June 5, 2019, https://www.global-connection.info/hr-articles/the-cross-cultural-competence-challenge/.

2. K. Amadeo, "US Imports and Exports with Components and Statistics," *The Balance*, July 9, 2020, https://www.thebalance.com/u-s-imports-and-exports-components-and-statistics-3306270.

3. "GDP Ranked by Country 2019," *World Population Review*, http://worldpopulationreview.com/countries/countries-by-gdp/ (accessed November 3, 2019).

4. K. Schwab, "Global Competitiveness Report 2019: How to End a Lost Decade of Productivity Growth," *World Economic Forum*, 2019, https://www.weforum.org/reports/how-to-end-a-decade-of-lost-productivity-growth.

5. W. Martin, "RANKED: The 29 Richest Countries in the World," *Business Insider*, May 22, 2018, https://www.businessinsider.com/the-richest-countries-in-the-world-2018-5.

6. *2019 Index of Economic Freedom*, https://www.heritage.org/index/ranking (accessed November, 2019).

7. Related discussion in J. McGregor and S. Hamm, "Managing the Global Workforce," *BusinessWeek*, January 28, 2008, p. 34. Also see C. Boles, "Last Call? Gates Pushes Globalism in Remarks," *The Wall Street Journal*, March 13, 2008, p. B3.

8. "Number of Smartphone Users Worldwide 2014–2020," *Statista*, https://www.statista.com/statistics/330695/number-of-smartphone-users-worldwide/ (accessed November 3, 2019).

9. "World Internet Users Statistics and 2019 World Population Stats," *Internet World Stats*, https://internetworldstats.com/stats.htm (accessed November 3, 2019).

10. "E-commerce in the United States—Statistics & Facts," *Statista*, https://www.statista.com/topics/2443/us-ecommerce/ (accessed November 3, 2019).

11. A. Lipsman, "US Ecommerce 2019," *eMarketer*, June 27, 2019, https://www.emarketer.com/content/us-ecommerce-2019.

12. M. Corkery and N. Wingfield, "Amazon Asked for Patience. Remarkably, Wall Street Complied," *The New York Times*, https://www.nytimes.com/2018/02/04/technology/amazon-asked-for-patience-remarkably-wall-street-complied.html (accessed December 12, 2019).

13. A. Levy, "The 7 Largest E-Commerce Companies in the World," *The Motley Fool*, August 23, 2019, https://www.fool.com/investing/the-7-largest-e-commerce-companies-in-the-world.aspx.

14. "Company Overview," *Alibaba Group*, http://www.alibabagroup.com/en/about/overview (accessed December 12, 2019). Also see "What Is Alibaba?" *The Wall Street Journal*, http://projects.wsj.com/alibaba/ (accessed December 12, 2019); N. McCarthy, "China Now Boasts More Than 800 Million Internet Users and 98% of Them Are Mobile," *Forbes*, August 23, 2018, https://www.forbes.com/sites/niallmccarthy/2018/08/23/china-now-boasts-more-than-800-million-internet-users-and-98-of-them-are-mobile-infographic/#173d06fd7092.

15. A. Levy, "The 7 Largest E-Commerce Companies in the World," *The Motley Fool*, August 23, 2019, https://www.fool.com/investing/the-7-largest-e-commerce-companies-in-the-world.aspx.

16. J. Summers, "Using WeChat or Alipay in China to Pay: Expat Guide," *Travel China Cheaper*, March 14, 2018, https://www.travelchinacheaper.com/using-wechat-alipay-china-expat-guide.

17. T. Ong, "Alibaba's Car Vending Machine in China Gives Free Test Drives to People with Good Credit Scores," *The Verge*, March 26, 2018, https://www.theverge.com/2018/3/26/17163478/ford-alibaba-cat-car-vending-machine-china.

18. C. Clifford, "Alibaba Billionaire Jack Ma: Almost 'Everybody Can Be Successful If You Really Try Hard,'" *CNBC*, June 4, 2019, https://www.cnbc.com/2019/06/04/alibabas-jack-ma-almost-everyone-can-be-successful.html.

19. R. M. Kantor, quoted in K. Maney, "Economy Embraces Truly Global Workplace," *USA Today*, December 31, 1998, pp. 1B, 2B.

20. C. Stief, "What Are the Positives and Negatives of Globalization?" *ThoughtCo*, June 24, 2019, https://www.thoughtco.com/globalization-positive-and-negative-1434946.

21. J. Kuepper, "How Globalization Impacts International Investors and Economic Growth," *The Balance*, July 29, 2019, https://www.thebalance.com/globalization-and-its-impact-on-economic-growth-1978843; J. Kuepper, "Globalization and Its Impact on Economic Growth," *The Balance*, June 19, 2017, https://www.thebalance.com/globalization-and-its-impact-on-economic-growth-1978843.

22. C. Stief, "What Are the Positives and Negatives of Globalization?" *ThoughtCo*, June 24, 2019, https://www.thoughtco.com/globalization-positive-and-negative-1434946.

23. J. Murray, "The Real Solution to Saving U.S. Automakers Isn't Tariffs, It's Empowering Workers," *The Washington Post*, August 14, 2019, https://www.washingtonpost.com/outlook/2019/08/14/real-solution-saving-american-automakers-isnt-tariffs-its-empowering-workers/.

24. A. Turner, "Japanese Automakers Tout US-Based Jobs at All-Time High as Trump Ramps Up Trade War," *CNBC*, May 21, 2019, https://www.cnbc.com/2019/05/21/japanese-automakers-tout-all-time-high-us-job-creation-pressure-on-trump.html.

25. J. Bucki, "Pros and Cons of Outsourcing," *The Balance*, February 4, 2018, https://www.thebalance.com/top-6-outsourcing-disadvantages-2533780.

26. J. Kuepper, "How Globalization Impacts International Investors and Economic Growth," *The Balance*, July 29, 2019, https://www.thebalance.com/globalization-and-its-impact-on-economic-growth-1978843.

27. "10 Benefits of Living Abroad," *Hamilton Recruitment*, https://www.hamilton-recruitment.com/portfolio-items/10-benefits-of-living-abroad/ (accessed November 3, 2019).

28. "Undeterred by Fears of Terrorism, Most 'Generation Z' College Seniors Want to Work Abroad, Driven by Personal Growth and Chance to

Travel," *PR Newswire*, September 13, 2017, https://www.prnewswire.com/news-releases/undeterred-by-fears-of-terrorism-most-generation-z-college-seniors-want-to-work-abroad-driven-by-personal-growth-and-chance-to-travel-300518532.html.

29. M. Sosby and L. League, "The 5 Things You'll Gain by Working Abroad Early in Your Career," *Fast Company*, January 12, 2016, https://www.fastcompany.com/3055265/the-5-things-youll-gain-by-working-abroad-early-in-your-career.

30. R. C. Carter, senior vice president for human resources at A&E Television Networks, quoted in H. Chura, "A Year Abroad (or 3) as a Career Move," *The New York Times,* February 26, 2006, www.nytimes.com/2006/02/25/business/worldbusiness/25abroad.html?pagewanted=all&_r=0.

31. A. Davies, D. Fidler, and M. Gorbis, "Future Work Skills," *Institute for the Future for the University of Phoenix Research Institute*, 2011, p. 9, http://www.iftf.org/futureworkskills.

32. "History," *McDonald's*, https://corporate.mcdonalds.com/corpmcd/about-us/history.html (accessed November 3, 2019).

33. A. B. Dhiraj, "These Are America's Top 10 Largest Companies by Revenue, 2019," *CEOWORLD Magazine*, July 26, 2019, https://ceoworld.biz/2019/07/26/these-are-americas-top-10-largest-companies-by-revenue-2019/.

34. "Global 500," *Fortune*, https://fortune.com/global500/2019/ (accessed November 3, 2019).

35. N. Rapp and Brian O'Keefe, "Here Are the 26 Big U.S. Companies with the Most Cash Stashed Overseas," *Fortune*, https://fortune.com/2018/02/22/us-companies-overseas-cash-tax-cut/ (accessed December 12, 2019).

36. M. Hanbury, "11 American Companies That Are No Longer American," *Business Insider*, January 13, 2018, http://www.businessinsider.com/american-companies-that-are-no-longer-american-2017-6/#ben-and-jerrys-2.

37. T. Andreas, "The Scope of Polycentric Governance Analysis and Resulting Challenges," *Journal of Self-Governance and Management Economics,* 2017, pp. 52–82. Also see D. G. Schmidt, "Geocentric Ethics: Using Bicultural Skills to Develop Global Organizational Culture," *Journal of International Business Ethics,* 2016, pp. 16–28.

38. C. A. Young, B. Haffejee, and D. L. Corsun, "The Relationship between Ethnocentrism and Cultural Intelligence," *International Journal of Intercultural Relations*, Vol. 58 (2017), pp. 31–41, https://doi.org/10.1016/j.ijintrel.2017.04.001.

39. S. Correa and A-M. Parente-Laverde, "Consumer Ethnocentrism, Country Image and Local Brand Preference: The Case of the Colombian Textile, Apparel and Leather Industry," *Global Business Review,* October 2017, pp. 1111–1123.

40. S. Costello, "Where Is the iPhone Made? (Hint: Not Just China)," *Lifewire*, April 8, 2019, https://www.lifewire.com/where-is-the-iphone-made-1999503.

41. L. Brennan. "How Netflix Expanded to 190 Countries in 7 Years," *Harvard Business Review*, October 12, 2018, https://hbr.org/2018/10/how-netflix-expanded-to-190-countries-in-7-years.

42. S. Masige, "Amazon Is Opening a Fulfilment Centre in Western Australia—the Company's 3rd Following Centres in Sydney and Melbourne," *Business Insider Australia*, October 30, 2019, https://www.businessinsider.com.au/amazon-western-australia-fulfilment-centre-2019-10. Also see L. He and S. Wang, "Costco's First China Store Was So Popular It Shut Down Traffic. But Can It Keep the Buzz Going?" *CNN*, August 28, 2019, https://www.cnn.com/2019/08/27/business/costco-shanghai-china-store/index.html.

43. "Mass Production of iPhones to Start in India, a Shift from China," *Live Mint*, https://www.livemint.com/industry/manufacturing/mass-production-of-iphones-to-start-in-india-1555317238257.html (accessed November 27, 2019).

44. L. Wei, "Goldman, China's Sovereign-Wealth Fund Begins Investing in U.S. Manufacturing," *The Wall Street Journal*, September 20, 2019, https://www.wsj.com/articles/goldman-chinas-sovereign-wealth-fund-begin-investing-in-u-s-manufacturing-11568978734.

45. L. Wei, "Goldman, China's Sovereign-Wealth Fund Begins Investing in U.S. Manufacturing," *The Wall Street Journal*, September 20, 2019, https://www.wsj.com/articles/goldman-chinas-sovereign-wealth-fund-begin-investing-in-u-s-manufacturing-11568978734.

46. "Companies Motivated to Reshore Says New Study," *Material Handling and Logistics (MHL News)*, https://www.mhlnews.com/global-supply-chain/companies-motivated-reshore-says-new-study#closeolyticsmodal (accessed November 27, 2019).

47. E. Comen, "Which Manufacturers Are Bringing the Most Jobs Back to America?" *USA Today*, June 28, 2018, https://www.usatoday.com/story/money/business/2018/06/28/manufacturers-bringing-most-jobs-back-to-america/36438051/.

48. D. Paletta, T. Telford, and M. B. Sheridan, "U.S. and Mexico Plan Summit in Washington on Wednesday in Bid to Head off Trade Dispute," *The Washington Post*, May 31, 2019, https://www.washingtonpost.com/business/2019/05/31/lawmakers-express-alarm-trump-forges-ahead-with-mexico-tariffs/.

49. K. Amadeo, "How Outsourcing Jobs Affects the U.S. Economy," *The Balance*, July 23, 2019, https://www.thebalance.com/how-outsourcing-jobs-affects-the-u-s-economy-3306279. Also see "Employment by Major Industry Sector," *U.S. Bureau of Labor Statistics*, September 4, 2019, https://www.bls.gov/emp/tables/employment-by-major-industry-sector.htm.

50. K. Bahler, "Americans See Job Outsourcing as Biggest Threat to U.S. Workers," *Money*, October 6, 2016, http://time.com/money/4521151/job-outsourcing-report/.

51. H. Johnson, "10 Hot Jobs That Simply Cannot Be Shipped Overseas." *The Simple Dollar*, September 27, 2019, https://www.thesimpledollar.com/10-hot-jobs-that-cannot-be-outsourced/.

52. K. Amadeo, "How Outsourcing Jobs Affects the U.S. Economy," *The Balance*, March 30, 2017, https://www.thebalance.com/how-outsourcing-jobs-affects-the-u-s-economy-3306279.

53. Bureau of Labor Statistics, "The Employment Situation—November 2019," https://www.bls.gov/news.release/pdf/empsit.pdf (accessed December 12, 2019). Also see A. Hess, "College Grads Expect to Earn $60,000 in Their First Job—Here's How Much They Actually Make," *CNBC*, February 20, 2019, https://www.cnbc.com/2019/02/15/college-grads-expect-to-earn-60000-in-their-first-job-few----do.html.

54. D. Workman, "United States Top 10 Exports," *World's Top Exports*, November 17, 2019, http://www.worldstopexports.com/united-states-top-10-exports/.

55. R. Bailey, "2019 Top 100 Franchises Report: Introduction and Overview," *Franchise Direct*, February 19, 2019, https://www.franchisedirect.com/information/2019-top-100-franchises-report-introduction-and-overview.

56. "American Airlines Receives Final Approval of Its Joint Business with Qantas and Announces New Routes," *Skift*, October 30, 2019, https://skift.com/2019/10/30/american-airlines-receives-final-approval-of-its-joint-business-with-qantas-and-announces-new-routes/.

57. "Mahindra and Ford Announce a Joint Venture to Drive Profitable Growth in India and Emerging Markets," *Ford Media Center*, October 1, 2019, https://media.ford.com/content/fordmedia/fna/us/en/news/2019/10/01/mahindra-ford-joint-venture-india.html.

58. "Mastercard Buys Nets For $3.19B," *PYMNTS.com*, August 6, 2019, https://www.pymnts.com/news/partnerships-acquisitions/2019/mastercard-buys-nets-payments-platform/.

59. "The US-China Trade War: A Timeline." *China Briefing News*, November 5, 2019, https://www.china-briefing.com/news/the-us-china-trade-war-a-timeline/.

60. C. Capozzi, "What Is the Difference between Tariffs & Import Quotas," *Bizfluent,* September 25, 2017, https://bizfluent.com/info-8458339-difference-between-tariffs-import-quotas.html.

61. "China Sets New Set of Scrap Aluminium Import Quotas to 9,844 Metric Tons through Year's End," *Aluminium Insider*, December 5, 2019, https://aluminiuminsider.com/china-sets-new-set-of-scrap-aluminium-import-quotas-to-9844-metric-tons-through-years-end/.

62. "U.S. Department of Commerce Initiates Antidumping Duty and Countervailing Duty Investigations of Imports of Glass Containers from

China," *U.S. Department of Commerce*, https://www.commerce.gov/news/press-releases/2019/10/us-department-commerce-initiates-antidumping-duty-and-countervailing (accessed November 27, 2019).

63. S. Jones, "U.S. Sanctions against Iran—History and Updates," *ThoughtCo*, January 29, 2019, https://www.thoughtco.com/a-history-of-u-s-sanctions-against-iran-3310088.

64. T. Zhao, "Why an Oil Embargo Won't Stop North Korea," *CNN*, December 1, 2017, https://www.cnn.com/2017/12/01/opinions/china-north-korea-oil-embargo/index.html.

65. E. Albert, "Understanding the China–North Korea Relationship." *Council on Foreign Relations*, June 25, 2019, https://www.cfr.org/backgrounder/china-north-korea-relationship.

66. These definitions are found in "What Are Embargoes and Sanctions?" *New York District Export Council*, www.newyorkdec.org/what-are-embargoes-and-sanctions.html (accessed March 13, 2016).

67. S. Azodi, "How US Sanctions Hinder Iranians' Access to Medicine," *Atlantic Council*, May 31, 2019, https://www.atlanticcouncil.org/blogs/iransource/how-us-sanctions-hinder-iranians-access-to-medicine/.

68. J. Bhagwati, *Protectionism* (Cambridge, MA: MIT Press, 1988).

69. S. Ben-Achour, "The Real Reason We Talk about NAFTA So Much," *Business Insider*, March 23, 2017, http://www.businessinsider.com/did-nafta-cost-or-create-jobs-2017-3.

70. "From NAFTA to USMCA," *Livingston International*, https://www.livingstonintl.com/usmca/ (accessed June 2, 2020).

71. K. Amadeo, "Largest Economies in the World," *The Balance*, July 21, 2020, https://www.thebalance.com/world-s-largest-economy-3306044.

72. N. Barkin and Y. Bayoumy, "On Eve of Trump Trip, EU Leaders Warn against Nationalism," *Reuters*, January 24, 2018, https://www.reuters.com/article/us-davos-meeting-europe/on-eve-of-trump-trip-eu-leaders-warn-against-nationalism-idUSKBN1FD28T?il=0.

73. V. Gunnella and L. Quaglietti, "The Economic Implications of Rising Protectionism: A Euro Area and Global Perspective," *European Central Bank*, March 2019, https://www.ecb.europa.eu/pub/economicbulletin/articles/2019/html/ecb.ebart201903_01~e589a502e5.en.html#toc2.

74. K. Tausche, "Can the US Rejoin TPP? Yes—with Permission," *CNBC*, January 26, 2018, https://www.cnbc.com/2018/01/26/can-the-us-rejoin-tpp-yes--with-permission.html

75. "Potential Macroeconomic Implications of the Trans-Pacific Partnership Agreement," *World Bank*, *Global Economic Prospects*, January 2016, www.worldbank.org/content/dam/Worldbank/GEP/GEP2016a/Global-Economic-Prospects-January-2016-Implications-Trans-Pacific-Partnership-Agreement.pdf.

76. J. Papier, "The Incredible Shrinking Dollar," *PWJohnson Wealth Management,* http://pwjohnson.com/wp-content/uploads/falling_dollar.pdf (accessed November 20, 2019).

77. "Compare Cost of Living between Cities," *Expatistan*, https://www.expatistan.com/cost-of-living (accessed November 10, 2019).

78. "Cost of Living in Chicago, Illinois, United States," *Expatistan*, https://www.expatistan.com/cost-of-living/chicago (accessed November 10, 2019).

79. "Cost of Living in London, United Kingdom," *Expatistan*, https://www.expatistan.com/cost-of-living/london?currency=USD (accessed November 10, 2019).

80. W. Bello, "The BRICS: Challengers to the Global Status Quo," *Foreign Policy in Focus*, August 29, 2014, http://fpif.org/brics-challengers-global-status-quo.

81. "Globalization Report 2018: What about the BRICS Countries?" *GED Blog*, June 13, 2018, https://ged-project.de/ged-blog/improving-public-understanding-of-economic-globalisation/globalization-report-2018-what-about-the-brics-countries/.

82. "Who Make Up China's Middle Class? We Asked 5 Simple Questions," *China Briefing News*, February 13, 2019, https://www.china-briefing.com/news/chinas-middle-class-5-questions-answered/.

83. "India Population (LIVE)," *Worldometers*, https://www.worldometers.info/world-population/india-population/ (accessed November 10,

2019). Also see N. Kwatra, "The Anatomy of India's Middle Class," *Livemint*, April 24, 2019, https://www.livemint.com/news/india/the-anatomy-of-india-s-middle-class-1556088919798.html; I. Bremmer, "The Mixed Fortunes of the BRICS Countries, in 5 Facts," *Time*, September 1, 2017, http://time.com/4923837/brics-summit-xiamen-mixed-fortunes/.

84. A. Kazmin, "India's Middle Class Loses Trust in the Economy," *OZY*, September 13, 2019, https://www.ozy.com/fast-forward/indias-middle-class-loses-trust-in-the-economy/96600/.

85. K. Amadeo, "How to Ruin an Emerging Market Success Story," *The Balance*, July 4, 2019, https://www.thebalance.com/brazil-s-economy-3306343.

86. "Brazil: Country at a Glance," *The World Bank,* www.worldbank.org/en/country/brazil (accessed March 13, 2016).

87. K. Allen, "Brazil's Economy Slumps to 25-Year Low," *The Guardian,* March 3, 2016, www.theguardian.com/business/2016/mar/03/brazil-economy-low-oil-prices-inflation (accessed March 13, 2016).

88. K. Amadeo, "How to Ruin an Emerging Market Success Story," *The Balance*, July 4, 2019, https://www.thebalance.com/brazil-s-economy-3306343.

89. O. Guo, "Aiming at China's Armpits: When Foreign Brands Misfire," *The New York Times*, February 2, 2018, https://www.nytimes.com/2018/02/02/business/china-consumers-deodorant.html.

90. "How Cultures Collide," *Psychology Today,* July 1976, p. 69.

91. N. Kathirvel and I.M.C. Febiula, "Understanding the Aspects of Cultural Shock in International Business Arena," *International Journal of Information, Business and Management,* May 2016, pp. 105–115. Also see F. Fitzpatrick, "Taking the 'Culture' Out of 'Culture Shock'—A Critical Review of Literature on Cross-Cultural Adjustment in International Relocations," *Critical Perspectives on International Business; Bradford,* 2017, pp. 278–296.

92. A summary of cross-cultural research is provided by M. J. Gelfand, Z. Aycan, M. Erez, and K. Leung, "Cross-Cultural Industrial Organizational Psychology and Organizational Behavior: A Hundred-Year Journey," *Journal of Applied Psychology,* March 2017, pp. 514–529.

93. For complete details, see G. Hofstede, *Culture's Consequences: International Differences in Work-Related Values,* abridged ed. (Newbury Park, CA: Sage, 1984).

94. M. L. Jones, "Hofstede—Culturally Questionable?" *Oxford Business & Economics Conference,* June 24, 2007, https://ro.uow.edu.au/cgi/viewcontent.cgi?article=1389&context=commpapers.

95. M. Javidan and R. J. House, "Cultural Acumen for the Global Manager: Lessons from Project GLOBE," *Organizational Dynamics,* Spring 2001, pp. 289–305. Also see R. J. House, P. J. Hanges, M. Javidan, P. W. Dorfman, and V. Gupta, eds., *Culture, Leadership, and Organizations: The GLOBE Study of 62 Societies* (Thousand Oaks, CA: Sage, 2004); M. Javidan, P. W. Dorfman, M. S. de Luque, and R. J. House, "In the Eye of the Beholder: Cross Cultural Lessons in Leadership from Project GLOBE," *Academy of Management Perspectives,* February 2006, pp. 67–90.

96. J. Marcus and H. Le, "Interactive Effects of Levels of Individualism–Collectivism on Cooperation: A Meta-Analysis," *Journal of Organizational Behavior,* August 2013, pp. 813–834.

97. S. Jang, W. Shen, T.D. Allen, and H. Zhang, "Societal Individualism-Collectivism and Uncertainty Avoidance as Cultural Moderators of Relationships between Job Resources and Strain," *Journal of Organizational Behavior* Vo. 39, No. 4 (2017), pp. 507–524, https://doi.org/10.1002/job.2253.

98. A. Smale et al., "Proactive Career Behaviors and Subjective Career Success: The Moderating Role of National Culture." *Journal of Organizational Behavior* Vol. 40, No. 1 (2018), pp. 105–122, https://doi.org/10.1002/job.2316.

99. B. S. Reiche, P. Cardona, Y.-T. Lee, et al., "Why Do Managers Engage in Trustworthy Behavior? A Multilevel Cross-Cultural Study in 18 Countries," *Personnel Psychology,* Vol. 67, No. 1 (2014), pp. 61–98.

100. M. Pauli, "How Many Languages Are There in the World?" *Babbel Magazine*, November 3, 2019, https://www.babbel.com/en/magazine/how-many-languages-are-there-in-the-world/. Also see M. Zagada, "The Most Useful Languages to Learn in 2019," *goFLUENT Blog*, November 19, 2018, https://www.gofluent.com/blog/most-useful-languages-2019/.

101.   J. Duffy, "The Best Free Language-Learning Apps for 2019," *PCMAG*, June 27, 2018, https://www.pcmag.com/roundup/358228/the-best-free-language-learning-apps.

102.   A. Sorokowska, P. Sorokowski, P. Hilpert, K. Cantarero, T. Frackowiak, K. Almadi et al., "Preferred Interpersonal Distances: A Global Comparison," *Journal of Cross-Cultural Psychology,* 2017, pp. 577–592.

103.   "Corona Virus Social Distancing around the World," *Los Angeles Times*, April 6, 2020, https://www.latimes.com/world-nation/story/2020-04-06/coronavi-social-distancing-around-the-world.

104.   J. B. Abugre, "Cross-Cultural Communication Imperatives," *Critical Perspectives on International Business*, Vol. 14, No. 2/3 (August 2018), pp. 170–187, https://doi.org/10.1108/cpoib-01-2017-0005.

105.   D. Marsh, *Doing Business in the Middle East* (London: Little, Brown Book Group, 2015).

106.   S. Bryant, "10 Cultural Differences between the Chinese and Americans," *Country Navigator*, July 17, 2019, https://countrynavigator.com/blog/global-talent/cultural-differences-us-vs-china/.

107.   C. Tam and T. Oliveira, "Understanding Mobile Banking Individual Performance: The DeLone & McLean Model and the Moderating Effects of Individual Culture," *Internet Research,* 2017, pp. 538–562.

108.   M. Daskin, "Linking Polychronicity to Hotel Frontline Employees' Job Outcomes: Do Control Variables Make a Difference," *EuroMed Journal of Business,* 2016, pp. 162–180.

109.   E. Olsson and M. Sundh, "Perception of Time in Relation to Work and Private Life among Swedish Social Workers—the Temporal Clash between the Organisation and the Individual," *European Journal of Social Work*, Vol. 22, No. 4 (2018), pp. 690–701, https://doi.org/10.1080/13691457.2018.1423549.

110.   J. Berg, "8 Things Planners Should Know about International Meetings," *Bizbash,* January 22, 2016, https://www.bizbash.com/8-things-planners-should-know-about-international-meetings/new-york/story/31675/#.WoMs_kxFx9B. Also see H. Jacobs, "I Forgot One Thing on My Trip to Japan—and Now I Have to Apologize to Every Person I Meet," *Business Insider,* January 17, 2017, http://www.businessinsider.com/japan-business-culture-etiquette-bring-business-cards-2017-1; K. Boyarsky, "5 Ways You Can Run More Effective International Meetings," *HubSpot Blog*, February 15, 2019, https://blog.hubspot.com/marketing/international-meetings.

111.   G. A. Smith, "A Growing Share of Americans Say It's Not Necessary to Believe in God to Be Moral," *Pew Research Center,* October 16, 2017, http://www.pewresearch.org/fact-tank/2017/10/16/a-growing-share-of-americans-say-its-not-necessary-to-believe-in-god-to-be-moral/. Also see "America's Changing Religious Landscape," *Pew Research Center*, May 12, 2015, http://www.pewforum.org/2015/05/12/americas-changing-religious-landscape/; "Religion in America: U.S. Religious Data, Demographics and Statistics," *Pew Research Center's Religion & Public Life Project*, https://www.pewforum.org/religious-landscape-study/ (accessed November 11, 2019).

112.   E. Green, "The Non-Religious States of America," *The Atlantic*, September 6, 2017, https://www.theatlantic.com/politics/archive/2017/09/no-religion-states-prri/538821/.

113.   W. Stueck, "Sahotas Push Back against Vancouver Expropriation Proposal, Dispute $1 Property Valuations." *The Globe and Mail*, November 7, 2019, https://www.theglobeandmail.com/canada/british-columbia/article-sahotas-push-back-against-vancouver-expropriation-proposal-dispute/.

114.   "Corruption Perceptions Index 2018," *Transparency.org*, https://www.transparency.org/cpi2018 (accessed November 11, 2019).

115.   "Paying for a Bus Ticket and Expecting to Fly: How Apparel Brand Purchasing Practices Drive Labor Abuses," *Human Rights Watch*, April 23, 2019, https://www.hrw.org/report/2019/04/23/paying-bus-ticket-and-expecting-fly/how-apparel-brand-purchasing-practices-drive.

116.   "Forced Labor: Modern Day Slavery," *End Slavery Now*, http://www.endslaverynow.org/learn/slavery-today/forced-labor (accessed November 11, 2019).

117.   P. Bump, "Millions of Americans Have Moved Overseas—and It's Not Because the U.S. Is a 'Shithole,'" *The Washington Post*, January 12, 2018, https://www.washingtonpost.com/news/politics/wp/2018/01/12/millions-of-americans-have-moved-overseas-and-its-not-because-the-u-s-is-a-shithole/.

118.   "What Living Abroad Will Cost You in These 13 Cities," *UBS Prices and Earnings*, https://www.ubs.com/microsites/prices-earnings/en/stories/10-what-living-abroad-will-cost-you-in-these-13-cities/ (accessed November 11, 2019).

119.   N. A. Raghavendra and A. Shivakanth Shetty, "Riding the Waves of Culture: An Empirical Study on Acclimatization of Expatriates in IT Industry," *Problems and Perspectives in Management*, Vol. 16, No. 3 (2018), pp. 432–442.

120.   M. Maclachlan, "The Return Home: How Companies Are Letting Expatriates Down," *Communicaid*, May 9, 2017, https://www.communicaid.com/cross-cultural-training/blog/return-home-expatriates/.

121.   A. Breitenmoser and B. Bader, "Repatriation Outcomes Affecting Corporate ROI: A Critical Review and Future Agenda," *Management Quarterly Review,* June 2016, pp. 195–234.

122.   J. W. Traphagan, "A Simple Way to Raise Your Cultural Awareness at Work," *Fast Company,* May 20, 2015, https://www.fastcompany.com/3043687/a-simple-way-to-raise-your-cultural-awareness-at-work.

123.   G. Johns, "Advances in the Treatment of Context in Organizational Research," in F. P. Morgeson, H. Aguinis, and S. J. Ashford, eds., *Annual Review of Organizational Psychology and Organizational Behavior* (Palo Alto: CA, Annual Reviews, 2017), pp. 21–46.

124.   B. Tulgan, *Bridging the Soft Skills Gap* (Hoboken, NJ: John Wiley & Sons, 2015).

125.   These suggestions were based on I. Sommerdorf, "60 Ways to Improve Your Cultural Awareness," *Odyssey,* April 26, 2016, https://www.theodysseyonline.com/60-ways-to-improve-your-cultural-awareness. Also see "How to Use the Cultural Awareness Definition to Better Yourself and the World," *Mindvalley Blog*, December 10, 2018, https://blog.mindvalley.com/cultural-awareness-definition/.

126.   L. Maizland, and A. Chatzky, "Huawei: China's Controversial Tech Giant," *Council on Foreign Relations*, June 12, 2019, https://www.cfr.org/backgrounder/huawei-chinas-controversial-tech-giant. Also see "Corporate Information," https://www.huawei.com/en/about-huawei/corporate-information (accessed November 22, 2019); "Milestones—About Huawei," https://www.huawei.com/en/about-huawei/corporate-information/milestone (accessed November 22, 2019).

127.   "Corporate Information," https://www.huawei.com/en/about-huawei/corporate-information (accessed November 12, 2019). Also see "Milestones—About Huawei," https://www.huawei.com/en/about-huawei/corporate-information/milestone (accessed November 12, 2019).

128.   F. J. Cilluffo and S. L. Cardash, "What's Wrong with Huawei, and Why Are Countries Banning the Chinese Telecommunications Firm?" *The Conversation*, January 29, 2019, https://theconversation.com/whats-wrong-with-huawei-and-why-are-countries-banning-the-chinese-telecommunications-firm-109036.

129.   A. Fitch and D. Strumpf, "Huawei Produce Phones without U.S. Part," *The Wall Street Journal*, December 2, 2019, pp. A1, A2.

130.   L. Hooker and D. Palumbo, "Huawei: The Rapid Growth of a Chinese Champion in Five Charts," *BBC News*, May 20, 2019, https://www.bbc.com/news/business-46480208.

131.   K. Rapoza, "Huawei Has Taken over Apple's Market Share in China; It Will Get Worse," *Forbes*, May 2, 2019, https://www.forbes.com/sites/kenrapoza/2019/05/02/huawei-has-taken-over-apples-market-share-in-china-it-will-get-worse/#3937b559385f.

132.   F. J. Cilluffo and S. L. Cardash, "What's Wrong with Huawei, and Why Are Countries Banning the Chinese Telecommunications Firm?" *The Conversation*, January 29, 2019, https://theconversation.com/whats-wrong-with-huawei-and-why-are-countries-banning-the-chinese-telecommunications-firm-109036.

133.   S. Segan, "What Is 5G?" *PCMAG*, October 31, 2019, https://www.pcmag.com/article/345387/what-is-5g.

134.   N. Lomas, "Germany Says It Won't Ban Huawei or Any 5G Supplier up Front," *TechCrunch*, October 15, 2019, https://techcrunch.com/2019/10/15/germany-says-it-wont-ban-huawei-or-any-5g-supplier-up-front/.

135. "Corporate Information," https://www.huawei.com/en/about-huawei/corporate-information (accessed November 13, 2019).

136. L. Maizland and A. Chatzky, "Huawei: China's Controversial Tech Giant," *Council on Foreign Relations*, June 12, 2019, https://www.cfr.org/backgrounder/huawei-chinas-controversial-tech-giant.

137. J. Horowitz, "What Is Huawei, and Why the Arrest of Its CFO Matters," *CNN*, December 9, 2018, https://www.cnn.com/2018/12/06/tech/what-is-huawei/index.html.

138. "Huawei Faces US Charges: The Short, Medium and Long Story," *BBC News*, May 7, 2019, https://www.bbc.com/news/world-us-canada-47046264. Also see J. Horowitz, "What Is Huawei, and Why the Arrest of Its CFO Matters," *CNN*, December 9, 2018, https://www.cnn.com/2018/12/06/tech/what-is-huawei/index.html.

139. Z. Doffman, "Huawei Just Launched 5G in Russia with Putin's Support: 'Hello Splinternet,'" *Forbes*, September 1, 2019, https://www.forbes.com/sites/zakdoffman/2019/09/01/hello-splinternet-huawei-deploys-5g-in-russia-with-putins-support/#545fb3ce199d.

140. S. Adghirni, "China Confident Huawei Will Build Brazil's 5G Mobile Network," *Bloomberg*, November 11, 2019, https://www.bloomberg.com/news/articles/2019-11-11/china-confident-huawei-will-build-brazil-s-5g-mobile-network.

141. Z. Doffman, "Huawei Just Launched 5G in Russia with Putin's Support: 'Hello Splinternet,'" *Forbes*, September 1, 2019, https://www.forbes.com/sites/zakdoffman/2019/09/01/hello-splinternet-huawei-deploys-5g-in-russia-with-putins-support/#545fb3ce199d.

142. C. Barfield, "Europe, Huawei, and 5G Wireless: Watch Germany," *American Enterprise Institute*, October 31, 2019, https://www.aei.org/technology-and-innovation/europe-huawei-and-5g-wireless-watch-germany/.

143. "World Cup Bribes, Death Threats: Corrupt World of FIFA," *USA Today*, November 20, 2017, https://www.usatoday.com/story/sports/soccer/2017/11/20/world-cup-bribes-death-threats-corrupt-world-of-fifa/107864644/.

144. "World Cup 2022: Will Qatar Be Stripped of Hosting the Finals by FIFA?" *Sporting News Canada*, August 15, 2019, https://www.sporting-news.com/ca/soccer/news/world-cup-2022-will-qatar-be-stripped-of-hosting-the-finals-by-fifa/1c561zhyt4v521qlwfgcmc0i78.

145. "World Cup Bribes, Death Threats: Corrupt World of FIFA," *USA Today*, November 20, 2017, https://www.usatoday.com/story/sports/soccer/2017/11/20/world-cup-bribes-death-threats-corrupt-world-of-fifa/107864644/.

146. G. Dunbar, "FIFA Corruption Culture Exposed in Trials," *Chicago Tribune*, December 22, 2017, https://www.chicagotribune.com/90minutes/ct-90mins-fifa-corruption-culture-exposed-in-trials-20171222-story.html.

147. "Middle East & North Africa: Corruption Continues as Institutions and Political Rights Weaken," *Transparency International*, January 29, 2019, https://www.transparency.org/news/feature/regional-analysis-MENA.

148. "United States of America," *Transparency International*, https://www.transparency.org/country/USA (accessed November 14, 2019).

CHAPTER 5

1. A. Doyle, "What Is the Career Planning Process?" *The Balance*, September 23, 2019, https://www.thebalancecareers.com/what-is-the-career-planning-process-2063709. Also see M. Caldwell, "Making It between College and Your First Job," *The Balance*, July 29, 2019, https://www.thebalance.com/making-it-between-college-and-your-first-job-2386193; "Make a Career Plan," *ge/cd MIT Global Education and Career Development*, https://gecd.mit.edu/explore-careers/career-first-steps/make-career-plan (accessed February 22, 2018); "7 Steps to Become a Better Planner," *The Ripenists*, http://www.theripenists.com/7-steps-become-better-planner/ (accessed February 22, 2018).

2. M. Caldwell, "Making It between College and Your First Job," *The Balance*, July 29, 2019, https://www.thebalance.com/making-it-between-college-and-your-first-job-2386193. Also see "Master It Monday: Landing Your First Job Out of College—7 Practical Tips for New Grads in 2019," *Xerox*, July 22, 2019, https://www.iot-xerox.com/2019/07/22/master-monday-landing-first-job-college-7-practical-tips-new-grads-2019.

3. I. Lapowsky, "Here's How Mark Zuckerberg Sees Facebook's New Era of Privacy," *Wired*, April 30, 2019, https://www.wired.com/story/f8-zuckerberg-future-is-private/.

4. R. Kreitner, *Management,* 11th ed. (Boston: Houghton Mifflin, 2008), p. 147.

5. A. A. Thompson Jr. and A. J. Strickland III, *Strategic Management: Concepts and Cases,* 13th ed. (New York: McGraw-Hill/Irwin, 2003).

6. D. J. Collis and M. G. Rukstad, "Can You Say What Your Strategy Is?" *Harvard Business Review*, April 2008, pp. 82–90.

7. M. Keynes, "Making Planning Work: Insights from Business Development," *International Journal of Entrepreneurship and Innovative Management,* 2018, pp. 33–56. Also see M. S. Ridwan, "Planning Practices: A Multiple Case Study in the High-Performing Banks," *Journal of Organizational Change Management,* 2017, pp. 487–500.

8. R. L. Martin, "The Big Lie of Strategic Planning," *Harvard Business Review,* January–February 2014, pp. 79–84.

9. "About Us," *Burger King*, https://company.bk.com/about-bk (accessed January 14, 2020).

10. C. Sorvino, "Whopper of a Turnaround," *Forbes*, April 30, 2019, https://www.forbes.com/sites/chloesorvino/2019/04/08/whopper-of-a-turnaround-at-burger-king-the-3g-capital-model-actually-worked/#ab4653f1ce67.

11. F. Simpson, "Burger Wars: How Burger King Is Taunting Its Biggest Rival Again," *Forbes*, May 3, 2019, https://www.forbes.com/sites/fionasimpson1/2019/05/03/burger-wars-how-burger-king-is-taunting-its-biggest-rival-again/#78cda03b7347.

12. C. Sorvino, "Plant-Based Protein Comes to Burger King: Meet the Impossible Whopper," *Forbes*, April 1, 2019, https://www.forbes.com/sites/chloesorvino/2019/04/01/plant-based-protein-comes-to-burger-king-meet-the-impossible-whopper/#ffa43f33758d.

13. C. Sorvino, "Whopper of a Turnaround," *Forbes*, April 30, 2019, https://www.forbes.com/sites/chloesorvino/2019/04/08/whopper-of-a-turnaround-at-burger-king-the-3g-capital-model-actually-worked/#ab4653f1ce67.

14. C. Sorvino, "Whopper of a Turnaround," *Forbes*, April 30, 2019, https://www.forbes.com/sites/chloesorvino/2019/04/08/whopper-of-a-turnaround-at-burger-king-the-3g-capital-model-actually-worked/#ab4653f1ce67.

15. H. Mintzberg, "The Strategy Concept II: Another Look at Why Organizations Need Strategies," *California Management Review,* Vol. 30, No. 1 (1987), pp. 25–32.

16. R. Arend, Y. L. Zhao, M. Song, and S. Im, "Strategic Planning as a Complex and Enabling Managerial Tool," *Strategic Management Journal*, Vol. 38, No. 8 (2015), pp. 1741–1752, https://doi.org/10.1002/smj.2420.

17. G. Hamel, with B. Breen, *The Future of Management* (Boston: Harvard Business School Press, 2007), p. 191.

18. A. Lashinsky, "Mattel CEO Ynon Kreiz Is Rewriting a Toy Story," *Fortune*, November 26, 2019, https://fortune.com/longform/mattel-ynon-kreiz/.

19. M. Ravindran, "Red Bull Hires Nat Geo's Bernadette McDaid as Global Head of Content Development," *Variety*, January 14, 2020, https://variety.com/2020/film/global/red-bull-hires-nat-geo-exec-bernadette-mcdaid-as-global-head-of-content-development-exclusive-1203466247/.

20. I. Lunden, "Taxify Rebrands as Bolt to Expand Its Transport Options beyond Private Cars," *TechCrunch*, March 6, 2019, https://techcrunch.com/2019/03/06/taxify-rebrands-as-bolt-as-it-expands-transport-options-beyond-private-cars/. Also see A. Wexler, "Taxify Overtakes Uber in Africa," *The Wall Street Journal,* September 17, 2018, p. B4.

21. E. Bernstein, "An Emotion We Need More of," *The Wall Street Journal*, March 22, 2016, pp. D1, D4.

22. P. F. Drucker, *The Practice of Management* (New York: Harper & Row, 1954), p. 122.

23. T. A. Stewart, "A Refreshing Change: Vision Statements That Make Sense," *Fortune*, September 30, 1996, pp. 195–196.

24. S. A. Kirkpatrick, "Understanding the Role of Vision, Mission, and Values in the HPT Model," *Performance Improvement*, Vol. 56, No. 3 (2017), pp. 6–14, https://doi.org/10.1002/pfi.21689.

25. "Company Information: At a Glance," The *Coca Cola Company*, https://www.coca-colacompany.com/policies-and-practices/company-information-at-a-glance (accessed January 15, 2020).

26. "Our Mission Statement & Company Values: Coca-Cola GB," *Coca-Cola*, https://www.coca-cola.co.uk/about-us/mission-vision-and-values (accessed January 15, 2020).

27. C. Christensen, "How Will You Measure Your Life?" *Harvard Business Review,* July–August 2010, pp. 46–51.

28. Adapted from H. L. Rossi, "7 Core Values Statements That Inspire," *Fortune.com,* March 13, 2015, http://fortune.com/2015/03/13/company-slogans/ (accessed March 21, 2016).

29. Eric Jacobson, quoted in H. L. Rossi, "7 Core Values Statements That Inspire," *Fortune.com,* March 13, 2015, http://fortune.com/2015/03/13/company-slogans/ (accessed March 21, 2016).

30. D. U. Irak and J. Mantler, "The Role of Temporal Flexibility on Person-Environment Fit and Job Satisfaction," *Journal of Management & Organization*, 2018, pp. 829–845. Also see Y-K. Lee, S-H. Kim, M-S. Kim, and H-S. Kim, "Person-Environment Fit and Its Effects on Employees' Emotions and Self-Rated/Supervisor-Rated Performances," *International Journal of Contemporary Hospitality Management*, 2017, pp. 1447–1467; and M. Rocziewska, S. Retowski, and E. T. Higgins, "How Person-Organization Fit Impacts Employees' *Perceptions of Justice and Well-Being*," *Frontiers in Psychology*, 2018, pp. 1–17.

31. "It's All About Powering the Curious," *SurveyMonkey*, https://www.surveymonkey.com/mp/aboutus/ (accessed January 15, 2020). Also see Z. Lurie, "SurveyMonkey's CEO on Creating a Culture of Curiosity," *Harvard Business Review*, January–February 2019, https://hbr.org/2019/01/surveymonkeys-ceo-on-creating-a-culture-of-curiosity; B. Çiçek and M. Deniz, "Liderlere Ve Organizasyonlara Değer Temelli Yaklaşım: Değer Merkezli Liderlik Ve Etik İklim İlişkisi Üzerine Bir Araştırma—Values-Based Approach to Leaders and Organizations: A Research on Value-Centered Leadership and Ethical Climate Relationship," *Journal of Business Research*, Turk 9, No. 2 (2017), pp. 150–168, https://doi.org/10.20491/isarder.2017.265; L. E. Paarlberg and J. L. Perry, "Values Management," *The American Review of Public Administration*, Vol. 37, No. 4 (2007), pp. 387–408, https://doi.org/10.1177/0275074006297238.

32. "10 Inspirational Bill Gates Quotes on How to Succeed in Business," *The Gentleman's Journal*, https://www.thegentlemansjournal.com/article/10-inspirational-bill-gates-quotes-on-how-to-succeed-in-business/ (accessed January 15, 2020).

33. "Investor Relations: Strategy," *The Coca-Cola Company*, https://investors.coca-colacompany.com/ (accessed January 28, 2020).

34. L. Bossidy and R. Charan, *Execution: The Discipline of Getting Things Done* (New York: Crown Business, 2002), p. 227.

35. "The World's Most Admired Companies—Southwest Airlines," *Fortune*, https://fortune.com/worlds-most-admired-companies/2020/southwest-airlines/ (accessed January 28, 2020). Also see "Southwest Airlines Reports 47th Consecutive Year of Profitability," January 23, 2020, http://investors.southwest.com/news-and-events/news-releases/2020/01-23-2020-112908345.

36. "Culture: Southwest," *Careers at Southwest*, https://careers.southwestair.com/culture (accessed January 16, 2020).

37. K. Arnold, "Southwest Airlines Profit-Sharing Pool Hits Record $667 Million—Thanks to the 737 Max Grounding," *The Dallas Morning New*, January 23, 2020, https://www.dallasnews.com/business/airlines/2020/01/23/southwest-airlines-profit-sharing-pool-hits-record-667-million-thanks-to-the-737-max-grounding/.

38. "Southwest Airlines Fleet Details and History," *Planespotters*, https://www.planespotters.net/airline/Southwest-Airlines (accessed January 15, 2020). Also see B. Spiegel, "What Kind of Planes Does Southwest Airlines Fly?" *USA Today*, April 24, 2018, http://traveltips.usatoday.com/kind-planes-southwest-airlines-fly-62394.html.

39. T. Rucinski, "Southwest Sees 737 MAX Costs Continuing to Lash Profits This Year," *Reuters*, January 23, 2020, https://www.reuters.com/article/us-southwest-results/southwest-sees-737-max-costs-continuing-to-lash-profits-this-year-idUSKBN1ZM1K9.

40. D. Gilbertson, "Southwest Adding New $99 Hawaii Flights in January: Sacramento-Honolulu, Oakland-Kona," *USA Today*, August 15, 2019, https://www.usatoday.com/story/travel/airline-news/2019/08/15/southwest-airlines-expands-hawaii-service-new-nonstop-flights/2012335001/.

41. "Southwest Airlines Reports 47th Consecutive Year of Profitability," *PR Newswire*, January 23, 2020, https://www.prnewswire.com/news-releases/southwest-airlines-reports-47th-consecutive-year-of-profitability-300991895.html.

42. J. Greathouse, "General Colin Powell's Leadership Precepts: Entrepreneurs Should Lead, Not Manage," *Forbes*, January 16, 2019, https://www.forbes.com/sites/johngreathouse/2019/01/16/general-colin-powells-leadership-precepts-entrepreneurs-should-lead-not-manage/#5b64aa8269dc.

43. K. Brenzel and D. Jeans, "Warped Lumber, Failed Projects: TRD Investigates Katerra, SoftBank's $4B Construction Startup," *The Real Deal New York*, December 16, 2019, https://therealdeal.com/2019/12/16/softbank-funded-construction-startup-katerra-promised-a-tech-revolution-its-struggling-to-deliver/. Also see "Vision," *Katerra*, https://www.katerra.com/vision/ (accessed January 16, 2020).

44. "About Us: We Are Driven," https://www.joinhandshake.com/about/ (accessed January 28, 2020). Also see J. Bauer-Wolf, "Handshake, Popular Career-Services Platform, Now Open to All Students," *Inside Higher Ed*, August 21, 2019, https://www.insidehighered.com/news/2019/08/21/handshake-popular-career-services-platform-now-open-all-students?mc_cid=7ec79b2d89&mc_eid=41c97f3492.

45. R. E. Riley-Topping, "The VA—A Decade in Review," *The Hill*, December 31, 2019, https://thehill.com/opinion/white-house/476317-the-va-a-decade-in-review. Also see B. Kesling and D. Nissenbaum, "Goal to Slash Wait Times Was 'Unrealistic,' Aide Said," *The Wall Street Journal,* May 24–25, 2014, p. A4.

46. P. F. Drucker, *The Practice of Management* (New York: Harper & Row, 1954).

47. G. Latham, G. Seijts, and J. Slocum, "The Goal Setting and Goal Orientation Labyrinth: Effective Ways for Increasing Employee Performance," *Organizational Dynamics*, October–December 2016, p. 275.

48. M. P. E. Cunha, L. Giustiniano, A. Rego, and S. Clegg, "Mission Impossible? The Paradoxes of Stretch Goal Setting," *Management Learning*, 2017, pp. 140–157. Also see G. Latham, G. Seijts, and J. Slocum, "The Goal Setting and Goal Orientation Labyrinth: Effective Ways for Increasing Employee Performance," *Organizational Dynamics*, October–December 2016, pp. 271–277.

49. M. A. Wolfson, S. I. Tannenbaum, J. E. Mathieu, and M. T. Maynard, "A Cross-Level Investigation of Informal Field-Based Learning and Performance Improvements." *Journal of Applied Psychology*, January 2018, p. 17.

50. "North Carolina Health Departments Address Opioid Crisis with New Plan," *NBC 12*, January 13, 2020, https://www.wxii12.com/article/north-carolina-health-departments-address-opioid-crisis-with-new-plan/30503948.

51. A. Fox, "Put Plans into Action," *HRMagazine,* April 2013, pp. 27–31.

52. S. S. Wang, "Never Procrastinate Again," *The Wall Street Journal,* September 1, 2015, pp. D1, D2.

53. G. Latham, G. Seijts, and J. Slocum, "The Goal Setting and Goal Orientation Labyrinth: Effective Ways for Increasing Employee Performance," *Organizational Dynamics,* October–December 2016, pp. 271–277.

54. R. Rodgers and J. E. Hunter, "Impact of Management by Objectives on Organizational Productivity," *Journal of Applied Psychology,* April 1991, pp. 322–336. Also see M. Johansen and D. P. Hawes, "The Effect of the Tasks Middle Managers Perform on Organizational Performance," *Public Administration Quarterly*, Fall 2016, pp. 580–616.

55. A. Kinicki, K. Jacobson, B. Galvin, and G. Prussia. "Multilevel Systems Model of Leadership," *Journal of Leadership and Organizational Studies*, Vol. 18 (2011), pp. 133–149.

56. This example was taken from a graphic illustration by A. Kinicki and is used for training managers in cascading; copyright ©2016 by Kinicki and Associates Inc. For more on goal cascading, see A. J. Kinicki, K. J. L. Jacobson, B. M. Galvin, and G. E. Prussia, "A Multilevel Systems Model of Leadership," *Journal of Leadership & Organizational Studies*, May 2011, pp. 133–149.

57. R. I. Williams Jr., S. C. Manley, J. R. Aaron, and F. Daniel, "The Relationship Between a Comprehensive Strategic Approach and Small Business Performance," *Journal of Small Business Strategy*, Vol. 28, No. 2 (2018), pp. 33–48.

58. "Small Businesses Generate 44 Percent of U.S. Economic Activity," *SBA's Office of Advocacy*, January 30, 2019, https://advocacy.sba.gov/2019/01/30/small-businesses-generate-44-percent-of-u-s-economic-activity/.

59. "Our Sustainability Story," *Great Lakes Brewing Company*, https://www.greatlakesbrewing.com/sustainability (accessed January 21, 2020).

60. "Facts Statistics: Wildfires," *Insurance Information Institute*, https://www.iii.org/fact-statistic/facts-statistics-wildfires (accessed January 17, 2020).

61. R. Gold, K. Blunt, and R. Smith, "PG&E Sparked at Least 1,500 California Fires. Now the Utility Faces Collapse," *The Wall Street Journal*, January 13, 2019, https://www.wsj.com/articles/pg-e-sparked-at-least-1-500-california-fires-now-the-utility-faces-collapse-11547410768. Also see "Company Profile," *PG&E*, https://www.pge.com/en_US/about-pge/company-information/profile/profile.page (accessed January 17, 2020).

62. M. McFall-Johnsen, "Over 1,500 California Fires in the Past 6 Years—Including the Deadliest Ever—Were Caused by One Company: PG&E. Here's What It Could Have Done but Didn't," *Business Insider*, November 3, 2019, https://www.businessinsider.com/pge-caused-california-wildfires-safety-measures-2019-10.

63. B. Rittiman, "Judge Orders PG&E Back to Criminal Court, May Add Terms to Probation," *KXTV*, January 16, 2020, https://www.abc10.com/article/news/local/wildfire/judge-orders-pge-back-to-criminal-court-may-add-terms-to-probation/103-604df0b9-2b40-4787-9c99-07184c545681.

64. L. Hepler, "As California Wildfire Season Looms, Finding Tree Trimmers Is a New Problem," *The New York Times*, May 23, 2019, https://www.nytimes.com/2019/05/23/business/energy-environment/pge-wildfire-trees.html.

65. M. Holcombe and S. Almasy, "California Utility PG&E to Pay $13.5 Billion to Settle Claims from Wildfire Victims," *CNN*, December 7, 2019, https://www.cnn.com/2019/12/07/us/pge-settlement/index.html.

66. P. Helsel, "PG&E Pleads Guilty to 84 Counts of Manslaughter in Devastating Camp Fire," *NBC News*, June 17, 2020, https://www.nbcnews.com/news/us-news/pg-e-pleads-guilty-84-counts-manslaughter-devastating-camp-fire-n1231256.

67. R. Nolan, "How to Be More Proactive: A Step-by-Step Guide," *Goalcast*, September 2, 2016, https://www.goalcast.com/2016/09/02/how-to-be-more-proactive-step-step-guide.

68. R. Umoh, "Billionaire Richard Branson Reveals the Simple Trick He Uses to Live a Positive Life," *CNBC*, January 16, 2018, https://www.cnbc.com/2018/01/16/richard-branson-uses-this-simple-trick-to-live-a-positive-life.html.

69. These recommendations were derived from R. Nolan, "How to Be More Proactive: A Step-by-Step Guide," *Goalcast*, September 2, 2016, https://www.goalcast.com/2016/09/02/how-to-be-more-proactive-step-step-guide.

70. The structure of this exercise was partially based on B. Tulgan, *Bridging the Soft Skills Gap* (Hoboken, New Jersey: John Wiley & Sons, 2015).

71. K. Cherry, "How to Become More Open-Minded," *Very Well Mind*, June 29, 2019, https://www.verywellmind.com/be-more-open-minded-4690673. Also see S. Vozza, "4 Ways to Train Your Brain to Be More Open-Minded," Fast Company, November 14, 2017, https://www.fastcompany.com/40494077/4-ways-to-train-your-brain-to-be-more-open-minded; S. Pavlina, "Suspending Judgment," June 3, 2010, https://www.stevepavlina.com/blog/2010/06/suspending-judgment.

72. "Improved Safety and Customer Experience Drive Record Amtrak Ridership," https://media.amtrak.com/2019/11/improved-safety-and-customer-experience-drive-record-amtrak-ridership/ (accessed January 29, 2020); "Amtrak Facts," https://www.amtrak.com/about-amtrak/amtrak-facts.html (accessed January 18, 2020).

73. J. Kim, "Amtrak Has Lost Money Every Year Since 1971. Here's Why Train Tickets Are So Expensive," *Business Insider*, March 27, 2019, https://www.businessinsider.com/amtrak-why-so-expensive-america-train-system-2019-3. Also see T. Mann, "Amtrak, Seeking to Break Even, Sees Some Light at the End of the Tunnel," *The Wall Street Journal*, November 8, 2019, https://www.wsj.com/articles/amtrak-seeking-to-break-even-sees-some-light-at-the-end-of-the-tunnel-11573223401.

74. J. Kim, "Amtrak Has Lost Money Every Year Since 1971. Here's Why Train Tickets Are So Expensive," *Business Insider*, March 27, 2019, https://www.businessinsider.com/amtrak-why-so-expensive-america-train-system-2019-3.

75. N. Oliver, "To Boost Amtrak Ridership, State Mulls Cutting Ticket Prices within Virginia, D.C," *Virginia Mercury*, December 5, 2018, https://www.virginiamercury.com/2018/12/05/to-boost-amtrak-ridership-state-mulls-cutting-ticket-prices-within-virginia-d-c/.

76. T. Mann, "Amtrak Has Lost Money for Decades. A Former Airline CEO Thinks He Can Fix It," *The Wall Street Journal*, July 6, 2019, https://www.wsj.com/articles/amtrak-has-lost-money-for-decades-a-former-airline-ceo-thinks-he-can-fix-it-11562385660?mod=article_inline.

77. R. O'Toole, "Amtrak's Big Lie," *Washington Examiner*, January 14, 2020, https://www.washingtonexaminer.com/opinion/amtraks-big-lie.

78. J. Hobson and A. Hagan, "Amtrak CEO Wants to Be a Good 'Steward' of the Country's Rail Corporation," *WBUR*, December 2, 2019, https://www.wbur.org/hereandnow/2019/12/02/amtrak-train-ceo-travel.

79. L. Lazo, "The End of an American Tradition: The Amtrak Dining Car," *The Washington Post*, September 21, 2019, https://www.washingtonpost.com/local/trafficandcommuting/the-end-of-an-american-tradition-the-amtrak-dining-car/2019/09/21/d63cca3a-d888-11e9-bfb1-849887369476_story.html.

80. J. Hobson and A. Hagan, "Amtrak Could Turn a Profit in 2020 for the 1st Time Ever," *WBUR*, November 15, 2019, https://www.wbur.org/hereandnow/2019/11/15/amtrak-profit-train-ceo-richard-anderson.

81. L. Lazo, "Amtrak Touts Record Ridership, Revenue for Fiscal 2019," *The Washington Post*, November 8, 2019, https://www.washingtonpost.com/transportation/2019/11/08/amtrak-touts-record-ridership-revenue-fiscal/.

82. L. Lazo, "Amtrak Chief Defends Decision to Kill the Traditional Dining Car on Some Long-Distance Trains," *The Washington Post*, November 13, 2019, https://www.washingtonpost.com/transportation/2019/11/13/amtrak-chief-defends-decision-kill-traditional-dining-car-some-long-distance-trains/.

83. D. Leonard, "Amtrak CEO Has a Plan for Profitability, and You Won't Like It," *Bloomberg*, November 20, 2019, https://www.bloomberg.com/news/features/2019-11-20/amtrak-ceo-has-no-love-lost-for-dining-cars-long-haul-routes.

84. T. Mann, "Surging Amtrak Seeks Green Light from Congress," *The Wall Street Journal*, January 1, 2020, https://www.wsj.com/articles/surging-amtrak-seeks-green-light-from-congress-11577889706.

85. C. Rowland, "Pfizer Had Clues Its Blockbuster Drug Could Prevent Alzheimer's. Why Didn't It Tell the World?" *The Washington Post*, June 4, 2019, https://www.washingtonpost.com/business/economy/pfizer-had-clues-its-blockbuster-drug-could-prevent-alzheimers-why-didnt-it-tell-the-world/2019/06/04/9092e08a-7a61-11e9-8bb7-0fc796cf2ec0_story.html.

86. J. D. Rockoff, "Pfizer Ends Hunt for Drugs to Treat Alzheimer's and Parkinson's," *The Wall Street Journal*, January 6, 2018, https://www.wsj.com/articles/pfizer-ends-hunt-for-drugs-to-treat-alzheimers-and-parkinsons-1515267654.

87. C. Rowland, "Pfizer Had Clues Its Blockbuster Drug Could Prevent Alzheimer's. Why Didn't It Tell the World?" *The Washington Post*, June 4, 2019, https://www.washingtonpost.com/business/economy/pfizer-had-clues-its-blockbuster-drug-could-prevent-alzheimers-why-didnt-it-tell-the-world/2019/06/04/9092e08a-7a61-11e9-8bb7-0fc796cf2ec0_story.html.

88. "Pharma Giant Pfizer Pulls Out of Research into Alzheimer's," *BBC News,* January 10, 2018, http://www.bbc.com/news/health-42633871.

89. D. Crow, "Big Pharma Efforts on Alzheimer's Tested by Pfizer Exit," *Financial Times*, January 18, 2018, https://www.ft.com/content/c4e1241e-f731-11e7-88f7-5465a6ce1a00.

90. J. D. Rockoff, "Pfizer Ends Hunt for Drugs to Treat Alzheimer's and Parkinson's," *The Wall Street Journal*, January 6, 2018, https://www.wsj.com/articles/pfizer-ends-hunt-for-drugs-to-treat-alzheimers-and-parkinsons-1515267654.

91. "Mission & Purpose," http://www.pfizer.com/careers/en/mission-purpose (accessed January 18, 2020).

92. D. Crow, "Big Pharma Efforts on Alzheimer's Tested by Pfizer Exit," *Financial Times*, January 18, 2018, https://www.ft.com/content/c4e1241e-f731-11e7-88f7-5465a6ce1a00.

93. D. Crow, "Big Pharma Efforts on Alzheimer's Tested by Pfizer Exit," *Financial Times*, January 18, 2018, https://www.ft.com/content/c4e1241e-f731-11e7-88f7-5465a6ce1a00.

CHAPTER 6

1. "Sneaky Veg, About," https://www.sneakyveg.com/about/ (accessed January 30, 2020). Also see K. Cook, "15 Inspiring Examples of Small Business Branding," *HubSpot*, https://blog.hubspot.com/marketing/inspiring-examples-of-small-business-branding (accessed March 5, 2018).

2. C. Castrillon, "Why Personal Branding Is More Important Than Ever," February 12, 2019, https://www.forbes.com/sites/carolinecastrillon/2019/02/12/why-personal-branding-is-more-important-than-ever/#f32af9824085.

3. "The Future of Talent," *Advertising Supplement to The Wall Street Journal*, 2017, p. 23.

4. M. Sweetwood, "8 Reasons a Powerful Personal Brand Will Make You Successful," *Entrepreneur*, March 27, 2017, https://www.entrepreneur.com/article/289278.

5. J. H. Hernandez and J. Arcand, "3 Steps to an Outstanding Personal Branding Statement," *Work It Daily*, October 23, 2019, https://www.workitdaily.com/how-to-write-personal-branding-statement. Also see L. Lake, "How to Write Your Personal Branding Statement," *The Balance*, June 10, 2017, https://www.thebalance.com/how-to-write-your-personal-branding-statement-2295809.

6. K. Lee, "The 5 Keys to Building a Social Media Strategy for Your Personal Brand," *Buffer*, https://buffer.com/resources/social-media-strategy-personal-branding-tips (accessed February 1, 2020). Also see E. Gross, "10 Ways to Build Your Personal Brand (and Why You Should)," *Skillcrush*, October 24, 2016, https://skillcrush.com/2015/02/20/10-ways-build-personal-brand/.

7. E. Gross, "10 Ways to Build Your Personal Brand (and Why You Should)," *Skillcrush*, October 24, 2016, https://skillcrush.com/2015/02/20/10-ways-build-personal-brand/.

8. M. E. Porter, "What Is Strategy?" *Harvard Business Review*, November–December 1996, pp. 61–78. Porter has updated his 1979 paper on competitive forces in M. E. Porter, "The Five Competitive Forces That Shape Strategy," *Harvard Business Review*, January 2008, pp. 79–93.

9. M. E. Porter, "What Is Strategy?" *Harvard Business Review*, November–December 1996, pp. 61–78.

10. J. Shabat, "The Reinvention of Allegiant Air," *Skift*, December 4, 2019, https://skift.com/2019/12/04/the-reinvention-of-allegiant-air/. Also see "Our Brand Manifesto," *buybuyBABY*, https://www.buybuybaby.com/store/static/BabyAboutUs (accessed February 1, 2020); "Fun Facts," *Crocs*, https://careers.crocs.com/about-us/default.aspx (accessed February 1, 2020).

11. P. Seifzadeh and W. G. Rowe, "The Role of Corporate Controls and Business-Level Strategy in Business Unit Performance," *Journal of Strategy and Management*, 2019, pp. 364–381.

12. P. Wadstrom, "Aligning Corporate and Business Strategy: Managing the Balance," *Journal of Business Strategy*, 2019, pp. 44–52.

13. "Fiat Chrysler and Foxconn Plan Chinese Electric Vehicle Joint Venture," *CNBC*, January 17, 2020, https://www.cnbc.com/2020/01/17/fiat-chrysler-and-foxconn-plan-chinese-electric-vehicle-joint-venture.html.

14. A. Starostinetskaya, "Dunkin' Expands beyond Breakfast Sandwich to All 9,000 Locations Nationwide," October 21, 2019, https://vegnews.com/2019/10/dunkin-expands-beyond-breakfast-sandwich-to-all-9000-locations-nationwide.

15. S. Taneja, M. G. Pryor, and M. Hayek, "Leaping Innovation Barriers to Small Business Longevity," *Journal of Business Strategy*, 2016, pp. 44–51. Also see G.N. Powell and K. A. Eddleston, "Family Involvement in the Firm, Family-to-Business Support, and Entrepreneurial Outcomes: An Exploration," *Journal of Small Business Management*, October 2017, pp. 614–631.

16. L. van Scheers and M. K. Makhitha, "Are Small and Medium Enterprises (SMEs) Planning for Strategic Marketing in South Africa?" *Foundations of Management*, 2016, pp. 243–250.

17. L. C. Bellamy, N. Amoo, K. Mervyn, and J. Hiddlestone-Mumford, "The Use of Strategy Tools and Frameworks by SMEs in the Strategy Formation Process," *International Journal of Organizational Analysis*, 2019, pp. 337–367.

18. I. Small, "Looking Ahead: Evernote's Priorities for 2019," *Evernote*, January 3, 2019, https://evernote.com/blog/looking-ahead-evernotes-priorities-2019/. Also see C. O'Brien, "Evernote's 5% Problem Offers a Cautionary Lesson to Tech Companies," *redhat*, January 5, 2016, https://venturebeat.com/2016/01/05/evernotes-5-problem-offers-a-cautionary-lesson-to-tech-companies/; A. Taylor, "Why Do the Best Companies in the World Use Strategic Planning?" *Strategy Management Consulting*, January 8, 2018, http://www.smestrategy.net/blog/why-do-the-best-companies-in-the-world-use-strategic-planning.

19. A. Turnbull, "What I Learned Rescuing Our Startup From Death," *Groove*, https://www.groovehq.com/blog/rescuing-startup-death (accessed February 1, 2020). Also see A. Turnbull, "Why I Almost Walked Away from the $500k/mo Company I Founded," *Groove*, https://www.groovehq.com/blog/almost-walked-away (accessed February 1, 2020).

20. J. Sedmak, "How Often Should Strategic Planning Be Done?" *SME Strategy Consulting*, https://www.smestrategy.net/blog/how-often-should-strategic-planning-be-done (accessed February 3, 2020).

21. T. Krisher, "Air Bag Woes Force Honda, Toyota, to Recall 6M Vehicles," *Detroit News*, January 22, 2020, https://www.detroitnews.com/story/business/autos/foreign/2020/01/21/air-bag-woes-force-honda-toyota-recall-vehicles/41040673/.

22. B. Miller, "Toyota Recalling Nearly 700,000 Vehicles Due to Faulty Fuel Pump," *L.A. Biz*, January 14, 2020, https://www.bizjournals.com/losangeles/news/2020/01/14/toyota-recalling-nearly-700-000-vehicles-due-to.html.

23. M. L. Engel, "Crafting the Ideal Mission Statement for Your Organization," *Hesselbein & Company*, 2018, pp. 7–12.

24. I. Alegre, J. Berbegal-Mirabent, A. Guerrero, and M. Mas-Machuca, "The Real Mission of the Mission Statement: A Systematic Review of the Literature," *Journal of Management & Organization*, Vol. 24, No. 4 (2018), pp. 456–473.

25. I. Alegre, J. Berbegal-Mirabent, A. Guerrero, and M. Mas-Machuca, "The Real Mission of the Mission Statement: A Systematic Review of the Literature," *Journal of Management & Organization*, Vol. 24, No. 4 (2018), pp. 456–473.

26. L. Gregory, "Microsoft's Mission Statement & Vision Statement (An Analysis)," *Panmore Institute*, February 24, 2019, http://panmore.com/microsoft-corporation-vision-statement-mission-statement-analysis.

27. "What We Value," *Microsoft*, https://www.microsoft.com/en-us/about/values (accessed February 3, 2020).

28. M. Janakiram, "A Look Back at Ten Years of Microsoft Azure," *Forbes*, February 3, 2020, https://www.forbes.com/sites/janakirammsv/2020/02/03/a-look-back-at-ten-years-of-microsoft-azure/#3a965a249292.

29. M. Janakiram, "A Look Back at Ten Years of Microsoft Azure," *Forbes*, February 3, 2020, https://www.forbes.com/sites/janakirammsv/2020/02/03/a-look-back-at-ten-years-of-microsoft-azure/#3a965a249292. Also see J. Tartakoff, "Ballmer: Microsoft 'Betting Our Company' on the Cloud," *GigaOm*, March 4, 2010, https://gigaom.com/2010/03/04/419-ballmer-microsoft-betting-our-company-on-the-cloud/.

30. E. Baylan, "Developing Strategy Evaluation Method Via Strategic Control System Based Risk Assessment," *Journal of International Trade, Logistics, and Law*, 2018, pp. 92–100.

31. A. Kinicki, K. Jacobson, B. Galvin, and G. Prussia, "A Multilevel Systems Model of Leadership," *Journal of Leadership & Organizational Studies*, May 2011, pp. 133–149.

32. T. Anning-Dorson, "Innovation and Competitive Advantage Creation: The Role of Organisational Leadership in Service Firms from Emerging Markets," *International Marketing Review*, 2018, pp. 580–600. Also see C. R. Breer, R. F. Lusch, and M. A. Hitt, "A Service Perspective for Human Capital Resources: A Critical Base for Strategy Implementation," *Academy of Management*, May 2017, pp. 137–158.

33. "Microsoft Strategy Teardown: Cloud, AI, & Subscriptions and the Next Trillion-Dollar Company," *CB Insights*, https://www.cbinsights.com/research/report/microsoft-strategy-teardown/ (accessed February 3, 2020).

34. "Diagnostics, Feedback, and Privacy in Windows 10," *Microsoft*, January 30, 2020, https://support.microsoft.com/en-us/help/4468236/diagnostics-feedback-and-privacy-in-windows-10-microsoft-privacy. Also see "About WER," *Microsoft*, May 31, 2018, https://docs.microsoft.com/en-us/windows/win32/wer/about-wer.

35. C. Duffy, "Microsoft's 'Blow Out' Fourth Quarter Beats Analyst Projections by $1 Billion," *CNN*, July 18, 2019, https://www.cnn.com/2019/07/18/tech/microsoft-fourth-quarter-earnings-2019/index.html.

36. W. R. Bigler, "A New Vista for Strategic Management: Continuously Aligning the Inside with the Outside," *Management Accounting Quarterly*, 2019, pp. 10–23.

37. "TMC Announces Financial Results for Fiscal Year Ended March 31, 2019," *Toyota*, May 8, 2019, https://pressroom.toyota.com/tmc-announces-financial-results-for-fiscal-year-ended-march-31-2019/. Also see P. Landers, "Toyota's Strong Performance in North America Fuels Profit," *The Wall Street Journal*, February 6, 2020, https://www.wsj.com/articles/toyotas-strong-performance-in-north-america-fuels-profit-11580979956; M. Toljagic, "These Are the 10 Biggest Automakers in the World," *Wheels*, August 20, 2019, https://www.wheels.ca/top-ten/these-are-ten-biggest-automakers-in-the-world/.

38. "Toyota Production System," *Toyota*, https://global.toyota/en/company/vision-and-philosophy/production-system/ (accessed February 6, 2020).

39. "2019 Toyota Awards," *J.D. Power*, https://www.jdpower.com/cars/ratings/toyota/2019 (accessed February 6, 2020).

40. "Leading Automotive Firms by Research and Development Spending Worldwide in FY 2018," *Statista*, https://www.statista.com/statistics/566060/automotve-firms-by-research-development-spending/ (accessed February 6, 2020). Also see "Toyota's Research and Development (R&D) Expenses from FY 2007 to FY 2019," *Statista*, https://www.statista.com/statistics/279648/research-and-development-spending-at-toyota/ (accessed February 6, 2020); "R&D Centers," Toyota, https://global.toyota/en/company/profile/facilities/r-d/ (accessed February 6, 2020).

41. J. Capparella, "Toyota RAV4 Topples Prius as Toyota's Best-Selling Hybrid," *Car and Driver*, January 3, 2020, https://www.caranddriver.com/news/a28262444/toyota-rav4-hybrid-prius-sales/. Also see "Toyota Cash on Hand 2006-2019," Macrotrends, https://www.macrotrends.net/stocks/charts/TM/toyota/cash-on-hand (accessed February 6, 2020).

42. O. Jurevicius, "SWOT Analysis of Toyota," *Strategic Management Insight*, December 10, 2016, https://www.strategicmanagementinsight.com/swot-analyses/toyota-swot-analysis.html. Also see "Voluntary Recalls," *Toyota USA Newsroom*, http://toyotanews.pressroom.toyota.com/section_display.cfm?section_id=639 (accessed March 5, 2018).

43. T. Krisher, "Air Bag Woes Force Honda, Toyota, to Recall 6M Vehicles," *Detroit News*, January 22, 2020, https://www.detroitnews.com/story/business/autos/foreign/2020/01/21/air-bag-woes-force-honda-toyota-recall-vehicles/41040673/.

44. See "Toyota Recalls Nearly 700K Vehicles to Fix Faulty Fuel Pumps," *Associated Press*, January 13, 2020, https://apnews.com/3f3f9 ee0c6926f3e96b5df2437019429. Also see "The Toyota Production System Is Not Nearly Enough," *Operational Excellence Society*, November 10, 2014, https://opexsociety.org/body-of-knowledge/the-toyota-production-system-is-not-nearly-enough/.

45. O. Jurevicius, "SWOT Analysis of Toyota," *Strategic Management Insight*, December 10, 2016, https://www.strategicmanagementinsight.com/swot-analyses/toyota-swot-analysis.html.

46. "Toyota to Use Advanced Self-driving Tech in Commercial Vehicles First," *Reuters*, December 17, 2019, https://www.reuters.com/article/us-toyota-autonomous/toyota-to-use-advanced-self-driving-tech-in-commercial-vehicles-first-idUSKBN1YL0G9. Also see N. Shirouzu and N. Tajitsu, "Toyota's Not Alone in the Slow Lane to Self-driving Cars," *Reuters*, October 25, 2019, https://www.reuters.com/article/us-autoshow-tokyo-toyota-technology/toyotas-not-alone-in-the-slow-lane-to-self-driving-cars-idUSKBN1X41XF.

47. O. Adeshokan, "Toyota Is Making a Small Bet on a Big Opportunity in African Mobility Startups," *Quartz Africa*, February 5, 2020, https://qz.com/africa/1797709/toyota-bets-on-african-mobility-startup-sendy-in-kenya/.

48. J. Dowling, "Beat the Price Rises: Currency Pressure Poised to Push up the Cost of Cars in 2020," *CarAdvice*, January 15, 2020, https://www.caradvice.com.au/818494/car-prices-to-go-up-in-2020/.

49. B. Foldy, "Idled Plants in China Add to Trouble for Auto Makers," *The Wall Street Journal*, February 8–9, 2020, p. B4. Also see S. Pham, "Toyota Won't Reopen China Plants for at Least Another Week as Coronavirus Shows Little Sign of Slowing Down," February 7, 2020, https://www.cnn.com/2020/02/07/business/toyota-factory-coronavirus/index.html.

50. A. Assensoh-Kodua, "The Resource-based View: A Tool of Key Competency for Competitive Advantage," *Problems and Perspectives in Management*, 2019, pp. 143–152.

51. J. B. Barney, "Firm Resources and Sustained Competitive Advantage," *Journal of Management*, Vol. 19 (1991), pp. 99–120.

52. K. Noonan, "What Does the Future Hold for Self-Driving Cars?" *The Motley Fool*, October 18, 2019, https://www.fool.com/investing/what-does-the-future-hold-for-self-driving-cars.aspx.

53. "40+ Corporations Working on Autonomous Vehicles," *CB Insights*, August 28, 2019, https://www.cbinsights.com/research/autonomous-driverless-vehicles-corporations-list/.

54. D. Geske, "A Look at the Investment in Self-Driving Cars: Who Has Spent the Most?" *International Business Times*, October 17, 2019, https://www.ibtimes.com/look-investment-self-driving-cars-who-has-spent-most-2848289.

55. P. Chatzoglou, D. Chatzoudes, L. Sarigiannidis, and G. Theriou, "The Role of Firm-Specific Factors in the Strategy-Performance Relationship," *Management Research Review*, 2017, pp. 46–73.

56. H. Greimel, "Toyota Will Have a Self-Driving Car for Sale in a Year," *Autoweek*, February 11, 2019, https://autoweek.com/article/autonomous-cars/report-toyota-will-have-self-driving-car-sale-year.

57. For forecasting related to public policy and political polling, see "Why Even the Best Forecasters Sometimes Miss the Mark," *Knowledge@Wharton*, April 19, 2016, http://knowledge.wharton.upenn.edu/article/why-even-the-best-forecasters- sometimes-miss-the-mark (accessed April 24, 2016).

58. A. Wieckowski, "Predicting the Future," *Harvard Business Review*, 2018, https://hbr.org/2018/11/predicting-the-future.

59. M. Niemimaa, J. Jarvelainen, M. Heikkila, and J. Heikkila, "Business Continuity of Business Models: Evaluating the Resilience of Business Models for Contingencies," *International Journal of Information Management*, 2019, pp. 208–216.

60. T. Mickle, "Apple Warns Coronavirus to Hit Sales," *The Wall Street Journal*, February 18, 2020, pp. A1, A7.

61. T. Mickle, "Apple Warns Coronavirus to Hit Sales," *The Wall Street Journal*, February 18, 2020, pp. A1, A7.

62. J. Oliver and E. Parrett, "Managing Future Uncertainty: Reevaluating the Role of Scenario Planning," *Business Horizons*, 2018, pp. 339–352.

63. N. Purnell, U.S. Tech Giants Bet Big on India. Now It's Changing the Rules," *The Wall Street Journal*, December 3, 2019, https://www.wsj .com/articles/u-s-tech-giants-bet-big-on-india-now-the-rules-are-changing-11575386675. Also see H. Chauhan, "Walmart's Shocking Retreat in India Could Prove Costly," The Motley Fool, January 15, 2020, https://www.fool.com/investing/2020/01/15/walmarts-shocking-retreat-in-india-could-prove-cos.aspx.

64. S. Rai, "Walmart Got a $10 Billion Surprise after Buying Flipkart," *Bloomberg*, July 9, 2019, https://www.bloomberg.com/news/articles/2019-07-09/walmart-payment-unit-is-raising-funds-at-up-to-10-billion-value.

65. "About Us," *Flipkart*, https://www.flipkart.com/about-us?otracker= undefined_footer_navlinks (accessed February 9, 2020).

66. A. Mediratta, "How Kiranas Have Weathered the Age of Ecommerce," *Forbes*, January 6, 2020, http://www.forbesindia.com/article/vision-2020/how-kiranas-have-weathered-the-age-of-ecommerce/56973/1.

67. J. Vincent, "Amazon and Walmart Hit Hard after New e-Commerce Rules in India Restrict Sales," *The Verge*, February 1, 2019, https://www .theverge.com/2019/2/1/18206538/amazon-walmart-flipkart-india-e-commerce-rules-regulation-chaos.

68. "Amazon, Walmart Face the Ire of 70 Million Indian Shopkeepers," *The Hindu Business Line*, December 2, 2019, https://www.thehindubusinessline .com/info-tech/amazon-walmart-face-the-ire-of-70-million-indian-shopkeepers/article30135455.ece#.

69. S. Dash, "Walmart Could Exit from Flipkart Because of India's New FDI Rules," *Business Insider India*, February 6, 2019, https://www .businessinsider.in/walmart-flipkart-acquisition-could-fall-through-report/articleshow/67849413.cms.

70. C. Goldwasser, "Benchmarking: People Make the Process," *Management Review*, June 1995, p. 40.

71. "Benchmarking," *Bain & Company*, November 7, 2017, www.bain .com/publications/articles/management-tools-benchmarking.aspx.

72. F. Reh, "The Importance of Benchmarking in Improving Business Operations," *The Balance Careers*, July 26, 2019, https://www .thebalancecareers.com/overview-and-examples-of-benchmarking-in-business-2275114.

73. See example in M. M. Yaseen, R. Sweis, A. B. Abdallah, and B. Y. Obeidat, "Benchmarking of TQM Practices in the Jordanian Pharmaceutical Industry (a comparative study)," *Benchmarking: An International Journal*, 2018, pp. 4058–4083. Also see D. C. Invernizzi, G. Locatelli, and N. J. Brookes, "A Methodology Based on Benchmarking to Learn across Megaprojects," *International Journal of Managing Projects in Business*, 2018, pp. 104–121.

74. "Research," *Charles Schwab*, February 2020, https://www.aboutschwab .com/research.

75. J. Spacey, "12 Examples of Benchmarking," *Simplicable*, July 4, 2017, https://simplicable.com/new/benchmarking.

76. S. McCartney, "The Best and Worst U.S. Airlines of 2019," *The Wall Street Journal*, January 15, 2020, https://www.wsj.com/articles/the-best-and-worst-u-s-airlines-of-2019-11579097301.

77. "History," *Lululemon*, https://info.lululemon.com/about/our-story/history (accessed February 10, 2020).

78. D. Sparks, "3 Things Investors Should Know about Lululemon," *The Motley Fool*, January 25, 2020, https://www.fool.com/investing/2020/01/25/3-things-investors-should-know-about-lululemon.aspx. Also see C. Scott," Lululemon Leans into Men's Apparel as Segment Expands," *The Wall Street Journal*, December 11, 2019, https://www.wsj.com/articles/lululemon-tests-how-far-men-will-stretch-11576069203.

79. "The History of Tabasco Brand," *Tabasco*, https://www.tabasco .com/tabasco-history/ (accessed February 10, 2020).

80. J. Montpetit, "How Once Mighty Bombardier Became Politically Toxic in Quebec," *CBC*, February 6, 2020, https://www.cbc.ca/news/canada/montreal/bombardier-what-happened-bailout-1.5453012. Also see "Bombardier's Future Looks Bleak, Wealth Manager Says," *CBC*, January 22, 2020, https://www.cbc.ca/news/canada/thunder-bay/bombardier-future-bleak-says-wealth-manager-1.5435162; J. McNish and

C. Lombardo, "Bombardier in Talks to Sell Business-Jet Unit to Textron," *The Wall Street Journal*, February 4, 2020, https://www.wsj.com/articles/bombardier-in-talks-to-sell-business-jet-unit-to-textron-11580835712.

81. Applications of the technique can be found in L. Norton, "4 Lessons to Learn from Declining Business Models: How to Prevent Your Organization from Going Extinct," *HRNews*, March 27, 2017. Also see G. Genoveva and T. S. Siam, "Analysis of Marketing Strategy and Competitive Advantage," *The International Journal of Economic Perspectives*, 2017, pp. 1571–1579.

82. "Dell Technologies Reports Fiscal Year 2019 Fourth Quarter and Full Year Financial Results," Dell, February 28, 2019, https://investors .delltechnologies.com/news-releases/news-release-details/dell-technologies-reports-fiscal-year-2019-fourth-quarter-and. Also see A. Kasi, "BCG Matrix of Dell," *BCG*, April 1, 2017, http://bcgmatrixanalysis .com/bcg-matrix-of-dell/.

83. "Keurig Dr Pepper to Acquire Core®, a Premium Enhanced Beverage Company," Keurig Dr Pepper, September 27, 2018, https://www .jabholco.com/documents/6/press-release-kdp-acquisition-of-core.pdf.

84. A. Berthene, "How Amazon's Whole Foods Acquisition Changed the Grocery Industry," *Digital Commerce 360*, June 21, 2019, https://www.digitalcommerce360.com/2019/06/21/how-amazons-whole-foods-acquisition-changed-the-grocery-industry/.

85. F. A. Hanssen, "Vertical Integration during the Hollywood Studio Era," *Journal of Law & Economics*, August 2010, pp. 519–543.

86. T. Haselton, "Apple Unveils Streaming TV Services," *CNBC*, March 25, 2019, https://www.cnbc.com/2019/03/25/apple-tv-channels-streaming-tv-service-announced.html. Also see "Starbucks' Closely Managed Supply Chain May Be the Key to the Premium Coffee Giant's Success," *Fronetics*, May 10, 2017, https://www.fronetics.com/supply-chain-putting-star-starbucks/

87. M. E. Porter, *Competitive Strategy* (New York: The Free Press, 1980). Also see M. E. Porter, "The Five Competitive Forces That Shape Strategy," *Harvard Business Review*, January 2008, pp. 79–93.

88. M. Lev-Ram, "Meet the Women Leading Netflix into the Streaming Wars," *Fortune*, September 23, 2019, https://fortune.com/longform/women-netflix-streaming-wars/. Also see A. Kasi, "Porter's Five Forces of Netflix," January 30, 2019, https://www.porteranalysis.com/porters-five-forces-of-netflix/.

89. A. Kasi, "Porter's Five Forces of Netflix," January 30, 2019, https:// www.porteranalysis.com/porters-five-forces-of-netflix/. Also see "How These Five Competitive Forces Can Shape Your Strategy," *Brightpod*, November 7, 2017; S. Gibbons, "What the Rise of Netflix's Original Content Can Teach Leaders about Diversity," *Forbes*, May 21, 2019, https://www.forbes.com/sites/serenitygibbons/2019/05/21/what-the-rise-of-netflixs-original-content-can-teach-leaders-about-diversity/#135477157a56.

90. "Netflix Inc, Competitive Position and Analysis," *Medium*, January 7, 2019, https://medium.com/@vik975/netflix-inc-competitive-position-and-analysis-7ea89a4bb356. Also see "How These Five Competitive Forces Can Shape Your Strategy," *Brightpod*, November 7, 2017.

91. M. Honorof, "Best Streaming Video Services 2020," *Tom's Guide*, February 4, 2020, https://www.tomsguide.com/us/best-streaming-video-services,review-2625.html. Also see "How These Five Competitive Forces Can Shape Your Strategy," *Brightpod*, November 7, 2017.

92. A. H. Gorondutse, "Testing the Effect of Business-Level Strategy on Performance of Hotels," *Global Business Review*, 2019, pp. 1141–1154.

93. A. Carr and K. Roache, "Warby Parker Wants to Be the Warby Parker of Contacts," *Bloomberg*, November 19, 2019, https://www .bloomberg.com/news/features/2019-11-19/warby-parker-launches-scout-daily-contact-lenses-at-440-a-year.

94. J. K. Willcox, "With Redbox on Demand, Kiosk Company Gives Streaming a Second Shot," *Consumer Reports*, February 16, 2018, https://www.consumerreports.org/streaming-video-services/with-redbox-on-demand-kiosk-company-gives-streaming-another-shot/.

95. "New Viking Cruise Ship Scheduled to Visit Great Lakes in 2022," *Fox Business*, February 9, 2020, https://www.foxbusiness.com/lifestyle/new-viking-cruise-ship-scheduled-to-visit-great-lakes-in-2022.

96. "About us," Viking Cruises, https://www.vikingcruises.com/about-us/history.html (accessed February 10, 2020). Also see L. Debter, "Viking Saga: The Tale of Tor Hagen and His Voyage from Ousted CEO to Cancer Survivor to Cruise Ship Billionaire," *Forbes*, April 15, 2019, https://www.forbes.com/sites/laurendebter/2019/04/15/meet-the-man-who-started-viking-cruises-in-his-50s-after-being-fired-losing-millions-and-surviving-cancer/#4651013e2652.

97. S. Iamratanakul, "A Conceptual Framework of Implementing Business Strategy for the NPD Process," *Review of Integrative Business & Economics Research*, 2017, pp. 116–123.

98. "Jack Welch," *Business Insider*, https://www.businessinsider.com/author/jack-welch (accessed February 10, 2020).

99. J. Welch, "Five Questions That Make Strategy Real," Jack Welch Management Institute, March 27, 2016, https://jackwelch.strayer.edu/winning/five-questions-make-strategy-real/. Also see A. Swaminathan; "'The Last of the 100-Year Breed': Here's What's Left of GE," *Yahoo Finance*, July 20, 2018, https://finance.yahoo.com/news/last-100-year-breed-heres-whats-left-ge-164237249.html.

100. P. Sawers, "Microsoft and Kroger to Create Data-Driven Connected Grocery Stores," *VB*, January 7, 2019, https://venturebeat.com/2019/01/07/microsoft-and-kroger-to-create-data-driven-connected-grocery-stores/.

101. L. Bossidy and Ram Charan, with C. Burck, *Execution: The Discipline of Getting Things Done* (New York: Crown Business, 2002).

102. C. Praeger and E. Assefa, "The CEO's Strategy Execution Gap... And How to Fix It," *Rhythm Systems*, November 30, 2019, https://www.rhythmsystems.com/blog/the-ceos-strategy-execution-gap.

103. J. Aten, "Boeing's CEO, Dennis Muilenburg, Is Out Over Failure to Contain the 737 Max Crisis," *Inc.*, December 23, 2019, https://www.inc.com/jason-aten/boeings-ceo-dennis-muilenburg-is-out-over-failure-to-contain-737-max-crisis.html.

104. R. Kaplan and D. Norton, "Mastering the Management System," *Harvard Business Review*, January 2008, pp. 66–77.

105. P. Economy, "Indeed Just Announced the 50 Top-Rated Workplaces for 2019 (Is Your Company on the List?)," *Inc.*, July 16, 2019, https://www.inc.com/peter-economy/indeed-just-announced-50-top-rated-workplaces-for-2019-is-your-company-on-list.html. Also see "World's Most Admired Companies," *Fortune*, https://fortune.com/worlds-most-admired-companies/ (accessed February 11, 2020).

106. J. Fechter, "Costco Employee Benefits Review: Are Their Careers Worth It?" *FutureFuel*, August 23, 2019, https://futurefuel.io/employee-benefits/costco-careers/.

107. C. Clifford, "How Costco Uses $5 Rotisserie Chickens and Free Samples to Turn Customers into Fanatics," *CNBC*, May 23, 2019, https://www.cnbc.com/2019/05/22/hooked-how-costco-turns-customers-into-fanatics.html.

108. Costco, "Corporate Profile," https://investor.costco.com/corporate-profile-2 (accessed February 26, 2020). Also see C. Clifford, "How Costco Uses $5 Rotisserie Chickens and Free Samples to Turn Customers into Fanatics," *CNBC*, May 23, 2019, https://www.cnbc.com/2019/05/22/hooked-how-costco-turns-customers-into-fanatics.html.

109. A. Kaul, "Culture vs Strategy: Which to Precede, Which to Align?" *Journal of Strategy and Management*, February 18, 2019, pp. 116–136.

110. Execution is also discussed by C. Montgomery, "Putting Leadership Back into Strategy," *Harvard Business Review*, January 2008, pp. 54–60; J. Lorsch and R. Clark, "Leading from the Boardroom," *Harvard Business Review*, April 2008, pp. 105–111.

111. V. Padmanabhan, "Functional Strategy Implementation—Experimental Study on Agile KANBAN," *SUMEDHA Journal of Management*, Vol. 7, No. 2 (2018).

112. C. A. Hartnell, A. J. Kinicki, L. S. Lambert, M. Fugate, and P. D. Corner, "Do Similarities or Differences between CEO Leadership and Organizational Culture Have a More Positive Effect on Firm Performance? A Test of Competing Predictions," *Journal of Applied Psychology*, 2016, https://doi.org/10.1037/apl0000083.

113. J. Zenger and J. Folkman, "4 Ways to Be More Effective at Execution," *Harvard Business Review*, May 23, 2016, https://hbr.org/2016/05/4-ways-to-be-more-effective-at-execution.

114. J. Zenger and J. Folkman, "4 Ways to Be More Effective at Execution," *Harvard Business Review*, May 23, 2016, https://hbr.org/2016/05/4-ways-to-be-more-effective-at-execution.

115. C. Ong, "5 Key Steps for Successful Strategy Execution," *Envisio*, September 14, 2017, http://www.envisio.com/blog/5-key-steps-for-successful-strategy-execution.

116. E. Barrows, "What Is Strategy Execution?" *American Management Association*, January 24, 2019, https://www.amanet.org/articles/what-is-strategy-execution/.

117. E. Barrows, "What Is Strategy Execution?" *American Management Association*, January 24, 2019, https://www.amanet.org/articles/what-is-strategy-execution/.

118. J. Zenger and J. Folkman, "4 Ways to Be More Effective at Execution," *Harvard Business Review*, May 23, 2016, https://hbr.org/2016/05/4-ways-to-be-more-effective-at-execution.

119. J. Berger, "How to Change Anyone's Mind," *The Wall Street Journal*, February 22–23, 2020, pp. C1, C2.

120. C. J. F. Candido and S. P. Santos, "Implementation Obstacles and Strategy Implementation Failure," *Baltic Journal of Managementi*, 2019, pp. 39–57.

121. B. W. Barry, "A Beginner's Guide to Strategic Planning," *The Futurist*, April 1998, pp. 33–36. Also see B. W. Barry, *Strategic Planning Workbook for Nonprofit Organizations*, revised and updated (St. Paul, MN: Amherst H. Wilder Foundation, 1997).

122. "A Simple Guide to Becoming a Better Business Strategist," *Macquarie*, December 12, 2016, https://www.macquarie.com/au/advisers/expertise/smart-practice/6-ways-you-can-improve-your-strategic-thinking.

123. N. Bowman, "4 Ways to Improve Your Strategic Thinking Skills," *Harvard Business Review*, December 27, 2016, https://hbr.org/2016/12/4-ways-to-improve-your-strategic-thinking-skills.

124. "5 Ways To Improve Your Strategic Thinking Skills Today," *Center for Management & Organization Effectiveness*, https://cmoe.com/blog/improve-strategic-thinking-skills/ (accessed February 11, 2020). Also see J. Sullivan, "6 Ways to Screen Job Candidates for Strategic Thinking," *Harvard Business Review*, December 13, 2016, https://hbr.org/2016/12/6-ways-to-screen-job-candidates-for-strategic-thinking; "How to Master Strategic Thinking Skills in 5 Simple Steps," *Fraser Dove*, February 1, 2019, https://www.fraserdove.com/master-strategic-thinking/.

125. D. Lacy, "Talent Management: Understand Your Employer's Business to Become Strategic Partner," *Dresser & Associates*, 2018, www.dresserassociates.com/knowledge-center/talent-management/Understand-Your-Employers-Business.php#.

126. W. R. Bigler, "A New Vista for Strategic Management: Continuously Aligning the Inside with the Outside," *Management Accounting Quarterly*, 2019, pp. 10–23.

127. D. Lacy, "Talent Management: Understand Your Employer's Business to Become Strategic Partner," *Dresser & Associates*, 2018, www.dresserassociates.com/knowledge-center/talent-management/Understand-Your-Employers-Business.php#.

128. "A Simple Guide to Becoming a Better Business Strategist," *Macquarie*, December 12, 2016, https://www.macquarie.com/au/advisers/expertise/smart-practice/6-ways-you-can-improve-your-strategic-thinking.

129. "LaCroix Sparkling Water Battles to Sizable Market Share in Category Then Owned by One Brand, Perrier, by Becoming the 'Anti-Perrier' Brand," *Meridian Associates Inc.*, http://www.meridianai.com/success_product_lacroix.html (accessed February 12, 2020). Also see A. Halpern, "The Secret History of the LaCroix Label," *Bon Appétit*, January 24, 2017, https://www.bonappetit.com/story/the-secret-history-of-the-lacroix-label.

130. E. Sweeney, "LaCroix's Massive Popularity Is Putting Major Pressure On Big Soda," *The Huffington Post*, July 17, 2018, https://www.huffpost.com/entry/lacroix-pressure-big-soda_n_5b464124e4b022fdcc555053.

131. L. Etter and C. Giammona, "Battle of the Bubbles," *Bloomberg*, August 22, 2019, https://www.bloomberg.com/features/2019-lacroix-sparkling-water-wars/.

132. J. Kosman, "'Sparkling' LaCroix Sales Drive Acquisition Talk," *New York Post*, December 3, 2015, https://nypost.com/2015/12/03/spar-kling-lacroix-sales-drive-acquisition-talk/.

133. D. Kalogeropoulos, "National Beverage Closes Out a Tough Year," *The Motley Fool*, July 10, 2019, https://www.fool.com/invest-ing/2019/07/10/national-beverage-closes-out-a-tough-year.aspx. Also see L. Sun, "Coca-Cola Declares War on National Beverage's La Croix," *The Motley Fool*, November 13, 2019, https://www.fool.com/investing/2019/11/13/coca-cola-declares-war-on-national-beverages-la-cr.aspx.

134. J. Pound, "LaCroix Parent Company's Stock Falls to Multiyear Low Following Lawsuit," *CNBC*, June 18, 2019, https://www.cnbc.com/2019/06/11/lacroix-parent-company-national-beverage-falls-to-multiyear-low-following-lawsuit.html.

135. J. Valinsky, "LaCroix Was the Millennial 'It' Brand. Now It Has Lost Its Way," *CNN*, May 30, 2019, https://www.cnn.com/2019/05/30/business/lacroix-sales/index.html.

136. E. Hapsis, "The Cult of LaCroix: Why Everyone's Gone Crazy over Canned Water," *KQED*, August 2, 2017, https://www.kqed.org/pop/37075/the-cult-of-lacroix-why-everyones-gone-crazy-over-canned-water.

137. E. Holodny, "The Epic Collapse of American Soda Consumption in One Chart," *Business Insider*, March 10, 2016, https://www.businessinsider.com/americans-are-drinking-less-soda-2016-3.

138. E. Hapsis, "The Cult of LaCroix: Why Everyone's Gone Crazy over Canned Water," *KQED*, August 02, 2017, https://www.kqed.org/pop/37075/the-cult-of-lacroix-why-everyones-gone-crazy-over-canned-water.

139. "LaCroix: Once a Favorite among Young People, Sales for the Carbonated Water Are Plummeting," *ABC News*, May 31, 2019, https://www.10news.com/news/national/lacroix-once-a-favorite-among-young-people-sales-for-the-carbonated-water-are-plummeting. Also see E. Hapsis, "The Cult of LaCroix: Why Everyone's Gone Crazy over Canned Water," *KQED*, August 02, 2017, https://www.kqed.org/pop/37075/the-cult-of-lacroix-why-everyones-gone-crazy-over-canned-water.

140. T. Forster, "Big Soda Might Be about to Crush Lacroix," *Eater*, August 22, 2019, https://www.eater.com/2019/8/22/20828068/lacroix-declining-sales-nick-caporella-pepsi-coca-cola-competition.

141. R. Arthur, "Billion Dollar Bubbles: Pepsico Wants to Make Bubly Its Next Billion Dollar Brand," *Beverage Daily*, July 18, 2019, https://www.beveragedaily.com/Article/2019/07/18/PepsiCo-wants-to-make-bubly-its-next-billion-dollar-brand.

142. E. J. Schultz, "Behind Coke's Move to Boost Sparkling Water Sales with New Aha Brand," *AdAge*, November 7, 2019, https://adage.com/article/cmo-strategy/behind-cokes-move-boost-sparkling-water-sales-new-aha-brand/2213846.

143. L. Ramsey, "Coca-Cola Is Coming Out with Its Own Seltzer and Getting Rid of Dasani Sparkling Water," *delish*, November 8, 2019, https://www.delish.com/food-news/a29739521/coca-cola-takes-on-la-croix-with-aha/.

144. G. Morabito, "Coca-Cola Acquires Topo Chico, the Sparkling Water for Cool People," *Eater*, October 2, 2017, https://www.eater.com/2017/10/2/16401848/coca-cola-topo-chico.

145. "Multiple Coke Brands Bubble Up in Fast-Growing Sparkling Water Category," The Coca-Cola Company, May 3, 2019, https://www.coca-colacompany.com/news/coke-brands-bubble-up-in-sparkling-water-category.

146. B. Avery, "When the Bubble's Bursting: Inside LaCroix's Decline," *BevNET*, July 15, 2019, https://www.bevnet.com/news/2019/when-the-bubbles-bursting-inside-lacroixs-decline.

147. B. Avery, "When the Bubble's Bursting: Inside LaCroix's Decline," *BevNet*, July 15, 2019, https://www.bevnet.com/news/2019/when-the-bubbles-bursting-inside-lacroixs-decline.

148. E. J. Schultz, "Behind Coke's Move to Boost Sparkling Water Sales with New Aha Brand," *AdAge*, November 7, 2019, https://adage.com/article/cmo-strategy/behind-cokes-move-boost-sparkling-water-sales-new-aha-brand/2213846.

149. T. Garcia, "LaCroix Sales Sink as Fans Break from the Brand But They Could Come Back This Summer," *MarketWatch*, June 5, 2019, https://www.marketwatch.com/story/lacroix-sales-are-down-now-but-could-pop-during-the-summer-2019-06-04. Also see J. Haden, "This Wild CEO Statement from the Maker of LaCroix Is One of the Most Bizarre We've Seen in a While," *CNBC*, March 8, 2019, https://www.cnbc.com/2019/03/08/lacroix-makers-ceo-blames-poor-performance-on-injustice.html.

150. M. Korn and C. Rexrode, "Banks Pay Big Bucks for Top Billing on College Campuses," *The Wall Street Journal*, January 28, 2018, https://www.wsj.com/articles/banks-pay-big-bucks-for-top-billing-on-college-campuses-1517148001.

151. A. Carrns, "Count Bank Overdraft Fees as a Holiday Expense, Too," *The New York Times*, January 5, 2018, https://www.nytimes.com/2018/01/05/your-money/bank-overdraft-fees.html.

152. R. Snyder, "Universities Collect Big Royalties while Students Pay Higher Banking Fees," *Sparks Tribune*, January 31, 2019, https://sparkstrib.com/2019/01/31/universities-collect-big-royalties-while-students-pay-higher-banking-fees/.

153. M. Korn and C. Rexrode, "Banks Pay Big Bucks for Top Billing on College Campuses," *The Wall Street Journal*, January 28, 2018, https://www.wsj.com/articles/banks-pay-big-bucks-for-top-billing-on-college-campuses-1517148001.

154. "U.S. Bank Student Checking Account," *U.S. Bank*, 2018, https://www.usbank.com/bank-accounts/checking-accounts/student-checking-account.html (accessed February 13, 2020).

155. M. Korn and C. Rexrode, "Banks Pay Big Bucks for Top Billing on College Campuses," *The Wall Street Journal*, January 28, 2018, https://www.wsj.com/articles/banks-pay-big-bucks-for-top-billing-on-college-campuses-1517148001.

156. M. Jarzemsky, "Cuomo Probes Cards' School Ties," *The Wall Street Journal*, September 4, 2010, https://www.wsj.com/articles/SB10001424052748704855104575470040614786402.

157. J. Silver-Greenberg and M.Pilon, "Cards Return to School," *The Wall Street Journal*, May 7, 2011, https://www.wsj.com/articles/SB10001424052748704322804576303652621312770.

LEARNING MODULE 2

1. "Number of Business Establishments Less than 1 Year Old in the United States, March 1994 to March 2019," *Statista*, https://www.statista.com/statistics/235494/new-entrepreneurial-businesses-in-the-us/ (accessed February 26, 2020).

2. "Small Businesses Drive Job Growth in United States; They Account for 1.8 Million Net New Jobs, Latest Data Show," *Small Business Association*, April 24, 2019, https://advocacy.sba.gov/2019/04/24/small-businesses-drive-job-growth-in-united-states-they-account-for-1-8-million-net-new-jobs-latest-data-show/#:~:text=The%202019%20Small%20Business%20Profiles,percent%20of%20the%20private%20workforce.

3. J. Rampton, "40 Inspirational Entrepreneurial Quotes," *Entrepreneur*, January 1, 2020, https://www.entrepreneur.com/slideshow/300234.

4. S. Stahl, "Five Steps to Pivoting into Entrepreneurship," *Forbes*, November 21, 2017, https://www.forbes.com/sites/ashleystahl/2017/11/21/five-steps-to-pivoting-into-entrepreneurship/#7d5f6507545c. Also see M. Murmann, "The Startups Most Likely to Succeed Have Technical Founders Who Quickly Hire Businesspeople," *Harvard Business Review*, November 6, 2017, https://hbr.org/2017/11/the-startups-most-likely-to-succeed-have-technical-founders-who-quickly-hire-businesspeople; B. Egeland, "Should You Hire Family and Friends for Your Small Business?" *Business Know-How*, April 22, 2019, https://www.businessknowhow.com/manage/hire-family.htm.

5. A. Y. Ou, D. A. Waldman, and S. J. Peterson, "Do Humble CEOs Matter? An Examination of CEO Humility and Firm Outcomes," *Journal of Management*, 2018, pp. 1147–1173.

6. H. Zhang, A.Y. Ou, A.S. Tsui, and H. Wang, "CEO Humility, Narcissism and Firm Innovation: A Paradox Perspective on CEO Traits," *The Leadership Quarterly*, 2017, http://dx.doi.org/10.1016/j.leaqua.2017.01.003.

7. S. Kumar, "List of Famous Entrepreneurs You Must Know About," *Startup Talky*, January 18, 2020, https://startuptalky.com/famous-entrepreneur-world/.

8. T. Loudenback and T. N. Rogers, "Elon Musk Made Almost $12 Billion in the Past Week as Tesla's Stock Soars. Here's How the Eccentric CEO Makes and Spends His $45.2 Billion Fortune," *Business Insider,* February 5, 2020, https://www.businessinsider.com/tesla-elon-musk-net-worth-2017-10.

9. T. Locke, "Elon Musk: 'I Really Didn't Want to Be CEO of Tesla'—Here's How He Says It Happened," *CNBC*, January 30, 2020, https://www.cnbc.com/2020/01/30/elon-musk-i-really-didnt-want-to-be-ceo-of-tesla.html.

10. "Elon Musk Biography," *Biography*, December 12, 2019, https://www.biography.com/business-figure/elon-musk.

11. R. K. Jain, "Entrepreneurial Competencies: A Meta-Analysis and Comprehensive Conceptualization for Future Research," *Vision,* 2011, p. 128.

12. Boston BBB, "The Difference between Entrepreneurs and the Self-Employed," *Malden Patch,* September 12, 2013, https://patch.com/massachusetts/malden/the-difference-between-entrepreneurs-and-the-selfemployed_0bb9c4b9.

13. Boston BBB, "The Difference between Entrepreneurs and the Self-Employed," *Malden Patch,* September 12, 2013, https://patch.com/massachusetts/malden/the-difference-between-entrepreneurs-and-the-selfemployed_0bb9c4b9.

14. "The Distinction between Entrepreneurship and Self-Employment," *Kenyaplex,* November 3, 2017, https://www.kenyaplex.com/resources/13730-the-distinction-between-entrepreneurship-and-self-employment.aspx.

15. N. Mavindidze, "Entrepreneurship vs Self-Employment," *The Herald,* March 27, 2018, https://www.herald.co.zw/entrepreneurship-vs-self-employment.

16. C. Davenport, "SpaceX Blames Faulty Valve for Dragon Spacecraft Explosion," *The Washington Post*, July 15, 2019, https://www.washingtonpost.com/technology/2019/07/15/spacex-blames-faulty-valve-dragon-spacecraft-explosion/.

17. N. Mavindidze, "Entrepreneurship vs Self-Employment," *The Herald,* March 27, 2018, https://www.herald.co.zw/entrepreneurship-vs-self-employment.

18. "The Distinction between Entrepreneurship and Self-Employment," *Kenyaplex,* November 3, 2017, https://www.kenyaplex.com/resources/13730-the-distinction-between-entrepreneurship-and-self-employment.aspx.

19. T. Gandhi and R. Raina, "Social Entrepreneurship: The Need, Relevance, Facets and Constraints," *Journal of Global Entrepreneurship Research*, 2018, https://doi.org/10.1186/s40497-018-0094-6.

20. "What Is Social Entrepreneurship?" American University School of International Service, November 14, 2017, https://ironline.american.edu/blog/social-entrepreneurship-degree/.

21. B. Groom, "A Third of Start-Ups Aim for Social Good," *Financial Times,* June 14, 2018, https://www.ft.com/content/d8b6d9fa-4eb8-11e8-ac41-759eee1efb74.

22. M. E. Porter and M. R. Kramer, "Creating Shared Value," *Harvard Business Review*, 2011, https://hbr.org/2011/01/the-big-idea-creating-shared-value.

23. M. Driver, "An Interview with Michael Porter: Social Entrepreneurship and the Transformation of Capitalism," *Academy of Management Learning & Education*, 2012, pp. 421–431.

24. Andriyansah and F. Zahra, "Student Awareness towards Social Entrepreneurship: A Qualitative Study," *International Journal of Civil Engineering and Technology,* 2017, pp. 457–464.

25. R. M. Saat, K. M. K. Bahador, and F. H. Rusly, "Social Entrepreneurial Traits Start-up Intention among Student Leaders," *Academy of Entrepreneurship Journal*, 2019, pp. 1–5.

26. "Meet Low Vision Visionaries Bradford and Bryan Manning from Two Blind Brothers," *Low Vision Specialists of Maryland and Virginia,* https://lowvisionmd.org/low-vision-visionaries-bradford-and-bryan-manning-two-blind-brothers/ (accessed February 22, 2020).

27. A. Thompson, "Inspiring America: Two Blind Brothers Curing Blindness with Clothing ," *NBC News*, January 24, 2017, https://www.nbcnews.com/feature/inspiring-america/inspiring-america-two-blind-brothers-curing-blindness-clothing-n711491. Also see "Meet Low Vision Visionaries Bradford and Bryan Manning from Two Blind Brothers," *Low Vision Specialists of Maryland and Virginia,* https://lowvisionmd.org/low-vision-visionaries-bradford-and-bryan-manning-two-blind-brothers/ (accessed February 22, 2020).

28. A. Arata, "Two Blind Brothers Launch a Viral 'Trust' Campaign, Encouraging Visitors to 'Shop Blind,'" *Vision Monday*, November 30, 2018, https://www.visionmonday.com/scene-and-heard/todays-read/article/two-blind-brothers-launch-a-viral-trust-campaign-encouraging-visitors-to-shop-blind/. Also see R. Laneri, "How Two Blind Brothers Became Clothing Designers," *New York Post*, April 7, 2017, https://nypost.com/2017/04/07/how-two-blind-brothers-became-clothing-designers/.

29. B. Leary, "Bryan Manning of Two Blind Brothers: Before It Was a Business, It Was a Mission," *Small Business Trends*, January 18, 2019, https://smallbiztrends.com/2019/01/mission-driven-two-blind-brothers.html.

30. A. Arata, "Two Blind Brothers Launch a Viral 'Trust' Campaign, Encouraging Visitors to 'Shop Blind,'" *Vision Monday*, November 30, 2018, https://www.visionmonday.com/scene-and-heard/todays-read/article/two-blind-brothers-launch-a-viral-trust-campaign-encouraging-visitors-to-shop-blind/.

31. H. Brandstätter, "Personality Aspects of Entrepreneurship: A Look at Five Meta-Analyses," *Personality and Individual Differences,* August 2011, pp. 222–230. Also see R. K. Jain, "Entrepreneurial Competencies: A Meta-Analysis and Comprehensive Conceptualization for Future Research," *Vision,* 2011, pp. 127–152; and H. Munir, C. Jianfeng, and S. Ramzan, "Personality Traits and Theory of Planned Behavior Comparison of Entrepreneurial Intentions between an Emerging Economy and a Developing Country," *International Journal of Entrepreneurial Behavior & Research*, 2019, pp. 554–580.

32. A. I. Voda, I. Martinez, C. G. Tiganas, L. G. Maha, and D. Filipeanu, "Examining the Effects of Creativity and Willingness to Take Risk on Young Students' Entrepreneurial Intention," *Transformations in Business and Economics*, 2019, pp. 469–488. Also see M. Memon, B. A. Soomro, N. Shah, "Enablers of Entrepreneurial Self-efficacy in a Developing Country," *Education + Training*, 2019, pp. 684–699; H. Munir, C. Jianfeng, and S. Ramzan, "Personality Traits and Theory of Planned Behavior Comparison of Entrepreneurial Intentions between an Emerging Economy and a Developing Country," *International Journal of Entrepreneurial Behavior & Research*, 2019, pp. 554–580; M. Markowska, D. Grichnik, J. Brinckmann, and D. Kapsa, "Strategic Orientations of Nascent Entrepreneurs: Antecedents of Prediction and Risk Orientation," *Small Business Economics*, 2019, pp. 859–878.

33. M. Memon, B. A. Soomro, N. Shah, "Enablers of Entrepreneurial Self-efficacy in a Developing Country," *Education + Training*, 2019, pp. 684–699. Also see Y. Yusuff, M. Mohamad, and N. Y. Ab Wahab, "The Influence of General Self-Efficacy on Women Entrepreneurs," *Academy of Entrepreneurship Journal*, 2019, 1528-2686-25-2-220; F. Sahin, H. Karadag, and B. Tuncer, "Big Five Personality Traits, Entrepreneurial Self-efficacy and Entrepreneurial Intention," *International Journal of Entrepreneurial Behavior & Research,* pp. 1188–1211.

34. S. Nikou, M. Brannback, A. Carsrud, "Entrepreneurial Intentions and Gender: Pathways to Start-up," *International Journal of Gender and Entrepreneurship*, 2019, pp. 348–372.

35. A. Ravenelle, "'We're Not Uber': Control, Autonomy, and Entrepreneurship in the Gig Economy," *Journal of Managerial Psychology*, 2019, pp. 269–285.

36. F. Sahin, H. Karadag, and B. Tuncer, "Big Five Personality Traits, Entrepreneurial Self-efficacy and Entrepreneurial Intention: A Configurational Approach," *International Journal of Entrepreneurial Behavior & Research*, 2019, pp. 1188–1211.

37. M. I. Lopez-Nunez, S. Rubio-Valdehita, M. E. Aparicio-Garcia, and E. M. Diaz-Ramiro, "Are Entrepreneurs Born or Made? The Influence of

Personality," *Personality and Individual Differences*, 2020, https://doi.org/10.1016/j.paid.2019.109699.

38. H. Munir, C. Jianfeng, and S. Ramzan, "Personality Traits and Theory of Planned Behavior Comparison of Entrepreneurial Intentions between an Emerging Economy and a Developing Country," *International Journal of Entrepreneurial Behavior & Research*, 2019, pp. 554–580.

39. R. K. Jain, "Entrepreneurial Competencies: A Meta-Analysis and Comprehensive Conceptualization for Future Research," *Vision*, 2011, p. 134.

40. D. R. Hidayat and A. Wibowo, "Do Big-Five Personality Impact on Youth Entrepreneurial Intention?" *Journal of Entrepreneurship Education*, 2019, 1528-2651-22-3-371.

41. H. Brandstätter, "Personality Aspects of Entrepreneurship: A Look at Five Meta-Analyses," *Personality and Individual Differences,* August 2011, pp. 222–230. Also see R. K. Jain, "Entrepreneurial Competencies: A Meta-Analysis and Comprehensive Conceptualization for Future Research," *Vision,* 2011, pp. 127–152.

42. R. Zitelmann, "Successful Entrepreneurs and Investors Are Nonconformists Who Swim against the Current," *Forbes*, September 23, 2019, https://www.forbes.com/sites/rainerzitelmann/2019/09/23/successful-entrepreneurs-and-investors-are-nonconformists-who-swim-against-the-current/#4bf7e4434fff.

43. T. Butler, "Hiring an Entrepreneurial Leader," *Harvard Business Review,* March–April 2017, pp. 85–93.

44. H. Munir, C. Jianfeng, and S. Ramzan, "Personality Traits and Theory of Planned Behavior Comparison of Entrepreneurial Intentions between an Emerging Economy and a Developing Country," *International Journal of Entrepreneurial Behavior & Research*, 2019, pp. 554–580. Also see S. Nikou, M. Brannback, and A. Carsrud, "Entrepreneurial Intentions and Gender: Pathways to Start-Up," *International Journal of Gender and Entrepreneurship*, 2019, pp. 348–372.

45. H. Munir, C. Jianfeng, and S. Ramzan, "Personality Traits and Theory of Planned Behavior Comparison of Entrepreneurial Intentions between an Emerging Economy and a Developing Country," *International Journal of Entrepreneurial Behavior & Research*, 2019, pp. 554–580. Also see S. Nikou, M. Brannback, and A. Carsrud, "Entrepreneurial Intentions and Gender: Pathways to Start-Up," *International Journal of Gender and Entrepreneurship*, 2019, pp. 348–372; I. Ajzen, "The Theory of Planned Behavior," *Organizational Behavior and Human Decision Processes,* 1991, pp. 179–211

46. A. Merkovich, "15 Entrepreneurship Statistics You Should Know," *Fit Small Business*, March 25, 2019, https://fitsmallbusiness.com/entrepreneurship-statistics/.

47. Definition by Paul Graham, head of business accelerator Y Combinator, cited in N. Robehmed, "What Is a Startup?" *Forbes,* December 16, 2013, www.forbes.com/sites/natalierobehmed/2013/12/16/what-is-a-strartup/print.

48. S. Adams, "Forbes Small Giants: The Best Small Companies of 2019," *Forbes*, April 30, 2019, https://www.forbes.com/sites/susanadams/2019/04/30/forbes-small-giants-the-best-small-companies-of-2019/#22332a3a382c.

49. "30 Companies Worth at Least $1 Billion That Didn't Exist 10 Years Ago," *Business Insider*, December 4, 2019, https://www.businessinsider.in/slideshows/miscellaneous/30-companies-worth-at-least-1-billion-that-didnt-exist-10-years-ago/slidelist/72357295.cms.

50. "Frequently Asked Questions," U.S. Small Business Administration Office of Advocacy, June 2016, http://www.sba.gov/sites/default/files/advocacy/SB-FAQ-2016_WEB.pdf.

51. "Frequently Asked Questions," U.S. Small Business Administration Office of Advocacy, January 2011, http://www.sba.gov/advo.

52. C. Tunstall, "Small Companies with Patents More Likely to Grow Rapidly than Those without," *Pinsent Masons*, June 4, 2019, https://www.pinsentmasons.com/out-law/news/small-companies-with-patents-more-likely-to-grow-rapidly-than-those-without.

53. "2019 Small Business Profile," U.S. Small Business Administration Office of Advocacy, 2019, https://cdn.advocacy.sba.gov/wp-content/uploads/2019/04/23142610/2019-Small-Business-Profiles-States-Territories.pdf. Also see "Frequently Asked Questions," U.S. Small Business Administration, 2019, https://cdn.advocacy.sba.gov/wp-content/uploads/2019/09/24153946/Frequently-Asked-Questions-Small-Business-2019-1.pdf.

54. T. Seth, "Standard of Living: Meaning, Factor and Other Details," *Economics Discussion,* http://www.economicsdiscussion.net/articles/standard-of-living-meaning-factor-and-other-details/1453 (accessed March 29, 2018).

55. "2018/2019 Global Report," *Global Entrepreneurship Monitor*, 2018/2019, https://www.gemconsortium.org/file/open?fileId=50213.

56. "Is 2019 the Year of the Inventor?" *Medium*, June 17, 2019, https://medium.com/dyson-on/is-2019-the-year-of-the-inventor-e7892541b47d.

57. A. Vance, "Polymath Who Dreams Up More Contraptions than Edison," *Bloomberg Businessweek,* October 26–November 1, 2015, pp. 57–61.

58. J. Tennenbaum, "Molten Salt and Traveling Wave Nuclear Reactors," *Asia Times*, February 4, 2020, https://asiatimes.com/2020/02/molten-salt-and-traveling-wave-nuclear-reactors/.

59. "Top 10 Sources of Business Ideas & Opportunities for 2018," *ProfitableVenture,* 2018, https://www.profitableventure.com/sources-of-business-ideas.

60. B. Ansberry, "An Entrepreneur with Autism Finds His Path," *The Wall Street Journal,* November 27, 2017, pp. R1–R2.

61. "Our Blog," *Green Bridge Growers*, https://www.greenbridgegrowers.org/ (accessed February 23, 2020).

62. A. Vance, "Celtic Tigers," *Bloomberg Businessweek,* August 7, 2017, p. 39.

63. "Stripe Expands Global Infrastructure with New Funding Round," *Stripe*, September 19, 2019, https://stripe.com/newsroom/news/stripe-expands-global-infrastructure-with-new-funding.

64. H. Zak, "How to Create Successful Products for Underserved Markets," *Inc.*, February 27, 2019, https://www.inc.com/heidi-zak/how-to-create-successful-products-for-underserved-markets.html. Also see "7 Ways to Discover a Winning Business Idea," *The Balance,* November 25, 2016, https://www.thebalance.com/create-winning-business-ideas-2947249.

65. I. Morris, "Apple Responds to iPhone Slowdown Complaints and Offers Solutions," *Forbes,* December 28, 2017, https://www.forbes.com/sites/ianmorris/2017/12/28/apple-responds-to-iphone-slowdown-complaints-and-offers-solutions/#5da610db79ee.

66. N. Gagliordi, "Apple Will Pay Up to $500 Million in iPhone Throttling Settlement," *ZDNet*, March 2, 2020, https://www.zdnet.com/article/apple-will-pay-up-to-500-million-in-iphone-throttling-settlement/.

67. M. Rosenburg, "Number of McDonald's Restaurants Worldwide," *ThoughtCo.*, February 5, 2020, https://www.thoughtco.com/number-of-mcdonalds-restaurants-worldwide-1435174. Also see "Number of Franchise Establishments in the United States from 2007 to 2020," *Statista*, February 19, 2020, https://www.statista.com/statistics/190313/estimated-number-of-us-franchise-establishments-since-2007/.

68. T. Minieri, "Is Franchising Right for Your Business?" *Forbes*, February 18, 2020, https://www.forbes.com/sites/theyec/2020/02/18/is-franchising-right-for-your-business/#2f742f20685f.

69. J. Wohl, "Subway Increases National Media Reach in Search of a Bigger Brand Voice," *AdAge,* January 10, 2020, https://adage.com/article/cmo-strategy/subway-increases-national-media-reach-search-bigger-brand-voice/2226306.

70. "What Are the Advantages and Disadvantages of Owning a Franchise?" *International Franchise Association*, https://www.franchise.org/faqs/basics/what-are-the-advantages-and-disadvantages (accessed February 23, 2020).

71. J. Wohl, "Subway Increases National Media Reach in Search of a Bigger Brand Voice," *AdAge,* January 10, 2020, https://adage.com/article/cmo-strategy/subway-increases-national-media-reach-search-bigger-brand-voice/2226306. Also see H. Peterson, "Subway Is One of the Cheapest Restaurant Chains to Open—Here's a Breakdown of All the Costs," *Business Insider*, July 11, 2019, https://www.businessinsider.com/what-it-costs-to-open-a-subway-2015-3.

72. "What to Consider before Opening a Franchise," *Wells Fargo,* August 2, 2019, https://wellsfargoworks.com/planning/article/what-to-consider-before-opening-a-franchise. Also see "Franchising FAQs," *McDonald's,* https://www.mcdonalds.com/us/en-us/about-us/franchising/franchising-faq.html (accessed February 24, 2019).

73. S. Robbins, "Why You Must Have a Business Plan," *Entrepreneur,* https://www.entrepreneur.com/article/74194 (accessed March 30, 2018). Also see F. J. Greene and C. Hopp, "Research: Writing a Business Plan Makes Your Startup More Likely to Succeed," *Harvard Business Review,* July 14, 2017, https://hbr.org/2017/07/research-writing-a-business-plan-makes-your-startup-more-likely-to-succeed.

74. S. Robbins, "Why You Must Have a Business Plan," *Entrepreneur,* https://www.entrepreneur.com/article/74194 (accessed February 23, 2020). Also see F. J. Greene and C. Hopp, "Research: Writing a Business Plan Makes Your Startup More Likely to Succeed," *Harvard Business Review,* July 14, 2017, https://hbr.org/2017/07/research-writing-a-business-plan-makes-your-startup-more-likely-to-succeed.

75. F. J. Greene and C. Hopp, "Are Formal Planners More Likely to Achieve New Venture Viability? A Counterfactual Model and Analysis," *Strategic Entrepreneurial Journal,* March 2017, pp. 36–60.

76. S. Ward, "One-Page Business Plan Templates," *The Balance,* April 10, 2017, https://www.thebalance.com/one-page-business-plan-templates-4135972. Also see N. Parsons, "How to Write a One-Page Business Plan," *Bplans,* https://articles.bplans.com/how-to-write-a-one-page-business-plan (accessed March 30, 2018).

77. "Business Plan Length: How Long Should Your Business Plan Be?" *GrowThink,* https://www.growthink.com/businessplan/help-center/ideal-length-your-business-plan (accessed February 23, 2020)

78. P. Hull, "10 Essential Business Plan Components," *Forbes,* February 21, 2013, https://www.forbes.com/sites/patrickhull/2013/02/21/10-essential-business-plan-components. Also see "7 Elements of a Business Plan," *Quickbooks,* 2017, https://quickbooks.intuit.com/r/business-planning/7-elements-business-plan.

79. S. Caramela, "How to Choose the Best Legal Structure for Your *Business," Business News Daily,* January 29, 2018, https://www.businessnewsdaily.com/8163-choose-legal-business-structure.html. Also see "IRS Business Structures," Internal Revenue Service, last updated December 14, 2017, https://www.irs.gov/businesses/small-businesses-self-employed/business-structures.

80. "Sole Proprietorships," *Internal Revenue Service,* last updated March 13, 2018, https://www.irs.gov/businesses/small-businesses-self-employed/sole-proprietorships.

81. "Partnerships," *Internal Revenue Service,* last updated on March 2, 2018, https://www.irs.gov/businesses/small-businesses-self-employed/partnerships.

82. "François Pelen, "POINT VISION," *HEC Paris,* https://www.hec.edu/en/stories/francois-pelen-point-vision (accessed February 23, 2020).

83. S. Caramela, "How to Choose the Best Legal Structure for Your Business," *Business News Daily,* January 29, 2018, https://www.businessnewsdaily.com/8163-choose-legal-business-structure.html.

84. S. Caramela, "How to Choose the Best Legal Structure for Your Business," *Business News Daily,* January 29, 2018, https://www.businessnewsdaily.com/8163-choose-legal-business-structure.html. Also see "Forming a Corporation," *Internal Revenue Service,* last updated December 15, 2017, https://www.irs.gov/businesses/small-businesses-self-employed/forming-a-corporation.

85. "Forming a Corporation," *Internal Revenue Service,* last updated December 15, 2017, https://www.irs.gov/businesses/small-businesses-self-employed/forming-a-corporation.

86. "S Corporations," *Internal Revenue Service,* last updated October 6, 2016, https://www.irs.gov/businesses/small-businesses-self-employed/s-corporations.

87. "2018 Small Business Taxation Survey," *National Small Business Association,* 2018, https://nsba.biz/wp-content/uploads/2018/04/Tax-Survey-2018.pdf.

88. H. R. Johnson, "What Is an LLC (Limited Liability Company)?" *Legal Zoom,* https://www.legalzoom.com/articles/what-is-a-limited-liability-company-llc?kid=0f29ecc7-72c8-4a58-8f23-c2193ac028c&utm_source=google&utm_medium=cpc&utm_term=what_is_an_llc&utm_content=247005141740&utm_campaign=BIZ_|_LLC&gclid=CjwKCAjwwPfVBRBiEiwAdkM0HYjZQSz6F3Q_BaPhdbJeQSC_ftlBJhH6m-prelPmnInJVyOxi1OH5_BoC92sQAvD_BwE (accessed March 30, 2018).

89. "2018 Small Business Taxation Survey," *National Small Business Association,* 2018, https://nsba.biz/wp-content/uploads/2018/04/Tax-Survey-2018.pdf.

90. A. Sweren, "Start-Up Costs: How Much Does It Cost to Start a Small Business?" *Lending Tree,* April 3, 2018, https://www.lendingtree.com/business/small/start-up-costs/. Also see G. Schmid, "17 Statistics Every Business Owner Needs to Be Well Aware of," *Fundera Ledger,* July 19, 2017, https://www.fundera.com/blog/small-business-statistics.

91. A. Andjelic, "42 Small Business Statistics: Everything You Need to Know," *SmallBizGenius,* December 15, 2019, https://www.smallbizgenius.net/by-the-numbers/small-business-statistics/#gref.

92. "2017 Mid-Year Economic Report," *National Small Business Association,* 2017, http://www.nsba.biz/wp-content/uploads/2017/09/Mid-Year-Economic-Report-2017.pdf.

93. "About the SBA," *U.S. Small Business Association,* https://www.sba.gov/about-sba/what-we-do/mission (accessed April 2, 1018).

94. "About the SBA," *U.S. Small Business Association,* https://www.sba.gov/about-sba/what-we-do/history (accessed April 2, 1018).

95. "7 Sources of Start-Up Financing," *bdc,* https://www.bdc.ca/en/articles-tools/start-buy-business/start-business/pages/start-up-financing-sources.aspx (accessed April 2, 1018).

96. "How Venture Capitalists Really Assess a Pitch," *Harvard Business Review,* May–June 2017, https://hbr.org/2017/05/how-venture-capitalists-really-assess-a-pitch.

97. K. Hassan, M. Varadan, and C. Zeisberger, "How the VC Pitch Process Is Failing Female Entrepreneurs," *Harvard Business Review,* January 13, 2020, https://hbr.org/2020/01/how-the-vc-pitch-process-is-failing-female-entrepreneurs.

98. M. Malmstrom, A. Voitkane, J. Johansson, and J. Wincent, "What Do They Think and What Do They Say? Gender Bias, Entrepreneurial Attitude in Writing and Venture Capitalists' Funding Decisions," *Journal of Business Venturing Insights*, 2020, https://doi.org/10.1016/j.jbvi.2019.e00154.

99. M. R. Zisser, S. L. Johnson, M. A. Freeman, and P. Staudenmaier, "The Relationship between Entrepreneurial Intent, Gender and Personality," *Gender in Management: An International Journal*, 2019, pp. 666–684.

100. "7 Sources of Start-Up Financing," *bdc,* https://www.bdc.ca/en/articles-tools/start-buy-business/start-business/pages/start-up-financing-sources.aspx (accessed April 2, 2018).

101. "How Venture Capitalists Really Assess a Pitch," *Harvard Business Review,* May–June 2017, https://hbr.org/2017/05/how-venture-capitalists-really-assess-a-pitch.

102. A. Camp, "Secure Funding from an Angel Investor to Grow Your Business," *finder,* September 18, 2019, https://www.finder.com/business-angel-investors.

103. "What Is Crowd Investing?" *SyndicateRoom,* https://www.syndicateroom.com/crowd-investing (accessed April 2, 2018).

104. "About GoFundMe," *GoFundMe,* https://www.gofundme.com/c/about-us (accessed February 23, 2020).

105. C. Hartnell, A. Kinicki, L. Lambert, M. Fugate, and P. Corner, "Do Similarities or Differences between CEO Leadership and Organizational Culture Have a More Positive Effect on Firm Performance? A Test of Competing Predictions," *Journal of Applied Psychology,* Vol. 101 (2016), pp. 846–861.

106. C. A Hartnell, A. Kinicki, A. Y. Ou, D. Choi, and E. P. Karam, "A Meta-Analytic Test of Organizational Culture's Association with Elements of an Organization's System and Its Relative Predictive Validity on Organizational Outcomes," *Journal of Applied Psychology*, 2019, pp. 832–850. Also see A. Y. Ou, C. Hartnell, A. Kinicki, E. Kram, and D. Choi, "Culture in Context: A Meta-Analysis of the Nomological Network of Organizational Culture," Presentation at Connecting Culture and Context:

Insights from Organizational Culture Theory and Research, 2016 National Academy of Management meeting, Anaheim, California.

107. M.T. Deane, "Top 6 Reasons New Businesses Fail," *Investopedia*, June 25, 2019, https://www.investopedia.com/financial-edge/1010/top-6-reasons-new-businesses-fail.aspx.

108. G. Dautovic, "Examining What Percentage of Small Businesses Fail," *Fortunly*, July 17, 2019, https://fortunly.com/blog/what-percentage-of-small-businesses-fail/. Also see "50 Reasons Why Some Businesses Fail While Others Succeed," *Success Harbor*, https://www.successharbor.com/why-some-businesses-fail-while-others-succeed-02132015/ (accessed February 23, 2020); P. Schaefer, "Why Small Businesses Fail: Top 7 Reasons for Startup Failure," *Business Know-How*, October 28, 2019, https://www.businessknowhow.com/startup/business-failure.htm.

CHAPTER 7

1. M. Schwantes, "5 CEOs Share 5 Leadership Tips for a Successful 2020," *Inc.*, January 21, 2020, https://www.inc.com/marcel-schwantes/5-ceos-share-5-leadership-tips-for-a-successful-2020.html.

2. J. R. Schultz, "Intuition: Make It More than a Roll of the Dice," *Performance Improvement*, 2019, https://doi.org/10.1002/pfi.21881.

3. C. Hook, "5 Ideas for Successful Leadership," *Deloitte*, April 30, 2019, https://www2.deloitte.com/au/en/blog/leadership-blog/2019/ideas-successful-leadership.html.

4. "To Infinity and Beyond: Harnessing the Power of Positive Thinking," *Business*, March 4, 2020, https://www.business.com/articles/the-power-of-positive-thinking-in-business/.

5. P. Hopper and K. Sakuja, "A 4-Step Process to Help Senior Teams Prioritize Decisions," *Harvard Business Review*, March 27, 2017, https://hbr.org/2017/03/a-4-step-process-to-help-senior-teams-prioritize-decisions.

6. J. R. Schultz, "Intuition: Make It More than a Roll of the Dice," *Performance Improvement*, 2019, https://doi.org/10.1002/pfi.21881.

7. J. Kabat-Zinn, "Mindfulness-Based Interventions in Context: Past, Present, and Future," *Clinical Psychology: Science and Practice*, Summer 2003, p. 145.

8. R. Hanson and R. Mendius, *Buddha's Brain* (Oakland, CA: New Harbinger Publications, Inc., 2009), p. 35.

9. L. Liang et al., "The Dimensions of Mindfulness in Regulating Aggressive Behaviors," *Journal of Applied Psychology*, March 2018, pp. 281–299. Also see D. Goleman, *Focus: The Hidden Driver of Excellence* (New York: Harper Collins, 2013).

10. J. Kabat-Zinn, *Wherever You Go There You Are* (New York: Hyperion, 1994), pp. 12–13.

11. C. Small and C. Lew, "Mindfulness, Moral Reasoning and Responsibility: Towards Virtue in Ethical Decision-Making," *Journal of Business Ethics*, 2019, https://doi.org/10.1007/s10551-019-04272-y.

12. S. Shapiro, H. Jazaeiri, and P. R. Goldin, "Mindfulness-Based Stress Reduction Effects on Moral Reasoning and Decision Making," *Journal of Positive Psychology*, 2012, pp. 504–515. Also see N. E. Ruedy and M. Schweitzer, "In the Moment: The Effect of Mindfulness on Ethical Decision Making," *Journal of Business Ethics*, 2010, pp. 73–87.

13. M. Daszko, "There Is a Way to Break the Decision-Making Logjam at the Top," *Silicon Valley Business Journal*, January 6, 2020, https://www.bizjournals.com/sanjose/news/2020/01/06/there-is-a-way-to-break-the-decision-making-logjam.html.

14. "Starbucks Reports Q4 and Full Year Fiscal 2019 Results," Starbucks, October 30, 2019, https://investor.starbucks.com/press-releases/financial-releases/press-release-details/2019/Starbucks-Reports-Q4-and-Full-Year-Fiscal-2019-Results/default.aspx.

15. H. Schultz, quoted in J. H. Ostdick, "Rekindling the Heart & Soul of Starbucks," *Success*, March 7, 2011, www.success.com/article/rekindling-the-heart-soul-of-starbucks.

16. J. Jargon, "Starbucks CEO to Focus on Digital," *The Wall Street Journal*, January 30, 2014, p. B6. Also see B. Gruley and L. Patton, "The Arabica Project," *Bloomberg Businessweek*, February 17–23, 2014, pp. 64–69; B. Horovitz, "Starbucks Serving Alcohol at More Locations," *USA Today*, March 21, 2014, p. 5B; Associated Press, "Boutique Coffee Shops Jolt Chains to Step Up Game," *San Francisco Chronicle*, March 26, 2016, p. D2.

17. B. Horowitz, "Starbucks Climbs to No. 2 in Sales," *Reno Gazette-Journal*, March 21, 2015, p. 4B, reprinted from *USA Today*.

18. K. Stankiewicz, "Starbucks CEO on Coronavirus: We Won't Hesitate to Close More Stores in China if Needed," *CNBC*, January 29, 2020, https://www.cnbc.com/2020/01/29/starbucks-ceo-kevin-johnson-on-coronavirus-and-store-closures-in-china.html. Also see "Coronavirus: Starbucks Closes 2,000 Chinese Branches," *BBC News*, January 20, 2020, https://www.bbc.com/news/business-51276317.

19. M. Flager, "Starbucks Announced Stores in 7 More Cities Will Replace Straws with Sippy Cup Lids by August," *delish*, July 26, 2019, https://www.delish.com/food-news/a22078798/starbucks-getting-rid-of-straws-2020/. Also see T. Koman, "Starbucks Responds to the Backlash from Their Plastic Straw Ban Announcement," *delish*, July 17, 2018, https://www.delish.com/food-news/a22223413/starbucks-responds-to-straw-ban-backlash/.

20. A. Cotler, "Creative Thinking: The Only Business Strategy You Need," *Forbes*, January 31, 2020, https://www.forbes.com/sites/ellevate/2020/01/31/creative-thinking-the-only-business-strategy-you-need/#2ae0b2967d43.

21. N. Malkawi, "How to Improve Decision Making Process through Decision Support Systems & Business Intelligence: Evidence from Jordan University Hospital," *Journal of Economic & Management Perspectives*, 2018, pp. 255–265.

22. J. Weller, A. Ceschi, L. Hirsch, R. Sartori, and A. Costantini, "Accounting for Individual Differences in Decision-Making Competence: Personality and Gender Differences," *Frontiers in Psychology*, 2018, https://doi.org/10.3389/fpsyg.2018.02258.

23. H. A. Simon, *Administrative Behavior*, 3rd ed. (New York: Free Press, 1996); H. A. Simon, "Making Management Decisions: The Role of Intuition and Emotion," *The Academy of Management Executive*, February 1987, pp. 57–63.

24. A. N. Gist-Mackey and A. Guy, "'You Get in a Hole, It's Like Quicksand': A Grounded Theory Analysis of Social Support amid Materially Bounded Decision-Making Processes," *Journal of Applied Communication Research*, 2019, pp. 237–259.

25. C. Lindig-Leon, S. Gottwald, and D. A. Braun, "Analyzing Abstraction and Hierarchical Decision-Making in Absolute Identification by Information-Theoretic Bounded Rationality," *Frontiers in Neuroscience*, 2019, https://doi.org/10.3389/fnins.2019.01230.

26. A. Sproten, C. Diener, C. J. Fiebach, and C. Schwieren, "Decision Making and Age: Factors influencing Decision Making under Uncertainty," *Journal of Behavioral and Experimental Economics*, 2018, pp. 43–54.

27. B. Carlin, L. Jiang, and S. Spiller, "Millennial-Style Learning: Search Intensity, Decision Making, and Information Sharing," *Management Science*, 2018, pp. 3313–3330.

28. K. Curran and D. Gamache, "Simply the Best: Organizational Hubris and Decision-Making Biases," *Academy of Management Proceedings*, 2018, https://doi.org/10.5465/AMBPP.2018.17352abstract.

29. I. Buruma, "Carlos Ghosn Was Too Big Not to Fail in Japan," *The New York Times*, February 5, 2020, https://www.nytimes.com/2020/02/05/opinion/carlos-ghosn-japan.html. Also see A. Hill, "Carlos Ghosn's Latest Quest Is Mission Impossible," *The Business Times*, January 15, 2020, https://www.businesstimes.com.sg/opinion/carlos-ghosns-latest-quest-is-mission-impossible.

30. J. McManus, "Hubris and Unethical Decision Making: The Tragedy of the Uncommon," *Journal of Business Ethics*, 2018, pp. 169–185.

31. F. Gonzalez-Valdes and J. de Dios Ortuzar, "The Stochastic Satisficing Model: A Bounded Rationality Discrete Choice Model," *Journal of Choice Modelling*, 2018, pp. 74–87.

32. S. Di Nuovo, and M. Sinatra, "Do Personality Traits and Self-Regulatory Processes Affect Decision-Making Tendencies?" *Australian Journal of Psychology*, 2018, pp. 284–294.

33. "Hallmark Exec Resigns after Same-Sex PR Fiasco," *blade*, January 22, 2020, https://www.losangelesblade.com/2020/01/22/hallmark-exec-resigns-after-same-sex-pr-fiasco/.

34. L. Alexander, "'It's All Intuition': How Hotelier Sharan Pasricha Built His Global Empire," *Robb Report*, February 23, 2020, https://robbreport.com/travel/hotels/how-hotelier-sharan-pasricha-built-global-empire-2898741/.

35. D. Kahneman and G. Klein, "Conditions for Intuitive Expertise: A Failure to Disagree," *American Psychologist*, September 2009, pp. 515–526.

36. K. Malewska, "The Profile of an Intuitive Decision Maker and the Use of Intuition in Decision-Making Practice," *Management*, 2018, pp. 31–44.

37. C. Julmi, "When Rational Decision-Making Becomes Irrational: A Critical Assessment and Re-Conceptualization of Intuition Effectiveness," *Business Research*, 2019, pp. 291–314. Also see J. Okoli and J. Watt, "Crisis Decision-Making: The Overlap between Intuitive and Analytical Strategies," *Management Decision*, 2018, pp. 1122–1134; H. Asvoll, "Developing a Framework of Reflective, Intuitive Knowing in Innovation Management," *Academy of Strategic Management Journal*, 2017, pp. 1–22; J. R. Schultz, "Intuition: Make It More than a Roll of the Dice," *Performance Improvement*, 2019, https://doi.org/10.1002/pfi.21881.

38. "About Us," https://www.virgin.com/virgingroup/content/about-us (accessed March 24, 2020). Also see "Richard Branson," *Biography*, June 25, 2019, https://www.biography.com/business-figure/richard-branson.

39. R. Branson, "Instinct in a World of Analytics," *Virgin*, November 27, 2019, https://www.virgin.com/richard-branson/instinct-world-analytics.

40. M. Potancok, "Role of Data and Intuition in Decision Making Processes," *Journal of Systems Integration*, 2019, pp. 31–3.

41. "Richard Branson: Billionaire Entrepreneur & Visionary," *Talkroute*, https://talkroute.com/richard-branson-billionaire-entrepreneur-visionary/ (accessed February 29, 2020).

42. R. Branson, "It's Okay to Trust Your Instincts, But Put People First," *Khaleej Times*, December 22, 2019, https://www.khaleejtimes.com/editorials-columns/its-okay-to-trust-your-instincts-but-put-people-first.

43. S. Lewin, "'Crazy Things Can Come True': Elon Musk Reacts to Falcon Heavy Launch Success," *Space.com*, February 7, 2018, https://www.space.com/39618-elon-musk-falcon-heavy-spacex-reaction.html.

44. R. Umoh, "Steve Jobs and Albert Einstein Both Attributed Their Extraordinary Success to This Personality Trait," *CNBC*, June 29, 2017, https://www.cnbc.com/2017/06/29/steve-jobs-and-albert-einstein-both-attributed-their-extraordinary-success-to-this-personality-trait.html.

45. R. Umoh, "Steve Jobs and Albert Einstein Both Attributed Their Extraordinary Success to This Personality Trait," *CNBC*, June 29, 2017, https://www.cnbc.com/2017/06/29/steve-jobs-and-albert-einstein-both-attributed-their-extraordinary-success-to-this-personality-trait.html.

46. R. Umoh, "Steve Jobs and Albert Einstein Both Attributed Their Extraordinary Success to This Personality Trait," *CNBC*, June 29, 2017, https://www.cnbc.com/2017/06/29/steve-jobs-and-albert-einstein-both-attributed-their-extraordinary-success-to-this-personality-trait.html.

47. E. Dane and M. G. Pratt, "Exploring Intuition and Its Role in Managerial Decision Making," *Academy of Management Review*, January 2007, pp. 33–54.

48. I. Gallo, S. Sood, T. C. Mann, and T. Giolovich, "The Heart and the Head: On Choosing Experiences Intuitively and Possessions Deliberately," *Journal of Behavioral Decision Making*, July 2017, pp. 754–768.

49. C. Julmi, "When Rational Decision-Making Becomes Irrational: A Critical Assessment and Re-Conceptualization of Intuition Effectiveness," *Business Research*, 2019, pp. 291–314. Also see J. Okoli and J. Watt, "Crisis Decision-Making: The Overlap between Intuitive and Analytical Strategies," *Management Decision*, 2018, pp. 1122–1134

50. L. B. Orlandi and P. Pierce, "Analysis or Intuition? Reframing the Decision-Making Styles Debate in Technological Settings," *Management Decision*, 2020, pp. 129–145.

51. These tips are based on A. Likierman, "The Elements of Good Judgment," *Harvard Business Review*, 2020, https://hbr.org/2020/01/the-elements-of-good-judgment.

52. J. McManus, "Emotions and Ethical Decision Making at Work: Organizational Norms, Emotional Dogs, and the Rational Tales They Tell Themselves and Others," *Journal of Business Ethics*, 2019, https://doi.org/10.1007/s10551-019-04286-6.

53. D. M. Rousseau, "Making Evidence-Based Organizational Decisions in an Uncertain World," *Organizational Dynamics*, 2018, pp. 135–146.

54. B. Allyn, "Top Reason for CEO Departures among Largest Companies Is Now Misconduct, Study Finds," *NPR*, May 20, 2019, https://www.npr.org/2019/05/20/725108825/top-reason-for-ceo-departures-among-largest-companies-is-now-misconduct-study-fi.

55. K. Rivera and P. Karlsson, "CEOs Are Getting Fired for Ethical Lapses More than They Used To," *Harvard Business Review*, June 6, 2017, https://hbr.org/2017/06/ceos-are-getting-fired-for-ethical-lapses-more-than-they-used-to.

56. M. J. Quade, R. L. Greenbaum, and O. V. Petrenko, "'I Don't Want to be Near You, Unless . . . ': The Interactive Effect of Unethical Behavior and Performance onto Relationship Conflict and Workplace Ostracism," *Personnel Psychology*, 2017, pp. 675–709.

57. J. Weber, "Understanding the Millennials' Integrated Ethical Decision-Making Process: Assessing the Relationship between Personal Values and Cognitive Moral Reasoning," *Business and Society*, 2019, pp. 1671–1706.

58. M. J. Lupoli, L. Jampol, and C. Oveis, "Lying Because We Care: Compassion Increases Prosocial Lying," *Journal of Experimental Psychology*, 2017, pp. 1026–1042. Also see Y. Liu, S. Zhao, R. Li, L. Zhou, and F. Tian, "The Relationship between Organizational Identification and Internal Whistle-Blowing: The Joint Moderating Effects of Perceived Ethical Climate and Proactive Personality," *Review of Managerial Science*, January 2018, pp. 113–134.

59. J. McManus, "Hubris and Unethical Decision Making: The Tragedy of the Uncommon," *Journal of Business Ethics*, 2018, pp. 169–185.

60. K. Alltucker, "A 'One-Off Opportunity': Drug Company Hikes Price of Blood Pressure Drugs after Competitors' Drugs Recalled," *USA Today*, January 30, 2019, https://www.usatoday.com/story/news/health/2019/01/30/blood-pressure-medicine-recall-alembic-teva-prinston-pharmaceuticals-price-hikes/2709633002/. Also see B. Mole, "879% Drug Price Hike Is One of 3,400 in 2019 So Far; Rate of Hikes Increasing," *ars Technica*, July 2, 2019, https://arstechnica.com/science/2019/07/big-pharma-raising-drug-prices-even-more-in-2019-3400-hikes-as-high-as-879/.

61. D. Yaffe-Bellany, " McDonald's C.E.O. Fired over a Relationship That's Becoming Taboo," *The New York Times*, November 4, 2019, https://www.nytimes.com/2019/11/04/business/mcdonalds-ceo-fired.html. Also see R. McHugh, "No One, Not Even Harvey Weinstein, Is Above the Law," *Vanity Fair*, February 25, 2020, https://www.vanityfair.com/news/2020/02/weinsteins-victims-speak-about-what-theyve-won-and-the-road-ahead.

62. M. Astor, "Florida Legislator's Aide Is Fired after He Calls Parkland Students 'Actors,'" *The New York Times*, February 20, 2018, https://www.nytimes.com/2018/02/20/us/florida-shooting-benjamin-kelly-actors.html.

63. C. Clifford, "These 14 Billionaires Just Promised to Give Away More Than Half of Their Money Like Bill Gates and Warren Buffett," *CNBC*, May 31, 2017, https://www.cnbc.com/2017/05/31/14-billionaires-signed-bill-gates-and-warren-buffetts-giving-pledge.html.

64. "A Commitment to Philanthropy," *The Giving Pledge*, https://givingpledge.org/ (accessed March 2, 2020).

65. N. Epley and A. Kumar, "How to Design an Ethical Organization," *Harvard Business Review*, 2019, https://hbr.org/2019/05/how-to-design-an-ethical-organization.

66. C. Small and C. Lew, "Mindfulness, Moral Reasoning and Responsibility: Towards Virtue in Ethical Decision-Making," *Journal of Business Ethics*, 2019, https://doi.org/10.1007/s10551-019-04272-y. Also see T. A. Paterson and L. Huang; "Am I Expected to Be Ethical? A Role-Definition Perspective of Ethical Leadership and Unethical Behavior," *Journal of Management*, 2019, pp. 2837–2860.

67. B. Weinstein, "What's The Difference between Compliance and Ethics?" *Forbes*, May 9, 2019, https://www.forbes.com/sites/bruceweinstein/2019/05/09/whats-the-difference-between-compliance-and-ethics/#4786b7b75249. Also see P. Lotich, "7 Ways to Demonstrate Ethics and Integrity in Your Business," *Thriving Small Business*, April 16, 2019, https://thethrivingsmallbusiness.com/examples-of-business-ethics-and-integrity/.

68. C. E. Bagley, "The Ethical Leader's Decision Tree," *Harvard Business Review*, February 2003, pp. 18–19.

69. L. Constantin, "Decision Trees," *Knowledge Horizons–Economics*, 2018, pp. 39–45.

70. C. E. Bagley, "The Ethical Leader's Decision Tree," *Harvard Business Review,* February 2003, p. 19.

71. C. E. Bagley, "The Ethical Leader's Decision Tree," *Harvard Business Review,* February 2003, p. 19.

72. The website YourMorals.org studies morality and values, offering questionnaires for readers to fill out. Some of the results are described in J. Haidt, *The Righteous Mind: Why Good People Are Divided by Politics and Religion* (New York: Random House, 2012).

73. N. Wetsman, "Coronavirus Cancellations Show Evidence-Based Decisions Are Rare during Epidemics," *The Verge*, February 14, 2020, https://www.theverge.com/2020/2/14/21136819/coronavirus-mwc-meetings-canceling-face-masks-evidence-risk.

74. K. D. A. Carillo, N. Galy, C. Guthrie, and A. Vanhems, "How to Turn Managers into Data-Driven Decision Makers: Measuring Attitudes towards Business Analytics," *Business Process Management Journal*, 2019, pp. 553–578. Also see A. M. Seoane Pardo, "Computational Thinking between Philosophy and STEM—Programming Decision Making Applied to the Behavior of 'Moral Machines' in Ethical Values Classroom," *Revista Iberoamericana de Tecnologias del Aprendizaje*, 2018, pp. 20–29.

75. H. Chang, C. Wang, and S. Hawamdeh, "Emerging Trends in Data Analytics and Knowledge Management Job Market: Extending KSA Framework," *Journal of Knowledge Management*, 2018, pp. 664–686. Also see A. Merendino, S. Dibb, M. Meadows, L. Quinn, D. Wilson, L. Simkin, and A. Canhoto, "Big Data, Big Decisions: The Impact of Big Data on Board Level Decision-Making," *Journal of Business Research*, 2018, pp. 67–78.

76. J. Pfeffer and R. I. Sutton, "Profiting from Evidence-Based Management," *Strategy & Leadership* Vol. 34, No. 2 (2006), pp. 35–42.

77. D. M. Rousseau, "Making Evidence-Based Organizational Decisions in an Uncertain World," *Organizational Dynamics*, 2018, pp. 135–146.

78. J. Pfeffer, *Leadership BS: Fixing Workplaces and Careers One Truth at a Time* (New York: HarperCollins, 2015).

79. J. Pfeffer and R. I. Sutton, "Profiting from Evidence-Based Management," *Strategy & Leadership* Vol. 34, No. 2 (2006), pp. 35–42.

80. "The Transformation 20: The Top Global Companies Leading Strategic Transformations," *Innosight*, September 2019, https://www.innosight.com/insight/the-transformation-20/.

81. S. Durcevic, "8 Big Data Examples Showing the Great Value of Smart Analytics in Real Life at Restaurants, Bars and Casinos," *datapine*, October 2, 2018, https://www.datapine.com/blog/big-data-examples-in-real-life/. Also see A. Datta, "Casinos Bet Large with Big Data," *aviana*, September 2, 2018, http://avianaglobal.com/casinos-bet-large-with-big-data/.

82. J. Pfeffer and R. I. Sutton, "Profiting from Evidence-Based Management," *Strategy & Leadership* Vol. 34, No. 2 (2006), pp. 35–42.

83. T. Acitelli, "The New Mall Tenant Is Your Office," *The New York Times*, April 30, 2019, https://www.nytimes.com/2019/04/30/business/the-new-mall-tenant-is-your-office.html. Also see "Data & Research," *Federal Aviation Administration*, https://www.faa.gov/data_research/ (accessed March 4, 2020).

84. J. Pfeffer and R. I. Sutton, "Profiting from Evidence-Based Management," *Strategy & Leadership* Vol. 34, No. 2 (2006), pp. 66–67.

85. "Data Analytics," *TechTarget*, https://searchdatamanagement.techtarget.com/definition/data-analytics (accessed March 19, 2020).

86. "Company Profile," https://www.netflixinvestor.com/ir-overview/profile/default.aspx (accessed March 24, 2020). Also see M. Dixon, "How Netflix Used Big Data and Analytics to Generate Billions," *Selerity*, April 5, 2019, https://seleritysas.com/blog/2019/04/05/how-netflix-used-big-data-and-analytics-to-generate-billions/.

87. "Data Mining in Healthcare," *USF Health*, https://www.usfhealthonline.com/resources/key-concepts/data-mining-in-healthcare/ (accessed March 4, 2020).

88. "$5.2Bn Sports Analytics Market—Global Forecast to 2024," *PR Newswire,* January 22, 2020, https://www.prnewswire.com/news-releases/5-2bn-sports-analytics-market---global-forecast-to-2024--300991148.html. Also see A. Ricky, "How Data Analysis in Sports Is Changing the Game," *Forbes*, March 4, 2020, https://www.forbes.com/sites/forbestechcouncil/2019/01/31/how-data-analysis-in-sports-is-changing-the-game/#42823c573f7b.

89. M. Lewis, *Moneyball: The Art of Winning an Unfair Game* (New York: W.W. Norton, 2004). For comment on the Oakland A's and *Moneyball*, see J. Manuel, "Majoring in Moneyball," *Baseball America Features*, December 23, 2003, www.baseballamerica.com/today/features/031223collegemoneyball.html.

90. M. Lockard, "How a Five-Person Analytics Department Keeps the A's on the Cutting Edge of Baseball's Numbers Game," *The Athletic*, September 22, 2019, https://theathletic.com/1229678/2019/09/22/how-a-five-person-analytics-department-keeps-the-as-on-the-cutting-edge-of-baseballs-numbers-game/. Also see D. Barron, "Houston's Sports Ties with NASA Go beyond Astros," *Houston Chronicle*, June 20, 2019, https://www.houstonchronicle.com/local/space/mission-moon/article/Houston-s-sports-ties-with-NASA-go-beyond-Astros-13998872.php.

91. B. Cohen, J. Diamond, and A. Beaton, "The Decade When Numbers Broke Sports," *The Wall Street Journal,* December 19, 2019, https://www.wsj.com/articles/2010s-decade-when-numbers-broke-sports-11576710216. Also see B. Cohen, "Remaking Basketball the Warriors' Way," *The Wall Street Journal,* April 7, 2016, pp. A1, A12; M. Johnson, "Now NBA Defenses Got Turned Inside Out," *The Wall Street Journal,* March 2, 2015, p. B8.

92. Joe Lacob, quoted in Schoenfeld, "Team Building."

93. "Warriors Secure 5th Consecutive NBA Finals Appearance," National Basketball Association, May 21, 2019, https://www.nba.com/article/2019/05/21/warriors-five-consecutive-finals-appearances.

94. S. Fortier, "The NFL's Analytics Movement Has Finally Reached the Sport's Mainstream," *The Washington Post*, January 16, 2020. Also see "The Atlanta Falcons Sleep Performance Program, FusionHealth," *YouTube.com*, https://www.youtube.com/watch?v=SHDEkZT0x2g (accessed March 4, 2020).

95. "Napoleon: War Is Ninety Percent Information: So All War Is Cyber War," *CTO Vision*, https://ctovision.com/quotes/war-is-ninety-percent-information-so-all-war-is-cyber-war/#:~:text=Napoleon%20was%20right%2C%20of%20course,all%20war%20is%20cyber%20war (accessed March 5, 2020).

96. "Volume of Data/Information Created Worldwide from 2010 to 2025," *Statista*, https://www.statista.com/statistics/871513/worldwide-data-created/ (accessed March 5, 2020). Also see A. Patrizio, "IDC: Expect 175 Zettabytes of Data Worldwide by 2025," *Network World*, December 3, 2018, networkworld.com/article/3325397/idc-expect-175-zettabytes-of-data-worldwide-by-2025.html.

97. "The Zettabyte Challenge," *Buckenhofer*, January 11, 2020, https://www.buckenhofer.com/2020/01/the-zettabyte-challenge/.17/where-is-the-world-supposed-to-put-all-of-its-data/#33e2a986112c (accessed May 13, 2016).

98. A. Brust, "Big Data: Defining Its Definition," *ZDNet*, March 1, 2012, www.zdnet.com/article/big-data-defining-its-definition.

99. S. Berinato, "Data Science & the Art of Persuasion," *Harvard Business Review*, January–February 2019, pp. 126–137.

100. McKinsey Global Institute report, May 2011, quoted in J. Temple, "Big Data Can Lead to Big Breakthroughs in Research," *San Francisco Chronicle,* December 9, 2011, www.sfgate.com/cgi-bin/article.cgi?f=/c/a/2011/12/08/BUDC1M9I8A.DTL (accessed June 14, 2014).

101. "Big Data Executive Survey 2018," *New Vantage Partners*, 2018, http://newvantage.com/wp-content/uploads/2018/01/Big-Data-Executive-Survey-2018-Findings.pdf.

102. T. Niebel, F. Rasel, and S. Viete, "BIG data–BIG gains? Understanding the LInk between Big Data Analytics and Innovation," *Economics of Innovation and New Technology*, 2019, pp. 296–316. Also see A. S. Aydiner, E. Tatoglu, E. Bayraktar, S. Zaim, and D. Delen, "Business Analytics and Firm Performance: The Mediating Role of Business Process Performance," *Journal of Business Research*, 2019, pp. 228–237; C. Fernandez-Marquez and F. Vazquez, "How Information and Communication Technology Affects Decision-Making on Innovation Diffusion: An Agent-Based Modelling Approach," *Intelligent Systems in Accounting Finance & Management*, 2018, https://doi.org/10.1002/isaf.1430.

103. "Coca-Cola Freestyle Unveils Next-Gen Fountain Dispenser, New Operating System and More," Coca-Cola Company, May 18, 2018, https://www.coca-colacompany.com/news/freestyle-unveils-new-dispenser-and-more#:~:text=More%20than%2050%2C000%20Coca%2DCola,a%20handful%20of%20other%20countries.

104. S. Chohan, "How Coca Cola Collects Consumer Insights with Creative Campaigns," *linkfluence*, https://www.linkfluence.com/blog/how-coca-cola-collects-consumer-insights-with-creative-campaigns (accessed March 19, 2020).

105. S. Berinato, "Data Science & the Art of Persuasion," *Harvard Business Review*, January–February 2019, pp. 126–137.

106. B. Marr, "The Top 10 Technology Trends in Retail: How Tech Will Transform Shopping in 2020," *Forbes*, November 25, 2019, https://www.forbes.com/sites/bernardmarr/2019/11/25/the-top-10-technology-trends-in-retail-how-tech-will-transform-shopping-in-2020/#185ca6484e03.

107. M. Wilson, "Infiniti Research: Four Hot Retail Trends," *CSA*, February 26, 2018, https://www.chainstoreage.com/store-spaces/infiniti-research-four-hot-retail-trends/.

108. C. Cutter, "Holding the Company Together," *The Wall Street Journal*, July 19, 2019, https://www.wsj.com/articles/the-secret-to-finding-the-quiet-employees-holding-your-company-together-11563528611.

109. S. Rickerd, "How Salesforce, Google, and Credit Suisse Apply Predictive Analytics to Hiring," *Up Work*, January 10, 2018, https://www.upwork.com/hiring/enterprise/salesforce-google-credit-suisse-apply-predictive-analytics-hiring/.

110. D. White, "Top 3 Examples of Predictive Analytics in HR," *Tech Funnel,* June 5, 2019, https://www.techfunnel.com/hr-tech/top-3-examples-of-predictive-analytics-in-hr/.

111. J. Smith, "Unilever Uses Virtual Factories to Tune Up Its Supply Chain," *The Wall Street Journal*, July 15, 2019, https://www.wsj.com/articles/unilever-uses-virtual-factories-to-tune-up-its-supply-chain-11563206402.

112. L. Hedges, "What Is Big Data in Healthcare and How Is It Already Being Used?" *Software Advice*, October 25, 2019, https://www.softwareadvice.com/resources/what-is-big-data-in-healthcare-and-whos-already-doing-it/.

113. S. Dash, S.K. Shakyawar, M. Sharma, and S. Kaushik, "Big Data in Healthcare: Management, Analysis and Future Prospects," *Journal of Big Data*, 2019, https://doi.org/10.1186/s40537-019-0217-0.

114. A. Bendix, "Dallas Is Saving $30 Million by Cutting Down on the Number of Mentally Ill People in Prison," *Business Insider*, August 29, 2018, https://www.businessinsider.com/mental-illness-in-prison-reduced-by-harrislogic-predictive-analytics-2018-8.

115. K. D. A. Carillo, N. Galy, C. Guthrie, and A. Vanhems, "How to Turn Managers into Data-Driven Decision Makers: Measuring Attitudes towards Business Analytics," *Business Process Management Journal*, 2019, pp. 553–578.

116. H. Chang, C. Wang, and S. Hawamdeh, "Emerging Trends in Data Analytics and Knowledge Management Job Market: Extending KSA Framework," *Journal of Knowledge Management*, 2018, pp. 664–686. Also see S. Berinato, "Data Science & the Art of Persuasion," *Harvard Business Review*, January–February 2019, pp. 126–137.

117. H. Chang, C. Wang, and S. Hawamdeh, "Emerging Trends in Data Analytics and Knowledge Management Job Market: Extending KSA Framework," *Journal of Knowledge Management*, 2018, pp. 664–686. Also see A. Merendino, S. Dibb, M. Meadows, L. Quinn, D. Wilson, L. Simkin, and A. Canhoto, "Big Data, Big Decisions: The Impact of Big Data on Board Level Decision Making, *Journal of Business Research*, 2018, pp. 67–78.

118. "Corporate Information," BBVA, https://www.bbva.com/en/corporate-information/#history-of-bbva (accessed March 22, 2020).

119. C. Semple, "BBVA Case Study Shows the Way in Data Science," BBVA, September 3, 2018, https://www.bbva.com/en/bbva-case-study-shows-the-way-in-data-science/.

120. "About UN Global Pulse," United Nations, https://www.unglobalpulse.org/about/ (accessed March 22, 2020). Also see C. Alvarez, "Big Data Contributes to the Sustainable Development Goals," BBVA, April 15, 2019, https://www.bbva.com/en/big-data-contributes-to-the-sustainable-development-goals/.

121. C. Semple, "BBVA Case Study Shows the Way in Data Science," BBVA, September 3, 2018, https://www.bbva.com/en/bbva-case-study-shows-the-way-in-data-science/.

122. "Measuring People's Economic Resilience to Natural Disasters," BBVA, https://www.bbvadata.com/odile/ (accessed March 22, 2020). Also see "Shaping Europe's Digital Future," European Commission, March 3, 2020, https://ec.europa.eu/digital-single-market/en/news/good-practices-b2g-data-sharing-bbva-and-un-global-pulse-measure-economic-resilience-disasters.

123. "BBVA, One of the Top Five European Banks for Sustainable Finance," BBVA, January 16, 2020, https://www.bbva.com/en/bbva-one-of-the-top-five-european-banks-for-sustainable-finance/.

124. N. De Marco, "An Introduction to Autonomous Devices," *Forbes*, August 16, 2019, https://www.forbes.com/sites/forbestechcouncil/2019/08/16/an-introduction-to-autonomous-devices/#7ca774bc6875.

125. B. J. Copeland, "Artificial intelligence," *Britannica*, March 5, 2020, https://www.britannica.com/technology/artificial-intelligence.

126. S. Huang, "Understanding AlphaGo: How AI Thinks and Learns (Fundamentals)," *Medium*, March 15, 2019, https://towardsdatascience.com/understanding-alphago-how-ai-think-and-learn-1-2-da07d3ec5278.

127. S. Huang, "Understanding AlphaGo: How AI Thinks and Learns (Fundamentals)," *Medium*, March 15, 2019, https://towardsdatascience.com/understanding-alphago-how-ai-think-and-learn-1-2-da07d3ec5278.

128. Y. Duan, J. S. Edwards, and Y. K. Dwivedi, "Artificial Intelligence for Decision Making in the Era of Big Data—Evolution, Challenges and Research Agenda," *International Journal of Information Management*, 2019, pp. 63–71.

129. J. Grill-Goodman, "How The Home Depot Is Employing Prescriptive Analytics," *RIS*, August 9, 2019, https://risnews.com/ris-exclusive-how-home-depot-employing-prescriptive-analytics. Also see "5 Technologies Changing How We Shop," *The Home Deposit*, August 20, 2018, https://corporate.homedepot.com/newsroom/5-technologies-changing-how-we-shop; T. Davenport and R. Ronanki, "Artificial Intelligence for the Real World," *Harvard Business Review*, 2018, pp. 108–117.

130. J. Edwards, "What Is Predictive Analytics? Transforming Data into Future Insights," *CIO*, August 16, 2019, https://www.cio.com/article/3273114/what-is-predictive-analytics-transforming-data-into-future-insights.html#:~:text=Predictive%20analytics%20is%20a%20category,a%20significant%20degree%20of%20precision.

131. B. Van Calster, L. Wynants, D. Timmerman, E. W. Steyerberg, and G. S. Collins, "Predictive Analytics in Health Care: How Can We Know It Works?" *Journal of the American Medical Informatics Association*, 2019, pp. 1651–1654.

132. S. Kumar, "The Differences between Machine Learning and Predictive Analytics," *D!gitalist*, March 15, 2018, https://www.digitalistmag.com/digital-economy/2018/03/15/differences-between-machine-learning-predictive-analytics-05977121.

133. R. Williams, "Forrester: Home Depot, Sephora Top Retail Mobile App Experiences," *Mobile Marketer*, March 8, 2019, https://www.mobilemarketer.com/news/forrester-home-depot-sephora-top-retail-mobile-app-experiences/550040/.

134. J. Sprovieri, "Collaborative Robots Help Finish Cars at Ford Assembly Plant in Germany," *Assembly Info Center*, November 20, 2019, https://www.assemblymag.com/articles/95317-collaborative-robots-help-finish-cars-at-ford-assembly-plant-in-germany. Also see "How to Make Your Resume Algorithm Ready," University of Maryland, May 23, 2019, https://www.rhsmith.umd.edu/faculty-research/smithbraintrust/insights/will-robots-your-resume; "Fraud Defenses," Wells Fargo, https://www.wellsfargo.com/com/fraud/fraud-defenses/#:~:text=Fraud%20detection&text=Wells%20Fargo%20employs%20multiple%20methods,on%20or%20at%20transaction%20submission (accessed March 7, 2020); A. Phaneuf, "Use of AI in Healthcare & Medicine Is Booming – Here's How the Market Is Benefiting from AI in 2020 and Beyond," *Business Insider*, July 31, 2019, https://www.businessinsider

.com/artificial-intelligence-healthcare; "What's a Robo-Advisor?" Morgan Stanley, January 16, 2019, https://www.morganstanley.com/articles/whats-a-robo-advisor; E. Siu, "9 Innovative Chatbot Examples from Top Brands," *Impact*, January 8, 2020, https://www.impactbnd.com/blog/marketing-chatbot-examples.

135. R. Tracy, "Tech Firms Seek to Head Off Bans on Facial Recognition," *The Wall Street Journal*, March 8, 2020, https://www.wsj.com/articles/tech-firms-seek-to-head-off-bans-on-facial-recognition-11583498034.

136. T. Davenport and R. Ronanki, "Artificial Intelligence for the Real World," *Harvard Business Review*, 2018, pp. 108–117. Also see J. Loucks, T. Davenport, and D. Schatsky, "State of AI in the Enterprise," 2nd Edition, *Deloitte Insights*, October 22, 2018, https://www2.deloitte.com/us/en/insights/focus/cognitive-technologies/state-of-ai-and-intelligent-automation-in-business-survey.html.

137. Y. R. Shrestha, "Organizational Decision-Making Structures in the Age of Artificial Intelligence," *California Management Review*, 2019, pp. 66–83.

138. A. Schroer, "AI and the Bottom Line," *Built In*, February 24, 2020, https://builtin.com/artificial-intelligence/ai-finance-banking-applications-companies.

139. J. Ross, "The Fundamental Flaw in AI Implementation," *MIT Sloan Management Review*, 2018, https://sloanreview.mit.edu/article/the-fundamental-flaw-in-ai-implementation/.

140. See J. Loucks, T. Davenport, and D. Schatsky, "State of AI in the Enterprise," 2nd Edition, *Deloitte Insights,* October 22, 2018, https://www2.deloitte.com/us/en/insights/focus/cognitive-technologies/state-of-ai-and-intelligent-automation-in-business-survey.html. Also see M. Beane, "Learning to Work with Intelligent Machines," *Harvard Business Review*, 2019, pp. 140–148.

141. "AI Pricing: How Much Does Artificial Intelligence Cost?" *WebFX*, https://www.webfx.com/page-speed-optimization-services.html (accessed March 8, 2020).

142. A. S. Rutschman, "AI Gave Stephen Hawking a Voice—and He Used It to Warn Us against AI," *Quartz*, March 16, 2018, https://qz.com/1231092/ai-gave-stephen-hawking-a-voice-and-he-used-it-to-warn-us-against-ai/. Also see S. Martin, "AI Warning: Machines Will Replace Humans at the Top—and Wipe Us Out If We Dare Resist," *Express,* September, 18, 2019.

143. C. Metz, "Good News: A.I. Is Getting Cheaper. That's also Bad News," *The New York Times,* February 20, 2018, https://www.nytimes.com/2018/02/20/technology/artificial-intelligence-risks.html.

144. C. Clifford, "Top A.I. Experts Warn of a 'Black Mirror'-esque Future with Swarms of Micro-Drones and Autonomous Weapons," *CNBC,* February 21, 2018, https://www.cnbc.com/2018/02/21/openai-oxford-and-cambridge-ai-experts-warn-of-autonomous-weapons.html.

145. A. Fitch, "Military Looks to AI to Improve Air Strikes," *The Wall Street Journal*, October 24, 2019, https://www.wsj.com/articles/military-looks-to-ai-to-improve-air-strikes-11571932283.

146. S. Martin, "AI Warning: Machines Will Replace Humans at the Top—and Wipe Us Out If We Dare Resist," *Express,* September 18, 2019, https://www.express.co.uk/news/science/1179569/ai-replace-human-what-is-ai-artificial-intelligence-machine-learning-end-times-elon-musk

147. N. Leiber, "For Job Security at the Factory, Learn How to Repair a Robot," *Bloomberg*, April 18, 2019, https://www.bloomberg.com/news/articles/2019-04-18/for-job-security-at-the-factory-learn-how-to-repair-a-robot.

148. H. J. Wilson and P. R. Daugherty, "Collaborative Intelligence: Humans and AI Are Joining Forces," *Harvard Business Review*, 2018, pp. 114–123.

149. S. Harrison, "AI May Not Kill Your Job—Just Change It," *Wired*, October 31, 2019, https://www.wired.com/story/ai-not-kill-job-change-it/.

150. E. Morath, "AI Is the Next Workplace Disrupter—and It's Coming for High-Skilled Jobs," *The Wall Street Journal*, February 23, 2020, https://www.wsj.com/articles/ai-is-the-next-workplace-disrupterand-its-coming-for-high-skilled-jobs-11582470000.

151. T. Chamorro-Premuzic, M. Wade, and J. Jordan, "As AI Makes More Decisions, the Nature of Leadership Will Change," *Harvard Business Review*, 2018, https://hbr.org/2018/01/as-ai-makes-more-decisions-the-nature-of-leadership-will-change. Also see H. Chang, C. Wang, and S.

Hawamdeh, "Emerging Trends in Data Analytics and Knowledge Management Job Market: Extending KSA Framework," *Journal of Knowledge Management*, 2018, pp. 664–686.

152. T. Chamorro-Premuzic, M. Wade, and J. Jordan, "As AI Makes More Decisions, the Nature of Leadership Will Change," *Harvard Business Review*, 2018, https://hbr.org/2018/01/as-ai-makes-more-decisions-the-nature-of-leadership-will-change.

153. R. Asif, "Resolving Ethical Dilemma in Artificial Intelligence," *Medium*, August 23, 2019, https://medium.com/@rizasif92/resolving-ethical-dilemma-in-artificial-intelligence-15c30087ad69.

154. The discussion of styles was based on material contained in A. J. Rowe and R. O. Mason, *Managing with Style: A Guide to Understanding, Assessing and Improving Decision Making* (San Francisco: Jossey-Bass, 1987), pp. 1–17.

155. K. Kelly, "Tribune Publishing's New CEO Cuts Executives in Bloodbath," *New York Post*, February 6, 2020, https://nypost.com/2020/02/06/tribune-publishings-new-ceo-cuts-executives-in-bloodbath/.

156. R. Pink, Some Inspiration: Ursula Burns and Six Pillars of Leadership," *Two West*, http://www.twowestcompanies.com/some-inspiration-ursula-burns-and-six-pillars-of-leadership/ (accessed March 20, 2020).

157. K. Remenova and N. Jankelova, "How Successfully Can Decision-Making Style Predict the Orientation toward Well- or Ill-Structured Decision-Making Problems," *Journal of Competitiveness*, 2019, pp. 99–115.

158. B. Morgan, "How a Humble Culture and Self-Deprecating CEO Fuels This $130M Tire Company," *Forbes*, April 23, 2018, https://www.forbes.com/sites/blakemorgan/2018/04/23/how-a-humble-culture-and-self-deprecating-ceo-fuels-this-130m-tire-company/#5535e61033d0.

159. K. Remenova and N. Jankelova, "How Successfully Can Decision-Making Style Predict the Orientation toward Well- or Ill-Structured Decision-Making Problems," *Journal of Competitiveness*, 2019, pp. 99–115.

160. R. Makgosa and O. Sangodoyin, "Retail Market Segmentation: The Use of Consumer Decision-Making Styles, Overall Satisfaction and Demographics," *The International Review of Retail,* February 2018, pp. 64–91.

161. J. Weller, A. Ceschi, L. Hirsch, R. Sartori, and A. Costantini, "Accounting for Individual Differences in Decision-Making Competence: Personality and Gender Differences," *Frontiers in Psychology,* 2018, https://doi.org/10.3389/fpsyg.2018.02258. Also see K. Remenova and N. Jankelova, "How Successfully Can Decision-Making Style Predict the Orientation toward Well- or Ill-Structured Decision-Making Problems," *Journal of Competitiveness*, 2019, pp. 99–115; S. Miceli, V. de Palo, L. Monacis, S. Di Nuovo, and M. Sinatra, "Do Personality Traits and Self-Regulatory Processes Affect Decision-Making Tendencies?" *Australian Journal of Psychology*, 2018, pp. 284–294.

162. B. de Langhe and P. Fernbach, "The Dangers of Categorical Thinking," *Harvard Business Review,* 2019, pp. 80–93. Also see D. Kahnemann and A. Tversky, "Judgment under Uncertainty: Heuristics and Biases," *Science* 185 (1974), pp. 1124–1131; A. Tversky and D. Kahneman, "The Belief in the Law of Numbers," *Psychological Bulletin,* Vol. 76 (1971), pp. 105–110; D. R. Bobocel and J. P. Meyer, "Escalating Commitment to a Failing Course of Action: Separating the Roles of Choice and Justification," *Journal of Applied Psychology,* June 1994, pp. 360–363.

163. C. Mims, "The World Isn't as Bad as Your Wired Brain Tells You," *The Wall Street Journal*, August 31, 2018, https://www.wsj.com/articles/the-world-isnt-as-bad-as-your-wired-brain-tells-you-1535713201. Also see "Odds of Dying," *Injury Facts*, https://injuryfacts.nsc.org/all-injuries/preventable-death-overview/odds-of-dying/?mod=article_inline (accessed March 9, 2020).

164. G. Phillips-Wren, D. J. Power, and M. Mora, "Cognitive Bias, Decision Styles, and Risk Attitudes in Decision Making and DSS," *Journal of Decision Systems*, 2019, pp. 63–66.

165. T. Huddleston, "1 Person Won the $768 Million Powerball—Here's Who Won the 5 Biggest US Lottery Prizes Ever," *CNBC,* March 28, 2019, https://www.cnbc.com/2019/03/25/powerball-hits-750-million-here-are-the-biggest-us-lottery-prizes.html. Also see K. Breuninger, "The Odds of Winning Those Record Powerball, Mega Millions Jackpots Are Beyond

Slim," *CNBC*, January 5, 2018, https://www.cnbc.com/2018/01/05/odds-of-winning-a-lottery-jackpot-are-worse-than-you-expect.html.

166. W. W. A. Sleegers, T. Proulx, and I. van Beest, "Confirmation Bias and Misconceptions: Pupillometric Evidence for a Confirmation Bias in Misconceptions Feedback," *Biological Psychology*, 2019, pp. 76–83.

167. J. Grohol, "The Psychology of Confirmation Bias," *PsychCentral*, February 10, 2020, https://psychcentral.com/blog/the-psychology-of-confirmation-bias/.

168. C. Ohlert and B. Weißenberger, "Debiasing Escalation of Commitment: The Effectiveness of Decision Aids to Enhance De-escalation, *Journal of Management Control*, 2019, https://doi.org/10.1007/s00187-019-00290-z. Also see C. Olivola, "The Interpersonal Sunk-Cost Effect," *Psychological Science*, 2018, pp. 1072–1083.

169. E. A. Meyers, M. Białek, J. A. Fugelsang, D. J. Koehler, and O. Friedman, "Wronging Past Rights: The Sunk Cost Bias Distorts Moral Judgment," *Judgement and Decision Making*, 2019, pp. 721–727.

170. E. Goode, "Mice Don't Know When to Let It Go, Either," *The New York Times*, July 12, 2018, https://www.nytimes.com/2018/07/12/health/sunk-costs-decisions.html.

171. "The Anchoring Effect and How It Can Impact Your Negotiation," *Harvard Law School*, November 26, 2019, https://www.pon.harvard.edu/daily/negotiation-skills-daily/the-drawbacks-of-goals/.

172. A. Ceschi, A. Costantini, R. Sartori, J. Weller, and A. Di Fabio, "Dimensions of Decision-Making: An Evidence-based Classification of Heuristics and Biases," *Personality and Individual Differences*, 2019, pp. 188–200.

173. J. Liu, H. Zhou, M. Wan, and L. Liu, "How Does Overconfidence Affect Decision Making of the Green Product Manufacturer?" *Mathematical Problems in Engineering*, 2019, https://doi.org/10.1155/2019/5936940. Also see J. M. Logg, U. Haran, and D. A. Moore, "Is Overconfidence a Motivated Bias? Experimental Evidence," *Journal of Experimental Psychology*, 2018, pp. 1445–1465.

174. R. Flavin, "Entrepreneur Cognitive Bias: 7 Biases That Kill Startups," *Founder Institute*, January 9, 2019, https://fi.co/insight/entrepreneur-cognitive-bias-7-biases-that-kill-startups. Also see T. Čuláková, P. Kotrus, A. Uhlířová, and Michal Jirásek, "The Overconfidence Bias and CEO: A Literature Overview," *Business Trends*, 2017, pp. 3–9.

175. J. Groß and T. Pachur, "Age Differences in Hindsight Bias: A Meta-Analysis," *Psychology and Aging*, 2019, pp. 294–310. Also see C. Bhattacharya and J. D. Jasper, "Degree of Handedness: A Unique Individual Differences Factor for Predicting and Understanding Hindsight Bias," *Personality and Individual Differences*, 2018, pp. 97–101.

176. C. Hollingworth and L. Barker, "Bias in the Spotlight: Framing," *Research World*, April 16, 2019, https://www.researchworld.com/bias-in-the-spotlight-framing/.

177. E. May, "Elizabeth May Asks, 'At What Cost, Canada?'" *National Observer*, February 12, 2020, https://www.nationalobserver.com/2020/02/12/opinion/elizabeth-may-asks-what-cost-canada.

178. H. Kalmanovich-Cohen, M. Pearsall, and J. S. Christian, "The Effects of Leadership Change on Team Escalation of Commitment," *The Leadership Quarterly*, 2018, pp. 597–608. Also see J. S. Lee, M. Keil, and K. F. E. Wong, "Does a Tired Mind Help Avoid a Decision Bias? The Effect of Ego Depletion on Escalation of Commitment," *Applied Psychology*, 2018, pp. 171–185; J. Ross and B. M. Staw, "Organizational Escalation and Exit: Lessons from the Shoreham Nuclear Power Plant," *Academy of Management Journal*, August 1993, pp. 701–732.

179. B. de Langhe and P. Fernbach, "The Dangers of Categorical Thinking," *Harvard Business Review*, 2019, pp. 80–93. Also see D. Massey, "Inequality, Social," *International Encyclopedia of the Social & Behavioral Sciences*, 2nd ed., 2015, pp. 908–913.

180. S. D. S. Walker and B. L. Bonner, "The Effects of Differing Knowledge Transfer Strategies on Group Decision Making and Performance," *Journal of Behavioral Decision Making*, 2018, pp. 115–126.

181. N. F. R. Maier, "Assets and Liabilities in Group Problem Solving: The Need for Integrative Function," *Psychological Review*, Vol. 74 (1967), pp. 239–249.

182. N. F. R. Maier, "Assets and Liabilities in Group Problem Solving: The Need for Integrative Function," *Psychological Review*, Vol. 74 (1967), pp. 239–249.

183. R. Sutton, "The Biggest Mistakes Bosses Make When Making Decisions—and How to Avoid Them," *The Wall Street Journal*, October 29, 2018, https://www.wsj.com/articles/the-biggest-mistakes-bosses-make-when-making-decisionsand-how-to-avoid-them-1540865340.

184. S. Cain, "The Rise of the New Groupthink," *The New York Times*, January 15, 2012, pp. WR1, WR6. Also see J. Lehrer, "Groupthink," *The New Yorker*, January 30, 2012, pp. 22–27.

185. F. Gonzalez-Valdes and J. de Dios Ortuzar, "The Stochastic Satisficing Model: A Bounded Rationality Discrete Choice Model," *Journal of Choice Modelling*, 2018, pp. 74–87. Methods for increasing group consensus were investigated by R. L. Priem, D. A. Harrison, and N. K. Muir, "Structured Conflict and Consensus Outcomes in Group Decision Making," *Journal of Management*, December 22, 1995, pp. 691–710.

186. J. P. Porck, D. van Knippenberg, M. Tarakci, N. Y. Ates, P. J. F. Groenen, and M. de Hass, "Do Group and Organizational Identification Help or Hurt Intergroup Strategic Consensus?" *Journal of Management*, 2020, pp. 234–260.

187. I. Janis, *Groupthink*, 2nd ed. (Boston: Houghton Mifflin, 1982), p. 9. Also see K. D. Lassila, "A Brief History of Groupthink," *Yale Alumni Magazine*, January–February 2008, pp. 59–61, www.philosophy-religion.org/handouts/pdfs/BRIEF-HISTORY_GROUPTHINK.pdf (accessed August 10, 2016).

188. J. DeMers, "How 'Groupthink' Can Cost Your Business (and 3 Corporate Examples)," *Entrepreneur*, April 16, 2018, https://www.entrepreneur.com/article/311864. Also see J. Kilhefner, "Groupthink Examples in Business," *Chron*, https://work.chron.com/groupthink-examples-business-21692.html (accessed March 10, 2020).

189. M. Clearly, D. Lees, and J. Sayers, "Leadership, Thought Diversity, and the Influence of Groupthink," *Issues in Mental Health Nursing*, 2019, pp. 731–733. Also see I. Janis, *Groupthink*, 2nd ed. (Boston: Houghton Mifflin, 1982), pp. 174–175.

190. D. D. Henningsen and M. M. Henningsen, "Nuanced Aggression in Group Decision Making," *International Journal of Business Communication*, 2020, pp. 145–158.

191. Surowiecki, quoted in Kemper, "Senate Intelligence Report: Groupthink Viewed as Culprit in Move to War". Also see J. A. LePine, "Adaptation of Teams in Response to Unforeseen Change: Effects of Goal Difficulty and Team Composition in Terms of Cognitive Ability and Goal Orientation," *Journal of Applied Psychology* 90 (2005), pp. 1153–1167.

192. A. Tarki, "How to Avoid Groupthink When Hiring," *Harvard Business Review*, August 13, 2019, https://hbr.org/2019/08/how-to-avoid-groupthink-when-hiring. Also see R. Sutton, "The Biggest Mistakes Bosses Make When Making Decisions—and How to Avoid Them," *The Wall Street Journal*, October 29, 2018, https://www.wsj.com/articles/the-biggest-mistakes-bosses-make-when-making-decisionsand-how-to-avoid-them-1540865340; C. R. Sunstein and R. Hastie, "How to Defeat Groupthink: Five Solutions," *Fortune*, January 13, 2015, http://fortune.com/2015/01/13/groupthink-solutions-information-failure/?iid=sr-link2#160.

193. G. Hamel, "The Advantages & Disadvantages of Group Decision-Making," *bizfluent*, October 18, 2018, https://bizfluent.com/info-8212675-advantages-disadvantages-group-decisionmaking.html.

194. D. L. Gladstein and N. P. Reilly, "Group Decision Making under Threat: The Tycoon Game," *Academy of Management Journal*, September 1985, pp. 613–627.

195. These conclusions were based on the following studies: J. H. Davis, "Some Compelling Intuitions about Group Consensus Decisions, Theoretical and Empirical Research, and Interpersonal Aggregation Phenomena: Selected Examples, 1950–1990," *Organizational Behavior and Human Decision Processes*, June 1992, pp. 3–38; J. A. Sniezek, "Groups under Uncertainty: An Examination of Confidence in Group Decision Making," *Organizational Behavior and Human Decision Processes*, June 1992, pp. 124–155.

196. See example in S. K. Lam, J. Karim, and J. Riedl, "The Effects of Group Composition on Decision Quality in a Social Production Community," *Proceedings of the 16th ACM International Conference on Supporting Group Work*, 2010, pp. 55–64; M. W. Blenko, M. C. Mankins, and P. Rogers, "The Decision-Driven Organization," *Harvard Business Review,* June 2010, pp. 55–62.

197. K. Cherry, "How Does Group Size Influence Problem Solving?" *Very Well Mind,* July 8, 2018, https://www.verywellmind.com/effects-of-group-size-on-problem-solving-2795678.

198. C. Lin, K. Chen, C. Liu, and C. Liao, "Assessing Decision Quality and Team Performance: Perspectives of Knowledge Internalization and Resource Adequacy," *Review of Managerial Science*, 2019, pp. 377–396.

199. Supporting results can be found in J. R. Hollenbeck, D. R. Ilgen, D. J. Sego, J. Hedlund, D. A. Major, and J. Phillips, "Multilevel Theory of Team Decision Making: Decision Performance in Teams Incorporating Distributed Expertise," *Journal of Applied Psychology,* April 1995, pp. 292–316.

200. "How the Sharing of Information Affects Team Performance," *Degarmo,* http://www.degarmo.com/how-the-sharing-of-information-affects-team-performance (accessed March 10, 2020). Also see D. H. Gruenfeld, E. A. Mannix, K. Y. Williams, and M. A. Neale, "Group Composition and Decision Making: How Member Familiarity and Information Distribution Affect Process and Performance," *Organizational Behavior and Human Decision Processes,* July 1996, pp. 1–15.

201. P. L. McLeod, R. S. Baron, M. W. Marti, and K. Yoon, "The Eyes Have It: Minority Influence in Face-to-Face and Computer-Mediated Group Discussions," *Journal of Applied Psychology,* Vol. 82 (1997), pp. 706–718.

202. Results can be found in C. K. W. De Dreu and M. A. West, "Minority Dissent and Team Innovation: The Importance of Participation in Decision Making," *Journal of Applied Psychology,* December 2001, pp. 1191–1201.

203. A. Pittampalli, "Difficult Decisions: The Costs of Consensus," *Psychology Today,* January 3, 2018, https://www.psychologytoday.com/us/blog/are-you-persuadable/201801/difficult-decisions-the-costs-consensus.

204. These recommendations were obtained from G. M. Parker, *Team Players and Teamwork: The New Competitive Business Strategy* (San Francisco: Jossey-Bass, 1990).

205. J. Mueller, S. Melwani, J. Loewenstein, and J. J. Deal, "Reframing the Decision-Makers' Dilemma: Towards a Social Context Model of Creative Idea Recognition," *Academy of Management Journal,* 2018, pp. 94–110. Also see A. F. Osborn, *Applied Imagination: Principles and Procedures of Creative Thinking,* 3rd ed. (New York: Scribner's, 1979). For an example of how brainstorming works, see P. Croce, "Think Brighter," *FSB,* January 2006, p. 35.

206. M. Oppezzo and D. L. Schwartz, "Give Your Ideas Some Legs: The Positive Effect of Walking on Creative Thinking," *Journal of Experimental Psychology: Learning, Memory, and Cognition,* Vol. 40, No. 4 (2014), pp. 1142–1152.

207. W. H. Cooper, R. Brent Gallupe, S. Pallard, and J. Cadsby, "Some Liberating Effects of Anonymous Electronic Brainstorming," *Small Group Research,* April 1998, pp. 147–178.

208. H. Al-Samarraie and S. Hurmuzan, "A Review of Brainstorming Techniques in Higher Education," *Thinking Skills and Creativity*, 2018, pp. 78–91.

209. H. Gregersen, "Managing People: Better Brainstorming," *Harvard Business Review,* 2018, pp. 64–71. Also see B. Nussbaum, "Brainstorming—Rules & Techniques for Idea Generation," *IDEO,* https://www.ideou.com/pages/brainstorming (accessed March 10, 2020); B. R. Johnson and C. J. D'Lauro, "After Brainstorming, Groups Select an Early Generated Idea as Their Best Idea," *Small Group Research*, 2018, pp. 177–194.

210. D. Meinert, "Brainstorming Gone Bad," *HR Magazine,* April 2016, p. 14.

211. "Dialectic Decisions Method," *Business Jargons,* https://business-jargons.com/dialectic-decisions-method.html (accessed March 10,

2020). Also see G. Katzenstein, "The Debate on Structured Debate: Toward a Unified Theory," *Organizational Behavior and Human Decision Processes,* June 1996, pp. 316–332.

212. P. Chen, "How to Hold a Productive Post-Mortem Meeting," *Forbes,* October 31, 2016, https://www.forbes.com/sites/forbestechcouncil/2016/10/31/how-to-hold-a-productive-post-mortem-meeting/2/#29bb22c077cf. Also see J. Fleming, "How to Conduct a Project Post-Mortem," *Bizfluent,* September 26, 2017, https://bizfluent.com/how-8421062-conduct-project-postmortem.html; M. Pretorius, "Business Rescue Decision-Making: Post-Mortem Evaluation of an 'Orgy,'" *South African Journal of Economic and Management Sciences,* 2018, https://doi.org/10.4102/sajems.v21i1.1622.

213. G. Guthrie, "How to Run an Incredibly Effective Post-Mortem Meeting," *Backlog Blog,* June 5, 2019, https://backlog.com/blog/run-incredibly-effective-post-mortem-meeting/.

214. M. Brunet and D. Forgues, "Investigating Collective Sensemaking of a Major Project Success," *International Journal of Managing Projects in Business*, 2019, pp. 644–665.

215. B. Tulgan, *Bridging the Soft Skills Gap: How to Teach the Missing Basics to Today's Young Talent* (Hoboken, NJ: John Wiley & Sons, 2015).

216. B. Tulgan, *Bridging the Soft Skills Gap: How to Teach the Missing Basics to Today's Young Talent* (Hoboken, NJ: John Wiley & Sons, 2015).

217. The idea for this exercise was based on B. Tulgan, *Bridging the Soft Skills Gap: How to Teach the Missing Basics to Today's Young Talent* (Hoboken, NJ: John Wiley & Sons, 2015).

218. These steps were based on M. Myatt, "6 Tips for Making Better Decisions," *Forbes,* March 28, 2012, https://www.forbes.com/sites/mikemyatt/2012/03/28/6-tips-for-making-better-decisions/#4206b32634dc.

219. These questions were based on L. Liaros, "Explaining Your Decision Making Process," *Interview Tips,* https://everydayinterviewtips.com/explaining-your-decision-making-process-during-an-interview/ (accessed March 19, 2018); L. Liaros, "How to Show You Have Quick Decision Making Skills," *Everyday Interview Tips,* https://everydayinterviewtips.com/how-to-show-you-have-quick-decision-making-skills/ (accessed March 19, 2018); L. Liaros, "Using Instincts vs. Data to Make Decisions," *Everyday Interview Tips,* https://everydayinterviewtips.com/using-instinct-data-to-make-decisions/ (accessed March 19, 2018).

220. O. Zaleski and E. Huet, "Juul Expects Skyrocketing Sales of $3.4 Billion, Despite Flavored Vape Restrictions," *Bloomberg,* February 22, 2019, https://www.bloomberg.com/news/articles/2019-02-22/juul-expects-skyrocketing-sales-of-3-4-billion-despite-flavored-vape-ban. Also see J. Maloney, "Juul to Cut about 500 Jobs," *The Wall Street Journal,* October 29, 2019, https://www.wsj.com/articles/juul-to-cut-about-500-jobs-11572301778; J. Kosman, "JUUL e-Cigarette Maker Sees Its Valuation Top $38B," *New York Post,* May 17, 2019, https://nypost.com/2019/05/17/juul-e-cigarette-maker-sees-its-valuation-top-38b/.

221. J. Kosman and K. Dugan, "Juul Stock Values Plummet amid Federal Crackdown," *New York Post,* September 13, 2019, https://nypost.com/2019/09/13/juul-profits-plummet-amid-federal-crackdown/. Also see A. Sircar, "E-Cigarette Sales Slow Dramatically in Wake of Vaping-Related Health Warnings," *Fortune,* October 15, 2019, https://fortune.com/2019/10/15/vaping-e-cigarette-sales-slowdown/; S. Klebnikov, "Juul Valuation Falls to $12 Billion as Altria Takes Another $4.1 Billion Hit," *Forbes,* January 30, 2020, https://www.forbes.com/sites/sergeiklebnikov/2020/01/30/juul-valuation-falls-to-12-billion-as-altria-takes-another-41-billion-hit/#1e209c13f4f2; J. Maloney, "Juul to Cut about 500 Jobs," *The Wall Street Journal*, October 29, 2019, https://www.wsj.com/articles/juul-to-cut-about-500-jobs-11572301778.

222. M. Padilla, "Robert Norris, Marlboro Man Who Didn't Smoke, Dies at 90," *The New York Times*, November 13, 2019, https://www.nytimes.com/2019/11/09/us/robert-norris-dead.html.

223. D. Thompson, "U.S. Smoking Rate Hits New Low, But Vaping Rises," *WebMD,* November 14, 2019, https://www.webmd.com/smoking-cessation/news/20191114/fewer-americans-than-ever-smoke-but-vaping-poses-a-growing-threat-cdc#1.

224. A. Capritto, "Juul Vape: What Is It, Why Are Teens Addicted, and Is It Safe?" *C-Net*, September 16, 2019, https://www.cnet.com/news/juul-what-is-it-how-does-it-work-and-is-it-safe/#:~:text=Developed%20by%20two%20former%20smokers,they%20used%20a%20Juul%20instead. Also see D. Thompson, "U.S. Smoking Rate Hits New Low, But Vaping Rises," *WebMD*, November 14, 2019, https://www.webmd.com/smoking-cessation/news/20191114/fewer-americans-than-ever-smoke-but-vaping-poses-a-growing-threat-cdc#1; L. Voytko, "FDA Investigates 127 Seizure Reports Potentially Linked to Vaping" *Forbes*, August 8, 2019, https://www.forbes.com/sites/lisettevoytko/2019/08/08/fda-investigates-127-seizure-reports-potentially-linked-to-vaping/#2e4408a0454b.

225. R. Miech, L. Johnston, Patrick M. O'Malley, and J. G. Bachman, "Trends in Adolescent Vaping, 2017–2019," *New England Journal of Medicine*, October 10, 2019, https://www.nejm.org/doi/pdf/10.1056/NEJMc1910739.

226. "6 Important Facts about JUUL," *Truth Initiative*, August 20, 2018, https://truthinitiative.org/research-resources/emerging-tobacco-products/6-important-facts-about-juul. Also see A. Capritto, "Juul Vape: What Is It, Why Are Teens Addicted, and Is It Safe?" *C-Net*, September 16, 2019, https://www.cnet.com/news/juul-what-is-it-how-does-it-work-and-is-it-safe/#:~:text=Developed%20by%20two%20former%20smokers,they%20used%20a%20Juul%20instead.

227. E. Brodwin, "The Precarious Path of e-Cig Startup Juul: From Silicon Valley Darling to $24 Billion Behemoth under Criminal Investigation," *Business Insider*, October 31, 2019, https://www.businessinsider.com/juul-timeline-from-startup-to-tobacco-company-challenges-bans-2019-9.

228. "Juul Labs Suspends Sale of Non-Tobacco, Non-Menthol-Based, Flavors in the U.S.," *Juul*, October 17, 2019, https://newsroom.juul.com/juul-labs-suspends-sale-of-non-tobacco-non-menthol-based-flavors-in-the-u-s/.

229. R. Jacklet et al., "JUUL Advertising over Its First Three Years on the Market," Stanford University School of Medicine, 2019, http://tobacco.stanford.edu/tobacco_main/publications/JUUL_Marketing_Stanford.pdf.

230. A. Aubrey, "Juul Suspends Sales of Flavored Vapes and Signs Settlement to Stop Marketing to Youth," *NPR*, October 17, 2019, https://www.npr.org/sections/health-shots/2019/10/17/771098368/juul-suspends-sales-of-flavored-vapes-and-signs-settlement-to-stop-marketing-to-.

231. E. Brodwin, "The Precarious Path of e-Cig startup Juul: From Silicon Valley Darling to $24 Billion Behemoth under Criminal Investigation," *Business Insider*, October 31, 2019, https://www.businessinsider.com/juul-timeline-from-startup-to-tobacco-company-challenges-bans-2019-9.

232. J. Maloney, "Juul Pitches Locked E-Cigarette in Bid to Stay on U.S. Market," *The Wall Street Journal*, February 24, 2020, https://www.wsj.com/articles/juul-pitches-locked-e-cigarette-in-bid-to-stay-on-u-s-market-11582576496. Also see R. Duprey, "Is Juul Labs' FDA Application Doomed?" *The Motley Fool*, November 19, 2019, https://www.fool.com/investing/2019/11/19/is-juul-labs-fda-application-doomed.aspx; K. Lyons, "New Juul Patent Application Hints at AI-Powered Vape to Help Users Quit Nicotine," *The Verge*, February 25, 2020, https://www.theverge.com/2020/2/25/21152436/juul-patent-e-cigarettes-vaping-ai-smartphone-quit-nicotine.

233. R. Duprey, "Is Juul Labs' FDA Application Doomed?" *The Motley Fool*, November 19, 2019, https://www.fool.com/investing/2019/11/19/is-juul-labs-fda-application-doomed.aspx.

234. L. Zumbach, "United Tightens Rules for Emotional Support Animals," *Chicago Tribune*, February 1, 2018, http://www.chicagotribune.com/business/ct-biz-united-tightens-rules-emotional-support-animals-0202-story.html.

235. L. Aratani, "Department of Transportation Proposes Ban on Emotional Support Animals on Planes," *The Washington Post*, March 11, 2020, https://www.washingtonpost.com/transportation/2020/01/22/department-transportation-proposes-ban-emotional-support-animals-planes/.

236. A. Sider, "U.S. Moves to Let Airlines Ban Emotional-Support Animals," *The Wall Street Journal*, January 22, 2020, https://www.wsj.com/articles/u-s-proposes-tighter-rules-for-emotional-support-animals-on-flights-11579720969.

237. L. Zumbach, "United Tightens Rules for Emotional Support Animals," *Chicago Tribune*, February 1, 2018, http://www.chicagotribune.com/business/ct-biz-united-tightens-rules-emotional-support-animals-0202-story.html.

238. "'Emotional Support Peacock Barred from United Airlines Plane," *BBC*, January 31, 2018, https://www.bbc.com/news/world-us-canada-42880690.

239. "What's New," U.S. Department of Transportation, January 22, 2020, https://cms8.dot.gov/airconsumer/latest-news.

240. A. Sider, "U.S. Moves to Let Airlines Ban Emotional-Support Animals," *The Wall Street Journal*, January 22, 2020, https://www.wsj.com/articles/u-s-proposes-tighter-rules-for-emotional-support-animals-on-flights-11579720969.

241. M. Goldstein, "Will 2020 Mark the End of Emotional Support Animals on Airlines?" *Forbes*, March 11, 2020, https://www.forbes.com/sites/michaelgoldstein/2019/12/19/will-2020-mark-the-end-of-emotional-support-animals-on-airlines/#ce90a82f7a87.

242. S. Gibbens, "Can Peacocks Be Emotional Support Animals? It's Complicated," *National Geographic*, January 31, 2018, https://news.nationalgeographic.com/2018/01/woman-brings-peacock-plane-emotional-support-animal-explained-spd/.

243. A. McCarren, "Delta Bites Back over Too Many Emotional Support Animals on Board," *WUSA*, January 19, 2018, http://www.wusa9.com/article/news/local/delta-bites-back-over-too-many-emotional-support-animals-on-board/509562359.

CHAPTER 8

1. C. Connley, "Suzy Welch: These Are the 2 Fastest Ways to Get Promoted," *CNBC*, April 2, 2019, https://www.cnbc.com/2019/04/01/suzy-welch-these-are-the-2-fastest-ways-to-get-promoted.html.

2. C. Dessi, "How to Sell Yourself in a Way That Won't Make You Cringe," *Inc*, September 28, 2017, https://www.inc.com/chris-dessi/how-to-sell-yourself-in-a-way-that-wont-make-you-cringe.html.

3. B. Swider, M. Barrick, and T. Harris, "Initial Impressions: What They Are, What They Are Not, and How They Influence Structured Interview Outcomes," *Journal of Applied Psychology*, Vol. 101, No. 5 (2016), pp. 625–638.

4. S. M. Heathfield, "Why 'Blink' Matters: The Power of First Impressions," *The Balance*, October 24, 2016, https://www.thebalance.com/why-blink-matters-the-power-of-first-impressions-1919374.

5. S. McCord, "4 Sneaky Ways to Determine Company Culture in an Interview," *The Muse*, https://www.themuse.com/advice/4-sneaky-ways-to-determine-company-culture-in-an-interview, accessed March 19, 2018.

6. A. Brooks and L. John, "The Surprising Power of Questions," *Harvard Business Review*, Vol. 96, No. 3 (2018), pp. 60–67.

7. J. Yoon, H. Blunden, A. Kristal, and A. Whillans, "Why Asking for Advice Is More Effective Than Asking for Feedback," *Harvard Business Review Digital Articles*, 2019, pp. 2–4.

8. K. Carrig and S. Snell, "Strategic Execution: Driving Breakthrough Performance in Business," 2019, Stanford University Press.

9. J. Trevor, J. and B. Varcoe, "How Aligned Is Your Organization," *Harvard Business Review*, Vol. 91, No. 1 (2017), pp. 2–6. Also see R. Carucci, "Executives Fail to Execute Strategy Because They're Too Internally Focused," *Harvard Business Review Digital Articles*, November, 2017, pp. 2–5.

10. For a thorough review of this process, see C. Ostroff, A. J. Kinicki, and R. S. Muhammad, "Organizational Culture and Climate," *Handbook of Psychology*, Vol. 12: *Industrial and Organizational Psychology* (Hoboken, NJ: John Wiley & Sons, 2012), pp. 643–676.

11. E. H. Schein, "Culture: The Missing Concept in Organization Studies," *Administrative Science Quarterly*, June 1996, p. 236.

12. B. Schneider, V. González-Roma, C. Ostroff, and M. A. West, "Organizational Climate and Culture: Reflections on the History of the Constructs in the Journal of Applied Psychology, *Journal of Applied Psychology*, March 2017, pp. 469–482.

13. T. Kim and J. Chang, "Organizational Culture and Performance: A Macro-Level Longitudinal Study," *Leadership & Organization Development Journal,* February 2019, pp. 65–84.

14. T. Harrison and J. Bazzy, "Aligning Organizational Culture and Strategic Human Resource Management," *Journal of Management Development*, November 2017, pp. 1260–1269. Also see A. Kaul, "Culture vs Strategy: Which to Precede, Which to Align?" *Journal of Strategy and Management*, Vol. 12 (1) 2018, pp. 116–136.

15. Z. Chen, S. Huang, C. Liu, M. Min, and L. Zhou, "Fit Between Organizational Culture and Innovation Strategy: Implications for Innovation Performance," *Sustainability,* September 2018, p. 3378. Also see D. Warrick, "What Leaders Need to Know about Organizational Culture," *Business Horizons*, May 2017 pp. 395–404.

16. M. della Cava, "Nadella Counts on Culture Shock to Drive Microsoft Growth," *USA Today Money,* February 20, 2017.

17. J. Thomson, "Company Culture Soars at Southwest Airlines," *Forbes,* December 18, 2018, https://www.forbes.com/sites/jeffthomson/2018/12/18/company-culture-soars-at-southwest-airlines/#383e2481615f.

18. H. Barbour, "The Beating Heart of Southwest Airlines' Culture," *The Digital Transformation People,* November 4, 2019, https://www.thedigitaltransformationpeople.com/channels/people-and-change/the-beating-heart-of-southwest-airlines-culture/.

19. T. Fountaine, B. McCarthy, and T. Saleh, "Building the AI-Powered Organization," *Harvard Business Review,* July-August 2019, pp. 63–73.

20. S. Sandhu and C. Kulik, "Shaping and Being Shaped: How Organizational Structure and Managerial Discretion Co-Evolve in New Managerial Roles," *Administrative Science Quarterly*, Vol. 64, No. 3 2019, pp. 619–658.

21. T. Giardino, "Is Your Company Struggling? It Might Be a Flaw in the Strategy-Structure Fit," *Forbes,* November 20, 2018, https://www.forbes.com/sites/forbeshumanresourcescouncil/2018/11/20/is-your-company-struggling-it-might-be-a-flaw-in-the-strategy-structure-fit/#25341c58591a. Also see S. Soderstrom and K. Weber, "Organizational Structure from Interaction: Evidence from Corporate Sustainability Efforts," *Administrative Science Quarterly*, Vol. 65, No. 1 2020, pp. 226–271; S. Sandhu and C. Kulik, "Shaping and Being Shaped: How Organizational Structure and Managerial Discretion Co-Evolve in New Managerial Roles," *Administrative Science Quarterly*, Vol. 64, No. 3 2019, pp. 619–658.

22. "Policies & Practices," Procter & Gamble, https://us.pg.com/policies-and-practices/purpose-values-and-principles/ (accessed March 24, 2020).

23. "Company Strategy," Procter & Gamble Investor, https://www.pginvestor.com/Company-Strategy/Index?KeyGenPage=1073753860#superiority-tag (accessed March 24, 2020).

24. Reuters, "P&G Restructures Operations, Creates Six Business Units," November 8, 2018, https://www.reuters.com/article/us-procter-gamble-strategy/pg-restructures-operations-creates-six-business-units-idUSKCN1ND37M.

25. A. Al-Muslim, "P&G Moves to Streamline Its Structure: CEO David Taylor Appoints Six Unit Chiefs with Oversight of Both Products and Sales," *The Wall Street Journal (Online)*, November 8, 2018, https://www.wsj.com/articles/p-g-moves-to-streamline-its-structure-1541713822.

26. J. Han, S. Kang, I. Oh, R. Kehoe, and D. Lepak, "The Goldilocks Effect of Strategic Human Resource Management? Optimizing the Benefits of a High-Performance Work System through the Dual Alignment of Vertical and Horizontal Fit," *Academy of Management Journal,* Vol. 62, No.5 2019, pp. 1388–1412. Also see B. Kuipers and L. Giurge, "Does Alignment Matter? The Performance Implications of HR Roles Connected to Organizational Strategy," *The International Journal of Human Resource Management*, Vol. 28, No. 22 2017, pp. 3179–3201. V. Khoreva and H. Wechtler, H., "HR Practices and Employee Performance: The Mediating Role of Well-Being," *Employee Relations,* Vol. 4, No. 2 2018, pp. 227–243.

27. C. Chadwick and C. Flinchbaugh, "Searching for Competitive Advantage in the HRM/Firm Performance Relationship," *Academy of Management Perspectives* (forthcoming).

28. T. Harrison and J. Bazzy, "Aligning Organizational Culture and Strategic Human Resource Management," *Journal of Management Development*, November 2017, pp. 1260-1269.

29. "Corporate Employment," In-N-Out Burger, https://www.in-n-out.com/employment/corporate/home (accessed March 25, 2020).

30. K. Beydler, "Six Ways In-N-Out Burger Is Excelling in Business—and Five Applications for Healthcare Today," *Becker's ASC Review,* May 22, 2017, https://www.beckersasc.com/asc-news/six-ways-in-n-out-burger-is-excelling-in-business-and-five-applications-for-healthcare-today.html.

31. "Restaurant Employment," In-N-Out Burger, https://www.in-n-out.com/employment/restaurant/home (accessed March 25, 2020).

32. C. Ostroff, A. Kinicki, and R. Muhammad, "Organizational Culture and Climate," *Handbook of Psychology,* 2nd ed, Vol. 12 (2012).

33. A. Lewis and J. Clark, "Dreams Within a Dream: Multiple Visions and Organizational Structure," *Journal of Organizational Behavior*, Vol. 41, No. 1 2020, pp. 50–76.

34. "UPS Board Appoints Carol Tomé as CEO; David Abney to Be Executive Chairman," *UPS GlobeNewswire,* March 12, 2020, https://www.globenewswire.com/news-release/2020/03/12/1999405/0/en/UPS-Board-Appoints-Carol-Tom%C3%A9-As-CEO-David-Abney-To-Be-Executive-Chairman.html.

35. M. Forde, "UPS Taps Former Home Depot CFO Carol Tomé to Succeed David Abney as CEO," *Supply Chain Dive,* March 12, 2020, https://www.supplychaindive.com/news/ups-carol-tome-ceo-effective-june-1/574011/

36. B. Groysberg, J. Lee, J. Price, and J. Cheng, "The Leader's Guide to Corporate Culture," *Harvard Business Review,* January–February 2018. Also see A. Lewis and J. Clark, "Dreams within a Dream: Multiple Visions and Organizational Structure," *Journal of Organizational Behavior*, Vol. 41, No. 1 2020, pp. 50–76.

37. N. Ateş, M. Tarakci, M., J. Porck, D. van Knippenberg, and P. Groenen, "The Dark Side of Visionary Leadership in Strategy Implementation: Strategic Alignment, Strategic Consensus, and Commitment," *Journal of Management,* January 2018, pp. 637–665.

38. V. Sonsev, "Patagonia's Focus on Its Brand Purpose Is Great for Business," *Forbes,* November 27, 2019, https://www.forbes.com/sites/veronikasonsev/2019/11/27/patagonias-focus-on-its-brand-purpose-is-great-for-business/#54d4120c54cb. Also see "Patagonia," *Great Place to Work 2019–2020,* https://www.greatplacetowork.com/certified-company/1000745 (accessed March 19, 2020); "1% For the Planet," Patagonia, https://www.patagonia.com/one-percent-for-the-planet.html (accessed March 19, 2020).

39. R. Feloni, "Patagonia's CEO Says 'Capitalism Needs to Evolve' If We Want to Save the Planet," *Business Insider,* April 15, 2019, https://www.businessinsider.com/patagonia-ceo-rose-marcario-says-capitalism-must-evolve-to-save-earth-2019-4.

40. F. Rattalino, "Circular Advantage Anyone? Sustainability-Driven Innovation and Circularity at Patagonia, Inc.," *Thunderbird International Business Review*, Vol. 60, No. 5 2018, pp. 747–755.

41. H. Watson, "HR Lessons From: Patagonia," *PeopleGoal,* June 18, 2019, https://www.peoplegoal.com/blog/hr-lessons-from-patagonia. Also see B. Anderson, "5 'Ridiculous' Ways Patagonia Has Built a Culture That Does Well and Does Good," *LinkedIn Talent Blog,* September 27, 2019, https://business.linkedin.com/talent-solutions/blog/talent-connect/2019/5-ways-patagonia-built-ridiculous-culture; https://www.greatplacetowork.com/certified-company/1000745; https://www.responsiveinboundmarketing.com/blog/13-companies-that-have-an-ideal-office-culture.

42. K. Margolin, "How Patagonia's Unique Leadership Structure Enabled Them to Thrive," *Virgin,* April 25, 2017, https://www.virgin.com/entrepreneur/how-patagonias-unique-leadership-structure-enabled-them-thrive.

43. D. Rock, "The NLI Interview: Patagonia's Dean Carter on How to Treat Employees like People," *Forbes,* January 9, 2020, https://www.forbes.com/sites/davidrock/2020/01/09/the-nli-interview-patagonias-dean-carter-on-how-to-treat-employees-like-people/#5bb08094188c.

44. H. Watson, "HR Lessons From: Patagonia," *PeopleGoal,* June 18, 2019, https://www.peoplegoal.com/blog/hr-lessons-from-patagonia. Also see B. Anderson, "5 'Ridiculous' Ways Patagonia Has Built a Culture That Does Well and Does Good," *LinkedIn Talent Blog,* September 27, 2019, https://business.linkedin.com/talent-solutions/blog/talent-connect/2019/5-ways-patagonia-built-ridiculous-culture; K. Margolin, "How Patagonia's Unique Leadership Structure Enabled Them to Thrive," *Virgin,* April 25, 2017, https://www.virgin.com/entrepreneur/how-patagonias-unique-leadership-structure-enabled-them-thrive.

45. D. Rock, "The NLI Interview: Patagonia's Dean Carter on How to Treat Employees like People," *Forbes,* January 9, 2020, https://www.forbes.com/sites/davidrock/2020/01/09/the-nli-interview-patagonias-dean-carter-on-how-to-treat-employees-like-people/#5bb08094188c.

46. D. O'Rourke and R. Strand, "Patagonia: Driving Sustainable Innovation by Embracing Tensions," *California Management Review,* Vol. 60, No. 1 2017, pp. 102–125.

47. K. Margolin, "How Patagonia's Unique Leadership Structure Enabled Them to Thrive," *Virgin,* April 25, 2017, https://www.virgin.com/entrepreneur/how-patagonias-unique-leadership-structure-enabled-them-thrive. Also see R. Feloni, "Patagonia's CEO Says 'Capitalism Needs to Evolve' if We Want to Save the Planet," *Business Insider,* April 15, 2019, https://www.businessinsider.com/patagonia-ceo-rose-marcario-says-capitalism-must-evolve-to-save-earth-2019-4.

48. N. Roulin and F. Krings, "Faking to Fit In: Applicants' Response Strategies to Match Organizational Culture," *Journal of Applied Psychology,* February 2020, pp. 130–145.

49. M. Perino, A. Cain, and R. Gillett, "Here's What Elon Musk, Richard Branson, and 53 Other Successful People Ask Job Candidates during Interviews," *Business Insider,* August 22, 2019, https://www.business insider.com/executives-favorite-job-interview-question-2014-11#can-you-tell-me-the-story-of-you-prior-successes-challenges-and-major-responsibilities-52.

50. J. A. Veitch, "How and Why to Assess Workplace Design: Facilities Management Supports Human Resources," *Organizational Dynamics,* 47 2018, pp. 78–87.

51. E. H. Schein, *Organizational Culture and Leadership,* 2nd ed. (San Francisco: Jossey-Bass, 1992). Also see E. T. Hall, *Beyond Culture* (New York, Anchor Books, 1976).

52. S. McLaren, "A 'No Shoes' Policy and 4 Other Unique Traditions That Make These Company Cultures Stand Out," *Linkedin Talent Blog,* November 12, 2018, https://business.linkedin.com/talent-solutions/blog/company-culture/2018/unique-traditions-that-make-these-company-cultures-stand-out.

53. "Services," Goldman Sachs, https://www.goldmansachs.com/careers/divisions/services/ (accessed March 21, 2020). Also see H. Son, "Goldman Won't Take Companies Public without 'At Least One Diverse Board Candidate,' CEO Says," *CNBC,* January 23, 2020, https://www.cnbc.com/2020/01/23/goldman-wont-take-companies-public-that-dont-have-at-least-one-diverse-board-candidate-ceo-says.html.

54. J. Craft, "Common Thread: The Impact of Mission on Ethical Business Culture: A Case Study," *Journal of Business Ethics,* Vol. 149, No. 1 2018, pp. 127–145. Also see M. Fotaki, S. Lioukas, and I. Voudouris, I., "Ethos Is Destiny: Organizational Values and Compliance in Corporate Governance," *Journal of Business Ethics,* September 2020, pp. 19–37.

55. S. Mlot, "Comcast Is America's Most Hated Company," *PC Mag,* January 12, 2017, https://www.pcmag.com/news/comcast-is-americas-most-hated-company. Also see T. Huddleston, "Comcast Tries Yet Again to Fix Its Customer Service (This Time, Online)," *Fortune,* March 23, 2015, https://fortune.com/2015/03/23/comcast-customer-service/; B. Snyder, "Comcast Pledges $300M to Fix its Terrible, Horrible, No Good, Very Bad Customer Service," *CIO,* May 8, 2015, https://www.cio.com/article/2920297/comcast-pledges-300m-to-fix-its-terrible-horrible-no-good-very-bad-customer-service.html.

56. M. Lev-Ram, "Beset by Big Customer Service Problems, Comcast Promises a Big Fix," *Fortune,* May 5, 2015, https://fortune.com/2015/05/05/comcast-hiring-call-center/.

57. M. Caffrey, "Jokes Aside, Comcast Has Moved Far from 'Most-Hated' Status—And a Recent Survey Confirms It," *BizJournals,* May 22, 2019, https://www.bizjournals.com/philadelphia/news/2019/05/22/jokes-aside-comcast-has-moved-far-from-most-hated.html.

58. K. Davis, "Why You Should Write Down Your Company's Unwritten Rules," *Harvard Business Review Digital Articles,* 2019, pp. 2–4.

59. J. Holt, "Facebook Has 5 'Core Values.' Guess Where 'Protect Users' Ranks," *Chicago Tribune,* December 20, 2018, https://www.chicagotribune.com/opinion/commentary/ct-perspec-facebook-privacy-zuckerberg-microsoft-amazon-1221-20181220-story.html.

60. J. Holt, "Facebook Has 5 'Core Values.' Guess Where 'Protect Users' Ranks," *Chicago Tribune,* December 20, 2018, https://www.chicagotribune.com/opinion/commentary/ct-perspec-facebook-privacy-zuckerberg-microsoft-amazon-1221-20181220-story.html.

61. M. Zetlin, "Here's Why Facebook's Former Employees Describe the Company as Cult-Like," *Inc,* January 11, 2019, https://www.inc.com/minda-zetlin/facebook-culture-cult-like-former-employees-report.html.

62. S. Frenkel, N. Confessore, C. Kang, M. Rosenberg, and J. Nicas, "Delay, Deny, Deflect: How Facebook Leaders Leaned Out in Crisis," *The New York Times,* November 15, 2018, section A, p. 1.

63. Editorial, "Facebook Fast Facts," *CNN,* February 3, 2020, https://www.cnn.com/2014/02/11/world/facebook-fast-facts/index.html. Also see H. Taneja, "The Era of 'Move Fast and Break Things' Is Over," *Harvard Business Review,* January 22, 2019; A. Burt, "Can Facebook Ever Be Fixed?" *Harvard Business Review Digital Articles,* 2019, pp. 2–5.

64. T. E. Deal and A. A. Kennedy, *Corporate Cultures: The Rites and Rituals of Corporate Life* (Reading, MA: Addison-Wesley, 1982), p. 22. See also T. E. Deal and A. A. Kennedy, *The New Corporate Cultures: Revitalizing the Workplace after Downsizing, Mergers, and Reengineering* (Cambridge, MA: Perseus, 2000).

65. "Building and Sustaining a Culture of Innovation," *Brand Culture,* https://brandculture.com/insights/building-and-sustaining-a-culture-of-innovation/ (accessed March 22, 2020).

66. "Lever's CEO Sarah Nahm on Building an Inclusive Culture Before Recruiting for Diversity," *Lever,* November 2, 2017, https://inside.lever.co/levers-ceo-sarah-nahm-on-building-an-inclusive-culture-before-recruiting-for-diversity-74be35523c06.

67. M. Taylor, J. Watts, and J. Bartlett, "Climate Crisis: 6 Million People Join Latest Wave of Global Protests," *The Guardian,* September 27, 2019, https://www.theguardian.com/environment/2019/sep/27/climate-crisis-6-million-people-join-latest-wave-of-worldwide-protests. Also see E. Felsenthal, "Person of the Year," *Time,* 2019, https://time.com/person-of-the-year-2019-greta-thunberg-choice/.

68. N. Hobson, J. Schroeder, J. Risen, D. Xygalatas, and M. Inzlicht, "The Psychology of Rituals: An Integrative Review and Process-Based Framework," *Personality and Social Psychology Review,* Vol 22, No. 3 2018, pp. 260–284.

69. L. Kane, "Why Every New Employee at a Billion-Dollar Glasses Brand Gets Kerouac and Pretzels as a Welcome Gift," *Business Insider,* April 14, 2017, https://www.businessinsider.com/how-warby-parker-builds-company-culture-2017-4

70. N. Hobson, N. Barr, and K. Peters, "Want to Make Your Brand Psychologically Capturing? Try Using the Power of Ritual," *Business Insider,* February 17, 2020, https://www.businessinsider.com/make-brand-psychologically-capturing-use-power-of-ritual#1-they-are-repeated-and-predictably-comforting-1.

71. J. Van Maanen, "Breaking In: Socialization to Work," in R. Dubin, ed., *Handbook of Work, Organization, and Society* (Chicago: Rand-McNally, 1976), p. 67.

72. J. Farid, "Organizational Socialization: The Role of Dual Supervisory Relationships in Newcomer Adjustment," *Advances in Management,* Vol. 12, No. 4 (2019), pp. 11–22. Also see S. Nifadkar, "Filling in the 'Blank Slate': Examining Newcomers' Schemas of Supervisors During Organizational Socialization," *Journal of Management,* May 2020, pp. 666–693; M. Jokisaari and J. Vuori, "Leaders' Resources and Newcomer Socialization: The Importance of Delegation," *Journal of Managerial Psychology,* March 2018 pp. 161–175.

73. D. C. Feldman, "The Multiple Socialization of Organization Members," *Academy of Management Review,* April 1981, pp. 309–381. Also see T. Allen, L. Eby, G. Chao, and T. Bauer, "Taking Stock of Two Relational Aspects of Organizational Life: Tracing the History and Shaping the Future of Socialization and Mentoring Research," *Journal of Applied Psychology*, Vol. 102, No. 3 (2017), pp. 324–337.

74. "New Employee Onboarding: Buddy Guidelines," https://www.nyu.edu/content/dam/nyu/hr/documents/managerguides/BuddyGuidelines.pdf (accessed March 19, 2018).

75. A thorough description of the competing values framework is provided in K. S. Cameron, R. E. Quinn, J. Degraff, and A. V. Thakor, *Creating Values Leadership* (Northhampton, MA: Edward Elgar, 2006). Also see C. Hartnell, A. Ou, A. Kinicki, D. Choi, and E. Karam, "A Meta-Analytic Test of Organizational Culture's Association with Elements of an Organization's System and Its Relative Predictive Validity on Organizational Outcomes," *Journal of Applied Psychology*, Vol. 104, No. 6 2019, pp. 832–850.

76. I. Suh, J. Sweeney, K. Linke, and J. Wall, "Boiling the Frog Slowly: The Immersion of C-Suite Financial Executives into Fraud," *Journal of Business Ethics,* Vol. 162 2020, pp. 645–673.

77. "Company Overview," https://www.wegmans.com/about-us/company-overview/ (accessed March 22, 2020).

78. S. Ciment, "8 Reasons Why People Are So Obsessed with Wegmans, According to the Store's Super Fans," *Business Insider,* October 8, 2019, https://www.businessinsider.com/8-reasons-people-love-wegmans-grocery-store-according-to-fanatics-2019-10#8-personal-store-experience-8.

79. B. Morgan, "10 Examples of How Employee Experience Impacted Business Performance," *Forbes,* November 7, 2019, https://www.forbes.com/sites/blakemorgan/2019/11/07/10-examples-of-how-employee-experience-impacted-business-performance/#a90c5147c916.

80. "Great Place to Work® and Fortune Name Wegmans One of the 2020 FORTUNE 100 Best Companies to Work For®, Ranking #3," February 18, 2020, https://www.wegmans.com/news-media/press-releases/great-place-to-work-and-fortune-name-wegmans-one-of-the-2020-fortune-100-best-companies-to-work-for-ranking/.

81. S. Gharib, "This CEO Believes That Innovation and Culture Are One and the Same," *Fortune,* February 14, 2018, http://fortune.com/2018/02/14/baxter-international-jose-almeida-/?iid=sr-link4.

82. Staff, "Baxter Health Recognized with Diversity Best Practices Award," *KTLO,* September 15, 2019, https://www.ktlo.com/2019/09/15/baxter-healthcare-recognized-with-diversity-best-practices-award/.

83. "Our Purpose," https://www.tysonfoods.com/who-we-are/our-story/purpose-values (accessed March 18, 2020).

84. G. Mickelson, "Tyson Foods: We're Activating the Ingredients for More Growth," *Tyson,* June 20, 2019, https://www.tysonfoods.com/news/news-releases/2019/6/tyson-foods-were-activating-ingredients-more-growth.

85. H. Chung, "Why Tyson Foods Pulled Its Beyond Meat Investment," *Yahoo Finance,* January 22, 2020, https://finance.yahoo.com/news/tyson-foods-ceo-on-the-companys-plantbased-meat-strategy-205755998.html.

86. G. Mickelson, "Tyson Foods Uniquely Positioned to Meet Global Protein Demand," *Globe Newswire,* February 19, 2020, https://www.globenewswire.com/news-release/2020/02/19/1987418/0/en/Tyson-Foods-Uniquely-Positioned-to-Meet-Global-Protein-Demand.html.

87. J. Trevor and B. Varcoe, "How Aligned Is Your Organization?" *Harvard Business Review Digital Articles*, Vol. 95, No. 1 (2017), pp. 2–6.

88. E. Day, "The Strike at McDonald's Is about More than Fighting Abuse—It's about Workplace Democracy," *Salon,* November 17, 2019, https://www.salon.com/2019/11/17/the-strike-at-mcdonalds-is-about-more-than-fighting-abuse-its-about-workplace-democracy_partner/.

89. A. Cain, "McDonald's Employees Share the 4 Things They Wish They Could Tell Management," *Business Insider,* July 5, 2018, https://www.businessinsider.com/mcdonalds-restaurant-employees-advice-for-management-2018-6#support-people-who-work-hard-4.

90. T. Kim and J. Chang, "Organizational Culture and Performance: A Macro-Level Longitudinal Study," *Leadership & Organization Development Journal*, February 2019, pp. 65–84. Also see B. Dyck, K. Walker, and A. Caza, "Antecedents of Sustainable Organizing: Relationships between Organizational Culture and the TBL," in *Academy of Management Proceedings,* Vol. 2017, No. 1, p. 14702).

91. C. Hartnell, A. Ou, A. Kinicki, D. Choi, and E. Karam, "A Meta-Analytic Test of Organizational Culture's Association with Elements of an Organization's System and Its Relative Predictive Validity on Organizational Outcomes," *Journal of Applied Psychology*, Vol. 104, No. 6 2019, pp. 832–850.

92. A. Kinicki, "'Fitting in' Important at Workplace," *Arizona Republic,* June 8, 2015, www.azcentral.com/story/money/business/career/2015/06/07/fitting-important-workplace/28592961/ (accessed May 18, 2016); Also see C. Boho, "How to Find the Right Cultural Fit," *Arizona Republic,* November 15, 2015, p. 4E.

93. E. Follmer, D. Talbot, A. Kristof-Brown, S. Astrove, and J. Billsberry, "Resolution, Relief, and Resignation: A Qualitative Study of Responses to Misfit at Work," *Academy of Management Journal*, Vol. 61, No. 2, 2018, pp. 440–465. Also see C. Schwepker, "Strengthening Customer Value Development and Ethical Intent in the Salesforce: The Influence of Ethical Values Person–Organization Fit and Trust in Manager," *Journal of Business Ethics*, Vol. 159 2019, pp. 913–925.

94. V. Maza, "What It Means to Hire for 'Culture Fit,' and How to Do It Right," *Forbes,* September 28, 2018, https://www.forbes.com/sites/forbeshumanresourcescouncil/2018/09/28/what-it-means-to-hire-for-culture-fit-and-how-to-do-it-right/#324798fe7986.

95. T. Higgins and R. Ballhaus, "Tesla General Counsel Makes a Quick Exit," *The Wall Street Journal,* February 21, 2019, pp. B1, B2.

96. The mechanisms are based on material contained in E. H. Schein, "The Role of the Founder in Creating Organizational Culture," *Organizational Dynamics,* Summer 1983, pp. 13–28.

97. "Home Page," https://www.hubspot.com/ (accessed March 26, 2020).

98. D. Shah, "What It Means to Hire for 'Culture Fit,' and How to Do It Right," *Hubspot Blog,* October 28, 2019, https://blog.hubspot.com/blog/tabid/6307/bid/34234/The-HubSpot-Culture-Code-Creating-a-Company-We-Love.aspx.

99. S. Marshall, "Leading with a Mission Mind-Set," *Strategy + Business,* August 7, 2019, https://www.strategy-business.com/article/Leading-with-a-mission-mind-set?gko=195e4.

100. T. Murray, "Beth Mooney to Retire as KeyCorp CEO; Chris Gorman Named Successor," *Cleveland.com,* September 19, 2019, https://www.cleveland.com/business/2019/09/beth-mooney-to-retire-from-keycorp.html.

101. "Mission and Values," https://www.key.com/about/careers/working-with-us/mission-value.jsp (accessed March 25, 2020).

102. K. Zhang, "Want a Killer Culture Like the Top Tech Firms? Start Some Company Rituals," *Entrepreneur,* May 23, 2019, https://www.entrepreneur.com/article/333495.

103. "He Warned of Coronavirus. Here's What He Told Us Before He Died," *The New York Times,* February 7, 2020, https://www.nytimes.com/2020/02/07/world/asia/Li-Wenliang-china-coronavirus.html.

104. N. Elegant, "Coronavirus Misinformation Is Fueled by a New Force in China: Government Mistrust," *Fortune,* February 19, 2020, https://fortune.com/2020/02/19/coronavirus-china-misinformation-mistrust/.

105. H. Zhang, "Grief and Weariness at a Vigil for Li Wenliang, the Doctor Who Tried to Warn China about the Coronavirus," *The New Yorker,* February 11, 2020, https://www.newyorker.com/news/news-desk/grief-and-wariness-at-a-vigil-for-li-wenliang-the-doctor-who-tried-to-warn-china-about-the-coronavirus.

106. K. Diss, "Troubled 737 MAX Boeing Airplane Had at Least 13 Other Safety Incidents, Ex-Employee Says," *ABC Australia,* February 15, 2020, https://www.abc.net.au/news/2020-02-15/ex-boeing-manager-says-one-in-25-737-max-had-safety-incident/11957634.

107. N. Kitreoff and D. Gelles, "'It's More Than I Imagined': Boeing's New C.E.O. Confronts Its Challenges," *The New York Times,* March 5,

2020, https://www.nytimes.com/2020/03/05/business/boeing-david-calhoun.html.

108. D. Shepardson, "New Boeing Chief Executive Takes Over with 737 MAX Crisis Unresolved," *Reuters,* January 13, 2020, https://www.reuters.com/article/boeing-737-max-ceo-calhoun/new-boeing-chief-executive-takes-over-with-737-max-crisis-unresolved-idUSL1N29I00J.

109. J. Jordan and M. Sorell, "Why Reverse Mentoring Works and How to Do It Right," *Harvard Business Review Digital Articles*, 2019, pp. 2–5.

110. T. Mellon, "3 Ways an Open Plan Office Drastically Changed My Company's Culture," *Inc.,* June 20, 2019, https://www.inc.com/tamara-mellon/3-ways-an-open-plan-office-drastically-changed-my-companys-culture.html.

111. D. Holger, "Clorox Will Attach Environmental, Animal-Testing Goals to Compensation," *Marketwatch,* October 2, 2019, https://www.marketwatch.com/story/clorox-will-attach-environmental-animal-testing-goals-to-executive-compensation-2019-10-02. Also see R. Gopalan, J. Horn, and T. Milbourn, "Shell Is Tying Executive Pay to Carbon Emissions. Here's Why It Could Create Real Impact," *CNN,* December 14, 2018, https://www.cnn.com/2018/12/14/perspectives/shell-executive-pay-carbon-emissions/index.html.

112. J. Cowan, "What Netflix's Corporate Culture Can Teach Us about Hiring—and Firing," *Canadian Business,* June 9, 2017, http://www.canadianbusiness.com/leadership/netflix-chief-talent-officer-patty-mccord/.

113. B. Murphy, "You Don't Just Get Fired at Netflix. What Happens Instead Is Brilliant. (Or Maybe Insane. There's a Raging Debate)," *Inc.,* October 27, 2018, https://www.inc.com/bill-murphy-jr/you-dont-just-get-fired-at-netflix-what-happens-instead-is-brilliant-or-maybe-insane-theres-a-raging-debate.html.

114. Bloomberg, "Barclays Installs Sensors to See which Bankers Are at Their Desks," *Independent,* August 19, 2017, https://www.independent.co.uk/news/barclays-bank-sensors-a7901566.html.

115. "Product Overview," *Sapience,* https://sapienceanalytics.com/product-overview/ (accessed March 26, 2020).

116. K. Earlay, "Barclays Scraps Tech That Warned Employees to 'Avoid Breaks,'" *Silicon Republic,* February 21 2020, https://www.siliconrepublic.com/companies/sapience-software-barclays-employee-data.

117. J. Useem, "Are Bosses Necessary?" *The Atlantic,* October 2015, pp. 28–32. Also see D. K. Berman, "The No-Boss Company," *The Wall Street Journal,* October 27, 2015, p. R3; B. Lam, "Why Are So Many Zappos Employees Leaving?" *The Atlantic,* January 15, 2016, www.theatlantic.com/business/archive/2016/01/zappos-holacracy-hierarchy/424173 (accessed May 25, 2016).

118. C. Albert-Deitch, "Zappos CEO Tony Hsieh's Biggest Management Experiment Is Evolving Again (in a Very Intriguing Way)," *Inc.,* January 30, 2020, https://www.inc.com/cameron-albert-deitch/zappos-tony-hsieh-holacracy-market-system.html.

119. J. Elias, "Google Will No Longer Hold Weekly All-Hands Meetings amid Growing Workplace Tensions," *CNBC,* November 15, 2019, https://www.cnbc.com/2019/11/15/google-cancels-tgif-weekly-all-hands-meetings.html.

120. K. Schreurs, "Why Cultural Change Fails," *HR News,* August, 2018, https://www.hrnews.be/2018/08/why-cultural-change-fails.html.

121. Canada Energy Regulator, "Advancing Safety in the Oil and Gas Industry—Statement on Safety Culture," Government of Canada, https://www.cer-rec.gc.ca/sftnvrnmnt/sft/sftycltr/sftycltrsttmnt-eng.html#ftn2 (accessed March 25, 2020).

122. H. de la Boutetière, J. Rose, and B. Spinoy, "Transforming Safety Culture: Insights from the Trenches at a Leading Oil and Gas Company," *McKinsey,* July 2019, https://www.mckinsey.com/business-functions/organization/our-insights/transforming-safety-culture-insights-from-the-trenches-at-a-leading-oil-and-gas-company.

123. B. Müller, S. Konlechner, K. Link, and W. Güttel, "The Emperor's New Clothes: How Dealing with Failure Prevents Cultural Change," *Organizational Dynamics,* Vol. 48, No. 4 (2019), p. 100672.

124. S. Shellenbarger, "A Checklist Before You Quit," *The Wall Street Journal,* January 3, 2018, p. A9. Also see E. Follmer, D. Talbot, A. Kristof-Brown, S. Astrove, and J. Billsberry, "Resolution, Relief, and Resignation: A Qualitative Study of Responses to Misfit at Work," *Academy of Management Journal,* Vol. 61, No. 2 2018, pp. 440–465.

125. Y. Hsieh, J. Weng, and T. Lin, "How Social Enterprises Manage Their Organizational Identification: A Theoretical Framework of Identity Management Approach through Attraction, Selection, and Socialization," *The International Journal of Human Resource Management,* Vol. 29, No. 20 2018 pp. 2880–2904.

126. C. I. Barnard, *The Functions of the Executive* (Cambridge, MA: Harvard University Press, 1938), p. 73.

127. E. H. Schein, *Organizational Psychology,* 3rd ed. (Englewood Cliffs, NJ: Prentice-Hall, 1980).

128. J. P. Friesen, A. C. Kay, R. P. Eibach, and A. D. Galinsky, "Seeking Structure in Social Organization: Compensatory Control and the Psychological Advantages of Hierarchy," *Journal of Personality and Social Psychology* 106 2014, pp. 590–609. This work on hierarchies existing within flat organizations is also described in M. Hutson, "Espousing Equality, but Embracing a Hierarchy," *The New York Times,* June 22, 2014, p. BU-3.

129. For an overview of the span of control concept, see D. D. Van Fleet and A. G. Bedeian, "A History of the Span of Management," *Academy of Management Review,* July 1977, pp. 356–372.

130. C. Thiel, J. Hardy III, D. Peterson, D. Welsh, and J. Bonner, "Too Many Sheep in the Flock? Span of Control Attenuates the Influence of Ethical Leadership," *Journal of Applied Psychology,* Vol. 103, No. 12 2018, p. 1324.

131. J. Mackey, J. Brees, C. McAllister, M. Zorn, M Martinko, and P. Harvey, "Victim and Culprit? The Effects of Entitlement and Felt Accountability on Perceptions of Abusive Supervision and Perpetration of Workplace Bullying," *Journal of Business Ethics,* Vol. 153, No. 3 2018, pp. 659–673.

132. M. Akinola, A. Martin, and K. Phillips, "To Delegate or Not to Delegate: Gender Differences in Affective Associations and Behavioral Responses to Delegation," *Academy of Management Journal,* Vol. 61, No. 4 2018, pp. 1467–1491.

133. D. Riegel, "8 Ways Leaders Delegate Successfully," *Harvard Business Review Digital Articles*, 2019, pp. 2–4.

134. D. Riegel, "8 Ways Leaders Delegate Successfully," *Harvard Business Review Digital Articles*, 2019, pp. 2–4.

135. J. Craven, "Great Leaders Perfect the Art of Delegation," *Forbes,* February 21, 2018, https://www.forbes.com/sites/forbescoachescouncil/2018/02/21/great-leaders-perfect-the-art-of-delegation/#681b47971eb2. Also see A. Acton, "Delegation Is a CEO's Secret Weapon: Here's How to Do It Right," *Forbes,* August 15, 2017, https://www.forbes.com/sites/annabelacton/2017/08/15/effective-delegation-is-a-ceos-secret-weapon-heres-how-to-do-it-right/#8ffca20433d1; D. Finkel, "Use This Little-Known Delegation Trick to Get Stuff Done the Right Way," *Inc.,* February 21, 2018, https://www.inc.com/david-finkel/use-this-little-known-delegation-trick-to-get-stuff-done-right-way.html?cid=search.

136. Z. Bakonyi, "Why Do Firms Centralise Their Strategic Decision-Making during Crisis?" *Journal of Organizational Change Management,* August 2018, pp. 1191–1205.

137. H. Treiblmaier, "Optimal Levels of (de) Centralization for Resilient Supply Chains," *The International Journal of Logistics Management,* February 2018, pp. 435–455.

138. R. Burton and B. Obel, "The Science of Organizatonal Design: Fit between Structure and Coordination," *Journal of Organization Design,* Vol. 8, No. 1 2018, pp. 1–13.

139. C. Miller, "Google's Chief Works to Trim a Bloated Ship," *The New York Times,* November 10, 2011 https://www.nytimes.com/2011/11/10/technology/googles-chief-works-to-trim-a-bloated-ship.html.

140. Editorial, "A Is for Alphabet," *San Francisco Chronicle,* August 12, 2015, p. A11.

141. F. Manjoo, "Google Seeks New Horizons: A Reorganization Gives the Founders Room to Dream Big beyond Search," *The New York Times,* August 11, 2015, pp. B1, B4. Also see N. Zipkin, "8 of the Coolest

Projects to Come Out of X, Google's Moonshot Factory," *Entrepreneur,* January 23, 2019, https://www.entrepreneur.com/article/326836.

142. M. Sullivan, "Will Alphabet's New Structure Make Google's Business More Transparent, or Less?" *Fast Company,* September 1, 2017, https://www.fastcompany.com/40462340/alphabet-google-xxvi-holdings-restructuring-reorganization-transparency. Also see R. Sharma, "Why Google Became Alphabet," *Investopedia,* October 24, 2019, https://www.investopedia.com/articles/investing/081115/why-google-became-alphabet.asp.

143. M. Meisenzahl, "Google Made a Small But Important Change in 2017 to How It Thinks about 'Googleyness,' a Key Value It Looks for in New Hires," *Business Insider,* October 31, 2019, https://www.businessinsider.com/google-googleyness-hiring-training-guide-change-2019-10. Also see R. Umoh, "The No. 1 Trait Google Looks for in 'Ideal' Job Candidates," *CNBC,* May 10, 2018, https://www.cnbc.com/2018/05/10/googles-ideal-job-candidate-has-this-trait.html.

144. J. D'Onfro, "Google Announces Reorg as It Moves to Make More Money off Assistant, App Store, Other Products," *Forbes,* May 2, 2019, https://www.forbes.com/sites/jilliandonfro/2019/05/02/google-global-partnerships-reorg-don-harrison/#414505864cfd.

145. This section was adapted from R. Kreitner and A. Kinicki, *Organizational Behavior,* 10th ed. (New York: McGraw-Hill/Irwin, 2013), pp. 503–508.

146. A. Cheng, "Two Years after Amazon Deal, Whole Foods Is Still Working to Shed Its 'Whole Paycheck' Image," *Forbes,* August 28, 2019, https://www.forbes.com/sites/andriacheng/2019/08/28/two-years-under-amazon-whole-foods-still-has-its-work-cut-out-to-erase-the-whole-paycheck-image/#3688ce574227.

147. S. Banker, "How Amazon Changed Whole Foods," *Forbes,* June 26, 2019, https://www.forbes.com/sites/stevebanker/2019/06/25/how-amazon-changed-whole-foods/#1ad2aad678dd. Also see "Amazon and Whole Foods: A Tale of Two Companies," *Qlicket,* October 21, 2019, https://www.qlicket.com/amazon-whole-foods-tale-two-companies/.

148. Adapted from "Boundaryless," *Encyclopedia of Small Business,* ed. K. Hillstrom and L. C. Hillstrom (Farmington Hills, MI: Thomson Gale, 2002; and Seattle, WA: eNotes.com, 2006), http://business.enotes.com/small-business-encyclopedia/boundaryless (accessed June 20, 2014).

149. R. Zitkiene and U. Dude, "The Impact of Outsourcing Implementation on Service Companies," *Entrepreneurship and Sustainability Issues,* September 2018, pp. 342–355.

150. 3M Supplier Direct, "Outsource Manufacturing Partners Systems Access," https://www.3m.com/3M/en_US/suppliers-direct/suppliers/outsource-mfg-partners-sys-access/ (accessed March 27, 2020).

151. S. Seth, "10 Major Companies Tied to the Apple Supply Chain," *Investopedia,* June 25, 2019, https://www.investopedia.com/articles/investing/090315/10-major-companies-tied-apple-supply-chain.asp.

152. L. Eadicicco, "The Coronavirus Outbreak Has Been Hurting Apple's iPhone Production, and One of the Most Accurate Analysts Says It Won't Get Better until the Second Quarter of 2020," *Business Insider,* March 2, 2020, https://www.businessinsider.com/apple-iphone-production-coronavirus-q2-kuo-2020-3.

153. R. Sher, "Making Virtual Teams Feel Like They're in the Same Room: The AppNeta Approach," *Forbes,* October 2, 2019, https://www.forbes.com/sites/robertsher/2019/10/02/making-virtual-teams-feel-like-theyre-in-the-same-room-the-appneta-approach/#5614d37a18bb.

154. See the related discussion in E. E. Makarius and B. Z. Larson, "Changing the Perspective of Virtual Work: Building Virtual Intelligence at the Individual Level," *Academy of Management Review,* 2017, pp. 159–178. Also see A. Asatiani and E. Penttinen, "Constructing Continuities in Virtual Work Environments: A Multiple Case Study of Two Firms with Differing Degrees of Virtuality," *Information Systems Journal,* Vol. 29. No. 2 2019, pp. 484–513.

155. "Home Page," https://articulate.com/ (accessed March 27, 2020).

156. G. Johns, "Advances in the Treatment of Context in Organizational Research," in F. P. Morgeson, H. Aguinis, and S. J. Ashford, eds., *Annual Review of Organizational Psychology and Organizational Behavior* (Palo Alto, CA: Annual Reviews, 2017), pp. 21–46.

157. Y. W. Chung, "The Role of Person–Organization Fit and Perceived Organizational Support in the Relationship between Workplace Ostracism and Behavioral Outcomes," *Australian Journal of Management,* May 2017, pp. 328–349. Also see J. Hu, S. J. Wayne, T. N. Bauer, B. Erdogan, and R. C. Liden, "Self and Senior Executive Perceptions of Fit and Performance: A Time-Lagged Examination of Newly Hired Executives," *Human Relations,* June 2016, pp. 1259–1286.

158. M. Corritore, A. Goldberg, and S. Srivastava, "The New Analytics of Culture: What Email, Slack, and Glassdoor Reveal about Your Organization," *Harvard Business Review,* January–February 2020.

159. See https://www.insidehighered.com/advice/2018/10/04/how-determine-if-prospective-job-good-fit-opinion. Also see R. Knight, "How to Tell If a Company's Culture Is Right for You," *Harvard Business Review Digital Articles,* 2017, pp. 2–6.

160. M. Fugate, A. J. Kinicki, and B. E. Ashforth, "Employability: A Psycho-Social Construct, Its Dimensions, and Applications," *Journal of Vocational Behavior,* August 2004, pp. 14–38.

161. V. Valet, "Working from Home During the Coronavirus Pandemic: What You Need to Know," *Forbes,* March 12, 2020, https://www.forbes.com/sites/vickyvalet/2020/03/12/working-from-home-during-the-coronavirus-pandemic-what-you-need-to-know/#3dde7a921421.

162. S. Ludwig, "9 Creative Ways Small Businesses Are Adapting to Coronavirus," U.S. Chamber of Commerce, March 18, 2929, https://www.uschamber.com/co/start/strategy/small-businesses-adapt-creatively-to-coronavirus.

163. T. Vinh, "From Whiskey, Gin and Vodka to Hand Sanitizer: Seattle-Area Distilleries Pivot to Fight Coronavirus," *Seattle Times,* March 26, 2020, https://www.seattletimes.com/life/food-drink/from-whiskey-gin-and-vodka-to-hand-sanitizer-seattle-area-distilleries-pivot-to-to-fight-coronavirus/.

164. M. Fugate, A. J. Kinicki, and B. E. Ashforth, "Employability: A Psycho-Social Construct, Its Dimensions, and Applications," *Journal of Vocational Behavior,* August 2004, pp. 14–38; Also see J. Boss, "14 Signs of an Adaptable Person," *Forbes,* September 3, 2015, https://www.forbes.com/sites/jeffboss/2015/09/03/14-signs-of-an-adaptable-person/#51b03aad16ea.

165. J. Boss, "14 Signs of an Adaptable Person," *Forbes,* September 3, 2015, https://www.forbes.com/sites/jeffboss/2015/09/03/14-signs-of-an-adaptable-person/#51b03aad16ea.

166. J. G. Berger, "4 Steps to Becoming More Adaptable to Change," *Fast Company,* March 9, 2015, https://www.fastcompany.com/3043294/4-steps-to-becoming-more-adaptable-to-change.

167. B. Mclean, "How Wells Fargo's Cutthroat Corporate Culture Allegedly Drove Bankers to Fraud," *Vanity Fair,* May 31, 2017, www.vanityfair.com/news/2017/05/wells-fargo-corporate-culture-fraud.

168. B. Mclean, "How Wells Fargo's Cutthroat Corporate Culture Allegedly Drove Bankers to Fraud," *Vanity Fair,* May 31, 2017, www.vanityfair.com/news/2017/05/wells-fargo-corporate-culture-fraud.

169. E. Glazer, "How Wells Fargo's High-Pressure Sales Culture Spiraled Out of Control," *The Wall Street Journal,* September 16, 2016, www.wsj.com/articles/how-wells-fargos-high-pressure-sales-culture-spiraled-out-of-control-1474053044.

170. C. Arnold, "Former Wells Fargo Employees Describe Toxic Sales Culture, Even at HQ," *NPR,* October 4, 2016, www.npr.org/2016/10/04/496508361/former-wells-fargo-employees-describe-toxic-sales-culture-even-at-hq.

171. E. Glazer, "How Wells Fargo's High-Pressure Sales Culture Spiraled Out of Control," *The Wall Street Journal,* September 16, 2016, www.wsj.com/articles/how-wells-fargos-high-pressure-sales-culture-spiraled-out-of-control-1474053044.

172. C. Arnold, "Former Wells Fargo Employees Describe Toxic Sales Culture, Even at HQ," *NPR,* October 4, 2016, www.npr.org/2016/10/04/496508361/former-wells-fargo-employees-describe-toxic-sales-culture-even-at-hq.

173. E. Glazer, "How Wells Fargo's High-Pressure Sales Culture Spiraled Out of Control," *The Wall Street Journal,* September 16, 2016, www.wsj.com/articles/how-wells-fargos-high-pressure-sales-culture-spiraled-out-of-control-1474053044.

174. M. Egan, "5,300 Wells Fargo Employees Fired over 2 Million Phony Accounts," *CNN Money,* September 9, 2016, http://money.cnn .com/2016/09/08/investing/wells-fargo-created-phony-accounts-bank-fees/index.html.

175. K. McCoy, "Wells Fargo Fined $185M for Fake Accounts; 5300 Were Fired," *USA Today,* September 8, 2016, www.usatoday.com/story/money/2016/09/08/wells-fargo-fined-185m-over-unauthorized-accounts/90003212/.

176. E. Glazer, "How Wells Fargo's High-Pressure Sales Culture Spiraled Out of Control," *The Wall Street Journal*, September 16, 2016, www.wsj.com/articles/how-wells-fargos-high-pressure-sales-culture-spiraled-out-of-control-1474053044.

177. E. Glazer and C. Rexrode, "Big U.S. Retail Bank Operations under Scrutiny after Wells Scandal," *The Wall Street Journal*, October 25, 2016, www.wsj.com/articles/big-u-s-retail-bank-operations-under-scrutiny-follow-wells-scandal-1477400747.

178. C. Arnold, "Former Wells Fargo Employees Describe Toxic Sales Culture, Even at HQ," *NPR,* October 4, 2016, www.npr.org/2016/10/04/496508361/former-wells-fargo-employees-describe-toxic-sales-culture-even-at-hq.

179. M. Egan, "I Called the Wells Fargo Ethics Line and Was Fired," *CNN Money*, September 21, 2016, www.money.cnn.com/2016/09/21/investing/wells-fargo-fired-workers-retaliation-fake-accounts/index.html.

180. "Wells Fargo Takes on Culture Change in Wake of Scandal," *CEB Global,* June 13, 2017, www.cebglobal.com/talentdaily/wells-fargo-takes-on-culture-change-in-wake-of-scandal/.

181. M. Egan, "Wells Fargo Accused of Lying to Congress about Auto Insurance Scandal," *CNN Money,* October 3, 2017, www.money.cnn .com/2017/10/03/investing/wells-fargo-lie-congress-hearing-auto-insurance/index.html.

182. G. Morgenson, "Regulator Blasts Wells Fargo for Deceptive Auto Insurance Program," *The New York Times*, October 20, 2017, www.nytimes.com/2017/10/20/business/wells-fargo-auto-insurance-comptroller.html.

183. G. Morgenson, "Wells Fargo, Awash in Scandal, Faces Violations over Car Insurance Refunds," *The New York Times*, August 7, 2017, www.nytimes.com/2017/08/07/business/wells-fargo-insurance.html.

184. G. Morgenson, "Regulator Blasts Wells Fargo for Deceptive Auto Insurance Program," *The New York Times*, October 20, 2017, www.nytimes.com/2017/10/20/business/wells-fargo-auto-insurance-comptroller.html.

185. M. Egan, "Wells Fargo Accused of Lying to Congress about Auto Insurance Scandal," *CNN Money,* October 3, 2017, www.money.cnn .com/2017/10/03/investing/wells-fargo-lie-congress-hearing-auto-insurance/index.html.

186. M. Egan, "Wells Fargo Accused of Lying to Congress about Auto Insurance Scandal," *CNN Money,* October 3, 2017, www.money .cnn.com/2017/10/03/investing/wells-fargo-lie-congress-hearing-auto-insurance/index.html.

187. M. Egan, "Wells Fargo Accused of Lying to Congress about Auto Insurance Scandal," *CNN Money,* October 3, 2017, www.money.cnn .com/2017/10/03/investing/wells-fargo-lie-congress-hearing-auto-insurance/index.html.

188. D. Borak, D. Wiener-Bronner, and J. Wattles, "The Fed Drops the Hammer on Wells Fargo," *CNN Money,* February 3, 2018, https://money.cnn .com/2018/02/02/news/companies/wells-fargo-federal-reserve/index.html.

189. B. Chappell, "Wells Fargo Hit with $1 Billion in Fines over Home and Auto Loan Abuses," *NPR,* April 20, 2018, https://www.npr.org/sections/thetwo-way/2018/04/20/604279604/wells-fargo-hit-with-1-billion-in-fines-over-consumer-abuses.

190. M. Bustillos, "The Robber Bank," *Slate,* March 9, 2020, https://slate.com/news-and-politics/2020/03/wells-fargo-fines-penalties-never-stop.html.

191. Banking Exchange Staff, "Authorities Shed New Light on Wells Fargo Fake Accounts Scandal," *Banking Exchange,* February 24, 2020, https://www.bankingexchange.com/community-banking/item/8138-authorities-shed-new-light-on-wells-fargo-fake-accounts-scandal1. Also

see P. Mattera, "Regulator Slaps Wells Fargo CEO with Biggest Fine Ever. It's Still Not Enough," *Inequality.org,* January 31, 2020, https://inequality.org/research/wells-fargo-ceo-fine/.

192. J. Liberto, "Wells Fargo CEO Quits in Wake of Consumer Financial Scandals," *NPR,* March 28, 2019, https://www.npr.org/2019/03/28/707738077/wells-fargo-ceo-quits-in-wake-of-consumer-financial-scandals.

193. C. Hudson, "Wells Fargo CEO Charles Scharf Hands Down Massive Business Restructure," *Biz Journals,* February 11, 2020, https://www.bizjournals.com/charlotte/news/2020/02/11/wells-fargo-ceo-hands-down-massive-business.html.

194. M. Henney, "Wells Fargo CEO Blames 'Broken' Culture on Consumer Abuses during Capitol Hill Testimony," *Fox Business,* March 10, 2020, https://www.foxbusiness.com/business-leaders/wells-fargo-ceo-blames-broken-culture-on-consumer-abuses-during-capitol-hill-testimony.

195. C. Beaton, "Bringing Work to the Bar: How to Put Fair Limits on the After-Work Hang," *Transparency,* August 3, 2017, https://transparency .kununu.com/how-to-put-fair-limits-to-socializing-after-work.

196. R. Gale, "Drinking with Co-Workers: Sexual Harassment Is Not the Only Reason We Should Rethink Pairing Drinks and Work," *Slate,* February 27, 2018, https://slate.com/human-interest/2018/02/harassment-isnt-the-only-reason-we-should-rethink-drinking-at-work.html.

197. A. Grandey, M. Frone, R. Melloy, and G. Sayre, "When Are Fakers Also Drinkers? A Self-Control View of Emotional Labor and Alcohol Consumption among US Service Workers," *Journal of Occupational Health Psychology,* Vol. 24, No. 4 2019, p. 482.

198. M. Kendall, "What's So Bad about Mandatory Work Socializing?" *qz.com,* February 24, 2016, http://qz.com/623260/whats-so-bad-about-mandatory-workplace-socializing/.

CHAPTER 9

1. B. Landry, "8 Tips for Acing Your Next Virtual Interview," Northeastern University Graduate Programs, February 1, 2018, https://www .northeastern.edu/graduate/blog/virtual-interview-tips/.

2. S. Joseph, "3 Tips for Acing Your Virtual Interviews," *Forbes,* March 28, 2020, https://www.forbes.com/sites/shelcyvjoseph/2020/03/28/4-tips-for-acing-your-virtual-interviews/#5ad3d07b4530. Also see B. Landry, "8 Tips For Acing Your Next Virtual Interview," *Northeastern University Graduate Programs,* February 1, 2018, https://www .northeastern.edu/graduate/blog/virtual-interview-tips/.

3. S. Joubert, "8 Tips to Prepare for Your Next Job Interview," *Northeastern University*, https://www.northeastern.edu/bachelors-completion/news/how-to-prepare-for-job-interview/ (accessed March 30, 2020).

4. M. Tews, K. Frager, A. Citarella, and R. Orndorff, "What Is Etiquette Today? Interviewing Etiquette for Today's College Student," *Journal of Advances in Education Research*, Vol. 3, No. 3 (2018), pp. 167–175.

5. M. Tews, K. Frager, A. Citarella, and R. Orndorff, "What Is Etiquette Today? Interviewing Etiquette for Today's College Student," *Journal of Advances in Education Research*, Vol. 3, No. 3 (2018), pp. 167–175.

6. M. Kuper, "Sticky Situations: How to Dodge Inappropriate Interview Questions," *University of Arizona Student Engagement & Career Development*, https://career.arizona.edu/cs-blog-post/sticky-situations-how-dodge-inappropriate-interview-questions (accessed March 30, 2020).

7. M. Tews, K. Stafford, and J. Michel, "Interview Etiquette and Hiring Outcomes," *International Journal of Selection and Assessment*, Vol. 26, No. 2-4 (2018), pp. 164–175.

8. A. Kiersz, "Here's Exactly What to Do If You Leave a Job Interview and Realize You Totally Flubbed a Question," *Business Insider,* August 20, 2018, https://www.businessinsider.com/job-interview-question-wrong-email-interviewers-2018-8.

9. "How Human Resource Professionals View the Use and Effectiveness of Background Screening Methods," *HR.com,* May, 2018, https://pubs .thepbsa.org/pub.cfm?id=9E5ED85F-C257-C289-9E8E-A7C7A8C58D00.

10. A. Doyle, "How to Answer Job Interview Questions About Your Grades," *The Balance Careers,* July 19, 2019, https://www.thebalance careers.com/how-to-answer-job-interview-questions-about-your-grades-2060516.

11. "6 Best Ways to Close an Interview," *Accenture Careers Blog,* https://www.accenture.com/us-en/blogs/blogs-careers/6-best-ways-to-close-an-interview (accessed March 30, 2020).

12. D. Marcroft, "Forbes Ranks Ultimate Software #6 on America's Best Employers for Diversity 2020 List," *Ultimate Software,* January 24, 2020, https://www.ultimatesoftware.com/PR/Press-Release/Forbes-Ranks-Ultimate-Software-6-on-Americas-Best-Employers-for-Diversity-2020-List. Also see M. Wiley, "The 5 Best Hotel Companies to Work For in 2020," *Business Insider,* February 20, 2020, https://www.business insider.com/best-hotel-companies-to-work-for-in-2020-hilton-fortune-2020-2; "*Fortune* Best Workplaces for Millennials 2020," *Great Place to Work,* https://www.greatplacetowork.com/best-workplaces/Millennials/2020 (accessed October 20, 2020).

13. "Three Charts and a Case Study to Spotlight the Value of Employees," *Accenture,* February 28, 2020, https://talentorganizationblog .accenture.com/financialservices/three-charts-and-a-case-study-to-spotlight-the-value-of-employees.

14. R. Sadun, N. Bloom, and J. van Reenen, 2017. "Why Do We Undervalue Competent Management?" *Harvard Business Review,* Vol. 95, No. 5 (2017), pp. 120–127.

15. J. Welch, quoted in N. M. Tichy and S. Herman, *Control Your Destiny or Someone Else Will: How Jack Welch Is Making General Electric the World's Most Competitive Corporation* (New York: Doubleday, 1993), p. 251.

16. "100 Best Companies to Work For," *Fortune,* 2020, https://fortune .com/best-companies/.

17. R. Hartman, "Companies with the Best Retirement Plans," *U.S. News,* February 5, 2020, https://money.usnews.com/money/retirement/401ks/articles/companies-with-the-best-retirement-plans. Also see "Benefits," *Workday,* https://www.workday.com/en-us/company/careers/benefits.html (accessed April 5, 2020); "Stryker," *Fortune 100 Best Companies to Work For 2020*, https://fortune.com/best-companies/2020/stryker (accessed April 6, 2020); and A. Adamczyk, "The Average Employer 401(k) Match Is at an All-Time-High—See How Yours Compares," *CNBC,* June 10, 2019, https://www.cnbc .com/2019/06/10/this-is-the-average-401k-employer-match.html.

18. N. Dries, "The Psychology of Talent Management: A Review and Research Agenda," *Human Resource Management Review,* Vol. 23, No. 4 (2013), pp. 272–285.

19. J. Delery and D. Roumpi, "Strategic Human Resource Management, Human Capital and Competitive Advantage: Is the Field Going in Circles?" *Human Resource Management Journal*, Vol. 27, No. 1 (2017), pp. 1–21.

20. J. Han, S. Kang, I. Oh, R. Kehoe, and D. Lepak, "The Goldilocks Effect of Strategic Human Resource Management? Optimizing the Benefits of a High-Performance Work System Through the Dual Alignment of Vertical and Horizontal Fit," *Academy of Management Journal,* Vol. 62, No. 5 (2019), pp. 1388–1412. Also see V. Khoreva and H. Wechtler, "HR Practices and Employee Performance: The Mediating Role of Well-Being," *Employee Relations,* Vol. 4, No. 2 (2018), pp. 227–243; and A. Glaister, G. Karacay, M. Demirbag, and E. Tatoglu, "HRM and Performance—The Role of Talent Management as a Transmission Mechanism in an Emerging Market Context," *Human Resource Management Journal*, Vol. 28, No. 1 (2018), pp. 148–166.

21. C. Chadwick and C. Flinchbaugh, "Searching for Competitive Advantage in the HRM/Firm Performance Relationship," *Academy of Management Perspectives* (forthcoming).

22. R. Kehoe and C. Collins, "Human Resource Management and Unit Performance in Knowledge-Intensive Work," *Journal of Applied Psychology,* 2017, pp. 1222–1236. Also see J. Korff, T. Biemann, and S. Voelpel, "Human Resource Management Systems and Work Attitudes: The Mediating Role of Future Time Perspective," *Journal of Organizational Behavior,* 2017, pp. 45–67.

23. D. Yohn, " What Happened When Airbnb Blew Up Its HR Department to Focus on 'Employee Experience,'" *Linkedin,* March 23, 2018, https://www.linkedin.com/pulse/what-happened-when-airbnb-blew-up-its-hr-department-focus-denise-yohn. Also see H. Ingwersen, "4 Effective, Innovative HR Practices You Can Adopt Today," *Capterra,* June 19, 2018, https://blog.capterra.com/innovative-hr-practices/.

24. M. Subramony, J. Segers, J., C. Chadwick, and A. Shyamsunder, "Leadership Development Practice Bundles and Organizational Performance: The Mediating Role of Human Capital and Social Capital," *Journal of Business Research*, Vol. 83 (2018), pp. 120–129.

25. M. Subramony, J. Segers, J., C. Chadwick, and A. Shyamsunder, "Leadership Development Practice Bundles and Organizational Performance: The Mediating Role of Human Capital and Social Capital," *Journal of Business Research*, Vol. 83 (2018), pp. 120–129.

26. M. Wiersema, Y. Nishimura, and K. Suzuki, "Executive Succession: The Importance of Social Capital in CEO Appointments," *Strategic Management Journal*, Vol. 39, No. 5 (2018), pp. 1473–1495.

27. M. Dixon, "Reinventing Customer Service," *Harvard Business Review,* Vol. 96, No. 6 (2018), pp. 82–90. Also see "Un-Conventional HR," *HRO Today,* August 15, 2019, https://www.hrotoday.com/news/innovation/un-conventional-hr/.

28. D. Collings, K. Mellahi, and W. Cascio, "Global Talent Management and Performance in Multinational Enterprises: A Multilevel Perspective," *Journal of Management,* Vol. 45, No. 2 (2019), pp. 540–566.

29. "Has CarMax Outpaced Other Retail-Wholesale Stocks This Year?" *Yahoo Finance,* November 21, 2019, https://finance.yahoo .com/news/carmax-kmx-outpaced-other-retail-143002056.html. Also see "CarMax Company Overview," *Great Place to Work,* https://www .greatplaceto work.com/certified-company/1000333 (accessed April 9, 2020).

30. T. Smith, "As CarMax Grows, It Is Training Employees to Work Across Multiple Functions Within a Store," *Richmond.com,* May 3, 2018, https://www.richmond.com/business/local/top-workplaces/as-carmax-grows-it-is-training-employees-to-work-across/article_8c39a013-a07a-5fc4-a56b-5fcd28f2abd0.html.

31. C. Hazard, "CarMax Career Can 'Take Employees to Places They Never Imagined,'" *Richmond.com,* May 2, 2019, https://www.richmond .com/business/local/top-workplaces/carmax-career-can-take-employees-to-places-they-never-imagined/article_815a5b5d-f8a0-501b-94b4-0accce858757.html.

32. M. Subramony, J. Segers, C. Chadwick, and A. Shyamsunder, "Leadership Development Practice Bundles and Organizational Performance: The Mediating Role of Human Capital and Social Capital," *Journal of Business Research*, Vol. 83 (2018), pp. 120–129.

33. G. De Boeck, M. Meyers, and M. Dries, "Employee Reactions to Talent Management: Assumptions versus Evidence," *Journal of Organizational Behavior*, Vol. 29, No. 2 (2018), pp. 199–213.

34. T. Chamorro-Premuzic and J. Kirschner, "How the Best Managers Identify and Develop Talent," *Harvard Business Review Digital Articles*, 2020, pp. 2–5.

35. M. Meyers, "The Neglected Role of Talent Proactivity: Integrating Proactive Behavior into Talent-Management Theorizing," *Human Resource Management Review*, 2019. Also see M. Crowley-Henry, M. and A. Al Ariss, "Talent Management of Skilled Migrants: Propositions and An Agenda for Future Research," *The International Journal of Human Resource Management*, Vol. 29, No. 3 (2018), pp. 2054–2079.

36. D. Collings, K. Mellahi, and W. Cascio, "Global Talent Management and Performance in Multinational Enterprises: A Multilevel Perspective," *Journal of Management,* Vol. 45, No. 2 (2019), pp. 540–566. Also see R. Brymer, C. Chadwick, A. Hill, and J. Molloy, "Pipelines and Their Portfolios: A More Holistic View of Human Capital Heterogeneity via Firmwide Employee Sourcing," *Academy of Management Perspectives*, Vol. 33, No. 2 (2019), pp. 207–233.

37. C. Cutter, "CEOs Hasten to Find Their Own Replacements as Coronavirus Spreads: Executives Say They're Making Plans Should They Need to Step Away or Hand the Company's Reins to a Lieutenant," *The Wall Street Journal,* April 3, 2020, https://www.wsj.com/articles/ceos-hasten-to-find-their-own-replacements-as-coronavirus-spreads-11585952869

38. K. Jiang and J. Messersmith, "On the Shoulders of Giants: A Meta-Review of Strategic Human Resource Management," *The International Journal of Human Resource Management*, Vol. 29, No. 1 (2018), pp. 6–33.

39. J. Schmidt, D. Pohler, and C. Willness, "Strategic HR System Differentiation Between Jobs: The Effects on Firm Performance and Employee Outcomes," *Human Resource Management*, Vol. 57, No. 1 (2018), pp. 65–81.

40. K. Jiang and J. Messersmith, "On the Shoulders of Giants: A Meta-Review of Strategic Human Resource Management," *The International Journal of Human Resource Management*, Vol. 29, No. 1 (2018), pp. 6–33.

41. A. Cain, "This $3.2 Billion Tech Company You've Never Heard of Has Insane Perks Including Massage Therapists, a Pool, and Woodside Yoga," *Business Insider,* October 21, 2017, https://www.businessinsider.com/sas-office-tour-2017-10.

42. P. Cappelli, "Your Approach to Hiring Is All Wrong," *Harvard Business Review*, Vol. 97, No. 3 (2019), pp. 48–58. Also see A. Zojceska, "Recruitment Metrics: Time-to-Hire," *TalentLyft,* January 17, 2019, https://www.talentlyft.com/en/blog/article/258/recruitment-metrics-time-to-hire.

43. "The Global Skills Shortage," *Society for Human Resource Management,* 2019, https://www.shrm.org/hr-today/trends-and-forecasting/research-and-surveys/Documents/SHRM%20Skills%20Gap%202019.pdf.

44. J. Puckett, V. Boutenko, L. Hoteit, K. Polunin, S. Perapechka, A. Stepanenko, E. Loshkareva, and G. Bikkulova, "Fixing the Global Skills Mismatch," *Boston Consulting Group,* January 15, 2020.

45. P. Cappelli, "Your Approach to Hiring Is All Wrong," *Harvard Business Review*, Vol. 97, No. 3 (2019), pp. 48–58.

46. P. Cappelli, "Your Approach to Hiring Is All Wrong," *Harvard Business Review*, Vol. 97, No. 3 (2019), pp. 48–58. Also see B. Anderson, "Make Internal Hiring a Success by Avoiding these 5 Pitfalls," *Linkedin Talent Blog,* February 5, 2020, https://business.linkedin.com/talent-solutions/blog/internal-mobility/2020/make-internal-hiring-successful-by-avoiding-these-pitfalls.

47. A. Fisher, "'Upskilling' Your Workforce? Start by Measuring the Skills They Have Now," *Fortune,* June 22, 2019, https://fortune.com/2019/06/22/upskilling-training-workforce-measure-skills/.

48. S. Hairston, D. Wu, and J. Yu, "Analyzing the LinkedIn Profiles of Audit Partners: A Snapshot of Firm Leadership," *The CPA Journal*, Vol. 89, No. 3 (2019), pp. 54–57. Also see L. Kim, "The 16 Best Job Search Engines in 2019," *Inc.,* May 17, 2019, https://www.inc.com/larry-kim/the-16-best-job-search-engines-in-2019.html.

49. B. Curtis, R. Ashford, K. Magnuson, and S. Ryan-Pettes, "Comparison of Smartphone Ownership, Social Media Use, and Willingness to Use Digital Interventions Between Generation Z and Millennials in the Treatment of Substance Use: Cross-Sectional Questionnaire Study," *Journal of Medical Internet Research*, Vol. 21, No. 4, p. e13050. Also see "2018 Recruiter Nation Survey," *Jobvite,* https://www.jobvite.com/wp-content/uploads/2018/11/2018-Recruiter-Nation-Study.pdf. M. A. Johnson and C. Leo, "The Inefficacy of LinkedIn? A Latent Change Model and Experimental Test of Using LinkedIn for Job Search," *Journal of Applied Psychology*, 2020.

50. M. Curtin, "54 Percent of Employers Have Eliminated a Candidate Based on Social Media. Time to Clean Up Your Feed (and Tags)," *Inc.,* January 9, 2020, https://www.inc.com/melanie-curtin/54-percent-of-employers-have-eliminated-a-candidate-based-on-social-media-time-to-clean-up-your-feed-and-tags.html.

51. The Hire Team, "10 Creative Candidate-Sourcing Strategies from Ikea, Spotify, Deloitte and More," *Hire by Google,* February 4, 2019, https://hire.google.com/articles/creative-candidate-sourcing-strategies/. Also see J. La Roche, "Goldman Kicks Off 'Ambitious' Recruitment Campaign to Attract New Talent," *Yahoo Finance,* September 10, 2019, https://finance.yahoo.com/news/goldman-sachs-new-recruiting-campaign-seeks-to-demystify-the-firm-134615712.html.

52. P. Cappelli, "Your Approach to Hiring Is All Wrong," *Harvard Business Review*, Vol. 97, No. 3 (2019), pp. 48–58.

53. S. Schlachter and J. Pieper, "Employee Referral Hiring in Organizations: An Integrative Conceptual Review, Model, and Agenda for Future Research," *Journal of Applied Psychology*, 104 (11), 2019, pp.1325–1346.

54. S. Sullivan and A. Al Ariss, "Making Sense of Different Perspectives on Career Transitions: A Review and Agenda for Future Research," *Human Resource Management Review*, 2019, p.100727.

55. S. Biswas, "Top 3 Innovative Corporate Recruitment Strategies for 2019," *HR Technologist,* https://www.hrtechnologist.com/articles/recruitment-onboarding/top-innovative-corporate-recruitment-strategies/.

56. R. Duncan, "Want Your People to Work Inspired? Be An Un-Leader," *Forbes,* November 26, 2018, https://www.forbes.com/sites/rodgerdeanduncan/2018/11/26/want-your-people-to-work-inspired-be-an-un-leader/#66e9ea211102. Also see "Kronos Scores Its Highest-ever Glassdoor Best Places to Work Ranking," *Business Wire,* December 11, 2019, https://www.businesswire.com/news/home/20191211005602/en/Kronos-Scores-Highest-ever-Glassdoor-Places-Work-Ranking.

57. C. Russell, "Who Are the 10 Biggest Retailers in the World?" *Forbes,* January 9, 2020, https://www.forbes.com/sites/callyrussell/2020/01/09/who-are-the-10-biggest-retailers-in-the-world/#6ceffa913802.

58. J. Bariso, "In a World Dominated by Amazon, Costco Continues to Thrive. Here's How They Do It," *Inc.,* March 18, 2019, https://www.inc.com/justin-bariso/in-a-world-dominated-by-amazon-costco-is-thriving-they-do-it-by-focusing-on-2-simple-things.html.

59. T. Relihan, "How Costco's Obsession with Culture Drove Success," *MIT Management,* May 11, 2018, https://mitsloan.mit.edu/ideas-made-to-matter/how-costcos-obsession-culture-drove-success.

60. J. Bariso, "In a World Dominated by Amazon, Costco Continues to Thrive. Here's How They Do It," *Inc.,* March 18, 2019, https://www.inc.com/justin-bariso/in-a-world-dominated-by-amazon-costco-is-thriving-they-do-it-by-focusing-on-2-simple-things.html.

61. T. Kim, S. Schuh, and Y. Cai, "Person or Job? Change in Person-Job Fit and Its Impact on Employee Work Attitudes over Time," *Journal of Management Studies*, 2018.

62. T. Sekiguchi and V. Huber, "The Use of Person–Organization Fit and Person–Job Fit Information in Making Selection Decisions," *Organizational Behavior and Human Decision Processes*, Vol. 116, No. 2 (2011), pp. 203–216.

63. J. Liu, "78% of Job Seekers Lie during the Hiring Process—Here's What Happened to 4 of Them," *CNBC,* February 20, 2020, https://www.cnbc.com/2020/02/19/how-many-job-seekers-lie-on-their-job-application.html.

64. J. O'Donnell, "85 Percent of Job Applicants Lie on Resumes. Here's How to Spot a Dishonest Candidate," *Inc.,* August 15, 2017, https://www.inc.com/jt-odonnell/staggering-85-of-job-applicants-lying-on-resumes-.html.

65. C. Henle, B. Dineen, and M. Duffy, "Assessing Intentional Resume Deception: Development and Nomological Network of a Resume Fraud Measure," *Journal of Business and Psychology,* Vol. 34, No. 1 (2019), pp. 87–106.

66. D. Winterton, "Is It Legal for My Employer to Fire Me for Lying on a Job Application or Resume?" *Legal Match,* April 11, 2018, https://www.legalmatch.com/law-library/article/lying-on-a-job-application-or-resume.html.

67. N. Bach, "Samsonite CEO Ramesh Tainwala Is Out after Being Accused of Padding His Resume," *Fortune,* June 1, 2018, https://fortune.com/2018/06/01/samsonite-ceo-ramesh-tainwala-resigns/.

68. J. Crowley, "Woman Imprisoned for Lying on Resume, Using Photo of Kate Upton as LinkedIn Profile to Land Job," *Newsweek,* December 4, 2019, https://www.newsweek.com/australian-woman-sentenced-deception-abuse-public-office-2019-1475499.

69. E. Relman, "A 24-Year-Old Trump Appointee Who Held a Top Drug Policy Job Despite Having No Relevant Experience Quit after an Investigation into His Credentials," *Business Insider,* January 25, 2018, http://www.businessinsider.com/taylor-weyeneth-office-of-national-drug-control-policy-lied-on-resume-2018-1. Also see R. O'Harrow Jr., "Trump's 24-Year-Old Drug Policy Appointee to Step Down by Month's End," *The Washington Post,* January 24, 2018, https://www.washingtonpost.com/investigations/trumps-24-year-old-drug-policy-appointee-to-step-down-by-months-end/2018/01/24/77ce5656-0159-11e8-8acf-ad2991367d9d_story.html?utm_term=.8316fdaec237.

70. N. Pesce, "These Are the Most Outrageous Lies People Have Put on Their Résumés," *MarketWatch,* August 30, 2019, https://www.marketwatch.com/story/these-are-the-most-hilarious-lies-people-have-put-on-their-resumes-2018-08-24.

71. M. Elliott, "Lying on Your Resume? Here's How You'll Get Caught," *Glassdoor,* November 19, 2018, https://www.glassdoor.com/blog/lying-on-your-resume/.

72. P. Cappelli, "Your Approach to Hiring Is All Wrong," *Harvard Business Review*, Vol. 97, No. 3 (2019), pp. 48–58.

73. K. Ryan, "Tesla and LinkedIn Think Resumes Are Overrated. They Use These Neuroscience-Based Games Instead," *Inc.,* June 6, 2018, https://www.inc.com/kevin-j-ryan/pymetrics-replacing-resumes-with-brain-games.html.

74. P. Barada, "What Can Former Employers Legally Say about Me?" *Monster,* accessed March 20, 2018, https://www.monster.com/career-advice/article/what-can-employers-legally-say.

75. A. Assad, "What Is HR Allowed to Ask from Previous Employers?" *Chron,* accessed March 20, 2018, http://work.chron.com/hr-allowed-ask-previous-employers-22431.html.

76. J. Bourdage, N. Roulin, and R. Tarraf, "I (Might Be) Just That Good: Honest and Deceptive Impression Management in Employment Interviews," *Personnel Psychology*, Vol. 71, No. 4 (2018), pp. 597–632.

77. J. Bourdage, N. Roulin, and R. Tarraf, "I (Might Be) Just That Good: Honest and Deceptive Impression Management in Employment Interviews," *Personnel Psychology*, Vol. 71, No. 4 (2018), pp. 597–632. Also see D. Zhang, S. Highhouse, M. Brooks, and Y. Zhang, "Communicating the Validity of Structured Job Interviews with Graphical Visual Aids," *International Journal of Selection and Assessment*, Vol. 26, No. 2-4 (2018), pp. 93–108.

78. E. Wilson, "Social Work, Cancer Survivorship and Liminality: Meeting the Needs of Young Women Diagnosed with Early Stage Breast Cancer," *Journal of Social Work Practice*, Vol. 34, No. 1 (2020), pp. 95–111. Also see D. Zhang, S. Highhouse, M. Brooks, and Y. Zhang, "Communicating the Validity of Structured Job Interviews with Graphical Visual Aids," *International Journal of Selection and Assessment*, Vol. 26, No. 2-4 (2018), pp. 93–108.

79. J. Levashina, C. Hartwell, F. Morgeson, and M. Campion, "The Structured Employment Interview: Narrative and Quantitative Review of the Research Literature," *Personnel Psychology*, Vol. 67, No. 1 (2014), pp. 241–293.

80. P. Gosselin, "Older Job Applicants Win $2.8 Million," *Forbes,* May 7, 2018, https://www.forbes.com/sites/nextavenue/2018/05/07/older-job-applicants-win-2-8-million/#4380bbaf31e6.

81. P. Cohen, "Nice Résumé. Wait, You're How Old?" *The New York Times*, June 8, 2019, Section B, p. 1.

82. P. Gosselin, "Older Job Applicants Win $2.8 Million," *Forbes,* May 7, 2018, https://www.forbes.com/sites/nextavenue/2018/05/07/older-job-applicants-win-2-8-million/#4380bbaf31e6.

83. J. Levashina, C. Hartwell, F. Morgeson, and M. Campion, "The Structured Employment Interview: Narrative and Quantitative Review of the Research Literature," *Personnel Psychology* Vol. 67, No. 1 (2014), pp. 241–293.

84. "A Guide to Conducting Behavioral Interviews with Early Career Job Candidates," *SHRM,* 2016, https://www.shrm.org/LearningAndCareer/learning/Documents/Behavioral%20Interviewing%20Guide%20for%20Early%20Career%20Candidates.pdf.

85. Y. Kim and R. Ployhart, "The Strategic Value of Selection Practices: Antecedents and Consequences of Firm-Level Selection Practice Usage," *Academy of Management Journal*, Vol. 61, No. 1 (2018), pp. 46–66.

86. L. Chierotti, "What Are the Top 2 Personality Traits of Leaders Across All Major Industries? IBM Supercomputer Watson Has the Results," *Inc.,* July 6, 2017, https://www.inc.com/logan-chierotti/supercomputer-discovers-top-2-personality-traits-o.html?cid=search.

87. "Candidate FAQs," *National Testing Network,* https://nationaltestingnetwork.com/publicsafetyjobs/faqs.cfm. (accessed April 14, 2020).

88. "A Guide to Taking the Physical Abilities Test," *SoCalGas,* https://www.socalgas.com/1443740394085/PhysicalTestBattery.pdf (accessed April 16, 2020).

89. M. Mullenweb, "The CEO of Automattic on Holding 'Auditions' to Build a Strong Team," *Harvard Business Review,* April 2014, pp. 39–42.

90. M. Kleinmann and P. Ingold, "Toward a Better Understanding of Assessment Centers: A Conceptual Review," *Annual Review of Organizational Psychology and Organizational Behavior*, Vol. 6 (2019), pp. 349–372.

91. P. Sackett, O. Shewach, and H. Keiser, "Assessment Center versus Cognitive Ability Tests: Challenging the Conventional Wisdom on Criterion-Related Validity," *Journal of Applied Psychology,* 2017, pp. 1435–1447.

92. P. Walmsley, P. Sackett, and S. Nichols, "A Large Sample Investigation of the Presence of Nonlinear Personality"Job Performance Relationships," *International Journal of Selection and Assessment*, Vol. 26, No. 2-4 (2018), pp. 145–163.

93. C. Rockwood, "How Accurate Are Personality Assessments?" *SHRM,* November 21, 2019, https://www.shrm.org/hr-today/news/hr-magazine/winter2019/pages/how-accurate-are-personality-assessments.aspx.

94. Y. Lee, C. Berry, and E. Gonzalez-Mulé, "The Importance of Being Humble: A Meta-Analysis and Incremental Validity Analysis of the Relationship Between Honesty-Humility and Job Performance," *Journal of Applied Psychology*, Vol. 104 (12), 2019, pp. 1534–1546. Also see C. Van Iddekinge, H. Aguinis, J. Mackey, and P. DeOrtentiis, "A Meta-Analysis of the Interactive, Additive, and Relative Effects of Cognitive Ability and Motivation on Performance," *Journal of Management*, Vol. 44, No. 1 (2018), pp. 249–279.

95. Y. Lee, C. Berry, and E. Gonzalez-Mulé, "The Importance of Being Humble: A Meta-Analysis and Incremental Validity Analysis of the Relationship between Honesty-Humility and Job Performance," *Journal of Applied Psychology*, Vol. 104 (12), 2019, pp. 1534–1546. Also see C. Rockwood, "How Accurate Are Personality Assessments?" *SHRM,* November 21, 2019, https://www.shrm.org/hr-today/news/hr-magazine/winter2019/pages/how-accurate-are-personality-assessments.aspx.

96. "Pre-Offer Personality Testing in the Selection of California Peace Officers," *CA.gov,* July 15, 2019, https://post.ca.gov/Pre-Offer-Personality-Testing-in-the-Selection-of-California-Peace-Officers. Also see "Pre-Offer Personality Testing in the Selection of Entry-Level California Peace Officers Resource Guide," *California Commission on Peace Officer Standards and Training—Resource Guide,* September 2015, https://post.ca.gov/Portals/0/Publications/Peace_Officer_Pre-Offer_Personality_Testing-Resource_Guide.pdf?ver=2019-07-12-131131-617.

97. M. Anderson, "Who Are You? The Legal Implications of Employee Personality Testing." *HR Law Matters,* April 10, 2018, https://www.hrlawmatters.com/2018/04/legal-implications-employee-personality-testing/. Also see C. O'Neil, "Personality Tests Are Failing American Workers," *The Charlotte Observer,* January 20, 2018, http://www.charlotteobserver.com/opinion/op-ed/article195668439.html.

98. "Types of Employment Tests," *Society for Industrial and Organizational Psychology,* http://www.siop.org/workplace/employment%20testing/testtypes.aspx (accessed March 21, 2018).

99. Y. Lee, C. Berry, and E. Gonzalez-Mulé, "The Importance of Being Humble: A Meta-Analysis and Incremental Validity Analysis of the Relationship between Honesty-Humility and Job Performance," *Journal of Applied Psychology*, Vol. 104 (12), 2019, pp. 1534–1546. Also see J. Bazzy and D. Woehr, "Integrity, Ego Depletion, and the Interactive Impact on Counterproductive Behavior," *Personality and Individual Differences*, Vol. 105 (2017), pp. 124–128.

100. S. Sajjadiani, A. Sojourner, J. Kammeyer-Mueller, and E. Mykerezi, "Using Machine Learning to Translate Applicant Work History into Predictors of Performance and Turnover," *Journal of Applied Psychology,* Vol. 104 (10), 2019, pp. 1207–1225.

101. "State Laws for Workplace Drug Testing," *NDS,* https://www.nationaldrugscreening.com/us-state-laws.php (accessed April 19, 2020).

102. M. Roosevelt, "In the Age of Legal Marijuana, Many Employers Drop 'Zero Tolerance' Drug Tests," *The Los Angeles Times,* April 12, 2019, https://www.latimes.com/business/la-fi-marijuana-drug-test-hiring-20190412-story.html.

103. K. Kuhn, "The Why and When of Background Checks: Situational Factors Moderate Effects of Criminal and Financial Stigma," *International Journal of Selection and Assessment*, September, 2020, pp. 283–296.

104. J. Ballance, R. Clifford, and D. Shoag, "'No More Credit Score': Employer Credit Check Bans and Signal Substitution," *Labour Economics*, Vol. 63 (2020), p.101769.

105. J. Baur, A. Hall, S. Daniels, M. Buckley, and H. Anderson, "Beyond Banning the Box: A Conceptual Model of the Stigmatization of Ex-Offenders in the Workplace," *Human Resource Management Review*, Vol. 28, No. 2 (2018), pp. 204–219.

106. J. Doleac and B. Hansen, "The Unintended Consequences Of 'Ban the Box': Statistical Discrimination and Employment Outcomes When Criminal Histories Are Hidden," *Journal of Labor Economics*, Vol. 38, No. 2 (2020), pp. 321–374.

107. J. Ballance, R. Clifford, and D. Shoag, "'No More Credit Score': Employer Credit Check Bans and Signal Substitution," *Labour Economics*, Vol. 63, April 2020.

108. "H.R.3621—Comprehensive CREDIT Act of 2020," *Congress.gov,* https://www.congress.gov/bill/116th-congress/house-bill/3621/text (accessed April 20, 2020).

109. B. Martinson and J. De Leon, "Testing Horizontal and Vertical Alignment of HR Practices Designed to Achieve Strategic Organizational Goals," *Journal of Organizational Effectiveness,* Vol. 5, No. 2 (2018), pp. 158–181.

110. "Employer Costs for Employee Compensation—December 2019," news release text, Bureau of Labor Statistics, https://www.bls.gov/news.release/pdf/ecec.pdf (accessed April 20, 2020).

111. C. Rudolph, R. Rauvola, and H. Zacher, "Leadership and Generations at Work: A Critical Review," *The Leadership Quarterly*, Vol. 29, No. 1 (2018), pp. 44–57.

112. C. Claire and S. Yar, "Young People Are Going to Save Us All from Office Life: The Office: An Analysis," *The New York Times (Online),* September 17, 2019.

113. L. Greco, S. Charlier, and K. Brown, "Trading Off Learning and Performance: Exploration and Exploitation at Work," *Human Resource Management Review*, Vol. 29, No. 2 (2019), pp. 179–195. Also see C. Nerstad, A. Dysvik, B. Kuvaas, and R. Buch, "Negative and Positive Synergies: On Employee Development Practices, Motivational Climate, and Employee Outcomes," *Human Resource Management*, Vol. 57, No. 5 (2018), pp. 1285–1302.

114. R. Carucci, "To Retain New Hires, Spend More Time Onboarding Them," *Harvard Business Review Digital Articles* (2018), pp.1–5.

115. M. Watkins, "7 Ways to Set Up a New Hire for Success," *Harvard Business Review Digital Articles*, 2019, pp. 2–5.

116. R. Maurer, "New Employee Onboarding Guide," *SHRM,* https://www.shrm.org/about-shrm/Documents/NewEmployeeOnboardingGuide.pdf (accessed April 23, 2020).

117. K. Becker and A. Bish, "A Framework for Understanding the Role of Unlearning in Onboarding," *Human Resource Management Review* (2019), p. 100730.

118. C. Caldwell and R. Peters, "New Employee Onboarding–Psychological Contracts and Ethical Perspectives," *Journal of Management Development*, 2018.

119. D. Zielinski, "How to Optimize Onboarding," *SHRM,* June 6, 2019, https://www.shrm.org/hr-today/news/hr-magazine/summer2019/pages/optimizing-onboarding.aspx.

120. R. Maurer, "New Employee Onboarding Guide," *SHRM,* https://www.shrm.org/about-shrm/Documents/NewEmployeeOnboardingGuide.pdf (accessed April 23, 2020).

121. S. Sunduram and N. Patel, "Essential Ingredients for an Effective Onboarding Program," *Gallup,* January 31, 2019, https://www.gallup.com/workplace/246242/essential-ingredients-effective-onboarding-program.aspx

122. R. Carucci, "To Retain New Hires, Spend More Time Onboarding Them," *Harvard Business Review Digital Articles*, 2018, pp. 1–5.

123. "Case Study—Netpeak Group—Academy Reduced Onboarding Time By 60%," *Academy Ocean,* https://academyocean.com/resources/case-study/netpeak-group (accessed April 28, 2020).

124. K. Robertson, "How to Design Your Employee Onboarding Process (step-by-step)," *The Predictive Index,* July 16, 2019, https://www.predictiveindex.com/blog/design-employee-onboarding-process/.

125. S. Sunduram and N. Patel, "Essential Ingredients for an Effective Onboarding Program," *Gallup,* January 31, 2019, https://www.gallup.com/workplace/246242/essential-ingredients-effective-onboarding-program.aspx.

126. M. Schneider, "Google Increased New Employee Productivity by 25 Percent with 1 Email. Here's What You Need to Know," *Inc.,* March 29, 2020, https://www.inc.com/michael-schneider/google-increased-new-employee-productivity-by-25-percent-with-1-email-heres-what-you-need-to-know.html.

127. S. Morrison, "Corporate Microlearning Examples: Real-World Case Studies," *Elearning Inside,* October 22, 2017, https://news.elearninginside.com/corporate-microlearning-examples/.

128. J. Meister, "Top 10 HR Trends That Matter Most in the 2020 Workplace," *Forbes,* January 15, 2020, https://www.forbes.com/sites/jeannemeister/2020/01/15/top-10-hr-trends-that-matter-most-in-the-2020-workplace/#48c827f77dfc.

129. J. Meister, "Top 10 HR Trends that Matter Most in the 2020 Workplace," *Forbes,* January 15, 2020, https://www.forbes.com/sites/jeannemeister/2020/01/15/top-10-hr-trends-that-matter-most-in-the-2020-workplace/#48c827f77dfc.

130. "Learning and Development," *Estee Lauder Companies,* https://www.elcompanies.com/talent/working-here/learning-and-development (accessed March 21, 2018).

131. P. Cappelli and A. Tavis, "The New Rules of Talent Management," *Harvard Business Review,* March–April 2018, https://hbr.org/2018/03/the-new-rules-of-talent-management.

132. N. Lewis, "Walmart Revolutionizes Its Training with Virtual Reality," *SHRM,* July 22, 2019, https://www.shrm.org/resourcesandtools/hr-topics/technology/pages/virtual-reality-revolutionizes-walmart-training.aspx.

133. "A Real Estate Powerhouse," *Keller Williams,* http://www.kw.com/kw/careers-in-real-estate.html (accessed March 21, 2018). Also see "Keller Williams Inducted into Training Magazine's Hall of Fame," *Business Wire,* https://www.businesswire.com/news/home/20180213006268/en/Keller-Williams-Inducted-Training-Magazine's-Hall-Fame (accessed March 21, 2018); "Tap into the Real Estate Industry's Brightest Minds and Top Producers," *Keller Williams,* http://www.kw.com/kw/education.html (accessed March 21, 2018); L. Freifeld, "Keller Williams Is at Home at No. 1," *Training,* https://trainingmag.com/trgmag-article/keller-williams-home-no-1 (accessed March 21, 2018). D. Blumberg, "It's Time to Take Command," *KW Outfront,* February 16, 2019, https://outfront.kw.com/technology/take-command/; E. Alberts, "Market Update 2019: A Sea Change in Real Estate," *KW Outfront,* August 13, 2019, https://outfront.kw.com/views/market-update-2019-a-sea-change-in-real-estate/; "Q3 2019: A Historic Quarter for Keller Williams," *KW Outfront,* November 12, 2019, https://outfront.kw.com/performance/kw-q3-2019-performance-report/; L. Freifeld, "Training Top 10 Hall of Fame 2018 Inductees," *Training,* https://trainingmag.com/trgmag-article/training-top-10-hall-of-fame-2018-inductees/ (accessed April 28, 2020); "Keller Williams Reports Year-End Results," *Business Wire,* March 7, 2019, https://www.businesswire.com/news/home/20190307005485/en/Keller-Williams-Reports-Year-End-Results; "Cydne Seymour," *KW,* https://www.cydneseymour.com/ (accessed April 27, 2020).

134. "2020 Workplace Learning Report," *LinkedIn Learning,* 2020, https://learning.linkedin.com/content/dam/me/learning/resources/pdfs/LinkedIn-Learning-2020-Workplace-Learning-Report.pdf.

135. E. Andersen, "Learning to Learn," *Harvard Business Review*, 2019, pp. 14–18.

136. J. Fuller, J. Wallenstein, M. Raman, and A. de Chalendar, "Your Workforce Is More Adaptable Than You Think," *Harvard Business Review*, Vol. 97, No. 3 (2019), pp. 118–126.

137. C. Brower and N. Dvorak, "Why Employees Are Fed Up with Feedback," *Gallup,* October 11, 2019, https://www.gallup.com/workplace/267251/why-employees-fed-feedback.aspx. Also see B. Wigert and N. Dvorak, "Feedback Is Not Enough," *Gallup,* May 16, 2019, https://www.gallup.com/workplace/257582/feedback-not-enough.aspx.

138. D. Schleicher, H. Baumann, D. Sullivan, and J. Yim, "Evaluating the Effectiveness of Performance Management: A 30-Year Integrative Conceptual Review," *Journal of Applied Psychology*, Vol. 104, No. 7 (2019), p. 851.

139. Adapted from A. J. Kinicki, K. J. L. Jacobson, S. J. Peterson, and G. E. Prussia, "Development and Validation of the Performance Management Behavior Questionnaire," *Personnel Psychology* 66 (2013), pp. 1–45.

140. "Corporate Overview," *Regeneron,* https://investor.regeneron .com/static-files/c1be21c5-bd18-45e4-b8ba-e09e3755fdf5 (accessed April 26, 2020). Also see "100 Best Companies to Work For—Regeneron Pharmaceuticals," *Fortune,* 2020, https://fortune.com/best-companies/ 2020/regeneron-pharmaceuticals/.

141. J. Courtney, "How Regeneron Built Their Performance Management System," *PerformYard,* November 20, 2018, https://blog.performyard .com/how-regeneron-built-their-performance-management-system.

142. P. Cappelli and A. Tavis, "HR Goes Agile," *Harvard Business Review*, Vol. 96, No. 2, pp. 46–52.

143. J. Courtney, "How Regeneron Built Their Performance Management System," *PerformYard,* November 20, 2018, https://blog.performyard .com/how-regeneron-built-their-performance-management-system.

144. "Foster a Culture of Integrity and Excellence," *Regeneron,* https:// www.regeneron.com/responsibility/corporate-integrity (accessed April 27, 2020).

145. "Director Statistical Programming," *Regeneron Careers,* https:// careers.regeneron.com/job/REGEA002619484BR5080/Director-Statistical-Programming (accessed April 26, 2020). Also see "Foster a Culture of Integrity and Excellence," *Regeneron,* https://www.regeneron .com/responsibility/corporate-integrity (accessed April 27, 2020); "2018 Responsibility Report, *Regeneron,* https://investor.regeneron .com/2018RR (accessed April 27, 2020).

146. D. Schleicher, H. Baumann, D. Sullivan, P. Levy, D. Hargrove, and B. Barros-Rivera, "Putting the System into Performance Management Systems: A Review and Agenda for Performance Management Research," *Journal of Management*, Vol. 44, No.6 (2018), pp. 2209–2245.

147. D. Schleicher, H. Baumann, D. Sullivan, and J. Yim, "Evaluating the Effectiveness of Performance Management: A 30-Year Integrative Conceptual Review," *Journal of Applied Psychology*, Vol. 104, No. 7 (2019), pp. 851–887.

148. M. Brown, M. Kraimer, and V. Bratton, "Performance Appraisal Cynicism among Managers: A Job Demands Resources Perspective," *Journal of Business and Psychology*, 2019, pp. 1–14.

149. E. Soltani and A. Wilkinson, "TQM and Performance Appraisal: Complementary or Incompatible?" *European Management Review,* VOL. 17 (1), 2018 pp. 57–82.

150. A. Croswell, "Why You Should Separate Performance Measurement and Development," *Culture Map,* https://www.cultureamp.com/ blog/performance-management-and-development/ (accessed April 26, 2020).

151. M. Schaerer and R. Swaab, "Are You Sugarcoating Your Feedback Without Realizing It?" *Harvard Business Review Digital Articles*, 2019, pp. 2–5.

152. P. Cappelli and A. Tavis, "The New Rules of Talent Management," *Harvard Business Review,* March–April 2018, https://hbr.org/2018/03/the-new-rules-of-talent-management. Also see C. Chambers, and W. Baker, "Robust Systems of Cooperation in the Presence of Rankings: How Displaying Prosocial Contributions Can Offset the Disruptive Effects of Performance Rankings," *Organization Science*, Vol. 31, No. 2 (2020), pp. 287–307.

153. "Why Adobe Ditched Its Annual Performance Reviews, *Engagedly,* December 13, 2018, https://engagedly.com/adobe-annual-performance-reviews/.

154. C. Chambers, and W. Baker, "Robust Systems of Cooperation in the Presence of Rankings: How Displaying Prosocial Contributions Can Offset the Disruptive Effects of Performance Rankings," *Organization Science*, Vol. 31, No. 2 (2020), pp. 287–307.

155. R. Carucci, "Giving Feedback to Someone Who Hasn't Had It in Years," *Harvard Business Review Digital Articles*, 2020, pp. 2–5.

156. P. Saxena, and E. Gupta, "Failure of Annual Performance Review and Way Forward: A Study of Few Select Companies," *Advance and Innovative Research*, 2018, p. 49.

157. M. Buckingham and A. Goodall, "Reinventing Performance Management," *Harvard Business Review*, Vol. 93, No. 4 (2015), pp. 40–50. Also see N. Sloan, "Performance Management: Does Your Process Serve Your Strategy?" *Deloitte,* https://www2.deloitte.com/us/en/pages/ finance/articles/cfo-insights-performance-management-process-strategy .html (accessed April 24, 2020); P. Saxena and E. Gupta, "Failure of Annual Performance Review and Way Forward: A Study of Few Select Companies," *Advance and Innovative Research*, 2018, p. 49.

158. "Activation Guide: Digital transformation through data: A Guide for News and Media Companies to Drive Value with Data," *Deloitte,* March, 2019, https://www2.deloitte.com/content/dam/Deloitte/us/Documents/ technology-media-telecommunications/us-digital-transformation-through-data-for-news.pdf.

159. J. Schmidt, "Do Trends Matter? The Effects of Dynamic Performance Trends and Personality Traits on Performance Appraisals," *Academy of Management Discoveries*, Vol. 4, No. 4 (2018), pp. 449–471.

160. "HCAHPS Scores: History, Goals, and Impacts," *Lippincott Solutions*, November 13, 2018, http://lippincottsolutions.lww.com/blog.entry .html/2018/11/30/hcahps_scores_histo-c3GP.html.

161. A. Jerant, J. Fenton, R. Kravitz, D. Tancredi, E. Magnan, K. Bertakis, and P. Franks, "Association of Clinician Denial of Patient Requests with Patient Satisfaction," *JAMA internal medicine*, Vol. 178, No. 1 (2018), pp. 85–91.

162. "New Report Shows Benefit of Modernizing HCAHPS Patient Experience Survey," *American Hospital Association,* July 25, 2019, https:// www.aha.org/press-releases/2019-07-25-new-report-shows-benefit-modernizing-hcahps-patient-experience-survey.

163. M. Kosoff, "Working at Netflix Sounds Absolutely Terrifying," *Vanity Fair,* October 16, 2018, https://www.vanityfair.com/news/2018/10/ working-at-netflix-sounds-absolutely-terrifying

164. "Netflix Culture," *Netflix,* https://jobs.netflix.com/culture (accessed April 26, 2020).

165. S. Denning, "The Netflix Pressure-Cooker: A Culture That Drives Performance," *Forbes,* October 26, 2019, https://www.forbes.com/ sites/stephaniedenning/2018/10/26/the-netflix-pressure-cooker-a-culture-that-drives-performance/#38d224d8151a.

166. S. Heathfield, "60 Degree Feedback: See the Good, the Bad and the Ugly," *The Balance,* January 4, 2018, https://www.thebalance .com/360-degree-feedback-information-1917537.

167. S. Karkoulian, J. Srour, and L. C. Messarra, "The Moderating Role of 360-Degree Appraisal Between Engagement and Innovative Behaviors," *International Journal of Productivity and Performance Management,* 2019.

168. J. Ghorpade, "Managing Five Paradoxes of 360-Degree Feedback," *Academy of Management Perspectives,* Vol. 14, No. 1 (2000), pp. 140–150.

169. A. Przystanski, "Performance Ranking Re-enters Legal Spotlight," *Namely,* February 10, 2016, https://hrnews.namely.com/hrnews/ blog/2016/2/10/performance-ranking-re-enters-legal-spotlight.

170. E. Pulakos, R. Mueller-Hanson, and S. Arad, "The Evolution of Performance Management: Searching for Value," *Annual Review of Organizational Psychology and Organizational Behavior*, Vol. 6 (2019), pp. 249–271.

171. T. Petrucci and M. Rivera, "Leading Growth through the Digital Leader," *Journal of Leadership Studies*, Vol. 12, No. 3 (2018), pp. 53–56.

172. G. Blau, T. Petrucci, M. Rivera, and R. Ghate, "Exploring the Impact of Receiving Sender-Based Negative and Positive Feedback on Team-Level Process Outcomes Using a Mobile Application," *Decision Sciences Journal of Innovative Education*, Vol. 17, No. 1 (2019), pp. 76–98.

173. G. Gupta, "Are You Still Using Force Rankings? Please Stop," *Forbes,* May 23, 2018, https://www.forbes.com/sites/johnkotter/ 2018/05/23/are-you-still-using-force-rankings-please-stop/#5b29e39334d2.

174. *"Woellecke et al. v. Ford Motor Company—2:19-cv-12430,"* *ClassAction.org,* August 16 2019, https://www.classaction.org/media/woellecke-et-al-v-ford-motor-company.pdf.

175. S. Thomason, A. Brownlee, A. Harris, and H. Rustogi, "Forced Distribution Systems and Attracting Top Talent," *International Journal of Productivity and Performance Management,* Vol. 67 (7), 2018, pp. 1171–1191.

176. "Break Free from Performance Management Shackles: Companies That Are Paving the Way," *business.com,* February 22, 2017, https://www.business.com/articles/performance-management-companies-that-are-breaking-free/.

177. M. Schaerer and R. Swaab, "Are You Sugarcoating Your Feedback Without Realizing It?" *Harvard Business Review Digital Articles,* 2019, pp. 2–5.

178. G. Leibowitz, "6 Ways Truly Effective Leaders Deliver Feedback," *Inc.,* February 13, 2018, https://www.inc.com/glenn-leibowitz/6-ways-truly-effective-leaders-deliver-feedback.html?cid=search. Also see P. Gasca, "Want to Deliver Effective Feedback? Try the 'You Suck Sandwich' Approach," *Inc.,* February 26, 2018, https://www.inc.com/peter-gasca/deliver-feedback-like-a-ninja-with-a-you-suck-sandwich.html?cid=search; J. Peterson, "Want to Be a Better Leader? Start by Giving Useful Feedback—Here's How," *Inc.,* January 12, 2018, https://www.inc.com/joel-peterson/3-ways-to-give-constructive-feedback-that-actually-works.html?cid=search; M. Schneider, "3 Steps to Give Tough but Effective Feedback to Your Employees," *Inc.,* September 27, 2017, https://www.inc.com/michael-schneider/3-steps-to-give-tough-but-effective-feedback-to-your-employees.html?cid=search.

179. E. Karam, J. Hu, R. Davison, M. Juravich, J. Nahrgang, S. Humphrey, and D. Scott DeRue, "Illuminating The 'Face' of Justice: A Meta-Analytic Examination of Leadership and Organizational Justice," *Journal of Management Studies,* Vol. 56, No.1 (2019), pp. 134–171.

180. C. Cast, "6 Ways to Take Control of Your Career Development If Your Company Doesn't Care about It," *Harvard Business Review Digital Articles,* 2018, pp. 1–4.

181. J. Ortakales and S. Lebowitz, "A BET Executive Used Self-Advocacy to Advance Her Career, Sending Emails to Her Boss' Boss. Here's How She Says to Make Yourself Stand Out," *Business Insider,* February 20, 2020, https://www.businessinsider.com/how-to-outline-your-accomplishments-email-boss-promotion-raise-2020-2.

182. P. Roth, J. Thatcher, P. Bobko, K. Matthews, J. Ellingson, and C. Goldberg, "Political Affiliation and Employment Screening Decisions: The Role of Similarity and Identification Processes," *Journal of Applied Psychology,* Vol. 105 (5), 2020, pp. 472–486.

183. S. Joseph, "Passed over for a Promotion? Here's What to Do Next" *Forbes,* January 24, 2020, https://www.forbes.com/sites/shelcyv joseph/2020/01/24/bypassed-for-a-promotion-heres-what-to-do-next/#3c8b437813df.

184. G. Moran, "The Simple Method to Keep Employees Happier at Their Jobs," *Fast Company,* June 7, 2018, https://www.fastcompany.com/40580641/the-simple-method-to-keeping-employees-happier-at-their-jobs.

185. A. Bibby, "7 Flexible Companies with Office Rotation Options," *FlexJobs,* March 3, 2018, https://www.flexjobs.com/blog/post/flexible-companies-office-rotation-options/. Also see A. Coolidge, "P&G and the Engine That Makes Leaders," *Cincinnati,* May 17, 2018, https://www.cincinnati.com/story/money/business/2017/05/17/procter-gamble-leaders/101565838/.

186. T. Verheyen and M. Guerry, "Motives For (Non) Practicing Demotion," *Employee Relations,* 2018.

187. A. Smith, "Demotions Can Often Lead to Departures but Also to Fresh Starts," *SHRM,* August 22, 2018, https://www.shrm.org/resourcesandtools/legal-and-compliance/employment-law/pages/demotions-departures-fresh-starts.aspx.

188. "How Layoffs Hurt Companies," *Knowledge@Wharton,* April 12, 2016, http://knowledge.wharton.upenn.edu/article/how-layoffs-cost-companies (accessed June 7, 2016).

189. "These 21 Prominent US Businesses Are among Those Temporarily Laying off the Most People," *USA Today,* April 25, 2020, https://www.usatoday.com/story/money/2020/04/25/21-american-businesses-temporarily-laying-off-the-most-people/111592432/. Also see R. Knight, "How to Manage Coronavirus Layoffs with Compassion," *Harvard Business Review,* April 2020, https://hbr.org/2020/04/how-to-manage-coronavirus-layoffs-with-compassion?ab=hero-main-text.

190. A. Schulz and M. Wiersema, "The Impact of Earnings Expectations on Corporate Downsizing," *Strategic Management Journal,* Vol. 39, No. 10 (2018), pp. 2691–2702.

191. T. Lee, "Fired CEOs 'Pursue Other Opportunities,'" *San Francisco Chronicle,* May 30, 2016, pp. A1, A6.

192. J. Sahadi, "Up to Half of Exiting CEOs Don't Quit. They Get Fired," *CNN,* July 19, 2019, https://www.cnn.com/2019/07/19/success/ceos-getting-fired/index.html

193. S. Heathfield, "The Effects of Downsizing on Employees Who Survive the Layoffs," *The Balance Careers,* July 1, 2019, https://www.thebalancecareers.com/how-employees-respond-to-change-after-layoffs-1918585.

194. E. Alterman, "Laid Off vs. Fired: What's the Difference and Why Does It Matter?" *The Muse,* accessed April 24, 2020, https://www.themuse.com/advice/laid-off-vs-fired-definition-meaning.

195. Y. Sharma, "A Healthy Reminder: Startups Need Employees More Than Employees Need Startups," *Entrackr,* July 2019, https://entrackr.com/2019/07/startups-and-employees/

196. T. West, "The Lies We Tell at Work—And the Damage They Do; Lying at Our Jobs Feels So Harmless. Honestly, It Isn't," *Wall Street Journal (Online),* March 27, 2020, https://www.wsj.com/articles/the-lies-we-tell-at-workand-the-damage-they-do-11585319160

197. E. Tippett, "Non-Disclosure Agreements and the #MeToo Movement," *ABA,* Winter 2019, https://www.americanbar.org/groups/dIspute_resolution/publications/dispute_resolution_magazine/2019/winter-2019-me-too/non-disclosure-agreements-and-the-metoo-movement/.

198. "At-Will Employment—Overview," National Conference of State Legislatures, April 15, 2008, https://www.ncsl.org/research/labor-and-employment/at-will-employment-overview.aspx.

199. "Title VII of the Civil Rights Act of 1964," *U.S. Equal Employment Opportunity Commission,* https://www.eeoc.gov/statutes/title-vii-civil-rights-act-1964 (accessed April 5, 2020).

200. A. Picchi, "The Federal Minimum Wage Sets a Record—for Not Rising," *CBS News,* June 15, 2019, https://www.cbsnews.com/news/federal-minimum-wage-sets-record-for-length-with-no-increase/. Also see "Minimum Wage," U.S. Department of Labor, https://www.dol.gov/general/topic/wages/minimumwage (accessed April 29, 2020); "State Minimum Wages | 2020 Minimum Wage by State," *NCSL,* January 6, 2020, https://www.ncsl.org/research/labor-and-employment/state-minimum-wage-chart.aspx.

201. S. Belskie, "The Progressive Case For and Against a $15 Minimum Wage," *Medium,* June 1, 2017, https://medium.com/@stevebelskie/15-dollar-minimum-wage-possible-4fffc280412c.

202. "FLSA Overtime Rule Resources," *SHRM,* https://www.shrm.org/resourcesandtools/legal-and-compliance/employment-law/pages/flsa-overtime-rule-resources.aspx (accessed April 27, 2020).

203. For more about legislation updating the Toxic Substances Control Act of 1976, see C. Davenport and E. Huetteman, "Deal Is Reached to Expand Rules on Toxic Chemicals," *The New York Times,* May 20, 2016, p. A3. Also see F. Krupp, "When Red and Blue in Congress Makes Green," *The Wall Street Journal,* June 10, 2016, p. A13.

204. C. Martin, "In the Health Law, an Open Door for Entrepreneurs," *The New York Times,* November 24, 2013, p. BU-3. Also see H. Knight, "Health Efforts Work—Experts," *San Francisco Chronicle,* November 30, 2013, pp. A1, A9; Associated Press, "Uninsured Rate Decreases as Law Takes Effect," *San Francisco Chronicle,* January 24, 2014, p. A13.

205. A. Nova, "How The Affordable Care Act Transformed Our Health-Care System," *CNBC,* December 29, 2019, https://www.cnbc.com/2019/12/29/how-the-affordable-care-act-transformed-the-us-health-care-system.html.

206. S. Paustian-Underdahl, A. Eaton, A. Mandeville, and L. Little, "Pushed Out or Opting Out? Integrating Perspectives on Gender Differences in Withdrawal Attitudes during Pregnancy," *Journal of Applied Psychology*, Vol. 104, No. 8 (2019), pp. 985–1002.

207. "EEOC Releases Fiscal Year 2019 Enforcement and Litigation Data," *U.S. Equal Employment Opportunity Commission*, https://www.eeoc.gov/eeoc/newsroom/release/1-24-20.cfm (accessed April 25, 2020).

208. K. Ryssdal and B. Bodnar, "The Next Steve Jobs Might Just Be Named Stephanie," *Marketplace,* November 4, 2019, https://www.marketplace.org/2019/11/04/the-next-steve-jobs-might-just-be-named-stephanie/. Also see S. Johari, "Stephanie Lampkin, Founder & CEO of Blendoor—All Raise's Enterprise SaaS #WomanCrushWednesday," *Medium,* May 22, 2019, https://medium.com/allraise/stephanie-lampkin-founder-ceo-of-blendoor-all-raises-enterprise-saas-womancrush wednesday-5b6990570a28.

209. "Affirmative Action Fast Facts," *CNN,* April 16, 2020, https://www.cnn.com/2013/11/12/us/affirmative-action-fast-facts/index.html.

210. F. Fallucchi and S. Quercia, "Affirmative Action and Retaliation in Experimental Contests," *Journal of Economic Behavior & Organization*, Vol. 156 (2018), pp. 23–40.

211. K. Reilly, "Federal Judge Upholds Harvard's Race-Conscious Admissions Policy in Trial over Asian-American Applicants," *Time,* October 1, 2019, https://time.com/5562334/judge-upholds-harvard-race-conscious-admissions-policy/.

212. C. Rubino, D. Avery, P. McKay, B. Moore, D. Wilson, M. Van Driel, L. Witt, and D. McDonald, "And Justice for All: How Organizational Justice Climate Deters Sexual Harassment," *Personnel Psychology*, Vol. 71, No. 4 (2018), pp. 519–544.

213. J. Bohr, "Employers Can Be Liable for Harassment Even with Policies in Place," *HR Daily Advisor,* October 15, 2019, https://hrdailyadvisor.blr.com/2019/10/15/employers-can-be-liable-for-harassment-even-with-policies-in-place/.

214. A. Almukhtar, M. Gold, and L. Buchanan, "After Weinstein: 71 Men Accused of Sexual Misconduct and Their Fall from Power," *The New York Times,* February 8, 2018, https://www.nytimes.com/interactive/2017/11/10/us/men-accused-sexual-misconduct-weinstein.html.

215. O. Rummler, "Global #MeToo Movement Has Resulted in 7 Convictions, 4 Charges of Influential Figures," *Axios,* March 11, 2020, https://www.axios.com/global-metoo-movement-convictions-charges-382ff226-7ad3-4b26-ac89-451788192578.html.

216. E. Bernstein, "The Role Power Plays in Sexual Harassment," *The Wall Street Journal,* February 6, 2018, p. A 13.

217. A. Anglin, M. Wolfe, J. Short, A. McKenny, and R. Pidduck, "Narcissistic Rhetoric and Crowdfunding Performance: A Social Role Theory Perspective," *Journal of Business Venturing*, Vol. 33, No. 6 (2018), pp.780–812.

218. T. Buyl, C. Boone, and J. Wade, "Ceo Narcissism, Risk-Taking, and Resilience: An Empirical Analysis in US Commercial Banks," *Journal of Management*, Vol. 45, No. 4 (2019), pp. 1372–1400.

219. E. Bernstein, "The Role Power Plays in Sexual Harassment," *The Wall Street Journal,* February 6, 2018, p. A 13.

220. M. Roehling and J. Huang, "Sexual Harassment Training Effectiveness: An Interdisciplinary Review and Call for Research," *Journal of Organizational Behavior*, Vol. 39, No. 2 (2018), pp. 134–150.

221. V. Bolden-Barrett, "Purple Campaign Creates Employer Certification to Address Harassment," *HR Dive,* July 18, 2019, https://www.hrdive.com/news/purple-campaign-creates-employer-certification-to-address-harassment/558960/.

222. "Corporate Certification," *The Purple Campaign,* https://www.purplecampaign.org/corporate-certification (accessed April 29, 2020).

223. N. Iqbal, "Donna Zuckerberg: 'Social Media Has Elevated Misogyny to New Levels of Violence,'" *The Guardian,* November 11, 2018, https://www.theguardian.com/books/2018/nov/11/donna-zuckerberg-social-media-misoyny-violence-classical-antiquity-not-all-dead-white-men.

224. Anti-harassment policies are discussed by J. A. Segal, "Upgrade Your Anti-Harassment Policy," *HRMagazine,* March 2018, pp. 64–65. Also see B. Robinson, "Bullying against Adults Has Risen," *Psychology Today,* January, 2020, https://www.psychologytoday.com/us/blog/the-right-mindset/202001/bullying-against-adults-has-risen.

225. G. Namie, "2017 Workplace Bullying Institute U.S. Workplace Bullying Survey," *Workplace Bullying Institute,* http://workplacebullying.org/multi/pdf/2017/2017-WBI-US-Survey.pdf (accessed March 21, 2018).

226. C. Magee, R. Gordon, L. Robinson, P. Caputi, and L. Oades, "Workplace Bullying and Absenteeism: The Mediating Roles of Poor Health and Work Engagement," *Human Resource Management Journal*, Vol. 27, No. 3 (2017), pp. 319–334.

227. P. Agarwal, "Here Is Why We Need to Talk about Bullying in the Work Place," *Forbes,* July 29, 2018, https://www.forbes.com/sites/pragyaagarwaleurope/2018/07/29/workplace-bullying-here-is-why-we-need-to-talk-about-bullying-in-the-work-place/#2dae46903259.

228. B. Robinson, "New Study Says Workplace Bullying on Rise: What You Can Do During National Bullying Prevention Month," *Forbes,* October 11, 2019, https://www.forbes.com/sites/bryanrobinson/2019/10/11/new-study-says-workplace-bullying-on-rise-what-can-you-do-during-national-bullying-prevention-month/#333dea812a0d.

229. B. Robinson, "New Study Says Workplace Bullying on Rise: What You Can Do During National Bullying Prevention Month," *Forbes,* October 11, 2019, https://www.forbes.com/sites/bryanrobinson/2019/10/11/new-study-says-workplace-bullying-on-rise-what-can-you-do-during-national-bullying-prevention-month/#333dea812a0d. Also see P. Agarwal, "Here Is Why We Need to Talk about Bullying in the Work Place," *Forbes,* July 29, 2018, https://www.forbes.com/sites/pragyaagarwaleurope/2018/07/29/workplace-bullying-here-is-why-we-need-to-talk-about-bullying-in-the-work-place/#2dae46903259.

230. P. Agarwal, "Here Is Why We Need to Talk about Bullying in the Work Place," *Forbes,* July 29, 2018, https://www.forbes.com/sites/pragyaagarwaleurope/2018/07/29/workplace-bullying-here-is-why-we-need-to-talk-about-bullying-in-the-work-place/#2dae46903259. Also see T. Xu, L. Magnusso, L. Hanson, T. Lange, L. Starkopf, H. Westerlund, I. Madsen, R. Rugulies, J. Pentti, S. Stenholm, J. Vahtera, and A. Hansen, "Workplace Bullying and Workplace Violence as Risk Factors for Cardiovascular Disease: A Multi-Cohort Study," *European Heart Journal*, Vol. 40, No. 14 (2019), pp. 1124–1134; M. Glambek, A. Skogstad, and S. Einarsen, "Workplace Bullying, The Development of Job Insecurity and the Role of Laissez-Faire Leadership: A Two-Wave Moderated Mediation Study," *Work & Stress*, Vol. 32, No. 3 (2018), pp. 297–312.

231. H. Benson, "Porters Found Road to Success Aboard Nation's 'Rolling Hotels,'" *San Francisco Chronicle,* February 11, 2009, pp. A1, A12.

232. J. Jones, "As Labor Day Turns 125, Union Approval Near 50-Year High," *Gallup,* August 28, 2019, https://news.gallup.com/poll/265916/labor-day-turns-125-union-approval-near-year-high.aspx.

233. H. Fingerhut, "More Americans View Long-Term Decline in Union Membership Negatively Than Positively," *Pew Research,* June 5, 2018, https://www.pewresearch.org/fact-tank/2018/06/05/more-americans-view-long-term-decline-in-union-membership-negatively-than-positively/.

234. D. Macaray, "Organized Labor and the Dreaded Two-Tier Contract," *CounterPunch,* December 1, 2017, https://www.counterpunch.org/2017/12/01/organized-labor-and-the-dreaded-two-tier-contract/. Also see "How Two-Tier Contracts Hurt Workers and Weaken Unions," June 1, 2018, http://www.tdu.org/how_two_tier_contracts_hurt_workers_and_weaken_unions.

235. S. Greenhouse, "'Bosses Take Note': Why GM's Strike Could Inspire More Collective Action," *The Guardian,* October 30, 2019, https://www.theguardian.com/us-news/2019/oct/30/general-motors-gm-strike-future-work-collective-action.

236. J. Silver-Greenberg and M. Corkery, "Bank Customers Likely to Regain Access to Courts," *The New York Times,* May 5, 2016, pp. A1, B3. Also see J. Silver-Greenberg and M. Corkery, "Start-Ups Turn to Arbitration in the Workplace," *The New York Times,* May 15, 2016, pp. News-1, News-4.

237. J. Silver-Greenberg and R. Gebeloff, "Arbitration Everywhere, Stacking Deck of Justice," *The New York Times,* November 1, 2015,

pp. News-1, News-22, News-23. Also see J. Silver-Greenberg and M. Corkery, "A 'Privatization of the Justice System,'" *The New York Times,* November 2, 2015, pp. A1, B4, B5.

238. M. Corkery and J. Silver-Greenberg, "'Scared to Death' by Arbitration: Companies Drowning in Their Own System," *The New York Times,* April 7, 2020, Section B, p. 1.

239. N. Torres, "Instant Feedback Hurts Our Performance," *Harvard Business Review,* Vol. 97, No. 4 (2019), pp. 32–33.

240. R. Blagoeva, T. Mom, J. Jansen, and G. George, "Problem-Solving or Self-Enhancement? A Power Perspective on How CEOs Affect R&D Search in the Face of Inconsistent Feedback," *Academy of Management Journal,* 2019.

241. A. Christensen, A. Kinicki, Z. Zhang, and F. Walumbwa, "Responses to Feedback: The Role of Acceptance, Affect, and Creative Behavior," *Journal of Leadership and Organizational Studies,* Vol. 25 (4), 2018, pp. 416–429.

242. J. Grenny, "How to Be Resilient in the Face of Harsh Criticism," *Harvard Business Review Digital Articles*, 2019, pp. 2–5.

243. "Conversation Is a Skill. Here's How to Be Better at It," *The Ladders,* May 22, 2018, https://www.theladders.com/career-advice/conversation-is-a-skill-heres-how-to-be-better-at-it.

244. C. Seiter, "How to Give and Receive Feedback at Work: The Psychology of Criticism," *Buffer,* September 14, 2018, https://open.buffer.com/how-to-give-receive-feedback-work/.

245. L. L. Holmer, "Understanding and Reducing the Impact of Defensiveness on Management Learning: Some Lessons from Neuroscience," *Journal of Management Education,* October 2014, pp. 618–641.

246. M. Parrish, T. Inagaki, K. Muscatell, K. Haltom, M. Leary, and N. Eisenberger, "Self-Compassion and Responses to Negative Social Feedback: The Role of Fronto-Amygdala Circuit Connectivity," *Self and Identity,* Vol. 17, No. 6 (2018), pp. 723–738.

247. J. Grenny, "How to Be Resilient in the Face of Harsh Criticism," *Harvard Business Review Digital Articles*, 2019, pp. 2–5.

248. E. Sherf and E. Morrison, "I Do Not Need Feedback! Or Do I? Self-Efficacy, Perspective Taking, and Feedback Seeking," *Journal of Applied Psychology*, February 2019, pp. 146–165.

249. A. Christensen, A. Kinicki, Z. Zhang, and F. Walumbwa, "Responses to Feedback: The Role of Acceptance, Affect, and Creative Behavior," *Journal of Leadership and Organizational Studies,* Vol. 25 (4), 2018; pp. 416–429. Also see J. Folkman, "You Can Take It! How to Accept Negative Feedback with Ease," *Forbes,* December 5, 2017, https://www.forbes.com/.../you-can-take-it-how-to-accept-negative-feedback-with-ease.

250. J. Kabat-Zinn, "Mindfulness-Based Interventions in Context: Past, Present, and Future," *Clinical Psychology: Science and Practice,* Summer 2003, p. 145.

251. M. Roche and J. Haar, "Adding Mindfulness to Psychological Capital: A Two Study Investigation into why Mindfulness Matters," *Academy of Management Proceedings*, Vol. 2019, No. 1 (July 2019).

252. "10 Reasons to Become a Nurse," *Purdue Global,* March 17, 2020, https://www.purdueglobal.edu/blog/nursing/10-reasons-become-nurse/.

253. J. Thew, "Want To Keep Nurses at The Bedside? Here's How," *Health Leaders,* March 27, 2019, https://www.healthleadersmedia.com/nursing/want-keep-nurses-bedside-heres-how.

254. "Top 10 Highest-Paying College Degrees," *Western Governors University*, December 13, 2019, https://www.wgu.edu/blog/top-10-highest-paying-college-degrees1912.html.

255. S. Miller, "Average Starting Salary for Recent College Grads Hovers Near $51,000," *SHRM,* August 22, 2019, https://www.shrm.org/resourcesandtools/hr-topics/compensation/pages/average-starting-salary-for-recent-college-grads.aspx. Also see "U.S. Median Household Income Up in 2018 from 2017," U.S. Census, September 26, 2019, https://www.census.gov/library/stories/2019/09/us-median-household-income-up-in-2018-from-2017.html.

256. "15 Highest Paying Nursing Careers [Infographic]," *Nurse.org,* March 6, 2020, https://nurse.org/articles/15-highest-paying-nursing-careers/.

257. A. Boyd, "The Insult of Saying We Get Paid WELL as a Nurse," *Thrive Global,* September 4, 2019, https://thriveglobal.com/stories/the-insult-of-saying-we-get-paid-well-as-a-nurse/.

258. M. DiMattio and A. Spegman, "Educational Preparation and Nurse Turnover Intention from the Hospital Bedside," *OJIN: The Online Journal of Issues in Nursing,* Vol. 24, No. 2 (April 30, 2019).

259. R. Hess, "We Work Hard for the Money: My Perspective on Nurse Salaries," *Nurse.com,* April 21, 2017, www.nurse.com/blog/2017/04/21/we-work-hard-for-the-money-my-perspective-on-nurse-salaries/.

260. K. Michek, "Nurses Not Immune to Gender Wage Gap," *Health Leaders,* June 20, 2018, https://www.healthleadersmedia.com/nursing/nurses-not-immune-gender-wage-gap.

261. B. Wilson, M. Butler, R. Butler, and W. Johnson, "Nursing Gender Pay Differentials in the New Millennium," *Journal of Nursing Scholarship,* 50 (2018), pp. 102–108.

262. "Physician-Led Health Care Teams," *AMA,* September 2018, https://www.ama-assn.org/system/files/2018-09/physician-led-teams-campaign-booklet.pdf.

263. "Why Nurses Deserve More Respect than Doctors," *Nurse Advisor,* http://nurseadvisormagazine.com/tn-exclusive/why-nurses-deserve-more-respect-than-doctors/.

264. "Bullying among Nurses, Other Healthcare Workers Harms Workplace Culture," *Relias Media,* April 1, 2019, https://www.reliasmedia.com/articles/144110-bullying-among-nurses-other-healthcare-workers-harms-workplace-culture. Also see A. Johnson and M. Benham"Hutchins, "The Influence of Bullying on Nursing Practice Errors: A Systematic Review," *AORN Journal*, Vol. 111, No. 2 (2020), pp. 199–210.

265. "Taking a Stand against Bullying," *HealthTrust,* Quarter 1, 2018, https://healthtrustpg.com/thesource/workplace-trends/taking-stand-bullying/.

266. S. Carroll, "Is Sexual Harassment of Nurses Prevalent in Health Care?" *ONSVoice,* March 7, 2018, https://voice.ons.org/stories/is-sexual-harassment-of-nurses-prevalent-in-health-care.

267. J. Gold, "For Nurses, the 'Patient's Always Right' Attitude Opens the Door for Abuse," *In Style,* February 28, 2019, https://www.instyle.com/times-up-nurse-patient-harassment-experience.

268. N. Carr, "Punches, Broken Bones and More: 1 In 4 Nurses Are Attacked on the Job, Study Says," *WSBTV,* November 12, 2019, https://www.wsbtv.com/news/2-investigates/punches-broken-bones-and-more-1-in-4-nurses-are-attacked-on-the-job-study-says/1007667127/.

269. "Injuries, Illnesses, and Fatalities," *U.S. Bureau of Labor Statistics*, 2018, https://www.bls.gov/iif/soii-chart-data-2017.htm#BLStable_2018_23_13_14_29_footnotes.

270. R. Tariq and T. Toney-Butler, "Back Safety," *StatPearls,* November 7, 2019, https://www.ncbi.nlm.nih.gov/books/NBK519066/.

271. A. Richardson, B. McNoe, S. Derrett, and J. Harcombe, "Interventions to Prevent and Reduce the Impact of Musculoskeletal Injuries among Nurses: A Systematic Review," *International Journal of Nursing Studies,* Vol. 82 (2018) pp. 58–67.

272. J. Palmer, "Lifting Patients Puts Nurses at Risk: Have You Tried These Alternatives?" *Health Leaders,* September 11, 2018, https://www.healthleadersmedia.com/nursing/lifting-patients-puts-nurses-risk-have-you-tried-these-alternatives.

273. A. Novitski-Juedes, "Standing on the Bottom Line: Nurses and Safe Patient Ratios," *The CT Mirror,* April 12, 2020, https://ctmirror.org/2020/04/12/standing-on-the-bottom-line-nurses-and-safe-patient-ratios-amanda-novitski-juedes/.

274. B. Covert, "'The Reality Is, It's Incredibly Hard,'" *The Atlantic,* April 14, 2020, https://www.theatlantic.com/health/archive/2020/04/women-fighting-covid-19-are-underpaid-and-overworked/609934/.

275. D. Dohrenwend, "Nurses Are the Coronavirus Heroes; They Marinate in Risk as They Spend More Time Than Anyone Else Tending to Patients," *The Wall Street Journal,* March 30, 2020, https://www.wsj.com/articles/nurses-are-the-coronavirus-heroes-11585608987.

276. A. Colvin and H. Shierholz, "Noncompete Agreements," *Economic Policy Institute,* December 10, 2019, https://www.epi.org/publication/noncompete-agreements/.

277. J. Heskett, "Should Non-Compete Clauses Be Abolished?" *Harvard Business School Working Knowledge,* November 1, 2019, https://hbswk.hbs.edu/item/should-non-compete-clauses-be-abolished.

278. J. Bennet, "'Money and Greed': How Non-Compete Clauses Force Workers to Fight for Rights," *The Guardian,* October 24, 2018, https://www.theguardian.com/us-news/2018/oct/24/non-compete-clause-low-wage-workers-lawsuits-rights.

279. L. Ohnesorge, "Citrix Sues Former Raleigh Employees over Non-compete Clause," *Triangle Business Journal,* October 20, 2017, www.bizjournals.com/triangle/news/2017/10/20/citrix-sues-former-raleigh-employees-over.html.

280. "The Delicate Nuances in New State Noncompete Laws," *Baker McKenzie,* January 7, 2020, https://www.bakermckenzie.com/en/insight/publications/2020/01/the-delicate-nuances-in-new-state-noncompete-laws. Also see M. Neville, "Competing with Noncompetes: Increasing Restrictions on the Use of Employment Noncompetition Agreements in New York," *Brooklyn Journal of Corporate, Financial, & Commercial Law,* Vol. 13, No. 2 (2019), p. 287.

281. N. Collamer, "Could a Noncompete Keep You from Getting Work?" *Forbes,* November 13, 2017, www.forbes.com/sites/nextavenue/2017/11/13/could-a-noncompete-keep-you-from-getting-work/#189c321967c.

CHAPTER 10

1. J. Shin and A. Grant, "When Putting Work Off Pays Off: The Curvilinear Relationship between Procrastination and Creativity," *Academy of Management Journal,* 2020.

2. H. Mercier, Y. Majima, and H. Miton, "Willingness to Transmit and the Spread of Pseudoscientific Beliefs," *Applied Cognitive Psychology,* Vol. 32, No. 4 (2018), pp. 499–505.

3. D. Pate, "The Skills Companies Need Most in 2020—And How to Learn Them," *LinkedIn Blog,* January 13, 2020, https://learning.linkedin.com/blog/top-skills/the-skills-companies-need-most-in-2020and-how-to-learn-them.

4. C. Mornata and I. Cassar, "The Role of Insiders and Organizational Support in the Learning Process of Newcomers during Organizational Socialization," *Journal of Workplace Learning,* Vol. September-October, 2018, pp. 562–575.

5. T. Zafar, "How to Be Innovative and Creative at Work," *Lifehack,* https://www.lifehack.org/819323/how-to-be-innovative (accessed May 6, 2020).

6. See "Hopelab," *The Omidyar Group,* https://www.omidyargroup.com/pov/organizations/hopelab/ (accessed April 3, 2018). Also see W. Racowich, "Treat Your Curious Culture Like a Product," *Walt Rakowich,* December 11, 2019, https://waltrakowich.com/treat-your-curious-culture-like-a-product/.

7. W. Hur, T. Moon, and S. Ko, "How Employees' Perceptions of CSR Increase Employee Creativity: Mediating Mechanisms of Compassion at Work and Intrinsic Motivation," *Journal of Business Ethics,* Vol. 153, No. 3 (2018), pp. 629–644.

8. P. Watkins, R. Emmons, M. Greaves, and J. Bell, "Joy Is a Distinct Positive Emotion: Assessment of Joy and Relationship to Gratitude and Well-Being," *The Journal of Positive Psychology,* Vol. 13, No. 5 (2018), pp. 522–539. Also see J. Emerson, S. Dunsiger, and D. Williams, "Reciprocal Within-Day Associations between Incidental Affect and Exercise: An EMA Study," *Psychology & Health,* Vol. 33, No. 1 (2018), pp. 130–143.

9. B. Robinson, "The Bitter Pill You Must Swallow If You Want Success," *Psychology Today,* June 10, 2019, https://www.psychologytoday.com/us/blog/the-right-mindset/201906/the-bitter-pill-you-must-swallow-if-you-want-success.

10. F. Gobet and G. Sala, "How Artificial Intelligence Can Help Us Understand Human Creativity," *Frontiers in Psychology,* Vol. 10 (2019), p. 1401.

11. Y. Gong, J. Wu, L. J. Song, and Z. Zhang, "Dual Tuning in Creative Processes: Joint Contributions of Intrinsic and Extrinsic Motivational Orientations," *Journal of Applied Psychology,* May 2017, pp. 829–844.

12. H. Meyer, "As Healthcare Changes, Systems Need to Broaden Search to Find Disruptive CEOs," *Modern Healthcare,* August 11, 2018, https://www.modernhealthcare.com/article/20180811/NEWS/180809909/as-healthcare-changes-systems-need-to-broaden-search-to-find-disruptive-ceos

13. P. Drucker, "The Future That Has Already Happened," *The Futurist,* November 1998, pp. 16–18.

14. "Intuit 2020 Report: Twenty Trends That Will Shape the Next Decade," *Intuit,* October 2010, http://http-download.intuit.com/http.intuit/CMO/intuit/futureofsmallbusiness/ intuit_2020_report.pdf (accessed June 15, 2016).

15. K. Albrecht, "Eight Supertrends Shaping the Future of Business," *The Futurist,* September–October 2006, pp. 25–29. Also see J. C. Glenn, "Scanning the Global Situation and Prospects for the Future," *The Futurist,* January–February 2008, pp. 41–46; "The Future Issue," *Fortune,* January 13, 2014; "The Future of Everything," *The Wall Street Journal,* July 8, 2014, pp. R1–R24.

16. J. Herrick, "This Marketing Strategy Is a Game Changer for Resource-Strapped Startups," *Entrepreneur,* March 25, 2018, https://www.entrepreneur.com/article/310762. Also see A. Freudmann, "Customers Want Customization, and Companies Are Giving It to Them," *The New York Times,* March 18, 2020, https://www.nytimes.com/2020/03/18/business/customization-personalized-products.html.

17. "Configurators," *The Configurator Database,* https://www.configurator-database.com/configurators#/ (accessed April 30, 2020).

18. "Xbox Design Lab," *Microsoft,* https://xboxdesignlab.xbox.com/en-ca (accessed April 30, 2020).

19. "How to Move Fast: Innovation at Speed And Scale," *McKinsey,* May, 2019, https://www.mckinsey.com/business-functions/strategy-and-corporate-finance/our-insights/how-to-move-fast-innovation-at-speed-and-scale.

20. P. Ziobro, "In Cutting Time to Market, Toy Companies Try on Fast-Fashion's Approach; Mattel, Hasbro and Smaller Firms Try to Spot Internet Memes, Collapse Production Times," *The Wall Street Journal,* February 18, 2018, https://www.wsj.com/articles/in-cutting-time-to-market-toy-companies-try-on-fast-fashion-1518958800

21. C. M. Christensen, *The Innovator's Dilemma: When New Technologies Cause Great Firms to Fail* (Boston: Harvard Business School Press, 1997). Also see J. Howe, "The Disruptor," *Wired,* March 2013, pp. 74–78; J. Lepore, "The Disruption Machine," *The New Yorker,* June 23, 2014, pp. 30–36.

22. T. Bureggemann, "Movie Theaters Endured Every Threat for over a Century, until Coronavirus Shut Them Down: A Timeline," *Indiewire,* March 18, 2020, https://www.indiewire.com/2020/03/coronavirus-american-movie-theaters-closed-1202217809/.

23. Staff, "When You Buy a Movie Ticket, Where Does That Money Go?" *The Week,* September 8, 2016, https://theweek.com/articles/647394/when-buy-movie-ticket-where-does-that-money.

24. N. Bilton, 'Why Hollywood as We Know It Is Already Over," *Vanity Fair,* January 29, 2017, https://www.vanityfair.com/news/2017/01/why-hollywood-as-we-know-it-is-already-over.

25. K. Shaver, "Why Developers Are Offering 'Experiences' to Attract Suburbanites," *The Washington Post,* January 3, 2019, https://www.washingtonpost.com/local/trafficandcommuting/why-developers-are-offering-experiences-to-attract-suburbanites/2019/01/03/02f7f490-031f-11e9-b6a9-0aa5c2fcc9e4_story.html

26. N. Evans, "AMC Theatres Says Movie Attendance Is Actually Up in 2019," *Cinemablend,* November 17, 2019, https://www.cinemablend.com/news/2484181/amc-theatres-says-movie-attendance-is-actually-up-in-2019.

27. J. Stoll, "The Movie Theater Isn't Taking Your Netflix Addiction Lying Down; A Theater Owner Explains the Math behind His Massive Expenditures on Reclining Chairs and Other Improvements to the Customer Experience," *The Wall Street Journal,* March 6, 2020, https://www.wsj.com/articles/the-movie-theater-isnt-taking-your-netflix-addiction-lying-down-11583446007?mod=searchresults&page=1&pos=1

28. Z. Sharf, "Edward Norton Says Spielberg Is Wrong: Netflix Isn't Destroying Movies, Theaters Are," *Indiewire,* October 15, 2019, https://www.indiewire.com/2019/10/edward-norton-spielberg-netflix-theaters-destroying-movies-1202181698/.

29. M. Hughes, "Disney's Great Future Will Change the Movie Theater Industry Forever," *Forbes,* April 22, 2020, https://www.forbes.com/sites/markhughes/2020/04/22/disneys-great-future-will-change-the-movie-theater-industry-forever/#a2ebe0474737.

30. E. Schwartzel, "Trolls World Tour' Breaks Digital Records and Charts a New Path for Hollywood," *The Wall Street Journal,* April 28, 2020, https://www.wsj.com/articles/trolls-world-tour-breaks-digital-records-and-charts-a-new-path-for-hollywood-11588066202?mod=searchresults&page=1&pos=2

31. "AMC Theatres Will No Longer Screen Universal Movies Due to 'Radical Change,'" *Blooloop,* April 29, 2020, https://blooloop.com/news/amc-theatres-universal-movies-trolls/.

32. J. Bariso, "Netflix Killed Blockbuster Video. The Movie Theater Is Next," *Inc.,* January 29, 2020, https://www.inc.com/justin-bariso/netflix-killed-blockbuster-video-movie-theater-is-next.html.

33. D. Ehrlich, "Movie Theaters Are Closed, but Their Value Isn't Lost to Us Yet—Analysis," *Indiewire,* March 22, 2020, https://www.indiewire.com/2020/03/movie-theaters-are-closed-but-their-value-isnt-lost-to-us-yet-analysis-1202219204/.

34. M. Oppenheimer, "Software Outsourcing: Why Uruguay?" *Medium,* June 13, 2019, medium.com/light-it/software-outsourcing-why-uruguay-4587a7056524. Also see C. Serron, "Uruguay: The Silicon Valley of South America," *Medium,* April 16, 2018, https://medium.com/bros/uruguay-the-silicon-valley-of-south-america-8cdef0bbcadc.

35. "Mercedes-Benz U.S. International," *Daimler,* https://supplier-portal.daimler.com/docs/DOC-1473 (accessed April 29, 2020).

36. S. Alway, G. Cathell, W. Wagstaff, J. Deskins, and B. Lego, "The Weirton Area Economic Outlook, 2019–2024," Spring 2019, *Bureau of Business & Economic Research, West Virginia University.*

37. T. Hansen, "The Future of Knowledge Work," *Intel Labs,* Tech. Rep., 2012.

38. D. Miller, "Technology Predictions for the Roaring '20s," *CMS Wire,* January 7, 2020, https://www.cmswire.com/digital-experience/technology-predictions-for-the-roaring-20s/. Also see "The Future of Work in America," *McKinsey Global Institute,* July 2019, https://www.mckinsey.com/~/media/McKinsey/Featured%20Insights/Future%20of%20Organizations/The%20future%20of%20work%20in%20America%20People%20and%20places%20today%20and%20tomorrow/MGI-The-Future-of-Work-in-America-Report-July-2019.ashx.

39. P. Daugherty and H. Wilson, "Using AI to Make Knowledge Workers More Effective," *Harvard Business Review,* April 19, 2019.

40. C. Roth, "2019: When We Exceeded 1 Billion Knowledge Workers," *Gartner,* December 11, 2019, https://blogs.gartner.com/craig-roth/2019/12/11/2019-exceeded-1-billion-knowledge-workers/.

41. S. Waite, "How Emerging Technology Is Empowering Knowledge Workers," *Forbes,* February 28, 2018, https://www.forbes.com/sites/forbescommunicationscouncil/2018/02/28/how-emerging-technology-is-empowering-knowledge-workers/#eb6829295f2d.

42. M. Simon, "The Tale of the Painting Robot That Didn't Steal Anyone's Job," *Wired,* February 8, 2018, https://www.wired.com/story/the-tale-of-the-painting-robot-that-didnt-steal-anyones-job/.

43. *Capitalizing on Complexity: Insights from the Global Chief Executive Officer Study,* International Business Machines, Somers, New York, 2010, www-01.ibm.com/common/ssi/cgi-bin/ssialias?htmlfid=GBE03301USEN&appname=wwwsearch. Also see *Leading through Connections: Insights from the IBM Global CEO Study,* International Business Machines, Somers, New York, 2012, www-935.ibm.com/services/us/en/c-suite/ceostudy2012; and *PwC's Annual Global CEO Survey,* PricewaterhouseCoopers, 2016, www.pwc.com/gx/en/ceo-agenda/ceosurvey/2016.html (all accessed June 17, 2016).

44. T. Bach, "COVID-19 Upends American Religious Life," *U.S. News,* March 13, 2020, https://www.usnews.com/news/national-news/articles/2020-03-13/americas-religious-communities-confront-coronavirus.

45. V. Taylor, "How Muslims Are Digitally Celebrating Ramadan under Quarantine and Protecting Themselves from Zoom-bombers," *Insider,* April 23, 2020, https://www.insider.com/ramadan-celebration-online-zoom-break-fast-pray-iftar-taraweeh-2020-4.

46. B. Sales, "Purim Is a Holiday for Partying. This Year, the Coronavirus Makes Things Different," *Jewish Telegraphic Agency,* March 4, 2020, https://www.jta.org/2020/03/04/global/purim-is-a-holiday-for-partying-this-year-coronavirus-makes-things-different.

47. J. Bates, "Local Police, Courts Caught Short as Louisiana Pastor Continues Holding Services amid COVID-19 Pandemic," *Time,* April 30, 2020, https://time.com/5829460/louisiana-pastor-tony-spell-services-arrests/.

48. P. Robertson, D. Roberts, and J. Porras, "Dynamics of Planned Organizational Change: Assessing Empirical Support for a Theoretical Model," *Academy of Management Journal* 36, no. 3 (1993), pp. 619–634.

49. "A Ballet of Airbus Jets," *Bloomberg Businessweek,* April 22, 2019.

50. A. Mohdin, "Nearly a Million More Young Adults Now Live with Parents—Study," *The Guardian,* February 7, 2019, https://www.theguardian.com/society/2019/feb/08/million-more-young-adults-live-parents-uk-housing.

51. N. Farrell, "Rometty Talks about the Fourth Industrial Revolution," *Fudzilla,* April 3, 2019, https://www.fudzilla.com/news/48440-rometty-talks-about-the-fourth-industrial-revolution.

52. B. Marr, "The Incredible Ways the 4th Industrial Revolution and AI Are Changing Winemaking," *Forbes,* July 3, 2019, https://www.forbes.com/sites/bernardmarr/2019/07/03/the-incredible-ways-the-4th-industrial-revolution-and-ai-are-changing-winemaking/#79bab40f1f61.

53. E. Terazono, "Winemakers Tackle Climate Change and Labour Shortages with Tech," *Financial Times,* February 24, 2020, https://www.ft.com/content/52fcff0e-53db-11ea-8841-482eed0038b1.

54. S. Corner, "Watson Makes Intelligent Wine Choices, Artificially," *Computer World,* September 18, 2019, https://www.computerworld.com/article/3478559/watson-makes-intelligent-wine-choices-artificially.html.

55. P. W. Moroz and E. N. Gamble, "Business Model Innovation as a Window into Adaptive Tensions: Five Paths on the B Corp Journey," *Journal of Business Research,* 2020, https://doi.org/10.1016/j.jbusres.2020.01.046. Also see L. Paine and S. Srinivasan, "A Guide to the Big Ideas and Debates in Corporate Governance," *Harvard Business Review,* October 14, 2019.

56. M. Leighton, "B Corps Are Businesses Committed to Using Their Profit for Good—These 14 Are Making Some Truly Great Products," *Business Insider,* March 23, 2020, https://www.businessinsider.com/b-corp-retail-companies#eileen-fisher-14.

57. A. Raval, "BP Shareholders Vote in Favour of Greater Climate Disclosure," *Financial Times,* May 21, 2019, https://www.ft.com/content/fcb14d66-7bcd-11e9-81d2-f785092ab560.

58. "Exxon Shareholders Say No to Climate Change Proposals," *Aljazeera,* May 29, 2019, https://www.aljazeera.com/ajimpact/exxon-shareholders-reject-climate-change-proposal-190529181834709.html.

59. J. Beer, "Why Brand Purpose Marketing Isn't Working with Young People," *Fast Company,* May 10, 2019, https://www.fastcompany.com/90347311/why-brand-purpose-marketing-isnt-working-with-young-people.

60. "Brand Activism Is Rising, Along with a Tool That's Social-Media Perfect," *Robert H. Smith School of Business,* July 1, 2019, https://www.rhsmith.umd.edu/faculty-research/smithbraintrust/insights/boycotts-are-rough-memes-may-be-worse.

61. C. Jin, "The Effects of Creating Shared Value (CSV) on the Consumer Self–Brand Connection: Perspective of Sustainable Development," *Corporate Social Responsibility and Environmental Management,* Vol. 25, No. 6 (2018), pp. 1246–1257.

62. "Our Leadership," https://shopretail.tothemarket.com/our-journey/our-leadership (accessed May 6, 2020).

63. M. Moore, "How CEOs Outside the Health Care Industry Decided to Get in on the Fight Against the Coronavirus," *Fortune,* April 28,

2020, https://fortune.com/2020/04/28/coronavirus-businesses-ventilators-ppe-bloom-energy-kr-sridhar-to-the-market-jane-mosbacher-morris/.

64. G. Galvin, "The U.S. Obesity Rate Now Tops 40%," *U.S. News,* February 7, 2020, https://www.usnews.com/news/healthiest-communities/articles/2020-02-27/us-obesity-rate-passes-40-percent. Also see "Childhood Obesity Facts," *CDC,* https://www.cdc.gov/obesity/data/childhood.html (accessed May 6, 2020).

65. C. Purdy, "A Handful of US Cities Have Passed Soda Taxes, But Are They Working?" *Yahoo Finance,* February 26, 2020, https://finance.yahoo.com/news/handful-us-cities-passed-soda-090006010.html.

66. G. Bridge, "Sugary Drinks Tax Is Working—Now It's Time to Target Cakes, Biscuits and Snacks," *The Conversation,* October 1, 2019, https://theconversation.com/sugary-drinks-tax-is-working-now-its-time-to-target-cakes-biscuits-and-snacks-124325. Also see C. Dewey, "Why the British Soda Tax Might Work Better than Any of the Soda Taxes That Came Before," *The Washington Post,* March 21, 2018, https://www.washingtonpost.com/news/wonk/wp/2018/03/21/why-the-british-soda-tax-might-work-better-than-any-of-the-soda-taxes-that-came-before-it/?utm_term=.84d7d0f540b1.

67. A. Raimonde, "The Number of Workers on Strike Hits the Highest since the 1980s," *CNBC,* October 21, 2019, https://www.cnbc.com/2019/10/21/the-number-of-workers-on-strike-hits-the-highest-since-the-1980s.html. Also see "Major Work Stoppages in 2019," Bureau of Labor Statistics, February 11, 2020, https://www.bls.gov/news.release/pdf/wkstp.pdf.

68. J. Stanier, "The Gig Economy's Unhappy Middle Class," *OneZero,* April 11, 2019, https://onezero.medium.com/the-unhappy-middle-of-the-gig-economy-5b845d2735ef.

69. Y. Khan, "Billionaire Ken Fisher Stunned an Audience by Saying Winning Clients Was Like 'Trying to Get into a Girl's Pants,'" *Business Insider,* October 10, 2019, https://markets.businessinsider.com/news/stocks/billionaire-ken-fisher-girls-pants-comment-stuns-conference-audience-2019-10-1028589600.

70. A. Riquier, "Wealth Manager Ken Fisher Apologizes after Backlash for Off-color Comments," *MarketWatch,* October 12, 2019, https://www.marketwatch.com/story/wealth-manager-ken-fisher-shocks-with-off-color-comments-doesnt-apologize-2019-10-10.

71. This three-way typology of change was adapted from discussion in P. C. Nutt, "Tactics of Implementation," *Academy of Management Journal,* June 1986, pp. 230–261.

72. Radical organizational change is discussed by T. E. Vollmann, *The Transformational Imperative* (Boston: Harvard Business School Press, 1996).

73. D. Waeger and K. Weber, "Institutional Complexity and Organizational Change: An Open Policy Perspective," *Academy of Management Review,* Vol. 44, No. 2 (2019), pp. 336–359.

74. T. Davenport, A. Guha, D. Grewal, and T. Bressgott, "How Artificial Intelligence Will Change the Future of Marketing," *Journal of the Academy of Marketing Science,* Vol. 48, No. 1 (2020), pp. 24–42.

75. E. Demaitre, "Bossa Nova CTO Explains Expansion to a Total of 1,000 Walmart Stores," *The Robot Report,* January 13, 2020, https://www.therobotreport.com/bossa-nova-cto-explains-expansion-1k-walmart-stores/.

76. A. Tiffany, "Walmart Says Its New Robots Will Make Human Employees Happier," *Vox,* April 11, 2019, https://www.vox.com/the-goods/2019/4/11/18306229/walmart-robot-job-automation-retail-labor-bossanova-robotics.

77. M. A. Wolfson, S. I. Tannenbaum, J. E. Mathieu, and M. T. Maynard, "A Cross-Level Investigation of Informal Field-Based Learning and Performance Improvements," *Journal of Applied Psychology,* January 2018, pp. 14–36. Also see S. Hussain, S.Lei, T. Akram, M. Haider, S. Hussain, and M. Ali, "Kurt Lewin's Change Model: A Critical Review of the Role of Leadership and Employee Involvement in Organizational Change," *Journal of Innovation & Knowledge,* Vol. 3, No. 3 (2018), pp. 123–127.

78. "AI Anxiety: An Ethical Challenge for Business," *Forbes,* March 27, 2019, https://www.forbes.com/sites/insights-intelai/2019/03/27/ai-anxiety-an-ethical-challenge-for-business/#28ff539d5788.

79. E. Winick, "Walmart's New Robots Are Loved by Staff—And Ignored by Customers," *Technology Review,* January 31, 2018, https://www.technologyreview.com/2018/01/31/145906/the-robots-patrolling-walmarts-aisles/.

80. E. Wee and M. Taylor, "Attention to Change: A Multilevel Theory on the Process of Emergent Continuous Organizational Change," *Journal of Applied Psychology,* Vol. 103, No. 1 (2018), pp. 1–13.

81. L. R. Hearld and J. A. Alexander, "Governance Processes and Change within Organizational Participants of Multi-Sectoral Community Health Care Alliances: The Mediating Role of Vision, Mission, Strategy Agreement, and Perceived Alliance Value," *American Journal of Community Psychology,* March 2014, pp. 185–197.

82. A. E. Rafferty, N. L. Jimmieson, and A. A. Armenakis, "Change Readiness: A Multilevel Review," *Journal of Management,* January 2013, pp. 110–135.

83. B. Hlalele, "Application of the Force-Field Technique to Drought Vulnerability Analysis: A Phenomenological Approach," *Journal of Disaster Risk Studies,* Vol. 11, No. 1 (2019), pp. 1–6.

84. J. Davis, "How Lego Clicked: The Super Brand That Reinvented Itself," *The Guardian,* June 4, 2017, https://www.theguardian.com/lifeandstyle/2017/jun/04/how-lego-clicked-the-super-brand-that-reinvented-itself. Also see L. Handley, "Lego Is the World's Most Reputable Company as Tech Giants Lag, Survey Says," *CNBC,* March 3, 2020, https://www.cnbc.com/2020/03/03/lego-is-the-worlds-most-reputable-company-disney-follows.html; "Value of the Leading Toy Brands Worldwide from 2017 to 2019," https://www.statista.com/statistics/399131/value-of-the-leading-global-toy-brands/ (accessed May 6, 2020).

85. E. Mason, "Innovating around the Box," *MIT Management,* June 6, 2018, https://mitsloan.mit.edu/ideas-made-to-matter/innovating-around-box.

86. J. Davis, "How Lego Clicked: The Super Brand That Reinvented Itself," *The Guardian,* June 4, 2017, https://www.theguardian.com/lifeandstyle/2017/jun/04/how-lego-clicked-the-super-brand-that-reinvented-itself.

87. B. Shimoni, "A Sociological Perspective to Organization Development," *Organizational Dynamics,* July–September 2017, pp. 165–170. Also see J. R. Austin and J. M. Bartunek, "Organization Change and Development: In Practice and in Theory," in N. W. Schmitt and S. Highhouse (eds.), *Handbook of Psychology,* vol. 12 (Hoboken, NJ: John Wiley & Sons, 2013), pp. 390–411.

88. B. Shimoni, "A Sociological Perspective to Organization Development," *Organizational Dynamics,* Vol. 46, No. 3 (2017), pp. 165–170.

89. "Founder Exposed: Opening Up about Startup Failures and Vulnerability," https://firstround.com/review/founder-exposed-opening-up-about-startup-failures-and-vulnerability/ (accessed May 6, 2020).

90. "4 Examples of Companies That Nailed Organizational Change," *Tiny Pulse,* https://www.tinypulse.com/blog/sk-examples-of-companies-that-nailed-organizational-change (accessed May 6, 2020).

91. M. Dao and F. Bauer "Human Integration Following M&A: Synthesizing Different M&A Research Streams," *Human Resource Management Review,* 2020, p. 100746.

92. "T-Mobile Hit by Layoffs amid Sprint Merger," *Market Watch,* March 2, 2020, https://www.marketwatch.com/press-release/t-mobile-hit-by-layoffs-amid-sprint-merger-2020-03-02. Also see A. Villasanta, "Sprint, T Mobile Merger Forces Layoffs; 30,000 Job Cuts Expected," *IB Times,* February 28, 2020, https://www.ibtimes.com/sprint-t-mobile-merger-forces-layoffs-30000-job-cuts-expected-2930673.

93. T. Williams, "ViacomCBS Lays Off Staff Across the Board as Part of Merger," *The Wrap,* April 29, 2020, https://www.thewrap.com/viacom-cbs-merger-bob-bakish-layoffs/.

94. E. Gilbert, T. Foulk, and J. Bono, "Building Personal Resources Through Interventions: An Integrative Review," *Journal of Organizational Behavior,* Vol. 39, No. 2 (2018), pp. 214–228.

95. C. Westfall, "Leadership Development Is a $366 Billion Industry: Here's Why Most Programs Don't Work," *Forbes,* June 20, 2019, https://www.forbes.com/sites/chriswestfall/2019/06/20/leadership-

development-why-most-programs-dont-work/#33f5ccd961de. Also see "Executive Coaching," *Oliver Group,* https://olivergroup.com/services/executive-coaching/ (accessed May 6, 2020).

96. E. De Haan, D. Gray, and S. Bonneywell, "Executive Coaching Outcome Research in a Field Setting: A Near-Randomized Controlled Trial Study in a Global Healthcare Corporation," *Academy of Management Learning & Education*, Vol. 18, No. 4 (2019), pp. 581–605.

97. E. Gilbert, T. Foulk, and J. Bono, "Building Personal Resources Through Interventions: An Integrative Review," *Journal of Organizational Behavior*, Vol. 39, No. 2 (2018), pp. 214–228.

98. "Change Management: The HR Strategic Imperative as a Business Partner," *Research Quarterly,* Fourth Quarter 2007, pp. 1–9. Also see D. A. Garvin, A. C. Edmondson, and F. Gino, "Is Yours a Learning Organization?" *Harvard Business Review,* March 2008, pp. 109–116.

99. B. Gleeson, "The Critical Role of Leadership Development During Organizational Change," *Forbes,* June 4, 2018, https://www.forbes.com/sites/brentgleeson/2018/06/04/leadership-developments-role-in-successful-organizational-change/#26fd9307fdd6.

100. M. Neill, L. Men, and C. Yue, "How Communication Climate and Organizational Identification Impact Change," *Corporate Communications: An International Journal,* November 2019, pp. 281–298.

101. J. Stouten, D. Rousseau, and D. De Cremer, "Successful Organizational Change: Integrating the Management Practice and Scholarly Literatures," *Academy of Management Annals*, Vol. 12, No. 2 (2018), pp. 752–788.

102. J. Bauer-Wolf, "Overconfident Students, Dubious Employers," *Inside Higher Ed,* February 23, 2018, https://www.insidehighered.com/news/2018/02/23/study-students-believe-they-are-prepared-workplace-employers-disagree.

103. "Building Tomorrow's Talent: Collaboration Can Close Emerging Skills Gap," *Bloomberg Next,* 2018, https://forms.workday.com/content/dam/web/en-us/documents/whitepapers/whitepaper-bloomberg-build-tomorrow-talent.pdf.

104. "Beyond Hiring: How Companies Are Reskilling to Address Talent Gaps," *McKinsey,* February 2020, https://www.mckinsey.com/business-functions/organization/our-insights/beyond-hiring-how-companies-are-reskilling-to-address-talent-gaps.

105. R. Chan, "Salesforce Will Sell Its Employee Training Tools to Other Companies So They Can Be More Like Salesforce," *Business Insider,* March 5, 2019, https://www.businessinsider.com/salesforce-launches-new-learning-platform-called-mytrailhead-2019-3.

106. "Work Ready Communities Help You Match Employees to Jobs Based on Verified Skill Levels," *ACT Work Ready Communities,* https://www.workreadycommunities.org/employers (accessed May 6, 2020).

107. "Employers Play Key Role in Career Readiness, Competency Development," *NACE,* November 18, 2019, https://www.naceweb.org/career-readiness/competencies/employers-play-key-role-in-career-readiness-competency-development/.

108. "Collaborating with Universities to Create Career-ready Graduates," *Intel,* https://www.intel.com/content/dam/www/public/us/en/documents/case-studies/brief-higher-education.pdf (accessed May 6, 2020).

109. S. Aldulaimi, "The Influence of National Culture on Commitment That Produces Behavioral Support for Change Initiatives," *International Journal of Applied Economics, Finance and Accounting*, Vol. 3, No. 2 (2018), pp. 64–73.

110. D. Howland, "Apparel Is Out of Fashion," *Retail Dive,* August 21, 2019, https://www.retaildive.com/news/apparel-is-out-of-fashion/561225/.

111. W. Purcell, "The Importance of Innovation in Business," *Northeastern University*, October 31, 2019, https://www.northeastern.edu/graduate/blog/importance-of-innovation/.

112. A. Fisher, "America's Most Admired Companies," *Fortune,* March 17, 2008, p. 66.

113. D. Bennett, "The Company Behind Gore-Tex Is Coming for Your Eyeballs," *Bloomberg Businessweek,* May 13, 2019, https://www.bloomberg.com/features/2019-gore-artificial-cornea/

114. "Keeping an Eye on Infection," *Wilmer Eye Institute: Johns Hopkins,* 2018, https://www.hopkinsmedicine.org/wilmer/about/publications/issues/cornea-concepts-18.pdf.

115. K. Krader, "Cloudy with a Chance of Big Macs," *Bloomberg Businessweek,* June 17, 2019, p. 66; Issue 4618.

116. H. Haddon, "To Speed Up, McDonald's Enlists Robots," *The Wall Street Journal,* June 21, 2019, https://www.wsj.com/articles/mcdonalds-tests-robot-fryers-and-voice-activated-drive-throughs-11561060920

117. P. Wahba, "Stitch Fix Thinks Outside the Box," *Fortune,* November 2019. Vol. 180 Issue 5, pp. 32–34.

118. D. Kessenides, "Interrogating the Planet," *Bloomberg Businessweek,* May 20, 2019. Issue 4615, pp. 20–22.

119. J. Ellis, "How Nike Started a Sneaker Arms Race," *Bloomberg Businessweek,* November 18, 2019. Issue 4637, pp. 16–27.

120. G. P. Pisano, "You Need an Innovation Strategy," *Harvard Business Review,* June 2015, p. 46.

121. N. Anderson, K. Potocnik, and J. Zhou, "Innovation and Creativity in Organizations: A Stateof-the-Science Review, Prospective Commentary, and Guiding Framework," *Journal of Management,* July 2014, pp. 1297–1333.

122. S. Erzurumlu, "What Can the Innovator Learn from the Operations Manager? An Operations View of Innovation Strategy," *IEEE Engineering Management Review*, Vol. 46, No. 2 (2018), pp. 97–102.

123. "Reevaluating Incremental Innovation," *Harvard Business Review,* September–October 2018. Vol. 96 Issue 5, pp. 22–25.

124. Y. Dong, K. M. Bartol, Z-X Zhang, and C. Li, "Enhancing Employee Creativity via Individual Skill Development and Team Knowledge Sharing: Influences of Dual-Focused Transformational Leadership," *Journal of Organizational Behavior,* 2017, pp. 439–458.

125. J. Weber, "Grant Reid, President and CEO, Mars Inc.," *Bloomberg Businessweek,* January 28, 2019. Issue 4601, pp. 40–43.

126. J. Hoppmann, F. Naegele, and B. Girod, "Boards as a Source of Inertia: Examining the Internal Challenges and Dynamics of Boards of Directors in Times of Environmental Discontinuities," *Academy of Management Journal*, Vol. 62, No. 2 (2019), pp. 437–468.

127. S. Pandolph, "Here's How Amazon May Have Led to Toys 'R' Us' Demise," *Business Insider,* September 20, 2017, https://www.businessinsider.com/heres-how-amazon-may-have-led-toys-r-us-demise-2017-9.

128. S. Anthony, P. Cobban, R. Nair, and N. Painchaud, "Breaking Down the Barriers to Innovation," *Harvard Business Review,* Vol. 97, No. 6 (November 2019), pp. 92–101.

129. A. Bos-Nehles and A. Veenendaal, "Perceptions of HR Practices and Innovative Work Behavior: The Moderating Effect of an Innovative Climate," *The International Journal of Human Resource Management*, Vol. 30, No. 18 (2019), pp. 2661–2683. Also see A. Oh, C. A. Hartnell, A. J. Kinicki, and D. Choi, "Culture in Context: A Meta-Analysis of the Nomological Network of Organizational Culture," paper presented at the 2016 National Academy of Management Meeting, Anaheim, California.

130. S. Thomke, "Building a Culture of Experimentation," *Harvard Business Review*, Vol. 98, No. 2 (2020), pp. 40–48.

131. J. Birkinshaw and M. Haas, "Increase Your Return on Failure," *Harvard Business Review,* May 2016, p. 90.

132. G. Pisano, "The Hard Truth about Innovative Cultures," *Harvard Business Review,* Vol. 97, No. 1 (2019), pp. 62–71.

133. "Enable Makeathon 2.0," *Global Disability Innovation Hub,* https://www.disabilityinnovation.com/practice/enable-makeathon-2-0 (accessed May 6, 2020).

134. "About IDEO," *IDEO,* https://www.ideo.com/about (accessed May 4, 2020).

135. "About IDEO," *IDEO,* https://www.ideo.com/about (accessed May 4, 2020).

136. T. Brown, "Design Thinking," https://designthinking.ideo.com/?page_id=1542 (accessed May 4, 2020).

137. "Designing Waste Out of the Food System," https://www.ideo.com/case-study/designing-waste-out-of-the-food-system (accessed May 4, 2020).

138. T. Wang and C. Zatzick, "Human Capital Acquisition and Organizational Innovation: A Temporal Perspective.," *Academy of Management Journal*, Vol. 62, No. 1 (2019), pp. 99–116. Also see X. Wang, Y. Fang, I. Qureshi, and O. Janssen, "Understanding Employee Innovative Behavior: Integrating the Social Network and Leader-Member Exchange Perspectives," *Journal of Organizational Behavior*, April 2015, pp. 403–420; F. C. Godart, W. W. Maddux, A. V. Shipilov, and A. D. Galinsky, "Fashion with a Foreign Flair: Professional Experiences Abroad Facilitate the Creative Innovations of Organizations," *Academy of Management Journal*, February 2015, pp. 195–220.

139. S. Melendez, "Hackerone Is Targeting Goldman Sachs, Uber, and the Pentagon—And Getting Paid for It," *Fast Company*, March 10, 2020, https://www.fastcompany.com/90457528/hacker-one-most-innovative-companies-2020.

140. H. Do, P. S. Budhwar, and C. Patel, "Relationship between Innovation-led HR Policy, Strategy, and Firm Performance: A Serial Mediation Investigation," *Human Resource Management*, Vol. 57, No. 5 (2018), pp. 1271–1284.

141. Y. Li, M. Wang, D. Van Jaarsveld, G. Lee, and D. Ma, "From Employee-Experienced High-Involvement Work System to Innovation: An Emergence-Based Human Resource Management Framework," *Academy of Management Journal*, Vol. 61, No. 5 (2018), pp. 2000–2019.

142. "John Kenneth Galbraith Quotes," *Brainy Quotes*, https://www.brainyquote.com/quotes/john_kenneth_galbraith_121862 (accessed May 6, 2020).

143. G. Kane, D. Palmer, A. Phillips, D. Kiron, and N. Buckley, "Accelerating Digital Innovation Inside and Out," *Deloitte*, June 4, 2019, https://www2.deloitte.com/us/en/insights/focus/digital-maturity/digital-innovation-ecosystems-organizational-agility.html.

144. "Amazon Pledges to Upskill 100,000 U.S. Employees for In-Demand Jobs by 2025," *Amazon Press Center*, July 11, 2019, https://press.aboutamazon.com/news-releases/news-release-details/amazon-pledges-upskill-100000-us-employees-demand-jobs-2025.

145. S. Oreg, J. M. Bartunek, G. Lee, and B. Do, "An Affect-Based Model of Recipients' Responses to Organizational Change Events," *Academy of Management Review*, January 2018, pp. 65–86. Also see B. Shimoni, "What Is Resistance to Change? A Habitus-Oriented Approach," *Academy of Management Perspectives*, November 2017, pp. 257–270.

146. J. Vos and J. Rupert, "Change Agent's Contribution to Recipients' Resistance to Change: A Two-Sided Story," *European Management Journal*, Vol 36, No. 4 (2018), pp. 453–462.

147. V. Amarantou, S. Kazakopoulou, D. Chatzoudes, and P. Chatzoglou, "Resistance to Change: An Empirical Investigation of Its Antecedents," *Journal of Organizational Change Management*, April 2018, pp. 426–450.

148. S. Efti, "Why Being Adaptable Is an Underrated Superpower in Business (and Life!)," *Forbes*, January 14, 2020, https://www.forbes.com/sites/steliefti/2020/01/14/why-being-adaptable-is-an-underrated-superpower-in-business-and-life/#5d7398f72c04.

149. J. Vos and J. Rupert, "Change Agent's Contribution to Recipients' Resistance to Change: A Two-Sided Story," *European Management Journal*, Vol 36, No. 4 (2018), pp. 453–462.

150. J. Vos and J. Rupert, "Change Agent's Contribution to Recipients' Resistance to Change: A Two-Sided Story," *European Management Journal*, Vol 36, No. 4 (2018), pp. 453–462.

151. Adapted in part from J. D. Ford, L. W. Ford, and A. D'Amelio, "Resistance to Change: The Rest of the Story," *Academy of Management Review*, April 2008, pp. 362–377.

152. S. Pir, "How Much Change Can Your Inner Child Take? Why We Need to Grow into Adulthood As Leaders of the 21st Century," *Forbes*, November 18, 2019, https://www.forbes.com/sites/sesilpir/2019/11/18/how-much-change-can-your-inner-child-take-why-we-need-to-grow-into-adulthood-as-leaders-of-the-21st-century/#f6577b06b7da. Also see S. Oreg, M. Bayazit, M. Vakola, L. Arciniega et al., "Dispositional Resistance to Change: Measurement Equivalence and the Link to Personal Values across 17 Nations," *Journal of Applied Psychology*, Vol. 23 (2008), pp. 935–944.

153. A. Kraft, J. Sparr, and C. Peus, "Giving and Making Sense about Change: The Back and Forth between Leaders and Employees," *Journal of Business and Psychology*, Vol. 33, No. 1 (2018), pp. 71–87.

154. R. Thakur and S. Srivastava, "From Resistance to Readiness: The Role of Mediating Variables," *Journal of Organizational Change Management*, 2018.

155. S. Lynch and M. Mors, "Strategy Implementation and Organizational Change: How Formal Reorganization Affects Professional Networks," *Long Range Planning*, Vol. 52, No. 2 (2019), pp. 255–270.

156. D. Bortz, "10 Behaviors That Will Sink Your Job Performance," *Monster*, https://www.monster.com/career-advice/article/the-terrible-10-behaviors-in-the-workplace-hot-jobs (accessed May 6, 2020).

157. J. Stouten, D. Rousseau, and D. De Cremer, "Successful Organizational Change: Integrating the Management Practice and Scholarly Literatures," *Academy of Management Annals*, Vol. 12, No. 2 (2018), pp. 752–788.

158. S. Gilbert, "The Movement of #MeToo," *The Atlantic*, October 16, 2017, https://www.theatlantic.com/entertainment/archive/2017/10/the-movement-of-metoo/542979. Also see K. Amadeo, "How Does Immigration Affect the Economy and You?" *The Balance*, October 31, 2017, https://www.thebalance.com/how-immigration-impacts-the-economy-4125413.

159. G. L. Cohen and D. K. Sherman, "Self-Affirmation Theory," in R. F. Baumeister and K. D. Vohns (eds.), *Encyclopedia of Social Psychology*, 2007, http://webcache.googleusercontent.com/search?q=cache:_dXcwuoXD80J:people.psych.ucsb.edu/sherman/david/cohernshermanency2007.pdf+&cd=14&hl=en&ct=clnk&gl=us, p. 787.

160. D.K. Sherman and G. L. Cohen, "The Psychology of Self-Defense: Self-Affirmation Theory," *Advances in Experimental Social Psychology*, 2006, pp. 183–242.

161. Z. Kinias and J. Sim, "Facilitating Women's Success in Business: Interrupting the Process of Stereotype Threat through Affirmation of Personal Values," *Journal of Applied Psychology*, Vol. 101, No. 11 (2016), pp. 1585–1597.

162. Z. Hereford, "Examples of Positive Affirmations," *Essential Life-Skills*, https://www.essentiallifeskills.net/positiveaffirmations.html (accessed April 4, 2018).

163. P. Onderko, "3 Tips to Open Your Heart, Mind and Life to Change," *Success*, August 6, 2015, https://www.success.com/article/3-tips-to-open-your-heart-mind-and-life-to-changeApply.

164. R. Brenner, D.Vogel, D. Lannin, K. Engel, A. Seidman, and P. Heath, "Do Self-Compassion and Self-Coldness Distinctly Relate to Distress and Well-Being? A Theoretical Model of Self-Relating," *Journal of Counseling Psychology*, Vol. 65, No. 3 (2018), pp. 346–357.

165. P. Onderko, "3 Tips to Open Your Heart, Mind and Life to Change," *Success*, August 6, 2015, https://www.success.com/article/3-tips-to-open-your-heart-mind-and-life-to-changeApply.

166. A. Abrams, "How to Cultivate More Self-Compassion," *Psychology Today*, March 3, 2017, https://www.psychologytoday.com/us/blog/nurturing-self-compassion/201703/how-cultivate-more-self-compassion.

167. K. Wong, "Why Self-Compassion Beats Self-Confidence," *The New York Times*, December 28, 2017, https://www.nytimes.com/2017/12/28/smarter-living/why-self-compassion-beats-self-confidence.html.

168. A. Abrams, "How to Cultivate More Self-Compassion," *Psychology Today*, March 3, 2017, https://www.psychologytoday.com/us/blog/nurturing-self-compassion/201703/how-cultivate-more-self-compassion.

169. L. Eby, T. Allen, K. Conley, R. Williamson, T. Henderson, and V. Mancini, "Mindfulness-Based Training Interventions for Employees: A Qualitative Review of the Literature," *Human Resource Management Review*, Vol. 29, No. 2 (2019), pp. 156–178.

170. A. Carr, C. Palmeri, J. Levin, M. Smith, and K. Oanh Ha. "Just Try And Social Distance This," *Bloomberg Businessweek*, April 20, 2020, pp. 40–45.

171. C. Tate, "Some Grand Princess Passengers Waited Weeks for Coronavirus Test Results, Or Never Got Tested," *USA Today*, April 20, 2020, https://www.usatoday.com.

172. M. Aspan, "Why Cruise Lines Are Fighting with Passengers—And Each Other—Over Safety Standards," *Fortune,* July 16, 2020, https://fortune.com/2020/07/16/cruise-companies-carnival-lawsuits-coronavirus-safety/.

173. C. Perrett, "A Company Started by an Aussie Took Billions of Photos from Social Media to Create a Facial-Recognition Database, and Police Are Already Using It," *Business Insider,* January 20, 2020, https://www.businessinsider.com.au/clearwater-ai-2020-1.

174. A. Wyrich, "What You Need to Know about Clearview AI and Its Facial Recognition App," *Daily Dot,* January 23, 2020, https://www.dailydot.com/layer8/clearview-ai-facial-recognition-app/.

175. T. Dukes, "Raleigh Police Abruptly End Use of Controversial Facial Recognition Tech," *WRAL,* February 12, 2020, https://www.wral.com/raleigh-police-abruptly-end-use-of-controversial-facial-recognition-tech/18933545/.

176. N. Statt, "Controversial Facial Recognition Firm Clearview AI Facing Legal Claims after Damning NYT Report," *The Verge,* January 24, 2020, https://www.theverge.com/2020/1/24/21079354/clearview-ai-nypd-terrorism-suspect-false-claims-facial-recognition.

CHAPTER 11

1. S. Shellenbarger, "The Next Step after a Bad First Impression at Work," *The Wall Street Journal,* August 22, 2017, https://www.wsj.com/articles/the-next-step-after-a-bad-first-impression-at-work-1503416463.
2. S. Shellenbarger, "The Mistakes You Make in a Meeting's First Milliseconds," *The Wall Street Journal,* January 31, 2018, p. A9.
3. A. Prossack, "How to Make a Great First Impression," *Forbes,* April 30, 2018, https://www.forbes.com/sites/ashiraprossack1/2018/04/30/how-to-make-a-great-first-impresson/#2ac4a7023398.
4. B. Brenberg, "Making a Good First Impression Really Matters—and Isn't as Easy as It Sounds," *Fox News,* https://www.foxnews.com/opinion/brian-brenberg-how-to-make-a-good-first-impression (accessed march 21, 2020). Also see H. Deutschendorf, "Do These 5 Things Your First Week at a New Job to Make a Good Impression," *Fast Company,* March 1, 2019, https://www.fastcompany.com/90304801/do-these-5-things-your-first-week-at-a-new-job-to-make-a-good-impression.
5. J. Jonson, "How to Make a Good First Impression at Work 2020," *Chart Attack,* February 28, 2020, https://www.chartattack.com/make-a-good-first-impression-at-work/. Also see K. Noel, "8 Body Language Tricks to Instantly Appear More Confident," *Business Insider,* March 31, 2016, http://www.businessinsider.com/body-language-tricks-appear-more-confident-2016-3.
6. "11 Tips for Making a Great First Impression with New Clients," *Forbes,* April 3, 2019, https://www.forbes.com/sites/theyec/2019/04/03/11-tips-for-making-a-great-first-impression-with-potential-new-clients/#41405e1cbd4f.
7. R. Knight, "How to Make a Great First Impression," *Harvard Business Review,* September 12, 2016, https://hbr.org/2016/09/how-to-make-a-great-first-impression.
8. B. Brenberg, "Making a Good First Impression Really Matters—and Isn't as Easy as It Sounds," *Fox News,* https://www.foxnews.com/opinion/brian-brenberg-how-to-make-a-good-first-impression (accessed March 21, 2020). Also see C. Brooks, "Starting a New Job? Don't Wait to Make a Good Impression," *Business News Daily,* March 28, 2016, https://www.businessnewsdaily.com/5831-new-hire-good-impression.html.
9. S. Shellenbarger, "The Next Step after a Bad First Impression at Work," *The Wall Street Journal,* August 22, 2017, https://www.wsj.com/articles/the-next-step-after-a-bad-first-impression-at-work-1503416463. Also see D. Clark, "4 Ways to Overcome a Bad First Impression," *Harvard Business Review,* May, 13, 2016, https://hbr.org/2016/05/4-ways-to-overcome-a-bad-first-impression.
10. For a thorough discussion of personality psychology, see P. R. Sackett, F. Lievens, C. H. Van Iddekinge, and N. R. Kuncel, "Individual Differences and Their Measurement: A Review of 100 Years of Research," *Journal of Applied Psychology,* March 2017, pp. 254–273.
11. S. A. Woods, F. Lievens, F. De Fruyt, and B. Wille, "Personality across Working Life: The Longitudinal and Reciprocal Influences of Personality on Work," *Journal of Organizational Behavior,* Vol. 34, No. S1 (2013), pp. S7–S25. Also see A. Oshio, K. Taku, M. Hirano, and G. Saeed, "Resilience and Big Five Personality Traits: A Meta-Analysis," *Personality and Individual Differences,* June 2018, pp. 54–60; M. P. Wilmot, C. R. Wanberg, J. D. Kammeyer-Mueller, and D. S. Ones, "Extraversion Advantages at Work: A Quantitative Review and Synthesis of the Meta-Analytic Evidence," *Journal of Applied Psychology,* 2019, pp. 1447–1470; P. Soni and K. M. Bakhru, "Understanding Triangulated Collaboration of Work-Life Balance, Personality Traits, and Eudaimonic Well-Being," *Problems and Perspectives in Management,* 2019, pp. 63–82; J. L. Pletzera, M. Bentvelzenb, J. K. Oostromc, R. E. de Vries, "A Meta-Analysis of the Relations between Personality and Workplace Deviance: Big Five versus HEXACO," *Journal of Vocational Behavior,* 2019, pp. 369–383.

12. J. M. Digman, "Personality Structure: Emergence of the Five-Factor Model," *Annual Review of Psychology,* Vol. 41 (1990), pp. 417–440.
13. N. van Bommel, "How to Use Psychometric Testing in Recruitment?" *Hire Thinking,* February 20, 2020, https://www.big5assessments.com/blog/2020/02/03/how-to-use-psychometric-testing-in-recruitment/. Also see R. O'Donnell, "In the Hunt for Soft Skills, Employers Look to Personality Tests," *HR Dive,* January 11, 2018, https://www.hrdive.com/news/in-the-hunt-for-soft-skills-employers-look-to-personality-tests/514572/.
14. "75% of Fortune 500 Companies Use Psychometric Testing in Recruitment," *Independent,* June 5, 2019, https://www.independent.com.mt/articles/2019-06-05/business-news/75-of-Fortune-500-companies-use-psychometric-testing-in-recruitment-6736209146.
15. "75% of Fortune 500 Companies Use Psychometric Testing in Recruitment," *Independent,* June 5, 2019, https://www.independent.com.mt/articles/2019-06-05/business-news/75-of-Fortune-500-companies-use-psychometric-testing-in-recruitment-6736209146. Also see N. van Bommel, "How to Use Psychometric Testing in Recruitment?" *Hire Thinking,* February 20, 2020, https://www.big5assessments.com/blog/2020/02/03/how-to-use-psychometric-testing-in-recruitment/.
16. J. L. Huang, R. Cropanzaano, A. Li, P. Shao, X-A. Zhang, and Y. Li, "Employee Conscientiousness, Agreeableness, and Supervisor Justice Rule Compliance: A Three-Study Investigation," *Journal of Applied Psychology,* November 2017, pp. 1564–1589. Also see A. Oshio, K. Taku, M. Hirano, and G. Saeed, "Resilience and Big Five Personality Traits: A Meta-Analysis," *Personality and Individual Differences,* June 2018, pp. 54–60; M. Egan, M. Daly, L. Delaney, C. J. Boyce, and A. M. Wood, "Adolescent Conscientiousness Predicts Lower Lifetime Unemployment," *Journal of Applied Psychology,* April 2017, pp. 700–709; M. Travers, "Which of the Big Five Personality Traits Best Predicts Job Performance?" *Forbes,* November 16, 2019, https://www.forbes.com/sites/traversmark/2019/11/16/which-of-the-big-five-personality-traits-best-predicts-job-performance/#7777b752c752.
17. D. Harari, B. W. Swider, L. B. Steed, and A. P. Breidenthal, "Is Perfect Good? A Meta-Analysis of Perfectionism in the Workplace," *Journal of Applied Psychology,* 2018, pp. 1121–1144.
18. S. Margolis and S. Lyubomirsky, "Experimental Manipulation of Extraverted and Introverted Behavior and Its Effects on Well-Being," *Journal of Experimental Psychology: General,* 2020, pp. 719–731. Also see M. P. Wilmot, C. R. Wanberg, J. D. Kammeyer-Mueller, and D. S. Ones, "Extraversion Advantages at Work: A Quantitative Review and Synthesis of the Meta-Analytic Evidence," *Journal of Applied Psychology,* 2019, pp. 1447–1470.
19. J. L. Pletzera, M. Bentvelzenb, J. K. Oostromc, R. E. de Vries, "A Meta-Analysis of the Relations between Personality and Workplace Deviance: Big Five versus HEXACO," *Journal of Vocational Behavior,* 2019, pp. 369–383.
20. Y. Zhang, J. Sun, C. Lin, and H. Ren, "Linking Core Self-Evaluation to Creativity: The Roles of Knowledge Sharing and Work Meaningfulness," *Journal of Business and Psychology,* 2020, pp. 257–270. Also see T. A. Judge, H. M. Weiss, J. D. Kammeyer-Mueller, and C. L. Hulin, "Job Attitudes, Job Satisfaction, and Job Affect: A Century of Continuity and of Change," *Journal of Applied Psychology,* March 2017, pp. 356–374;

Z. Wang, X. Bu, S. Cai, "Core Self-Evaluation, Individual Intellectual Capital and Employee Creativity," *Current Psychology*, 2018, https://doi.org/10.1007/s12144-018-0046-x; H. Ding, X. Lin, "Exploring the Relationship between Core Self-Evaluation and Strengths Use: The Perspective of Emotion," *Personality and Individual Differences*, 2020, https://doi.org/10.1016/j.paid.2019.109804; S. S. Kirmani, S. Attiq, H. Bakari, and M. Irfan, "Role of Core Self Evaluation and Acquired Motivations in Employee Task Performance," *Pakistan Journal of Psychological Research*, 2019; J. Ahn, S. Lee, and S. Yun, "Leaders' Core Self-Evaluation, Ethical Leadership, and Employees' Job Performance: The Moderating Role of Employees' Exchange Ideology," *Journal of Business Ethics*, 2018, pp. 457–470.

21. T. A. Judge, A. Earez, and J. A. Bono, "The Power of Being Positive: The Relation between Positive Self-Concept and Job Performance," *Journal of Human Performance,* June 1998, pp. 167–187.

22. S. Machmud and S. Pasundan, "The Influence of Self-Efficacy on Satisfaction and Work-Related Performance," *International Journal of Management Science and Business Administration*, 2018, pp. 43–47. Also see A. Byars-Winston, J. Diestelmann, J. N. Savoy, and W. T. Hoyt, "Unique Effects and Moderators of Effects of Sources on Self-Efficacy: A Model-Based Meta-Analysis," *Journal of Counseling Psychology,* November 2017, pp. 645–658; K. Shoji, R. Cieslak, E. Smoktunowicz, A. Rogala, and C. C. Benight, "Associations between Job Burnout and Self-Efficacy: A Meta-Analysis," *Anxiety, Stress, and Coping,* July 2016, pp. 367–386; F. Cetin, D. Askun, "The Effect of Occupational Self-Efficacy on Work Performance through Intrinsic Work Motivation," *Management Research Review,* 2018, pp. 186–201; P. R. Sackett, F. Lievens, C. H. Van Iddekinge, and N. R. Kuncel, "Individual Differences and Their Measurement: A Review of 100 Years of Research," *Journal of Applied Psychology,* March 2017, pp. 254–273; Z. A. Green, "The Mediating Effect of Well-Being between Generalized Self-Efficacy and Vocational Identity Development," *International Journal for Educational and Vocational Guidance,* 2019, https://doi.org/10.1007/s10775-019-09401-7; K. Talsma, B. Schuz, R. Schwarzer, and K. Norris, "I Believe, Therefore I Achieve (and Vice Versa): A Meta-Analytic Cross-Lagged Panel Analysis of Self-Efficacy and Academic Performance," *Learning and Individual Differences,* 2018, pp. 136–150; D. De Clercq, I. Ul Haq, and M. U. Azeem, "Self-Efficacy to Spur Job Performance," *Management Decision,* 2018, pp. 891–907; A. D. Stajkovic, A. Bandura, E. A. Locke, D. Lee, and K. Sergent, "Test of Three Conceptual Models of Influence of the Big Five Personality Traits and Self-Efficacy on Academic Performance: A Meta-Analytic Path-Analysis," *Personality and Individual Differences,* 2018, pp. 238–245; J. W. Beck and A. M. Schmidt, "Negative Relationships between Self-Efficacy and Performance Can Be Adaptive: The Mediating Role of Resource Allocation," *Journal of Management,* 2018, pp. 555–588.

23. P. R. Lyons and R. P. Bandura, "Exploring Linkages of Performance with Metacognition," *Journal of Management Development,* 2019, pp. 195–207.

24. W. S. Silver, T. R. Mitchell, and M. E. Gist, "Response to Successful and Unsuccessful Performance: The Moderating Effect of Self-Efficacy on the Relationship between Training and Newcomer Adjustment," *Journal of Applied Psychology,* April 1995, pp. 211–225.

25. J. V. Vancouver, K. M. More, and R. J. Yoder, "Self-Efficacy and Resource Allocation: Support for a Nonmonotonic, Discontinuous Model," *Journal of Applied Psychology,* January 2008, pp. 35–47.

26. V. Mattias, L. Bjørn, and R. Torleif, "Predictors of Return to Work 6 Months after the End of Treatment in Patients with Common Mental Disorders: A Cohort Study," *Journal of Occupational Rehabilitation,* December 2017, pp. 1–11. Also see Z. Millman, "Taking Control: Training in Verbal Self-Guidance to Enhance One's Performance," *Organizational Dynamics,* 2017, pp. 182–188; M. R. Chowdhury, "4 Ways To Improve and Increase Self-Efficacy," *Positive Psychology,* February 18, 2020, https://positivepsychology.com/3-ways-build-self-efficacy/.

27. M. J. Martinko and W. L. Gardner, "Learned Helplessness: An Alternative Explanation for Performance Deficits," *Academy of Management Review,* April 1982, pp. 195–204. Also see C. R. Campbell and M. J.

Martinko, "An Integrative Attributional Perspective of Employment and Learned Helplessness: A Multimethod Field Study," *Journal of Management,* Vol. 2 (1998), pp. 173–200.

28. P. Filippello, C. Buzzai, S. Costa, S. Orecchio, and L. Sorrenti, "Teaching Style and Academic Achievement: The Mediating Role of Learned Helplessness and Mastery Orientation," *Psychology in the Schools,* 2019, https://doi.org/10.1002/pits.22315; C. H. Van Iddekinge, and N. R. Kuncel, "Individual Differences and Their Measurement: A Review of 100 Years of Research," *Journal of Applied Psychology,* March 2017, pp. 254–273.

29. Y. Z. Yusuff, M. Mohamad, and N.Y. Ab Wahab, "The Influence of General Self-Efficacy on Women Entrepreneurs," *Academy of Entrepreneurship Journal,* 2019, DOI: 1528-2686-25-2-220. Also see R. Head, "Self-Efficacy and Sports Performance," *Sport Psychology Today,* October 8, 2019, http://www.sportpsychologytoday.com/youth-sports-psychology/self-efficacy-and-sports-performance/.

30. V. Gecas, "The Self-Concept," in R. H. Turner and J. F. Short Jr. (eds.), *Annual Review of Sociology,* Vol. 8 (Palo Alto, CA: Annual Reviews, 1982).

31. S. B. Dust, J. C. Rode, M. L. Arthaud-Day, S. S. Howes, A. Ramaswami, "Managing the Self-Esteem, Employment Gaps, and Employment Quality Process: The Role of Facilitation- and Understanding-Based Emotional Intelligence," *Journal of Organizational Behavior,* 2018, pp. 680–693. Also see C. E. Whelpley and M. A. McDaniel, "Self-Esteem and Counterproductive Work Behaviors: A Systematic Review," *Journal of Managerial Psychology,* 2016, pp. 850–863; K. Matzler, F. A. Bauer, and T. A. Mooradian, "Self-Esteem and Transformational Leadership," *Journal of Managerial Psychology,* 2015, pp. 815–831; U. Orth, R. W. Robins, L. L. Meier, and R. D. Conger, "Refining the Vulnerability of Low Self-Esteem and Depression: Disentangling the Effects of Genuine Self-Esteem and Narcissism," *Journal of Personality and Social Psychology,* January 2016, pp. 133–149.

32. B. R. Schlenker, M. F. Weigold, and J. R. Hallam, "Self-Serving Attributions in Social Context: Effects of Self-Esteem and Social Pressure," *Journal of Personality and Social Psychology,* May 1990, pp. 855–863. Also see P. Sellers, "Get over Yourself," *Fortune,* April 2001, pp. 76–88.

33. D. A. Stinson, C. Logel, M. P. Zanna, J. G. Holmes, J. V. Wood, and S. J. Spencer, "The Cost of Lower Self-Esteem: Testing a Self- and Social-Bonds Model of Health," *Journal of Personality and Social Psychology,* March 2008, pp. 412–428.

34. J. W. McGuire and C. V. McGuire, "Enhancing Self-Esteem by Directed-Thinking Tasks: Cognitive and Affective Positivity Asymmetries," *Journal of Personality and Social Psychology,* June 1996, pp. 1117–1125.

35. For an overall view of research on locus of control, see B. M. Galvin, A. E. Randel, B. J. Collins, and R. E. Johnson, "Changing the Focus of Locus (of Control): A Targeted Review of the Locus of Control Literature and Agenda for Future Research," *Journal of Organizational Behavior,* 2018, pp. 820–833. Also see M. Wilding, "Successful People Have a Strong 'Locus of Control.' Do You?" *Forbes,* March 2, 2020, https://www.forbes.com/sites/melodywilding/2020/03/02/successful-people-have-a-strong-locus-of-control-do-you/#5582d17d7af3.

36. C. Wu, M. Griffin, and S. Parker, "Developing Agency through Good Work: Longitudinal Effects of Job Autonomy and Skill Utilization on Locus of Control," *Journal of Vocational Behavior* Vol. 89 (2015), pp. 102–108.

37. J. D. Mayer, R. D. Roberts, and S. G. Barsade, "Human Abilities: Emotional Intelligence," *Annual Review of Psychology,* January 2008, http://papers.ssrn.com/sol3/papers.cfm?abstract_id=1082096 (accessed July 1, 2016).

38. K. Schlegel and M. Mortillaro, "The Geneva Emotional Competence Test (GECo): An Ability Measure of Workplace Emotional Intelligence," *Journal of Applied Psychology,* 2019, pp. 559–580.

39. D. Voisin, "Emotional Intelligence: Why Companies Are Seeking Higher EQ over IQ," *Lead Managing,* February 21, 2019, https://www.leadmanaging.com/blog/emotional-intelligence.

40. Results are based on C. Miao, R. H. Humphrey, and S. Qian, "A Meta-Analysis of Emotional Intelligence and Work Attitudes," *Journal of Occupational and Organizational Psychology,* June 2017, pp. 177–202; C. Miao, R. H. Humphrey, and S. Qian, "Are the Emotionally Intelligent Good Citizens or Counterproductive? A Meta-Analysis of Emotional Intelligence and Its Relationships with Organizational Citizenship and Counterproductive Work Behavior," *Personality and Individual Differences,* October 2017, pp. 144–156. Also see A. Minbashian, N. Beckmann, and R. E. Wood, "Emotional Intelligence and Individual Differences in Affective Processes Underlying Task-contingent Conscientiousness," *Journal of Organizational Behavior*, 2018, pp. 1182–1196; S. B. Dust, J. C. Rode, M. L. Arthaud-Day, S. S. Howes, A. Ramaswami, "Managing the Self-Esteem, Employment Gaps, and Employment Quality Process: The Role of Facilitation- and Understanding-Based Emotional Intelligence," *Journal of Organizational Behavior*, 2018, pp. 680–693.

41. D. Goleman, "What Makes a Leader," *Harvard Business Review,* November–December 1998, pp. 93–102.

42. S. Coté, "Enhancing Managerial Effectiveness via Four Core Facets of Emotional Intelligence: Self-Awareness, Social Perception, Emotion Understanding, and Emotion Regulation," *Organizational Dynamics,* 2017, pp. 140–147.

43. A. Chapman, "Empathy, Trust, Diffusing Conflict and Handling Complaints," *Businessballs.com*, www.businessballs.com/empathy.htm (accessed July 19, 2016).

44. M. Thakrar, "How (and Why) to Develop Your Emotional Intelligence," *Forbes,* March 22, 2018, www.forbes.com/sites/forbescoachescouncil/2018/03/22/how-and-why-to-develop-your-emotional-intelligence/2/#3695cf4921b3. Also see V. Zarya, "Can VR Help Your Coworkers Be More Empathetic?" *Fortune,* April 25, 2017, www.fortune.com/2017/04/25/workplace-empathy-translator-app/?iid=sr-link10.

45. "Empathy," *Wikipedia,* https://en.wikipedia.org/wiki/Empathy (accessed March 28, 2018).

46. M. Schwantes, "5 Masterful Ways That People with Emotional Intelligence Avoid Drama and Conflict," *Inc.,* December 12, 2017, www.inc.com/marcel-schwantes/5-masterful-ways-that-people-with-emotional-intelligence-will-avoid-drama-conflict.html?cid=search. Also see V. Zarya, "Can VR Help Your Coworkers Be More Empathetic?" *Fortune,* April 25, 2017, www.fortune.com/2017/04/25/workplace-empathy-translator-app/?iid=sr-link10.

47. M. Thakrar, "How (and Why) to Develop Your Emotional Intelligence," *Forbes,* March 22, 2018, www.forbes.com/sites/forbescoachescouncil/2018/03/22/how-and-why-to-develop-your-emotional-intelligence/2/#3695cf4921b3.

48. G. Tredgold, "How to Improve your Emotional Intelligence and Be a Better Leader," *Huffington Post,* December 6, 2017, www.huffingtonpost.com/gordon-tredgold/how-to-improve-your-emotional-intelligence_b_9119398.html.

49. T. Oesch, "Developing Employee Empathy Using Virtual Reality," *Training Industry*, May 30, 2018, https://trainingindustry.com/articles/learning-technologies/developing-employee-empathy-using-virtual-reality/.

50. T. Oesch, "Developing Employee Empathy Using Virtual Reality," *Training Industry*, May 30, 2018, https://trainingindustry.com/articles/learning-technologies/developing-employee-empathy-using-virtual-reality/.

51. K. U. Phillips, "The Empathy Gap, and What It's Like Being Trans in the Workplace," *Salon*, February 16, 2020, https://www.salon.com/2020/02/16/the-empathy-gap-and-what-its-like-being-trans-in-the-workplace/. Also see V. Zarya, "Can VR Help Your Coworkers Be More Empathetic?" *Fortune,* April 25, 2017, www.fortune.com/2017/04/25/workplace-empathy-translator-app/?iid=sr-link10.

52. "The Random App of Kindness App," *Random App of Kindness,* http://www.rakigame.com/home (accessed March 21, 2020). Also see S. Konrath, "Empathy: There's an App for That!" *Psychology Today,* March 14, 2017, www.psychologytoday.com/us/blog/the-empathy-gap/201703/empathy-there-s-app.

53. M. Rokeach, *Beliefs, Attitudes, and Values* (San Francisco: Jossey-Bass, 1968), p. 168.

54. S. H. Schwartz, "An Overview of the Schwartz Theory of Basic Values," *Online Readings in Psychology and Culture*, December 1, 2012, http://dx.doi.org/10.9707/2307-0919.1116.

55. H. N. Ismail, S. Karkoulian, and S. K. Kertechian, "Which Personal Values Matter Most? Job Performance and Job Satisfaction across Job Categories," *International Journal of Organizational Analysis*, 2019, pp. 109–124. Also see J. Weber, "Understanding the Millennials' Integrated Ethical Decision-Making Process: Assessing the Relationship between Personal Values and Cognitive Moral Reasoning," *Business and Society*, 2019, pp. 1671–1706.

56. M. Fishbein and I. Ajzen, *Belief, Attitude, Intention and Behavior: An Introduction to Theory and Research* (Reading, MA: Addison-Wesley Publishing, 1975), p. 6.

57. M. Reid and A. Wood, "An Investigation into Blood Donation Intentions among Non-Donors," *International Journal of Nonprofit and Voluntary Sector Marketing,* February 2008, pp. 31–43. Also see J. Ramsey, B. J. Punnett, and D. Greenidge, "A Social Psychological Account of Absenteeism in Barbados," *Human Resource Management Journal,* April 2008, pp. 97–117.

58. T. A. Judge, C. J. Thoresen, J. E. Bono, and G. K. Patton, "The Job Satisfaction–Job Performance Relationship: A Qualitative and Quantitative Review," *Psychological Bulletin,* May 2001, pp. 376–407.

59. "15Five Study Finds That Supporting Mental and Emotional Wellness Improves Retention and Engagement of Gen Z Employees," *PR Web*, September 9, 2019, http://www.prweb.com/releases/15five_study_finds_that_supporting_mental_and_emotional_wellness_improves_retention_and_engagement_of_gen_z_employees/prweb16553552.htm.

60. J. S. Becker, "Empirical Validation of Affect, Behavior, and Cognition as Distinct Components of Attitude," *Journal of Personality and Social Psychology,* May 1984, pp. 1191–1205. Also see A. P. Brief, *Attitudes in and around Organizations* (Thousand Oaks, CA: Sage, 1998), pp. 49–84.

61. K. Lowden, S. Hall, D. Elliot, and J. Lewin, "Employers' Perceptions of the Employability Skills of New Graduates," 2011, www.gla.ac.uk/faculties/education/scre.

62. S. Shahid and M.K. Muchiri, "Positivity at the Workplace," *International Journal of Organizational Analysis*, Vol. 27 (3) 2019, pp. 494–523.

63. P. S. Thompson and M. C. Bolino, "Negative Beliefs about Accepting Coworker Help: Implications for Employee Attitudes, Job Performance, and Reputation," *Journal of Applied Psychology*, 2018, pp. 842–866. Also see C. Barbaranell, M. Paciello, V. Biagioli, R. Fida, C. Tramontano, "Positivity and Behaviour: The Mediating Role of Self-Efficacy in Organisational and Educational Settings," *Journal of Happiness Studies*, 2019, pp. 707–727.

64. L. Festinger, *A Theory of Cognitive Dissonance* (Stanford, CA: Stanford University Press, 1957).

65. M. Cicerchia, "Learning Disabilities and Self-Esteem," *Touch-Type Read and Spell,* December 18, 2017, www.readandspell.com/us/learning-disabilities-and-self-esteem.

66. M. Alvord, "For Teens Knee-Deep in Negativity, Reframing Thoughts Can Help," *NPR,* September 9, 2017, www.npr.org/sections/health-shots/2017/09/09/549133027/for-teens-knee-deep-in-negativity-reframing-thoughts-can-help.

67. V. MacGill, "Reframing Cognitive Behaviour Theory from a Systems Perspective," *Systemic Practice and Action Research*, 2018, pp. 495–507. Also see C. Ackerman, "CBT's Cognitive Restructuring (CR) for Tackling Cognitive Distortions," *Positive Psychology Program,* February 12, 2018, www.positivepsychologyprogram.com/cbt-cognitive-restructuring-cognitive-distortions/.

68. E. Scott, " How to Reframe Situations So They Create Less Stress," *Very Well Mind*, October 2, 2019, https://www.verywellmind.com/cognitive-reframing-for-stress-management-3144872.

69. S. Hookway, M. F. Johansson, A. Svensson, and B. Heiden, "The Problem with Problems: Reframing and Cognitive Bias in Healthcare Innovation," *The Design Journal*, 2019, pp. 553–574.

70. O. Williams, "Why Virgin Group Will No Longer Ask for Your Exam Results When Hiring," *Forbes,* October 15, 2019, https://www.forbes.com/sites/oliverwilliams1/2019/10/15/why-virgin-group-will-no-longer-ask-for-your-exam-results-when-hiring/#1b8734b456be. Also see C. Gallo, "How Richard Branson Uses a Simple, Psychologically Proven Brain Trick to Turn a 'Disorder' into a Strength," *Inc.,* January 25, 2018, www.inc.com/carmine-gallo/richard-bransons-letter-to-his-dyslexic-self-reveals-a-powerful-psychological-trait-of-ultra-successful-leaders.html?cid=search.

71. C. Gallo, "How Richard Branson Uses a Simple, Psychologically Proven Brain Trick to Turn a 'Disorder' into a Strength," *Inc.*, January 25, 2018, www.inc.com/carmine-gallo/richard-bransons-letter-to-his-dyslexic-self-reveals-a-powerful-psychological-trait-of-ultra-successful-leaders.html?cid=search.

72. A. Kinicki and M. Fugate, *Organizational Behavior: A Practical, Problem-Solving Approach,* 2nd ed. (New York: McGraw-Hill, 2018).

73. A. H. Tangari, J. Kees, J. C. Andrews, and S. Burton, "Can Corrective Ad Statements Based on *U.S. v. Philip Morris USA Inc.* Impact Consumer Beliefs about Smoking?" *Journal of Public Policy & Marketing.* Vol. 29, No. 2 (2010), pp. 153–169.

74. Adapted from R. Kreitner and A. Kinicki, *Organizational Behavior,* 10th ed. (New York: McGraw-Hill/Irwin, 2013), Figure 7-1, p. 181.

75. Definition adapted from C. M. Judd and B. Park, "Definition and Assessment of Accuracy in Social Stereotypes," *Psychological Review,* January 1993, p. 110.

76. E. V. Hall, A. V. Hall, A. D. Galinsky, and K. W. Phillips, "Mosaic: A Model of Stereotyping through Associated and Intersectional Categories," *Academy of Management Review*, July 2019, pp. 643–672.

77. S. Hedreen, "'Gendered' Jobs Are on the Decline, But Stereotypes Remain," *Business News Daily*, August 14, 2019, https://www.businessnewsdaily.com/10085-male-female-dominated-jobs.html.

78. P. Agarwal, "Are Women and Men Being Treated the Same in the Workplace?" *Forbes*, March 3, 2020, https://www.forbes.com/sites/pragyaagarwaleurope/2020/03/03/are-women-and-men-being-treated-the-same-in-the-workplace/#7fd9462942eb.

79. K. Hassan, M. Varadan, and C. Zeisberger, "How the VC Pitch Process Is Failing Female Entrepreneurs," *Harvard Business Review*, January 13, 2020, https://hbr.org/2020/01/how-the-vc-pitch-process-is-failing-female-entrepreneurs. Also see M. Malmstrom, A. Voitkane, J. Johansson, and J. Wincent, "What Do They Think and What Do They Say? Gender Bias, Entrepreneurial Attitude in Writing and Venture Capitalists' Funding Decisions," *Journal of Business Venturing Insights*, 2020, https://doi.org/10.1016/j.jbvi.2019.e00154; "How Venture Capitalists Really Assess a Pitch," *Harvard Business Review*, May–June 2017, https://hbr.org/2017/05/how-venture-capitalists-really-assess-a-pitch.

80. M. A. McCord, D. L. Joseph, L. Y. Dhanani, and J. M. Beus, "A Meta-Analysis of Sex and Race Differences in Perceived Workplace Mistreatment," *Journal of Applied Psychology,* February 2018, pp. 137–163.

81. V. K. Gupta, S. C. Mortal, S. Han, and S. Silveri, "Do Women CEOs Face Greater Threat of Shareholder Activism Compared to Male CEOs? A Role Congruity Perspective," *Journal of Applied Psychology,* February 2018, pp. 228–236.

82. J. B. Evans, J. E. Slaughter, A. P. J. Ellis, and J. M. Rivin, "Gender and the Evaluation of Humor at Work," *Journal of Applied Psychology*, August 2019, pp. 1077–1087.

83. N. Ellemers, "Gender Stereotypes," *Annual Review of Psychology,* 2018, pp. 275–298.

84. L. D. Sheppard and S. K. Johnson, "The Femme Fatale Effect: Attractiveness Is a Liability for Businesswomen's Perceived Truthfulness, Trust, and Deservingness of Termination," *Sex Roles*, March 2019, pp. 779–796.

85. See examples in P. T. Rocks, "Addressing and Removing Common Stereotypes About Older Workers," *Forbes*, August 14, 2019, https://www.forbes.com/sites/forbescommunicationscouncil/2019/08/14/addressing-and-removing-common-stereotypes-about-older-workers/#3cac71f96e4c. Also see "Older Consumers: Redefining Health and Wellness as They Age," *Forbes*, October 31, 2017, https://www.forbes.com/sites/thehartmangroup/2017/10/31/older-consumers-redefining-health-and-wellness-as-they-age/#391edb7815fd; J. Bersin and T. Chamorro-Premuzic, "The Case for Hiring Older Workers," *Harvard Business Review*, September 26, 2019, https://hbr.org/2019/09/the-case-for-hiring-older-workers.

86. Bersin and T. Chamorro-Premuzic, "The Case for Hiring Older Workers," *Harvard Business Review*, September 26, 2019, https://hbr.org/2019/09/the-case-for-hiring-older-workers. Also see Transamerica Center for Retirement Studies, "Perspectives on Retirement: Baby Boomers, Generation X, Millennials," https://www.transamericacenter.org/retirement-research/17th-annual-retirement-survey/17th-annual-infographics/perspectives-on-retirement-by-generation-infographic (accessed April 19, 2020).

87. K. Terrell, "Who's Working More? People Age 65 and Older," *AARP*, November 22, 2019, https://www.aarp.org/work/working-at-50-plus/info-2019/surging-older-workforce.html; K. Hannon, "Reaping the Benefits of an Aging Work Force," *The New York Times,* March 2, 2018, https://www.nytimes.com/2018/03/02/business/retirement/aging-workers-opportunity.html.

88. "Aptive Environmental," *Entrepreneur*, October 23, 2019, https://www.entrepreneur.com/company/aptive-environmental. Also see "Careers at Aptive Environmental," *Aptive*, https://careers.smartrecruiters.com/AptiveEnvironmental1 (accessed March 24, 2020); "10 Companies That Really Care about Their Older Workers," *Monster*, monster.com/career-advice/article/companies-friendly-toward-older-workers-1217 (accessed March 24, 2020).

89. D. Reddy, "How Doctors Deal with Racist Patients," *The Wall Street Journal,* January 23, 2018, p. A11.

90. T. DeAngelis, "Unmasking 'Racial Micro Aggressions,'" *Harvard Business Review,* February 2009, pp. 42–46.

91. M. D. C. Triana, M. Jayasinghe, and J. R. Pieper, "Perceived Workplace Racial Discrimination and Its Correlates: A Meta-Analysis," *Journal of Organizational Behavior,* May 2015, pp. 491–513.

92. T. Essig, "13 Things White Men with Black Bosses Should Know," *Forbes,* March 7, 2016, https://www.forbes.com/sites/toddessig/2016/03/07/13-things-white-men-with-black-bosses-should-know/#340ed11f1ebe.

93. Z. Greenbaum, "Countering Stereotypes about Asian Americans," *Monitor on Psychology*, December 1, 2019, https://www.apa.org/monitor/2019/12/countering-stereotypes. Also see "Study Shows Positive Impact of Numeric Diversity and Diversity Climate on Psychological Outcomes for Faculty of Color," *Human Resource Management International Digest*, 2019, pp. 26–28.

94. A. Rattan and C. S. Dweek, "What Happens after Prejudice Is Confronted in the Workplace? How Mindsets Affect Minorities' and Women's Outlook on Future Social Relations," *Journal of Applied Psychology*, June 2018, pp. 676–687.

95. K. Payne, L. Niemi, and J. M. Doris, "How to Think about 'Implicit Bias,'" *Scientific American*, March 27, 2018, https://www.scientificamerican.com/article/how-to-think-about-implicit-bias/.

96. "Explicit Bias," *Perception Institute*, https://perception.org/research/explicit-bias/ (accessed April 9, 2020).

97. T. DeAngelis, "How Does Implicit Bias by Physicians Affect Patients' Health Care?" *Monitor on Psychology*, March 2019, https://www.apa.org/monitor/2019/03/ce-corner.

98. B. Kurdi et al., "Relationship between the Implicit Association Test and Intergroup Behavior: A Meta-Analysis," *American Psychologist*, 2019, pp. 569–586.

99. H. R. Roberts, "Implicit Bias and Social Justice," *Open Society Foundations*, December 18, 2011, https://www.opensocietyfoundations.org/voices/implicit-bias-and-social-justice.

100. K. P. Jones, I. E. Sabat, E. B. King, A. Ahmad, T. C. Mccausland, and T. Chen, "Isms and Schisms: A Meta-Analysis of the Prejudice—Discrimination Relationship across Racism, Sexism, and Ageism," *Journal of Organizational Behavior,* September 2017, pp. 1076–1110.

101. L. Mackenzie , J. Wehner and S.J. Correll, "Why Most Performance Evaluations Are Biased, and How to Fix Them," *Harvard Business*

Review, January 11, 2019, https://hbr.org/2019/01/why-most-performance-evaluations-are-biased-and-how-to-fix-them.

102. D. McGrath, "What's to Be Done about the Implicit Racial Bias I Found in My English Class Textbook?" *Chicago Sun-Times*, January 30, 2020, https://chicago.suntimes.com/2020/1/30/21115791/implicit-racial-bias-black-history-month-leonard-pitts-david-mcgrath. Also see "Bias on the Bench," *Online Journalism Awards*, https://awards.journalists.org/entries/bias-on-the-bench/ (accessed March 24, 2020).

103. K. D. Elsbach and I. Stigliani, "New Information Technology and Implicit Bias," *Academy of Management Perspective*, May 2019, pp. 185–206.

104. R. D. Godsil, "Breaking the Cycle: Implicit Bias, Racial Anxiety, and Stereotype Threat," *Poverty & Race,* January/February 2015, www.prrac.org/newsletters/janfeb2015.pdf (accessed July 13, 2016).

105. C. N. Macrae and S. Quadflieg, "Perceiving People," in S. T. Fiske, D. T. Gilbert, and G. Lindzey (eds.), *Handbook of Social Psychology* (New York: John Wiley & Sons, 2010), pp. 428–463. Also see M. Snyder and A. A. Stukas Jr., "Interpersonal Processes: The Interplay of Cognitive, Motivational, and Behavioral Activities in Social Interaction," in J. T. Spence, J. M. Darley, and D. J. Foss (eds.), *Annual Review of Psychology* (Palo Alto, CA: Annual Review, 1999), pp. 273–303.

106. A. Akhtar and D. Baer, "11 Scientific Reasons Why Attractive People Are More Successful in Life," *Business Insider*, October 8, 2019, https://www.businessinsider.com/beautiful-people-make-more-money-2014-11.

107. "When Did Americans Begin to Get Obsessed with Weight Loss?" *Daily History,* https://dailyhistory.org/index.php?title=When_did_Americans_begin_to_get_obsessed_with_weight_loss%3F&mobileaction=toggle_view_mobile (accessed March 24, 2020). Also see J. Carpenter, "A Woman to Know: Lulu Hunt Peters," *A Woman to Know*, March 2, 2017, https://awomantoknow.substack.com/p/a-woman-to-know-lulu-hunt-peters.

108. C. Sandvick and A. Gutierrez-Romine, "When Did Americans Begin to Get Obsessed with Weight Loss?" *DailyHistory.org*, www.dailyhistory.org/When_did_Americans_begin_to_get_obsessed_with_weight_loss%3F (accessed March 24, 2020).

109. J. Carpenter, "A Woman to Know: Lulu Hunt Peters," *A Woman to Know*, March 2, 2017, https://awomantoknow.substack.com/p/a-woman-to-know-lulu-hunt-peters.

110. Obesity Society, "Facts about Obesity," www.obesity.org/obesity/resources/facts-about-obesity/bias-stigmatization (accessed March 30, 2018). Also see R. Alexander, "Only 15% of Hiring Managers Would Consider Hiring an Overweight Woman," *Moneyish,* December 9, 2017, www.moneyish.com/ish/only-15-of-hiring-managers-would-consider-hiring-an-overweight-woman/.

111. S. Lebowitz, "Science Says People Determine Your Competence, Intelligence, and Salary Based on Your Weight," *Business Insider,* September 9, 2015, www.businessinsider.com/science-overweight-people-less-successful-2015-9.

112. S. Bevan, "Half of Employers Say They Are Less Inclined to Recruit Obese Candidates—It's Not OK," *The Conversation,* January 21, 2019, https://theconversation.com/half-of-employers-say-they-are-less-inclined-to-recruit-obese-candidates-its-not-ok-109821. Also see S. Flint, M. Čadek, S. Codreanu, V. Ivić, C. Zomer, and A. Gomoiu, "Obesity Discrimination in the Recruitment Process: 'You're Not Hired!'" *Frontiers in Psychology,* Vol. 7 (May 3, 2016), p. 647, www.ncbi.nlm.nih.gov/pmc/articles/PMC4853419/; B. Nowrouzi, A. McDougall, B. Gohar, B. Nowrouz-Kia, J. Casole, and A. Fizza, "Weight Bias in the Workplace: A Literature Review," *Occupational Medicine & Health Affairs,* Vol. 3, No. 3 (2015).

113. C. Ross, "I See Fat People," *Psychology Today*, August 7, 2013, www.psychologytoday.com/us/blog/real-healing/201308/i-see-fat-people.

114. See example about traits in X. Fang, G. A. van Kleef, and D. A. Sauter, "Person Perception from Changing Emotional Expressions: Primacy, Recency, or Averaging Effect?" *Cognition and Emotion*, 2018, pp. 1597–1610. Also see S. Guéraud, E. K. Walsh, A. E. Cook, and E. J. O'Brien, "Validating Information during Reading: The Effect of Recency," *Journal of Research in Reading*, 2018, pp. S85–S101.

115. T. Odean and B. M. Barber, "All That Glitters: The Effect of Attention and News on the Buying Behavior of Individual and Institutional Investors," *The Review of Financial Studies,* Vol. 21, No. 2 (2008), pp. 785–818. Also see P. Sullivan, "Want an Active Investment Manager? Here's What to Look For," *The New York Times,* March 30, 2012, p. B8.

116. J. Denrell, C. Fang, and C. Liu, "In Search of Behavioral Opportunities from Misattributions of Luck," *Academy of Management Review*, October 2019, pp. 896–915.

117. S. Wen, "The Effect of Result Publicity on Self-serving Attributional Bias—a Social Comparison Perspective," *Frontiers of Business Research in China*, 2018, https://doi.org/10.1186/s11782-018-0028-8.

118. K. Cherry, "How the Self-Serving Bias Protects Self-Esteem," *Verywellmind,* February 12, 2018, https://www.verywellmind.com/what-is-the-self-serving-bias-2795032.

119. J. Weaver, J. F. Moses, and M. Snyder, "Self-Fulfilling Prophecies in Ability Settings," *Journal of Social Psychology,* Vol. 156, no 2 (2016), pp. 179–189.

120. S. Madon et al., "The Accumulation of Stereotype-Based Self-Fulfilling Prophecies," *Journal of Personality and Social Psychology*, 2018, pp. 825–844. Also see D. Nolkemper, H. Aydin, and M. Knigge, "Teachers' Stereotypes about Secondary School Students: The Case of Germany," *Quality and Quantity,* March 2018, pp. 1–21.

121. These recommendations were adapted from J. Keller, "Have Faith—in You," *Selling Power*, June 1996, pp. 84, 86. Also see R. W. Goddard, "The Pygmalion Effect," *Personnel Journal*, June 1985, p. 10; J. S. Livingston, "Pygmalion in Management," *Harvard Business Review,* January 2003, https://hbr.org/2003/01/pygmalion-in-management; R. E. Riggio, "Pygmalion Leadership: The Power of Positive Expectations," *Psychology Today,* April 18, 2009, https://www.psychologytoday.com/blog/cutting-edge-leadership/200904/pygmalion-leadership-the-power-positive-expectations; G. Swanson, "The Pygmalion Effect: How It Drives Employee Performance," *LinkedIn,* September 24, 2014, https://www.linkedin.com/pulse/20140924142003-9878138-the-pygmalion-effect-how-it-drives-employees-performance.

122. "About Erik," *Erik Weihenmayer*, https://erikweihenmayer.com/about-erik/ (accessed April 18, 2020).

123. N. Angley, "All of Us in a Way Are Climbing Blind," *CNN,* May 11, 2016, www.cnn.com/2016/05/11/health/turning-points-erik-weihenmayer/index.html.

124. *No Barriers,* https://www.nobarriersusa.org/?gclid=EAIaIQobChMIgvGlhNWU2gIVVpN-Ch2G2Q4vEAAYASAAEgLtMvD_BwE (accessed April 11, 2018).

125. "Erik Weihenmayer," *MedStar National Rehabilitation Network*, https://www.medstarnrh.org/tag/erik-weihenmayer/ (accessed March 24, 2020).

126. T. Pupic, "Overcoming Adversity: Erik Weihenmayer on "Quitters, Campers, and Climbers," *Entrepreneur*, October 14, 2019, https://www.entrepreneur.com/article/340769.

127. *No Barriers,* https://www.nobarriersusa.org/?gclid=EAIaIQobChMIgvGlhNWU2gIVVpN-Ch2G2Q4vEAAYASAAEgLtMvD_BwE (accessed April 11, 2018).

128. M. Dabney, "At No Barriers Summit: Aira Is Showcased as the Novel Technology Service That Helps the Blind Become Even More 'Adventurous'," *Medium,* July 6, 2016, https://medium.com/aira-io/at-no-barriers-summit-aira-is-showcased-as-the-novel-technology-service-that-helps-the-blind-become-5a98845242ce.

129. T. Pupic, "Overcoming Adversity: Erik Weihenmayer on 'Quitters, Campers, and Climbers,'" *Entrepreneur*, October 14, 2019, https://www.entrepreneur.com/article/340769; "Climbs," *Alpine Ascents International,* https://www.alpineascents.com/climbs/seven-summits/ (accessed March 24, 2020).

130. "About Erik," *Touch the Top*, www.touchthetop.com/about-erik (accessed March 24, 2020).

131. C. Marshall, "How the First Blind Man to Summit Mount Everest Changed My Perspective on Fear," *Huffington Post,* May 25, 2017,

www.huffingtonpost.com/entry/how-the-first-blind-man-to-summit-mount-everest-changed_us_59161939e4b02d6199b2ef04.

132. E. Weihenmayer, interview with the American Foundation for the Blind, https://www.afb.org/node/11132?page=13 (accessed March 24, 2020).

133. A. B. Bakker, "Strategic and Proactive Approaches to Work Engagement," *Organizational Dynamics,* April–June 2017, p. 67.

134. M. A. Uddin, M. Mahmood, and L. Fan, "Why Individual Employee Engagement Matters for Team Performance?" *Team Performance Management: An International Journal,* March 2019, pp. 47–67. Also see B. Schneider, A. B. Yost, A. Kropp, C. Kind, and H. Lam, "Workforce Engagement: What It Is, What Drives It, and Why It Matters for Organizational Performance," *Journal of Organizational Behavior,* May 2018, pp. 462–480; "A. M. Saks, "Translating Employee Engagement Research into Practice," *Organizational Dynamics,* April–June 2017, pp. 76–86; J. P. Meyer, "Has Engagement Had Its Day: What's Next and Does It Matter," *Organizational Dynamics,* April–June 2017, pp. 87–95; R. Muller, E. Smith, and R. Lillah, "The Impact of Employee Engagement on Organisational Performance: A Balanced Scorecard Approach," *International Journal of Economics and Finance Studies,* 2018, pp. 22–38; A. Madden and C. Bailey, "Engagement: Where Has All the 'Power' Gone?" *Organizational Dynamics,* 2017, pp. 113–119; M. R. Antony, "Paradigm Shift in Employee Engagement—A Critical Analysis on the Drivers of Employee Engagement," *International Journal of Information, Business and Management,* 2018, pp. 32–46.

135. M. Hayes, F. Chumney, C. Wright, and M. Buckingham, "The Global Study of Engagement Technical Report," *ADP Research Institute,* 2019, https://www.adp.com/-/media/adp/resourcehub/pdf/adpri/adpri0102_2018_engagement_study_technical_report_release%20ready.ashx. Also see M. Perry, "Engagement Around the World, Charted," *Harvard Business Review,* May 15, 2019, https://hbr.org/2019/05/engagement-around-the-world-charted.

136. "Gallup Q12® Meta-Analysis Report," *Gallup,* https://news.gallup.com/reports/191489/q12-meta-analysis-report-2016.aspx (accessed March 25, 2020).

137. M. A. Uddin, M. Mahmood, and L. Fan, "Why Individual Employee Engagement Matters for Team Performance?" *Team Performance Management: An International Journal,* March 2019, pp. 47–67. Also see B. Schneider; R. Muller, E. Smith, and R. Lillah, "The Impact of Employee Engagement on Organisational Performance: A Balanced Scorecard Approach," *International Journal of Economics and Finance Studies,* July 2018, pp. 22–38; M. Christian, A. Garza, and J. Slaughter, "Work Engagement: A Quantitative Review and Test of Its Relations with Task and Contextual Performance," *Personnel Psychology,* March 2011, pp. 89–136; A. M. Saks, "Translating Employee Engagement Research Into Practice," *Organizational Dynamics,* April–June 2017, pp. 76–86; A. Madden and C. Bailey, "Engagement: Where Has All the 'Power' Gone?" *Organizational Dynamics,* April 2017, pp. 113–119; L. Wang, K. S. Law, M. J. Zhang, Y. N. Li, and Y. Liang, "It's Mine! Psychological Owner of One's Job Explains Positive and Negative Workplace Outcomes of Job Engagement," *Journal of Applied Psychology,* Vol. 104 (2) 2019, pp. 229–246; M. R. Antony, "Paradigm Shift in Employee Engagement—A Critical Analysis on the Drivers of Employee Engagement," *International Journal of Information, Business and Management,* May 2018, pp. 32–46.

138. S. Walker, "If You Can Manage a Waffle House, You Can Manage Anything," *The Wall Street Journal,* November 2, 2019, https://www.wsj.com/articles/if-you-can-manage-a-waffle-house-you-can-manage-anything-11572667205.

139. B. A. Allan, J. R. Rolniak, and L. Bouchard, "Underemployment and Well-Being: Exploring the Dark Side of Meaningful Work," *Journal of Career Development,* February 2020, pp. 111–125.

140. J. Kelly, "If Your Work Lacks Purpose, Make It More Meaningful Through Job Crafting," *Forbes,* April 6, 2019, https://www.forbes.com/sites/jackkelly/2019/08/06/if-your-work-lacks-purpose-make-it-more-meaningful-through-job-crafting/#4c1886336416.

141. M. Christian, A. Garza, and J. Slaughter, "Work Engagement: A Quantitative Review and Test of Its Relations with Task and Contextual Performance," *Personnel Psychology,* March 2011, pp. 89–136. Also see B. Schneider, "Workforce Engagement: What It Is, What Drives It, and Why It Matters for Organizational Performance," *Journal of Organizational Behavior,* May 2018, pp. 462–480; "Examining the Impact of Managerial Coaching on Employee Job Performance: Mediating Role of Work Engagement, Leader-Member-Exchange Quality, Job Satisfaction, and Turnover Intentions," *Pakistan Journal of Commerce and Social Sciences,* Vol. 12 (1) 2018, pp. 253–282; D. Pandita and S. Ray, "Talent Management and Employee Engagement—A Meta-Analysis of Their Impact on Talent Retention," *Industrial and Commercial Training,* April 2018, pp. 185–199; S. Blount and P. Leinwand, "Why Are We Here?" *Harvard Business Review,* 2019, https://hbr.org/2019/11/why-are-we-here; G. Matthews, "Employee Engagement: What's Your Strategy?" *Strategic HR Review,* June 2018, pp. 150–154; S. Kim, Y. Park, and L. Headrick, "Daily Micro-Breaks and Job Performance: General Work Engagement as a Cross-Level Moderator," *Journal of Applied Psychology,* July 2018, pp. 772–786.

142. D. Geddes, R. R. Callister, and D. E. Gibson, "A Message in the Madness: Functions of Workplace Anger in organizational Life," *Academy of Management Perspectives,* February 2020, pp. 28–47.

143. "Top 60 Employee Engagement Ideas from the Experts," *PageUp,* June 30, 2019, https://www.pageuppeople.us/resource/top-60-employee-engagement-ideas-from-the-experts/.

144. C. Brennan, "New Data: How Learning Impacts Engagement and Productivity," *HR Dive,* November 6, 2018, https://www.hrdive.com/spons/new-data-how-learning-impacts-engagement-and-productivity/541080/.

145. A. Croswell, "10 Companies with Great Learning and Development Programs," https://www.cultureamp.com/blog/10-companies-with-great-learning-and-development-programs/ (accessed April 9, 2020).

146. C. Liu and H. Li, "Stressors and Stressor Appraisals: the Moderating Effect of Task Efficacy," *Journal of Business and Psychology,* February 2018, pp. 141–154; S. Sonnentag, E. Mojza, E. Demerouti, and A. Bakker, "Reciprocal Relations between Recovery and Work Engagement: The Moderating Role of Job Stressors," *Journal of Applied Psychology,* July 2012, pp. 842–853.

147. K. Weise, "Doctors Fear Bringing Coronavirus Home: 'I Am Sort of a Pariah in My Family,'" *The New York Times,* March 17, 2020, https://www.nytimes.com/2020/03/16/us/coronavirus-doctors-nurses.html.

148. These five job dimensions are developed by researchers at Cornell University as part of the Job Descriptive Index. For a review of the development of the JDI, see P. C. Smith, L. M. Kendall, and C. L. Hulin, *The Measurement of Satisfaction in Work and Retirement* (Skokie, IL: Rand McNally, 1969).

149. J. Abate, T. Schaefer, and T. Pavone, "Understanding Generational Identity, Job Burnout, Job Satisfaction, Job Tenure, and Turnover Intention," *Journal of Organizational Culture, Communications and Conflict,* January 2018, pp. 1–12. Also see C. Wu, I. Chen, and J. Chen, "A Study Into the Impact of Employee Wellness and Job Satisfaction on Job Performance," *The International Journal of Organizational Innovation,* October 2017, pp. 252–269; A. J. Kinicki, F. M. McKee-Ryan, C. A. Schriesheim, and K. P. Carson, "Assessing the Construct Validity of the Job Descriptive Index: A Review and Meta-Analysis," *Journal of Applied Psychology,* February 2002, pp. 14–32.

150. D. Spiegel, "85% of American Workers Are Happy with Their Jobs, National Survey Shows," *CNBC,* April 2, 2019, https://www.cnbc.com/2019/04/01/85percent-of-us-workers-are-happy-with-their-jobs-national-survey-shows.html.

151. T. A. Judge, C. J. Thoresen, J. E. Bono, and G. K. Patton, "The Job Satisfaction–Job Performance Relationship: A Qualitative and Quantitative Review," *Psychological Bulletin,* May 2001, pp. 376–407; R. Kreitner and A. Kinicki, *Organizational Behavior,* 10th ed. (New York: McGraw-Hill/Irwin, 2013), pp. 168–170.

152. T. A. Judge, H. M. Weiss, J. D. Kammeyer-Mueller, and C. L. Hulin, "Job Attitudes, Job Satisfaction, and Job Affect: A Century of

Continuity and of Change," *Journal of Applied Psychology,* March 2017, pp. 356–374.

153. A. Shahjehan, B. Afsar, and S. I. Shah, "Is Organizational Commitment–Job Satisfaction Relationship Necessary for Organizational Commitment–Citizenship Behavior Relationships? A Meta-Analytical Necessary Condition Analysis," *Economic Research,* August 2019, pp. 2657–2679. Also see A. Berberoglu, "Impact of Organizational Climate on Organizational Commitment and Perceived Organizational Performance: Empirical Evidence from Public Hospitals," *BMC Health Services Research,* June 2018, https://doi.org/10.1186/s12913-018-3149-z; A. H. Kabins, X. Xu, M. E. Bergman, C. M. Berry, and V. L Wilson, "A Profile of Profiles: A Meta-Analysis of the Nomological Net of Commitment Profiles," *Journal of Applied Psychology,* June 2016, pp. 881–904.

154. For a review of commitment research, see the entire May 2016 issue of *Journal of Organizational Behavior,* May 2016, pp. 489–632. Also see S. Belwalkar, V. Vohra, and A. Pandey, "The Relationship between Workplace Spirituality, Job Satisfaction and Organizational Citizenship Behaviors—An Empirical Study," *Social Responsibility Journal,* June 2018, pp. 410–430.

155. N. Eisenberg, S. K. VanSchyndel, and T. L. Spinrad, "Prosocial Motivation: Inferences from an Opaque Body of Work," *Child Development,* November 2016, pp. 1668–1678.

156. M. Bolino and A. M. Grant, "The Bright Side of Being Prosocial at Work, and the Dark Side, Too: A Review and Agenda for Research on Other-Oriented Motives, Behavior, and Impact on Organizations," *The Academy of Management Annals,* 2016, p. 599.

157. "Who We Are," Bill and Melinda Gates Foundation, https://www.gatesfoundation.org/Who-We-Are/General-Information/Foundation-Factsheet (accessed April 21, 2020).

158. "9 Bill Gates Leadership Style Traits, Skills and Qualities," *Future of Working,* https://futureofworking.com/9-bill-gates-leadership-style-traits-skills-and-qualities/ (accessed April 21, 2020).

159. T. Huddleston, "These Are Bill Gates' 2 Superpowers, According to Bill Gates," *CNBC,* October 9, 2019, https://www.cnbc.com/2019/10/09/bill-gates-says-these-are-his-superpowers.html. Also see K. Piper, "Bill Gates's Efforts to Fight Coronavirus, Explained," *Vox,* April 16, 2020, https://www.vox.com/future-perfect/2020/4/14/21215592/bill-gates-coronavirus-vaccines-treatments-billionaires.

160. M. Owens, "4 Personality Traits That All Effective Leaders Share," *Business Insider,* April 30, 2015, https://www.businessinsider.com/traits-that-effective-leaders-share-2015-4.

161. C. Li and Y. Bao, "Ethical Leadership and Positive Work Behaviors: A Conditional Process Model," *Journal of Managerial Psychology,* March 2020, pp. 155–168. Also see A. Grant and J. M. Berg, "Prosocial Motivation at Work: When, Why, and How Making a Difference Makes a Difference," *Handbook of Positive Organizational Scholarship,* 2010.

162. R. D. Lebel and S. V. Patil, "Proactivity Despite Discouraging Supervisors: The Powerful Role of Prosocial Motivation," *Journal of Applied Psychology,* July 2018, pp. 724–737. Also see J. F. B. Ong, J. M. T. Tan, R. F. C. Villareal, and J. L. Chiu, "Impact of Quality Work Life and Prosocial Motivation on the Organizational Commitment and Turnover Intent of Public Health Practitioners," *Review of Integrative Business & Economics Research,* January 2019, pp. 24–43; A. M. Kjeldsen and L. B. Andersen, "How Pro-social Motivation Affects Job Satisfaction: An International Analysis of Countries with Different Welfare State Regimes," *Scandinavian Political Studies,* June 2013, pp. 153–176;

163. L. Ganli, L. Ye, and G. Ming, "Effect of High Performance Work System on Organizational Citizenship Behaviors fom China New Generation Employees," *Pakistan Journal of Statistics,* 2014, pp. 911–922.

164. I. Thielmann, G. Spadaro, and D. Balliet, "Personality and Prosocial Behavior: A Theoretical Framework and Meta-Analysis," *Psychological Bulletin,* January 2020, pp. 30–90.

165. Y. Xiong and N. Gan, "This Chinese Doctor Tried to Save Lives, But Was Silenced. Now He Has Coronavirus," *CNN,* February 4, 2020, https://www.cnn.com/2020/02/03/asia/coronavirus-doctor-whistle-blower-intl-hnk/index.html. Also see V. Yu, "'Hero Who Told the Truth': Chinese Rage over Coronavirus Death of Whistleblower Doctor," *The Guardian,* February 7, 2020, https://www.theguardian.com/global-development/2020/feb/07/coronavirus-chinese-rage-death-whistleblower-doctor-li-wenliang.

166. R. D. Lebel and S. V. Patil, "Proactivity Despite Discouraging Supervisors: The Powerful Role of Prosocial Motivation," *Journal of Applied Psychology,* July 2018, pp. 724–737. Also see J. F. B. Ong, J. M. T. Tan, R. F. C. Villareal, and J. L. Chiu, "Impact of Quality Work Life and Prosocial Motivation on the Organizational Commitment and Turnover Intent of Public Health Practitioners," *Review of Integrative Business & Economics Research,* January 2019, pp. 24–43; A. M. Kjeldsen and L. B. Andersen, "How Pro-social Motivation Affects Job Satisfaction: An International Analysis of Countries with Different Welfare State Regimes," *Scandinavian Political Studies,* June 2013, pp. 153–176.

167. A. C. Klotz, M. C. Bolino, H. Song, and J. Stornelli, "Examining the Nature, Causes, and Consequences of Profiles of Organizational Citizenship Behavior," *Journal of Organizational Behavior,* June 2018, pp. 629–647.

168. S. Belwalkar, V. Vohra, and A. Pandey, "The Relationship between Workplace Spirituality, Job Satisfaction and Organizational Citizenship Behaviors—an Empirical Study," *Social Responsibility Journal,* June 2018, pp. 410–430. Also see N. P. Podsakoff, S. W. Whiting, P. M. Podsakoff, and B. D. Blume, "Individual- and Organizational-Level Consequences of Organizational Citizenship Behaviors: A Meta-Analysis," *Journal of Applied Psychology,* January 2009, pp. 122–141; D. S. Whitman, D. L. Van Rooy, and C. Viswesvaran, "Satisfaction, Citizenship Behaviors, and Performance in Work Units: A Meta-Analysis of Collective Relations," *Personnel Psychology,* Spring 2010, pp. 41–81; A. C. Klotz, M. C. Bolino, H. Song, and J. Stornelli, "Examining the Nature, Causes, and Consequences of Profiles of Organizational Citizenship Behavior," *Journal of Organizational Behavior,* June 2018, pp. 629–647.

169. K. J. Lin, K. Savani, R. Ilies, "Doing Good, Feeling Good? The Roles of Helping Motivation and Citizenship Pressure," *Journal of Applied Psychology,* August 2019, pp. 1020–1035.

170. R. D. Lebel and S. V. Patil, "Proactivity despite Discouraging Supervisors: The Powerful Role of Prosocial Motivation," *Journal of Applied Psychology,* July 2018, pp. 724–737. Also see J. F. B. Ong, J. M. T. Tan, R. F. C. Villareal, and J. L. Chiu, "Impact of Quality Work Life and Prosocial Motivation on the Organizational Commitment and Turnover Intent of Public Health Practitioners," *Review of Integrative Business & Economics Research,* January 2019, pp. 24–43; A. M. Kjeldsen and L. B. Andersen, "How Pro-social Motivation Affects Job Satisfaction: An International Analysis of Countries with Different Welfare State Regimes," *Scandinavian Political Studies,* June 2013, pp. 153–176.

171. I. Odermatt et al., "Incivility in Meetings: Predictors and Outcomes," *Journal of Business and Psychology,* March 2018, pp. 263–282. Also see P. E. Spector and S. Fox, "Theorizing about the Deviant Citizen: An Attributional Explanation of the Interplay of Organizational Citizenship and Counterproductive Work Behavior," *Human Resource Management Review,* June 2010, pp. 132–143; J. Wu and J. M. Lebreton, "Reconsidering the Dispositional Basis of Counterproductive Work Behavior: The Role of Aberrant Personality," *Personnel Psychology,* Vol. 64 (2011), pp. 593–626; L. L. Meier and P. E. Spector, "Reciprocal Effects of Work Stressors and Counterproductive Work Behavior: A Five-Wave Longitudinal Study," *Journal of Applied Psychology,* May 2013, pp. 529–539; T. Mankodi, "Workplace Incivility and Rudeness Needs to Stop. Here's Why," *Harvard Business Review,* https://hbrascend.org/topics/workplace-incivility-and-rudeness-needs-to-stop-heres-why/ (accessed March 26, 2020); J. J. Lavelle et al., "Multifoci Effects of Injustice on Counterproductive Work Behaviors and the Moderating Roles of Symbolization and Victim Sensitivity," *Journal of Organizational Behavior,* October 2018, pp. 1022–1039.

172. T. Mankodi, "Workplace Incivility and Rudeness Needs to Stop. Here's Why," *Harvard Business Review,* https://hbrascend.org/topics/workplace-incivility-and-rudeness-needs-to-stop-heres-why/ (accessed March 26, 2020).

173. A. M. Abubakar, T. F. Yazdian, and E. Behravesh, "A Riposte to Ostracism and Tolerance to Workplace Incivility: A Generational Perspective," *Personnel Review*, March 2018, pp. 441–457.

174. N. C. Carpenter, B. Rangel, G. Jeon, and J. Cottrell, "Are Supervisors and Coworkers Likely to Witness Employee Counterproductive Work Behavior? An Investigation of Observability and Self-Observer Convergence," *Personnel Psychology*, Winter 2017, pp. 843–889.

175. Z. Yuan, C.M. Barnes, and Y. Li, "Bad Behavior Keeps You Up at Night: Counterproductive Work Behaviors and Insomnia," *Journal of Applied Psychology*, April 2018, pp. 383–398.

176. S. Dilchert, D. S. Ones, R. D. Davis, and C. D. Rostow, "Cognitive Ability Predicts Objectively Measured Counterproductive Work Behaviors," *Journal of Applied Psychology*, May 2007, pp. 616–627; B. Iliescu, D. Ispas, C. Sulea, and A. Ilie, "Vocational Fit and Counterproductive Work Behaviors: A Self-Regulation Perspective," *Journal of Applied Psychology*, Vol. 100, No. 1 (2015), pp. 21–39.

177. J. J. Lavelle et al., "Multifoci Effects of Injustice on Counterproductive Work Behaviors and the Moderating Roles of Symbolization and Victim Sensitivity," *Journal of Organizational Behavior*, October 2018, pp. 1022–1039. Also see J. R. Detert, L. K. Treviño, E. R. Burris, and M. Andiappan, "Managerial Modes of Influence and Counterproductivity in Organizations: A Longitudinal Business-Unit-Level Investigation," *Journal of Applied Psychology*, July 2007, pp. 993–1005; Z. E. Zhou, E. M. Eatough, and D. R. Wald, "Feeling insulted? Examining end-of-work anger as a mediator in the relationship between daily illegitimate tasks and next-day CWB," *Journal of Organizational Behavior*, January 2018, pp. 911–921; J. Yang and D. C. Treadway, "A Social Influence Interpretation of Workplace Ostracism and Counterproductive Work Behavior," *Journal of Business Ethics*, April 2018, pp. 879–891.

178. I. M. Jawahar, B. Schreurs, "Supervisor Incivility and How It Affects Subordinates' Performance: A Matter of Trust," *Personnel Review*, April 2018, pp. 709–726.

179. S. Braun, N. Aydin, D. Frey, and C. Peus, "Leader Narcissism Predicts Malicious Envy and Supervisor Targeted Counterproductive Work Behavior: Evidence from Field and Experimental Research," *Journal of Business Ethics*, May 2018, pp. 725–741.

180. C. Porath, "How to Avoid Hiring a Toxic Employee," *Harvard Business Review*, February 3, 2016, https://hbr.org/2016/02/how-to-avoid-hiring-a-toxic-employee.

181. C. Porath, "How to Avoid Hiring a Toxic Employee," *Harvard Business Review*, February 3, 2016, https://hbr.org/2016/02/how-to-avoid-hiring-a-toxic-employee.

182. T. Foulk, quoted in R. E. Silverman, "Workplace Rudeness Is as Contagious as a Cold," *The Wall Street Journal*, August 12, 2015, p. B7. Also see T. Foulk, A. Woolum, and A. Erez, "Catching Rudeness Is Like Catching a Cold: The Contagion Effects of Low-Intensity Negative Behaviors," *Journal of Applied Psychology*, Vol. 101, No. 1 (2016), pp. 50–67.

183. G. Spreizer, quoted in B. Hyslop, "Bad Attitudes Can Sap Workers' Energy and Productivity," *Providence Journal*, July 4, 2015. Also see P. Korkki, "Thwarting the Jerk at Work," *The New York Times*, November 22, 2015, p. BU-4; C. L. Porath and A. Erez, "Does Rudeness Really Matter? The Effects of Rudeness on Task Performance and Helpfulness," *Academy of Management Journal*, Vol. 50, No. 5 (2007), pp. 1181–1197; A. Gerbasi, C. L. Porath, A. Parker, G. Spreitzer, and R. Cross, "Destructive De-energizing Relationships: How Thriving Buffers Their Effect on Performance," *Journal of Applied Psychology*, Vol. 100, No. 5 (2015), pp. 1423–1433; C. L. Porath, A. Gerbasi, and S. L. Schorch, "The Effects of Civility on Advice, Leadership, and Performance," *Journal of Applied Psychology* 100, no. 5 (2015), pp. 1527–1541.

184. C. Rosen, J. Koopman, A. Gabriel, and R. Johnson, "Who Strikes Back? A Daily Investigation of When and Why Incivility Begets Incivility," *Journal of Applied Psychology*, Vol. 101, No. 11 (2016), pp. 1620–1634.

185. D. Walker, D. van Jaarsveld, and D. Skarlicki, "Sticks and Stones Can Break My Bones but Words Can Also Hurt Me: The Relationship between Customer Verbal Aggression and Employee Incivility," *Journal of Applied Psychology*, Vol. 102, No. 2 (2017), pp. 163–179.

186. C. Porath, "No Time to Be Nice," *The New York Times*, June 21, 2015, p. SR–1.

187. A. S. Gabriel, M. M. Butts, Z. Yuan, R. L. Rosen, and M. T. Sliter, "Further Understanding Incivility in the Workplace: The Effects of Gender, Agency, and Communion," *Journal of Applied Psychology*, April 2018, pp. 362–382.

188. S. G. Taylor, D. H. Kluemper, W. M. Bowler and J. R. B. Halbesleben, "Why People Get Away with Being Rude at Work," *Harvard Business Review*, July 10, 2019, https://hbr.org/2019/07/why-people-get-away-with-being-rude-at-work.

189. M. Housman and D. Minor, "Toxic Workers," *Harvard Business School*, Working Paper 16-057, November 2015, www.hbs.edu/faculty/Publication%20Files/16-057_d45c0b4f-fa19-49de-8f1b-4b12fe054fea.pdf.

190. N. Torres, "It's Better to Avoid a Toxic Employee Than Hire a Superstar," *Harvard Business Review*, December 9, 2015, https://hbr.org/2015/12/its-better-to-avoid-a-toxic-employee-than-hire-a-superstar.

191. A. Di Fabio and M. Duradoni, "Fighting Incivility in the Workplace for Women and for All Workers: The Challenge of Primary Prevention," *Frontiers in Psychology*, August 2019, https://doi.org/10.3389/fpsyg.2019.01805.

192. M. Hershcovis, B. Ogunfowora, T. Reich, and A. Christie, "Targeted Workplace Incivility: The Roles of Belongingness, Embarrassment, and Power," *Journal of Organizational Behavior*, Vol. 38 (2017), pp. 1057–1075.

193. C. Penman, "The Cost of Incivility in the Workplace," *NAVEX Global*, February 21, 2019, https://www.navexglobal.com/blog/article/the-cost-of-incivility-in-the-workplace/.

194. A. M. Grant and J. J. Sumanth, "Mission Possible? The Performance of Prosocially Motivated Employees Depends on Manager Trustworthiness," *Journal of Applied Psychology*, July 2009, pp. 927–944. Also see A. Grant and J. M. Berg, "Prosocial Motivation at Work: When, Why, and How Making a Difference Makes a Difference," *Handbook of Positive Organizational Scholarship*, 2010; S. Livi, A. Theodorou, M. Rullo, L. Cinque, and G. Alessandri, "The Rocky Road to Prosocial Behavior at Work: The Role of Positivity and Organizational Socialization in Preventing Interpersonal Strain," *PLoS One*, https://doi.org/10.1371/journal.pone.0193508.

195. M. C. Kocakulah, A. G. Kelley, K. M. Mitchell, and M. P. Ruggieri, "Absenteeism Problems and Costs: Causes, Effects, and Cures," *International Business & Economics Research Journal*, May/June 2016, pp. 81–88. Also see C. R. S. de Carvalho, M. A. R. Castro, L. P. da Silva, and L. O. P. de Carvalho, "The Relationship between Organizational Culture, Organizational Commitment and Job Satisfaction," *Revista Brasileira de Estrategia*, January 2018, pp. 201–215.

196. "Faking It: Why Employees Call in 'Sick,'" *Business News Daily*, January 22, 2020, https://www.businessnewsdaily.com/7353-employees-faking-sick.html. Also see M. R. Barrick and R. D. Zimmerman, "Reducing Voluntary Turnover through Selection," *Journal of Applied Psychology*, January 2005, pp. 159–166.

197. M. Zivkovic, The True Cost of Hiring an Employee in 2020," *Toggle Hire*, May 22, 2018, https://toggl.com/blog/cost-of-hiring-an-employee.

198. S. McFeely and B. Wigert, "This Fixable Problem Costs U.S. Businesses $1 Trillion," *Gallup*, March 13, 2019, https://www.gallup.com/workplace/247391/fixable-problem-costs-businesses-trillion.aspx.

199. F. De Stefano, R. Bonet, and A. Camuffo, "Does Losing Temporary Workers Matter?" *Academy of Management Journal*, August 2019, pp. 979–1002.

200. T. Arnold, "Ramping Up Onboarding," *HR Magazine*, May 2010, pp. 75–76; D. Robb, "New-Hire Onboarding Portals Provide a Warmer Welcome," *HR Magazine*, December 2015/January 2016, pp. 58–60.

201. C. M. Porter, S. E. Woo, D. G. Allen, M. G. Keith, "How Do Instrumental and Expressive Network Positions Relate to Turnover? A Meta-Analytic Investigation," *Journal of Applied Psychology*, April 2019, pp. 511–536; C. M. Porter et al., "On-the-Job and Off-the-Job Embeddedness Differentially Influence Relationships between Informal Job Search

and Turnover," *Journal of Applied Psychology*, May 2019, pp. 678–689.

202. T. W. Lee, P. Hom, M. Eberly, and J. Li, "Managing Employee Retention and Turnover with 21st Century Ideas," *Organizational Dynamics,* April 2018, pp. 88–98. Also see P. W. Hom, T. W. Lee, J. D. Shaw, and J. P. Hausknecht, "One Hundred Years of Employee Turnover Theory and Research," *Journal of Applied Psychology,* March 2017, pp. 530–545; J. Hornickel, "Retain Employees and Lower Turnover Costs," *Training Magazine*, 2019, https://trainingmag.com/trgmag-article/retain-employees-and-lower-turnover-costs/.

203. I. Thielmann, G. Spadaro, and D. Balliet, "Personality and Prosocial Behavior: A Theoretical Framework and Meta-Analysis," *Psychological Bulletin,* January 2020, pp. 30–90. Also see A. Grant and J. M. Berg, "Prosocial Motivation at Work: When, Why, and How Making a Difference Makes a Difference," *Handbook of Positive Organizational Scholarship*, 2010; J. Stollberger, M. L. Heras, Y. Rofcanin, and M. J. Bosch, "Serving Followers and Family? A Trickle-Down Model of How Servant Leadership Shapes Employee Work Performance," *Journal of Vocational Behavior*, June 2019, pp. 158–171; M. van Dijke, D. De Cremer, G. Langendijk, and C. Anderson, "Ranking Low, Feeling High: How Hierarchical Position and Experienced Power Promote Prosocial Behavior in Response to Procedural Justice," *Journal of Applied Psychology*, February 2018, pp. 164–181.

204. A. Grant and J. M. Berg, "Prosocial Motivation at Work: When, Why, and How Making a Difference Makes a Difference," *Handbook of Positive Organizational Scholarship*, 2010.

205. A. Grant and J. M. Berg, "Prosocial Motivation at Work: When, Why, and How Making a Difference Makes a Difference," *Handbook of Positive Organizational Scholarship*, 2010.

206. J. M. Krogstad, J. S. Passel, and D. Cohn, "5 Facts about Illegal Immigration in the U.S.," *Pew Research Center*, June 12, 2019, https://www.pewresearch.org/fact-tank/2019/06/12/5-facts-about-illegal-immigration-in-the-u-s/.

207. "Racial Wage Gap for Men," *PayScale*, May 7, 2019, https://www.payscale.com/data/racial-wage-gap-for-men.

208. K. Little, "Restaurant Tabs and Weddings Aren't Keeping Millennials from Reaching Financial Milestones. Here's What Is," *Bankrate*, November 26, 2018, https://www.bankrate.com/personal-finance/millennials-earning/.

209. B. Reiners, "80+ Diversity in the Workplace Statistics You Should Know," *Built In*, February 24, 2020, https://builtin.com/diversity-inclusion/diversity-in-the-workplace-statistics. Also see A. Cilluffo and D. Cohn, "6 Demographic Trends Shaping the U.S. and the World in 2019," *Pew Research Center*, April 11, 2019; S. W. Kight, "Future Foretold: A New America in 2040," *Axios*, May 21, 2019, https://www.axios.com/being-30-in-2040-future-new-world-us-diversity-2d3ba6db-3345-4ec4-97a8-9282fe1cee67.html; P. Mohan, "How the End of the White Majority Could Change Office Dynamics in 2040," *Fast Company*, January 27, 2020, https://www.fastcompany.com/90450018/how-the-end-of-the-white-majority-could-change-office-dynamics-in-2040.

210. Quote found in J. L. Turnock, "Diversity at the Top: Leading with Purpose," *Forbes*, October 31, 2019.

211. L. M. Leslie, "Diversity Initiative Effectiveness: A Typological Theory of Unintended Consequences," *Academy of Management Review*, July 2019, pp. 538–563; S. McCallaghan, L. Jackson, and M. Heyns, "Exploring organisational diversity climate with associated antecedents and employee outcomes," *SA Journal of Industrial Psychology*, Vol. 45 2019, https://doi.org/ 10.4102/sajip.v45i0.1614. Also see N. Luanglath, M. Ali, and K. Mohannak, "Top Management Team Gender Diversity and Productivity: The Role of Board Gender Diversity," *Equality, Diversity and Inclusion: An International Journal*, February 2019, pp. 71–86.

212. M. Dennissen, Y. Benschop, and M. van den Brink, "Rethinking Diversity Management: An Intersectional Analysis of Diversity Networks," *Organizational Studies*, Vol. 41 (2) 2020, pp. 219–240. Also see J. A. Clair, B. K. Humberd, E. D. Rouse, and E. B. Jones, "Loosening Categorial Thinking: Extending the Terrain of Theory and Research on Demographic Identities in Organizations," *Academy of Management*

Review, 2019, pp. 592–617; S. M. Nkomo, M. P. Bell, L.M. Roberts, A. Joshi, and S. M. B. Thatcher, "Diversity at a Critical Juncture: New Theories for a Complex Phenomenon," *Academy of Management Review*, July 2019, pp. 498–517; S. Tasheva and A. J. Hillman, "Integrating Diversity at Different Levels," *Academy of Management Review*, October 2019, pp. 746–765; M. Janssens and C. Steyaert, "A Practice-Based Theory of Diversity," *Academy of Management Review*, July 2019, pp. 518–537; G. Cachat-Rosset, K. Carillo, and A. Klarsfeld, "Reconstructing the Concept of Diversity Climate–A Critical Review of Its Definition, Dimensions, and Operationalization," *European Management Review*, September 2019, pp. 863–885.

213. M. Loden, *Implementing Diversity* (Chicago: Irwin, 1996), pp. 14–15.

214. Y. Serhan and T. McLaughlin, "The Other Problematic Outbreak," *The Atlantic*, March 13, 2020, https://www.theatlantic.com/international/archive/2020/03/coronavirus-covid19-xenophobia-racism/607816/.

215. D. Holger, "PepsiCo Puts Military Veterans to Work," *The Wall Street Journal*, October 26, 2019, https://www.wsj.com/articles/pepsico-puts-military-veterans-to-work-11572091211.

216. K. Bialik and R. Fry, "Millennial Life: How Young Adulthood Today Compares with Prior Generations," *Pew Research Center*, February 14, 2019, https://www.pewsocialtrends.org/essay/millennial-life-how-young-adulthood-today-compares-with-prior-generations/.

217. L. Plews, "Older Americans in the Workforce," *United Income*, April 22, 2019, https://unitedincome.capitalone.com/library/older-americans-in-the-workforce.

218. M. Wisniewski, "Why Retirees Are Unretiring—and No, It's Not Only for the Money," *Bankrate*, February 22, 2019, https://www.bankrate.com/retirement/why-retirees-are-unretiring/.

219. P. Span, "Many Americans Try Retirement, Then Change Their Minds," *The New York Times,* March 30, 2018, https://www.nytimes.com/2018/03/30/health/unretirement-work-seniors.html.

220. C. Hymowitz, "Older Workers Have a Big Secret: Their Age," *The Wall Street Journal*, November 17, 2019, https://www.wsj.com/articles/older-workers-have-a-big-secret-their-age-11574046301.

221. H. Zacher, D. Kooij, and M.E. Beier, "Active Aging at Work," *Organizational Dynamics*, January 2018, pp. 37–45.

222. J. Kelly, "Women Now Hold More Jobs Than Men in the U.S. Workforce," *Forbes*, January 13, 2020, https://www.forbes.com/sites/jackkelly/2020/01/13/women-now-hold-more-jobs-than-men/#6c3c644c8f8a.

223. L. Searing, "The Big Number: Women Now Outnumber Men in Medical Schools," *The Washington Post*, December 23, 2019, https://www.washingtonpost.com/health/the-big-number-women-now-outnumber-men-in-medical-schools/2019/12/20/8b9eddea-2277-11ea-bed5-880264cc91a9_story.html. Also see I. Pisarcik, "Women Outnumber Men in Law School Classrooms for Third Year in a Row, but Statistics Don't Tell the Full Story," *Jurist*, March 5, 2019, https://www.jurist.org/commentary/2019/03/pisarcik-women-outnumber-men-in-law-school/.

224. M. Shepherd, "Women-Owned Businesses: Statistics and Overview (2020)," *Fundera*, March 18, 2020, https://www.fundera.com/resources/women-owned-business-statistics.

225. "List: Women CEOs of the S&P 500," *Catalyst*, April 6, 2020, https://www.catalyst.org/research/women-ceos-of-the-sp-500/.

226. U.S. Census, "Equal Pay Day: March 31, 2020," https://www.census.gov/newsroom/stories/2020/equal-pay.html (accessed April 14, 2020).

227. S. J. Glynn, "Breadwinning Mothers Continue to Be the U.S. Norm," *Center for American Progress*, May 10, 2019, https://www.americanprogress.org/issues/women/reports/2019/05/10/469739/breadwinning-mothers-continue-u-s-norm/.

228. N. Graf, A. Brown, and E. Patten, "The Narrowing, But Persistent, Gender Gap in Pay," *Pew Research Center*, March 22, 2019, https://www.pewresearch.org/fact-tank/2019/03/22/gender-pay-gap-facts/.

229. M. Baker, Y. Halberstam, K. Kroft, A. Mas, and D. Messacar, "Can Transparency Laws Fix the Gender Wage Gap?" *Harvard Business Review*, February 26, 2020, https://hbr.org/2020/02/can-transparency-laws-fix-the-gender-wage-gap.

CHAPTER NOTES

230. "Women More Likely Than Men to Have Earned a Bachelor's Degree by Age 31," *U.S. Bureau of Labor Statistics*, December 6, 2018, https://www.bls.gov/opub/ted/2018/women-more-likely-than-men-to-have-earned-a-bachelors-degree-by-age-31.htm.

231. R. J. Ely and I. Padavic, "What's Really Holding Women Back?" *Harvard Business Review*, March-April 2020, https://hbr.org/2020/03/whats-really-holding-women-back.

232. I. Hideg, A. Krstic, R.N.C. Trau, and T. Zarina, "The Unintended Consequences of Maternity Leaves," *Journal of Applied Pscyhology*, October 2018, pp. 1155–1164.

233. L. M. Little, A. S. Hinojosa, S. Paustian-Underdahl, and K. P. Zipay, "Managing the Harmful Effects of Unsupportive Organizations during Pregnancy," *Journal of Applied Psychology*, June 2018, pp. 631–643.

234. A. Beard, "Ideal Worker or Perfect Mom," *Harvard Business Review*, January-February 2019, pp. 150–151; J. Burnford, "Is Organizational Culture Holding Women Back in the Workplace?" *Forbes*, January 29, 2019, https://www.forbes.com/sites/joyburnford/2019/01/29/is-organizational-culture-holding-women-back-in-the-workplace/#135721c1655a.

235. J. Burnford, "Is Organizational Culture Holding Women Back in the Workplace?" *Forbes*, January 29, 2019, https://www.forbes.com/sites/joyburnford/2019/01/29/is-organizational-culture-holding-women-back-in-the-workplace/#135721c1655a.

236. K. Sawyer and A. M. Valerio, "Making the Case for Male Champions for Gender Inclusiveness at Work," *Organizational Dynamics*, January 2018, pp. 1–7. Also see H. Aguinis, Y. H. Ji, and H. Joo, "Gender Productivity Gap Among Star Performers in STEM and Other Scientific Fields," *Journal of Applied Psychology*, December 2018, pp. 1283–1306.

237. J. Burnford, "Is Organizational Culture Holding Women Back in the Workplace?" *Forbes*, January 29, 2019, https://www.forbes.com/sites/joyburnford/2019/01/29/is-organizational-culture-holding-women-back-in-the-workplace/#135721c1655a. Also see C. H. Tinsley and R. J. Ely, "What Most People Get Wrong About Men and Women," *Harvard Business Review*, May-June 2018, https://hbr.org/2018/05/what-most-people-get-wrong-about-men-and-women.

238. S. Reddy, "In Published Work, Male Scientists Sing Their Own Praises More," *The Wall Street Journal*, December 16, 2019, https://www.wsj.com/articles/in-published-work-male-scientists-sing-their-own-praises-more-11576539053.

239. A. Gupta, "Women Leaders and Organizational Diversity: Their Critical Role in Promoting Diversity in Organizations," *Development and Learning in Organizations*, March 2019, pp. 8–11.

240. N. Luanglath, M. Ali, and K. Mohannak, "Top Management Team Gender Diversity and Productivity: The Role of Board Gender Diversity," *Equality, Diversity and Inclusion: An International Journal*, February 2019, pp. 71–86. Also see J. Chen, W. S. Leung, W. Song, and M. Goergen, "Research: When Women Are on Boards, Male CEOs Are Less Overconfident," *Harvard Business Review*, September 12, 2019, https://hbr.org/2019/09/research-when-women-are-on-boards-male-ceos-are-less-overconfident.

241. J. Burns, "The Results Are In: Women Are Great for Business, But Still Getting Pushed Out," *Forbes*, September 22, 2017, https://www.forbes.com/sites/janetwburns/2017/09/22/2016-proved-women-are-great-for-business-yet-still-being-pushed-out/#962c55e188b6.

242. J. Vespa, L. Medina, and D. M. Armstrong, "Demographic Turning Points for the United States: Population Projections for 2020 to 2060," *U.S. Census*, February 2020, https://www.census.gov/content/dam/Census/library/publications/2020/demo/p25-1144.pdf.

243. "Income and Wealth in the United States: An Overview of Recent Data," *Peter G. Peterson Foundation*, October 4, 2019, https://www.pgpf.org/blog/2019/10/income-and-wealth-in-the-united-states-an-overview-of-data.

244. M. Hernandez, D. R. Avery, S. D. Volpone, and C. R. Kaiser, "Bargaining While Black: The Role of Race in Salary Negotiations," *Journal of Applied Psychology*, April 2019, pp. 581–592.

245. U.S. Equal Employment Opportunity Commission, "Race-Based Charges FY 1997–FY 2019," www.eeoc.gov/eeoc/statistics/enforcement/race.cfm (accessed March 30, 2020). Also see B. Leonard, "Web, Call Center Fuel Rise in EEOC Claims," *HR Magazine*, June 2008, p. 30; M. Luo, "In Job Hunt, Even a College Degree Can't Close the Racial Gap," *The New York Times*, December 1, 2009, pp. A1, A4.

246. K. Sherrer, "What Is Tokenism, and Why Does It Matter in the Workplace?" Vanderbilt University, February 26, 2018, https://business.vanderbilt.edu/news/2018/02/26/tokenism-in-the-workplace/.

247. M. B. Watkins, A. Simmons, and E. Umphress, "It's Not Black and White: Toward a Contingency Perspective on the Consequences of Being a Token," *Academy of Management Perspectives*, August 2019, pp. 334–365. Also see "Study Shows Positive Impact of Numeric Diversity and Diversity Climate on Psychological Outcomes for Faculty of Color," *Human Resource Management International Digest*, 2019, pp. 26–28.

248. M. Busine, "How to Overcome the Barriers to Diversity in Your Organization," *Development Dimensions International*, July 10, 2019, https://www.ddiworld.com/blog/july-2019/how-to-overcome-the-barriers-to-diversity.

249. P. Jain-Link, J. T. Kennedy, and T. Bourgeois, "5 Strategies for Creating an Inclusive Workplace," *Harvard Business Review*, January 13, 2020, https://hbr.org/2020/01/5-strategies-for-creating-an-inclusive-workplace.

250. J. McCarthy, "Americans Still Greatly Overestimate U.S. Gay Population," *Gallup*, June 27, 2019, https://news.gallup.com/poll/259571/americans-greatly-overestimate-gay-population.aspx.

251. "Lesbian, Gay, Bisexual, and Transgender Workplace Issues: Quick Take," *Catalyst*, June 17, 2019, https://www.catalyst.org/research/lesbian-gay-bisexual-and-transgender-workplace-issues/.

252. K. Paul, "Nearly 50% of LGBTQ Americans Are in the Closet at Work," *Market Watch*, October 11, 2019, https://www.marketwatch.com/story/half-of-lgbtq-americans-are-not-out-to-co-workers-2018-06-27.

253. J. J. Mohr et al., "Affective Antecedents and Consequences of Revealing and Concealing a Lesbian, Gay, or Bisexual Identity," *Journal of Applied Psychology*, October 2019, pp. 1266–1282. Also see K. Sawyer and C. Thoroughgood, "Gender Non-conformity and the Modern Workplace," *Organizational Dynamics*, January 2017, pp. 1–8; K. W. Phillips, Tracy L. Dumas, and N. P. Rothbard, "Diversity & Authenticity," *Harvard Business Review*, March-April 2018, pp. 132–136.

254. M. Huston, "None of the Above," *Psychology Today*, March/April 2015, pp. 28–30.

255. T. Butler, "What Percentage of the US Population Is Transgender?" *Pink News*, April 2, 2019, https://www.pinknews.co.uk/2019/04/02/percentage-us-population-transgender-statistics/.

256. "Gay and Lesbian Rights," *Gallup*, https://news.gallup.com/poll/1651/gay-lesbian-rights.aspx (accessed March 30, 2020).

257. Kennedy, quoted in W. Richey, "Supreme Court Declares Same-Sex Couples' 'Fundamental Right' to Marry," *The Christian Science Monitor*, June 26, 2015, www.csmonitor.com/USA/Justice/2015/0626/Supreme-Court-declares-same-sex-couples-fundamental-right-to-marry (accessed June 27, 2016).

258. P. Varathan, "Gay Men Now Earn More than Straight Men in the US," *Quartz at Work*, December 6, 2017, https://work.qz.com/1147659/gay-men-now-earn-more-than-straight-men-in-the-us-according-to-a-vanderbilt-study/.

259. N. Thirani Bagri, "New Research Confirms the 'Sexuality Pay Gap' Is Real," *Quartz*, January 12, 2017, https://qz.com/881303/eight-million-americans-are-affected-by-a-pay-gap-that-no-one-talks-about/.

260. S. Singh and L. E. Durso, "Widespread Discrimination Continues to Shape LGBT People's Lives in Both Subtle and Significant Ways," Center for American Progress, May 2, 2017, https://www.americanprogress.org/issues/lgbt/news/2017/05/02/429529/widespread-discrimination-continues-shape-lgbt-peoples-lives-subtle-significant-ways/.

261. C. N. Thoroughgood, K. B. Sawyer, and J. R. Webster, "Creating a Trans-Inclusive Workplace," *Harvard Business Review*, March-April 2020, https://hbr.org/2020/03/creating-a-trans-inclusive-workplace. Also see A. Powell, "The Problems with LGBTQ Health Care," *Harvard Gazette*, March 23, 2018, https://news.harvard.edu/gazette/story/2018/03/health-care-providers-need-better-understanding-of-lgbtq-patients-harvard-forum-says/.

262. S. Singh and L. E. Durso, "Widespread Discrimination Continues to Shape LGBT People's Lives in Both Subtle and Significant Ways," *Center for American Progress*, May 2, 2017, https://www.americanprogress .org/issues/lgbt/news/2017/05/02/429529/widespread-discrimination-continues-shape-lgbt-peoples-lives-subtle-significant-ways/.

263. S. Singh and L. E. Durso, "Widespread Discrimination Continues to Shape LGBT People's Lives in Both Subtle and Significant Ways," *Center for American Progress*, May 2, 2017, https://www.americanprogress .org/issues/lgbt/news/2017/05/02/429529/widespread-discrimination-continues-shape-lgbt-peoples-lives-subtle-significant-ways/.

264. "1 in 4 US Adults Live with a Disability," *Centers for Disease Control and Prevention*, August 16, 2018, https://www.cdc.gov/media/releases/2018/p0816-disability.html.

265. "Persons with a Disability: Labor Force Characteristics Summary," *U.S. Bureau of Labor Statistics*, February 26, 2020, https:// www.bls.gov/news.release/disabl.nr0.htm. Also see "nTIDE January 2020 Jobs Report: Year Begins with Good News for People with Disabilities," *American Association for the Advancement of Science*, February 7, 2020, https://www.eurekalert.org/pub_releases/2020-02/kf-nj2020720.php.

266. D. C. Baldridge and M. L. Swift, "Withholding Requests for Disability Accommodation: The Role of Individual Differences and Disability Attributes," *Journal of Management*, March 2013, pp. 743–762.

267. M. Ameri et al., "The Disability Employment Puzzle," *ILR Review*, June 2017, pp. 329–364.

268. H. Ramer, "Survey: Only 28 Percent of Companies Have Disability Hiring Goals," *Inc.*, October 10, 2017, https://www.inc.com/associated-press/missed-employment-opportunities-workers-with-disabilities-2017.html?cid=search.

269. Z. Henry, "Why More Tech Companies Should Hire People with Disabilities," *Inc.*, August 23, 2017, https://www.inc.com/zoe-henry/aapd-disability-equality-index-2017.html?cid=search.

270. S. Lindsay, E. Cagliostro, M. Albarico, N. Mortaji, and L. Karon, "A Systematic Review of the Benefits of Hiring People with Disabilities," *Journal of Occupational Rehabilitation*, February 2018, pp. 634–655.

271. P. M. A. Baker, M. A. Linden, S. S. LaForce, J. Rutledge, and K. P. Goughnour, "Barriers to Employment Participation of Individuals with Disabilities: Addressing the Impact of Employer (Mis)Perception and Policy," *American Behavioral Scientist*, May 2018, pp. 657–675.

272. E. Redden, "41% of Recent Grads Work in Jobs Not Requiring a Degree," *Inside Higher Ed*, February 18, 2020, https://www .insidehighered.com/quicktakes/2020/02/18/41-recent-grads-work-jobs-not-requiring-degree.

273. J. Kolko, "What the Job Market Looks Like for Today's College Graduates," *Harvard Business Review*, May 9, 2019, https://hbr .org/2019/05/what-the-job-market-looks-like-for-todays-college-graduates.

274. "Dropout Rates," *National Center for Education Statistics*, https:// nces.ed.gov/fastfacts/display.asp?id=16 (accessed March 30, 2020).

275. "What's the Latest U.S. Literacy Rate?" *Wylie Communications*, https://www.wyliecomm.com/2019/03/us-literacy-rate/. Also see A. Bernstein, "The Time Bomb in the Workforce: Illiteracy," *BusinessWeek*, February 25, 2002, p. 122; M. Kutner, M. Greenberg, and J. Baer, *National Assessment of Adult Literacy (NAAL): A First Look at the Literacy of America's Adults in the 21st Century* (Washington, DC: National Center for Educational Statistics, 2005); D. F. Mellard, E. Fall, and K. L. Woods, "A Path Analysis of Reading Comprehension for Adults with Low Literacy," *Journal of Learning Disabilities*, March–April 2010, pp. 154–165.

276. M. Loden, *Implementing Diversity* (Chicago: Irwin, 1996); E. E. Spragins, "Benchmark: The Diverse Work Force," *Inc.*, January 1993, p. 33; A. M. Morrison, *The New Leaders: Guidelines on Leadership Diversity in America* (San Francisco: Jossey-Bass, 1992).

277. E. Chuck, "James Damore, Google Engineer Fired for Writing Manifesto on Women's 'Neuroticism,' Sues Company," *NBC News*, January 8, 2018, https://www.nbcnews.com/news/us-news/google-engineer-fired-writing-manifesto-women-s-neuroticism-sues-company-n835836.

278. L. Weber, "Diversity Efforts Challenged," *The Wall Street Journal*, March 15, 2018, p. B5.

279. R. Umoh, "Meet America's Best Employers for Diversity 2020," *Forbes*, January 21, 2020, https://www.forbes.com/sites/ruthumoh/2020/01/21/meet-americas-best-employers-for-diversity-2020/#478de5bb5739.

280. J. A. Gonzalez and A. DeNisi, "Cross-Level Effects of Demography and Diversity Climate on Organizational Attachment and Firm Effectiveness," *Journal of Organizational Behavior*, January 2009, p. 24.

281. Y. Chung, H. Liao, S. E. Jackson, M. Subramony, S. Colakoglu, and Y. Jiang, "Cracking but Not Breaking: Joint Effects of Faultline Strength and Diversity Climate on Loyal Behavior," *Academy of Management Journal*, October 2015, pp. 1495–1515. Also see S. A. Boehm, F. Kunze, and H. Bruch, "Spotlight on Age-Diversity Climate: The Impact of Age-Inclusive HR Practices on Firm-Level Outcomes," *Personnel Psychology*, September 2013, pp. 667–704.

282. Y. Chung, H. Liao, S. E. Jackson, M. Subramony, S. Colakoglu, and Y. Jiang, "Cracking but Not Breaking: Joint Effects of Faultline Strength and Diversity Climate on Loyal Behavior," *Academy of Management Journal*, October 2015, pp. 1495–1515. Also see S. A. Boehm, F. Kunze, and H. Bruch, "Spotlight on Age-Diversity Climate: The Impact of Age-Inclusive HR Practices on Firm-Level Outcomes," *Personnel Psychology*, September 2013, pp. 667–704.

283. Interview with Amy Edmondson in "Creating Psychological Safety in the Workplace," *Harvard Business Review*, January 22, 2019, https:// hbr.org/podcast/2019/01/creating-psychological-safety-in-the-workplace.

284. S. Jha, "Team Psychological Safety and Team Performance," *International Journal of Organizational Analysis*, Vol. 27 (4) 2019, pp. 903–924. Also see L. Delizonna, "High-Performing Teams Need Psychological Safety. Here's How to Create It," *Harvard Business Review*, August 24, 2017, https://hbr.org/2017/08/high-performing-teams-need-psychological-safety-heres-how-to-create-it; M. Chism, "Improve Performance through Psychological Safety," *SmartBrief*, November 4, 2019, https://www.smartbrief.com/original/2019/11/improve-performance-through-psychological-safety; "Creating Psychological Safety in the Workplace," *Harvard Business Review*, January 22, 2019, https://hbr.org/podcast/2019/01/creating-psychological-safety-in-the-workplace.

285. W. Wang, "The Majority of U.S. Children Still Live in Two-Parent Families," *Institute for Family Studies*, October 4, 2018, https://ifstudies .org/blog/the-majority-of-us-children-still-live-in-two-parent-families.

286. "Table 4, Families with Own Children: Employment Status of Parents by Age of Youngest Child and Family Type, 2017–2018 Annual Averages," *Bureau of Labor Statistics*, April 18, 2019, www.bls.gov/news.release/famee.t04.htm.

287. C. Cain Miller, "Walmart and Now Starbucks: Why More Big Companies Are Offering Paid Family Leave," *The New York Times*, January 24, 2018, https://www.nytimes.com/2018/01/24/upshot/parental-leave-company-policy-salaried-hourly-gap.html.

288. N. Ogrysko, "Questions about the New Paid Parental Leave Law? You're Not Alone," *Federal News Network*, January 10, 2020, https:// federalnewsnetwork.com/benefits/2020/01/questions-about-the-new-paid-parental-leave-law-youre-not-alone/.

289. L. Peppard, "Hostile Environment for Female Firefighter Upheld," *HR Magazine*, March 2015, p. 70.

290. R. Boczkiewicz, "Colo. Sexual Harassment Case Urges Brinker Corp. to Update Policy," *The Pueblo Chieftain*, March 5, 2020, https:// www.chieftain.com/news/20200305/colo-sexual-harassment-case-urges-brinker-corp-to-update-policy.

291. "EEOC Releases Fiscal Year 2019 Enforcement and Litigation Data," *U.S. Equal Employment Opportunity Commission*, January 24, 2020, https://www.eeoc.gov/eeoc/newsroom/release/1-24-20.cfm.

292. "Ultimate Software Ranks #2 on Fortune's 100 Best Companies to Work For 2020 List," *Ultimate Software*, February 18, 2020, https:// www.ultimatesoftware.com/PR/Press-Release/Ultimate-Software-Ranks-2-on-Fortunes-100-Best-Companies-to-Work-For-2020-List.

293. "Forbes Names Ultimate Software to America's Best Employers for Diversity 2019 List," *Ultimate Software*, January 29, 2019, https://www.ultimatesoftware.com/PR/Press-Release/Forbes-Names-Ultimate-Software-to-Americas-Best-Employers-for-Diversity-2019-List.

294. "Ultimate Software Ranks #2 on Fortune's 100 Best Companies to Work For 2020 List," *Ultimate Software*, February 18, 2020, https://www.ultimatesoftware.com/PR/Press-Release/Ultimate-Software-Ranks-2-on-Fortunes-100-Best-Companies-to-Work-For-2020-List.

295. "Ultimate Software," *Great Place to Work,* http://reviews.greatplacetowork.com/ultimate-software (accessed April 2, 2018). Also see D. Marcroft, "Ultimate Software Named #3 Best Company to Work for by Fortune [Press Release]," February 20, 2018, www.ultimatesoftware.com/PR/Press-Release/Ultimate-Software-Named-3-Best-Company-to-Work-For-by-Fortune; "Our Culture," *Ultimate Software*, https://www.ultimatesoftware.com/Ultimate-Company-Culture (accessed March 30, 2020).

296. "HEAT to Host Second Annual Loud and Proud Dance Party Presented by Ultimate Software," *NBA,* March 4, 2018, www.nba.com/heat/heat-host-second-annual-loud-and-proud-dance-party-presented-ultimate-software.

297. D. Marcroft. "Ultimate Software Ranked #2 Best Workplace for Women by Fortune [Press Release]," September 15, 2017, www.ultimatesoftware.com/PR/Press-Release/Ultimate-Software-Ranked-2-Best-Workplace-for-Women-by-Fortune.

298. "Products," *Ultimate Software*, https://www.ultimatesoftware.com/products (accessed March 30, 2020) "Ultipro Reviews," *Trust Radius,* www.trustradius.com/products/ultipro/reviews/pros-and-cons?f=175 (accessed March 30, 2020).

299. D. Marcroft, "Ultimate Software Extends Talent Management with Career Development and Succession Management in UltiPro Fall 2011 Release [Press Release]," January 12, 2012, www.ultimatesoftware.com/PR/Ultimate-Software-Extends-Talent-Management-with-Career-Development-and-Succession-Management-in-UltiPro-Fall-2011-Release.

300. "Reporting, Workforce Analytics, and Business Intelligence Tools," *Ultimate Software,* www.ultimatesoftware.com/UltiPro-Solution-Features-Reporting-Workforce-Analytics-Business-Intelligence-Tools (accessed March 30, 2018).

301. "Solution Features," *Ultimate Software,* www.ultimatesoftware.com/UltiPro-Solution-Features (accessed March 30, 2018).

302. "Financial Services Company Uses UltiPro Perception to Give Managers Faster, Better Employee Insight," *Business Wire,* January 12, 2018, www.businesswire.com/news/home/20180112005424/en/Financial-Services-Company-UltiPro-Perception-Give-Managers.

303. R. S. Lazarus, *Psychological Stress and Coping Processes* (New York: McGraw-Hill, 1966); R. S. Schuler, "Definition and Conceptualization of Stress in Organizations," *Organizational Behavior and Human Performance,* April 1980, pp. 184–215.

304. "Work Related Stress on Employees Health," *EKU Online,* https://safetymanagement.eku.edu/resources/infographics/work-related-stress-on-employees-health/ (accessed March 31, 2020). Also see "Workplace Stress," *The American Institute of Stress*, https://www.stress.org/workplace-stress (accessed March 31, 2020).

305. A. Day, S. A. Penney, N. Hartling, "The Psychology, Potential Perils, and Practice of Leading Healthy Workplaces," *Organizational Dynamics,* July 2019, pp. 75–84. Also see "42 Worrying Workplace Stress Statistics," The American Institute of Stress, September 25, 2019, https://www.stress.org/42-worrying-workplace-stress-statistics; J. Pfeffer, "The Hidden Costs of Stressed-Out Workers," *The Wall Street Journal,* February 28, 2019, https://www.wsj.com/articles/the-hidden-costs-of-stressed-out-workers-11551367913.

306. "Workplace Stress: A Silent Killer of Employee Health and Productivity," *Corporate Wellness Magazine,* https://www.corporatewellnessmagazine.com/article/workplace-stress-silent-killer-employee-health-productivity (accessed March 31, 2020). Also see E. Scott, "How to Deal With Stress-Related Insomnia," *Very Well Mind,* January 28, 2020, https://www.verywellmind.com/stress-related-insomnia-3144827.

307. C. Zhang, D. M. Mayer, and E. Hwang, "More Is Less: Learning But Not Relaxing Buffers Deviance under Job Stressors," *Journal of Applied Psychology*, February 2018, pp. 123–136; P. D. Bliese, J. R. Edwards, and S. Sonnentag, "Stress and Well-Being at Work: A Century of Empirical Trends Reflecting Theoretical and Societal Influences," *Journal of Applied Psychology,* March 2017, pp. 380–402.

308. R. Koerber, M. Rouse, K. Stanyar, M. Pelletier, "Building Resilience in the Workforce," *Organizational Dynamics*, April 2018, pp. 124–134.

309. M. Akinola, C. Kapadia, J. G. Lu, and M. F. Mason, "Incorporating Physiology into Creativity Research and Practice," *Academy of Management Perspectives*, June 2019, pp. 163–184; "Researchers Explore the Benefits of Stress and Anxiety," The American Institute of Stress, August 23, 2019, https://www.stress.org/researchers-explore-the-benefits-of-stress-and-anxiety.

310. B. H. Cheng and J. M. McCarthy, "Understanding the Dark and Bright Sides of Anxiety: A Theory of Workplace Anxiety," *Journal of Applied Psychology*, May 2018, pp. 537–560.

311. P. D. Bliese, J. R. Edwards, and S. Sonnentag, "Stress and Well-Being at Work: A Century of Empirical Trends Reflecting Theoretical and Societal Influences," *Journal of Applied Psychology,* March 2017, pp. 380–402.

312. C. M. Barnes, "Sleep Well, Lead Better," *Harvard Business Review,* September-October 2018, https://hbr.org/2018/09/sleep-well-lead-better.

313. R. Cross, S. Taylor, and D. Zehner, "Collaboration without Burnout," *Harvard Business Review*, July-August 2018, pp. 134–137.

314. W. B. Schaufeli, "Applying the Job Demands-Resources Model," *Organizational Dynamics*, April 2017, pp. 120–132.

315. H. Selye, *Stress without Distress* (New York: Lippincott, 1974), p. 27.

316. R. S. Lazarus and S. Folkman, "Coping and Adaptation," in W. D. Gentry (ed.), *Handbook of Behavioral Medicine* (New York: Guilford, 1982).

317. L. Zhou, M. Wang, C-H. Chang, S. Liu, Y. Zhan, and J. Shi, "Commuting Stress Process and Self-Regulation at Work: Moderating Roles of Daily Task Significance, Family Interference with Work, and Commuting Means Efficacy," *Personnel Psychology,* Vol. 70 (4) 2017, pp. 891–922.

318. J. Zweig, "This Is Your Brain on a Crashing Stock Market," *The Wall Street Journal*, March 19, 2020, https://www.wsj.com/articles/this-is-your-brain-on-a-crashing-stock-market-11584615601.

319. H. Selye, *Stress without Distress* (New York: Lippincott, 1974), pp. 28–29.

320. M. B. Hargrove, D. L. Nelson, and C. L. Cooper, "Generating Eustress by Challenging Employees: Helping People Savor Their Work," *Organizational Dynamics,* Vol. 42 (2013), pp. 61–69; M. Akinola, C. Kapadia, J. G. Lu, and M. F. Mason, "Incorporating Physiology into Creativity Research and Practice," *Academy of Management Perspectives*, June 2019, pp. 163–184.

321. M. Beck, "When Fretting Is in Your DNA: Overcoming the Worry Gene," *The Wall Street Journal,* January 15, 2008, p. D1. Also see W-D. Li, Z. Zhang, Z. Song, and R. D. Arvey, "It Is Also in Our Nature: Genetic Influences on Work Characteristics and in Explaining Their Relationships with Well-Being," *Journal of Organizational Behavior,* August 2016, pp. 868–888.

322. M. Friedman and R. H. Rosenman, *Type A Behavior and Your Heart* (Greenwich, CT: Fawcett Publications, 1974), p. 84.

323. M. S. Taylor, E. A. Locke, C. Lee, and M. E. Gist, "Type A Behavior and Faculty Research Productivity: What Are the Mechanisms?" *Organizational Behavior and Human Performance,* December 1984, pp. 402–418; S. D. Bluen, J. Barling, and W. Burns, "Predicting Sales Performance, Job Satisfaction, and Depression by Using the Achievement Strivings and Impatience–Irritability Dimensions of Type A Behavior," *Journal of Applied Psychology,* April 1990, pp. 212–216.

324. S. Booth-Kewley and H. S. Friedman, "Psychological Predictors of Heart Disease: A Quantitative Review," *Psychological Bulletin,* May 1987, pp. 343–362; S. A. Lyness, "Predictors of Differences between Type A and B Individuals in Heart Rate and Blood Pressure Reactivity," *Psychological Bulletin,* September 1993, pp. 266–295; T. Q. Miller, T. W. Smith, C. W. Turner, M. L. Guijarro, and A. J. Hallet, "A Meta-Analytic

Review of Research on Hostility and Physical Health," *Psychological Bulletin,* March 1996, pp. 322–348.

325. 2016 study by CareerCast, reported in C. Brooks, "Most (and Least) Stressful Jobs for 2016," *Business News Daily,* January 7, 2016, www.businessnewsdaily.com/1875-stressful-careers.html (accessed July 11, 2016).

326. J. O'Donnell, "Wanted: Retail Managers," *USA Today,* December 24, 2007, pp. 1B, 3B. Also see A. Salario, "Retail Manager Stressed by 'Never Enough' Sales Strategy," *Womensenews,* July 15, 2013, http://womensenews.org/2013/07/retail-manager-stressed-never-enough-sales-strategy/ (accessed July 1, 2016).

327. M. Richtel, "In Web World of 24/7 Stress, Writers Blog Till They Drop," *The New York Times,* April 6, 2008, news section, pp. 1, 23.

328. S. Diestel, W. Rivkin, and K.-H. Schmidt, "Sleep Quality and Self-Control Capacity as Protective Resources in the Daily Emotional Labor Process: Results from Two Diary Studies," *Journal of Applied Psychology,* Vol. 100, No. 3 (2015), pp. 809–827.

329. "Stressful Jobs That Pay Badly," *CNN Money,* March 7, 2014, http://money.cnn.com/gallery/pf/jobs/2013/03/07/jobs-stress-pay (accessed July 19, 2016).

330. See Key Workplace Factors from G. Tinline and C. Cooper, "Work-related Stress: The Solution Is Management, Not Mindfulness," *Organizational Dynamics*, Vol. 48 (3) 2019, pp. 93–97.

331. E. Gonzalex-Mulé and B. Cockburn, "Worked to Death: The Relationships of Job Demands and Job Control with Mortality," *Personnel Psychology,* Vol. 70 (1) 2017, pp. 73–112.

332. W. B. Schaufeli, "Applying the Job Demands-Resources Model: A 'How to' Guide to Measuring and Tackling Work Engagement and Burnout," *Organizational Dynamics,* April–June 2017, pp. 120–132; E. Gonzalex-Mulé and B. Cockburn, "Worked to Death: The Relationships of Job Demands and Job Control with Mortality," *Personnel Psychology,* Vol. 70 (1) 2017, p. 73.

333. E. Reid and L. Ramarajan, "Managing the High Intensity Workplace," *Harvard Business Review,* June 2016, pp. 85–90.

334. J. H. Wayne, M. M. Butts, W. J. Casper, and T. D. Allen, "In Search of Balance: A Conceptual and Empirical Integration of Multiple Meanings of Work-Family Balance," *Personnel Psychology,* Vol. 70 (1) 2017, pp. 167–210. Also see S. J. Wayne, G. Lemmon, J. M. Hoobler, G. W. Cheung, and M. S. Wilson, "The Ripple Effect: A Spillover Model of the Detrimental Impact of Work-Family Conflict on Job Success," *Journal of Organizational Behavior,* July 2017, pp. 876–894.

335. D. S. Carlson, M. J. Thompson, and K. M. Kacmar, "Double Crossed: The Spillover and Crossover Effects of Work Demands on Work Outcomes through the Family," *Journal of Applied Psychology*, February 2019, pp. 214–228. Also see S. Gisler et al., "Work–Life Conflict and Employee Health: A Review," *Journal of Applied Biobehavioral Research*, December 2018, https://doi.org/10.1111/jabr.12157.

336. W. S. Crawford, M. J. Thompson, and B. E. Ashforth, "Work-Life Events Theory: Making Sense of Shock Events in Dual-Earner Couples," *Academy of Management Review,* January 2019, pp. 194–212.

337. A. Hirschi, K. M. Shockley, and H. Zacher, "Achieving Work-Family Balance: An Action Regulation Model," *Academy of Management Review,* January 2019, pp. 150–171. Also see A. Cazan, C. Truță, M. Pavalache-Ilie, "The Work-Life Conflict and Satisfaction with Life: Correlates and the Mediating Role of the Work-Family Conflict," *Romanian Journal of Applied Psychology*, June 2019, pp. 3–10; R. Ilies, X-Y. Liu, Y. Liu, and X. Zheng, "Why Do Employees Have Better Family Lives When They Are Highly Engaged at Work?" *Journal of Applied Psychology,* June 2017, pp. 956–970; J. I. Menges, D. V. Tussing, A. Wihler, and A. M. Grant, "When Job Performance Is All Relative: How Family Motivation Energizes Effort and Compensates for Intrinsic Motivation," *Academy of Management Journal,* April 2017, pp. 695–719; J. Choi et al., "Antecedents and Consequences of Satisfaction with Work-Family Balance: A Moderating Role of Perceived Insider Status," *Journal of Organizational Behavior,* January 2018, pp. 1–11.

338. G. N. Powell, J. H. Greenhaus, T. D. Allen, and R. E. Johnson, "Advancing and Expanding Work-Life Theory from Multiple Perspectives," *Academy of Management Review,* January 2019, pp. 54–71. Also see S. Bourdeau, A. Ollier-Malaterre, and N. Houlfort, "Not All Work-Life Policies Are Created Equal: Career Consequences of Using Enabling versus Enclosing Work-Life Policies," *Academy of Management Review,* January 2019, pp. 172–193.

339. A. Kidwai, "Chipotle to Expand Paid Parental Leave, Test Unlimited PTO," *HR Dive*, March 6, 2020, https://www.hrdive.com/news/chipotle-to-expand-paid-parental-leave-test-unlimited-pto/573585/. Also see S. Pollack, "6 Companies Redefining Parental Leave," *NBC News*, March 20, 2019, https://www.nbcnews.com/know-your-value/feature/6-companies-redefining-parental-leave-ncna984946.

340. J. Alpert, "Yes, Secondhand Stress Is a Thing. Here's How to Protect Yourself—And Others," *Inc.,* March 31, 2017, https://www.inc.com/jonathan-alper/what-you-need-to-know-about-secondhand-stress.html.

341. J. Kim, "8 Traits of Toxic Leadership to Avoid," *Psychology Today,* July 6, 2016, https://www.psychologytoday.com/us/blog/culture-shrink/201607/8-traits-toxic-leadership-avoid.

342. R. Cross, S. Taylor, and D. Zehner, "Collaboration without Burnout," *Harvard Business Review*, July-August 2018, pp. 134–137. Also see M. Thomas, "Protecting Company Culture Means Having Rules for Email," *Harvard Business Review*, September 17, 2018, https://hbr.org/2018/09/protecting-company-culture-means-having-rules-for-email.

343. C. Pazzanese, "The High Price of Workplace Stress," *Harvard Gazette,* July 12, 2016, https://news.harvard.edu/gazette/story/2016/07/the-high-price-of-workplace-stress/.

344. A. Peters, "One Trick to Make Employees Happy: Ban Emails on Nights and Weekends," *Fast Company,* June 1, 2016, https://www.fastcompany.com/3060349/one-trick-to-make-employees-happy-ban-emails-on-nights-and-weekends.

345. D. Z. Morris, "New French Law Bars Work Email after Hours," *Fortune,* January 1, 2017, http://fortune.com/2017/01/01/french-right-to-disconnect-law/.

346. L. Albrecht, "Banning Access to Work Emails after Hours Can Harm Your Mental Health (Seriously)," *Market Watch*, October 22, 2019, https://www.marketwatch.com/story/banning-access-to-work-emails-can-harm-employees-mental-health-seriously-2019-10-22. Also see S. Christie, "Porsche Could Ban Out-of-Hour Emails—but What Other Companies Already Have These Policies in Place?" *The Telegraph,* December 20, 2017, https://www.telegraph.co.uk/business/2017/12/20/porsche-could-ban-out-of-hour-emails-companies-already-have/; B. Chignell, "How to Manage email Overload at Work," *CIPHR*, August 6, 2019, https://www.ciphr.com/advice/email-overload/.

347. L. Albrecht, "Banning Access to Work Emails after Hours Can Harm Your Mental Health (Seriously)," *Market Watch*, October 22, 2019, https://www.marketwatch.com/story/banning-access-to-work-emails-can-harm-employees-mental-health-seriously-2019-10-22. Also see D. Z. Morris, "New French Law Bars Work Email after Hours," *Fortune,* January 1, 2017, http://fortune.com/2017/01/01/french-right-to-disconnect-law/.

348. S. Milligan, "Wellness Blows Up," *HRMagazine,* September 2017, pp. 61–67.

349. R. Koerber, M. Rouse, K. Stanyar, and M. Pelletier, "Building Resilience in the Workforce," *Organizational Dynamics*, April 2018, pp. 124–134.

350. I. T. Roberson, C. L. Cooper, M. Sarkar, and T. Curran, "Resilience Training in the Workplace from 2003 to 2014: A Systematic Review," *Journal of Occupational and Organizational Psychology,* September 2015, pp. 533–562.

351. S. Cao, "Dyson Curling Iron Hype Has Made Its Inventor the Richest Man in the UK," *Observer*, January 26, 2019, https://observer.com/2019/01/james-dyson-richest-uk-man-dyson-airwrap/. Also see "Inventor James Dyson Now UK's Wealthiest Person after Dyson Vacuum Cleaner Firm Cleans Up," *Bloomberg*, January 23, 2019, https://www.scmp.com/magazines/style/people-events/article/2183307/inventor-james-dyson-now-uks-wealthiest-person-after.

352. G. Tinline and C. Cooper, "Work-Related Stress: The Solution Is Management Not Mindfulness," *Organizational Dynamics*, Vol. 48 (3) 2019, pp. 93–97. Also see E. Dane, "Where Is My Mind? Theorizing

Mind Wandering and Its Performance-Related Consequences in Organizations," *Academy of Management Review,* April 2018, pp. 179–197; K. M. Kiburz, T. D. Allen, and K. A. French, "Work-Family Conflict and Mindfulness: Investigating the effectiveness of a Brief Training Intervention," *Journal of Organizational Behavior,* September 2017, pp. 1016–1037; E. Bernstein, "A Daily Workout for the Brain," *The Wall Street Journal,* December 5, 2017, p. A13.

353. T. Parker-Pope, "How to Build Resilience in Midlife," *The New York Times,* July 25, 2017, https://www.nytimes.com/2017/07/25/well/mind/how-to-boost-resilience-in-midlife.html. Also see P. R. Pietromonaco and N. L. Collins, "Interpersonal Mechanisms Linking Close Relationships to Health," *American Psychologist,* September 2017, pp. 531–542; B. Litwiller, L. A. Snyder, W. D. Taylor, and L. M. Steele, "The Relationship between Sleep and Work: A Meta-Analysis," *Journal of Applied Psychology,* April 2017, pp. 682–699.

354. K. Charles-Collins, "COVID-19: How Businesses Can Prepare for the Aftermath," *Thrive Global,* March 31, 2020, https://thriveglobal.com/stories/covid-19-how-businesses-can-prepare-for-the-aftermath/. Also see K. Pho, "Do Corporate Wellness Programs Really Work?" *USA Today,* September 12, 2013, p. 10A; S. Hananel, "A Workout during Work," *Reno Gazette-Journal,* September 12, 2013, p. 7F; N. Hellmich, "Healthy, Wellness, and Wise about Costs," *USA Today,* December 13, 2013, p. 8B; A. Lukits, "Take Your Bike to Your Desk to Improve Health," *The Wall Street Journal,* May 27, 2014, p. D2; A. Bruzzese, "Mindful Eating, Exercise Boost Work Performance," *Reno Gazette-Journal,* January 18, 2014, p. 9A.

355. "US Population by Age and Generation in 2020," *Knoema,* https://knoema.com/egyydzc/us-population-by-age-and-generation-in-2020 (accessed March 31, 2020). Also see B. Reiners, "A Recruiter's Guide to Preparing for the Gen Z Workforce," *Built In,* January 15, 2020, https://builtin.com/recruiting/gen-z-workforce/.

356. "10 Companies with Amazing Workplace Wellness Programs," *Rise,* March 30, 2017, www.risepeople.com/blog/10-companies-with-amazing-workplace-wellness-programs/.

357. L. Martis, "7 Companies with Great Wellness Programs," *Fortune,* August 17, 2017, http://fortune.com/2017/08/17/companies-great-wellness-programs/.

358. L. Bradford, "13 Tech Companies That Offer Cool Work Perks," *Forbes,* July 27, 2016, www.forbes.com/sites/laurencebradford/2016/07/27/13-tech-companies-that-offer-insanely-cool-perks/#723db7d979d1. Also see M. Wilkinson, "18 of Google's Employee Perks You're Missing Out On," *Coburg Banks,* https://www.coburgbanks.co.uk/blog/friday-funnies/googles-employee-perks/ (accessed March 31, 2020).

359. S. Thieroff, "Wellness Case Study: Google," *Healthyworks,* October 6, 2015, www.healthyworksofpa.com/wellness-case-study-google/.

360. L. Bradford, "13 Tech Companies That Offer Cool Work Perks," *Forbes,* July 27, 2016, www.forbes.com/sites/laurencebradford/2016/07/27/13-tech-companies-that-offer-insanely-cool-perks/#723db7d979d1.

361. L. Martis, "7 Companies with Great Wellness Programs," *Fortune,* August 17, 2017, http://fortune.com/2017/08/17/companies-great-wellness-programs/.

362. J. D'Onfro & K. Smith, "Google Employees Reveal Their Favorite Perks about Working for the Company," *Business Insider,* July 1, 2014, www.businessinsider.com/google-employees-favorite-perks-2014-7#.

363. M. Wilkinson, "18 of Google's Employee Perks You're Missing Out On," *Coburg Banks,* https://www.coburgbanks.co.uk/blog/friday-funnies/googles-employee-perks/ (accessed March 31, 2020).

364. "10 Companies with Amazing Workplace Wellness Programs," *Rise,* March 30, 2017, www.risepeople.com/blog/10-companies-with-amazing-workplace-wellness-programs/.

365. "10 Companies with Amazing Workplace Wellness Programs," *Rise,* March 30, 2017, www.risepeople.com/blog/10-companies-with-amazing-workplace-wellness-programs/. Also see L. Bradford, "13 Tech Companies That Offer Cool Work Perks," *Forbes,* July 27, 2016, www.forbes.com/sites/laurencebradford/2016/07/27/13-tech-companies-that-offer-insanely-cool-perks/#723db7d979d1.

366. M. Wilkinson, "18 of Google's Employee Perks You're Missing Out On," *Coburg Banks,* https://www.coburgbanks.co.uk/blog/friday-funnies/googles-employee-perks/ (accessed March 31, 2020).

367. M. Wilkinson, "18 of Google's Employee Perks You're Missing Out On," *Coburg Banks,* https://www.coburgbanks.co.uk/blog/friday-funnies/googles-employee-perks/ (accessed March 31, 2020).

368. L. Martis, "7 Companies with Great Wellness Programs," *Fortune,* August 17, 2017, http://fortune.com/2017/08/17/companies-great-wellness-programs/.

369. M. Gill and T. Roulet, "Stressed at Work? Mentoring a Colleague Could Help," *Harvard Business Review,* March 1, 2019, https://hbr.org/2019/03/stressed-at-work-mentoring-a-colleague-could-help. Also see H. Aguinis, Y. H. Ji and H. Joo, "Gender Productivity Gap Among Star Performers in STEM and Other Scientific Fields," *Journal of Applied Psychology,* December 2018, pp. 1283–1306; "Mentors Help Reduce Stress, Burnout," *San Francisco Chronicle,* February 26, 2016, p. C2, reprinted from *Pittsburgh Post-Gazette.*

370. S. Lucas, "Companies Are Reducing Employee Stress by Doing This 1 Simple Thing," *Inc.,* February 22, 2018, https://www.inc.com/suzanne-lucas/companies-are-reducing-employee-stress-by-doing-this-one-simple-thing.html?cid=search.

371. See Key Workplace Factors in G. Tinline and C. Cooper, "Work-related Stress: The Solution Is Management, Not Mindfulness," *Organizational Dynamics,* Vol. 48 (3) 2019, pp. 93–97.

372. These questions were adapted from B. Tulgan, *Bridging the Soft Skills Gap* (Hoboken, NJ: John Wiley & Sons, 2015).

373. These steps were based on material in B. Tulgan, *Bridging the Soft Skills Gap* (Hoboken, NJ: John Wiley & Sons, 2015).

374. D. Meinert, "Are You an Emotional Genius?" *HRMagazine,* March 2018, pp. 17–19.

375. S. Côte, "Enhancing Managerial Effectiveness via Four Core Facets of Emotional Intelligence: Self-Awareness, Social Perception, Emotion Understanding, and Emotional Regulation," *Organizational Dynamics,* July–September 2017, pp. 140–147; R. Hanson and R. Mendius, *Buddha's Brain* (Oakland, CA: Harbinger Publications, 2009).

376. D. Auten and C. Fritz, "Mental Health at Work: How Mindfulness Aids in More Ways than One," *Organizational Dynamics,* 2019, pp. 98–104; G. Tinline and C. Cooper, "Work-Related Stress: The Solution Is Management Not Mindfulness," *Organizational Dynamics,* Vol. 48 (3) 2019, pp. 93–97.

377. D. Auten and C. Fritz, "Mental Health at Work: How Mindfulness Aids in More Ways than One," *Organizational Dynamics,* Vol. 48 (3) 2019, pp. 98–104.

378. A. Feldman, "Away Luggage Hits $1.4B Valuation after $100M Fundraise," *Forbes,* May 14, 2019, https://www.forbes.com/sites/amyfeldman/2019/05/14/at-a-valuation-as-high-as-145b-valuation/#4efebb7a33d7.

379. M. Meisenzahl, "Away Warns Employees Not to Interact with Criticism of the Company's Workplace Culture after the CEO's Public Apology," *Business Insider,* December 6, 2019, https://www.businessinsider.com/away-steph-korey-apology-toxic-company-culture-report-2019-12. Also see N. Mascarenhas and M. A. Azevedo, "Away CEO Korey Resigns after Abusive Practice Allegations," *Crunchbase News,* December 9, 2019, https://news.crunchbase.com/news/away-ceo-korey-resigns-after-abusive-practice-allegations/.

380. Z. Schiffer, "Emotional Baggage," *The Verge,* December 5, 2019, https://www.theverge.com/2019/12/5/20995453/away-luggage-ceo-steph-korey-toxic-work-environment-travel-inclusion.

381. A. Holmes, "Some Away Workers Were Reportedly Fired after Bosses Caught Them Complaining in a Secret Slack Channel," *Business Insider,* December 5, 2019, https://www.businessinsider.com/away-employees-fired-complaining-secret-slack-channel-report-2019-12. Also see C. Newton and Z. Schiffer, "The Away Scandal Is a Moment of Reckoning for Slack," *The Verge,* December 10, 2019, https://www.theverge.com/2019/12/10/21002881/away-steph-korey-resigns-slack-platform-incentives.

382. S. G. Carmichael, "You Could Fill a Suitcase with Bad Boss Behavior," *Bloomberg*, December 11, 2019, https://www.bloomberg.com/opinion/articles/2019-12-11/away-s-ceo-departure-shows-lessons-toxic-bosses-need-to-learn.

383. C. Newton and Z. Schiffer, "The Away Scandal Is a Moment of Reckoning for Slack," *The Verge*, December 10, 2019, https://www.theverge.com/2019/12/10/21002881/away-steph-korey-resigns-slack-platform-incentives. Also see A. Holmes, "Some Away Workers Were Reportedly Fired after Bosses Caught Them Complaining in a Secret Slack Channel," *Business Insider*, December 5, 2019, https://www.businessinsider.com/away-employees-fired-complaining-secret-slack-channel-report-2019-12; C. Lagorio-Chafkin, "A Scathing New Report Alleges Away Mistreats Its Employees. Here's Why Slack May Be to Blame," *Inc.*, December 5, 2019, https://www.inc.com/christine-lagorio-chafkin/away-jen-rubio-steph-korey-verge-report.html.

384. M. Meisenzahl, "Away Warns Employees Not to Interact with Criticism of the Company's Workplace Culture after the CEO's Public Apology," *Business Insider*, December 6, 2019, https://www.businessinsider.com/away-steph-korey-apology-toxic-company-culture-report-2019-12; J. Roeder, "Away Co-Founder to Split Leadership Role with Incoming Stuart Haselden," *Bloomberg*, January 13, 2020, https://www.bloomberg.com/news/articles/2020-01-13/away-co-founder-to-split-leadership-role-with-incoming-haselden.

385. A. Stych, "Away CEO Is Back, 'Exploring Legal Options' in Response to Negative Press," *Biz Journals*, January 14, 2020, https://www.bizjournals.com/bizwomen/news/latest-news/2020/01/away-ceo-is-back-exploring-legal-options-in.html?page=all.

386. J. Shen, "'People Are Getting Soft': How the Away Scandal Exposed a Silicon Valley Culture War," *Fast Company*, December 11, 2019, https://www.fastcompany.com/90442083/people-are-getting-soft-how-the-away-scandal-exposed-a-silicon-valley-culture-war.

387. Z. Schiffer, "Emotional Baggage," *The Verge*, December 5, 2019, https://www.theverge.com/2019/12/5/20995453/away-luggage-ceo-steph-korey-toxic-work-environment-travel-inclusion.

388. J. Shen, "'People Are Getting Soft': How the Away Scandal Exposed a Silicon Valley Culture War," *Fast Company*, December 11, 2019, https://www.fastcompany.com/90442083/people-are-getting-soft-how-the-away-scandal-exposed-a-silicon-valley-culture-war.

389. J. Shen, "'People Are Getting Soft': How the Away Scandal Exposed a Silicon Valley Culture War," *Fast Company*, December 11, 2019, https://www.fastcompany.com/90442083/people-are-getting-soft-how-the-away-scandal-exposed-a-silicon-valley-culture-war. Also see C. Lagorio-Chafkin, "A Scathing New Report Alleges Away Mistreats Its Employees. Here's Why Slack May Be to Blame," *Inc.*, December 5, 2019, https://www.inc.com/christine-lagorio-chafkin/away-jen-rubio-steph-korey-verge-report.html.

390. R. Radka, "U.S. Airlines with the Widest Seats in Coach," *Airfare Watch Dog*, June 22, 2018, https://www.airfarewatchdog.com/blog/44255063/u-s-airlines-with-the-widest-seats-in-coach/. Also see B. Wilson, "Seat Pitches and Widths on the Top 6 U.S. Carriers," *Trip Savvy*, June 26, 2019, https://www.tripsavvy.com/everything-you-want-to-know-about-airline-seat-pitch-53282.

391. Excerpted from K. Mayo, "Economy Plus Size," *Bloomberg Businessweek*, May 6–May 12, 2013, p. 81.

392. J. Serra, "Plus Size Air Travel Tips," *Love to Know*, https://travel.lovetoknow.com/wiki/Plus_Size_Air_Travel# (accessed April 1, 2020).

393. J. Wattles, "Judges Order FAA to Review Airplane Seat Sizes," *CNN Money*, July 29, 2017, http://money.cnn.com/2017/07/29/news/companies/faa-airline-seat-sizes/index.html.

394. C. Morris, "The FAA May Put an End to Shrinking Airline Seats and Cramped Leg Room," *Fortune*, February 26, 2018, http://fortune.com/2018/02/26/faa-airline-seats-regulation-safety-comfort/.

395. A. Schmertz, "Senator Schumer's Silly Idea about Airline Seat Sizes," *Huffington Post*, March 7, 2016, http://www.huffingtonpost.com/andrew-schmertz/senator-schumers-silly- d_b_9400796.html.

396. K. Dark, "Planes Weren't Built for Big People Like Me. Here's What I Want My Seatmates to Know," *Time*, September 23, 2019, https://time.com/5683972/big-people-on-plane/.

397. S. McCartney, "When the Plane Seat Doesn't Fit," *The Wall Street Journal*, November 20, 2019, https://www.wsj.com/articles/when-the-plane-seat-doesnt-fit-11574245801.

398. "Facts and Figures," *Airbus*, February 2020, file:///C:/Users/Patrick/Desktop/Backgrounder-Airbus-Commercial-Aircraft-A220-Facts-and-Figures-EN.pdf.

CHAPTER 12

1. J. Suárez, A. Fernández, and Á Zamora, "The Use of Classmates as a Self-Motivation Strategy from the Perspective of Self-Regulated Learning," *Frontiers in Psychology*, Vol. 10 (2019), p. 1314.

2. K. Wong, "How to Motivate Employees: 13 Simple Ways," *Business2Community*, May 5, 2020, https://www.business2community.com/human-resources/how-to-motivate-employees-13-simple-ways-02307153.

3. "How to Stay Self-Motivated, According to Science," *World Happiness Summit*, January 7, 2019, https://www.happinesssummit.world/index.php/2019/01/07/how-to-stay-self-motivated-according-to-science/.

4. C. Moore, "How to Set and Achieve Life Goals the Right Way," *Positive Psychology*, April 29, 2020, https://positivepsychology.com/life-worth-living-setting-life-goals/.

5. E. Kaplan, "How to Stay Insanely Self-Motivated, According to Science," *Medium.com*, September, 15, 2017, https://medium.com/the-mission/how-to-create-insane-change-in-your-life-according-to-science-bb3cddd1022.

6. G. Matthews, "Study Focuses on Strategies for Achieving Goals, Resolutions," *Dominican University of California*, https://www.dominican.edu/dominicannews/study-highlights-strategies-for-achieving-goals (accessed April 23, 2018).

7. S. Shellenbarger, "Women Try New Strategies to Boost Career Confidence," *The Wall Street Journal*, March 20, 2018, p. A13.

8. K. Tyko, "Top Companies Offer Perks like Free Gym Memberships, Meals and Unlimited Paid Time Off," *USA Today*, October 3, 2019, https://www.usatoday.com/story/money/careers/2019/10/03/top-companies-perks-microsoft-facebook-google-top-comparably-list/3838377002/.

9. A. Hirsch, "How to Set and Achieve Life Goals the Right Way," *SHRM*, July 30, 2018, https://www.shrm.org/ResourcesAndTools/hr-topics/benefits/Pages/employers-explore-repaying-student-loan-debt.aspx.

10. Y. Noguchi, "A New Benefit: Some Companies Help Workers Pay Down Student Loans," *NPR*, February 25, 2019, https://www.npr.org/2019/02/25/696355143/come-work-for-us-well-help-pay-down-your-student-loans. Also see C. von Schilling, "Penguin Random House Ranks #1 on Forbes List," *Bertelsmann*, https://www.bertelsmann.com/corporate-responsibility/projects-worldwide/project/penguin-random-house-ranks-1-on-forbes-list.jsp (accessed May 13, 2020).

11. K. Hagen, "20 Companies That Pay Off Employees' Student Loans," *The Motley Fool*, February 6, 2020, https://www.fool.com/student-loans/20-companies-pay-off-employees-student-loans/.

12. Adapted from definition in T. R. Mitchell, "Motivation: New Directions for Theory, Research, and Practice," *Academy of Management Review*, January 1982, p. 81.

13. R. Ryan and E. Deci, "Intrinsic and Extrinsic Motivations: Classic Definitions and New Directions," *Contemporary Educational Psychology*, January 2000, pp. 54–67.

14. D. Onu, L. Oats, and E. Kirchler, "The Dynamics of Internalised and Extrinsic Motivation in the Ethical Decision-Making of Small Business Owners," *Applied Psychology*, Vol. 68, No. 1 (2019), pp. 177–201.

15. J. Sammer, "Employer Incentives Encourage Employees to Quit Smoking," *SHRM*, October 29, 2019, https://www.shrm.org/hr-today/news/hr-magazine/1118/pages/employer-incentives-encourage-employees-to-quit-smoking.aspx.

16. S. Halpern, M. Harhay, K. Saulsgiver, C. Brophy, A. Troxel, and K. Volpp, "A Pragmatic Trial of E-Cigarettes, Incentives, and Drugs for Smoking Cessation," *New England Journal of Medicine*, Vol. 378, No. 24 (2018), pp. 2302–2310.

17. R. Derfler-Rozin and M. Pitesa. "Motivation Purity Bias: Expression of Extrinsic Motivation Undermines Perceived Intrinsic Motivation and Engenders Bias in Selection Decisions," *Academy of Management Journal*, 2020.

18. S. Eisenberg, "Intrinsic vs. Extrinsic Motivation: How to Drive People to Do Amazing Work," *Wrike,* July 30, 2019, https://www.wrike.com/blog/intrinsic-vs-extrinsic-motivation/.

19. S. Shaaban, "The Impact of Motivation on Organisational Citizenship Behaviour (OCB): The Mediation Effect of Employees' Engagement," *Journal of Human Resource Management*, Vol. 6, No. 2 (2018), pp. 58–66. Also see F. Philippe, M. Lopes, N. Houlfort, and C. Fernet, "Work-Related Episodic Memories Can Increase or Decrease Motivation and Psychological Health at Work," *Work & Stress*, Vol. 33, No. 4 (2019), pp. 366–384; Q. Miao, A. Newman, G. Schwarz, and B. Cooper, "How Leadership and Public Service Motivation Enhance Innovative Behavior," *Public Administration Review*, Vol. 78, No. 1 (2018), pp. 71–81.

20. A. Maslow, "A Theory of Human Motivation," *Psychological Review,* July 1943, pp. 370–396.

21. A. Poddar, "Social Responsibility: The New Competitive Advantage," *The HR Business Partner Story,* March 6, 2020, https://thehrbpstory.com/2020/03/06/social-responsibility-the-new-competitive-advantage/.

22. V. Valet, "The World's Most Reputable Companies for Corporate Responsibility 2019," *Forbes,* September 17, 2019, https://www.forbes.com/sites/vickyvalet/2019/09/17/the-worlds-most-reputable-companies-for-corporate-responsibility-2019/#2b026d8f679b.

23. T. Bridgman, S. Cummings, and J. Ballard, "Who Built Maslow's Pyramid? A History of the Creation of Management Studies' Most Famous Symbol and Its Implications for Management Education," *Academy of Management Learning & Education*, Vol. 18, No. 1 (2019), pp. 81–98.

24. A. Janssen, "Work Culture: Engaged and Committed," *Auto Service World,* October 23, 2019, https://www.autoserviceworld.com/work-culture-engaged-and-committed/.

25. C. Connley, "Amazon, Facebook and 8 Other Companies That Have Committed to Raising Their Minimum Wage," *CNBC,* May 24, 2019, https://www.cnbc.com/2019/05/24/glassdoor-10-companies-that-have-committed-to-raising-minimum-wage.html.

26. D. C. McClelland, *Human Motivation* (Glenview, IL: Scott, Foresman, 1985).

27. J. Schüler, N. Baumann, A. Chasiotis, M. Bender, and I. Baum, "Implicit Motives and Basic Psychological Needs," *Journal of Personality,* Vol. 87, No. 1 (2019), pp. 37–55.

28. O. Saracho, "Motivation Theories, Theorists, and Theoretical Conceptions," *Contemporary Perspectives on Research in Motivation in Early Childhood Education*, 2019, p. 21.

29. C. Chen, A. Elliot, and K. Sheldon, "Psychological Need Support as a Predictor of Intrinsic and External Motivation: The Mediational Role of Achievement Goals," *Educational Psychology*, Vol. 39, No. 8 (2019), pp. 1090–1113.

30. J. Schüler, N. Baumann, A. Chasiotis, M. Bender, and I. Baum, "Implicit Motives and Basic Psychological Needs," *Journal of Personality,* Vol. 87, No. 1 (2019), pp. 37–55.

31. J. Hofer and H. Busch, "Women in Power-Themed Tasks: Need for Power Predicts Task Enjoyment and Power Stress," *Motivation and Emotion*, Vol. 43, No. 5 (2019), pp. 740–757.

32. R. Rybnicek, S. Bergner, and A. Gutschelhofer, "How Individual Needs Influence Motivation Effects: A Neuroscientific Study on Mc Clelland's Need Theory," *Review of Managerial Science*, Vol. 13, No. 2 (2019), pp. 443–482.

33. J. E. Ramsay, "Authoritative Maternal Parenting Associates with the Explicit Need for Autonomy," *Journal of Individual Differences*, Vol. 41, No. 2 (2020), pp. 110–116.

34. C. Burk and B. Wiese, "Professor or Manager? A Model of Motivational Orientations Applied to Preferred Career Paths," *Journal of Research in Personality*, Vol. 75 (2018), pp. 113–132.

35. R. M. Ryan and E. L. Deci, "Self-Determination Theory and the Facilitation of Intrinsic Motivation, Social Development, and Well-Being," *American Psychologist,* January 2000, pp. 68–78.

36. Y. Zhang, J, Zhang, J. Forest, and Z. Chen, "A Dynamic Computational Model of Employees Goal Transformation: Using Self-Determination Theory," *Motivation and Emotion,* Vol. 43, No. 3 (2019), pp. 447–460. Also see S. van Schie, A.Gautier, A. Pache, and S. Güntert, "What Keeps Corporate Volunteers Engaged: Extending the Volunteer Work Design Model with Self-Determination Theory Insight," *Journal of Business Ethics,* Vol. 160, No. 3 (2019), pp. 693–712.

37. H. Fang, H. Fu, X. Li, and L. Meng, "Trapped in the Woods: High Performance Goal Orientation Impedes Competence Restoration," *Personality and Individual Differences,* Vol. 150 (2019).

38. R. Tripathi, D. Cervone, and K. Savani, "Are the Motivational Effects of Autonomy-Supportive Conditions Universal? Contrasting Results Among Indians and Americans," *Personality and Social Psychology Bulletin*, Vol. 44, No. 9 (2018), pp. 1287–1301.

39. A. Divine, P. Watson, S. Baker, and C. Hall, "Facebook, Relatedness and Exercise Motivation in University Students: A Mixed Methods Investigation," *Computers in Human Behavior*, Vol. 91 (2019), pp. 138–150.

40. K. W. Rockmann and G. A. Ballinger, "Intrinsic Motivation and Organizational Identification Among On-Demand Workers," *Journal of Applied Psychology,* September 2017, pp. 1305–1316.

41. "Education," *Mascoma Bank*, https://www.mascomabank.com/careers/education/ (accessed May 13, 2020).

42. "2019 Benefits Guide," *Appriss,* June 2018, https://apprissbenefits.com/wp-content/uploads/sites/6/2018/10/CORP-2019-Benefits-Guide-FINAL-v2.pdf.

43. T. Russell, "15 Practice Areas Critical to Achieving a Great Workplace," *Great Place to Work,* April 23, 2019, https://www.greatplacetowork.com/resources/blog/15-practice-areas-critical-to-achieving-a-great-workplace.

44. F. Herzberg, B. Mausner, and B. B. Snyderman, *The Motivation to Work* (New York: Wiley, 1959). Also see F. Herzberg, "One More Time: How Do You Motivate Employees?" *Harvard Business Review,* January–February 1968, pp. 53–62. For a modern look at the application of Herzberg's theory, see C. Christensen, "Clayton Christensen on How to Find Work That You Love," *Fast Company,* May 14, 2012, www.fastcompany.com/1836982/clayton-christensen-how-find-work-you-love (accessed July 9, 2016).

45. P. Padma and J. Ahn, "Guest Satisfaction & Dissatisfaction in Luxury Hotels: An Application of Big Data," *International Journal of Hospitality Management*, Vol. 84 (2020).

46. "100 Best Companies to Work For 2020: REI," *Fortune,* https://fortune.com/best-companies/2020/rei/ (accessed May 13, 2020).

47. A. Cain, "The Best Way to Stand Out in a Job Interview at One of the Most Beloved Companies in America," *Dallas News,* February 27, 2018, https://www.businessinsider.com/rei-jobs-biggest-mistake-2018-2.

48. J. Haden, "When a Southwest Airlines Flight Was Delayed, Passengers Got Increasingly Frustrated. Then the Gate Agent Did Something Remarkable," *Inc.,* August 26, 2019, https://www.inc.com/jeff-haden/a-southwest-airlines-flight-was-delayed-passengers-grew-frustrated-unthen-gate-agent-did-something-remarkable.html.

49. P. O'Donnell, "Southwest Airlines' Annual Tradition: It's Sharing $544 Million in Profits with Employees," *Dallas News,* February 13, 2019, https://www.dallasnews.com/business/local-companies/2019/02/13/southwest-airlines-annual-tradition-it-s-sharing-544-million-in-profits-with-employees/.

50. Survey by the Conference Board, reported in P. Korkki, "With Jobs Few, Most Workers Aren't Satisfied," *The New York Times,* January 10, 2009, Business section, p. 2. Also see P. Coy, "Are Your Employees Just Biding Their Time?" *BusinessWeek,* November 16, 2009, p. 27.

51. Staff, "Excerpts from @Work Talent + HR Conference," *CNBC,* April 5, 2019, https://www.cnbc.com/2019/04/05/excerpts-from-work-talent-hr-conference.html.

52. "State of the Global Workplace," *Gallup,* May 14, 2019, https://www.gallup.com/workplace/257552/state-global-workplace-2017.aspx.

53. M. Burke, "The Power of Play at Work," September 14, 2016, https://www.huffpost.com/entry/the-power-of-play-at-work_b_12011462. Also see T. Cummings, "Pets and Productivity: Does Having an Animal in the Office Make You a Better Worker?" *Lifehack,* May 12, 2020, https://www.lifehack.org/articles/productivity/pets-and-productivity-does-having-an-animal-in-the-office-make-you-a-better-worker.html.

54. "Google Benefits," *Glassdoor,* https://www.glassdoor.com/Benefits/Google-US-Benefits-EI_IE9079.0,6_IL.7,9_IN1.htm (accessed May 13, 2020).

55. D. Widiss, "One Thing the U.S. Can Do to Treat Single Moms More Fairly," *Fast Company,* May 10, 2020, https://www.fastcompany.com/90502816/one-thing-the-u-s-can-do-to-treat-single-moms-more-fairly.

56. J. Andrews, "Perhaps Money Can Buy You Happiness—At Least, At Work," *CNBC,* July 16, 2019, https://www.cnbc.com/2019/07/16/perhaps-money-can-buy-you-happiness-at-least-at-work.html.

57. J. S. Adams, "Toward an Understanding of Inequity," *Journal of Abnormal and Social Psychology,* November 1963, pp. 422–436; J. S. Adams, "Injustice in Social Exchange," in L. Berkowitz (ed.), *Advances in Experimental Social Psychology,* 2nd ed. (New York: Academic Press, 1965), pp. 267–300.

58. D. Gerdeman, "If the CEO's High Salary Isn't Justified to Employees, Firm Performance May Suffer," *Forbes,* January 22, 2018, https://www.forbes.com/sites/hbsworkingknowledge/2018/01/22/if-the-ceos-high-salary-isnt-justified-to-employees-firm-performance-may-suffer/#59cdc9e8433d.

59. L. Greco, J. Whitson, E. O'Boyle, C. Wang, and J. Kim, "An Eye for An Eye? A Meta-Analysis of Negative Reciprocity in Organizations," *Journal of Applied Psychology,* Vol. 104, No. 9 (2019), p. 1117.

60. D. Larcker and B. Tayan, "Pay for Performance . . . But Not Too Much Pay," *Stanford Closer Look Series,* November 25, 2019, https://www.gsb.stanford.edu/sites/gsb/files/publication-pdf/cgri-closer-look-80-pay-for-performance.pdf.

61. R. Zitelmann, "Why Do So Many People Think That CEOs Earn Too Much?" *Forbes,* October 7, 2019, https://www.forbes.com/sites/rainerzitelmann/2019/10/07/why-do-so-many-people-think-that-ceos-earn-too-much/#2d3f9385152e.

62. M. Sajko, C. Boone, and T. Buyl, "CEO Greed, Corporate Social Responsibility, and Organizational Resilience to Systemic Shocks," *Journal of Management* (2020). Also see https://www.forbes.com/sites/hbsworkingknowledge/2018/01/22/if-the-ceos-high-salary-isnt-justified-to-employees-firm-performance-may-suffer/#59cdc9e8433d.

63. Perceptions of fairness are discussed by L. J. Barclay, M. R. Bashshur, and M. Fortin, "Motivated Cognition and Fairness: Insights, Integration, and Creating a Path Forward," *Journal of Applied Psychology,* June 2017, pp. 867–889.

64. R. Cropanzano, D. Rupp, C. Mohler, and M. Schminke, "Three Roads to Organizational Justice," in G. R. Ferris (ed.), *Research in Personnel and Human Resources Management,* Vol. 20 (New York: JAI Press, 2001), pp. 269–329.

65. E. Marescaux, S. De Winne, and L. Sels, "Idiosyncratic Deals from a Distributive Justice Perspective: Examining Co-Workers' Voice Behavior," *Journal of Business Ethics*, Vol. 154, No. 1 (2019), pp. 263–281.

66. C. Xiang, C. Li, K. Wu, and L. Long, "Procedural Justice and Voice: A Group Engagement Model," *Journal of Managerial Psychology*, September 2019, pp. 491–503.

67. M. van Dijke, D. De Cremer, G. Langendijk, and C. Anderson, "Ranking Low, Feeling High: How Hierarchical Position and Experienced Power Promote Prosocial Behavior in Response to Procedural Justice," *Journal of Applied Psychology,* Vol. 103, No. 2 (2018), pp. 164–181. Also see M. Valentine, "When Equity Seems Unfair: The Role of Justice Enforceability in Temporary Team Coordination," *Academy of Management Journal,* Vol. 61, No. 6 (2018), pp. 2081–2105.

68. J. Colquitt, D. Conlon, M. Wesson, C. Porter, and K. Ng, "Justice at the Millennium: A Meta-Analytic Review of 25 Years of Organizational Justice Research," *Journal of Applied Psychology,* June 2001, pp. 425–445.

69. M. van Dijke, M. Joost, T. Wildschut, and C. Sedikides, "Nostalgia Promotes Intrinsic Motivation and Effort in the Presence of Low Interactional Justice," *Organizational Behavior and Human Decision Processes*, Vol. 150 (2019), pp. 46–61.

70. J. Norman, "Four in 10 U.S. Workers Think They Are Underpaid," *Gallup,* August 18, 2018, https://news.gallup.com/poll/241682/four-workers-think-underpaid.aspx.

71. Z. Small, "Meow Wolf Is Being Sued by Former Employees for Unfair Labor Practices," *Hyperallergic,* July 3, 2019, https://hyperallergic.com/508005/meow-wolf-former-employees/. Also see https://www.cpr.org/2019/07/10/meow-wolf-responds-to-lawsuit-discrimination-allegations/.

72. R. Outlaw, J. Colquitt, M. Baer, and H. Sessions, "How Fair versus How Long: An Integrative Theory-Based Examination of Procedural Justice and Procedural Timeliness," *Personnel Psychology*, Vol. 72, No. 3 (2019), pp. 361–391.

73. S. Tangirala and R. Ramanujam, "Ask and You Shall Hear (but Not Always): Examining the Relationship between Manager Consultation and Employee Voice," *Personnel Psychology* 65, No. 2 (2012), pp. 251–252.

74. T. Kochan, D. Yang, W. Kimball, and E. Kelly, "Worker Voice in America: Is There a Gap between What Workers Expect and What They Experience?" *ILR Review,* Vol. 72, No. 1 (2019), pp. 3–38.

75. "HSBC: Giving Your Employees a Seat at the Table," *Rebel Playbook,* http://www.rebelplaybook.com/bonus-plays/giving-your-employees-a-seat-at-the-table-hsbc (accessed May 13, 2020).

76. "Grade Appeal Policy and Process," *ASU Mary Lou Fulton Teachers College*, https://education.asu.edu/sites/default/files/grade_appeal_policy_and_process_9-12-17_0.pdf.

77. E. Sherf, V. Venkataramani, and R. Gajendran, "Too Busy to Be Fair? The Effect of Workload and Rewards on Managers' Justice Rule Adherence," *Academy of Management Journal*, Vol. 62, No. 2 (2019), pp. 469–502.

78. J. Webber, "Oprah Winfrey Interviews Whole Foods Vegan Founder about Conscious Capitalism," *Live Kindly,* November 28, 2018, https://www.livekindly.co/oprah-winfrey-whole-foods-vegan-founder-john-mackey/.

79. R. Gillett and M. Perino, "13 Top Executives Who Earn a $1 Salary or Less," *Business Insider,* July 22, 2019, https://www.businessinsider.com/ceos-who-take-1-dollar-salary-or-less-2015-8#edward-lampert-9.

80. M. Ambrose, D. Rice, and D. Mayer. "Justice Climate and Workgroup Outcomes: The Role of Coworker Fair Behavior and Workgroup Structure," *Journal of Business Ethics*, November 2019, pp. 1–21.

81. "EEOC Releases Fiscal Year 2019 Enforcement and Litigation Data," *EEOC,* January 24, 2020, https://www.eeoc.gov/newsroom/eeoc-releases-fiscal-year-2019-enforcement-and-litigation-data.

82. R. Sharp, "Breaking the Silence: Employee Voice," *HR Magazine,* July 9, 2018, https://www.hrmagazine.co.uk/article-details/breaking-the-silence-employee-voice.

83. K. Gilchrist, "How Millennials and Gen Z Are Reshaping the Future of the Workforce," *CNBC,* March 5, 2019, https://www.cnbc.com/2019/03/05/how-millennials-and-gen-z-are-reshaping-the-future-of-the-workforce.html.

84. P. Cappelli, "What to Make of the New Employee Activism," *HR Executive,* December 6, 2019, https://hrexecutive.com/what-to-make-of-the-new-employee-activism/.

85. I. Ivanova, "Wayfair Employees Walk Out after Company's Sales to Migrant Children Holding Facility," *Fortune,* November 3, 2018, https://www.cbsnews.com/news/wayfair-employees-plan-walkout-after-companys-sales-to-detention-centers/.

86. L. Segarra, "More Than 20,000 Google Employees Participated in Walkout over Sexual Harassment Policy," *Fortune,* November 3, 2018, https://fortune.com/2018/11/03/google-employees-walkout-demands/.

87. J. Bhuiyan, "Walkout Rippled beyond Google; A Year Ago, 20,000 Workers Staged a Global Protest—and Inspired Activism across the

Industry," *Los Angeles Times*, November 6, 2019, https://www.latimes.com/business/technology/story/2019-11-06/google-employee-walkout-tech-industry-activism

88. T. Casey, "Lush: A Business Model Built on Campaigns," *Triple Pundit*, September 25, 2019, https://www.triplepundit.com/story/2019/lush-business-model-built-campaigns/85021.

89. R. Sharp, "Breaking the Silence: Employee Voice," *HR Magazine*, July 9, 2018, https://www.hrmagazine.co.uk/article-details/breaking-the-silence-employee-voice.

90. K. Gee, "The New Labor Movement: Pushing Employers to Be Socially Active; Workers Are Banding Together to Influence Their Company's Policies toward the Environment and Social Issues," *The Wall Street Journal*, June 25, 2019, https://www.wsj.com/articles/the-new-labor-movement-pushing-employers-to-be-socially-active-11561476199.

91. V. H. Vroom, *Work and Motivation* (New York: Wiley, 1964).

92. M. Langfelder, "Did One of America's Largest Corporations Just Switch to a Pay-for-Performance Model?" *Connex Partners*, March 23, 2018, https://www.connexpartners.com/blog/did-one-of-americas-largest-corporations-just-switch-to-a-pay-for-performance-model.

93. J. Rampton, "Different Motivations for Different Generations of Workers: Boomers, Gen X, Millennials, and Gen Z," *Inc*, October 17, 2017, https://www.inc.com/john-rampton/different-motivations-for-different-generations-of-workers-boomers-gen-x-millennials-gen-z.html. Also see J. Desjardins, "How Different Generations Approach Work," *Visual Capitalist*, May 30, 2019, https://www.visualcapitalist.com/generations-approach-workplace/. Also see https://www.skillsportal.co.za/content/what-motivates-each-generation-work.

94. M. Maltarich, A. Nyberg, G. Reilly, D. Abdulsalam, and M. Martin, "Pay-for-Performance, Sometimes: An Interdisciplinary Approach to Integrating Economic Rationality with Psychological Emotion to Predict Individual Performance," *Academy of Management Journal*, December 2017, pp. 2155–2174.

95. M. Majerczyk, R. Sheremeta, and Y. Tian, "Adding Tournament to Tournament: Combining Between-Team and within-Team Incentives," *Journal of Economic Behavior & Organization*, Vol. 166 (2019), pp. 1–11.

96. L. Greco and M. Kraimer, "Goal-Setting in the Career Management Process: An Identity Theory Perspective," *Journal of Applied Psychology*, Vol. 105, No. 1 (2020), p. 40.

97. C. Groening and C. Binnewies, ""Achievement Unlocked!"—The Impact of Digital Achievements as a Gamification Element on Motivation and Performance," *Computers in Human Behavior*, Vol. 97 (2019), pp. 151–166.

98. N. Green, "4 Ways 'Stretch Goals' Can Bring Your Company Greater Gains," *Business Journals*, September 8, 2017, https://www.bizjournals.com/bizjournals/how-to/growth-strategies/2017/09/4-ways-stretch-goals-can-bring-your-company.html.

99. F. Schneider, "The Stretch Goal Myth: When More Ambition Is Really Better," *Workpath*, https://www.workpath.com/en/magazine/the-stretch-goal-myth-when-more-ambition-is-really-better/ (accessed May 13, 2020).

100. I. Hamilton, "Meet the Coding Prodigy Who Has Prince Harry and Meghan Markle on Her Side in the Fight to Boost Women in Tech," *Business Insider*, October 4, 2018, https://www.businessinsider.com/anne-marie-imafidon-coding-prodigy-fighting-for-women-in-tech-2018-10.

101. "Anne-Marie Imafidon MBE," *Anne-Marie Imafidon*, https://aimafidon.com/ (accessed May 13, 2020).

102. "About Us," *Stemettes*, https://stemettes.org/about-us/ (accessed May 13, 2020).

103. Z. Ziemtus, "'Get Dot to Do a PhD': Stemettes Co-Founder Wants EastEnders to Lead Women into Tech," *The Guardian*, October 4, 2018, https://www.theguardian.com/careers/2018/oct/04/get-dot-to-do-a-phd-stemettes-co-founder-wants-eastenders-to-lead-women-into-tech.

104. I. Hamilton, "Meet the Coding Prodigy Who Has Prince Harry and Meghan Markle on Her Side in the Fight to Boost Women in Tech," *Business Insider*, October 4, 2018, https://www.businessinsider.com/anne-marie-imafidon-coding-prodigy-fighting-for-women-in-tech-2018-10.

105. M. Egan, "Wells Fargo Uncovers Up to 1.4 Million More Fake Accounts," *CNN Money*, August 31, 2017, http://money.cnn.com/2017/08/31/investing/wells-fargo-fake-accounts/index.html?iid=EL. Also see J. Wattles, B. Geier, and M. Egan, "Wells Fargo's 17-Month Nightmare," *CNN Money*, February 5, 2018, http://money.cnn.com/2018/02/05/news/companies/wells-fargo-timeline/index.html.

106. M. Gaim, S. Clegg, and M. Cunha, "Managing Impressions Rather Than Emissions: Volkswagen and The False Mastery of Paradox," *Organization Studies*, December 2019

107. K. Roose and W. Williams, "An Evaluation of the Effects of Very Difficult Goals," *Journal of Organizational Behavior Management*, Vol. 38, No. 1 (2018), pp. 18–48.

108. D. Vandewalle, "Goal Orientation: Why Wanting to Look Successful Doesn't Always Lead to Success," *Organizational Dynamics*, November 2001, pp. 162–171. Also see P. R. Sackett, C. H. Van Iddekinge, F. Lievens, and N. R. Kuncel, "Individual Differences and Their Measurement: A Review of 100 Years of Research," *Journal of Applied Psychology*, March 2017, pp. 254–273.

109. J. Lindzon, "10 Wildly Successful People on How They View Failure," *Fortune*, March 25, 2016, http://fortune.com/2016/03/25/successful-people-failure/.

110. J. Schroeder and A. Fishbach, "How to Motivate Yourself and Others? Intended and Unintended Consequences," *Research in Organizational Behavior*, Vol. 35 (2015), pp. 123–141. Also see E. Locke and G. Latham, "Building a Practically Useful Theory of Goal Setting and Task Motivation," *American Psychologist*, September 2002, pp. 705–717.

111. G. Latham and E. Locke, "Enhancing the Benefits and Overcoming the Pitfalls of Goal Setting," *Organizational Dynamics*, November 2006, pp. 332–340.

112. "PG&E's 2020 Wildfire Mitigation Plan Expands, Enhances Community Wildfire Safety Program, Reduces Impacts of Public Safety Power Shutoffs," *PG&E External Communications*, February 7, 2020, https://www.pge.com/en/about/newsroom/newsdetails/index.page?title=20200207_pges_2020_wildfire_mitigation_plan_expands_enhances_community_wildfire_safety_program_reduces_impacts_of_public_safety_power_shutoffs.

113. G. Shinkle, C. Jackson, B. McCann, M. Goudsmit, and F. Yang, "How to Establish Legitimate Organizational Goal Targets," *Organizational Dynamics*, Vol. 48, No. 4 (2019).

114. D. Morisano, J. Hirsh, J. Peterson, R. Phil, and B. Shore, "Setting, Elaborating, and Reflecting on Personal Goals Improves Academic Performance," *Journal of Applied Psychology*, March 2010, pp. 255–264.

115. "Strategic Action Plan 2017–2020," *Calvary Care*, https://www.calvarycare.org.au/public-hospital-bruce/wp-content/uploads/sites/2/2016/04/CPHB_Strategic-Plan_2017_2020.pdf (accessed May 13, 2020).

116. A. Bartz, "This Healthcare Company Is Determined to Have the Healthiest Employees in the World," *Johnson & Johnson*, February 25, 2018, https://www.jnj.com/innovation/how-johnson-johnson-is-improving-workplace-wellness-for-healthiest-employees.

117. C. Steinhorst, "Why Your Workforce Is Bored Out of Their Minds," *Forbes*, January 28, 2020, https://www.forbes.com/sites/curtsteinhorst/2020/01/28/why-your-workforce-is-bored-out-of-their-minds/#6320c418208d.

118. G. Oldham and J. Hackman, "Not What It Was and Not What It Will Be: The Future of Job Design," *Journal of Organizational Behavior*, February 2010, pp. 463–479. Also see Garg, Pooja, and Ki-Soon Han. "High Performance Work Practices: The Trending Approaches in India," *IUP Journal of Organizational Behavior*, Vol. 17, No. 3 (2018), pp. 74–90.

119. E. Lawrie, M. Tuckey, and M. Dollard, "Job Design for Mindful Work: The Boosting Effect of Psychosocial Safety Climate," *Journal of Occupational Health Psychology*, Vol. 23, No. 4 (2018), pp. 483–495.

120. M. Campion and C. McClelland, "Follow-Up and Extension of the Interdisciplinary Costs and Benefits of Enlarged Jobs," *Journal of Applied Psychology*, June 1993, pp. 339–351. Also see R. Cote, "Motivating Multigenerational Employees: Is There a Difference?" *Journal of Leadership, Accountability and Ethics*, Vol. 16, No. 2 (2019).

121. F. Herzberg, B. Mausner, and B. B. Snyderman, *The Motivation to Work* (New York: Wiley, 1959).

122. N. Alias, R. Othman, L. Hamid, N. Salwey, N. Romaiha, K. Samad, and N. Masdek, "Managing Job Design: The Roles of Job Rotation, Job Enlargement and Job Enrichment on Job Satisfaction," *Journal of Economic & Management Perspectives*, Vol. 12, No. 1 (2018): pp. 397–401.

123. D. Weis, "Giving Employees Permission to Fail Is a Formula for Innovation At 3M," *AEM,* June 21, 2018, https://www.aem.org/news/giving-employees-permission-to-fail-is-a-formula-for-innovation-at-3m/.

124. J. Hackman and G. Oldham, *Work Redesign* (Reading, MA: Addison-Wesley, 1980).

125. D. Simonet, and C. Castille, "The Search for Meaningful Work: A Network Analysis of Personality and the Job Characteristics Model," *Personality and Individual Differences*, Vol. 152 (2020).

126. S. Achor, A. Reece, G. Kellerman, and A. Robichaux, "9 Out of 10 People Are Willing to Earn Less Money to Do More-Meaningful Work," *Harvard Business Review*, November 6, 2018.

127. G. De Boeck, N. Dries, and H. Tierens, "The Experience of Untapped Potential: Towards a Subjective Temporal Understanding of Work Meaningfulness," *Journal of Management Studies*, Vol. 56, No. 3 (2019), pp. 529–557.

128. G. Nagrath, "Work Motivation of School Teachers: An Application of Job Characteristics Model," *Journal of Strategic Human Resource Management*, Vol. 8, No. 2 (2019), pp. 26–30.

129. S. Pipes, "Government Policies Are Driving Doctors to Quit Health Care," *Forbes,* October 15, 2018, https://www.forbes.com/sites/sallypipes/2018/10/15/government-policies-are-driving-doctors-to-quit-health-care/#dd11a6c2bf36.

130. "The CARES Act," *Direct Primary Care Coalition,* https://www.dpcare.org/ (accessed May 13, 2020).

131. K. Huffman, "Our Restaurants Can't Reopen Until August; Employees Refuse to Return to Work as Long as They're Getting an Extra $600 a Week," *The Wall Street Journal*, April 21, 2020, https://www.wsj.com/articles/our-restaurants-cant-reopen-until-august-11587504885.

132. E. Thorndike, *Educational Psychology: The Psychology of Learning*, Vol. II (New York: Columbia University Teachers College, 1913). Also see B. Skinner, *Walden Two* (New York: Macmillan, 1948); B. Skinner, *Science and Human Behavior* (New York: Macmillan, 1953); D. Mozingo, "Contingencies of Reinforcement," in F. R. Volker (ed.), *Encyclopedia of Autism Spectrum Disorders* (New York: Appleton-Century-Crofts, 1969), p. 799.

133. E. Thorndike, *Educational Psychology: The Psychology of Learning*, Vol. II (New York: Columbia University Teachers College, 1913).

134. H. Martin, "Airlines Are Paying Fewer Fines. Are Regulators More Lenient or Are Airlines More Law Abiding?" *MSN,* January 13, 2020, https://www.msn.com/en-us/news/us/airlines-are-paying-fewer-fines-are-regulators-more-lenient-or-are-airlines-more-law-abiding/ar-BBYUyQ0.

135. C. Elliott, "Airline Fines Have Fallen to Historic Lows. That Could Be Bad News for Travelers; The U.S. Transportation Department Sees No Connection; Consumer Advocates Don't Agree," *Washington Post Blogs,* December 4, 2019.

136. H. Martin, "Airlines Push to Roll Back Consumer-Protection Rules," *The Seattle Times,* March 23, 2018, https://www.seattletimes.com/business/boeing-aerospace/airlines-push-to-roll-back-consumer-protection-rules/.

137. These recommendations were based on S. Achor, A. Reece, G. Kellerman, and A. Robichaux, "9 Out of 10 People Are Willing to Earn Less Money to Do More-Meaningful Work," *Harvard Business Review*, November 6, 2018, https://hbr.org.

138. G. James, "10 Things Employees Want More Than a Raise," *Inc.,* October 7, 2013, https://www.inc.com/geoffrey-james/10-things-employees-want-more-than-a-raise.html, Also see A. Gostick and C. Elton, "Opinion: The 1 Thing Workers Want More Of—And It's Not Money," *Market Watch,* March 5, 2020, https://www.marketwatch.com/story/the-1-thing-workers-want-more-of-and-its-not-money-2020-03-05.

139. A. Kohll, "What Employees Really Want at Work," *Forbes,* July 10, 2018, https://www.forbes.com/sites/alankohll/2018/07/10/what-employees-really-want-at-work/#131b8dee5ad3.

140. D. Bortz, "5 Things You Need to Be Happy at Work," *Monster,* https://www.monster.com/career-advice/article/5-things-you-need-to-be-happy-at-work-0417 (accessed May 13, 2020).

141. "2019 Job Seeker Nation Survey," *Jobvite,* April 2019, https://www.jobvite.com/wp-content/uploads/2019/04/2019_Job_Seeker_Nation.pdf.

142. V. Fuhrmans, "CEO Pay and Performance Often Don't Match Up; the S&P 500 CEOs Who Received the Biggest Pay Increases Scored Middling Shareholder Returns," *The Wall Street Journal*, May 14, 2018, https://www.wsj.com/articles/ceo-pay-and-performance-dont-match-up-1526299200

143. "Minimum Wage," *Worker.gov,* https://www.worker.gov/concerns/pay-minimum-wage/ (accessed May 13, 2020).

144. "Financial Advisor Compensation Package," *Edward Jones Careers,* http://careers.edwardjones.com/explore-opportunities/new-financial-advisors/compensation/compensation.html (accessed May 11, 2020).

145. C. Connley, "13 Companies Offering Hiring Bonuses up to $20,000 Right Now," *CNBC,* July 26, 2019, https://www.cnbc.com/2019/07/26/13-companies-offering-hiring-bonuses-up-to-20000-right-now.html.

146. J. B., "In The Words of Mr. George," *Publix Blog,* April 16, 2018, https://blog.publix.com/publix/in-the-words-of-mr-george/.

147. M. Atih, "Using 'Gainsharing' to Achieve Sustainability Goals," *HDT Truckinginfo,* April 2, 2014, www.truckinginfo.com/blog/market-trends/story/2014/04/using-gainsharing-to-achieve-sustainability-goals.aspx.

148. "The Progressive Corporation 2019 Gainsharing Plan," *SEC,* December 31, 2018, https://www.sec.gov/Archives/edgar/data/80661/000008066119000008/pgr-20181231exhibit103.htm.

149. J. Kramer, "15 Companies with Awesome 401k Plans Hiring Now," *Glassdoor,* March 10, 2020, https://www.glassdoor.com/blog/companies-401k-plan/. Also see R. Safier, "29 Work from Home Companies with Incredible Employee Benefits," *Remote Bliss,* December 12, 2019, https://remotebliss.com/26-legit-work-from-home-companies-hiring/; W. Rose, "Apple Employee Benefits Review: Are Their Careers Worth It?" *Future Fuel,* August 12, 2019, https://futurefuel.io/employee-benefits/apple-careers/; "Proxy Statement: Nordstrom," *SEC,* April 12, 2019, https://www.sec.gov/Archives/edgar/data/72333/000007233319000098/jwn2019-def14a.htm.

150. J. Richard and E.Kang, "Culture, Competencies and Compensation: A Framework for Pay for Performance Incentives," *American Journal of Management*, Vol. 18, No. 4 (2018), pp. 33–48.

151. E. Veksler, "Work Life Balance: Everything You Need to Know to Stay Sane," *The Ladders,* April 27, 2020, https://www.theladders.com/career-advice/work-life-balance-everything-you-need-to-know-to-stay-sane.

152. "The Importance of Work-Life Balance," *Rewire,* https://www.rewireinc.com/work-life-balance#The_Struggle_Is_Real_Work-Life_Balance_Obstacles__Benefitswidget_5596380223 (accessed May 13, 2020).

153. Definition from I. Tatara, *Work-Life Benefits: Everything You Need to Know to Determine Your Work-Life Program* (Chicago: CCH KnowledgePoint, 2002), p. 2.

154. M. Bush and S. Lewis-Kulin, "100 Best Companies to Work For 2018," *Fortune,* March 1, 2018, pp. 55–78.

155. C. Miller, "Leaps in Leave, if Only Parents Would Take It," *The New York Times,* September 2, 2015, pp. A1, A3. Also see R. Lieber, "Paid Leave for Fathers. Any Takers?" *The New York Times,* August 8, 2015, pp. B1, B5; R. E. Silverman, "Challenges of the 'Daddy Track,'" *The Wall Street Journal,* September 2, 2015, pp. B1, B5.

156. K. Bucholz, "The Countries with the Best Work-Life Balance," *Statista,* September 26, 2019, https://www.statista.com/chart/12977/countries-with-the-best-work-life-balance/.

157. "50 Best Workplaces for Flexibility," *Fortune,* 2020, https://fortune.com/best-workplaces-flexibility/.

158. E. Howard, "Is Flextime in Your Company's Future?" *Employment Law Handbook,* October 31, 2019, https://www.employmentlawhandbook.com/flextime/is-flextime-in-your-companys-future/.

159. T. Chandola, C. Booker, M. Kumari, and M. Benzeval, "Are Flexible Work Arrangements Associated with Lower Levels of Chronic Stress-Related Biomarkers? A Study of 6025 Employees in the UK Household Longitudinal Study," *Sociology*, Vol. 53, No. 4 (2019), pp. 779–799.

160. Glassdoor Team, "20 Companies Offering Unlimited PTO," *Glassdoor,* January 17, 2020, https://www.glassdoor.com/blog/cool-companies-offering-unlimited-vacation/.

161. D. Sitar, "These 7 Unexpected Companies Will Actually Let You Take Sabbatical Leave," *The Penny Hoarder,* December 18, 2019, https://www.thepennyhoarder.com/make-money/career/sabbatical-leave/.

162. A. Hess, "LinkedIn: 94% of Employees Say They Would Stay at a Company Longer for This Reason—And It's Not a Raise," *CNBC,* February 27, 2019, https://www.cnbc.com/2019/02/27/94percent-of-employees-would-stay-at-a-company-for-this-one-reason.html.

163. L. Freifeld, "2019 Industry Training Report," *Training Magazine,* 2019, https://trainingmag.com/trgmag-article/2019-training-industry-report/.

164. M. E. Seligman, *Flourish* (New York: Free Press, 2011).

165. B. L. Fredrickson and M. F. Losada, "Positive Affect in the Complex Dynamics of Human Flourishing," *American Psychologist,* 2005, pp. 678–686.

166. See K. Redelinghuys, S. Rothmann, and E. Botha, "Workplace Flourishing: Measurement, Antecedents and Outcomes," *SA Journal of Industrial Psychology*, Vol. 45, No. 1 (2019), pp. 1–11. Also see K. Redelinghuys, S. Rothmann, and E. Botha, "Flourishing-At-Work: The Role of Positive Organizational Practices," *Psychological Reports*, Vol. 122, No. 2 (2019), pp. 609–631.

167. P. Brussard, "Workplace Stress Has Reached Near-Epidemic Levels. These 4 Tips Can Keep You Sane," *CNBC,* May 31, 2019, https://www.cnbc.com/2019/05/31/workplace-stress-is-reaching-epidemic-levels-4-tips-to-keep-you-sane.html.

168. P. Brussard, "Workplace Stress Has Reached Near-Epidemic Levels. These 4 tips Can Keep You Same," *CNBC,* May 31, 2019, https://www.cnbc.com/2019/05/31/workplace-stress-is-reaching-epidemic-levels-4-tips-to-keep-you-sane.html.

169. D. Ganegoda and P. Bordia, "I Can Be Happy for You, But Not All The Time: A Contingency Model of Envy and Positive Empathy in the Workplace," *Journal of Applied Psychology*, Vol. 104, No. 6 (2019), p. 776.

170. K. Sun, "How to Create a Culture of Gratitude in the Workplace," *Charney & Associates,* https://nscharney.com/how-to-create-a-culture-of-gratitude-in-the-workplace/(accessed May 14, 2020).

171. M. Robbins, "Why Employees Need Both Recognition and Appreciation," *Harvard Business Review,* November 12, 2019, https://hbr.org.

172. H. Lee, J. Bradburn, R. Johnson, S. Lin, and C. Chang, "The Benefits of Receiving Gratitude for Helpers: A Daily Investigation of Proactive and Reactive Helping at Work," *Journal of Applied Psychology,* Vol. 104, No. 2 (2019), pp. 197–213. Also see M. Patil, S. Biswas, and R. Kaur, "Does Gratitude Impact Employee Morale in the Workplace?" *Journal of Applied Management–Jidnyasa,* Vol. 10, No. 2 (2018), pp. 21–36.

173. J. Baldoni, "Gratitude: A Lesson in Two Parts," *Forbes,* April 4, 2018, https://www.forbes.com/sites/johnbaldoni/2018/04/04/gratitude-a-lesson-in-two-parts/#421cb7784414.

174. C. Albert-Deitch, "These Tech Companies Want to Help You Reopen Your Office Safely," *Inc,* May 11, 2020, https://www.inc.com/cameron-albert-deitch/reopening-software-health-safety-maptician-salesforce-gensler.html.

175. L. Hirsch, "Business Appreciation: Adding Gratitude to Company Culture in 2020," *Winstead,* January 21, 2020, https://www.winstead-businessdivorce.com/2020/01/business-appreciation-adding-gratitude-to-company-culture-in-2020/.

176. J. Steinfeld, "5 Ways to Show Gratitude at Work," *Inc,* June 8, 2017, https://www.inc.com/jay-steinfeld/5-ways-gratitude-improves-your-bottom-line.html.

177. D. DeSteno, "How to Cultivate Gratitude, Compassion, and Pride on Your Team," *Harvard Business Review,* February 20, 2018, https://hbr.org.

178. S. Jared, "A Witness for Gratitude," *The Well,* November 26, 2019, https://thewell.unc.edu/2019/11/26/a-witness-for-gratitude/.

179. "Cheers for Peers," *UC Davis Human Resources,* https://hr.ucdavis.edu/departments/worklife-wellness/events/cheers-peers (accessed May 13, 2020).

180. N. Jha, P. Sareen, and R. Potnuru, "Employee Engagement for Millennials: Considering Technology as an Enabler," *Development and Learning in Organizations: An International Journal,* January 2019, pp. 9–11.

181. N. Beheshti, "Don't Underestimate the Impact (and Business Value) of a Simple 'Thank You' Note," *Forbes,* November 15, 2019, https://www.forbes.com/sites/nazbeheshti/2019/11/15/dont-underestimate-the-impact-and-business-value-of-a-simple-thank-you-note/#7bbb1b753672.

182. J. Baldoni, "Gratitude: A Lesson in Two Parts," *Forbes,* April 4, 2018, www.forbes.com/sites/johnbaldoni/2018/04/04/gratitude-a-lesson-in-two-parts/#46bfa7724414.

183. F. Reh, "How to Give Positive Feedback," *The Balance Careers,* October 15, 2018, https://www.thebalancecareers.com/giving-positive-feedback-2275335.

184. G. Tredgold, "Don't Make This Common Mistake about Giving Praise," *Inc.,* February 16, 2018, https://www.inc.com/gordon-tredgold/the-thing-that-many-people-get-wrong-about-giving-praise.html.

185. T. Manning, "The Boldest and Best Leaders Lead with Heart," *Bold Business,* February 22, 2019, https://www.boldbusiness.com/human-achievement/boldest-best-leaders-lead-with-heart/.

186. J. Meister, "Survey: What Employees Want Most from Their Workspaces," *Harvard Business Review Digital Articles,* August 26, 2019, https://hbr.org/2019/08/survey-what-employees-want-most-from-their-workspaces.

187. T. Bradberry, "9 Bad Manager Mistakes That Make Good People Quit," *The Ladders,* February 13, 2020, https://www.theladders.com/career-advice/9-bad-manager-mistakes-make-good-people-quit.

188. M. Abbajay, "What to Do When You Have a Bad Boss," *Harvard Business Review*, September 7, 2018, https://hbr.org/2018/09/what-to-do-when-you-have-a-bad-boss.

189. M. Abbajay, "What to Do When You Have a Bad Boss," *Harvard Business Review*, September 7, 2018, https://hbr.org/2018/09/what-to-do-when-you-have-a-bad-boss, https://hbr.org/2018/09/what-to-do-when-you-have-a-bad-boss.

190. S. Achor, A. Reece, G. Kellerman, and A. Robichaux, "9 Out of 10 People Are Willing to Earn Less Money to Do More-Meaningful Work," *Harvard Business Review,* November 6, 2018, https://hbr.or.

191. "The 25 Most Meaningful Jobs That Pay Well," *Forbes,* accessed April 24, 2018, https://www.forbes.com/pictures/efkk45elhld/the-25-most-meaningful-jobs-that-pay-well-2/#52fb6a264e55.

192. V. E. Frankl, *Man's Search for Meaning* (New York: Pocket Books, 1959).

193. L. Garrad and T. Premuzic, "How to Make Work More Meaningful for Your Team," *Harvard Business Review,* August 9, 2017, https://hbr.org/2017/08/how-to-make-work-more-meaningful-for-your-team.

194. M. E. Seligman, *Flourish* (New York: Free Press, 2011).

195. L. Schumer, "Why Following Your Passions Is Good for You (and How to Get Started)," *The New York Times*, October 3, 2018, Section A, p. 3.

196. M. Schwantes, "The Traditional Job Interview Is Dead. Here's What Top Companies Are Doing Instead," *Inc.,* January 21, 2019, https://www.inc.com/marcel-schwantes/end-frustration-of-interviewing-job-candidates-with-5-simple-methods.html.

197. M. E. Seligman, *Flourish* (New York: Free Press, 2011).

198. J. McLaren, "Making This One Thing Part of Your Company Culture Will Boost Employee Engagement and Retention," *LinkedIn,* July 30, 2018, https://business.linkedin.com/talent-solutions/blog/company-culture/2018/companies-volunteering-culture.

199. J. Porter, "How to Move from Self-Awareness to Self-Improvement," *Harvard Business Review*, November 2019, pp. 37–38.

200. "Productivity Stop Checking Off Easy To-Dos," *Harvard Business Review*, November-December 2017, p. 24.

201. B. Wigert and S. Agrawal, "Employee Burnout, Part 1: The 5 Main Causes," *Gallup*, July 12, 2018, https://www.gallup.com/workplace/237059/employee-burnout-part-main-causes.aspx.

202. E. Saunders, "Working Parents, Give Yourself Permission to Recharge," *Harvard Business Review Digital Articles*, February 2020, pp. 1–5. Also see https://www.healthline.com/health/how-to-recharge#overview.

203. C. Jewett and L. Szabo, "True Toll of COVID-19 on U.S. Health Care Workers Unknown," *Kaiser Health News*, April 15, 2020, https://khn.org/news/true-toll-of-covid-19-on-u-s-health-care-workers-unknown/.

204. W. Eadie, "Navigating Nurse Burnout in Response to COVID-19," *MedCityNews*, April 2020, https://medcitynews.com/2020/04/navigating-nurse-burnout-in-response-to-covid-19/.

205. K. Wells, "New York Is Offering Nurses Up to $7k a Week. Michigan Is Offering Way Less," *Michigan Radio*, April 8, 2020, https://www.michiganradio.org/post/new-york-offering-nurses-7k-week-michigan-offering-way-less.

206. B. Mann, "Nurses Left Vulnerable to COVID-19: 'We're Not Martyrs Sacrificing Our Lives,'" *NPR*, May 2, 2020, https://www.npr.org/2020/05/02/848997142/nurses-left-vulnerable-to-covid-19-we-re-not-martyrs-sacrificing-our-lives.

207. R. Parry, "Exclusive: 'We Wouldn't Send Our Soldiers into Biological Warfare without Gas Masks.' Illinois Nurse Sobs after Quitting Her Job because Hospital Didn't Have Enough Masks, as She Demands More Protection for Medical Workers," *Daily Mail*, April 2, 2020, https://www.dailymail.co.uk/news/article-8180255/Nurse-sobs-quitting-hospital-didnt-PPE.html.

208. T. Gill, "Arkansas Plans to Pay Nurses Up to $2,000 Per Month During Pandemic," *Fayetteville Flyer*, March 27, 2020, https://www.fayettevilleflyer.com/2020/03/27/arkansas-to-pay-nurses-up-to-2000-per-month-during-pandemic/.

209. K. Wells, "New York Is Offering Nurses Up to $7k A Week. Michigan Is Offering Way Less," *Michigan Radio*, April 8, 2020, https://www.michiganradio.org/post/new-york-offering-nurses-7k-week-michigan-offering-way-less.

210. J. Jung, H. Freger, and A. Myers, "ICU Nurse Talks How Covid-19 Has Changed Her Life," *ABC News*, April 18, 2020, https://abcnews.go.com/Health/icu-nurse-life-changed-battle-zone/story?id=70207389.

211. D. Cuellar, "Fatigue Setting In for Nurses on Front Lines of COVID-19 Outbreak," *ABC6 Action News*, April 14, 2020, https://6abc.com/crozer-chester-medical-center-covid19-nurses-coronavirus-tips/6101243/.

212. K. Shamus, "Tales from the Front Lines: Health Care Workers Share Coronavirus Fears and Triumphs," *Detroit Free Press*, April 5, 2020, https://www.freep.com/story/news/local/michigan/2020/04/05/coronavirus-covid-19-front-lines-nurses-doctors-michigan/2943297001/.

213. K. Shamus, "Tales from the Front Lines: Health Care Workers Share Coronavirus Fears and Triumphs," *Detroit Free Press*, April 5, 2020, https://www.freep.com/story/news/local/michigan/2020/04/05/coronavirus-covid-19-front-lines-nurses-doctors-michigan/2943297001/.

214. K. Shamus, "Tales from the Front Lines: Health Care Workers Share Coronavirus Fears and Triumphs," *Detroit Free Press*, April 5, 2020, https://www.freep.com/story/news/local/michigan/2020/04/05/coronavirus-covid-19-front-lines-nurses-doctors-michigan/2943297001/.

215. D. Cuellar, "Fatigue Setting In for Nurses on Front Lines of COVID-19 Outbreak," *ABC6 Action News*, April 14, 2020, https://6abc.com/crozer-chester-medical-center-covid19-nurses-coronavirus-tips/6101243/.

216. L. Painter, "Mental, Physical Risks Pose Challenges for Medical Workers amid COVID-19 Crisis," *WWMT*, April 27, 2020, https://wwmt.com/features/first-42/mental-physical-risks-pose-challenges-for-medical-workers-amid-covid-19-crisis.

217. K. Shamus, "Tales from the Front Lines: Health Care Workers Share Coronavirus Fears and Triumphs," *Detroit Free Press*, April 5, 2020, https://www.freep.com/story/news/local/michigan/2020/04/05/coronavirus-covid-19-front-lines-nurses-doctors-michigan/2943297001/.

218. "Wellness Programs," *Healthcare.gov*, www.healthcare.gov/glossary/wellness-programs/ (accessed April 23, 2018).

219. J. Appleby, "How Well Do Workplace Wellness Programs Work?" *NPR*, April 16, 2019, https://www.npr.org/sections/health-shots/2019/04/16/713902890/how-well-do-workplace-wellness-programs-work.

220. "Wellness Programs," *The Workplace Solution*, https://www.theworkplacesolution.com/wps-solutions/wellness-programs/ (accessed May 13, 2020).

221. "Workplace Health Glossary," *Centers for Disease Control and Prevention*, www.cdc.gov/workplacehealthpromotion/tools-resources/glossary/glossary.html (accessed April 23, 2018).

222. S. Wadyka, "Are Workplace Wellness Programs a Privacy Problem?" *Consumer Reports*, January 16, 2020, https://www.consumerreports.org/health-privacy/are-workplace-wellness-programs-a-privacy-problem/.

223. M. Torres, "Everyone Cheats on Fitness Trackers. But Who's Really Being Cheated?" *Huffpost*, November 20, 2019, https://www.huffpost.com/entry/activity-tracker-hack-employee-discount_l_5dd2cfbce4b02947481bc860.

224. V. Sandercock and J. Andrade, "Evaluation of Worksite Wellness Nutrition and Physical Activity Programs and Their Subsequent Impact on Participants' Body Composition," *Journal of Obesity*, December 2018, pp. 1–14.

CHAPTER 13

1. "Ways to Deal with Team Conflict Effectively," *Sandler Blog*, October 18, 2018, https://www.sandler.com/blog/professional-development-blog/ways-to-deal-with-team-conflict-effectively/. Also see Forbes Coaches Council, "11 Ways You Can Better Resolve Conflicts," *Forbes*, November 14, 2017, https://www.forbes.com/sites/forbescoachescouncil/2017/11/14/11-ways-you-can-better-handle-conflict-resolution/#65f142202854; E. Aguilar, " Managing Conflict in School Leadership Teams," *Edutopia*, March 22, 2016, https://www.edutopia.org/blog/managing-conflict-school-leadership-teams-elena-aguilar; T. Bradberry, "6 Ways Nice People Can Master Conflict," *Inc.*, April 20, 2017, https://www.inc.com/travis-bradberry/6-ways-nice-people-can-master-conflict.html?cid=search.

2. T. A. O'Neill, M. J. W. McLarnon, G. C. Hoffart, H. J. R. Woodley, and N. J. Allen, "The Structure and Function of Team Conflict State Profiles," *Journal of Management*, April 2018, pp. 811–836. Also see M. A. Maltarich, M. Kukenberger, G. Reilly, and J. Mathieu, "Conflict in Teams: Modeling Early and Late Conflict States and the Interactive Effects of Conflict Processes," *Group & Organization Management*, December 2018, pp. 6–37; T. A. O'Neill and M. J. W. McLarnon, "Optimizing Team Conflict Dynamics for High Performance Teamwork," *Human Resource Management Review*, December 2018, pp. 378–394.

3. P. F. Drucker, "The Coming of the New Organization," *Harvard Business Review*, January–February 1988, pp. 45–53.

4. A. Stansell, "The Next Generation of Talent: Where Gen Z Wants to Work," *Glassdoor*, February 20, 2019, https://www.glassdoor.com/research/gen-z-workers/.

5. B. Reiners, "Culture Kings: 25 Company Culture Examples to Get You Inspired," *Built In*, January 22, 2020, https://builtin.com/company-culture/company-culture-examples.

6. J. Diehl and D. Witt, "Work Team Training and Performance Goals," *Training*, July/August 2017, pp. 20–23.

7. "Inside Out Culture," *Xero*, https://www.xero.com/us/about/investors/financial-info/annual-report-2018/inside-out-culture/ (accessed April 10, 2020).

8. B. Atherton, "How Xero's Culture Enables Engineers to Do the Best Work of Their Lives," *Xero Blog*, https://www.xero.com/blog/2018/04/xero-culture-best-work/ (accessed April 10, 2020).

9. This definition is based in part on one found in D. Horton Smith, "A Parsimonious Definition of 'Group': Toward Conceptual Clarity and Scientific Utility," *Sociological Inquiry,* Spring 1967, pp. 141–167.

10. J. R. Katzenbach and D. K. Smith, *The Wisdom of Teams: Creating the High- Performance Organization* (Boston: Harvard Business School Press, 1993), p. 45.

11. M. Nevins, "Why 'Swim Lanes' Won't Help Your Team," *Forbes,* March 10, 2020, https://www.forbes.com/sites/hillennevins/2020/03/10/why-swim-lanes-wont-help-your-team/#38350af012ea.

12. See "H2M's Commitment to Professional Development," *H2M,* July 25, 2019, https://www.h2m.com/news/h2ms-commitment-to-professional-development/; L. Le Phan, "Top 10 Companies in the U.S with Awesome Teamwork Culture," *kununu,* July 30, 2019, https://transparency.kununu.com/the-top-10-companies-in-the-u-s-with-awesome-teamwork-culture/; corporate website, "About," *H2M,* https://www.h2m.com/about/#tab-charitable-giving (accessed April 10, 2020).

13. R. Cross, N. Nohria, and A. Parker, "Six Myths about Informal Networks—and How to Overcome Them," *MIT Sloan Management Review,* Spring 2002, pp. 67–75; C. Shriky, "Watching the Patterns Emerge," *Harvard Business Review,* February 2004, pp. 34–35.

14. C. Fisher, "How Informal Groups Emerge in the Workplace," *The Nest,* https://woman.thenest.com/informal-groups-emerge-workplace-20758.html (accessed April 11, 2020); R. Cross and L. Prusack, "The People Who Make Organizations Go—or Stop," *Harvard Business Review,* June 2002, pp. 104–112; R. McDermott and D. Archibald, "Harnessing Your Staff's Informal Networks," *Harvard Business Review,* March 2010, pp. 82–89.

15. M. Bennett, "The Benefits of Informal Social Networks in the Workplace," *The Telegraph,* March 10, 2017, https://www.telegraph.co.uk/business/ready-and-enabled/benefits-of-informal-social-networks/.

16. A. A. Abbas, "Influence of Informal Groups on Productivity: A Case Study on Philadelphia Pharmaceuticals Company," *International Journal of Academic Research in Business and Social Sciences,* August 2018, pp. 421–435; "Getting across Cross-Functional Teams: Case Study Based in the Public Sector," *Human Resource Management International Digest,* March 2019, pp. 31–33.

17. "Getting across Cross-Functional Teams: Case Study Based in the Public Sector," *Human Resource Management International Digest,* March 2019, pp. 31–33.

18. C. Field, "How T-Mobile's Team of Experts Reinvented Customer Support," *Forbes,* November 14, 2019, https://www.forbes.com/sites/tmobile/2019/11/14/how-t-mobiles-team-of-experts-reinvented-customer-support/#2f8ff4c73700; M. Dixon, "Reinventing Customer Service," *Harvard Business Review,* November-December 2018, https://hbr.org/2018/11/reinventing-customer-service.

19. M. Dixon, "Reinventing Customer Service," *Harvard Business Review,* November-December 2018, https://hbr.org/2018/11/reinventing-customer-service; R. Cheng, "How T-Mobile Rebuilt Its Customer Service to Be Less Sucky and More about You," *C-Net,* August 15, 2018, https://www.cnet.com/news/t-mobile-rebuilds-customer-service-with-you-and-happiness-in-mind-uncarrier/.

20. R. Jacobson, S. Jautelat, J. Raabe, and L. Wienke, "Bringing Agile to Customer Care," *McKinsey & Company,* February 2019, https://www.mckinsey.com/business-functions/operations/our-insights/bringing-agile-to-customer-care; M. Dixon, "Reinventing Customer Service," *Harvard Business Review,* November-December 2018, https://hbr.org/2018/11/reinventing-customer-service.

21. M. Dixon, T. McKenna, and G. de la O, "Supporting Customer Service through the Coronavirus Crisis," *Harvard Business Review,* April 8, 2020, https://hbr.org/2020/04/supporting-customer-service-through-the-coronavirus-crisis.

22. C. Field, "How T-Mobile's Team of Experts Reinvented Customer Support," *Forbes,* November 14, 2019, https://www.forbes.com/sites/tmobile/2019/11/14/how-t-mobiles-team-of-experts-reinvented-customer-support/#2f8ff4c73700; M. Dixon, "Reinventing Customer Service," *Harvard Business Review,* November-December 2018, https://hbr.org/2018/11/reinventing-customer-service.

23. "T-Mobile's Latest Un-carrier Move: Real People, Not Robots Introducing T-Mobile Team of Experts," *T-Mobile,* August 15, 2018, https://www.t-mobile.com/news/introducing-tex.

24. A. Wagner, "T-Mobile Named No. 1 in Customer Service Satisfaction by Nielsen," *Tmo News,* February 1, 2017, https://www.tmonews.com/2017/02/t-mobile-no-1-customer-service-satisfaction-nielsen/.

25. "T -Mobile & Metro by T-Mobile Nab J.D. Power's Top Spots for Wireless Customer Care," *T-Mobile,* February 6, 2020, https://www.t-mobile.com/news/jdp-care-jan-2020.

26. L. MacDonald, "What Is a Self-Managed Team," *Chron,* March 7, 2019, https://smallbusiness.chron.com/selfmanaged-team-18236.html.

27. R. Starr, "What Are Self-Managed Teams and How Can They Serve Your Business?" *Small Business Trends,* November 8, 2018, https://smallbiztrends.com/2018/11/self-managed-teams.html.

28. Based on three meta-analyses covering 70 studies. See P. S. Goodman, R. Devadas, and T. L. Griffith Hughson, "Groups and Productivity: Analyzing the Effectiveness of Self-Managed Teams," in J. P. Campbell, R. J. Campbell, and Associates (eds.), *Productivity in Organizations* (San Francisco: Jossey-Bass, 1998), pp. 295–327; S. Kauffeld, "Self-Directed Work Groups and Team Competence," *Journal of Occupational and Organizational Psychology,* March 2006, pp. 1–21.

29. J. Hu, Z. Zhang, K. Jiang, W. Chen, "Getting Ahead, Getting Along, and Getting Prosocial: Examining Extraversion Facets, Peer Reactions, and Leadership Emergence," *Journal of Applied Technology,* November 2019, pp. 1369–1386. Also see J. Lim, Navigating the Pathway to Leader Emergence in Self-Managed Work Groups over Time: Should I Self-Promote and Try to Emerge Initially as a Leader?" *Sex Roles,* April 2019, pp. 489–502.

30. "Remote Work Statistics: Shifting Norms and Expectations," *Flex Jobs,* February 13, 2020, https://www.flexjobs.com/blog/post/remote-work-statistics/.

31. "The IWG Global Workplace Survey," *International Workplace Group,* March 2019, http://assets.regus.com/pdfs/iwg-workplace-survey/iwg-workplace-survey-2019.pdf.

32. C. Reddy, "Virtual Teams: Meaning, Types, Advantages & Disadvantages," *Wisestep,* https://content.wisestep.com/virtual-teams-meaning-types-advantages-disadvantages/ (accessed April 11, 2020); L. Gilson, M. Maynard, N. Young, M. Varianien, and M. Hakonen, "Virtual Teams Research: 10 Years, 10 Themes, and 10 Opportunities," *Journal of Management,* July 2015, pp. 1313–1337.

33. E. E. Makarius and B. Z. Larson, "Changing the Perspective of Virtual Work: Building Virtual Intelligence at the Individual Level," *Academy of Management Perspectives,* May 2017, pp. 159–178.

34. "Challenges to Managing Virtual Teams and How to Overcome Them," *Harvard Extension School,* https://www.extension.harvard.edu/professional-development/blog/challenges-managing-virtual-teams-and-how-overcome-them (accessed April 11, 2020).

35. E. E. Makarius and B. Z. Larson, "Changing the Perspective of Virtual Work: Building Virtual Intelligence at the Individual Level," *Academy of Management Review,* March 2017, pp. 159–178.

36. "10 Common Virtual Team Challenges," *EZ Talks,* https://www.ez-talks.com/telecommuting/virtual-team-challenge.html (accessed April 11, 2020). Also see J. E. Hoch and S. W. Kozlowski, "Leading Virtual Teams: Hierarchical Leadership, Structural Supports, and Shared Team Leadership," *Journal of Applied Psychology,* Vol. 99 2012, pp. 1–13.

37. "What Are the Challenges of Working in Virtual Teams?" *Experteer,* July 20, 2018, https://us.experteer.com/magazine/what-are-the-challenges-of-working-in-virtual-teams/. Also see "How-to Guide: How to Manage Team Time Zone Challenges," *1 Million for Work Flexibility,* https://www.workflexibility.org/how-to-manage-team-time-zone-challenges/ (accessed April 11, 2020).

38. W. Vanderbloemen, "Best Practices on Running Virtual Teams from Founder of Company with 1,000 Remote Employees," *Forbes,* March 22, 2020, https://www.forbes.com/sites/williamvanderbloemen/2020/03/20/leading-teams-virtually/#71af03bd5b8b.

39. S. McLaren, "4 Ways You Can Give Your Remote Workforce a Sense of Togetherness," *LinkedIn,* March 16, 2020, https://business.linkedin

.com/talent-solutions/blog/work-flexibility/2020/ways-you-can-make-remote-workers-feel-included.

40. A. Ravichandran, "Trust: The Hidden Dividend of Working from Home," *Forbes*, April 6, 2020, https://www.forbes.com/sites/forbestechcouncil/2020/04/06/trust-the-hidden-dividend-of-working-from-home/#2e3ba1172d92. Also see E. E. Makarius and B. Z. Larson, "Changing the Perspective of Virtual Work: Building Virtual Intelligence at the Individual Level," *Academy of Management Review*, May 2017, pp. 159–178; C. Tate, "5 Ways to Make Working Remotely Actually Work," *Fast Company*, July 28, 2015, https://www.fastcompany.com/3048953/5-ways-to-make-working-remotely-actually-work.

41. W. Vanderbloemen, "Best Practices on Running Virtual Teams from Founder of Company with 1,000 Remote Employees," *Forbes*, March 22, 2020, https://www.forbes.com/sites/williamvanderbloemen/2020/03/20/leading-teams-virtually/#71af03bd5b8b. Also see J. Schiefelbein, "Smart Tips for Working with Your Virtual Teams," *Entrepreneur*, May 24, 2017, https://www.entrepreneur.com/article/292734; M. J. W. McLarnon et al., "Global Virtual Team Communication, Coordination, and Performance across Three Peer Feedback Strategies," *Canadian Journal of Behavioural Science*, October 2019, pp. 207–218.

42. P. La Gioia, " Top 9 Characteristics of Successful Remote Workers," *Thrive Global*, February 18, 2020, https://thriveglobal.com/stories/top-9-characteristics-of-successful-remote-workers/.

43. "What Is Remote Work & How to Find It," *Hub Staff*, https://hubstaff.com/remote_work (accessed April 11, 2020).

44. S. Hill and K. Bartol, "Three Behaviors for High-Performing Virtual Teams," *AACSB*, January 2, 2018, https://bized.aacsb.edu/articles/2018/january/three-behaviors-for-high-performing-virtual-teams.

45. N. S. Maduka, H. Edwards, D. Greenwood, A. Osborne, and S. O. Babatunde, "Analysis of Competencies for Effective Virtual Team Leadership in Building Successful Organisations," *Benchmarking: An International Journal*, March 2018, pp. 696–712.

46. R. Boyd, "Virtual Meetings versus Face to Face Meetings: Which to Choose?" *Bright Hub*, https://www.brighthubpm.com/resource-management/123148-opting-for-a-face-to-face-meeting-with-virtual-teams/ (accessed April 11, 2020). Also see E. E. Makarius and B. Z. Larson, "Changing the Perspective of Virtual Work: Building Virtual Intelligence at the Individual Level," *Academy of Management Review*, May 2017, pp. 159–178.

47. E. Martinez-Moreno, A. Zornoza, P. Gonzalez-Navarro, and L. F. Thompson, "Investigating Face-to-Face and Virtual Teamwork over Time: When Does Early Task Conflict Trigger Relationship Conflict?" *Group Dynamics: Theory, Research, and Practice*, September 2012, pp. 159–171.

48. S. Kahan, "Five Keys to Building a High-Performing Virtual Team," *Forbes*, July 25, 2019, https://www.forbes.com/sites/forbescommunicationscouncil/2019/07/25/five-keys-to-building-a-high-performing-virtual-team/#754dca73256a. Also see M. J. W. McLarnon et al., "Global Virtual Team Communication, Coordination, and Performance Across Three Peer Feedback Strategies," *Canadian Journal of Behavioural Science*, October 2019, pp. 207–218; N. S. Maduka, H. Edwards, D. Greenwood, A. Osborne, and S. O. Babatunde, "Analysis of Competencies for Effective Virtual Team Leadership in Building Successful Organisations," *Benchmarking: An International Journal*, March 2018, pp. 696–712.

49. C. Breuer, "Trust in Teams: A Taxonomy of Perceived Trustworthiness Factors and Risk-Taking Behaviors in Face-to-Face and Virtual Teams," *Human Relations*, Vol. 73 2020, pp. 3–34. Also see K. Jaakson, A. Reino, and P. B. McClenaghan, "The Space between—Linking Trust with Individual and Team Performance in Virtual Teams," *Team Performance Management: An International Journal*, October 2018, pp. 30–46.

50. B. W. Tuckman, "Developmental Sequence in Small Groups," *Psychological Bulletin*, June 1965, pp. 384–399; B. W. Tuckman and M.A.C. Jensen, "Stages of Small-Group Development Revisited," *Group & Organization Studies*, December 1977, pp. 419–427.

51. M. Kiweewa, D. Gilbride, M. Luke, and T. Clingerman, "Tracking Growth Factors in Experiential Training Groups through Tuckman's Conceptual Model," *The Journal for Specialists in Group Work*, July 2018, pp. 274–296.

52. C. Lin and J. Shih, "Analysing Group Dynamics of a Digital Game–Based Adventure Education Course," *Education Technology & Society*, 2018, pp. 51–63.

53. D. Meinert, "Team Troubles," *HRMagazine*, February 2017, p. 18.

54. J.-L. Farh, C. Lee, and C. I. C. Farh, "Task Conflict and Team Creativity: A Question of How Much and When," *Journal of Applied Psychology* 95, no. 6 (2010), pp. 1173–1180; B. R. Smyth, "Successfully Navigate the Four Stages of Team Development," *SkillPath*, August 22, 2019, https://skillpath.com/blog/successfully-navigate-the-four-stages-of-team-development.

55. J. Lim, "Navigating the Pathway to Leader Emergence in Self-Managed Work Groups over Time: Should I Self-Promote and Try to Emerge Initially as a Leader?" *Sex Roles*, April 2019, pp. 489–502.

56. M. Kankousky, "6 Ways to Help New Employees Mesh Well with Their Team," *Insperity*, https://www.insperity.com/blog/6-ways-help-new-employees-mesh-well-team/ (accessed April 12, 2020).

57. C. Lin and J. Shih, "Analysing Group Dynamics of a Digital Game–Based Adventure Education Course," *Education Technology & Society*, October 2018, pp. 51–63.

58. P. Alleyne, R. Haniffa, and M. Hudaib, "Does Group Cohesion Moderate Auditors' Whistleblowing Intentions?" *Journal of International Accounting, Auditing and Taxation*, March 2019, pp. 69–90; Y. Zhang, "Functional Diversity and Group Creativity: The Role of Group Longevity," *Journal of Applied Behavioral Science*, March 2016, pp. 97–123.

59. J. M. Kiweewa, D. Gilbride, M. Luke, and T. Clingerman, "Tracking Growth Factors in Experiential Training Groups through Tuckman's Conceptual Model," *The Journal for Specialists in Group Work*, July 2018, pp. 274–296. Also see T. Hall, "Does Cohesion Positively Correlate to Performance in All Stages of a Group's Life Cycle," *Journal of Organizational Culture, Communications and Conflict*, January 2015, pp. 58–69.

60. M. S. Cole, H. Bruch, and B. Vogel, "Energy at Work: A Measurement Validation and Linkage to Unit Effectiveness," *Journal of Organizational Behavior*, May 2012, pp. 445–467.

61. For an application, see S. Kwak, "'Windows of Opportunity,' Revenue Volatility, and Policy Punctuations: Testing a Model of Policy Change in the American States," *Policy Studies Journal*, May 2017, pp. 265–288.

62. A. Sandford, "Brexit Timeline 2016–2020: Key Events in the UK's Path from Referendum to EU Exit," *Euro News*, January 30, 2020, https://www.euronews.com/2020/01/30/brexit-timeline-2016-2020-key-events-in-the-uk-s-path-from-referendum-to-eu-exit. Also see T. Edgington, "Brexit: What Is the Transition Period?" *BBC News*, January 31, 2020, https://www.bbc.com/news/uk-politics-50838994.

63. Based on J. E. Mathieu, J. R. Hollenbeck, D. van Knippenberg, and D. R. Ilgen, "A Century of Work Teams," *Journal of Applied Psychology*, March 2017, pp. 452–467. Also see D. D. Warrick, "What Leaders Can Learn about Teamwork and Developing High Performance Teams from Organizations Development Practitioners," *Performance Improvement*, March 2016, pp. 13–21; T. Daniel, B. Gleeson, "15 Characteristics of High-Performance Teams," *Forbes*, March 14, 2019, https://www.forbes.com/sites/brentgleeson/2019/03/14/15-characteristics-of-high-performance-teams/#50ac4b906ae0; D. Roach, "8 Attributes of High-Performance Teams," *Like a Team*, https://likeateam.com/8-attributes-of-high-performance-teams/ (accessed April 13, 2020).

64. For a review of related research, see J. E. Mathieu, J. R. Hollenbeck, D. van Knippenberg, and D. R. Ilgen, "A Century of Work Teams," *Journal of Applied Psychology*, March 2017, pp. 452–467; N. D. Oldfield, "Building a High-Performance Team in Three Steps," *Forbes*, January 23, 2020, https://www.forbes.com/sites/forbescoachescouncil/2020/01/23/building-a-high-performance-team-in-three-steps/#4b94468e5d55.

65. M. Smirnova, V. A. Rebiazina, and S. G. Khomich, "When Does Innovation Collaboration Pay Off? The Role of Relational Learning and the Timing of Collaboration," *Industrial Marketing Management*, October 2018, pp. 126–137. Also see K. Löhr, M. Weinhardt, F. Graef, and S. Sieber, "Enhancing Communication and Collaboration in Collaborative Projects through Conflict Prevention and Management Systems," *Organizational Dynamics*, October 2018, pp. 259–264.

66. J. Hu and R. Liden, "Making a Difference in the Teamwork: Linking Team Prosocial Motivation to Team Processes and Effectiveness," *Academy of Management Journal*, August 2015, pp. 1102–1127.

67. J. Hüffmeier, M. Filusch, J. Mazei, G. Hertel, A. Mojzisch, and S. Krumm, "On the Boundary Conditions of Effort Losses and Effort Gains in Action Teams," *Journal of Applied Psychology,* December 2017, pp. 1673–1685.

68. "Realigning Incentives along the Value Chain to Reform Health Care," *Harvard Business Review,* May 2020.

69. L. Handrick, "Top 25 Employee Incentive Programs from the Pros," *Fit Small Business,* July 18, 2018; see "About Us," *BubbleBum,* https://www.bubblebum.co/us/about-us/ (accessed April 13, 2020).

70. C. Duhigg, "What Google Learned from Its Quest to Build the Perfect Team," *The New York Times Magazine,* February 25, 2016, http://www.nytimes.com/2016/02/28/magazine/what-google-learned-from-its-quest-to-build-the-perfect-team.html?_r=0.

71. T. A. O'Neill, M. J. W. McLarnon, G. Hoffart, D. Onen, and W. Rosehart, "The Multilevel Nomological Net of Team Conflict Profiles," *International Journal of Conflict Management,* February 2018, pp. 24–46. Also see C. Sime, "What Makes a Successful Team?" *Forbes,* March 26, 2019, https://www.forbes.com/sites/carleysime/2019/03/26/what-makes-a-successful-team/#5b83d2da2348; J. Harvey, K. J. Johnson, K. S. Roloff, and A. C. Edmondson, "From Orientation to Behavior: The Interplay between Learning Orientation, Open-Mindedness, and Psychological Safety in Team Learning," *Human Relations,* January 2019, pp. 1726–1751.

72. S. Shellenbarger, "The Invisible Walls at Work," *The Wall Street Journal,* November 29, 2017, p. A11.

73. D. Maloney, "The Ultimate Guide to Effective Collaboration in the Workplace," *Slack,* April 16, 2019, https://slackhq.com/ultimate-guide-collaboration-in-the-workplace.

74. "Our Leadership Principles," *Amazon,* https://www.aboutamazon.com/working-at-amazon/our-leadership-principles (accessed April 13, 2010).

75. F. Gino, "Cracking the Code of Sustained Collaboration," *Harvard Business Review,* November 2019, pp. 73–81.

76. R. Brühl, J. S. Basel, and M. F. Kury, "Communication after an Integrity-Based Trust Violation: How Organizational Account Giving Affects Trust," *European Management Journal,* April 2018, pp. 161–170.

77. A. C. Costa, C. A. Fulmer, and N. R. Anderson, "Trust in Work Teams: An Integrative Review, Multilevel Model, and Future Directions," *Journal of Organizational Behavior,* February 2018, pp. 169–184. Also see B. A. De Jong, K. T. Dirks, and N. Gillespie, "Trust and Team Performance: A Meta-Analysis of Main Effects, Moderators, and Covariates," *Journal of Applied Psychology,* August 2016, pp. 1134–1150; M. J. Burtscher, B. Meyer, K. Jonas, S. Feese, and G. Troster, "A Time to Trust? The Buffering Effect of Trust and Its Temporal Variations in the Context of High-Reliability Teams," *Journal of Organizational Behavior,* November 2018, pp. 1099–1112.

78. T. Kim, J. Wang, and J. Chen, "Mutual Trust between Leader and Subordinate and Employee Outcomes," *Journal of Business Ethics*, June 2018, pp. 945–958.

79. F. X. Frei and A. Morriss, "Begin with Trust," *Harvard Business Review,* May 2020, https://hbr.org/2020/05/begin-with-trust.

80. F. X. Frei and A. Morriss, "Begin with Trust," *Harvard Business Review,* May 2020, https://hbr.org/2020/05/begin-with-trust.

81. C. Gallo, "Marriott's CEO Demonstrates Truly Authentic Leadership in a Remarkably Emotional Video," *Forbes,* March 21, 2020, https://www.forbes.com/sites/carminegallo/2020/03/21/marriotts-ceo-demonstrates-truly-authentic-leadership-in-a-remarkably-emotional-video/#229a2edf1654. Also see C. Karmin and E. Fung, "Marriott, Hotel Owners Furlough Thousands of Workers, Cut Staff," *The Wall Street Journal,* March 22, 2020, https://www.wsj.com/articles/marriott-to-furlough-thousands-of-corporate-jobs-in-u-s-and-abroad-in-response-to-travel-collapse-11584834631.

82. A. Brown, "5 Reasons Why Great Leaders Admit Their Mistakes," *Engagement Multiplier,* October 30, 2019, https://www.engagementmultiplier.com/blog/5-reasons-why-great-leaders-admit-their-mistakes/. Also see G. Llopis, "4 Reasons Great Leaders Admit Their Mistakes," *Forbes,* July 23, 2015, https://www.forbes.com/sites/glennllopis/2015/07/23/4-reasons-great-leaders-admit-their-mistakes/2/#54037f8d6038.

83. "Don't Be Afraid to Be Vulnerable: 6 Ways to Build Trust with Your Team," *Inc.com,* January 22, 2018, https://www.inc.com/young-entrepreneur-council/dont-be-afraid-to-be-vulnerable-6-ways-to-build-trust-with-your-team.html?cid=search.

84. "Don't Be Afraid to Be Vulnerable: 6 Ways to Build Trust with Your Team," *Inc.com,* January 22, 2018, https://www.inc.com/young-entrepreneur-council/dont-be-afraid-to-be-vulnerable-6-ways-to-build-trust-with-your-team.html?cid=search.

85. M. Levin, "8 Ways to Build a Culture of Trust Based on Harvard's Neuroscience Research," *Inc.com,* October 5, 2017, https://www.inc.com/marissa-levin/harvard-neuroscience-research-reveals-8-ways-to-build-a-culture-of-trust.html?cid=search.

86. D. Williams, "How to Ask for Help When You're the Boss and You're Supposed to Know Everything," *Forbes,* October 10, 2016, https://www.forbes.com/sites/davidkwilliams/2016/10/10/how-to-ask-for-help-when-youre-the-boss-and-youre-supposed-to-know-everything/#5b66c9001f0a.

87. M. Levin, "8 Ways to Build a Culture of Trust Based on Harvard's Neuroscience Research," *Inc.com,* October 5, 2017, https://www.inc.com/marissa-levin/harvard-neuroscience-research-reveals-8-ways-to-build-a-culture-of-trust.html?cid=search.

88. "The Science of Trust," *Science of People,* December 13, 2017, https://www.scienceofpeople.com/the-science-of- trust/.

89. T. L. Rapp, D. G. Bachrach, A. A. Rapp, and R. Mullins, "The Role of Team Goal Monitoring in the Curvilinear Relationship between Team Efficacy and Team Performance," *Journal of Applied Psychology,* September 2014, pp. 976–987.

90. J. Schaubroeck, S. S. K. Lam, and S. E. Cha, "Embracing Transformational Leadership: Team Values and the Impact of Leader Behavior on Team Performance," *Journal of Applied Psychology,* July 2007, pp. 1020–1030.

91. E. Bernstein, J. Bunch, N. Canner, and M. Lee, "Beyond the Holacracy Hype," *Harvard Business Review,* July–August 2016, p. 43.

92. S. H. Courtright, G. R. Thurgood, G. L. Stewart, and A. J. Pierotti, "Structural Interdependence in Teams: An Integrative Framework and Meta-Analysis," *Journal of Applied Psychology,* November 2015, pp. 1825–1846.

93. S. H. Courtright, G. R. Thurgood, G. L. Stewart, and A. J. Pierotti, "Structural Interdependence in Teams: An Integrative Framework and Meta-Analysis," *Journal of Applied Psychology,* November 2015, pp. 1825–1846.

94. J. Garrett and S. Gopalakrishna, "Sales Team Formation: The Right Team Member Helps Performance," *Industrial Marketing Management*, February 2019, pp. 13–22.

95. L. Chin, "How Interdependence in Team Task Structure Impacts Evaluations of Members' Work Contributions: Examining Resource versus Process Interdependence," *The Sociological Quarterly,* January 2018, pp. 250–278.

96. L. M. Leslie, "Diversity Initiative Effectiveness: A Typological Theory of Unintended Consequences," *Academy of Management Review,* July June 2019, pp. 538–563. Also see S. McCallaghan, L. Jackson, and M. Heyns, "Exploring Organisational Diversity Climate with Associated Antecedents and Employee Outcomes," *SA Journal of Industrial Psychology,* June 2019, https://doi.org/10.4102/sajip.v45i0.1614; N. Luanglath, M. Ali, and K. Mohannak, "Top Management Team Gender DIversity and Productivity: The Role of Board Gender Diversity," *Equality, Diversity and Inclusion: An International Journal,* January 2019, pp. 71–86.

97. J. Morgan, "The Chief People Officer of Cisco Shares Her Top Three Tips for Building High-Performing Teams," *Forbes,* June 6, 2016, http://www.forbes.com/sites/jacobmorgan/2016/04/06/the-chief-people-officer-of-cisco-shares-her-top-three-tips-for-building-high-preforming-teams/#3c3d3b1051ce.

98. J. Y. Seong, W-W. Park, D-S. Hong, and Y. Shin, "Person-Group Fit: Diversity Antecedents, Proximal Outcomes, and Performance at the Group Level," *Journal of Management,* May 2015, pp. 1184–1213. Also see S. T. Bell, S. G. Brown, and J. A. Weiss, "A Conceptual Framework for Leveraging Team Composition Decisions to Build Human Capital," *Human Resource Management Review,* December 2018, pp. 450–463; Z. Lalegani, A. N. Isfahani, A. Shahin and A. Safari, "Developing a Model

for Analyzing the Factors Influencing Interpersonal Conflict," *Management Decision*, May 2019, pp. 1127–1144.

99. L. L. Gilson, M. T. Maynard, N. C. J. Young, M. Vartiainen, and M. Hakonen, "Virtual Team Research: 10 Years, 10 Themes, and 10 Opportunities," *Journal of Management,* July 2015, pp. 1313–1337. Also see S. T. Bell, S. G. Brown, and J. A. Weiss, "A Conceptual Framework for Leveraging Team Composition Decisions to Build Human Capital," *Human Resource Management Review*, December 2018, pp. 450–463.

100. Y. Tu, Y. Hong, Y. Jiang, and W. Zhang, "Team Ability Disparity and Goal Interdependence Influence Team Members' Affective and Informational States," *Group Dynamics: Theory, Research, and Practice*, March 2020, pp. 6–25. Also see S. T. Bell, S. G. Brown, A. Colaneri, and N. Outland, "Team Composition and the ABCs of Teamwork," *American Psychologist*, May-June 2018, pp. 349–362; "Teams: Another Argument for Cognitive Diversity," *Harvard Business Review,* July–August 2017, p. 32.

101. E. R. Crawford, C. J. Reeves, G. L. Stewart, and S. L. Astrove, "To Link or Not to Link? Multiple Team Membership and Unit Performance," *Journal of Applied Psychology*, March 2019, pp. 341–356.

102. J. Chen and D. Houser, "When Are Women Willing to Lead? The Effect of Team Gender Composition and Gendered Tasks," *The Leadership Quarterly*, December 2019, https://doi.org/10.1016/j.leaqua.2019.101340.

103. C. Bicchieri and A. Funcke, "Norm Change: Trendsetters and Social Structure," *Social Research,* April 2008, pp. 1–21.

104. D. C. Feldman, "The Development and Enforcement of Group Norms," *Academy of Management Review,* January 1984, pp. 47–53.

105. A. Schecter, A. Pilny, A. Leung, M.S. Poole, and N. Contractor, "Step by Step: Capturing the Dynamics of Work Team Process through Relational Event Sequences," *Journal of Organizational Behavior*, November 2018, pp. 1163–1181. Also see T. Friehe, "Predicting Norm Enforcement: The Individual and Joint Predictive Power of Economic Preferences, Personality, and Self-control," *European Journal of Law and Economics*, February 2018, pp. 127–146.

106. D. C. Feldman, "The Development and Enforcement of Group Norms," *Academy of Management Review,* January 1984, pp. 47–53.

107. S. Baker, "How To Define Your Team's Norms (And Why It's Important)," *Forbes*, July 1, 2019, https://www.forbes.com/sites/forbeshumanresourcescouncil/2019/07/01/how-to-define-your-teams-norms-and-why-its-important/#595a3cd11000.

108. Jacob Morgan, "4 Things You Need to Know to Build a High Performing Team," *Inc.com*, April 7, 2017, https://www.inc.com/jacob-morgan/4-things-you-need-to-know-to-build-a-high-performing-team.html?cid=search.

109. S. Nawaz, "How to Create Executive Team Norms—and Make Them Stick," *Harvard Business Review*, January 15, 2018, https://hbr.org/2018/01/how-to-create-executive-team-norms-and-make-them-stick.

110. "Collaborative Team Structures: Norms," *Missouri EduSAIL,* http://www.moedu-sail.org/lessons/collaborative-team-structures-norms/ (accessed April 14, 2020).

111. S. Nawaz, "How to Create Executive Team Norms—and Make Them Stick," *Harvard Business Review,* January 15, 2018, https://hbr.org/2018/01/how-to-create-executive-team-norms-and-make-them-stick.

112. " Establish Norms for How Your Team Will Work Together," *Harvard Business Review*, May 30, 2018, https://hbr.org/tip/2018/05/establish-norms-for-how-your-team-will-work-together.

113. S. Nawaz, "How to Create Executive Team Norms—and Make Them Stick," *Harvard Business Review,* January 15, 2018, https://hbr.org/2018/01/how-to-create-executive-team-norms-and-make-them-stick.

114. S. Baker, "How to Define Your Team's Norms (And Why It's Important)," *Forbes*, July 1, 2019, https://www.forbes.com/sites/forbeshumanresourcescouncil/2019/07/01/how-to-define-your-teams-norms-and-why-its-important/#595a3cd11000.

115. See A. Schecter, A. Pilny, A. Leung, M. S. Poole, and N. Contractor, "Step by Step: Capturing the Dynamics of Work Team Process through Relational Event Sequences," *Journal of Organizational Behavior*, November 2018, pp. 1163–1181.

116. M. A. Marks, J. E. Mathieu, and S. J. Zaccaro, "A Temporally Based Framework and Taxonomy of Team Processes," *Academy of Management Review,* July 2001, pp. 356–376, p. 357.

117. J. E. Mathieu and T. L. Rapp, "Laying the Foundation for Successful Team Performance Trajectories: The Roles of Team Charters and Performance Strategies," *Journal of Applied Psychology,* January, pp. 90–103 2009, p. 92.

118. S. T. Bell, S. G. Brown, A. Colaneri, and N. Outland, "Team Composition and the ABCs of Teamwork," *American Psychologist*, May-June 2018, pp. 349–362. Also see S. H. Courtright, B. W. McCormick, S. Mistry, and J. Wang, "Quality Charters of Quality Members? A Control Theory Perspective on Team Charters and Team Performance," *Journal of Applied Psychology,* October 2017, pp. 1462–1470.

119. J. Chen, P. A. Bamberger, Y. Song, and D. R. Vashdi, "The Effects of Team Reflexivity on Psychological Well-Being in Manufacturing Teams," *Journal of Applied Psychology,* April 2018, pp. 443–462.

120. M. Yang et al., "Why and When Team Reflexivity Contributes to Team Performance: A Moderated Mediation Model," *Frontiers in Psychology*, January 2020, https://doi.org/10.3389/fpsyg.2019.03044. Also see S. Rauter, M. Weiss, and M. Hoegl, "Team Learning from Setbacks: A Study in the Context of Start-up Teams," *Journal of Organizational Behavior*, March 2018, pp. 783–795; R. Tesler, S. Mohammed, K. Hamilton, V. Mancuso, and M. McNeese, "Mirror, Mirror: Guided Storytelling and Team Reflexivity's Influence on Team Mental Models," *Small Group Research*, August, 2017, pp. 267–305; P. Rong, C. Li, and J. Xie, "Learning, Trust, and Creativity in Top Management Teams: Team Reflexivity as a Moderator," *Social Behavior and Personality: An International Journal*, May 2019, https://doi.org/10.2224/sbp.8096.

121. J. Chen, P. A. Bamberger, Y. Song, and D. R. Vashdi, "The Effects of Team Reflexivity on Psychological Well-Being in Manufacturing Teams," *Journal of Applied Psychology*, April 2018, pp. 443–462.

122. G. Guthrie, "How to Run an Incredibly Effective Post-Mortem Meeting," *Backlog Blog*, June 5, 2019, https://backlog.com/blog/run-incredibly-effective-post-mortem-meeting/.

123. M. Brunet and D. Forgues, "Investigating Collective Sensemaking of a Major Project Success," *International Journal of Managing Projects in Business*, September 2019, pp. 644–665.

124. A. N. Li, H. Liao, and B. M. Firth, "The Content of the Message Matters: The Differential Effects of Promotive and Prohibitive Team Voice on Team Productivity and Safety Performance Goals," *Journal of Applied Psychology,* August 2017, p. 1259.

125. J. Warström, "Stop Managersplaining on Video Calls and Give People a Voice," *Forbes*, April 6, 2020, https://www.forbes.com/sites/johnnywarstrom/2020/04/06/stop-managersplaining-on-video-calls-and-give-people-a-voice/#1c07a3391f20.

126. Q. Ye, D. Wang, and W. Guo, "Inclusive Leadership and Team Innovation: The Role of Team Voice and Performance Pressure," *European Management Journal*, August 2019, pp. 468–480. Also see E. N. Sherf, R. Sinha, S. Tangirala, and N. Awasty, "Centralization of Member Voice in Teams: Its Effects on Expertise Utilization and Team Performance," *Journal of Applied Psychology*, April 2018, pp. 813–827.

127. "Top 4 Causes of Conflict in the Workplace and How to Overcome It," *Xponents*, https://www.xponents.com/resources/white-pages-and-articles/top-4-causes-of-conflict (accessed April 14, 2020); E. Bernstein, "When a Co-worker Is Stressed Out," *The Wall Street Journal*, August 26, 2008, pp. D1, D2.

128. J. A. Wall Jr. and R. Robert Callister, "Conflict and Its Management," *Journal of Management* Vol. 3 (1995), p. 517.

129. L. Beachum, "CEO Fired by Company He Founded after Video Showed Him Shouting Racial Slur at Uber Driver," *The Washington Post*, February 6, 2020, https://www.washingtonpost.com/business/2020/02/06/hans-berglund-fired-uber-video/. Also see Z. Crenshaw, "Valley CEO Forced Out after Racial Slur: 'My Life Has Been Ruined,'" *ABC 15 Arizona*, February 6, 2020, https://www.abc15.com/news/region-southeast-valley/tempe/valley-ceo-forced-out-after-racial-slur-my-life-has-been-ruined.

130. Z. Crenshaw, "Valley CEO Forced Out after Racial Slur: 'My Life Has Been Ruined,'" *ABC 15 Arizona*, February 6, 2020, https://www.abc15.com/news/region-southeast-valley/tempe/valley-ceo-forced-out-after-racial-slur-my-life-has-been-ruined.

131. D. Tjosvold, *Learning to Manage Conflict: Getting People to Work Together Productively* (New York: Lexington, 1993); D. Tjosvold and D. W. Johnson, *Productive Conflict Management Perspectives for Organizations* (New York: Irvington, 1983).

132. T. A. O'Neill, G. C. Hoffart, M. M. J. W. Mclarnon, H. J. Woodley, M. Eggermont, W. Rosehart, and R. Brennan, "Constructive Controversy and Reflexivity Training Promotes Effective Conflict Profiles and Team Functioning in Student Learning Teams," *Academy of Management Learning & Education,* June 2017, pp. 257–276.

133. N. Lehmann-Willenbrock and M. M. Chiu, "Igniting and Resolving Content Disagreements During Team Interactions: A Statistical Discourse Analysis of Team Dynamics at Work," *Journal of Organizational Behavior*, November 2018, pp. 1142–1162.

134. "The Top 20 Valuable Facebook Statistics—Updated April 2020," *Zephoria Digital Marketing,* https://zephoria.com (accessed April 22, 2020). Also see R. Prior, "This Breast Cancer Advocate Says She Discovered a Facebook Flaw That Put the Health Data of Millions at Risk," *CNN*, March 6, 2020, https://www.cnn.com/2020/02/29/health/andrea-downing-facebook-data-breach-wellness-trnd/index.html; K. Yurieff, "Your Facebook Data Scandal Questions Answered," *CNN Tech,* April 11, 2018, http://money.cnn.com/2018/04/11/technology/facebook-questions-data-privacy/index.html; "If Facebook Will Not Fix Itself, Will Congress?" *The Economist,* April 11, 2018, https://www.economist.com/news/united-states/21740387-if-facebook-will-not-fix-itself-will-congress-fit-it-mr-zuckerberg-goes-washington.

135. M.-L. Chang, "On the Relationship between Intragroup Conflict and Social Capital in Teams: A Longitudinal Investigation in Taiwan," *Journal of Organizational Behavior,* January 2017, pp. 3–27; A. M. O'Leary-Kelly, R. W. Griffin, and D. J. Glew, "Organization-Motivated Aggression: A Research Framework," *Academy of Management Review,* January 1996, pp. 225–253.

136. D. Lovric and T. Chamorro-Premuzic, "Too Much Team Harmony Can Kill Creativity," *Harvard Business Review,* June 28, 2018, https://hbr.org/2018/06/too-much-team-harmony-can-kill-creativity.

137. A. Di Fabio and M. Duradoni, "Fighting Incivility in the Workplace for Women and for All Workers: The Challenge of Primary Prevention," *Frontiers in Psychology*, August 2019, https://doi.org/10.3389/fpsyg.2019.01805. Also see L. Batista and T. G. Reio, "Occupational Stress and Instigator Workplace Incivility as Moderated by Personality: A Test of an Occupational Stress and Workplace Incivility Model," *Journal of Organizational Psychology*, June 2019, pp. 38–49; K. Holm, E. Torkelson, and M. Bäckström, "Exploring Links between Witnessed and Instigated Workplace Incivility," *International Journal of Workplace Health Management*, June 2019, pp. 160–175; Y. Chen et al., "The Multidimensionality of Workplace Incivility: Cross-Cultural Evidence," *International Journal of Stress Management*, November 2019, pp. 356–366.

138. D. B. Ganegoda and P. Bordia, "I Can Be Happy for You, but Not All the Time: A Contingency Model of Envy and Positive Empathy in the Workplace," *Journal of Applied Psychology*, June 2019, pp. 776–795.

139. L. Yu, M. K. Duffy, and B. J. Tepper, "Why Supervisors Envy Their Employees," *Harvard Business Review*, September 13, December 2018, https://hbr.org/2018/09/why-supervisors-envy-their-employees.

140. M. Y. Ghadi, "Empirical Examination of Theoretical Model of Workplace Envy: Evidences from Jordan," *Management Research Review*, December 2018, pp. 1438–1459.

141. "Jussie Smollett Staged Attack Because He Was Unhappy with Salary, Police Say," *The Guardian*, February 21, 2019, https://www.theguardian.com/us-news/2019/feb/21/actor-jussie-smollett-arrested-in-chicago-say-police. Also see Khal, "A Timeline of Jussie Smollett's Case," *Complex*, February 25, 2020, https://www.complex.com/pop-culture/jussie-smollett-case-timeline.

142. M.Y. Ghadi, "Empirical Examination of Theoretical model of workplace envy: evidences from Jordan," *Management Research Review*, 2018, pp. 1438–1459.

143. H. Purank, J. Koopman, H.C. Vough, and D.L. Gamache, "They Want What I've Got (I Think): The Causes and Consequences of Attributing Coworker Behavior to Envy," *Academy of Management Review*, Vol. 44 2019, pp. 424–449.

144. K. Lee and M.K. Duffy, "A Functional Model of Workplace Envy and Job Performance: When Do Employees Capitalize on Envy by Learning from Envied Targets?" *Academy of Management Journal*, August 2019, pp. 1085–1110.

145. D.B. Ganegoda and P. Bordia, "I Can Be Happy for You, but Not All the Time: A Contingency Model of Envy and Positive Empathy in the Workplace," *Journal of Applied Psychology*, June 2019, pp. 776–795.

146. E. Boehm, "To Enforce Social Distancing Rules, Cops Fined a Pennsylvania Woman Who Was Driving Alone," *Reason*, April 7, 2020, https://reason.com/2020/04/07/to-enforce-social-distancing-rules-cops-fined-a-pennsylvania-woman-who-was-driving-alone/.

147. S. Jang, W. Shen, T.D. Allen, and H. Zhang, "Societal Individualism-Collectivism and Uncertainty Avoidance as Cultural Moderators of Relationships between Job Resources and Strain," *Journal of Organizational Behavior*, December 2017, pp. 507–524.

148. G. Alteren and A. A. Tudoran, "Open-Mindeness and Adaptive Business Style," *International Marketing Review*, May 2019, pp. 365–390.

149. M. Seitchik, "The Goldilocks Approach to Team Conflict: How Leaders Can Maximize Innovation and Revenue Growth," *The Psychologist-Manager Journal,* February 2019, pp. 37–45.

150. S. G. Katzenstein, "The Debate on Structured Debate: Toward a Unified Theory," *Organizational Behavior and Human Decision Processes,* June 1996, pp. 316–332.

151. "Speak Up! Dissension Is Key to Successful Teamwork," *Business News Daily*, March 6, 2020, https://www.businessnewsdaily.com/8594-dissenting-voice-teamwork.html.

152. J. Winter, "How to Play the Devil's Advocate (without Being Evil)," *The Muse,* https://www.themuse.com/advice/how-to-play-the-devils-advocate-without-being-evil (accessed April 8, 2018).

153. J. Winter, "How to Play the Devil's Advocate (without Being Evil)," *The Muse,* https://www.themuse.com/advice/how-to-play-the-devils-advocate-without-being-evil (accessed April 8, 2018).

154. C. Mui, "3 Key Design Factors for an Effective Devil's Advocate," *Forbes,* April 23, 2014, https://www.forbes.com/sites/chunkamui/2014/04/23/3-keys-to-an-effective-devils-advocate/#2ce099fb83d1.

155. "Speak Up! Dissension Is Key to Successful Teamwork," *Business News Daily*, March 6, 2020, https://www.businessnewsdaily.com/8594-dissenting-voice-teamwork.html.

156. C. Mui, "3 Key Design Factors for an Effective Devil's Advocate," *Forbes,* April 23, 2014, https://www.forbes.com/sites/chunkamui/2014/04/23/3-keys-to-an-effective-devils-advocate/#2ce099fb83d1.

157. "Speak Up! Dissension Is Key to Successful Teamwork," *Business News Daily*, March 6, 2020, https://www.businessnewsdaily.com/8594-dissenting-voice-teamwork.html.

158. J. Winter, "How to Play the Devil's Advocate (without Being Evil)," *The Muse,* https://www.themuse.com/advice/how-to-play-the-devils-advocate-without-being-evil (accessed April 8, 2018).

159. J. Winter, "How to Play the Devil's Advocate (without Being Evil)," *The Muse,* https://www.themuse.com/advice/how-to-play-the-devils-advocate-without-being-evil (accessed April 8, 2018).

160. J. Fey, "Resolve Conflicts in the Workplace with These 12 Techniques," *DPM*, March 4, 2018, https://thedigitalprojectmanager.com/12-conflict-resolution-techniques-workplace/.

161. M. A. Rahim, "A Strategy for Managing Conflict in Complex Organizations," *Human Relations,* January 1985, p. 84. Also see M. A. Rahim and N. R. Magner, "Confirmatory Factor Analysis of the Styles of Handling Interpersonal Conflict: First-Order Factor Model and Its Invariance across Groups," *Journal of Applied Psychology,* February 1995, pp. 122–132.

162. M. Benitez, F.J. Medina, and L. Munduate, "Buffering Relationship Conflict Consequences in Teams Working in Real Organizations," *International Journal of Conflict Management*, April 2018, pp. 279–297.

163. S. Murphy, "10 Leadership Focus Areas That Build High Performing Teams," *Inc.*, January 15, 2018, https://www.inc.com/shawn-murphy/10-leadership-focus-areas-that-build-high-performing-teams.html. Also see M. K. Stewart, "How Can You Be a More Effective Team Member," *Meeteor*, August 11, 2016, http://blog.meeteor.com/blog/effective-team-member.

164. K. Cherry, "What Is the Norm of Reciprocity?" *VeryWellMind*, April 21, 2018, https://www.verywellmind.com/what-is-the-rule-of-reciprocity-2795891.

165. J. Folkman, "The Four Behavior Patterns That Enable Collaboration," *Forbes*, February 25, 2020, https://www.forbes.com/sites/joefolkman/2020/02/25/the-four-behavior-patterns-that-enable-collaboration/#808afeb2da03. Also see J. Peñalver, M. Salanova, I.M. Martínez, and W.B. Schaufeli, "Happy-Productive Groups: How Positive Affect Links to Performance through Social Resources," *The Journal of Positive Psychology*, Vol. 14 2019, pp. 377–392; N. Pillay, G. Park, Y. K. Kim, and S. Lee, "Thanks for Your Ideas: Gratitude and Team Creativity," *Organizational Behavior and Human Decision Processes*, January 2020, pp. 69–81.

166. R. Serban, "The Teamwork Guide: How to Be a Better Team Player (Part 1)," *Hubgets*, May 16, 2017, https://www.hubgets.com/blog/teamwork-guide-better-team-player-part-1.

167. M. K. Stewart, "How Can You Be a More Effective Team Member," *Meeteor*, August 11, 2016, http://blog.meeteor.com/blog/effective-team-member.

168. J. Keyser, "Active Listening Leads to Business Success," *T+D*, July 2013, pp. 26–28.

169. G. Alteren and A. A. Tudoran, "Open-Mindedness and Adaptive Business Style," *International Marketing Review*, May 2019, pp. 365–390. Also see J. Harvey, K. J. Johnson, K. S. Roloff, and A. C. Edmondson, "From Orientation to Behavior: The Interplay between Learning Orientation, Open-mindedness, and Psychological Safety in Team Learning," *Human Relations*, January 2019, pp. 1726–1751.

170. J. Faulkner, "Beyond the Brainstorm: How to Be a Better Collaborator," *Proposify*, May 10, 2016, https://www.proposify.com/blog/collaborative-workplace.

171. R. Molla, R. Lightner, and C. Tovar, "As Colbert Ascends 'The Late Show' Throne, a Look Back at Late Night TV Show Ratings," *The Wall Street Journal*, September 9, 2015, http://graphics.wsj.com/late-night-tv-show-ratings-and-hosts/.

172. B. Steinberg, "How Stephen Colbert, Jimmy Fallon, Jimmy Kimmel, Trevor Noah and Other Late-night TV Shows Are Adapting to Coronavirus Chaos," *Chicago Tribune*, March 31, 2020 https://www.chicagotribune.com/entertainment/tv/ct-ent-late-night-tv-changes-coronavirus-20200331-u3ikeu6dqjcqhb6vogx63hbxpa-story.html.

173. D. Itzkoff, "Late-Night TV Is Back: No Studios, No Audiences, No Problems (Mostly)," *The New York Times*, April 1, 2020, https://www.nytimes.com/2020/04/01/arts/television/late-night-tv-coronavirus.html.

174. D. Itzkoff, "Late-Night TV Is Back: No Studios, No Audiences, No Problems (Mostly)," *The New York Times*, April 1, 2020, https://www.nytimes.com/2020/04/01/arts/television/late-night-tv-coronavirus.html.

175. D. Itzkoff, "Late-Night TV Is Back: No Studios, No Audiences, No Problems (Mostly)," *The New York Times*, April 1, 2020, https://www.nytimes.com/2020/04/01/arts/television/late-night-tv-coronavirus.html.

176. P. White, "As Late-Night Shows Zoom to Air, Producers Hope to Harness Quarantine Creativity Once Shutdown Ends," *Deadline*, April 6, 2020, https://deadline.com/2020/04/late-night-tv-coronavirus-changes-producers-jimmy-fallon-jimmy-kimmel-seth-meyers-samantha-bee-1202901977/.

177. P. White, "As Late-Night Shows Zoom to Air, Producers Hope to Harness Quarantine Creativity Once Shutdown Ends," *Deadline*, April 6, 2020, https://deadline.com/2020/04/late-night-tv-coronavirus-changes-producers-jimmy-fallon-jimmy-kimmel-seth-meyers-samantha-bee-1202901977/.

178. D. Reilly, "How to Produce a Late-Night Show During a Global Pandemic in 6 Steps," *Vulture*, April 6, 2020, https://www.vulture.com/2020/04/late-night-shows-during-a-global-pandemic.html.

179. D. Reilly, "How to Produce a Late-Night Show During a Global Pandemic in 6 Steps," *Vulture*, April 6, 2020, https://www.vulture.com/2020/04/late-night-shows-during-a-global-pandemic.html.

180. M. Vulpo, "Here's Proof Jimmy Fallon's Daughters Are the True Stars of The Tonight Show," *E News*, April 9, 2020, https://www.eonline.com/news/1139174/here-s-proof-jimmy-fallon-s-daughters-are-the-true-stars-of-the-tonight-show. Also see E. Zemler, "Watch Samantha Bee Broadcast 'Full Frontal' from a Woodshed," *Rolling Stone*, March 19, 2020, https://www.rollingstone.com/tv/tv-news/samantha-bee-full-frontal-woodshed-969533/.

181. T. Teodorczuk, "If Its Ratings Don't Really Matter, Why Is Netflix Suddenly Canceling So Many Shows?" *Market Watch*, May 25, 2018, https://www.marketwatch.com/story/if-its-ratings-dont-really-matter-why-is-netflix-suddenly-canceling-so-many-shows-2018-05-24.

182. J. Berke and S. Gould, "Legal Marijuana Just Went on Sale in Illinois. Here Are All the States Where Cannabis Is Legal," *Business Insider*, January 1, 2020, https://www.businessinsider.com/legal-marijuana-states-2018-1.

183. "Legal Marijuana and Workplace Drug Testing," *FindLaw*, October 2, 2019, https://employment.findlaw.com/workplace-privacy/legal-marijuana-and-workplace-drug-testing.html.

CHAPTER 14

1. J. Galvin, "Why You Should Focus on Developing Yourself as a Leader—and 5 Ways to Start," *Inc.*, April 13, 2018, https://www.inc.com/joe-galvin/5-tough-questions-to-ask-yourself-to-become-a-better-leader.html?cid=search.

2. J. Griffith, C. Gibson, K. Medeiros, A. MacDougall, J. Hardy III, and M. Mumford, "Are You Thinking What I'm Thinking?: The Influence of Leader Style, Distance, and Leader–Follower Mental Model Congruence on Creative Performance," *Journal of Leadership & Organizational Studies*, Vol. 25, No. 2 (2018), pp. 153–170.

3. USC Price, "Leadership Style Quiz: Identify Your Style," *USC Price Sol Price School of Public Policy*, March 21, 2018, https://eml.usc.edu/blog/leadership-style-quiz.

4. C. Shum, A. Gatling, and S. Shoemaker, "A Model of Hospitality Leadership Competency for Frontline and Director-Level Managers: Which Competencies Matter More?" *International Journal of Hospitality Management*, Vol. 74 (2018), pp. 57–66.

5. B. Green, "This Is How Elon Musk Handles Bad Situations. Every Business Leader Should Take Note," *Inc.*, January 23, 2018, https://www.inc.com/bill-green/elon-musk-other-leaders-should-handle-all-situations-good-bad-like-this.html?cid=search.

6. B. Green, "This Is How Elon Musk Handles Bad Situations. Every Business Leader Should Take Note," *Inc.*, January 23, 2018, https://www.inc.com/bill-green/elon-musk-other-leaders-should-handle-all-situations-good-bad-like-this.html?cid=search.

7. R. Power, "Acing Leadership: How to Make Your Employees Feel Valued," *Inc.*, January 9, 2018, https://www.inc.com/rhett-power/acing-leadership-how-to-make-your-employees-feel-valued.html?cid=search.

8. F. Frei, and A. Morriss, "Begin with Trust," *Harvard Business Review*, Vol. 98, No. 3 (2020), pp. 112–121.

9. Y. Stedham, W. Kuechler, and T. Skaar, "Mindfulness and Transformational Leadership Practices," *Frontiers in Psychology*, Vol. 10 (2019), p. 1588.

10. J. Scheltgen, "This 10 Minute Daily Exercise Can Make You a Surprisingly Better Leader," *Inc.*, March 13, 2018, https://www.inc.com/jordan-scheltgen/this-10-minute-daily-exercise-can-make-you-a-surprisingly-better-leader.html?cid=search.

11. L. Garnett, "5 Leadership Rules from the Past That Don't Work Now (If You're Doing Any of These, Stop)," *Inc.*, April 2, 2018, https://www.inc.com/laura-garnett/5-leadership-rules-from-past-that-dont-work-now-if-youre-doing-any-of-these-stop-now.html?cid=search.

12. P. G. Northouse, *Leadership: Theory and Practice*, 6th ed. (Thousand Oaks, CA: Sage, 2012), p. 3.

13. E. De Haan, D. Gray, and S. Bonneywell, "Executive Coaching Outcome Research in a Field Setting: A Near-Randomized Controlled Trial Study in a Global Healthcare Corporation," *Academy of Management Learning and Education*, Vol. 18, No. 4 (2019), pp. 581–605. Also see M. Subramony, J. Segers, C. Chadwick, and A. Shyamsunder, "Leadership Development Practice Bundles and Organizational Performance: The Mediating Role of Human Capital and Social Capital," *Journal of Business Research*, Vol. 83 (2018), pp. 120–129; K. Lanaj, T. Foulk, and A. Erez, "Energizing Leaders via Self-Reflection: A Within-Person Field Experiment," *Journal of Applied Psychology*, Vol. 104, No. 1 (2019), p. 1.

14. "What Is Leadership Coaching (And How to Use It for Career Development)?" *Cleverism*, February 21, 2017, https://www.cleverism.com/leadership-coaching-and-career-development.

15. U. Venkatesh, "Coaching Industry—Statistics!" *LinkedIn*, September 11, 2019, https://www.linkedin.com/pulse/coaching-industry-statistics-umesh-venkatesh.

16. T. J. Quigley and D. C. Hambrick, "Has the 'CEO Effect' Increased in Recent Decades? A New Explanation for the Great Rise in America's Attention to Corporate Leaders," *Strategic Management Journal*, 2015, pp. 21–830.

17. B. M. Bass and R. Bass, *The Bass Handbook of Leadership: Theory, Research, and Managerial Applications*, 4th ed. (New York: Free Press, 2008), p. 654.

18. R. Cross, N. Nohria, and A. Parker, "Six Myths about Informal Networks—and How to Overcome Them," *MIT Sloan Management Review*, Spring 2002, pp. 67–75. Also see C. Shriky, "Watching the Patterns Emerge," *Harvard Business Review*, February 2004, pp. 34–35.

19. C. Lieber, "Lululemon Employees Report a Toxic 'Boy's Club' Culture," *Racked*, February 14, 2018, https://www.racked.com/2018/2/14/17007924/lululemon-work-culture-ceo-laurent-potdevin.

20. "Enterprise Holdings CEO Pam Nicholson to Retire at Year's End," *Enterprise Holdings*, October 4, 2019, https://www.enterpriseholdings.com/en/press-archive/2019/10/enterprise-holdings-ceo-pam-nicholson-to-retire-at-years-end.html.

21. C. Voegtlin, C. Frisch, A. Walther, and P. Schwab, "Theoretical Development and Empirical Examination of a Three-Roles Model of Responsible Leadership," *Journal of Business Ethics*, April 2019, pp. 1–21.

22. G. A. Yuki, *Leadership in Organizations*, 7th ed. (Upper Saddle River, NJ: Prentice Hall, 2008), p. 8.

23. L. Parmer and J. Dillard Jr., "The Way Employees Are Treated Predicts Power Feelings," *Leadership & Organization Development Journal*, February 2019, pp. 2–16.

24. "Recognizing the Best of the Best: Introducing Tallgrass Freight's Club 200," *Tallgrass Freight*, 2018, https://tallgrassfreight.com/recognizing-best-of-the-best-introducing-tallgrass-freights-club-200/.

25. H. Milnes, "Tapestry CEO Ousted for Poor Performance, per Internal Email," *Vogue Business*, September 4, 2019, https://www.voguebusiness.com/companies/tapestry-kate-spade-coach-stuart-weitzman-removes-chief-executive.

26. S. Behrmann, "Study: Americans Trust Fauci More than Trump or Their Own Governors," *USA Today*, April 29, 2020, https://www.usatoday.com/story/news/politics/2020/04/29/coronavirus-public-trusts-fauci-over-governors-trump-survey-says/3044867001/.

27. J. Gmoser, "Dr. Anthony Fauci Warned in a Senate Hearing on Tuesday about the Dangers of States Reopening without Following Federal Guidelines. Here's How He Became the Nation's Top Disease Expert," *Business Insider*, May 12, 2020, https://www.businessinsider.com/how-anthony-dr-fauci-became-nations-top-disease-expert-2020-4.

28. Bill, "The Keys to Her Success? Character, Core Values, Vision and Energy!" *Branding For Results*, August 18, 2018, https://brandingforresults.com/angela-ahrendts/.

29. B. Raven, J. Schwarzwald, and M. Koslowsky, "Conceptualizing and Measuring a Power/Interaction Model of Interpersonal Influence," *Journal of Applied Social Psychology*, Vol. 28, No. 4 (1998), pp. 307–332.

30. E. Landells and S. Albrecht, "Organizational Political Climate: Shared Perceptions about the Building and Use of Power Bases," *Human Resource Management Review*, Vol. 23, No. 4 (2013), pp. 357–365.

31. M. Reeves, S. Levin, T. Fink, and A. Levina, "Taming Complexity," *Harvard Business Review*, Vol. 98, No.1 (2020), pp. 112–121.

32. E. Harrell, "Persuasion—And Resistance," *Harvard Business Review*, Vol. 97, No. 6 (2019), pp. 162–163.

33. K. Cullen, A. Gerbasi, and D. Chrobot-Mason, "Thriving in Central Network Positions: The Role of Political Skill," *Journal of Management*, Vol. 44, No. 2 (2018), pp. 682–706. Also see L. Maher, V. Gallagher, A. Rossi, G. Ferris, and P. Perrewé, "Political Skill and Will as Predictors of Impression Management Frequency and Style: A Three-Study Investigation," *Journal of Vocational Behavior*, Vol. 107 (2018), pp. 276–294; E. Lvina, G. Johns, and C. Vandenberghe. "Team Political Skill Composition as a Determinant of Team Cohesiveness and Performance," *Journal of Management*, Vol. 44, No. 3 (2018), pp. 1001–1028.

34. A. Simpson, "Confessions of a Diehard Fan of Insurance Data: Part 1," *Insurance Journal*, November 24, 2019, https://www.insurancejournal.com/news/national/2019/11/24/549386.htm.

35. M. Abad, "Indya Moore Gives Powerful Speech after Accepting Award," *Paper Magazine*, September 5–6, 2019, https://www.paper-mag.com/indya-moore-cover-speech-awards-2640234191.html?rebelltitem=2#rebelltitem2.

36. M. Curtin, "A Top-Rated CEO on Glassdoor Says This Is Her Secret to Success," *Inc.*, June 29, 2018, https://www.inc.com/melanie-curtin/the-no-1-rated-ceo-on-glassdoor-says-this-is-secret-to-her-success.html.

37. F. Schoutten, T. Barrett, and L. Fox, "A Top-Rated CEO on Glassdoor Says This Is Her Secret to Success," *CNN*, March 12, 2019, https://www.cnn.com/2019/03/12/politics/boeing-capitol-hill-lobbying/index.html.

38. S. Horsley, "Airplane Grounding Tests Boeing's Influence in Washington," *NPR*, March 14, 2019, https://www.npr.org/2019/03/14/703165860/airplane-grounding-tests-boeings-influence-in-washington.

39. S. Horsley, "Airplane Grounding Tests Boeing's Influence in Washington," *NPR*, March 14, 2019, https://www.npr.org/2019/03/14/703165860/airplane-grounding-tests-boeings-influence-in-washington.

40. C. Fairchild, "Are Your Friendships at Work Holding You Back?" *LinkedIn*, November 6, 2019, https://www.linkedin.com/pulse/your-friendships-work-holding-you-back-caroline-fairchild.

41. J. Kelly, "Prominent CEOs Promise That They Will Not Lay off Workers in 2020," *Forbes*, May 27, 2020, https://www.forbes.com/sites/jackkelly/2020/03/27/prominent-ceos-promise-that-they-will-not-layoff-workers-in-2020/#1b5e83fa9a61.

42. "Attend or Sponsor an Event," *Graham*, https://www.graham-windham.org/attend-or-sponsor-an-event/.

43. A. Chatterji and M. Toffel, "The New CEO Activists," *Harvard Business Review*, Vol. 96, No. 1 (2018), pp. 78–89.

44. P. Chesser, "Moralizing CEOs Exert Pressure over Guns and Abortion Laws," *NLPC*, June 7, 2019, https://nlpc.org/2019/06/07/moralizing-ceos-exert-pressure-guns-abortion/.

45. C. Madigan, K. Way, M. Capra, and K. Johnstone, "Influencing Organizational Decision-Makers—What Influence Tactics Are OHS Professionals Using?" *Safety Science*, Vol. 121 (2020), pp. 496–506.

46. C. Kininmonth, "Glass Ceiling Alive and Well—6 Left at the Very Top in 2019," *The Growth Faculty*, January 21, 2019, https://www.thegrowthfaculty.com/blog/Glassceilingaliveandwell6leftattheverytopin2019.

47. A. Root, "The Captains of Industry Are Still Mostly Men—but Not in Defense," *Barron's (Online)*, June 20, 2019.

48. R. M. Stogdill, *Handbook of Leadership* (New York: Free Press, 1974). Also see B. M. Bass and R. Bass, *The Bass Handbook of Leadership: Theory, Research, and Managerial Applications*, 4th ed. (New York: Free Press, 2008). An update on the role of intelligence can be found in M. Daly, M. Egan, and F. O'Reilly, "Childhood General Cognitive Ability Predicts Leadership Role Occupancy across Life: Evidence from 17,000 Cohort Study Participants," *The Leadership Quarterly*, 2015, pp. 323–341.

49. B. M. Bass and R. Bass, *The Bass Handbook of Leadership: Theory, Research, and Managerial Applications*, 4th ed. (New York: Free Press, 2008).

50. J. Vergauwe, B. Wille, J. Hofmans, R. Kaiser, and F. Fruyt, "The Double-Edged Sword of Leader Charisma: Understanding the Curvilinear Relationship between Charismatic Personality and Leader Effectiveness," *Journal of Personality and Social Psychology*, Vol. 114, No.1 (2018), pp. 110–130.

51. These results are based on D. S. DeRue, J. D. Nahrgang, N. Wellman, and S. E. Humphrey, "Trait and Behavioral Theories of Leadership: An Integration and Meta-Analytic Test of Their Relative Validity," *Personnel Psychology,* Vol. 64 (2011), pp. 7–52. Also see D. L. Joseph, L Y. Dhanani, W. Shen, B. C. McHugh, and M. A. McCord, "Is a Happy Leader a Good Leader? A Meta-Analytic Investigation of Leader Trait Affect and Leadership," *The Leadership Quarterly,* 2015, pp. 558–577; E. H. O'Boyle Jr., D. F. Forsyth, G. C. Banks, and M. A. McDaniel, "A Meta-Analysis of the Dark Triad and Work Behavior: A Social Exchange Perspective," *Journal of Applied Psychology,* May 2012, pp. 557–579.

52. M. Cannon, A. Vedel, and P. Jonason, "The Dark and Not So Humble: School-Type Effects on the Dark Triad Traits and Intellectual Humility," *Personality and Individual Differences*, Vol. 163, September 2020, p. 110068.

53. D. Simonet, R. Tett, J. Foster, A. Angelback, and J. Bartlett, "Dark-Side Personality Trait Interactions: Amplifying Negative Predictions of Leadership Performance," *Journal of Leadership & Organizational Studies*, Vol. 25, No. 2 (2018), pp. 233–250.

54. D. Montano, A. Reeske, F. Franke, and J. Hüffmeier, "Leadership. Followers' Mental Health and Job Performance in Organizations: A Comprehensive Meta-Analysis from an Occupational Health Perspective," *Journal of Organizational Behavior,* March 2017, pp. 509–537. Also see O'Boyle et al., "A Meta-Analysis of the Dark Triad and Work Behavior," *Journal of Applied Psychology* Vol. 97, No. 3 (May 2012), pp. 557–579.

55. J. Hogan, R. Hogan, and R. Kaiser, "Management Derailment," in S. Zedeck (ed.), *APA Handbook of Industrial and Organizational Psychology* (Washington, DC: American Psychological Association, 2011), pp. 555–575. Also see S. Braun, A. Nilüfer, D. Frey, and C. Peus, "Leader Narcissism Predicts Malicious Envy and Supervisor-Targeted Counterproductive Work Behavior: Evidence from Field and Experimental Research," *Journal of Business Ethics*, Vol. 151, No. 3 (2018), pp. 725–741.

56. H. Liu, J. T-J. Chiang, R. Fehr, M. Xu, and S. Wang, "How Do Leaders React When Treated Unfairly? Leader Narcissism and Self-Interested Behavior in Response to Unfair Treatment," *Journal of Applied Psychology,* November 2017, pp. 1590–1599.

57. C. Castille, J. Buckner, and C. Thoroughgood, "Prosocial Citizens without a Moral Compass? Examining the Relationship between Machiavellianism and Unethical Pro-Organizational Behavior," *Journal of Business Ethics*, Vol. 149, No. 4 (2018), pp. 919–930.

58. K. Landay, P. Harms, and M. Credé, "Shall We Serve the Dark Lords? A Meta-Analytic Review of Psychopathy and Leadership," *Journal of Applied Psychology,* Vol. 104, No. 1 (2019), p. 183.

59. T. Charmrro-Premuzic, "Could Your Personality Derail Your Career?" *Harvard Business Review,* September–October 2017,pp. 138–141; D. Meinert, "Why Leaders Fail," *HR Magazine,* October 2017, p. 18.

60. S. Roberts, K. Weisman, J. Lane, A. Williams, N. Camp, M. Wang, M. Robison, K. Sanchez, and C. Griffiths, "God as a White Man: A Psychological Barrier to Conceptualizing Black People and Women as Leadership Worthy," *Journal of Personality and Social Psychology*, January 2020. Also see J. Napolitano, "Women Earn More College Degrees and Men Still Earn More Money," *Forbes,* September 4, 2018, https://www.forbes.com/sites/janetnapolitano/2018/09/04/women-earn-more-college-degrees-and-men-still-earn-more-money/#64ceffa939f1; L. Italiano, "There Are Now More Woman in the Workforce Than Men: Feds," *New York Post,* January 10, 2020, https://nypost.com/2020/01/10/there-are-now-more-woman-in-the-workforce-than-men-feds/.

61. C. Zillman and M. Hinchliffe, "The Fortune 500 Gets Another Female CEO," *Fortune,* March 13, 2020, https://fortune.com/2020/03/13/fortune-500-female-ceo-ups-carol-tome/.

62. C. Duffy, "From the Brink of Bankruptcy to a 1,300% Stock Gain: How This CEO Turned Around Her Company," *CNN,* March 22, 2020, https://www.cnn.com/2020/03/27/tech/lisa-su-amd-risk-takers/index.html.

63. S. Gharib, "AMD CEO Lisa Su on 2020 Outlook: 'The Best Is Yet to Come,'" *Fortune,* October 30, 2019, https://fortune.com/2019/10/30/amd-ceo-lisa-su-outlook-on-leading/.

64. For examples see E. McClean, S. Martin, K. Emich, and Col T. Woodruff, "The Social Consequences of Voice: An Examination of Voice Type and Gender on Status and Subsequent Leader Emergence," *Academy of Management Journal,* Vol. 61, No. 5 (2018), pp. 1869–1891. Also see P. Dwivedi, A. Joshi, and V. Misangyi, "Gender-Inclusive Gatekeeping: How (Mostly Male) Predecessors Influence the Success of Female CEOs," *Academy of Management Journal*, Vol. 61, No. 2 (2018), pp. 379–404.

65. Based on the following studies, meta-analyses, and leadership research reviews: W. Shen and D. Joseph, "Gender and Leadership: A Criterion-Focused Review and Research Agenda," *Human Resource Management Review,* 2020. Also see J. Mackey, R. Frieder, J. Brees, and M. Martinko, "Abusive Supervision: A Meta-Analysis and Empirical Review," *Journal of Management,* Vol. 43 (2017), pp. 1940–1965; A. Eagly, M. Johannesen-Schmidt, and M. van Engen, "Transformational, Transactional, and Laissez-Faire Leadership Styles: A Meta-Analysis Comparing Men and Women," *Psychological Bulletin*, Vol. 129 (2003), pp. 569–591; S. Paustian-Underdahl, L. Walker, and D. Woehr," Gender and Perceptions of Leadership Effectiveness: A Meta-Analysis of Contextual Moderators," *Journal of Applied Psychology*, Vol. 99 (2014), pp. 1129–1145; K. Badura, E. Grijalva, D. Newman, T. Yan, and G. Jeon, "Gender and Leadership Emergence: A Meta-Analysis and Explanatory Model," *Personnel Psychology*, Vol. 71 (2018), pp. 335–367.

66. J. Huang, A. Krivkovich, I. Starikova, L. Yee, and D. Zanoschi, "Women in the Workplace 2019," *McKinsey,* October 15, 2019, https://www.mckinsey.com/featured-insights/gender-equality/women-in-the-workplace-2019.

67. Bloomberg, "You May Want to Buy Stock in Companies Run by Female CEOs. Here's Why," *Fortune,* August 1, 2017, http://fortune.com/2017/08/01/female-ceo-stock-returns/?iid=sr-link2.

68. S. Jeong and D. Harrison, "Glass Breaking, Strategy Making, and Value Creating: Meta-Analytic Outcomes of Women as CEOs and TMT Members," *Academy of Management Journal,* August 2017, pp. 1219–1252.

69. L. Fincher, "Women Leaders Are Doing a Disproportionately Great Job at Handling the Pandemic. So Why Aren't There More of Them?" *CNN,* April 14, 2020, https://www.cnn.com/2020/04/14/asia/women-government-leaders-coronavirus-hnk-intl/index.html.

70. K. Sergent and A. Stajkovic, "Women's Leadership Is Associated with Fewer Deaths during the Covid-19 Crisis: Quantitative and Qualitative Analyses of United States Governors," *Journal of Applied Psychology,* August 2020, pp. 771–783.

71. H. Marcoux, "Female Leaders Are Winning the COVID-19 Wars," *Motherly,* April 23, 2020, https://www.mother.ly/news/response-to-covid-19-proves-what-can-happen-we-we-let-moms-lead/taiwan-president-tsai-ing-wens-win-she-started-fighting-the-virus-in-december.

72. J. Hassan and S. O'Grady, "Female World Leaders Hailed as Voices of Reason During Coronavirus Chaos," *Anchorage Daily News* April 21, 2020, https://www.adn.com/nation-world/2020/04/21/female-world-leaders-hailed-as-voices-of-reason-amid-the-coronavirus-chaos/.

73. H. Marcoux, "Female Leaders Are Winning the COVID-19 Wars," *Motherly,* April 23, 2020, https://www.mother.ly/news/response-to-covid-19-proves-what-can-happen-we-we-let-moms-lead/taiwan-president-tsai-ing-wens-win-she-started-fighting-the-virus-in-december.

74. A. Horn, "After Days of No New Coronavirus Cases, New Zealand Reopens Most Businesses," *NPR,* May 14, 2020, https://www.npr.org/sections/coronavirus-live-updates/2020/05/14/856093586/after-days-of-no-new-coronavirus-cases-new-zealand-reopens-most-businesses.

75. N. Aspinwall and E. Rauhala, "Taiwan Beat Covid-19 and Won Friends. At the WHO, It's Still Fighting for a Seat at the Table," *The Washington Post,* May 15, 2020, https://www.washingtonpost.com/world/asia_pacific/taiwan-beat-covid-19-and-won-friends-at-the-who-its-still-fighting-for-a-seat-at-the-table/2020/05/15/d924b082-9025-11ea-9322-a29e75effc93_story.html.

76. R. Hass, "Taiwan's Tsai Ing-Wen Enters Second Term with a Strong Political Mandate, But No Room for Complacency," *Brookings*, May 13, 2020, https://www.brookings.edu/blog/order-from-chaos/2020/05/13/taiwans-tsai-ing-wen-enters-second-term-with-a-strong-political-mandate-but-no-room-for-complacency/.

77. R. Hass, "Taiwan's Tsai Ing-Wen Enters Second Term with a Strong Political Mandate, But No Room for Complacency," *Brookings*, May 13, 2020, https://www.brookings.edu/blog/order-from-chaos/2020/05/13/taiwans-tsai-ing-wen-enters-second-term-with-a-strong-political-mandate-but-no-room-for-complacency/.

78. A. Somvichian-Clausen, "Countries Led by Women Have Fared Better against Coronavirus. Why?" *The Hill*, April 18, 2020, https://thehill.com/changing-america/respect/equality/493434-countries-led-by-women-have-fared-better-against.

79. A. Somvichian-Clausen, "Countries Led by Women Have Fared Better against Coronavirus. Why?" *The Hill*, April 18, 2020, https://thehill.com/changing-america/respect/equality/493434-countries-led-by-women-have-fared-better-against.

80. A. Taub, "Why Are Women-Led Nations Doing Better with Covid-19?" *The New York Times* May 15, 2020, https://www.newyorktimes.com.

81. L. Champoux-Paillé and A. Croteau, "Why Women Leaders Are Excelling during the Coronavirus Pandemic," *The Conversation*, May 13, 2020, https://theconversation.com/why-women-leaders-are-excelling-during-the-coronavirus-pandemic-138098.

82. S. Spencer, E. Blazek, and J. Orr, "Bolstering the Female CEO Pipeline: Equalizing the Playing Field and Igniting Women's Potential as Top-Level Leaders," *Business Horizons*, Vol. 62, No. 5 (2019), pp. 567–577.

83. J. Huang, A. Krivkovich, I. Starikova, L. Yee, and D. Zanoschi, "Women in the Workplace 2019," *McKinsey*, October 15, 2019, https://www.mckinsey.com/featured-insights/gender-equality/women-in-the-workplace-2019.

84. J. Horowitz, R. Igielnik, and K. Parker, "Women and Leadership 2018," *Pew Research Center*, September 20, 2018, https://www.pewsocialtrends.org/2018/09/20/women-and-leadership-2018/.

85. K. Charles, J. Guryan, and J. Pan, "The Effects of Sexism on American Women: The Role of Norms vs. Discrimination," *National Bureau of Economic Research*, No. w24904 (2018).

86. N. Montgomery and A. Cowen, "How Leader Gender Influences External Audience Response to Organizational Failures," *Journal of Personality and Social Psychology*, April 2019, pp. 639–660.

87. C. Tinsley and R. Ely, "What Most People Get Wrong about Men and Women," *Harvard Business Review*, Vol. 96, No. 3 (2018), pp. 114–121.

88. V. Gupta, S. Han, S. Mortal, S. Silveri, and D. Turban, "Do Women CEOs Face Greater Threat of Shareholder Activism Compared to Male CEOs? A Role Congruity Perspective," *Journal of Applied Psychology*, February 2018, p. 232.

89. P. Banerjee, "Shy, Intelligent Student with 'Big Handwriting': IIT Professors Remember Google CEO Sundar Pichai," *Hindustan Times*, August 26, 2018, https://www.hindustantimes.com/india-news/20-years-of-google-iit-kgp-remembers-sundar-the-student/story-m1A6akTDILWQszk7uLBTIN.html.

90. J. Austin, "15 Company Culture Examples That Deserve Your Attention," *Atlassian*, April 3, 2020, https://www.atlassian.com/blog/leadership/15-company-culture-examples-that-deserve-your-attention. Also see P. Eggen, "Reflecting on the Zoom Investment: Getting It Right & Wrong," *LinkedIn*, April 26, 2019, https://www.linkedin.com/pulse/reflecting-zoom-investment-getting-right-wrong-patrick-eggen.

91. F. Gino, "The Business Case for Curiosity," *Harvard Business Review*, September–October 2018.

92. A. Collins, "Ulta Beauty's Mary Dillon Talks Leadership," *Women's Wear Daily*, October 29, 2019, https://www.herbertmines.com/media/ulta-beautys-mary-dillon-talks-leadership.

93. M. Curtin, "Billionaire CEO Sara Blakely Says These 7 Words Are the Best Career Advice She Ever Got," *Thrive Global*, April 26, 2018, https://thriveglobal.com/stories/billionaire-ceo-sara-blakely-says-these-7-words-are-the-best-career-advice-she-ever-got/.

94. R. G. Lord, D. V. Day, S. J. Zaccaro, B. J. Avolio, and A. H. Eagly, "Leadership in Applied Psychology: Three Ways of Theory and Research," *Journal of Applied Psychology*, March 2017, pp. 434–451.

95. A. and J. Bornstein, "22 Qualities That Make a Great Leader," *Entrepreneur*, March 22, 2016, https://www.entrepreneur.com/article/270486 (accessed July 2016).

96. "Our Railroad," https://www.bnsf.com (accessed May 26, 2020).

97. C. O'Reilly III, B. Doerr, and J. Chatman, "See You in Court": How CEO Narcissism Increases Firms' Vulnerability to Lawsuits," *The Leadership Quarterly*, Vol. 29, No. 3 (2018), pp. 365–378.

98. D. Levine, "In Trade-Secrets Trial, Subdued Kalanick Says Uber Trailed in Self-Driving Cars," *Yahoo Finance*, February 6, 2018, https://finance.yahoo.com/news/waymo-calls-ex-uber-ceo-202048572.html.

99. E. Newcomer and B. Stone, "The Fall of Travis Kalanick," *Bloomberg Businessweek*, No. 4555 (January 2018), pp. 46–51.

100. T. Shingal, "10 Companies Who Use Psychometric Testing," *Mettl*, https://blog.mettl.com/talent-hub/10-companies-using-psychometric-testing (accessed May 25, 2020).

101. "Personality Assessment: Helping Leaders Blame Less, Help More," *Inc.*, January 23, 2018, https://www.inc.com/entrepreneurs-organization/personality-assessment-helping-leaders-blame-less-help-more.html.

102. K. Rockwood, "Assessing Personalities," *Society for Human Resource Management*, February 29, 2020, https://www.shrm.org/hr-today/news/all-things-work/pages/personality-assessments.aspx.

103. M. Andresen and F. Bergdolt, "Individual and Job-Related Antecedents of a Global Mindset: An Analysis of International Business Travelers' Characteristics and Experiences Abroad," *International Journal of Human Resource Management*, April 2019, pp. 1–33.

104. D. Menabney, "Why Emotional Intelligence Needs Cultural Intelligence When Working across Borders," *Forbes*, December 30, 2019, https://www.forbes.com/sites/darrenmenabney/2020/12/30/why-emotional-intelligence-needs-cultural-intelligence-when-working-across-borders/#1149f2a161a7. Also see Y. Yehia, "The Importance of Cultural Intelligence in International Business," *Global Edge*, February 16, 2018, https://globaledge.msu.edu/blog/post/55562/the-importance-of-cultural-intelligence.

105. G. Yukl, "Effective Leadership Behavior: What We Know and What Questions Need More Attention," *Academy of Management Perspectives*, November 2012, pp. 66–85.

106. G. Anderson, "Can Old Navy's Boss Lead a Turnaround at Gap Inc.?" *Retail Wire*, March 6, 2020, https://retailwire.com/discussion/can-old-navys-boss-lead-a-turnaround-at-gap-inc/.

107. G. Yukl, R. Mahsud, G. Prussia, and S. Hassan, "Effectiveness of Broad and Specific Leadership Behaviors," *Personnel Review*, Vol. 48, No. 3 (2019), pp. 774–783.

108. G. Yukl, "Effective Leadership Behavior: What We Know and What Questions Need More Attention," *Academy of Management Perspectives*, November 2012, pp. 66–85.

109. N. Van Quaquebeke and W. Felps, "Respectful Inquiry: A Motivational Account of Leading through Asking Questions and Listening," *Academy of Management Review*, January 2018, pp. 5–27.

110. C. Becker, "TIAA CEO Roger W. Ferguson Jr.: 'Never Stop Learning and Growing,'" Wisconsin School of Business, April 2, 2018, https://wsb.wisc.edu/news/school-news-blog/2018/04/02/tiaa-ceo-roger-w-ferguson-jr-never-stop-learning-and-growing.

111. G. Yukl, R. Mahsud, G. Prussia, and S. Hassan, "Effectiveness of Broad and Specific Leadership Behaviors," *Personnel Review*, Vol. 48, No. 3 (2019), pp. 774–783.

112. F. Fiedler, "Assumed Similarity Measures as Predictors of Team Effectiveness," *Journal of Abnormal and Social Psychology*, Vol. 49 (1954), pp. 381–388. Also see F. Fiedler, *Leader Attitudes and Group Effectiveness* (Urbana, IL: University of Illinois Press, 1958); F. Fiedler, *A Theory of Leadership Effectiveness* (New York: McGraw-Hill, 1967).

113. B. Oc, "Contextual Leadership: A Systematic Review of How Contextual Factors Shape Leadership and Its Outcomes," *The Leadership Quarterly*, Vol. 29, No. 1 (2018), pp. 218–235.

114. N. Rüzgar, "The Effect of Leaders' Adoption of Task-Oriented or Relationship-Oriented Leadership Style on Leader-Member Exchange (LMX), in the Organizations That Are Active in Service Sector: A Research on Tourism Agencies," *Journal of Business Administration Research*, Vol. 7, No. 1 (2018), pp. 50–60.

115. M. V. Vugt, R. Hogan, and R. Kaiser, "Leadership, Followership, and Evolution," *American Psychologist*, April 2008, pp. 182–196.

116. R. J. House, "A Path-Goal Theory of Leader Effectiveness," *Administrative Science Quarterly*, September 1971, pp. 321–338.

117. P. M. Podsakoff, S. B. MacKenzie, M. Ahearne, and W. H. Bommer, "Searching for a Needle in a Haystack: Trying to Identify the Illusive Moderators of Leadership Behaviors," *Journal of Management,* 1995, pp. 422–470; J. Domingues, V. Afonso, and R. Agnihotri, "The Interactive Effects of Goal Orientation and Leadership Style on Sales Performance," *Marketing Letters,* December 2017, pp. 637–649.

118. C. Smith, "'I'm a Chief Executive Who Has to Get Stuff Done': How Andrew Cuomo Became the Coronavirus Trump Antidote," *Vanity Fair,* April 30, 2020, https://www.vanityfair.com/news/2020/04/cover-story-how-andrew-cuomo-became-the-coronavirus-trump-antidote.

119. C. Smith, "'I'm a Chief Executive Who Has to Get Stuff Done': How Andrew Cuomo Became the Coronavirus Trump Antidote," *Vanity Fair,* April 30, 2020, https://www.vanityfair.com/news/2020/04/cover-story-how-andrew-cuomo-became-the-coronavirus-trump-antidote.

120. C. Cillizza, "Everyone Needs to See Andrew Cuomo's Inspiring Words on the Fight Against Coronavirus," *CNN,* March 24, 2020, https://www.cnn.com/2020/03/24/politics/andrew-cuomo-new-york-coronavirus/index.html.

121. J. Turner, R. Baker, and F. Kellner, "Theoretical Literature Review: Tracing the Life Cycle of a Theory and Its Verified and Falsified Statements," *Human Resource Development Review,* January 2018, pp. 34–61.

122. G. Wang, I. Oh, S. Courtright, and A. Colbert, "Transformational Leadership and Performance Across Criteria and Levels: A Meta-Analytic Review of 25 Years of Research," *Group & Organization Management,* Vol. 36, No. 2 (2011), pp. 223–270.

123. Based on P. M. Podsakoff, S. B. MacKenzie, M. Ahearne, and W. H. Bommer, "Searching for a Needle in a Haystack: Trying to Identify the Illusive Moderators of Leadership Behaviors," *Journal of Management,* Vol. 21, No. 3 (1995), pp. 423–470.

124. G. Sidhu, "Impact of Coaching on Employee Performance Mediated by Rewards and Recognition," *International Journal of Education, Learning and Training*, Vol. 4, No. 2 (2019). Also see Z. Mwangi, G. Wario, J. Nzulwa, and R. Odhiambo, "Effect of Coaching on Employee Performance in State Corporations in Kenya," *Strategic Journal of Business & Change Management*, Vol. 5, No. 1 (2018).

125. The steps were developed by H. P. Sims Jr., S. Faraj, and S. Yun, "When Should a Leader Be Directive or Empowering? How to Develop Your Own Situational Theory of Leadership," *Business Horizons,* March–April 2009, pp. 149–158.

126. For a complete description of the full-range leadership theory, see B. J. Bass and B. J. Avolio, *Revised Manual for the Multi-Factor Leadership Questionnaire* (Palo Alto, CA: Mindgarden, 1997).

127. G. Curtis, "Connecting Influence Tactics with Full-Range Leadership Styles," *Leadership & Organization Development Journal*, March 2018, pp. 2–13.

128. A definition and description of transactional leadership is provided by B. M. Bass and R. Bass, *The Bass Handbook of Leadership: Theory, Research, and Managerial Applications,* 4th ed. (New York: Free Press), 2008), pp. 618–648.

129. S. Kimmorley, "Here's How 12 Successful CEOs Set Their Goals for the Year," *Business Insider,* January 31, 2018, https://www.businessinsider.com.au/how-ceos-set-goals-2018-1.

130. D. DeRue, J. Nahrgang, N. Wellman, and S. Humphrey, "Trait and Behavioral Theories of Leadership," *Personnel Psychology,* Vol. 64 (2011), pp. 7–52.

131. U. R. Dundum, K. B. Lowe, and B. J. Avolio, "A Meta-Analysis of Transformational and Transactional Leadership Correlates of Effectiveness and Satisfaction: An Update and Extension," in B. J. Avolio and F. J. Yammarino (eds.), *Transformational and Charismatic Leadership: The Road Ahead* (New York: JAI Press, 2002), p. 38.

132. L. Xie, "The Impact of Servant Leadership and Transformational Leadership on Learning Organization: A Comparative Analysis," *Leadership & Organization Development Journal,* April 2020, pp. 220–236. Also see U. Raja, D. Bouckenooghe, F. Syed, and S. Naseer, "Interplay between PO Fit, Transformational Leadership and Organizational Social Capital," *Personnel Review,* June 2018, pp. 913–930.

133. E. McDowell, "The 45 Most Beloved CEOs in America, According to Employees," *Business Insider,* July 17, 2019, https://www.businessinsider.com/best-ceos-ranking-glassdoor-companies-employees-2019-7.

134. V. Salemi, "How Good CEOs Make Personal Connections with Employees," *New York Post,* May 19, 2019, https://nypost.com/2019/05/19/how-good-ceos-make-personal-connections-with-employees/.

135. G. Demetriou, "An Interview with Michael Dowling, CEO of Northwell Health," *Greg's Corner Office,* February 2018, https://gregscorneroffice.com/wp-content/uploads/2018/02/An-Interview-with-Michael-Dowling.pdf.

136. Supportive results can be found in I. Buil, E. Martínez, and J. Matute, "Transformational Leadership and Employee Performance: The Role of Identification, Engagement and Proactive Personality," *International Journal of Hospitality Management*, Vol. 77 (2019), pp. 64–75. Also see B. McCormick, R. Guay, A. Colbert, and G. Stewart, "Proactive Personality and Proactive Behaviour: Perspectives on Person–Situation Interactions," *Journal of Occupational and Organizational Psychology,* Vol. 92, No. 1 (2019), pp. 30–51; W. Lam, C. Lee, M. Taylor, and H. Zhao, "Does Proactive Personality Matter in Leadership Transitions? Effects of Proactive Personality on New Leader Identification and Responses to New Leaders and Their Change Agendas," *Academy of Management Journal,* Vol. 61, No. 1 (2018), pp. 245–263; T. Judge and J. Bono, "Five-Factor Model of Personality and Transformational Leadership," *Journal of Applied Psychology,* October 2000, pp. 751–765; S. Oreg and Y. Berson, "Leadership and Employees' Reactions to Change: The Role of Leaders' Personal Attributes and Transformational Leadership," *Personnel Psychology,* Vol. 64 (2011), pp. 627–659.

137. Supportive research is summarized by Antonakis and House, "The Full-Range Leadership Theory: The Way Forward"; Monographs in Leadership and Management, Vol. 5, (Emerald Group Publishing Limited), 2013), pp. 3–33; W. Zhu, R. E. Riggio, B. J. Avolio, and J. J. Sosik, "The Effect of Leadership on Follower Moral Identity: Does Transformational/Transactional Style Make a Difference?" *Journal of Leadership & Organizational Studies,* Vol. 18 (2011), pp. 150–163.

138. "Most Powerful Women: 2019," *Fortune,* https://fortune.com/most-powerful-women/.

139. "Bold Leader Spotlight: Ann-Marie Campbell, EVP Stores for the Home Depot Inc.," *Bold Business,* October 11, 2018, https://www.bold-business.com/human-achievement/bold-leader-spotlight-ann-marie-campbell-home-depot-inc/.

140. "Home Depot's Ann-Marie Campbell for Destination Experience Summit," *Jamaica Observer,* February 20, 2019, http://www.jamaicaobserver.com/business-observer/_157517?profile=1008.

141. "Ann-Marie Campbell," *AACSB,* 2019, https://www.aacsb.edu/influential-leaders/honorees/2019/ann-marie-campbell.

142. "WE Interviews: Ann-Marie Campbell," *The Kinlin Company,* https://www.kinlin.com/we-interviews-ann-marie-campbell/.

143. "Ann-Marie Campbell Nomination," *Leaderhip Character Awards,* April 2018, https://www.leadershipcharacterawards.org/wp-content/uploads/2018/04/Ann-Marie-Campbell-Nomination.pdf.

144. A. Gumbs, "This Jamaican Immigrant Went from Home Depot Cashier to Running All U.S. Stores," *Black Enterprise*, November 20, 2017, https://www.blackenterprise.com/jamaican-immigrant-home-depot/.

145. B. Tepper, N. Dimotakis, L. Lambert, J. Koopman, F. Matta, H. Park, and W. Goo, "Examining Follower Responses to Transformational Leadership from a Dynamic, Person–Environment Fit Perspective," *Academy of Management Journal*, Vol. 61, No. 4 (2018), pp. 1343–1368.

146. G. Curtis, "Connecting Influence Tactics with Full-Range Leadership Styles," *Leadership & Organization Development Journal,* March 2018, pp. 2–13.

147. Charisma is defined and discussed by K. O. Tskhay, R. Zhu, C. Zou, and N. O. Rule, "Charisma in Everyday Life: Conceptualization and Validation of the General Charisma Inventory," *Journal of Personality and Social Psychology,* January 2018, pp. 131–152.

148. B. Nanus, *Visionary Leadership* (San Francisco: Jossey-Bass, 1992), p. 8.

149. M. S. Malone, "The Secret to Midcareer Success," *The Wall Street Journal,* February 12, 2018, p. A17.

150. D. Hoffeld, "7 Scientifically Proven Habits of Charismatic Leaders," *Fast Company,* February 3, 2016, http://www.fastcompany .com/3056232/how-to-be-a-success-at-everything/7-scientifically-proven-habits-of-charismatic-leaders.

151. J. Eads, "Tony Bennett Rejects a Raise and Teaches a Powerful Lesson in Leadership. The Raise Was Well Deserved, But He Knew It Could Be Used In Better Ways," *Inc.,* September 18, 2019, https://www .inc.com/john-eades/esteemed-basketball-coach-tony-bennett-just-rejected-a-major-raise-its-a-powerful-lesson-in-leadership.html.

152. A. Cain, "The 34 Most Beloved CEOs in 2018," *Business Insider*, June 20, 2018, https://www.businessinsider.com/glassdoor-most-popular-ceos-2018-6#34-steve-beauchamp-paylocity-1.

153. "A Great Company for Most," *Paylocity Review,* September 2018, https://www.kununu.com/us/paylocity/review/4f2e8982-8d9a-439a-aa98-2c5f0a70cbf6.

154. M. Blanding, "Concerned by the Scarcity of Girls in Computer Science Classrooms, Saujani Launched Girls Who Code. Already, the Organization Has Helped 40,000 Girls Learn How to Code," *Winder,* 2018, https://www.hks.harvard.edu/more/alumni/alumni-stories/computer-science-has-girl-problem-and-reshma-saujani-mpp-1999-fixing-it.

155. R. G. Lord, D. V. Day, S. J. Zaccaro, B. J. Avolio, and A. H. Eagly, "Leadership in Applied Psychology: Three Ways of Theory and Research," *Journal of Applied Psychology,* March 2017, pp. 434–451. Also see J. Duan, C. Li, Y. Xu, and C.-H. Wu, "Transformational Leadership and Employee Voice Behavior: A Pygmalion Mechanism," *Journal of Organizational Behavior,* June 2017, pp. 650–670; S. J. Ashford, N. Wellman, M. S. de Luque, and K. E. M. De Stobbeleir, "Two Roads to Effectiveness: CEO Feedback Seeking, Vision Articulation, and Firm Performance," *Journal of Organizational Behavior,* January 2018, pp. 82–95.

156. R. Frieder, G. Wang, and I. Oh, "Linking Job-Relevant Personality Traits, Transformational Leadership, and Job Performance via Perceived Meaningfulness at Work: A Moderated Mediation Model," *Journal of Applied Psychology*, Vol. 103, No. 3 (2018), pp. 324–333.

157. S. E. Seibert, L. D. Sargent, M. L. Kraimer, and K. Kiazad, "Linking Developmental Experiences to Leader Effectiveness and Promotability: The Mediating Role of Leadership Self-Efficacy and Mentor Network," *Personnel Psychology,* April 2017, pp. 357–397.

158. G. Graen and J. F. Cashman, "A Role-Making Model of Leadership in Formal Organizations: A Developmental Approach," in J. G. Hunt and L. L. Larson (eds.), *Leadership Frontiers* (Kent, OH: Kent State University Press, 1975), pp. 143–165. Also see F. Dansereau Jr., G. Graen, and W. J. Haga, "A Vertical Dyad Linkage Approach to Leadership within Formal Organizations: A Longitudinal Investigation of the Role-Making Process," *Organizational Behavior and Human Performance,* February 1975, pp. 46–78; K. S. Wilson, H.-P. Sin, and D. E. Conlon, "What about the Leader in Leader–Member Exchange? The Impact of Resource Exchanges and Substitutability in the Leader," *Academy of Management Review,* July 2010, pp. 358–372.

159. R. Martin, G. Thomas, A. Legood, and S. Russo, "Leader–Member Exchange (LMX) Differentiation and Work Outcomes: Conceptual Clarification and Critical Review," *Journal of Organizational Behavior*, Vol. 39, No. 2 (2018), pp. 151–168.

160. J. Seo, J. Nahrgang, M. Carter, and P. Hom, "Not All Differentiation Is the Same: Examining the Moderating Effects of Leader-Member Exchange (LMX) Configurations," *Journal of Applied Psychology*, Vol. 103, No. 5 (2018), p. 478.

161. A. Yu, F. Matta, and B. Cornfield, "Is LMX differentiation Beneficial or Detrimental for Group Effectiveness? A Meta-Analytic Investigation and Theoretical Integration," *Academy of Management Journal*, Vol. 61, No. 3 (2018), pp. 1158–1188.

162. R. G. Lord, D. V. Day, S. J. Zaccaro, B. J. Avolio, and A. H. Eagly, "Leadership in Applied Psychology: Three Ways of Theory and Research," *Journal of Applied Psychology*, March 2017, pp. 434–451. Also see R. Martin, G. Thomas, A. Legood, and S. D. Russo, "Leader-Member Exchange (LMX) Differentiation and Work Outcomes: Conceptual Clarification and Critical Review," *Journal of Organizational Behavior,* February 2018, pp. 151–168.

163. R. K. Gottfredson and H. Aguinis, "Leadership Behaviors and Follower Performance: Deductive and Inductive Examination of Theoretical Rationales and Underlying Mechanisms," *Journal of Organizational Behavior,* May 2017, pp. 558–591.

164. S. Shellenbarger, "The Right and Wrong Ways to Manage Up," *The Wall Street Journal*, April 11, 2018, p. A9.

165. A summary of servant leadership is provided by L. Spears, *Reflections on Leadership: How Robert K. Greenleaf's Theory of Servant-Leadership Influenced Today's Top Management Thinkers* (New York: Wiley, 1995).

166. M. Schwantes, "The World's 10 Top CEOs (They Lead in a Totally Unique Way). A Leadership Philosophy That's Been around for Centuries Is Only Practiced by a Few Wildly Successful Global Leaders," *Inc.,* March 29, 2017, https://www.inc.com/marcel-schwantes/heres-a-top-10-list-of-the-worlds-best-ceos-but-they-lead-in-a-totally-unique-wa.html.

167. N. Eva, M. Robin, S. Sendjaya, D. van Dierendonck, and R. Liden, "Servant Leadership: A Systematic Review and Call for Future Research," *The Leadership Quarterly*, Vol. 30, No. 1 (2019), pp. 111–132.

168. G. Lemoine, C. Hartnell, and H. Leroy, "Taking Stock of Moral Approaches to Leadership: An Integrative Review of Ethical, Authentic, and Servant Leadership," *Academy of Management Annals*, Vol. 13, No. 1 (2019), pp. 148–187.

169. A. Y. Ou, A. S. Tsui, A. J. Kinicki, D. A. Waldman, Z. Xiao, and L. J. Song, "Humble Chief Executive Officers' Connections to Top Management Team Integration and Middle Managers' Responses," *Administrative Science Quarterly,* March 2014, pp. 34–72.

170. "The Best-Performing CEOs in the World, 2019 Edition," *Harvard Business Review*, November–December 2019, https://hbr.org.

171. "Microsoft CEO Satya Nadella: How Empathy Sparks Innovation," *Knowledge@Wharton*, February 22, 2018, https://knowledge.wharton .upenn.edu/article/microsofts-ceo-on-how-empathy-sparks-innovation/.

172. G. Freeland, "Microsoft CEO Satya Nadella: Finding Success Out of the Spotlight," *Forbes*, March 18, 2019, https://www.forbes.com/sites/grantfreeland/2019/03/18/microsoft-ceo-satya-nadellas-success-secret/#27c736667efd.

173. D. Ancona, E. Backman, and K. Isaacs, "Nimble Leadership," *Harvard Business Review*, Vol. 97, No. 4 (2019), pp. 74–83.

174. Based on research in B. Oc, M. Daniels, J. Diefendorff, M. Bashshur, and G. Greguras, "Humility Breeds Authenticity: How Authentic Leader Humility Shapes Follower Vulnerability and Felt Authenticity," *Organizational Behavior and Human Decision Processes,* May 2020, pp. 112–125. Also see J. Hu, B. Erdogan, K. Jiang, T. Bauer, and S. Liu, "Leader Humility and Team Creativity: The Role of Team Information Sharing, Psychological Safety, and Power Distance," *Journal of Applied Psychology*, Vol. 103, No. 3 (2018), p. 313.

175. L. Wang, B. Owens, J. Li, and L. Shi, "Exploring the Affective Impact, Boundary Conditions, and Antecedents of Leader Humility," *Journal of Applied Psychology*, Vol. 103, No. 9 (2018), pp. 1019–1038.

176. K. Goldin, "'I Would Never Hire The Smartest Person in the Room,' Says One Ceo—Here's Why," *CNBC,* August 22, 2019, https://www .cnbc.com/2019/08/22/never-hire-the-smartest-person-in-the-room-says-hint-ceo-kara-goldin.html.

177. Based on results found in: M. Mayo, "If Humble People Make the Best Leaders, Why Do We Fall for Charismatic Narcissists?" *Harvard Business Review*, April 7, 2017, https://hbr.org/2017/04/if-humble-people-make-the-best-leaders-why-do-we-fall-for-charismatic-narcissists. Also see J. Hu, B. Erdogan, K. Jiang, T. Bauer, and S. Liu, "Leader Humility

and Team Creativity: The Role of Team Information Sharing, Psychological Safety, and Power Distance," *Journal of Applied Psychology*, Vol. 103, No. 3 (2018), p. 313; J. Mao, C. Chiu, B. Owens, J. Brown, and J. Liao, "Growing Followers: Exploring the Effects of Leader Humility on Follower Self-Expansion, Self-Efficacy, and Performance," *Journal of Management Studies*, Vol. 56, No. 2 (2019), pp. 343–371.

178. B. Oc, M. Daniels, J. Diefendorff, M. Bashshur, and G. Greguras, "Humility Breeds Authenticity: How Authentic Leader Humility Shapes Follower Vulnerability and Felt Authenticity," *Organizational Behavior and Human Decision Processes,* May 2020, pp. 112–125.

179. N. Van Quaquebeke and W. Felps, "Respectful Inquiry: A Motivational Account of Leading through Asking Questions and Listening," *Academy of Management Review,* January 2018, pp. 5–27. Also see H. Gregersen, "Bursting the CEO Bubble," *Harvard Business Review,* March–April 2017, pp. 76–83.

180. T. Maldonado, D. Vera, and N. Ramos, "How Humble Is Your Company Culture? And, Why Does It Matter?" *Business Horizons*, Vol. 61, No. 5 (2018), pp. 745–753.

181. A. Lee, S. Willis, and A. W. Tian, "Empowering Leadership: A Meta-Analytic Examination of Incremental Contribution, Mediation, and Moderation," *Journal of Organizational Behavior,* March 2018, pp. 306–325. Also see M. Chamberlin, D. Newton, and J. LePine, "A Meta-Analysis of Empowerment and Voice as Transmitters of High-Performance Managerial Practices to Job Performance," *Journal of Organizational Behavior*, Vol. 39, No. 10 (2018), pp. 1296–1313.

182. J. Wingard, "Bernard Tyson: Lessons from a Great American CEO," *Forbes*, November 15, 2019, https://www.forbes.com/sites/jasonwingard/2019/11/15/bernard-tyson-lessons-from-a-great-american-leader/#22950a8643a4.

183. J. Wingard, "Bernard Tyson: Lessons from a Great American CEO," *Forbes*, November 15, 2019, https://www.forbes.com/sites/jasonwingard/2019/11/15/bernard-tyson-lessons-from-a-great-american-leader/#22950a8643a4.

184. C. Beam, "Petra Reflects on an Admired Healthcare Leader, Kaiser Permanente CEO Bernard Tyson," *Petra*, November 27, 2019, https://petra.pro/petra-kaiser-bernard-tyson/.

185. P. Michelman, "The Question Every Executive Should Ask," *MIT Sloan Management Review*, May 22, 2017, https://sloanreview.mit.edu/article/the-question-every-executive-should-ask/.

186. S. Berger, "Top Reason CEOs Were Ousted in 2018 Was Because of Scandal," *CNBC,* May 15, 2019, https://www.cnbc.com/2019/05/15/pwc-strategy-report-top-reason-ceos-were-ousted-in-2018-was-scandals.html.

187. T. Ng and D. Feldman, "Ethical Leadership: Meta-Analytic Evidence of Criterion-Related and Incremental Validity," *Journal of Applied Psychology,* May 2015, pp. 948–965.

188. B. Weinstein, "Seven Bold Leaders Reveal How Ethical Leadership Is a Boon to Business," *Forbes*, October 14, 2019, https://www.forbes.com/sites/bruceweinstein/2019/10/14/seven-bold-leaders-reveal-how-ethical-leadership-is-a-boon-to-business/#3741f3b5454c.

189. As demonstrated in C. Thiel, J. Hardy III, D. Peterson, D. Welsh, and J. Bonner, "Too Many Sheep in the Flock? Span of Control Attenuates the Influence of Ethical Leadership," *Journal of Applied Psychology,* Vol. 103, No. 12 (2018), p. 1324. Also see C. Moore, D. Mayer, F. Chiang, C. Crossley, M. Karlesky, and T. Birtch, "Leaders Matter Morally: The Role of Ethical Leadership in Shaping Employee Moral Cognition and Misconduct," *Journal of Applied Psychology,* Vol. 104, No. 1 (2019), p. 123; M. Kuenzi, D. Mayer, and R. Greenbaum, "Creating an Ethical Organizational Environment: The Relationship between Ethical Leadership, Ethical Organizational Climate, and Unethical Behavior," *Personnel Psychology,* Vol. 73, No. 1 (2020), pp. 43–71; J. E. Hoch, W. H. Bommer, J. H. Dulebohn, and D. Wu, "Do Ethical, Authentic, and Servant Leadership Explain Variance above and beyond Transformational Leadership? A Meta-Analysis," *Journal of Management,* February 2018, pp. 501–529.

190. L. Dunn, "Women in Business Q&A: Lauren Bush Lauren, Founder and CEO, FEED," *Huffington Post,* October 24, 2017, www.huffington-post.com/entry/women-in-business-qa-lauren-bush-lauren-founder_us_59ef70bee4b04809c0501185.

191. D. Fenn, "Lauren Bush Lauren: Social Enterprise Is Her Bag," *Inc.,* August 21, 2013, www.inc.com/donna-fenn/feed-lauren-bush-lauren-social-enterprise.html.

192. K. Schmookler, "Lauren Bush Lauren of Feed Shares Her Motivations and Advice for Social Ventures," *Conscious Magazine,* http://consciousmagazine.co/lauren-bush-lauren-feed-world-hunger/ (accessed April 24, 2018).

193. L. Dunn, "Women in Business Q&A: Lauren Bush Lauren, Founder and CEO, FEED," *Huffington Post,* October 24, 2017, www.huffington-post.com/entry/women-in-business-qa-lauren-bush-lauren-founder_us_59ef70bee4b04809c0501185.

194. D. Fenn, "Lauren Bush Lauren: Social Enterprise Is Her Bag," *Inc.,* August 21, 2013, www.inc.com/donna-fenn/feed-lauren-bush-lauren-social-enterprise.html.

195. "Feeding the World through FEED Products," *Medium*, May 21, 2019, https://medium.com/@Miigle/feeding-the-world-through-feed-products-e0881489314.

196. "About Feed," *FEED,* www.feedprojects.com/about-feed (accessed April 24, 2018).

197. K. Schmookler, "Lauren Bush Lauren of Feed Shares Her Motivations and Advice for Social Ventures," *Conscious Magazine,* http://consciousmagazine.co/lauren-bush-lauren-feed-world-hunger/ (accessed April 24, 2018).

198. "About Feed," *FEED,* www.feedprojects.com/about-feed (accessed April 24, 2018).

199. "Giving Back with Lauren Bush Lauren," *Shoppe Salt,* June 10, 2019, https://www.shoppesalt.com/blogs/news/lauren-bush-lauren.

200. D. Fenn, "Lauren Bush Lauren: Social Enterprise Is Her Bag," *Inc.,* August 21, 2013, www.inc.com/donna-fenn/feed-lauren-bush-lauren-social-enterprise.html.

201. L. Dunn, "Women in Business Q&A: Lauren Bush Lauren, Founder and CEO, FEED," *Huffington Post,* October 24, 2017, www.huffington-post.com/entry/women-in-business-qa-lauren-bush-lauren-founder_us_59ef70bee4b04809c0501185.

202. G. Wang, C. Van Iddekinge, L. Zhang, and J. Bishoff, "Meta-Analytic and Primary Investigations of the Role of Followers in Ratings of Leadership Behavior in Organizations," *Journal of Applied Psychology,* Vol. 104, No. 1 (2019), p. 70.

203. D. Pietraszewski, "The Evolution of Leadership: Leadership and Followership as a Solution to the Problem of Creating and Executing Successful Coordination and Cooperation Enterprises," *The Leadership Quarterly,* June 2019, p.101299.

204. Based on T. O'Driscoll, "5 Foundational Elements of Followership," *Training,* May/June 2017, p. 56. Also see D. Ciampa, "Why New Leaders Should Be Wary of Quick Wins," *Harvard Business Review*, June 5, 2018, https://hbr.org.

205. B. M. Bass and R. Bass, *The Bass Handbook of Leadership: Theory, Research, and Managerial Applications,* 4th ed. (New York: Free Press, 2008).

206. L. Bossidy, "What Your Leader Expects of You and What You Should Expect in Return," *Harvard Business Review,* April 2007, pp. 58–65.

207. Based on B. Schroeder, "To Be a Great Leader, Learn How to Be a Great Follower: The Four Rules of Following," *Forbes,* December 5, 2019, https://www.forbes.com/sites/bernhardschroeder/2019/12/05/to-be-a-great-leader-learn-how-to-be-a-great-follower-the-four-rules-of-following/#1c6b06c07325. Also see R. Riggio, "You Can Lead, But Are You a Good Follower?" *Psychology Today,* March 16, 2014, https://www.psychologytoday.com/us/blog/cutting-edge-leadership/201403/you-can-lead-are-you-good-follower; K. Peters and A. Haslam, "Research: To Be a Good Leader, Start by Being a Good Follower," *Harvard Business Review Digital Articles*, August 2–4 (2018); G. Moran, "5 Ways Being a Good Follower Makes You a Better Leader," *Fast Company,* April 30, 2014, http://www.fastcompany.com/3029840/bottom-line/5-ways-being-a-good-follower-makes-you-a-better-leader.

208. B. Tepper, "Consequences of Abusive Supervision," *Academy of Management Journal*, Vol. 43, No. 2 (2000), pp. 178–190.

209. M. Gonzalez-Morales, M. Kernan, T. Becker, and R. Eisenberger, "Defeating Abusive Supervision: Training Supervisors to Support Subordinates," *Journal of Occupational Health Psychology*, Vol. 23, No. 2 (2018), p. 151.

210. For a thorough review of the abusive supervision literature, see B. Tepper, L. Simon, and H. Park, "Abusive Supervision," *Annual Review of Organizational Psychology and Organizational Behavior*, Vol. 4 (2017), pp. 123–152.

211. J. Mackey, R. Frieder, J. Brees, and M. Martinko, "Abusive Supervision: A Meta-Analysis and Empirical Review," *Journal of Management*, Vol. 43 (2017), pp. 1940–1965.

212. "Confronting Workplace Bullying," *Society for Human Resource Management*, 2016, https://www.shrm.org/resourcesandtools/tools-and-samples/presentations/pages/confrontingworkplacebullying.aspx.

213. T. Eurich, "What Self-Awareness Really Is (And How to Cultivate It)," *Harvard Business Review*, January 4, 2018, https://hbr.org.

214. K. Lanaj, T. Foulk, and A. Erez, "Energizing Leaders Via Self-Reflection: A Within-Person Field Experiment," *Journal of Applied Psychology*, Vol. 104, No. 1 (2019), p. 1.

215. These questions were taken from B. Gardner, "Become a Better Leader with Disciplined Reflection," *Forbes*, December 28, 2015, https://www.forbes.com/sites/forbescoachescouncil/2015/12/28/become-a-better-leader-with-disciplined-reflection/#f60ae9f65c39.

216. These questions were taken from B. Gardner, "Become a Better Leader with Disciplined Reflection," *Forbes*, December 28, 2015, https://www.forbes.com/sites/forbescoachescouncil/2015/12/28/become-a-better-leader-with-disciplined-reflection/#f60ae9f65c39.

217. H. M. Kraemer, "How Self-Reflection Can Make You a Better Leader," *Kellogg Insight*, December 2, 2016, https://insight.kellogg.northwestern.edu/article/how-self-reflection-can-make-you-a-better-leader.

218. A. Abell, "How to Break Free from the Imposter Syndrome Zone," *LinkedIn*, November 10, 2018, https://www.linkedin.com/pulse/how-break-free-from-imposter-syndrome-zone-alexander-abell.

219. M. Murphy, "The Dunning-Kruger Effect Shows Why Some People Think They're Great Even When Their Work Is Terrible," *LSA Psychology: University of Michigan*, January 26, 2017, https://lsa.umich.edu/psych/news-events/all-news/faculty-news/the-dunning-kruger-effect-shows-why-some-people-think-they-re-gr.html.

220. T. Herrera, "How to Spot and Overcome Your Hidden Weaknesses," *The New York Times*, April 23, 2018, https://www.nytimes.com/2018/04/23/smarter-living/how-to-spot-and-overcome-your-hidden-weaknesses.html.

221. E. Brown, "How Adam Neumann's Over-the-Top Style Built WeWork. 'This Is Not the Way Everybody Behaves,'" *The Wall Street Journal*, September 18, 2019, https://www.wsj.com.

222. A. Lowrey, "Curse of the Cult of the Founder," *The Atlantic*, September 25, 2019, https://www.theatlantic.com/ideas/archive/2019/09/curse-cult-of-the-founder/598753/.

223. E. Brown, "How Adam Neumann's Over-the-Top Style Built WeWork. 'This Is Not the Way Everybody Behaves,'" *The Wall Street Journal*, September 18, 2019, https://www.wsj.com.

224. D. Schuster, "Ousted WeWork CEO Adam Neumann Is a 'Phony' Who 'Thinks He Is a Jesus Figure,'" *New York Post*, September 28, 2019, https://nypost.com/2019/09/28/ousted-wework-ceo-adam-neumann-is-a-phony-who-thinks-he-is-a-jesus-figure-insiders/.

225. E. Brown, "How Adam Neumann's Over-the-Top Style Built WeWork. 'This Is Not the Way Everybody Behaves,'" *The Wall Street Journal*, September 18, 2019, https://www.wsj.com.

226. D. Schuster, "Ousted WeWork CEO Adam Neumann Is a 'Phony' Who 'Thinks He Is a Jesus Figure,'" *New York Post*, September 28, 2019, https://nypost.com/2019/09/28/ousted-wework-ceo-adam-neumann-is-a-phony-who-thinks-he-is-a-jesus-figure-insiders/.

227. D. Schuster, "Ousted WeWork CEO Adam Neumann Is a 'Phony' Who 'Thinks He Is a Jesus Figure,'" *New York Post*, September 28, 2019, https://nypost.com/2019/09/28/ousted-wework-ceo-adam-neumann-is-a-phony-who-thinks-he-is-a-jesus-figure-insiders/.

228. D. Schuster, "Ousted WeWork CEO Adam Neumann Is a 'Phony' Who 'Thinks He Is a Jesus Figure,'" *New York Post*, September 28,

2019, https://nypost.com/2019/09/28/ousted-wework-ceo-adam-neumann-is-a-phony-who-thinks-he-is-a-jesus-figure-insiders/.

229. D. Schuster, "Ousted WeWork CEO Adam Neumann Is a 'Phony' Who 'Thinks He Is a Jesus Figure,'" *New York Post*, September 28, 2019, https://nypost.com/2019/09/28/ousted-wework-ceo-adam-neumann-is-a-phony-who-thinks-he-is-a-jesus-figure-insiders/.

230. B. Gilbert, "WeWork Paid Its Own CEO $8.7 Million to Use the Name 'We'—Now He's Giving It Back," *The Sydney Morning Herald*, September 16, 2019, https://www.smh.com.au/business/companies/wework-paid-its-own-ceo-8-7-million-to-use-the-name-we-now-he-s-giving-it-back-20190905-p52o5l.html.

231. J. Aten, "WeWork's Fall Was a Disaster. A Full-Page Ad Isn't Going to Change That," *Inc.*, December 19, 2019, https://www.inc.com/jason-aten/weworks-fall-was-a-disaster-a-full-page-ad-isnt-going-to-change-that.html.

232. E. Brown, "How Adam Neumann's Over-the-Top Style Built WeWork. 'This Is Not the Way Everybody Behaves,'" *The Wall Street Journal*, September 18, 2019, https://www.wsj.com.

233. D. Schuster, "Ousted WeWork CEO Adam Neumann Is a 'Phony' Who 'Thinks He Is a Jesus Figure,'" *New York Post*, September 28, 2019, https://nypost.com/2019/09/28/ousted-wework-ceo-adam-neumann-is-a-phony-who-thinks-he-is-a-jesus-figure-insiders/.

234. J. Wingard, "The WeWork Disaster: Three Signs a Leader's Time Is Up," *Forbes*, October 3, 2019, https://www.forbes.com/sites/jasonwingard/2019/10/03/the-wework-disaster-three-signs-a-leaders-time-is-up/#69c90bfd75fe.

235. G. Sherman, "You Don't Bring Bad News to the Cult Leader: Inside The Fall of WeWork," *Vanity Fair*, November 21, 2019, https://www.vanityfair.com/news/2019/11/inside-the-fall-of-wework.

236. R. Molla, "WeWork Is Still Growing. That's Not Necessarily a Good Thing," *Vox*, January 8, 2020, https://www.vox.com/recode/2020/1/8/21052001/wework-growth-us-new-york-real-estate.

237. T. Huddleston Jr., "How WeWork's Infamous Co-Founder Adam Neumann Just Lost His Billionaire Status," *CNBC*, April 2, 2020, https://www.cnbc.com/2020/04/02/softbank-pulls-deal-costing-weworks-adam-neumann-nearly-1-billion.html.

238. L. Fruen, "Ousted WeWork Ceo Adam Nuemann Sues Softbank for Walking Away from $3 Billion Bailout and 'Secretly Taking Actions to Undermine' Troubled Startup," *Daily Mail*, May 5, 2020, https://www.dailymail.co.uk/news/article-8289087/Ousted-WeWork-CEO-Adam-Nuemann-sues-SoftBank-walking-away-3-billion-bailout.html.

239. A. González, "New Starbucks Campaign Touts Role as Global Hangout," *Seattle Times*, September 29, 2014, www.seattletimes.com/business/new-starbucks-campaign-touts-role-as-global-hangout/.

240. M. Gajanan, "Want to Use the Starbucks Bathroom? These Are Your Rights," *Time*, April 16, 2018, http://time.com/5241671/starbucks-philadelphia-bathroom-rights/.

241. B. Hutchinson and M. Stone, "Starbucks Manager Who Made Call Resulting in Black Men's Arrests No Longer Works for Company," *ABC News*, April 16, 2018, https://abcnews.go.com/Business/starbucks-ceo-kevin-johnson-orders-unconscious-bias-training/story?id=54496139.

242. B. Hutchinson and M. Stone, "Starbucks Manager Who Made Call Resulting in Black Men's Arrests No Longer Works for Company," *ABC News*, April 16, 2018, https://abcnews.go.com/Business/starbucks-ceo-kevin-johnson-orders-unconscious-bias-training/story?id=54496139.

243. E. Whack, "Black Men Arrested at Starbucks Settle for $1 and $200K Youth Program," *ABC News*, May 2, 2018, https://abcnews.go.com/US/wireStory/black-men-arrested-starbucks-settle-200k-program-54882092.

244. B. Hutchinson and M. Stone, "Starbucks Manager Who Made Call Resulting in Black Men's Arrests No Longer Works for Company," *ABC News*, April 16, 2018, https://abcnews.go.com/Business/starbucks-ceo-kevin-johnson-orders-unconscious-bias-training/story?id=54496139.

245. B. Hutchinson and M. Stone, "Starbucks Manager Who Made Call Resulting in Black Men's Arrests No Longer Works for Company," *ABC News*, April 16, 2018, https://abcnews.go.com/Business/starbucks-ceo-kevin-johnson-orders-unconscious-bias-training/story?id=54496139.

246. E. Whack, "Black Men Arrested at Starbucks Settle for $1 and $200K Youth Program," *ABC News,* May 2, 2018, https://abcnews.go.com/US/wireStory/black-men-arrested-starbucks-settle-200k-program-54882092.

247. G. Marks, "Starbucks Is Now Open for Loitering and It's a Terrible Business Decision," *Entrepreneur,* May 22, 2018, https://www.entrepreneur.com/article/313735.

CHAPTER 15

1. R. Maurer, "These 3 Talent Trends for 2020 Focus on Empathy," *SHRM Daily Newsletter*, January 31, 2020, https://www.shrm.org/resourcesandtools/hr-topics/talent-acquisition/pages/shrm-talent-trends-2020-empathy-employee-experience.aspx.

2. M. A. Clark, M. M. Robertson, and S. Young, "'I Feel Your Pain': A Critical Review of Organizational Research on Empathy," *Journal of Organizational Behavior*, February 2019, pp. 166–192.

3. B. Tait, "The Importance of Empathy in Leadership," *Forbes*, February 6, 2020, https://www.forbes.com/sites/forbescoachescouncil/2020/02/06/the-importance-of-empathy-in-leadership/#761e6b712d16. Also see Ö. N. Yalcin and S. DiPaola, "Modeling Empathy: Building a Link between Affective and Cognitive Processes," *Artificial Intelligence Review*, August 2019, pp. 2983–3006.

4. A. König, J. Bundy, and L. M. Little, "A Blessing and a Curse: How CEOs' Trait Empathy Affects Their Management of Organizational Crises," *Academy of Management Review*, January 2020, pp. 130–153.

5. O. L. Klimecki, "The Role of Empathy and Compassion in Conflict Resolution," *Emotion Review*, July 2019, https://journals.sagepub.com/doi/10.1177/1754073919838609.

6. B. Boyce, "Going Deeper," *Mindful*, April 2020, pp. 44–53.

7. S. Domet, "Adventure Inward," *Mindful*, April 2020, pp. 38–43.

8. J. A. Hall and R. Schwartz, "Empathy Present and Future," *The Journal of Social Psychology*, May 2019, pp. 225–243.

9. D. Carpenter, "Why Perspective Taking Is an Essential Skill for Success," *Lifehack*, December 18, 2019, https://www.lifehack.org/842058/perspective-taking.

10. M. A. Clark, M. M. Robertson, and S. Young, "'I Feel Your Pain': A Critical Review of Organizational Research on Empathy," *Journal of Organizational Behavior*, February 2019, pp. 166–192.

11. P. Bregman, "Empathy Starts with Curiosity," *Harvard Business Review*, April 27, 2020, https://hbr.org/2020/04/empathy-starts-with-curiosity?ab=hero-subleft-1.

12. "Career Readiness Defined," *NACE Center*, 2020, https://www.naceweb.org/career-readiness/competencies/career-readiness-defined.

13. S. Bilkha, "What Do Employers Mean by 'Good Communication Skills'?" *Entrepreneur*, April 3, 2019, https://www.entrepreneur.com/article/331660.

14. R. S. Wyer Jr. and L. J. Shrum, "The Role of Comprehension Processes in Communication and Persuasion," *Media Psychology*, April 2015, pp. 163–195.

15. J. Bauer-Wolf, "Overconfident Students, Dubious Employers," *Inside Higher Ed*, February 23, 2018, https://www.insidehighered.com/news/2018/02/23/study-students-believe-they-are-prepared-workplace-employers-disagree.

16. J. Kotter, "Power, Dependence, and Effective Management," *Harvard Business Review*, Vol. 55 (1977), pp. 125–136.

17. N. Oseland and P. Hodsman, "A Psychoacoustical Approach to Resolving Office Noise Distraction," *Journal of Corporate Real Estate*, November 2018, pp. 260–280.

18. These sources are discussed by A. Ahmed, "Noise in Business Communication," *bizfluent*, April 25, 2019, https://bizfluent.com/facts-6757500-noise-business-communication.html.

19. L. Rolfö, J. Eklund, and H. Jahncke, "Perceptions of Performance and Satisfaction after Relocation to an Activity-Based Office," *Ergonomics*, November 2017, pp. 644–657.

20. N. Oseland and P. Hodsman, "A Psychoacoustical Approach to Resolving Office Noise Distraction," *Journal of Corporate Real Estate*, November 2018, pp. 260–280.

21. Supporting findings can be found in "Mama Was Right! Study Shows Students Learn Better When They Take Handwritten Notes," *Daily Health Post*, January 29, 2020, https://dailyhealthpost.com/student-learn-better-handwritten-notes. Also see A. Wignall, "Laptop vs. Notebook: Which Is Better to Take Notes On?" *College Raptor*, December 18, 2019; https://www.collegeraptor.com/find-colleges/articles/tips-tools-advice/laptop-vs-notebook-better-take-notes.

22. C. Siemaszko, "Language Barriers Helped Turn Smithfield Foods Meat Plant into COVID-19 Hotspot," April 23, 2020, https://www.nbcnews.com/news/us-news/language-barriers-helped-turn-smithfield-foods-meat-plant-covid-19-n1190736.

23. J. Lussenhop, "Coronavirus at Smithfield Pork Plant: The Untold Story of America's Biggest Outbreak," April 17, 2020, https://www.bbc.com/news/world-us-canada-52311877.

24. C. Siemaszko, "Language Barriers Helped Turn Smithfield Foods Meat Plant into COVID-19 Hotspot," April 23, 2020, https://www.nbcnews.com/news/us-news/language-barriers-helped-turn-smithfield-foods-meat-plant-covid-19-n1190736.

25. C. Woolston, "Jargon Shuts Readers Out," *Nature*, March 12, 2020, p. 309.

26. T. Musbach, "The Most Annoying, Overused Words in the Workplace," *San Francisco Chronicle*, October 11, 2009, p. A1.

27. M. Gafni and J. Garofoli, "Exclusive: Captain of Aircraft Carrier with Growing Coronavirus Outbreak Pleads for Help from Navy," *San Francisco Chronicle*, April 9, 2020, https://www.sfchronicle.com/bayarea/article/Exclusive-Captain-of-aircraft-carrier-with-15167883.php.

28. E. Livni, "The Navy Captain Fired for Sounding Coronavirus Alarms Broke No Law—Just Protocol," April 4, 2020, https://qz.com/1831969/coronavirus-fired-navy-captain-brett-crozier-broke-no-laws-just-protocol.

29. B. Odom, "Navy Captain Fired Over Coronavirus Memo Is a Calm, Honorable Leader. He's Also My Friend," *USA Today*, April 7, 2020, https://www.usatoday.com/story/opinion/2020/04/07/navy-fired-defamed-my-friend-over-coronavirus-letter-column/2960627001.

30. An application to social media was conducted by S. Tanupabrungsun and J. Hemsley, "Studying Celebrity Practices on Twitter Using a Framework for Measuring Media Richness," *Social Media + Society*, March 2018, pp. 1–11.

31. C-H. Tseng and L-F. Wei, "The Efficiency of Mobile Media Richness Across Different Stages of Online Consumer Behavior," *International Journal of Information Management*, February 2020, pp. 353–364.

32. R. L. Daft and R. H. Lengel, "Information Richness: A New Approach to Managerial Behavior and Organizational Design," in B. M. Staw and L. L. Cummings (eds.), *Research in Organizational Behavior* (Greenwich, CT: JAI Press, 1984), p. 196. Also see R. H. Lengel and R. L. Daft, "The Selection of Communication Media as an Executive Skill," *Academy of Management Executive*, August 1988, pp. 225–232.

33. M. Lipowski and I. Bondos, "The Influence of Perceived Media Richness of Marketing Channels on Online Channel Use," *Baltic Journal of Management*, January 2018, pp. 169–190.

34. D. R. Dunaetz, T. C. Lisk, and M. M. Shin, "Personality, Gender, and Age as Predictors of Media Richness Preference," *Advantages in Multimedia*, October 2015, pp. 1–9.

35. S-H. Chao, J, Jiang, C-H. Hsu, Y-T. Chiang, E. Ng, and W-T. Fang, "Technology-Enhanced Learning for Graduate Students: Exploring the Correlation of Media Richness and Creativity of Computer-Mediated Communication and Face-to-Face Communication," *Applied Sciences*, Vol. 10 (2020), p. 1602, https://www.mdpi.com/journal/applsci. Also see F-C. Tseng, T. Cheng, P-L. Yu, T-L. Huang, and C-I. Teng, "Media Richness, Social Presence and Loyalty to Mobile Instant Messaging," *Industrial Management & Data Systems*, July 2019, pp. 1357–1373.

36. T. Neeley, "What Managers Need to Know about Social Tools," *Harvard Business Review*, November–December 2017, pp. 118–126. Also see T. Harbert, "Let's Chat," *HR Magazine*, November 2017, pp. 46–51.

37. "What to Say and How to Say It: Executives Discuss Crisis Communication in the Heat of a Pandemic," *Catholic Health World*, April–May 2020, https://www.chausa.org/publications/catholic-health-world/archives/issues/pandemic-coverage/what-to-say-and-how-

to-say-it-executives-discuss-crisis-communication-in-the-heat-of-a-pandemic.

38. This case was based on "What to Say and How to Say It: Executives Discuss Crisis Communication in the Heat of a Pandemic," *Catholic Health World*, April–May 2020, https://www.chausa.org/publications/catholic-health-world/archives/issues/pandemic-coverage/what-to-say-and-how-to-say-it-executives-discuss-crisis-communication-in-the-heat-of-a-pandemic.

39. C. Cutter and J. Maloney, "With Business Turned Upside Down, CEOs Face Monumental Leadership Challenge," *The Wall Street Journal*, March 22, 2020, https://www.wsj.com/articles/with-business-turned-upside-down-ceos-face-monumental-leadership-challenge-11584891047?mod=searchresults&page=2&pos=2.

40. A. Blank, "Don't Lose Contact with These 5 People During Coronavirus Isolation," *Forbes*, April 7, 2020, https://www.forbes.com/sites/averyblank/2020/04/07/dont-lose-contact-with-these-5-people-during-coronavirus-isolation/#6e64245b7b56.

41. S. Subhakaran and L. Dyaram, "Interpersonal Antecedents to Employee Upward Voice: Mediating Role of Psychological Safety," *International Journal of Productivity and Performance Management*, November 2018, pp. 1510–1525.

42. X. Peng, G. Hendrikse, and W. Deng, "Communication and Innovation in Cooperatives," *Journal of the Knowledge Economy*, December 2018, pp. 1184–1209.

43. C. Samuelson, "How Companies Are Leading with Empathy," *Entrepreneur*, April 30, 2020, https://theconversation.com/lead-with-empathy-during-the-covid-19-crisis-135175.

44. See the related discussion in A. Bencsik and T. Juhasz, "Impacts of Informal Knowledge Sharing (Workplace Gossip) on Organisational Trust," *Economics and Sociology*, March 2020, pp. 249–270.

45. C. K. Goman, "I Heard It through the Grapevine," *American Management Association*, January 24, 2019, https://www.amanet.org/articles/i-heard-it-through-the-grapevine.

46. These recommendations were based on "How to Stop Workplace Gossip," *Robert Half blog*, January 6, 2020, https://www.roberthalf.com/blog/management-tips/managing-the-rumor-mill-6-tips-on-dealing-with-office-gossip.

47. J. Humphrey "Why You Need to Master In-Person Conversations in Your Slack-Driven Office," *Fast Company*, July 1, 2016, http://www.fastcompany.com/3061470/how-to-be-a-success-at-everything/why-you-need-to-master-in-person-conversations-in-your-sla.

48. E. Hardy, "Apple CEO Tells Employees He's 'Optimistic' in Stressful Times," *Cult of Mac*, April 16, 2020, https://www.cultofmac.com/702807/apple-ceo-tells-employees-hes-optimistic-in-stressful-times.

49. P. Economy, "A New Study of 19 Million Meetings Reveals That Meetings Waste More Time Than Ever (but There Is a Solution)," *Inc.*, February 24, 2020, https://www.inc.com/peter-economy/a-new-study-of-19000000-meetings-reveals-that-meetings-waste-more-time-than-ever-but-there-is-a-solution.html.

50. A quote from Paul Axtell in S. Hyken, "Six Ways to Have Effective and Successful Meetings," *Forbes*, May 10, 2020, https://www.forbes.com/sites/shephyken/2020/05/10/six-ways-to-have-effective-and-successful-meetings/#1a50cd838b94.

51. M. Abbajay, "9 Ways to Make Your Meetings Matter," *Forbes*, January 20, 2020, https://www.forbes.com/sites/maryabbajay/2020/01/20/9-ways-to-make-your-meetings-matter/#19a4a3203831.

52. These recommendations were largely based on Abbajay, "9 Ways to Make Your Meetings Matter," *Forbes*, January 20, 2020, https://www.forbes.com/sites/maryabbajay/2020/01/20/9-ways-to-make-your-meetings-matter/#19a4a3203831. Also see S. Hyken, "Six Ways to Have Effective and Successful Meetings," *Forbes*, May 10, 2020, https://www.forbes.com/sites/shephyken/2020/05/10/six-ways-to-have-effective-and-successful-meetings/#1a50cd838b94.

53. H. Field, "Survey: Here's How U.S. Workers Really Feel about Meetings," *Entrepreneur*, February 25, 2020, https://www.entrepreneur.com/article/346742.

54. K. Hedges, "Why Great Leaders Do These 5 Things in Every Meeting," *Inc.com*, December 19, 2017, https://www.inc.com/the-muse/how-to-stand-out-crowded-meeting-great-leaders-run-meetings-like-this.html.

55. E. Bernstein and B. Waber, "The Truth About Open Offices." *Harvard Business Review*, Vol. 97 (2019), pp. 82–91.

56. R. Sanson-Fisher, B. Hobden, A. Waller, N. Dodd, and L. Boyd, "Methodological Quality of Teaching Communication Skills to Undergraduate Medical Students: A Mapping Review," *BMC Medical Education*, Vol. 18, No. 1 (2018), p. 151.

57. C. Rogers and F. Roethlisberger, "Barriers and Gateways to Communication," *Harvard Business Review*, July–August 1952, pp. 46–52.

58. S. Heathfield, "The Components of Communication in the Workplace," *The Balance Careers*, April 29, 2020, https://www.thebalancecareers.com/communication-in-the-workplace-1918089.

59. C. Yue, L. Men, and M Ferguson, "Bridging Transformational Leadership, Transparent Communication, and Employee Openness to Change: The Mediating Role of Trust," *Public Relations Review*, Vol. 45, No. 3 (2019). Also see H. Jiang and Y. Luo, "Crafting Employee Trust: From Authenticity, Transparency to Engagement," *Journal of Communication Management*, May 2018, pp. 138–160.

60. J. Folkman, "How Trust Affects Your Ability to Communicate and How to Fix It," *Forbes*, April 7, 2020, https://www.forbes.com/sites/joefolkman/2020/04/07/how-trust-effects-your-ability-to-communicate-and-how-to-fix-it/#4b98b704acae.

61. E. Langer, "Minding Matters: The Consequences of Mindlessness—Mindfulness," *Advances in Experimental Social Psychology*, Vol. 22 1989, pp. 137–173.

62. V. Greenwood, "Focus and the Organized Mind: A Cheat Sheet to Boost Productivity and Cope with Information Overload," *The Washington Center for Cognitive Therapy*, https://washingtoncenterforcognitivetherapy.com/focus-and-the-organized-mind/(accessed May 30, 2020).

63. "How Smartphones Are Killing Conversation," *Greater Good Magazine*, December 7, 2015, https://greatergood.berkeley.edu/article/item/how_smartphones_are_killing_conversation.

64. S. Kang and T. Kurtzberg, "Reach for Your Cell Phone at Your Own Risk: The Cognitive Costs of Media Choice for Breaks," *Journal of Behavioral Addictions*, Vol. 8, No. 3 (2019), pp. 395–403.

65. Bernie Sanders, https://twitter.com/SenSanders (accessed May 24, 2020).

66. J. Brandon, "Please Stop Sending So Many Emails All Day Long. It's Not Working Anyway," *Inc.*, October 15, 2019, https://www.inc.com/john-brandon/please-stop-sending-so-many-emails-all-day-long-its-not-working-anyway.html.

67. M. Finnegan, "Want a More Digital Workplace? You'll Have to Overcome Resistance to Tech," *Computer World*, June 27, 2018, https://www.computerworld.com/article/3284940/want-a-more-digital-workplace-youll-have-to-overcome-resistance-to-tech.html.

68. George Ritzer, *Introduction to Sociology* (Thousand Oaks, CA: Sage Publications, 2013), p. 116.

69. T. Jiang, H. Li, and Y Hou, "Cultural Differences in Humor Perception, Usage, and Implications," *Frontiers in Psychology*, Vol. 10 (2019), p. 123.

70. "YouGov Survey: British Sarcasm 'Lost on Americans,'" *BBC*, January 11, 2019, https://www.bbc.com/news/world-us-canada-46846467.

71. "The Value of Cultural Training for Expatriates," *GLOBAL LT*, https://global-lt.com/wp-content/uploads/2017/07/Value-of-Cultural-Training.pdf?2e5101.

72. "Strategies to Improve Intercultural Communication," *Notre Dame Online*, March 13, 2020, https://www.notredameonline.com/resources/intercultural-management/strategies-to-improve-intercultural-communication/.

73. Based on: "What Is Cultural Fluency? And Why Is It Important?" *NBC News*, October 15, 2019, https://www.nbcnews.com/better/lifestyle/what-cultural-fluency-why-it-important-ncna1061656. Also see "Strategies to Improve Intercultural Communication," *Notre Dame*

Online, March 13, 2020, https://www.notredameonline.com/resources/intercultural-management/strategies-to-improve-intercultural-communication/; V. Gambhir, "Building Cultural Fluency," *LinkedIn*, May 13, 2019, https://www.linkedin.com/pulse/building-cultural-fluency-vivek-gambhir.

74. "What Is Cultural Fluency? And Why Is It Important?" *NBC News*, October 15, 2019, https://www.nbcnews.com/better/lifestyle/what-cultural-fluency-why-it-important-ncna1061656.

75. M. Nesic and V. Nesic, "Neuroscience of Nonverbal Communication," in A. Kostic and D. Chadee (eds.), *The Social Psychology of Nonverbal Communication* (New York: Palgrave Macmillan, 2015), pp. 30–64.

76. S. Anders, "What Are You Really Saying? The Importance of Nonverbal Clues," *American Association for Physician Leadership*, December 5, 2018, https://www.physicianleaders.org/news/what-are-you-really-saying-importance-nonverbal-clues.

77. S. Rogers, O. Guidetti, C. Speelman, M. Longmuir, and R. Phillips, "Contact Is in the Eye of the Beholder: The Eye Contact Illusion," *Perception*, Vol. 48, No. 3 (2019), pp. 248–252.

78. J. Hannan, M. Fonseca, E. Lara, M. Braithwaite, F. Irving, and E. Azutillo, "Coaching Nurses to Care: Empathetic Communication in Challenging Situations," in *Teaching Empathy in Healthcare: Building a New Core Competency* (New York: Springer, 2019), pp. 193–209.

79. O. Khazan, "Why Americans Smile So Much," *The Atlantic*, May 3, 2017, https://www.theatlantic.com/science/archive/2017/05/why-americans-smile-so-much/524967/.

80. T. Talhelm, S. Oishi, and X. Zhang, "Who Smiles While Alone? Rates of Smiling Lower in China Than US," *Emotion*, Vol. 19, No. 4 (2019), p. 741.

81. L. Ko, "An American Woman Quits Smiling," *The New York Times*, April 21, 2018, https://www.nytimes.com/2018/04/21/opinion/sunday/an-american-woman-quits-smiling.html.

82. "Russia Training Their People to Smile for World Cup," *OHO Feed*, June 21, 2018, https://www.ohofeed.com/russia-training-people-smile-fifa-world-cup/.

83. S. Lebowitz and A. Akhtar, "19 Science-Backed Tricks for Reading Body Language So You Can Avoid Awkward Situations," *Business Insider*, August 8, 2019, https://www.businessinsider.com/how-to-read-body-language-2017-5#an-expansive-pose-signals-power-and-a-sense-of-achievement-9.

84. K. Vasel, "To Hug or Not to Hug: A 5-Step Guide to Embracing at Work," *CNN*, July 12, 2019, https://www.cnn.com/2019/07/12/success/hugging-at-work/index.html.

85. Based on "Why You Shouldn't Hug Your Colleagues," *BBC*, October 16, 2018, https://www.bbc.com/news/business-45680670. Also see K. Vasel, "To Hug or Not to Hug: A 5-Step Guide to Embracing at Work," *CNN*, July 12, 2019, https://www.cnn.com/2019/07/12/success/hugging-at-work/index.html.

86. T. Taciano and C. Sibley, "Empathic and Social Dominance Orientations Help Explain Gender Differences in Environmentalism: A One-Year Bayesian Mediation Analysis," *Personality and Individual Differences*, Vol. 90 (2016), pp. 85–88. Also see T. Lorenz, "Are Male and Female Brains Biologically Different?" *The Atlantic*, June 25, 2018, https://www.theatlantic.com/science/archive/2018/06/male-female-brains-biologically-different/563702/.

87. D. Tannen, "The Power of Talk: Who Gets Heard and Why," in R. J. Lewicki and D. M. Saunders (eds.), *Negotiation: Readings, Exercises, and Cases*, 3rd ed. (Burr Ridge, IL: Irwin/McGraw-Hill, 1999), pp. 147–148.

88. P. Cooper, "140+ Social Media Statistics That Matter to Marketers in 2020," *Hootsuite*, February 20, 2020, https://blog.hootsuite.com/social-media-statistics-for-social-media-managers/#general. Also see J. Zote, "55 Critical Social Media Statistics to Fuel Your 2020 Strategy," *Sprout Social*, https://sproutsocial.com/insights/social-media-statistics/ (accessed May 16, 2020); G. Pickard-Whitehead, "73% of Small Businesses Invest in Social Media Marketing, Survey Finds," *Small Business Trends*, March 10, 2020, https://smallbiztrends.com/2019/04/2019-social-media-statistics.html.

89. A. Poulis, I. Rizomyliotis, and K. Konstantoulaki, "Do Firms Still Need to Be Social? Firm Generated Content in Social Media," *Information Technology & People*, April 2019, pp. 387–404. Also see Y. Bilgin, "The Effect of Social Media Marketing Activities on Brand Awareness, Brand Image and Brand Loyalty," *Business & Management Studies: An International Journal*, April 2018, pp. 128–148.

90. B. Davis, "30 Brands with Excellent Social Media Strategies," *Econsultancy*, November 20, 2018, https://econsultancy.com/30-brands-with-excellent-social-media-strategies/.

91. M. Saito, "Tear Gas and Water Cannons: Hong Kong Students Brave the Front Lines to Livestream the Protests," *U.S. News and World Report*, January 9, 2020, https://www.usnews.com/news/world/articles/2020-01-09/tear-gas-and-water-cannons-hong-kong-students-brave-the-front-lines-to-livestream-the-protests. Also see "The Hong Kong Protests Explained in 100 and 500 Words," *BBC*, November 28, 2019, https://www.bbc.com/news/world-asia-china-49317695.

92. H. Gardner, "Livestreaming Funerals Becomes Increasingly Common in Age of Coronavirus," *Louisville Courier Journal*, April 15, 2020, https://www.courier-journal.com/story/news/local/2020/04/15/covid-19-kentucky-livestreaming-funerals-age-coronavirus/2990874001/.

93. E. Roth, "The Top 9 Russian Social Networks," *MUO*, February 4, 2020, https://www.makeuseof.com/tag/top-8-russian-social-networks-makes-great/. Also see T. DeGennaro, "10 Most Popular Social Media Sites in China (2019 Updated)," *Dragon Social*, https://www.dragonsocial.net/blog/social-media-in-china/ (accessed May 17, 2020); A. Carrasquilla, "A Marketer's Handbook to Social Media Usage in Latin America," *Colibri*, August 21, 2019, https://www.colibricontent.com/social-media-latin-america/.

94. "Recruiting in the New Age: Social Media and Recruitment Statistics," *Career Arc*, May 31, 2019, https://www.careerarc.com/blog/2019/05/social-media-and-recruitment-statistics-for-today/.

95. J. Chu, "20 Mind-Blowing Social Recruiting Statistics [2020]," *Career Arc*, July 24, 2019, https://www.careerarc.com/blog/2019/07/20-mind-blowing-social-recruiting-statistics/. Also see J. Clement, "Number of Facebook Users Worldwide 2008–2020," *Statista*, April 30, 2020, https://www.statista.com/statistics/264810/number-of-monthly-active-facebook-users-worldwide/; J. Gallant, "50+ LinkedIn Statistics for 2020 (User Stats, Demographics, Usage & More)," *Foundation Inc.*, https://foundationinc.co/lab/b2b-marketing-linkedin-stats/ (accessed May 18, 2020).

96. A. Hrab, "How to Select New Employees Through Social Media Recruiting," *eSkill*, https://www.eskill.com/blog/recognize-skills-social-media/ (accessed May 18, 2020).

97. A. Doyle, "Tips for Text Messaging and Interviewing with Recruiters," *The Balance Careers*, November 22, 2019, https://www.thebalancecareers.com/tips-for-texting-with-recruiters-2060584.

98. T. Kunsman, "17 Social Recruiting Statistics and the Impact on Hiring Top Talent," *Everyone Social*, February 12, 2020, https://everyonesocial.com/blog/social-recruiting-statistics/.

99. "Why GitHub," *GitHub*, https://github.com/about (accessed May 18, 2020). Also see "Microsoft Acquires GitHub," *Microsoft*, https://news.microsoft.com/announcement/microsoft-acquires-github/ (accessed May 18, 2020); "About," *Mediabistro*, https://www.mediabistro.com/about/ (accessed May 18, 2020); "About," *Dribbble*, https://dribbble.com/about (accessed May 18, 2020).

100. H. K. Aggerholm and S. E. Andersen, "Social Media Recruitment 3.0: Toward a New Paradigm of Strategic Recruitment Communication," *Journal of Communication Management*, Vol. 22, No. 2 (2018), pp. 122–137.

101. "More Than Half of Employers Have Found Content on Social Media That Caused Them NOT to Hire a Candidate, According to Recent CareerBuilder Survey," *PR Newswire*, August 9, 2018, https://www.prnewswire.com/news-releases/more-than-half-of-employers-have-found-content-on-social-media-that-caused-them-not-to-hire-a-candidate-according-to-recent-careerbuilder-survey-300694437.html.

102. J. Foster, "SEO Guide to Optimizing Your LinkedIn Profile for More Connections, Better Leads," *Search Engine Land*, April 24, 2019,

https://searchengineland.com/seo-guide-to-optimizing-your-linkedin-profile-for-more-connections-better-leads-315882.

103. M. De Silva, "What to Delete from Social Media before You Start Job Hunting," *Quartz*, April 17, 2019, https://qz.com/work/1597042/what-to-delete-from-social-media-before-you-start-job-hunting/.

104. S. Gunel, "How to Build a Strong Brand on Social Media in 2020," *Medium*, January 9, 2020, https://medium.com/better-marketing/how-to-build-a-strong-brand-on-social-media-in-2020-ff56fa51b4ca.

105. R. Maurer, "Screening Candidates' Social Media May Lead to TMI, Discrimination Claims," *Society for Human Resource Management*, April 23, 2018, https://www.shrm.org/resourcesandtools/hr-topics/talent-acquisition/pages/screening-social-media-discrimination-claims.aspx.

106. M. Krauter, "Gen Z Overuses Social Media," *The Daily Illini*, April 14, 2020, https://dailyillini.com/opinions/2020/04/14/opinion-gen-z-overuses-social-media/.

107. R. M. S. Jafar, S. Geng, W. Ahmad, B. Niu, and F. T. S. Chan, "Social Media Usage and Employee's Job Performance: The Moderating Role of Social Media Rules," *Industrial Management & Data Systems*, October 2019, pp. 1908–1925. Also see T. Wushe and J. Shenje, "The Relationship between Social Media Usage in the Workplace and Employee Productivity in the Public Sector: Case Study of Government Departments in Harare," *SA Journal of Human Resource Management*, November 2019, https://doi.org/ 10.4102/sajhrm.v17i0.1116.

108. T. Ogink and J. Q. Dong, "Stimulating Innovation by User Feedback on Social Media: The Case of an Online User Innovation Community," *Technology Forecasting & Social Change*, July 2019, pp. 295–302; H. Bhimani, A. Mention, and P. Barlatier, "Social Media and Innovation: A Systematic Literature Review and Future Research Directions," *Technology Forecasting & Social Change*, July 2019, pp. 251–269; G. Corral de Zubielqui, H. Fryges, and J. Jones, "Social Media, Open Innovation & HRM: Implications for Performance," *Technology Forecasting & Social Change*, July 2019, pp. 334–347; B. W. Robertson and K. F. Kee, "Social Media at Work: The Roles of Job Satisfaction, Employment Status, and Facebook Use with Co-Workers," *Computer in Human Behavior*, May 2017, pp. 191–196.

109. S. Patel, "How to Boost Productivity as a Remote Employee," *Forbes*, March 2, 2016, http://www.forbes.com/sites/sujanpatel/2016/03/02/how-to-boost-productivity-as-a-remote-employee/5/#1adc908752d9.

110. N. Burton, "14 Habits of the Most Productive Remote Workers," *Fast Company*, June 8, 2015, http://www.fastcompany.com/3060650/your-most-productive-self/14-habits-of-the-most-productive-remote-workers. Also see D. Aamoth, "25 Free Chrome Extensions to Make You an Incredibly Productive Person," *Fast Company*, June 15, 2016, http://www.fastcompany.com/3060764/app-economy/25-free-chrome-extensions-to-make-you-an-incredibly-productive-person.

111. J. Martin, "How to Unplug from Work During the Holidays: 7 Tips to Help You Achieve Work Life Balance," *CloudApp*, May 9, 2020, https://www.getcloudapp.com/blog/unplug-during-holidays.

112. J. Crowley, "How an After Hours Email Policy Might Work in Practice," *People HR*, January 30, 2019, https://www.peoplehr.com/blog/2019/01/30/hours-email-policy-might-work-practice/.

113. S. Baer, "Social Media Proves to Boost Employee Engagement," *Forbes*, February 13, 2018, https://www.forbes.com/sites/forbesagencycouncil/2018/02/13/social-media-proves-to-boost-employee-engagement/#5a4da4d54db5. Also see M. Stevenson, "Embracing Social Media as a Means to Achieve Employee Engagement," *HR Exchange Network*, March 13, 2018, https://www.hrexchangenetwork.com/employee-engagement/articles/embracing-social-media-as-a-means-to-achieve.

114. J. C. Searls, "Forward-Thinking Financial Institutions Need to Be Aware of Social Media Compliance Risks," *Bradley*, August 16, 2019, https://www.bradley.com/insights/publications/2019/08/forwardthinking-financial-institutions-need-to-be-aware-of-social-media-compliance-risks. Also see R. E. Ployhart, "Social Media in the Workplace: Issues and Strategic Questions," *SHRM Executive Briefing*, November 2011, www.shrm.org/about/foundation/products/documents/social%20media%20briefing-%20final.pdf. Also see "Should Companies Monitor Their Employees' Social Media?" *The Wall Street Journal*, May 12, 2014, pp. R1, R2.

115. A. Huntsberger, "How Much Do People Spend on Fantasy Football?" *Opp Loans*, April 22, 2020, https://www.opploans.com/blog/how-much-do-people-spend-on-fantasy-football/.

116. P. Ausick, "How Much the $7 Billion Fantasy Football Business Costs Other Employers," *24/7 Wall Street*, August 15, 2019, https://247wallst.com/economy/2019/08/15/how-much-the-7-billion-fantasy-football-business-costs-other-employers/.

117. "Rethinking Crowdsourcing," *Harvard Business Review*, November–December 2017, pp. 20–22.

118. "4 Companies That Are Killing It with Crowdsourcing," *Planbox*, https://www.planbox.com/4-companies-that-are-killing-it-with-crowdsourcing/ (accessed May 19, 2020). Also see "LEGO Ideas Sets Record with First 2020 rRview," *Brick Fanatics*, May 5, 2020, https://www.brickfanatics.com/lego-ideas-sets-record-with-first-2020-review/.

119. K. B. Wilson, V. Bhakoo, and D. Samson, "Crowdsourcing: A Contemporary Form of Project Management with Linkages to Open Innovation and Novel Operations," *International Journal of Operations & Production Management*, Vol. 38 (6) 2018, pp. 1467–1494.

120. F. R. Assis Neto and C. A. S. Santos, "Understanding Crowdsourcing Projects: A Systematic Review of Tendencies, Workflow, and Quality Management," *Information Processing and Management*, July 2018, pp. 490–506. Also see L. Dahlander and H. Piezunka, "Why Some Crowdsourcing Efforts Work and Others Don't," *Harvard Business Review*, February 21, 2017, https://hbr.org/2017/02/why-some-crowdsourcing-efforts-work-and-others-dont.

121. These four conclusions were based on N. Jones, R. Borgman, and E. Ulusoy, "Impact of Social Media on Small Businesses," *Journal of Small Business and Enterprise Development*, Vol. 22 (2015), pp. 611–632.

122. A. Poulis, I. Rizomyliotis, and K. Konstantoulaki, "Do Firms Still Need to Be Social? Firm Generated Content in Social Media," *Information Technology & People*, April 2019, pp. 387–404. Also see Y. Bilgin, "The Effect of Social Media Marketing Activities on Brand Awareness, Brand Image and Brand Loyalty," *Business & Management Studies: An International Journal*, April 2018, pp. 128–148; Y. Liu and R. A. Lopez, "The Impact of Social Media Conversations on Consumer Brand Choices," *Marketing Letters*, August 2014, pp. 1–13; A. Dwivedi, L. W. Johnson, D. C. Wilkie, and L. De Araujo-Gil, "Consumer Emotional Brand Attachment with Social Media Brands and Social Media Brand Equity," *European Journal of Marketing*, June 2019, pp. 1176–1204.

123. M. Dibenedetto, "Our Favourite Social Media Campaigns of 2019," *Moon Dust*, November 28, 2019, https://www.moondustagency.com/knowledge-center/best-social-campaigns-2019.

124. R. Guesalaga, "The Use of Social Media in Sales: Individual and Organizational Antecedents, and the Role of Customer Engagement in Social Media," *Industrial Marketing Management*, April 2016, pp. 71–79. Also see L. Collier, "Should You Let Your Employees Shop Online at Work?" Office-Depot Solutions Center, October 26, 2015, http://solutions.officedepot.com/leadership/article/should-you-let-your-employees-shop-online-at-work.

125. D. Baasiri, "How to Boost Your Brand through an Effective Social Media Strategy," *Forbes*, December 15, 2016, https://www.forbes.com/sites/forbescommunicationscouncil/2016/12/15/how-to-boost-your-brand-through-an-effective-social-media-strategy/#1dd3be8b7334.

126. "The 9 Best Brands on Social Media," *e-clincher*, September 27, 2019, https://eclincher.com/blog/the-9-best-brands-on-social-media/.

127. M. Etter, D. Ravasi, and E. Colleoni, "Social Media and the Formation of Organizational Reputation," *Academy of Management Review*, January 2019, pp. 28–52.

128. A. Triantafillidou and P. Yannas, "Social Media Crisis Communication in Racially Charged Crises: Exploring the Effects of Social Media and Image Restoration Strategies," *Computers in Human Behavior*, May 2020, https://doi.org/10.1016/j.chb.2020.106269.

129. P. Cooper, "How to Write a Social Media Policy for Your Company (Free Template)," *Hootsuite*, July 29, 2019, https://blog.hootsuite.com/social-media-policy-for-employees/.

130. M. Gollin, "15 Cringeworthy Instagram Marketing Mistakes," *Falcon*, January 2, 2020, https://www.falcon.io/insights-hub/topics/social-media-strategy/15-brands-most-embarrassing-instagram-marketing-mistakes/.

131. "How to Successfully Apologize on Social Media," *Creative Label*, https://itscreativelabel.com/how-to-successfully-apologize-on-social-media/ (accessed May 20, 2020).

132. B. Cherry, "The Dos and Don'ts of Responding to Negative Social Media Comments," *BlueLeadz*, December 31, 2018, https://www.bluleadz.com/blog/the-dos-and-donts-of-responding-to-negative-social-media-comments.

133. B. Cherry, "The Dos and Don'ts of Responding to Negative Social Media Comments," *BlueLeadz*, December 31, 2018, https://www.bluleadz.com/blog/the-dos-and-donts-of-responding-to-negative-social-media-comments.

134. "Social Media in the Workplace: Encouraging Employees to be Active on Platforms," *SOJCSSM*, February 12, 2019, http://sojcssm.com/2019/02/social-media-in-the-workplace-encouraging-employees-to-be-active-on-platforms/.

135. S. Pindek, A. Krajcevska, and P. E. Spector, "Cyberloafing as a Coping Mechanism: Dealing with Workplace Boredom," *Computers in Human Behavior*, September 2018, pp. 147–152. Also see K. Koay and P. C. Soh, "Should Cyberloafing Be Allowed in the Workplace?" *Human Resource Management International Digest*, October 2018, pp. 4–6.

136. "2018 Workplace Distraction Report," *Udemy*, 2018, https://research.udemy.com/wp-content/uploads/2018/03/FINAL-Udemy_2018_Workplace_Distraction_Report_links.pdf. Also see C. Stokel-Walker, "Cyberloafing: The Line between Rejuvenating and Wasting Time," *BBC*, February 7, 2020, https://www.bbc.com/worklife/article/20200206-cyberloafing-the-line-between-rejuvenating-and-wasting-time.

137. C. Goerner, "Practical Advice on Work and Careers from Dr. Carolyn Goerner," *Practical Paradigms*, April 24, 2019, https://www.practicalparadigms.com/blog-content/2019/4/22/stop-the-cyberloafing.

138. L. Khansa, R. Barkhi, S. Ray, and Z. Davis, "Cyberloafing in the Workplace: Mitigation Tactics and Their Impact on Individuals' Behavior," *Information Technology Management*, September 2017, pp. 197–215.

139. B. A. Allan, J. R. Rolniak, and L. Bouchard, "Underemployment and Well-Being: Exploring the Dark Side of Meaningful Work," *Journal of Career Development*, February 2020, pp. 111–125.

140. C. Goerner, "Practical Advice on Work and Careers from Dr. Carolyn Goerner," *Practical Paradigms*, April 24, 2019, https://www.practicalparadigms.com/blog-content/2019/4/22/stop-the-cyberloafing.

141. N. Nair, D. C. Good, and A. J. Murrell, "Microaggression Experiences of Different Marginalized Identities," *Equality, Diversity and Inclusion: An International Journal*, November 2019, pp. 870–883.

142. N. Goodman, "Micro-Aggressions and Phubbing in the Age of FoMO," *Training*, https://trainingmag.com/trgmag-article/micro-aggressions-and-phubbing-age-fomo/ (accessed May 20, 2020).

143. A. Ivanova et al., "Mobile Phone Addiction, Phubbing, and Depression among Men and Women: A Moderated Mediation Analysis," *Psychiatric Quarterly*, September 2020, https://doi.org/10.1007/s11126-020-09723-8. Also see Ö. Çikrikci, M. D. Griffiths, and E. Erzen, "Testing the Mediating Role of Phubbing in the Relationship between the Big Five Personality Traits and Satisfaction with Life," *International Journal of Mental Health and Addiction*, July 2019, https://doi.org/10.1007/s11469-019-00115-z.

144. N. Goodman, "Micro-Aggressions and Phubbing in the Age of FoMO," *Training*, https://trainingmag.com/trgmag-article/micro-aggressions-and-phubbing-age-fomo/ (accessed May 20, 2020). Also see J. Ducharme, "'Phubbing' Is Hurting Your Relationships. Here's What It Is," *Time*, March 29, 2018, http://time.com/5216853/what-is-phubbing/.

145. J. Ducharme, "'Phubbing' Is Hurting Your Relationships. Here's What It Is," *Time*, March 29, 2018, http://time.com/5216853/what-is-phubbing/.

146. N. Goodman, "Micro-Aggressions and Phubbing in the Age of FoMO," *Training*, https://trainingmag.com/trgmag-article/micro-aggressions-and-phubbing-age-fomo/ (accessed May 20, 2020). Also see J. Ducharme, "'Phubbing' Is Hurting Your Relationships. Here's What It Is," *Time*, March 29, 2018, http://time.com/5216853/what-is-phubbing/.

147. N. Goodman, "Micro-Aggressions and Phubbing in the Age of FoMO," *Training*, https://trainingmag.com/trgmag-article/micro-aggressions-and-phubbing-age-fomo (accessed May 14, 2018).

148. K. Weir, "(Dis)connected," *Monitor on Psychology*, March 2017, pp. 42–48.

149. M. Milyavskaya, M. Saffran, N. Hope, and R. Koestner, "Fear of Missing Out: Prevalence, Dynamics, and Consequences of Experiencing FOMO," *Motivation and Emotion*, March 2018, pp. 725–737.

150. K. Weir, "(Dis)connected," *Monitor on Psychology*, March 2017, pp. 42–48.

151. S. Reid, "5 Questions for Adam Alter," *Monitor on Psychology*, July/August 2017, p. 32.

152. J. L. Ledbord, "Could a Cyber Attack Knock Out Your Computer?" *Lifewire*, February 8, 2018, https://www.lifewire.com/cyber-attacks-4147067. Also see J. Belbey, "How to Avoid Cyber Attacks: 5 Best Practices from SEC and FINRA," *Forbes*, June 30, 2017, https://www.forbes.com/sites/joannabelbey/2017/06/30/how-to-avoid-cyberattacks-5-best-practices-from-sec-and-finra/#71e32e0a1a16.

153. C. Crane, "33 Alarming Cybercrime Statistics You Should Know in 2019," *Hashed Out*, November 14, 2019, https://www.thesslstore.com/blog/33-alarming-cybercrime-statistics-you-should-know/. Also see A. Bera, "Terrifying Cybercrime Statistics," *Safe At Last*, March 12, 2019, https://safeatlast.co/blog/cybercrime-statistics/.

154. *Norton Cyber Security Insights Report 2017 Global Results*, Norton, https://www.symantec.com/content/dam/symantec/docs/about/2017-ncsir-global-results-en.pdf (accessed May 14, 2018).

155. A. Blau, "Better Cybersecurity Starts with Fixing Your Employees' Bad Habits," *Harvard Business Review*, December 11, 2017, https://hbr.org/2017/12/better-cybersecurity-starts-with-fixing-your-employees-bad-habits.

156. "Password Recklessness Leaves American Millennials at Risk of Data Theft," *Associated Press*, May 6, 2020, https://apnews.com/PR%20Newswire/b8047f31a654b22e143a2fb3d4c1a4ba.

157. S. Courtney, "What Is Social Proof? The Ultimate Guide (2020)," *Nudgify*, January 22, 2020, https://www.nudgify.com/social-proof/. Also see A. Blau, "Better Cybersecurity Starts with Fixing Your Employees' Bad Habits," *Harvard Business Review*, December 11, 2017, https://hbr.org/2017/12/better-cybersecurity-starts-with-fixing-your-employees-bad-habits.

158. Derived from B. K. Williams and S. C. Sawyer, *Using Information Technology: A Practical Introduction*, 11th ed. (New York: McGraw-Hill Education, 2015), pp. 94, 100, 101, 357, 478.

159. "What Is Encryption & How Does It Work?" *Medium*, November 27, 2017, https://medium.com/searchencrypt/what-is-encryption-how-does-it-work-e8f20e340537.

160. I. Rijnetu, "The Most Popular Free Encryption Software Tools to Protect Your Data," *Heimdal Security*, April 15, 2019, https://heimdalsecurity.com/blog/free-encryption-software-tools/.

161. A. Bhatia, "Two Years Since Cambridge Analytica: What Has Changed?" *CPO Magazine*, May 20, 2020, https://www.cpomagazine.com/data-privacy/two-years-since-cambridge-analytica-what-has-changed/.

162. A. Dixon, "America's 15 Largest Banks," *Bankrate*, May 30, 2019, https://www.bankrate.com/banking/biggest-banks-in-america/.

163. H. Pawar, "Will Capital One's Latest Data Breach Upend Its Reputation as a Digital Transformation Darling?" *Delphix*, August 1, 2019, https://www.delphix.com/blog/capital-one-breach-upend-reputation. Also see "Information on the Capital One Cyber Incident," *Capital One*, September 23, 2019, https://www.capitalone.com/facts2019/.

164. A. Bhatia, "Two Years Since Cambridge Analytica: What Has Changed?" *CPO Magazine*, May 20, 2020, https://www.cpomagazine.com/data-privacy/two-years-since-cambridge-analytica-what-has-changed/.

165. R. Reed, "Workplace Monitoring Gets Personal, and Employees Fear It's Too Close for Comfort. They're Right," *Chicago Tribune*, March 2, 2018, http://www.chicagotribune.com/business/columnists/reed/ct-biz-amazon-workplace-privacy-dilemma-robert-reed-0304-story.html.

166. E. Sheng, "Employee Privacy in the US Is at Stake as Corporate Surveillance Technology Monitors Workers' Every Move," *CNBC*, July 22, 2019, https://www.cnbc.com/2019/04/15/employee-privacy-is-at-stake-as-surveillance-tech-monitors-workers.html.

167. " More Than Half of Employers Have Found Content on Social Media That Caused Them NOT to Hire a Candidate, According to Recent CareerBuilder Survey," *Career Builder*, August 9, 2018, http://press.careerbuilder.com/2018-08-09-More-Than-Half-of-Employers-Have-Found-Content-on-Social-Media-That-Caused-Them-NOT-to-Hire-a-Candidate-According-to-Recent-CareerBuilder-Survey.

168. K. Litman-Navarro, "We Read 150 Privacy Policies. They Were an Incomprehensible Disaster," *The New York Times*, June 12, 2019, https://www.nytimes.com/interactive/2019/06/12/opinion/facebook-google-privacy-policies.html.

169. A. Koohang, J. Paliszkiewicz, and J. Goluchowski, "Social Media Privacy Concerns: Trusting Beliefs and Risk Beliefs," *Industrial Management & Data Systems*, July 2018, pp. 1209–1228. Also see A. K. Fox and M. B. Royne, "Private Information in a Social World: Assessing Consumers' Fear and Understanding of Social Media Privacy," *Journal of Marketing Theory and Practice*, March 2018, pp. 72–89.

170. "Journalism, 'Fake News' and Disinformation: A Handbook for Journalism Education and Training," *UNESCO*, https://en.unesco.org/fightfakenews (accessed May 22, 2020).

171. F. Stroud, "Fake News," *Webopedia*, https://www.webopedia.com/TERM/F/fake-news.html (accessed May 22, 2020).

172. "The Real Story of 'Fake News,'" *Merriam-Webster*, https://www.merriam-webster.com/words-at-play/the-real-story-of-fake-news (accessed May 22, 2020).

173. M. Wendling, "The (Almost) Complete History of 'Fake News,'" *BBC*, January 22, 2018, https://www.bbc.com/news/blogs-trending-42724320.

174. J. Waterson, "Democracy at Risk Due to Fake News and Data Misuse, MPs Conclude," *The Guardian*, July 27, 2018, https://www.the-guardian.com/technology/2018/jul/27/fake-news-inquiry-data-misuse-deomcracy-at-risk-mps-conclude. Also see J. Carson, "Fake News: What Exactly Is It—and How Can You Spot It?" *The Telegraph*, November 20, 2019, https://www.telegraph.co.uk/technology/0/fake-news-exactly-has-really-had-influence/.

175. "Fake News," *COM Library*, https://libguides.com.edu/c.php?g=649902&p=4556540 (accessed May 21, 2020).

176. N. Berman, "The Victims of Fake News," *Columbia Journalism Review*, 2017, https://www.cjr.org/special_report/fake-news-pizzagate-seth-rich-newtown-sandy-hook.php.

177. C. Binham, "Companies Fear Rise of Fake News and Social Media Rumours," *Financial Times*, September 29, 2019, https://www.ft.com/content/4241a2f6-e080-11e9-9743-db5a370481bc.

178. C. Binham, "Companies Fear Rise of Fake News and Social Media Rumours," *Financial Times*, September 29, 2019, https://www.ft.com/content/4241a2f6-e080-11e9-9743-db5a370481bc.

179. S. Vosoughi, D. Roy, and S. Aral, "The Spread of True and False News Online" *Science*, 2018, pp. 1146–1151.

180. C. Atkinson, "Fake News Can Cause 'Irreversible Damage' to Companies—and Sink Their Stock Price," *NBC News*, April 25, 2019, https://www.nbcnews.com/business/business-news/fake-news-can-cause-irreversible-damage-companies-sink-their-stock-n995436.

181. C. Keown, "Facebook, Twitter, Google and Other Tech Giants Join Forces to Fight Coronavirus Fake News," *Market Watch*, March 17, 2020, https://www.marketwatch.com/story/facebook-twitter-google-and-other-tech-giants-join-forces-to-fight-coronavirus-fake-news-2020-03-17.

182. E. Stoycheff, "4 Easy Ways to Protect Yourself from Today's Avalanche of Fake News," *Fast Company*, February 28, 2020, https://www.fastcompany.com/90469490/4-easy-ways-to-protect-yourself-from-todays-avalanche-of-fake-news.

183. E. Dreyfuss, "Want to Make a Lie Seem True? Say It Again. And Again. And Again," *Wired*, February 11, 2017, https://www.wired.com/2017/02/dont-believe-lies-just-people-repeat/.

184. A. Mitchell, J. Gottfried, M. Barthel, and N. Sumida, "Distinguishing between Factual and Opinion Statements in the News," *Pew Research Center*, June 18, 2018, https://www.journalism.org/2018/06/18/distinguishing-between-factual-and-opinion-statements-in-the-news/.

185. K. Ashford, "Employees Feel Guilty for Texting at Work (Do You?)," *Forbes*, April 27, 2015, http://www.forbes.com/sites/kateashford/2015/04/27/guilty-for-texting/ #72616c678397.

186. L. Bizzi, "Employees Who Use Social Media for Work Are More Engaged—but Also More Likely to Leave Their Jobs," *Harvard Business Review*, May 17, 2018, https://hbr.org/2018/05/employees-who-use-social-media-for-work-are-more-engaged-but-also-more-likely-to-leave-their-jobs. Also see D. Kline, "Here's What People Are Using Social Media for at Work," *The Motley Fool*, June 27, 2016, http://www.fool.com/investing/2016/06/27/heres-what-people-are-using-social-media-for-at-wo.aspx.

187. S. Weingartner and T. Hunter, "Creating Effective Corporate Social Media Policies," *Ivey Business Journal*, May 2019, pp. 1–10.

188. "Intel Social Media Guidelines," *Intel*, http://www.intel.com/content/www/us/en/legal/intel-social-media-guidelines.html (accessed July 2016).

189. "IBM Social Computing Guidelines," *IBM*, https://www.ibm.com/blogs/zz/en/guidelines.html (accessed May 22, 2018).

190. J. Bouman, "Need Social Media Policy Examples? Here Are 7 Terrific Social Policies to Inspire Yours," *Everyone Social*, March 15, 2019, https://everyonesocial.com/blog/need-sample-social-media-policies-here-are-7-to-inspire-yours/.

191. "Best Buy Social Media Policy," *Best Buy*, https://forums.bestbuy.com/t5/Welcome-News/Best-Buy-Social-Media-Policy/td-p/20492 (accessed May 22, 2020).

192. J. Bouman, "Need Social Media Policy Examples? Here Are 7 Terrific Social Policies to Inspire Yours," *Everyone Social*, March 15, 2019, https://everyonesocial.com/blog/need-sample-social-media-policies-here-are-7-to-inspire-yours/.

193. "Walmart Policies and Guidelines," *Walmart*, https://corporate.walmart.com/policies (accessed April 27, 2018).

194. E. Duffin, "The World's 50 Largest Companies Based on Number of Employees in 2018," *Statista*, July 31, 2019, https://www.statista.com/statistics/264671/top-20-companies-based-on-number-of-employees/.

195. "Walmart Policies and Guidelines," *Walmart*, https://corporate.walmart.com/policies (accessed May 22, 2020).

196. "Policies and Standards," *The Washington Post*, January 1, 2016, https://www.washingtonpost.com/policies-and-standards/?utm_term=.a4df65b9fdf8. Also see A. Beaujon, "The Washington Post Needs a New Social Media Policy. Or Maybe Some Better Guidelines," *Washingtonian*, January 31, 2020, https://www.washingtonian.com/2020/01/31/the-washington-post-needs-a-new-social-media-policy-or-maybe-some-better-guidelines/.

197. A. Beaujon, "The Washington Post Needs a New Social Media Policy. Or Maybe Some Better Guidelines," *Washingtonian*, January 31, 2020, https://www.washingtonian.com/2020/01/31/the-washington-post-needs-a-new-social-media-policy-or-maybe-some-better-guidelines/.

198. K. D'angelo, "5 Terrific Examples of Company Social Media Policies," *Hire Rabbit*, http://blog.hirerabbit.com/5-terrific-examples-of-company-social-media-policies/ (accessed May 22, 2020).

199. M. Porter and N. Nohria, "How CEOs Manage Time," *Harvard Business Review*, Vol. 96, No. 4 (July 2018), pp. 42–51. Also see L. Weaver, "Highly Effective Communication Habits for Those Who Want to Succeed," *Thrive Global*, August 20, 2019, https://thriveglobal.com/stories/highly-effective-communication-habits-for-those-who-want-to-succeed/.

200. "The Four Career Competencies Employers Value Most," *NACE*, March 29, 2019, https://www.naceweb.org/career-readiness/competencies/the-four-career-competencies-employers-value-most/.

201. "5 Ways to Stop Talking So Much," *Leader Motiv*, https://leader-motiv.com/blog/5-ways-to-stop-talking-so-much.

202. L. Adelman and N. Dasgupta, "Effect of Threat and Social Identity on Reactions to Ingroup Criticism: Defensiveness, Openness, and a Remedy," *Personality and Social Psychology Bulletin*, Vol. 45, No. 5 (2019), pp. 740–753.

203. N. Van Quaquebeke and W. Felps, "Respectful Inquiry: A Motivational Account of Leading through Asking Questions and Listening," *Academy of Management Review*, January 2018, pp. 5–27. Also see E. Bernstein, "This Conversation Doesn't . . . Have to Be So Hard," *The Wall Street Journal*, July 18, 2017, p. A10.

204. M. Zwilling, "Entrepreneurs Face Serious Communication Barriers," *Forbes*, July 7, 2013, http://www.forbes.com/sites/martinzwilling/2013/07/07/entrepreneurs-face-serious-communication-barriers/#15cde9605398.

205. Newsroom, "Empathy? In Denmark They're Learning It in School," *Morning Future*, April 26, 2019, https://www.morningfuture.com/en/article/2019/04/26/empathy-happiness-school-denmark/601/.

206. A. König, L. Graf-Vlachy, J. Bundy, and L. Little. "A Blessing and a Curse: How CEOs' Trait Empathy Affects Their Management of Organizational Crises," *Academy of Management Review*, Vol. 45, No. 1 (2020), pp. 130–153.

207. These definitions were taken from "Nice Guys Finish First," *Mindful*, October 2017, p. 32.

208. L. Rollins, "Does Mindfulness Support Empathy?" *Scholar Works: University of Massachusetts Boston*, August 31, 2018, https://scholarworks.umb.edu/doctoral_dissertations/418.

209. Thomas Jefferson University, "Medical Students Become Less Empathic Toward Patients Throughout Medical School," *Medical Express*, February 5, 2020, https://medicalxpress.com/news/2020-02-medical-students-empathic-patients-school.html.

210. A. Light, T. Gupta, A. Burrows, M. Nandakumar, A. Daniel, and S. Karthikeyan, "Learning Empathy: The Medical Student Perspective," *The Clinical Teacher*, Vol. 16, No. 1 (2019), pp. 76–77.

211. Young Entrepreneur Council, "Speak Like a Leader: 7 Effective Communication Skills," *Inc.*, December 18, 2018, https://www.inc.com/young-entrepreneur-council/7-communication-secrets-of-great-leaders.html.

212. "Listening," *GSB Comms*, https://www.gsbcomms.co.uk/listening (accessed May 28, 2020).

213. K. J. Lloyd, D. Boer, J. W. Keller, and S. Voelpel, "Is My Boss Really Listening to Me? The Impact of Perceived Supervisor Listening on Emotional Exhaustion, Turnover Intention, and Organizational Citizenship Behavior," *Journal of Business Ethics*, June 2014, pp. 509–524.

214. C. Wofford, "Are Most Managers Bad Listeners?" *Cornell 360*, January 26, 2018, https://blog.ecornell.com/are-most-managers-bad-listeners/.

215. S. Spataro, and J. Bloch, "'Can You Repeat That?' Teaching Active Listening in Management Education," *Journal of Management Education*, Vol. 42, No. 2 (2018), pp. 168–198.

216. M. Hagerty, "5 Things to Know about the Lost Art of Listening," *Houston Public Media*, February 26, 2020, https://www.houstonpublicmedia.org/articles/shows/houston-matters/2020/02/26/361969/listening-a-skill-that-takes-effort-and-practice/.

217. C. Headlee, "10 Ways to Have a Better Conversation," *TED*, https://www.ted.com/talks/celeste_headlee_10_ways_to_have_a_better_conversation?language=en (accessed May 28, 2020).

218. J. Kavanaugh, "'Pro Listener' and NPR Guest Faith Salie Coming to Annual Meeting," *MMA*, September 16, 2019, https://www.mma.org/pro-listener-and-npr-guest-faith-salie-coming-to-annual-meeting/.

219. F. Salie, "All I Really Need to Know in Life I Learned from My Kid's Online Kindergarten," *USA Today*, May 19, 2020, https://www.usatoday.com/story/opinion/voices/2020/05/19/virtual-classrooms-coronavirus-zoom-kindergarten-lessons-column/5214597002/.

220. P. D'Arcy, "How to Listen to People You Disagree With," *Emerson Collective*, November 2019, https://www.emersoncollective.com/articles/2019/11/how-to-listen-to-people-you-disagree-with/. Also see C. Headlee, "10 Ways to Have a Better Conversation," *TED*, https://www.ted.com/talks/celeste_headlee_10_ways_to_have_a_better_conversation?language=en (accessed May 28, 2020).

221. Based on advice in J. Kerr, "How to Talk to People, According to Terry Gross," *The New York Times*, November 17, 2018, https://www.nytimes.com.

222. Based on C. Headlee, "10 Ways to Have a Better Conversation," *TED*, https://www.ted.com/talks/celeste_headlee_10_ways_to_have_a_better_conversation?language=en (accessed May 28, 2020). Also see K. Murphy, "Talk Less. Listen More. Here's How," *The New York Times*, January 9, 2020, https://www.nytimes.com.

223. C. Headlee, "10 Ways to Have a Better Conversation," *TED*, https://www.ted.com/talks/celeste_headlee_10_ways_to_have_a_better_conversation?language=en (accessed May 28, 2020). Also see M. Hagerty, "5 Things to Know about the Lost Art of Listening," *Houston Public Media*, February 26, 2020, https://www.houstonpublicmedia.org/articles/shows/houston-matters/2020/02/26/361969/listening-a-skill-that-takes-effort-and-practice/.

224. J. Stich, M. Tarafdar, and C. Cooper, "Electronic Communication in the Workplace: Boon or Bane?" *Journal of Organizational Effectiveness: People and Performance*, March 2018, pp. 98–106.

225. C. Gallo, "Public Speaking Is No Longer a 'Soft Skill.' It's Your Key to Success in Any Field," *Inc.*, January 4, 2019, https://www.inc.com/carmine-gallo/public-speaking-is-no-longer-a-soft-skill-its-your-key-to-success-in-any-field.html.

226. S. Sheth, "America's Top Fears 2019," *Chapman University*, 2019, https://www.chapman.edu/wilkinson/research-centers/babbie-center/_files/americas-top-fears-2019.pdf.

227. T. Smedley, "Your Fear of Public Speaking May Be Holding You Back at Work. Here's What You Can Do about It," *BBC*, March 22, 2017, http://www.bbc.com/capital/story/20170321-is-public-speaking-fear-limiting-your-career.

228. C. Anderson, "TED Talks: The Official TED Guide to Public Speaking," *Blumz Books Briefly*, April 4, 2020, https://blumzbooksbriefly.wordpress.com/2020/04/04/ted-talks-the-official-ted-guide-to-public-speaking/.

229. G. Genard, "How to Open a Presentation: Tell 'Em What You're Going to Say," November 22, 2015, http://www.genardmethod.com/blog/bid/192061/How-to-Open-a-Presentation-Tell-Em-What-You-re-Going-to-Say.

230. IESE Business School, "12 Tips for Public Speaking," *Forbes*, April 18, 2016, http://www.forbes.com/sites/iese/2016/04/18/12-tips-for-public-speaking/ #3fae354d5af3.

231. G. Belli, "Everyone's a Storyteller: Learn to Tell Your Story and Supercharge Your Career," *Payscale*, May 9, 2019, https://www.payscale.com/career-news/2019/05/everyones-a-storyteller-learn-to-tell-your-story-and-supercharge-your-career. Also see S. Olenski, "Storytelling, Brands and Some Words of Wisdom," *Forbes*, April 6, 2018, https://www.forbes.com/sites/steveolenski/2018/04/06/storytelling-brands-and-some-words-of-wisdom/#77fc2a655ae1.

232. "TED Talk Takeaways: 8 Ways to Hook Your Audience," July 30, 2014, https://blog.slideshare.net/2014/07/30/set-your-hook-to-capture-your-audience.

233. S. Bagdadli and M. Gianecchini, "Organizational Career Management Practices and Objective Career Success: A Systematic Review and Framework," *Human Resource Management Review*, September 2019, pp. 353–370.

234. S. McClear, "How Will You Find Your Next Job? Networking, Probably?" *Ladders*, January 31, 2019, https://www.theladders.com/career-advice/how-will-you-find-your-next-job-networking-probably.

235. D. Burkus, "Networking for Actual Human Beings," *The Wall Street Journal*, April 21–22, 2018, p. C3.

236. J. E. Kobara and M. Smith, "Job Networking Tips," *HelpGuide*, March 2020, https://www.helpguide.org/articles/relationships-communication/job-networking-tips.htm.

237. "Network Marketing: How a Positive Attitude Determines Your Success," *Teamzy*, December 30, 2019, https://teamzy.com/network-marketing-how-a-positive-attitude-determines-your-success.

238. "Top Networking Skills You Should Have (And How to Improve Them)," *Indeed Career Guide*, February 25, 2020, https://www.indeed.com/career-advice/resumes-cover-letters/networking-skills-on-resume.

239. D. Burkus, "Networking for Actual Human Beings," *The Wall Street Journal*, April 21–22, 2018, p. C3.

240. S. Shellenbarger, "Save Yourself from Tedious Small Talk," *The Wall Street Journal*, May 24, 2017, p. A13.

241. S. Shellenbarger, "Save Yourself from Tedious Small Talk," *The Wall Street Journal*, May 24, 2017, pp. A13, A15.

242. "Networking Skills: Six Ways Beginners Can Build Better Connections," *Forbes*, September 18, 2018, https://www.forbes.com/sites/theyec/2018/09/18/networking-skills-six-ways-beginners-can-build-better-connections/#40a67932fede.

243. M. Castillo, "Festival-Goers Paid Up to $49,000 for Ja Rule's Bash in the Bahamas, and Got Chaos Instead," *CNBC*, April 28, 2017, www.cnbc.com/2017/04/28/fyre-festival-debacle-in-the-bahamas.html.

244. B. Burrough, "Fyre Festival: Anatomy of a Millennial Marketing Fiasco Waiting to Happen," *Vanity Fair*, August 2017, www.vanityfair.com/news/2017/06/fyre-festival-billy-mcfarland-millennial-marketing-fiasco.

245. B. Burrough, "Fyre Festival: Anatomy of a Millennial Marketing Fiasco Waiting to Happen," *Vanity Fair*, August 2017, www.vanityfair.com/news/2017/06/fyre-festival-billy-mcfarland-millennial-marketing-fiasco.

246. L. Wamsley, "Paradise Lost: Luxury Music Festival Turns Out to Be Half-Built Scene of Chaos," *NPR*, April 28, 2017, www.npr.org/sections/thetwo-way/2017/04/28/526019457/paradise-lost-luxury-music-festival-turns-out-to-be-half-built-scene-of-chaos.

247. G. Tolentino, "The Fyre Festival Was a Luxury Nightmare," *The New Yorker*, April 28, 2017, www.newyorker.com/culture/jia-tolentino/the-fyre-festival-was-a-luxury-nightmare.

248. G. Bluestone, "Let's Just Do It and Be Legends, Man: Fyre Festival Organizers Blew All Their Money Early on Models, Planes, and Yachts," *Vice News*, May 3, 2017 https://news.vice.com/en_ca/article/7xwabq/fyre-fest-organizers-blew-all-their-money-months-early-on-models-planes-and-yachts.

249. B. Burrough, "Fyre Festival: Anatomy of a Millennial Marketing Fiasco Waiting to Happen," *Vanity Fair*, August 2017, www.vanityfair.com/news/2017/06/fyre-festival-billy-mcfarland-millennial-marketing-fiasco.

250. L. Wamsley, "Paradise Lost: Luxury Music Festival Turns Out to Be Half-Built Scene of Chaos," *NPR*, April 28, 2017, www.npr.org/sections/thetwo-way/2017/04/28/526019457/paradise-lost-luxury-music-festival-turns-out-to-be-half-built-scene-of-chaos.

251. T. Murray, "It Was Designed for Terrible Things to Happen: We Spoke to Someone Who Said She Was 'Locked Indoors' with 'No Food or Water' at the Chaotic Fyre Festival," *Business Insider*, April 28, 2017, www.businessinsider.com/we-spoke-to-someone-with-no-food-or-water-at-the-chaotic-fyre-festival-2017-4.

252. G. Tolentino, "The Fyre Festival Was a Luxury Nightmare," *The New Yorker*, April 28, 2017, www.newyorker.com/culture/jia-tolentino/the-fyre-festival-was-a-luxury-nightmare.

253. G. Kaufman, "Fyre Festival Fiasco: Timeline of a Disaster," *Billboard*, May 2, 2017, www.billboard.com/articles/columns/music-festivals/7777047/fyre-festival-timeline-fiasco.

254. A. Greenblatt, "Eight Things You Need to Know before You Start a Music Festival," *NPR*, April 27, 2010, www.npr.org/sections/therecord/2010/08/26/129449645/starting-a-music-festival-eight-things-you-need-to-know. Also see M. Woodward, "Outdoor Music Festival Planning Tips," *The Balance*, October 16, 2017, www.thebalancesmb.com/planning-an-outdoor-music-festival-1223340; Conferences and Events, "Logistical Planning," Yale University, https://conferencesandevents.yale.edu/services/logistical-planning (accessed May 11, 2018).

255. B. Burrough, "Fyre Festival: Anatomy of a Millennial Marketing Fiasco Waiting to Happen," *Vanity Fair*, August 2017, www.vanityfair.com/news/2017/06/fyre-festival-billy-mcfarland-millennial-marketing-fiasco.

256. C. Gordon, "I Worked at Fyre Festival. It Was Always Going to Be a Disaster," *The Cut*, April 28, 2017, www.thecut.com/2017/04/fyre-festival-exumas-bahamas-disaster.html.

257. G. Kaufman, "Fyre Festival Fiasco: Timeline of a Disaster," *Billboard*, May 2, 2017, www.billboard.com/articles/columns/music-festivals/7777047/fyre-festival-timeline-fiasco.

258. G. Tolentino, "The Fyre Festival Was a Luxury Nightmare," *The New Yorker,* April 28, 2017, www.newyorker.com/culture/jia-tolentino/the-fyre-festival-was-a-luxury-nightmare.

259. A. Flanagan, "Fyre Festival Co-Founder Billy McFarland Sentenced to 6 Years in Prison," *NPR*, October 11, 2018, https://www.npr.org/2018/10/11/656480640/fyre-festival-co-founder-billy-mcfarland-sentenced-in-manhattan. Also see J. Blistein, "Fyre Festival Attendees Win $5 Million Lawsuit," *Rolling Stone*, July 3, 2018, https://www.rollingstone.com/music/music-news/fyre-festival-attendees-win-5-million-lawsuit-695806/.

260. J. Blistein, "Fyre Festival Trustee Files 14 Lawsuits over Payments to Blink-182, Kendall Jenner, Pusha T," *Rolling Stone*, December 16, 2019, https://www.rollingstone.com/music/music-news/fyre-festival-14-lawsuits-talent-agencies-927897/.

261. J. R. Miller, "Nurse Sues Hospital for Firing Her after Speaking Out on Poor Conditions," *New York Post*, April 22, 2020, https://nypost.com/2020/04/22/detroit-nurse-fired-for-highlighting-equipment-staffing-issues/.

262. A. Court, "Nurse at Detroit Hospital Which Had 'Dead Bodies Lined Up on the Floor' Files Lawsuit Claiming She Was Wrongfully Fired for Blowing the Whistle about Unsafe Working Conditions," *Daily Mail*, April 24, 2020, https://www.dailymail.co.uk/news/article-8246025/Nurse-fired-Detroit-hospital-files-lawsuit-claiming-blew-whistle-unsafe-conditions.html.

263. "Sinai Grace Nurse Fired for Facebook Post; Attorney Says It Was for Union Organizing," *Fox 2 Detroit*, April 15, 2020, https://www.fox2detroit.com/news/sinai-grace-nurse-fired-for-facebook-post-attorney-says-it-was-for-union-organizing.

264. Q. Klinefelter, "Fired Sinai Grace Nurse Files Whistleblower Lawsuit, Says Hospital Is Overwhelmed," *NPR*, April 16, 2020, https://wdet.org/posts/2020/04/16/89501-fired-sinai-grace-nurse-files-whistleblower-lawsuit-says-hospital-is-overwhelmed/. Also see J. R. Miller, "Nurse Sues Hospital for Firing Her after Speaking Out on Poor Conditions," *New York Post*, April 22, 2020, https://nypost.com/2020/04/22/detroit-nurse-fired-for-highlighting-equipment-staffing-issues/.

265. A. Court, "Nurse at Detroit Hospital Which Had 'Dead Bodies Lined Up on the Floor' Files Lawsuit Claiming She Was Wrongfully Fired for Blowing the Whistle about Unsafe Working Conditions," *Daily Mail*, April 24, 2020, https://www.dailymail.co.uk/news/article-8246025/Nurse-fired-Detroit-hospital-files-lawsuit-claiming-blew-whistle-unsafe-conditions.html.

266. P. P. Murphy and T. Waldrop, "Detroit Hospital Workers Say People Are Dying in the ER Hallways before Help Can Arrive," *CNN*, April 9, 2020, https://www.cnn.com/2020/04/09/us/detroit-hospital-workers-sinai-grace-coronavirus/index.html.

267. J. R. Miller, "Nurse Sues Hospital for Firing Her after Speaking Out on Poor Conditions," *New York Post*, April 22, 2020, https://nypost.com/2020/04/22/detroit-nurse-fired-for-highlighting-equipment-staffing-issues/.

268. E. Loop, "A Detroit Nurse Was Fired After Speaking Out about Her Hospital's Handling of the Coronavirus Outbreak. Now She's Fighting Back," *Buzz Feed*, April 21, 2020, https://www.buzzfeednews.com/article/emmaloop/detroit-nurse-fired-lawsuit-coronavirus-sinai-grace.

CHAPTER 16

1. This definition is based on M. Higgins and K. Kram, "Reconceptualizing Mentoring at Work: A Developmental Network Perspective," *Academy of Management Review*, April 2001, pp. 264–288.

2. "Top 10 Tips for Being a Good Mentee," *Insala*, June 3, 2019, https://www.insala.com/blog/how-to-be-a-good-mentee. Also see A. Prossack,

"How to Be a Great Mentee," *Forbes,* April 27, 2018, https://www.forbes.com/sites/ashiraprossack1/2018/04/27/how-to-be-a-great-mentee/#6dc49feb512b; L. Bradford, "8 Tips for an Amazing Mentor Relationship," *Forbes,* January 31, 2018, https://www.forbes.com/sites/laurencebradford/2018/01/31/8-tips-for-an-amazing-mentor-relationship/#584602c221e2; S. Mautz, "12 Keys to Being a SuperMentee (the Kind of Mentee Every Mentor Loves)," *Inc.,* May 17, 2017, https://www.inc.com/scott-mautz/12-keys-to-being-a-supermentee-the-kind-of-mentee-every-mentor-loves.html; B. P. Hardy, "How to Get Mentors (and How to Know if Your Mentors Are Any Good)," *Inc.,* February 26, 2018, https://www.inc.com/benjamin-p-hardy/how-to-get-mentors-and-how-to-know-if-your-mentor-is-any-good.html?cid=search.

3. D. Goldman, "Fed Chair Says This Is the Worst Economy in History," *CNN,* April 29, 2020, https://www.cnn.com/us/live-news/us-coronavirus-update-04-29-20/h_20ffee0c7ad410075e8110c32442527c.

4. K. Carey, "Everybody Ready for the Big Migration to Online College? Actually, No," *The New York Times,* March 13, 2020, https://www.nytimes.com/2020/03/13/upshot/coronavirus-online-college-classes-unprepared.html.

5. A. A. Smith, "College Faculty in California Scramble to Adapt as Classes Move to Online Instruction," *EdSource,* March 13, 2020, https://edsource.org/2020/instructors-adapt-online-learning-coronavirus/625519.

6. E. Bary, "'This Is Online Education's Moment' as Colleges Close during Coronavirus Pandemic," *Market Watch,* March 18, 2020, https://www.marketwatch.com/story/this-is-online-educations-moment-as-colleges-close-during-coronavirus-pandemic-2020-03-17.

7. C. Enloe, "Pennsylvania Forced to Remove Hundreds from COVID-19 Death Count over Glaring Irregularities," *The Blaze,* April 26, 2020, https://www.theblaze.com/news/pennsylvania-forced-to-remove-hundreds-from-covid-19-death-count-over-glaring-irregularities.

8. S. Simon, "Pa. Coroners, Health Department at Odds over How to Handle Suspected Coronavirus Cases, Potentially Affecting Death Count," *The Philadelphia Inquirer,* April 10, 2020, https://www.inquirer.com/news/pennsylvania/spl/pennsylvania-coronavirus-coroners-testing-communication-health-department-20200410.html.

9. A. Root, "American Industry Declares War on Covid-19. Here's What That Means," *Barron's,* April 1, 2020, https://www.barrons.com/articles/industry-ventilators-oxygen-training-industrial-gas-health-care-coronavirus-covid-19-51585690537. Also see "Ford Works with 3M, GE, UAW to Speed Production of Respirators for Healthcare Workers, Ventilators for Coronavirus Patients," *Ford,* March 24, 2020, https://media.ford.com/content/fordmedia/fna/us/en/news/2020/03/24/ford-3m-ge-uaw-respirators-ventilators.html.

10. N. Vitezic and V. Vitezic, "A Conceptual Model of Linkage between Innovation Management and Controlling in the Sustainable Environment," *Journal of Applied Business Research,* January/February 2015, pp. 175–184.

11. P. Seitz, "Covid-19 Crisis Could Be Time for Warehouse Robots to Shine," *Investor's Business Daily,* April 9, 2020, https://www.investors.com/news/technology/industrial-automation-opportunity-seen-coronavirus-crisis/.

12. D. Rezania, R. Baker, and A. Nizon, "Exploring Project Managers' Accountability," *International Journal of Managing Projects in Business,* December 2019, pp. 919–937. Also see M. Schröder, S. Schmitt, and R. Schmitt, "Design and Implementation of Quality Control Loops," *TQM Journal,* April 2015, pp. 294–302.

13. A. Christensen, A. Kinicki, Z. Zhang, and F. Walumbwa, "Responses to Feedback: The Role of Acceptance, Affect, and Creative Behavior," *Journal of Leadership and Organizational Studies,* February 2018, pp. 416–429.

14. S. Nawaz, "How Managers Can Support Remote Employees," *Harvard Business Review,* April 1, 2020, https://hbr.org/2020/04/how-managers-can-support-remote-employees.

15. C. Wijethilake, R. Munir, and R. Appuhami, "Environmental Innovation Strategy and Organizational Performance: Enabling and Controlling Uses of Management Control Systems," *Journal of Business Ethics,* July 2018, pp. 1139–1160.

16. S. Heath, "How Coronavirus Sparked Industry Collaboration, Team-Based Care," *Patient Engagement Hit*, March 27, 2020, https://patientengagementhit.com/features/how-coronavirus-sparked-industry-collaboration-team-based-care.

17. D. Cechova, "How to Measure Performance Management Effectiveness and Efficiency," *People Goal*, March 2, 2020, https://www.peoplegoal.com/blog/how-to-measure-performance-management-effectiveness-and-efficiency. Also see L. Katz, "Monitoring Employee Productivity: Proceed with Caution," *SHRM*, June 1, 2015, https://www.shrm.org/publications/hrmagazine/editorialcontent/2015/0615/pages/0615-employee-monitoring.aspx.

18. C. McWhirter, "Congrats, You Finished the Race! Sorry, We Measured It Wrong!" *The Wall Street Journal,* December 23–24, 2017, p. A1.

19. M. Frey, "5 Factors That Affect Calorie Count Accuracy," *Very Well Fit*, January 21, 2020, https://www.verywellfit.com/the-number-not-to-trust-on-the-nutrition-label-3495626.

20. C. Berardinelli, "A Guide to Control Charts," *i Six Sigma,* https://www.isixsigma.com/tools-templates/control-charts/a-guide-to-control-charts/ (accessed May 15, 2018). Also see A. Foley, "Control Charts: Everything You Need to Know," *Clear Point Strategy,* July 18, 2016, https://www.clearpointstrategy.com/control-charts-everything-you-need-to-know/.

21. R. M. Walter, M. M. Higgins, and H. P. Roth, "Our Greatest Hits: Applications of Control Charts," *CPA Journal,* November 2017, https://www.cpajournal.com/2017/12/08/greatest-hits-applications-control-charts/. Also see "Control Chart," ASQ, http://asq.org/learn-about-quality/data-collection-analysis-tools/overview/control-chart.html.

22. A. G. Abdulaziz, C. S. Ribas, and G. S. Weheba, "Application of Group Control Charts for Multiple Parts Manufacturing," *Journal of Management and Engineering Integration*, Vol. 12, No. 2 (Winter 2019), pp. 41–48.

23. H. Peterson, "Inside a UPS Training School Where Workers Haul Boxes across Slick 'Ice,' Perform High-Stakes Driving Drills, and Deliver Packages to Empty Homes in a Mock Neighborhood," *Business Insider*, February 25, 2020, https://www.businessinsider.com/ups-school-drivers-deliver-fake-packages-walk-on-ice-2020-2.

24. "UPS Integrad Fact Sheet," *UPS Pressroom,* https://pressroom.ups.com/pressroom/ContentDetailsViewer.page?ConceptType=FactSheets&id=1460489309501-709 (accessed May 2, 2020).

25. H. Peterson, "Inside a UPS Training School Where Workers Haul Boxes across Slick 'Ice,' Perform High-Stakes Driving Drills, and Deliver Packages to Empty Homes in a Mock Neighborhood," *Business Insider*, February 25, 2020, https://www.businessinsider.com/ups-school-drivers-deliver-fake-packages-walk-on-ice-2020-2. Also see D. McMackin, "UPS Driver Training Center Opens in Lake Mary, Florida," *GlobeNewswire,* October 5, 2017, https://globenewswire.com/news-release/2017/10/05/1141510/0/en/UPS-Driver-Training-Center-Opens-In-Lake-Mary-Florida.html.

26. "UPS Integrad Fact Sheet," *UPS Pressroom,* https://pressroom.ups.com/pressroom/ContentDetailsViewer.page?ConceptType=FactSheets&id=1460489309501-709 (accessed May 2, 2020).

27. D. DiPiero, "How Does a UPS Driver Spend a Workday?" *Career Trend,* September 3, 2019, https://careertrend.com/info-8591213-job-helper-united-parcel-service.html. Also see "UPS Sets Efficiency Standards by Monitoring Drivers' Every Move," *WDRB,* March 24, 2015, http://www.wdrb.com/story/28604605/ups-sets-efficiency-standards-by-monitoring-drivers-every-move.

28. "ORION Backgrounder," *UPS,* https://www.pressroom.ups.com/pressroom/ContentDetailsViewer.page?ConceptType=Factsheets&id=1426321616277-282 (accessed May 2, 2020). Also see "UPS Sets Efficiency Standards by Monitoring Drivers' Every Move," *WDRB,* March 24, 2015, http://www.wdrb.com/story/28604605/ups-sets-efficiency-standards-by-monitoring-drivers-every-move.

29. T. Yates, "What UPS Can Teach Fleets about Driver Safety," *Work Truck,* https://www.worktruckonline.com/145703/what-ups-can-teach-fleets-about-driver-safety (May 2, 2020).

30. P. Kozodoy, "The New Trick Brilliant Managers Use to Provide Effective Feedback," *Inc.*, September 26, 2017, https://www.inc.com/peter-kozodoy/the-new-trick-brilliant-managers-use-to-provide-ef.html.

31. L. Liu, S. Tian, D. Xue, T. Zhang, and Y. Chen, "Industrial Feedforward Control Technology: A Review," *Journal of Intelligent Manufacturing*, December 2019, pp. 2819–2833.

32. C. Dyer, "Fail Well: How to Handle Business Mistakes," *Management Today,* April 16, 2018, https://www.managementtoday.co.uk/fail-well-handle-business-mistakes/reputation-matters/article/1462189.

33. J. Magoci, "Why Delivery Companies Are Using GPS Tracking?" *Fuel Loyal*, January 16, 2018, https://www.fueloyal.com/why-delivery-companies-are-using-gps-tracking/.

34. "4 Companies That Are Shaking Up Their Performance Review Process," *Tiny Pulse*, https://www.tinypulse.com/blog/4-companies-that-are-changing-performance-reviews (accessed May 2, 2020).

35. R. K. Martin, "The High Price of Efficiency," *Harvard Business Review*, 2019, https://hbr.org/2019/01/rethinking-efficiency. Also see V. Page, "Walmart's Biggest Liability: Labor Costs (WMT)," *Investopedia*, March 26, 2020, https://www.investopedia.com/articles/investing/020916/walmarts-biggest-liability-labor-costs-wmt.asp.

36. C. Rickert, "Airlines Insist on Vouchers—Not Refunds—for Passengers Canceling due to COVID-19 Pandemic," *Wisconsin State Journal*, May 4, 2020, https://madison.com/wsj/business/airlines-insist-on-vouchers-not-refunds-for-passengers-canceling-due-to-covid-19-pandemic/article_0173ca6e-d8aa-57ef-a14f-0ec6d114c21f.html.

37. R. S. Kaplan and D. P. Norton, "The Balanced Scorecard—Measures That Drive Performance," *Harvard Business Review,* January–February 1992, pp. 71–79.

38. N. Hamid, "Use Balanced Scorecard for Measuring Competitive Advantage of Infrastructure Assets of State-Owned Ports in Indonesia: Case in Pelindo IV, Indonesia," *Journal of Management Development,* Vol. 37 (2) 2018, pp. 114–126. Also see A. Kshatriya, V. Dharmadhikari, D. Srivastave, and P. C. Basak, "Strategic Performance Measurement Using Balanced Scorecard: A Case of Machine Tool Industry," *Foundations of Management,* February 2017, pp. 75–86.

39. R. S. Kaplan and D. P. Norton, "The Balanced Scorecard—Measures That Drive Performance," *Harvard Business Review,* January–February 1992, pp. 71–79.

40. N. Hamid, "Use Balanced Scorecard for Measuring Competitive Advantage of Infrastructure Assets of State-Owned Ports in Indonesia: Case in Pelindo IV, Indonesia," *Journal of Management Development,* Vol. 37 (2) 2018, pp. 114–126. Also see A. Kshatriya, V. Dharmadhikari, D. Srivastave, and P. C. Basak, "Strategic Performance Measurement Using Balanced Scorecard: A Case of Machine Tool Industry," *Foundations of Management,* February 2017, pp. 75–86.

41. R. Malagueño, E. Lopez-Valeiras, and J. Gomez-Conde, "Balanced Scorecard in SMEs: Effects on Innovation and Financial Performance," *Small Business Economics*, June 2018, pp. 221–244. Also see I. Kefe, "The Determination of Performance Measures Using a Balanced Scorecard Framework," *Foundations of Management*, March 2019, pp. 43–56; O. Brui, "Implementation of Strategic Management Based on the Balanced Scorecard in a University Library," *Library Management*, November 2018, pp. 530–540; R. Kaplan, S. Sikochi, and J. Steimle, "Performance Management at Afreximbank," *Harvard Business School*, March 22, 2020.

42. C. Vollmer, The Revenue Stream Revolution in Entertainment and Media," *Strategy+Business*, May 7, 2018, https://www.strategy-business.com/article/The-Revenue-Stream-Revolution-in-Entertainment-and-Media.

43. S. Garg, "Macy's to Shutter 125 Stores, Confirms Closure of Valley Call Center," *Phoenix Business Journal*, February 5, 2020, https://www.bizjournals.com/phoenix/news/2020/02/05/macys-to-shutter-125-stores-confirms-closure-of.html.

44. J. Shon, G. A. Porumbescu, and R. K. Christensen, "Can Budget Ambiguity Crowd Out Intrinsic Motivation? Longitudinal Evidence from Federal Executive Departments," *Public Administration*, August 2020, pp. 194–209.

45. J. DeMuro, B. Turner, and R. Clymo, "Best Budgeting Software of 2020: Easily Manage Your Money and Debt," *Tech Radar Pro*, April 22, 2020, https://www.techradar.com/best/best-budgeting-software.

46. "Types of Budgets," *Corporate Finance Institute*, https://corporatefinanceinstitute.com/resources/knowledge/accounting/types-of-budgets-budgeting-methods/ (accessed May 21, 2020).

47. X. Nensi, A. Marioara, and I. Maria-Andreia, "Annual Financial Statements and Their Role in Financial Communication," *Studia Universitatis Petru Maior. Series Oeconomica*, January 2018, pp. 8–14. Also see G. Voss, "Information and Strategic Aspects of Financial Statements in the Assessment of Their Users," *Folia Oeconomica Stetinensia*, December 2019, pp. 176–187.

48. J. Derrick, "Exxon's CEO on How Oil Giant Plans to Maintain Dividend, Focus on Balance Sheet," *Yahoo Finance*, April 7, 2020, https://finance.yahoo.com/news/exxons-ceo-oil-giant-plans-182506244.html.

49. H. Averkamp, "Cash Flow Statement," *Accounting Coach*, https://www.accountingcoach.com/cash-flow-statement/explanation (accessed May 3, 2020).

50. E. Yoon and C. Lochhead, "5 Ways to Stimulate Cash Flow in a Downturn," *Harvard Business Review*, April 8, 2020, https://hbr.org/2020/04/5-ways-to-stimulate-cash-flow-in-a-downturn.

51. S. Biswas and S. Kapner, "J.Crew Tumbles into Bankruptcy in the Wake of Coronavirus," *The Wall Street Journal*, May 4, 2020, https://www.wsj.com/articles/j-crew-files-for-bankruptcy-protection-reaches-debt-swap-deal-11588583196.

52. "Financial Ratios," *Inc.*, https://www.inc.com/encyclopedia/financial-ratios.html (accessed May 3, 2020).

53. L. Kierczak, "Customer Satisfaction: 5 Reasons Why It Is Important in 2020," *Survicate*, https://survicate.com/customer-satisfaction/importance-customer-satisfaction/ (accessed May 4, 2020).

54. "'Sorry' Is Not Enough," *Harvard Business Review*, January-February 2018, pp. 20–22.

55. V. Krieg, "A Customer Experience to Watch: Learn 5 Examples of Good Customer Service from Alaska Airlines," *Sharpen*, January 15, 2020, https://sharpencx.com/blog/examples-of-good-customer-service/.

56. D. McCarthy and P. Fader, "How to Value a Company by Analyzing Its Customers," *Harvard Business Review*, 2020, pp. 51–55.

57. M. Galetto, "What Is Customer Retention?" *NG Data*, June 25, 2015, https://www.ngdata.com/what-is-customer-retention/. Also see C. Morin, "How the Ritz-Carlton Creates a 5 Star Customer Experience," *CRM*, December 13, 2019, https://crm.org/articles/ritz-carlton-gold-standards.

58. "Go the Extra Mile: Providing Outrageous Customer Service," *Content Bacon*, October 30, 2019, https://www.contentbacon.com/blog/go-the-extra-mile-providing-outrageous-customer-service.

59. "60+ Customer Loyalty Statistics for 2020," *ProProfs*, April 21, 2020, https://www.proprofs.com/c/customer-support/customer-loyalty-statistics/.

60. R. S. Kaplan and D. P. Norton, "Having Trouble with Your Strategy? Then Map It," *Harvard Business Review*, October 2000, https://hbr.org/2000/09/having-trouble-with-your-strategy-then-map-it.

61. P. Gleeson, "Examples of Benchmarking," *Chron*, March 4, 2019, https://smallbusiness.chron.com/examples-benchmarking-81426.html.

62. "Best Practices," *Investopedia,* https://www.investopedia.com/terms/b/best_practices.asp (accessed May 16, 2018).

63. H. Stringer, "Boosting Productivity," *Monitor on Psychology*, September 2017, pp. 54–58.

64. "The Balanced Scorecard—Who's Doing It?" *Balanced Scorecard Institute*, http://www.balancedscorecard.org/BSC-Basics/Examples-Success-Stories (accessed May 15, 2018). Also see "National Marrow Donor Program (NMDP) Case Study," Balanced Scorecard Institute, http://www.theinstitutepress.com/uploads/7/0/0/1/7001740/nmdp_case_study_cr7_october_2013.pdf (accessed May 4, 2020).

65. S. Quain, "Why Is Quality Important for a Business?" *Chron*, February 12, 2019, https://smallbusiness.chron.com/quality-important-business-57470.html.

66. C. Henry, "iPhone Users Have Most Brand Loyalty," *The Mac Observer*, August 21, 2019, https://www.macobserver.com/news/iphone-users-have-most-brand-loyalty/.

67. "What Is Quality in a Business?" *Indeed*, January 3, 2020, https://www.indeed.com/career-advice/career-development/what-is-quality-in-a-business.

68. B. Hill, "What Is Social Responsibilty for an Organization?" *Chron*, https://smallbusiness.chron.com/social-responsibilty-organization-26140.html (accessed May 7, 2020).

69. "How a Good Workplace Safety Program Got Even Better," *Industrial Safety and Hygiene News*, November 20, 2018, https://www.ishn.com/articles/109806-how-a-good-workplace-safety-program-got-even-better.

70. V. Vohra, and A. Pandey, "The Relationship between Workplace Spirituality, Job Satisfaction and Organizational Citizenship Behaviors—an Empirical Study," *Social Responsibility Journal, June* 2018, pp. 410–430; J. Abate, T. Schaefer, and T. Pavone, "Understanding Generational Identity, Job Burnout, Job Satisfaction, Job Tenure, and Turnover Intention," *Journal of Organizational Culture, Communications and Conflict*, 2018. Also see C. Wu, I. Chen, and J. Chen, "A Study Into the Impact of Employee Wellness and Job Satisfaction on Job Performance," *The International Journal of Organizational Innovation*, October 2017, pp. 252–269; A. J. Kinicki, F. M. McKee-Ryan, C. A. Schriesheim, and K. P. Carson, "Assessing the Construct Validity of the Job Descriptive Index: A Review and Meta-Analysis," *Journal of Applied Psychology, February* 2002, pp. 14–32; M. A. Uddin, M. Mahmood, and L. Fan, "Why Individual Employee Engagement Matters for Team Performance?" *Team Performance Management: An International Journal, March* 2019, pp. 47–67.

71. A. H. Ozkan et al., "Antecedents of Turnover Intention: A Meta-Analysis Study in the United States," *E+M Ekonomie a Management*, January 2020, pp. 93–110. Also see P. W. Hom, T. W. Lee, J. D. Shaw, and J. P. Hausknecht, "One Hundred Years of Employee Turnover Theory and Research," *Journal of Applied Psychology*, March 2017, pp. 530–545.

72. W. Clark, "Difference Between Functional & Dysfunctional Employee Turnover," *Biz Fluent*, September 26, 2017, https://bizfluent.com/info-8154593-difference-functional-dysfunctional-employee-turnover.html. Also see C. R. Williams, "Reward Contingency, Unemployment, and Functional Turnover," *Scholarship and Professional Work–Business*, 2000, https://digitalcommons.butler.edu/cob_papers/1.

73. P. W. Hom, T. W. Lee, J. D. Shaw, and J. P. Hausknecht, "One Hundred Years of Employee Turnover Theory and Research," *Journal of Applied Psychology*, March 2017, pp. 530–545.

74. "Exit Interview," *Entrepreneur*, https://www.entrepreneur.com/encyclopedia/exit-interview (accessed May 12, 2020).

75. C. Fishman, "'We Were Made for This': How Slack Became King of the Remote-Work World," *Fast Company*, April 23, 2020, https://www.fastcompany.com/90490741/we-were-made-for-this-how-slack-became-king-of-the-remote-work-world.

76. C. Hazard, "CarMax Career Can 'Take Employees to Places They Never Imagined,'" *Richmond Times-Dispatch*, May 2, 2019, https://www.richmond.com/business/local/top-workplaces/carmax-career-can-take-employees-to-places-they-never-imagined/article_815a5b5d-f8a0-501b-94b4-0accce858757.html. Also see "CarMax Celebrates 15 Years as One of FORTUNE Magazine's 100 Best Companies to Work For," *CarMax*, February 14, 2019, http://investors.carmax.com/news-releases/news-releases-details/2019/CarMax-Celebrates-15-Years-as-One-of-FORTUNE-Magazines-100-Best-Companies-to-Work-For/default.aspx.

77. A sample map for a university can be found in S. Han and Z. Zhong, "Strategy Maps in University Management: A Comparative Study," *Educational Management Administration & Leadership,* November 2015, pp. 939–953.

78. I. Adeinat, "Mediating Effects between Perspectives in Strategy Maps," *Administrative Sciences*, February 2019, https://doi.org/10.3390/admsci9010014. Also see R. Lueg, "Strategy Maps: the Essential Link between the Balanced Scorecard and Action," *Journal of Business Strategy*, April 2015, pp. 34–40. Also see R. Armstrong, "Revisiting Strategy Mapping for Performance Management: A Realist Synthesis," *International Journal of Productivity and Performance Management*, April 2019, pp. 721–752.

79. An example of creating scorecards for projects is illustrated in M. Scheiblich, M. Maftei, V. Just, and M. Studeny, "Developing a Project Scorecard to Measure the Performance of Project Management in Relation to EFQM Excellence Model," *Total Quality Management,* November 2017, pp. 966–980.

80. "Adventist Health White Memorial," *NIST*, https://www.nist.gov/baldrige/adventist-health-white-memorial (accessed May 7, 2020).

81. The Foundation for the Malcolm Baldrige National Quality Award, *baldrige.org,* http://www.baldrigepe.org/ (accessed May 7, 2020). Also see K. R. Thompson and M. L. Blazey, "What We Can Learn from the Baldrige Criteria: An Integrated Management Model to Guide Organizations," *Organizational Dynamics*, January 2017, pp. 21–29.

82. "Adventist Health White Memorial," *NIST*, https://www.nist.gov/baldrige/adventist-health-white-memorial (accessed May 7, 2020).

83. "Adventist Health White Memorial," *NIST*, https://www.nist.gov/baldrige/adventist-health-white-memorial (accessed May 7, 2020).

84. W. E. Deming, *Out of the Crisis* (Cambridge, MA: MIT Press, 1986), p. 5.

85. R. N. Lussier, *Management: Concepts, Applications, Skill Development* (Cincinnati, OH: South-Western College Publishing, 1997), p. 260.

86. "About TMMK," *Toyota Kentucky,* http://toyotaky.com/boutdex.asp (accessed May 7, 2020).

87. "All-New 2019 Kentucky-Assembled Lexus Rolls off the Line," *Lexus Newsroom*, August 3, 2018, https://pressroom.lexus.com/all-new-2019-kentucky-assembled-lexus-rolls-off-the-line/.

88. M. Jaeger and D. Adair, "Perception of TQM Benefits, Practices and Obstacles," *TQM Journal,* March 2016, pp. 317–336.

89. N. Bomey, "These Are the 10 Best Cars, SUVs and Pickups of 2020, According to Consumer Reports," *USA Today*, February 20, 2020, https://www.usatoday.com/story/money/cars/2020/02/20/consumer-reports-top-picks-new-cars-trucks-suvs-2020/4797858002/

90. G. Coppola, "Luxury-Car Ranks Upended as Genesis Tops Germany's Stalwarts," *Bloomberg.com,* February 22, 2018, https://www.bloomberg.com/news/articles/2018-02-22/korean-cars-pull-ahead-of-german-brands-consumer-reports-says.

91. A. Honeyman, "How Did Hyundai Do It with Genesis?—Quality, the Only Game in Town," *Torque News,* June 28, 2017, https://www.torque-news.com/3793/hyundai-genesis-quality-game-town.

92. D. Levin, "How Korean Car Makers Beat Out the Japanese," *Fortune,* June 29, 2015, http://fortune.com/2015/06/29/korean-japanese-cars-quality/.

93. A. Honeyman, "How Did Hyundai Do It with Genesis?—Quality, The Only Game in Town," *Torque News,* June 28, 2017, https://www.torque-news.com/3793/hyundai-genesis-quality-game-town.

94. A. Honeyman, "How Did Hyundai Do It with Genesis?—Quality, The Only Game in Town," *Torque News,* June 28, 2017, https://www.torque-news.com/3793/hyundai-genesis-quality-game-town.

95. D. Levin, "How Korean Car Makers Beat Out the Japanese," *Fortune,* June 29, 2015, http://fortune.com/2015/06/29/korean-japanese-cars-quality/.

96. V. Vijayenthiran, "Genesis Tops 2020 J.D. Power Vehicle Dependability Study," *Motor Authority*, February 13, 2020, https://www.motor-authority.com/news/1127099_genesis-tops-2020-j-d-power-vehicle-dependability-study.

97. S. Richmond, "How KIA Motors Is Reinventing Itself," *Investopedia*, https://www.investopedia.com/articles/personal-finance/062315/how-kia-motors-reinventing-itself.asp (accessed May 15, 2018).

98. J. Garcia-Bernal and M. Ramirez-Aleson, "Why and How TQM Leads to Performance Improvements," *Quality Management Journal*, November 2017, pp. 23–37.

99. "Smart Data Analytics: BMW Group Relies on Intelligent Use of Production Data for Efficient Processes and Premium Quality," *BMW Group*, August 31, 2017, https://www.press.bmwgroup.com/global/article/detail/T0273931EN/smart-data-analytics:-bmw-group-relies-on-intelligent-use-of-production-data-for-efficient-processes-and-premium-quality?language=en.

100. A. Choudhury, "Kaizen with Six Sigma Ensures Continuous Improvement," *isixsigma.com,* https://www.isixsigma.com/methodology/kaizen/kaizen-six-sigma-ensures-continuous-improvement/ (accessed July 2016).

101. L. Flory, "How 5 Companies Used Kaizen Effectively," *Effex Management Solutions,* October 7, 2014, http://blog.effexms.com/how-5-companies-used-kaizen-effectively.

102. "Wagamama Creates the First 'Walk Out and Pay' App with Mastercard," *Mastercard,* March 21, 2018, https://newsroom.mastercard.com/eu/press-releases/wagamama-creates-the-first-walk-out-and-pay-app-with-mastercard/.

103. Jack Stewart, "How Boeing Builds a 737 in Just 9 Days," *Wired,* September 27, 2016, https://www.wired.com/2016/09/boeing-builds-737-just-nine-days/.

104. S. Wilhelm, "Boeing to Meet 2017 Goal to Stop Growth of Greenhouse Gas Emissions," *Business Journals,* May 28, 2016, https://www.bizjournals.com/seattle/news/2016/03/28/boeing-to-meet-2017-goal-to-stop-growth-of.html.

105. A. Choudhury, "Kaizen with Six Sigma Ensures Continuous Improvement," *isixsigma.com,* https://www.isixsigma.com/methodology/kaizen/kaizen-six-sigma-ensures-continuous-improvement/ (accessed July 2016).

106. "Training," *Publix,* https://corporate.publix.com/careers/stores/training (accessed May 7, 2020).

107. "No Second Chances: New Northridge Group Study Reveals 72% of Consumers Will Likely Switch Brands After Just One Bad Service Experience," *Business Wire,* November 12, 2019, https://www.businesswire.com/news/home/20191112005268/en/Chances-New-Northridge-Group-Study-Reveals-72.

108. "About Us," *Nordstrom,* https://shop.nordstrom.com/c/about-us (accessed May 7, 2020).

109. N. Sinclair, "Why Nordstrom Is Beating All of Its Department Store Competitors," *Yahoo! Finance,* August 12, 2017, https://finance.yahoo.com/news/nordstrom-beating-department-store-competitors-125704786.html.

110. B. Taylor, "Trust Your Employees, Not Your Rule Book," *Harvard Business Review,* April 20, 2017, https://hbr.org/2017/04/trust-your-employees-not-your-rulebook.

111. "Reimagining Our Approach to Supply Chain," *Nordstrom,* https://press.nordstrom.com/news-releases/news-release-details/reimagining-our-approach-supply-chain (May 7, 2020). Also see B. Morgan, "Nordstrom Revamps Customer Experience with New Supply Chain Strategy," *Forbes,* January 2, 2020, https://www.forbes.com/sites/blakemorgan/2020/01/02/nordstrom-revamps-customer-experience-with-new-supply-chain-strategy/#34f4822e23a4.

112. "Our Story," *Trader Joe's,* https://www.traderjoes.com/our-story (accessed May 7, 2020).

113. K. Johnston, "Trader Joe's and Costco Top Amazon in Customer Satisfaction, ACSI Data Show," *ACSI,* February 26, 2019, https://www.theacsi.org/news-and-resources/press-releases/press-2019/press-release-retail-and-consumer-shipping-2018-2019.

114. "Careers," *Trader Joe's,* https://www.traderjoes.com/careers/meet-our-crew (accessed May 7, 2020); V. Jaiswal, "How Trader Joe's Provides EXCELLENT Customer Experience CONSISTENTLY—4 Key Takeaways," *CustomerThink,* September 27, 2017, https://customerthink.com/how-trader-joes-provides-excellent-customer-experience-consistently-4-key-takeaways/.

115. V. Jaiswal, "How Trader Joe's Provides EXCELLENT Customer Experience CONSISTENTLY—4 Key Takeaways," *CustomerThink,* September 27, 2017, https://customerthink.com/how-trader-joes-provides-excellent-customer-experience-consistently-4-key-takeaways/.

116. S. Bakhtiari, "Productivity, Outsourcing and Exit: The Case of Australian Manufacturing," *Small Business Economics,* 2015, pp. 425–447.

117. A. Asatiani, E. Penttinen, and A. Kumar, "Uncovering the Nature of the Relationship between Outsourcing Motivations and the Degree of Outsourcing: An Empirical Study on Finnish Small and Medium-Sized Enterprises," *Journal of Information Technology,* March 2019, pp. 39–58.

Also see O. A. Awe, N. Kulangara, and D. F. Henderson, "Outsourcing and Firm Performance: A Meta-Analysis," *Journal of Strategy and Management,* August 2018, pp. 371–386.

118. "Job Overseas Outsourcing Statistics," *Statistic Brain Research Institute,* https://www.statisticbrain.com/outsourcing-statistics-by-country/ (accessed May 15, 2018). Also see G. Dautovic, "15 Must-Know Outsourcing Statistics (2020 Update)," *Fortunly,* August 1, 2019.

119. C. Chien, C. Kuo, and C. Yu, "Tool Allocation to Smooth Work-in-Process for Cycle Time Reduction and an Empirical Study," *Annals of Operations Research,* September 2018, pp. 1009–1033.

120. M. Heric and P. Doddapaneni, "Intelligent Automation: Getting More Bang from the Bots," *CFO,* May 7, 2020, https://www.cfo.com/applications/2020/05/intelligent-automation-getting-more-bang-from-the-bots/.

121. M. Sagnak and Y. Kazancoglu, "Fuzzy Analytic Hierarchy Process Integrated Statistical Process Control: An Application of Demerit Chart at Furniture Manufacturing Company," *Journal of Multi-Criteria Decision Analysis,* May 2020, pp. 96–103.

122. R. Merriman, "A Review of Current Implementations of Statistical Process Control in Large Organizations," *Journal of Management and Engineering Integration,* January 2018, pp. 46–54.

123. "Great Ways Companies Can Use Six Sigma," *Villanova University,* January 17, 2020, https://www.villanovau.com/resources/six-sigma/ways-companies-use-six-sigma/. Also see B. Burnseed and E. Thornton, "Six Sigma Makes a Comeback," *Bloomberg Businessweek,* September 10, 2009, www.businessweek.com/magazine/content/09_38/b4147064137002.htm.

124. B. W. Jacobs, M. Swink, and K. Linderman, "Performance Effects of Early and Late Six Sigma Adoptions," *Journal of Operations Management,* May 2015, pp. 244–257.

125. M. Poppendieck, "Why the Lean in Lean Six Sigma?" *The Project Management Best Practices Report,* June 2004, www.poppendieck.com/pdfs/Lean_Six_Sigma.pdf.

126. "Companies Turn to Lean Six Sigma to Better Handle COVID-19," *Six Sigma Daily,* April 23, 2020, https://www.sixsigmadaily.com/lean-six-sigma-coronavirus/.

127. A. Rongala, "Top 10 Reasons Why Organizations Do Not Use Lean Six Sigma," *Invensis,* November 19, 2015, http://www.invensislearning.com/blog/top-10-reasons-why-organizations-do-not-use-lean-six-sigma/.

128. "ISO 9000 & ISO 9001 DIFFERENCES," *The British Assessment Bureau,* May 8, 2011, http://www.british-assessment.co.uk/guides/whats-the-difference-between-iso-9000-9001/.

129. B. Kumar, "What's the Differences between ISO 9000 & ISO 9001?" *Quora,* May 25, 2015, https://www.quora.com/What%E2%80%99s-the-difference-between-ISO-9000-9001.

130. "ISO 9000 Family: Quality Management," *ISO,* https://www.iso.org/iso-9001-quality-management.html (accessed May 8, 2020).

131. ISO 4000 Family: Environmental Management," *ISO,* https://www.iso.org/iso-14001-environmental-management.html (accessed May 21, 2020).

132. L. L. Bernardino, F. Teixeira, A. R. de Jesus, A. Barbosa, M. Lordelo, and H. A. Lepikson, "After 20 Years, What Has Remained of TQM?" *International Journal of Productivity and Performance,* March 2016, pp. 378–400.

133. L. L. Bernardino, F. Teixeira, A. R. de Jesus, A. Barbosa, M. Lordelo, and H. A. Lepikson, "After 20 Years, What Has Remained of TQM?" *International Journal of Productivity and Performance,* March 2016, pp. 378–400. Also see R. Merriman, "A Review of Current Implementations of Statistical Process Control in Large Organizations," *Journal of Management and Engineering Integration,* January 2018, pp. 46–54.

134. "Product Recall—Managing the Impact of the New Risk Landscape," *Allianz,* https://www.agcs.allianz.com/news-and-insights/reports/product-recall.html (accessed May 10, 2020).

135. "Officials Say C.D.C. Errors Caused Testing Delays," *The New York Times,* April 20, 2020, https://www.nytimes.com/2020/04/18/us/coronavirus-live-news.html.

136. "About Us," *Siemens*, https://new.siemens.com/global/en/company/about.html (accessed May 10, 2020).

137. B. Ramsey, "How Machine Learning Is Poised to Revolutionize Manufacturing," *Medium*, July 9, 2018, https://medium.com/supplyframe-hardware/how-machine-learning-is-poised-to-revolutionize-manufacturing-7e72b4ba8e5f.

138. "2018 AI Predictions," *PwC*, https://www.pwc.com/us/en/services/consulting/library/artificial-intelligence-predictions.html (accessed May 10, 2020).

139. S. Bose, "How Artificial Intelligence Can Increase Your Business Productivity," *Digitalist*, March 19, 2018, https://www.digitalistmag.com/future-of-work/2018/03/19/how-artificial-intelligence-can-increase-your-business-productivity-05978998. Also see R. Daws, "TrenItalia Is the Next Train Operator to Adopt the IoT," *IoT News*, October 12, 2016, https://iottechnews.com/news/2016/oct/12/trenitalia-next-train-operator-adopt-iot/.

140. L. Sorokanich, "This Cold-Storage Company That Works with Walmart and McDonald's Cut Its Energy Consumption 34% and Saves Millions of Dollars a Year," *Fast Company*, February 19, 2019, https://www.fastcompany.com/90299025/lineage-logistics-most-innovative-companies-2019. Also see B. Morgan, "5 Examples of How AI Can Be Used Across the Supply Chain," *Forbes*, September 17, 2018, https://www.forbes.com/sites/blakemorgan/2018/09/17/5-examples-of-how-ai-can-be-used-across-the-supply-chain/#238f7679342e.

141. C. Steele, "The Quantified Employee: How Companies Use Tech to Track Workers," *PC*, February 14, 2020, https://www.pcmag.com/news/the-quantified-employee-how-companies-use-tech-to-track-workers.

142. K. Hernandez, "Even If You're Working from Home, Your Employer Is Still Keeping Track of Your Productivity—Here's What You Need to Know," *CNBC*, March 20, 2020, https://www.cnbc.com/2020/03/19/when-working-from-home-employers-are-watching---heres-what-to-know.html.

143. B. Miller, "Pros and Cons of Employee Monitoring," *HR Daily Advisor*, September 25, 2019, https://hrdailyadvisor.blr.com/2019/09/25/pros-and-cons-of-employee-monitoring/.

144. "Three Square Market," *Three Square Market*, https://www.32market.com/public/ (accessed May 10, 2020).

145. R. Metz, "This Company Embeds Microchips in Its Employees, and They Love It," *MIT Technology Review*, August 17, 2018, https://www.technologyreview.com/2018/08/17/140994/this-company-embeds-microchips-in-its-employees-and-they-love-it/. Also see A. Miller, "More Companies Are Using Technology to Monitor Employees, Sparking Privacy Concerns," *ABC News*, March 10, 2018, https://abcnews.go.com/US/companies-technology-monitor-employees-sparking-privacy-concerns/story?id=53388270.

146. A. Miller, "More Companies Are Using Technology to Monitor Employees, Sparking Privacy Concerns," *ABC News*, March 10, 2018, https://abcnews.go.com/US/companies-technology-monitor-employees-sparking-privacy-concerns/story?id=53388270.

147. R. Metz, "This Company Embeds Microchips in Its Employees, and They Love It," *MIT Technology Review*, August 17, 2018, https://www.technologyreview.com/2018/08/17/140994/this-company-embeds-microchips-in-its-employees-and-they-love-it/.

148. B. Miller, "Pros and Cons of Employee Monitoring," *HR Daily Advisor*, September 25, 2019, https://hrdailyadvisor.blr.com/2019/09/25/pros-and-cons-of-employee-monitoring/.

149. A. Shirish, S. Chandra, and S.C. Srivastava, "Watch Out—It's My Private Space! Examining the Influence of Technology Driven Intrusions on Employee Performance," *Proceedings of the 50th Hawaii International Conference on System Sciences*, 2017, DOI: 10.24251/HICSS.2017.699. Also see S. Morrison, "Just Because You're Working from Home Doesn't Mean Your Boss Isn't Watching You," *Recode*, April 2, 2020, https://www.vox.com/recode/2020/4/2/21195584/coronavirus-remote-work-from-home-employee-monitoring.

150. I. Kohen, "How to Embrace Employee Monitoring without Compromising Culture," *Forbes*, March 12, 2019, https://www.forbes.com/sites/theyec/2019/03/12/how-to-embrace-employee-monitoring-without-compromising-culture/#1e4b73944e1f.

151. B. Kropp, "Employers Are Increasingly Using Nontraditional Employee Monitoring Tools, and Employees Are Growing More Comfortable with It—If You Tell Them What You're Doing and Why," *Gartner*, May 3, 2019, https://www.gartner.com/smarterwithgartner/the-future-of-employee-monitoring/.

152. S. Bond, "Your Boss May Soon Track You at Work for Coronavirus Safety," *NPR*, May 8, 2020, https://www.npr.org/2020/05/08/852896051/your-boss-may-soon-track-you-at-work-for-coronavirus-safety.

153. K. Granville, "How to Manage Your Career," *The New York Times*, https://www.nytimes.com/guides/business/manage-your-career (accessed May 8, 2018).

154. S. B. McKinney, "How to Manage Your Career in 8 Steps," *BlueSteps*, March 31, 2017, https://www.bluesteps.com/blog/how-manage-your-career-8-steps.

155. B. Aeon and H. Aguinis, "It's about Time: New Perspectives and Insights on Time Management," *Academy of Management Perspectives*, November 2017, pp. 309–330. Also see A. Rastogi, "10 Essential Time Management Strategies," *GreyCampus*, December 19, 2017, https://www.greycampus.com/blog/project-management/ten-essential-time-management-strategies.

156. "Productivity Stop Checking Off Easy To-Dos," *Harvard Business Review*, November–December 2017, p. 24.

157. K. Granville, "How to Manage Your Career," *The New York Times*, https://www.nytimes.com/guides/business/manage-your-career (accessed May 8, 2018).

158. These suggestions were derived from J. Garfinkle, "The Keys to Effective Self-Promotion," *Garfinkle Executive Coaching*, https://garfinkleexecutivecoaching.com/articles/self-promotion-spread-the-word-about-you/the-keys-to-effective-self-promotion (accessed May 11, 2020).

159. A. Doyle, "How Often Do People Change Jobs during a Lifetime?" *The Balance Careers*, January 20, 2020, https://www.thebalancecareers.com/how-often-do-people-change-jobs-2060467.

160. M. Wang and C. Wanberg, "100 Years of Applied Psychology Research on Individual Careers: From Career Management to Retirement," *Journal of Applied Psychology*, March 2017, pp. 546–563.

161. D. Sitar, "5 Ways to Instantly Ruin a Job Interview, According to Hiring Managers," *The Penny Hoarder*, January 9, 2019, https://www.thepennyhoarder.com/make-money/career/job-interview-deal-breakers/.

162. R. Molla, "Tech Companies Tried to Help Us Spend Less Time on Our Phones. It Didn't Work," *Vox*, January 6, 2020, https://www.vox.com/recode/2020/1/6/21048116/tech-companies-time-well-spent-mobile-phone-usage-data.

163. "6 Ways to Use Technology for Personal Development," *Brantley Agency*, https://www.brantleyagency.com/technology-for-personal-development/ (accessed May 10, 2020). Also see "Explore Your Creativity," *Skill Share*, https://www.skillshare.com/?via=header (accessed May 10, 2020).

164. J. Duffy, "The Best Fitness Apps for 2020," *PC*, January 7, 2020, https://www.pcmag.com/news/the-best-fitness-apps-for-2020.

165. B. Green, "How to Build a Business Around Your Passion," *Medium*, November, 9, 2018, https://medium.com/swlh/how-to-build-a-business-around-your-passion-cc0f06cf393a. Also see "Hound and Co: A New Dog-Centric Online Marketplace," *The Broke Dog*, https://www.thebrokedog.com/hound-and-co/.

166. B. Scott, "Diane Von Furstenberg on Self-Discovery, Acceptance, and the American Dream," *Inc.*, http://www.inc.com/bartie-scott/diane-von-furstenberg-and-seth-meyers- on-becoming-the-woman-you-want-to-be.html (accessed July 2016).

167. V. Lipman, "The Hardest Thing for New Managers," *Forbes*, http://www.forbes.com/sites/victorlipman/2016/06/01/the-hardest-thing-for-new-managers/#2d3a7bca218f (accessed July 2016).

168. R. Reiss, "Amid This Pandemic, Women CEOs Share That Leadership and Culture Matter Most," *Forbes*, May 11, 2020, https://www.forbes.com/sites/robertreiss/2020/05/11/amid-this-pandemic-women-ceos-share-that-leadership-and-culture-matter-most/#1b6f1fb43293.

169. R. Chan, "How to Stand Out from the Crowd and Land Your Dream Job," *Forbes*, February 13, 2020, https://www.forbes.com/sites/forbestechcouncil/2020/02/13/how-to-stand-out-from-the-crowd-and-land-your-dream-job/#7b88b70e4f89.

170. C. Liu, "4 Easy Ways to Become a Better Leader at Work," *Inc.*, http://www.inc.com/the-muse/develop-leadership-skills-4-easy-steps.html (accessed July 2016).

171. "The Way You Treat People Matters," *Brian Mitchell*, https://www.bmitch30.com/blog/the-way-you-treat-people-matters.cfm (accessed May 15, 2020).

172. J. Benjamin, "For Bryce Drew, People Matter More Than Results," *Forbes*, http://www.forbes.com/sites/joshbenjamin/2016/03/29/for-bryce-drew-people-matter-more-than-results/#1eddcba07648 (accessed July 2016).

173. D. Overbye, "Stephen Hawking Dies at 76; His Mind Roamed the Cosmos," *The New York Times*, March 14, 2018, https://www.nytimes.com/2018/03/14/obituaries/stephen-hawking-dead.html.

174. M. P. Seligman, *Flourish* (New York: Free Press, 2011).

175. J. Clemente, "The Middle East's Growing Oil Demand Problem," *Forbes*, March 29, 2015, https://www.forbes.com/sites/judeclemente/2015/03/29/the-middle-easts-growing-oil-demand-problem/#196c9d9944af.

176. K. Amadeo, "US Shale Oil Boom and Bust," *The Balance*, May 1, 2020, https://www.thebalance.com/us-shale-oil-boom-and-bust-3305553.

177. M. Egan, "Oil Prices Turned Negative. Hundreds of US Oil Companies Could Go Bankrupt," *CNN*, April 20, 2020, https://www.cnn.com/2020/04/20/business/oil-price-crash-bankruptcy/index.html. Also see J. Hiller and L. Hampton, "Oil in the Age of Coronavirus: A U.S. Shale Bust Like No Other," *Reuters*, April 15, 2020, https://www.reuters.com/article/us-global-oil-shale-bust-insight/oil-in-the-age-of-coronavirus-a-u-s-shale-bust-like-no-other-idUSKCN21X0HC.

178. K. Amadeo, "Shale Oil and the Pros and Cons of Fracking," *The Balance*, January 31, 2020, https://www.thebalance.com/what-is-shale-oil-and-how-is-it-produced-3306195. Also see A. Beattie, "Shale Oil vs. Conventional Oil: What's the Difference?" *Investopedia*, August 8, 2019, https://www.investopedia.com/articles/active-trading/051215/cost-shale-oil-versus-conventional-oil.asp.

179. A. Beattie, "Shale Oil vs. Conventional Oil: What's the Difference?" *Investopedia*, August 8, 2019, https://www.investopedia.com/articles/active-trading/051215/cost-shale-oil-versus-conventional-oil.asp. Also see A. Truong, "How Far Underground Are Oil Deposits?" *How Stuff Works*, https://science.howstuffworks.com/environmental/energy/underground-oil-deposits.htm (accessed May 11, 2020).

180. K. Amadeo, "US Shale Oil Boom and Bust," *The Balance*, May 1, 2020, https://www.thebalance.com/us-shale-oil-boom-and-bust-3305553.

181. K. Amadeo," US Shale Oil Boom and Bust," *The Balance*, May 1, 2020, https://www.thebalance.com/us-shale-oil-boom-and-bust-3305553.

182. J. Hiller, "Few U.S. Shale Firms Can Withstand Prolonged Oil Price War," *Reuters*, March 16, 2020, https://www.reuters.com/article/us-global-oil-shale-costs-analysis/few-u-s-shale-firms-can-withstand-prolonged-oil-price-war-idUSKBN2130HL. Also see W. Englund, "Oil Drops below $0, Signaling Extreme Collapse in Demand. But You're Still Going to Have to Pay for Gas," *The Washington Post*, April 20, 2020, https://www.washingtonpost.com/business/2020/04/20/oil-barrel-below-zero/.

183. "Top 500 List," *Top 500*, https://www.top500.org/list/2019/06/ (accessed May 13, 2020).

184. M. Park, "Drillers Turn to Big Data in the Hunt for More, Cheaper Oil," *Financial Times*, February 12, 2018, https://www.ft.com/content/19234982-0cbb-11e8-8eb7-42f857ea9f09

185. D. Zaidi, "Role of Data Analytics in the Oil Industry," *Toward Data Science*, October 25, 2017, https://towardsdatascience.com/here-is-how-big-data-is-changing-the-oil-industry-13c752e58a5a.

186. M. Park, "Drillers Turn to Big Data in the Hunt for More, Cheaper Oil," *Financial Times*, February 12, 2018, https://www.ft.com/content/19234982-0cbb-11e8-8eb7-42f857ea9f09. Also see D. Zaidi, "Role of Data Analytics in the Oil Industry," *Toward Data Science*, October 25, 2017, https://towardsdatascience.com/here-is-how-big-data-is-changing-the-oil-industry-13c752e58a5a.

187. D. Zaidi, "Role of Data Analytics in the Oil Industry," *Toward Data Science*, October 25, 2017, https://towardsdatascience.com/here-is-how-big-data-is-changing-the-oil-industry-13c752e58a5a.

188. M. Park, "Drillers Turn to Big Data in the Hunt for More, Cheaper Oil," *Financial Times*, February 12, 2018, https://www.ft.com/content/19234982-0cbb-11e8-8eb7-42f857ea9f09. Also see D. Zaidi, "Role of Data Analytics in the Oil Industry," *Toward Data Science*, October 25, 2017, https://towardsdatascience.com/here-is-how-big-data-is-changing-the-oil-industry-13c752e58a5a.

189. "The Complete Guide to Workplace GPS Tracking and Location-Aware Tech 2019," *Quickbooks*, https://www.tsheets.com/gps-survey/2019-survey (accessed May 12, 2020).

190. J. Scott, "Park Hills to Begin Tracking City Vehicles," *Daily Journal News*, April 8, 2018, https://dailyjournalonline.com/news/local/park-hills-to-begin-tracking-city-vehicles/article_b9a36c68-2a04-502b-9287-6fbaa4ee0d71.html.

191. "Is It Legal to Track Employee Location via GPS in 2020?" *Hub Staff*, March 6, 2020, https://blog.hubstaff.com/employee-tracking-policy/.

192. "What Do Workers Really Think about GPS Monitoring?" *TSheets*, https://www.tsheets.com/gps-survey (accessed May 12, 2020).

193. H. Kelly, "Amazon's Idea for Employee-Tracking Wearables Raises Concerns," *CNNMoney*, February 2, 2018, http://money.cnn.com/2018/02/02/technology/amazon-employee-tracker/index.html.

194. E. Spitznagel, "Inside the Hellish Workday of an Amazon Warehouse Employee," *New York Post*, July 13, 2019, https://nypost.com/2019/07/13/inside-the-hellish-workday-of-an-amazon-warehouse-employee/.

195. "12 Most Asked Questions on U.S. Employee Monitoring Laws," *WorkTime*, https://www.worktime.com/what-are-the-u-s-employee-monitoring-laws-get-updated-in-2020 (accessed May 12, 2020). Also see K. Waddell, "Why Bosses Can Track Their Employees 24/7," *The Atlantic*, January 6, 2017, https://www.theatlantic.com/technology/archive/2017/01/employer-gps-tracking/512294/.

Note: Page numbers in *italics* represent figures, tables, and illustrations. Page numbers in **bold** represent glossary terms.

Behavioral appraisals, 388

Behavioral complexity, 600

Behavioral component of an attitude *Also known as intentional component, this refers to how one intends or expects to behave toward a situation,* **466**

Behavioral decision-making style, 293–294

Behavioral-description interview *Type of structured interview in which the interviewer explores what applicants have done in the past,* **374**

Behavioral leadership approaches *Attempts to determine the distinctive styles used by effective leaders, 611,* **611**–613
   task-oriented, 611

Behaviorally anchored rating scale (BARS) *Employee gradations in performance rated according to scales of specific behaviors,* **388**

Behavioral objectives, *194*

Behavioral science approach *Relies on scientific research for developing theories about human behavior that can be used to provide practical tools for managers,* **54**

Behavioral signs, stress, 496

Behavioral viewpoint *Emphasizes the importance of understanding human behavior and of motivating employees toward achievement,* 52–55

Behavior modification, 542
   to motivate employees, 544–545
   types of, 542–545, *543*

Benchmarking *A process by which a company compares its performance with that of high-performing organizations,* **221**–222, *222,* 712

Benefits *Additional nonmonetary forms of compensation,* **378**–379, 396

Best practices *A set of guidelines, ethics or ideas that have been shown to produce optimal results,* **712**

Bias
   anchoring and adjustment, 296
   availability, 295
   categorical thinking, 297
   confirmation, 295
   decision making, 294–297
   in decision making, 266
   escalation of commitment, 297
   explicit, 472
   framing, 296–297
   fundamental attribution, 474
   hindsight, 296
   implicit, 471–472
   judicial, 472, *472*
   overconfidence, 296
   representativeness, 295
   self-serving, 474
   sunk-cost, 296

Big data *Stores of data so vast that conventional database management systems cannot handle them,* **23,** 23–24, **282**–286, *285*

Big Five personality dimensions *They are (1) extroversion, (2) agreeableness, (3) conscientiousness, (4) emotional stability,*

and (5) openness to experience, 250–251, **458**–459

Blockchain, 87

Board of directors *Group of people elected to oversee the firm's activities and ensure that management acts in the shareholders' best interests,* 77, **79**

Body language, 457, 641, 659

Bonuses *Cash awards given to employees who achieve specific performance objectives,* 334, **547**

Boomerangs *Former employees who return to the organization,* **370**

Boundaryless organization *A fluid, highly adaptive organization whose members, linked by information technology, come together to collaborate on common tasks; the collaborators may include competitors, suppliers, and customers,* 349–351, *350*

Bounded rationality *One type of nonrational decision making; the ability of decision makers to be rational is limited by numerous constraints,* **272**

Brainstorming *Technique used to help groups generate multiple ideas and alternatives for solving problems; individuals in a group meet and review a problem to be solved, then silently generate ideas, which are collected and later analyzed,* 301–302, *302*

Brand recognition, 209, 667–669

Brazil, emerging economy of, 160, *160*

Bribes, 168–169

BRICS countries, 160, *160*

Broader stakeholders, 425–426

Budgets *A formal financial projection,* 179, **707**–708

Buffers *Administrative changes that managers can make to reduce the stressors that lead to employee burnout,* **499**

Bullying *Repeated mistreatment of one or more persons by one or more perpetrators. It's abusive, physical, psychological, verbal, or nonverbal behavior that is threatening, humiliating, or intimidating,* **401**–403, *402, 403,* 413

Bureaucracy, 51

Burnout *State of emotional, mental, and even physical exhaustion,* **496**

Business, core processes of, 231–233, *232*

Business ethics, 275–277

Business-level strategy *Focuses on individual business units or product/service lines, 211,* **211**–212

Business model *Outline of need the firm will fill, the operations of the business, its components and functions, as well as the expected revenues and expenses,* **181**

Business plan *A document that outlines a proposed firm's goals, the strategy for achieving them, and the standards for measuring success,* **181,** 257–258

Business skills, *609*

Buyers, bargaining power of, 227

Buzzwords, 645

CAFTA-DR. *See* Central America Free Trade Agreement

Canada
   individualism in, 162
   in NAFTA, 156

Career counseling, 501

Career readiness *Represents the extent to which you possess the knowledge, skills, and attributes desired by employers,* **30**
   competencies needed for, 32, *32–33*
   critical thinking/problem solving and, 304
   cross-cultural awareness and, 141, 170–172
   development of, 35–36
   emotional regulation and, 504
   interventions, 437
   levels of, 30, *30*
   management of, 37–39, 65–67, 731–734
   model of, *31,* 31–35
   networking skills and, 686–688
   openness to change and, 448–450
   personal adaptability and, 170
   positive approach and, 502–503
   process for developing, 37, *38*
   professionalism and work ethic in, 107–108
   receiving feedback, 408–410
   self-awareness and, 170, 633–634
   strategic thinking and, 235–237
   task-based/functional knowledge and, 237
   understanding business and personal adaptability, *351,* 351–353
   understanding the business and, 236

Cascading goals *Objectives are structured in a unified hierarchy, becoming more specific at lower levels of the organization,* 195–**196**

Cash cows, 224

Categorical thinking bias *Tendency of decision makers to classify people or information based on observed or inferred characteristics,* **297**

Causal attribution *The activity of inferring causes for observed behavior,* **474**

C corporations, 258

Cell phones, 656

Central America Free Trade Agreement (CAFTA-DR), *157*

Centralized authority *Organizational structure in which important decisions are made by upper managers—power is concentrated at the top,* **342**

Certifications, 437

Challenger space shuttle disaster, *92,* 92–93

Change. *See* Organizational change

Change agent *A person inside or outside the organization who can be a catalyst in helping deal with old problems in new ways,* **434,** 446

Change and acquisition phase, organizational socialization, 324

Content perspectives *Also known as need-based perspectives; theories that emphasize the needs that motivate people,* **516**
  Deci and Ryan's self-determination theory, 519–521, *521*
  Herzberg's two-factor theory, 521–524, *522*
  Maslow's hierarchy of needs, 53–54, 516–518, *517*
  McClelland's acquired needs theory, *518,* 518–519

Context *The situational or environmental characteristics that influence our behavior,* **171**

Contingency factors, 540–541

Contingency leadership model *A model that determines if a leader's style is (1) task-oriented or (2) relationship-oriented and if that style is effective for the situation at hand,* **613**–615, *614*

Contingency planning *Also known as scenario planning and scenario analysis; the creation of alternative hypothetical but equally likely future conditions,* **220**–221

Contingency viewpoint *The belief that a manager's approach should vary according to-that is, be contingent on-the individual and the environmental situation,* **60**–61

Continuous improvement *Ongoing, small, incremental improvements in all parts of an organization,* **721**–722

Contract negotiation, *404,* 404–405

Control charts *A visual statistical tool used for quality-control purposes,* **700**–702, *701–702*

Control/control systems. *See also* Total quality management (TQM)
  balanced scorecard and, 705–707, *706*
  contemporary issues, 727–731
  need for, 696–698, *697, 699*
  productivity and, 697–698
  strategy map and, 715–717, *716*
  types of, 703–704

Controlling *Monitoring performance, comparing it with goals, and taking corrective action as needed,* **10, 696,** *696*

Control process steps *The four steps in the process of controlling: (1) establish standards; (2) measure performance; (3) compare performance to standards; and (4) take corrective action, if necessary,* **699,** *699*–703

Control standard *The first step in the control process; the performance standard (or just standard) is the desired performance level for a given goal,* **700**

Coordinated effort *The coordination of individual efforts into a group or organization-wide effort,* **339**

Core influence tactics, 604

Core self-evaluation (CSE) *Represents a broad personality trait comprising four positive individual traits: (1) self-efficacy, (2) self-esteem, (3) locus of control, and (4) emotional stability,* **459**–462

Core values statement, 66

Coronavirus (COVID-19) pandemic. *See* COVID-19 pandemic

Corporate culture *Set of shared taken-for-granted implicit assumptions that group holds and that determines how it perceives, thinks about, and reacts to its various environments,* 66, **315,** *315. See also* Organizational culture

Corporate governance *The system of governing a company so that the interests of corporate owners and other stakeholders are protected,* **105**–107
  failure in, 106–107
  and social responsibility, 105–106

Corporate-level strategy *Focuses on the organization as a whole,* **211,** *211*

Corporate loitering policy, 638–639

Corporate reputation, 668–669

Corporate social responsibility (CSR) *The notion that corporations are expected to go above and beyond following the law and making a profit, to take actions that will benefit the interests of society as well as of the organization,* **99**
  climate change and, 102
  effects of, 102–103, *104*
  philanthropy and, 102–103
  pyramid of, 100, *100*
  viewpoints on, 100–101

Corporate wellness programs, 559–560

Corporation *An entity that is separate from its owners, meaning it has its own legal rights, independent of its owners-it can sue, be sued, own and sell property, and sell the rights of ownership in the form of stocks,* **258**–259

Corruption, 93, 168–169

Cost-focus strategy *One of Porter's four competitive strategies; keeping the costs, and hence prices, of a product or service below those of competitors and to target a narrow market,* **228**

Cost-leadership strategy *One of Porter's four competitive strategies; keeping the costs, and hence prices, of a product or service below those of competitors and to target a wide market,* **228**

Cost-of-living adjustment (COLA) clause *Clause in a union contract that ties future wage increases to increases in the cost of living,* **406**–407

Counterproductive work behavior (CWB) *Type of behavior that harms employees and the organization as a whole,* **482**–483

Counterthrusters, 432, 433

Countertrading *Bartering goods for goods,* **152**

Courage *Taking intentional action in a worthy cause and enduring in this act despite the risk of serious personal consequences,* **75**

Courtroom, implicit bias in, 472

COVID-19 pandemic
  and contact tracing, 730
  contingency approach to communication during, 647–648
  downward communication during, 649
  fake news about, 674

gender and leadership during, 608
  health care workers and, 414, 558–559
  managers' resistance to change, 452–453
  need for control during, 696–698
  religious practices during, 422–423
  and U.S. health care system, 692

Creativity, 251, 417

Credibility, 655

Crime, white-collar, 95–97

Criminal background checks, 377

Crises, responses to organizational, 332–333, *333*

Critical thinking, 200, 304

Cross-cultural awareness *The ability to operate in different cultural settings,* 141, **146,** 170–172

Cross-cultural communication barriers, 657–658

Cross-cultural conflict, 584–585

Cross-functional teams *A team that is staffed with specialists pursuing a common objective,* 347, **567**

Crowdfunding *Raising money for a project or venture by obtaining many small amounts of money from many people ("the crowd"),* **83,** 666

Crowd investing *Allows a group of people–the crowd–to invest in an entrepreneur or business online,* **260**

Crowdsourcing *The practice of obtaining needed services, ideas, or content by soliciting contributions from a large group of people and especially from the online community, such as Facebook and Twitter users,* **443,** 666–667

CSR. *See* Corporate social responsibility

CSR contracting *Linking executive compensation to CSR criteria such as environment and social performance,* **106**

Cultural differences. *See also* Diversity
  communication and, 165
  competitive advantage and, 164–165
  dimensions of, 162–164, *163–164*
  GLOBE project and, 162–164, *163–164*
  interpersonal space and, 165, *166*
  language and, 165
  law and political stability and, 167–169
  meetings and, 167
  national culture and, 161–162
  overview of, 161
  religion and, 167, *168*
  stereotypes and, 469–471
  time orientation and, 166
  tipping customs and, *161*
  in workforce, 490

Culture Code, 330, *330*

Culture of secrecy, 107

Culture *The shared set of beliefs, values, knowledge, and patterns of behavior common to a group of people,* **161**–162. *See also* Organizational culture
  adhocracy, 325–326
  business travel and, 141

drive down the price of a competing domestic product, 154

Dunning-Kruger effect *A cognitive bias whereby people who are incompetent at something are unable to recognize their own incompetence. And not only do they fail to recognize their incompetence, they're also likely to feel confident that they actually are competent,* **634,** 695

Dysfunctional conflict *Conflict that hinders the organization's performance or threatens its interests,* **582**

Dysfunctional turnover, 714

EAPs. *See* Employee assistance programs

E-business *Using the Internet to facilitate every aspect of running a business,* **22**

E-commerce *Electronic commerce—the buying and selling of goods or services over computer networks,* **22,** **143**

Economic community. *See* Trading bloc

Economic forces *General economic conditions and trends—unemployment, inflation, interest rates, economic growth—that may affect an organization's performance,* **85**

Economy, global, 144–145

EEOC. *See* Equal Employment Opportunity Commission

Effectiveness *To achieve results, to make the right decisions, and to successfully carry them out so that they achieve the organization's goals,* 5–6

Efficiency *To use resources-people, money raw materials, and the like-wisely and cost effectively,* **5,** 22, 712
  big data and, 284
  effectiveness *vs.,* 5–6
  social responsibility and, 102

Effort-to-performance expectancy, 531

Electronic brainstorming *Technique in which members of a group come together over a computer network to generate ideas and alternatives,* 301–302

Embargoes *A complete ban on the import or export of certain products,* **155**

Emotional empathy, 680

Emotional intelligence *The ability to cope, to empathize with others, and to be self-motivated,* 462, **462**–463, 587

Emotional regulation, 504

Emotional stability *Is the extent to which people feel secure and unworried and how likely they are to experience negative emotions under pressure,* 458, **462**

Empathy *Represents the ability to recognize and understand another person's feelings and thoughts,* 463, 575, 641–642, **680,** *680*

Employee assistance programs (EAPs) *Host of programs aimed at helping employees to cope with stress, burnout, substance abuse,* health-related problems, family and marital issues, and any general problems that negatively influence job performance, **500**

Employee-centered leader behaviors *Emphasize relationships with subordinates and attention to their individual needs,* **612**

Employee engagement *A mental state in which a person performing a work activity is full immersed in the activity, feeling full of energy and enthusiasm for the work,* 476, **476**–478

Employee referrals *Tap into existing employees' social networks to fill open positions with outside applicants,* **369**–370

Employee Retirement Income Security Act (ERISA) (1974), *396*

Employee-run mini-businesses, 567

Employees. *See also* Human resource management (HRM)
  activism, 530–531
  AI to engage, 288
  foreign, 147
  GPS tracking of, 739–740
  insubordination of, 71
  noncompete agreements and, 414–415
  as owners, 79
  perceptions, 528–529
  productivity, social media and, 664–665
  profiles, 368
  promotion of, 392
  resistance to change in, *445,* 445–447
  social media policy for, 668
  social responsibility effect on, *104*
  as stakeholders, 78, *78*
  voice of, 529

Employee socialization, 379

Employee tracking and monitoring
  advantages of, 729
  disadvantages of, 730–731
  overview, 729

Employment at will *Governing principle of employment in the great majority of states, that anyone can be dismissed at any time for any reason at all-or for no reason,* **395**

Employment interviews, 66–67, 306, 361, 373–374

Employment tests *Tests legally considered to consist of any procedure used in the employment selection process,* **374**–378

Empowering leadership *A form of leadership that represents the extent to which a leader creates perceptions of psychological empowerment in others,* **628**–629

Empowerment
  leadership and, 628–629
  quality and, 720

Enacted values *Values and norms actually exhibited in the organization,* **321**–322

Encoding barrier, *653*

Encoding *Translating a message into understandable symbols or language,* **643**

Encounter phase, organizational socialization, 324

Entrepreneurship *The process of taking risks to try to create a new enterprise,* 245–248, 246
  global importance of, 252–254
  innovation and, 253
  self-employment *vs.,* 247–248
  social, 248–249
  standard of living and, 253–254

Entrepreneurs *Someone who sees a new opportunity for a product or service and launches a business to try to realize it,* **246**
  characteristics of, 249–251, *250*
  examples of, 245
  supporting, 101, *101*
  types of, 246

Envy-based conflicts, 583–584

Epiphany, 274

Equal employment opportunity, 397–398

Equal Employment Opportunity Commission (EEOC) *U.S. panel whose job it is to enforce anti-discrimination and other employment related laws,* **397,** 493–494

Equal Pay Act (1963), *396*

Equity theory *In the area of employee motivation, the focus on how employees perceive how fairly they think they are being treated compared with others,* **525**–531, *526*

ERISA. *See* Employee Retirement Income Security Act

Escalation of commitment bias *When decision makers increase their commitment to a project despite negative information about it,* **297**

Espoused values *Explicitly stated values and norms preferred by an organization,* **321**–322

Esteem needs, 516, *517*

Ethical behavior *Behavior that is accepted as "right" as opposed to "wrong" according to those standards,* **91,** 98

Ethical climate *A term that refers to employees' perceptions about the extent to which work environments support ethical behavior,* **97**

Ethical dilemma *A situation in which you have to decide whether to pursue a course of action that may benefit you or your organization but that is unethical or even illegal,* **89**–90, 94–95

Ethical leadership *Directed by respect for ethical beliefs and values for the dignity and rights of others,* **629**–630

Ethical/legal issues
  airline accommodation for overweight individuals, 509
  approaches to, 94–95
  Clearview's technology, 454
  corporate loitering policy, 638–639
  emotional support animals, 310–311
  GPS tracking of employees, 739–740
  in human resource management, 395–403
  insubordinate employees, 71
  for managers, 26–27
  marijuana use, 594
  noncompete agreements, legality of, 414–415

Focused-differentiation strategy *One of Porter's four competitive strategies; offering products or services that are of unique and superior value compared to those of competitors and to target a narrow market,* **228**

Followers, 630–631

FOMO *Fear of missing out or of being out of touch with something happening in your social network,* **670**, 688

Forced ranking performance review systems *Performance review systems whereby all employees within a business unit are ranked against one another, and grades are distributed along some sort of bell curve, like students being graded in a college course,* 390–391

Force-field analysis *A technique to determine which forces could facilitate a proposed change and which forces could act against it,* **432**

Forcing, conflict and, 588

Forecast *A vision or projection of the future,* **220**–221

Foreign Corrupt Practices Act (1978) *Act that makes it illegal for employees of U.S. companies to make "questionable" or "dubious" contributions to political decision makers in foreign nations,* 168–169

Formal communication channels *Communications that follow the chain of command and are recognized as official,* **648**–650, *649*

Formal group *A group, headed by a leader, that is established to do something productive for the organization,* **566**

Formal statements, 330

Forming *The first of the five stages of forming a team, in which people get oriented and get acquainted,* **570**–571

For-profit organizations, 13

Fortune 500, 4, 118, 120, 180, 390, 394, 436, 458, 607

Fortune 1000, 547, 568,

Fortune (magazine), 4, 29, 46, 78, 105, 120, 128, 135, 186, 190, 323, 325, 362, 367, 370, 386, 520, 523, 605, 720

Four management functions *The management process that "gets things done": planning, organizing, leading, and controlling,* **9**

Framing bias *The tendency of decision makers to be influenced by the way a situation or problem is presented to them,* **296**–297

Franchising *A form of licensing in which a company allows a foreign company to pay it a fee and a share of the profit in return for using the first company's brand name and a package of materials and services,* **153**, 256

Free trade *The movement of goods and services among nations without political or economic obstruction,* **154**

Fringe benefits. *See* Benefits

Full-range leadership *Approach that suggests that leadership behavior varies along a full range of leadership styles, from take-no-responsibility (laissez-faire) "leadership" at one extreme through transactional leadership, to transformational leadership at the other extreme,* **619**–623

Functional conflict *Conflict that benefits the main purposes of the organization and serves its interests,* **582**

Functional knowledge, 200

Functional-level strategy *Plan of action by each functional area of the organization to support higher level strategies,* 211, **212**

Functional manager *Manager who is responsible for just one organizational activity,* **12**

Functional strategy, 230

Functional structure *The second type of organizational structure, whereby people with similar occupational specialties are put together in formal groups,* **345**, *345*

Functional turnover, 714

Fundamental attribution bias *Tendency whereby people attribute another person's behavior to his or her personal characteristics rather than to situational factors,* **474**

Future orientation, 163, *164*

Gainsharing *The distribution of savings or "gains" to groups of employees who reduce costs and increase measurable productivity,* **547**

Gender
pay inequality and, 413, 489
traits and, 606–609
in workforce, 488–490

Gender differences
as communication barrier, 659–660, *660*

Gender egalitarianism, 163, *163*

General and Industrial Management (Fayol), 51

General environment *Also called macroenvironment; in contrast to the task environment, it includes six forces: economic, technological, sociocultural, demographic, political-legal, and international,* 84–89

Generalized self-efficacy *Represents the belief in one's general ability to perform across different situations,* **459**–460

General manager *Manager who is responsible for several organizational activities,* **13**

Generational differences, communication and, 656–657

Genetic Information Nondiscrimination Act, 560

Genuine sense of curiosity, 641–642, 658, 682

Gen Y. *See* Millennials

Gen Z, 45, 77, 85, 87, 130, 145, 379, 425, 465, 500, 564

Geocentric managers *Managers who accept that there are differences and similarities between home and foreign personnel and practices and that they should use whatever techniques are most effective,* **148**

Geographic divisions *Divisional structures in which activities are grouped around defined regional locations,* **346**, *346*

Gestures, 659

Gig economy, 724

Givebacks *Negotiation tactic in which the union agrees to give up previous wage or benefit gains in return for something else,* **407**

Giving Voice to Values (GVV), 96

Glass ceiling *The metaphor for an invisible barrier preventing women and minorities from being promoted to top executive jobs,* **489**

Global economy *The increasing tendency of the economies of the world to interact with one another as one market instead of many national markets,* **144**–145

Globalization *The trend of the world economy toward becoming a more interdependent system,* **142**
competition and, 142, *142*
cultural awareness and, 141, 146, 170–172
managing for, 25–26

Global management
attitudes and, 148
benefits of learning about, 146–148
BRICS countries, 160, *160*
cross-cultural awareness and, 141, 146, 170–172
cultural differences and, 161–169
electronic commerce, 143
exchange rates and, 158–159, *159*
expansion methods and, 149–153, *150*
expatriates and, 169
global competition, 142, *142*
global economy, 144–145
international markets, growing, 149–153
most favored nation trading status and, 158
organizations promoting trade and, 155, *156*
trade issues and, 153–160
trading blocs and, 156–158, *157*
travel issues and, 141

Global mind-set *Your belief in your ability to influence dissimilar others in a global context,* **611**

Global outsourcing *Also called offshoring; use of suppliers outside the United States to provide labor, goods, or services,* **151**

Global village *The "shrinking" of time and space as air travel and the electronic media have made it easier for the people around the globe to communicate with one another,* **143**

Global warming *One aspect of climate change, refers to the rise in global average temperature near the Earth's surface, caused mostly by increasing concentrations in the atmosphere of greenhouse gases, such as carbon emissions from fossil fuels,* **102**

GLOBE project *A massive and ongoing cross-cultural investigation of nine cultural dimensions involved in leadership and organizational processes,* **162**–164, *163–164*

Identity theft *A violation of privacy in which thieves hijack your name and identity and use your good credit rating to get cash or buy things,* **672**–673

Illusory truth effect *When our brain equates repetition with trust,* **675**

Imitability (in VRIO framework), 219, *219*

Immigration Reform & Control Act (1986), *396*

Impersonal sexuality, 400

Implementation
artificial intelligence, 290
in evidence-based decision making, 280–281
in rational model of decision making, 270–271

Implicit bias *Is the attitudes or beliefs that affect our understanding, actions, and decisions in an unconscious manner,* 471–**472**

Importing *Buying goods outside the country and reselling them domestically,* **151**

Import quotas *A trade barrier in the form of a limit on the numbers of a product that can be imported,* **154**, *155*

Improvement innovations, 439

Improvement orientation, 721–722

Incentives, 378

Income statement *Summary of an organization's financial results—revenues and expenses—over a specified period of time,* **708**, *709*

Incremental budgeting *Allocating increased or decreased funds to a department by using the last budget period as a reference point; only incremental changes in the budget request are reviewed,* **707**

India
emerging economy of, 160, *160*
offshoring to, 151

Individual approach *One of four approaches to solving ethical dilemmas; ethical behavior is guided by what will result in the individual's best long-term interests, which ultimately are in everyone's self-interest,* **94**–95

Individualism, 162

Industrial engineering, 49–50

Industrial psychology, 52

Influence tactics *Are conscious efforts to affect and change behaviors in others,* **602**–605, *603–604*

Informal communication channels *Communication that develops outside the formal structure and does not follow the chain of command,* **650**–652

Informal group *A group formed by people seeking friendship that has no officially appointed leader, although a leader may emerge from the membership,* **566**

Informal influence, 566, *566*

Informal nominations, 368

Informational power *Power deriving from one's access to information,* **602**

Informational roles *Managers as monitors, disseminators, and spokespersons,* **17**, *18*

Information oversimplification, 647

Information processing, 655

Information technology application skills *The extent to which you can effectively use information technology and learn new applications on an ongoing basis,* **22**

Ingratiation, *603,* 605

In-group collectivism, 163, *163*

In-group exchange, 624

In-house training, 437

Initiating-structure leadership *A leadership behavior that organizes and defines—that is, "initiates the structure for"—what employees should be doing to maximize output,* **611**–612

Innovation *Introduction of something new or better, as in goods or services,* **22**, 183. See also Organizational change
balanced scorecard and, 251, 713–715
control function of, 698
crowdsourcing and, 666–667
culture of, 417
disruptive, 419
employee attitudes, 713
employee turnover, 713–714
entrepreneurship and, 253
focus of, 439–440
human capital and, 444
organizational culture, 714–715
process, 439
product, 438–439, *439,* 440, *440*
resource capabilities, 714
resources and, 444
structure and processes for, 442–443
type of, 438–439, *439*

Innovation strategy *Grows market share or profits by innovating improvements in products or services,* **223**, **440**–441

Innovation system *A set of mutually reinforcing structures, processes, and practices that drive an organization's choices around innovation and its ability to innovate successfully,* **440**–444, *441*

Innovative change *The introduction of a practice that is new to the organization,* **428**

The Innovator's Dilemma (Christensen), 419

In-person meetings, 651

Inputs *The people, money, information, equipment, and materials required to produce an organization's goods or services,* **58**, *59,* 430–431

In Search of Excellence (Peters), 46

Insider trading *The illegal trading of a company's stock by people using confidential company information,* **95**

Inspirational appeals, *603*

Instability, international, 168

Institutional collectivism, 163, *163*

Institutional power, 518

Instrumentality *The expectation that successful performance of the task will lead to the outcome desired,* **532**

Integrating, conflict and, 588

Integrity tests, 376

Intelligence, emotional, *462,* **462**–463

Interactional justice *Relates to how organizational representatives treat employees in the process of implementing procedures and making decisions,* **527**

Intergroup conflicts, 584

Internal business perspective, 711–713
efficiency, 712
productivity, 711–712

Internal dimensions of diversity *Differences that exert a powerful, sustained effect throughout every stage of people's lives,* **486**–487

Internal fit, strategic HRM, 363

Internal job postings, 368

Internal locus of control, 251, 461

Internal recruiting *Hiring from the inside, or making people already employed by the organization aware of job openings,* **368**–369

Internal stakeholders *Employees, owners, and the board of directors, if any,* **77**–80, *78*

International forces *Changes in the economic, political, legal, and technological global system that may affect an organization,* **88**–89

International management. *See* Global management

Internet of Things (IoT), 86–87

Interpersonal roles *Of the three types of managerial roles, the roles in which managers interact with people inside and outside their work units. The three interpersonal roles include figurehead, leader, and liaison activities,* **17**, *18*

Interpersonal skills, *609*

Interpersonal space, 165, *166*

Intervention *Interference in an attempt to correct a problem,* **436**

Interviews
employment, 306, 361, 373–374
exit, 394–395

Intrapreneurs *Someone who works inside an existing organization who sees an opportunity for a product or service and mobilizes the organization's resources to try to realize it,* **247**

Intrinsic rewards *The satisfaction, such as a feeling of accomplishment, a person receives from performing a task,* **514**

Intuition *Making a choice without the use of conscious thought or logical inference,* **273**–275

Inverted U-shaped relationship, 495

Investment activities, 709

IoT. *See* Internet of Things

LMX model. *See* Leader-member exchange model of leadership

Local communities, as stakeholders, 83

Locus of control *Measure of how much people believe they control their fate through their own efforts,* 251, **461**

Logic, 575

Loitering policy, 638–639

Long-term goals *Tend to span 1 to 5 years and focus on achieving the strategies identified in a company's strategic plan,* **190**, 190–191, 554

Love needs, 516, *517*

Low-context culture *Culture in which shared meanings are primarily derived from written and spoken words,* **162**

Low-control situation, *614,* 615

Lying, 372

Machiavellianism *A cynical view of human nature and condoning opportunistic and unethical ways of manipulating people, putting results over principles,* **606**

Machine learning *An extension of predictive analytics, occurs when systems or algorithms automatically improve themselves based on data patterns, experiences, and observations,* **287–288**

Macroenvironment *In contrast to the task environment, it includes six forces: economic, technological, sociocultural, demographic, political–legal, and international,* **84**–89

Maintenance role *Relationship-related role consisting of behavior that fosters constructive relationships among team members,* *578,* **579**

Management by exception *Control principle that states that managers should be informed of a situation only if data show a significant deviation from standards,* **702**

Management by objectives (MBO) *Four-step process in which (1) managers and employees jointly set objectives for the employee, (2) managers develop action plans, (3) managers and employees periodically review the employee's performance, and (4) the manager makes a performance appraisal and rewards the employee according to results,* **193**–195, *194*
- types of objectives in, *194*

Management theory
- administrative management, 48, 50–51
- behavioral science viewpoint, 54
- behavioral viewpoint, 52–55
- classical viewpoint, 48–51
- contingency viewpoint, 60–61
- human relations movement, 53–54
- learning organization, 61–63, *62*
- operations management, 56–57
- perspectives on, 48, *48*
- quantitative viewpoints, 56–57
- reasons to study, 47–48

scientific management, 49–50
systems viewpoint, 58–60

Management *The pursuit of organizational goals efficiently and effectively by integrating the work of people through planning, organizing, leading, and controlling the organization's resources,* 4, **5**
- areas of, 10, *11,* 12–13
- leadership *vs.,* 598–599, *599*
- levels of, 10, *11,* 11–12
- organization types and, 13–14
- origins of modern management, 46
- perspectives, progression of, 48, *48*
- perspectives of, 48, *48*
- process of, 9, *9*
- rewards of practicing, 7–8
- rewards of studying, 7
- skills, 3

Managerial leadership *Involves both influencing followers to internalize and commit to a set of shared goals, and facilitating the group and individual work that is needed to accomplish those goals,* **600**

Managers
- challenges facing, 21–29
- and communication, 15
- communication channels and, 648–652, *649*
- and control of organizational effectiveness, 705–717
- demands for, 15
- expatriate, 169
- international, 148
- leaders *vs.,* 598–599, *599*
- multiplier effect, 6–7
- organizational change and behavior of, 426–427
- rewards for, 7–8
- roles of, 14–18, *18*
- skill requirements for, 18–21
- stress created by, 498
- thoughtfulness of, 551
- and time management, 15–16
- traits in, 21

Man's Search for Meaning (Frankl), 551

Maquiladoras *Foreign-owned manufacturing plants allowed to operate in Mexico with special privileges in return for employing Mexican citizens,* **150**

Marijuana, 87, *88,* 594

Market culture *Type of organizational culture that has a strong external focus and values stability and control,* 325, **326,** 328

Markets
- access to new markets, 149–150

Masculinity *vs.* femininity, 162

Matrix structure *Fourth type of organizational structure, which combines functional and divisional chains of command in a grid so that there are two command structures—vertical and horizontal,* **346**–347, *347*

MBO. *See* Management by objectives

Meaningfulness *Is characterized by a sense of being part of something you believe is bigger than yourself,* **28**–29, **552**

Means-end chain *A hierarchy of goals; in the chain of management (operational, tactical, strategic), the accomplishment of low-level goals are the means leading to the accomplishment of high-level goals or ends,* **190**

Measurable and controllable activities, 334–335

Measurable goals, 192–193

Media richness *Indication of how well a particular medium conveys information and promotes learning,* 646, **646**–647

Mediation *The process in which a neutral third party, a mediator, listens to both sides in a dispute, makes suggestions, and encourages them to agree on a solution,* **407**

Medium *The pathway by which a message travels,* **644**

Meetings, 167, 651–652

Men. *See* Gender

Mentor *An experienced person who provided guidance to someone new in the work world,* **8,** 695

Mercosur, *157*

Mergers and acquisitions (M&A), 435

Message, 643, *643*

#MeToo movement, 277, 395

Mexico
- collectivism in, 162
- imports from, 151
- maquiladoras in, 150
- masculinity in, 162
- in NAFTA, 156

Microaggressions *Acts of unconscious bias; include a number of seemingly tiny but repeated actions, like interrupting others, mispronouncing or mistaking someone's name, and avoiding eye contact,* **670**

Microlearning *Also called bite-size learning, which segments learning into bite-size content, enabling a student to master one piece of learning before advancing to anything else,* **382**

Middle managers *One of four managerial levels; they implement the policies and plans of the top managers above them and supervise and coordinate the activities of the first-line managers below them,* **12**

Millennials, 77, 485
- industries affected by, 87
- learning opportunities desired by, 62
- technological adoption by, 418

Mindfulness *is the state of being fully aware of what is happening in the present moment without reacting or applying judgment,* **16**–17, 267–268, 504, 597, 641, 680, 682–683, 688

Mindlessness *A state of reduced attention expressed in behavior that is rigid, or thoughtless,* **656**

Minority dissent *Dissent that occurs when a minority in a group publicly opposes the beliefs, attitudes, ideas, procedures, or policies assumed by the majority of the group,* **301**

Problem solving, 200, 304, 417

Procedural justice *The perceived fairness of the process and procedures used to make allocation decisions,* **527**

Process *A series of actions or steps followed to bring about a desired result,* **37**

Process innovation *A change in the way a product or service is conceived, manufactured, or disseminated,* **439**

Process perspectives *Theories of employee motivation concerned with the thought processes by which people decide how to act: expectancy theory, equity theory, and goal-setting theory,* **524**
   equity/justice theory, 525–531, *526*
   expectancy theory, 531–533, *532*
   goal-setting theory, 533–537

Product divisions *Divisional structures in which activities are grouped around similar products or services,* **345,** *346*

Product innovation *A change in the appearance or the performance of a product or a service or the creation of a new one,* **438**–439, *439,* 440, *440*

Production-centered leader behaviors *Emphasize the technical or task-related aspects of employees' roles,* **611**

Productivity, 483, 711
   artificial intelligence and, 728
   benchmarking and, 712
   best practices and, 712
   control systems and, 697–698
   digital tools, 665
   social media use and, 664–666

Professionalism, 107–108

Profit, social responsibility and, *104*

Profit sharing *The distribution to employees of a percentage of the company's profits,* **547**

Programmed conflict *Conflict designed to elicit different opinions without inciting people's personal feelings,* **585**–586

Project management software *Programs for planning and scheduling the people, costs, and resources to complete a project on time,* **25**

Project post-mortem *A review of recent decisions in order to identify possible future improvements,* **302**–304

Project teams, 566–567

Promotions, 334, 392

Prosocial behavior (PSB) *Voluntary behavior intended to benefit another, such as helping, donating, sharing, and comforting,* **479,** *480,* 481
   increasing, 484

Prosocial motivation (PSM) *The desire to promote the well-being of others,* **479**–481

Protective tariffs, 154

Psychological capital *Positive state of psychological development that is characterized by high levels of hope, resiliency, optimism, and self-efficacy,* **410**

Psychological empowerment *Employees' belief that they have control over their work,* **628**–629

Psychological noise, 644

Psychological safety *Reflects the extent to which people feel free to express their ideas and beliefs without fear of negative consequences,* **493**

Psychological signs, stress, 496

Psychopathy *A lack of concern for others, impulsive behavior, and a dearth of remorse when the psychopath's actions harm others,* **606**

Public policy, 284

Punctuated equilibrium *Establishes periods of stable functioning until an event causes a dramatic change in norms, roles, and/or objectives resulting in the establishment and maintenance of new norms of functioning, returning to equilibrium,* **573,** *573*

Punishment *The process of weakening behavior by presenting something negative or withdrawing something positive,* **544**–545

Purple Campaign, 400, *400*

Pygmalion effect, *474*–475

Quality assurance *A means of ensuring quality that focuses on the performance of workers, urging employees to strive for "zero defects,"* **718**

Quality control *A means of ensuring quality whereby errors are minimized by managing each stage of production,* **718**

Quality *The total ability of a product or service to meet customer needs,* 22, *712,* **718**
   Deming management and, 718–719

Quantitative management *The application to management of quantitative techniques, such as statistics and computer simulations. Two branches of quantitative management are management science and operations management,* **56**

Quantitative viewpoint, 56–57

Questions
   closed-ended, 682
   curious, 682
   judgmental, 682
   noncurious, 682
   nonjudgmental, 682
   open-ended, 681–682

Quid pro quo harassment, 401

Quotas
   avoidance of, 150
   import, 154, *155*

Race/ethnicity stereotypes, 471

Radically innovative change *Introduces a practice that is new to the industry,* **428**

Rarity (in VRIO framework), 219, *219*

Rational model of decision making *Also called the classical model; the style of decision making that explains how managers should make decisions; it assumes that managers will make logical decisions that are the optimal means of furthering the organization's best interests,* **269**
   assumptions of, *271*
   problems related to, 271, *271*
   stages in, *269,* 270–271

Rational persuasion, *603*

Reactive change *Change made in response to problems or opportunities as they arise; compare proactive change,* **422**–423, 445

Readiness for change *The beliefs, attitudes, and intentions of the organization's staff regarding the extent of the changes needed and how willing and able they are to implement them,* 431

Receiver barrier, *653*

Receiver *The person wanting to share information,* **643,** *643*

Recency effect *The tendency of people to remember recent information better than earlier information,* **473**

Recharging, self-motivation strategy, 555

Recruiting *The process of locating and attracting qualified applicants for jobs open in the organization,* **366**–371

Reduced cycle time *The reduction of steps in the work process,* **724**

Referent power *One of five sources of a leader's power deriving from personal attraction,* **601**

Reflection, 304–305

Refreezing stage of organizational change, *428,* 429

Refugees, 157

Reinforcement *Anything that causes a given behavior to be repeated or inhibited; the four types are positive, negative, extinction, and punishment*

Reinforcement theory *The belief that behavior reinforced by positive consequences tends to be repeated, whereas behavior reinforced by negative consequences tends not to be repeated,* **542**

Related diversification *When a company purchases a new business that is related to the company's existing business portfolio,* **226**

Relatedness needs, 520

Relationship management, *462*

Relationship-oriented leadership *Form of leadership that is primarily concerned with the leader's interactions with his or her people,* **612**

Relationship-oriented role, 579

Reliability *Degree to which a test measures the same thing consistently, so that an individual's score remains about the same over time, assuming the characteristics being measured also remain the same,* **371**

Self-management, *462*, 503–504

Self-motivation, 417, 511

Self-serving bias *The attributional tendency to take more personal responsibility for success than for failure,* **474**

Semantic noise, 644–645

Sender barrier, *653*

Sender *The person wanting to share information,* **643**, *643*

Servant leadership *Focuses on providing increased service to others—meeting the goals of both followers and the organization—rather than to yourself,* **625–626**, *626*

Services companies, 722–723

Sex-role stereotype, 470

Sexual harassment *Unwanted sexual attention that creates an adverse work environment,* 93, **399**–401, *401*
   actions to prevent, 401
   types of, 401
   at work, 400

Sexual orientation, 87, 490–491

Sham participation *Occurs when powerless, but useful individuals are selected by leaders to rubber stamp decisions and work hard to implement them,* **298**

Shared values, 64–65

Shareholders, 707–710

Short-term goals *Tend to span 12 month and are connected to strategic goals in a hierarchy known as a means-end chain,* **190**, 191, 554

Simple structure *The first type of organizational structure, whereby an organization has authority centralized in a single person, as well as a flat hierarchy, few rules, and low work specialization,* 344, **344**–345

Situational approaches *An approach to leadership where it is believed that effective leadership behavior depends on the situation at hand,* **613**–618

Situational interview *A structured interview in which the interviewer focuses on hypothetical situations,* **374**

Six Sigma *A rigorous statistical analysis process that reduces defects in manufacturing and service-related industries,* **725**

Skills. *See also* Soft skills
   business, *609*
   and communication, 655
   conceptual, 19–20, *610*
   human, 20
   interpersonal, *609*
   listening, 590, 641, 681–683
   management, 3
   soft, 20
   speaking, 684–685, *685*
   technical, 19
   writing, 683

Skill variety, 539

Slogans, 331

Small businesses, 244, *253*

Smart devices, 87

SMART goals *A goal that is Specific, Measurable, Attainable, Results oriented, and has Target dates,* **192**–193

Smart manufacturing, 727

Social audit *A systematic assessment of a company's performance in implementing socially responsible programs, often based on predefined goals,* **76**

Social awareness, 462

Social capital *Economic or productive potential of strong, trusting, and cooperative relationships,* **365**

Social entrepreneurship *Consists of improvising systems, devising new approaches, grasping opportunities others miss and generating solutions to change society for the better,* **248**–249

Social intelligence, 587

Socialized power *Power directed at helping others,* **600**

Social media *Internet-based and mobile technologies used to generate interactive dialogue with embers of a network,* 209, **660**–677
   age distribution of usage, 662, *662*
   brand recognition and, 667–669
   crowdsourcing and, 666–667
   downsides of, 669–674
   as external recruitment source, 369
   hiring decisions and, 361, 663–664
   impact of, 661–662
   innovation in, 666–667
   networks, 663
   personal brand, building, 664
   policy creation for, 675–677, *676*
   productivity and, 664–666
   sales and, 667–669

Social media policy *Describes the who, how, when, and for what purposes of social media use, and the consequences for noncompliance,* **675**–677, *676*

Social responsibility *A manager's duty to take actions that will benefit the interests of society as well as of the organization,* **99**
   climate change and, 102
   corporate, 100, *100*
   effects of, 102–103, *104*
   philanthropy and, 102–103
   viewpoints on, 100–101

Social Security Act of 1935 *Established the U.S. retirement system,* **397**

Social support, 76

Society for Human Resource Management (SHRM), 368

Sociocultural forces *Influences and trends originating in a country's, a society's, or a culture's human relationships and values that may affect an organization,* **87**

Soft skills *Ability to motivate, to inspire trust, and to communicate with others,* **20**, 34

Sole proprietor *Someone who owns an unincorporated business by himself or herself,* 79, **258**

South Africa, emerging economy of, 160, *160*

Span of control *The number of people reporting directly to a given manager,* **340**, *340*

Speaking skills, 684–685, *685*

Special-interest groups *Groups whose members try to influence specific issues,* **84**

Specificity of goals, 192, 536

Stability strategy *One of three grand strategies, this strategy involves little or no significant change,* **223**, 224

Stakeholders *People whose interests are affected by an organization's activities,* 77, 425–426
   external, *78*, 81–89
   internal, 77–80, *78*
   social media for connecting with, 666

Standard of living *Is the level of necessaries, comforts and luxuries that a person is accustomed to enjoy,* **253**–254

Start-up *Newly created company designed to grow fast,* **252**
   considerations for, 244–245
   culture and design for, 261–262
   failure, causes for, 262–263
   financing for, 259–260
   ideas for, 254–256
   legal structure for, 258–259
   plans for, 257–258
   trends for, 244, *244*

Statement of cash flows *Reports the cash generated and used over a specific period of time,* **708**–710

Static budget, 707

Statistical process control *A statistical technique that uses periodic random samples from production runs to see if quality is being maintained within a standard range of acceptability,* 724–**725**

Stereotyping *The tendency to attribute to an individual the characteristics one believes are typical of the group to which that individual belongs,* **469**–471, 489, 492

Stockholders, 79

Stock options *The right to buy a company's stock at a future date for a discounted price,* **547**

Storming *The second of five stages of forming a team in which individual personalities, roles, and conflicts within the group emerge,* **571**

Story *A narrative based on true events, which is repeated—and sometimes embellished upon—to emphasize a particular value,* **323**, 331

Strategic allies *The relationship of two organizations who join forces to achieve advantages neither can perform as well alone,* **82**

Strategic control *Monitoring performance to ensure that strategic plans are being implemented and taking corrective action as needed,* **215**, 235

Strategic goals *Goals that are set by and for top management and focus on objectives for the organization as a whole,* **190**, 190–191

Practical Skills. Relevant Theory. Purposeful Application.

A bridge to student success

The study of management is an essential crossing on the road to achievement. The cover shows the striking Infinity Bridge located in Stockton-on-Tees, England. It is a pedestrian and cycle footbridge that spans about 787 feet. The bowstring bridge was built in 18 months and was opened in May 2009. The Infinity Bridge received the Institution of Structural Engineers' Supreme Award for Structural Excellence, the premier structural engineering award in the UK, among others.

Some great achievements of history were accomplished by individuals working quietly by themselves, such as scientific discoveries or works of art. But so much more has been achieved by people working together for a common goal or cause, such as building the Infinity Bridge. Managers had to plan, organize, lead, and control the work of 530 workers, who used 450 tons of Corus steel, 1.5 km of locked coil steel cable, 780 lights, and 5,472 bolts to assemble this architectural wonder. The bridge could not have been built on time and within budget without effective management.

ISBN 978-1-264-26368-4
MHID 1-264-26368-6

EAN

9 781264 263684

90000

mheducation.com/highered